WORK PSYCHOLOGY

Visit the *Work Psychology*, fifth edition Companion Website at **www.pearsoned.co.uk/workpsych** to find valuable **student** learning material including:

- Multiple-choice questions to help test your learning
- Links to relevant sites on the web
- Online glossary to explain key terms

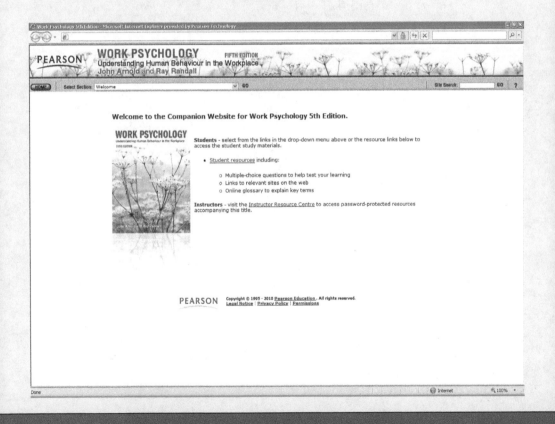

WORK PSYCHOLOGY

Understanding Human Behaviour in the Workplace

FIFTH EDITION

John Arnold and Ray Randall

with Fiona Patterson, Joanne Silvester, Ivan Robertson, Cary Cooper, Bernard Burnes, Stephen Swailes, Don Harris, Carolyn Axtell and Deanne Den Hartog

**Financial Times
Prentice Hall
is an imprint of**

PEARSON

Harlow, England • London • New York • Boston • San Francisco • Toronto • Sydney • Singapore • Hong Kong
Tokyo • Seoul • Taipei • New Delhi • Cape Town • Madrid • Mexico City • Amsterdam • Munich • Paris • Milan

Pearson Education Limited
Edinburgh Gate
Harlow
Essex CM20 2JE
England

and Associated Companies throughout the world

Visit us on the World Wide Web at:
www.pearsoned.co.uk

First published 1991
Second edition 1995
Third edition 1998
Fourth edition 2005
Fifth edition published 2010

© Financial Times Professional Limited 1998
© Pearson Education Limited 1991, 1995, 2005, 2010

ISBN: 978-0-273-71121-6

British Library Cataloguing-in-Publication Data
A catalogue record for this book is available from the British Library

Library of Congress Cataloging-in-Publication Data

Arnold, John, 1958–
    Work psychology : understanding human behaviour in the workplace / John Arnold and Ray Randall; with Joanne Silvester . . [et al.]. — 5th ed.
      p. cm.
    ISBN 978-0-273-71121-6 (pbk.)
  1. Psychology, Industrial. 2. Work—Psychological aspects. I. Randall, Ray. II. Title.
    HF5548.8.A78 2010
    158.7—dc22

2010000883

ARP impression 98

Typeset in 9.5/12 Stone Serif by 73.

Printed and bound by Ashford Colour Press Ltd.

CONTENTS

Supporting resources

Visit **www.pearsoned.co.uk/workpsych** to find valuable online resources:

Companion Website for students

- Multiple-choice questions to help test your learning
- Links to relevant sites on the web
- Online glossary to explain key terms

For instructors

- PowerPoint slides that can be downloaded and used for presentations
- Complete, downloadable Instructor's Manual

Also: The Companion Website provides the following features:

- Search tool to help locate specific items of content
- E-mail results and profile tools to send results of quizzes to instructors
- Online help and support to assist with website usage and troubleshooting

For more information please contact your local Pearson Education sales representative or visit **www.pearsoned.co.uk/workpsych**

LIST OF TABLES

LIST OF FIGURES

LIST OF CASE STUDIES

LIST OF EXERCISES

PREFACE

Work psychology is about people's behaviour, thoughts and emotions related to their work. It can be used to improve our understanding and management of people (including ourselves) at work. By work, we mean what people do to earn a living. However, much of the content of this book can also be applied to study, voluntary work and even leisure activities.

All too often, work organisations have sophisticated systems for assessing the costs and benefits of everything except their management of people. It is often said by senior managers that 'our greatest asset is our people', but sometimes the people do not feel that they are being treated as if they were valuable assets. People are complicated, and their views of themselves and their worlds differ. They do not necessarily do what others would like them to do. One reaction to all this is for managers to focus on things that don't talk back, such as profit and loss accounts or organisational strategy. Another is to adopt a highly controlling 'do as I say' approach to dealing with people at work. Either way, the thinking behind how people in the workplace function, and how they might be managed, tends to be rather careless or simplistic. Work psychologists seek to counter that tendency by carefully studying people's behaviour, thoughts and feelings regarding work. As well as developing knowledge and understanding for its own sake, this also leads to insights about motivation, leadership, training and development, selection and many other people-related aspects of management. Work psychologists are also concerned about the ethical use of psychological theories and techniques, and their impact on the well-being and effectiveness of individuals, groups and organisations.

This book is designed to appeal to readers in many different countries, especially in Europe and Australasia. Judging by the feedback and sales figures for previous editions, we seem to have generally been successful in appealing to a range of people in a range of places. We have tried to make the book suitable both for people encountering the subject for the first time and for those who already have some familiarity with it. Specifically, and in no particular order, we intend that this book should be useful for:

- undergraduate students in psychology, taking one or more modules with names such as work psychology, work and organisational psychology, organisational psychology, occupational psychology, and industrial-organisational psychology;

- undergraduate students in business and management taking one or more modules that might have titles such as organisational behaviour, managing people or human resource management;

- postgraduate (MSc, MBA, MA) and post-experience students in psychology or business/management taking one or more modules with any or all of the titles listed above;

- students taking professional qualifications, particularly (in the United Kingdom) those of the Chartered Institute of Personnel and Development (CIPD);

- students on undergraduate or postgraduate courses in other vocational subjects such as engineering, whose curriculum includes some elements to do with managing people at work.

We aim to give clear and straightforward – but not simplistic – accounts of many key areas of contemporary work psychology. More specifically, we try to achieve several objectives in order to make this book as useful as possible to its readers.

First, we seek to blend theory and practice. Both are important. Without good theory, practice is blind. Without good practice, theory is not being properly used. We therefore describe key theories and evaluate them where appropriate. We also discuss how the concepts described can find practical application. We provide case studies and exercises to which material in the book can readily be applied. These can be used as classroom exercises, or as assignments for individual students. Some guidance and suggestions about how to use these are included on the website for this book.

Second, we try to present material at a level the reader should find intellectually stimulating, but not too difficult. It is all too easy to use a slick, glossy presentation at the expense of good content. There is always the temptation to resort to over-simple 'recipes for success' that insult the reader's intelligence. On the other hand, it is equally easy to lose the reader in unnecessarily complex debates. We hope that we avoid both these fates (and that you will let us know if we do not!).

Third, we try to help the reader to gain maximum benefit from the book by providing several more aids to learning. Each chapter begins with clearly stated learning outcomes, and concludes with some short self-test questions and longer suggested assignments that reflect these outcomes. At the end of each chapter we provide a small number of suggestions for further reading. Throughout the text we specify key learning points that express succinctly the main message of the preceding two or three pages of text. We include a number of diagrams as well as text, in recognition that pictures can often express complex ideas in an economical and memorable way. At the end of the book there is a comprehensive glossary explaining in a concise way the meaning of lots of key words and phrases. There is also a very long list of references, to enable interested readers to find more material if they wish – for more advanced study for example.

Fourth, we have chosen topics that we judge to be the most useful to potential readers of this book. Some usually appear in organisational behaviour texts, whereas others are generally found in books of a more specifically psychological orientation. We believe we have found a helpful balance between these two overlapping but different worlds, so that there should be plenty of relevant material both for people who want to be psychologists and those who do not. The topics we cover in chapters or parts of chapters include individual differences, employee selection, assessing work performance, attitudes at work, training and development, teamwork, work motivation, stress and well-being at work, designing workplaces for humans, managing diversity, leadership, careers, organisational change, the nature of work psychology as a discipline and profession and how to design, conduct and understand research studies in work psychology.

Fifth, we provide up-to-date coverage of our material. There are currently exciting advances in many areas of work psychology, and we try to reflect these. At the same time, where the old stuff is best and still relevant, we include it. There is nothing to be gained by discussing recent work purely because it is recent.

Sixth, we attempt to use material from many different parts of the world, and to point out cross-national and cross-cultural differences where these seem particularly important. Much of the best research and practice in work psychology originate from North America, but it is possible to go too far and assume that nowhere else has contributed anything. No doubt we have our own blinkers, but we try to include perspectives from places other than North America, especially the United Kingdom and other European countries. Nevertheless, the United States and Canada provide much valuable material. We therefore also make use of research and theory originating in those countries.

Developments from the fourth edition

Readers familiar with the fourth edition of this text, published in 2005, may find it helpful if we describe the changes we have made. These are quite substantial, though more evident in some parts of the book than others. Readers familiar with previous editions will readily recognise this book as a direct descendant of the others, but will also notice quite a few differences. The scale of the changes from the fourth edition and the expanded team of authors are among the reasons (or excuses!) why this edition has taken longer to produce than we would have liked. We apologise for this, not least because we know that some readers have been waiting a long time, and might justifiably have been losing patience with us.

The changes from the fourth edition reflect the fact that quite a lot has happened in work psychology over the last few years. Reviewers commissioned by the publisher (plus users' comments made direct to us) helped us to see where re-thinks were required.

Perhaps the most noticeable change is the change in lead author. John Arnold handed over overall responsibility for this text to me (Ray Randall) in 2008. I used the first edition as a student, and subsequent editions as a lecturer, so I felt the pressure that often comes with understanding the demanding consumer perspective. Therefore I took on the task with equal amounts of excitement and trepidation. It has been a steep learning curve and the patience of the team at Pearson has been much appreciated. As with the fourth edition, Fiona Patterson (Chapters 3, 4 and 5) and Joanne Silvester (Chapters 6 and 11) took a major role in this edition. Bernard Burnes has again contributed a chapter on organisational change and culture. This edition also sees some new authors, Stephen Swailes and Deanne Den Hartog provided specialist input into the updating of the chapters on teamwork and leadership respectively. Don Harris (Chapter 9) and Carolyn Axtell (Chapter 10) produced the new chapters on technology and human factors for this book. We believe these fresh new perspectives have helped to enliven the text, and hope that you agree. John Arnold invited these authors to get involved and I (Ray Randall) am certainly grateful that they agreed. John Arnold is now the contributor of two chapters (8 and 14). Ivan Robertson and Cary Cooper have taken more of a back seat this time. Ray Randall is responsible for the book as a whole though, so any errors, omissions, etc. are primarily his responsibility.

All contributors are excellent researchers with an international reputation in their field. Importantly, all are also practitioners, with extensive experience of intervention in organisations and this allows them to describe how theory can be put into practice. Our intention has been to make sure the links between theory and practice are even more apparent than they have been in previous editions. We are proud of this fifth edition, but as with all preceding editions, your opinion is the one that really matters!

Feedback from readers of previous editions clearly indicated that they appreciated the clarity of style and the combination of theoretical and practical considerations. They also very much valued the substantial list of references, many quite recent. Naturally, we have tried to preserve these features. The style remains the same and the reference lists have been revised and updated. We are grateful for the feedback we have received from readers of the earlier editions, and wherever possible we have reflected it in this edition.

So, apart from routine updating, adjustment and internationalising of material, what specifically is new about this fifth edition?

From positive feedback provided by reviewers we have kept the large number of exercises and case studies. The majority of case studies have been updated to highlight the relevance that psychology has when dealing with contemporary issues in the workplace. Where we feel the case studies from the fourth edition still have a strong relevance these have been retained. You will also notice that the results of meta-analyses are used more in this edition. This is in response to comments about the fourth edition that some of the focus on specific research findings led students to overestimate the importance of the results of single studies. Of course, the danger is that the detail is lost, so we have retained more in-depth accounts of illustrative pieces of research where we feel that a piece of research makes some particularly important points.

You will also notice the inclusion of 'stop to consider' boxes. There are 2–4 of them in most chapters. These are designed to encourage students to pause to reflect on their learning. Their content points the reader towards controversies or debates in the literature, in order to foster critical thinking and cement learning. We hope these prove useful for students who wish to go beyond an understanding of content to attempt further analysis and integration of the issues described.

Chapter 1 retains the introductory material of previous editions, but gives some more coverage to the topics of work–life balance, diversity and cross-cultural issues. The former is certainly a topic of growing interest and some important research is highlighted to show how psychologists can make a contribution to helping people to balance the demands of different aspects of their lives. Diversity is a thread that runs throughout the text, and the material in Chapter 1 is designed to orientate the reader to how the concept relates to more established topics such as equal opportunities. As with diversity, cross-cultural issues are discussed throughout the text, and we provide some early illustrations of how important it is to consider culture when studying work psychology. It would also be remiss of us not to mention the impact of major global economic upheaval in describing the context within which work psychologists practise. This is covered not only in Chapter 1 but reflected throughout the text (most notably in some of the new case studies). Our view is that while these events have impacted on the agenda for work psychology by bringing certain issues into sharper focus, the potential for work psychologists to make a difference in organisations is as good now as it has ever been.

Chapter 2 now has less coverage of specific statistical techniques. The content is designed to be less technical than before but to give the reader a basic understanding of why different methods of analysis are used to deal with various theoretical and practical questions. Some of this more technical material is now available on the website that accompanies this book. There is also more coverage of the issue of the academic–practitioner divide to cement students' understanding of how the transition can be made between theory and practice. Qualitative methods also receive more attention than before, and we believe this reflects their growing importance and frequency of use. Of course, this text is not a research methods book, but we hope that Chapter 2 orientates students to the methodologies that we use in our discipline.

Chapter 3 on individual differences had changed a lot and I am very grateful to Fiona Patterson for all her hard work on this. In the fourth edition this chapter was out of kilter with the rest of the book: it was too technical and not easily accessible. While tackling these issues has been the focus of the revision, there is also more detailed coverage of important topics such as emotional intelligence, the potential to innovate and creativity.

Chapters 4 and 5 on personnel selection have been well-received in previous editions of the book. So the structure and coverage remain similar, but as with the rest of the text a lot has happened in five years of research so it is updated extensively. The updates describe many recent debates and controversies in selection and assessment, as well as giving coverage to emerging techniques such as situational judgement tests.

Chapter 6 on assessing people at work has been re-focused. The emphasis is now on what performance is, and how it is measured. This includes a description of extra-role performance, such as organisational citizenship behaviours. There is also more detailed analysis of multi-source feedback and more about the difficulties involved in obtaining reliable and valid measures of performance. We now include a discussion of how the contribution of work psychology can be important from a human resource management perspective.

Chapter 7 on attitudes at work and employee relations has changed quite a lot from the fourth edition. The basic social psychology material that dominated this chapter in the fourth edition now takes a back seat (especially the material on attitude change and persuasion). Space is still given over to the theory of attitude formation but this quickly develops into an updated description and discussion of job satisfaction and organisational commitment. The focus of this is now very much on the links between attitudes and behaviour, an issue for which there is much recent research to report. This chapter has two new sections on employee turnover and unemployment. These are intended to show how attitudes to work come to life in situations where they have heightened significance for people and organisations. The section on the psychological contract now appears here (and not in the careers chapter) and has wider coverage than in previous editions: the breadth of coverage reflects the prominence of this topic in work psychology research. The material on negotiation and employee relations has been re-positioned within this chapter.

Chapter 8 (what was Chapter 9 in the fourth edition on motivation and job design) has been extensively updated and revised. These are solid topics in work psychology and much of the existing material from the fourth edition retains its relevance. The same applies to Chapter 11, Training and development. However, this chapter now also includes coverage of contemporary topics such as e-learning, communities of practice and the concept of learning organisations. With these chapters the challenge has been to retain their core coverage, while giving enough analysis of emerging issues.

Two new chapters, Chapter 9, Design at work, and Chapter 10, Communication technology, have been added. These cover more 'traditional' aspects of human-centred design as well as important issues raised by computer-based communications. The new chapters draw on several case studies which look at the design of equipment in high-risk work environments and communication within virtual teams. We believe that this fulfils an important need for the reader to understand how design issues integrate with other topics in occupational psychology. Workplace redesign is an important intervention option when dealing with many problem organisations and we hope that these chapters help students to appreciate this. These chapters have replaced Chapter 8 from the fourth edition on the analysis and modification of work behaviour (part of which is now presented within Chapter 6). We believe this reflects one of the most common use of such methods in organisations today, but removing material is always a tough call and we have made the Chapter 8 from the fourth edition available to download from the website that accompanies this book.

Chapter 12 on stress and well-being at work is approximately 75 per cent new. We have responded to reviewers' comments on previous editions and included much more coverage of the theories of work stress, but retained a critical analysis of the concept itself. We also include a wider discussion of emotions at work that examines how well-designed work can lead to the experience of positive emotions at work. There is also a much more detailed account of measurement issues that we hope helps to demystify this topic for the reader. In our experience students appreciate seeing how theory translates to intervention, therefore various different approaches to intervention receive detailed coverage illustrated with high-quality examples drawn from the recent literature.

Chapters 13 (Groups, teams and teamwork), 14 (Leadership) and 16 (Understanding organisational change and culture) have received good reviews so their structures remain largely unchanged. The content has been updated to reflect new developments, and Chapter 14 on leadership now includes more explicit coverage of cross-cultural issues. Chapter 15 on careers has undergone a major rewrite to reflect not only recent developments on existing topics, but also the changing nature of the careers' landscape bought about by economic upheaval and changes to the demographic composition of the workforce.

Overall, then, the average length of each chapter is greater, and we hope that the coverage is contemporary and more integrated than before. Lecturers using the book may want to recommend parts of certain chapters, rather than whole chapters, to support a particular lecture topic, so it is worth having a close look at the contents pages to check what is where.

As before, we welcome feedback and dialogue about this book. Please direct it to Ray Randall, School of Psychology, University of Leicester, Leicester, LE1 7EA, UK (rjr15@le.ac.uk). Thank you for reading this preface, and please now carry on into the rest of the book!

GUIDED TOUR

The **full colour design** and **photographs** that open each chapter make for a more stimulating read. Have fun guessing why each image was selected to represent its chapter!

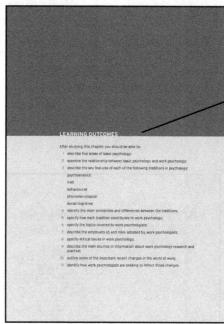

Learning outcomes open each chapter, enabling you to focus on what you should have achieved by the end of the chapter and helping to structure your learning.

LEARNING OUTCOMES

After studying this chapter, you should be able to:

1 describe five areas of basic psychology;

2 examine the relationship between basic psychology and work psychology;

3 describe the key features of each of the following traditions in psychology:
  psychoanalytic
  trait
  behaviourist
  phenomenological
  social cognitive;

4 identify the main similarities and differences between the traditions;

5 specify how each tradition contributes to work psychology;

6 specify the topics covered by work psychologists;

7 describe the employers of, and roles adopted by, work psychologists;

8 specify ethical issues in work psychology;

9 describe the main sources of information about work psychology research and practice;

10 outline some of the important recent changes in the world of work;

11 identify how work psychologists are seeking to reflect those changes.

Chapter opening case studies set a real-life context to which the theory can be related.

Opening Case Study   Working from a distance

More and more people are now working remotely, but what happens to team dynamics when colleagues are based hundreds – or even thousands – of miles apart?

It's hard enough for people to work as a team when they are based in the same building. But for a virtual team of IT developers at Eli Lilly the challenges were much greater.

The 15-strong team was split across a larger group in the centre-west of Germany (Giessen) and two smaller satellites: one in north-east Germany (Berlin) and one in London, England. An added complication was that team members communicated with each other in English, which for many was a second language.

Small wonder, then, that despite the team's shared professional background there were misunderstandings – especially when the software developers used e-mail to convey complex information to each other. Task coordination also became a problem as new members arrived. With role boundaries not always clearly defined and the added problem of distance, uncertainty arose as to who was supposed to carry out activities such as updating the project database. Some tasks fell in the cracks because team members assumed that someone else was dealing with them.

The team responded to these problems by clarifying and modifying individuals' roles. Team-building events also helped cement working relations between colleagues based at the different locations. As one software developer said, the larger group at Giessen all know each other well, but communications between those working at different sites could initially be a bit cold and impersonal. The team-building events, which were held around three times a year and included workshops and meetings, as well as fun activities such as go-karting, helped break the ice, and over time led to improved communications between team members. Telephone conversations between those who had met several times began to include the social chat that goes on between people who really are part of the same team.

However, there were a number of other problems that needed to be addressed.

The software developers needed to liaise with customers throughout Eli Lilly's European sites. A misunderstanding between a German developer and a Spanish customer illustrates the problem. When the customer took delivery of a product she had ordered, it turned out that there had been confusion about some of the system requirements and their cost. This was partly because of the difficulty of exchanging information about complex technical issues via telephone or e-mail. It didn't help that the customer did not share the developer's technical know-how and that they had been communicating in English, which was neither party's first language.

The IT developers also ran into difficulties when dealing with the UK-based 'server management' team, which was responsible for putting software onto the appropriate server – for example, for testing or development purposes. The development team blamed the server team for causing delays and could not

Where possible ideas are illustrated by **figures** and **tables** to appeal to all learning styles.

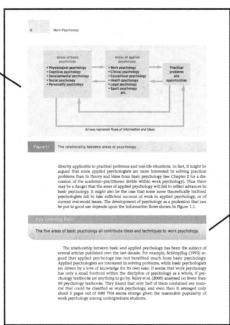

Key learning points emphasise the crucial building blocks of the subject, whilst the **glossary** at the end of the book is useful for revision purposes.

The **stop to consider** box briefly takes you away from the main text to help review the chapter, helping you to map your progress and re-examine the key concepts.

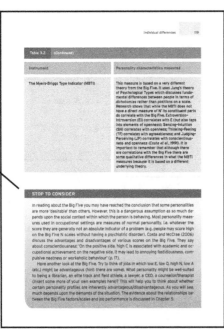

Short-answer questions and **suggested assignments** test your understanding and allow you to track your progress.

Regular **exercises** throughout the chapters enable students to apply their knowledge and own experience to what they have learned.

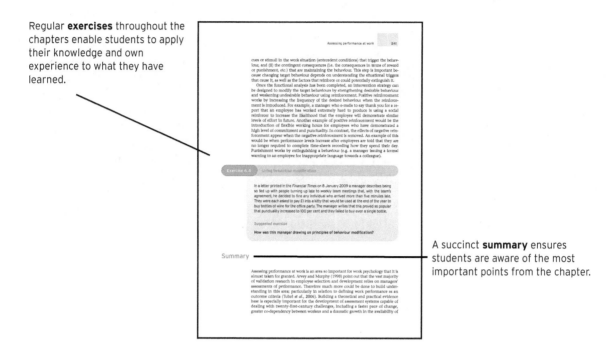

A succinct **summary** ensures students are aware of the most important points from the chapter.

A **chapter closing case study** with an exercise contextualises the theory and relates it to the world of work.

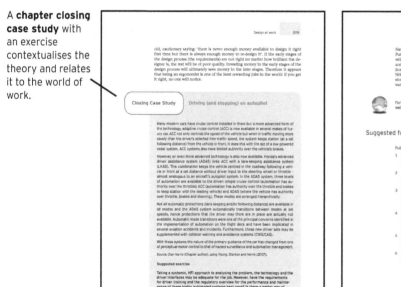

Further reading offers opportunities for you to take your studies further.

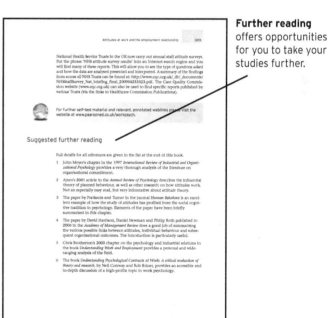

Visit the Companion Website at **www.pearsoned.co.uk/workpsych** to find valuable teaching and learning material. See page viii for full details.

ACKNOWLEDGEMENTS

We thank Gabrielle James, Sarah Wild and Matthew Walker at Pearson Education for their immense patience in waiting for the manuscript, and for doing anything they could to help it along without putting the authors under pressure, even when we thoroughly deserved it. Ray Randall would like to thank his wife Kirsty, children Izzy and Owen, and his parents Lal and Bob for their patience, advice, understanding, support and, especially Kirsty, for the occasional bit of proof-reading and sense-checking. He would also like to thank Sue Harrington for her contribution of the content in Chapter 12 (the material about workplace bullying) and Danny Sharples for his help with some of the material on rater bias in Chapter 6. John Arnold would also like to thank his parents Ann and Rev, and his wife Helen, for their love, wisdom and support.

Publisher's acknowledgements

We are grateful to the following for permission to reproduce copyright material:

Figures

Figures 2.1, 2.2 from 'The role of psychologists in enhancing organizational effectiveness' in *Organizational Effectiveness: The Role of Psychology* (Hodgkinson, G.P. & Herriot, P. eds Robertson, I.T., Callinan, M. and Bartram, D. 2002) pp. 48-49, copyright © Wiley-Blackwell 2002; Figure 4.1 adapted from *Selection into Medical Education and Training*, ASME monographs, Edinburgh (Patterson, F. and Ferguson, E. 2007), copyright © ASME; Figures 6.1, 6.5 from Randy Glasbergen, Glasbergen Cartoons, www.glasbergen.com; Figure 7.1 from 'Prediction of goal-directed behaviour: attitudes, intentions, and perceived behavioural control', *Journal of Experimental Social Psychology*, Vol 22, pp. 453-741 (Ajzen, I. and Madden, J.T. 1986), copyright © Elsevier Science, 1986; Figure 7.2 adapted from 'Some possible relationships between job satisfaction (JS) and job performance (JP)' in 'The job satisfaction - job performance relationship: a qualitative and quantitative review', *Psychological Bulletin*, 127, pp. 376-401 (Judge, T.A., Thoreson, C.J., Bono, J.E. and Patton, G.K. 2001) (Figure 1, p. 377), copyright © American Psychological Association; Figure 7.3 from 'Job satisfaction as a reflection of disposition: a multiple source causal analysis', *Organizational Behaviour and Human Decision Processes*, Vol 56, pp. 388-421 (Judge, T.A. and Hulin, C.L. 1993), copyright © Elsevier Science 1993; Figure 7.5 adapted from *Psychological*

Contracts in Organizations (Rousseau, D.M. 1995) p. 118, copyright © Sage Publications Inc, permission conveyed through Copyright Clearance Centre; Figure 7.6 adapted from "Negotiator concerns and characteristic strategies", *Annual Review of Psychology*, Vol 43 (Carnevale and Pruitt 1992), copyright © Annual Reviews, Inc. permission conveyed by Copyright Clearance Centre; Figure 7.7 adapted from 'Psychology in employee relations' in *International Review of Industrial and Organizational Psychology*, Vol 7, John Wiley (Cooper, C.L. & Roberston, I.T. eds, 1992) copyright © Wiley-Blackwell 1992; Figure 8.5 adapted from *Work Redesign*, Pearson Education, Inc. (Hackman, J.R. and Oldman, G.R. 1980) copyright © Pearson Education, Inc.; Figure 8.6 adapted from 'An elaborated model of work design', *Journal of Occupational & Organizational Psychology* (Parker, S. *et al.*, 2001), British Psychology Society, copyright © Parker *et al.*, 2001; Figure 8.7 from 'A circular and dynamic model of the process of job design' p. 324, *Journal of Occupational and Organizational Psychology*, Vol 80, pp. 321-339 (Clegg & Spencer 2007), Reproduced with permission from the Journal of Occupational and Organizational Psychology, copyright © The British Psychological Society; Figure 8.8 adapted from 'What should we do about motivation theory? Six recommendations for the twenty-first century', p. 390, *Academy of Management Review*, Vol 29, pp. 388-403 (Locke, E.A. and Latham, G.P. 2004), copyright © Academy of Management, permission conveyed through Copyright Clearance Center; Figure 9.1 from 'Evaluating the transfer of technology between application domains: a critical evaluation of the human component in the system', *Technology in Society*, Vol 26(4), pp. 551-565 (Harris, D. and Harris, F.J. 2004), Copyright © 2004, Elsevier; Figure 9.2 from 'Using SHERPA to predict design-induced error on the flight deck', *Aerospace Science and Technology* Vol 9(6), pp. 525-532 (Harris, D., Stanton, A., Marshall, A., Young, M.S., Demagalski, J.M., And Salmon, P. 2005), Copyright © Elsevier 2005; Figure 11.3 from 'Application of cognitive skill based and affective theories of learning outcomes to new methods of training evaluation', *Journal of Applied Psychology*, Vol 78, pp. 311-328 (Kraiger, K. Ford, J. and Salas, E. 1993), copyright © American Psychological Association; Figure 12.1 from 'A cybernetic framework for the study of occupational stress', *Human Relations*, Vol 32, pp. 395-419 (Cummings, T. and Cooper, C.L. 1979); Figure 12.2 'Medical extension of Yerkes-Dodson law' Figure 6.3, from *Executive Health*, Random House Business books (Dr Andrew Melhuish 1978) p. 85, Reproduced by permission of The Random House Group Ltd; Figure 13.4 adapted from 'What a mess! Participation as a Simple Managerial Rule to "Complexify" Organizations', *Journal of Management Studies*, Vol 39(2), pp. 189-206 (Ashmos, D.P., Duchon, D., McDaniel Jr, R.R. and Huonker, J.W. 2002), John Wiley and Sons. Copyright © 2002, Blackwell Publishers Ltd; Figure 13.5 adapted from 'Does decision process matter? A study of strategic decision-making effectiveness', *Academy of Management Journal*, Vol 39, pp. 368-396 (Dean, J.W. and Sharfman, M.P. 1996), copyright © Academy of Management, permission conveyed through Copyright Clearance Center; Figure 15.2 from 'Career Success: Constructing a Multidimensional Model', *Journal of Vocational Behavior*, Vol 73(2), pp. 254-267 (Dries, N., Pepermans, R. and Carlier, O. 2008), Copyright © 2008, Elsevier; Figure 15.3 adapted from 'Predictors of Objective and Subjective Career Success: A Meta-Analysis', *Personnel Psychology*, Vol 58(2), pp. 367-408 (Ng, T. *et al.*, 2005), John Wiley and Sons. Copyright © 2005, by Blackwell Publishing Inc.; Figure 15.4 from *Making Vocational Choices*, 3rd edition (Holland, J. 1997) copyright © 1973, 1985, 1992, 1997 Psychology Assessment Resources Inc.

Tables

Table 3.1 from 'Some questions from an intelligence test - The AH5 Test.' by Heim, A.W., Copyright © 1968 A.W Heim. Reproduced with permission of the publisher, ASE, College Lane, Hatfield, Herts, AL10 9AA, UK; Table 7.1 adapted from 'Experiencing work: values, attitudes and moods', *Human Relations*, Vol 50, pp. 393-416 (George J.M. and Jones, G.R. 1997), copyright © The Tavistock Institute; Table 7.3 from 'A Job satisfaction measure' *Occupational Stress Indicator* (Cooper, C.L.,Sloan, S. and Williams, S. 1998), Copyright © 1988 Cooper, Sloan and Williams. Reproduced with permission of the publisher, ASE, College Lane, Hatfield, Herts, AL10 9AA, UK; Table 8.2 adapted from 'Decline and stabilization of managerial motivation over a 20 year period' p. 298, *Journal of Applied Psychology*, Vol 67, pp. 297-305 (Miner & Smith 1982), copyright © American

automation: Learning from aviation about design philosophies', *International Journal of Vehicle Design,* Vol 45(3), pp. 323-338 (Young, M.S., Stanton, N.A. and Harris, D), based on. Reproduced with permission from Inderscience Enterprises Ltd and Michael Young; Case Study on pages 386-7 adapted from 'From a Distance', *People Management*, 25 March 2004, p. 39-40 (Carolyn Axtell, Jo Wheeler, Malcolm Patterson and Anna Leach (Anna Meachin) 2004), copyright © People Management, reproduced by permission of People Management and the authors Carolyn Axtell, Jo Wheeler, Malcolm Patterson and Anna Meachin; Case Study on pages 432-433 from "Workplaces cause depression in one in 20 adults", *The Times*, 1 August 2007 (Henderson, M.), copyright © The Times, 2007, www.nisyndication.com; Case Study on pages 492-493 adapted from *Case study: Establishing the business case for investing in stress prevention activities and evaluating their impact on sickness absence levels RR295.*, HSE Books (Tasho, W., Jordan, J., & Robertson, I. 2005); Exercise 12.5 from 'Minister welcomes practical help to tackle stress at work' Press release from UK Government's Health & Safety Executive HSE, 30 October 2003 © Crown copyright; Case Study on pages 583-585 adapted from "Lion King and the Politics of Pain", *The Guardian*, 1 September 2001 (Watts, J.), Copyright © Guardian News & Media Ltd 2001; Case Study on pages 643-644 from "Charities: Passion and skills in aid of a good cause", *The Financial Times*, 13 October 2008 (Murray, S.), copyright © Sarah Murray; Exercise 16.2 adapted from *Managing Change*, 3rd edition, FT/Prentice Hall (Burnes, B. 2000) copyright © Pearson Education Limited.

The Financial Times

Case Study on pages 134-135 adapted from "The Civil Service: There's a price to be paid for job security and a fat pension", *The Financial Times*, 13 October 2008 (Tieman, R.), Copyright © The Financial Times Ltd; Case Study on pages 165-166 adapted from "Russia bids to find new elite breed", *The Financial Times*, 6 Aug 2008 (Clover, C.), Copyright © The Financial Times Ltd; Case Study on pages 308-309 after "Inside Track: Land Rover frees its creative assets", *The Financial Times*, 27 October 2000 (Burt, T.), Copyright © The Financial Times Ltd; Case Study on page 552 after "Inside Track: Executive search: Corporate Leadership", *The Financial Times*, 21 September 2001 (Maitland, A.), Copyright © The Financial Times Ltd; Case Study on pages 592-593 from "A life after redundancy", *The Financial Times*, 24 September 2008 (Clegg, A.), Copyright © The Financial Times Ltd; Case Study on page 650 after "Nardelli's style helps to seal his fate", *The Financial Times*, 4 January 2007, p. 22 (Ward, A. and Politi, J.), Copyright © The Financial Times Ltd; Exercise 16.1 from "Culture is key to CPA professional development", *The Financial Times*, 12 November 2007 (Newing, R.), Copyright © The Financial Times Ltd; Exercise 16.3 adapted from "Birth of the living company", *The Financial Times*, 21 August 2003, p. 11 (Witzel, M.), Copyright © The Financial Times Ltd.

In some instances we have been unable to trace the owners of copyright material, and we would appreciate any information that would enable us to do so.

CHAPTER 1

Work psychology: an initial orientation

LEARNING OUTCOMES

After studying this chapter, you should be able to:

1 describe five areas of basic psychology;

2 examine the relationship between basic psychology and work psychology;

3 describe the key features of each of the following traditions in psychology:

psychoanalytic

trait

behaviourist

phenomenological

social cognitive;

4 identify the main similarities and differences between the traditions;

5 specify how each tradition contributes to work psychology;

6 specify the topics covered by work psychologists;

7 describe the employers of, and roles adopted by, work psychologists;

8 specify ethical issues in work psychology;

9 describe the main sources of information about work psychology research and practice;

10 outline some of the important recent changes in the world of work;

11 identify how work psychologists are seeking to reflect those changes.

Introduction

In this chapter we aim to help the reader gain a broad understanding of the nature of work psychology and the context within which it operates before tackling more specific topics later in the book. We start with a brief description of the discipline of psychology as a whole and discuss the links between what we call basic and applied psychology, with work psychology positioned as one branch of applied psychology. Then we provide a brief analysis of images of the person offered by five traditions within basic psychology. These are psychoanalytic, trait, phenomenological, behaviourist and social cognitive. Each of these traditions has influenced work psychology: in some respects they contradict each other and in some circumstances they complement each other. As you read this text you will see that some of the issues we know most about have been examined using a variety of traditions and approaches and this can help to enrich greatly our understanding. The nature of their contribution is briefly outlined in this chapter and the portions of this book that examine those contributions in more detail are identified. We then recount briefly some history of work psychology before moving to coverage of work psychology today. Here we give an account of the different labels sometimes given to work psychology, the topics it covers, what work psychologists do and ethical issues that arise in practice. We also alert readers to the best sources of good knowledge about work psychology (apart from this book of course!).

In the latter part of this chapter we examine how the world of work is changing. We identify some key issues that are thrown up by these changes, and point out some of the ways in which people in work psychology and related disciplines have tried to (i) investigate the impact of those changes and (ii) reflect those changes in the way they go about their own work. In so doing we examine how psychology can be used to tackle problems, but also how it might help to release potential or help organisations to build on the good things they are doing. We also take a close look at the role of work psychology in understanding the nature of diversity in the workforce and how that diversity can be managed (this is a thread that weaves its way through the various chapters of this book).

Basic psychology and work psychology

Psychology has been defined in various ways. Perhaps the simplest yet most informative definition is that provided long ago by Miller (1966): 'the science of mental life'. Mental life refers to three phenomena: behaviours, thoughts and emotions. Most psychologists these days would agree that psychology involves all three.

The notion that psychology is a science is perhaps rather more controversial. Science involves the systematic collection of data under controlled conditions, so that theory and practice can be based on verifiable evidence rather than on the psychologist's intuition. The aims are to describe, explain and predict behaviours, thoughts and emotions (*see* Chapter 2 for more on psychological theory). Not everyone agrees that it is appropriate to study behaviours, thoughts and emotions in a scientific manner. Some argue that human behaviour is too complex for that, and anyway people's behaviour changes in important ways when they are being observed or experimented upon (*see also* Chapter 2). The scientific approach has a large influence on most courses and training in psychology, and is perhaps most evident in the emphasis given to research design and statistical analysis in many university psychology courses.

The discipline of psychology can be divided into several subdisciplines, each with its own distinctive focus. Collectively they can be termed *basic psychology*. There are several ways of splitting psychology. Perhaps the most helpful of these is as follows:

- *Physiological psychology* concerns the relationship between mind and body. For example, physiological psychologists might investigate the activity in the brain associated with particular behaviours, thoughts and emotions, or they might be interested in the bodily changes associated with feeling stressed at work.

- *Cognitive psychology* focuses on our cognitive functioning; that is, our thought processes. This includes topics such as how well we remember information under various conditions, how we weigh up information when making decisions, or how quickly and accurately we deal with questions in a psychometric test.

- *Developmental psychology* concerns the ways in which people grow and change psychologically. This includes issues such as how and when children become able to understand particular concepts, and how they learn language. Also, developmental psychology is beginning to pay more attention to change and growth throughout adult life.

- *Social psychology* concerns how our behaviours, thoughts and emotions affect, and are affected by, other people. Topics include how groups of people make decisions, and the extent to which a person's attitudes towards particular groups of people influence his or her behaviour towards them.

- *Personality psychology* focuses on people's characteristic tendency to behave, think and feel in certain ways. It is concerned with issues such as how people differ from each other psychologically, and how those differences can be measured. It also increasingly recognises that situations as well as personality influence a person's behaviour, thoughts and emotions. Hence some attention is also paid to defining how *situations* differ from each other.

Work psychology is defined in terms of its context of application (*see* Figure 1.1), and is not in itself one of the subdisciplines of psychology defined above. It is an area of applied psychology. As you will see this throughout this textbook, work psychologists use concepts, theories and techniques derived from all areas of basic psychology. These areas are not mutually exclusive: studying people at work from a number of different perspectives is often necessary in order to understand fully the issue being examined. The same is true of psychologists working in other applied contexts such as education and health.

As shown in Figure 1.1, areas of applied psychology use ideas and information from basic psychology. Conversely, they can also contribute ideas and information to the development of basic psychology. Sometimes theory from basic psychology can directly contribute to the solution of real-world problems, and conversely those problems can also stimulate developments in basic psychology. More often, applied psychology rather than basic psychology offers theories and techniques

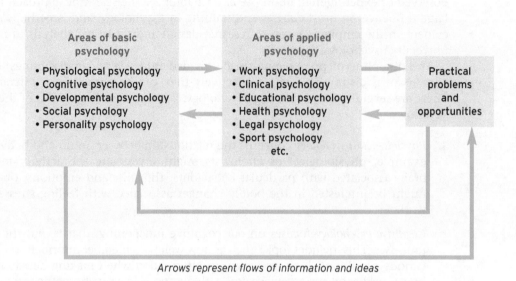

Arrows represent flows of information and ideas

Figure 1.1	The relationship between areas of psychology

directly applicable to practical problems and real-life situations. In fact, it might be argued that some applied psychologists are more interested in solving practical problems than in theory and ideas from basic psychology (see Chapter 2 for a discussion of the academic–practitioner divide within work psychology). Thus there may be a danger that the areas of applied psychology will fail to reflect advances in basic psychology. It might also be the case that some more theoretically inclined psychologists fail to take sufficient account of work in applied psychology, or of current real-world issues. The development of psychology as a profession that can be put to good use depends upon the information flows shown in Figure 1.1.

Key Learning Point

The five areas of basic psychology all contribute ideas and techniques to work psychology.

The relationship between basic and applied psychology has been the subject of several articles published over the last decade. For example, Schönpflug (1993) argued that applied psychology has not benefited much from basic psychology. Applied psychologists are interested in solving problems, while basic psychologists are driven by a love of knowledge for its own sake. It seems that work psychology has only a small foothold within the discipline of psychology as a whole, if psychology textbooks are anything to go by. Raley *et al.* (2003) analysed no fewer than 60 psychology textbooks. They found that only half of them contained *any* material that could be classified as work psychology, and even then it averaged only about 5 pages out of 600! This seems strange given the reasonable popularity of work psychology among undergraduate students.

Whatever the strength of these diverse and sometimes contradictory viewpoints, it can be said that work psychology, as one branch of applied psychology, does have its own theories and techniques. The following chapters will demonstrate this. Some draw upon basic psychology a lot, others less so.

It would be dishonest to pretend that psychology is a well-integrated discipline with generally accepted principles. Underlying it are several competing and quite different concepts of the person. These are most apparent in personality psychology – not surprisingly since personality psychology is the subdiscipline most concerned with the essence of human individuality. These competing conceptions of humanity will now be examined briefly. The interested reader can find much fuller coverage of each in texts such as Ewen (2003) and Schultz and Schultz (2001). Table 1.1 summarises some of the differences and similarities between the five traditions reviewed in the next section.

Key Learning Point

Psychology is a discipline that includes many different views of what a person is. Some of these views contradict each other. However, in studying people at work, drawing on a variety of traditions can help to increase the depth and breadth of knowledge about an issue.

Table 1.1   Key characteristics of five theoretical traditions in psychology

	Behaviour	Emotion	Thinking/reasoning	Self-actualisation	The unconscious	Biologically based needs/drives	Personal change	Self-determination
Psychoanalytic (Freud)	O	✓	✗	✗	✓	✓	✗	✗
Trait	✓	✓	✓	✗	✗	✓	✗	✗
Phenomenological (Rogers)	O	✓	O	✓	O	O	✓	✓
Behaviourist (Skinner)	✓	✗	✗	✗	✗	✗	✓	✗
Social cognitive	✓	O	✓	O	O	✗	O	✓

✓ = Emphasised   O = Acknowledged but not emphasised   ✗ = De-emphasised or considered unimportant

Five traditions in psychology

The psychoanalytic tradition

This approach, also sometimes known as *psychodynamic*, was developed by Sigmund Freud (1856–1939). He developed a completely new approach to human nature which has had a great influence on many areas of pure and applied social science, literature and the arts. Perhaps in reaction to the stilted Viennese society in which he spent much of his life, Freud proposed that our psychological functioning is governed by instinctive forces (especially sex and aggression), many of which exert their effect outside our consciousness. He developed his ideas in a series of famous published works (e.g. Freud, 1960).

Freud identified three facets of the psyche:

1   The *id*: the source of instinctual energy. Prominent among those instincts are sex and aggression. The id operates on the *pleasure principle*: it wants gratification and it wants it now. It has no inhibitions, and cannot distinguish between reality and fantasy.

2   The *ego*: this seeks to channel the id impulses so that they are expressed in socially acceptable ways at socially acceptable times. It operates on the *reality principle*. It can tolerate delay, and it can distinguish between reality and fantasy. However, it cannot eliminate or block the id impulses, only steer them in certain directions.

3   The *superego*: the conscience – the source of morality. It develops during childhood and represents the internalised standards of the child's parents. It defines ideal standards and operates on the principle of *perfection*.

According to Freud, these parts of the psyche are in inevitable and perpetual conflict. Much of the conflict is unconscious. Indeed, Freud's concept of the psyche has often been likened to an iceberg, of which two-thirds is under water (unconscious) and one-third above water (conscious). When conflicts get out of hand we experience anxiety, though often we cannot say *why* we feel anxious.

Because anxiety is unpleasant, people try to avoid it. One way to do this is to distort reality and push unwelcome facts out of consciousness. Freud proposed a number of *defence mechanisms* that accomplish this. For example, *projection* occurs when we see in other people what we do not like in ourselves. It is easier to cope with righteous indignation about somebody else's faults than to come to terms with our own. *Denial* is when we pretend things are not as they really are.

Defence mechanisms consume energy, and impair realism. They therefore detract from a person's capacity to live a full life. When asked what a psychologically healthy person should be able to do, Freud replied 'love and work'. Even many people who have little time for his general approach regard this as a valid point.

For Freud, the key to understanding a person is to uncover unconscious conflicts. Most of these have their origins in childhood and are very difficult to change. They are revealed most clearly when the person's guard is down – for example, in dreams or in apparently accidental slips of the tongue ('Freudian slips') where the person expresses what they *really* feel. Freud believed that virtually no behaviour is truly accidental, but that people can rarely account for it accurately. Some psychologists working from other perspectives in psychology would agree that people cannot report accurately the causes of their own behaviour (Nisbett and Wilson, 1977). If correct, this would make a mockery of current work psychology, much of which is based on self-reports (e.g. using questionnaires, *see* Chapter 2) which are taken more or less at face value. Fortunately, there are research methods that allow us to examine the quality of self-report data.

Key Learning Point

The psychoanalytic tradition places a high emphasis on unconscious psychological conflicts which can reduce personal effectiveness at work.

Some psychologists who initially followed Freud subsequently broke away from him, though they remained within the psychoanalytic school of thought. Their biggest quarrels with Freud were that the drives he proposed were too few and too negative, and that the ego was more powerful than he gave it credit for. They tended to place greater emphasis than Freud on social behaviour, and believed that strivings for ideals reflect something more noble than rationalisation of instincts. Perhaps the best known of these post-Freudian psychoanalytic psychologists is Carl Jung. He extended the concept of the unconscious to include the *collective unconscious* as well as the personal unconscious. Jung saw the collective unconscious as an inherited foundation of personality. It contains images that have never been in consciousness such as God, the wise old person and the young hero. Jung (1933) also examined the ways in which different people relate to the world. He distinguished between *introversion* (a tendency to reflect on one's own experiences) and *extroversion* (a preference for social contact). He identified *sensing, intuition, feeling* and *thinking* as other ways of experiencing the world. Some of these concepts have been taken up in trait-based approaches to personality (*see* next section and Chapter 3).

Within psychology as a whole, the psychoanalytic school of thought lost its earlier domination around the 1950s, and has never regained it. Critics complain that it is highly interpretative, incapable of being proved or disproved, and therefore unscientific. They argue that Freud was a product of his time (but aren't we all?), and was over-influenced by hang-ups about sex. Many also claim that he does not account for women's psychological functioning nearly as well as men's.

Nevertheless, the psychoanalytic approach is far from dead. Freudian terms and concepts (e.g. defence mechanisms) have found their way into common parlance, and some psychologists have used psychoanalytic concepts in the world of work. Much work of this kind seeks to demonstrate that individual and collective behaviour in business is not driven by straightforward pursuit of profit but by the conflicts, defence mechanisms and personal concerns of the people involved. For example, Schneider and Dunbar (1992) analysed media coverage of hostile takeover bids, where one business makes an unwelcome attempt to take over another one. They identified several different themes in media accounts of these events (e.g. growth, control, dominance and synergy) and related these to developmental themes identified by psychoanalytic psychologists, including dependency, control, mastery and intimacy. Also, Vince (2002) applies psychoanalytic ideas to the ways in which major organisational change was understood and managed in a large company.

The psychoanalytic tradition tries to explain why behaviour at work can often seem irrational, hostile or self-defeating.

The trait tradition

This approach is essentially concerned with measuring a person's psychological characteristics. These characteristics, which include intellectual functioning, are generally assumed to be quite stable. That is, a person's personality is unlikely to change much, especially during adulthood (McCrae and Costa, 1990). Some theorists have developed personality types, or 'pigeonholes', in which any individual can be placed. One good example dates back to ancient Greek times when Hippocrates wrote of four types: phlegmatic (calm); choleric (quick-tempered); sanguine (cheerful, optimistic); and melancholic (sad, depressed).

These days psychologists more often think in terms of traits than types. A trait is an underlying dimension along which people differ one from another. Hence rather than putting people into a pigeonhole, trait theorists place them on a continuum, or rather a number of continua. Trait psychologists such as Eysenck (1967) and Cattell (1965) did pioneering work by identifying specific traits through much careful experimental and statistical investigation. Some of this work is covered in more detail in Chapter 3. Favoured assessment devices of trait psychology are personality questionnaires, which consist of a number of questions about people's behaviour, thoughts and emotions. The better questionnaires are painstakingly developed to ensure that the questions are clear and responses to them are stable over short and medium time periods (*see also* Chapters 3 and 4). Of course, ideally one would collect information about a person's actual behaviour rather than *reports* of their behaviour. Indeed, Cattell among others did just this. However, normally that would be too time-consuming. Personality questionnaires are the best alternative and are used quite extensively in selection and assessment at work.

Most trait psychologists argue that the same traits are relevant to everyone, though for any individual some traits (usually those on which they have extreme scores) will be more evident than others in their behaviour. However, some trait psychologists have taken a rather more flexible approach. Allport (1937) long ago argued that for any given person, certain traits may be *cardinal* (that is, pervasive across all situations), *primary* (evident in many situations) or *secondary* (evident only in certain quite restricted situations). So if we wanted to predict a person's behaviour, it would be important to identify their cardinal traits. These traits would be different for different people.

In recent years there has been a growing consensus among trait theorists that there are five fundamental dimensions of personality – the so-called 'Big Five' or five-factor model (FFM) (Digman, 1990; *see also* Chapter 3). These are:

1   extroversion, e.g. sociability, assertiveness;

2   emotionality, e.g. anxiety, insecurity;

3   agreeableness, e.g. conforming, helpful to others;

4 conscientiousness, e.g. persistent, organised;

5 openness to experience, e.g. curiosity, aesthetic appreciation.

Key Learning Point

Recent research by trait theorists suggests that there are five fundamental personality dimensions.

Most advocates of the trait approach argue that traits are at least partly genetically determined, which is one reason why they are stable. Research comparing the personalities of identical and non-identical twins tends to support this conclusion, though it is very difficult to separate the effects of environment from those of genes. About one-quarter of the variation in personality seems to be due to genetic factors (Bouchard and McGue, 1990). This of course means that three-quarters of the variation is due to other factors.

Trait theory carries the danger of circularity. Advocates of behaviourism (see the section after next) have always been keen to point this out. How do we know somebody scores high on a particular personality trait? Because they behave in a certain way. Why does the person behave in that way? Because they score high on that personality trait. Behaviour is therefore taken as a sign of certain traits, which is all very well so long as the underlying traits not only exist but also determine behaviour. However, there is also plenty of evidence that situations, as well as personality, influence behaviour (see Cervone and Mischel, 2002). In situations where social rules are strict and widely understood, personality will influence behaviour less than in unstructured situations that lack clearly defined codes of behaviour. For example, in selection interviews usually the candidate must answer questions fully, and avoid interrupting the interviewer. Thus the demands of this situation dictate the candidate's behaviour to a considerable extent. This makes it difficult for the interviewer to make inferences about the candidate's personality.

In spite of such caveats, the trait tradition has had a great influence in work psychology. This is particularly evident in selection (*see* Chapters 4 and 5) and vocational guidance (*see* Chapter 15), where the aim is to match individuals to work they will enjoy and in which they will work effectively. Salgado (2003), among others, has produced some evidence that people's scores on personality tests based on the FFM are linked to their work performance.

Key Learning Point

The trait tradition emphasises the importance of stable and measurable psychological differences between people which are frequently reflected in their work behaviour.

Large sums of money are spent on the development and marketing of personality measures such as the NEO PI-R (published in the UK by Hogrefe), the 16PF (Oxford Psychologists Press; *see also* Cattell and Cattell, 1995), The Hogan Personality Inventory (PCL Ltd.) and the Occupational Personality Questionnaires (Saville and Holdsworth Ltd). The last was developed specifically for use in work settings by the British consultancy firm Saville and Holdsworth with the backing of many large organisations. Such ventures testify to the continuing prominence of the trait approach in work psychology.

The phenomenological tradition

Phenomenology concentrates on how people experience the world around them. It emphasises our capacity to construct our own meaning from our experiences (Spinelli, 1989). With roots in philosophy as well as psychology, phenomenologists assert that our experience of the world is made up of an interaction between its 'raw matter' (i.e. objects) and our mental faculties. Thus, for example, a piece of music exists in the sense that it consists of a series of sounds, but has meaning only when we place our own interpretation on it.

Phenomenologists argue that what appears to be objectively defined reality is in fact merely a widely agreed *interpretation* of an event. They also assert that many interpretations of events are highly individual and not widely agreed. Thus phenomenology places a high value on the integrity and sense-making of individuals. That general sentiment underlies many somewhat different perspectives that can loosely be called phenomenological. Several of these perspectives also portray the person as striving for personal growth or *self-actualisation*; that is, fulfilment of his or her potential. This optimistic variant of phenomenological theory is often called *humanism*.

A good example of humanism is provided by Carl Rogers (e.g. Rogers, 1970). He argued that if we are to fulfil our potential, we must be *open to our experience*. That is, we must recognise our true thoughts and feelings, even if they are unpalatable. Unfortunately we are often not sufficiently open to our experience. We may suppress experiences that are inconsistent with our self-concept, or that we feel are in some sense morally wrong. Rogers has argued that often we readily experience only those aspects of self that our parents approved of when we were children. Parents define *conditions of worth* – in effect, they signal to children that they will be valued and loved only if they are a certain sort of person.

For Rogers, the antidote to conditions of worth is *unconditional positive regard* (UPR). In order to become a fully functioning person, we need others to accept us as we are, 'warts and all'. This does not mean that anything goes. Rogers argues for a separation of person and behaviour, so that it is all right (indeed desirable) to say to somebody 'that was not a sensible thing to do', and if necessary punish them for it. But it is not all right to say 'you are not a sensible person', because that signals disapproval of the person, not just their behaviour. Only when people realise that their inherent worth will be accepted whatever their actions can they feel psychologically safe enough to become open to their experience. Further, since Rogers believes that people are fundamentally trustworthy, he has argued that they will not take advantage of UPR to get away with murder. Instead, UPR encourages more responsible behaviour.

Key Learning Point

The phenomenological tradition puts high emphasis on personal experience and the inherent potential of people to develop and act responsibly.

Humanism has been criticised for being naive. Certainly in the authors' experience some business/management students do not find it convincing. Social workers and others in the caring professions are, however, much more sympathetic, and so are psychology students. As far as work psychology is concerned, the basic point that people's *interpretations* of events are crucial has been heeded to some extent. Many questionnaire-based measures of people's experiences at work (for example, their supervision) have been developed (*see* Cook *et al.*, 1981). On the other hand, people's responses on such questionnaires are often taken as approximations of an objective reality rather than as a product of the individual's interpretative faculties, which rather contradicts the humanist position.

Phenomenological approaches find expression in some theories of work stress, work motivation and the design of jobs (*see* Chapter 8). The idea that people strive to express and develop themselves at work is quite a popular one, though by no means universally held. Trends in management towards empowerment of employees and total quality management (TQM) are based on the assumption that people can and will use their skills to help their organisation, not sabotage it. Phenomenology has also contributed to career development (Chapter 15). Many counsellors make extensive use of Rogers' ideas when working with clients on career decisions and other work-related issues. They work on the assumption that showing a client unconditional positive regard will allow them to bring true career interests and ambitions into consciousness. By and large, though, phenomenological approaches are not currently dominant in work psychology. Chapter 2 includes some further discussion of how phenomenological approaches can be bought to life in organisational research.

The behaviourist tradition

In its more extreme forms, behaviourism makes no inferences whatever about what is going on inside the organism. It is concerned only with observable behaviour and the conditions (situations) that elicit particular behaviours. A person, and their personality, is a set of behaviours; nothing more and nothing less. There is no need to invoke invisible concepts such as traits or defence mechanisms when what we are really interested in – behaviour – can be observed directly. A leading advocate of this position was B.F. Skinner (1904–1990) (*see*, for example, Skinner, 1971). He and other learning theorists argued that our behaviour is environmentally controlled. He used the concept of *reinforcer* to refer to any favourable outcome of behaviour. Such an outcome reinforces that behaviour, i.e. makes it more likely to occur again in a similar situation. *Punishment* is where a behaviour is followed by an unpleasant outcome. Behavioural modification (see Chapter 6) is an example of this theory being applied to the management of performance at work (although as Chapter 6 shows this is a very simplistic way of influencing human behaviour).

Behaviourists therefore argue that the behaviour a person performs (which is their personality) is behaviour that has been reinforced in the past. If a child is consistently reinforced for being polite, they will behave in a polite manner. Abnormal behaviour is the result of abnormal reinforcement. If a child's parents pay attention to them only when they misbehave, the child may learn to misbehave because parental attention is a reinforcer. Behaviour problems can also rise from *conflicts*. One is an *approach–avoidance conflict*. This occurs when a particular behaviour is associated with both reinforcement and punishment. For example, a person may find that volunteering to take on extra tasks at work is reinforced by a pay rise, but also punished by the disapproval of workmates.

The behaviourist approach to personality implies that behaviour (and therefore personality) can be changed if reinforcement changes. The introduction of a reward for arriving at work on time is likely to lead to greater frequency of staff arriving on time. This change in behaviour would *not* mean that staff had changed their position on a personality trait of punctuality or conscientiousness. Behaviourists do not believe in traits. The change would simply be the result of reinforcement.

Of course, when we ask *why* a particular outcome reinforces a particular behaviour, it becomes difficult to avoid reference to a person's internal states. We might say a person liked or wanted that outcome, and then we would probably enter a debate about *why* they liked or wanted it. Some behavioural psychologists have acknowledged the necessity of taking internal states into account, and have suggested that biologically based drives or needs are the bases for reinforcement (Hull, 1952). Skinner's reliance solely on observable behaviour may perhaps have been viable for the rats and pigeons with which he performed many of his experiments. Most psychologists these days agree that it is insufficient for human beings, though there are also some claims that Skinner made more allowance for cognitive processes than he was given credit for (Malone and Cruchon, 2001).

One interesting and controversial implication of Skinner's version of behaviourism is that we do not plan for the future, even though we talk about plans. Our behaviour is governed by what has happened to us in the past, not what might happen in the future. Although all this might sound very negative and demeaning of people, Skinner did show a real concern for the future of humanity and the planet. He also believed there were ways of organising society that could protect both human welfare and the environment, as illustrated in his novel *Walden Two* (Skinner, 1948).

Key Learning Point

Behaviourism focuses on what people do, and how rewards and punishments influence that.

A major development of behaviourist theory is *social learning* (e.g. Bandura, 1977b). This differs from traditional learning theory in a number of ways, and is one basis of the social cognitive tradition described in the next section. Briefly, advocates of social learning theory stress our capacity to learn from the reinforcements and punishments experienced by other people as well as ourselves. Other people may *model* certain behaviours, and we notice the reinforcements that follow for them. They also point out that we do not necessarily *immediately* do something that will obtain reinforcement. We may choose to delay that behaviour if we would prefer to be reinforced at some other time. In short, social learning ideas portray people as much more self-controlled and thinking than traditional behaviourist theory.

Concepts from learning and social learning have been used quite a lot in work psychology. They appear quite frequently throughout this book. In training (*see* Chapter 11), rewards can be used to reinforce the desired behaviours when trainees perform them. Trainees can also learn appropriate behaviours if they are performed (modelled) for them by a competent performer. More generally, in *organisational behaviour modification*, rewards are used to reinforce behaviours such as arriving for work on time or taking appropriate safety precautions (*see* Chapter 6). Some organisations make extensive use of *mentoring* in their career development (*see* Chapter 15), based partly on the social learning idea that the experienced mentor will model desirable behaviours that the less experienced young employee will learn. Some motivation theories (Chapter 8) draw upon social learning theory. Social learning has in recent years developed further into what is now termed social cognition (*see* next section).

The social cognitive tradition

From around the mid-1970s, psychology has become increasingly influenced by a fusion of ideas, chiefly from social psychology and cognitive psychology but also from behaviourism and to a lesser extent phenomenology. *Social cognition* focuses on how our thought processes are used to interpret social interaction and other social–psychological phenomena such as the self. There is also a recognition that our thought processes reflect the social world in which we live, as well as formal logic. As noted in the previous section, one major root of the social cognitive tradition is social learning. Advocates of social cognition see the person as motivated to understand both self and the social world in order to establish a sense of order and predictability. The existence of other people (whether or not they are actually physically present) affects the nature of thought processes.

Bandura (1986) among others has argued that although the person is partly a product of their environment (including reinforcement history), the person can also influence that environment. This is the principle of *reciprocal determinism*. It can apply to groups of people and whole societies as well as to individuals. For example, we can administer our own rewards and punishments rather than relying on the environment to do it. Thus I might decide that I will allow myself a cup of coffee when I have finished rewriting this section, and not before. The coffee becomes a self-administered reward for my work. In the process of observational learning, we notice the behaviour of other people and the reinforcement that follows, but we do not necessarily copy them even if the reinforcement is positive. Instead, we consider our own goals and our values (for example, concerning what reinforcements we most want, or what we consider acceptable behaviour) before acting.

Advocates of the social cognitive tradition also pay a great deal of attention to *information processing* (Schneider, 1991). High emphasis is placed on memory, and it is assumed that the ways in which people process information are general – that is, the same across different kinds of situation. It is assumed that how we store new information depends partly upon how our existing knowledge is structured, and that we are biased towards preserving existing cognitive structures. In other words, although we can assimilate new information, we are normally unwilling to let it change our general outlook.

Also, conceptions of self act as a filter through which information is processed. For example, we tend to process information about ourselves which is consistent with our self-concept more readily than inconsistent information. We also remember it better. Indeed the *self* is seen by some social cognitive psychologists as playing a very important regulatory role in behaviour. Our ideas about the type of person we are, and about our goals and interests (i.e. our self-concept), influence the type of situations we seek and the behaviours we choose to perform. One especially important concept here is *self-efficacy* (Bandura, 1997), which concerns the extent to which a person believes they can perform the behaviour required in any given situation. Self-efficacy is frequently a good predictor of behaviour. People with a high sense of self-efficacy are more likely than others to set challenging goals for themselves, and to keep trying in the face of setbacks.

The *schema* is another key concept in social cognition. It is a knowledge structure that a person uses to make sense of situations. An example of a schema is a stereotype of what members of a certain group of people are like. If, for example, we believe soccer fans are violent thugs, we will interpret their behaviour accordingly, and behave towards them in certain ways. Schemas are in effect ready-made frameworks into which one's experiences can be fitted. Schemas that involve sequences of actions are termed *scripts* (Abelson, 1981). For example, we might have a script of the sequence of events we expect to happen when we enter a restaurant. Scripts guide our own behaviour and also enable us to develop expectations about the behaviour of other people in any given type of situation. Events that cannot be accommodated within our schemas and scripts are experienced as puzzling, and may lead us to revise them. This is analogous to scientists changing their theories in the light of new evidence (Kelly, 1951).

Key Learning Point

Social cognition examines the ways in which people think about and regulate themselves and their behaviour.

The impact of social cognition on work psychology has not yet been very great, though it is growing. As a general rule, work psychology is slow to incorporate new theoretical perspectives (Webster and Starbuck, 1988). This is partly because it usually takes some time to identify how new theories can be applied. In the case of social cognition, however, there is also the 'problem' that its relative complexity limits its capacity to generate straightforward 'off-the-shelf' techniques that can be applied across a range of situations.

Nevertheless, ideas from social cognition are certainly highly relevant to the world of work. In several chapters, this can be seen in the context of the way people are perceived (for example in selection and performance appraisal). In Chapters 11 and 12, the importance of self-efficacy in work settings is examined. Other work has shown how social cognitive phenomena can enhance our understanding of work behaviour. For example, Gioia and Manz (1985) argued that scripts play a key part in learning behaviour from others (vicarious learning) at work. Akgün *et al.* (2003) discuss how concepts drawn from social cognition can help us understand how whole organisations learn, as well as individuals and groups. Social cognition is becoming more prominent in work psychology, especially when coupled with social learning.

The origins of work psychology

Work psychology has at least two distinct roots within applied psychology. One resides in a pair of traditions that have often been termed 'fitting the man [sic] to the job' (FMJ) and 'fitting the job to the man [sic]' (FJM). The FMJ tradition manifests itself in employee selection, training and vocational guidance. These endeavours have in common an attempt to achieve an effective match between job and person by concentrating on the latter. The FJM tradition focuses instead on the job, and in particular the design of tasks, equipment and working conditions that suit a person's physical and psychological characteristics. You will see the influence of both approaches throughout this text.

Much early work in these traditions was undertaken in response to the demands of two world wars. In the United Kingdom, for example, there was concern about the adverse consequences of the very long hours worked in munitions factories during the First World War and again in the Second World War (Vernon, 1948). The extensive use of aircraft in the Second World War led to attempts to design cockpits that optimally fitted pilots' capacities (and as Chapter 9 shows the processes used in designing military equipment have found their way into the design of other work environments). In both the United Kingdom and the United States, the First World War highlighted the need to develop methods of screening people so that only those suitable for a post were selected for it. This need was met through the development of tests of ability and personality. One major source of such work in the United Kingdom was the National Institute of Industrial Psychology (NIIP), which was established in 1921 by the influential psychologist C.S. Myers and a business colleague named H.J. Welch, and survived in various forms until 1977. The brief of the NIIP was 'to promote and encourage the practical application of the sciences of psychology and physiology to commerce and industry by any means that may be found practicable'. The UK Civil Service began to employ a considerable number of psychologists after the Second World War. Their brief was, and largely still is, to improve civil service procedures, particularly in selection and training. Especially in the 1960s and 1970s, some other large organisations also employed psychologists. Organisational and labour market trends since the 1980s have reduced the proportion of work psychologists employed in large organisations, and increased the proportion who are self-employed or employed by small consultancy firms.

Key Learning Point

Two important traditions in work psychology concern how jobs can be fitted to people and how people can be fitted to jobs.

The FMJ and FJM traditions essentially concern the relationship between individuals and their work. The other root of work psychology can be loosely labelled *human relations* (HR). It is concerned with the complex interplay between individuals, groups, organisations and work. It therefore emphasises social factors at work much more than FMJ and FJM. The importance of human relations was highlighted in some famous research now known as the *Hawthorne studies*. These were conducted in the 1920s at a large factory of the Western Electric Company at Hawthorne, near Chicago, USA. The studies were reported most fully in Roethlisberger and Dickson (1939). Originally, they were designed to assess the effect of level of illumination on productivity. One group of workers (the experimental group) was subjected to changes in illumination, while another (the control group) was not. The productivity of both groups increased slowly during this investigation; only when illumination was at a small fraction of its original level did the productivity of the experimental group begin to decline. These strange results suggested that other factors apart from illumination were determining productivity.

This work was followed up with what became known as the *relay assembly test room study*. A small group of female assembly workers was taken from the large department, and stationed in a separate room so that working conditions could be controlled effectively. Over a period of more than a year, changes were made in the length of the working day and working week, the length and timing of rest pauses, and other aspects of the work context. Productivity increased after every change, and the gains were maintained even after all conditions returned to their original levels.

Why did these results occur? Clearly, factors other than those deliberately manipulated by the researchers were responsible. For example, the researchers had allowed the workers certain privileges at work, and had taken a close interest in the group. Hence some factor probably to do with feeling special, or guessing what the researchers were investigating, seemed to be influencing the workers' behaviour. The problem of people's behaviour being affected by the knowledge that they are being researched has come to be called the *Hawthorne effect*. The more general lessons here are: (i) it is difficult to experiment with people without altering some conditions other than those intended and (ii) people's behaviour is substantially affected by *their interpretation* of what is happening around them (Adair, 1984).

These conclusions were extended by a study of a group of male workers who wired up equipment in the bank wiring room. A researcher sat in the corner and observed the group's activities. At first this generated considerable suspicion, but apparently after a time the men more or less forgot about the researcher's presence. Once this happened, certain phenomena became apparent. First, there were social *norms*; that is, shared ideas about how things should be. Most importantly, there was a norm about what constituted an appropriate level of production. This was high enough to keep management off the men's backs, but less than they were capable of. Workers who either consistently exceeded the productivity norm or fell short of it were subjected to social pressure to conform. Another norm concerned supervisors' behaviour. Supervisors were expected to be friendly and informal with the men: one who was more formal and officious was strongly disapproved of. Finally, there were two informal groups in the room, with some rivalry between them.

The bank wiring room showed clearly how social relationships between workers were important determinants of work behaviour. These relationships were often more influential than either official company policy or monetary rewards.

Key Learning Point

The human relations tradition in work psychology emphasises individuals' experiences and interpretations at work.

Highhouse (1999) has argued that one outcome of the Hawthorne studies was a huge increase in the use of personal counselling in American workplaces during the middle part of the twentieth century. This included Hawthorne itself, where in 1941 55 counsellors served 21,000 workers. The idea was that counsellors were available to every member of the workforce, and indeed would often circulate amongst them. They would help employees solve personal problems, which in turn was thought to lead to an increase in their productivity. However, Highhouse also notes that personal counselling had virtually disappeared from workplaces by the 1960s. He identified several reasons for this. Some of them reflect continuing and general problems for work psychologists almost half a century later:

- It was difficult to demonstrate the contribution of counsellors to company profitability.

- Senior managers thought that counsellors were on the side of the workers.

- Trade union officials thought that counsellors were trying to win workers' loyalty to their employer.

- Counsellors were loaded with administrative work.

- Managers and supervisors were increasingly trained in human relations and could do (or thought they could do) any counselling required.

There has been much criticism of the experimental methods used by the Hawthorne researchers and considerable debate about the exact reasons for their findings. However, subsequent research by other social scientists confirmed and extended the general message that human relations matter. For example, Trist and Bamforth (1951), working in British coalmines, showed that if technology is introduced that disrupts existing social groups and relationships, then there are serious consequences for productivity, industrial relations and employee psychological well-being. Their work gave birth to the *socio-technical systems* approach to work design (*see also* Chapters 8 and 9).

Work psychology today

What is work psychology?

One source of confusion is that work psychology has a lot of different names. In the United Kingdom and the United States, the old-established term (still sometimes used) is *industrial psychology*. The newer label in the United States is *industrial/ organisational psychology* (or *I/O psychology* for short). In the United Kingdom, it is often called *occupational psychology*, but this term is uncommon in most other countries. Throughout Europe, increasing use is made of *the psychology of work and organisations* and *work and organisational psychology* to describe the area. Just to confuse things further, some specific parts of the field are given labels such as *vocational psychology*, *managerial psychology* and *personnel psychology*. Meanwhile, there are also some bigger areas of study to which psychology contributes greatly. These include *organisational behaviour* and *human resource management*.

Our advice for the confused reader is: don't panic! The differences between these labels do mean something to some people who work in the field, but should not unduly worry most of us. The main distinction mirrors that made in the earlier section between individually oriented versus group- or organisation-oriented topics. In the United Kingdom, the label 'occupational psychology' is most commonly applied to the first, and 'organisational psychology' to the second (Blackler, 1982), but many psychologists in the workplace regularly cross this rather artificial boundary. We use the term *work psychology* because of its simplicity, and because to us it encompasses both the individual and organisational levels of analysis.

A reading of this chapter so far should have given the reader a reasonable idea of what work psychology is. In order to be more specific, we now list eight areas (or knowledge dimensions) in which work psychologists operate as teachers, researchers and consultants. This list is adapted from information about the Qualification in Occupational Psychology published on the British Psychological Society website (http://www.bps.org.uk).

1   *Personnel selection and assessment*: for all types of job by a variety of methods, including tests and interviews.

2   *Training*: identification of training needs and the design, delivery and evaluation of training.

3   *Performance appraisal and career development*: identification of key aspects of job performance; design of systems for accurate performance assessment and development; training in the use of appraisal and development interventions such as personal development plans.

4   *Organisational development and change*: analysis of systems and relationships, leadership and negotiation skills; analysis and change of organisational culture and/or climate.

5   *Human–machine interaction*: analysis and design of work equipment and environments to fit human physical and cognitive capabilities.

6   *Counselling and personal development*: techniques of listening and counselling regarding work- and career-related issues; assessment and analysis of people's career interests and aspirations.

7   *Design of environments and work – health and safety*: the assessment of existing and preferred features of the environment such as light levels, workspace positioning and sources of danger, risk or stress.

8   *Employee relations and motivation*: allocation and design of jobs that are as motivating and satisfying as possible; team-building; negotiating and bargaining; techniques for analysing and improving inter-group relations.

These are the content areas of work psychology. It is also expected that qualified work psychologists will not only know about these areas, but also possess generic skills such as questionnaire design, interviewing, report writing, presentation skills and data analysis methods that they have developed when using their knowledge. In addition in several of these areas they need to have substantial experience of conducting problem diagnoses, research, consultancy, intervention, evaluation and be able to deliver training.

Key Learning Point

Work psychology concerns all aspects of human behaviour, thoughts, feelings and experiences concerning work.

The qualifications and roles of work psychologists

How can one tell whether somebody who claims to be a work psychologist is in fact appropriately qualified? In the United Kingdom, the British Psychological Society (BPS) oversees the professional practice of psychologists. To become a Chartered Psychologist (C. Psychol.) a person must possess not only an approved degree in psychology (or the equivalent), but also several years of appropriate specialist postgraduate training and/or work experience. It is also possible to be a Chartered *Occupational* Psychologist, though some people who could become one prefer to stick with the generic C. Psychol. To be a Chartered Occupational Psychologist, a person must be eligible for full membership of the Division of Occupational Psychology of the BPS. This means obtaining the Qualification in Occupational Psychology (QOccPsych). To obtain the QOccPsych requires *practical expertise* and both breadth and depth of experience in several of the areas listed above – *knowledge* is not enough. Certain tests of ability and personality can be administered only by Chartered Psychologists or (in some cases) by people who have been awarded a Certificate of Competence in Occupational Testing after training from a Chartered Psychologist. In August 2009 in the UK the Health Professions Council began to keep the register of psychologists in the UK. As a consequence of this, the title of Occupational Psychologist is now protected in law in the UK, meaning that only appropriately qualified persons can use the title *occupational psychologist*.

Chartered Psychologists and Chartered Occupational Psychologists in the UK are bound by BPS ethical guidelines and disciplinary procedures. Information on all of these matters, including lists of Chartered Psychologists, can be obtained from the BPS via their website.

The ethical code of conduct produced by the BPS (British Psychological Society, 2006) covers a range of topics. They include the ways in which work psychologists are allowed to advertise their services, guidelines for the use of non-sexist language, and guidelines on conduct in professional practice and in psychological research. The code of conduct requires practising psychologists to be guided by four principles:

1　*Respect*: Psychologists value the dignity and worth of all persons, with sensitivity to the dynamics of perceived authority or influence over clients, and with particular regard to people's rights including those of privacy and self-determination.

2　*Competence*: Psychologists value the continuing development and maintenance of high standards of competence in their professional work, and the importance of preserving their ability to function optimally within the recognised limits of their knowledge, skill, training, education and experience.

3　*Responsibility*: Psychologists value their responsibilities to clients, to the general public and to the profession and science of psychology, including the avoidance of harm and the prevention of misuse or abuse of their contributions to society.

4　*Integrity*: Psychologists value honesty, accuracy, clarity, and fairness in their interactions with all persons, and seek to promote integrity in all facets of their scientific and professional endeavours.

From *BPS Code of Ethics and Conduct* (2006)

In practical terms, this means that psychologists are required to consider, amongst other things, the following:

- *Consent*: those who participate in the research should normally be made aware beforehand of all aspects of it that might reasonably be expected to influence their willingness to participate.

- *Deception*: deception of those who participate in the research should be avoided wherever possible. If deception is necessary for the effective conduct of the research, it should not be the cause of significant distress when participants are debriefed afterwards.

- *Debriefing*: after participation, the participants should be given any information and other support necessary to complete their understanding of the research, and to avoid any sense of unease their participation might have engendered.

- *Withdrawal from the investigation*: the psychologist should tell participants of their right to withdraw from the research.

- *Confidentiality*: subject to the requirements of legislation, including (in the United Kingdom) the Data Protection Act, information obtained about a participant is confidential unless agreed otherwise in advance. This is in some ways especially important in work psychology where, for example, a senior member of an organisation may put pressure on the researcher to reveal what a junior member has said.

- *Protection of participants*: the investigator must protect participants from physical and mental harm during the investigation. The risk of harm should normally be no greater than that posed by the participant's normal lifestyle.

Key Learning Point

Work psychologists are required to demonstrate their academic and practical competence, and also to adhere to ethical principles. This is partly to protect the rights and well-being of people who pay for their services and/or participate in their research.

Whatever country they live in, work psychologists can be teachers, researchers and consultants. Many are found in academic institutions, where they tend to engage in all three activities, especially of course the first two. Shimmin and Wallis (1994), among others, have noted that work psychologists in academia are now much more often employed in departments of business and management than in departments of psychology. This reflects both a tendency for work psychology to be used primarily to achieve management goals, and a mixing of psychology with other disciplines in a subject that has come to be called organisational behaviour (OB). Other work psychologists operate as independent consultants, advising organisations and individuals who seek their services on a fee-paying basis. There are also some specialist firms of psychologists and/or management consultants. Some psychologists are employed full-time by such firms. Others work for them on an occasional basis as independent associates. Still other psychologists are employed by larger organisations to give specialist advice, in effect acting as internal consultants.

In the UK, the Civil Service, the armed forces and the postal and telecommunications industries have been prominent in this regard.

Another issue concerns the influence of work psychologists on organisations which purchase their services. Many tend to see themselves as technical experts (Blackler and Brown, 1986), able to advise on the detail of specific procedures – for example, psychometric tests, stress management training, ergonomics and so on. On the other hand, human resource managers are attempting to play an increasingly central and strategic role in their organisations. If work psychologists are to influence organisational functioning, they need to move away from a technical specialist role toward that of a general business consultant (Anderson and Prutton, 1993). They must understand the organisational impact of their techniques, be able to work on 'macro' issues such as organisational change and human resource planning, and be able to demonstrate the likely financial impact of their recommendations. They must be able to speak the language of business, and to communicate with a wide range of people. They need to be open to new ideas and techniques, including those originating outside psychology (Offermmann and Gowing, 1990). They need to recognise the politics of doing work psychology – that is, the power relationships between individuals and organisations involved in it. Regarding research, this means being able to 'sell' a research proposal so that practical benefits for the potential sponsoring organisation are apparent (and exceed the costs), to be prepared to negotiate and renegotiate on how the research will be conducted, and to develop and maintain contacts within the organisation. All of this must be done without contravening the ethical guidelines described earlier. Some would, however, argue that ethical and practical issues go deeper than this. Who, exactly, is the psychologist working for? Many see occupational psychologists as working partners with senior managers. Effectiveness and efficiency (concepts related to profitability) are often seen as the key deliverables of an occupational psychologist's work (rather than, for example, employee satisfaction). This is *not* to argue that psychologists' intentions and effects are malign, only that their agendas are often most heavily influenced by concerns that might be described as managerial.

Reading about work psychology

Where can one find out about advances in work psychology? Some can be found in books. General texts such as this give a necessarily brief account of major developments. Other specialist books are devoted to particular topics and sometimes even to particular theories. Many new theoretical developments, and also tests of established theories, can be found in certain academic journals. Leading journals of work psychology include *Journal of Occupational and Organizational Psychology* (published in the UK), *Journal of Applied Psychology* (USA), *Journal of Occupational Health Psychology* (USA), *Journal of Organizational Behavior* (USA/UK), *Applied Psychology: An International Review* (The International Association of Applied Psychology), *Organizational Behavior and Human Decision Processes* (USA), *Personnel Psychology* (USA), *Human Relations* (UK), *Work and Stress* (EU) and *Journal of Vocational Behavior* (USA). There are also other prestigious journals which include work psychology along with other disciplines applied to work behaviour. These include *Academy of Management Journal* (USA), *Academy of Management Review* (USA), *Administrative Science Quarterly* (USA), *Organizational Research Methods* (USA) and *Journal of Management Studies* (UK). Some other journals concentrate more on the concerns of practitioners; that is, people who earn their living by supplying work psychology to organisations (e.g. *The Industrial–Organizational Psychologist* [USA]).

This is a long list of journals, and plenty more could be added to it, but there are subtle differences among journals in content and approach, which soon become evident to the observant reader. This makes information search easier if one has carefully defined the topic one wishes to explore. Also, online literature searches can be accomplished through databases such as ISI Web of Knowledge, PsychInfo, IngentaConnect and EBSCO. Electronic searches have helped to make the quest for knowledge much quicker and less tedious. Most of the journals listed above publish reports of carefully designed evaluations of theories or psychological techniques. They also publish review articles summarising the current position and perhaps proposing new directions: recent reviews can be an excellent starting point for those wishing to know more about a particular topic.

Sometimes people feel that when they read about psychology (including work psychology) what they get is common sense dressed up with jargon. Indeed, one of the better jokes about psychologists is that they tell you what you already know, in words that you do not understand. Like most good jokes, it has a grain of truth – but only a grain. To see why, let us look a little more at the notion of common sense.

Common sense is sometimes expressed in proverbs such as 'look before you leap'. Yes, one says, that is common sense – after all, it would be stupid to proceed with something without checking first to see if it was wise. But the reader may already have called to mind another proverb: 'He who hesitates is lost'. Well, yes, that is common sense too. After all, in this life we must take our chances when they come, otherwise they will pass us by. This example illustrates an important characteristic of common sense: it can be contradictory. Interestingly, one research study found that students sometimes endorsed pairs of contradictory proverbs of this kind as both having high 'truth value' (Halvor Teigen, 1986). And so they should. Both *are* true – sometimes, and in some circumstances. Psychologists are in the business of working out when, and in what circumstances. For example, when do high levels of job demands become a problem and for whom, and under what circumstances? Even so, psychologists' claims about common sense can sometimes undermine their credibility. Kluger and Tikochinsky (2001) suggest that, over the years, psychologists have often too readily claimed that their research findings on specific topics contradict common sense, only to find later that they have over-generalised from the results of a single study.

Key Learning Point

Work psychology seeks to go beyond 'common-sense' views of work behaviour, thoughts and feelings.

Because most research, training and consultancy in organisations are paid for by senior managers, it is likely that the agenda will be driven by their perspectives and priorities. Obtaining the informed consent of people at lower levels of the organisation does not really get round that reality. An alternative is to work only on behalf of individuals or groups and communities with low power and resources. Decisions such as this have obvious links with the psychologist's own values and political stance, and equally obvious consequences for the level of financial rewards they enjoy. Most work psychologists take the view that usually organisations are sufficiently unitarist (that is, united in objectives and values) to permit all constituencies within them to gain from the psychologist's interventions, or at least not lose. Some might argue that this is a convenient assumption, as opposed to a carefully considered and justified position, and that ensuring that a person or group is not harmed by the work psychologist's activities is not the same as actively working for their interests.

Key Learning Point

Many work psychologists wish to influence top managers, but they may be seen as technicians, not strategists. Also, it is important for the work psychologist to consider their impact on all parties, not just senior managers.

The changing world of work

Workplace trends

It is probably true to say that nobody has ever lived at a time when they felt that not very much was happening or changing in their world. At the time of writing, many economies are emerging from a recession that was a result of the turmoil in the global money markets. This has had a major impact on almost every organisation as credit or demand for products and services slows. No doubt this changes the agenda for work psychologists as organisations cut back on initiatives that are seen as desirable rather than essential. This may place even more onus on practitioners to demonstrate their worth to organisations while – or most likely before – they win contracts for their work. There may be a shift of emphasis away from employee welfare issues to more performance- and productivity-related issues. In such circumstances it is easy to overestimate the impact that these changes might have on what work psychologists actually do. However, as Donaldson-Feilder (2009) points out, economic difficulty can strengthen the case for interventions that might not otherwise be perceived by management as essential. Donaldson-Feilder argues that there are three reasons why there is a stronger case for focusing on staff well-being during a financial downturn:

1   Because the need to save money and enhance performance is greater, organisations need to pay greater attention to issues such as improving employee engagement, reducing staff turnover (so that they do not lose good staff), improving employee performance, enhancing teamworking, cutting absence, etc. The argument is that if these issues are properly dealth with then the organisation is better placed to grow in a challenging environment.

2   The risks to employee well-being are higher so more attention needs to be paid to 'people issues'. Employees may have more fear for their own jobs, they may experience negative emotions when they see colleagues being made redundant, they may have more work to deal with and their traditional support networks in the workplace may be disrupted.

3   When the upturn comes, organisations need to be a strong position to capitalise on the opportunities that this will offer. By putting effort into managing staff well-being companies are more likely to have an engaged, committed, healthy, creative and productive workforce ready to exploit new opportunities. This last argument also points to the importance of continued employee training and development – which is often one of the first victims when severe financial pressures occur.

Even without seismic economic events, there is a lot of consensus that the last part of the twentieth century saw some quite radical changes in the nature of work, and that these are continuing in the early part of the twenty-first century (Sparrow, 2003). Many of these changes arise from a combination of technological advances and economic trends, which themselves go hand in hand to some extent. Improved communication and information technologies mean that, for example, it is now much easier than it used to be to work away from a physical location yet still keep in touch with what is going on. In response to this, Chapter 10 of this text focuses on the issues generated by technology-mediated communication. Some companies now provide customer services from call centres in countries far away from their main markets. This can bring some problems, such as when the call centre staff perhaps do not know enough about the culture and people of the country or countries they are dealing with, but nevertheless moves of this kind are happening and may well continue (Batt, 2000). For some time, many companies have been reducing their workforces, partly by outsourcing functions such as catering, premises security and sometimes human resources, IT and other functions too. In some companies (though by no means all), only staff who are core to the company's business have full-time employment contracts with the company. Others come and go, often employed short-term via an agency or as independent contractors. The psychological contract that companies have with their employees is very different as a result of some of these changes (see Chapter 7).

A longer-term trend is the relocation of manufacturing operations from developed countries to developing ones where wages are lower. This means the export of some jobs (predominantly, but not only, relatively low-skilled work) from rich countries to poorer ones. In order to find ways of competing, governments and companies in northern and western Europe, Japan, Australasia and North America are emphasising both cost-cutting and the need to stay ahead of the game in advanced skills and knowledge. Again in order to cut costs and improve performance, some Western governments have privatised some public services and industries. These changes have led to what is sometimes referred to as the intensification of work in the developed countries: increasing work hours and pressure, the need for lifelong learning, the ability and willingness to change the type of work one does, perhaps several times in one career (Delbridge *et al.*, 1992). Some people who during the middle-to-late part of the twentieth century were able to jog along in seemingly secure jobs without much need to change or work very hard, now find themselves in a far less comfortable position (*see also* Chapter 15, on careers). It is important to recognise that these changed demands can have both positive and negative effects (see Chapters 8 and 12).

In many developed countries there are also changes in the working population brought about by demographic patterns. For example, for some years there have been trends toward smaller families which means that now there are relatively small numbers of people starting work and in early career than there were in some earlier times, and more people are working past retirement age (Office for National Statistics, 2009a). Hence the average age of the working population is increasing. Life expectancy is also on the rise in most of the developed countries. This may

necessitate increases in the retirement age (how lucky we are!) and changes in pension provision in order to ensure that economies produce enough wealth to remain competitive while also sustaining social care.

Other changes to working populations arise from changing views about the rights and roles of various groups within societies. Often these views are backed up with legislation to try to ensure that those rights are upheld. During nearly all of the twentieth century many countries saw sustained moves towards equality of provision and treatment for men and women. Many would argue that there is still a long way to go on that score, but it is equally clear that big changes have occurred, at least in terms of what people are doing with their lives. For example, in the United Kingdom in 1971 less than 60 per cent of women were economically active; in 2008 it was nearer 70 per cent (Office for National Statistics, 2009b). This change has several interrelated causes, including many women's wish to be employed, changing expectations about the roles of women in society, the introduction of legislation to promote equal opportunities, maternity leave (etc.), a wish for higher material standards of living for households, and a realisation in many organisations that competitiveness depends on having the right people in the right jobs, whatever their gender (Cassell, 2000). Less optimistically, there is still a clear tendency for women to be segregated in certain kinds of work (e.g. caring, teaching, secretarial), and for their work to be paid less (by about 17 per cent according to the UK Labour Force Survey, 2007). Commenting on these figures in 2007, the CIPD's chief economist expressed concern that the narrowing of the gender pay gap had 'stalled'. This suggests that although progress has been made, there is still some way to go, even to conform to legislation, let alone to transform social attitudes. At the same time, there is also concern that the role of home-maker (whether a woman or a man) should be recognised as valuable, and definitely not an easy ride. There is perhaps a danger that admiration for people who can make a success of dual-career family life makes home-makers feel like second class citizens.

Gender is not the only basis for potential discrimination. Most countries have quite ethnically diverse populations. There are numerous statistics and specific incidents that show clearly how people with ethnic minority affiliations tend to get a raw deal in the labour market. Legislation to promote equality of opportunity has been introduced of course, and strong cases have been made for the value to organisations of having a diverse workforce (Kandola and Fullerton, 1994). These measures have arguably reduced bias against people with ethnic minority affiliations, but they have not eliminated it. The issues underlying this are complex, and include not just overt prejudice, but also more subtle phenomena of social perception of individuals and groups (*see also* Chapter 13).

Another potential basis for discrimination is disability, and again many countries now have legislation to protect and promote the rights of people with a disability to live a full life, including in employment where possible. Attitudes towards people with a disability have moved away somewhat from a so-called medical model of illness and lifelong child-like dependence (Oliver, 1990). This attitude was illustrated by the saying 'does he take sugar?' which was allegedly a question asked frequently by a well-meaning but insensitive tea-maker to an able-bodied person accompanying a person with a disability, even though that person was well able to answer for themselves. Indeed, it became the title of a long-running UK radio programme about issues to do with disability. In recent years there has been a shift towards recognising that people with a disability are, in many respects, just as able to do worthwhile work as anybody else, and sometimes more so. In many countries, legislation now puts an onus on workplaces and educational institutions to take on and then cater properly for people with a disability, even though this may mean some additional

cost and inconvenience in providing appropriate equipment and adjustments to physical layout. Again, though, much depends on how individuals (especially those who have power in a workplace) perceive people with a disability.

Key Learning Point

The world of work is changing rapidly because of technological advances, global competition, and societal demographic and cultural trends. Work psychology can examine the human consequences of these changes, and in many areas is already doing so.

Workplace trends and work psychology

Work psychology formed and rapidly developed as a discipline and profession before most of the economic and technological trends described above became apparent, and before some of the population and cultural changes described above had gained full momentum. Also, we have already noted in this chapter that work psychology tends to ask whether the techniques being used to manage people at work, and/or their implementation, are effective in enhancing productivity and/or satisfaction (a managerial perspective). There is little investigation of the wider power relations and control mechanisms of the workplace, or asking whether these should change. Some argue that all this is readily apparent in the way that work psychologists carry out and report their research, even when that research concerns the changes in the workplace noted above (Legge, 2003). It is probably true that work psychology has some historical baggage arising from its development in workplaces which were:

- predominantly male;

- predominantly large organisations;

- concerned with manufacturing more than service provision (although this seems to be changing quite quickly as service industry grows and manufacturing industry shrinks within many developed economies);

- relatively ethnically homogeneous, and located in rich countries (especially the United States);

- populated by people with full-time permanent employment contracts;

- characterised by clear and stable structures and practices.

Nevertheless, there is no doubt that many work psychologists have been keen to investigate the consequences of some of the workplace changes described above. This is shown by the number of articles on (for example) advanced manufacturing technology, virtual working, work–life balance, agency workers, the psychological contract and women in management, among other topics. However, the changing nature of the workplace implies wide and deep changes of emphasis across most areas of work psychology. In Table 1.2 we note some of the world of work changes and suggest some consequences for what are, or should be, hot topics within work

Table 1.2	World of work changes and their implications for work psychology

World of work changes	Implications for work psychology (i.e. topics of increasing importance)
Ageing working population	Learning, performance, satisfaction and engagement with work of older people
Increasing labour market participation and equality for historically disadvantaged groups, including ethnic minorities and people with a disability	Further development of fair selection procedures; the work experiences of members of disadvantaged groups; impact of diversity on workplaces and organisational performance; diversity policies; inter-group relations at work
Increasing workloads for people in work	Stress and pressure at work; burnout and mental health; balance between work and other aspects of life; effects of workload on thinking and behaviour
More people working remotely (e.g. at home) using information and communication technologies (ICT)	Selection of people suited to home working; supervision and leadership of people not physically present; impact of isolation on work performance and satisfaction; effective virtual communication and teamwork; recruitment and selection via the Internet
Pressures on organisations both to cut costs and to use knowledge well	Impact of these competing pressures (including new technology) on the design of jobs; organisational learning and knowledge management; stress and pressure at work; innovation and creativity; organisational change
Downsized, delayered and outsourced organisations	Fewer and more ambiguous organisational career paths; individual coping with change and uncertainty; relations between 'core' and 'peripheral' workers; working life in small organisations; entrepreneurship
(Slow) increase in women's participation in traditionally male-dominated high-status work	The experience of being a woman in a man's world; gender stereotypes; women's career success, rewards and costs relative to men's; 'feminine' ways of working
Reduction in availability of manual work; growth of low-skill service sector jobs; growing divide between those with marketable skills and qualifications and those without	The psychological and societal impact of income and wealth differences; the experience and consequences of unemployment and underemployment
Increasing internationalisation of organisations and markets	Cross-cultural comparisons of workplaces; working abroad; interpersonal and intercultural influence; the appropriateness of selection, etc. procedures across cultures

psychology. Without highlighting them using 'bells and whistles' throughout this text, you will notice that research and practice of direct relevance to these issues can be found throughout this textbook.

Changes in workplace technology

Many people adopt a fairly fatalistic approach to technology, feeling they have to adapt to the new and different demands placed on them by it. One of the best-known examples of how technology has changed work is call centres. These have been defined by Holman (2003, p. 116), drawing on the Health and Safety Executive (1999), as a work environment in which the main business is mediated by computer and telephone-based technologies that enable the efficient distribution of incoming calls (or allocation of outgoing calls) to available staff, and permit the use of display-screen information when customer–employee calls are in progress. Worries have been expressed that call centre work is likely to be alienating because it is designed to minimise costs and skill requirements (i.e. so-called Taylorism, *see* Chapter 8). Often the workers have to stick to a script and a call time limit, and their adherence to both is monitored closely. This can make for stressful and unfulfilling work (Holman *et al.*, 2002). However, it is also clear that it is possible to give workers more freedom about how they deal with such demands (Bond *et al.*, 2008). It is also possible to make interactions more like relationships than encounters (Gutek, 1995). Although customer resistance to this can occur when they perceive that a sales pitch is masquerading as a relationship, on the whole people (both customers and call centre workers) seem to prefer being treated as individuals rather than in a standardised way. It also seems to be possible to use monitoring systems in ways that support the development of call centre workers, rather than as a disciplinary device to catch workers who deviate from the script and/or deal with calls too slowly (Aiello and Kolb, 1995).

Thus it seems that, in call centres, the technology does not have *inevitable* consequences. It does not necessarily deskill and dehumanise people who work there. This should not surprise us, because exactly the same conclusion was drawn by work psychologists investigating the impact of changes in manufacturing technology (especially computer-controlled machine tools) in the 1970s and 1980s (Wall *et al.*, 1987). How new technology affects jobs, well-being and individual and organisational performance depends not just on how clever the technology is, but also on the motives of those who introduce it, the processes by which it is introduced, and how well it fits with existing social systems in the workplace (Blackler and Brown, 1986; Burnes, 1989). Chapter 9 of this book tackles these issues head-on by examining how the design and implementation of new technology can be best managed (using a human-centred approach to design). Blackler and Brown (1986) pointed out that companies often muddled through the implementation of new technology, and perhaps unsurprisingly the results were not always as good as had been planned. Human-centred approaches tend to produce good results because they make use of the knowledge of system operators and have the best chance of securing their commitment (because they have been consulted). Commenting on advanced manufacturing technology (AMT), Chase and Karwowski (2003) argue:

> One of the ironies of AMT is that human and organizational factors become more, not less, important . . . Of course, AMT may be implemented and used in such a way that it reduces the skill of the operators and reduces role breadth and job control. It would

appear that not only will this increase the level of employee stress, but it will not permit the efficient use of AMT. Rather, the full benefits of AMT may only be realised when accompanied by appropriate job designs that include wide job roles and high levels of operator control.

Key Learning Point

Recent research on new technology at work reinforces earlier conclusions that the introduction of new technology does not inevitably deskill jobs. However, the impact of new technology on organisational success is often less positive than anticipated because the technology is not well-suited to the psychological characteristics of individuals, nor to the patterns of social interaction in the workplace.

Some similar ideas about the importance of individual and social/cultural factors also emerge from the literature on knowledge management (KM), which has been defined by Bassi (1997) as 'the process of creating, capturing, and using knowledge to enhance organizational performance'. Given the emphasis in advanced economies on the importance of competitiveness through superior knowledge, it is not surprising that KM has attracted a lot of attention from managers. The basic idea of KM is to capture the local and tacit (i.e. unspoken, unformalised) knowledge held within an organisation, to express it in formal terms and to share it with other members of the organisation. Information technology is usually seen as a key to this endeavour, because it allows the storage, presentation and dissemination of a lot of information to a lot of people (Scarbrough, 2003). Certainly technology is no longer a barrier: company intranets are now relatively common and the advent of Web 2.0 technology enables employees to publish their work in such environments, even without the need for specialist skills. But of course it is not as simple as that. In spite of incentives or even requirements to do so, people in organisations are often reluctant to share their knowledge with all and sundry. They may see it as undermining their value to the organisation. It may run counter to organisational culture, custom and practice, which might emphasise the sharing of information in small groups of people who do similar tasks, or who have special friendships with each other (McKinlay, 2000). This is another reminder that psychological and social factors often override the impact of an IT system. Some organisations, including Shell, have tried to get round this by encouraging what are called communities of practice (see Chapter 11 for more detailed discussion of these groups). These are informal groups of people who share their learning and experience in order to learn from each other. This is likely to work well if it builds upon existing patterns of interaction between people, but less so if it forces together people who have not hitherto had much to do with each other. Of course, it might be very helpful if they did share information more, but in workplaces governed by short-term performance goals, talking to people who may or may not tell you something useful is not necessarily seen as a priority.

One of the consequences of ICTs is that people are able to work in a variety of different locations (this usually means working at home or some other remote location, and communicating and conducting other work activities using the Internet, Wi-Fi technology and increasingly sophisticated mobile telephones). There are many potential benefits of such arrangements for both individuals and employing organisations (Cascio, 2000). These include cost reduction and improved productivity for organisations, and better coordination between work and non-work lives, less commuting and greater autonomy for individuals. There may also be wider benefits, such as more community cohesion and less pollution. But there are also dangers, including less opportunity for supervision, social isolation and possible difficulties in keeping work and non-work separate. Perhaps the acid test is whether a person experiences more or fewer interruptions at home than they would in a 'normal' workplace. Estimates vary, but it seems that only very small proportions of the workforce spend significant amounts of time working at home (less than about 10 per cent in developed countries). An interesting issue is whether employers trust employees to work effectively from home. Recent surveys by the CIPD (2008a) suggest that many managers are reluctant to give employees the opportunity to work from home.

Lamond *et al.* (2003) provide a review of the literature of remote working. Among the points they make is that certain personality types may be better suited to it than others. For example, conscientious individuals (i.e. those who are inclined to take a well-organised and diligent approach to their work) may be at an even bigger advantage than when in a more traditional workplace, but Lamond *et al.* also repeatedly make the point that much depends on the exact nature of the job. Not all remote working is the same. What might be termed 'telejobs' differ in terms of:

- location – at home or elsewhere; same place or nomadic;
- the amount and sophistication of IT usage required;
- how much knowledge is required to do the work;
- how much communication is required within the organisation;
- how much communication is required outside the organisation.

Chapter 10 shows how psychology can be used to understand better the challenges that are presented by technology-mediated communication: it shows how these challenges can be better understood and dealt with.

Key Learning Point

A rapidly growing minority of employees carry out significant amounts of their work away from the office. The consequences of these changes, when made, are quite profound and complicated. Again, much depends on how managers decide to let technology change the nature of jobs.

Another technology-driven influence on the nature of work is the advent of e-business. Wright and Dyer (2001) distinguish between four aspects of e-business. First is e-commerce, which is links between businesses and customers, i.e. online marketing and selling. The customers can be individuals or other organisations. Second is the use of intranets to improve within-company integration and communication. The third aspect is supply-chain management, which involves relationships with suppliers and increasing speed of order delivery. Finally there is what they term 'integrated e-business', which is doing all of these. The more a company is into e-business, the more likely it is that some employees and contractors will have to work with sophisticated ICT, and the more likely they will get a chance to work at flexible times and locations, but need to rely more on electronic communications (see Chapter 10).

Understanding and managing workplace diversity

Ever since major civil rights legislation was enacted in the United States, the United Kingdom and many other European countries in the 1960s and 1970s, considerable attention has been devoted in work psychology to fairness in selection and other organisational procedures, especially regarding women and ethnic minorities. Work psychologists are seen (or at least, see themselves) as having a lot to offer in the systematic evaluation of techniques (such as selection interviews) and instruments (such as psychometric tests), including how to make them free from bias. Chapters 3, 4 and 5 contain more on these topics. Managers in organisations were said to be motivated to implement equal opportunities by (i) support for the ethical principle of fairness (Kandola and Fullerton, 1994) and (ii) fear of prosecution (Werner and Bolino, 1997).

From around the late 1980s onwards, however, the thinking and language began to change somewhat. The term 'managing diversity' became popular, and it still is (Cassell, 2000). The motivation for this is still partly ethical and partly to avoid prosecution, but now it is also argued that diversity is good for business, and that it makes for good publicity for the organisation.

> The basic concept of managing diversity accepts that the workforce consists of a diverse population of people. The diversity consists of visible and non-visible differences which will include sex, age, background, race, disability, personality and workstyle. It is founded on the premise that harnessing these differences will create a productive environment in which everybody feels valued, where their talents are fully utilised and in which organisational goals are met.
>
> *Kandola and Fullerton (1994, p. 19).*

Konrad (2003) provided a concise summary of the three most often cited reasons as to why paying attention to diversity is beneficial to organisations:

- The workforce is becoming more diverse, and therefore to attract and retain the best employees organisations need to recruit from all demographic groups.

- A more diverse workforce might help organisations sell to a more diverse client/customer base (especially as organisations sell their products and services in a global marketplace).

- There is evidence that, in certain circumstances, diverse groups can outperform homogeneous groups because they bring a greater variety of knowledge, skills, experiences and attitudes to the tasks they are working with.

At first glance the evidence seems to suggest that increasing diversity in a workforce is a 'win–win' situation for employees and organisations. However, most writers acknowledge that there are problems in making the business case for managing diversity. It is difficult to demonstrate a clear impact on profitability, for example (Cassell, 2000). There is some research that links workforce diversity to important organisational outcomes. One study found a tendency for companies with conspicuous diversity initiatives to fare better than others on the stock market (Wright *et al.*, 1995). Frink *et al.* (2003) provide strong evidence that having a workforce where the gender composition was unbalanced placed organisational performance at risk. Welbourne *et al.* (2007) found that gender diversity in top management teams had a direct association with financial performance of a large number of US-based companies. On the whole it seems that management teams with diverse membership do perform better than others, at least on tasks that require the generation and evaluation of ideas (Jackson and Joshi, 2001). This may be the case because diversity could help to avoid problems such as 'groupthink' (see Chapter 13). However, this does depend quite a lot on the ways in which conflicts within the team arise and are handled.

Avery *et al.* (2007) found that employees from ethnic minority groups who perceived their employer as not adequately valuing diversity reported significantly higher absence than those from the white majority group. If organisations are successful in conveying that they value diversity there is evidence that this makes them a more attractive employer, particularly to minority groups and those who value racial tolerance (Ng and Burke, 2005; Brown *et al.*, 2006). This 'marketing approach' has replaced affirmative action in many organisations because of the legal problems they encountered when attempting to use quota systems to hire more employees from minority groups (Kravitz, 2008). It also seems that diverse workforces are associated with the good levels of retention of employees from minority groups (Zatzik *et al.*, 2003). Perhaps what should be of equal concern to organisations is that there is overwhelming evidence that when people perceive they are discriminated against they are more likely to develop a number of problems with their physical and psychological health (Pascoe and Smart Richman, 2009).

One of the challenges for work psychology is to examine why diversity does not always give good results. Williams and O'Reilly (1998) found evidence that diversity had a negative relationship with performance, with damaging effects on relationships between employees and the cohesiveness of groups. Richard and Johnson (1999) have argued that in general the connection between diversity and organisational financial performance has not been proven. Cassell (2000) suggests that an emphasis on more local financial criteria such as cost savings through decreased staff turnover and decreased litigation may appeal to many managers, though in fact evidence suggests that on the whole turnover is (or at least, has been) higher in more diverse workplaces than less diverse ones (Jackson *et al.*, 1991).

Janssens and Zanoni (2005) argue that early reviews of diversity struggled to explain these inconsistencies because diversity was reduced to the study of the impact of demographic differences *without* sufficient analysis of the impact that these differences had on human perceptions and the interactions employees had with each other. In other words, they underestimated the psychology of diversity. Taking a psychological perspective allows us to see how diversity is perceived by employees within organisations. Ely and Thomas (2001) re-examined the concept of diversity and identified three different perspectives on diversity that may be found in organisations.

- *The integration-and-learning perspective.* In this perspective the different skills, knowledge, experiences and attitudes that accompany the demographic diversity in the team are perceived as being helpful to employees when they are working together.

- *The access-and-legitimacy perspective* occurs when organisation's customers are culturally diverse. The perception is that having a diverse workforce helps the organisation gain access to a diverse market. Janssens and Zanoni (2005) argues that this form of diversity can be beneficial in work environments where the similarity between the customer/client and employee impacts upon job performance.

■ *The discrimination-and-fairness perspective* is based upon the perception that diversity is a moral issue to ensure fair treatment for all employees. This perception is often in evidence when the organisation focuses on equal opportunities and eliminating discrimination.

Ely and Thomas (2001) argue that when diversity is perceived within the integration-and-learning perspective, outcomes are positive (i.e. there is improved task performance). However, when employees take the discrimination-and-fairness perspective, divisions and segregation are highlighted. Van Knippenberg and Schippers (2007, p. 517) provide a simpler dichotomy that does a good job in summarising the possible outcomes of diversity:

■ *Social categorisation perspective*: differences between work group members may engender the classification of others as either ingroup/similar or outgroup/dissimilar, categorisations that may disrupt group process.

■ *Information/decision-making perspective*: diversity may introduce differences in knowledge, expertise and perspectives that may help work groups reach higher quality and more creative and innovative outcomes.

Proudford and Smith (2007) conclude that if demographic differences have some salience to the job role and/or task itself then diversity is more likely to have a positive impact on the task. For example, young employees may assume that older workers have old-fashioned attitudes to work when compared to younger workers (i.e. diversity is perceived as a basis for separation). Or they may perceive that older workers have more knowledge, experience and wisdom than younger workers (i.e. diversity is associated with a perceived variety of skills and experience that could prove useful). Work psychology has allowed us to see that it is not necessarily the demographic differences themselves that have an impact on the way employees behave, but rather how employees perceive and identify the implications of these differences. This also suggests that the aspects of difference between people that matter may well vary a lot between contexts (Jackson and Joshi, 2001). In one workplace (for example a hospital serving a highly multi-ethnic local population) it might be ethnicity, and in another (e.g. the research laboratory of a pharmaceutical company) it might be whether one's qualifications are in pharmacy, biochemistry or medicine.

This opens up the possibility that organisations might intervene to influence how employees perceive diversity in order to increases the chances of diversity interventions having positive outcomes. Harrison (2007) suggests that positive outcomes are more likely if employees see demographic differences as a source of variety (of skills, attitudes, values, etc.) rather than as a basis for separation.

On the whole it looks as if interventions that aim solely to increase awareness of other groups' qualities and their perspectives do not make much difference (*see also* Chapter 13). Pettigrew (1998) suggests that contact between groups can improve relations, but only if the nature of the contact: (i) encourages *learning* about the other group as opposed to just coexisting; (ii) requires behaving differently towards the other group; (iii) creates positive emotions associated with the other group; and

(iv) enables new insights about one's own group. This last point is interesting and important, because arguably empathy with members of other groups is possible only if one can appreciate that the worldviews of group(s) to which one belongs are just one way of looking at things rather than the absolute truth. Situations that meet these four criteria can sometimes be engineered in workplaces, and sometimes they occur naturally. Probably their key features are that they require members of different groups to work cooperatively towards a common goal, that goal-achievement is a real possibility and that nobody is allowed to opt out of the endeavour.

Key Learning Point

Effective management of diversity requires attention to many kinds of difference between people, not just the obvious ones such as gender and ethnic origin. It is also involves understanding how differences are perceived by employees.

Jackson and Joshi (2001) point out that a lot depends on historical context too. They give the example of the United States, where in the 1940s and 1950s black youngsters tended to value a white identity higher than a black one. In the 1960s civil rights movements began to emphasise that being black was nothing to be ashamed of. The campaign was successful in changing the preferred identity of young black people, and not only in the United States. People of that generation are now in leading and established positions in their workplaces. Their identities are likely to influence their attitudes to managing diversity. This example also points to another aspect of diversity. It is not just a person's racial or national background that matters, but also how they see themselves – i.e. their ethnic identity.

Lau and Murnighan (1998) have pointed out that how differences are distributed also matters. For example, suppose a six-person team consists of three middle-aged white male senior managers without university degrees who have all been production managers, and three young black female women managers with Ph.D.s who have all been marketing managers. In this case, the many differences all stack up together and find expression in the same people. Lau and Murnighan refer to this as a 'faultline'. If, for example, seniority had been mixed up a bit so that one of the men was a middle manager and one of the women was a senior manager, then perhaps the dynamics of the group would have changed significantly. Although the group would be equally diverse, the distribution of the differences would have been different, and the 'faultline' less deep and wide.

It should be fairly apparent by now that work psychology has quite a lot to offer to theory and practice in managing diversity. Problems in managing diversity often stem from perceptions of dissimilarity between individuals and/or groups. On the whole, people tend to feel more attracted to people who are similar to themselves than to those who are dissimilar. They also tend to be more generous towards them, and happier to cooperate with them. These and other findings about interpersonal perception and inter-group relations are well-established ones within psychology. The identification of these tendencies, and the analysis of the circumstances in which they occur and their consequences for behaviour, have wide implications for many aspects of working life. Following on from this, work psychology should also offer the tools to evaluate the impact of attempts to manage diversity. Ellis and Sonnenfeld (1994) identified the following common forms of diversity management in organisations:

- multicultural workshops designed to improve understanding and communication among members of different groups;

- support groups, mentoring and networks for minority and/or disadvantaged groups;

- advisory councils reporting to top management;

- rewarding managers for their development of members of minority and/or disadvantaged groups;

- fast-track developmental programmes and special training opportunities for minority and/or disadvantaged groups.

However, one of the main reasons for focusing on diversity so early in this text is that it is an issue that weaves through the majority of this book. Enhancing the management of diversity is often about following best practice that has been identified in a number of aspects of work psychology. These include:

- Ensuring that selection processes are based on the proper job analysis so that the criteria for selection are related to the potential, or ability, to do the job (and not irrelevant factors such as age or gender). This includes training employees in the use of fair selection techniques and methods (see Chapters 4 and 5) and has implications for career development (Chapter 15). In addition, organisations wishing to transform their culture (see Chapter 16) by recruiting tolerant employees, need to communicate clearly that they value diversity (Kim and Gefland, 2003).

- Designing physical work environments that allow people to perform to their full potential (see Chapter 9).

- Establishing and developing teams that include people with the skills, knowledge, abilities and attitudes that are needed to get the job done (rather than a group of people who are all good friends because they are similar in some way – see Chapter 13).

- Ensuring that training and development interventions allow a diverse workforce to develop (see Chapter 11).

- Ensuring that the criteria for measuring performance advancement are open to all employees and having formal induction processes for all employees (see Chapter 6).

- Allowing flexible working for all employees (and not just for working mothers), and introducing policies on harassment and discrimination (see Chapter 12).

Of course, there are significant dangers in attempts to manage diversity. There is some evidence that attempts to increase contact and understanding can sometimes backfire, and make stereotypes more entrenched (Nemetz and Christensen, 1996). Also, it is important not to equate being a minority group with being disadvantaged in all respects. For example, there is evidence that Asian Americans achieve more in education and earn more than European Americans, though on the other hand the average boost to earnings provided by education is less for Asian Americans that European Americans, which shows the complexity of the phenomena involved (Friedman and Krackhardt, 1997). As discussed in the next section on cross-cultural issues, perhaps the biggest danger is of treating individuals as if they were identikit members of one or more groups. Even if different groups (for example men and women) are different on average, this does not mean that all men are the same. Nor are they different from all women in the same way.

Key Learning Point

Work psychology has a lot to offer the management of diversity, particularly in understanding how individuals and groups perceive, and relate to, each other.

Gender, ethnicity and disability

It is also worth making some additional points about three specific elements of diversity: gender, ethnicity and disability. They have been selected because at present they are the aspects of diversity (alongside age, religion and sexual orientation) that most often feature in legislation, and they affect large numbers of people.

For all three group differences discussed below, it is noticeable that:

- the position of women, ethnic minority groups, and people with a disibility in the labour market (e.g. ability to get jobs, the types of jobs they get, how successful they are in their occupation) is improving somewhat;

- their position still does not match that of the majority group (in this case, white able-bodied males);

- this appears not to be entirely attributable to possibly legitimate factors such as differences in qualifications and experience;

- their disadvantage has not been entirely eradicated by legislation; it is probably due partly to subtle or not-so-subtle prejudice and/or discrimination;

- in some instances, people's sense of identity (i.e. how they see themselves) may matter as much as their objective group membership.

Chapter 15, on careers, explores some of the factors that affect the extent and nature of career success that people experience. It is highly relevant to this section, particularly regarding the career success experienced by women.

Key Learning Point

Women, ethnic minorities and people with a disability are all seeing moves towards better recognition in the labour market, but still do not enjoy equality, and legislation to protect them is not always fully effective.

Gender

Women constitute on average 14.7 per cent of board members on Fortune 500 companies in the United States. This is up from a figure of about 10 per cent reported in the 1990s (Catalyst, 1996). In the UK, women hold 11 per cent of FTSE 100 directorships, according to the UK Equality and Human Rights Commission (2008). Although this figure is also increasing, it is still too low, from the points of view of both fairness and the effective deployment of national human resources.

Women's earnings are lower than men's too, in spite of equal pay for equal work legislation. In the United Kingdom, average earnings for women are between 70 and 80 per cent of those for men, depending on occupation. The pay gaps are bigger than that in some other European countries, and smaller in yet others, but the gap is always present. They cannot be entirely explained away by women being in less skilled employment than men. Even if they could, it is necessary to ask why women (whose educational achievements are on average higher than men's) are in less highly skilled and/or highly paid employment than men. According to the UK government's update on the 2008 Labour Force Survey, men achieved their highest weekly wage (£598) between the age of 40 and 49 years. However, while women achieved the highest weekly wage somewhat sooner (between 30 and 39 years), the average was much lower (£480). As an aside (rather depressingly for this author) salaries rose up to these age ranges, but dropped afterwards. The picture is similar in the US: in 2008 figures showed women earned around 80 per cent of what men earned.

In terms of what people are capable of doing in the workplace, these findings appear unjust. Most gender-related differences in ability and personality are really quite small, or even non-existent. In Chapters 4–6 we discuss, among other things, ways of assessing people for selection and appraisal that avoid biases that may stem from assessors' beliefs about how men and women differ. In Chapter 14, on leadership, we comment briefly on leaders might be perceived as different as a result of their gender, and the consequences of that. So it might be a mistake to focus purely on a person's biological sex (i.e. their genes) or their gender (i.e. whether they live as a man or a woman).

As a general statement, women's more communal as opposed to individualistic orientation should be well suited to teamwork, and to workplaces where relationships and social networks are said to be more important than rules and procedures. Women's apparent advantage in (and often more experience of) multitasking and flexibility should also prove an advantage over men, who are often thought to be more single-task focused and less able to switch between tasks at short notice. It could be argued that while men are in most of the positions of power such qualities may not be as valued as they should be.

One consistent finding from research is that when both a woman and her male partner are in employment, it is the woman who does most of the housework and (if relevant) childcare (Barnett and Shen, 1997), particularly the elements that are most time-pressured such as getting the children ready for school. This could be one reason why, many more women managers than men managers are unmarried or married but childless. One might think also that men and women experience different kinds of stress at work, and/or cope with it differently. As discussed later in this chapter women may experience more interference of home life with work, but this depends on how much men and women think they should be working in the first place. In fact, although some studies have shown differences, others have failed to find them (Nelson and Burke, 2000). One of the more persistent findings, though still not universal, is that women cope with stress by expressing their feelings about it, and seeking social support, while men treat it as a problem to be solved, usually through individual effort (Ptacek *et al.*, 1994). Nelson and Burke (2000) suggest that a halfway position of problem-solving through discussion with supportive colleagues and friends might suit both men and women.

There are nevertheless some sources of stress that clearly are more relevant to women than to men. Women are more likely to experience sexual harassment than men. Women are more likely than men to suffer from anxiety and depression, and this is sometimes attributable to stresses at work. On the other hand, men are more likely to suffer from more life-threatening stress-related illnesses such as heart problems (see Chapter 12 for more on stress).

Key Learning Point

Although it is clear that women are still paid less and have lower-status jobs than men, arguments rage about whether women are oppressed, or whether they are free to make choices never previously available to them.

Finally, Travers and Pemberton (2000) among others, discuss the role of social networking in women's working lives. A problem for women in male-dominated environments is the difficulty of being part of social networks where up-to-date information about what is going on, what jobs are coming up, etc. is shared informally. It seems that people tend to network with people like themselves. Furthermore, men network a lot with colleagues in the same organisation or close to it, and in an instrumental task-focused way, whereas women are more inclined to network with other women, perhaps in other organisations, and use these contacts for mutual support rather than, for example, getting known by the people at the top (Vinnicombe and Colwill, 1996). It may also be the case that women tend to have relatively small networks of people they know quite well, whereas men have larger numbers of contacts, each of whom they know only slightly. Most of the research suggests that the latter is better for 'getting on', but it might also be suggested that the former is better for quality of life. Nevertheless, it is important not to generalise too readily. Travers and Pemberton (2000) report a survey they conducted which found significant, though not huge, differences between women from different countries regarding how they viewed networking. American women seemed to see it in quite instrumental masculine terms, British women in terms of their development, and Spanish women on socialising and enjoying the company and support of other women.

Ethnic minorities

Many anecdotal reports, 'fly on the wall' television programmes and research studies indicate clearly that people from ethnic minorities in any given country are at a disadvantage relative to members of the majority when it comes to getting jobs and other opportunities. High-quality reviews such as Huffcutt and Roth (1998), McKay and McDaniel (2006) and Dean *et al.* (2008) offer confirmatory scientific evidence of this. These impressive studies show that the mean ratings for black candidates in employment interviews, assessments of job performance and assessment centre ratings are lower than those for whites. The authors of these reviews cite many reasons for these differences that reside in problems with the way performance is measured (in general) and specific biases that operate in the assessment of people at work.

Given the evidence described in the previous paragraph, perhaps it is not surprising that members of ethnic minorities seem less likely to enter high-prestige occupations than members of the majority, and even if they get there, they often do not progress as far. This is in spite of legislation in many countries to ensure equal rights. Cokley *et al.* (2004) summarise statistical evidence from the US Census Bureau which shows that white men's earnings are 25 per cent or more higher than the salaries of black and Hispanic men. They also note that the higher the proportion of black people in an occupation, the lower its salary.

People from ethnic minorities cope in different ways with working in white-dominated environments. Cross developed and later refined a theory to try to describe and explain how black people's identities develop in different ways (Cross, 1995). Some remain what Cross called 'pre-encounter'. These are people who feel more white than black. Then there are those who encounter a jolting experience that makes their ethnic identity salient, usually because the experience is unpleasant. Some of those who take on a black identity by this or other means may be described as 'immersed' because they are very focused on their black identity. As discussed earlier in this chapter it is likely that people's identity status will be a major determinant of how easy or difficult they find it to function around others with different 'identities'. Perhaps those 'immersed' in particular will be inclined to leave or never join in the first place, and this in turn might lead white people to believe there is less of a culture gap than there actually is (Cokley *et al.*, 2004). Cross's theory is a good example of how it is important to look beyond factual information such as skin colour in defining groups.

Key Learning Point

Members of ethnic minorities tend to be at a disadvantage in the labour market relative to the majority. This is mostly due to aspects of person perception and identity that lead majority and minority groups to hold certain opinions about themselves and each other, sometimes without realising it.

The kinds of social networks that people build up are also probably partly a consequence of their identities, as well as the opportunities that they are given. People in minorities tend to form networks that consist of other members of minorities, and members of the majority also stick together. Usually, members of the majority hold most of the powerful positions, and the people who get to know them also tend to be from the majority. To the extent that decisions such as who gets which job are made on the basis of the decision-maker knowing the people concerned, then these social networks will become self-perpetuating (Ibarra, 1995). One way round this is to institute mentoring or other schemes where members of the (powerful) majority take some responsibility for the development of one or members of a minority. There is more about the roles of social networks and mentoring (among other things) in Chapter 15, on careers.

People with a disability

Barnes (1991) defines disability as 'the loss of opportunities to take part in the normal life of the community on an equal level with others due to physical and social barriers'. This definition highlights the social element of disability – it is not simply a physical phenomenon. How disability and disabled people are viewed by society as a whole affects the opportunities available to people with disabilities (McHugh, 1991). It is clear that, although the lot of people with a disability in the workplace is improving, they are still at a disadvantage compared with people with no disability. The introduction in many countries of laws protecting and enhancing the rights of people with a disability has reduced the gap, but not eliminated it. It seems that the image of disabled people as ill, dependent on others, child-like and asexual does persist, even though much of the medical and other provision for people with a disability has moved away from treating people in that way (Oliver, 1990). Yet many of the technological advances outlined earlier make it easier for people with a disability to work productively, because they compensate for any limitations people may have in physical coordination and mobility. Much of the provision required to make workplaces usable for people with a disability is hardly rocket science, which is one reason why the UK Disability Discrimination Act, which came into force in 1996, insists that employers make 'reasonable accommodations' where the working arrangements and/or physical features of the workplace put people with a disability at a significant disadvantage.

Even so, the UK Labour Force Survey in 2008 (Office for National Statistics, 2009b) recorded 51 per cent of disabled people as being economically active (quite a substantial increase from previous surveys), compared with 80 per cent of people without a disability. Of course, some of this difference may be due to fewer disabled than non-disabled people looking for work, but that is not the whole story because the UK unemployment rate (which includes only those seeking work) is approaching twice as high for disabled people than non-disabled ones.

As is the case with other diversity issues, legislation does not in itself override human perceptions, beliefs and prejudices about people with a disability. So it is likely to remain difficult for disabled people to rise to the top of their professions. Numerous studies in the 1980s confirmed that disabled people tend to be concentrated in lower-status occupations and if they did get into higher-status occupations, they tended to be at junior levels within them (Walker, 1982). There is now much more concern than there used to be with identifying ways in which disabled people can be supported in achieving independence. Furthermore, this is increasingly being done by finding out the experiences of disabled people themselves, rather than simply implementing what able-bodied people think would be good for them (Hendey and Pascall, 2001).

Key Learning Point

The talents of people with a disability are being increasingly recognised in employment and education, and this is supported by laws upholding their rights in many countries. However, there is still some disadvantage relative to people without a disability.

The persistent difficulties of disabled people in the labour market are not only due to real limitations in their capabilities, nor to unreasonable employers. It also seems clear that gender, ethnicity and social class play their parts, through the ways in which children with a disability are socialised. In fact, in some respects, these factors may be more important than disability in shaping what a disabled person expects of themself. Shah *et al.* (2004a) for example have shown that, among a group of disabled professionals who had achieved considerable career success, those raised in middle class professional households recalled rarely being allowed to use their disability as an excuse for failure. Education is also a key factor. Some people with a disability are educated in separate schools whereas others are in mainstream schools. Which of these two forms of schooling is more successful has been debated at length over many years (e.g. Jenkinson, 1997), and it is likely that much depends on the personal resources of the young person in dealing with whichever environment they are in. As a generalisation, it seems that mainstream schools offer a relatively challenging curriculum, but sometimes not much social support, while segregated schools tend to be the other way round (Shah *et al.*, 2004b).

Cross-cultural issues

An important aspect of diversity is nationality. This is associated with ethnicity of course, but is not always the same. Hofstede (2001) and Trompenaars (1993), among others, have found systematic cultural differences between people from different countries. Cross-national differences crop up quite a lot in this book, most notably in Chapters 8 (motivation), 13 (groups and teams), 14 (leadership) and 15 (careers).

Students of occupational psychology are often confused by the array of different populations and research settings that they encounter when studying the academic literature. Inconsistencies in research findings are often difficult to fathom or explain (just take a look at the discussion section of many research papers to see how baffling these can be for even the most experienced academics). One very important issue that drives some of these inconsistencies in work psychology is that of cultural differences.

Gelfand and colleagues (2007) provide a neat summary of the meaning of culture, drawing together a range of definitions. They state that culture is the human-generated part of the environment that is transmitted across time and generations; culture results in people from the same culture have a set of shared meanings (they see things in a similar way and share similar patterns of thinking); culture gives us 'standard operating procedures' or ways of doing things.

In other words, the culture we grow up in, or spend some time in, gives us a 'lens' through which we see and interpret the world around us. Culture can have many different dimensions: it may be a national culture, a historical religious culture, or it may even be an organisational culture (*see* Chapter 16). As far as possible we have tried to give this text an international feel, to subtly raise the issue of culture as you study each topic. Still it is worth noting early on in your reading of this text that various dimensions of culture can have a quite profound impact on the way people think and behave in the workplace.

Extensive research has consistently shown that people from different national cultures look for different things in the environment. People from different cultural backgrounds also have different interpretations of the same events or situations and culture determines our norms and standards. What is seen as right in one culture might be seen wrong in another, and different cultures have different sources of self-worth (what makes us feel worthwhile and valued is highly affected by the culture we develop and live in). These norms provide a number of very useful functions. For example they help us to manage our anxiety. If we know a course of action is acceptable within a cultural norm we are less anxious about acting in that way.

Key Learning Point

The culture that a person develops within, or lives in, has a strong impact on what they notice, how they make sense of what they notice, and the impact that external events have on them.

Chapter 14 gives an in-depth description of a number of different dimensions of culture and how they relate to leadership (e.g. what is important for people from different cultures). For now we will look at one of the most frequently studied cultural dimensions: individualistic vs. collectivistic (Hofstede, 1980, 2001). The former reflects a belief that individuals should be self-sufficient while the latter emphasises people's belongingness to groups in which there is mutual support.

Two recent reviews published in the *Annual Review of Psychology* provide elegant summaries of the importance of culture for anyone using psychology in organisational settings. Reviewing a wide range of research (only a small amount of it drawn from work psychology), Lehman *et al.* (2004) identify a number of important effects of culture that have an obvious relevance for work psychology. Their review focused on comparing the East Asian culture (collectivistic) and the European North American culture (individualistic). Gelfand *et al.* (2007) looked more closely at how some of these effects translate into important differences in the workplace (the words in italics). A summary of the key findings is presented in Table 1.3.

At this stage it is important to not read too much into the content of Table 1.3. There are huge individual differences within cultures and neither cultural perspective is inherently right or wrong. For example, there are circumstances where it is helpful to investigate and attribute personal responsibility for work problems. In other situations it might be better to identify systematic causes for problems, but culture means that the environment shapes employees' preferences to some degree.

Peter Warr (2008) looked at a different dimension of culture, that of historical religious values. Almost 21,000 employees were asked what they valued about their job. Although good pay was important across various cultures, it seems particularly important in historically communist cultures. Having pleasant people to work with, or a job with high levels of responsibility, was seen as important by significantly fewer people in communist countries than it was in Catholic and Protestant countries.

All of this might have you thinking that cultural differences threaten the idea that good psychological theories can generalise across cultures (the idea of *psychological universals*). They may, but to simplify things a little what we generally find is that similar issues affect most cultures. There is evidence that the Big Five personality factors (*see* Chapter 3) exist across cultures but that culture influences the way people respond to questionnaire items that measure them (Thompson, 2008). Job satisfaction, motivation, leadership and so on are clearly important to some extent to the vast majority of the global working population. However, culture might play

Table 1.3	The impact of a national cultural difference

Individualistic culture European North American	Collectivistic culture East Asian
Tend to develop an analytical thinking style, focusing on the 'hard facts'. They tend to be troubled when logic fails to make accurate predictions *Employees tend to seek facts and figures on which to base their efforts to solve work problems*	Tend to use holistic thinking styles, using subjective impressions to solve problems, rather than relying on formal logic *Employees tend to seek and use a range of different information (e.g. hard facts and subjective impressions) in decision-making*
Prefer to attribute causes of events to individuals rather than to situational factors *Employees tend to attribute personal blame to others when others fail (and personal credit for others' successes)*	Prefer to attribute causes of events to a wide range of environmental, group and social factors *Employees take a complex and multifaceted view when looking at reasons for success and failure*
View themselves and others as independent beings (i.e. people are independent, self-contained and autonomous) *Employees highly motivated by jobs that provide autonomy*	See people as being interdependent (i.e. people have value in society as part of a group) *Employees highly motivated by jobs that involve co-dependency with colleagues*
Tend to seek knowledge for its own sake, with their motivation for learning being to fulfil their own potential *Employees tend to value job demands, training and development that helps them as an individual*	Knowledge is sought that will serve the 'wider good' with personal development being less important *High value is placed on job demands and training that will help the employees to make a stronger contribution to team or company performance*
Individual, positively focused feedback tends to be important *Employees likely to be motivated by feedback about their own performance rather than by feedback about the performance of the group they work in*	Feedback on poor performance, and how it impacts on those around them tends to be a powerful motivator *Negative feedback likely to create a strong response, especially if it is about group performance*

(Continued)

Table 1.3	The impact of a national cultural difference (*Continued*)
Individualistic culture **European North American**	**Collectivistic culture** **East Asian**
Life satisfaction tends to be quite dependent on self-esteem, personal freedom and pursuit of individual goals	Social standing/reputation tends to be closely linked to person's feelings of self-worth. Group failures tend to be ego-threatening and pursuit of team goals and good interpersonal relationships contributes strongly to self-worth
Employees are likely to be motivated by goals that they choose themselves that help them realise their own potential	*Employees are likely to be motivated by the goals sets for the work group they are in, especially when these goals are set for them by figures of authority and when achievement is measured in terms of contribution to a group*
Biases such as unrealistic optimism and self-enhancement are common	Tend to be quite self-critical, getting their self-esteem instead from being a valued member of the group and being connected to other group members
Self-perceptions/appraisals might present an overly positive estimate of performance and this need to be validated with other sources of information	*Self-appraisals may be overly harsh, but optimistic biases may operate when employees evaluate the performance of the group they are in*

an important role in determining the factors that have an impact on these issues. For example, Warr (2008) shows that, in general, job satisfaction is determined by a range of different factors that are all relevant across different cultures. It is the relative importance of these factors that becomes different because of cultural influences. In a similar vein, motivation tends to be related to job performance but what motivates people may differ from one culture to another. This helps to explain why some working practices with their origin in Asian cultures have proved difficult to implement in Europe.

Culture may sometimes force us to re-examine the meaning of some of the concepts we use. Meyer *et al.* (2002) found that outside of the US, organisational commitment (see Chapter 7) may be more about perceived support from the organisation that it is to do with age and tenure (age and tenure have stronger relationships with organisational commitment in the USA than they do elsewhere).

Lehman *et al.* (2004) also argue that there is ample evidence to indicate that developing cultural experience is a bit like a building a toolkit. When we experience different cultures we grow to appreciate a wider range of normative values, and we gather up more 'lenses' (tools) which we can then use to see the world in different ways. It seems that travel really does broaden the mind. The authors called this 'contextual priming' and it is a principle already being put to use by companies whose workers operate across cultures. Many organisations use cultural acclimatisation periods to prepare their employees for work overseas. Employees who have experienced the culture they are working in are more likely to understand the cultural norms that are operating and appreciate how their actions will be viewed by others.

Work-life integration

People have lives outside work (most of us anyway!). There are many reasons why the interface between home and work lives has become increasingly prominent in work psychology (Frone, 2002). These include the following:

- The increasing proportion of women in the workforce – traditionally women have tended to shoulder most of the responsibility for managing the home and caring for children, so fitting home and work lives together is seen as an important issue (Greenhaus and Parasuraman, 1999).

- The rise of the so-called boundaryless career (*see* Chapter 15), where work and home lives are thought of as intertwined and (ideally) existing in harmony with each other.

- The increasing pressure that some people feel to work harder and/or for longer hours than was formerly the case.

- The increasing number of dual-career households, where the total burden of employment and domestic responsibilities tends to be high, and personal resources stretched.

It is clear that in many countries, individuals are becoming more aware of, and sometimes less satisfied with, the imbalance between the amount of time they spend at work and the amount of time they spend away from it. Arguably this then becomes an important issue for employers that want to attract the best employees and ensure that their workforce is satisfied and committed. Given the demands most of us face in our lives, achieving a balance between work and non-work activities can be an issue for any employee (not just women with young families).

The interactions (or overlaps) between the work and non-work domains are at the heart of most work-life integration research. Kopelman *et al.* (1983) described the negative aspects of these interactions as 'inter-role conflict'. This occurs when the pressures and demands of one role *conflict* with the pressures and demands of the other. For example, working late because of an urgent deadline might conflict with an arrangement to socialise with friends or with childcare commitments. The individual's perception of a *problematic conflict* also plays a key role in determining the impact that the situation has on an employee's well-being and satisfaction (Van Steenbergen *et al.*, 2008). We discuss such perceptions in more detail in Chapter 12.

The argument put forward in much of the research is in that having incompatible or conflicting work and non-work commitments places the individual at risk. Sometimes, however, *positive spillover* can occur. Some have argued that the skills or knowledge gained in one domain can positively enhance performance in the other domain (e.g. Grzywacz and Marks, 2000). For example someone who is required to be very organised at work might use similar skills in planning their social or leisure activities, thus enhancing the quality of their non-work time. However, the evidence shows that poor work-life integration appears to be associated with stress and ill-health (Geurts and Demerouti, 2003; Hurst and Baker, 2007). Greenhaus and Beutell (1985) suggested that three types of conflict commonly occur:

- Time-based conflict: pressures from one domain (e.g. work) make it physically impossible to meet demands from the other domain (e.g. home).

- Strain-based conflict: the impact of engagement in one domain reduces the resources (e.g. energy) available for the person to meet demands in the other domain.

- Behaviour-based conflict: in this type of conflict the person finds themselves taking on a different role at work from the one they take on at home (e.g. a hard negotiator at work, and a sensitive friend, or spouse outside of it).

Work psychologists have tended to concentrate on the problematic interactions between perceived work pressures and perceived family pressures. Inevitably issues such as long working hours and working away from home have been the focus of the research (which has a great deal of overlap with work stress, *see* Chapter 12). There is also a growing interest in the potential impact of family life on work, such as sudden and unexpected family commitments demanding an employee's attention (Gutek *et al.*, 1991). Recent studies (e.g. Westman *et al.*, 2008) consider the impact of work on the family (work–family conflict) separately to the impact of the family on work (family–work conflict). This is why the term 'work–life integration' is useful: it captures the dynamics of employees trying to balance a wide range of work and non-work activities (Lewis and Cooper, 2005).

It also appears that work–life integration is a complex issue and the results of research are not always predictable. For example, the impact of interventions designed to achieve better work–life integration may be determined by historical factors and social norms. For some groups in society (e.g. lower income families) the quality of work–life balance depends upon the availability of good childcare support amongst family and friends (Kossek *et al.*, 2008). It might not always be that time away from family demands is stressful. For some women working away from home, it was the return home that was most stressful (Westman *et al.*, 2008). Interestingly this study found that during the business trip, female workers' psychological health improved, indicating that they were benefiting from some 'respite' during the trip. It may also be that *role diversity* could enrich the lives of many people by exposing them to a wider range of experiences than they would experience either at work or at home. This is illustrated by research into unemployment which shows the many positive benefits the work environment can hold for people (*see* Chapter 12).

Key Learning Point

Work–life integration is a complex phenomenon. What is clear is that what happens at work can influence people's lives outside of work and vice versa. This influence can be both positive and negative.

In terms of interventions to help employees, changes to working practices include different working patterns such as part-time working or flexible hours. These may have a profound positive impact on the psychological contract between the employee and the employer (*see* Chapter 7). Compressed hours/working weeks (e.g. working a small amount of extra time each day so that employees could have one day off work every two weeks), on-site provision for childcare, and maternity and paternity benefits have also all been used to help employees. As well as these formal arrangements, research suggests that a culture of flexibility (i.e. the availability of informal flexible working arrangements) is very important (Lewis and Taylor, 1996). As you might expect, large companies tend to be more active than smaller ones in the level of formal supporting mechanisms they offer to employees that are juggling work–life responsibilities (Geurts and Grundemann, 1999).

Although intervention research on work–life integration is still in its infancy, several studies show that flexible working and/or working from home can have positive outcomes for employees (Bond *et al.*, 2005; Hogarth *et al.*, 2001). More intervention research is needed to examine the effects of the range of possible interventions discussed above. As you can see work–life integration is another cross-cutting issue for this text. It will crop up again in Chapters 7 (Attitudes at work and the employment relationship), 12 (Stress and well-being at work) and 15 (Careers and career management).

Summary

Modern psychology can be divided into several subdisciplines which reflect different facets of human psychological functioning. Cutting across these divisions are competing theoretical traditions in psychology. These are the psychoanalytic, trait, behaviourist, phenomenological and social cognitive traditions. None of them can be described as correct, though the social cognitive tradition is the most recent, and makes most use of other traditions. The traditions make some contradictory assumptions about the fundamental nature of the person. Their differences and similarities are summarised in Table 1.1. Each tradition finds some expression in work psychology. The differences between them emphasise that any apparent coherence of work psychology is due to the fact that it always takes place in the work setting. It does not possess a generally agreed view of human nature.

Work psychology concerns both the interaction between an individual and their work, and the relationships between people in the work setting. This includes personnel selection and assessment, training, performance appraisal, career development, organisational change and development, human–machine interaction, counselling, the design of work environments and employee relations and motivation, among other things. Work psychologists act as researchers, teachers and consultants in these areas. In the United Kingdom, the British Psychological Society oversees the professional qualifications and conduct of work psychologists. Many other countries have equivalent bodies.

We also believe it is important to examine the context in which work psychology is operating. Changes have been occurring over the past two decades or so which mean that many work organisations are more pressured than they were, with flatter structures, fewer employees and more varied terms and conditions. Employees may well be required to be flexible to suit employers' needs, but there is also often a chance for them to work flexibly to suit their own needs. It is clear that new technology in the workplace does not have inevitable consequences – its effects on people, jobs and organisations depend a lot on how it is introduced and subsequently used. The changing mix of people in the labour force in terms of their gender, ethnic affiliation, (dis)ability, religion, nationality, age, sexual orientation and other factors presents both challenges and opportunities for work psychology. So does the increasing awareness of diversity issues, independent of the changing nature of the workforce. Work psychology needs to ensure that it moves well beyond its roots in large manufacturing organisations with predominantly white male workforces and stable structures. It should be analysing and answering questions such as 'how do different groups at work relate to each other?', 'how can fairness be achieved at work?', 'how can the potential value of a diverse workforce be made a reality?' and 'how can small organisations with limited resources make use of what work psychology can offer?'

Test your learning

Short-answer questions

1 What are the areas of basic psychology, and what kind of issues does each area address?

2 Draw a diagram to show the relationship between basic psychology and work psychology.

3 In psychoanalytic psychology, what are (i) the id, (ii) the ego, (iii) the superego and (iv) defence mechanisms?

4 What is a trait? Briefly describe two key features of the trait approach to personality.

5 In behaviourism, what is reinforcement? Why do behaviourist psychologists think that personality can be changed?

6 In phenomenological psychology, what are (i) conditions of worth, (ii) unconditional positive regard and (iii) self-actualisation?

7 Why is the self an important concept in the social cognitive tradition?

8 What were the key lessons learned by work psychologists from the Hawthorne studies?

9 Name and briefly describe eight areas of work undertaken by work psychologists.

10 If you were a manager considering buying the services of a work psychologist, what would you want to know about the psychologist's qualifications and experiences?

11 How would you evaluate whether the research undertaken by a work psychologist was ethical?

12 Specify five ways in which workplaces tend to be different now from 30 years ago.

13 Choose one of these (from question 12), and comment on what work psychology can contribute to understanding its impact.

14 Suggest three ways in which work psychology should be able to help in the management of diversity.

15 Choose one way in which people at work differ from each other, and specify three insights from work psychology about this difference.

Suggested assignments

1 Compare and contrast any two approaches to personality.

2 Select any two traditions in personality. Imagine two managers. One believes one tradition is correct; the other supports the other tradition. Examine the probable impact of their beliefs on the way they deal with other people at work.

3 Examine whether the ethical codes of practice governing work psychologists adequately reflect all the ethical issues that can arise in work psychology research and practice.

4 Why are the links between work and home-life important? How can organisations ensure that the home–work interface is well-managed?

5 How can work psychology help to ensure that workplace diversity is healthy and productive?

6 What role does culture play in understanding workplace behaviour?

Relevant websites

Professional psychology associations offer considerable information about the theory and practice of psychology, including work psychology. Three good ones are The International Association for Applied Psychology (IAAP) at http://www.iaapsy.org, The European Association of Work and Organizational Psychology (EAWOP) at http://www.eawop.org/ and the British Psychological Society at http://www/bps.org.uk/.

The Chartered Institute for Personnel and Development (CIPD) has an excellent website that provides access to reports and surveys on a range of important workplace issues. It is at http://www.cipd.co.uk.

One of a number of websites devoted to supporting people who experience disadvantage in the workplace is http://www.wide-network.org/. This is a European network for women, with a particular interest in training and development.

The UK's Equality and Human Rights Commission has a broad mission to support equality in all aspects of life. The organisation is taking increasing interest in workplace issues, and you can find out about current activities, including advice for employers, at http://www.equalityhumanrights.com/.

For further self-test material and relevant, annotated weblinks please visit the website at **www.pearsoned.co.uk/workpsych**

Suggested further reading

Full details for all references are given in the list at the end of this book.

1   Two papers from the *Annual Review of Psychology* are accessible and useful. These are the articles on (i) culture (Gelfand, Erez and Aycan, 2007) and (ii) diversity (Van Knippenberg and Schippers, 2007).

2   The sixth edition of Robert Ewen's book *An Introduction to Theories of Personality* provides a thorough but readable account of different traditions in psychology, particularly concerning how each tradition has construed the nature of the person and personality. Although Ewen majors on the psychoanalytic tradition, his coverage of the other traditions is clear and informative.

3   The 2004 book edited by David Holman and colleagues called *The Essentials of the New Workplace – A guide to the human impact of modern working practices,* published by WileyBlackwell, offers a really good detailed look at the human side of nearly every technology-driven workplace change that has happened over the last two decades.

4   Binna Kandola and Johanna Fullerton's book titled *Managing the Mosaic: Diversity in action* provides a down-to-earth but not oversimple account of some of the practical issues in managing a diverse workforce, and is written by two of the UK's leading consultants in this area.

CHAPTER 2

Theory, research and practice in work psychology

LEARNING OUTCOMES

After studying this chapter, you should be able to:

1 describe the main elements of a psychological theory, and explain the links between those elements;

2 distinguish between two opposing philosophies in the conduct of psychological research;

3 describe the various methods of data collection used in research by work psychologists;

4 describe the key features, advantages and disadvantages of different research designs used by work psychologists;

5 define the null and alternative hypotheses in psychological research;

6 explain the concept of statistical significance;

7 explain the concepts of power and effect size in statistical testing;

8 define in words the circumstances in which the following statistical techniques would be used:

   t-test,

   analysis of variance,

   chi-square,

   correlation,

   multiple regression,

   meta-analysis,

   structural equation modelling;

9 describe how qualitative data can be collected and analysed;

10 describe how interventions can be evaluated;

11 describe the divide that can occur between researchers and practitioners.

Introduction

In this chapter we build on the previous one by looking more closely at how theories in work psychology can be developed, evaluated and used. We start with an examination of the nature of theory and we provide a concrete example to show the factors that a good theory needs to take into account. Then we turn to the relationship between theory and practice. We argue that good practice requires good theory, and we discuss the problem that all too often theory-oriented and practice-oriented work psychologists find it difficult to communicate with (and learn from) each other. Then we take a look at the ways in which work psychologists conduct research, from the point of view of the overall strategy (research design) and also specific techniques (research methods). We consider how work psychologists' assumptions about the nature of knowledge and theory influence how they go about their research work, the kinds of data they obtain and how they interpret their data. Finally, we explain how statistical and qualitative techniques for analysing data can be utilised in order to draw conclusions about what the data mean. Many complex issues are involved in the appropriate use and interpretation of research data, and psychologists sometimes ignore them (Judd *et al.*, 1995). This chapter attempts, in a straightforward way, to help the reader avoid some of the more common pitfalls.

The nature of theory in work psychology

A theory in psychology can be defined as an organised collection of ideas that serves to describe, explain or predict what a person will do, think or feel. To be successful, it needs to specify the following five elements (*see also* Figure 2.1):

1　The particular behaviours, thoughts or emotions in question. These should have significance for human affairs.

2　Any differences between people in the degree to which they characteristically exhibit the behaviours, thoughts or emotions in question.

3　Any situational factors that might influence whether or when the behaviours, thoughts or emotions in question occur.

4　Any consequences of the interaction between 2 and 3 for the behaviours, thoughts or emotions.

5　Any ways in which the occurrence of particular behaviours, thoughts or emotions might feed back to produce change in 2 and 3.

To take an example, let us suppose that a psychologist wishes to develop a theory to explain and predict the occurrence of arriving late for work. Relevant individual characteristics might include a person's job satisfaction and the extent to which they tend to be well organised. Relevant past experiences might include punishments for being late. Situational features might include the distance from home to work, the simplicity or complexity of travel between home and work, and the expectations of the person's workmates. They may also include factors that

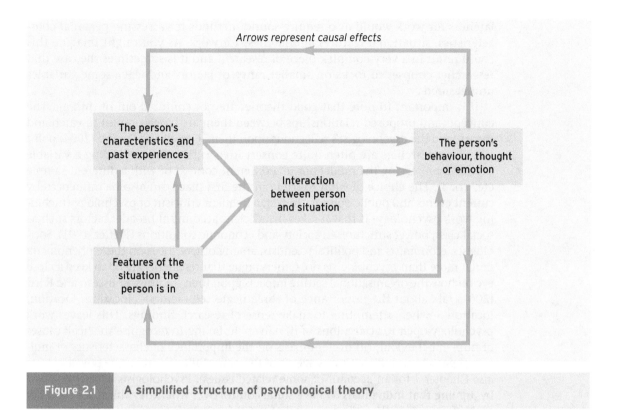

Arrows represent causal effects

The person's characteristics and past experiences

Interaction between person and situation

The person's behaviour, thought or emotion

Features of the situation the person is in

Figure 2.1   A simplified structure of psychological theory

change day by day such as the weather. These might all directly affect the person's actual incidence of arriving late for work, but so might the *interaction* between person and situation. For example, a well-organised person may have no difficulty making complex travel arrangements between home and work. For such a person, complexity of travel arrangements might *not* have much effect on time of arrival at work. A poorly organised person may be able to cope with straightforward travel arrangements but not complex ones. For that person, the complexity of travel to work could make a big difference to punctuality. This is an example of an *interaction effect* – the travel between work and home affects the lateness of some people but not others. In this case the interaction appears to be between the person and the environment.

Just to make things more complicated, it is likely that person and situation influence each other (this is sometimes referred to as the person–environment *transaction*). This can occur in at least three ways. Two of these will have happened before the specific events of interest to the psychologist. First, people's characteristics can affect the types of situation they expose themselves to. In this example, a badly organised person might not think carefully about travel to work when deciding where to live. Second, people may be able to change features of their situation, or features of their situation may change them. Third, a person's behaviour right now may lead him or her to change ('I'm late again; I must become a better organised person') or may cause a change in their situation (in an extreme case, being dismissed for being late once too often).

Naturally, it is possible to suggest many other personal characteristics and situational features that could influence lateness for work. The choice of which to investigate might itself be guided by theory. Testing and applying a theory of lateness for work would also require sound methods for assessing personal characteristics, situational features and lateness for work. As you might imagine this could result in a very complex piece of research, and it is sometimes the case that researcher chooses to focus on smaller range of factors and leave some variables unmeasured.

It is important to note that good theories are not conjured out of thin air. The concepts and proposed relationships between them are based on past research and theory, and the psychologist's reflections upon them. Cassell and Symon (2004) point out that researchers are often quite conservative in this respect 'adding a variable here or there, trying the model out in a different context or with a different sample etc.' (p. 4). The choice of what to study in the first place can also be influenced by current events and public opinion. In fact, a frequent criticism of psychology (including work psychology) is that it takes insufficient account of broader factors such as social class, power structures in society and economic conditions (Pfeffer, 1991). Sociologists, economists and political scientists, among others, focus on those phenomena much more than psychologists do. Others argue that researchers need to keep a close eye on how the organisational setting impacts upon their findings. Rousseau and Fried (2001) talk about the importance of three neglected factors – 'location, location, location' – when attempting to make sense of research findings. This leaves work psychology open to accusations of (i) naivety in failing to recognise the 'real' causes of human behaviour; (ii) overemphasis on the importance of characteristics of individual people; and (iii) acting as agents of the powerful rather than the powerless (*see also* Chapter 1 for an account of some related issues). Psychologists usually respond by arguing that individuals *do* have some control over what they think, feel and do. Each of us is more than the sum total of social forces acting upon us. To avoid bland generalisations, or those based on naive or simplistic notions of what it is to be human, it is crucial to examine individuals and their immediate environments.

Key Learning Point

The conventional view of good theory in work psychology is that the theory should be precise in specifying the behaviour, thoughts or feelings it is designed to predict, and the individual and situational characteristics which influence them.

The point was made in Chapter 1 that psychology is not a united or unified discipline. The multiplicity of views certainly extends to what research and theory are about and how research should be conducted. The most fundamental polarity has been described nicely by, among others, Easterby-Smith *et al.* (2002, Chapter 3) as positivism versus social constructionism. Each of these positions has distinct and very different philosophical roots. Easterby-Smith and colleagues stress that in practice nowadays much research includes a bit of both, and that they represent two extremes.

Positivism assumes that the social world exists objectively, i.e. that it has an objective reality. This usually (but not always) implies measuring things using quantitative (i.e. numerical) data. Science is seen as advancing by making hypotheses about laws and causes of human behaviour and then testing those hypotheses, preferably by simplifying the problem of interest as much as possible. It is also assumed that the researcher can investigate without influencing what is being investigated: that is, their presence and actions are assumed not to alter how people would naturally behave, think or feel.

The other extreme is labelled social constructionism by Easterby-Smith *et al*. It might also be termed phenomenological (*see* Chapter 1). This viewpoint suggests that reality is not objective. Instead, the meaning of events, concepts and objectives is constructed and interpreted by people, through their thought processes and social interactions. The discussion of cross-cultural issues in Chapter 1 shows how different people can interpret similar events in different ways. Research conducted on the basis of this philosophy will aim 'to understand and explain why people have different experiences, rather than search for external causes and fundamental laws to explain their behaviour' (Easterby-Smith *et al*., 2002, p. 30). So instead of measuring how often certain behaviours occur, the aim of research is to examine the different ways in which people interpret and explain their experience. The data produced by such research tend to be harder to obtain and to summarise than those produced by positivist research, but tend to be richer in meaning, detail and explanation.

To extend this principle one step further, if we collect data on people's interpretations of things, then we as researchers do some interpreting as well (we interpret our participants' interpretations: this is a sentence that is probably not best read late at night!). In other words, we cannot really gain direct access to the way participants view things because we have to interpret others' views. If we are going to collect data about someone's view of the world we will need to interact with them and interpret what they say. This means that the data produced are always an interpretation of the participant's experience, and hence the term interpretative phenomenological analysis (Willig, 2008). Reflexivity is an important concept in phenomenological research: researchers often go to great lengths to reflect upon their own point of view and how it has influenced the way they tackled the research question and interpreted research findings. Therefore, data are not viewed as some objective reality that exists independent of the view of the researcher or the views of the research participants.

Many topics in work psychology can be investigated from both perspectives and all points in between. To continue the example of arriving late for work, a positivist research project (which was the sort implied in the example given earlier) would assess the frequency of this behaviour and try to link it with objective factors such as distance from work as well as perhaps more subjective factors such as job satisfaction. The assumption would be that such factors may *cause* lateness for work, irrespective of the sense individuals might make of their situation. On the other hand, social constructionist research on lateness at work would focus much more on how individuals thought and felt about being late for work, and how they explained their own behaviour in this area. The general theoretical framework outlined in Figure 2.1 would still have some relevance, but aspects of the person and situation to be examined would be treated as part of people's ways of understanding and/or explaining their own behaviour rather than as objectively verifiable forces causing it. Ways of understanding and explaining might be researched by asking people about them directly, or alternatively by observing their behaviour and making inferences from the observations. For example they might look at what distance to work *meant* to the employee (did they see it as a challenge to be tackled through planning, or as a good source of excuses for being late?). The researcher might also consider how their own views on lateness had impacted upon the data collection and analysis.

Work psychology research published in academic journals such as those listed in Chapter 1 is mostly positivist. This probably reflects psychology's attempts to position itself as a science subject, with consequences for the ways in which work psychologists are trained, as well as the kinds of people it attracts in the first place. Some psychologists (e.g. Johnson and Cassell, 2001) have, however, criticised the highly positivist and quantitative orientation of work psychology. They argue strongly that phenomenological studies have many advantages over positivist ones, and deserve a more prominent place in work psychology. Cassell and Symon (2004) state that qualitative non-positivist studies 'hold out the promise of new insights by adopting a critical stance on accepted practices and approaching research topics with different objectives' (p. 4).

Key Learning Point

There is an important philosophical disagreement in psychology between positivism and phenomenological approaches. The former emphasises objectively verifiable causes of behaviour, thoughts and emotions; the latter focuses more on people's subjective explanations and accounts.

Theory and practice in work psychology

Some might argue that theory has little to offer practice. There are various reasons for advancing that argument. Theories in a particular area may not be very good, in the sense that they do not adequately or accurately specify the phenomena portrayed in Figure 2.1. A psychologist may find that a particular technique seems to work well, and not be concerned about theoretical reasons *why* it works. Work psychology is predominantly problem-centred. There is no single dominant theoretical perspective, and (again as noted earlier) work psychology has sometimes been somewhat isolated from theoretical developments in mainstream psychology. Sparrow (1999), for example, criticised work psychologists for ignoring theoretical developments in social psychology in their study of people at work. The present authors firmly believe that a good theory is essential to *good* practice. It is incorrect to say, as people sometimes do, that an idea is good in theory but not in practice. A good theory does a good job of describing, explaining and predicting behaviour, thoughts or emotions which have important outcomes. Basing practice on good theory *is* better than basing it on superstition, guesswork or an inferior theory. As the distinguished social psychologist Kurt Lewin (1945) long ago argued, there is nothing so practical as a good theory.

In an excellent article, Gary Johns (Johns, 1993) analysed why techniques advocated by work psychologists (e.g. in personnel selection or job design) are not always adopted in organisations, even if they seem to be based on good research and have potential to save (or make) money. He argued that work psychologists often neglect the political and social contexts of organisations. Organisational context can be defined as 'situational opportunities and constraints that affect the occurrence and meaning of organizational behaviour as well as functional relationships between variables' (Johns, 2006; p. 386). Context considerations (such as 'I am under pressure to make money') loom larger in managers' minds than the finer points of a psychologist's arguments concerning the technical merit of, for example, a particular personality measure. Managers are likely to respond to such factors as how rival companies do things, what legislation requires and what their bosses are likely to find readily acceptable. Evidence for the effectiveness of a psychological theory or technique is often derived from quite complex, abstract research, where the social and political context in which the research was carried out is either not adequately reported or non-existent. The sorts of contextual variables Johns (2001, 2006) has in mind include an organisation's recent history, the state of the labour market (e.g. how much unemployment there is) and cultural influences on what constitutes appropriate behaviour at work.

Johns (1993) argued that if work psychologists want to influence management practice, they should also be prepared to publicly name organisations that adopt good practice, since permission to do so is usually granted, and managers are more impressed by information about named organisations than unnamed ones. Perhaps this is one reason why articles in popular management journals have more impact within organisations than those published in psychology journals. Work psychologists should also actively seek to publish their work in managers' journals as well as academic ones. Unfortunately many academics are not accustomed to writing for manager audiences. In addition, the reward system in academia rarely gives them sufficient encouragement to do so.

In recent years work psychologists and their professional bodies have become increasingly concerned about an apparent lack of communication between those who produce new knowledge (researchers) and those who might put it to use in real workplaces (consultants and managers). It seems that researchers often believe that consultants and managers fail to make proper use of existing knowledge, preferring instead to follow their 'gut feeling' or established practice. Managers and consultants commonly think that researchers fail to produce information that is relevant to their day-to-day concerns, and even if they do, they fail to communicate it well.

Hodgkinson and Herriot (2002) distinguish between two ways of doing research in work psychology: scientific enquiry and problem-solving. These are shown in Figure 2.2. It can be seen that the latter involves much more engagement than the

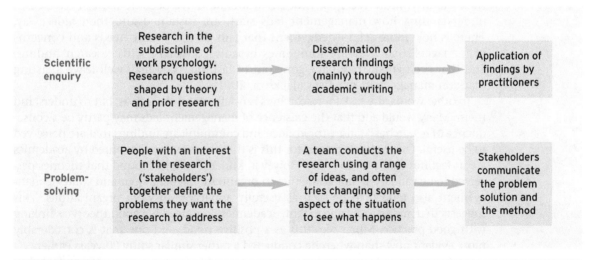

Figure 2.2   **Two ways of doing research in work psychology**
Source: **adapted from Hodgkinson and Herriot (2002). Copyright John Wiley & Sons Ltd. Reproduced with permission.**

former with people in the workplace(s) being researched. However, Hodgkinson and Herriot also argue for the importance of conducting problem-solving research rigorously using careful methods and relevant theory, rather than just chatting to a few people or 'getting the feel of things'.

Much has been made of an 'academic–practitioner' divide that seems to exist in work psychology. What this is divide is, and how such a gap can be bridged, has been the subject of much debate from both sides of the divide. By now you might have formed your own views about psychology as a science. Certainly there are some aspects of psychology that are like the 'hard sciences' (such as physics or chemistry) where variables are carefully measured and manipulated in controlled settings. Experimental studies of visual and auditory perception are examples of this. When we use psychological theory in organisations, things are generally less clear-cut. As Johns (2006) and Cox *et al.* (2007) argue, work psychologists often practise in fairly chaotic environments, where there are a number of different influences on what is achievable and acceptable. This leads many psychologists who come from an experimental background to question the scientific rigour of research carried out in organisational settings.

Anderson *et al.* (2001b) provide a useful categorisation of four types of enquiry that work psychologists might engage in. In *popularist science* the relevance of the research is very high: its addresses a pressing organisational problem. However, in the dash to solve the problem, scientific rigour is sacrificed. The latest fads in organisational research might fall into this category. There is always a risk that organisations will be drawn to practitioners of this type of science, because of its perceived relevance. Academics worry that concepts developed in this way often fail to deliver on the promises made by those who develop them. Researchers often complain that managers and consultants are far more keen on management fads (i.e. the latest popular ideas about how to do management) than on the findings of rigorous research. Academics tended at one time to be very dismissive of so-called fads such as business process re-engineering (BPR), total quality management (TQM) and emotional intelligence (EI), because they were not based on good research showing their validity. More recently, though, academics have become more interested in understanding how management fads start, are sustained and then fade away. There is now more acknowledgement that fads do meet some needs and concerns of managers, that they are sometimes broadly consistent with research findings and that even when they have gone out of fashion, they may well leave a lasting mark on management practices (Jackson, 2001).

In other words, the task for researchers is not to moan about fads, but to understand them. Many would add that the existence of management fads may partly be a consequence of researchers' failure to produce and communicate findings that are perceived to be useful. One possible reason for this is that theories most favoured by academics are in fact not very easy to apply. However, Miner (2003) has found that theories perceived to be valid by senior academics in organisational behaviour and strategic management also tended to be seen as usefully applicable in work organisations. This suggests that, at least to some extent, academics do indeed see good theory as linking with good practice. Miner sees this as a positive trend, and one that is considerably more evident now than when he conducted a rather similar study 20 years earlier.

At the other extreme Anderson *et al.* (2001b) identify two other approaches to science: *puerile science* and *pedantic science*. These forms of research have limited use because they fail to address problems that have practical relevance. Pedantic science addresses issues well enough to satisfy the hard-nosed academic through well-designed and executed research, but the results are of limited use because there are few opportunities to apply them. An excellent study about the relationship between scuba-diving experience and the performance of bee-keepers in a call centre environment might constitute pedantic science. This is an extreme (and to the best of our knowledge hypothetical) example. In puerile science the methodological rigour is poor (perhaps only one bee-keeper was studied and a poorly designed questionnaire was used) and the issue being addressed is unimportant. Fortunately, such information rarely finds its way into the work psychologist's toolkit.

The approach that many work psychologists aim for is what Anderson *et al.* (2001b) refer to as *pragmatic science*. This type of work addresses problems of practical importance and does so using rigorous methodology. We have tried to ensure that, where possible, the vast majority of the material cited in this text falls into this category. It refers to research that is done well, that has been subject to review and critique, and stood up to such tests of its quality. At the same time, the research is useful and relevant: it helps organisations. Linley (2006, p. 3) summarises the benefits of this approach:

> Good research questions have the potential to bridge the academic–practitioner divide very effectively, because they catalyse the interests, needs, and aspirations of both parties through delivering findings that are not only academically sound and valued, but that also offer practical application and advancement.

Key Learning Point

Pragmatic science gives us the best of both worlds: good research that has clear practical relevance.

In pragmatic science good research and practice are almost indistinguishable. Bond *et al.* (2008) report an excellent example of pragmatic science. They implemented an intervention designed to improve working conditions in a call centre. The study had a control group (that did not receive the intervention, so the effects on the group receiving the intervention could be adequately examined) and collected data over a reasonably long period of time. The study examined the impact of the intervention on issues that were important to the organisation (e.g. absence levels). From a theoretical perspective the study was also strong because it looked at how changes in perceptions of working conditions and individual differences (and the interactions between them) are linked to employee well-being.

However, there are tensions that can draw researchers and practitioners away from pragmatic science. The vast majority of research published in academic journals is carried out by academics (written by academics for academics). One might suspect that academics do not always have an intimate understanding of the issues that are currently vexing managers and practitioners. The organisational context can also ration the opportunities for carrying out rigorous work in organisations. In intervention research it is often difficult (though not impossible) to persuade organisations to use control groups. Managers might sensibly ask why, if an intervention is likely to be effective, should it be denied to a large proportion of employees through the use of a control group? Managers might also be concerned that if there is a need for a control group, there might be some doubt as to whether the intervention is effective at all. Rigour in real-world research is more difficult to establish and maintain, meaning that talented academics also need to develop strong consultancy skills in order to carry out pragmatic research. It is also the case that ethical considerations mean that some manipulations are not possible in functioning organisations. For example, it would not be ethical to attempt the controlled manipulation of the information provided to a manager about their employees' performance because this could result in irrecoverable damage to manager–subordinate relationships. This is one of the reasons why many controlled investigations into the dynamics of performance appraisals are carried out in simulated appraisal settings (quite often using samples of willing undergraduate students). Of course, there is likely to be some debate as to whether such findings will be valid in the 'real world' (i.e. whether the results demonstrate *ecological validity*).

Rynes *et al.* (1999) have examined how research projects can have an impact on practice within work organisations. They found that the amount of time spent by the researcher on site and whether the organisation contracted the research (as opposed to simply helping a work psychologist conduct their research) both appeared to influence whether the research findings were implemented. Both of these factors are consistent with a 'problem-solving' rather than 'scientific enquiry' approach to research. Yet the most common form of work psychology research is the use of questionnaires designed on the basis of the researcher's knowledge and interests and completed by employees with minimal researcher involvement in the organisation. We should not be surprised if this research has little practical impact.

Key Learning Point

If work psychology is to have a substantial influence on organisational and public policy, work psychologists must get involved in the organisations they research, and address the political acceptability as well as the technical merit of their recommendations.

Finally in this section, we should note that the effective application of theory and research is rarely straightforward. It depends on many broader factors such as policy priorities, values and demographics. Two examples can illustrate this well. First, Gardner (2003) points out that the finding that it is difficult to change intelligence as measured by psychometric tests (*see* Chapter 3) could mean that (i) it is not worth trying or (ii) we need to try extra hard and devote lots of resources to the effort. The choice depends on many factors, including what we think intelligence test scores say about an individual's behaviour and quality of life, and what value we ascribe to those potential consequences of intelligence.

The second example arises from the work of one of the authors (Arnold). He and colleagues conducted research for the UK Government's Department of Health, investigating why people did or did not want to work for the UK's National Health Service (NHS) as nurses, radiographers or physiotherapists. Two of the findings were as follows:

1 People who were already qualified in one of those three professions and had chosen to leave the NHS were unlikely to return.

2 After allowing for factors such as whether someone is already qualified, and their perceptions of NHS work, older people were less inclined to work for the NHS than younger people.

On the face of it, two implications for the Department of Health in its attempts to raise NHS staffing levels might be: do not target already-qualified people, and target younger people more than older ones. However, it is possible to draw quite different conclusions. On the first point, it can be argued that already-qualified people are quite easy to find (for example via professional associations) and do not require extensive training, so even a low success rate in attracting them back to the NHS might be a worthwhile investment. On the second point, given that the general population of the United Kingdom (like most countries) is ageing, it would be unwise to stop trying to recruit older people. Instead extra efforts and new strategies should be devised to attract older people.

Key Learning Point

A schematic summary of some key points of this section is shown in Figure 2.3. The formulation, conduct, output and utilisation of research in work psychology are all part of a complex process.

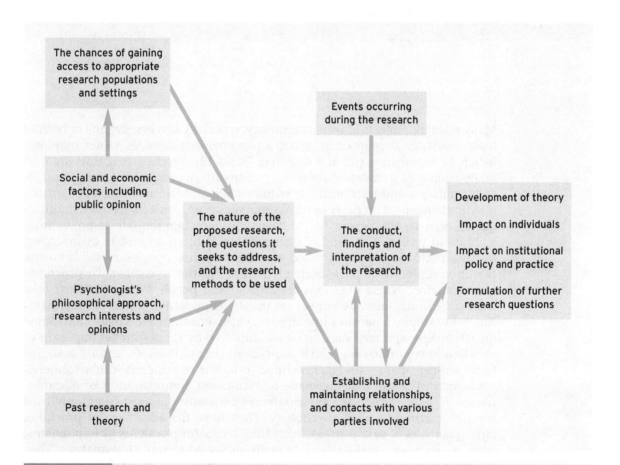

| Figure 2.3 | The research process in work psychology |

Research methods in work psychology

Work psychologists use a variety of techniques in their research on human behaviour, thoughts and emotions in the workplace. In considering these techniques, it is helpful to distinguish between research *designs* and research *methods*. The former concern the overall research strategy employed. This strategy depends on the researcher's beliefs about scientific investigation as well as the nature of the phenomena being researched. Research methods are the specific ways in which information is gathered within the overall research strategy. Drawing on Bryman (2001), a number of designs and methods can be identified. There is more than one way of carrying out each design and each method. The designs are discussed later in this chapter. First, it is necessary to make a few points about each of the research methods.

Key Learning Point

Research design refers to the overall strategy in conducting research, whereas research methods are the procedures by which information is collected.

Questionnaires and psychometric tests

Many research projects in work psychology, especially surveys, use one or both of these. Questionnaires are often used to assess a person's attitudes, values, opinions, beliefs or experiences (*see also* Chapters 7 and 12). Psychometric tests are normally employed to measure ability or personality (*see also* Chapters 3, 4 and 5). Questionnaires and tests normally require a person to answer a series of written questions presented on paper or on a computer screen. Answers are often multiple-choice; that is, the person has to select the most appropriate response from a choice of several. This kind of questionnaire is often referred to as *structured*, because both the questions asked and the response options available to the person completing it have been predefined by the researcher. Unstructured questionnaires, where questions are broader and people respond in their own words, are much rarer. Responses are usually expressed as a number representing, for example, a person's intelligence, extroversion or job satisfaction. Some questionnaires and tests need to be administered by the researcher in person or in a tightly controlled way (such as psychometric testing). Others are designed to be self-explanatory and can be filled in by the respondent without supervision. Increasing use is being made of Web-based administration of questionnaires and tests. Structured questionnaires are easily the most commonly used research method in work psychology. They have the advantage of providing large quantities of data with relatively little hassle for researcher or respondents. Also, the data are usually relatively easily subjected to statistical analysis. They are often used in a positivist way. This means that they may fail to reflect important aspects of respondents' experiences, and be (mis)used by the researcher as a way of getting quick and easy information rather than truly engaging with people in the setting being researched (*see also* the previous section of this chapter).

Interviews

A work psychologist may conduct one or more interviews, normally with an individual, but sometimes with a group of people. Group interviews are often designed to encourage discussion among interviewees about one or more topics, and are often referred to as focus groups (Millward, 2000). The work psychologist asks questions and records responses, either by making notes or using a voice recorder. The questions may be specified in advance, in which case it is a *structured interview*. On the other hand, the interviewer may define only the general topic they wish to investigate and permit respondents to talk about whatever they wish within that topic. This is an *unstructured interview*.

Interview data, and some forms of archival data (see below), are particularly open to alternative forms of analysis. The type of analysis that is to be carried out should be reflected in the design of the interview. Content analysis usually involves assigning interviewee responses to one or more categories or types, according to what the interviewee said when asked a particular question. This is probably the most common way of analysing interview data in work psychology. One of the authors of this text and colleagues used this form of analysis (template analysis) to better understand the experiences that nurses had when they were given more office hours to reduce the stress caused by the conflict between their administrative and clinical workloads (Randall *et al.*, 2007). Discourse analysis and conversation analysis involve a closer look at sequences of interviewee statements, often including information about the length of pauses, voice intonation and perhaps (if videotaped) other aspects of non-verbal behaviour. The aim here would usually be to show how the interviewee is seeking to present themself in certain ways, and/or to construct plausible accounts. The researcher might also be interested in how the normal rules of conversation are reflected (or not) in the interviewee's talk. An example of how interview data can be analysed appears later in this chapter. Grounded theory (see Lansisalmi *et al.*, 2004) is a technique that is used to generate new theories from data. In this approach to data analysis, the researcher seeks to identify categories or concepts within qualitative data and take this a step further by examining the linkages and relationships between those categories.

Psychophysiological and psychophysical measures

Psychophysiological and psychophysical measures involve assessing a person's neurological, biological, physical or physiological state or performance. So, for example, in a study of work stress, blood samples may be taken to gauge the concentration of fatty acids in a person's bloodstream. Other types of measures (see Barrett and Sowden, 2000) include muscle activity, eye movements and electrical activity in the brain (by electroencephalogram [EEG]). These methods of data collection are less common in work psychology than in some other areas of psychology. This is partly because collecting such data is invasive, and organisations and their employees are often reluctant to engage in such research. Moreover, although research of this type yields 'hard data', organisations are rarely concerned about blood corti-sol levels, and much more concerned with issues such as performance, absence and turnover.

Observation

A work psychologist may observe people's behaviour by stationing themselves as un-obtrusively as possible, and recording the frequency, source and timing of behav-iour. This can be termed *structured observation*. Alternatively, the work psychologist may participate in the events they are studying. For example, King (1992) investi-gated innovations on a hospital ward while also working as a nursing assistant. This is *participant observation*. Observations are often used in the development of competency frameworks for use in selection and training. Patterson *et al.* (2008) describe how observations of doctors were used to help choose and design appro-priate selection methods and to identify the knowledge, skill and attitudes that needed to be assessed during selection. Where people are being observed in their workplace, they are normally informed, or asked about it in advance. Their aware-ness may itself affect their behaviour (*see* Chapter 1), but that is usually preferable to the alternatives of secrecy or even deception. Observation may also include observing the consequences of behaviour; for example, a person's work productiv-ity. Silverman (2001) emphasises that observation is not simply seeing and hearing what is 'out there'. The researcher's observations will inevitably be influenced by their theoretical orientation and the focus of their research. This is not bad in itself, but needs to be acknowledged: *reflexivity* is often used to describe this process of introspection whereby the researcher analyses how their own perspectives influence on the way the data were collected and recorded. Observation without some focus or goals will in any case lead to an unmanageable amount of uninterpretable data. Clearly, a strength of observation is that it allows the researcher to form impressions of what is said and done in a workplace at first hand (without having to rely upon *potentially* biased data from employees). It also allows access to everyday mundane events, not just 'big' events, and not just the kind of summary of a person's opinions and perceptions that is usually obtained from questionnaires and interviews. One possible disadvantage of observation is that if people know they are being observed, they may behave, think or feel differently from how they otherwise would.

Key Learning Point

Observational data should not be interpreted as 'hard facts'. This is because employees are likely to be aware that they are being observed, and the observer will have their own per-spective on what they are observing.

Diaries

People may be asked to keep a diary of key events and/or their behaviour, thoughts and feelings. It is normally necessary to give people a fair amount of structure to help them to focus their written comments, and to stay in contact with them as an encouragement to keep up the diary-filling. For example, in a study of the impact of achieving goals on people's sense of emotional well-being, Harris *et al.* (2003) obtained diary data from 22 call centre workers twice a day for 12 days. Most of these data consisted of workers' responses to questions about their goals and their mood – in effect, a questionnaire in diary form. Respondents were e-mailed each day to remind them to complete their diary. One important advantage of the diary method is the ability to track the detailed and fast-moving developments of people's day-to-day lives. One disadvantage is that, almost inevitably, some people on some occasions will forget to complete their diary, or simply not bother.

Experience sampling methodology (ESM) is a mixture of questionnaire and diary methods. Often ESM studies use electronic hand-held devices that are issued to participants. Alarms on these devices sound a number of times during the day: when the alarm sounds the participant answers questions presented on the electronic device. This approach helps researchers to investigate the relationships between variables (for example if a person reported feeling happy at work at lunchtime, might it be that their experiences at work in the morning offered an explanation for their happiness?). Because data collection is more 'instant' the data collected may be more accurate than data collected once a day (*see* Daniels *et al.*, 2009).

Archival sources

As Bryman (2001) has pointed out, archival sources are a potentially rich but sometimes neglected form of data. This is, strictly speaking, a source of data rather than a method of collecting it. Archival information is anything that already exists in organised form before the work psychologist's investigation. Examples include absenteeism data, company accounts, productivity records, human resource policy documents, accident statistics, minutes of meetings and many others. Data from archival sources are most often used either to provide a context for a particular research project, or to investigate the impact of an event on the functioning of an organisation.

Archival sources are important in pragmatic science. Research that shows how interventions impact upon 'hard' organisational outcomes such as absence, performance or turnover are seen as providing good evidence to support theories and as having a direct (often monetary) benefit to organisations. Archival sources often yield quantitative data such as how much a workgroup has produced or how many people were promoted in a particular year. There is a temptation to view such data as being inherently free from bias and as objective criteria upon which to judge the validity of a theory or success of an intervention. However, this is not always the case. In Chapter 6 we discuss the difficulties in obtaining reliable, valid and fair objective measures of performance. Unfortunately, organisations do not always keep accurate records of absence (e.g. is someone who is 'working at home' actually absent from work?). We also know that turnover is a very complex phenomenon and extremely difficult to influence through a single intervention (see Chapter 7). The same could also be said of absence and performance data. Nonetheless, if such measures can be shown to be accurate, explaining and influencing them is often seen as the 'holy grail' of pragmatic research.

Archival methods can also produce qualitative data, which may be the main focus of a particular research study. For example, in research on media coverage of a particular topic, newspaper stories often *are* the data. A researcher may wish to examine what kinds of narrative structures are present in the articles, what purposes they are designed to achieve and so on. Delgado (2003) analyses press coverage in the United States of the soccer match between the United States and Iran in the 1998 World Cup, and discusses how political and ideological issues, as well as sporting ones, affected how the match was reported.

Research methods and philosophical stances

We noted earlier that there is a broad distinction between two kinds of research in work psychology (Easterby-Smith *et al.*, 2002). One (easily the most common in published work psychology research) is based on the proposition that the data collected reflect (albeit imperfectly) an objective reality. This research is sometimes referred to as positivist research. The other kind is based on the assumption that most or all of what work psychologists study is best seen as *socially constructed* – that is, it reflects subjective experience that is made sense of by individuals and groups through their own thought processes and social interactions.

In work psychology, most of the first kind of research tends to use questionnaires and tests because these tend to produce the most 'ready-made' quantitative data, and because the researchers believe that they will yield data that approximate to an objectively verifiable reality. There is also some use of psychophysical and psychophysiological methods – these are quite rare in most areas of work psychology, but where they are used, they are almost always in research of the positivist kind. The other methods listed above may also be used in that kind of research, but tend not to be. Qualitative researchers tend to use interviews, observations and/or archival material, and possibly unstructured questionnaires and recorded naturally occurring conversations.

The same method may be viewed in different ways by researchers from the two traditions. It is important to note that a particular approach to science is not wedded to particular research methods. For example, a positivist researcher who uses interview data will aim to obtain facts about the interviewee's behaviour, thoughts or emotions. If there is some other information that appears to contradict what the interviewee said, or if researchers analysing the interview data do not agree on what an interviewee's response means, the validity of the data is seen as being open to question. Positivist researchers will often use qualitative methods to gather information about an issue that is poorly understood: the qualitative data will then be used to design a questionnaire so as to understand the issue better (e.g. Randall *et al.*, 2009).

Non-positivist researchers, on the other hand, are more likely to treat the interviewee's talk as reflecting their authentic experiences, or as something mutually constructed in conversation with the interviewer. For example, Millward (2006) used interpretative phenomenological analysis to explore women's experiences of maternity leave through to their return to the organisation. Shepherd (2006) used an interpretative approach to explore how the implementation of technology was described in organisations as a means of understanding how such changes could be successfully implemented.

Either way, the existence of other information which contradicts what the interviewee said (possibly even other information from the interviewee themself) may be seen as interesting or as inconsequential, but not usually as a problem (*see* Silverman, 2001, Chapter 4).

A work psychologist's research data can be obtained using questionnaires, psychometric tests, interviews, observation of behaviour, measurement of bodily activity and existing data banks.

Research designs

The survey design

The key distinguishing feature of a survey is that it does not intervene in naturally occurring events, nor does it control them. It simply takes a snapshot of what is happening, usually by asking people about it. The aim is usually to gather (mostly) quantitative information about certain phenomena (for example, events, attitudes) from a large number of people. On occasions this will be done simply to ascertain the frequency of occurrence of a certain event, such as feeling anxious at work. More commonly, a survey will attempt to discover the relationships of variables with each other – for example, whether anxiety at work tends to be accompanied by low job satisfaction (this does not mean that anxiety causes satisfaction, but just that the two tend to occur together).

The survey design could involve use of any of the methods described above. However, it most commonly involves questionnaires. Questionnaires cannot be just thrown together (as they are in some popular magazines) if they are to do a proper job. Consistent with the positivist research philosophy, they must be carefully devised so that they unambiguously measure what they are supposed to measure – i.e. so that they are *valid* (*see* Chapter 4). It is important to ask the right people to participate in the survey. Ideally, the respondents should be a *representative sample* of all those people to whom the survey is relevant. Sometimes random sampling is used along with checks and balances to ensure that the random sample is representative of the group being studied. This means that everyone to whom the survey was relevant would have an equal chance of participating in it. In practice, of course, this is rarely the case.

This leads to another point: exactly what information should be collected in the survey? Questionnaires set the boundaries for the data collection: if the question is not asked, the employee cannot respond to it. What is included in the questionnaire and the way questions are worded are often driven by the researcher's interpretation of theory. The work psychologist might ask about any number of things. If we were interested in the relationship between the type of work a person did and their job satisfaction, then age, sex, work experience, educational attainment, abilities required by work, job status, supervision, friendships at work, wage levels and working conditions are just a few of the things we might ask about. There is always the possibility that some *third variable* (a factor we had not considered and measured), such as prior work experience, determined *both* a person's job satisfaction *and* the kind of work he or she did. Unless we knew about their prior experience, we could not examine its importance.

Thus the survey has both advantages and disadvantages (*see* Bryman, 2001). It can be used with people directly involved in the issues to be investigated. It can investigate their experiences in their day-to-day setting. It is normally fairly easy to conduct, and makes relatively low demands on people's time. On the other hand, the survey does not involve any manipulation of the variables being investigated. This makes it very difficult to establish cause and effect. The survey takes the world as it is. The world is complicated, and unless the survey takes all relevant factors into account, it may lead the psychologist to draw incorrect conclusions. Various sophisticated data analysis techniques (see later in this chapter, especially the sections on regressions and structural equation modelling) can reduce this danger, but not eliminate it entirely. Having said all of that, surveys often provide a good jumping off point for further research. They provide quick tests of relationships between variables that can then be examined more rigorously with more complex research designs.

Key Learning Point

Surveys are relatively easy to conduct and they investigate the real world in which people work. However, it is often difficult to be sure about causes and effects.

Longitudinal surveys can help to clarify cause and effect relationships. In a longitudinal survey, data are gathered on more than one occasion. This contrasts with *cross-sectional* surveys, where data are collected on one occasion only. Longitudinal data can help to tease out possible causal connections. Conditions pertaining at time 1 may cause those at time 2 but not, presumably, vice versa. Again, though, there remains the danger of key information not being collected. Also, even if event A happens before event B, that does not necessarily mean that A *causes* B: our research design would also need to gather data on other possible causes of B and examine their effects.

Sometimes survey research involves collection of information from sources other than the people concerned (for example, archival data from the personnel records of a company), but often *all* the data consist of people's *self-reports* of their behaviour, thoughts and/or emotions. These may not be accurate or complete, and in any case the questions asked of respondents may not reflect what matters most to them. Data that are entirely self-reported are also subject to a problem called *common method variance*, which is where the relationship between variables is artificially high simply because all of the data are obtained by the same method. For example, if we found that having lots of control at work was linked to high job satisfaction, this relationship could be partly due to the fact that the respondents responded to all questionnaire items in a similar way, rather than there being some psychological mechanism that linked control at work and job satisfaction. To avoid this problem, researchers suggest that where possible more than one source of data should be used to capture information.

Finally, survey information can be collected using interviews (*see* previous section). Market researchers and social researchers often conduct them. The interview is in effect often used as a talking questionnaire. However, it can also be employed to explore issues with respondents in more depth than a questionnaire allows. Conducting research interviews is a skilled business. From a positivist point of view, care must be taken to gain the trust of the respondent, to explore issues to the extent required and to avoid accidentally influencing the respondent's answers. All these are in order to maximise the accuracy of the data and reflect the true state of affairs. Of course, work psychologists who are not sympathetic to positivist research would say that there is no absolute truth out there to find, and that while establishing a good relationship with the interviewee might be ethically desirable, it inevitably influences what is said in the interview.

The experimental design

The claim of psychology to be a science rests partly on its extensive use of experiments. One key advantage of an experiment is that it allows the psychologist *control* over what happens and rules out alternative explanations for the research findings. This in turn permits inference about causes and effects. On the other hand, there are some disadvantages too. These are discussed below, but first let us examine a concrete example.

The most controlled environment is the psychologist's laboratory. For example, the psychologist might set up a conveyor belt in the laboratory. They would probably choose a task typical of conveyor belt work – perhaps checking that boxes of chocolates have been properly packed. The boxes travel along the conveyor belt at a set speed, and the worker has to remove any faultily packed ones. People might be asked to work on this task for a period of several weeks, and to indicate their job satisfaction at various points during that period.

All of this would, of course, cost a lot of money. A large research grant would be required. The psychologist would probably also take the opportunity to record other things apart from job satisfaction, such as work performance (proportion of incorrectly packed boxes identified) and perhaps some physiological measures of stress (e.g. heart rate, blood cholesterol levels).

This would not be enough on its own. It would also be necessary to include a *control group* as well as the *experimental group* already described. People in the control group should as far as possible do the same job as the experimental group, except that their task would not be machine-paced. Hence, the control group would perhaps be given piles of boxes of chocolates, and instructed to check them. Data on job satisfaction, etc. would be collected from members of the control group in the same way and at the same times as from the experimental group.

The work psychologist would try to ensure that the conditions experienced by the experimental and control groups differed *only* in whether or not their task was machine-paced. The two groups have the same task. They perform it in the same laboratory (though the groups may not see each other or even be aware of each other's existence). They can be paid the same amount with the same pay rules, and be supervised in the same way, though the difference between paced and non-paced work may make these last two similarities difficult to achieve in practice. The groups can be given the same opportunities (or lack of them) for interaction with other workers. It would not be easy to ensure that the two groups did the same *amount* of work. The control group could be told that they had to check the same number of boxes per day or week as the experimental group. This would introduce some degree of pacing, though not nearly as much as a conveyor belt running at a constant speed.

Two key terms in experimental jargon are as follows. The *independent variable* is what the psychologist manipulates in order to examine its effect on the *dependent variable*. In this example, therefore, the independent variable is whether or not the work is machine-paced, and the dependent variable is job satisfaction. More complex experiments often have more than one independent variable (in the example above we might also adjust the volume of work to examine its effects), and more than one dependent variable (in the example above we could look at job satisfaction, self-reported well-being, blood pressure, etc.).

Another important point concerns the people who undertake the work for the sake of the experiment (who used to be called the *subjects* but are now more often *participants*). Ideally, they would be typical of people who do that kind of work. If so, this would increase the confidence with which experimental results could be applied to the 'real world'. An attempt to recruit such people to the experiment could be made by advertising in local newspapers. This might not be successful, however. Since most researchers work in higher education, they would be tempted to recruit students because they are easy to find – and they usually need the money that is often paid for participation in experiments! But because students are unlikely to work at conveyor belts for much of their career, their reactions in the experiment might not be typical of those who do. Whoever participates in the experiment, individuals would normally be *assigned at random* to either the experimental group or the control group. This random assignment helps to ensure that the people in the two groups do not differ in systematic ways.

It should now be clear that the laboratory experiment allows the psychologist to make unambiguous inferences about the effects on job satisfaction of machine-paced work. Or does it? The psychologist's control necessarily makes it an artificial situation because the real world is rarely so neat and tidy. Unless the psychologist indulges in a huge (and unethical) deception, the experimental participants will know that they are not in a real job, and that the experiment will last only a few weeks. This could crucially affect their reactions to the work. So could the guesses they make about what the psychologist is investigating. These guesses will be influenced by unintentional cues from the experimenter via (for example) tone of voice and body posture. Such cues are termed *demand characteristics*. Every experiment has them. In running experiments something is gained – control – but something is lost – realism. Arguments rage over the use of experimental approaches to investigate organisational phenomena. Some argue that it is only by finding out things in controlled settings first that one can begin to study them in more applied settings. Others argue that the experimental situation produces results that wouldn't be discovered in the 'real world' because they do not exist there.

Key Learning Point

Laboratory experiments allow the work psychologist to control and manipulate the situation in order to establish whether there are causal relationships between variables, but it is often not clear whether the same relationships would occur in real-life situations.

Sometimes it is possible to conduct a *field experiment* instead. *Quasi-experiments* (see Cook and Campbell, 1979) of varying degrees of sophistication are often used in work psychology. For a work psychologist these experiments would take place in a real work setting, probably with the people who worked there. Such experiments rarely have 'perfect' designs. Even if managers and union officials at a factory were prepared to allow the psychologist to create an experimental and control group on the factory floor, they would probably not allow random assignment of subjects to groups. Also, they probably could not arrange things such as identical supervision and identical opportunities to interact with co-workers even if they wanted to. And even if they did, it would be unlikely that the researcher could maintain control over these things throughout the whole study.

Occasionally, it is possible for psychologists to conduct a field experiment using events that are occurring anyway. This is sometimes called a *natural experiment*. For example some groups may engage in interventions to improve their working conditions while other groups who will get the intervention some time later act as a 'waiting list' control. For example, a chocolate factory may be changing some, but not all, of its chocolate inspection from self-paced work to conveyor belts (*see* Kemp *et al.*, 1983, for a rather similar situation). The psychologist could use this profitably, especially if they were able to obtain data on job satisfaction, etc. both before and after the change was made. Here again, though, the gain in realism is balanced by a loss of control and the consequent presence of confounding factors. For example, the people working at the factory might have some choice of which form of work they undertook. This immediately violates the principle of random allocation to groups. On the other hand, one might argue that if this is the way the world works, there is nothing to be gained by trying to arrange conditions that do not reflect it. Random allocation established groups of employees to interventions is sometimes possible (e.g. department A gets the intervention while department B does not).

Key Learning Point

It is occasionally possible to conduct experiments in real-world settings, though usually the work psychologist has far less control over the situation than in laboratory experiments.

Evaluating interventions

As described in Chapter 1, one of the key aims of work psychologists is to make a difference in organisations (as well as coming up with interesting and exciting new theories!). Quasi-experimental research designs are often used to help us identify whether an intervention works or not. For example, we might be interested in whether training employees to use a new piece of equipment helped them to develop more knowledge about how that piece of equipment worked. The simplest solution would be to train all employees and to see if their knowledge changed (i.e. to measure knowledge before the training, and then again after the training).

However, could we be sure that it was the training that had an effect? Could it be that by just working with the new equipment their knowledge had developed? What if completing the knowledge test before the training sparked some employees' interest and they went to do some of their own research about the new equipment, and it was this that helped them to develop new knowledge?

Research designs of varying degrees of sophistication are used to evaluate interventions, and as a general rule of thumb, the more sophisticated the design, the more alternative explanations for change are tested. Table 2.1 shows some of the designs available to researchers.

Table 2.1	Some research designs for the evaluation of interventions

Pre-post single intervention group, no control group design.

	Measure before intervention?	Intervention delivered?	Measure after intervention?
Group 1	Yes	Yes	Yes

Pre-post single control group intervention design (for an example see Bond et al., 2008).

	Measure before intervention?	Intervention delivered?	Measure after intervention?
Group 1	Yes	Yes	Yes
Group 2	Yes	No	Yes

Solomon four-group design (for an example see Jackson, 1983).

	Measure before intervention?	Intervention delivered?	Measure after intervention?
Group 1	Yes	Yes	Yes
Group 2	Yes	No	Yes
Group 3	No	Yes	Yes
Group 4	No	No	Yes

A very strong design for organisational interventions is known as the Solomon four-group design as shown in Table 2.1. This design is the 'gold standard' in quasi-experimental research. It is well known that the process of being observed can impact on intervention outcomes (see Chapter 1). The Solomon four-group design can identify whether this is occurring. If there are changes that occur independent of the impact of the intervention repeated tests without intervention (Group 2) will show significant change over time. If measuring before the intervention was having an effect then the after-intervention measure for Group 2 would be different from the after-intervention scores for Group 4 (no pre-intervention measure). By the same logic, pre-testing would also be having an impact if the after-intervention scores for Group 3 were different from the after-intervention scores for Group 1 (i.e. the change was biggest in an intervention group that had been measured before the intervention).

Clearly, establishing such a design requires a considerable degree of goodwill and flexibility on the part of the client organisation and favourable organisational context. The rarity of this design in intervention research shows how infrequently such opportunities present themselves to researchers. Students should not be critical of organisational research that does not follow this design!

The simple pre–post design without a control group (*see* Table 2.1) is used often. Unfortunately, the lack of a control group means that it is not possible to rule out alternative explanations for change without gathering more data (Cook and Campbell, 1979). Studies that use a single control group are, in many cases, the most complex that can be achieved. Fortunately, such studies can be extremely informative since data analysis techniques and the measurement of a range of variables allow for some alternative explanations for change to be tested. In the training example mentioned above, if we only have one control group we might gather additional data about whether employees had previous experience of the equipment they were being trained on and we might also investigate whether variables such as self-confidence were related to training outcomes.

One often-cited criticism of the use of quasi-experiments to evaluate organisational interventions is that they focus on measuring what changes, at the expense looking at why something changed (Griffiths, 1999; Randall *et al.*, 2005). This is especially problematical if an intervention fails because we don't know whether (i) the intervention is useless or (ii) the intervention is fine, it's just that it was poorly implemented. Returning to our earlier example, the training might fail because the trainer delivered the course in a very bland and uninteresting way. Cook and Shadish (1994) point out that if we are interested in why interventions work or fail then we need to gather more data about the *processes* of change (e.g. we might collect some data about what the trainees thought of the trainer's style of delivery and the course content). This might involve the use of a range of data collection methods, but qualitative methods have often been used to carry out process evaluation. Qualitative methods offer a flexibility and breadth of data collection that can be useful when the researcher is not sure what process factors might have influenced intervention outcomes (Randall *et al.*, 2007). A detailed discussion of process evaluation in relation to stress management interventions can be found in Chapter 12.

Key Learning Point

Quasi-experiments can be used to evaluate interventions in the workplace. These focus on the outcomes of change so additional data collection and analysis are often needed to examine the processes of change.

Qualitative design

Both surveys and experiments normally express data using numbers (i.e. quantitatively). They allow the people participating in the research little chance to express their opinions in their own words, since the work psychologist investigates a limited number of variables of their own choice, selected in advance. Hence surveys and experiments do not obtain a detailed picture of any individual's world. They both involve the psychologist in a fairly detached, quasi-scientific role, and tend to reflect the positivist research philosophy described earlier. As discussed later in this chapter, the strength of findings from quantitative research is usually governed to some extent by the number of research participants. It is generally agreed that qualitative methods produce more data per participant than quantitative methods, and that smaller samples of participants support rigorous data analysis. This is not just of theoretical concern: small organisations may not be able to make use of methods that rely upon huge participant samples.

Qualitative research often (though not always) involves a much greater emphasis on seeing the world from the point of view of the people who participate in it (Cassell and Symon, 2004). That is, it tends to reflect the phenomenological research philosophy described earlier. This normally means collecting detailed information using observation and/or unstructured interviews from a fairly small number of individuals or organisations – perhaps only one. This information is intended to paint a picture rather than measure a limited number of specific phenomena. Therefore, rather than *testing hypotheses*, qualitative methods deal with *research questions*. Drawing on Gubrium and Holstein (1997), Silverman (2001, pp. 38–9) has identified four kinds of qualitative research:

1 *Naturalism*: the emphasis is on observing what goes on in real-life settings. This tends to produce rich descriptions of behaviour and events, but little insight into how those things are understood by the people involved.

2 *Ethnomethodology*: focuses on a close analysis of interactions between people and how these maintain and reflect social order. This can show how social groups and cultures work, but runs the risk of neglecting the role of broader contextual factors such as economic conditions.

3 *Emotionalism*: here the primary interest is in establishing a close rapport with the people being researched, and finding out about their experiences and feelings. This differs from the previous two categories in giving priority to people's personal opinions, rather than the researcher's frame of reference, but runs the risk of overemphasising emotion.

4 *Postmodernism*: rejects the notion that there is an objective truth, focusing instead on how people portray themselves and their contexts in order to achieve personal goals and/or affirm their sense of identity.

Rather than testing a prespecified theory, a work psychologist who conducts qualitative research may well begin the research with some loose theoretical ideas, and then develop and perhaps later test theory in the light of the data obtained during the course of the research. Data collection should also be influenced by developing theoretical ideas as the research proceeds (as in *grounded theory*).

Returning to our earlier example, a work psychologist engaging in qualitative research would most likely be interested in how people working on paced and/or unpaced inspection of boxes of chocolates made sense of their situation, and how they coped with it. The psychologist might work on the task as a participant observer, and might also interview individuals or groups about it.

Key Learning Point

Qualitative research often involves an attempt to describe and analyse how individuals make sense of the situations they are in. The focus may be on behaviour, social interaction, personal experience or self-presentation.

Qualitative research usually produces a large amount of data, which requires some editing and interpretation by the researcher. It is time-consuming and difficult to carry out. Even obtaining the necessary access to people in their workplace can prove impossible. It leaves researchers vulnerable to the accusation that they have simply discovered in the data what they expected to find. Because this research is usually conducted with relatively small numbers of people, it is often not clear whether the findings would be repeated with a bigger, different sample. These are some of the reasons why there are relatively few articles reporting qualitative research in leading work psychology journals. On the other hand, many qualitative researchers reject positivist criteria for evaluating research (such as generalisability and objectivity). They argue that the results of qualitative research are often intended to resonate with others in a similar situations (rather than to generalise in the traditional scientific sense of the word).

They point out that qualitative work has the advantages already outlined in this section. It is becoming more popular as dissatisfaction with the shortcomings of surveys and experiments slowly grows. Some journals (for example the *Journal of Occupational and Organizational Psychology*) explicitly state an editorial policy encouraging qualitative research.

There is a wide variety of qualitative research methods. Cassell and Symon's (2004) text provides an excellent description of many such techniques, including 'worked examples'. Some have already been mentioned. Other techniques include:

■ Case study research: this involves the collection of data from a number of teams, organisations or individuals in order to better understand how the research context influences the research findings. Case studies can be aggregated in order to identify some of the general findings that apply across different research settings.

■ Ethnography where the researcher participates in the research setting in order to collect data that reflects the meaning of events, behaviours or activities in the research setting (rather than the meaning that might be attached to things by some 'detatched' observer). For example, one of the authors of this text spent some time with various sewage workers in order to better understand their working conditions (and who said the work psychologist's life wasn't very glamorous?).

■ Repertory grid technique, which is sometimes used to identify the knowledge, skills and competencies of effective (and ineffective) employees in job analysis (*see* Chapter 4).

■ Attributional coding, which can be used, for example, to analyse how people describe the causes of the events that occur in their working lives (*see* Chapter 5).

By far the most commonly used technique is the qualitative interview and this is discussed in some detail later in this chapter.

Action research design

Lewin (1946) coined the term *action research* to describe research where the researcher and the people being researched participate jointly in it. Action research is intended both to solve immediate problems for the people collaborating with the researcher, and to add to general knowledge about the topic being researched. It involves not only diagnosing and investigating a particular problem, but also making changes in a work organisation on the basis of research findings, and evaluating the impact of those changes. Increasingly, it also involves the development of an organisation's capacity to solve problems without external help in the future (Eden and Chisholm, 1993).

Action research can involve any of the research methods described earlier but, like qualitative research, is most likely to use interviews and participant observation (*see* Meyer, 2001). Much more than other research designs, it focuses on a specific problem in an organisation and what to do about it. It abandons the detachment of survey and experimental designs. Like qualitative research, it seeks to examine how people participating in the research see things, and it usually covers fairly long periods of time. Unlike much qualitative research, it involves attempting to solve a problem, and monitoring the success of that attempt.

From the point of view of the researcher, action research can be exciting, difficult and unpredictable. Because of its problem orientation, it requires close involvement with an organisation. This in turn requires careful negotiation and renegotiation of the researcher's role in the organisation, particularly concerning who in the organisation (if anyone) the researcher is 'working for'. Also, people in the organisation may reject the researcher's recommendations for dealing with a problem. This creates obvious difficulties for the evaluation of attempts to deal with the problem, though the researcher may be permitted to evaluate the success of any alternative strategy produced by organisation members. In action research, therefore, the process of conducting the research can become as much a focus of interest as the problem it was originally designed to address.

Key Learning Point

In action research, the psychologist and the people involved in the situation being researched work together to define the aims of the research and solve practical problems.

Mixed methods approaches

An increasing amount of research in work psychology is beginning to draw upon a number of methods used in combination, or sequence, to strengthen research designs. This mixed methods approach is used to make the best of both worlds, drawing on the advantages of a number of different techniques to offset the disadvantages of each. It is common that this 'mixing' refers to the use of both qualitative and quantitative methods in the same study. Bryman (2006, p. 105, citing Greene *et al.*, 1989) describes a number of ways this can be done and the benefits of each:

1 *Triangulation*: convergence, corroboration, correspondence or results from different methods.

2 *Complementarity*: 'seeks elaboration, enhancement, illustration, clarification of the results from one method with the results from another' (Greene *et al.*, 1989, p. 259).

3 *Development*: 'seeks to use the results from one method to help develop or inform the other method, where development is broadly construed to include sampling and implementation, as well as measurement decisions' (Greene *et al.*, 1989, p. 259).

4 *Initiation*: 'seeks the discovery of paradox and contradiction, new perspectives of [sic] frameworks, the recasting of questions or results from one method with questions or results from the other method' (Greene *et al.*,1989, p. 259).

5 *Expansion*: 'seeks to extend the breadth and range of enquiry by using different methods for different inquiry components' (Greene *et al.*, 1989, p. 259).

Bryman (2007) expands on this list somewhat, pointing out the numerous advantages offered by mixed methods. He also notes that too few quasi-experimental studies have included mixed methods to strengthen the results (only 5 out of 232 reviewed).

Key principles in hypothesis testing using quantitative data

Much research in work psychology, particularly in the positivist tradition, examines one or both of the following questions:

■ Do two or more groups of people *differ* from each other?

■ Do two or more variables *covary* (that is, go together, or are related to each other) within a particular group of people? Often we test linear relationships (e.g. as one thing goes up so does the other), although as you will see throughout this text, relationships beteen variables are often not quite as simple as that.

Work psychologists ask these questions because the answers to them enhance our understanding of human behaviour in the workplace. For example, a researcher might be interested in the relationship between machine-paced work and job satisfaction. They would obtain job satisfaction data from each individual within the experimental group (which experienced machine-paced work) and the control group (which experienced self-paced work). Clearly, to establish the effect of machine-pacing on job satisfaction, it is necessary to compare the job satisfaction scores of the two groups. This could be done using a statistical technique called a *t*-test, which is described later in this chapter.

To move on to the second question, a psychologist might conduct a survey in order to establish whether or not people's age is associated with the amount of job satisfaction they experience. It would be possible to divide people into age-groups (e.g. 20–29; 30–39, etc.) and compare pairs of groups using a *t*-test. But this would lose information about people's ages – for example, 29-year-olds would be lumped together with 20-year-olds (variance, as discussed later in this chapter, would be lost). Also, the age groupings would be arbitrarily defined. It would be better to see whether age and job satisfaction go together by means of a *correlation*. This essentially plots each person's age against their job satisfaction on a graph, and assesses the extent to which as age increases, job satisfaction either increases or decreases. Correlation is discussed further below.

Key Learning Point

Work psychologists use statistics to assess whether two or more groups of people differ psychologically in some way, or whether two or more aspects of people's psychological functioning tend to go together.

Psychologists often test *hypotheses* in their research. An important concept here is the *null hypothesis* (H_0). Essentially, this is the hypothesis that there is 'nothing going on' (or at least what the researcher predicted would happen, did not happen!). Thus, if a psychologist is investigating whether two or more groups differ in their job satisfaction, the null hypothesis would be that they do not. If the psychologist is investigating whether age and job satisfaction tend to go together, the null hypothesis would be that they do not. That is, knowing someone's age would tell you nothing about their level of job satisfaction, and vice versa.

In each case, we can also make an *alternative* or *experimental hypothesis* (H_1). This can either be directional or non-directional. For example, a directional alternative hypothesis would specify whether people doing machine-paced work would experience higher or lower job satisfaction than those doing self-paced work, or whether job satisfaction increases or decreases as age increases. Non-directional hypotheses would be less specific. They would simply state that there was a difference between groups in levels of job satisfaction (but not which group was higher) or that age and job satisfaction do go together (but not whether older people are more satisfied or less satisfied).

Hypotheses refer to the *population(s)* from which the sample(s) of people who participate in research are drawn. They do *not* refer to those samples alone. In essence, then, when doing research, a psychologist is asking: 'given the data I have obtained from my research sample, is the null hypothesis or the alternative hypothesis more likely to be true for the population as a whole?' Note that 'population' does not mean everyone in the whole world, or even in a particular country. It should refer to those people to whom the psychologist wishes to generalise the results. This might be, for example, 'production line workers in Denmark' or 'people currently employed in the Netherlands'.

Interestingly, researchers are sometimes not very specific concerning what population they wish to draw conclusions about. Also, they sometimes use *samples of convenience* – that is, people they can get data from easily. Ideally, from a statistical point of view, those who participate in the research should be a *random sample* of the population of interest (*see* 'The survey design' section earlier in this chapter). Surveys may involve questionnaires being sent to a *random sample* of people from a given population, but of course not everybody replies. One inevitably wonders whether responders differ in important ways from non-responders. Responders may, for example, be more conscientious/conforming, or simply have more time on their hands: sometimes researchers attempt to test whether there is any systematic bias underpinning failure to respond.

Therefore, rather than attempting to obtain a random sample, it is more common for researchers to try to show that their inevitably non-random sample is reasonably *representative* (for example in age, sex, type of employment, location) of the population as a whole. Even when random sampling is used the researcher needs to check that the sample obtained is representative. Put another way, the proportions of people of each age, sex and so on among those participating in the research should not differ much from those in the wider population. But it is still possible that participants differ from non-participants in other respects, including those of interest in the research. So, for example, it may be that people high on the conscientiousness dimension of personality are more likely to respond than others. This obviously matters if, for example, the research concerns overall levels of conscientiousness in the population.

Statistical analysis of data in work psychology most often involves assessment of *the probability of accepting the alternative hypothesis when the null hypothesis is in fact true for the population*. The lower this probability, the more confident the psychologist can be that the alternative hypothesis can be accepted, and the null hypothesis can be rejected. This probability is also called *statistical significance* – a crucial concept in psychology. Typically, psychologists are not prepared to accept the alternative hypothesis (thus rejecting the null hypothesis) unless there is only a probability of 0.05 (a 5 per cent or 1 in 20 chance) or less that the null hypothesis is true given the data the psychologist has collected. Erroneously rejecting the null hypothesis is sometimes called *type I error*.

Key Learning Point

The concept of statistical significance refers to the probability of the null hypothesis being true, given the data obtained.

The psychologist is therefore saying 'I must be at least 95 per cent sure that I can reject the null hypothesis before I am prepared actually to do so'. This might be considered pretty conservative – perhaps *too* conservative. After all, how many of us wait until we are 95 per cent certain of something before we act on the basis of it in our day-to-day lives? There is also the other side of the coin, less often considered by psychologists: the probability of accepting the null hypothesis when the alternative hypothesis is in fact true. Erroneously accepting the null hypothesis is sometimes called *type II error*.

If the psychologist finds that, on the basis of their data, there is less than a 0.05 (i.e. 1 in 20) chance of mistakenly rejecting the null hypothesis, they will usually declare that the result is *statistically significant at the 0.05 level*. If the probability is less than 0.01 (i.e. 1 in 100), the result is *statistically significant at the 0.01 level*. A similar rule applies for a probability of 0.001 (1 in 1000). These are, of course, arbitrary cut-off points. Basically, the lower the probability, the more confident the psychologist is in rejecting the null hypothesis. Notice also that the lower the probability, the more 'highly statistically significant' the result is said to be.

As an aside (albeit quite an important one) there is another less well-known error to be aware of. The *type III error* can occur in intervention research. When interventions fail it is easy to conclude that the intervention is ineffective. However, the intervention might not have been implemented as it should have been, or something about the organisational context might have prevented it from working as it should. Erroneously concluding that an intervention is ineffective when there are other explanations for a lack of change is a type III error. This is discussed further in Chapter 12.

But how do psychologists calculate statistical significance given their research data? They use one or more techniques referred to collectively as *statistical tests* of the data. We now briefly examine some of these in general terms. There are some worked examples on the website associated with this book. Doing worked examples is an excellent way of understanding the principles of statistical testing. However, there are several commercially available software packages for conducting statistical analyses, and normally these are used. The most commonly used is called SPSS – the Statistical Package for Social Sciences (see www.spss.com).

Some common statistical tests

In this section we look at some of the most common tests used in work psychology. They are discussed briefly here in order that you may gain an understanding of their purpose. We begin by examining the *t*-test in some detail: not because it is the most important test, but because it helps us to describe the principles that apply across a range of statistical tests.

The *t*-test

Suppose for a moment that a psychologist is interested in seeing whether production managers are more or less numerate than accountants. They administer a test of numeracy to (say) 20 of each and obtains a mean score of 25 for the production managers and 30 for the accountants. Clearly, the accountants score higher on average, but what other information is required before deciding whether to accept or reject the null hypothesis that the populations of production managers and accountants do not differ in their numeracy? No measure of ability is 100 per cent accurate, so we need to know if there is enough 'clear blue water' between the two scores so that we can be more comfortable that other factors (such as errors in the measures used) do not account for all of the difference between scores. Typically, in order to assess whether two mean scores show a statistically significant difference, psychologists use a *t*-test.

First, we need to consider whether the difference between sample means is large relative to the overall range of scores. After all, if scores in the sample ranged from 10 to 50, a difference of 5 between the two means might not mean very much. However, if scores ranged only from (say) 20 to 35 that difference of 5 might seem quite large in comparison.

The most commonly used numerical measure of the spread of scores is the *standard deviation*. The bigger the standard deviation, the more variable the individual scores are. The standard deviation is a function of the differences between each in-dividual score and the overall mean score, and of the sample size. Hence if all scores were exactly the mean, the standard deviation would be zero because there would be no differences between individual scores and the mean (this would mean there was not much spread in the data). Apart from this exceptional case, we can normally expect about 68 per cent of all individual scores to be within one stan-dard deviation either side of the mean (as one might expect on a lot of measures, most people are about average). About 96 per cent of scores are within two stan-dard deviations of the mean.

Sample size is also important in evaluating the significance of a difference between two means. Suppose for a moment that the null hypothesis was in fact true. If a psychologist repeatedly took samples of 20 production managers and 20 account-ants, they would *on average* expect their mean scores to be equal, but of course in small samples, it takes only one or two exceptional scores to make quite a big dif-ference between the two group means. Thus, although on average the mean scores for the samples should be equal, in some samples there could be quite big differ-ences. If the psychologist repeatedly took bigger samples (say 100 production man-agers and accountants), then the influence of a few extreme scores would be more diluted. If the null hypothesis was in fact true, we would again expect the difference between the two group means to be zero, but this time there would be less varia-tion from that figure between samples.

So, to evaluate the statistical significance of a difference between two mean scores in a research study, we need to consider not only the magnitude of that difference, but also the *standard deviation* and the *sample size*. For any given difference between means, the smaller the standard deviation, and the larger the sample size, the more likely it is that the psychologist could reject the null hypothesis. The result of the number-crunching behind the *t*-test is a single number (the bigger it is the more likely it is to be significant).

Key Learning Point

The *t*-test assesses the significance of a difference between two group mean scores, taking into account the sample sizes and the amount of variation in scores within each group.

Of course, the *t*-test requires that the data are *quantitative*. That is, the data should reflect scores on a dimension along which people vary, not different types, or pigeon-holes, into which they fall. Strictly, the data should also be such that a difference of a given number of units between two scores should reflect the same amount of dif-ference no matter what the absolute level of the scores. So, a score of 100 should be the same amount more than 90 as 20 is more than 10. This may seem straightforward, but with many self-report measures (e.g. job satisfaction) we cannot strictly be sure whether it is the case (although in practice in work psychology we often assume that it is). Further, scores should approximate to a *normal distribution* (*see* Figure 2.4). This is a technical term for a bell-shaped distribution of scores, which peaks at the mean, and drops off at equal rates on either side of it, with that rate being linked to the standard deviation i.e. 68 per cent of scores within one standard deviation of the mean.

Fortunately, the *t*-test is not usually invalidated if the data do not approximate a normal distribution (Sawilowsky and Blair, 1992). In the jargon, it is a *robust* test.

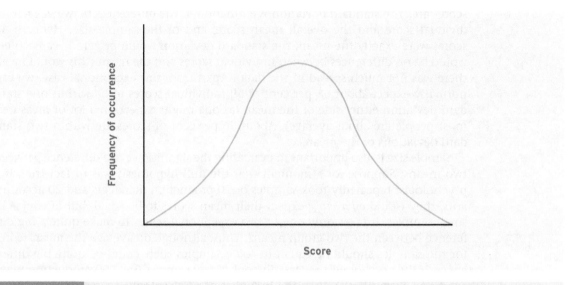

Figure 2.4   **The normal distribution**

This is just as well, because the research data obtained by psychologists are often very unlike the normal distribution (Micceri, 1989). Some data are not very 'spread' at all. For example, in employee performance appraisals it is common to find that almost all employees get high scores (especially if selection and management processes are working well so that very able staff are selected and then trained and developed to a high standard). The *restriction of range* we find in some data makes life a little more difficult – but not impossible – for researchers. The reason for raising this is issue is that many students skim over the topic of the normal distribution, thinking it to be of only statistical importance. However, it can tell us quite a lot about the variables we are interested in.

A somewhat different version of the *t*-test can be employed if we wish to see whether the means of two sets of scores from the *same* people differ significantly. So, for example, we might be interested in assessing people's performance at a task before and after training. The formula is somewhat different, but most of the principles for this *t*-test for *related samples* are the same as those for the independent samples *t*-test described earlier.

Analysis of variance

What happens when the scores of more than two groups are to be compared? In this situation, another very common statistical test is performed – it is called *analysis of variance*. Essentially, it is an extension of the *t*-test procedure. The resulting statistic is called *F*, and the principles concerning statistical significance are applied to *F* in the same way as to *t* (see above). The same limitations to the use of *t* also apply to *F*. *F* can also be used instead of *t* to compare just two means.

F reflects the ratio of variation in scores between groups to variation in scores within groups. The greater the former relative to the latter, the higher the *F* value, and the more likely it is that the population means differ (i.e. there is a low probability of obtaining our results if the null hypothesis is in fact true for the population). If a statistically significant F value is obtained, we can reject the null hypothesis that the population means are identical. If we wish, we can then use a modified form of the t-test to identify which particular pair or pairs of groups differ significantly from each other.

Data from more complex research designs can be analysed using analysis of variance. Suppose, for example, the psychologist was interested in the effects of both machine-paced work *and* style of supervision on job satisfaction. They run an experiment with four groups of people. One group does machine-paced work under close supervision. Another does the same work under distant supervision. The third does self-paced work under close supervision, and the fourth performs self-paced work under distant supervision. Analysis of variance can be used to examine the statistical significance of the separate effects of each factor (pacing of work and style of supervision) on job satisfaction. It can also identify *interaction effects*. For example, the impact on job satisfaction of close versus distant supervision might be greater when work is self-paced than when it is machine-paced.

Key Learning Point

The statistical technique called analysis of variance extends the principles of the t-test to more than two groups and can be used to identify interaction effects.

Chi-square

As indicated earlier, data are sometimes qualitative rather than quantitative. Suppose, for example, that a psychologist wishes to examine whether women are more likely or less likely than men to be unemployed. The psychologist cannot use t or F because the data are *categorical*. The psychologist is therefore interested in determining whether there is a statistically significant difference in employment status that could be linked to gender. The statistical test employed in this instance is known as chi-square (χ^2). The more the groups differ, the higher the chi-square figure for the data, and the less likely it is that the null hypothesis is true. As with t and F, critical values of chi-square at various levels of statistical significance can be checked in tables in most statistics texts. Unlike t and F, these critical values do not depend directly on sample size. Instead, they depend on the number of rows and columns in the data when tabulated. In the above example, the table would contain four cells altogether: 2 (gender) $\times$ 2 (employment status). The figure in each cell would be the number of participants falling into that category. The chi-square procedure compares the observed numbers with those that would be expected if the proportions reporting unemployment/employment were the same for each gender. A worked example of chi-square appears on the website for this book.

Key Learning Point

The statistical technique called chi-square is used to test differences between groups in the frequency with which group members fall into defined categories.

Correlation

The second question posed at the start of this section concerned whether two or more variables tend to go together. Correlation is most commonly used in survey research. Thus, for example, a psychologist might wish to find out whether job satisfaction and intention to leave one's job are connected. Alternatively, they might be interested in seeing whether self-esteem and salary are connected. In other words, the researcher wishes to find out whether the two variables correlate (co-relate).

There are several different but similar statistical tests of correlation, each of which produces a *correlation coefficient*. The most common of these is Pearson's product–moment correlation coefficient, or *r* for short. Correlation coefficients cannot exceed a value of 1, and cannot be lower than −1. A Pearson's *r* of 1 would mean that when scores on the two variables of interest were plotted on a graph, a straight line could be drawn that would go through all of the plotted points (*see* Figure 2.5a). This line

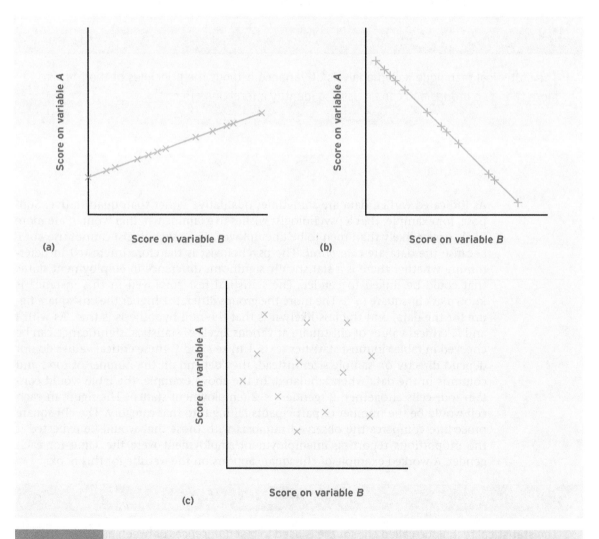

| Figure 2.5 | Correlation: (a) a correlation of 1; (b) a correlation of −1; (c) a correlation of 0 (each x represents data collected from one person) |

would rise from left to right, indicating that as variable *A* increased, so did variable *B*. This line would not need to be at any particular angle, nor would it necessarily go through the origin. An *r* of −1 would also mean that a straight line could be drawn through all of the plotted points, but this time it would slope the other way, so that as *A* increased, *B* decreased (*see* Figure 2.5b). An *r* of 0 would mean that there was no tendency whatever for scores on either of the two variables to rise or fall with scores on the other one (*see* Figure 2.5c).

The psychologist therefore typically asks 'Does the correlation coefficient I have obtained with my sample differ sufficiently from 0 for me to reject the null hypothesis?' Just as with other statistics, for any given sample, size dictates the point at which a correlation becomes significant. Thus, for example, with a sample size of 20, the critical value of *r* for significance at the 0.05 level is ±0.444. Corresponding values at the 0.01 and 0.001 levels are 0.590 and 0.708.

Another form of correlation is the *Spearman rank correlation (rho, ρ)*. This is used when the data do not reflect absolute scores, but only a rank order. This would mean that we know, for example, that score *x* is greater than score *y*, but not by how much. The formula for calculating rho looks different from that for *r*, but in fact it boils down to the same thing. Rho can also be useful when the data deviate a great deal from the normal distribution (*see* Figure 2.4) and when there are a few scores hugely different from the others.

Key Learning Point

The statistical technique called correlation tests the extent to which scores on two variables tend to go together (i.e. covary).

Whatever the exact correlation technique, it is important to remember the old maxim *correlation does not imply causality* (see also the earlier section on survey design). Often, a psychologist would like to infer that the reason why two variables are correlated is that one causes the other. This may seem plausible, but it is hard to be sure. Suppose that a psychologist finds a highly significant positive correlation between self-esteem and salary. If both are measured at the same time, there is no basis on which to decide whether self-esteem causes salary or salary causes self-esteem. It is fairly easy to think of possible explanations for either causal direction. It is also possible that some other variable(s) (e.g. social status, educational attainment) cause both self-esteem and salary, but unless we have measured them, we can only speculate. There is one slight caveat to this and it applies when one of our variables is a demographic. For example if we find that age correlates with self-esteem, it would be difficult to argue that self-esteem causes age, but we would still need to be cautious because other variables that correlate with age might be the things that are driving self-esteem.

As noted earlier in this chapter, obtaining data over time (a *longitudinal study*) can help, in so far as it may uncover whether scores on one variable at time 1 predict scores on the other at time 2, but even then, the fact that phenomenon A happens before B does not necessarily mean that A *causes* B: more evidence and good theory would be needed before such conclusions could be drawn.

Multiple regression

Just as analysis of variance is an extension of the *t*-test for more than two groups, so multiple regression is an extension of correlation for more than two variables. In other words it is a 'posh correlation'. Suppose a psychologist wishes to assess the correlation with self-esteem of each of salary, educational attainment and social status. They might well find that the latter three variables are all correlated with each other, and also with self-esteem. In this case, the psychologist might wonder which one(s) really matter in predicting self-esteem.

Multiple regression is a statistical technique that allows the social scientist to assess the *relative* importance of each of salary, educational attainment and social status as predictors of self-esteem. It involves estimation of the correlation of each of the three with self-esteem *independent of the other two* (the technique can of course be extended to larger numbers of variables). In this way the researcher can end up with an equation that specifies the weighting to be given to each predictor variable in predicting self-esteem, as well as an overall indication of just how predictable self-esteem is using all of the predictor variables. But note: just because variables are designated 'predictors' in multiple regression analyses, it does not mean that they are necessarily 'causes' of the variable to be predicted.

Another advantage of multiple regression is that it allows demographic variables to be controlled for in the analysis (usually within a hierarchical multiple regression). To continue with the example given above, the social scientist might want to control for the effects of age and gender on self-esteem before considering the other variables. These demographics could then be entered in a 'block' before a second block of variables (salary, educational attainment and social status). The social scientist could then make things even more complicated if they so wished by including a third block of variables that looked at the interactions between the variables entered in the first two blocks (for example whether social status was less of a predictor of self-esteem for older people). This type of interaction is often called a moderating effect: a moderator variable is one that alters the strength of the relationship between two other variables.

Regressions are also used to test for mediated relationships. For example, we may find that machine-paced work is linked to low job satisfaction. But is it machine-paced work per se, or the fact that machine-paced work results in fewer opportunities for the employee to exercise control at work (i.e. control at work mediates, or acts as a 'bridge' in the relationship between machine-pacing and low job satisfaction)? If we find that it is control that is mediating the relationship we might look for ways of introducing more control into the employees' work (rather then abandoning machine-paced work altogether).

Because it can test so much, multiple regression is a much-used technique in work psychology. It is quite complex. Its intricacies are beyond the scope of this book, but the interested reader can find out more by consulting Baron and Kenny (1986), Licht (1997) or Cohen *et al.* (2003). Factor analysis is also based on correlational techniques, but rather than testing relationships between variables it looks to find structures within data (e.g. it was used extensively to identify the five clusters of personality variables, the 'Big Five'). Kline (1993) provides a good description of this technique.

If regression is a posh correlation, then structural equation modelling (SEM) is positively regal. This method of data analysis has gained popularity because it enables researchers to disentangle the many different relationships between variables in applied research that uses lots of variables. It is not for the faint-hearted, but fortunately most researchers who use it provide clear explanations of the meaning of SEM results in research papers.

Other phenomena in statistical testing

Effect size

The reader may have wondered whether statistical significance is necessarily the same as significance for practical purposes. At least one behavioural science statistics text (Rosenthal and Rosnow, 1984) repeatedly reminds its readers that statistical significance depends on the size of the effect (e.g. the difference in means between two groups relative to the standard deviation; or the value of *r* for two variables) *multiplied by* the size of the study. Thus, when research uses large samples, quite small effect sizes can lead us to reject the null hypothesis – probably correctly, of course, *but* if the effect is so small, albeit detectable, are we going to worry about it? For example, a psychologist might find that, in a large sample, marketing managers score on average 58 out of 100 on a numeracy test whereas production managers score on average 59.5 out of 100, and that this difference is highly statistically significant. So what? How much does this tell us about, for example, the relative effectiveness of marketing and production managers? Clearly although production managers do slightly better, there are many marketing managers who score higher than many production managers. One way of addressing this issue is to assess the relationship between numeracy and work performance, focusing particularly on the extra work performance one could expect given a specified increase in numeracy, and then translating this into practical benefits (*see* Chapter 4 concerning utility analysis).

However, it is also useful to consider effect size in more abstract terms. We can think of it as *the degree to which the null hypothesis is false*. For *t*, we can consider the difference between group means as a proportion of the standard deviation of scores (*d*) to be a measure of effect size. For *r*, we can use the proportion of variance in scores common to both variables. This is r^2. Thus, a correlation of 0.60 indicates that $0.60 \times 0.60 = 0.36$, or 36 per cent of the variance in one variable is 'accounted for' by scores in the other. With large samples, it is often possible for a correlation of only 0.2 or less to be statistically significant. In this case, the variables share just 4 per cent of variance. This sounds small, but Rosenthal and Rosnow (1984, pp. 207–11) have demonstrated that it can nevertheless reflect practical outcomes of real importance. For example, if one form of treatment for depression is 4 per cent better than another, over a whole nation that could amount to a lot more happy people.

Key Learning Point

Effect size goes beyond statistical significance by assessing the magnitude of the relationship obtained, rather than how confident one can be that the relationship is not zero.

For F, one often-used indicator of effect size is called *eta* (η). It reflects the proportion of total score variation that is accounted for by group membership. Like r^2, eta can be considered an indicator of the proportion of total variance accounted for.

There is nothing mysterious about indices of effect size. They are often quite simply derived, and are sometimes even routinely calculated on the way to a test of statistical significance. Examples appear on http://www.booksites.net/arnold_workpsych.

Statistical power

Statistical power refers to the probability of rejecting the null hypothesis when it is indeed false and therefore should be rejected. It is, in other words, the probability of avoiding making a type II error. Like all probability estimates, it can vary from 0 to 1. The level of power operating in any particular research study depends on the level of statistical significance the psychologist wishes to work at, the size of the sample and the size of the effect under examination. The chief practical lesson to be learned is that small sample sizes have very low power – that is, a high probability of missing a relationship that does exist in the population from which the sample is drawn.

Cohen (1977) has produced tables that specify the sample sizes required to achieve certain levels of power for particular statistical tests at specified significance levels and effect sizes. These tables are a useful guide for researchers wondering how many participants they need for their study.

These observations about statistical power are very important. Often in research, one investigator reports a statistically significant finding with a moderate to large sample size. Then another researcher attempts to replicate the result with a smaller sample, fails to find a statistically significant effect, and declares that the original finding must have been a fluke. Close examination shows that the *effect size* in the second study is as large as the first – it is just that the smaller sample prevents statistical significance being achieved.

Key Learning Point

There is a high probability that small-scale studies will fail to find effects which exist in the population of interest.

Meta-analysis

Some published research articles report a *meta-analysis* of findings from a number of studies. This type of article is quite common, especially in topic areas where a lot of research has been conducted. The aim of meta-analysis is to provide an overview and summary of what general conclusions can be drawn from a body of research. Using concepts such as effect size and statistical power (see the previous section of this chapter), a researcher conducting a meta-analysis extracts (and if necessary adjusts) measures of association (usually correlation) between variables of interest from each relevant research study, and weights them according to the sample size. Other information may well also be recorded – for example whether the people studied were managers or blue-collar workers, how variables of interest were measured, and whether the study was an experiment or a survey. Then the person conducting the meta-analysis is in a position to make some general statements about the extent to which two or more variables are statistically associated with each other, and whether the strength of the association depends partly on factors such as the measures used and the populations studied.

Meta-analysis has been criticised by some as being something of a blunt instrument that cannot capture important details of how particular research studies were carried out. Others have defended meta-analysis. Rosenthal and DiMatteo (2000) have reviewed these arguments and conclude that many of the criticisms are invalid. An example of meta-analysis is provided by Lee *et al.* (2000). They examined the relationships between occupational commitment (the extent to which a person feels a sense of belonging and loyalty to the type of work they do) and other variables, including organisational commitment and job involvement (*see* Chapter 7 for more about work-related attitudes such as these). Lee and colleagues aggregated the results of 77 different studies, with a total sample size of nearly 16,000 people, so their conclusions were based on a great deal of data.

Analysing qualitative data

Just as there are many techniques for analysing numerical data, so the same is also true for qualitative data. Just as statisticians sometimes disagree about which statistical techniques are appropriate in which circumstances, so qualitative researchers sometimes disagree about the best ways to analyse qualitative data. But statistical arguments are usually about technical issues, whereas disagreements over how to analyse qualitative data are more often to do with the researcher's philosophical and theoretical position. Much qualitative data analysis is conducted by hand, but here too there are computer packages (e.g. NVivo) available to help locate and code data according to categories nominated by the researcher.

Table 2.2 shows an extract from a research interview conducted by the one of the authors of this book. The interview was one of 80 conducted by the author and colleagues as part of an investigation of how lawyers and architects see their work, and in particular how they, as professionals, view management and being managed. In this extract, the interviewer (I) and respondent (R – a lawyer working for a large firm of solicitors) discuss how the respondent's work is evaluated.

First of all notice that this is not a highly structured interview. To some extent the interviewer follows up what the respondent says, for example when he asks 'But it doesn't sound like you feel that way about your PDR?' A highly structured interview would not include such a specific question based on what the interviewee just said, since all or virtually all of the questions would be specified in advance. However, the interview was semi-structured rather than unstructured because there was a list of topic areas to be covered, but also scope to adjust the depth in which each was covered. Second, notice how the interviewer to some extent adopts what Silverman (2001) terms an 'emotionalist' position. This is evident in the question mentioned a few sentences back. Also, in his first question of this extract he is clearly interested in the respondent's opinion as well as trying to elicit what might be thought of as factual information about the way the respondent's work performance was evaluated. On the other hand, the interviewer also wants to use the interview

Table 2.2	An excerpt from a research interview

A lawyer discusses assessment of work performance

Note: I = Interviewer, R = Respondent

I: How is your performance evaluated here and what do you think of that?

R: They have an annual PDR, which is Personal Development Review. You are given a form to complete a short time before and then you meet with whoever's undertaking it generally – the partner that you report to – and you sit in a room and discuss it.

I: And is that a fruitful discussion or is it going through the motions?

R: For me it was fruitful because I think the . . . The difficulty I have with these is that more senior people can see the benefit and the relevance of them. When you get down to the secretaries, they view it very, very much as a . . . almost as a disciplinary matter. It's their annual kicking from the boss because they haven't been up to standard.

I: But it doesn't sound like you feel that about your PDR?

R: No. I think it's the only true way of finding out your own standing and seriously expressing ambitions and what you have to achieve to reach those.

I: And is it sufficiently candid and open to achieve that?

R: It was for me, yes.

I: There's a couple of indications that it might not be for everybody. Is that . . . ? Or am I reading too much into that?

R: No, you're right. There are some people who I've been told on the quiet have reached as far as they will go, but having spoken to those individuals – not directly about their PDRs, but you know, just generally – I don't think they've actually been told that clearly.

I: Okay.

R: I think that's more a function of whoever's actually doing the PDR because I had two very forthright speakers who will tell you exactly whereas others are a little bit more political.

I: Okay. There would have been a time when having your performance assessed and working in a managed system was a bit of an insult for a professional person, but it sounds like that comes with the territory now.

R: It does. I've only had them since I've been here. It was a new concept to me. And yes, I was very nervous before it. But unless you do get some form of independent view, I don't think you're the best judge of your own performance.

to go beyond the interviewee's own experiences. This is demonstrated by his observation 'There's a couple of indications that it might not be for everybody.' That could be seen as an attempt to gain a more general picture of performance assessment in that firm, but it could also arguably be an extension of the emotionalist position because the interviewer is seeking to access indirectly the experiences of other people in the firm.

How might these data be analysed? What general statements can be made, and conclusions drawn, on the basis of data such as these? This depends heavily both on the research questions being asked (together with the theoretical and/or practical basis for considering those questions important), and on the philosophical assumptions of the researcher. Excellent coverage of the range of methods available for analysing qualitative data (including interviews) can be found in Cassell and Symon (2004).

One way of analysing this transcript would in effect involve turning qualitative data into quantitative data. The researcher could attempt to assess how positively the interviewee felt about the firm's methods for assessing the work performance of employees, perhaps on a numerical scale. Another researcher could be asked to do the same, partly in order to check that the scoring of the interviewee's opinion about the performance assessment showed interrater reliability.

While such a scoring procedure might be useful, it would of course be a huge waste of information if that was all that was done with these data. Another approach would be to conduct a *content analysis* of what the interviewee says. Bryman (2001, p. 180) defines content analysis as 'an approach to the analysis of documents and texts that seeks to quantify content in terms of predetermined categories and in a systematic and replicable manner'. So in this case, the researcher might have prepared the content categories shown in Table 2.3 based on prior theory and research.

Table 2.3   An example of content analysis categories

Respondent's name: Content category	Coding option (tick as applicable)
1. Frequency of assessment	Less frequently than annual Annual More frequently than annual
2. Prior preparation	Thinking only Some written None specified
3. Who does the assessment?	Boss Other more senior person(s) Peer(s) Other

The researcher would study the interview transcript and decide, for each content category, which response option(s) were evident in what the interviewee said. Probably another researcher would do the same, in order to establish interrater reliability. Notice that agreement between raters is normally considered a sign that their 'scoring' of the interview is getting at objective truth, though it might also be argued that such agreement simply means the two raters share similar perceptions (sometimes referred to as *intersubjective agreement*).

Sometimes the categories for a content analysis are specified in advance of the data being gathered. This is consistent with the idea that the categories are 'systematic' and 'predetermined' (see the definition above). However, it is usually very difficult to anticipate the kind of responses interviewees will offer. Categories are therefore defined in some studies by the researchers doing an initial reading of interview transcripts and then devising content categories that reflect as much as possible the things the interviewees chose to focus on. Template analysis (N. King, 2004b) is one method whereby a predetermined set of codes can be reviewed and changed in response to the analysis of data. This can achieve a good balance between deductive reasoning (that is, deducing what types of response are important on the basis of prior theory and research) and inductive reasoning (that is, starting with the data and trying to develop theory on the basis of it). Some themes that might be recorded in this example are:

- description of personal experience of the performance assessment system;
- differences in perception between staff at different levels;
- belief that PDRs have value;
- variation in PDR process and outcome according to who conducts it;
- existence of 'off the record' communications about people's performance.

These themes would probably do better than a very detailed content analysis at capturing the meaning of what was said in the interview. On the other hand the themes, in themselves, might miss some of the more precise points made.

It might also be said that thematic analysis still does not get at the complex and dynamic nature of what is going on in talk and text. Some researchers might use *discourse analysis* (Potter, 1997; Dick, 2004) to try to access this. Researchers have used several different approaches to discourse analysis. They have in common a desire to analyse in detail the versions of reality offered by a person, and their purposes in presenting themselves and their worlds in the way they do. Often this endeavour requires quite a lot of interpretation. It rests partly on subtle elements of what is said, and indeed what is not said. Some versions of discourse analysis use features such as voice intonation and the existence and length of pauses, as well as what is actually said. Researchers who use discourse analysis frequently (though not always) take the view that reality is entirely defined by people through their talk, interaction and thought (social constructionist rather than positivist). Most now consider their own interpretation of what is said to be an important factor in shaping the analysis (reflexivity).

An analysis of the discourse in Table 2.2 might lead to the following conclusions about what the interviewee is trying to do: through expressing appreciation of the PDR (some methods might note facial expressions, such as if the person smiles or nods when they mention something and attach meaning to these), he is showing himself to be a loyal company man who is valued by the firm, and who is concerned to perform well and advance his career. His depiction of himself as initially nervous about the PDR could be taken to indicate an attempt to show how the firm's benevolence had convinced a sceptic about the integrity of the performance assessment system, to the benefit of both parties. His points about how secretaries experience PDR might serve to emphasise the difference in status between them and him, yet also show his good-hearted concern for their situation. Being the recipient of 'on the quiet' information about the performance of others could be offered as a sign that he is well-placed in informal company social networks.

This is, of course, quite speculative and focused more on the motives and purposes that could lie behind what was said than on the content of what was said. This analysis, then, entirely avoids the kinds of conclusions that might be reached by positivist or realist researchers, particularly if a number of interviewees and not just this one come up with the same point. These conclusions might be that the PDR is experienced as disciplinary by secretaries but as developmental by lawyers, and that nevertheless PDRs still on occasions fail to deliver open and honest feedback. Instead, the discourse analyst draws conclusions about the broad nature of the realities offered by interviewees and about their reasons for presenting those realities in the way they do.

All of this points to interviews being a very flexible and data rich technique. Sometimes students use them in their research because they see interviews as the 'easy option' when it would take time and effort (and lots of reading around) to identify variables of interest and source questionnaires. Many late nights spent transcribing and analysing qualitative data eventually persuades them that this is not the case. Interviews are time-consuming (but generally enjoyable) for participants, so care needs to be taken over recruitment and retention (N. King, 2004a).

Summary

Research designs used by work psychologists include surveys, experiments, qualitative research and action research. These designs vary in the amount of control exerted by the work psychologist, the degree of difficulty in carrying out the research, the role of theory and the nature of the data obtained. Perhaps most importantly, work psychologists using different designs often have different philosophical positions about the nature of knowledge and the existence (or not) of an objective reality. Research designs can be distinguished from methods of data collection. Methods include questionnaires, tests, interviews, observation, psychophysiological measures and archival sources. The characteristics of research published in leading journals of work psychology have been summarised by Schaubroeck and Kuehn (1992, p. 107):

> a majority of published studies were conducted in the field, although laboratory work comprises nearly one-third of the research. Half of the published research was experimental . . . most studies minimized common method factors by using diverse data sources. On the down side, a majority of field studies were cross-sectional in nature, there was very little cross-validation of findings, 'hard' data such as physiological measures and archival records were used infrequently . . . Researchers appeared to invest in particular design strengths and compromise on others.

Statistical techniques are available to help draw appropriate conclusions from quantitative data. Collectively, these techniques are intended to address two general situations. Firstly, where there are comparisons between two or more groups of people (*t*-test; analysis of variance; chi-square), and secondly where two or more variables are being examined within a participant group to see whether they tend to go together (correlation, multiple regression). The concept of statistical significance is important in interpreting the results produced by statistical tests. So is the notion of effect size. Techniques for analysing qualitative data are many and varied and offer a degree of flexibility that can be attractive when dealing with a number of issues in work psychology.

Test your learning

Short-answer questions

1 Briefly describe a psychological study of your own invention and specify a null hypothesis and an alternative hypothesis suitable for that study.

2 Explain the concepts of statistical significance, statistical power and effect size.

3 Explain (in one sentence) the type of data and research question to which each of the following techniques can be applied:

   t-test

   correlation

   chi-square

   regression

   content analysis

   factor analysis.

4 Imagine that you are trying to develop a theory to explain successful performance in telephone sales work. For each box in Figure 2.1, suggest at least two possible factors.

5 List three important differences between positivist research and social constructionist research.

6 How do work psychologists tend to evaluate interventions?

7 List five methods by which work psychologists obtain research information.

8 Write a short paragraph on the differences between experimental, quasi-experimental and survey research in work psychology.

9 What is action research?

10 What are the advantages and disadvantages of the interview as a research method?

Suggested assignments

1 Choose any issue in work psychology that interests you. Examine how different research designs (both qualitative and quantitative) might be used to tackle that issue. Is any one design better than the others?

2   'It is not worth distinguishing between research designs and research methods in work psychology because the choice of research design dictates the choice of method.' Discuss why you agree or disagree with this statement.

3   Find an article in an academic work psychology journal. Check that it reports research in which some kind(s) of data were collected. Identify the underlying research philosophy (e.g. was it positivist?), the research design, methods and data analysis techniques used and discuss (i) whether these were appropriate given the research hypotheses or questions specified, *and* (ii) whether you think the research hypotheses/questions were appropriate.

Relevant websites

The publisher Sage produces many books on research methods in psychology and the social sciences more generally. There are both general books about a range of methods, and specific books about one or a small number of similar methods. Check out the following address for their latest offerings: http://www.sagepub.com/ and go to the section on research methods and evaluation.

To do with the results of research more than method, the American Psychological Association (APA) publicises recent research in various fields of psychology. To see recent research on psychology, much of it applied, go to http://www.apa.org/monitor/.

Statistics at Square One provides descriptions and worked examples of a variety of common statistical methods including many of those mentioned in this chapter. Although aimed at medical researchers, the examples given are clear and useful. http://www.bmj.com/collections/statsbk/. If you are feeling more adventurous you might also want to visit David Kenny's site http://davidakenny.net/kenny.htm which looks at some of the more advanced methods mentioned in this chapter (such as regression and SEM).

A neat article discussing the possible dangers in the workplace of applying so-called 'pop' psychology (i.e. ideas that people can relate to, but which have not necessarily been tested or thought through) can be found at http://performance-appraisals.org/Bacalsappraisalarticles/articles/poppsych.htm.

For further self-test material and relevant, annotated weblinks please visit the website at **www.pearsoned.co.uk/workpsych**

Suggested further reading

Full details for all references are given in the list at the end of this book.

1   The book by Sylvia Shimmin and Don Wallis, *Fifty Years of Occupational Psychology in Britain*, provides a well-written description of how work psychology has evolved in the United Kingdom and the topics it focuses on. Although the

historical details are of course specific to the UK context, much of the content of this book can be generalised to other countries.

2   Cathy Cassell and Gillain Symon's *Essential Guide to Qualitative Methods in Organizational Research* is a superb, focused introduction to a wide range of qualitative methods and how they are used in organisational research.

3   Although about management rather than work psychology, the 2002 book by Mark Easterby-Smith, Richard Thorpe, Paul Jackson and Andy Lowe, *Management Research: An introduction*, gives a clear and practical guide to key issues in formulating and doing research.

4   Alan Bryman's book, *Social Research Methods*, is in many respects a rather more advanced and detailed version of Easterby-Smith *et al.*, with slightly greater emphasis on conceptual as well as practical issues. Bryman's 2006 article 'Integrating quantitative and qualitative research: how is it done?', *Qualitative Research*, 6, 97–113 is also very useful.

5   The book by Adamantios Diamantopoulos and Bodo Schlegelmilch, *Taking the Fear out of Data Analysis*, is a gentle and entertaining introduction for those who feel they are not particularly numerate but want to understand how to apply basic statistics appropriately. The examples used are not confined to psychology.

6   *Discovering Statistics Using SPSS* (Introducing Statistical Methods series) by Andy Field is a very accessible text that shows how to understand and use the SPSS software package. It is peppered with a good amount of humour to lighten the load.

CHAPTER 3

Individual differences

LEARNING OUTCOMES

After studying this chapter, you should be able to:

1 outline contemporary theories of human intelligence and intelligence testing;

2 compare conventional approaches to intelligence with system models;

3 describe the main conceptualisations of emotional intelligence;

4 describe the research evidence for emotional intelligence and how it is assessed;

5 define the 'Big Five' personality constructs;

6 describe the characteristics and behaviours associated with innovation at work;

7 describe socio-cognitive approaches to understanding behaviour at work.

Mention Slough these days and the BBC comedy *The Office,* headed by the crassly insensitive David Brent, springs to mind. But Slough council, rather than take offence at this unprovoked slight, has responded by embracing one of the latest concepts in workplace psychology: emotional intelligence, known as EI – something for which Brent is hardly famous.

The term emotional intelligence was coined by American psychologists Dr Peter Salovey and Dr John Mayer as 'a type of social intelligence that involves the ability to monitor one's own and others' emotions, to discriminate among them, and to use the information to guide one's thinking and actions'. Their research led them to assert in 1990 that EI is a quantifiable form of intelligence that can be measured through an ability test.

The American management guru Daniel Goleman, who developed and popularised the concept, has suggested that applying it can bring dramatic improvements in the workplace. He believes the contribution of EI to 'effective performance' is 66 per cent for all jobs and 85 per cent in leadership roles. Another leading EI figure, Reuven Bar-On, is more cautious. His research suggests that the difference EI brings to effective performance is an average of 27 per cent across all jobs and sectors.

Slough council turned to EI after it identified a specific need to improve the performance of its front-line staff, who spend most of their time facing the public. Rosemary Westbrook, director of Slough's housing and neighbourhood services, says:

> There was nothing wrong with our staff, but because there is less investment in the public sector we have struggled to supply the level of customer-service standards that people now expect and receive from private-sector organisations. There has been so much focus in the private sector on getting customer care right; it forces us to raise our game.

The council commissioned the Hay Group to run a two-day EI course for its staff as a pilot project to improve performance. Hay applied the Goleman EI model, which groups together four so-called 'emotional competences' – self-awareness, self-management, social awareness and social skills.

Westbrook says:

> We felt some of the ideas behind emotional intelligence were helpful, because so much in customer service depends on people skills. We sent some front-line staff and first-line supervisors, and they all got different things from it. But they all said the points about self-awareness and tuning in to the customer were useful. We felt it was a model that had an explanation and a theory behind it that fitted quite well into the customer-service environment.

Some detractors have described EI as 'neo-psycho babble', a philosophy that reveals nothing but a common-sense way of working, one that mature, sensible employees should be putting into practice without being told.

Dilum Jirasinghe of the Hay Group says:

Yes, these techniques do come anyway, with experience, but this programme is aimed at personal development. It gets people to work at their skills, so instead of leaving it to chance and waiting for time and maturity to take their course, they have a chance to acquire them now. EI helps you recognise how you are feeling at that precise moment; through that awareness you can manage your feelings. Although you've had a stressful day, you use that awareness and understanding to change the way you engage with a particular person you are dealing with.

Source: The Sunday Times, *9 February 2003, (Davies, G.H.), copyright © The Sunday Times 2003, www.nisyndication.com*

Introduction

The case study demonstrates that there is a growing interest in intelligence, personality and emotion in relation to job performance in many different settings. Some key questions are: does emotional intelligence exist? What do intelligence tests actually measure? How does an individual's personality relate to performance at work? In this chapter we explore theories of intelligence and personality and provide a brief historical overview of the research literature in these areas. Traditionally, studies of intelligence and of personality have been treated separately but more contemporary theories of individual differences have begun to integrate these approaches in order to explain behaviour. As the opening case study illustrates, recent research explores whether 'emotional' intelligence is a critical factor in explaining performance at work. This has been a topic of fierce debate and current research evidence is reviewed in this chapter.

Historically, in attempts to explain personality, psychologists have tended to emphasise the role of either internal (person) factors or external (situational) factors. It is important to understand that debate about the relative importance of people and situations in determining behaviour is a long-standing issue within psychology. Many previous approaches have focused on the structure and measurement of individual differences without emphasising the role of situational factors in determining behaviour. It would be a mistake, however, to conclude that the approaches described do not recognise the potential for situations to influence how people behave. Recent theoretical and research work has developed an important, more sophisticated concept than the idea that both people and situations are important.

Given recent global economic uncertainty, the topic of innovation at work has become a vital research question for work psychologists. In this chapter we explore the individual level resources that are important in predicting innovative working in organisations. The evidence shows that innovation is multifaceted and research has explored the role of intellect, personality, motivation and other social resources (such as teamworking) in predicting innovation at work. Here, by exploring the topic of innovation in organisations, our review shows how both the people level resources and situations at work are important.

Traditional models of cognitive ability

Some people are better at processing information than others. We are constantly exposed to evidence that, when it comes to cognitive (thinking) ability, there are significant variations among people. It is equally clear that some of these differences are the result of differences in opportunities to learn (i.e. they are situationally or environmentally determined). Psychologists have invested a great deal of time and effort into trying to understand and measure differences in cognitive ability. One approach to the issues involved has a long history and is particularly relevant to personnel selection and assessment. The core of this approach involves the use of carefully designed tests to assess people's levels of cognitive ability. Such tests need to be administered under standardised conditions and require people to attempt to answer written questions, all of which have been evolved through a highly technical process of trialling and analysis (*see* Table 3.1 for illustrative questions). The standardisation of tests (in terms of administration and test content) means that, in theory, everyone is given the same opportunity to perform. However, because of the need for standardisation, this approach cannot assess people on their capacity to conduct everyday, real-life tasks. This is seen by some psychologists as a serious weakness. Also, note that cognitive ability is often tested within a maximal performance paradigm (i.e. the very best you can do within a set time frame) rather than a typical performance paradigm (i.e. what you tend to do).

In the early years of the twentieth century, two French psychologists, Alfred Binet and Theodore Simon, developed what is generally accepted as the first satisfactory test of human intelligence. At the turn of the nineteenth century, France, in common with other industrialised nations, had introduced compulsory education. Most of the children entering the schools seemed well able to benefit from the regular mainstream schools. Some were perhaps in need of special help, but could still be dealt with by the regular system. A third group, however, did not demonstrate sufficient ability to be able to benefit from the regular system. It was not always easy to identify the children in need of special intervention, and the test developed by Binet and Simon was intended to help in identifying these children by assessing their intellectual capabilities.

The approach adopted by Binet and Simon is still the basis for contemporary intelligence tests. In essence, they considered that intelligence could be measured by assessing a person's ability to answer a carefully selected collection of questions. Although the questions in modern tests (*see* Table 3.1) sometimes differ from the type of questions used by Binet and Simon, the principle of sampling behaviour on a carefully selected set of tasks is still at the core of most tests. Clearly, by sampling behaviour one runs the risk of drawing false conclusions about a person – perhaps

Table 3.1	Some questions from an intelligence test

Q7 Mountain is to molehill as valley is to . . .

1	2	3	4	5
hollow	chasm	hill	plain	mound

Q8 The third member of this series is omitted. What is it?
0.1, 0.7, . . . , 34.3, 240.1

Q9 Which one of the five words on the right bears a similar relation to each of the two words on the left?

	1	2	3	4	5
Class; shape	Rank	Grade	Analyse	Size	Form

Q10 Here are five classes. Write down the number of the class which contains two, and two only, of the other four classes:

1	2	3	4	5
Terriers	Mammals	'Scotties'	Dogs	Canines

Q11 Sniff is to handkerchief as shiver is to . . .

1	2	3	4	5
blow	fire	catarrh	burn	sneeze

Q12 How many members of the following series are missing?
1, 2, 5, 6, 7, 11, 12, . . . , 20, 21, 22, 23

Q13 Which one of the five words on the right bears a similar relation to each of the two words on the left?

	1	2	3	4	5
Stream; tolerate	Brook	Contribute	Bear	Support	Pour

Q14 Working from the left, divide the fourth whole number by the fifth fraction:
8, 6, 5/7, 3, 9, 2/9, 3/8, 1, 17/31, 4/9

Source: The AH5 Test. Copyright © 1968, A. W. Heim. Reprinted by permission of the publisher ASE, College Lane, Hatfield, Herts, AL10 9AA, UK.

because of the particular questions asked, the circumstances in which the test is taken, or various other reasons. Binet and Simon certainly recognised that test scores alone were not enough and they proposed that, before any decision about a child was taken, other types of assessment should also be made.

Intelligence testing

Since the pioneering work of Binet and Simon, psychologists have carried out a considerable amount of work in their attempts to measure intelligence and to understand its structure. So far we have managed to discuss the underlying structure of intelligence without directly confronting the problem of what intelligence actually is! Defining intelligence presents problems for psychologists, and to this day there is no universally accepted definition. Many psychologists will settle for the definition first proposed by Boring (1923, p. 35): *'Intelligence is what intelligence tests measure.'* In fact, this definition is not as meaningless as it seems at first sight. Tests of general intelligence are designed to examine the innate ability of people to carry out certain *mental operations* (e.g. to manipulate data, solve problems, interpret information, and so on). Refer back to Table 3.1 for examples of intelligence test questions. Don't worry if you find them difficult – they are! The various tests of general intelligence (which Spearman labelled 'g') are all interrelated and people obtain similar scores in different tests. Thus, 'g' is a quality that can be measured reliably and with some precision. Regardless of whether the available tests measure what we think of as intelligence or some other qualities, tests of intelligence and specific abilities have been used with some success in personnel selection (*see* Chapters 4 and 5).

Tests of intelligence have been criticised on various grounds. One criticism is based on the argument that intelligence tests do not measure pure underlying intelligence, but a mixture of it and of taught or acquired knowledge (sometimes referred to as crystallised intelligence). For example, the questions in Table 3.1 require the test taker to have knowledge of the English language (although it could be argued that the vast majority of test takers would possess enough knowledge of the English language engage in the mental processes required to tackle the questions). Unfortunately, it is one thing to make such a distinction in writing but quite another to put it into practice by developing tests that are 'pure' tests of one or other factor. Proponents of intelligence tests believe that this can be done; others consider that it has not been done properly and is probably impossible.

In the personnel selection context, tests are also criticised because they are biased in favour of certain ethnic or cultural groups. The argument of cultural bias asserts that the intellectual development that takes place naturally is dependent on the specific environmental and cultural background in which a person develops. This means that perfectly bright and intelligent people from certain socio-economic or ethnic backgrounds will fail to develop the normal qualities assessed in the tests. The consequence will be that, despite their underlying intelligence, the tests will label them as unintelligent.

A rational and unbiased examination of the advantages and disadvantages of psychological tests is important to both the science of psychology and society as a whole. The criticism that intelligence tests are biased against certain ethnic groups is, at least in part, based on the frequently replicated research finding that ethnic minority groups (mostly black Americans) obtain lower scores on cognitive tests than whites (*see* Sackett *et al.*, 2008 for a review of evidence and Chapter 5). Despite these subgroup differences, the prevailing view of the scientific community is that it is not unfair to use such tests for selection decision-making. In essence this conclusion is based on the finding that although there are consistent differences between subgroups in mean scores, the accuracy of prediction of the tests (i.e. the prediction of future levels of work performance) is the same for different ethnic groups. Of course there are wider, societal issues to consider here (e.g. whether certain ethnic groups have better access to better schools) which need to be kept in mind, but these fall outside the remit of this book.

There is a wide range of different tests available to measure 'g' and various specific abilities (mechanical, spatial, numerical, etc.) and several publishers of psychological tests are operating globally. There is plenty of evidence to indicate that 'g' determines performance across different job roles. A widely used test of 'g' which requires minimal special experience or training is Raven's progressive matrices: this test measures 'g' through a series of abstract diagrammatic problems (Raven *et al.*, 1996).

However, specific abilities tend to predict performance when they are 'matched' to the demands of the job role (e.g. verbal ability predicting the performance of a journalist, numerical ability predicting the performance of an accountant, etc.). Indeed, measures of specific abilities appear to predict variability in performance that is not predicted by 'g' (i.e. they can offer some useful additional information). Evidence concerning the value of cognitive tests and the fairness of such tests is discussed in Chapter 5.

Key Learning Point

There are consistent differences in the general mental ability test scores obtained by different subgroups.

Systems models of intelligence

Unlike previous structural models of intelligence, systems models expand the concepts underlying intelligence to include concepts other than cognitive abilities. Three contemporary approaches are briefly reviewed. Several 'new' approaches to intelligence theory have become fairly widespread in both their acceptance and application. Two prominent approaches are Gardner's Theory of Multiple Intelligences (Gardner, 1983) and the Triarchic Theory of Intelligence (Sternberg, 1985). An emerging approach is that of emotional intelligence (*see* Goleman, 1995; Bar-On, 2000; and Mayer *et al.*, 2001).

Gardener's Multiple Intelligences

Drawing on studies of giftedness and brain injury deficits, Howard Gardner (1983) proposed a theory of multiple intelligences (MI). Gardener argued that there is more than a single, general factor of intelligence. His theory has attracted a great deal of attention, particularly in the media, and it has some intuitive appeal. Gardner proposes seven different types of intelligence as follows:

1. *linguistic* – a mastery of language, the ability to effectively manipulate language to express oneself;

2. *spatial* – ability to manipulate and create mental images in order to solve problems;

3. *musical* – capability to recognise and compose musical pitches, tones and rhythms;

4. *logical-mathematical* – ability to detect patterns, reason deductively and think logically;

5. *bodily kinaesthetic* – ability to use one's mental abilities to coordinate one's own bodily movements;

6   *interpersonal* – ability to understand and discern the feelings and intentions of others;

7   *intrapersonal* – ability to understand one's own feelings and motivations.

Each of these seven intelligences is derived from Gardner's subjective classification of human abilities based on a set of scientific criteria such as neuropsychological evidence (e.g. speech and language functions appear to reside in the left cerebral hemisphere in the brain), support from experimental psychology and from psychometric findings. For example, there is evidence that some individuals may perform very poorly on IQ tests, yet demonstrate exceptional talent in other domains such as music. Gardner claims that although the seven intelligences are anatomically separated from each other, they rarely operate independently. In other words, the intelligences are hypothesised to operate concurrently thereby complementing one another as individuals develop skills or solve problems. For example, the theory suggests that a dancer can perform well only if they have (1) strong musical intelligence to understand the rhythm of the music, (2) interpersonal intelligence to understand how they can inspire their audience, and (3) bodily-kinaesthetic intelligence to provide them with the dexterity and coordination to complete the movements successfully.

Although many educationalists have used Gardner's theory in schools, MI theory has been criticised by many academics. Criticisms include the observation that MI theory is subjective, and is incompatible with the well-established concept of 'g' and with the likely impact of environmental influences. Gardner (1995) has vehemently defended MI theory by referring to various laboratory and field studies for support, arguing that researchers should be interested in understanding intellectual processes that are not explained by 'g'. Matthews *et al.* (2003a) argue that there are some potentially serious omissions in MI theory. For example, the primary mental abilities associated with intelligence such as word fluency, inductive reasoning, memory and perceptual speed cannot be classified in his system. They also argue that MI theory has some limitations:

> for example, assuming bodily kinaesthetic intelligence is a distinct domain, do we take it that one should also distinguish tennis intelligence, athletic intelligence, football intelligence, dance intelligence, and golf intelligence? If not, one might assume that an individual who turns out to be highly proficient at football might equally have turned that talent to performing in a classical ballet production.
>
> *(p. 121)*

Sternberg's Triarchic Theory of Intelligence

Robert Sternberg's Triarchic Theory (Sternberg, 1985, called *Beyond IQ: A triarchic theory of human intelligence*) builds on Spearman's 'g' and the underlying information processing components of intelligence. The theory consists of three parts (also known as subtheories) used to describe and measure intelligence. The three facets (or subtheories) are: *analytical* (componential), *creative* (experiential) and *practical* (contextual). Each is defined as follows:

■   *Analytical (componential) subtheory*: analytical intelligence refers to academic problem-solving (such as solving puzzles) and reflects how an individual relates to their internal world. Sternberg suggests that analytical intelligence (problem-solving skills) is based on the joint operations of 'metacomponents', 'performance' components and 'knowledge acquisition' components of intelligence. *Metacomponents* control, monitor and evaluate cognitive processing. These are the executive functions that help to organise strategies for performance and the process of knowledge acquisition. In other words, metacomponents decide what to do. *Performance* components are the basic operations that execute the strategies governed by the metacomponents. They are the cognitive processes that enable us to encode information, hold information in short-term memory, perform mental operations and recall information from long-term memory. *Knowledge acquisition* components are the processes used in gaining and storing (memorising) new knowledge (i.e. the capacity for learning).

■ *Creative (experiential) subtheory*: creative intelligence involves the insights people have, their ability to synthesise (e.g. have new ideas) and their ability to react to novel situations and stimuli. Sternberg suggests that this experiential aspect of intelligence reflects how an individual associates their internal world to the external world. Creative intelligence comprises the ability to think creatively *and* the ability to adapt creatively and effectively to new situations.

■ *Practical (contextual) subtheory*: practical intelligence involves the ability to understand and deal with everyday tasks. It is referred to as 'real-world intelligence'. This contextual facet of intelligence reflects how the individual relates to the external world. People with high levels of this type of intelligence can adapt to, or shape their environment. Sternberg and Wagner's test of Practical Managerial Intelligence includes measures of the ability to write effective memos, to motivate people, to identify when to delegate and so on. In contrast to structural models of intelligence, measures of practical intelligence go beyond mental skills and include assessment of attitudes and emotional factors (Sternberg and colleagues, 2000). In this way, one of Sternberg's most important contributions to intelligence theory has been the redefinition of intelligence to incorporate practical knowledge. Sternberg's discoveries and theories have influenced cognitive science, and have resulted in the re-thinking of conventional methods of evaluating an individual's intelligence.

Key Learning Point

Sternberg's Triarchic Theory of Intelligence redefines intelligence to incorporate a practical knowledge component.

Emotional intelligence

As described in the opening case study in this chapter, there has been an explosion of interest in the concept of emotional intelligence (EI), in both the media and the academic literature. Since Daniel Goleman's book *Emotional Intelligence* was published in 1995, many researchers have initiated studies of EI, believing that EI fills a gap in knowledge. Not surprisingly, this has led to heated debate among researchers and practitioners, who are keen to define EI and understand how EI differs from established theories of intelligence, and how it is best measured. For practitioners, a key question is whether EI provides incremental validity in predicting job performance over and above measures of cognitive ability (*see* Chapter 5 for a discussion of validity in assessment).

Early research described three main conceptualisations of EI appearing in the research literature: one proposed by Goleman, one by Bar-On, and the third by Mayer and Salovey (e.g. Bar-On, 2000; Goleman, 1995, 1998; Mayer and Salovey, 1997). Although there is some obvious commonality, there exists some significant divergence of thought in these three approaches to EI. Each is briefly reviewed in turn. For a thorough review of the emotional intelligence literature see Matthews *et al.* (2003a) and Zeidner *et al.* (2008).

Goleman defined EI as:

> abilities such as being able to motivate oneself and persist in the face of frustrations; to control impulse and delay gratification; to regulate one's moods and keep distress from swamping the ability to think; to empathize and to hope.
>
> *(Goleman, 1995, p. 34)*

Goleman's conceptualisation has been criticised on the basis that the definition is overinclusive and that it is 'old wine in new bottles'. In other words, some have argued that EI is a repackaging of previous literature on personality and intelligence and nothing 'new' has been identified (Chapman, 2000). Matthews *et al.* (2003a) suggest that Goleman's conceptualisation of EI rests on gathering up various aspects of what psychologists today would describe as cognition, motivation, personality, emotions, neurobiology and intelligence. However, Goleman has insisted that EI is an ability that differs from other more established abilities (although there is limited empirical evidence to support some of his claims). In later publications, Goleman (1998, 2001) suggests how his EI theory represents a framework of an individual's potential for mastering the skills in four key domains: of self-awareness, self-management, social awareness and relationship management. Unlike other conceptualisations of EI, Goleman's framework (2001) specifically refers to behaviours in the workplace and is based on content analyses of competencies in several organisations. He defines an emotional 'competence' as 'a learned capability based on emotional intelligence that results in outstanding performance at work'. In this way, each EI domain is viewed as a competency. For example, in considering the EI domain of self-awareness, this provides the underlying basis of the extent to which an individual is accurate (competent) in their self-assessment of personal strengths and limitations.

Equally influential in this area is the work of Reuven Bar-On (1997, 2000). He defines EI as 'an array of non-cognitive capabilities, competencies and skills that influence one's ability to succeed in coping with environmental demands and pressures' (1997, p. 14). He produced the first commercially available measure of EI, based on a self-assessment instrument called the *Emotional Quotient Inventory* (EQi; similar to the concept of IQ). Bar-On (2000) defines his model in terms of an array of traits and abilities related to emotional and social knowledge: these influence our ability to cope effectively with environmental demands. In this way, he views EI as a model of *psychological well-being and adaptation*. His model includes four domains including the ability to (1) be aware of, to understand and to express oneself (intrapersonal intelligence); (2) be aware of, to understand and relate to others (interpersonal intelligence); (3) deal with strong emotions and control one's impulses (stress management); and (4) adapt to change and to solve problems of a personal or social nature (adaptability). Bar-On has reported several validation studies of the EQi and there is reasonable evidence that it predicts academic success and diagnosis of some clinical disorders. However, as with Goleman's work, one of the main criticisms of the EQi centres around the question of whether is captures any construct that is unique and is not already captured in existing personality measures (see Mayer *et al.*, 2000). Further research is clearly warranted in this area to explore whether the EQi is measuring personal qualities beyond personality as it is currently understood (see the latter part of this chapter).

The research of Jack Mayer and Peter Salovey (1997) has perhaps been the most influential in this area, and they were first to publish their accounts of EI in scientific peer-reviewed journal articles. Unlike other approaches, Mayer and Salovey describe EI as extending traditional models of intelligence. They define EI as 'a concept of intelligence that processes and benefits from emotions. From this perspective, EI is composed of mental abilities, skills or capacities' (Mayer *et al.*, 2000, p. 105). They suggest that traditional measures of intelligence fail to measure individual differences in the ability to perceive, process and manage emotions and emotional information effectively. In this way, the Mayer and Salovey approach defines EI as the ability to perceive emotions, to access and generate emotions to assist thought, to understand emotions and emotional knowledge and to reflectively regulate emotions to promote emotional and intellectual growth (Mayer and Salovey, 1997). For measurement purposes Mayer *et al.* (1999) have produced a Multifactor Emotional Intelligence Scale (MEIS) to assess facets of EI, comprising 12 subscales. Unlike other approaches, this model attempts to measure EI as a *distinct concept*, i.e. something that is not captured in established measures of personality. Vernon *et al.* (2008) found evidence to support the possible existence of a genetic component of EI. However, the evidence on the validity of the MEIS is mixed.

Clearly there are some similarities, but also some important differences, between the three approaches. Bar-On has tried to develop a general measure of social and emotional intelligence associated with psychological well-being and adaptation. Mayer and Salovey attempt to establish the validity of a new form of intelligence, whereas Goleman's approach is specific to behaviour in organisations based on the ability to demonstrate social and emotional competencies. Emmerling and Goleman (2003) argue that EI is something unique that helps to explain performance over and above measures of general mental ability. This kind of reasoning has led practitioners to believe that EI is a useful concept in assisting decisions about promotion to leadership positions, for example. Ashkanasy and Daus (2005) argue that the 'abilities' model of EI is an important concept for understanding how emotion affects the behaviour of individuals at work. However, Locke (2005) argues EI cannot strictly be classed as a type of intelligence: he suggests that the vast number of factors found in definitions of EI renders it too broad a concept to be properly measured, understood and used in a meaningful way.

Conte (2005) reviewed the research evaluating the most prominent measures of EI, including Goleman's Emotional Competence Inventory (ECI), Bar-On's Emotional Quotient Inventory (EQ-i), and Mayer and Salovey's Multifactor Emotional Intelligence Scale (MEIS). Conte (2005) argued there are 'serious concerns' regarding all three measures, for example, with the way ability-based EI tests are scored and the discriminant validity of self-report EI measures. As a result of his findings, Conte (2005) cautioned against the use of EI measures for selection purposes, until further research has shown EI to be a valid concept.

A review of the EI literature from the last 20 years has recently been conducted by Zeidner *et al.* (2008). This review identifies what is generally agreed about EI as a concept, and the contentious issues which are at the core of the ongoing debate. In terms of the 'conceptualisation' of EI, there is general agreement that

EI is a concept comprising multiple facets; though there is still a lack of agreement over *which* facets are part of EI. Zeidner *et al.* (2008) argue that EI can be seen to encompass other established aspects of cognition (including personality and general intelligence). However, there is debate over the extent to which this overlap can be seen, and which measures of EI, personality and general intelligence overlap with each other. The review concludes that it is still unclear whether EI is predictive of important outcomes. Indeed, there is still much debate about the type of outcomes that may depend upon EI (i.e. whether EI should influence task performance, managerial performance, psychological well-being, etc.).

Key Learning Point

The existence of emotional intelligence as a new construct, distinct from other established constructs, has been vigorously debated. Although there is an acceptance that EI is multi-faceted, there is still disagreement about what these facets are.

Zeidner *et al.*'s (2008) review argues that EI has traditionally been conceptualised using a 'mixed model', i.e. it has been viewed as a *trait* and measured using self-report methods, or as an observable *ability* and assessed using objective methods. This has fuelled even more debate about which assessment methods *should* be used to measure EI. It can be argued that responses to self-report measures can can be faked, coached and manipulated by individuals. Zeidner *et al.*'s conclusion is that the different measures of EI do not converge: different measures have been found to be measuring different concepts.

If we look back to the concept of EI we can see that it is appealing to organisations who want to recruit employees who can work effectively with colleagues and customers. However, Zeidner *et al.* (2008) highlight three key problems with EI research in occupational settings. These are:

1 The approach to measuring EI in occupational settings has been generic (i.e. it has not been specific to particular occupations). Different jobs have different emotional demands (compare those of a nurse to those of an accountant). Generic measurement means that the emotional demands of various jobs are not well understood, and therefore it is difficult to identify how the various aspects of EI relate to performance in a variety of different job roles.

2 Few measures of EI have extensive norm (comparison) groups which show how EI varies across different occupational groups. If we do accept that EI exists, then we might reasonably assume that different jobs require different 'levels' of it.

3 Perhaps most important of all, there is a lack of evidence that shows measures of EI are linked to future job performance (although the concept is relatively new and this evidence may emerge with time – absence of proof is not the same a proof of absence!). Several commentators have argued that EI cannot be used reliably to make decisions in organisations because of the lack of rigorous research that has been carried out into the properties of the EI construct.

In order to address some of these highlighted problems, Zeidner *et al.* (2008) call for the use of 'emotional task analysis'. This is rather like job analysis (*see* Chapter 4) but focuses on the emotional demands in the workplace. This would help us to understand exactly which emotional demands are made by particular occupations and organisational contexts. Such analysis would make it possible for us to identify which aspects of EI are required in different occupational settings.

More research is required to answer many questions about EI. There is no doubt that the debate associated with EI has begun to challenge previous assumptions of what leads to success in organisations. Many of these questions centre around one fundamental issue. The work reviewed in this section treats EI as if it was a 'thing' – that is, as if it was a definable entity that exists *independently* of the minds of the people who try to define and measure it. An alternative approach would be to adopt an *interpretivist* perspective (see Chapter 2). This would see EI as a phenomenon constructed by those who are interested in it, with arguments about its definition and measurement reflecting their personal preferences rather than a search for objective truth (Fineman, 2003). This perspective encourages us to be more interested in questions such as:

- ▇ Why has the notion of EI has come to prominence at this time?
- ▇ Why it is defined in the ways it is?
- ▇ How are different groups of people (e.g. academics, consultants, managers) seeking to use it?

Of course, this alternative perspective can be applied to many different phenomena in work psychology, not just EI.

Key Learning Point

Emotional intelligence is seen by many as an exciting concept because it encompasses thought, emotion and interpersonal awareness more than earlier models of intelligence.

Trait views of personality

Psychoanalytic theories of human personality (e.g. the work of Freud that you may well have heard something about!) are often criticised by other psychologists. They argue that these theories often lack of scientific rigour, or fail to clearly define their key concepts (i.e. the main ingredients of the theory). From a scientific perspective, the most fundamental criticisms are that these theories either do not generate testable predictions about human behaviour or, if they do, when predictions are made they do not work out in practice. Trait theories perhaps come closest to describing the structure of personality in a way that matches our everyday use of the term personality. Trait theories use words such as *shy, outgoing, tense* and *extroverted* to describe the basic factors of human personality. These basic elements – traits – represent predispositions (or tendencies) to behave in certain ways, in a variety of different situations.

Over several decades academic debate, research has produced some fairly consistent evidence of the existence of five – the so-called 'Big Five' – major personality factors. A fairly high degree of consensus has emerged and investigators have agreed that a five-factor structure represents an almost universal template for describing the basic dimensions of personality (Digman, 1990; McCrae and Costa, 1990; Costa and McCrae, 1992). The Big Five dimensions of personality are described below. Costa and McCrae's work found that within each of these dimensions there appear to be a number of facets (or subdimensions). These facets help us to understand the breadth of each of the Big Five and to appreciate how the model attempts to measures the richness of individual differences in personality. These facets are also listed after each of the Big Five labels below:

Extroversion – warmth, gregrariousness, assertiveness, activity (energy), excitement-seeking, and the experience of positive emotions. People who report themselves to have high levels of E tend to describe themselves as outgoing, gregarious, lively and sociable.

Neuroticism – anxiety, angry hostility, depression, self-consciousness, impulsiveness and vulnerability. People who report themselves to have high levels of N tend to describe themselves as prone to worry and self-doubt, and being highly affected by their emotions in stressful situations.

Conscientiousness – competence (i.e. feeling capable), preference for order, dutifulness, achievement striving, self-discipline, deliberation (e.g. giving thorough and careful thought to tasks). People who report themselves to have high levels of C tend to describe themselves as being highly organised and thorough in their approach to tasks.

Agreeableness – trust, straightforwardness, altruism, compliance, modesty, tender-mindedness. People who report themselves to have high levels of A tend to describe themselves as being helpful to others and mindful of others' feelings, and as preferring cooperation to competition.

Openness to experience – fantasy, aesthetics, feelings, actions, ideas, values. People who report themselves to have high levels of O tend to like working with ideas and possibilities (as opposed to established methods), and they are ready to re-examine their attitudes and values.

Key Learning Point

The 'Big Five' has become a widely accepted template for understanding the structure of human personality.

Substantial evidence exists that the Big Five structure is consistent across various national groups. For example, McCrae and Costa (1997) reported results comparing six diverse samples (German, Portuguese, Hebrew, Chinese, Korean and Japanese) showing all to have substantial similarity in a Big Five structure when compared with a large American sample. This and other evidence suggests very strongly that the Big Five structure is a useful general framework although, as McCrae and Costa acknowledge, this may be limited to modern, literate, industrialised cultures. It also seems that the 'openness to experience' dimension is less well defined than the others (Ferguson and Patterson, 1998).

The identification of the Big Five personality factors is an important development in the trait-factor analytic approach. It is important to realise, though, that the establishment of the Big Five does not mean that other conceptualisations of personality become redundant (Hough and Oswald, 2000). The Big Five provide a useful view of the minimum factors that must be included in any description of human personality. In many circumstances it may make sense to use a more detailed set of dimensions. Hough and Ones (2001), for example, make an important distinction between the use of personality variables for *description* and their use for *predicting job performance*. In other words, while the Big Five may be a useful framework for describing the different aspects of personality, they may not be as accurate when predicting job performance. Lee and Ashton (2004) suggest that there may be a sixth factor called honesty-humility (with facets of sincerity, fairness, greed avoidance and modesty), a measure of which is found in their HEXACO personality questionnaire.

Recent meta-analytic studies have examined the stability of personality over individuals' lifespan. Roberts *et al.* (2006) conducted a meta-analysis of longitudinal studies which included a total of 92 participants in order to investigate the changeability of mean levels of personality traits throughout their lives. Findings showed that as people grew older social dominance (an aspect of extroversion), emotional stability (an aspect of extroversion) and conscientiousness all increased (this trend was most notable between the ages of 20 and 40). Rantanen *et al.* (2007) conducted a meta-analysis into Big Five trait stability in an adult sample, using structural equation modelling (see Chapter 2). Findings show that between the ages of 33 and 42, there was a significant increase in mean levels of extroversion, openness to experience, agreeableness and conscientiousness. Levels of neuroticism fell between ages 33 and 42. In the same study it was found that extroversion and neuroticism changed less over time in the male sample, compared to the female sample.

The role of personality in personnel selection decision-making is discussed further in Chapters 4 and 5. For the moment it is sufficient to recognise that the Big Five provide a level of description for personality that dominates the research literature.

Personality measures

Although several studies have shown that the factors measured by many personality measures can be related to the Big Five, the tests themselves provide data on a variety of personality dimensions. Table 3.2 gives some information on the better-known personality questionnaires available in the United Kingdom.

As with all kinds of psychological measures, personality questionnaires need to satisfy various well-established psychometric criteria before they can be considered to be acceptable measuring instruments. These criteria are concerned with assessing the extent to which the test measures what it is intended to measure (the issue of validity) and the precision or consistency of measurement that the test achieves (reliability). The British Psychological Society has produced a detailed review of all of the most widely used personality tests in the United Kingdom (http://www.psychtesting.org.uk). These reviews give thorough technical evaluations of each test.

As a light-hearted illustration, Table 3.3 provides descriptions of the 16PF scales together with examples of historical or literary figures who are supposed to exemplify the person qualities described. You may want to think of some other famous (or infamous) individuals who display such qualities!

Table 3.2	Personality questionnaires

Instrument	Personality characteristics measured
Eysenck Personality Questionnaire (EPQ; Eysenck and Eysenck, 1964)	Extroversion, neuroticism (or emotional stability), psychoticism
The Sixteen PF5 (16PF; Cattell *et al.*, 1970). Several versions of short/long forms are available and measure second-order personality factors, etc., in addition to the 16 factors mentioned here	Sixteen personality factors, e.g. submissiveness (mild, humble, easily led, docile, accommodating); self-assurance (placid, serene, secure, complacent); tender-mindedness (sensitive, clinging, over-protected)
The Occupational Personality Questionnaire (OPQ; SHL, 1990)	Thirty personality dimensions are measured in the most detailed version of the OPQ (the concept model). The questions have their origins in descriptions of people's behaviour in the workplace. Other versions/models of the questionnaires are available. Illustrative personality dimensions are: ■ caring (considerate to others, helps those in need, sympathetic, tolerant) ■ emotional control (restrained in showing emotions, keeps feelings back, avoids outbursts) ■ forward planning (prepares well in advance, enjoys target-setting, forecasts trends, plans projects)
The Hogan Personality Inventory	Its seven primary scales are: adjustment, ambition, sociability, agreeability, prudence, intellectance and scholarship. It was designed specifically for use in occupational settings and hence questionnaire responses can also be scored on six occupational scales: service orientation, stress tolerance, reliability, clerical potential, sales potential and managerial potential. The measure is based on the Big Five model, but also socioanalytic theory. This means that the questionnaire's items are designed to measure how people present themselves to others (rather than how they would describe themselves).
The revised NEO Personality Inventory (NEO PI-R, Costa and McCrae, 1992)	The Big Five personality factors, plus facet scores for six subscales within each of the Big Five domains. This measure is designed for a wide range of purposes (e.g. clinical, research and occupational uses).

Table 3.2	*(Continued)*
Instrument	**Personality characteristics measured**
The Myers-Briggs Type Indicator (MBTI)	This measure is based on a very different theory from the Big Five. It uses Jung's theory of Psychological Types which discusses fundamental differences between people in terms of *dichotomies* rather than positions on a scale. Research shows that while the MBTI does not have a direct measure of N, its constituent parts do correlate with the Big Five. Extroversion-Introversion (EI) correlates with E (but also taps into elements of openness); Sensing-Intuition (SN) correlates with openness; Thinking-Feeling (TF) correlates with agreeableness; and Judging-Perceiving (JP) correlates with conscientiousness and openness (Costa *et al.*, 1991). It is important to remember that although there are correlations with the Big Five there are some qualitative differences in what the MBTI measures because it is based on a different underlying theory.

STOP TO CONSIDER

In reading about the Big Five you may have reached the conclusion that some personalities are more 'desirable' than others. However, this is a dangerous assumption as so much depends upon the social context within which the person is behaving. Most personality measures used in occupational settings are measures of normal personality, i.e. whatever the score they are generally not an absolute indicator of a problem (e.g. people may score high on the Big Five N scales without having a psychiatric disorder). Costa and McCrae (2006) discuss the advantages and disadvantages of various scores on the Big Five. They say about conscientiousness: 'On the positive side, high C is associated with academic and occupational achievement; on the negative side, it may lead to annoying fastidiousness, compulsive neatness or workaholic behaviour' (p. 17).

Have another look at the Big Five. Try to think of jobs in which low E, low O, high N, low A (etc.) might be advantageous (hint: there are some). What personality might be well-suited to being a librarian, an elite track and field athlete, a lawyer, a CEO, a counsellor/therapist (insert some more of your own examples here)? This will help you to think about whether certain personality profiles are inherently advantageous/disadvantageous. As you will see, much depends upon the demands of the situation. The evidence about the relationships between the Big Five factors/scales and job performance is discussed in Chapter 5.

Table 3.3	The personality traits assessed by the 16PF with examples of famous individuals exemplifying the traits			
Factor	Trait descriptions		Famous individuals	
	High	Low	High	Low
A	Outgoing Warm-hearted	Reserved Detached	Falstaff	Greta Garbo
C	Unemotional Calm	Emotional Changeable	George Washington	Hamlet
E	Assertive Dominant	Humble Cooperative	Genghis Khan	Jesus
F	Cheerful Lively	Sober Taciturn	Groucho Marx	Clint Eastwood
G	Conscientious Persistent	Expedient Undisciplined	Mother Teresa	Casanova
H	Venturesome Socially bold	Shy Retiring	Columbus	Sylvia Plath
I	Tough-minded Self-reliant	Tender-minded Sensitive	James Bond	Robert Burns
L	Suspicious Sceptical	Trusting Accepting	De Gaulle	Pollyanna
M	Imaginative Bohemian	Practical Conventional	Van Gogh	Henry Ford
N	Shrewd Discreet	Forthright Straightforward	Machiavelli	Joan of Arc
O	Guilt prone Worrying	Resilient Self-assured	Dostoevsky	Stalin
Q1	Radical Experimental	Conservative Traditional	Karl Marx	Queen Victoria
Q2	Self-sufficient Resourceful	Group-dependent Affiliative	Copernicus	Marilyn Monroe
Q3	Controlled Compulsive	Undisciplined Lax	Margaret Thatcher	Mick Jagger
Q4	Tense Driven	Relaxed Tranquil	Macbeth	Buddha

Note: Dimension B (intelligence) is omitted.
Sources: from Conn and Rieke (1994), Matthews and Deary (1998).

Creativity and innovation

Over the past two decades there has been an explosion of interest in innovation as organisations have recognised that creating new processes, products and procedures is vital for productivity and growth in all sectors. With more dispersed and virtual working, role innovation is essential, since clearly defined job descriptions no longer exist for many jobs. The research literature on creativity and innovation is immense. The case study below illustrates the 'business case' for enhancing innovative working in organisations.

Exercise 3.1   Creativity pays, says the iPod generation

The Design Council's recent report, *Design in Britain*, says that while much of corporate Britain is treading water, companies, such as Apple and its all-conquering iPod, that use design to innovate and to differentiate themselves, are growing faster than their competitors.

In fact, almost half of companies who regard design as integral to their operations have increased turnover, profits and competitiveness, compared with only 10 per cent of companies overall.

One such company is Clipper Teas. In 2000, it relaunched its range by employing Williams Murray Hamm, the designers. A 'cohesive' design strategy was introduced and packaging was adorned with 'museum pieces' you might find in the V&A. The results were astonishing. Paul Machin, PR manager at the firm, estimates that business has improved by 90 per cent. Mike Brehme, co-founder and director says: 'The new identity has, without question, been the single most important activity we have undertaken in our 20-year history.' Machin says that brand awareness has 'gone through the roof' with the company now positioning itself as the thinking person's brand. 'At consumer shows we have designers who approach us and ask us to do their design, and, of course, we have to turn them away,' he adds.

But design is not just a case of prettifying existing product and waiting for the bucks to roll in. Design and innovation, as is the case with Apple and Dyson, go hand in hand. For people such as Matt Stevenson, founder of fish tank makers Reef One, functionality allied with design at premium prices has reaped rich rewards. The 29-year-old entrepreneur and designer decided to delve into a market that 'no one had looked to improve' and sought to combine the simplicity of a goldfish bowl with the welfare aspects of the large, square glass tanks. The result was the beautiful biOrb.

'James Dyson is a good role model for people like me, where technological advancement is the reason for inventing something. We are always looking for a better product,' he says. The look and therefore the allure of the biOrb has been key to the company's success. Turnover has almost doubled in every year of its existence. Having sold products worth £3 billion around the world, Dyson himself puts his success down 'to the creation of well-engineered machines'. 'I am still heavily involved in design and engineering, working alongside 350 like-minded people in our R&D centre,' he says. 'Innovation is integral to our business and our success. In fact, everybody at Dyson is encouraged to think creatively.' It took him five years and 5,127 prototypes before he produced the world's first bagless vacuum cleaner.

In his eyes style does not really matter in the long run:

> People buy Dysons because they work better, though of course I am happy if they like the machine's looks too. You can quickly fall out of love with a styled object that doesn't work, but you learn to love an unstyled product that works well.

Source: The Times, *13 January 2005 (Bjontomt, O.), copyright © The Times 2005, www.nisyndication.com*

Suggested exercise

Imagine you were the chief executive of Dyson. How would you ensure that creativity and innovation are valued by employees and managers? How would you encourage creative thinking in your employees? How would you ensure creative thinkers are attracted to your organisation? What challenges are might there be in managing creative people?

So, what is known about the individual level resources associated with innovative working? The concepts of creativity and innovation are often confused and used interchangeably in the literature. The concepts do overlap, but the main distinction can be seen as novelty. Creativity is concerned with generating new and entirely original ideas. Innovation is a broader concept because it also encompasses the application and implementation of new ideas to produce something new and useful (in the context of groups, organisations or societies). Innovation is often referred to as a process, because implementing new ideas necessarily involves influencing others (whereas creativity could be achieved in isolation).

One of the most widely accepted definitions of innovation is West and Farr (1990), emphasising the positive nature of innovation; 'the intentional introduction and application within a role, group or organization of ideas, processes, products or procedures, new to the relevant unit of adoption, designed to significantly benefit the individual, the group, the organization or wider society' (p. 9). In the UK, the Department for Business Enterprise and Regulatory Reform offer a more concise definition of innovation as 'the successful exploitation of new ideas'. Authors commonly agree that innovation in organisations is a complex, iterative process. Numerous approaches and process models have been proposed, but two main stages are common to all. First, there is a suggestion phase and second, an implementation phase. Innovation is not a linear process: it involves several cycles of activities such as initiation, reappraisal, adaptation, implementation and, finally, stabilisation. Innovation is a result of both person level resources and various environmental factors such as feedback, leadership style, resource availability and organisational climate. In terms of the measurement of innovative potential, there are various measures available that claim to assess the propensity to innovate, such as Patterson's (2002) Innovation Potential Indicator.

Innovation involves multiple components at the individual level. In her reviews on individual differences, Patterson (2002, 2004) suggests that the research literature can be classified into studies of the links between innovation and:

■ intelligence;

■ knowledge;

- personality; or

- motivation.

Early research claimed that creativity was equivalent to high intelligence. The best-known researcher in this field is Guilford. In his theory of the Structure of Intellect (SI) published in the 1950s, he claimed that creative thinking was a mental ability, involving *divergent production (i.e. thinking that goes off in different directions)*. Many researchers followed Guilford's work by producing evidence that ideational fluency (i.e. the quantity of new ideas) underlies divergent thinking test scores. This is akin to Edward De Bono's 'lateral' thinking concept. However, review studies have cast doubt on this conclusion: divergent thinking scores often fail to correlate significantly with various indices of innovation. Some authors doubt whether divergent thinking tests are adequately measuring the abilities actually involved in creative thinking.

Other authors suggest that *genius*, as the most obvious manifestation of high intelligence, is closely tied to the propensity for innovation. However, despite the substantial amount of research carried out, there has been a substantial lack of evidence to support a direct relationship between innovation and intelligence. Recent studies conclude that intelligence and innovation potential are moderately related, but once IQ scores go over 115 the relationship is near zero. This finding has been described as 'threshold theory': once intelligence reaches a certain point, its relationship to innovation breaks down. It seems that instead of being twin or even sibling constructs, intelligence and innovation potential may be more like 'cousins'.

Finke *et al.* (1992) suggest that in order to understand the role of cognitive abilities in idea generation, we must draw upon cognitive psychology. These researchers have used experimentally based observations of the processes that underlie generative (creative) tasks. Their work follows a framework called the *'geneplore model'*. The model proposes that many creative activities can be described in terms of:

- an initial generation of ideas or solutions *followed by*

- an extensive exploration of those ideas.

They suggest that individual differences occur due to variations in the use and application of these two generative processes, together with the sophistication of an individual's memory and knowledge in the domain they are working in. In summary, findings showed that the capacity for creative cognition is normally distributed among the general population (*see* Chapter 2) and therefore, highly creative people do not have minds that operate in any fundamentally different way from other individuals.

Exercise 3.2   Test your creative thinking

Task 1. The nine dots puzzle

Look at the nine dots below. Draw no more than four straight lines (without lifting the pencil from the paper) which will cross through all nine dots.   ▶

• • •

• • •

• • •

Task 2. One-minute idea generator

Your task is to ask yourself the following question:

How many uses are there for a teaspoon?

Go for quantity not quality of ideas. Write down every idea. Do not judge or criticise! Stay relaxed, playful, even silly. Adapt your point of view. For example, look at the teaspoon as if you were an insect or as a designer or as an electrician or in the middle of the desert. Ask yourself 'What if . . . ?' questions. What if the teaspoon were flattened out and one end was sharpened to a point? What if several of them were linked together somehow? Time yourself for one minute.

STOP TO CONSIDER

After reading the section on creativity and innovation and trying the two tasks above, ask yourself the following questions:

1   What individual-level factors do you feel influenced your performance on the above tasks?

2   What group-level factors may have influenced your performance if you had been working as part of a team in an organisation to complete the tasks?

3   Do you think these are robust tests to assess an individual's creativity?

Almost all researchers in this field have assumed that knowledge is a key variable in both generative thinking and innovation. An essential condition for innovation is being immersed in domain-specific *knowledge*, as one must develop an accurate sense of the domain before one can hope to change it for the better. For example, it would be difficult to design the world's best car if you did not know what a car was! However, on the other hand, the literature highlights that too much expertise in one area can also be a block to innovation within that domain. This is illustrated by research by Simonton (2004), who studied the lives of over 300 eminent people to explore lifespan development of innovation. They found that both a lack of, and an excess of, familiarity within a subject domain, can be detrimental to innovation. It seems that knowing too much can stifle innovation.

From several decades of research on the association between innovation and *personality*, a consistent set of characteristics has emerged. Innovative people tend to be imaginative, inquisitive, have high energy, a high desire for autonomy, social rule independence and high self-confidence. Research suggests that (of the Big Five) openness to experience is perhaps the most important personality dimension to predict the propensity for innovation. Research also shows that *low conscientiousness* is associated with innovation. Defined by terms such as fastidious, ordered, neat and methodical, the evidence shows that individuals high on conscientiousness are more resistant to changes at work, and are more likely to comply with current organisational norms.

Research shows that high levels of *motivation* are required for innovation and innovators are viewed as displaying a devotion and total absorption in their work. In the 1980s, Amabile suggested a three-component model of innovation that included intrinsic task motivation, domain-relevant skills (i.e. expertise) and innovation relevant process skills (cognitive skills and work styles conducive to novelty). Intrinsic motivation is clearly a prerequisite for innovation but the role of extrinsic motivators is less clear. The impact of environmental influences on motivation, and therefore, innovation is important. The evidence suggests that constructive evaluation (i.e. feedback that is informative, supportive and recognises accomplishment) can enhance innovation. In related studies, results showed that individuals who received positive feedback given in an informational style, and who worked in a high task autonomy environment, generated the most innovative solutions (*see* Zhou and Shalley, 2008).

Exercise 3.3   Assessing the propensity to innovate at work

A long-standing problem for HR managers has been how to select and develop innovative individuals effectively. Getting the right raw material in the first place is a critical issue. The propensity to innovate is often listed as a key competency in person specifications, but there has been little available to assess it in a reliable way. Traditional measures of creative thinking have been of the kinds that ask 'How many uses for a paper clip can you think of?' in say, three minutes. Such measures may indicate some level of conceptual thinking, but are of limited use in identifying individuals who are innovative in the workplace. Organisations are interested in the successful introduction of new products and processes in a competitive marketplace to generate revenue. This necessarily involves influencing others in the organisation to adopt the ideas suggested. Some organisations use trait-based personality questionnaires to assess the propensity to innovate.

Previous literature has been confused as to whether the propensity to innovate is predicted by an individual's level of intelligence or whether it is more concerned with personality. Early research suggested that innovative potential was an aspect of general intelligence. However, many authors have demonstrated that aspects of intelligence may be a necessary, but not a sufficient, condition for innovation to occur. Later research focused on the propensity to innovate as an aspect of personality. More recently, researchers have noted that motivation and job-specific knowledge are key components in predicting the propensity to innovate at work. Although there has been a vast amount of work examining these characteristics, this has lacked an integrative model with which to understand how all these aspects interrelate.

Socio-cognitive approaches to individual differences

The beginnings of this approach were evident in the debate about whether it is individual differences or the situations that people find themselves in that determine
people's behaviour. To most of us it is clear from everyday experience that our behaviour is not completely at the mercy of situational influences. There is some
cross-situational consistency in how we behave from one setting to another, particularly in terms of key features of our psychological make-up, such as extroversion,
agreeableness and anxiety. On the other hand most people will behave quite differently at a lively party and at a very important formal business event. The relative
influence of person and situation variables has been a topic of considerable controversy. Some people have argued very strongly for the predominance of situational
influences, suggesting that stable individual differences in psychological make-up
have a relatively small role to play (e.g. Mischel, 1968). Despite these historical differences of opinion, it is clear that modern psychology allows for the influence of
both person and situation variables. Eysenck captured the essential futility of trying to
identify a single cause by writing,

> Altogether I feel that the debate is an unreal one. You cannot contrast persons and
> situations in any meaningful sense . . . No physicist would put such a silly question
> as: which is more important in melting a substance – the situation (heat of the flame)
> or the nature of the substance?
>
> *Quoted by Pervin (1980, p. 271)*

Situations influence our behaviour because we think about how we should respond
to them. We could argue that work psychologists are equally guilty of ignoring the
thought processes that underlie behaviour. For example, most selection research has
sought to determine *whether* various selection methods predict job performance,
rather than *why* these methods predict. For example, we know that personality traits
predict work performance (*see* Chapters 4 and 5), but we know much less about how
personality traits influence behaviour. Moreover, it is highly unlikely that there is a
direct relationship between personality traits and behaviour (Skarlicki *et al.*, 1999).
After all, individuals will have their own way of *appraising* the situation that they
find themselves in and *decide* how they should best respond.

Hodgkinson (2003) found that senior managers, particularly CEOs and senior
executives, all have their own way of explaining key organisational events (such
as company performance) and this way of thinking influences strategic decisions
(Sparrow and Hodgkinson, 2002). This is just one example of how individual differences in cognitive style may play a significant role in job performance.

A number of cognitive-based personality characteristics have been developed
and investigated over the years, including: proactive personality, personal initiative,

self-efficacy, attributional style, and locus of control (e.g. Bandura, 1982; Frese *et al.*, 1997; Silvester *et al.*, 2003). Interestingly, all of these appear to relate to motivation – a construct that has been notoriously difficult to pin down in terms of a personality trait explanation. Kanfer and Ackerman's (2002) work on motivational traits acknowledges the importance of cognition in motivation. This raises the intriguing possibility that the impact of personality traits on work performance will be mediated by individual differences in cognitive style. Evidence for this can be found in work examining the relationship between attributional style and the performance of sales personnel. For example, Corr and Gray (1996) found that:

- male insurance sales agents who attributed positive outcomes (such as making a sale) to internal, stable and global causes (such as their own personality) were more successful than . . .

- individuals who externalised the cause to more unstable causes (e.g. luck, or being in a good mood that day).

Silvester *et al.* (2003) also found that individuals who perceived themselves to have more control over sales outcomes (both successful and unsuccessful) were rated as more successful by their managers. These findings indicate that even in the case of failure, individuals who attribute the outcome to more *internal controllable causes* (e.g. using the wrong sales strategy) will be more likely to maintain a higher level of motivation and effort than sales staff who typically put the failure down to external uncontrollable causes (e.g. the customer had seen a cheaper version of the product elsewhere). Clearly there is tremendous potential for selection researchers to explore how individual differences in sense-making and cognition impact upon work performance.

Key Learning Point

Stable individual differences in cognitive style represent another potential source of variance in job behaviour.

Summary

Individual differences in personality and cognitive ability have been the subject of much psychological research. Research has uncovered stable, underlying structures for both cognitive ability (a general factor and specific abilities) and personality (five major factors). Measures have been developed for cognitive ability and personality. To be of value in work psychology, such measures need to be both reliable and valid (*see* Chapter 4). At the moment there is a great deal of interest in exploring the concept of emotional intelligence and whether it might offer something new in terms of our understanding of behaviour at work. Recently, there has been an increase in research into possible biological, neurological and physiological correlates of intelligence. For example, McDaniel (2005) conducted a meta-analysis of 37 participant samples encompassing 1530 individuals and found a correlation of 0.33 between individuals' intelligence and the volume of their brain, a finding that was consistent across all gender and age groups in the sample. Beaujean (2005) conducted a meta-analysis of studies that have investigated the relationship between individuals' genetics and the speed at which they are able to process information: this showed that genetics played a role in mental processing speed, with the impact of genetics being most important when tasks were difficult. The closing case study illustrates the growing interest in neuroscience and exploring the biological aspects of brain functions and how these relate to behaviour. However, there is also increasing recognition that understanding individual differences means that we also need to understand how factors such as learned patterns of social interaction and features of the situation impact on work behaviour.

Closing Case Study

Give in to temptation and fail in life: the secret of how some of us can resist temptation may soon be unlocked

A psychologist who found he could predict children's prospects by testing whether they could resist eating a marshmallow, is to scan their brains to find the neurological roots of temptation. The 'marshmallow test', one of the world's simplest and most successful behavioural experiments, was developed by Professor Walter Mischel. He proved conclusively that the longer a four-year-old child was able to wait before taking a sweet, the better were their chances of a happy and successful life. Mischel has been monitoring the lives of dozens of his subjects since he started the marshmallow experiments at a nursery on the campus of Stanford University, California, in the 1960s.

His findings have proved so compelling that 40 of his original subjects, now in their forties, are preparing to undergo scans in the hope of answering a perplexing human question: why are some of us better than others at resisting temptation? 'Brain imaging provides a very exciting and important new tool,' said Mischel, who now works at Columbia University in New York. By examining the differences between the brains of subjects who turned out to be good at controlling their impulses and those who wolfed down the marshmallow the moment it was offered, researchers hope to come up with new ways of teaching the benefits of delayed gratification. Mischel's marshmallows have become a cornerstone of research into what is now known as emotional intelligence (EI), a human quality more to do with feelings than education and rationality.

His experiments began with a simple proposition. He placed a marshmallow on a plate in front of his subjects and told them they could eat it if they wanted to. But if they could wait while he left the room for a few minutes, he would give them a second marshmallow. Mischel would then leave the room for 10 to 15 minutes. He found that about a third of his subjects would grab the marshmallow immediately, a third would wait for his return to claim two marshmallows and the rest would try to wait but give up at varying times. It was not until 14 years later, when his earliest subjects were leaving school and going on to university or to work, that Mischel began to confirm a dramatic correlation between marshmallow munching and success in life. The children who grabbed the sweets immediately turned into teenagers who lacked self-esteem and experienced difficult relations with their peers. Those who waited for a second marshmallow turned out to be more socially competent, self-assertive and academically successful. In their school exams, the 'waiters' scored an average of 210 points more than the 'grabbers'.

Mischel continues to monitor the progress of his original subjects and his broad findings have entered American academic lore – the ability to delay gratification turns children into successful adults. This lesson has since been embraced in all walks of American life. Preachers refer to the marshmallow test when urging worshippers to suppress sinful impulses. Business gurus cite marshmallows when telling chief executives to resist short-term strategies that boost the share price but risk long-term problems. Sceptics have suggested Mischel might have had different results had he replaced the marshmallow with a more tempting treat, such as a Jelly Tot or a toffee. Many others, however, cite Mischel's work as evidence that EI – or what some refer to simply as 'grit' – plays a crucial role in child development.

One study by Martin Seligman and Angela Duckworth concluded that an individual's IQ, or intelligence quotient, accounts for only a third of any difference in academic performance when compared with peers. The rest has to do with qualities such as perseverance, self-discipline, hard work, creativity and luck. One impediment to developing grit, another study concluded, was a parent's overindulgent praise of a child. For Mischel and other researchers, the question now is whether neuroscience can identify the part of the brain that processes marshmallow desire.

Source: The Sunday Times, *2 November 2008 (Allen-Mills, T.), copyright © The Sunday Times 2008, www.nisyndication.com*

Suggested exercise

1   What factors are important to consider in exploring the reliability of Mischel's research findings?

2   If the researchers are successful in identifying the 'neurological roots to temptation', what does that imply for interventions by work psychologists?

3   Do you agree with Seligman and Duckworth that an individual's IQ accounts for 'only a third' of any difference in academic performance when compared with peers?

Test your learning

Short-answer questions

1   Give examples of how cognitive ability can be assessed.

2   Are a person's scores on tests of different cognitive abilities likely to be similar? Explain your answer.

3   What are Gardner's multiple intelligences?

4   What are the 'Big Five' personality factors?

5   What is emotional intelligence?

6   Suggest three general reasons why a person's scores on personality and intelligence tests might influence their work performance.

7   What tools are available to assess creative thinking at work?

Suggested assignments

1   What evidence is there that emotional intelligence is distinct from traditional conceptualisations of personality and intelligence?

2   Discuss the extent to which the 'Big Five' provide a comprehensive picture of human personality.

3   What are the individual level resources associated with innovation in organisations?

Relevant websites

A directory of just some of the many consultancy firms that offer psychometric testing products and services in the workplace can be found at http://directory.google.com/Top/Regional/Europe/United_Kingdom/Business_and_Economy/Human_Resources/Psychometric_Profiling/.

A very useful site for learning about psychometric testing from the points of view of both the tester and the person being tested is provided by the British Psychological Society at http://www.psychtesting.org.uk/.

If you are interested in intelligence testing, Indiana University, USA, hosts a site with material you may find helpful. It is not specifically about the workplace, but much here is relevant to the workplace. Find it at http://www.indiana.edu/~intell/.

For further self-test material and relevant, annotated weblinks please visit the website at **www.pearsoned.co.uk/workpsych**

Suggested further reading

Full details for all references are given in the list at the end of this book.

1   Paul Kline's book *Handbook of Psychological Testing* (1999) provides a good overview of the theoretical underpinnings of personality and intelligence and how it translates into measurement. Also see *The New Psychometrics: Science, psychology and measurement* (2000) by Paul Kline.

2   Matthews, Deary and Whiteman's book on *Personality Traits* provides an excellent overview of the research literature in personality and provides a summary of evidence relevant to work psychology.

3   Matthews, Zeidner and Roberts' book called *Emotional Intelligence: Science and myth* provides an in-depth analysis of the evidence on emotional intelligence.

CHAPTER 4

The foundations of personnel selection

Analysing jobs, competencies and selection effectiveness

After studying this chapter, you should be able to:

1 outline the personnel selection design and validation process;

2 name and describe four different job analysis techniques;

3 define competencies and competency models in organisations;

4 describe the outputs from competency analysis and how they are used as assessment criteria;

5 describe the relative advantages and disadvantages of different job analysis techniques;

6 in the context of personnel selection, define reliability and five different types of validity:

faith

face

content

construct

criterion-related validity;

7 outline the criterion problem and the practical difficulties associated with conducting validation studies in organisations;

8 describe the roles that validity, selection ratio and other factors play in determining financial utility.

The civil service: there's a price to be paid for job security and a fat pension

Getting into the fast stream of Britain's civil service is not easy. Imagine an exam where new e-mails arrive, requiring decisions, even as you are trying to figure out the best solution to the previous problem e-mail. Sound like real life? Welcome to online recruitment and assessment, version 2.1. Yet every year, about 20,000 candidates apply for 400–500 vacancies in the civil service programme for its most talented graduate recruits.

In France, where mistrust of business remains strong, demand for safe state jobs never palls. According to one survey, 75 per cent of parents would like their offspring to work for the government. Every year, 800,000 applicants compete for 60,000 vacancies. And if you cannot get a job at home, why not try Brussels? The European Personnel Selection Office in Brussels handles tens of thousands of applications every year. It acts as the gateway to careers in the full range of European institutions.

The entry barriers are high. Last year, 13,562 people applied for 'graduate' jobs as administrators, linguists and similar at the European Commission and related bodies, and 1630 were accepted. So far this year, 661 administrators and linguists have been offered posts, from 9534 applicants.

Though selection procedures are becoming more open, they continue to require huge commitment and patience. To get a job at the Commission, you not only need to have a degree, but must feed yourself for up to two years while the selection process winds its leisurely course.

The good news is that state recruiters are aware that inefficient procedures discourage many quick-witted graduates, and are tackling the problem. In a world where bureaucrats, rather than chief executives, are increasingly deciding the fate of financial institutions, bureaucracies are going to need more of the kind of brains that previously wound up in investment banks.

But there is a price to pay. Job security and a fat pensions are the pay-offs for a bread-and-water diet in the early years. The starting salary of a London-based graduate recruited into fast stream is just £25,000 (€28,000) a year, pretty much in line with UK average earnings, and the opportunities for prosperity will never match those in the private sector: the average permanent secretary running a government department had a basic salary in 2007 of £162,000 (approx. €182,000). Civil service salaries in continental Europe, too, tend to be comfortable rather than extravagant. Though the European Commission's tables are a little out of date, a mid-ranking official would command a basic salary of about €66,000 (£59,000), rising to €193,000 (approx. £173,000) for the very top posts. Allowances of one kind or another could help pay for a BMW, though.

The fast stream recruitment procedure was massively modernised in 2004. One objective was that it will no longer be the preserve just of the well-educated middle class from the south of England. To achieve a fairer and more efficient selection process, much of the weeding-out now takes place online. Candidates undertake a series of tests, which simultaneously give them insights into what the career entails. About half the applicants quit after feedback.

The EPSO in Brussels, which historically has used the French 'Concours' model of massive examinations leading to selection of candidates with the highest marks, is overhauling its process, refocusing on personal and professional competence, and taking advantage of online technology. By 2010, it aims to cut the selection competition time to between five and nine months. Even in France, where competition for posts is being intensified by a policy of replacing only half the civil servants who retire, the Internet is beginning to play a big role in selection.

Recruitment reforms are part of a sweeping civil service overhaul. A spokesman for André Santini, the civil service minister, says that the quality of applicants remains as high as ever, but 'our challenge is to ensure the civil service is attractive for reasons other than job security'.

Source: Adapted from an article at FT.com, 13 October 2008, by Ross Tieman.

Introduction

The research and practice of work psychology have important contributions to make in many areas of organisational life. Personnel selection and assessment probably constitute the area where the biggest and most consistent contribution has been made (see Patterson, 2001, for a review of developments in work psychology). In fact, the contribution of psychology to this area of activity is distinctive and complements the work of other professional groups, such as human resources personnel in organisations. Whereas others may have interests in administrative or managerial issues, such as the collection and storage of information about the competencies of employees, the focus of attention for psychologists has always been the assessment process itself. The opening case study shows the complexity of the task for large-scale recruitment within the context such as the civil service. Changes and improvements to selection processes are ongoing in many large organisations as they respond to the needs of the applicant pool and to make use of the developing technologies. The case study also points to attraction of applicants and self-selection following feedback on performance in the selection process. All of these are important aspects in the selection process to which psychological knowledge and theory can make an important contribution.

Research and development work has concentrated on the production and evaluation of technically sound assessment procedures. Given the centrality of psychological measurement to psychological science in general, psychologists are recognised as experts in the design and validation of selection processes. This chapter and the two following it focus on different aspects of selection and related processes. In this chapter we examine some building blocks of good selection, namely the careful analysis of jobs and competencies, and ways of checking on the effectiveness of any selection process. Then in Chapter 5 we examine some specific selection techniques in more detail, and in doing so we apply some of the concepts introduced in this chapter. In Chapter 6 we take a closer look at the psychology of how people's performance in everyday work can be assessed.

Two main principles underlie the roles that personnel selection and assessment procedures play in organisational settings. The first principle is that there are individual differences between people in aptitudes, skills and other personal qualities. This simple principle leads to the very important conclusion that people are not equally suited to all jobs, and suggests that procedures for matching people and jobs could have important organisational benefits. The second principle is that future behaviour is, at least partly, predictable. The goal of selection and assessment activities is to match people to jobs and ensure the best possible levels of future job performance; the belief that *future job performance* can be estimated is an important facet of the second principle mentioned above. The essential function of personnel selection and assessment procedures (e.g. interviews, psychometric tests) is to provide means of estimating the likely future job performance of candidates.

Over several decades, work psychology research has had a significant influence on the way people are recruited into jobs, through rigorous development and evaluation of personnel selection procedures. Since the early part of the twentieth century a great deal of research has concentrated on the development and evaluation of personnel selection procedures. Much of this work will be considered in the next chapter. The present chapter is *not* concerned with a detailed analysis of alternative personnel selection methods. Instead, it focuses on those aspects of psychological theory and practice that underlie the successful application of personnel selection procedures. The main topics covered in this chapter are related to the two principles given above. First, since personnel selection has traditionally involved the matching of people to the requirements of jobs, job analysis is covered (individual differences between people were discussed in Chapter 3). The second part of the chapter concentrates on topics concerned with the development of procedures for predicting future job performance; specifically, validation studies and associated issues regarding the practicalities of conducting research in organisations.

The design and validation process in selection

Figure 4.1 provides an outline of the main elements involved in designing and implementing a personnel selection procedure. The process begins with a *job analysis* to define a *competency model* and create a *person specification*. This information is used to identify the *selection and assessment criteria* and may also be used for *advertising* the job role. The job analysis information is used to decide which *selection methods* to use to access applicant behaviour related to the selection criteria. Selection methods can then be *piloted* and where possible validated and candidate reactions assessed. In attracting a pool of applicants, prospective candidates will engage in self-selection where they can make an informed judgement about whether the particular role suits their skills and abilities. Once candidates have applied, a *selecting out* process may take place based on eligibility (e.g. essential criteria such as educational qualifications) before the *selecting in* process is undertaken using the chosen selection methods. Following the selection decisions and the accepted applicants enter the organisation (assuming they accept the organisation's offer). After some time has elapsed, information on the work performance of job holders (i.e. measures of performance related to the original competency model) can then used to examine

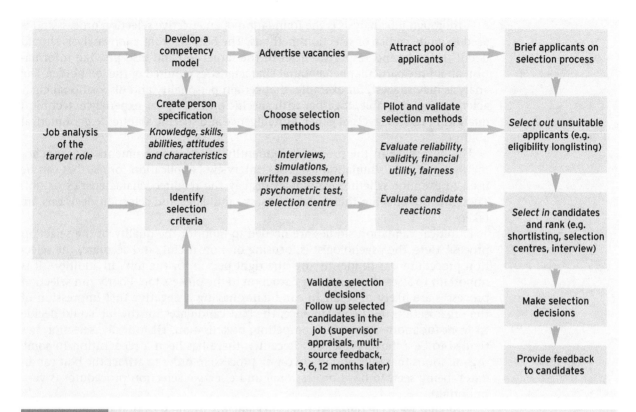

The personnel selection, design and validation process
Source: Adapted from Patterson and Ferguson (2007).

the *validity* of the selection methods and decisions (i.e. whether high and low scores on the selection instruments are associated with good and poor work performance respectively). This information in turn can help to inform changes to the original competency model. Feedback to candidates (both successful and unsuccessful) may be provided which is useful for development, although many organisations have practical and legal reasons for not always providing detailed feedback.

Key Learning Point

Personnel selection is one of the most prominent topic areas in work and organisational psychology, and research findings have had a major impact on recruitment practice.

Organisations have become increasingly aware that it is important to evaluate candidates' reactions to the selection process, particularly in relation to fairness. Since many organisations spend a great deal of time and resources in selection procedures, the financial costs and benefits of selection may also be evaluated. The information collected at selection is also invaluable in helping to design training and development plans and activities for individuals entering the organisation.

A thorough job analysis is the foundation of an effective selection process and is used to guide choice of selection methods. The outputs from a job analysis should detail the tasks and responsibilities in the target job and also provide information about the particular behavioural characteristics required of the job holder. The analysis may suggest, for example, that certain personality and dispositional characteristics are desirable, together with specific previous work experience, technical qualifications and levels of general intelligence and specific abilities (e.g. numerical ability).

The next stage in the process is to identify selection instruments (e.g. psychometric tests, work simulation exercises, interviews, application forms) that can be used to examine whether candidates display the required characteristics or not. These instruments are then used to assess candidates and selection decisions are taken.

Empirical validation studies are needed to monitor the quality of the selection process. Here, the psychologist is focusing on how useful (and accurate) the selection procedure was in identifying 'the right person for the job'. In addition, it is important to assess the candidates' reaction to the process too. Poorly run selection processes are likely to result in candidates having a negative first impression of the organisation. As a consequence, the best candidates for the job could decide to work for another (possibly competing) organisation. Historically, selection has tended to be a 'buyers' market'. Recently, there has been a recognition in some organisations that selection is a two-way process: in order to attract the best candidates, being seen to have professional and effective selection procedures is very important.

Although we have outlined the core elements in the selection process, in practice there are two elements in the process that are often not conducted effectively. First, in many organisations there is no thorough job analysis to identify precisely the key knowledge, skills and behaviours associated with successful performance in the target job role. Part of the problem is that these techniques require specialist training, and few human resources departments have this expertise within the organisation. Second, validation studies are rarely conducted in organisations because they can be time-consuming and costly. Validating a selection process often means tracking the performance of new recruits over several months or years. Validation studies are usually only possible with large-scale recruitment programmes and many organisations do not recruit large numbers of people into one specific job role to allow a statistical validation study to be carried out. As a result, organisations often employ work psychologists to advise on best practice procedures in selection.

In overview, research clearly demonstrates that best practice selection is an iterative process. In other words, the results from evaluation and validation studies are used to reassess the original thinking behind the job analysis and choice of selection methods. Therefore, feedback is used continually to improve the selection system to enhance accuracy and fairness.

Key Learning Point

Best practice personnel selection involves thorough job analysis and using feedback from validation studies to continually improve accuracy and fairness.

Job analysis

Job analysis procedures are designed to produce systematic information about jobs, including the nature of the work performed, responsibilities, equipment used, the working conditions and the position of the job within the organisation. The outputs from a job analysis are often used to generate a job description and/or a person specification for the job role. It is worth noting that satisfactory job analyses are prerequisites for many decisions and activities that have a crucial influence on the lives of employees within the organisation (including the design and validation of selection procedures, training and career development schemes, job design or redesign, job evaluation and safety). There is a wide range of techniques and procedures available. Robertson and Smith (2001) and Voskuijl (2005) provide detailed critical examinations of the principal techniques that will be introduced in this chapter. Job analysis also has an important role to play in the design on work environments (see Chapter 9) and in training needs analysis (*see* Chapter 11).

Although not always clear cut, there is an important distinction between *job-oriented* and *worker-oriented* job analysis procedures. As the term suggests, job-oriented (or task-oriented) procedures focus on the work itself, producing a description in terms of the equipment used, the end results or purposes of the job, resources and materials utilised. In contrast, worker-oriented (or person-oriented) analyses concentrate on describing the psychological or behavioural requirements of the job, such as communicating, decision-making and reasoning (*see* Sandberg, 2000, for a detailed review). There has been little research reported on task-oriented job analysis (*see* Robertson and Smith, 2001). The majority of authors have tended to focus on use of future-oriented job analysis for newly created job roles, focusing on the knowledge, skills and abilities associated with new job roles. The reason for this is because many organisations are, or have been, involved in business process re-engineering where downsizing and reorganising job roles is commonplace. In this way, many jobs are now 'newly created job roles' (NCJs) where there are no pre-existing job descriptions nor indeed current job holders who can provide information during the job analysis.

There has also been a shift in the research literature towards considering models of work performance that distinguish between *task performance* (focusing on specific responsibilities in the job) and *contextual performance* (for example organisational citizenship behaviours such as courtesy, prosocial behaviour and being altruistic towards others at work (*see* Viswesvaran and Ones, 2000, and *also* Chapter 6). Each of these might imply using different selection criteria and related techniques to assess them. In general, there still tends to be more emphasis on the discrete *task performance*-oriented analyses rather than considering the contextual aspects in job analysis research and practice (although recent research by Diedorff and Morgeson, 2007, has begun to consider the impact of the occupational context on role expectations).

Traditional job analysis approaches in personnel selection are aimed at 'fitting the person to the job'. With recent changes in the nature of work and employee work patterns, this approach is becoming less relevant and other techniques are being introduced including the suggestion for a more proactive and strategic approach to job analysis (Singh, 2008). There is some debate as to whether these are 'new' techniques or a variation of existing job analysis techniques (see Voskuijl, 2005, for an overview), but competency modelling and analysis has become the most widely used alternative to traditional job analysis.

Key Learning Point

Job analysis procedures are generally either worker-oriented or job-oriented, and much research now focuses on the future requirements of the job role.

Competencies and competency analysis

Traditionally, job analyses have aimed to identify the tasks and responsibilities associated with a job role. In general, job analysis is an umbrella term for many different analyses and involves analysing *job tasks*. In practice, it is sometimes difficult to translate the information into describing observable behaviours that underpin the tasks and responsibilities. For example, it is difficult to describe the behaviours associated with writing a complex financial report. As a result, *competency analysis* has become very popular in organisations to help define the person-focused assessment criteria. Research to compare and contrast competency analysis and job analysis attempted to assess the benefits of each approach (Schippman *et al.*, 2000). While each has its strengths and weaknesses, there is some agreement that competency analysis goes beyond rigid boundaries of the job title by taking into account the organisation's objectives, visions and strategy in the formulation of staffing requirements (Sanchez and Levine, 2001; Lievens and Sanchez, 2007). A *competency* can be defined as the cluster of specific characteristics and behaviour patterns a job holder is required to demonstrate in order to perform the relevant job tasks with competence. Many organisations now use competency analysis to identify the required knowledge, skills and behaviours that are essential to perform a specific job role. The main aim of competency analysis is to derive a *competency model* for the target role. A competency model comprises a comprehensive list of all the relevant competencies associated with a given job role. For more detailed discussions *see* Sparrow and Hodgkinson (2002) and Schippman *et al.* (2000).

To illustrate the use of competency analysis, imagine you are examining the person-focused requirements for the job of a sales assistant, in a large retailing company. A key competency of a sales assistant might be called 'customer service'. The observable behaviours (or *behavioural indicators*) that underlie this competency could be:

- actively listens to customers and attempts to understand their needs;
- proactively seeks feedback and involvement of customers in decision-making processes;
- ensures that customers feel at ease and in control of a sales interaction.

Note that these are all *positively* associated with job performance. Many competency models also detail the negative behavioural indicators, i.e. what job holders are expected to avoid doing. Competency analysis is used to build a competency model for each job role, where a model may define several competencies with associated behavioural indicators. In practice, a specific job may have between six and twelve competencies in a competency model, although there is wide variation depending on the target job role.

Competencies can be used as assessment criteria which have a whole variety of different applications including selection, but also performance appraisal, management development, careers counselling and so on, as you will see in several chapters in this book. One of the key advantages in using competencies as assessment criteria is that competencies can become a common language shared by employees in the organisation to describe the desired (and undesirable) behaviours during performance appraisal and career development activities. In this way, the competency analysis outputs can directly inform the design of the assessment criteria in selection.

For example, if demonstrating positive communication skills is a key job requirement for sales assistants, the researcher could design a competency-based interview question for selection purposes such as: 'Describe a time when you have encountered an angry customer and had to use your communications skills to deal with the situation. What did you do and what was the outcome?' An applicant's response could then be assessed on predefined behavioural criteria derived from the competency model. Exercise 4.1 provides further opportunities to explore the use of competencies and behavioural indicators in defining assessment criteria.

Exercise 4.1   Competency analysis and defining behavioural indicators

A key competency for the job of retail sales assistant is *team involvement*. An initial job analysis indicates that a sales assistant is required to use a collaborative style and value the contribution of others in the workgroup. Some example behavioural indicators are illustrated below.

Example positive behavioural indicators:

- Accepts and promotes new ways of working.
- Treats other team members as equals and recognises people as individuals.
- Demonstrates a cooperative interaction style and views success in terms of the team rather than individual outcomes.
- Seeks to understand other people in the team and values their contribution.

Example negative behavioural indicators:

- Demonstrates a competitive interaction style, and focuses on individual successes.
- Criticises individual differences in style.
- Treats group members differently according to status.
- Is openly critical of others' suggestions and actions.

Suggested exercises

1   Imagine the role of a sales assistant in a large retailing organisation. Describe additional behavioural indicators associated with team involvement (both positive and negative) in this context.

2   Think about your own experiences as a customer/shopper. Describe other competencies that might be associated with the job role of sales assistant. For each, suggest some example positive and negative behavioural indicators.

Although the use of competencies and competency modelling has become commonplace in organisations, there is considerable confusion about what competencies actually are and how they differ from other job analysis outputs. As we have seen, competency models define the relevant behavioural indicators or behaviour patterns that indicate competence. However, in many organisations competency models for a job role have been developed *but* appropriate psychological techniques have not been used to identify precisely the requirements in terms of behavioural indicators. This is important because it is these indicators that can be targeted for measurement purposes in selection, and other contexts. Further, in some organisations a generic *competency framework* has been developed: this often comprises a set of core competencies relevant to many job roles in the organisation. Although this approach is appealing for ease of interpretation, generic competency frameworks often lack sufficient behavioural specificity for many job roles. In other words, the behavioural indicators in a competency model should be directly relevant to the job role and the context within which the employee operates. By adopting a tailor-made approach, the assessment criteria can be more accurately defined, which in turn may optimise their use at selection.

In a job analyses of the role of doctors, Patterson *et al.* (2000) suggest that organisations rely too often on off-the-shelf competency models: the more specific the competency analysis is to the target job, the more useful (and potentially more accurate) the behavioural indicators are as assessment criteria. In Table 4.1 we provide an example of three competencies in a competency model for a family physician (a General Practitioner in the UK). In the example, each competency heading is defined by a series of behavioural indicators. Note that the behavioural indicators (assessment criteria) associated with communication skills share some similarities with those of the retail sales assistant, but the content is qualitatively (and significantly) different. Similarly, recent research evidence demonstrates that when comparing communication skills output from a job analysis *across* different medical roles and specialties, the content is reflective of the context of the specialties. Different medical specialties exhibit slightly different, context-specific, behavioural indicators of the same competency (Patterson *et al.*, 2008).

Key Learning Point

Competency models define the key behaviours associated with performance in the target job role.

It is important to note that competency models are not static documents: best practice personnel selection is characterised by a continuous improvement cycle. Over time, as the needs of the organisation evolve (possibly in response to a range of external influences such as changes in legislation or customer demand), the job requirements and competencies required for a specific role may also change. For example, in the UK General Practitioner doctors have experienced significant changes in their role: familiarity with information technology, financial acumen and legal awareness are now core requirements for the job. The evidence suggests that competency models and outputs from job analyses should be regularly reviewed (especially after a selection programme has been implemented) to evaluate the original assessment criteria. There

Table 4.1	Three competencies from a competency model for family physicians	

Competency	Definition	Example positive behavioural indicators
(1) Empathy and sensitivity	Patient is treated with sensitivity and personal understanding, asks patient about feelings. GP is empathetic, in control but not dominating, and creates atmosphere of trust and confidence. Focuses on the positive rather than negative, works to involve the patient, shows interest in the individual, gives reassurance and checks patient needs are satisfied	■ Generates an atmosphere where the patient feels safe ■ Patient is taken seriously, treated confidentially ■ Picks up on patient's emotions and feelings ■ Encourages patient, gives reassurances ■ Use of 'I understand what you're saying' ■ Focuses on the positive ■ Is sensitive to feelings ■ Treats individuals as people ■ Checks patient needs are satisfied ■ Demonstrates a caring attitude
(2) Communication skills	Active listening to patients, understands and interprets body language. Able to use different questioning styles and probe for information to lead to root cause. Matches patient language, uses analogy to explain, engages in social conversation, confident style. Clarity in both verbal and written communication	■ Demonstrates active listening skills ■ Is not patronising ■ Confident in approach ■ Able to form relationships with people and build rapport easily ■ Uses analogy to explain problems/complex issues ■ Re-states information for understanding ■ Open body language and direct eye contact ■ Matches patient's language ■ Allows patients time to talk ■ Engages in social conversation ■ Refers to the patient by name
(3) Clinical expertise	Able to apply and trust their judgement (and others) in diagnosing problems. Fully investigates problem before prescribing, able to anticipate rather than just react and to maintain knowledge of current practice. Does not allow patient to develop a dependency	■ Trust in your clinical judgement ■ Clinical competence ■ Provides anticipatory care ■ Guards against dependency ■ Has courage to make decisions ■ Seeks to update clinical skills ■ Gives clear decision and diagnosis ■ Prescribes and checks medication ■ Provides clear explanation of facts and systems ■ Gets to the root of the problem ■ Encourages patient compliance

are now legal reasons for ensuring accurate selection procedures are used and it is essential for compliance with current employment law. Organisations could be asked to demonstrate that they have used fair and accurate selection processes that assess candidates on competencies that are relevant to the job role.

Job analysis data

Sources of job analysis data may be divided into four categories: written material, job holders' reports, colleagues' reports and direct observation.

Written material and existing documentation

Until the 1990s, many organisations held written job descriptions available for many job roles, which provided the researcher with useful information, particularly for more blue-collar job roles. Unfortunately, in many organisations existing job descriptions are rarely up to date, comprehensive or detailed enough. With the rapid pace of organisational change caused by the introduction of technology (*see* Chapter 1), there has been a dramatic change in the nature of various job roles and work patterns in general. The introduction of highly technical equipment has made many jobs different and more complex. For other employees, in many manufacturing job roles for example, their role has become that of an equipment monitor in which they follow set procedures, rather than having cognitively demanding tasks. The assessment criteria for use in selection procedures must reflect these changes, and must be updated regularly.

In some organisations, rather than having precise job descriptions, job holders may have 'performance contracts' that detail the broad objectives and responsibilities for the job that are to be fulfilled within a prescribed time frame. Where this approach is used for appraising job performance, expectations are documented and an employee is assessed on the extent to which they have met the specified objectives. In general, published analyses of jobs may provide useful leads but are of limited value: jobs analysed elsewhere are likely to be similar but not identical to the one under consideration. An accountant's, secretary's or production manager's job will vary considerably from one organisation to another, perhaps in ways that are crucial to the selection process. Other written material such as production data, organisation charts, training manuals, job aids and so on may also provide useful additional information.

Job holders' reports

Interviews in which job holders are asked, through careful questioning, to give a description of their main tasks and how they carry them out, provide extremely useful information. Such interviews are usually an essential element in any job analysis. On the other hand, it is difficult to be sure that all of the important aspects of the job have been covered by the interview and that the information provided by the job holder is not too subjective, biased (owing to faulty memory, perhaps) or even deliberately misleading. Therefore, it is usual that several job holders are interviewed to get a consistent picture of the target job role. However, this can be problematic for newly created jobs that have no incumbents to interview: in this case it is likely that senior personnel would be consulted to describe the key responsibilities and performance indicators for the target job role, using a future-oriented approach.

Where there are existing job holders, reports may be obtained by asking them to complete a diary or activity record. This can be done on a regular basis as the job is being carried out to avoid problems associated with faulty memory and so forth. The advantage here is that the psychologist can gain an insight into the temporal components to the job (e.g. the sequences in which different tasks occur), and the information can offer a useful level of detail on the job activities. Work diaries, however, are a difficult and time-consuming procedure, for both the job holder and the analyst. The diaries have to be constructed in such a way as to provide the appropriate level of detail. For example, Exercise 4.2 illustrates a hypothetical work diary for a finance manager working in a large manufacturing company. The diary is a record of daily events and is only structured through time spent on different tasks. In this example, the information gathered is limited as it lacks specificity and can be difficult to translate into behavioural indicators that could be used in the selection process.

Exercise 4.2	Excerpt from an unstructured work diary

8.00–8.20	Examined e-mail and related correspondence.
8.20–8.30	Met with secretary to plan priorities and responses to correspondence. Organised diary of events and had to reschedule two meetings.
8.30–10.00	Attended strategy meeting with the Executive. Presented a 15-minute summary of the new product launch and projected impact report. Responded to technical questions about calculation of the key performance indicators and profit margin.
10.00–12	Analysed data tables of departmental expenditure for 1st quarter and sketched out a draft report to go to senior management for the forthcoming business process re-engineering review. Involved calculating spend versus income and forecasting total year spend, both for staff salaries and associated costs. Highlighted key figures in the report and illustrated in graphical format.
12–12.20	Grabbed sandwich!
12.20	Made telephone call to key supplier to negotiate pricing of materials for product launch.
12.30–1.30	Chaired a team meeting with my staff. Presented news update and business figures. Discussed implications of restructure of job roles.

Suggested exercises

1   Examine the extract from the work diary shown above and create a list of behaviours that appear to be associated with successful performance in this finance manager's job role. (Hint: you may find it useful to highlight particular words that refer to behaviours, e.g. 'prioritise', or 'negotiate'.)

2   Having created your list, comment on how the information you have gathered can be used. Suggest ways in which the work diary could be improved to provide additional information in order to design relevant assessment criteria.

To improve the collection of data from job holders Flanagan (1954) developed a procedure known as the *critical incident technique* (CIT). In brief, using this technique involves asking the interviewee to recall specific incidents of job behaviour that are characteristic of either highly effective or highly ineffective performance in the job. A critical incident is defined as 'any observable human activity that is sufficiently complete in itself to permit inferences and predictions to be made about the person performing the act'. By describing the behaviours and characteristics that led to the incident, the analyst can get an excellent insight into the relevant job behaviour(s) that are important. Not only will this information enable the analyst to differentiate between good and poor job holders, it can provide some contextual information that might be helpful in designing the actual selection methods (such as work sample tests: see Chapter 5). CIT is a versatile technique that can be conducted either during interviews with individuals or with groups of job holders. A group-based CIT can be very useful to get initial 'cross-validation' of information, where job holders might have experienced or witnessed similar incidents (see Patterson *et al.*, 2000, 2008). One potential drawback with using this method is that it might lead to job holders focusing on the extreme behaviours (good or bad) that influence performance, at the expense of a detailed analysis of the more routine but important elements of job performance. However, a skilled practitioner can use CIT in a way that avoids this problem.

The *position analysis questionnaire* (PAQ) produced by McCormick *et al.* (1972) remains an often mentioned example of a structured, and standardised, questionnaire approach to job analysis. The elements in the questionnaire are worker-oriented in that they focus on generalised aspects of human behaviour and are not closely tied to the technology of specific jobs. This means the questionnaire can be used, without being tailored, to analyse a wide variety of jobs. The PAQ consists of nearly 200 items organised into six broad categories. These questions ask about what the job involves, including (1) the information input components of the job, (2) the mediation processes (i.e. the mental processes of reasoning, decision-making, etc.) involved in the work, (3) work output, (4) interpersonal activities associated with the work (i.e. relationships with others), (5) the work situation and job context, (6) miscellaneous aspects of the job (i.e. things not covered by 1–5). The results of the PAQ then points directly to specific abilities and skills the job holder would require. One problem with the PAQ is that it requires a fairly high level of reading ability on the part of respondents (some of the questions are quite complex). Nevertheless, the PAQ is a well-researched and valuable means of analysing jobs using a standardised and well-established technique.

Key Learning Point

Generic job analysis questionnaires are available. They can be used to analyse a wide variety of jobs.

McCormick and others carried out the original development work for the PAQ in the United States, and there has also been development of British job analysis questionnaires such as that by Banks and colleagues (Banks *et al.*, 1983; Banks, 1988) who produced the *job components inventory* (JCI). This inventory focuses on both the job and the worker, and, as with the PAQ, the outputs from the analysis include quantified profiles of the skills required for the job under investigation. Another British questionnaire is the work profiling system (WPS) (produced by UK occupational psychology consultants SHL). This consists of a set of over 800 items. A subset of about 200 items is usually used for any particular job, depending on the level of complexity of the job being analysed.

Functional job analysis (FJA) is job-oriented rather than worker-oriented (Fine and Wiley, 1974). This approach makes use of standardised language to describe what job holders do and provides a means of examining both the complexity and the *orientation* of the job. Orientation here is described as the extent to which the job is directed towards 'data', 'people' or 'things': as a result of analysis, this orientation can be expressed in percentage terms. The basic unit of analysis in FJA is the task – that is, an action or action sequence organised over time and designed to contribute to a specific end result or objective. Using a very similar definition of the task, Annett and others (Annett *et al.*, 1971; Shepherd, 1976) have developed a means of analysis known as *hierarchical task analysis* (HTA): this is described in more detail in Chapters 9 and 11. A more recent development is the use of flexible, large-scale, computer-driven databases that contain information not just about the work behaviours but also the associated worker attributes including information on the personality, behavioural and situational variables (see Hough and Oswald, 2000).

A procedure for collecting job analysis information that still remains popular involves the use of Kelly's (1955) *repertory grid technique*. This approach provides systematic worker-oriented data. It has an advantage over other means of obtaining worker-oriented data such as PAQ in that it does not limit the responses of the job holder by providing a predetermined set of categories. Repertory grid technique is based on Kelly's Personal Construct Theory and works by eliciting an individual's personal constructs. Kelly describes a personal construct as 'a reference axis, a basic dimension of appraisal, often unverbalised, frequently unsymbolised'. Metaphorically, the theory suggests that individuals view the world through their own personal 'spectacles', and hold a set of mental models and beliefs about how the world works. Using repertory grid in job analysis aims to get job holders to reveal and describe their mental models of the work they do and what is required to perform the job effectively. Repertory grid technique involves a highly structured interviewing process to elicit mental models. The theory assumes that behind any act of judgement (conscious or unconscious) lies an *implicit theory* about the domain of events within which the individual is making the judgement. In addition, it is assumed that these implicit theories are unique to an individual but that similar constructs may occur between individuals (so there may be common mental models about what is required for effective job performance among a group of workers doing a similar job). For job analysis purposes, repertory grid technique is often used to interview job holders about the knowledge, skills and abilities involved in the target role and provides a rich source of qualitative data (Fransella and Bannister, 1977). It has a powerful advantage over many other techniques in that job holders may describe constructs that they have never verbalised before. In practice, repertory grid technique is most useful as a starting point in a job analysis because it helps to explore the breadth of the job domain (particularly if the range of activities and tasks involved in the job it is not well known). In this way, the technique avoids predetermining the domain of questioning, unlike structured work profiling questionnaires. It is also a useful technique for analysing the cognitive components of the job (e.g. expert decision-making processes) that are opaque to someone observing the worker doing the job.

Colleagues' reports

In addition to gleaning information directly from job holders, it can be useful to obtain data from direct reports, peers and supervisors. For example, when collecting critical incident data, the views of a job holder, a direct report and a supervisor on the nature of such critical incidents might provide for interesting comparisons. It might also be useful to gain information from customers or the *user group* of the intended job holders. For example, in a job analysis of family physicians (Patterson *et al.*, 2000), information was collected not just from the physicians themselves, but also from patients. An important part of this study was to compare the patient perceptions to doctor perceptions of the job role (i.e. it identified aspects of job performance that were important from the perspective of established experts, but also from those for whom they provided care). In this way, the user group perspective can be reflected in the assessment criteria in both selection and performance management applications. In another study Patterson *et al.* (2008) collected information from other health care professionals who worked alongside doctors: this significantly increased the accuracy of the job analysis.

Direct observation

In any job analysis some direct observation of the job being carried out is invariably helpful. It is, of course, possible that the presence of the researcher may alter the job holder's behaviour, and as with the approaches described earlier the data obtained cannot be perfect. Yet data derived from observation, perhaps even from participant observation (where the analyst does all or some of the job) can provide insights that no other method can. Observation is most useful for jobs where there is a manual or visible component such as a factory line worker, as the tasks conducted can be viewed clearly by the observer. For managerial jobs however, where there are extended periods of time spent working on a computer or on the telephone, observation may not add a great deal of useful information for the job analysis.

A variety of different techniques for job analysis have been introduced and it is often useful to conduct an analysis using a variety of methods rather than just one. On this basis, as well as being useful for personnel selection, the outputs may be helpful in other applications, such as training and development or job evaluation.

Key Learning Point

No single method of job analysis is perfect. Job analyses are usually best developed by using as many different approaches and means of data collection as possible and pooling the results.

When deciding which approach (or approaches) to adopt in conducting a job analysis in practice, Table 4.2 provides a checklist of questions or criteria that you may wish to consider when deciding which methods to use in a given setting.

Table 4.2	A checklist of considerations for conducting a job analysis

- Is my purpose to conduct a task-oriented or worker-oriented analysis (i.e. precise tasks and responsibilities or primarily psychological factors)?
- What level of expertise is required for the analyst?
- What is the level of job proximity in using this technique (direct observation versus remote analysis of self-report on a questionnaire)? How will this influence the quality of data I collect?
- What type of data does this technique provide and how will this be analysed?
- How can I best validate my initial findings?
- What is the capacity of using this technique to generate usable outcomes?
- What is the cost (both in terms of time and resource) of using this technique?
- Are there issues regarding employee sensitivity and access to job holders that need to be addressed?

Using job analysis information

The job analysis information is used in a number of ways. A job description can be prepared from the job analysis data to give an outline of the key responsibilities. The job analysis also provides information that might be used when recruitment advertisements and so forth are prepared to attract candidates for the job (and so that candidates can decide whether the job will suit them before they decide to enter the selection process). Naturally it is essential for designing and/or choosing appropriate selection tools. It can also be used within the organisation to provide information for training, job evaluation and other purposes.

A personnel specification represents the demands of the job translated into human terms. It involves listing the essential criteria that candidates must satisfy and also those criteria that would exclude candidates from consideration. As described earlier, job analysis information may also be used to define a competency model for the job role. However, moving from a job analysis to a clear specification of the psychological qualities thought to be required by a successful job holder is a difficult process. Various procedures have been suggested and used to make this step, but it is important to remember that none of them is entirely objective and that some inferences and judgements are required.

It is also worth noting that the inferential steps needed and the nature of these inferences are different, depending on whether one is designing a *sign- or sample-based* selection procedure. Wernimont and Campbell (1968) made this important distinction between what they described as *signs* and *samples* of behaviour. Consider, for example, how a candidate for a sales position may react to being asked to complete a personality questionnaire, containing questions such as 'Do you often wish that your life was more exciting?' Consider also how the same candidate may react to being required to conduct a role-play exercise and expected to persuade a client to make a purchase. The relevance of the role-play exercise and its potential to provide the selection decision-makers with a realistic *sample* of the candidate's behaviour is obvious. Although it may not be so obvious to the candidate, the results of the personality questionnaire may also provide important *signs* relating to certain job-relevant psychological characteristics. For example, success in sales jobs may be more likely when someone is extroverted (high extroversion), emotionally stable (low neuroticism) and seeks to avoid conflict and help others (high agreeableness).

Job analysis data may be used in two broadly different ways in the design of selection procedures depending on whether the selection procedure will be used to assess samples or signs of behaviour.

Key Learning Point

Job analysis information may be used to design sign- or sample-based personnel selection procedures.

The more traditional use of job analysis involves moving from the analysis to make inferences about the kind of psychological characteristics (signs) needed for successful job performance. By contrast, the sample approach involves focusing on the job tasks and designing selection procedures that provide representative samples of the actual behaviour needed for successful jobs. With the rapid pace of change in modern organisations and with it the increased prevalence of newly created job roles, traditional job analysis techniques may be less relevant as current job holders may not exist. In this way, the challenge of psychologists is to find new ways of conducting future-oriented job analysis techniques (see Hough and Oswald, 2000). There are also challenges and opportunities in using technology to collect and inform the job analysis process. McEntire *et al.* (2006) and Reiter-Palmon *et al.* (2006) describe how web-based job analysis process and applications (such as O*NET) can be more flexible and less resource-intensive than traditional job analysis methods. They argue that there are benefits of this approach that meet the needs of today's dynamic workforce. Sometimes conducting an in-depth job analysis with multiple techniques will provide excellent information: unfortunately it may take so long that the job role which was analysed is no longer needed by the organisation.

Exercise 4.3 presents a case study based on a real example of the issues that psychologists face in conducting job analysis in organisations today.

Exercise 4.3   Using job analysis procedures in organisations

Background

Specs-R-Us are a well-established UK-based opticians company, specialising in eyesight testing and the sale of related eyewear. There are 350 stores throughout the country. The company has been the market leader for several years but has recently experienced tough competition from other optical sales providers coming into the market. The competition is fierce and is primarily based on cost and 'express delivery' of spectacles and eyewear. Specs-R-Us has been a trusted brand over the years and has established a reputation for expertise in optometry and quality service delivery. In each store there is usually one optometrist, who conducts the eye examinations and produces a prescription for the customer. Depending on the size of the store, the optometrist is supported by several optical assistants. The optical assistants' role is to conduct initial eye screening tests and to advise on choice of frames and lenses, based on the customer's prescription. Historically, Specs-R-Us optical assistants have tended to treat people coming into the stores as 'patients' with a prescription, and there has been little or no emphasis on generating sales and selling goods with a higher profit margin.

The job analysis issue

Given increased competition in the market, Specs-R-Us have been losing revenue to other organisations that are generating higher profit through increased sales. In response, the executive has decided to restructure the organisation and create a new job role called sales advisers. This represents a major cultural change in the organisation, where sales performance is now a core requirement of the job role. The new sales adviser's role is designed specifically to increase revenue based on sales in store. These advisers will work alongside the optical assistants, where the optical assistants will conduct the 'technical' elements, such as pre-screening eye tests, before customers see the optometrist. Once customers have their prescription, the sales advisers will focus on guiding customers in their choice of frames and lenses. For sales advisers, a key performance indicator is based on sales revenue, and they will be encouraged to sell goods that carry a high profit margin such as designer frames and lenses.

Suggested exercises

In light of these changes, you have been asked by the executive to conduct two job analyses, one for the role of optical assistants and the other for sales advisers. Prepare an outline of the process you would conduct for the job analysis for each role. In your response:

1 Explain why it is important for Specs-R-Us to conduct the job analyses (in terms that the executive in the organisation could understand).

2 Describe how the job analysis information could be used in the organisation.

3 Outline the various techniques you might employ to conduct the analyses: what would be the ideal approach, and what approach might be more realistic given the demands the organisation is facing?

4 Outline any potential difficulties in accessing the data.

STOP TO CONSIDER

In the preceding section we have looked at job analysis in quite a lot of detail. What are the possible consequences of not carrying out a thorough job analysis before designing and implementing a new selection process? Do you think that these offset the costs of carrying out the job analysis? Why?

You may also have noticed that many jobs change quickly and the boundaries of many job roles are not clearly defined. Are there some job analysis techniques that might be better than others for these types of jobs? What might be some of the advantages of using more than one technique/method to analyse a job?

Validation processes

The pivotal stage in the personnel selection process occurs when the selection decision is taken and a candidate is either offered a position within the organisation, or turned away. At this point various pieces of evidence concerning the current or past performance of candidates (e.g. behaviour at an interview, psychological test scores or references), usually referred to as predictors, are used to decide whether or not a candidate is suitable for the job in question. Although job analysis may suggest that certain candidate characteristics might be desirable, on its own the job analysis data cannot *prove* that candidates with these characteristics will do better than others on the job. This evaluation of the accuracy of the selection methods is obtained by assessing the *criterion-related validity* of the predictors. In essence, validation is about finding out whether the various parts of the selection process were effective. There are a number of ways of examining the effectiveness of a selection process, and these will be described over the next few pages: the interested reader will also find Sackett and Lievens (2008) a useful reference with regard to these issues.

Criterion-related validity

Criterion-related validity refers to the strength of the relationship between the predictor (e.g. psychological test scores or interview ratings) and the criterion (e.g. subsequent work behaviour indicated by measures such as output figures or supervisor's ratings). Criterion-related validity is high if candidates who obtain high predictor scores obtain high criterion scores *and* candidates who obtain low scores on a predictor also obtain low criterion scores. Figure 4.2 shows a scatter plot of some hypothetical data obtained by using two predictors:

1   a job knowledge test score; and

2   a cognitive ability test score;

and one criterion: an average number of units produced per day.

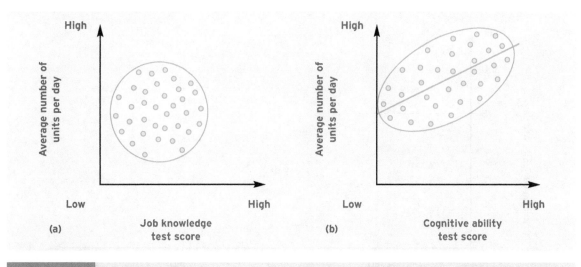

Figure 4.2   **Some hypothetical predictor and criterion scores: (a) a job knowledge test; (b) a cognitive ability test**

Inspection of the scatter plot in Figure 4.2b shows that the criterion-related validity of the cognitive ability test appears to be quite good. Participants' scores in this test correspond closely with the number of units produced. Although the predictor and criterion scores are obviously closely related, it is worth noting that the correspondence is not perfect. For perfect correspondence all of the points would lie exactly on the diagonal line drawn in on Figure 4.2b. For the job knowledge test there is no correspondence at all and, as Figure 4.2a clearly shows, the points are distributed more or less in a circle and high scores on one variable can be associated with either high or low scores on the other variable.

The strength of the relationship between predictor scores and criterion scores is usually expressed as a correlation coefficient (referred to as a validity coefficient. *See also* Chapter 2 for an explanation of correlation.) Perfect correlation between two variables will produce a correlation of 1. No correlation at all, as in Figure 4.2a, will produce a coefficient of zero.

Key Learning Point

The criterion-related validity of a selection procedure is normally indicated by the magnitude of the validity coefficient (the correlation between the predictor and criterion scores).

When the correlation between two variables is high it is possible to predict the score of one when supplied with the score on the other. Consider, for example, Figure 4.3, where the predictor–criterion relationship is perfect (i.e. a validity (correlation) coefficient of +1.0). In the case of a new candidate, it would be possible to obtain their score on predictor A and thus predict a score on the criterion. For example, if the organisation wished to select staff who would produce an average of at least 75 units per day, what should be done?

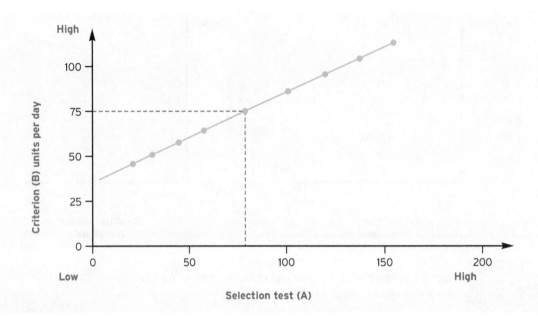

Figure 4.3 Prediction of criterion scores from selection test scores

As Figure 4.3 shows, if only people who obtained a score of above 80 on selection test A were offered jobs by the organisation, all future employees would be likely to produce 75 units (or more) per day. Unfortunately, in practice selection can rarely be conducted in such an idealised and clear-cut fashion and there are several practical problems that must be considered.

Research has shown that it is most unusual in practical situations to obtain validity coefficients much in excess of +0.5, let alone the coefficient of +1.0 that will allow perfect prediction (e.g. Patterson and Ferguson, 2007; Salgado *et al.*, 2001). Nevertheless, validity coefficients of considerably less than +1.0 can provide a basis for improved personnel selection. Theoretically the ideal way to collect criterion-related validity data is to use a predictive (or follow-up) design. This design involves collecting predictor information (e.g. interview ratings, test scores) for candidates during the selection process and then following up the candidates (e.g. during their first year of employment) to gather criterion data on their work performance (*see* for example Patterson *et al.*, 2005). Recent reviews of the various dimensions of job performance suggest that what might be assessed as the predictor criterion needs careful consideration (Sackett and Lievens, 2008; Rotundo and Sackett, 2002). These reviews found that task performance, citizenship performance and counterproductive work behaviour are the three major domains of job performance. Cognitively loaded predictors (e.g. cognitive ability) tend to be the strongest correlates of task performance and non-cognitive predictors tend to be the best predictors in the citizenship and counterproductive behaviour domains. This indicates that careful attention needs to be paid to the criterion of interest to the organisation: this should be a critical determinant of the eventual make-up and success of a selection system (Sackett and Lievens, 2008). Clearly it would be unwise to have a selection system that predicted perfectly aspects of performance that were irrelevant to the organisation.

Similarly, the role of the human raters in the measurement of performance is also an important consideration. Viswesvaran *et al.*'s (2005) meta-analysis compared correlations between ratings on various different performance dimensions made by different raters with those made on various performance dimensions by the same rater. This analysis showed the positive impact that rater training and experience within the organisation are likely to have on the quality of performance measurement, and hence predictive validity (especially when the selection process has been running for more than one year). When selection processes are new, the way performance measures are identified and designed improves predictive validity, but as the selection process matures, the qualities of the rater tend to become increasingly important.

An alternative design for conducting criterion-related validity studies is the *concurrent* design. In the concurrent design, predictor data are obtained from existing employees on whom criterion data are already available. Ideally, in a study of predictive validity the predictor scores should not be used to take selection decisions until after a validation study has been conducted. In other words, until the relationship between predictor and criterion is firmly established, candidates should be offered employment regardless of their performance on the predictors. Understandably, this is a difficult step for an organisation to take. If job analysis and other information (in the absence of validity data) suggest that the use of certain predictors should improve their selection decisions, in many organisations managers would not be willing to permit candidates with low scores on these predictors to enter employment. Sometimes it is possible to convince them not to use the results of potential predictors and to continue to use their existing methods while a validation study is carried out. Often, however, they cannot accept the constraints of a complete predictive validity design (because it takes considerable time to follow-up enough candidates) and some compromise is needed.

Another design problem with the predictive validity design is that of ensuring that the predictor results obtained by new employees are not revealed to other members of the organisation before a validity study has been conducted. Obviously a supervisor who is allocated a new employee with either a high or low predictor score could be affected by these results. The supervisor's behaviour towards the new employee might be influenced and/or estimates of the new employee's work performance could be biased.

Key Learning Point

Predictive validity designs are more rigorous than concurrent validity designs but their implementation usually presents a number of practical problems.

One advantage of the concurrent design is that the organisation is not required to collect predictor data from candidates (for employment) and then somehow ignore that data during selection decision-making. Predictor data are collected from existing employees only. A second advantage of the concurrent design is that there is no time delay between the collection of predictor and criterion data. Existing employees' predictor scores are correlated with their criterion performance. The criterion data are likely to be available already, or at least can be collected quickly. There is certainly no need to wait for the lengthy follow-up period involved with

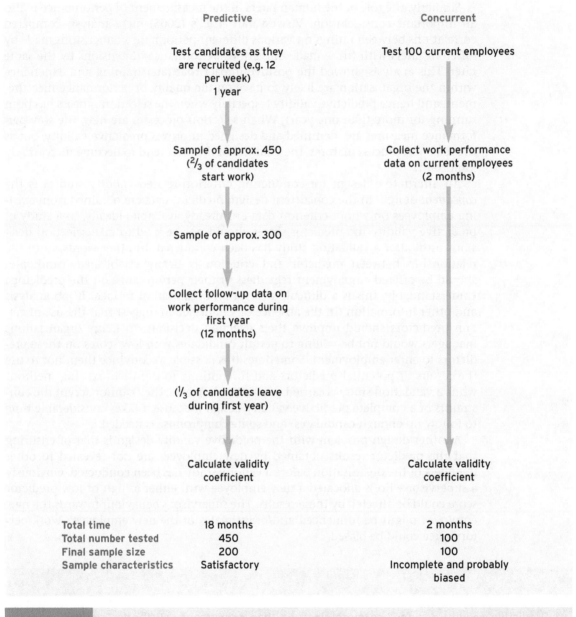

	Predictive	Concurrent
	Test candidates as they are recruited (e.g. 12 per week) 1 year	Test 100 current employees
	Sample of approx. 450 ($^2/_3$ of candidates start work)	Collect work performance data on current employees (2 months)
	Sample of approx. 300	
	Collect follow-up data on work performance during first year (12 months)	
	($^1/_3$ of candidates leave during first year)	
	Calculate validity coefficient	Calculate validity coefficient
Total time	18 months	2 months
Total number tested	450	100
Final sample size	200	100
Sample characteristics	Satisfactory	Incomplete and probably biased

Figure 4.4   A comparison of predictive and concurrent designs

the predictive design. Figure 4.4 compares the two designs in a hypothetical situation and indicates the considerable differences in timescales and data collection effort that can occur.

Because of these advantages the concurrent design is attractive to many organisations. However, there are disadvantages. The workers presently employed by an organisation provide a population that may be very different from the population of job applicants. Current job holders have already survived existing company selection procedures and represent a preselected group of people who have been with the organisation for some time. No data are available on people who were not hired by the company, or on those who were hired but have subsequently left. It is very likely that the concurrent sample is incomplete and not representative of the potential workforce. If, as a result of a concurrent validity study, a link between, say, scores in an arithmetic test and job performance is established, it is difficult to be sure if the people tested come to the job with such skills or whether arithmetic skills are acquired as a result of training and job experience. It would not be fair or informative to test new applicants for skills that could only be acquired through training and experience within the company. Such problems make it hard to be certain about the actual predictive value of results derived from a concurrent validity study.

As we have already seen, once people are in the job their performance may be measured across a number of different criteria. Therefore, validation studies can quickly become very complex in practical terms because organisations rarely use one single predictor to make selection decisions. Given the multifaceted nature of job analysis information, recruiters are likely to design multiple selection tools to assess these criteria. Therefore, recruiters must decide whether a job applicant must score highly on all assessment criteria (i.e. take a non-compensatory approach to selection) or whether high scores on some criteria can make up for low scores on another (i.e. a compensatory approach to selection). In practice, recruiters might assign different weightings to various assessment criteria, depending on the nature of the job role. For example, in the sales assistant job role, it might be decided that customer service skill is the most important criterion and applicants who do not achieve a certain score will not be considered further.

Most selection systems combine several predictors (selection tools), such as an applicant's score on an interview and on a cognitive ability test. In validation studies, a key question is how much does adding another predictor increase the predictive power of the selection process? This is known as *incremental validity*. In other words, recruiters might want to know how much accuracy is improved as a result of using a psychometric test (rather than relying solely on interview scores). Information on the incremental validity of a specific selection tool is extremely valuable as it allows organisations to conduct a cost–benefit analysis of using additional tools. Recent research including meta-analysis has attempted to estimate the incremental validity of one predictor over another. Much of this research attempts to better understand the relationships among predictors and dimensions of job performance to enhance the practical choice of selection methods (*see* Sackett and Lievens, 2008, for a summary of incremental validity studies and limitations to these). The typical levels of predictive validity for various selection methods are examined in Chapter 5.

Another significant practical difficulty in today's organisations is that of accessing an adequate sample size in order to perform certain statistical analyses on the data. The design and sample of the study need to be sufficiently robust to allow the analyst to draw firm conclusions about the validity of various selection techniques. Most organisations are not involved in large-scale recruitment programmes and usually it is sizeable graduate recruitment initiatives that are the focus of validation studies (i.e. several hundred applicants from which at least a hundred begin working for the organisation).

One important point to make about any validity study, regardless of whether predictive or concurrent procedures are used, is that the initial validity study should always be followed by a 'cross-validation' study on a second sample of people to cross-check the results obtained. For studies that involve relatively few predictors this requirement is perhaps not essential and represents a 'counsel of perfection'.

However, when a study has investigated many possible predictors and those with the strongest predictor–criterion relationship are to be used for selection purposes, cross-validation is more important. The more potential predictors are used, the more likely it becomes that random or chance variations will produce apparent relationships between some of these predictors and the criterion measure(s). Relationships due to chance would be unlikely to occur again in the cross-validation sample – only 'real' relationships would produce the same results in both samples.

Some additional important points about validity appear in the next chapter, in the context of interpreting evidence about the validity of specific selection techniques.

Key Learning Point

Cross-validation is necessary to be confident of the results from a validation study, unless the sample is very large.

STOP TO CONSIDER

In this section we have discussed how we can examine whether test scores at selection are related to job performance. Now consider how well the performance measures used by organisations (e.g. manager appraisals, sales performance, number of mistakes, etc.) provide a true reflection of job performance. Is the care taken in the design and use of selection measures matched by the care taken in the design and use of performance measures?

Also consider the challenges facing small organisations (e.g. of fewer than 25 employees) when they attempt to validate their selection processes. How would their situation differ from that faced by large organisations carrying out high-volume recruitment? What implications might this have for small organisations seeking to improve their selection processes?

Other types of validity

Criterion-related validity is the most important type of validity as far as selection is concerned, but there are other important types of validity as well. The first two are not 'real' forms of validity, in the sense that they refer to appearance rather than substance.

Faith validity

Sometimes organisations might believe that a selection method (e.g. a psychometric ability test) is valid because a reputable company sells it, and it is packaged in a very expensive-looking way. However, Cook (2004, 2009) suggests that money spent on 'gloss' could mean less money has been spent on research and development of the instrument. He suggests that organisations must be wary of blindly accepting the validity of an instrument without thorough inspection of all supporting data and documentation.

Face validity

A selection test or procedure displays face validity if it 'looks right'. For example, requiring an applicant for a carpenter's job to make a T-joint from two pieces of wood would show face validity. On the other hand asking the applicant to carry out a test of general intelligence would probably have much less face validity for the candidate, since the link between that test and job performance would probably be less obvious to the candidate. One key advantage of face validity is the positive impact it has upon user acceptability: candidates are less likely to feel unfairly treated and challenge the outcomes of selection processes if they believe that the selection process looks relevant to the job role.

Content validity

Content validity is established on a logical basis rather than by calculating validity coefficients or following other technical statistical procedures. A predictor shows content validity when it covers a representative sample of the behaviour domain being measured. For example, a content-valid test of car-driving ability would be expected to cover all of the essential activities that a competent driver should be able to carry out. A test that did not include an emergency stop and a reversing exercise would be lacking in content validity (and most likely result in higher car insurance premiums and more work for accident compensation lawyers!).

Construct validity

This involves identifying the psychological characteristics (or constructs) such as intelligence, emotional stability or manual dexterity that underlie successful performance of the task (such as a test or performance on the job) in question. Since construct validity involves relationships between predictors and characteristics that are not directly observable (e.g. cognitive processes), it can be assessed only by indirect means. Often this is achieved by correlating a well-established measure of a construct with a new measure of the same construct. A poor relationship would suggest that the new measure may lack construct validity. For example, if a new measure of extroversion had been developed, one would expect that scores this new measure would be highly correlated with scores on other well-established measures of extroversion (we might also reasonably expect that correlations between the new measure and other, very different constructs, should be low). Exploring the construct validity of any psychological instrument is an important facet of understanding what the instrument actually measures (i.e. 'does it do what it says on the tin?'). As material in Chapter 5 shows, the construct validity of several frequently used personnel selection methods is not well understood.

Exercise 4.4 gives an opportunity to reflect upon your own experiences of selection processes, particularly in relation to your perceptions of the validity of the process.

Exercise 4.4   The validity of selection processes

In this exercise you are asked to reflect upon your own experience(s) of selection and recruitment processes. Think about a job in which you have been, or are currently, employed (whether full-time or part-time) and consider the following issues:

Suggested exercises

1   What are the key responsibilities of the role?
2   Describe the elements of the recruitment process. From your perspective as the applicant, did the selection procedures display face validity and content validity at each stage?
3   In general, what is your impression of the accuracy of the selection process?
4   What recommendation would you make to improve the likely validity of this selection process?

Reliability

Any measuring instrument (whether predictor or criterion) used in a selection procedure must be both valid and reliable. The reliability of a selection instrument is an extremely important characteristic and refers to the extent to which it *measures consistently under varying conditions*. If the same candidate produces very different scores when they take a test on two different occasions, the reliability of the test must be questioned. In technical terms, if a selection tool has high reliability it is relatively free from errors of measurement (i.e. the score that we obtain is close to the *true* score). Of course, this means that a test cannot be valid unless it is reliable. There are number of different types of reliability.

If we want to assess the reliability for an ability test we could calculate the *test–retest reliability* (where participants are administered the same test on two separate occasions with a significant time lag between administrations). If the test was reliable we would expect the scores to not change very much over time. If the test had high reliability we would expect a strong positive correlation between scores at time 1 and time 2 administrations. In assessing this form of reliability it would be very important to ensure that the testing conditions were the same on both occasions, and that the construct being measured was thought to be relatively stable.

Another form of reliability is *parallel forms*, where test developers might design two tests to be equivalent, including items of similar content and equal difficulty. Test publishers might develop 50 high-quality questions for a test and use 25 in version A and the other 25 in version B. For example, organisations involved in graduate recruitment often use similar psychometric ability tests. In order to prevent practice effects, test publishers produce parallel forms of the same ability test. In designing parallel forms of the same test, the test developers assess the external reliability between scales, where high reliability is characterised by a strong positive correlation between participant scores on both tests. Not all tests will have parallel forms because of the increased costs in involved in development (i.e. developing double the number of test items that are actually needed).

Test–retest and parallel forms can both be described as *external* forms of reliability, because scores on the measure in question are compared with an external reference point, even if that is scores on the same measure at a different time.

The *internal* reliability of a scale can be assessed by a variety of different statistical methods and formulae (*see* Smith and Robertson, 1993; Kline, 1999, for relevant formulae and further technical information). The common feature is that internal reliability always concerns the extent to which different parts of the same measure produce results consistent with each other. In essence it is a measure of the extent to which questions designed to measure the same thing produce similar, i.e. consistent, results. The type of scale and its content determine the specific approach to assessing internal reliability. Common approaches to assessing the internal reliability of scales include Cronbach's coefficient alpha, the 'split half' method (where the researcher can examine the association between scores on two halves of a test, for example) and KR20 (which is used for questions that have right or wrong answers). Clearly it is desirable to find consistency across different items that are measuring the same thing: as a rule of thumb high internal consistency reliabilities (e.g. Cronbach's coefficient alpha of 0.7 or above) are desirable. However, if internal consistency reliability is too high (above about 0.95) then the test may be inefficient because it is asking the same questions (and therefore gathering the same data) over and over again.

Key Learning Point

To be effective, personnel selection methods must be both valid and reliable.

Financial utility

Like many organisational practices, personnel selection procedures cost money to implement. Using selection procedures with good predictive validity is always important but, unfortunately, procedures with good predictive validity alone do not guarantee that a selection procedure will be cost-effective. Two important factors determining cost-effectiveness (usually referred to as utility) are:

1   the selection ratio, i.e. $\frac{\text{number of jobs}}{\text{number of candidates}}$;
2   the financial benefit of improved job performance.

Let us now examine in a little more detail the role that validity, selection ratio and the other factors play in determining utility. Figure 4.5a shows the situation for a validity coefficient of 0.1. The shaded areas (B and C) identify people who will be hired by the organisation. Notice, however, that although all of these people achieve the minimum score on the predictor, only a proportion of them (B) also show satisfactory work performance. Similarly, although all of the people in the unshaded areas (A and D) fail to achieve the cut-off score on the predictor, some of them are capable

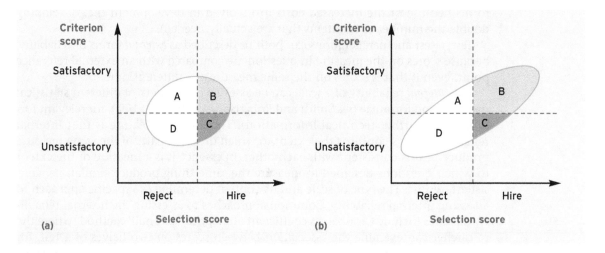

Figure 4.5

**The effect of different validity coefficients on the proportion hired:
(a) validity coefficient = 0.1; (b) validity coefficient = 0.5**

of satisfactory work performance (those in area A). Areas B and D represent correct selection decisions; area D contains people who have justifiably been rejected, known as true negatives. Area C contains the false positives; that is, people who would be hired but produce unsatisfactory work performance. Area A contains the false negatives; that is, people who would not be hired but are capable of satisfactory work performance. Areas A and C represent errors in the selection process. Note that unless the validity coefficient is 1.0 there will *always* be errors of selection.

As Figure 4.5b shows, when validity increases (0.5), the proportions in areas A and C decrease and the proportion of correct decisions (areas B and D) increases. Thus, as validity increases, the quality of selection decisions also increases.

If validity was perfect, error-free selection could be achieved and the relative performance of candidates on the selection method would be reproduced in their work performance. Thus, a group of candidates with selection scores in the top 10 per cent would deliver work performance scores at the same level (remember that in perfect selection, work performance is perfectly correlated with selection score).

If the assumption that candidates' scores are normally distributed is made, then it is possible to use statistical tables to calculate the average standard score (z-score) of any group of candidates (e.g. the top 10 per cent). With *perfect selection*, the average z-score of the selected candidates would also be their average work performance score:

Average selection score (z_s) = average work performance score (z_w)

Of course, in reality, selection is never perfect and the predictive accuracy of the selection score is proportional to the magnitude of the validity coefficient. The work performance that can be expected of selected candidates will be dependent on the accuracy of selection:

(z_s)(validity coefficient) = z_w

The next step in the process is to consider how much value can be assigned to different levels of work performance. Several investigators have tackled this problem, and although there is no accepted solution (*see* Boudreau, 1989), a very conservative rule of thumb is to assign a value of 40 per cent of salary to each standard deviation of performance. Once this step has been made, it is a simple matter to derive an estimate of the financial gain that can be expected from different selection situations. Since z-scores are already expressed in standard score units, the estimate of z_w gives a direct estimate of financial gain. The cost of the procedure needs to be subtracted and account taken of the expected tenure of recruits and the number of people selected. The final equation is:

$$(z_s)(r)(T)(N) = \text{financial benefit}$$

where: z_s = average z-score of selected group
 r = validity coefficient for the selection procedure
 T = number of years recruits will stay
 N = number of recruits taken in one year

This equation has many potential uses. It could be used, for instance, to calculate the gain to be derived from changing from one selection method to another. To make the relevant calculations it is often necessary to make some estimates of the various terms in the equation. For example, if a company was considering the use of assessment centres to replace a procedure that involved only unstructured interviews, it would be necessary to make estimates of the likely validity for the new procedure. Given the wealth of research on most selection methods (*see* Chapter 5) such estimates can be made with reasonable confidence. Similarly, the equation could be used to estimate the gain that could be derived from the attraction of a bigger field of candidates (e.g. by extensive advertising). The financial gain derived from the improved selection ratio (see below) may then be set against the cost of the advertising campaign.

Key Learning Point

Utility calculations can be used to address a variety of problems and assist organisations in determining recruitment advertising strategies, etc., as well as indicating the direct benefits to be derived from selection procedures.

Clearly, when the selection ratio is greater than 1 (i.e. there are more available jobs than applicants), the use of any selection procedure is likely to be of relatively little benefit. In this situation the organisation may be forced to accept anyone who applies for a job. In practice, even with a selection ratio of more than 1, it may still be sensible for an organisation to apply stringent selection criteria and leave jobs empty rather than hire totally unsuitable employees. When the selection ratio is less than 1 (i.e. more applicants than jobs), the organisation can gain obvious benefits from using selection. Consider the situation for two different selection ratios. If the selection ratio is 0.7 (i.e. seven jobs for every ten applicants), the organisation can afford to refuse jobs to people with the lowest 30 per cent of scores on the predictor. If, however, the selection ratio is 0.4 (i.e. four jobs for every ten applicants), the bottom 60 per cent of applicants can be rejected and the group of applicants selected will have a much higher score. In turn, as the material presented above shows, this will translate into financial gain.

Other factors

Burke (2005) and DeCorte (2000) provide more detailed discussion on utility models and their applications. Studies where selection utility has been estimated have shown very clearly that, even with modest validity coefficients, striking financial gains may be made. Schmidt *et al.* (1984), for example, showed that gains of over US$1 million per annum could be expected if cognitive ability tests were used to select the large numbers of US Park Rangers recruited each year. Schmidt *et al.* (1979) showed that even more dramatic gains could be obtained if the *computer programmer aptitude test* (Hughes and McNamara, 1959) was used to select computer programmers in the United States. With a selection ratio of 0.5 (i.e. two applicants per job), gains of between US$13 and 37 million could be expected: a figure certain to grab the attention of any company's finance director!

Key Learning Point

The cost-effectiveness of a personnel selection procedure is not dependent on validity alone.

STOP TO CONSIDER

Measuring utility will be seen as important by many organisations. You will have seen some quite complex equations in this section. Anderson *et al.* (2001b) have argued that study utility theory has 'witnessed an ever-increasing pre-occupation by some researchers active in this area over the minutiae of formulaic expressions' (p. 395). They argue that this pedantic approach damaged the practical relevance of utility theory. How precise and complex do you think that utility calculations need to be? What are some of the variables that are very difficult to measure when attempting to estimate the utility of a selection process? Is it possible to gather enough information to make a very precise calculation of the return on investment for a selection process?

Summary

Selection processes are designed on the assumption that there are job-relevant, individual differences between people, which can be assessed. Assessment in organisational settings is a common activity, which can have a useful impact on individual and organisational success and well-being. The cornerstone of effective selection processes is the job analysis, which defines the assessment criteria that form the basis for many human resource activities in organisations, and it is particularly important in personnel selection. More recently, organisations have used competency analysis to define the key behaviours that underpin successful performance in the target job role. A range of approaches to job analysis is available, including qualitative and quantitative techniques. Job analysis information may be used to develop sign- or sample-based selection procedures.

Given significant changes in the nature of work and work patterns in recent years, many jobs do not have specific, prescribed job descriptions. This presents a variety of challenges for the job analyst, particularly in deciding which job analysis techniques to employ. As a result, many analysts are trying to use more future-oriented approaches. Since the reliability and validity of such procedures determine the quality of personnel entering the organisation it is crucial that selection procedures provide valid assessments of future work behaviour. Several different (e.g. predictive or concurrent) validation processes are available for assessing validity.

Closing Case Study — Russia bids to find new elite breed

The Kremlin has begun a recruitment drive to find a new elite after complaints by Dmitry Medvedev, Russia's president, that the country has a shortage of talented civil servants, managers and politicians. Regional governors have received letters from both Mr Medvedev and Vladimir Putin, prime minister, in the past couple of days, asking them to contribute names to a database of the country's 'reserve of manpower'.

A database was begun last year but after painstaking research, it contains just 7000 names, according to the newspaper *Nezavisimaya Gazeta*. In a speech on 23 July, Mr Medvedev criticised the effort, saying there was a 'famine' of talent in Russia in both government and business. Outlining plans to replace several Russian regional governors, he said: 'We don't have a bench of fresh reserves. We have to bash our heads against a wall every time we must replace high officials.'

Civil service used to be a prestigious profession in Russia, ever since the Tsar Peter the Great created 14 ranks of the civil service in 1722. During the Soviet Union, state service was the route to the best lifestyle in the country, and high-ranking civil service jobs came with cars, large apartments and country houses as perks. Since the collapse of communism, however, the prestige of the bureaucracy has fallen drastically as talented managers find better-paying work in the private sector or have emigrated.

The project of compiling a list of prospective officials is being managed by United Russia, the political party headed by Mr Putin that has become a quasi state institution, but party representatives have said the database would be open to everyone, not just party members. Yuri Kotler, coordinator of the database project, says his team is only just starting to grapple with the immensity of the project. 'We are specifying criteria,' he said. 'We are discussing which capabilities and leadership qualities ▶

the aspiring leaders must have, which ideology they should be guided by in life, and also – do they plan to live in Russia or not. We are developing a sophisticated selection system to find people who are interesting to us.'

The database will not be open to anyone over 47 years old, he said, and the target for the end of the year is to have 50,000 names.

Source: Adapted from FT.com, August 6 2008 by Charles Clover in Moscow

Suggested exercise

You have been asked by the Russian Government to provide recommendations that will help to begin the development of a selection system for civil servants. Produce a two-page report that provides recommendations for:

1 A systematic approach to assessing the competencies required, and
2 How the validity and reliability of the new system should be examined once it is in operation.
3 Highlight any issue to consider in applying your approach in a Russian context.

Test your learning

Short-answer questions

1 Outline three job analysis techniques and describe the relative advantages and disadvantages of each.
2 For what purposes can job analysis outputs be used in organisations?
3 Draw a diagram of the personnel selection design and validation system.
4 What are competencies and competency analysis? Describe how they are used in organisations and for what purposes.
5 What are behavioural indicators in competency models and how are they used?
6 Describe the criteria you would use to make the decisions about which job analysis technique to use in practice.
7 Describe a predictive validity study for a selection process and explain the associated practical problems they present in organisations.
8 What are the differences between face, content and construct validity, and how is each type of validity assessed?
9 What are the main items of information needed in order to calculate the financial utility of a selection procedure?

Suggested assignments

1   Given recent changes in the nature of work and the increasing number of newly created job roles in organisations, discuss the relative effectiveness of job analysis techniques and suggest how psychologists might improve them.

2   You have been asked to design a job analysis process for the role of a politician. Describe the techniques you might use and how this will inform the selection process.

3   Outline the key stages in the selection process. Discuss the practical problems associated with validating selection procedures in organisations.

Relevant websites

There is a lot of useful information about job analysis at http://www.job-analysis. net/. This is a site for human resource managers and consultants, but it also offers quite a lot of general information about what job analysis is, how it can be done and how to do it legally.

For further self-test material and relevant, annotated weblinks please visit the website at **www.pearsoned.co.uk/workpsych**

Suggested further reading

Full details of all references are given in the list at the end of this book.

1   For more depth on the issues raised in this chapter, consult a comprehensive text on personnel selection, such as *The Blackwell Handbook on Personnel Selection* by Evers, Anderson and Voskuijl (2005), or *Personnel Selection: Adding value through people*, Cook (2004), *Personnel Selection: A theoretical approach* by Schmitt and Chan (1998).

2   A very detailed treatment of validity and reliability is given in Anastasi's book, *Psychological Testing*, or Kline's *Handbook of Psychological Testing*.

CHAPTER 5

Personnel selection and assessment methods

What works?

LEARNING OUTCOMES

After studying this chapter, you should be able to:

1 list seven personnel selection methods and describe three in more detail;

2 state the major evaluative standards for personnel selection procedures;

3 name the chief sources of distortion in validation studies;

4 explain the contribution of meta-analysis to personnel selection research;

5 specify advantages and disadvantages of several selection methods, including:

   interviews

   psychometric tests

   situational judgement tests

   assessment centres;

6 specify which selection methods tend to be (i) most valid and (ii) most acceptable to applicants;

7 explain how some selection techniques could lead to bias and unfairness to some subgroups;

8 explain some of the issues associated with the increasing use of technology in personnel selection.

Made for the job? Is recruiting by star sign any more ludicrous than most normal hiring policies?

See, all this time we thought working like a dog was a bad thing. How wrong can you be? A company in northern China has announced that not only does it approve of dog-like behaviour in its employees – it positively insists upon it. According to a recruitment advert, it will only hire employees born in the Chinese year of the dog, which, as there are 12 signs in Chinese astrology, is certainly going to limit the amount of post that HR has to deal with.

As luck would have it, the next Chinese New Year, which begins on Sunday, heralds another dog year, so babies born over the next 12 months will one day have the chance to work for Jilin Jiangshan HR Development Company Limited. Mr Dong, a spokesperson for the company, said it thought dogs were more suited to corporate culture, given that they are loyal, faithful, honest and ethical.

And while you might think hiring people, or not, on the basis of a fluke of birth is the total opposite of 'ethical', you'll be interested to know that Chinese law does forbid discrimination in hiring – but doesn't say what constitutes an offence. Apparently, eliminating eleven-twelfths of the population is OK, and Mr Dong says he doesn't see how his company's rule could hurt anyone. Although people born in a year that isn't 1994, 1982, 1970, 1958 or 1946 – I think you see the pattern here – might disagree. It's hard to see the trend catching on here. For one thing, Western astrology is so nuanced, it would be hard to enforce blanket bans. You could easily talk round an anti-bull recruitment manager with: 'I admit I'm a Taurus, but I'm right on the cusp, I've got Scorpio rising and my moon's in Aquarius, so you'd hardly know.'

Of course, that's not why the story raises eyebrows. Really, we're just amused by the superstition, and maybe just a tad envious. Rather than wading your way through endless psychometric testing and profiling questionnaires, wouldn't it be nice to be able to say: 'I'm the perfect employee, and here's my birth certificate to prove it'? However, apart from the horoscope element you'd have a hard time convincing me it's that different to hiring policy in this country.

I once spoke to the HR manager of a company lots of people wanted to work for. He told me that, of the applicants they saw, a proportion were so terrible, they would leave the interviewer slack-jawed with wonderment, and a rejection letter would have been dispatched from the building almost before the interviewee was. A similar proportion were similarly astounding, but for more positive reasons, and it would be all the interviewer could do to stop themselves offering up their first-born child in exchange for the candidate deigning to take a job. The majority, however, were simply good. Perfectly acceptable. The company attracted so many good applicants that there was normally a handful for each job who were similarly matched in qualifications, aptitude and experience. 'So how do you choose between them?' I asked. 'Well, we just decide whom we like the most,' I was told. 'Who's going to fit in the best.' Nothing too controversial there – finding a fit is one of the purposes of holding interviews, after all – but you might feel a bit peeved if you were the one who'd just missed out on your dream job for a reason no more substantial than that one of the other applicants supported the same football team as their new boss. And, despite discrimination laws, which probably would come down quite heavily on someone for-mulating their hire and fire policy according to star sign, certain workers – disabled people, people from ethnic minorities, for example – could probably tell you how often they have failed to 'fit in'.

The fact is, most companies recruit in their own image. If you want to design trainers or computer games, you'll probably get further if you've got a trendy haircut, a working knowledge of street slang and a pair of jeans round your knees. It's hard to picture a balding 50-something father of three working on a beauty counter. And when you get to the august institutions that form the Establishment – the City, the law, academia, the media – who could argue that you won't be better placed if the person interviewing you happens to be good chums with Daddy from their Cambridge days? So laugh at the Chinese story all you like, but remember that accidents of birth can rule recruitment here, too.

Source: office.hours@guardian.co.uk accessed 2006.

Introduction

There is over a century's research literature exploring how best to select a person for a job. Work psychologists have had a major influence on the way selection processes are designed and implemented across many organisations in all sectors of industry across the world. Over the past three decades, the research shows that although there are a variety of personnel selection methods available to use in organisational settings, not all of the methods are equally useful or appropriate in some selection processes. The opening case study illustrates some complex issues such as how to assess a candidate's 'organisational fit'. The case study highlights the importance of rigorous research evidence in evaluating various approaches to personnel selection. Approaches to recruitment do differ across the globe: this is due in part to employment law regarding selection practices differing significantly. A recent review of selection practices in 22 countries clearly shows this to be the case (Moyrs *et al.*, 2008).

For high-volume graduate recruitment the use of technology in selection processes has transformed how people apply for jobs. The use of technology may have improved efficiencies for organisations, but the 'candidate experience' is now a key research topic. Over the past decade organisations have become increasingly concerned about how to attract and retain the best candidates in a competitive marketplace. With the recent economic downturn, the global labour market may change again, with per-haps more competition for fewer jobs in some locations. Perceptions of fairness are key to exploring applicant reactions to selection methods: they also indicate the potential for legal challenges by unsuccessful candidates. From an organisational perspective, there are concerns regarding plagiarism and cheating when it comes to screening applicants, especially when using the Internet.

This chapter describes the main personnel selection procedures that are used fre-quently in organisations and examines their relative accuracy at determining who is 'the best person for the job'. The opening case study illustrates that although we now know a great deal about the accuracy of different selection techniques, psy-chologists need to address how the various methods are implemented in practice.

There is a growing need to understand issues regarding fairness and how adverse reactions could lead to challenges in the law courts. After examining the evidence concerning the validity of each of the main methods, this chapter explores the extent to which the various methods are used.

An overview of personnel selection methods

Table 5.1 shows the major personnel selection methods that are available for use and also gives a brief explanation of what the methods involve. Most of the methods are well known, and many readers will have first-hand experience of some of them.

When using predictors such as interviews, psychometric tests or work-sample tests, the specific areas to be investigated in the interview or test should be derived from job analysis data (*see* Chapter 4). The information from the job analysis provides a basis for deciding which factors (e.g. numerical ability, communication skills, organisational skills) might be important for job success.

Biographical data are often developed in a different way. When candidates apply for a job with an organisation it is likely that they will complete an application form and other documents in which they are expected to provide certain verifiable biographical information concerning factors such as previous employment, personal career history and education. The basic procedure for using biographical data is to collect information on a number of candidates and correlate it with subsequent performance. Items of information that predict subsequent performance can then be identified and perhaps used in selection decision-making. Items of information chosen on this basis do not necessarily have any obvious link with the job; it has merely been demonstrated, on a statistical basis, that they predict future performance.

In most practical situations it is not sensible to base selection decisions on the use of one predictor only (such as the results of one test) or even on one type of predictor. As you will see in this chapter, each predictor has its own strengths and weaknesses and none is perfect. When several different predictors are used together, the basic aim should be to ensure that the various predictors *complement* one another rather than duplicate each other. One successful method of selection that makes use of many different predictors is the 'assessment centre'. Assessment centres typically include interviews, psychological tests, in-basket exercises and group discussions. They usually extend for a period of two to three days, although they may be as short as a day or as long as a week. Candidates are usually assessed by trained assessors, who are often senior managers in the organisation. A typical assessment centre would involve groups of 12 candidates being assessed by 6 assessors. Assessment centres are used frequently to evaluate people who already work within an organisation. The information gained from the assessment centre is then used to help take decisions concerning promotion and career development (i.e. it becomes a development centre).

Key Learning Point

In most situations it is best to use a combination of several personnel selection techniques to ensure fairness and accuracy.

Table 5.1	Personnel selection methods

1 Interviews
Many involve more than one interviewer. When several interviewers are involved, the term *panel interview* is used. The most important features of an interview are the extent to which a pre-planned structure is followed and the proportion of questions that are directly related to the job.

2 Psychometric tests
This category includes tests of cognitive ability (such as general intelligence, verbal ability, numerical ability), self-report measures of personality* and situational judgement tests.

3 References
Usually obtained from current or previous employers, these are used often in the final stages of the selection process. The information requested may be specific or general and open-ended.

4 Biodata
Specifications of biographical information about a candidate's life history. Some biodata inventories may contain many (e.g. 150+) questions and ask objective questions, such as which professional qualifications are held by the applicant, and more subjective ones, such as preferences for different job features.

5 Work-sample tests
Such tests literally use samples of the job in question (e.g. the contents of an in-tray for an executive position, specific kinds of typing for a secretarial post or interacting with a customer for a sales position). The applicant is given instructions and then a specific amount of time to complete the tasks.

6 Handwriting analysis (graphology)
Inferences are made about candidates' characteristics by examining specific features of their handwriting (e.g. slant, letter shapes). Obviously, a reasonably lengthy sample of the candidate's normal writing is required.

7 Assessment centres
This procedure involves a combination of several of the previously mentioned techniques (e.g. psychometric tests, interviews, work samples). Candidates are usually dealt with in groups and some of the techniques used require the candidates to interact (e.g. in simulated group decision-making exercises or group presentations).

*The term personality test is used here for simplicity. However, *measures* of personality are not really tests because they do not have 'right or wrong' answers. Personality questionnaire and personality measure are appropriate terms.

How well do selection methods work?

Before it is feasible to consider how well selection methods work it is necessary to be clear about what it means for a selection method to work. The previous chapter introduced the concept of criterion-related validity and demonstrated how this could be evaluated by means of validation procedures. Obviously, criterion-related validity is an essential requirement for a selection method but other features are also important. Table 5.2 lists a number of other features of personnel selection methods that are also vital. A comprehensive evaluation of any selection method would require a thorough examination of the method in relation to each of the features given in Table 5.2. In the interests of clarity and simplicity, the evaluation of selection methods that follows concentrates on criterion-related validity.

Key Learning Point

One of the key evaluative standards for personnel selection methods is criterion-related validity (i.e. is performance at selection linked to job performance?).

Estimating the validity of personnel selection procedures

As the previous chapter explained, predictive or concurrent validation processes may be used to estimate the criterion-related validity of a selection procedure. Most of the selection procedures mentioned so far in this chapter have been examined in this way: investigators have conducted a huge number of validation studies on many selection procedures in many industries. Any single validation study is unlikely to provide a definitive answer on the validity of a selection method. This is because any particular study can be conducted on only a sample of relevant people and, of course, has to be conducted in a specific organisation, at a particular time, using particular measures. There may be specific factors – to do with the sample of people used, the measures, the timing of the study and so on – which influence the study and bias the results in some way.

It is obvious, then, that to estimate the validity of a particular selection procedure more than one study is needed, so that any bias due to specific features of any particular study will not have an unduly large influence on the findings. How many studies are required and how can we summarise and aggregate the results of several studies in order to draw conclusions? Various statistical techniques have been developed to resolve the problem: these are now discussed within the context of personnel selection but you will see them mentioned throughout this book, as they have applications in many areas of work psychology.

An example will help to illustrate the way in which the results of validation studies may be cumulated and summarised. A researcher may, for example, be interested in the extent to which a particular individual difference characteristic, such as intelligence, achievement motivation or verbal ability (call this factor X) is predictive of managerial performance. As already noted, any individual study, using a particular sample of managers, will not give a definitive result for the validity of factor X. Consider for a moment why this is so. In other words consider what things might cause the results of any specific study to be less than perfectly accurate.

Table 5.2	Major evaluative standards for personnel selection procedures

1 Discrimination
The measurement procedures involved should provide for clear discrimination between candidates. If candidates all obtain similar assessments (i.e. scores, if a numerical system is used), selection decisions cannot be made. Of course, this discrimination should be based on job-relevant criteria and not irrelevant factors such as gender or ethnicity.

2 Validity and reliability
The technical qualities of the measurement procedures must be adequate (*see* Chapter 4).

3 Legality and fairness
The measures must not discriminate *unfairly* against members of any specific subgroup of the population (e.g. ethnic minorities).

4 Administrative convenience/practicality
The procedures should be acceptable within the organisation and capable of being implemented effectively within the organisation's administrative structure. Those administering the procedures may need appropriate training. For example, to administer a personality inventory or cognitive ability tests, professional qualifications are required.

5 Cost and development time
Given the selection decisions (e.g. number of jobs, number of candidates, type of jobs) involved, the costs involved and the time taken to develop adequate procedures need to be balanced with the potential benefits. This is essentially a question of utility.

6 Applicant reactions
Applicant reactions have important consequences for an organisation. If the best candidates reject the job offer, then the utility of the selection system is reduced. The best candidates may decide to work for competitor organisations and speak negatively about their treatment. In addition, dissatisfied candidates at selection are more likely to take legal action to challenge the outcome.

7 Generates appropriate information for feedback
When using selection tools such as psychometric tests, it is good practice to ensure that candidates receive appropriate and useful feedback. Sometimes, giving detailed feedback is difficult to achieve in high-volume recruitment. However, most candidates will expect some level of feedback after the selection process, especially those who have reached the latter stages of the selection process but have not been offered the job.

Table 5.3 provides a list of these features, with a brief explanation of how they may influence the accuracy of the result obtained from any study. If you need a reminder of the meaning of the word 'correlation', refer back to Chapter 2. As Table 5.3 makes clear, some of the problems are caused by sampling error (item 1) and imperfect reliability in the selection method, imperfect reliability in the criterion

Table 5.3	Major sources of distortion in validation studies

1   Sampling error
The small samples (e.g. 50-150) used in many validation studies mean that the results obtained may be unduly influenced by the effects of small numbers of people within the sample whose results are unusual. As sample size increases, these irregularities usually balance each other out and a more reliable result is obtained.

2   Poor measurement precision
The measurement of psychological qualities at both the predictor (i.e. selection method) and criterion (i.e. job performance) stage of the validation process is subject to unsystematic error. No selection or performance measure is infallible: the result we get from a selection method comprises the candidate's true score *plus* error. The error (unreliability) in the scores obtained will *reduce* the maximum possible observed correlation between predictor and criterion: the error is unsystematic and random, thus this element of the predictor or criterion score will not correlate systematically with anything. This means that as reliability decreases, the maximum possible correlation between predictor and criterion will decrease.

3   Restricted range of scores
The sample of people used in a validation study may not provide the full (theoretically possible) range of scores on the predictor and/or criterion measures. A restricted range of scores has a straightforward statistical effect: it limits the size of the linear correlation between two variables. So, just like unreliability, range restriction in a sample serves to reduce the magnitude of the observed correlation coefficient.

measure (item 2) and range restriction in the selection method scores (item 3). Consider these sources of error in relation to our example of the predictive validity of factor X. The sources of error are usually referred to as *artefacts* because they are not part of the natural relationship under investigation, but are a consequence of the particular investigative procedures used in the study (carrying out research in functioning organisations is very different from carrying out research in the laboratory setting). If the researcher in our example was able to identify 10 studies of the predictive validity of factor X, each study would be inaccurate due to the artefacts that impacted upon that study. Sampling error would be present because in each study the sample involved would not be perfectly representative of the population (studies with larger samples would of course be less prone to sampling error, because the sample is a bigger percentage of the available population).

Exercise 5.1   The importance of sample characteristics

To get a clearer idea of the importance of sampling error, think about how confident you would be that a random sample of six people from your family gave a good estimate of the average height of human beings. Then consider what you would need to do - and how large the sample would need to be - to get a good estimate.

Now consider your fellow students, or work colleagues. Select a random sample of 10 per cent of them. Think about their academic or work performance. If you just looked at the performance of this sample how good an estimate would you have of the whole population of students or work colleagues? Again, what you would need to do - and how large the sample would need to be - to get a good estimate of the average work/academic performance in these groups?

As far as unreliability and range restriction are concerned, these artefacts will adversely affect observed validity coefficients (i.e. the validity will appear to be less than it actually is). Test reliability may be calculated and expressed in a numerical form, with zero indicating total unreliability (e.g. in a totally unreliable test someone's score on a second administration could not be predicted with any accuracy whatever from his or her score on the first). To illustrate the impact of even modest deviations from reliability (0.8 is usually taken as the ideal, acceptable lower limit), Table 5.4 shows how the confidence interval for estimating an individual's *true* score on the test gets wider and wider as test reliability decreases.

Key Learning Point

Studies with larger sample sizes are less prone to sampling error and more likely to give reliable results.

Even with good reliability (0.8), two apparently quite different observed scores such as 94 and 112 could, because of a lack of measurement precision, have identical true scores. When data from unreliable tests are used to calculate correlation coefficients, the effect is clear. An unreliable test contains a large amount of random error. Obviously these random factors will not vary systematically (i.e. correlate) with any other factors; hence, as the reliability of a measure decreases,

Table 5.4   The impact of different reliabilities on an estimated true score

	Reliability		
	0.9	0.8	0.6
Observed score	100	100	100
Probable (95% confidence) range for candidate's true score	91-109	87-113	81-119

the opportunity for the measure to correlate with any other variable also decreases. Indeed, in technical terms the reliability of a measure sets a precise limit on the possible magnitude of its correlation with any other variable: the square root of the reliability is the maximum possible level of correlation (*see* Moser and Schuler, 1989). Similarly, the availability of only a restricted range of scores will set an artificially low ceiling on the magnitude of any observed correlation.

Consider what tends to happen in a predictive validity study. The candidates who score badly on the selection tests are (quite sensibly) not offered employment. If these low-scoring candidates were offered jobs (i.e. if the organisation was inexplicably benevolent!) they would be expected to perform badly. This link between people with low selection test scores producing low job performance scores is an important element in producing high validity coefficients. However, we almost never get to collect the performance scores from those who do badly at selection: the low scorers are excluded from the sample in the validation study. The resulting validity coefficient can be based only on high and average scorers, where differences in job performance will be much less extreme. The resulting validity coefficient will thus be limited in magnitude.

The main strategy for managing this problem of *range restriction* is to apply a statistical correction using formulas to estimate the correlation in the population of interest (*see* Sackett and Yang, 2000, for a detailed summary). This issue has been debated recently and the most accurate estimates of range restriction occur when the researcher can identify the mechanism by which restriction occurred (e.g. *direct* restriction is due to the use of the test for selection versus *indirect* restriction due to use of another predictor that is correlated with the test as the basis for selection; *see* Hunter *et al.*, 2006, for a detailed review). In other words, if the researcher has information about the standard deviation of test scores in the population of interest (e.g. the applicant pool where there will be low, average and high scores) as well as in the restricted sample, estimates can be made of the correlation in the population of interest. This correction for restriction of range is often needed in validation studies: it usually raises the validity coefficient (i.e. the corrected coefficient is often higher than the observed coefficient). However, Hunter and colleagues (2006) concluded that, in general, corrections for restriction of range may produce conservative *underestimates* of the actual validity of selection methods.

Key Learning Point

Restriction of range in scores will artificially limit the size of validity coefficients and give misleadingly low results. Failure to take range restriction into account can dramatically distort research findings, underestimating the predictive validity of selection methods and processes.

The statistical procedures of meta-analysis (Oswald and Converse, 2005; Hermelin and Robertson, 2001) involve methods for estimating the amount of sampling error in a set of studies and hence calculating a more accurate estimate of the validity coefficient in question. As explained in Chapter 2, meta-analysis is a statistical procedure for aggregating the results from many separate studies in order to obtain a more stable indication of the effect under investigation. More complex meta-analysis formulae also allow the estimation of validity coefficients corrected for unreliability and range restriction (Hunter and Schmidt, 2004). Notice that removing the effect of sampling error does not change the magnitude of the validity coefficients; it changes the estimated variance (i.e. the spread) in observed coefficients and hence narrows the confidence interval around the average coefficient (i.e. we can be more confident about what the true coefficient actually is). As you might expect, correcting for unreliability and range restriction will increase the magnitude of the mean validity coefficients. The development and use of meta-analytic procedures have had a considerable impact on personnel selection. Research findings from meta-analyses have allowed researchers to see past the problems associated with conducting research on functioning selection processes and isolate the extent to which different personnel selection methods predict job performance.

Hermelin and Robertson (2001) demonstrated that around 50 per cent of variance in the meta-analytic coefficients was explained by the correctable experimental artefacts of sampling error, *direct* range restriction in the predictor variable and criterion unreliability. Therefore, when interpreting results from meta-analytic studies, remember that statistical corrections are likely to have been applied so that the 'operational' or 'true' validity coefficients are reported.

Key Learning Point

Meta-analysis has been used extensively to derive estimates of the validity of personnel selection procedures.

One of the most often referenced meta-analysis studies reported is by Schmidt and Hunter (1998), who based their results on 85 years of research in personnel selection. This study separated the results of selection studies into two categories: (i) training performance used as criteria and (ii) overall job performance used as criteria to examine employee performance. The results showed that the predictive validity for each selection method is broadly similar in predicting both training and overall job performance criteria. Since this study there have been several other meta-analytic studies on the relative accuracy of different selection methods. The significant research evidence on each of the techniques listed in Table 5.5 is discussed next in this chapter. Also included is an estimate of the extent of usage, and likely applicant reaction to, each technique.

STOP TO CONSIDER

Have a close look at Table 5.5. You will see that the best selection methods are not always the most widely used. Also, there are some quite weak methods that are widely used. Why do you think this might be? Think about how different stakeholders in the selection process might view the various selection methods (e.g. might there be some that managers prefer to use). Table 5.2 lists some practical issues that might also help you with this task. Is it always practical or necessary to use the selection methods with the highest validity - and if not, why not?

Table 5.5	A summary of studies on the validity of selection procedures		
Selection method	Evidence for criterion-related validity	Applicant reactions	Extent of use*
Structured interviews	High	Moderate to positive	High
Cognitive ability tests	High	Negative to moderate	Moderate
Personality measures	Moderate	Negative to moderate	Moderate
Situational judgement tests	High	Moderate to positive	Low
Biodata	Can be high	Moderate	Moderate
Work sample tests	High	Positive	Low
Assessment centres	Can be high	Positive	Moderate
Handwriting	Low	Negative to moderate	Low
References	Low	Positive	High

*Note that there are international differences in the extent of usage for various techniques. For example, assessment centres are used more frequently in the United Kingdom than in the United States.

Interviews

Interviews have long been the most popular form of personnel selection (e.g. Keenan, 1995). They are used by nearly every organisation and for selecting employees at all levels. However, despite this popularity, interviews have been criticised for being subjective, unreliable and vulnerable to bias. This was probably fair criticism 30 years ago, when interviews were often little more than an informal chat between an interviewer and a prospective employee. However, we now know considerably more about how selection decisions are reached, and the potential sources of error and bias, so there is the potential to design and execute better interviews. There have been several reviews of the literature on selection interviews in recent years (e.g. Dipboye, 2005; Posthuma *et al.*, 2002). These reviews show that interviews can be structured, and interviewers trained, in ways that considerably enhance their validity. Therefore an important point to remember is that the employment interview can represent an extremely important and valid means of selecting employees *if* it is structured to ensure that (i) interviewer questions are based on a job analysis, (ii) questions are consistent across interviewers and interviewees, and (iii) the interviewers use a consistent set of criteria to evaluate interviewee responses. In fact, a meta-analysis by Huffcutt *et al.* (2001) found that criterion-related validities for interviews compared favourably with other forms of personnel selection such as cognitive ability tests.

However, while there is considerable evidence to support the use of structured interviews in selection, there is much less agreement as to *why* selection interviews predict work performance. In a recent review, Dipboye (2005) notes that the majority of previous research on interviews has focused on (i) analysing the way interviewers process information, (ii) the social processes involved in the interaction between the interviewer and the candidate, and (iii) the quality of interviewer assessments. Investigations of these issues have found that factors such as non-verbal and verbal cues and impression management can play an important role in determining the evaluation that a candidate receives in the interview. These issues are discussed a little later. However, what this research suggests is that great care needs to be taken in the design and execution of interviews for them to have a chance of exhibiting good reliability and validity.

The two most common forms of structured interview used in selection are behavioural interviewing (e.g. Janz, 1989) and situational interviewing (e.g. Maurer *et al.*, 1999). Also known as Behavioural Pattern Description Interviews (BPDIs), behavioural interviewing involves asking interviewees to describe previous behaviour in past situations that are relevant to the job they are being interviewed for. This type of interviewing is based upon the central premise that past behaviour predicts future behaviour. In essence, interviewers are looking for evidence that an individual has demonstrated behaviour that would suggest they are capable of similar behaviour in a job situation. This type of interviewing forms the foundation of much of the competency-based interviewing that is popular today. For example, an interviewer may ask an interviewee: 'Can you please describe a time when you have been able to persuade someone to do something that they had initially been unsure about?' This could provide an opportunity to demonstrate behavioural indicators for a competency concerned with *persuasion and negotiating skills*. In both competency and BPDI interviews, interviewers use a behaviourally anchored rating scale (BARS. *See* Table 5.6) to rate interviewee responses, thereby helping to ensure consistency of rating across interviews.

Key Learning Point

Situational interviews and competency-based structured interviews produce good criterion-related validity.

In contrast, situational interviews are based on goal-setting theory. These interviews present interviewees with hypothetical job-related situations and ask them to indicate how they would respond. They are based on the assumption that *intention to behave predicts future behaviour*. For example, imagine you are applying for a place on a graduate recruitment programme with a national retail organisation. During the interview you may be asked what you would do if you were the acting manager for a supermarket who arrived one morning to discover that nearly 25 per cent of your staff had called in sick because of a 'flu epidemic. How would you respond? Of course there are a number of different possible responses. However, the interviewer will compare your response with those provided by a group of experts who have

Table 5.6	Example situational interview question and response anchors to assess initiative

'You are the new personnel officer in a large car manufacturing plant and the boiler is not working properly. The temperature has dropped below the legal minimum and the shop floor workers are threatening to walk out at any minute. The trade union representative is demanding an urgent meeting with the managing director. The managing director is playing golf with the chairman today (they are using the opportunity to discuss a hostile takeover of a competitor organisation). Production is way behind schedule for the week and the costs of stopping the line could be enormous. What would you do in this situation?'

Behavioural indicators and score points (Poor, Satisfactory, Excellent)

Poor	Stop the line immediately.
	Send the workers home.
	Call the managing director on her mobile phone to ask advice.
	Tell the union representative that the meeting will have to wait.
Satisfactory	Ask the employees to stop work immediately.
	Call all employees together including the union representative for a public meeting.
	Arrange for the technicians to repair the boiler on emergency call-out.
	Text the managing director asking her to get in touch when she finishes playing golf with the chairman.
Excellent	Ask the employees to continue working on the line, arrange for portable heaters to be installed immediately. Ask catering to provide free hot drinks for all employees.
	Meet the union representative to discuss your actions and arrange a time later that day to review the situation.
	Log the incident and actions you took and leave a note on the managing director's desk to discuss when she comes into the office.

Note: The indicators reflect an excellent, average and poor response reflective of initiative. They were previously agreed by the personnel department in the car manufacturing company. Note that what constitutes poor, satisfactory or excellent responses may be quite highly organisation-specific.

been asked to indicate the type of responses they would expect from good, average and poor performers in this role. Interviewers will often use a behaviourally anchored rating scale to rate a response and compare it with those provided by others. Table 5.6 provides an illustration of a situational interview question and a scoring key using behavioural indicators.

A key problem with situational interviewing, however, is that it takes no account of different levels of experience. For example, there may be recent graduates with no relevant previous experience who are competing alongside other applicants with several years' experience. One might therefore expect the experienced applicants to have a better understanding of what is required in terms of a 'good' answer. Individuals with little experience yet great potential to learn may be disadvantaged. A further potential problem, which besets both behavioural and situational interviewing, is the criticism that what interviewees *say* in selection interviews may bear very little relation to what they actually *do* once in the job.

While no personnel selection will demonstrate absolute comparability between what is assessed during selection and subsequent work behaviour, interviews are particularly vulnerable to criticism. One reason for this is that interviewers are often worried about being deceived by candidates engaging in impression management. That is, individuals once appointed may demonstrate altogether different patterns of behaviour once in the job. It assumes that the task of the interviewer is to peel away layers of impression management in order to uncover the true person underneath.

However, this may be an overly simplistic notion. Indeed, certain researchers have argued that personality is itself socially constructed, and that there is no 'true' persona hiding beneath layers of presentation waiting to be discovered. As such, individuals adapt proactively to different situations and people according to needs.

It could also be argued that this ability to understand different contexts and adapt one's behaviour to meet their varying needs is an exceptionally useful skill, one that can be useful in helping an individual to navigate their work environment successfully (Rosenfeld *et al.*, 2002). However, recent research suggests that the way in which individuals choose to present themselves during interviews (their impression management) may reflect cognitive personality characteristics associated with motivation. For example, Silvester *et al.* (2002) found that more successful applicants demonstrated an attributional style also found in higher performers at work. Individuals who explained past behaviour in terms of causes that they were able to control tended to be rated more favourably by interviewers (e.g. 'I didn't do well in the exam because I left my revision until too late') than those explained performance in terms of uncontrollable causes (e.g. 'The lecturer didn't like us so he made the examination question too difficult'). Interestingly, the interviewer's own attributional style was also important in determining how they evaluated the attributions made by the interviewee (i.e. impression management is the result of an interaction between what the interviewer sees as desirable behaviour and what the interviewee sees as desirable behaviour). More recent research has also found that coaching interviewees to perform in interviews can influence scores. Maurer *et al.* (2008) examined coaching interventions designed to help interviewees focus on interview-relevant content and to help them convey the content accurately (as opposed to interventions designed to teach interviewees to manipulate their scores). Using a predictive validation study of a situational panel interview, Maurer *et al.* (2008) showed that the predictive validity of interview performance was *higher* in a sample of coached interviewees compared to a sample of uncoached interviewees.

A summary of lessons learned from the huge amount of research on selection interviews appears in Table 5.7.

Table 5.7	Tips for best practice structured interview design

- Base questions on a thorough job analysis
- Ask exactly the same questions of each candidate, limit prompting, use follow-up questions but limit elaboration
- Use relevant questions and design them as either situational, competency-based, biographical or knowledge questions
- Use longer interviews or larger number of questions, control the input of ancillary information (e.g. CV [résumé], references)
- Do not allow questions from the candidate until after the interview (when the data have been collected)
- Rate each answer using multiple rating scales
- Use detailed anchored rating scales and take detailed notes
- Use multiple interviewers where possible
- Use the same interviewer(s) across all candidates and provide extensive interviewer training to enhance reliability
- Use statistical rather than clinical prediction

Psychometric tests and measures of personality

In the 1980s, Cronbach described psychometric tests as providing 'a standardized sample of behaviour which can be described by a numerical scale or category system'. In other words, psychometric tests offer a quantitative assessment of some psychological attribute, (such as verbal reasoning ability, general intelligence, numerical reasoning ability, etc.). For personnel selection purposes psychometric tests may be divided into two categories: cognitive ability tests (e.g. general intelligence, spatial ability, numerical ability) and personality measures (*see* Chapter 3 for more information on specific tests). The research for both categories can be considered in relation to their validity for selection purposes in organisations.

Cognitive ability tests in selection

In the past 30 years, there has been an explosion in the use of cognitive ability tests for selection purposes. For many practitioners conducting large-scale recruitment programmes, ability tests are relatively cost-effective selection tools. Unlike most other selection techniques, to purchase and administer psychometric tests in many countries you have to demonstrate a specific level of competence in administration, scoring tests and interpreting test scores (e.g. the British Psychological Society's certificates of competence in occupational testing).

In the 1970s, particularly in the United States, cognitive ability testing became increasingly unpopular and it was common for people to argue that such tests had no useful role in personnel selection. The meta-analytic work and the evidence for validity generalisation (i.e. the generalisation of validity across different types of jobs and different organisational settings) caused work psychologists to revise these views. In general, cognitive ability tests have been shown to be the single best predictor of job performance (e.g. Sackett *et al.*, 2008; Ones *et al.*, 2005; Gottfredson, 2002; Salgado *et al.*, 2003; Schmidt and Hunter, 1998) with validity coefficients generally shown to be approximately 0.50 (i.e. explaining an impressive 25 per cent of the variance in the test-taker's future job performance). Recent meta-analysis studies have demonstrated consistently that cognitive ability accurately predicts future job performance across almost all occupations and organisations. In their large-scale review of many meta-analytic studies (a meta-analysis of meta-analyses), Ones *et al.* (2005) show that the evidence for the validity of cognitive ability tests in predicting job performance is overwhelming. In this respect, many researchers argue that cognitive ability tests are perhaps the best and most widely applicable predictor in personnel selection because all jobs require some cognitive ability to learn the job and perform effectively. Ones and Viswesvaran (2003) suggest that the predictive validity of cognitive ability tests tends to be higher for high-complexity jobs (0.58) than for low-complexity jobs (0.23), but still significant regardless of the level of complexity. A high-complexity job (such as, believe it or not, a professor in work psychology) involves *denser* processing of information than a lower-complexity job (such as a taxi driver).

In addition to tests developed to assess general cognitive ability ('*g*') (*see* Chapter 3), sometimes referred to as general mental ability (GMA), there are tests tailored to assess specific abilities such as mechanical comprehension, or spatial ability. Such tests measure '*g*' to some extent, but also have a specific ability component which means that tests of specific abilities could be more predictive for specific jobs. For example, spatial ability might be more important in mechanical engineering jobs than it would be for a journalist or author. However, Ones and Viswesvaran (2003) suggest that the predictive validity of specific abilities stems from their assessment of a general information-processing ability (i.e. the general cognitive ability required to perform well on the test). Thus, if the general cognitive ability is held constant, most of the predictive power of specific ability tests disappears. On the other hand, in considering the practical application of tests in organisations, specific ability tests may have more face validity and generate positive candidate reactions in a selection context.

Bertua and colleagues (2005) report a meta-analysis that compares the validity of tests of general mental ability (GMA) and specific cognitive abilities when predicting job performance and training success in the UK. The analyses were based on a data set of 283 independent samples with job performance as the criterion, and 223 with training success as the criterion: by any standard this is an impressive number of studies. The results showed that GMA and specific ability tests are valid predictors of job performance and training success, with validity coefficients in the region of 0.5–0.6. As anticipated, the highest validities were found between cognitive tests and various performance criteria (i.e. job performance and training success) in occupational groups with greater job complexity. Similar studies that use data from a number of different countries and cultures have found similar results. Salgado and colleagues (2003) examined the validity of GMA and other specific cognitive abilities, including verbal, numerical, spatial–mechanical, perceptual and memory across 10 European countries (with N ranging from 946 to 16,065). Once again, GMA and specific cognitive ability were found to be very good predictors of job performance and training success across Europe.

Key Learning Point

Cognitive ability tests produce good criterion-related validities for a wide range of jobs in various countries and cultures.

Arguments against the use of cognitive tests in personnel selection are often based on the belief that such tests are unfair to ethnic minorities. The evidence on this issue is reviewed briefly in a separate section on fairness later in this chapter. In overview, the evidence suggests cognitive ability testing does not provide differentially 'unfair' predictions for people from different ethnic minority groups (*see* Ones *et al.*, 2007b), although it may not be appropriate to use ability tests for all selection purposes. A second argument against the use of cognitive tests is that candidate reactions to them can be less than positive. Both test publishers and users would agree that how the tests are used is critical to their effectiveness as selection tools. Port and Patterson (2003) suggest that best practice guidelines in using tests in selection are not always followed, and some test users are 'less than thorough' in their use of tests in selection (e.g. they may neglect to explain why tests are being used or fail to provide full feedback on the test results). Therefore, the way tests are used, rather than the tests themselves, might be responsible for candidates' negative reactions to them.

In reviewing large-scale review of many meta-analytic studies, Sackett *et al.* (2008) address many of the criticisms commonly levelled against cognitive ability tests. These criticisms are listed in Exercise 5.2.

Criticisms made against the use of cognitive tests *(adapted from Sackett* et al.*, 2008).*

Assertion 1:   Tests predict badly, if at all. Correlations with commonly used criteria are small.

Assertion 2:   Even if tests do predict to the modest degree outlined above, they predict performance in the short-term only.

Assertion 3:   Even if tests have some predictive value, they are valuable only for screening out individuals with low scores. Above a certain threshold, higher scores do not matter.

Assertion 4:   Tests serve merely as a proxy for wealth and privilege; they reflect socio-economic status (SES) rather than developed abilities.

Assertion 5:   Tests are readily coached; those with knowledge of this fact and the financial resources to pay for coaching programmes can substantially increase their scores.

Assertion 6:   Tests are biased against members of racial and ethnic minority groups, and sometimes against women as well.

Assertion 7:   While minority group members obtain lower mean scores on tests, they perform just as well as majority group members once admitted or hired.

Assertion 8:   Motivational mechanisms explain majority–minority group mean differences.

Suggested exercises

In turn, consider each of the assertions above.

1   Do you agree with any or all of the assertions?

2   What are the implications if an assertion is true?

3   What evidence exists to support your view? Use this part of the task to review this part of the chapter.

What do the experts say?

Based on large-scale studies, Sackett *et al.* (2008) conclude that none of the assertions above is supported by the evidence. By contrast, the evidence suggests a very positive review in that (a) ability tests are generally valid for their intended uses in predicting a wide variety of aspects of short-term and long-term job performance, (b) validity is not an artefact of SES, (c) coaching is not a major determinant of test-performance, (d) tests do not generally exhibit bias by under-predicting the performance of minority group members, and (e) test-taking motivational mechanisms are not major determinants of test performance in these high-stakes settings. Sackett *et al.* (2008) is an excellent review article for those interested in this topic.

In summary, the research findings clearly demonstrate the validity of cognitive ability tests for selection purposes. However, there are two main issues to consider for future research. First, while selection research is focusing on a unitary trait of general mental ability, research into intelligence itself is moving away from this simple conceptualisation and developing multifaceted models of intelligence (*see* Chapter 3). Second, in the last decade, the amount of research investigating the use of new technology in personnel selection procedures (particularly Internet testing) has dramatically increased. The widespread use of the Internet is likely to transform personnel selection procedures in the future. In their review, Lievens and Harris (2003) suggest although Internet recruitment is now being used on a global basis, the research literature cannot keep pace with its proliferation (see also Sackett and Lievens, 2008). The limited evidence available suggests that applicants have more positive reactions to cognitive ability tests administered via the Internet than they do to 'pencil and paper' equivalents. The issues surrounding the impact of technology on selection procedures is discussed in more detail later in this chapter.

Personality measures

The personality measures used in selection activities are usually based on some kind of trait-factor analytic model of personality (described in Chapter 3). For more than two decades the status of personality measures as predictors of performance was low. However, some authors have argued persuasively that personality is an important determinant of behaviour at work and there has been a resurgence of interest in personality assessment in the past three decades.

Results from various meta-analytic studies (*see* Salgado *et al.*, 2003) suggest that conscientiousness is a valid predictor of performance across most jobs and organisational settings, with an average criterion-related validity of 0.23. Ones *et al.* (2007a) report that particular facets of conscientiousness are predictive of job performance, for example, the facet 'achievement' is predictive of 'overall job performance' and 'task performance' ($r = 0.18$ and $r = 0.22$, respectively). Openness to experience tends to be positively correlated with training performance across many job roles. Emotional stability has been shown to be positively associated with job performance across many organisational settings. Extroversion is generally found to correlate positively with performance in jobs such as sales, where performance is judged within an interpersonal environment.

Hough and Furnham (2003) highlight that validity of personality variables varies according to the type of performance being measured and job type. For example, conscientiousness correlates most highly with overall job performance, compared to all other Big Five personality dimensions. However, conscientiousness is negatively correlated with creativity (a competency for many job roles). In this way, depending on the job, the facets of conscientiousness are *differentially* important. Hough and Furnham (2003) report that the dependability facet of conscientiousness correlates 0.18 with overall job performance in sales jobs and 0.03 with overall job performance in managerial jobs. In addition, when comparing the validity for facets of conscientiousness for managerial jobs, results show that the achievement facet correlates 0.17 with overall job performance but the dependability facet only correlated 0.03 (more or less zero, or no relationship) with overall job performance. In other studies, research suggests that agreeableness is positively associated with job performance in some job roles, but chief executives of organisations tend to be low on agreeableness (as you might have noticed!).

Conscientiousness tends to predict overall job performance over a range of occupational settings. However, when exploring validity at the facet level, results are criterion dependent. For other personality factors, their relationship with job performance tends to depend upon the nature of the job being carried out.

In a recent debate, Ones *et al.* (2007a) cite meta-analytic data to suggest that, in contrast to ability testing, the predictive validity of personality measures for 'overall job performance' is not seen across all occupational areas and settings. Instead, only the trait of conscientiousness is predictive of 'overall job performance' over a range of occupations; the predictive traits for other occupations vary along with the occupations themselves. For example, for managerial roles, it is the 'achievement' and 'dependability' facets of conscientiousness that predict job performance. Morgeson *et al.* (2007a) contributed to the debate by expressing concern over the lack of consistent evidence for the predictive validity of personality measures in the selection context. Ones *et al.* (2007a) responded to Morgeson *et al.* (2007a), arguing that there is supporting evidence from many meta-analytic studies for the predictive validity of personality measures for various organisational outcomes, including 'overall job performance' ($r = 0.27$), 'individual teamwork' and 'leadership criteria'. Ones and colleagues concluded that the evidence is 'substantial' and that the valid use of personality measurement in selection is confirmed. Tett and Christiansen (2007) also responded to the concerns of Morgeson *et al.* (2007a), suggesting the individuality of different measures of personality (i.e. they are all a bit different) and each measure's relationship to relevant organisational behaviour (i.e. different jobs have different performance criteria) should be considered: therefore, the predictive validity of personality measurement is often underestimated. Tett and Christiansen (2007) argue that research should focus on identifying the specific circumstances that yield strong (or weak), and positive (or negative) relationships between personality traits and job performance. Morgeson *et al.* (2007b) responded by arguing that the statistical correction methods applied to the ('very low') validity coefficients for personality measures (remember such corrections tend to raise the validity coefficient) are not appropriate, meaning that evidence for the validity of personality measures is poor. They also suggest that only the 'job proficiency' outcomes (i.e. measures of how good someone is at their job) are relevant, thus arguably rendering Ones *et al.*'s (2007a) inclusion of outcomes such as 'leader emergence' unimpressive.

This shows the ongoing debate about using personality measures in selection: you might therefore find it difficult to reach conclusions! However, it would be fair to say that the research indicates that personality variables can be useful in predicting job performance. Perhaps it is more important to recognise that their predictive accuracy is increased when the predictor and criterion variables are closely matched (e.g. in terms of their complexity, or job type).

Personality measures used in selection can add significant incremental validity for some job roles, particularly when predictor and criterion variables are carefully matched.

A common concern for practitioners involved in recruitment is whether job applicants could fake (or intentionally distort) their responses on a personality measure and present themselves in a socially desirable manner. Morgeson *et al.* (2007a) questioned whether the potential for applicant faking in the completion of personality measures limits their usefulness for selection purposes. Many authors have debated this issue of faking and response distortion in recent years. Hough and Furnham (2003) suggest that when instructed to do so (in a laboratory setting, for example), people can distort their responses to self-report personality measures in either a positive or negative direction, depending on the instruction they are given. However, in real-world settings, the majority of the evidence suggests that intentional distortion *does exist but it does not have a substantial influence on the criterion-related validity of personality measures*. The research suggests that in real-life settings distortion is reduced when warnings about the detection of faking and the potential negative consequences of faking are included in the administration instructions to applicants. In practice, most personality measures used in selection will include a scale to assess social desirability and intentional distortion. Ones *et al.* (2007) argue that experimental manipulation of conditions in laboratory-based studies of faking is very likely to exaggerate the actual effect of faking on validity (as seen in the real world): they urge researchers to conduct more studies of faking in real-life settings. Tett and Christiansen (2007) suggest that of those predictive validity studies conducted in real-life settings, results demonstrate that faking might have an effect on validity, but does not remove validity entirely.

In overview, the literature suggests that when used appropriately, personality measures can add significant incremental validity in a selection process because they measure something unique that also predicts performance. However, we illustrate here the ongoing debate. Morgeson *et al.* (2007b) cite Guion (1965): '*In view of the problems . . . one must question the wisdom . . . of using personality as instruments of decision in employment procedures*' (p. 379), but Ones *et al.* (2007) argue that the abandoning of personality measurement in selection would be senseless, as evidence proves its value. Future research is likely to consider cross-cultural differences in personality testing. With an increasingly global marketplace there is much work to be done to explore the use of personality testing on an international basis.

Exercise 5.3	Personalities and jobs

Think about the five different jobs listed below:

- Sales job in a large international advertising agency.
- Teacher in a secondary school.
- A plumber running a business independently.
- A pharmacist working in a small shop in the local community.
- Financial controller in a large manufacturing organisation.

Suggested exercise

For each role, suggest which personality factors might be important in performing the job. Using the information from Chapter 3 on personality, discuss the personality factors that might help or hinder effectiveness in each role. You may also like to think of how people with very different personalities could do a job equally well – but in very different ways.

Assessment centres

An assessment centre (AC) is a popular and effective method of recruitment consisting of a multifaceted assessment process. An AC is not a place, as the name assessment *centre* may suggest, but instead is a term used to describe the setting of multiple assessments of individuals using different methods, and involving multiple observers called assessors. In a typical AC, numerous applicants are invited together for between half a day and three days of assessment. Assessment methods can include: work sample exercises, group exercise, presentation, in-tray exercise, role play, practical skills, interviews (competency and/or situational) and psychometric tests (aptitude, personality, knowledge-based, situational judgement); the particular combination depends on the target job role. ACs profile an applicant's ability across a range of competencies and job-related contexts. The appeal of ACs lies in their generally good levels of criterion-related validity and face validity (Hough and Oswald, 2000). Although there has been much debate regarding the predictive validity of ACs, meta-analytic studies show the average validity of AC studies to be very good.

There are certain criteria that an assessment process must fulfil in order to be defined as an AC. These include: (1) explicit dimensions (now more commonly referred to as competencies: see Chapter 4) derived from a job analysis which define the key knowledge, skills and abilities required by a candidate in order to perform the role they are being assessed for; (2) multiple techniques (methods) to provide information relevant to the dimensions to be assessed and the context in which those dimensions are to be demonstrated (e.g. different aspects of the role); (3) multiple, trained assessors to observe and evaluate each candidate; and (4) a systematic procedure to record and rate specific behaviours as they occur. Independent assessor ratings and reports are then brought together to form an overall rating for each candidate at what is often referred to as the 'wash-up' or moderation session: this is where candidates' performance is discussed and selection decisions are made.

Key Learning Point

Assessment centres assess an applicant on multiple competencies using multiple job-related exercises and multiple trained assessors.

The design of an AC reflects the need to assess the extent to which applicants can demonstrate a range of competencies. Consequently a series of exercises and assessment tools are developed that: (1) are able to elicit the required behaviours; (2) reflect the actual content of the role; (3) assess applicants' performance in a variety of job-related situations; and (4) allow for different assessors to assess these competencies over different exercises.

Typically competencies are assessed multiple times within each selection centre, using different exercises to assess the same competencies. Typically each exercise assesses multiple competencies. For instance, a group exercise may be assessing leadership skills and communication skills. However, exercises should never attempt to assess *all* of the competencies, as this would overload assessors with too many sets of behavioural criteria to assess (Sackett and Tuzinski, 2001). Assessors are human and there are limits to their cognitive abilities. Certain exercises are best suited to assessing particular competencies. For example, a communication skills competency can be assessed in a presentation exercise and a group exercise, rather than in a psychometric test.

There is a substantial body of research debating the traditional assumptions that dimensions (competencies) are central to how ACs work. Lance (2008) conducted a review of the last 25 years of research into this so-called *'construct validity problem'*. This problem has plagued the AC literature and can be described as follows. It has generally been assumed that assessors look for evidence that candidates can or cannot demonstrate competence in each of the dimensions across the varying work-related situations in different exercises. However, a common finding is that performance ratings on individual AC component exercises often reflect factors associated with the *exercises, as opposed to the traits,* or 'constructs' that the AC is designed to measure. This relates to the problem of convergent validity versus discriminant validity: performance tends to be more consistent across dimensions (or competencies) within an exercise, than it is within a competency across different exercises (Lance, 2008).

The problem can be illustrated as follows. If dimensions are of central importance in assessor decision-making, one would expect relatively high correlations between different assessors' ratings of a candidate for the same competence (say communication skills) across different exercises. This would mean that the applicant demonstrates good communication skills in a presentation, in a group exercise and in an in-tray exercise. However, they may not score highly for all competencies within a particular exercise. Cross-situational consistency across exercises rather than within exercises indicates that the AC has discriminant validity, i.e. that different traits are evaluated separately in each exercise. However, researchers have found that in most ACs assessors are more likely to provide similar ratings for an individual across different dimensions within the same exercise, rather than for the same competency across different exercises (Robertson and Smith, 2001). This represents *convergent validity* and suggests that exercises, not dimensions, are the important construct behind candidate ratings. Another recent meta-analysis of 24 studies into the construct validity of ACs was conducted by Bowler and Woehr (2006), who found that AC exercises explain more variance in candidate performance than do AC dimensions.

This poses several challenges to work psychologists. Are ACs measuring what they are supposed to measure (i.e. a dimension or competency that drives performance across a range of situations)? If not, does it matter as long as they predict job performance? What other mechanisms might contribute to the validity of ACs? Some argue that the tasks that assessors have to undertake when observing and rating a candidate's behaviour are complex and demanding and that in general it is easier to provide an overall evaluation of effectiveness in a particular exercise. There has been much recent discussion around the construct validity problem. Arthur and colleagues (2008) responded to Lance (2008), suggesting that dimension-based AC construct validity should not be abandoned. Instead a more representative sample of constructs must be taken to represent the job content. They argue that the AC is theoretically sound and that the construct validity of AC dimensions may still stand up if the appropriate constructs (i.e. competencies that are relevant to the job role) are measured in the AC, and they are defined in the appropriate way. This is an important point as it represents a possible explanation for the problems associated with AC construct validity. Rather than viewing construct validity as problematic for ACs, there may be good reasons why performance on the same dimension can differ between exercises. For example, a person may be much more effective at communicating on a one-to-one basis than presenting information in a public speaking context: a competency/dimension such as communication skills might be assessed in both contexts, with the same individual achieving different scores in the two different contexts. It may be that defining the competency differently (e.g. defining presentational communication skills and individual communication skills as two separate dimensions) might lead to greater consistency across exercises.

Key Learning Point

When designed appropriately, assessment centres are valid predictors of job performance. Construct validity is enhanced by ensuring the content is directly relevant to the target job role.

The AC is generally assumed to have good predictive validity because assessment is based upon direct observation of job-relevant behaviours. This enables assessors to predict how candidates will behave in the job by observing them engaging in job-relevant behaviour. Hermelin *et al.* (2007) conducted a meta-analysis of 26 studies into the predictive validity of ACs with performance ratings provided by participants' supervisors as the criteria. They found a correlation of 0.28 between 'overall assessment ratings' and ratings of performance by supervisors, providing recent evidence for the predictive validity of ACs. Another explanation for why ACs work is that incremental validity is achieved by using many different methods that assess separate and distinct aspects of performance. Therefore an AC is a better predictor because each exercise adds something to the predictive power of the process. Research has been conducted into the predictive validity of particular assessment methods used within ACs. Slivinski (2008) investigated the predictive validity of AC pencil-and-paper tests compared with the predictive validity of AC situational test measures: both tests were equally valid, but used together, both types of measures added incremental validity. Meriac *et al.* (2008) conducted a meta-analysis of 38 studies to find out whether seven particular AC dimensions (organising and planning, influencing others, drive, problem solving, stress tolerance, consideration/awareness of others and communication) were distinct from cognitive ability and personality. They found that although there was some overlap between performance on the AC dimensions and cognitive ability and personality, the relationship was small, showing that AC dimensions are, in the main, distinct from cognitive ability and personality. This indicates that AC dimensions add something unique to the prediction of performance over and above that offered by cognitive tests and personality measures.

In terms of the cost-effectiveness of ACs, Crail (2007) reported on the research findings of a survey carried out by *Employment Review*, which contacted individuals in personnel roles within 91 different private and public sector organisations. Although ACs are known for being a very expensive method of recruitment, 53 per cent of those surveyed felt this level of cost was 'justified'. Furthermore, Crail's results showed that over nine out of ten employers felt that ACs are effective for use in recruitment and, 47 per cent of employers surveyed felt that ACs are 'very effective' in recruiting new employees.

Exercise 5.4   Designing an assessment centre to recruit brain surgeons

This exercise describes the development of a new selection system to recruit neurosurgeons in the UK. The selection system consists of three phases. Firstly, applicants are 'longlisted' – in other words, there are checks on whether the applicant is a qualified and a registered doctor. Second, applicants are shortlisted on the basis of their application form, and finally, suitable applicants were invited to attend a one-day assessment centre. The assessment centre comprises seven exercises designed to measure a variety of competencies in a range of scenarios. Exercises consist of three interviews; two situational interviews, with one focusing on management scenarios and the other relating to clinical scenarios. The third interview is a competency-based structured interview.

The remaining four exercises consist of various work sample exercises including a telephone consultation exercise, a simulated doctor–patient consultation, an X-ray diagnosis and interpretation test and a practical skills assessment. The telephone consultation exercise consisted of a scenario whereby the candidate and a senior doctor engage in a role play regarding a medical emergency. The patient simulation exercise requires the candidate to engage in a conversation with an upset relative. The role of the relative is played by a trained actor. The X-ray diagnosis and interpretation exercise provided candidates with an image of a brain scan and candidates were asked to interpret the image and answer questions about the diagnosis and management of the case presented on the scan. The practical skills assessment is an objective structured assessment of technical skills, requiring candidates to demonstrate suturing and knot tying.

An illustration of the selection process, the weighting of the marks for the assessment centre, and the number of candidates participating at each stage of the process, is shown in Figure 5.1.

Selecting neurosurgeons is an example of a high-stakes selection process, meaning that the consequences of making the wrong decisions about who to appoint are

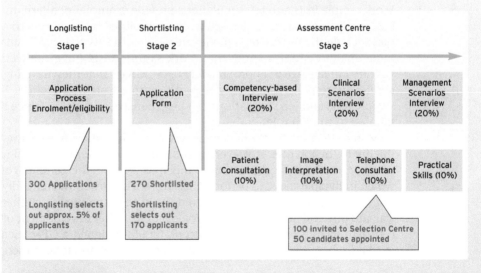

Figure 5.1   Selection process stages

higher than in the general selection context. This makes evaluation and validation processes even more essential. A psychometric evaluation of the new selection system will need to be conducted, by running tests to explore the reliability and validity of the exercises and the assessment centre overall. Candidates and assessors will be invited to complete an evaluation feedback questionnaire at the end of the assessment centre. The candidate evaluation questionnaire will contain items to measure candidates' (dis)agreement with a number of statements based on the concept of procedural and distributive justice (Gilliland, 1993). For example, questions will include the extent to which candidates felt they had sufficient opportunity to provide evidence of their abilities/achievements in the assessment centre, and the extent to which they felt well-treated throughout the process.

Suggested exercises

How do you select brain surgeons? From what you have read in the case study presented above:

1   Do you think the marks for each assessment centre exercise are weighted appropriately?

2   Why is it important to evaluate the selection process from the candidate perspective? Imagine you are a candidate attending the assessment centre.

3   How would you feel about the assessments used in this selection centre: would you think that they were fair and appropriate?

Work sample tests and job simulations

Work sample tests and job simulations provide examples of alternatives to the 'sign-based' approach to personnel selection exemplified by psychometric testing. Examples include the in-tray tests mentioned earlier in this chapter. Results from various meta-analytic studies show that work sample tests have high criterion-related validity (an average of approximately 0.55). Given that they have high face validity, applicants respond favourably to work sample tests in selection. However, work sample tests and job simulations can be expensive to develop (since they have to be tailored to the job role).

Many selection methods are criticised on the grounds that they have limited fidelity to the job role. However, work sample tests attempt to build realism into the selection methods by simulating as much as possible the genuine conditions under which individuals have to perform their work. They test how well individuals perform in those simulations. Simulations can differ in the extent to which there is psychological and physical fidelity to reality. For example, in her development of an assessment centre to recruit doctors, Patterson *et al.* (2005) designed a GP–patient consultation exercise, where medical actors play the role of patient and follow a script.

Key Learning Point

Work sample tests and job simulations show good criterion-related validity.

Situational judgement tests

An example of an assessment method with lower physical fidelity is where applicants are presented with paper-based scenarios in a written exercise. Here, applicants might be asked to indicate how they would respond in the situations described, and to justify their decisions. These types of assessments are sometimes referred to as *situational judgement tests* (SJTs). SJTs are designed to assess an applicant's judgement regarding situations where hypothetical work-based scenarios are presented to applicants, who make judgements about possible responses, and these responses are then assessed against a predetermined scoring key (Lievens *et al.*, 2008).

Scenarios are often created on the basis of job analysis findings and applicants can be required to make their judgements in the format of choosing the best option, worst option, or asked to rate effectiveness of alternatives. Their responses are typically scored by comparing them to the judgements of experts in the respective field (Bergman *et al.*, 2006). Some similarities can be seen between SJTs and situational interviews, assessment centre exercises and work samples, but there are key differences in terms of presentation (usually because SJTs are written), how options are presented, and how options are scored (i.e. predetermined scoring from a set of predetermined options), and the type of responses given.

Over the last 15 years, SJTs have become increasingly more popular (*see* Weekley and Ployhart, 2006, for a detailed review), though they actually date back to at least 1926, in the form of the George Washington Social Intelligence Test. The popularity of SJTs is seen most in large-scale selection, often at the shortlisting stage (Patterson *et al.*, 2009). There are a number of benefits from using SJTs. They are relatively easy and cost-effective to develop, administer and score. SJTs are also versatile in their presentation, and can be written, Web or video-based (Lievens *et al.*, 2008). However, although SJTs have become popular for practical reasons, their construct validity has remained elusive (and there remains uncertainty over how SJTs work and what they actually measure). That said, there is an emerging consensus that they are a measurement method for job-relevant attributes that reflect complex situations and events, are tailored to the particular context, and can be designed to measure a variety of cognitive and non-cognitive constructs (Lievens *et al.*, 2005).

Correlations between SJTs and personality are to be expected, due to the types of situations included in SJTs (e.g. many situations include interpersonal aspects of situations and tap into work preferences/styles). McDaniel and Nguyen (2001) conducted a meta-analysis and found that SJT scores are significantly related to the Big Five personality traits ($r = 0.31$ between SJTs and emotional stability; $r = 0.26$ for conscientiousness; $r = 0.25$ for agreeableness). Other researchers have found similar but not entirely consistent patterns (Clevenger *et al.*, 2001). This is likely to reflect the wide variation in content of the SJTs and the range of contexts in which they are used. In relation to cognitive ability, the McDaniel *et al.* (2001) meta-analysis shows a mean correlation of $r = 0.34$ with SJTs, although they note that this masks a wide variation of results. McDaniel *et al.* (2007) more recently highlighted the importance of the type of response instructions in determining the link between SJT scores and cognitive ability, i.e. whether the test has knowledge or behavioural tendency related questions. With regards to predictive validity, meta-analyses show moderate to good criterion-related validity of SJTs. Importantly, SJTs have incremental validity over ability and personality measures (e.g. Oswald *et al.*, 2004; McDaniel *et al.*, 2007). However, most of this research was not conducted in operational (real-life) settings, although in two key studies, Patterson *et al.* (2009) and Lievens *et al.* (2005) have found evidence of the predictive and incremental validity of SJTs in operational settings.

Exercise 5.5   Designing an SJT to recruit doctors (see Patterson *et al.*, 2009)

The following question comes from a research study to develop a new SJT for recruiting doctors. An example question using a multiple best-answer response format is:

You are looking after Mrs Sandra Jones, who is being investigated in hospital. You are asked by her family not to inform Mrs Jones if the results confirm cancer.

Choose the three most appropriate actions to take in this situation:

A   *Ignore the family's wishes*

B   *Agree not to tell Mrs Jones*

C   *Explain to the family that it is Mrs Jones' decision*

D   *Ask Mrs Jones whether she wishes to know the test results*

E   *Ask Mrs Jones whether she wishes you to inform the family*

F   *Inform Mrs Jones that her family do not wish her to have the results*

G   *Give the results to the family first*

H   *Give the results to the next of kin first*

Suggested exercises

1   **What do you think this question is testing?**

2   **Could anyone answer this question? What does a candidate need to know before they can answer the question?**

3   **Try to create another question that is relevant for recruiting doctors. What is difficult in developing the question? What skills do you need to do question writing?**

In terms of fairness and adverse impact, findings show there are generally smaller subgroup differences using SJTs than using cognitive ability tests (Jensen, 1998, as cited in Lievens *et al.*, 2008). Research also shows that fairness and adverse impact may vary with the way that constructs are measured, e.g. it may vary in accordance with the presentation format. Kanning *et al.* (2006) also found that multimedia SJTs are more face valid, more enjoyable and tend to invoke better applicant reactions.

Key Learning Point

Situational judgement tests are a valid selection method. Applicant reactions tend to be positive. Further research is needed to explore the construct validity of SJTs.

Other methods

The use of biographical data (referred to as biodata) as a selection procedure is an interesting and sometimes controversial topic. The underlying principle in the use of biodata is that past behaviour is a good predictor of future performance. The fundamentals of the biodata approach involve identifying correlations between items of biographical information and criterion measures (e.g. work performance, absenteeism). These correlations are established empirically by conducting a predictive or (more often) concurrent validation study.

Biodata items that predict the criterion are then combined into a questionnaire which may be administered to applicants. Information from the prior validation stage can then be used to provide a scoring procedure. For example, items may be assigned weights based on their ability to predict the relevant criterion. It should be stressed at this point that the correlations observed between biodata items and the criterion could be influenced by chance factors that only occur in a single data set. It is not uncommon for one source of biodata (e.g. educational qualifications) to show predictive validity in one recruitment process, but not in another (this is sometimes referred to as 'shrinkage' in the validity coefficient). Before using the results of a biodata validation study for selection purposes, cross-validation, preferably using a second sample, is needed. It is also clear from empirical research that the validity of biodata items is not always stable over time and it is advisable for them to be revalidated from time to time.

Biodata items can be described as 'hard' or soft' items. A hard item might include verifiable information such as educational qualifications, whereas a soft item might be an applicant's preferred interests or hobbies. Results from meta-analytic studies report good predictive validity of biodata in general with validity coefficients of approximately 0.48. For example, education-related biodata items can be used for selection purposes to indicate literacy, and some argue (somewhat controversially) that is a reasonable proxy measure of intelligence. Items asking candidates about any social positions they held at university could indicate certain personality characteristics. Most of the problems with the use of biodata arise from the uncritical use of empirically derived items. In other words, many biodata studies have involved the identification of items that predict the criterion, with no attempt to consider *why* the items are predictive. In this respect, some biodata are atheoretical and are entirely empircally derived. For example, why should it be that living in a particular area of town or having had a newspaper delivery round as a child is associated with job success? Two problems may be associated with this kind of *raw empiricism*. One problem is that the observed biodata item may be a surrogate for some other variable; for example, what if the area of the town in question is predominantly inhabited by a particular social or ethnic group? The other, more general, problem is that while they may provide predictive value, such items provide no help in *understanding* the determinants of job success.

Key Learning Point

The uncritical use of empirically derived items in biodata questionnaires can lead to problems with equal opportunities. Rationally derived items are a safer option.

With these problems in mind the rational approach (*rational empiricism*) to the development of biodata has been utilised. This approach reflects attempts to develop a theoretical rationale for the predictive validity of biodata. Using the rational approach involves clear hypotheses about specific job-relevant constructs such as ability to work in a team, which may be tapped by specific biodata items (e.g. membership of clubs and societies being linked to certain personality factors). Only items with a potential rational connection with the criterion will then be tried out, even in the pre-validation version of the biodata questionnaire. This approach is clearly much more appealing from the explanatory point of view, although evidence to date suggests that it has slightly poorer validity than the empirical approach. Gains in fairness and understanding of employee performance may, however, outweigh this loss of validity. Stokes and Reddy (1992), after reviewing the evidence, suggest that a combination of raw empiricism and rational empiricism might produce the best and most interpretable results.

References

Reference reports are widely used methods for obtaining information on candidates, although it seems likely that in many situations potential employers take up references only when they are about to make a job offer. This high level of usage is not, however, matched by a comparable amount of research on references. In general, the validity evidence for reference reports is not particularly good (see Salgado *et al.*, 2001, for a review). One reason for the poor validity of references may be that they are not reliable and referees do not give consistent views on candidates. Further, there has been no analysis of whether reference reports add any incremental validity over cognitive ability tests, for example. Given their high level of usage, further research into references would seem to be important.

Other methods

Other potential selection methods not mentioned so far in this chapter include graphology (handwriting analysis), astrology and polygraphy (the use of the so-called lie detector test). In brief, none of these procedures is used to any great extent in the United Kingdom, although some continental European companies make extensive use of graphology (see Ryan *et al.*, 1999). As far as validity is concerned there is relatively little research available on the use of these methods for personnel selection but the clear balance of available evidence is that none of the methods shows any useful criterion-related validity. Summaries of the evidence on graphology and polygraphy may be found in the review paper by Salgado *et al.* (2001).

Key Learning Point

There is no evidence for the criterion-related validity of graphology in selection procedures.

STOP TO CONSIDER

In the preceding sections we have considered the properties of a range of different selection methods. What do the best selection methods have in common? What do the worst methods have in common? Is good selection just about the predictive validity of measure? If not, what other factors contribute to the effectiveness of a selection method?

The impact of selection procedures on applicants

Fairness

Until recently, there has been relatively little work in personnel selection which has looked at the issues involved from the perspective of candidates. The main area of work concerns the extent to which selection procedures are fair to different subgroups (such as ethnic minorities or women) of the population. This issue has stimulated a large amount of research. A variety of terms such as bias, adverse impact, fairness and differential validity are used in the literature on this issue, and a clear grasp of the meanings and definitions of some of these terms is crucial to an understanding of the research results.

First, it needs to be made clear that a test is not unfair or biased simply because members of different subgroups obtain different average scores on the tests. Men and women have different mean scores for height; this does not mean that rulers are unfair measuring instruments. However, it would be unfair to use height as a selection criterion for a job, if the job could be done by people of any height, since it is important for selection criteria to be job-related. Normally, of course, the extent to which a selection method is related to job performance can be estimated by validation research, and it is clear therefore that fairness and validity are closely related.

Unfortunately, it is possible for tests to appear to be valid and yet be biased against some subgroups. This may happen if the relationship between the test score and job performance is not the same for the two subgroups. For example, it is possible to imagine that the link between job performance and certain personality or ability factors could be different for two subgroups of the population (e.g. the personality factor predicts performance for men but not for women). A validity study based on a mixed sample of people would produce results that were somewhat incorrect for both subgroups; if the results were used to develop a selection procedure the predictions of candidates' work performance would be in error. Of course, the situation would be even worse if the validity study was based on only one subgroup but was then used to select members of another. Unfair direct discrimination is where the selection process treats an individual less favourably because of their gender or ethnic group, for example. Indirect discrimination is usually unintended and difficult to prove. It occurs when an employer applies a requirement for applicants (e.g. score on a test) which one group (defined by gender/race) finds it considerably harder to comply with, i.e. a larger proportion of one group cannot meet this requirement. This is known as *adverse impact*.

Key Learning Point

Indirect discrimination occurs when an employer applies a requirement for applicants (e.g. score on a test) which one group (defined by gender or race) finds it considerably harder to comply with.

This description of possible unfairness leads to the definition of test bias that is accepted by most work psychologists: 'A test is biased for members of a subgroup of the population if, in the prediction of a criterion for which the test was designed, consistent non-zero errors of prediction are made for members of the subgroup' (Cleary, 1968, p. 115). When, triggered by civil rights movements in the United States, fairness first became an issue in personnel selection research, it was felt that many selection procedures, including tests, were unfair. This was because of consistent differences in mean scores between different subgroups of the population (*see* Schmitt, 1989). As the discussion above makes clear, subgroup equality in mean scores is not the same as fairness. A procedure is biased or unfair when it shows different validity for different groups.

In using a selection test, the test designers would need to ensure that the difficulty level of items (percentage of applicants getting the item right) is not significantly different across different ethnic groups sitting the test. If differences are found, then there is said to be *differential item functioning*. There are sophisticated statistical procedures that can be applied to assess differential item functioning for tests. In general, the research evidence suggests that for professionally developed selection tests there is little or no evidence of differential item functioning across ethnic groups. The fact that the scientific research provides little evidence of differential validity for well-established selection procedures does not imply that all selection methods are unbiased, nor does it imply that unfair discrimination does not take place. It is clear, for example, that despite the 1976 Race Relations Act, unfair discrimination still takes place in the United Kingdom. Robertson and Smith (2001) note that cognitive ablity testing is the method that has created the most frequent problems with adverse impact in selection processes (*also see* Ones and Viswesvaran, 1998; Bobko *et al.*, 1999).

Assessment centres make use of several selection methods and this may minimise the impact of bias in one component. Dean *et al.* (2008) conducted a meta-analysis with 27 research studies to explore adverse impact in ACs. They looked at 'standardised subgroup differences' produced by ACs for three particular subgroups (namely black people, Hispanic people and females). They found a subgroup difference of 0.52 between black and white individuals, showing that in contrast to the traditional assumption of low subgroup difference effects in ACs, there is still a significant difference between the ratings of black and white individuals in ACs. In the same study, a lower level of subgroup difference was found between Hispanic and white individuals than between black and white individuals. There was also evidence of a negative subgroup difference between female and male individuals, as females tended to perform better in ACs. Anderson *et al.* (2006) conducted a study into gender differences in AC performance using a military sample, and found that females achieved higher ratings than males on interpersonal leadership style traits, including 'oral communication and interaction' and 'drive and determination'. The studies conducted by Dean *et al.* (2008) and Anderson *et al.* (2006) can be taken alongside other studies of diversity and fairness to illustrate the mixed picture of evidence that exists regarding potential discrimination arising from the use of ACs. It is also worth remembering that candidates taking part in an AC are a small proportion of the general population, that is they have chosen to apply for the job and have been selected for the AC based on the information provided in application form (and perhaps some other pre-AC assessments). Therefore, it might be that some of the effects observed at ACs are a result of events that occur before the AC. For example, it may be that only very able female candidates apply for the job and make it through the pre-AC assessments. In contrast, males of all levels of ability may apply for the job and some of the pre-AC assessments may favour males, thus resulting in males from across the ability spectrum being assessed at the AC.

Applicant reactions

As the opening case study to this chapter illustrates, applicant reactions to a selection system are crucially important. In recent years, there has been more emphasis placed on applicants' decision-making where selection is now viewed as a two-way process. Attracting applicants to apply for a job is the first important step. If offered the job, an applicant with a negative reaction is likely to refuse a job offer (and the best applicants could work for a competing organisation). In an extreme case, an applicant who has a negative reaction to a selection procedure could make a legal challenge on the basis of unfair discrimination. Applicants who have negative experiences with an organisation's selection system could boycott the organisation's products and encourage their friends and acquaintances to do the same.

Adverse reactions from candidates can lead to a legal challenge. The Head of Equality and Employment in the TUC (Trades Union Congress) in the United Kingdom, Sarah Veale, says

There is nothing intrinsically wrong with tests but there is an over-reliance on them to the exclusion of other means of assessment. Lots of employers are not very good – they're quite sloppy, particularly smaller businesses. We have complaints from unions about employers relying on tests, using them to justify not taking somebody on, and they worry the real reason was potentially discriminatory.

Financial Times, *FT.com, 19 June 2003*

Exercise 5.6   Adverse impact in selection

A large organisation was found to have discriminated against ethnic minority applicants after an employment tribunal. Following a restructuring of the organisation, 100 new middle management posts were created. Approximately 30 per cent of employees are of ethnic minority origin, and currently, 3 per cent of management are of ethnic minority origin. The personnel department decided to use a structured interview and two cognitive ability tests (a measure of verbal reasoning and a measure of numerical reasoning).

Of the 600 employees applied for management posts, 30 per cent were of ethnic origin. However, only 10 per cent of the job offers were made to ethnic candidates. The tribunal ruled that the tests were inappropriate in terms of the time allowed, the level of difficulty, the skills tested and the content covered. There was evidence of adverse impact and unlawful discrimination. The organisation conceded there was unintentional and indirect discriminatory impact on ethnic minority candidates and suggested compensation.

Suggested exercises

1   What is the difference between fair and unfair selection testing?
2   How can unfair discrimination be recognised?
3   What needs to be considered in evaluating the fairness of the test?

Research has tended to explain the different factors that affect applicant reactions using theories of organisational justice (*see also* Chapter 8). Distributive justice focuses on perceived fairness regarding equity (where the selection outcome is consistent with the applicant's expectation) and equality (the extent to which applicants have the same opportunities in the selection process). Procedural justice refers to the formal characteristics of the selection process such as the level and quality of information and feedback offered, job-relatedness of the procedures and methods and recruiter effectiveness. For an early review of these theories see Anderson *et al.* (2001a) and Gilliland (1993). Anderson *et al.* (2001a) suggest that four main factors seem to account for positive or negative applicant reactions to selection methods. These are: (1) the selection method is based on a thorough job analysis and appears more job-relevant; (2) the selection method is less personally intrusive; (3) the method does not contravene procedural or distributive justice expectations; and (4) the method allows applicants to meet in person with the recruiters. Other literature suggests that applicants prefer multiple opportunities to demonstrate their skills, that they prefer assessment that allows them to talk about their potential, and that the selection system is administered consistently for all applicants.

Of course, perceptions of injustice can depend partly on whether the person is successful in the selection process. For example, Robertson and Smith (2001) suggest that if the selection decision is in the candidate's favour, then the procedure is likely to be viewed as fair. However, 'if the decision goes against the candidate, it is unlikely to be viewed as fair . . . it seems that the concepts of fairness and self-interest are closely entwined!' (p. 452). Hausknecht *et al.* (2004) conducted a meta-analysis of the applicant reactions literature, using 86 studies, providing a summary of their main findings as follows. The organisational outcomes of: intentions to accept a job offer; intentions to recommend the organisation to people; and positive opinion of the organisation are more likely to be reported by those individuals who perceived the selection process in a positive light. Applicants' perceptions of the selection process were found to be related to their actual level of performance *and* the level of performance they believe they have achieved. Hausknecht *et al.* (2004) reported that applicants' perceptions of predictive validity and the face validity of the selection method were strongly linked to many aspects of candidates' perceptions of the selection process (e.g. predictive and distributive justice and applicant attitudes towards selection and its component tests).

In terms of the relative popularity of different types of selection tests, Hausknecht *et al.*'s (2004) meta-analysis showed that applicants held favourable perceptions of interviews, CVs, work sample tests and references, whereas cognitive ability tests were moderately popular among applicants, with tests such as graphology, biodata, honesty tests and measures of intelligence following as less popular. However, Sackett and Lievens (2008) critiqued Hausknecht *et al.*'s (2004) findings, arguing that the sampling and methodological weaknesses of their meta-analysis cast doubts over the usefulness of the results. This criticism was mainly because only a small number of studies were included, because the studies used have relied heavily upon hypothetical contexts and that in real selection settings, a different picture could exist. Sackett and Lievens (2008) are generally critical about research on applicant reactions and suggest that because of the lack of studies focusing on important organisational outcomes (e.g. applicants actually choosing to withdraw from selection processes, or refusing to take the job offer), there are some weaknesses in this field of research, especially when it is applied to real selection settings.

Organisational justice theories are used to understand applicant reactions to selection methods.

STOP TO CONSIDER

It might be argued (although not by the authors of this textbook) that if a selection method predicts job performance then applicant reactions are of little importance. From what you have read in the preceding sections, what is it about a selection method that shapes candidates' perceptions of it? You might want to consider your own experiences of selection processes to help you think about this question.

Is it possible that a selection method that generally prompts positive candidate reactions might, if it is not delivered in a professional manner, provoke negative candidate reactions? When delivering a selection process, what needs to be done in order to ensure that candidates do not have neagtive reactions to it?

The use of technology in selection

The rapid advances that have been made in the world of technology and telecommunications have presented selection practitioners and researchers with new opportunities and challenges. In an edition of the *International Journal of Selection and Assessment* devoted to technology and selection, a range of potentially important issues were raised (Viswesvaran, 2003). Not the least of these was how to balance the tremendous potential of technology to increasing the pool of potential applicants to an organisation, with the possibility that technology itself may influence the decisions that are reached (Anderson, 2003). Let us take the example of Internet-based application forms. There has been a dramatic increase in the number of organisations advertising via the Internet and expecting applicants to complete and submit online application forms (Bartram, 2000). The advantages for the organisation include:

- the ability to create interactive application forms;
- the possibility of providing additional information to potential applicants by signposting other relevant web pages;
- the capacity to request information from applicants in a standard format that can be processed and assessed by computer technology.

For example, it is now possible for the first stage of a selection process involving analysis of biodata to be completed by computer without any member of the organisation gaining sight of the application form.

Some applicants may approve of online application forms, which could be perceived as easier and faster to complete and send (even up to seconds before the deadline). Others may experience technical difficulties that may lead to negative applicant reactions. In this topic, researchers have been left trailing in the wake of advances that have been made in practice. For example, Internet-based forms are often cited as a way of improving international recruitment in global organisations. However, we do not know as yet whether cultural differences and familiarity with technology will impact upon the way in which applicants present themselves in these applications. Certainly, by restricting application to Internet-based procedures, those with reduced access to computer technology, or who are less familiar with it, will be at a disadvantage. This may well include older workers and could be discriminatory under the new legislation being brought in within the United Kingdom.

In his review of applicants and recruiter reactions to the use of technology on selection, Anderson (2003) identifies three main themes to consider including (i) applicant reactions, (ii) equivalence (e.g. is an applicant's score on a selection test administered online equivalent to the same test administered using paper and pencil?) and (iii) adverse impact. For some selection methods there has already been extensive research (e.g. cognitive ability testing via computer), but for others there is very little evidence yet available (for a detailed review of this literature *see* Lievens and Harris, 2003). It is possible that interviews conducted using technology such as telephones or videoconferencing could result in negative applicant perceptions and could even put potential applicants off from applying (Sackett and Lievens, 2008).

The concept of equivalence is a critical question since there is increasing usage of the Internet for use in recruitment in general, and legal concerns are of importance. Research investigating the equivalence across different selection methods has produced mixed results. Sackett and Lievens (2008) report that using Internet-based testing produces 'lower means (average scores), larger variances (more spread in the data), more normal distributions, and larger internal consistencies (i.e. internal reliability)' (p. 1619). Potosky and Bobko (2004) argue that one advantage of tests delivered via the Internet is that they do not allow candidates to flick through the test items and make strategic decisions about the way they distribute their time across the test items.

Key Learning Point

Applicant reactions, equivalence and adverse impact are key themes in investigating the use of technology in selection.

One important area where there is certain to be further development is that of interactive testing. At the moment test publishers are working on questionnaires that are able to make interim assessments of the ability level of respondents and alter the difficulty of subsequent questions accordingly. Similarly, a number of organisations (e.g. a number of police organisations) are already using interactive computer technology to present intelligent training scenarios. For example, police officers undergoing firearms training are presented with realistic large-screen video scenarios depicting armed criminals. Using guns fitted with lasers and a light-sensitive screen, their decision to shoot and their shooting accuracy can be monitored and the endings of the scenarios changed accordingly. The potential for interactive work sample assessments is only beginning to be uncovered and there will undoubtedly be interesting developments ahead.

There is evidence that technology can change the way in which individuals are perceived. Although the telephone might be considered relatively old technology, there is surprisingly little research that has considered how interacting by phone might influence the way we perceive others. For example, research investigating the comparability of selection decisions made by interviewers in face-to-face and telephone interviews suggests that telephone ratings are lower (harsher) than face-to-face ratings (Silvester *et al.*, 2000). However, it is also suggested that ratings in telephone interviews may be more valid because there is a tendency for interviewers to focus on task-relevant information when visual information is absent. In a more recent study of telephone interviews Silvester and Anderson (2003) found that interviewers tended to focus on applicants' accounts of more personal and unique aspects of themselves: this may have made it easier for interviewers to discriminate more easily among interviewees whom they could not see.

Sackett and Lievens (2008) recommend that future research should explore the utility of technology-based selection methods, and uncover *if and how* Internet-based selection may impact upon the type of candidates completing these tests, and the predictive validity of these tests. As you may imagine, there are potential dangers involved with the use of *'unproctored Internet testing'* (which is Internet-based testing without a person physically administering the test to candidates). These dangers include the possibility that the identity of candidates may be revealed and the test may not be securely stored. Some suggest that the latter may be overcome but the former will present a problem until more advanced identification technology enters mainstream use. Tippins *et al.* (2006) suggest that given these concerns, unprotected Internet testing should be restricted to use on 'low-stakes' selection.

In summary, a great deal of further research is needed to explore the various ways in which technology can influence the personnel selection process from both the organisation's and the applicant's perspective.

Exercise 5.7 Applicants' reactions to online application forms in graduate recruitment

A study was conducted by Price and Patterson (2003) to examine applicant reactions to the use of online application forms as opposed to paper and pencil application forms. A small number of structured interviews were used to elicit applicant reactions to the use of online application forms in graduate recruitment. The results showed positive and negative applicant reactions. The negative applicant reactions are themed under the factors presented below. Each factor is listed with a corresponding quotation that illustrates the nature of the factor.

Factor	Quotation from participant
Dehumanisation	'[A paper-based form allows you to] put more of your-self into it . . . online is more cold.'
Feedback	'Everyone else had e-mail acknowledgement, but I didn't. I rang up but they never got back to me.'
Technical issues	'I spent hours typing information, and the page expired. It hadn't saved properly and I lost it all. I ended up in tears absolutely frustrated and didn't apply in the end.'
Attitude	'Using an online application form means they have got more scope to make themselves look bad. It puts me off the company if I have technical problems.'
Motivation	'I got that sick of the technical problems that I just wanted to finish it and send it off.'
Fairness	'It feels like I haven't done justice to myself in the space provided.'
Satisfaction	'Online application forms have the potential to be better and quicker, but they are more frustrating, and I think they've got a long way to go on the design issues.'

Suggested exercise

Consider the applicants' reactions to on-line application forms for graduates. List the possible advantages of using online application forms for recruiters and applicants. To what extent do you think these outweigh the possible advantages? What advice and practical recommendations would you offer organisations involved in on-line recruitment?

Summary

A variety of personnel selection procedures is available for use in organisational settings. Research over the past three decades has provided a much clearer picture of the criterion-related validity of these procedures. Some of the methods, such as cognitive ability tests, seem to have broad applicability across a range of situations. As well as examining the validity of personnel selection procedures, research has also concentrated on the impact of the procedures on candidates. One area that has been reasonably well researched involves an examination of the fairness (to different subgroups) of the various techniques. Preliminary research suggests that the assessment experience itself (e.g. the way the test is delivered) may have an impact on the measurement of candidates' psychological characteristics. Further research is required to assess the impact of the use of technology for both organisations and applicants in personnel selection procedures.

Closing Case Study

Broken legs, knots and CVs: interviewing, army-style

For more than 60 years the army's Regular Commissions Board has been recognised as one of the most rigorous recruiting systems in the UK. But has its reputation for thoroughness stood the test of time and do its selection methods have relevance for private sector recruitment, where command and control has given way to the arts of gentle persuasion?

To find out I took the opportunity last week to revisit a selection process I first encountered at first hand as a teenage candidate. This time, however, I watched from the sidelines. On that first encounter 30 years ago I was 18 years old and fresh out of school. I had abandoned a holiday with a couple of friends who dropped me outside the gates before heading for St Ives in Cornwall. Wearing a denim shirt, jeans and a cracked pair of glasses with a crumpled suit in my rucksack I can see now that I might not have created the best of impressions from the off.

I was sharing a room with a viscount. I can't recall his name but in speech and appearance we must have looked like the Odd Couple. He was wearing a sports jacket, striped tie and a slick parting plastered across his forehead. I had long hair and flared trousers. His accent was cut glass. Mine was beer glass. But within minutes of our arrival we were issued with identical pairs of overalls with numbered bibs that removed most outward differences. Today candidates are also handed a light helmet for safety's sake.

Helmet aside, what struck me most about today's board was how little it appears to have changed from the system it employed more than a generation ago. Candidates still take psychometric tests looking at various abilities, although these days the tests are taken in an earlier session when potential candidates are briefed on the processes and basic skills that will be helpful in the full board. In addition to seeking leadership potential, the army is looking for strong evidence of practical skills. This is why a substantial portion of the selection is based on outside exercises in which teams of candidates are asked to negotiate obstacles using planks and pieces of rope. A two-day pre-board briefing, introduced about 10 years ago, explains knots and lashings plus a few engineering principles such as the fulcrum and the cantilever, each of ▶

which come in handy during the team exercises. The briefings were introduced to re-move a perceived advantage for those with cadet force experience, for example, who would be familiar with such techniques. 'A big brain is not necessarily what we want. Sometimes it is possible to find a highly intelligent candidate who lacks any practical skills. It is also possible that someone might score highly on abstract reasoning and turn out to be bone idle, so the intelligence tests don't tell us everything,' says Lieu-tenant Ashton-Wickett.

Beyond the psychometrics, candidates are also tested on their knowledge of current affairs, the armed services and general knowledge. Added to this are interviews, often based on their CV offerings. I recall being asked about my interest in sport. 'What's your handicap?' asked the interviewer. Unfortunately they didn't play golf much where I lived. That didn't seem fair at the time but I'm assured that it's not the questions that matter so much as how you handle them and how you express your-self. A popular misconception about the board is that it is looking for future gener-als. This is not the case. The selection board for the Royal Military Academy, Sandhurst, is looking for those who have the potential to be a second lieutenant leading a platoon or a troop. This is only the start of an officer career. A lot more se-lection is going to happen down the line and a percentage of candidates will drop out of Sandhurst.

Another mistaken belief is that the army needs to fill quotas. In fact all candidates are assessed against a single standard. If they reach that standard, their qualifica-tion is valid for seven years should they wish to delay their entry.

Some of the exercises, particularly one that looks at a scenario in which candidates must form a plan to achieve various aims, are designed to put individuals under pres-sure so that assessors can witness their ability to perform under stress. These paper exercises have changed very little over the years. A typical scenario puts you some-where in the wilds when your friend breaks a leg, just as some other crisis develops which also needs your attention. This leaves you to work out the best way to priori-tise and deal with competing emergencies.

Times have changed and so has the army but, fundamentally, the qualities sought in an officer 30 years ago have changed very little. It is difficult to see how the selec-tion system could be any fairer or any more scrupulous than it is now. But does it need to be so thorough? The process is expensive in time and manpower, ensuring the performance of every candidate is subjected to detailed scrutiny. 'You have to consider the cost of getting it wrong,' says Mr Ashton-Wickett.

Source: FT.COM, 6 October 2005. Copyright © Richard Donkin.

Suggested exercise

1   For this job role, how would you begin to calculate the costs of getting the selection decision wrong?

2   How would you convince an organisation that, in terms of the investment in time and resources, using an assessment centre is worth it?

3   Why do you think the content of the assessment process hasn't changed much over 30 years (as the case study suggests)?

Test your learning

Short-answer questions

1 What selection methods are used in assessment centres?

2 How does sampling error distort validation studies?

3 What is an adverse impact in personnel selection?

4 What stages are involved in developing a situational judgement test (SJT)?

5 What can be done to ensure that selection interviews are as effective as possible?

6 What problems may apply to designing and implementing work sample tests?

7 Are candidate reactions to SJTs generally positive or negative? Why?

8 What are the advantages and disadvantages of online application forms for (a) applicants, (b) organisations?

9 What is unprotected Internet-based testing?

Suggested assignments

1 Critically review the validity evidence for three of the following contemporary personnel selection methods: personality assessment, tests of cognitive ability, interviews, assessment centres.

2 Discuss the advantages and disadvantages of using technology for personnel selection and assessment.

3 What do situational judgement tests measure? What are their advantages and disadvantages compared to other selection methods?

Relevant websites

The UK-based consultancy SHL offers some advice about how to manage various selection techniques effectively and ethically. Go to http://www.shl.com/Our Science/BestPractice/ and follow the links to Best Practice in Assessment Practice.

The Recruitment and Employment Federation offers quite a practical site about how to select, and how to get selected. Find it at http://www.rec.uk.com/home.

For further self-test material and relevant, annotated weblinks please visit the website at **www.pearsoned.co.uk/workpsych**

Suggested further reading

Full details for all references are given in the list of references at the end of this book.

1   Sackett and Lievens (2008). This article presents an excellent review of the state of the art in personnel selection. Some of the language used is a little complex but it is an excellent source for use throughout your study of personnel selection.

2   Patterson *et al.* (2009). 'Evaluation of three short-listing methodologies'. This article shows how important it is that shortlisting is done well. It provides a good analysis of the impact on selection decisions of using different shortlisting methods.

3   Schmidt and Hunter's (1998) review article explores the validity and utility of selection methods over 85 years of research. It analyses a huge amount of data to examine the links between performance during selection and in the job itself.

CHAPTER 6

Assessing performance at work

LEARNING OUTCOMES

After studying this chapter, you should be able to:

1 understand the importance of defining work performance;

2 recognise different methods of measuring and rating performance;

3 understand the strengths and weaknesses of different methods of assessing performance;

4 identify how bias can influence performance ratings;

5 compare different methods of assessing performance in the workplace;

6 understand the qualities of various different performance rating scales;

7 recognise good practice in the design and execution of performance appraisals;

8 describe the properties of multi-source feedback systems and understand the strengths and weaknesses of these systems;

9 be aware of the current issues and future directions in performance assessment research.

Credit crunch performance

Imagine the scene. It is November 2006 – just before the global banking crisis and the term 'credit crunch' has yet to enter everyday language. We are in the London headquarters of an international investment bank and the time has come to assess the annual performance of all junior level investment bankers. Six middle managers are meeting to rate the people who work for them. This information will be used by senior managers to decide who should be promoted and what bonuses will be paid. These six managers are responsible for market sectors in different parts of the world. Some of the people they manage sit next to them at the trading desk in London, allowing the managers to observe those working for them managing large investment portfolios. Others work in Paris, Tokyo, Singapore, Frankfurt, New York, Beijing or Moscow and the managers see them only occasionally (but hear about the losses and profits on their portfolios on a regular basis).

Today the atmosphere in the meeting is buoyant. Global headquarters in Zurich have announced pre-tax profits of $3 billion, but the rest of the banking sector has done well too and managers are keen to retain their top performers. They know that these juniors will be actively courted by competitors offering them lucrative deals to move jobs. The managers also know that their own individual bonuses depend on how well their teams perform.

Today they must rate 24 junior investment bankers as either 'underperforming', 'performing as expected' or 'performing above expectation'. The first manager is asked to run through his three juniors. After consulting his notes he begins by describing Junior A as 'a safe pair of hands, somebody who is technically excellent, and who does a lot behind the scenes'. Junior B is described as 'delightful, helpful to colleagues, has an exceptional focus on detail, not always aggressive and tends to avoid risks'. Finally, Junior C is described as 'a rock star, one of the best juniors I've ever seen, unbelievable presence, someone who kicks ass and is undoubtedly a future leader'. After asking for comments from other managers who might have come across these individuals, the meeting decide to rank Junior A as 'performing', Junior B as 'underperforming' and Junior C as 'performing above expectation' and someone who should be promoted.

Two years later, it is mid-credit crunch. Around the world major banks have collapsed, merged or been rescued by governments through part or full nationalisation. The question being asked by governments, media and members of the public all around the world is 'why did the banks get it so wrong?' Whilst many factors may have led to the banking crisis, could the way in which individual performance was assessed and rewarded have contributed? Could work psychology help managers to assess performance more accurately and manage performance better? Keep this case study in mind as you read this chapter: do you think that more rigorous and informed assessment processes could have resulted in better financial decision-making?

Source: Prof. Jo Silvester, City University (2009).

Introduction

The global financial crisis of 2008 has brought performance assessment firmly into the spotlight. Many have argued that the bonus culture has contributed to the collapse of the banking sector. Rightly or wrongly, there are few better illustrations of why studying how we assess and reward work performance is an important field for research and practice in work psychology. Performance assessment exists as a mechanism to evaluate employee performance, provide feedback about how individuals are performing relative to their colleagues and relative to their managers' expectations, and to provide managers with information to guide strategic decisions about performance management. As such, assessment is part of the broader arena of performance management that exists to enhance individual performance and ultimately organisational performance to help achieve business goals.

As the example illustrates, however, performance assessment is a complex interpersonal phenomenon where the interests of managers often conflict with the interests of their employees or the organisation itself. Assessment decisions can also have profound and long-lasting implications for individual workers. Individuals judged to have 'high potential' may receive increased financial rewards and the opportunity to join high flier programmes, whereas those judged 'poor performers' may have their promotion prospects blocked or find themselves managed out of organisations. Fair and objective assessment is therefore important to workers and managers, and much of the research and practice in work psychology has focused on the design of assessment processes that capture accurate information. This information can then be used to guide evidence-based decisions about how the capabilities of individual workers can be employed, developed and rewarded.

Performance assessment systems also play an important part in wider organisational systems, because data collected from different parts of a company can be used to inform strategic decisions about investing in or supporting human capital (e.g. it may identify a training need in a particular part of the organisation). It can also be used to compare levels of performance across groups in different parts of an organisation. Technology has made it possible to collect large quantities of performance data, making performance assessment an important resource, but it is important to remember that most derives from interpersonal judgements made by managers rating the work of those individuals they supervise. It is therefore not surprising that Campbell (2008) cites individual work performance as the most critical dependent variable in applied psychology. He argues that efforts to build a better understanding of work performance and how it can be assessed are among the most important challenges for work psychologists today. In this chapter we begin by considering what is meant by work performance, how we can define it and how we can measure it. The chapter then describes how work psychologists have contributed to the development of objective, reliable and useful systems of performance assessment and performance management. It concludes by looking at future challenges for researchers and practitioners in this area.

Defining work performance

At the core of performance assessment lie two fundamental questions: 'what do we mean by performance at work' and 'how do we measure it?' These have come to be known as the 'criterion problem' (Austin and Crespin, 2006; Bennett *et al.*, 2006) and constitute an ongoing challenge for researchers and practitioners in work psychology. Measurement is integrally linked to definition: accurate measurement depends on first determining what needs to be measured – which in the case of work performance is more difficult than it may first seem. Take the case of three people with different jobs: an actor playing a lead role in a stage production of *Macbeth*, a high-school mathematics teacher and a journalist working for a local newspaper. It may seem obvious that good performance for the actor is being able to act well, but what do we mean by this, and can it be measured objectively? What would we use as our criteria of acting well and how would we assess this? Good performance may therefore be further defined as the actor behaving in a way that leads members of an audience see a character that they believe in and empathise with (and this may rely upon a subjective evaluation by the audience or theatre critics). In contrast, good performance for the journalist might involve writing an article that leads readers to request a follow-up story. Good work performance for the teacher may involve marking homework assignments on time (which could be assessed using objective criteria) and preparing lessons that capture the curiosity of pupils (pupil evaluations would be a subjective criteria).

These examples suggest that there are many different ways that role incumbents can demonstrate good and poor work performance (Murphy and Jackson, 1999). This means that performance assessment requires clarity on the part of both the worker and the manager about what a job incumbent is expected to do and the standards to which they are expected to perform.

Exercise 6.1   Performance on TV

Think of a popular TV presenter. How would you define good and poor performance for them? How would you capture information about different types of performance? What criteria (if any) might provide an objective assessment of their performance, and what criteria could be used to provide a subjective measure of their performance?

Generic models of work performance

One way in which researchers have tried to deal with the complexity and diversity of work performance has been to ask whether there may be underlying components of work performance that are common to all work roles. Campbell (1990) argues that attempts to map the underlying (latent) structure of work performance are just as important as past efforts to understand the latent structure of intelligence and personality. For example, personality theorists have identified five traits that appear to explain personality (see Chapter 3). In a similar way, work psychologists like Campbell have undertaken research to identify common components of job performance and develop a theory that could inform the design of assessment tools. In one of the first large-scale investigations Campbell and colleagues (1993) identified eight general factors of job performance, each of which is made up of several more specific factors (see Table 6.1 and Campbell *et al.*, 1996). According to the researchers all eight general factors will be useful in describing performance across different types of work: of course some will be more useful for some job roles than they will be for others. However, three factors – core task proficiency, demonstrating

Table 6.1	Job performance factors	
Campbell		**Bartram**

Campbell	Bartram
1 Job-specific 'core' task proficiency*	1 Enterprising and performing
2 Non-job specific proficiency	2 Interacting and presenting
3 Written and oral communication	3 Analysing and reporting
4 Demonstrating effort*	4 Creating and conceptualising
5 Maintaining discipline*	5 Adapting and coping
6 Facilitating peer/team performance	6 Supporting and cooperating
7 Supervision/leadership	7 Leading and deciding
8 Management/administration	8 Organising and executing

*Important for all job roles.

effort and maintaining discipline – are important for all job roles. As an aside, this is consistent with the research discussed in Chapter 3 which showed the consistent links between conscientiousness and job performance. Campbell and other researchers have found evidence to support this eight-factor model in a variety of research studies. However, they also call for more research to clarify the construct validity of individual factors (i.e. there is a still a need provide more accurate definitions of each of the factors).

Bartram (2005) has attempted to map the latent structure of work performance by examining competencies exhibited in a range of different jobs in different organisations. Competencies relate to the observable skills or abilities that an individual requires in order to perform a task or role effectively, and competency frameworks describe the behaviours associated with good and poor performance for each competency. His starting point was to examine competency frameworks developed by many different companies for a variety of different jobs. He looked at whether there were similar competencies in similar jobs in different companies, and whether similar competencies were found in different job roles. By doing this he was able to identify whether there were any common factors among many different independent sources of competency data. Interestingly, Bartram's meta-analysis of 29 validation studies using line manager performance ratings also found evidence for eight 'great' factors of job performance. These are listed next to Campbell's eight factors in Table 6.1 and despite the fact that both researchers identify the same number of factors, there are intriguing differences. For example, Bartram does not identify the factors associated with core task performance, effort or motivation that Campbell identifies. However, Bartram identifies other factors like creativity (innovation), conceptualising and analysing (cognitive ability) that are not identified by Campbell, but have become increasingly recognised as important to job performance. As Table 6.1 shows, used together the two models provide a comprehensive description of the breadth and depth of work performance.

Viswesvaran *et al.* (2005) provide a contrary view. Their research found evidence of 25 conceptually distinct categories of job performance. However, they argue that statistical analysis of their data shows there could well be a single factor of job performance (i.e. that good performance in one category is usually associated with good performance in the other categories, and that poor performance in one category tends to be associated with poor performance in other categories). Therefore, rather than an eight factor model (similar to the 'Big Five' factor model of personality), they suggest that job performance is better understood in terms of a single general factor in much the same way as general mental ability ('g'). Given ongoing efforts to understand and map the latent structure of job performance, debate as to whether there is one, or more than one, common underlying component is likely to continue as a focus of attention for researchers and practitioners in future.

Extra-role performance

The work discussed in this chapter so far has concentrated on job performance as defined, or expected, by managers. In the early 1980s Organ and his colleagues coined the term 'organisational citizenship behaviour' (OCB) to describe what might be considered extra-role performance undertaken by workers in their jobs. In their research Smith *et al.* (1983) asked supervisors to describe behaviour they might expect from good workers, but which they could not reward or force them to do. Managers listed behaviours such as employee helpfulness, conscientiousness, courtesy, sportsmanship (i.e. tolerating impositions without complaining) and civic virtue or positive political behaviour at work. These were all actions that were not requested directly by managers and not listed on job descriptions or appraisal forms. However, all contributed to making the workplace a better environment (Organ, 1997). For example, whereas one employee might fulfil traditional performance expectations by producing accurate and detailed reports on time, a second might do the same but also offer to help other colleagues who might be struggling. OCB has been defined as 'individual behaviour that is discretionary, not directly or explicitly recognised by the formal reward system, and that in the aggregate promotes the effective functioning of the organisation' (Organ, 1988, p. 4). This explains its absence from models of work performance developed from the analysis of organisational competency frameworks.

From its definition it is easy to see that OCB may be important for creating positive work climates and improved group performance. This has prompted greater research interest in other aspects of job performance that may not be captured by traditional job descriptions or models of work performance. Borman and Motowidlo (1997) draw a useful distinction between 'task' performance (defined as the effectiveness with which an employee completes a set of technical or role-specific objectives) and 'contextual' performance (which impacts indirectly on organisational climate and improved work satisfaction). They argue that whilst task performance contributes to the organisation's technical objectives, contextual performance is important for broader organisational performance because it impacts indirectly on the work climate and other employees' perceptions of support. Contextual performance is conceptually similar to OCB. Borman and Motowidlo identify seven types of behaviour associated with contextual performance, including volunteering to take on responsibilities that are not formally part of their role, supporting and defending organisational decisions, persisting with enthusiasm and following rules even when they may be personally inconvenienced. This research on contextual performance has helped to identify and reward behaviours that have hitherto been neglected. However, as the opening case study illustrates, it is unlikely that managers will view

OCB or contextual behaviour as anywhere near as important as task performance. In the opening case study OCB does not appear to be a valued behaviour in this organisation; worse it may be viewed as indicating that an individual is too 'soft' to succeed in such a competitive banking culture. However, in most jobs good OCB is unlikely to compensate for poor task performance (although perhaps you can think of an examples where poor performance is tolerated because an employee demonstrates OCB). Hanson and Borman (2006) conclude that we need to broaden both our conceptualisations of job performance and our methods of measuring it: neither task performance nor OCB on their own provide a sufficient framework for understanding work performance.

STOP TO CONSIDER

'Real performance is going beyond what is expected; it is setting one's own highest standards, invariably standards that surpass what others demand or expect' (Whitmore, 2004, p. 97).

John Whitmore defines 'real' work performance as that which exceeds what managers expect. This presents something of difficulty for those developing rating scales. Can or should extra-role behaviour be included as something to be reviewed as part of an appraisal process? Does this mean that the unexpected becomes an expected part of an employee's contribution to the workplace?

Key Learning Point

For performance assessment to be successful in any work context two questions need to be answered: (1) what constitutes good and poor performance, and (2) how can performance be measured?

Measuring work performance

Our ability to define work performance is important because it impacts on how performance is measured and assessed. In the case of an actor, if audience perception is used as a criterion of good or poor performance, we need to ask the audience to rate the actor. We also need to consider what rating scales might be used and how we can be sure that members of the audience are rating aspects of performance in a similar way. There are many different criteria and some are easier to quantify than others; for example, performance criteria for a retail sales person might include the number of successful sales they make, their customer satisfaction ratings, absenteeism rate or the number of mistakes they make. These types of information are often viewed as more objective measures of performance than ratings by managers, which can be influenced by bias or insufficient opportunity to observe a worker. However, no performance criterion is likely to be completely accurate. Volume of sales may be influenced by the product area for which an employee is responsible (there may be fewer opportunities to sell foot spas than there are to sell hair products), or whether

"I always give 110% to my job.
40% on Monday, 30% on Tuesday, 20% on
Wednesday, 15% on Thursday, and 5% on Friday."

Figure 6.1	An example of how the timing of a manager's observations of an employee (e.g. Monday or Friday) might affect their rating of the employee's performance *Source*: Randy Glasbergen, Glasbergen Cartoons, www.glasbergen.com

an employee is working in a store in a deprived area or one in an economically vibrant area. In order to overcome problems associated with any one type of performance data, data from several different performance criteria can be collected and the findings triangulated (i.e. examined together) to build a more comprehensive picture of how an individual or work group is performing. To date, however, the most common form of performance data is still derived from managers' direct or indirect observation of individuals in the workplace (Arvey and Murphy, 1998).

Observing and judging performance

There is considerable evidence that interpersonal judgements are often selective and biased. For example, individuals tend to make generally favourable or unfavourable evaluations of people based on initial judgements or prior information; a bias often referred to as 'halos and horns'. Managers rating employees can also be vulnerable to primacy and recency effects, where information presented early or late in a sequence dominates memory and judgement. For example, how a new employee performs in their early days can play an important role in determining managers' expectations about their long-term potential. Managers also tend to overlook the influence of the work environment or their own actions on employee behaviour because of the *fundamental attributional* error. This means that they attribute performance to the qualities of the individual rather than the influence of the environment such as the equipment an employee has to do the job or the amount of support they receive from their colleagues). Similarly, managers may demonstrate a 'like me' or similarity effect, where they rate more highly those employees whom they see as similar to themselves. Schneider (1987) argues that over time this can result in organisational cloning. According to his attraction-selection-attrition (ASA) model, there is a tendency for managers in organisations to develop and manage systems that serve to attract, select and promote those people with similar personality and values.

However, these types of bias are often unconscious and result from the cognitive shortcuts (better known as cognitive heuristics) that our brains use to quickly make sense of and respond to complex situations, people and surroundings. For example, stereotyping arises when we rely on automatic processing of cognitive schemata in long-term memory (LTM) that have been developed as a consequence of past experiences (Klimoski and Donahue, 2001). Stereotypes guide decisions about new situations and people; they speed up the way we deal with the world, enabling us to make rapid decisions about people and their actions without devoting too much conscious effort or cognitive capacity. These benefits come with two important costs: accuracy and fairness. In broad terms, stereotypes are too simple; they develop relatively early on in a relationship and can therefore contaminate subsequent judgements about performance (Barnes-Farrell, 2001). A manager may hold a stereotype of new graduates as being 'clever but poor at understanding client needs'. This stereotype may have the advantage of leading the manager to prioritise training in client liaison. It could also have the disadvantage of leading a manager to wrongly attribute a client's complaint to the graduate's lack of experience rather than a failure of another work group to deliver a report on time. The consequences of stereotyping vary in severity. This may be a relatively innocuous example, but stereotypes based on racial categories or gender can lead to occupational segregation and economic disadvantage for groups involved (see also Chapter 1 where the issue of diversity at work is examined).

An important use of performance judgements is in making decisions about leadership potential. According to Lord and Maher (1991) becoming a leader is as much about being perceived to be a leader as it is to do with possessing certain qualities or characteristics (*see* Chapter 14). At work those individuals judged by managers to have the potential to become a leader can find themselves singled out to receive additional training and development, provided with greater access to mentors and networks, and therefore more opportunity to build skills required for leadership. However, Lord and Maher also point out that most people base their judgements about leadership potential on their prototype schema of leader characteristics. This develops over time through their personal encounters with leaders and their exposure to leader images in the media, education and work. As such, prototype schemas are more likely to resemble the traditional view of who or what makes a good leader. For example, in most Western cultures a majority of individuals in leadership or more powerful positions are white and male, as such decisions influenced by leadership prototypes are likely to perpetuate this bias. Virginia Schein has illustrated the way in which women and minority groups can be disadvantaged by leadership prototypes in her work on 'think manager – think male' (Schein, 1975; Schein *et al.*, 1996). Schein has shown that automatic processing of leadership prototypes, combined with stereotypes of women and minorities, reduces the likelihood of being judged to have leadership potential. It is therefore important to train managers who are responsible for performance assessment to be aware of unconscious bias that can differentially impact on the progression of different groups.

Finally, the relative power of an observer can exert an unconscious influence on assessment decisions, thereby reducing its reliability and validity. David Kipnis and his colleagues have shown that power-holders typically fail to take full account of their own power and status when explaining why others agree or disagree with them (e.g. Kipnis *et al.*, 1980). Leaders are more likely to think that those who work for them agree with their decisions because they think the decisions are good; consequently, leaders overlook other potential factors such as subordinates' motivation to curry favour with a powerful individual who can influence their future. Kipnis argues that power corrupts because over time power-holders come to believe that their own views are superior and devalue the worth of those held by their subordinates. More recently Fiske (2001) has developed these arguments and in her power-as-control theory claims that powerful people at work stereotype less powerful people for three reasons. First, power-holders already have influence and resources and therefore have less need to expend the cognitive effort required to overcome stereotypes and individuate others. Secondly, individuals at higher organisational levels often manage large numbers of people, which means that they would need to make greater effort to pay individual attention to all the people they are responsible for. Thirdly, those people who self-select for positions of power, or who are appointed to them, may have personal characteristics that mean they are simply less interested in, or motivated to individuate, those lower in a hierarchy.

Although Conway (1999) suggests we still have much to learn about how managers make judgements about work performance, studies have identified factors that can help achieve more objective performance assessment. We know that simply holding people accountable for assessment decisions can make them more careful and less likely to engage in automatic stereotypic thinking. We also know that requiring assessors to record their observations, and to explain their decisions, leads them to engage in more controlled processing of information (Pendry and Macrae, 1996). Finally, bias is more likely when there are no clear or shared criteria regarding good and poor performance (Graves and Powell, 1988). All of these point to the need for work psychologists to continue in their efforts to develop robust, valid and fair assessment procedures.

Key Learning Point

In order to maximise fairness and validity, raters need to be aware of the ways in which unconscious bias can impact upon the way they perceive and rate the performance of others.

Rating performance

Designing rating scales that make it possible to quantify and compare different aspects of job performance is an area where work psychologists have had much to contribute. Figure 6.2 shows several graphical rating scales that vary in their effectiveness at eliciting performance appraisal data. Like many forms of psychological measurement, key issues concern problems of reliability and validity. For example, scales should provide a clear indication of the meaning that can be assigned to each point on the scale (validity) so that the rater, and anyone who needs to interpret the rating on the scale, can make a valid inference. Clear and unambiguous interpretation is impossible with the scales in Figure 6.2a and b, since they provide so little information. It is also important that scales are used consistently, either by different raters, or by the same rater on different occasions. The scale in Figure 6.2c poses problems, because with so much subjective judgement required judgements may well change from rater to rater or from trial to trial. Although the scales in

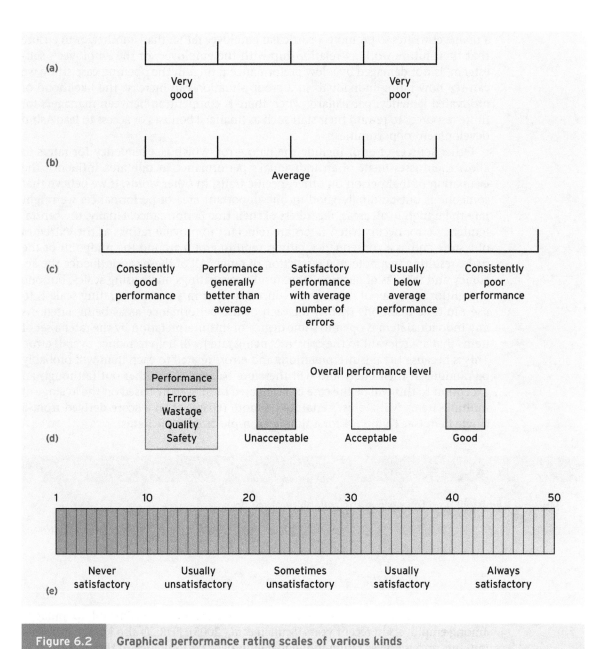

Figure 6.2 Graphical performance rating scales of various kinds

Figure 6.2d and e provide a better basis for validity and reliability, such graphical rating scales are still vulnerable to many possible sources of error. One of these, leniency, is a characteristic of the person doing the rating. Some people appear to be 'easy' raters and tend to provide a greater proportion of high scores (positive leniency). Others can be harsh or severe raters (negative leniency). Leniency effects can often be observed when the results of two or more assessors are compared. Although leniency effects may be the result of unconscious bias on the part of the rater, there is also a potential for motivated leniency, which occurs when a rater is motivated to favour one assessee over another. Motivated leniency might occur when a manager wishes to promote a particular employee rather than another, or to ensure that their future working relationship with the employee, or the employee's self-esteem, is not damaged by a low performance rating. In the opening case study we can see how rating individuals in a group situation can increase the likelihood of motivated leniency; particularly when there is competition between managers for finite resources to reward their staff such as financial bonuses or access to leadership development opportunities.

Other sources of error include the halo error, which is a tendency for raters to allow their assessment of an individual's performance in one area influence the evaluation of that person on other specific traits. In other words, if we believe that someone is outstandingly good in one important area of performance, we might rate them high in all areas, regardless of their true performance. Finally, the central tendency error occurs when raters are reluctant to provide ratings at the extremes of a scale and as a consequence ratings tend to group around the midpoint of the scale, resulting in a potential restriction of range. All of these can influence the accuracy and fairness of decisions that result from ratings made using scales, but one straightforward way of helping to reduce the error in any type of rating scale is to use multiple questions (items) for each of the performance areas being rated. As any individual item is open to some degree of misinterpretation by the rater a set of items that are relevant to the construct being rated will help to reduce overall error. This is because the misinterpretations and errors related to each item will probably be random in their effect and will therefore balance each other out (although an exception to this will be the case of motivated bias). A score based on the average of multiple items will almost certainly be more reliable than a score derived from a single item (see Figure 6.4 for a simple example of multiple items).

Key Learning Point

Multiple items will help to improve the reliability of rating scales.

Forced distribution rating systems

Forced distribution rating systems (FDRS) have achieved considerable popularity among employers in recent years (Scullen *et al.*, 2005). FDRS is also known as forced ranking, and involves rating individual employee performance so that it is directly compared to that of other workers in a group. FDRS is based on the idea that the performance of a group of employees is likely to be normally distributed: there will be lots of average performers, and relatively few high and low performers. However, managers are more likely to show a central tendency (where more employees than expected receive a middle-ranking) or positive bias when rating their own staff. In FDRS managers are required to identify the 20 per cent of their staff who are 'top performers', the 70 per cent who are 'average performers' and the bottom 10 per cent who are 'low performers' (see Figure 6.3). Managers are also expected to act on these ratings by rewarding top performers (e.g. with increased wages or promotions) and dealing with underperformers by setting explicit expectations regarding improved performance or potentially by firing the bottom 5–10 per cent. As such FDRS is seen as a way of encouraging managers to take a more critical look at the people

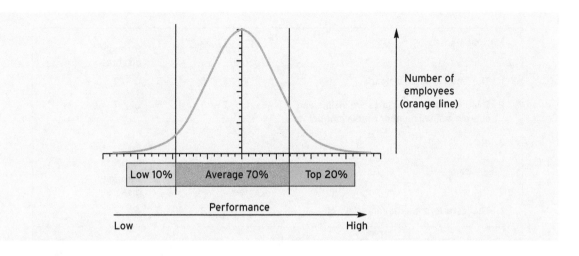

Figure 6.3   **Typical bell curve distribution for FDRS**

that work for them: by constraining the distribution of ratings it is designed to reduce leniency.

Perhaps not surprisingly, FDRS is not always popular among managers and staff. A common complaint from managers is that because they can allocate top grades to only 20 per cent of their staff, the system forces them to downgrade other excellent performers, making them appear like mediocre performers. In fact there are situations where it may not be valid to assume that the performance of a group of employees is normally distributed – for example when there are relatively few people in a group, or when the company is facing challenging market conditions. It is also difficult to implement FDRS when the performance of a group member is co-dependent on that of others. Consequently, FDRS may be better suited to situations where managers supervise larger numbers of relatively independent employees.

Behaviourally anchored rating scales

As we have seen, a common problem with unsatisfactory rating scales concerns the failure to define sufficiently the 'anchors' points. Broad, generalised descriptions of anchors such as 'average', 'good' or 'excellent' make it impossible to be sure that everyone who uses the scales will interpret them similarly. One popular means of providing unambiguous anchor points on a scale is to use behaviourally anchored rating scales (BARS), where anchors describe a specific behaviour which is critical in determining a particular level of job performance (Smith and Kendall, 1963). An example BARS is shown in Figure 6.4. BARS are developed using a four-step procedure:

1   With the aid of a group of 'experts' (these are people who understand the role in detail, e.g. employees, supervisors or senior managers) define the factors needed for successful job performance.

2   Use a second group of 'experts' to provide examples of specific behaviour associated with high, average or low performance on the factors.

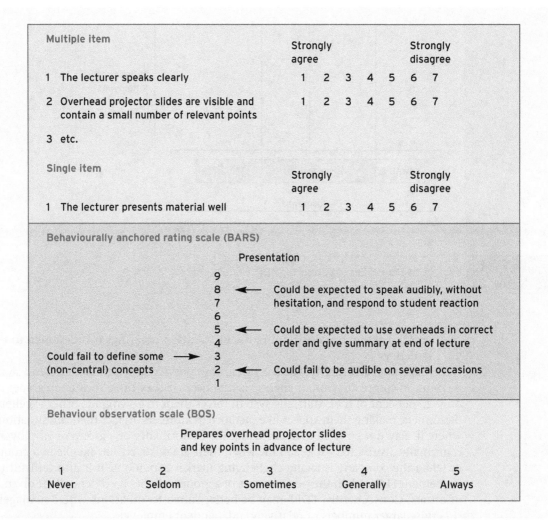

3   A third group takes the examples from step 2 and independently matches them with the factors from step 1. This retranslation acts as a cross-check on the two previous steps. Examples that are not assigned correctly to the aspect for which they were written do not provide unambiguous behavioural anchors for that aspect of job performance and should not be used.

4   The final step involves using more 'experts' to assign scale values to the surviving items, which then serve as the behavioural anchors for the scale.

Research suggests that BARS produce results that are only slightly better than well-constructed graphic rating scales, leading some people to question whether the effort involved in constructing BARS is worth the trouble. However, two points are worth bearing in mind here. First, a well-constructed graphic scale may require an amount of effort equal to that involved in constructing BARS. Second, with planning, it is possible to combine the process of eliciting information required to compile a BARS with undertaking a job analysis, which minimises both cost and effort. Figure 6.4 also shows another scale called a behaviour observation scale (BOS) (e.g. Weirsma and Latham, 1986). BOS development procedures will also ensure the development of reasonably sound scales. In essence BOS, like BARS, are based on critical examples of behaviour. With BOS the rater assesses the ratee in terms of the frequency of occurrence of the relevant behaviour. Some research has shown that there is a preference among users for BOS in the case of appraisal. BOS are seen as better for providing feedback, determining training needs, setting goals and overall ease of use (*see* Latham *et al.*, 1993). Somewhat disappointingly, however, no procedures have been able to produce scales immune to rating errors. Rating behaviour still remains one of the most difficult tasks that managers must undertake when assessing employee performance.

Key Learning Point

Rating scales can be improved by using behavioural anchors that define the types of behaviours that raters might expect someone to demonstrate for each point on the rating scale.

STOP TO CONSIDER

As you have seen, there are various different rating scales that can be used to assess performance, and some are reported to be more accurate than others. Is accuracy the only criterion when choosing a rating scale to assess work performance? In which work situations might accuracy be paramount? In which work situations might it be less important? Do you think that using rating scales overcomes some of the problems that were identified with the use of 'objective' measures of performance, such as sales performance, quality of work and so on?

Performance assessment at work

The first part of this chapter has looked at efforts by work psychologists to define and measure work performance. The latter part considers how this has been applied in practice to the design, implementation and evaluation of performance assessment systems. Before doing so it is worth reflecting on how work has changed over the past 50 years and how this has influenced performance assessment. For example, increased automation has resulted in a simplification of many production-level jobs. The speed of innovation in computer and communication technologies has not only changed the way people work, but where they work and even how organisations are structured. With organisations becoming more global, managers are likely to be responsible for managing and assessing employees who work in different geographical areas, different countries or even different time zones. Teleworking and virtual offices mean that employees can work from home and be supervised by their manager via e-mail or the telephone (Dambrin, 2004), and international work teams frequently depend on videoconferencing to facilitate group meetings. Today's work environments require employees to cope with a faster pace of work, greater levels of change, and demonstrate the flexibility to work with multiple partners and shifting work relationships within flatter and more flexible organisations. These changes also make performance assessment more challenging for managers, many of whom now have a broader span of control, which means more people to assess (London and Tornow, 1998a,b). Fortunately, technological innovation has also brought new ways of shaping assessment systems capable of collecting and comparing performance data across larger numbers of employees over time.

Performance monitoring

Performance monitoring has existed since work first began. Traditionally an overseer or a 'gaffer' would have watched people work and no doubt acted quickly if he thought performance was dropping. Monitoring performance through direct observation of employees is still important, but now electronic methods are increasingly popular, particularly in new types of work environment like call centres. Call centre work involves the use of computer and telephone-based technologies to distribute incoming calls from customers or clients to available staff (Holman, 2005). Electronic performance monitoring is common in call centre environments. Computers can record and store information about every keystroke made by a call centre worker responding to customer enquiries. Computerised tracking can also be used to determine when a worker begins work, as well as when they take comfort breaks (and for how long!). In addition, telephone calls can be recorded so that a third party can check whether a worker has followed a script, the accuracy of information they provide or their helpfulness, enthusiasm and empathy. Managers often undertake spot checks on the quality of an employee's work by listening in to conversations between workers and customer; perhaps without the worker knowing. Holman (2005) reports that, typically, a third of call centres monitor individual worker conversations once a week and another third monitor conversations at least once a month.

There are clearly advantages to be gained by employers who use electronic monitoring. For example, performance data can be collected over periods of time and from large numbers of workers. This makes it possible to look at questions like 'do workers respond less well to difficult customers when they have been working for longer periods of time?', or 'does the performance of new recruits improve after a training programme?' Such data can therefore be an important source of information for evaluating development or selection procedures. However, electronic monitoring can also benefit employees, because performance data that are collected over time are generally more resistant to rater error, and less vulnerable to the effects of one-off events such as employee illness or a problem at work. That said, electronic monitoring can be unpopular, with some researchers and unions claiming that it is overly intrusive and stressful. Yet studies investigating its impact on employees have yielded mixed findings. Bakker *et al.* (2003) found that performance feedback from electronic monitoring reduced emotional exhaustion among employees, possibly because it helped them to understand how to improve their performance and develop new skills. But Holman and colleagues (2002) found that these positive effects were cancelled out if monitoring was perceived as intense or intrusive. These findings point to the need for management to take care in considering how electronic and other forms of monitoring are used in the workplace and explained to employees.

Exercise 6.2   Monitoring your performance

How would you feel if you were continually monitored at work? Would you see this as an infringement of your rights, or do you think you would soon forget that you were being recorded? Now put yourself in a manager's position. How would you reassure employees that this type of monitoring was justified? How else might you capture relevant performance-related data?

Performance assessment and human resource management

Another important change over the past 20 years has been the rapid evolution of human resource management (HRM). During this period HRM has emerged to replace traditional personnel functions in many organisations, with HR managers taking responsibility for organisational activities concerned with recruiting, developing and managing employees. HRM plays a strategic role in organisations and is in sharp contrast with personnel management, which focused on providing support and services such as payroll and contracts. According to the HRM philosophy employees are an important business resource (sometimes referred to as human capital) which needs to be managed carefully to maximise return on investment (ROI) and achieve business objectives. HR managers therefore seek to align HR strategy with business strategy by designing systems such as recruitment, development and performance management that can help to achieve business objectives (Hendry and Pettigrew, 1986). A good example of this can be found in the recent popularity of 'talent pipelines' where efforts are made to identify at a very early stage those individuals with the potential to achieve leadership positions. Once identified, these individuals are provided with additional support and development opportunities to help them rise through the pipeline and achieve higher organisational positions. Repositioning HRM as a strategic driver central to business success has meant that it has become a more powerful area of operations within many larger corporations (Guest, 1997; Novicevic and Harvey, 2004).

HRM has had a big influence on performance assessment. For example, information gained from HRM systems can be used to inform and justify business decisions about investment in many different areas such as leadership development or coaching. That said, some researchers have questioned the assumption that implementing such systems will inevitably lead to business improvement. Wall and Wood (2005), for example, argue that we should be cautious about placing too much faith in the effectiveness of HRM. They reviewed the evidence from existing studies and found that in many cases conclusions drawn about causal links between HRM and business performance were limited by poor research design, a failure to capture longitudinal data and a reliance on findings from single organisations. Wall and Wood argue that it is premature to conclude that HRM processes inevitably lead to organisational performance gains. They call for researchers to undertake more rigorous research, in order to identify the specific factors that lead HRM approaches to deliver improved individual or business performance. Their research also reminds us of the importance of paying attention to the type of performance data used and to ensure that individual performance assessment judgements are valid and reliable.

After all, aggregated business performance data often relies on individual judgements made by managers about their workers: as we have already seen, these can be subject to bias.

Key Learning Point

Human resource management (HRM) aligns people strategies with business strategies by designing performance assessment systems that identify, develop and reward talent to achieve business objectives.

Performance appraisal

One of the most important contexts for performance assessment is employee appraisal. Performance assessment exists to capture information about how well an individual is meeting the requirements of a role so that the best strategies for maintaining or improving performance can be determined. Key to this process is the opportunity for a manager to provide feedback to an employee and engage in a dialogue about what they could be doing differently. By far the most common method for doing this is the performance appraisal (PA) meeting between manager and employee, which can serve many purposes including:

- providing an employee with feedback about how they have performed;
- determining whether an employee has development needs;
- identifying areas where performance can be improved;
- establishing future performance goals or objectives;
- making appropriate performance-related rewards;
- identifying individuals with potential to move to more senior or challenging roles;
- determining the reasons for poor performance;
- comparing individual performance with that of other employees.

In broad terms, PA is a mechanism for ensuring that an individual's performance is contributing to business goals. In reality PA involves a complex social interaction between individuals with different, possibly competing needs and views. Therefore the PA meeting is an opportunity for managers to help employees understand how their personal objectives link to the overall business strategy (Williams, 2002), thereby building a shared understanding about wider organisational needs and how to achieve them. In his review of current research and practice on PA, Fletcher (2008, p. 5) makes an important point; he argues that the most important question that those intending to develop and implement an appraisal process must answer is 'what's the aim?' 'Get this bit wrong and you can bet that . . . the appraisal system will not run smoothly – if at all.' Indeed, one third of the people in Kluger and DeNisi's (1996) study demonstrated reduced performance following appraisal, illustrating

"Before we begin your performance review,
I took the liberty of ordering you some comfort food."

Figure 6.5	The impact that performance appraisal could have on an employee
	Source: Randy Glasbergen, Glasbergen Cartoons, www.glasbergen.com

that, if not done properly, performance appraisal also has the ability to demotivate employees.

A common problem occurs when PA systems are designed for both development and reward. Performance-related pay (PRP) or 'merit pay' is one of the most difficult and contentious areas that managers encounter in their roles, but efforts to discuss reward alongside employee developmental needs compound the difficulty still further. Few individuals are willing to be open and frank about areas they need to improve if they also know that the PA meeting will determine how much they are paid. As Fletcher (2008) points out, people might like the idea of linking pay to performance, but they also tend to believe that their own performance is better than most of their peers. This perception can be even more prevalent at senior levels (Wright, 1991) and may be one explanation for the prevalence of 'fat cat' bonuses at executive levels! For this reason, it is often better to keep assessment processes for the purposes of employee development separate from those concerning reward.

Advantages and disadvantages of performance appraisal

Traditional PA meetings usually involve a discussion between the manager and employee about the employee's performance over the past 6–12 months. The manager provides feedback about how the employee has performed relative to expectations, plus evidence of good or poor performance to support their assessment. Employees are usually asked to provide a self-review describing what they see as their main achievements over the period and identifying areas where they might develop further. This enables the manager and employee to discuss any differences that may emerge, and agree future performance objectives. One advantage of PA meetings is that they can be adaptable, providing an opportunity for reflective dialogue between employee and manager. This two-way discussion helps to enhance the employee' sense of control over the review process and can encourage employee engagement.

However, PA can also be stressful and a source of considerable dissatisfaction for both employees and managers. Managers often find it difficult to deliver feedback to underperforming employees or meet the expectations of those who are performing very well. Some employees also find it difficult to present a good impression of themselves and their work. There are a number of difficulties with traditional PA that are worth exploring. For example, performance ratings and decisions are usually heavily reliant on a single source (the manager) in PA. This can make them more vulnerable to bias and error, because managers may only observe a small fraction of the work undertaken by an employee, and this fraction may not be an accurate reflection of their overall performance. Managers' ratings can also be influenced by their prior experience of an employee, whether they like that person as well as how 'valuable' the employee is to the manager in other ways (Arvey and Murphy, 1998).

There is evidence that employees and managers act to consciously distort the outcomes of appraisal. It is not surprising that employees are keen to present favourable impression in PA settings Rosenfeld et al. (2002) argue that some individuals are more motivated and skilled at engaging in impression management (IM) than others. It is possible that IM reduces the validity and accuracy of managers' decisions, and according to Frink and Ferris (1998) evaluation systems where employees set performance goals are particularly prone to this. Klimoski and Inks (1990) found that performance ratings were significantly higher when raters were made aware that the ratee had made a high self-assessment. Murphy and Cleveland (1995) argue that when an employee overestimates their own performance, raters are more likely to give lenient ratings to protect the subordinate's self-esteem or the manager–subordinate relationship. However, if IM is itself an important skill for leadership roles, it may be that IM improves the validity of PA judgements (Silvester et al., 2002). A less frequently discussed issue, however, is the fact that managers can also be motivated to distort performance appraisal processes for their own needs (Gioia and Longenecker, 1994). This can occur if a manager is keen to retain a valuable team member or lose a difficult or poor performer. In fact, promotion and reward decisions generate most of the incidents described as political in organisations (Ferris and King, 1991) and Murphy and Cleveland (1995) argue that organisational and political factors exert a stronger influence on performance ratings than appraiser capabilities and limitations.

Relatively few studies have investigated motivated distortion – possibly because managers may be less forthcoming about the 'darker' side of PA. However, managers' concerns about harming their relationship with a subordinate appear to influence PA ratings (Murphy and Cleveland, 1995; Murphy et al., 2004). Murphy and Cleveland (1995) argue that raters make accurate private judgements about performance, but often distort these in their public ratings of performance. In cases of poor employee performance, managers may use lenient PA ratings to enhance employee self-efficacy (i.e. to help the employee feel more positive about their skills) or to avoid post-appraisal conflict with the employee (Harris, 1994). It has also been shown that a manager's personality can also influence the ratings they give. Rater conscientiousness has been shown to be linked to accurate ratings (Tziner et al., 2005). In contrast, high-agreeableness individuals show a propensity to value conflict-free, harmonious relationships with others and have a willingness to compromise their own interests for the sake of others (*see* Chapter 3). This means they are more likely to give lenient ratings (Bernardin *et al.*, 2000). Yun and colleagues (2005) found a significant link between rater agreeableness and performance ratings when poor performance was being evaluated. This suggests that ratings may be more accurate if managers are given the skills and confidence that they need to manage difficult discussions with an employee who is not performing well.

Another problem is that work has become increasingly co-dependent (Griffin *et al.*, 2007). This means that the performance of many individual workers will depend as much on how others perform as it does on their own efforts. A problem for PA is therefore to determine how the efforts of individuals can be separated from those of their colleagues, or how individuals should be rewarded if they have performed well, but their team or the company has not. Although work psychologists have begun to explore how assessment and appraisal systems can be adapted for use with teams or other areas where work is co-dependent there is still much work to be done in this area.

Villanova and Bernardin (1991) list some of the ways in which PA can be structured to help avoid some of these problems. They suggest that it is important to:

- make sure that the performance criteria used by managers in PA are relevant to the job and essential or at least important to job performance;
- provide clear definitions for performance criteria so that both managers and employees have a shared understanding of what is being assessed;
- train appraisers and appraisees so that they know how to use the system;
- ensure that appraisal happens frequently to avoid managers relying too much on memory or generic impressions;
- aggregate individual performance to a group or team level when the performance of employees is co-dependent on others;
- increase the number of people who provide performance ratings and combine ratings from these raters statistically;
- hold appraisers accountable for their ratings.

Exercise 6.3   Isolating individual performance

There are many situations where an individual worker performs well because of situational factors rather than their own efforts. A good example of this is the case of equity traders who buy and sell shares on the stock market. It is usually easier to make a profit buying and selling shares in a bull market (where the price of shares are moving up) than in a bear market (when prices are falling). Yet the bonus payments made to traders in bull markets are higher than those made in bear markets. Why might this be the case, and can anything be done to separate the effects of the market on individual trader performance?

Multi-source feedback

Multi-source feedback (MSF) has emerged in response to many of the criticisms levelled at traditional PA – as Fletcher (2008) puts it MSF 'is an idea whose time has come' (p. 69). MSF is often referred to as 360-degree feedback because individuals are rated anonymously by several different raters including their manager, work colleagues, people who they supervise (direct reports) and potentially their clients (see Figure 6.6). Although there have been various surveys exploring the use of MSF in business (e.g. Church, 2000; CIPD, 2008b; Kandola and Galpin, 2000) there is general consensus that its use is increasing. For example, a survey of UK companies by the Chartered Institute of Personnel Development (CIPD, 2005a) found that the proportion of companies using MSF rose from 11 per cent in 1997 to 14 per cent in 2005. Reasons for this success include the potential for MSF to provide a more rounded, and therefore possibly more accurate, picture of an individual's performance (London and Smither, 1995). As many different people provide performance ratings, each can observe a slightly different aspect of the person's work, thereby

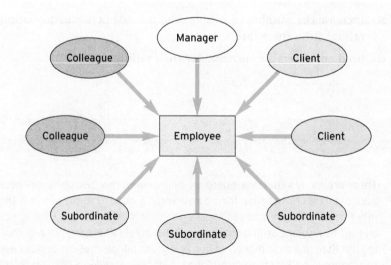

Figure 6.6   **Feedback sources for multi-source feedback**

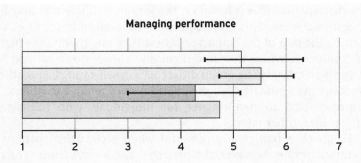

Managing performance

| Figure 6.7 | Comparison of ratings from different sources |

contributing to the validity of an assessment. For example, work colleagues may be better able to judge how well someone engages with other team members; customers can provide a different perspective on service interactions, and direct reports on their manager's ability to manage.

MSF typically involves 8–10 people who individually rate a target person on a series of behaviours relevant to the job (e.g. 'responds quickly to customer needs' or 'provides clear instructions to colleagues') using 5 or 7-point Likert-type scales (such as those shown earlier in Figures 6.3 and 6.4). Early forms of MSF were paper-based, requiring that information be collated and analysed by hand, but more recently online systems make it possible to collect and analyse large amounts of performance feedback, and translate these into feedback reports, quickly and with relatively little effort (Stanton, 2000). Figure 6.7 illustrates how feedback from different sources (self [in blue], manager, colleagues and subordinates) might be summarised and presented in a report.

Each bar indicates the mean rating provided by individuals in a rater group to items relating to a competency, in this case 'managing performance' where 1 = well below average and 7 = well above average. The bottom bar represents how the individual has rated themselves, the second bar up shows ratings from senior managers, the third bar ratings from colleagues, and the top bar ratings from subordinates. The lines on each of the bars show maximum and minimum ratings from that group, which provide an indication of how varied the ratings were from individuals within that group. Comparing ratings from different groups helps employees understand where they might need to change: for example, if they rate themselves higher than others on an area such as 'listens to customer's needs', feedback helps the individual to understand that this is an area they need to develop. A discrepancy between self- and other-ratings can occur because individuals lack self-awareness (Atwater *et al.*, 1998) and therefore, feedback provides them with a means of more effectively calibrating their own efforts and performance against that of others and the expectations of their manager. Some individuals may overrate their performance, whereas others underestimate their performance. Researchers have investigated systematic group differences in self-assessment, with some arguing that women typically underestimate their performance relative to men (Wohlers and London, 1989). In reality, however, findings have been mixed with most studies demonstrating few consistent gender differences (Ibarra and Obodaru, 2009).

The discrepancy between self-ratings and ratings from others is also an area of interest, because it is assumed that feedback can help individuals to act to reduce the discrepancy. This is based on the idea that differences may be caused by a lack of self-awareness. This may require a recalibration in terms of a change in behaviour on the part of the employee, where they rate themselves higher than others, or in confidence where they rate themselves lower (Johnson and Ferstl, 1999). However, there may also be group differences in self-ratings, and other individuals may typically overestimate their own performance relative to others. They found bigger improvements in performance for individuals who initially rated themselves higher than other raters.

Feedback is particularly powerful when a consistent pattern emerges from all feedback groups; however, the pattern is not always consistent and differences between ratings provided by different groups and between self and others are more complex than may at first appear. For example, if an individual is rated high on customer service by their colleagues and by customers, but not by their manager, which ratings should they believe? This raises interesting questions about the validity of assessments, because it is quite possible that while each set of ratings may be an accurate reflection of the views of that particular group, each group may have a slightly different construction of what good performance entails for that particular performance area. For example, a manager's view of how the individual should undertake customer service may reflect broader organisational demands that customer service should always link to a sale, whereas customers and colleagues may view customer service entirely in terms of helping behaviour (such as OCBs). Neither is right or wrong except that certain sources may have more power and legitimacy in terms of what employees should pay attention to. Source credibility determines what feedback employees are most likely to pay attention to and relates to both trust in, and perceived level of influence of, a particular feedback source (Kluger and DeNisi, 1996). Bailey and Fletcher (2002) found that although feedback from direct reports was the most accurate, individuals paid most attention to the feedback that came from their boss!

Key Learning Point

Multiple performance ratings from different sources can provide a more rounded picture of an individual's work performance.

Does MSF work?

According to Smither and colleagues (2005) evidence that MSF leads to enhanced work performance is mixed. In their meta-analysis of 24 longitudinal studies Smither *et al.* found only modest improvements in employee behaviour and attitudes following the introduction of MSF systems. Fletcher (1998) also found that most organisations that introduced MSF for PA dropped it again within two years. Atwater *et al.* (2007) suggest a number of key factors are likely to impact on the success of an MSF system, including clarity of purpose, the level of trust participants have in the system, individual characteristics of those receiving feedback and organisational factors like post-feedback support.

MSF appears to be more successful if it is implemented first as an employee development tool rather than for evaluation. For this reason London (2001a) suggests that the first 2–4 rounds of MSF should be used for developmental purposes and that, at least initially, individuals should not be expected to share their feedback with their bosses. This helps to foster trust in the system, a factor identified as important by Bolton *et al.* (2004) who also found that online feedback helped to promote anonymity for raters. This anonymity increased the level of trust that individuals had in the system. Of course, it may also be that the lack of accountability provided by anonymous ratings may have an impact on the quality of the rating.

Individual differences also appear to be important determinants of reactions to feedback. Smither *et al.* (2005) found that subsequent improvement in ratings provided by direct reports, peers and supervisors were greater among individuals with a positive orientation to feedback, who perceived a need to change and believed that change was possible, and set realistic goals for themselves. Colquitt and colleagues (2000) also found that individuals with high conscientiousness and self-efficacy, low anxiety and an internal locus of control were more motivated to use feedback for development. Interestingly, Smither *et al.* (2005) found that although leaders who received unfavourable feedback reacted negatively at first, after six months this group had set more performance goals than other leaders who had received more favourable feedback. This suggests that MSF may have a delayed effect on performance, with recipients taking a little time to process and respond to the feedback, and that researchers and practitioners need to consider when evaluation data are collected in order to properly evaluate the impact of MSF.

Finally, it appears that follow-up support also enhances the likelihood that performance will improve among feedback recipients. Mabey (2001) found that individuals who believed that co-workers and supervisors supported their development reacted more positively towards feedback, and that simply discussing their feedback with managers resulted in significantly greater improvement over five years (Walker and Smither, 1999). Providing post-MSF coaching has also been found to increase the benefits of feedback through improved job satisfaction and reduced intentions to leave the organisation (Tyson and Ward, 2004).

Clearly there are many interesting questions that arise from the development and utilisation of MSF systems. Not the least of these has been the opportunity to collect large amounts of performance data very quickly and easily. Future developments are likely to focus on the design and utilisation of even more efficient systems. However, the most exciting opportunities may well lie in using MSF to aid our understanding of what we mean by work performance and how this is constructed and shared by different groups within organisational settings.

Key Learning Point

MSF can lead to improvements in employee performance provided there is trust in the process, and support is provided post-feedback to help individuals understand and act on identified development needs.

Improving performance

Performance assessment exists to inform strategies for improving employee performance and achieving business objectives. One aspect of this involves identifying the most effective way of rewarding people for good performance. An obvious form

Table 6.2	Examples of rewards	
Social context	**Job-related**	**Personal**
■ Private office ■ Desk near a window ■ Company parties ■ Club privileges ■ Access to personal learning opportunities (not job-related) ■ Introduction to senior personnel ■ Membership of 'high potential' group	■ Flexible working hours and/or breaks ■ Job with more responsibility ■ Control over work content (e.g. choice of clients, projects) ■ Access to a mentor or coach ■ Home-working ■ Job rotation	■ Saying 'thank you' ■ Compliments on work in progress ■ Friendly greetings ■ Soliciting advice, views or suggestions ■ Non-verbal recognition (smile) ■ Formal recognition of achievement (letter, in-house journal)

of reward is pay, but there are many other rewards that managers can use with staff that do not necessarily involve substantial financial outlay (see Table 6.2).

The study of work motivation is of direct relevance to employee reward. Chapter 8 discusses the various models of motivation in some detail and describes their implications for the reward and management of employee performance. Many of these theories describe the employee as someone who processes information about rewards (i.e. they actively appraise rewards) and there are individual differences in what different employees find rewarding, or feel to be important to them. However, there are some approaches to reward that argue that behaviour can be modified through the delivery of timely rewards after instances of desirable behaviour. One such approach, behaviour modification, is discussed below.

Behaviour modification

Rewards are an important component of behaviour modification (OBMod), the theory and practice of which have been used as part of behaviour change programmes for several decades (Hellervik *et al.*, 1992). The essence of behaviour modification involves focusing on critical behaviours that are important for satisfactory work performance and the application of reinforcement principles to strengthen desired behaviour patterns. According to Luthans and Kreitner (1975), the first step is to identify the desired behaviour and then specify the critical behaviours that need changing and how. This can be done in a number of ways, such as through discussion with relevant personnel, systematic observation or via focus groups. The second component of OBMod involves creating a baseline measure of the frequency of critical behaviours, either by direct observation or recording, or perhaps from existing company records. This is important for two reasons: the baseline provides an objective view of the current situation and acts as a basis for examining any change that may take place. The third step involves a functional analysis that identifies (i) the cues or stimuli in the work situation (antecedent conditions) that trigger the behaviour, and (ii) the contingent consequences (i.e. the consequences in terms of reward or punishment, etc.) that are maintaining the behaviour. This step is important because changing target behaviour depends on understanding the situational triggers that cause it, as well as the factors that reinforce or could potentially extinguish it.

Once the functional analysis has been completed, an intervention strategy can be designed to modify the target behaviours by strengthening desirable behaviour and weakening undesirable behaviour using reinforcement. Positive reinforcement works by increasing the frequency of the desired behaviour when the reinforcement is introduced. For example, a manager who e-mails to say thank you for a report that an employee has worked extremely hard to produce is using a social reinforcer to increase the likelihood that the employee will demonstrate similar levels of effort in future. Another example of positive reinforcement would be the introduction of flexible working hours for employees who have demonstrated a high level of commitment and punctuality. In contrast, the effects of negative reinforcement appear when the negative reinforcement is removed. An example of this would be when performance levels increase after employees are told that they are no longer required to complete time-sheets recording how they spend their day. Punishment works by extinguishing a behaviour (e.g. a manager issuing a formal warning to an employee for inappropriate language towards a colleague).

Exercise 6.4   Using behaviour modification

In a letter printed in the *Financial Times* on 8 January 2009 a manager describes being so fed up with people turning up late to weekly team meetings that, with the team's agreement, he decided to fine any individual who arrived more than five minutes late. They were each asked to pay £1 into a kitty that would be used at the end of the year to buy bottles of wine for the office party. The manager writes that this proved so popular that punctuality increased to 100 per cent and they failed to buy even a single bottle.

Suggested exercise

How was this manager drawing on principles of behaviour modification?

Summary

Assessing performance at work is an area so important for work psychology that it is almost taken for granted. Arvey and Murphy (1998) point out that the vast majority of validation research in employee selection and development relies on managers' assessments of performance. Therefore much more could be done to build understanding in this area; particularly in relation to defining work performance as an outcome criteria (Tubré *et al.*, 2006). Building a theoretical and practical evidence base is especially important for the development of assessment systems capable of dealing with twenty-first-century challenges, including a faster pace of change, greater co-dependency between workers and a dramatic growth in the availability of information fuelled by an increasing use of technology. Whilst technological innovations have generated many opportunities for fast large-scale assessment systems there is still a need for a better understanding of what the technology is measuring.

Another area that has received relatively little attention concerns the role of power and politics in assessment (Gioia and Longenecker, 1994). The opening case study involving the assessment of junior bankers' performance reveals several potential problems: there is little evidence that senior managers are assessing the performance of these juniors using shared performance criteria or even that their judgements are based on evidence of performance. Neither does there appear to be any account taken of potential cultural differences (these juniors may be drawn from different parts of the world), or any consideration of whether they are doing comparable jobs. These problems aside, one of the most notable features of this assessment scenario is that a group of senior managers are competing with each other in a public arena to reward their juniors from a finite pool of resources. This automatically brings into play concerns about the seniors' own performance and their desire to create a positive impression of their own sectors. Combine competition for resources (bonus payments) with an investment banking corporate culture that generally promotes aggressive rivalry and free market conditions, and the scene is set for motivated distortion and/or selective presentation of performance information rather than objective assessment. In reality many situations involving performance assessment and promotion decisions, particularly at senior levels, occur in similar public settings. They are therefore rife with opportunities for political manoeuvring and game-playing among decision-makers (Bozionelos, 2005) that can have a much more powerful influence on decisions than carefully and systematically collected objective evidence. This is an area that deserves far more attention from psychologists, as does recognition of performance assessment and HRM as political systems (Novicevic and Harvey, 2004), because they formalise and legitimise a managerial perspective and increase managers' power to control performance (Ferris and Judge, 1991). Hollway (1991) argues that it is important for work and organisational psychologists to recognise and acknowledge the social and political conditions that underpin their work. In the case of assessment, it is therefore also important to recognise the importance of power in shaping a shared understanding of what good and poor performance looks like in different settings, as well as the role played by political motivations in assessment decisions.

Closing Case Study   Using bonuses

You are the manager of a team of 16 software specialists responsible for designing new software for client-owned mobile phone networks. The team represents the end-point in the design process. Team members interface with client users and help them to implement the new technology. They are ultimately responsible for making sure that there are no problems or glitches with the new software, and that implementation occurs smoothly. Most of the work involves final-stage testing of the software and client liaison, either remotely, or by travelling to the client's location, which can be anywhere in the world.

Although there are some very good team members, who consistently put in extra effort, others are less committed and 3-4 frequently underperform. One of the underperformers has been suffering from depression and as a result has had to take several weeks off work (although the reason is unknown to the team). You have also received complaints from some of your team that another team is responsible for getting a virtually finished product to your team to work on, but they have often produced poor work or missed deadlines.

Suggested exercise

This year the company has decided to allocate a bonus of £30,000 to be divided between you and your team. Your task is to decide how to divide this bonus up and explain why you have reached your decision. How would you make the process fairer next year?

Test your learning

Short-answer questions

1 Define job performance.

2 What is organisational citizenship behaviour?

3 What factors can lead to bias when managers rate the performance of their employees?

4 How would you create a behaviourally anchored rating scale?

5 What does FDRS stand for?

6 What is 'electronic monitoring'?

7 Why is the HRM approach different from that taken by personnel functions?

8 What are the main differences between traditional performance appraisal and MSF?

9 What is meant by 'source credibility' in MSF?

10 List five ways that managers can reward staff (don't include money).

Suggested assignments

1 Why does Campbell believe that mapping the latent structure of job performance is akin to understanding personality or cognitive ability?

2 How can we make interpersonal assessment more objective and reliable?

3   What advice would you give to an organisation keen to implement a new performance appraisal process that is rigorous, fair and objective?

4   Electronic monitoring is an important tool for managers. Discuss.

5   Employees often prefer traditional performance appraisal to feedback from MSF. Are they right to do so?

6   How might individual differences influence an appraisee's response to feedback?

7   If performance assessment depends on managers' views of what constitutes good and bad performance, can it ever be a democratic process?

Relevant websites

An interesting and provocative site developed by the American consultant Robert Bacal can be found at http://performance-appraisals.org/. It contains a lot of information (and honest opinion!) about how to do – and how not to do – performance appraisal.

The Chartered Institute for Personnel and Development website contains lots of practical information about performance appraisal which draws upon both scientific research and the experience of practitioners. It is also a good link to other resources on the topic: http://www.cipd.co.uk/subjects/perfmangmt/appfdbck/perfapp.htm.

For further self-test material and relevant, annotated weblinks please visit the website at **www.pearsoned.co.uk/workpsych**

Suggested further reading

Full details for all the references are given in the list at the back of this book.

1   Clive Fletcher provides an excellent review of the key elements of performance appraisal and the practical steps involved in developing appraisal schemes and multimethod multisource (360-degree) rating schemes in his book *Appraisal, Feedback and Development: Making performance review work*, 4th edition.

2   *How People Evaluate Others in Organizations* edited by Manuel London, published in 2001, is a detailed review of some of the research concerned with assessing people at or for work that expands on many of the themes in this chapter.

CHAPTER 7

Attitudes at work and the employment relationship

LEARNING OUTCOMES

After studying this chapter, you should be able to:

1 briefly describe two ways in which attitudes have been divided into three components;

2 specify two functions of attitudes for the person who holds them;

3 describe the theory of planned behaviour;

4 explain why attitudes and behaviour are not always consistent;

5 describe three features of attitudes that increase the probability that they will influence behaviour;

6 define job satisfaction and identify three general propositions about what affects it;

7 describe one research study that has suggested that a person's job satisfaction is not simply a function of the nature of their work;

8 define organisational commitment and its component parts;

9 specify the factors that appear to strengthen a person's organisational commitment, and outline its consequences;

10 understand the main causes of employee turnover;

11 describe different explanations of why unemployment has negative consequences;

12 explain the psychological contract and understand what influences it and how breaches of it affect employees and employers;

13 describe the factors that affect the success of attempts to change attitudes;

14 define negotiation and distinguish between different types of negotiator behaviour;

15 define the main features of interest-based negotiation.

Opening Case Study

CIPD survey showing rise in job satisfaction suggests that worried workers' response to the recession is to grin and bear it

Job satisfaction has surprisingly increased since 2006 despite the impact of the recession, according to the new quarterly Employee Outlook survey of more than 3,000 employees by the Chartered Institute of Personnel and Development. The survey finds that the net proportion of people satisfied with their job has increased to +46 from +26 in 2006 and the proportion of people who say their job makes them feel cheerful most or all of the time has also gone up.

However, the survey suggests that fault lines are developing that will undermine employee well-being, morale and commitment if not addressed. Exactly three-quarters of respondents report their organisation has been affected by the recession with half (52 per cent) citing increases in work-related stress as a consequence and nearly four in ten (38 per cent) agreeing there has been a rise in office politics.

The proportion of people who say their jobs make them worried or tense has also increased since the CIPD's 2006 employee attitudes and engagement survey and nearly six in ten employees say they are worried by the future. Ben Willmott, Senior Public Policy Adviser and co-author of the survey, CIPD, says:

> Job satisfaction may have edged up – but this could be the employee opinion survey equivalent of a fixed grin. Employees grateful to have a job at all are less likely to grumble, and more likely to see scorched earth rather than greener grass on the other side of the fence.

> Beneath this positive glow, however, our survey highlights the impact the recession is having on the workplace. Without action to tackle some of the stresses and strains that are clear in our survey, employers could find employee health and well-being deteriorating, and employee engagement tailing off at precisely the time they need all hands to the pump to survive the recession and thrive in the recovery.

The research shows a third (37 per cent) of employees worry about being made redundant as a result of the recession and most believe finding a new job would be difficult. Almost four in ten (36 per cent) employees report that their organisation has made redundancies or is planning to make job cuts and just under a fifth say their employer has cut back on training (17 per cent), or frozen pay (18 per cent).

The survey, conducted by YouGov, also highlights problems with how people are managed. Although most people feel supported and treated fairly by their line manager they are much less happy with the extent their manager discusses their training and development, gives feedback or coaches them.

Employees are particularly critical of senior managers, with less than a fifth agreeing that they trust them and only a quarter agreeing that they consult employees about important decisions.

Source: 'CIPD survey showing rise in job satisfaction suggests that worried workers' response to the recession is to grin and bear it' from CIPD press release, 5 May 2009, http://www.cipd.co.uk/pressoffice/_articles/EmployeeOutlook050509.htm, with the permission of the publisher, the Chartered Institute of Personnel and Development, London (www.cipd.co.uk).

Introduction

This press release is typical of many that describe the results of an attitude survey. Such surveys are a common feature of twenty-first century life. The press release makes some assumptions and claims that are common. First, it assumes that attitudes are not neutral. They include an element of emotion and or evaluation. In this case happiness (or lack of it) about feedback from management (amongst other things), and the 'grin and bear it' attitude to the recession influence how cheerful their jobs make employees feel. Second, attitudes are linked to behaviour: in this case it is suggested that underperformance is a possible outcome of employees becoming less engaged in their work. Third, there is an implication that attitudes can be changed, perhaps by managers consulting more with employees. Fourth, it is assumed that the view expressed by a person in an attitude survey reflects something more long-term than a momentary opinion.

It is well over half a century since attitude surveys become a standard tool for managers to check on what employees thought of their work and their workplace (Schneider *et al.*, 1996). The design, analysis and reporting of attitude surveys have been prominent activities of work and organisational psychologists ever since. Over the same period, more theoretically minded academic social psychologists have developed some sophisticated analyses of the nature of attitudes, how they change, and how they predict behaviour (or fail to). In this chapter we first provide a discussion of what an attitude is, with particular reference to the work situation. Second, we briefly describe the ways in which attitudes can be measured. Then we will look at two of the attitudes that are particularly important in work psychology – job satisfaction and organisational commitment. We will also take a look at what work means to people by examining the issues of turnover and unemployment.

Then attention turns to the question of what factors affect the formation and change of attitudes at work. A particularly important concept in work psychology is the psychological contract, so we look at this in some detail. We also look at how attitudes can be changed and the process of negotiation in the workplace. Attitude change might not be very important if it is not reflected in behaviour change, so the connection between attitudes and behaviour is a recurrent theme in this chapter.

What is an attitude?

Attitudes were defined by Secord and Backman (1969) as 'certain regularities of an individual's feelings, thoughts and predispositions to act toward some aspect of his [sic] environment'. Feelings represent the *affective component* of an attitude, thoughts the *cognitive component* and predispositions to act the *behavioural component*. Attitudes are evaluative; that is, they reflect a person's tendency to feel, think or behave in a positive or negative manner towards the object of the attitude. Evaluative dimensions of attitudes include good–bad, harmful–beneficial, pleasant–unpleasant and likeable–dislikeable (Ajzen, 2001). Attitudes refer to a particular *target*, or *object* – a person (e.g. boss), group of people (e.g. close colleagues, senior management), object (e.g. work equipment) or concept (e.g. performance-related pay). Because of this, attitudes are different from personality which reflects a person's predispositions across a range of situations. Everyone holds attitudes, not least because it seems that we usually attach an evaluation to our perceptions of people and things around us

(Ajzen and Fishbein, 2000). However, some people hold some attitudes more strongly than others. This is because the strength of the tendency to evaluate is partly an individual difference variable (Jarvis and Petty, 1996).

The affective component of an attitude (how we feel about something) is reflected in a person's physiological responses (e.g. increased blood pressure might rise when the computer crashes – again) and/or in what the person says about how they feel about the object of the attitude. The cognitive component refers to a person's *perception* of the object of the attitude, and/or what the person says they believe about that object (e.g. that computers are unreliable). The behavioural component is reflected by a person's observable *behaviour* toward the object of the attitude and/or what they say about that behaviour (e.g. furiously clicking the mouse button in frustration!). In practice, the term 'attitude' is usually taken to mean the cognitive and/or affective components. Behaviour is most often construed as an outcome of attitudes (*see* below, Attitudes and behaviour).

Key Learning Point

Attitudes are a person's predisposition to think (cognitive component), feel (affective component) or behave (behavioural component) in certain ways towards certain defined targets. Attitudes are different to personality because they focus on particular object/target.

Is it worth noting that there can be some differences between these three components (Breckler, 1984). Hence, it is possible for a person to feel positive about their job (affective component) but to believe that the job has few attractive elements (cognitive component). Which attitude is expressed, and which one will influence behaviour on any given occasion, may therefore depend on whether the person is concentrating on emotions or on beliefs at that time (Millar and Tesser, 1989). Later in this chapter we look at employee turnover and you will see that because someone does not like a job, it does not mean that they will resign (especially if they see 'scorched earth' elsewhere, as described in the opening case study).

It is also important to distinguish attitudes from other related concepts. George and Jones (1997) analyse the relationships between attitudes, values and moods. Values are a person's beliefs about what is good or desirable in life. They are long-term guides for a person's choices and experiences. As the opening case study shows, it might be that a worker does not like their boss but what they value the most are the money and security that the job provides, and that a harmonious working relationship with their boss is relatively unimportant to them. Moods, on the other hand, are 'generalized affective states that are not explicitly linked to particular events or circumstances which may have originally induced the mood' (George and Jones, 1997, p. 400).

Values, attitudes and moods differ in terms of (i) whether they concern the past, present or future; (ii) their stability over time; and (iii) whether they are general or specific. These differences are summarised in Table 7.1. The three concepts are linked. In the long run, attitudes can change values. For example, being dissatisfied with one's job for a long time may change a person's beliefs about the importance of work in life. A consideration of values and moods also helps to explain why attitudes do not always predict behaviour at work. A person may have negative attitudes towards their job and colleagues but still help out others at work because they place a high value on being responsible and cooperative. The link (or lack of it) between attitudes and behaviour is discussed further later in this chapter.

Table 7.1	Values, attitudes and moods		
	Values	**Attitudes**	**Moods**
Time perspective	Future (how things should be)	Past (my past experience of a target)	Present (how I feel right now)
Dynamism	Stable (little change over long periods)	Evolving (slow or steady change)	Fluctuating (substantial change over short periods)
Focus	General (guides approach to life)	Specific (directed towards a specific target)	General (how I feel about everything right now)

Source: Adapted from J. M. George and G. R. Jones (1997) 'Experiencing work: values, attitudes and moods', *Human Relations*, vol. 50, pp. 393–416. Adapted with permission.

Exercise 7.1   Attitudes to this book

Consider your attitude (if any) to this book. How positively or negatively do you *feel* about it (affective component)? How positive or negative are your *thoughts* about it (cognitive component)? How positively or negatively do you *behave* towards it (e.g. how often do you read it and for how long?) (behavioural component)? In each case, describe what your feelings, thoughts and behaviours are.

Consider whether the extent to which you use this book is influenced by your values, attitudes and moods. What other factors affect your behaviour towards the book?

Pratkanis and Turner (1994) and Cialdini and Trost (1998) among others asked why we have attitudes – in other words, what purposes do they serve? There seem to be three general answers to this:

Key Learning Point

Attitudes are related to, but distinguishable from, values, moods and personality.

1   Attitudes can help us to make sense of our environment and act effectively within it. For example, people who are dissatisfied with their job are more likely than others to believe that ambiguous events are sure to end in disaster. Also, knowing our own attitudes and those of others helps us to categorise people into groups (see the section in Chapter 1 on understanding and managing workplace diversity).

2   Attitudes can help us to define and maintain our sense of self-identity (who we are) and self-esteem (a sense of personal value). It seems to be important to most people to have a clear sense of who they are, and to feel reasonably positive about it.

3   Attitudes can help us maintain good relations with other people, particularly those who have the power to reward or punish us. By holding and expressing attitudes similar to another person, we can often make ourselves more attractive to them, and more able to understand and empathise with them.

Pratkanis and Turner (1994) have argued that an attitude is stored in memory as a 'cognitive representation', which consists of three components:

1   An object label and rules for applying it. For example, if one is concerned about attitudes to colleagues, it is necessary to be clear about who counts as a colleague.

2   An evaluative summary of that object, i.e. whether it is broadly 'good' or 'bad'.

3   A knowledge structure supporting the evaluative summary. This can be simple or complex, and may include technical knowledge about the domain, arguments for or against a given proposition, or a listing of the advantages and disadvantages of a target.

Key Learning Point

Attitudes are cognitive representations which help us to structure our social world and our place within it.

As an example of some research on attitudes, let us take an article by Furnham *et al.* (1994). They used their academic contacts in 41 countries to obtain a total sample of more than 12,000 young people, who completed a questionnaire concerning their attitudes to work and economic issues. Furnham *et al.* assessed, among other things, the following attitudes, each of which was measured with several statements and a Likert response scale (*see* next section) asking the respondent to what extent they agreed or disagreed with each statement.

- *Work ethic* – Example statement: 'I like hard work'.
- *Competitiveness* – Example statement: 'I feel that winning is important in both work and games'.
- *Money beliefs* – Example statement: 'I firmly believe money can solve all my problems'.

They found quite marked differences between countries in the extent to which young people held these attitudes. Work ethic was higher in America than in Europe or the East and Asia. The reverse was true for competitiveness. Money beliefs were highest in the East and Asia, lower in America, and lower again in Europe. At the level of individual countries, those with high economic growth tended to score higher on both competitiveness and money beliefs. However, it is not clear whether the attitudes caused the economic growth, were caused by it, both, or neither. This illustrates one of the problems of the survey method, as discussed in Chapter 2.

How are attitudes measured?

Attitudes are almost always assessed using self-report questionnaires. In other words, attitude measurement usually depends upon what people say about their feelings, beliefs and/or behaviour towards the particular object in question. Thurstone scaling and Likert scaling are frequently used to measure attitudes (there is information about Thurstone scaling on the website that accompanies this book). Likert scales are easier to understand and use, and tend to be more widely used in research, so we will concentrate on those.

The *Likert technique* is sometimes known as the summated scale. In this approach, the psychologist selects a large number of statements that relate to the attitude object concerned. They should either be clearly in favour of the object, or clearly against it. Respondents indicate their agreement or disagreement with each statement. Statements are included in the final scale only if they: (i) tend to be responded to in the same way as others covering apparently similar ground, and (ii) elicit the same responses on two occasions. A five-, seven- or ten-point response scale is utilised for each statement, usually in terms of strongly agree to strongly disagree. For example, with a five-point response scale, respondents might have the options 'strongly agree' (score 4), 'agree' (score 3), 'neither agree nor disagree' (score 2), 'disagree' (score 1) and 'strongly disagree' (score 0). Scores are reversed (i.e. 4 changes to 0, 3 to 1, etc.). Some statements are worded negatively to check that the respondent is not simply agreeing or disagreeing with everything for the sake of it, or perhaps not reading the items properly. For example in a questionnaire to measure attitudes to overtime, a positively worded item could be 'overtime is the best part of my job' and a negatively worded item could be 'overtime is a real nuisance'. The person's overall attitude score is the sum or mean of their responses to the statements. In the case of the overtime example used above, because the scores for negatively worded statements have been reversed, a high score indicates a favourable attitude.

One difficulty with using questionnaire measures of attitudes is that they are subject to the *social desirability effect* – that is, to respondents giving the socially desirable answer, such as, for instance, 'Of course I have never driven faster than the speed limit' when, in fact, they have (actually, almost everyone has). There are techniques available to minimise this effect. *Social desirability scales* contain questions that almost everyone responds to in the same way *if* they are telling the truth. To return to the example, almost everyone who drives has broken a speed limit at least once, so the vast majority of people who drive say they have broken the speed limit if they are telling the truth. Therefore if the responses a person gives to a series of questions like this consistently goes against that of the majority, there is an increased likelihood they are trying to present in a socially desirable way on the questionnaire. Another way of dealing with the problem is given in the questionnaire in Table 7.2. One of the authors wanted to find out what people thought about male and female managers.

Table 7.2	Stereotyped attitudes towards male versus female managers

Description of a character you may know

Is 21 years old
Graduate
Trainee manager
Woman/man*
Unmarried
Enjoys films

Whereabouts on these scales would you place this character? Please put a tick in the appropriate box according to where you think she/he* would most probably be best described on the scale.

Will be a high flyer				Will not necessarily be a high flyer
Is inclined to be bossy				Is inclined to be meek
Is a good mixer socially				Is rather shy socially
Is very studious				Is not very studious
Would assume leadership in groups				Would not assume leadership in groups
Contains emotions				Expresses emotions freely
Is self-confident				Is not self-confident
Is ambitious				Is not particularly ambitious
Is assertive				Is not particularly assertive

How much do you think he/she* will be earning   (a) when he/she* is 30? £ ...../p.a.
                                                  (b) when he/she* is 60? £ ...../p.a.

*One or the other given on each form.

Instead of asking them directly, he devised two questionnaires that were exactly alike, except that in each version a single line was different – 'man' and 'woman'. The two versions of the questionnaire were distributed among a random sample of the general public and the differences between the two forms were assessed, without the issue of male versus female stereotypes ever being raised on the questionnaire. Forced choice items can also be used to address the problem. In these questions, the respondent chooses between two desirable responses. An example would be: 'Is it better to be (a) helpful to colleagues or (b) well-organised in your approach to work?'

Key Learning Point

Attitude measurement is systematic and quantitative. In line with the positivist research philosophy (*see* Chapter 2), it is usually assumed that attitudes exist independently of attempts to articulate or measure them (*i.e. they are real and not just a pattern of responses on a questionnaire*).

The result of attitude measurement is normally a measure of how *extreme* a person's attitude is: for example, whether they strongly like, mildly like, are indifferent towards, mildly dislike or strongly dislike studying work psychology. Petty and Krosnick (1992) have argued for the more general concept of attitude *strength*. As well as extremity, this includes the amount of certainty people feel about their attitude, its importance to them, how intensely they hold the attitude and how knowledgeable they are about it. Petty and Krosnick suggested that consideration of these factors will improve the predictability of behaviour from attitudes. Along the same lines, Pratkanis and Turner (1994) have referred to attitude *salience*, which concerns the extent to which an attitude is clearly relevant to the situation at hand. Their definition of a strong attitude is one that comes easily to mind. This definition seems quite appropriate because research suggests that beliefs that are important to a person are remembered more completely and more quickly than those that are not (van Harreveld *et al.*, 2000). In fact, some psychologists believe that the speed with which a person reacts to a stimulus could be the most valid indicator of their attitude (Greenwald *et al.*, 1998).

But to what extent are attitudes measurable? Verkuyten (1998) argues that it is a mistake to see attitudes as quantitatively measurable phenomena that in some sense exist inside a person's head. Like other discursive social psychologists, Verkuyten argues that attitudes are expressed in conversation as part of an attempt to achieve the personal goals of the speaker. These might be to convince others of one's correctness, morality, acceptability, rationality and so on. They might be very transient, and they might depend very much on how the object of the attitude is defined. Verkuyten analysed a transcript from a Dutch television programme in which the organisers of an erotic fair in Utrecht debated with a group called Christians for Truth which objected to the fair. Verkuyten (p. 314) commented:

> The fact that the nature of the attitude object was subject to debate also implies that it would be difficult to compare the attitudes of the participants using traditional measures. For some participants the fair was about pornography, whereas for others it represented eroticism and lifestyle. Their views about eroticism [good] and pornography [bad] did not seem to differ, but their attitudes toward the fair were difficult to compare because of the different ways that the fair was defined.

Key Learning Point

Strength and certainty, as well as extremity, are important properties of attitudes.

What this rather colourful example illustrates is that our attitude to something depends very much on the meaning we attach to it, or how it fits into our lives. Your attitudes toward this book are most likely the result of your seeing it as an aid to your studies (well, that's what we hope!). For the publishers of this book, their attitudes towards it are more likely to be the result of their seeing it as a product. Senior management attitudes towards a trade union representative might develop from a view of the representative as an adversary. Employees' attitudes toward the same representative are more likely to be based upon the view that the representative is an advocate. What all of this means is that the complexity of attitudes can be difficult to pin down using a questionnaire survey.

Attitudes and behaviour

So far we have looked at what attitudes are and hinted that they might be important in organisational settings, but it could be argued that attitudes only matter if they influence actual behaviour. For example, racial prejudice in the workplace is damaging to the extent that it finds expression in discrimination or other negative behaviour towards minority groups. To what extent do attitudes predict behaviour? It appears that they do to some extent, but not often very much. People's avowed feelings and beliefs about someone or something seemed only very loosely related to how they behaved towards that person or object.

If true, this would mean that people who say they like their job do not necessarily work harder or better, work longer hours, or relate better to customers than people who say they do not like their job. It would also mean that all the many attitude surveys conducted in workplaces were a waste of time.

A number of possible reasons were suggested for this lack of correspondence. One was social pressures of various kinds: laws, societal norms and the views of specific people can all prevent a person behaving consistently with their attitudes. So can other attitudes, limitations on a person's abilities, and, indeed, a person's general activity levels. There was also some suggestion that the research on this issue was badly designed, and therefore failed to find correspondences that did in fact exist between attitudes and behaviour. In particular, it was argued that measures of attitude were often general (e.g. attitudes about law-breaking) whereas measures of behaviour were specific, reflecting only one of many elements of the attitude (e.g. committing motoring offences). Also, behaviour was assessed on only one occasion or over a short time period. Longer-term assessments of multiple instances of the behaviour would be a fairer test of whether attitudes predict behaviour.

Pratkanis and Turner (1994) identified four of the factors they suggest will increase the correspondence between attitudes and behaviour:

1   When the object of the attitude is both well-defined and salient. An example of a poorly defined object would be where a person was not sure whether their immediate supervisor should be classed as a member of management. This would make it uncertain whether that person's attitudes to management would affect their behaviour towards the supervisor. Salience concerns the extent to which the object of the attitude is perceived as relevant to the situation at hand.

2   When attitude strength is high – that is, when the attitude comes easily to mind.

3   When knowledge supporting the attitude is plentiful and complex. This increases a person's certainty about what they think, as well as their ability to act effectively towards the object of the attitude.

4   When the attitude supports important aspects of the self. For example, an accountant may have positive attitudes towards other accountants because they believe that accountants (and therefore by extension themself) perform an important role in the national economy.

The lack of correspondence between attitudes and behaviour found in much research is due partly to poor research design, and partly to a neglect of cognitive processes concerning attitudes.

Ajzen and Fishbein (1980) developed a model of the relationship between attitudes and behaviour designed to overcome these difficulties. This model was called the *theory of reasoned action*. It assumed that actions are best predicted by intentions, and that intentions are in turn determined by a person's attitude and their perception of social pressure. For example, in the work context, we might look at how well intention to leave predicted actual turnover.

The theory of reasoned action was then adapted by Ajzen and Madden (1986), and its name was changed to the *theory of planned behaviour* (Figure 7.1). It now includes the concept of perceived behavioural control. This reflects the extent to which the person believes that they can perform the necessary behaviours in any given situation. It can affect both intention and the extent to which intention translates into actual behaviour.

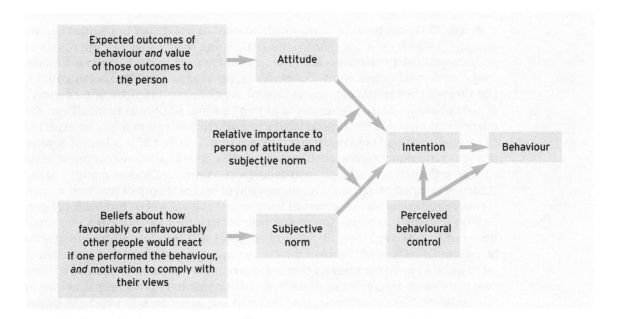

Figure 7.1	Theory of planned behaviour

Source: Reprinted from *Journal of Experimental Social Psychology*, 22, Ajzen, I. and Madden, J.T., 'Prediction of goal-directed behavior: attitudes, intentions, and perceived behavioral control', pp. 453-74. Copyright (1986), with permission from Elsevier.

Note that in the theory of planned behaviour, 'attitude' is defined in precise and rather unusual terms – it concerns beliefs and personal values about the consequences of a specific behaviour, and not general beliefs or feelings about an object or person. This is similar to expectancy theories of motivation (*see* Chapter 8). Note also that 'subjective norm' takes into account both the opinions of other people and the person's wish (or lack of it) to comply with those opinions. Therefore this model allows us to consider the influence of culture in determining thought and action (*see* Chapter 1). The theory of planned behaviour also acknowledges that people vary in the relative importance of attitude and subjective norm in determining their intentions. The theory has proved quite successful in predicting behaviour in a wide range of settings. However, relatively few of these directly concern work behaviour (though many concern consumer behaviour). This is perhaps an example of how work psychology sometimes neglects theoretical advances in social psychology.

Key Learning Point

The theory of planned behaviour takes ideas from cognitive theories of motivation in proposing that actions are the product of attitudes, social pressures and intentions. It is effective in explaining both intentions and actual behaviour.

Ajzen (1991) has provided a thorough account of the theory of planned behaviour and research on it. He pointed out that, as the theory suggests, intentions to perform particular behaviours are often accurately predicted by attitudes towards the behaviour, subjective norms and perceived behavioural control. Also, intentions, together with perceived behavioural control, are quite good at predicting a person's actual behaviour. Ajzen also draws attention to some additional points. First, the relative importance of the various factors in predicting intention might be expected to vary with different behaviours and different situations, but little is known beyond this very general proposition about how particular situations/behaviours might exert such an influence. Second, perceived behavioural control really does matter – so the theory of planned behaviour is an improvement on the theory of reasoned action. However, the usefulness of perceived behavioural control will be limited if the perception is wildly inaccurate. If a person believes that they are in control of a situation, but is mistaken, then no amount of belief will translate an intention into behaviour. Third, the influence of subjective norms on intentions and behaviour is often quite weak. Ajzen suggests that some people may be more responsive to their own perceptions of moral obligations than to the opinions of other people, at least in individualistic Western cultures. These observations suggest areas in which the theory of planned behaviour may be improved in future. Also, comparison of the theory of planned behaviour with material presented earlier in this chapter shows that it ignores factors such as the salience of the attitude and the extent to which it is supported by knowledge.

Reviews of the theory of planned behaviour by Ajzen (2001) and Armitage and Conner (2001) have reinforced many of the points already made. Armitage and Conner conducted a meta-analysis of tests of the theory. Based on a total sample of nearly a million people across many research studies, they found that the combination of attitude, subjective norm and perceived behavioural control correlated 0.63

with behavioural intention. They also found that intention plus perceived behavioural control correlated 0.52 with actual behaviour. These are impressive findings. Subjective norm appeared to be a relatively weak link. Armitage and Conner considered that this was partly due to a tendency to measure it with only one question, but there may also be other reasons. For example, in Western culture we may be unwilling to admit that the opinions of other people influence us, even if they really do. Also, we may surround ourselves with people who generally agree with us, so that subjective norm is not much different from attitude.

Another issue concerns the evaluation of alternative courses of action. In a research study, a person may score quite high on intention to pursue action A, but what we do not know (because we did not ask) is that they score even higher on intention to pursue action B. Finally, there is considerable debate about the nature of perceived behavioural control. Is it, in effect, self-efficacy, or does it include external factors such as lack of opportunity?

The theory of planned behaviour can easily be used in the workplace, even though it is not used very often. For example, a person may have the opportunity to apply for promotion. Their attitude to doing so will be determined by an assessment of the potential consequences of doing so (both good and bad), the probability that those consequences might include increased pay, a better car, a more interesting job, a requirement to work longer hours, and the risk of being turned down. For a person with fragile self-esteem and/or a concern about personal image, this last possibility might be extremely important. Subjective norm would reflect whether other people (for example partner and colleagues) thought it was a good idea to apply for promotion, and how much the person cared about their opinions. Perceived behavioural control should not be a problem, since it refers simply to the person's ability to apply for the promotion, not to do so effectively. Intention should lead fairly reliably to behaviour in this instance, unless for example the promotion opportunity is unexpectedly withdrawn.

Exercise 7.2   A lunchtime drink

Jerry Lander felt that there was nothing wrong with drinking a glass or two of beer during his lunch break. He could afford it easily enough. He claimed that he had never seen any evidence that a lunchtime drink harmed his work performance during the afternoon. He found that it helped him feel more relaxed and happy at work. Nevertheless, he could do without a drink without much difficulty if he had to. Jerry liked the friendship and approval of other people, and at lunchtime the nearby bar was full of acquaintances he could chat to. Work was an important part of Jerry's life and he was keen to gain promotion. Unfortunately his boss did not approve of alcoholic drink at lunchtime – or indeed at any other time. Nor did most of his colleagues, with whom he had to work closely. They seemed to view it as a sign of personal inadequacy.

Suggested exercise

Use the theory of planned behaviour to decide whether Jerry Lander is likely to drink a glass of beer during his lunch break on most working days.

What all of this means is that the link between attitudes and behaviour is often quite complex. Nonetheless, the link is there, and models exist to help us make sense of it. This makes it worthwhile examining attitudes at work. So far in this chapter we have deliberately avoided discussing specific attitudes, in order to ensure that we cover the important general points. Now it is time to be more specific. We now look at two concepts of great importance in work psychology: job satisfaction and organisational commitment. In the first the object of the attitude is the job. The second reflects how attached the employee is to the employing organisation (the object of the attitude is the organisation). These have been the subject of much research and practical interest over many years.

STOP TO CONSIDER

From what you have read so far, how concerned do you think managers should be about their employees' attitudes? To what extent might they be able to alter employee attitudes (and how could they do this)?

Job satisfaction

Job satisfaction has been seen as important for two main reasons. First, it is one indicator of a person's psychological well-being, or mental health. As such it is often used in stress research (see Chapter 12). It is unlikely (though not impossible) that a person who is unhappy at work will be happy in general. So psychologists and others who are concerned with individuals' welfare are keen to ensure that high job satisfaction is experienced. Second, it is often assumed that job satisfaction will lead to motivation and good work performance. We have already noted that such simple connections between attitudes and behaviour do not necessarily occur. The link between job satisfaction and work performance is a good example of how it is often assumed that attitudes affect behaviour, but it is not easy to demonstrate that this is indeed the case.

What is job satisfaction?

Locke (1976) defined job satisfaction as a 'pleasurable or positive emotional state resulting from the appraisal of one's job or job experiences'. The concept generally refers to a variety of aspects of the job that influence a person's levels of satisfaction with it. These usually include attitudes toward pay, working conditions, colleagues and boss, career prospects and the intrinsic aspects of the job itself. Even as long ago as 1976, job satisfaction had been the topic of huge amounts of research. Locke found well over 3000 published studies.

Judge and Hulin (1993), among others, have suggested that in the field of job satisfaction there are three different approaches. The first is that work attitudes such as job satisfaction are dispositional in nature; that is, they are 'stable positive or negative dispositions learned through experience' (Griffin and Bateman, 1986; Staw et al., 1986) or based on a person's genetic inheritance. If this was the case, job satisfaction might be considered more a personality characteristic than an attitude, and attempts to improve satisfaction by changing jobs would be doomed to failure (see Chapter 12 for a discussion of the role of individual differences in the stress process). The second approach is the 'social information processing' model, which suggests that job satisfaction and other workplace attitudes are developed or constructed out of experiences and information provided by others at work (Salancik and Pfeffer, 1978; O'Reilly and Caldwell, 1985). In other words, at least in part, job satisfaction is a function of how other people in the workplace interpret and evaluate what goes on. The third approach is the information-processing model, which is based on the accumulation of cognitive information about the workplace and one's job. In a sense, this is the most obvious approach – it argues that a person's job satisfaction is influenced directly by the characteristics of their job (Hackman and Oldham, 1976; *see also* Chapter 8), and the extent to which those characteristics match what that person wants in a job.

Key Learning Point

Job satisfaction can be seen in three ways - as a function of (i) a person's general personality or disposition; (ii) the opinions of other people in the person's workplace; or (iii) the features of a person's job.

Measuring job satisfaction

There have been many measures of job satisfaction in the workplace. Examples include the very widely used Job Description Index (JDI; Smith *et al.*, 1969), the Job Satisfaction Scales of Warr *et al.* (1979), the Overall Job Satisfaction scale (Brayfield and Rothe, 1951) and the job satisfaction scale of the Occupational Stress Indicator (OSI; Cooper *et al.*, 1987). They all involve questions or statements asking respondents to indicate what they think and/or feel about their job as a whole (so-called global satisfaction) and/or specific aspects of it, such as pay, work activities, working conditions, career prospects, relationship with superiors and relationships with colleagues (so-called facet satisfaction). Likert scaling (see earlier in this chapter) is usually employed. In Table 7.3 we provide an example of a measure of job satisfaction from the OSI, which contains all of the elements that usually make up a job satisfaction measure.

It is generally assumed in attitude measurement that it is better to ask lots of questions than only one. The argument is that this increases accuracy, for example by including many different facets of the attitude concerned and by avoiding the possibility that a careless response to a single question will mess everything up. However, Nagy (2002) has shown that having just one question to measure global job satisfaction, and/or one question to measure each facet of job satisfaction, can be just as good. Nagy's point is that people generally know how satisfied they are, and do not need a whole set of questions to express this.

Taber and Alliger (1995) have investigated the extent to which overall job satisfaction can be thought of as the *total* or *average* of people's opinions about each task in their job. They asked over 500 employees of a US medical college to describe the tasks of their job, and to rate each task according to its importance, complexity, level of supervision, level of concentration required, how much they enjoyed it, and the amount of time spent on it each week. Taber and Alliger found that the percentage of time spent in enjoyable tasks correlated 0.40 with satisfaction with the work itself, and 0.28 with global job satisfaction. The importance of the task, closeness of supervision and concentration required did not have much impact on job satisfaction. The correlations show that the accumulation of enjoyment across the various tasks involved in the job did, not surprisingly, say something about

Table 7.3	A job satisfaction measure

How you feel about your job

Very much satisfaction	6	Much satisfaction	5
Some satisfaction	4	Some dissatisfaction	3
Much dissatisfaction	2	Very much dissatisfaction	1

1	Communication and the way information flows around your organisation	6 5 4 3 2 1
2	The relationships you have with other people at work	6 5 4 3 2 1
3	The feeling you have about the way you and your efforts are valued	6 5 4 3 2 1
4	The actual job itself	6 5 4 3 2 1
5	The degree to which you feel motivated by your job	6 5 4 3 2 1
6	Current career opportunities	6 5 4 3 2 1
7	The level of job security in your present job	6 5 4 3 2 1
8	The extent to which you may identify with the public image or goals of your organisation	6 5 4 3 2 1
9	The style of supervision that your superiors use	6 5 4 3 2 1
10	The way changes and innovations are implemented	6 5 4 3 2 1
11	The kind of work or tasks that you are required to perform	6 5 4 3 2 1
12	The degree to which you feel that you can personally develop or grow in your job	6 5 4 3 2 1
13	The way in which conflicts are resolved in your company	6 5 4 3 2 1
14	The scope your job provides to help you achieve your aspirations and ambitions	6 5 4 3 2 1
15	The amount of participation which you are given in important decision-making	6 5 4 3 2 1
16	The degree to which your job taps the range of skills which you feel you possess	6 5 4 3 2 1
17	The amount of flexibility and freedom you feel you have in your job	6 5 4 3 2 1
18	The psychological 'feel' or climate that dominates your organisation	6 5 4 3 2 1
19	Your level of salary relative to your experience	6 5 4 3 2 1
20	The design or shape of your organisation's structure	6 5 4 3 2 1
21	The amount of work you are given to do, whether too much or too little	6 5 4 3 2 1
22	The degree to which you feel extended in your job	6 5 4 3 2 1

Source: Copyright © 1988 Cooper, Sloan and Williams. Reproduced with permission of the publisher ASE, College Lane, Hatfield, Herts, AL10 9AA, UK.

overall job satisfaction, but the correlations were also low enough to indicate that other factors also matter. As the authors noted (p. 118):

> Perhaps workers form a gestalt – a perception of pattern – about their jobs that is not a simple linear function of task enjoyment . . . a worker might perform 15 different enjoyable tasks; nevertheless, the worker's global job satisfaction still could be low if the 15 tasks were so unrelated to one another that the total job was not meaningful, or did not relate clearly to the mission of the organization.

The coverage of attitudes earlier in this chapter suggests that job satisfaction is likely to be used by people to help make sense of their work, and to define who they are, or are not. So in a brief reply to Taber and Alliger, Locke (1995) pointed out that job satisfaction will depend partly on how well people's tasks fit their long-term purposes, how much their self-esteem depends on their job and which job experiences are processed most thoroughly in their memory. One could add that the opinions of others, as discussed by O'Reilly and Caldwell (1985), will also influence a person's overall feelings about their job. How people appraise various aspects of their job is discussed in some depth in Chapter 12.

Key Learning Point

Job satisfaction is more than how much the person enjoys the job tasks. It also depends on how important the job is to the person, and how well it fits in with their long-term aims.

Another issue, particularly for global organisations, is whether questionnaire measures of job satisfaction (or indeed anything else) travel well across cultures. Possible problems are that translations between languages are imperfect, that people in different countries understand the same words in the questions (e.g. 'stress') in different ways, and that they interpret response scale options such as 'quite' or 'often' in different ways. These problems are difficult to identify, let alone solve, but they might matter to managers who want to know, for example, whether employees working in a factory in one country are more satisfied than those in a factory in another country. Ryan *et al.* (1999) give an example, using complex statistics, of how some of the problems of comparing across cultures can be investigated. They found only relatively minor differences between data obtained from employees of one large company in the United States, Spain, Mexico and Australia.

Causes and consequences of job satisfaction

The major determinants of job satisfaction seem to derive from all three of the theoretical approaches identified earlier. Thus, regarding the job itself, for most people the major determinants of global job satisfaction derive from the intrinsic features of the work itself. These are most commonly based on the Hackman and Oldham (1976) core constructs of skill variety, task identity, task significance, autonomy and feedback (*see also* Chapter 8). Hackman and Oldham (1976) defined their constructs as:

- *skill variety*: the extent to which the tasks require different skills;

- *task identity*: the extent to which the worker can complete a 'whole' piece of work, as opposed to a small part of it;

- *task significance*: the extent to which the work is perceived as influencing the lives of others;

- *autonomy*: the extent to which the worker has freedom within the job to decide how it should be done;

- *feedback*: the extent to which there is correct and precise information about how effectively the worker is performing.

In addition, as Griffin and Bateman (1986) observed, 'in general, most studies find significant and positive correlations between leader behaviours such as initiating structure and consideration, and satisfaction'. So leader behaviour is also important in satisfaction at work (*see* Chapter 14). Of course, it is also possible that job satisfaction causes job perceptions. People who are satisfied may be given the more interesting tasks to do by their bosses, and/or they may optimistically rate their job more favourably than those who are dissatisfied. Wong *et al.* (1998) collected data over a two-year period and found both that perceived job characteristics lead to job satisfaction and vice versa.

Other social factors have more subtle influences on job satisfaction, as predicted by the social information processing approach. For example, Agho *et al.* (1993) found that perceptions of distributive justice (the fairness with which rewards were distributed in the organisation) predicted job satisfaction. O'Reilly and Caldwell (1985) demonstrated that both task perceptions and job satisfaction of workers were influenced by the opinions of others in their workgroups.

Of particular interest to researchers has been whether the saying 'A happy worker is a productive worker' is true. Work and organisational psychologists have usually examined this in the form of whether job satisfaction (happiness) correlates with work performance (productivity). For some years the general consensus was that there was little connection. Iaffaldano and Muchinsky (1985) conducted a meta-analysis and found a mean correlation of 0.17, which is pretty low, but Judge *et al.* (2001) have pointed out several things that were wrong with Iaffaldano and Muchinsky's analysis. They discovered that the mean correlation corrected for measurement unreliability between job satisfaction and job performance was 0.30. As they point out, this still is not huge but is comparable to correlations between some of the more valid employment selection techniques and job performance. Correlations tended to be highest for complex jobs, i.e. those requiring a range of skills. Harrison and colleagues (2006) found that job satisfaction was not only linked to job performance but also outcomes such as absence and lateness: these effects were small-to-modest, but they were significant. If you think back to the description of attitudes earlier in this chapter, this makes sense. Job satisfaction is a non-specific attitude in terms of action, so it would be expected to influence a wide range of unrelated work behaviours. It could be a *common cause* for a lot of different employee behaviours.

Judge *et al.* (2001) identify six possible reasons why job satisfaction and job performance might be related. These are shown and briefly explained in Figure 7.2. The last of the six abandons the usual pattern of treating job satisfaction as the measure of happiness and reflects the idea we have already explored that job satisfaction may partly reflect a person's disposition. This has both an advantage and a disadvantage. The advantage is that it recognises that job satisfaction is only one aspect of happiness. The disadvantage is that it risks repeating the old problem in attitude–behaviour research of having one measure (happiness) that is more general than the other (job performance).

Of course, demonstrating that two variables are correlated is not the same as demonstrating that one *causes* the other. Riketta (2008) chose to re-examine the satisfaction–performance relationship but his meta-analysis included 14 studies that used strong longitudinal research designs. After controlling for initial levels of performance, this revealed a much weaker link between job satisfaction and later performance than the relationship between job satisfaction and performance found by Judge *et al.* (2001). This may be because Judge *et al.* had included many studies with cross-sectional survey designs. There was also no evidence that good

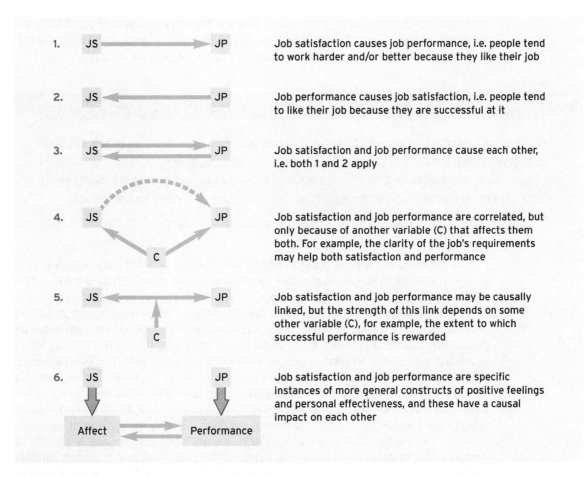

1. JS ⟶ JP   Job satisfaction causes job performance, i.e. people tend to work harder and/or better because they like their job

2. JS ⟵ JP   Job performance causes job satisfaction, i.e. people tend to like their job because they are successful at it

3. JS ⇄ JP   Job satisfaction and job performance cause each other, i.e. both 1 and 2 apply

4. JS   JP   Job satisfaction and job performance are correlated, but only because of another variable (C) that affects them both. For example, the clarity of the job's requirements may help both satisfaction and performance
      C

5. JS ⟷ JP   Job satisfaction and job performance may be causally linked, but the strength of this link depends on some other variable (C), for example, the extent to which successful performance is rewarded
      C

6. JS   JP   Job satisfaction and job performance are specific instances of more general constructs of positive feelings and personal effectiveness, and these have a causal impact on each other
   Affect ⟷ Performance

Figure 7.2 **Some possible relationships between job satisfaction (JS) and job performance (JP)**
Source: Adapted from Judge *et al.* Copyright © 2001 by the American Psychological Association. Adapted with permission.

performance consistently caused higher job satisfaction as Judge had suggested. Interestingly, Riketta also found that the link between satisfaction and performance was strongest when there was a short time gap between the measurement of satisfaction and performance, indicating that any effect of satisfaction on performance could be instant but short-lived, perhaps helping to explain why correlations are higher in cross-sectional survey studies. This short-lived connection may occur because high performers develop higher expectations of the rewards that are due to them – when these are unmet, performance levels may soon drop. As Riketta acknowledges, meta-analyses do sometimes gloss over important effects within particular studies: in some situations the satisfaction–performance link might be strong, but it does not appear to be consistently strong across a range of different longitudinal studies.

It is also worth noting that even if job satisfaction is related to performance, we cannot be sure that it is the cause of it. Wright and Staw (1999) reported two studies in social services settings that strongly suggest that people's characteristic tendency to experience positive emotion (i.e. happiness) does predict their subsequent work performance as assessed by supervisory ratings. These people would have high job satisfaction because of their disposition, but these studies showed that the characteristic tendency to be happy was a better predictor of performance than mood.

Key Learning Point

Happiness and productivity have often been investigated using measures of job satisfaction and work performance. There is some evidence that people who are satisfied at work perform better, are less absent and more punctual. However, recent research looking at the results of well-designed studies suggests that this link could be small and short-lived.

The dispositional approach to job satisfaction has also received some support. That is, there is some evidence that some people are simply more satisfied than others by their nature. In a review of research, Arvey *et al.* (1991) suggested that somewhere between 10 and 30 per cent of the variation in job satisfaction depends on genetic factors. They argued that 'there is less variability in job satisfaction between genetically identical people [i.e. identical twins] who hold different jobs than there is among genetically unrelated people who hold the same job' (p. 374). However, it is difficult to be sure about what proportion of job satisfaction is a function of a person's disposition. Most research has construed it as what is left over when situational factors have been considered, but this assumes that all of the important situational factors have been taken into account – surely an optimistic assumption. According to Judge and Hulin (1993), research has also tended to use small samples and/or data originally collected for other purposes, and has been unclear about what aspects of a person's disposition might be expected to affect their job satisfaction.

Judge and Hulin (1993) obtained data from 255 people working in medical clinics, and for 160 of them they also got the opinions of other individuals who knew them well. The researchers wanted to examine the linkages between affective disposition (that is, a person's tendency to feel positive or negative about life), subjective well-being (how they feel about life right now), job satisfaction and job characteristics. Their data were most consistent with the causal model shown in Figure 7.3. Affective disposition not surprisingly had a substantial effect upon subjective well-being. That is, a person's tendency to take an optimistic and happy approach to life influenced how optimistic and happy they felt day to day. Subjective well-being (and therefore, indirectly, affective disposition) had a substantial impact on job satisfaction, and job satisfaction had almost as much effect upon subjective well-being. Intrinsic job characteristics affected job satisfaction, as one would expect, but scarcely more strongly than subjective well-being.

Bowling *et al.* (2006) present one of the few recent longitudinal studies of the role of disposition in determining job satisfaction. They found that job satisfaction was fairly stable (which suggests disposition is important), but that it changes when people change jobs (which suggests the situation is important). Perhaps more significantly they found that when people change jobs, people with a positive disposition tended to experience gains in job satisfaction, while those with a negative disposition tended to experience losses in job satisfaction. The researchers argue that this is because people with a positive disposition are more likely to look for, be aware of,

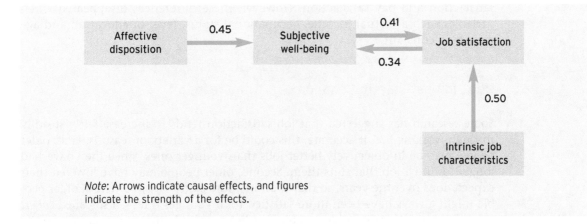

Note: Arrows indicate causal effects, and figures
indicate the strength of the effects.

Figure 7.3	A causal model of job satisfaction
	Source: Reprinted from *Organizational Behavior and Human Decision Processes*, 56, Judge, T.A. and Hulin, C.L., 'Job satisfaction as a reflection of disposition: a multiple source causal analysis', pp. 388–421. Copyright (1993), with permission from Elsevier.

and remember positive experiences. In other words some people are likely to seek
and find jobs of certain kinds, and that the nature of these jobs then affects job satisfaction. Findings such as these indicate that the impact of a person's disposition
on their job satisfaction is largely *indirect*.

Dormann and Zapf (2001) reviewed studies reported up to September 1997 and
found that, on average, people's job satisfaction on one occasion was quite highly
correlated (about 0.5) with their job satisfaction on a later occasion (on average,
three years later). This finding might suggest that personality, being relatively stable, is linked to job satisfaction. However, in their own study of people in the Dres-
den area of Germany, Dormann and Zapf found a correlation for job satisfaction
over 5 years of 0.26 among people who changed jobs during that time. When they
adjusted statistically for changes in those people's job characteristics, the stability
of job satisfaction scores fell virtually to zero.

So it would seem that (i) the nature of the job really does matter for job satisfaction; (ii) so, indirectly, does a person's disposition; and (iii) job satisfaction has an
impact on more general well-being – work does spill over, psychologically, into
other areas of life. This is issue is discussed in more depth in Chapter 12.

Another angle on the idea that job satisfaction is more a feature of the person than
the job is expressed in research on gender differences in job satisfaction. A number of
studies have, for example, found that on average women's job satisfaction is lower
than men's. This has fuelled stereotypical views of women as being less interested
and involved in work than men. Often this is assumed to be because women's
earnings are, or have been, the subsidiary income of the household, whereas men
tend to be the main breadwinners. On the other hand, a less often considered
possibility is that women might be less satisfied simply because they tend to have
less good jobs than men. Indeed, this was what Lefkowitz (1994) found. Lefkowitz
obtained a diverse sample of 371 men and 361 women from nine organisations.
As predicted, men scored significantly higher on average than women on work

satisfaction and pay satisfaction. However, these differences disappeared when variables such as actual income, occupational status, level of education and age were held constant.

Does job satisfaction change over the lifespan?

Some research has suggested that job satisfaction tends to increase fairly steadily through working life. If accurate, this could be for a variety of reasons. First, older people may be in objectively better jobs than younger ones, since they have had longer to find a job that suits them. Second, older people may have lowered their expectations over the years, so that they are more easily satisfied. Third, older people might always have been more satisfied than younger ones – a so-called *cohort effect*. Fourth, dissatisfied older people may be more likely than younger ones to opt for early retirement or voluntary redundancy, so that those remaining in employment represent a biased sample of older people. Clarke *et al.* (1996) found in a sample of over 5000 UK employees that job satisfaction started fairly high in a person's teens, then dipped in the 20s and 30s, then rose through the 40s (back to teenage levels) and further in the 50s and 60s. After controlling for various factors, Clarke *et al.* reckoned that, on average, job satisfaction bottomed-out at age 36. The dip and subsequent rise were more marked for men than for women. Because the study was cross-sectional, the researchers were, however, unable to rule out any of the first three possible explanations described above.

Key Learning Point

Job satisfaction is partly determined by a person's general disposition, but not so much so that it is constant over a person's working life.

Organisational commitment

What is organisational commitment?

The concept of organisational commitment has generated huge amounts of research from the 1980s onwards. This is no doubt partly because it is what some employers say they want from employees – organisational commitment is a managerial agenda to a greater extent than job satisfaction. In recent years particularly, this can be seen as exceptionally one-sided: as Hirsh *et al.* (1995) have pointed out, what some employers now appear to want is totally committed but totally expendable staff. Exactly *why* employers should want committed staff is less obvious, partly because, as we shall see below, commitment does not guarantee high work performance.

Organisational commitment has been defined by Mowday *et al.* (1979) as 'the relative strength of an individual's identification with and involvement in an organisation'. This concept is often thought to have three components (Griffin and Bateman, 1986): (i) a desire to maintain membership in the organisation, (ii) belief in and acceptance of the values and goals of the organisation, and (iii) a willingness to exert effort on behalf of the organisation. If a person is committed to an organisation, therefore, they have a strong identification with it, value membership, agree with its objectives and value systems, are likely to remain in it, and, finally, are prepared to work hard on its behalf. It has also been suggested that commitment will lead to so-called organisational citizenship behaviours, such as helping out others and being particularly conscientious (*see* Chapter 6). We look more closely at the validity of these claims later in this section.

Some work psychologists have divided organisational commitment slightly differently from the way described above. For example, Allen and Meyer (1990) have distinguished between the following:

■ *Affective commitment*: essentially concerns the person's emotional attachment to their organisation.

■ *Continuance commitment*: a person's perception of the costs and risks associated with leaving their current organisation. There is considerable evidence that there are two aspects of continuance commitment: the personal sacrifice that leaving would involve, and a lack of alternatives available to the person.

■ *Normative commitment*: a moral dimension, based on a person's felt obligation and responsibility to their employing organisation.

There is good evidence for the distinctions between these forms of commitment (Dunham *et al.*, 1994). Interestingly, they approximate respectively to the affective, behavioural and cognitive components of attitudes identified at the start of this chapter. Critics of the model have argued that this concept of organisational commitment is a little muddled because it combines an attitude toward a target (the organisation) with attitudes toward a behaviour (leaving or staying), and is therefore best used as a means of predicting turnover (Solinger *et al.*, 2008). Unfortunately there is little research on the validity of alternative models of organisational commitment so we will stick with the very influential three-component model for now.

Other observers have pointed out that people feel multiple commitments at work – not only to their organisation, but also perhaps to their location, department, workgroup or trade union (Reichers, 1985; Barling *et al.*, 1990). There is also a wider issue here: what exactly *is* the organisation? Complexities such as parent companies and franchises can make it difficult to identify exactly which organisation one belongs to. More than that, some psychologists (e.g. Coopey and Hartley, 1991) have been critical of the whole notion of organisational commitment because it implies that the organisation is unitarist – that is, it is one single entity with a united goal. A moment's thought reveals that most organisations consist of various factions with somewhat different and possibly even contradictory goals. Faced with these ambiguities, it seems that most people think of the term organisation as meaning top management. This is clearly different from commitment to (for example) one's supervisor or workgroup, which employees may also feel (Becker and Billings, 1993). Further, it is possible to distinguish between (yet more) different bases of commitment to the various constituencies in an organisation. Two such bases are identification and internalisation. As Becker *et al.* (1996, p. 465) have put it:

> Identification occurs when people adopt attitudes and behaviours in order to be associated with a satisfying, self-defining relationship with another person or group . . . Internalization occurs when people adopt attitudes and behaviours because their content is congruent with their value systems.

Organisational commitment concerns a person's sense of attachment to their organisation. It has several components, and is only one of a number of commitments a person may feel.

Measuring organisational commitment

A number of questionnaires have been developed to measure the various aspects or theories of commitment discussed above. For example, a widely used scale is the Organisational Commitment Questionnaire (OCQ), which was developed by Mowday *et al.* (1979). It is a 15-item questionnaire which has been used as a total commitment scale, but has also been broken down into subscales by various researchers (Bateman and Strasser, 1984). The OCQ comprises items such as 'I feel very little loyalty to this organisation', 'I am willing to put in a great deal of effort beyond that normally expected in order to help this organisation be successful' and 'I really care about the fate of this organisation'. The OCQ was designed before the distinctions between affective, normative and continuance commitment were articulated in the literature. Subsequent research has clearly shown that the OCQ chiefly reflects affective commitment. There are other scales in use as well. For example, Warr *et al.* (1979) developed a nine-item scale. An example item is 'I feel myself to be part of the organisation'. This measure also tends to concentrate on affective commitment. Allen and Meyer (1990) have developed their own questionnaire measure of affective, normative and continuance commitment, with each of the three components assessed by eight items. Although not perfect, this measure has stood up well to psychometric scrutiny, and is now commonly used. There are also plenty of other questionnaire measures designed to measure other components and concepts of commitment.

All the commonly used measures of commitment are self-report: that is, a person indicates how committed they are. In many ways this makes good sense. After all, the person is in the best position to comment on their own commitment. Yet perhaps we are biased. Perhaps other people could provide a more dispassionate view of how committed we are. Goffin and Gellatly (2001) found that self-ratings of commitment were only moderately correlated with ratings given by supervisors and work colleagues. In line with much other research on self vs. other ratings, ratings of people's commitment made by their supervisors and colleagues were more similar to each other than either was to self-ratings. This suggests that an external perspective is providing something over and above self-perceptions. It is also likely that the word commitment means different things to different people. Singh and Vinnicombe (2000) have shown that, for many people, it has more to do with taking a creative and assertive approach to one's work than with involvement in and loyalty to one's employing organisation.

Like job satisfaction, organisational commitment is usually measured with questionnaires using Likert scaling.

Causes and consequences of organisational commitment

Much research has investigated how organisational commitment relates to other experiences, attitudes and behaviour at work. This is discussed below. Some of this has presented quite complex models indicating causal connections between commitment, satisfaction, motivation, job characteristics and other variables (*see*, for example, Eby *et al*.,1999). Figure 7.4 represents our attempt to summarise what is known, and what seems likely.

As with job satisfaction, there are several distinct theoretical approaches to organisational commitment. One of these, the behavioural approach, sees commitment as being created when a person does things publicly, of their own free will, and that would be difficult to undo (Kiesler, 1971). Rather like Bem's (1972) self-perception approach, it is suggested that people examine their own behaviour and conclude that since they did something with significant consequences in full view of others, when they could have chosen not to do so, they really must be committed to it. So if a person freely chooses to join an organisation, and subsequently performs other committing behaviours (e.g. voluntarily working long hours), they

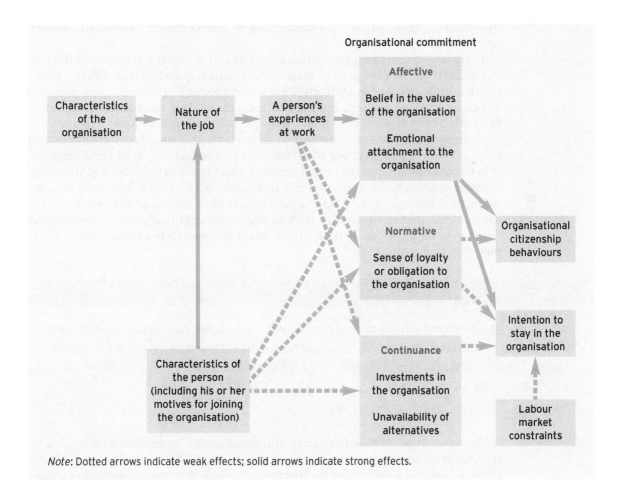

Note: Dotted arrows indicate weak effects; solid arrows indicate strong effects.

| Figure 7.4 | **A model of organisational commitment** |

will feel more committed to it. This is a neat theory and there is a certain amount of evidence in favour of it (Mabey, 1986).

More commonly, however, it has been suggested that people's commitment can be fostered by giving them positive experiences. This reflects a kind of social exchange approach. The person is essentially saying 'if this work organisation is nice to me, I will be loyal and hardworking'. Many researchers have tried to identify exactly which pleasant experiences matter most for organisational commitment. On the whole, it seems that factors intrinsic to the job (e.g. challenge, autonomy) are more important in fostering commitment than extrinsic factors such as pay and working conditions (Mathieu and Zajac, 1990; Arnold and Mackenzie Davey, 1999). This seems especially true for the affective component of commitment (i.e. commitment based on emotional attachment). On the other hand, continuance commitment (that is, the extent to which leaving would be costly for the person) is more influenced by the person's perception of their past contributions to the organisation and present likely attractiveness (or lack of it) to other employers (Meyer et al., 1989). Finegan (2000) reported an interesting study of how organisational values might affect commitment. The extent to which the organisation was perceived to value 'humanity' (e.g courtesy, fairness) and 'vision' (e.g. initiative, openness) was correlated with affective commitment, while the value of 'convention' (e.g cautiousness) was correlated with continuance commitment.

There is also some suggestion that commitment is partly a function of the person rather than what happens to them at work (Bateman and Strasser, 1984). That is, perhaps some people are, through their personality or disposition, more prone to feel committed than others, just as some seem more likely than others to feel satisfied with their job. Given the research on job satisfaction, that looks like a reasonable proposition. The small amount of research on this issue suggests that factors such as positive and negative affect (defined in Chapter 12) show some relationship to organisational commitment. Positive affect tends to be associated with high levels of organisational commitment, and negative affect with low levels of commitment (Thoresen et al., 2003). Similar results have been found in well-designed longitudinal studies which also tend to show that organisational commitment is stable over long periods of time, which again suggests dispositional factors are at play (Bowling et al., 2006).

Key Learning Point

It is usually assumed that organisational commitment is fostered by positive experiences at work, and to a lesser extent by the circumstances in which the person joined the organisation. The possibility that some people may be more predisposed to be committed than others is less often investigated.

The distinction between affective and continuance commitment may also be significant for work performance. Meyer et al. (1989, 1993) and Goffin and Gellatly (2001) found that workers high on affective commitment to their organisation tended to be better performers than those low on affective commitment. The opposite pattern of results was observed for continuance commitment. This makes sense: high continuance commitment is based partly on a perceived lack of employment options, and one reason for people lacking options may be that they are not much good at their work! On the other hand, some other research has failed to find these links between commitment and performance. As with job satisfaction, it seems that many factors intervene between attitude and behaviour. One of these might be ability. A person is unlikely to perform well at a task that they are not able to do, even if highly committed to the organisation. Therefore, one might expect a stronger link between commitment and performance for aspects of performance that depend more on motivation than ability.

Consistent with this, Harrison *et al.* (2006) reviewed relevant longitudinal research and found a significant link between commitment and subsequent contextual performance (which is more or less organisational citizenship behaviours as described in Chapter 6) of about 0.28, compared to 0.16 for focal (core) job performance. These correlations are quite small, but significant, and the evidence is mounting that organisational commitment predicts future performance. However, the research remains equivocal about the size and specificity of the relationship. A more recent meta-analysis of five longitudinal studies (Riketta, 2008) suggests that the correlations are somewhat smaller than that found in earlier studies, with the links between organisational commitment on the one hand and focal and contextual performance on the other hand being about the same.

Key Learning Point

Organisational commitment has only loose links with overall job performance. However, highly committed people are more likely than less committed people to help others in the organisation.

It may also be worth taking into account commitment to other constituencies. Wasti and Can (2008) showed that employees distinguish between different targets of their commitment, i.e. commitment to the organisation, their colleagues and their supervisors. This is particularly important because the same study showed that the type of commitment determined its impact: commitment to the organisation predicted organisational outcomes (such as turnover), and commitment to the supervisor predicted citizenship behaviours. Becker *et al.* (1996) also found that commitment to the supervisor (especially commitment based on internalisation) is more highly correlated with job performance than is organisational commitment. Interactions between these different commitments can be important too. Vandenberghe and Bentein (2009) found that low affective commitment to the supervisor was a good predictor of turnover, but that when coupled with low affective commitment to the organisation the chance of employee turnover was significantly increased.

This brings us on to a relatively consistent finding in the research literature: a person who does not feel committed to their employing organisation is more likely to want to leave it, and actually to do so, than a person who feels more committed (Mathieu and Zajac, 1990). In fact, intention to leave the organisation is the strongest and most often reported correlate of low organisational commitment (Solinger *et al.*, 2008). However, as we discuss later in this chapter, intention to leave does not necessarily translate into actual leaving.

People may be committed to different objects (their employer, their manager or their peers) and the object of the commitment may be important in determining how commitment impacts upon behaviour.

Exercise 7.3   Satisfaction and commitment

Using your own experience of work, what factors most affect your job satisfaction? And what factors affect how committed you feel towards an employer? Are they the same things?

Consider the extent to which you think people can be 'made' more satisfied and/or committed by changing things in their work environment. In your experience, are some people just contented (or not) by nature, almost no matter what happens to them?

Employee turnover

For organisations employee turnover can have significant costs. There is the cost of hiring new staff, training new staff, disruption to teamwork, organising people to cover the work done by people who have left and so on. It is an issue that organisations like to monitor, and employee turnover is an important piece of data for most organisations. One of the problems with collecting data on turnover is that once employees have left the organisation, there is little that can be done to get them back.

This is where measures of intention to leave become important. These can provide the organisation with some early warning signs. Thinking about leaving the organisation is something that has obvious links to eventual turnover (Mobley *et al.*, 1978) and for a long time now research has shown this is often the case (Steers and Mowday, 1981).

As we saw earlier in the theory of planned behaviour, intentions can sometimes be quite good predictors of behaviour. If the theory were correct, *attitudes to the act* of leaving would influence intention to leave the company. This would involve asking employees whether they agreed with statements such as 'leaving the organisation would be good for me'. *Subjective norms* would also come into the equation. This might mean finding out whether other people that were important to the employee (e.g. partner, colleagues, friends, etc.) thought it was acceptable for the employee to leave the job.

Breukelen and colleagues (2004) point out that the state of the employment market is an indicator of *actual behavioural control*. This is the essence of many *labour market theories* of turnover: these state that people are all essentially the same and turnover is mostly influenced by objective labour market conditions (Morrell *et al.*, 2001). Psychological theories that have used the theory of planned behaviour focus more on a person's perception of the amount of employment opportunities. This is an indicator of *perceived behavioural control* (i.e. an employee's view of their chances of getting another job in the labour market). A logical prediction from the model is that the better people see their chances in the labour market, the stronger their intention to leave *and* the more likely that their intention to leave will lead to them handing in their resignation.

Key Learning Point

The theory of planned behaviour has been used to understand how intention to leave develops, and how this intention translates into actually leaving the organisation.

Is turnover really as simple as all that? Although the theory of planned behaviour has some validity, factors that sit outside the theory have been implicated. Research has shown that intention to leave is not only influenced by attitudes towards the act of leaving, but also attitudes towards objects (the job itself and the employing organisation). By now, you can probably see where this is going: because they are attitudes toward very broad objects (the job and the organisation) it appears that organisational commitment and job satisfaction influence lots of organisational outcomes including turnover (Harrison *et al.*, 2006). As discussed in the previous section, meta-analyses tend to indicate that there are some significant but modest links between organisational commitment and job satisfaction on the one hand, and turnover on the other hand (e.g. Griffeth *et al.*, 2000).

Breukelen and colleagues (2004) studied turnover intentions and actual turnover in part of the Netherlands' navy. They found that job satisfaction and organisational commitment had no significant direct effect on *actual* turnover. However, job satisfaction did have a significant effect on turnover intention (this was in addition to the influence of the factors set out in the theory of planned behaviour). This intention was then a significant predictor of actual turnover. They also found that tenure was important (as tenure increased, intention to leave weakened). This is probably because tenure is a measure of the strength of the relationship between the employee and the organisation, and an indicator of the employees' past behaviour (e.g. that they have turned down opportunities to leave in the past). Results such as these point to turnover as a planned act and something that people give a lot of consideration to.

Morrell *et al.* (2004) examined turnover among nursing staff using a rather different theoretical approach. They hypothesised that people have a relatively high degree of inertia when it comes to leaving their job, and that in order to leave they have to be 'shocked' out of this inertia. They use the concept of *image theory* to describe the turnover process. Image theory proposes that people develop habitual ways of perceiving events (schemas) and that we tend to see things in a way that fits with these schemas. For example, if you feel the organisation is a very good employer, but one of your colleagues says something at work that upsets you a little, it might not be enough to challenge your view of the company as a good employer. However, if something extreme happens, either at work or at home, this might be enough of a shock to break this habitual interpretation that you have a very good employer. For example, if you think your current employer pays a good salary, and you hear that a friend has a similar job that pays double your salary, that may be a significant enough shock to change the way you see things. This might then get you thinking about leaving your current employment (i.e. changing your habitual behaviour). Morrell *et al.* (2004) found that negative shocks at work (e.g. a perceived unfairness after being passed over for promotion) tended to lead to people looking for other jobs. Positive shocks from outside the workplace (e.g. the opportunity for a new challenge elsewhere) were linked to people actually leaving the organisation. The implication of this is that organisations may be able to intervene to stop employees leaving as a result of some types of work-related shocks. It also tells us that in some cases turnover is the inevitable consequence of events that happen in people's lives.

Key Learning Point

Events that jolt people out of their habitual way of thinking about their job and their employer have been implicated as causes of turnover.

What about the content of the job itself? Chapter 12 discusses the issue of work stress in some detail, and stressful working conditions are often significant 'push' factors in an employees' decision to leave the organisation. Podsakoff *et al.* (2007) carried out a meta-analysis of studies that had looked at the links between positive and negative aspects of jobs and employee turnover. Positive job characteristics are those that employees often interpret as challenges that give them opportunities to develop (*challenge stressors*). These include the level of attention required by the job, the demands of the role, having to work quickly and dealing with interesting tasks. Meta-analysis showed that these factors were largely *unrelated* to turnover intentions and actual turnover. The results were very different for *hindrance stressors* (the constraints that the work situation placed on employees, hassles, organisational politics, role conflict, role ambiguity and lack of resources – *see* Chapter 12). These were linked to both turnover intentions and actual turnover, as well as being linked to other predictors of turnover intention such as organisational commitment and job satisfaction. These results suggest that problems with job content are significant *push factors* for employee turnover. In terms of the *context* within which people work, a lack of fit between the values and needs of employees and what can be provided by the organisation also seems to play a small, but significant, role in employee turnover (Hoffman and Woehr, 2006).

As with most topics in work psychology, it is also worth considering the role of individual differences in determining employee turnover. Ng and Feldman (2009) present a huge meta-analysis of the relationship between age and turnover, finding a small but significant relationship between the two ($r = -0.14$) with increases in age being linked to decreases in the likelihood of turnover. This relationship is a little stronger among those with few, or no, formal educational qualifications. Ng and Feldman argue that there could be a number of reasons for these findings, including:

- Age tends to be linked to tenure, and when tenure is higher the relationship between the employee and the employer tends to be stronger.

- Compared to younger adults, older adults tend to have less intense emotional experiences in the face of problems and, to coin a phrase, tend to 'accentuate the positive'.

- For older adults, perceptions about job insecurity have only a weak link to turnover. This is probably partly because of anxiety about re-entering the job market and because they are not as skilled in moving between jobs as younger workers might be.

- Older adults also tend to have lower self-efficacy than younger adults and hence have more doubts about their ability to adjust to a new job role.

- Compared to younger adults, older adults strive for high-quality interpersonal relationships which might be provided by long-term employment. In other words they are more focused on social needs and work fulfils some social needs.

These factors bring us back to an issue discussed earlier in this chapter, the relationship between age and job satisfaction. It might be that by comparing the job satisfaction of older workers with that of younger workers we are comparing apples with oranges: the two groups might be drawing their job satisfaction from very different elements of their work.

There is also plenty of research that shows another individual difference, personality, has an impact on both turnover intentions and actual turnover. In his meta-analysis, Zimmerman (2008) found a significant relationship between emotional stability (or neuroticism, *see* Chapter 3) and turnover intention: the higher emotional stability, the less likely the intention to leave. This is logical because people who report low levels of emotional stability experience more problems than most when dealing with stressful situations and experience and display more negative emotions than most. Almost always there is a certain level of stress involved in being a new employee, and a person's propensity to express negative emotions at work may also lead to a lack of support from colleagues. Interestingly, Zimmerman's analysis showed this effect of personality on *turnover intention to be direct*, meaning that the increased likelihood of turnover was not because people with low emotional stability were performing less well or were less satisfied with their job. Agreeableness and conscientiousness were related to *actual* turnover (the higher levels of these, the less likely people were to leave). Again, these relationships make sense. Those low on agreeableness are more likely to *act on impulse* and have less concern about the impact that their departure will have on others. People who have high levels of conscientiousness prefer to see things through and tend to make careful plans when decision-making. What was particularly interesting about Zimmerman's findings was that the link between agreeableness and conscientiousness and actual turnover was *not* dependent on turnover intentions. This indicates that those low on agreeableness and conscientiousness are more likely than most people to act on impulse and leave their job without planning. This challenges the theory of planned behaviour. The effects were not huge, but add an extra dimension to how we might think about the causes of employee turnover.

Key Learning Point

Numerous factors are implicated as causes of employee turnover. These include some aspects of personality, age and job design, as well as attitudes to the job and the organisation and the state of the labour market. There are numerous different psychological processes through which these factors have an effect.

STOP TO CONSIDER

From what you have read so far how important is it for organisations to have a satisfied and committed workforce? Are there certain circumstances when it becomes especially important for organisations to worry about such issues?

Unemployment

As we have seen there are a number of factors that influence a person's decision to leave an organisation. What about when this decision is made for them and they do not have an alternative job ready for them to go to? We have positioned unemployment in this chapter to highlight its contrast with voluntary turnover. We could have just as easily positioned it in Chapter 12: unemployment is often argued to be a far bigger source of stress than any of the problems people experience while at work.

Ever since the high levels of unemployment in the United Kingdom and many other countries throughout the 1980s, into the early 1990s, the consequences of being unemployed have been a major topic of concern. It is a problem faced by many, from the unskilled to the professional worker. Reviews of the research on the psychological experience of being unemployed (e.g. Winefield, 1995; Fryer, 1998; Wanberg *et al.*, 2001) conclude that people who experience unemployment tend to suffer from lower levels of personal happiness, life satisfaction, self-esteem and psychological well-being than (i) people who are employed and (ii) when they themselves were in employment. They also tend to report increased depression, difficulty in concentrating and other minor to severe behavioural and physical problems.

In what is probably the largest meta-analysis reported in this textbook, Paul and Moser (2009) analysed 323 studies that compared the mental health of employed people with unemployed people and 86 longitudinal studies (in total data from around half a million people drawn from across a wide range of different countries). They found that the mental health of unemployed people was, on average, half a standard deviation lower (*see* Chapter 2) than that of employed people. In practical terms they conclude that this equates to 34 per cent of unemployed people reporting psychological health problems of clinical severity, compared to 16 per cent in the employed group.

These findings tally with earlier meta-analyses such as Murphy and Athanasou (1999), showing that unemployment still has as much of an impact on people now as it did over a decade ago. They conducted a meta-analysis of 16 longitudinal studies of unemployment published between 1986 and 1996. It was found that moving involuntarily from employment to unemployment was associated with a fall, on average, of 0.36 standard deviations on measures of well-being. Regaining employment brought, on average, an improvement in well-being of 0.54 standard deviations. Paul and Moser (2009) found a similar effect: when people moved back into employment mental health improvements were bigger than the deteriorations associated with job loss. This suggests that, at least for a time, regaining employment may lead to better well-being than the person had experienced in their pre-unemployment job.

There is of course the possibility that poor mental health raises the likelihood of unemployment (i.e. reverse causality). Paul and Moser (2009) tested for this and found the effect of *mental health on unemployment* to be significant (i.e. those with impaired mental health were more likely to lose their job and find it more difficult to get another), but this effect was small in comparison to the impact of *unemployment on mental health*. One specific finding that supported this conclusion was the significant increase in school leavers' mental health when they found employment. In summary there is strong evidence that unemployment *causes* poor mental health. In addition there are some studies (e.g. Stansfeld and Candy, 2006) that have found that the possibility of unemployment (i.e. poor job security) also places psychological well-being at risk.

Key Learning Point

Becoming unemployed tends to have a negative impact on a person's mental health, but the damage is often repaired when the person finds a another job that is at least as satisfying as the one they left behind.

Although there are differences of opinion about the relationship between unemployment and mortality, evidence is emerging of a positive association, with studies indicating that long-term unemployment may adversely affect the longevity of the unemployed by as much as two to three years, depending on when the person had been made redundant. Gunnell and colleagues (2009) summarise evidence from numerous studies carried out in several countries that show significant increases in suicide rates during economic recessions which resulted in high levels of unemployment.

However, much depends on the coping strategies of the individual (Kinicki *et al.*, 2000). It seems that problem-based coping (e.g. trying to find a job) rather than emotion-focused coping (e.g. telling oneself that employment is not very important) does not necessarily help people feel better at the time, but it does help them find a new job. This, as we have already noted, leads to a recovery of mental and physical health. Creed *et al.* (2009) carried out a longitudinal study of the predictors of the intensity of job search (i.e. the amount of time, effort and resources spent preparing CVs, contacting employers, looking for job advertisements, etc.). You will probably not be surprised to read that job search intensity is good predictor of re-employment (and hence an increased likelihood of improved mental health). People who held a strong belief that their efforts would lead to self-improvement (a *learning goal orientation*) tended to also carry out the most intense job searches, much more so than those who believed their capabilities were fixed (*a performance goal orientation*). They also found that this relationship was mediated (*see* Chapter 2) by self-regulation. This meant that those who were goal oriented were more intense in their job search because they were more active in monitoring their own emotions and behaviour. They were also more active in critically evaluating whether how they were behaving, thinking and feeling was helping them to achieve their goals. It was learning goal orientation that led to more self-regulation, and this in turn led to more intense job searching.

Of course, some people experience more than average falls and rises in well-being when their employment status changes while others experience less. What determines this? Researchers have investigated a number of factors (Wanberg *et al.*, 2001) and have mostly reported unsurprising findings. Greater financial hardship is associated with lower well-being, and so is the extent to which a person feels committed to the idea of being employed. High levels of social support and a high ability to structure time tend to reduce the impact of unemployment on well-being. Paul and Moser's (2009) analysis also revealed a number of other important moderators (*see* Chapter 2) of the relationship between unemployment and well-being:

- The effects of unemployment were felt most by men, those in blue-collar jobs and by people who had been unemployed for a long time. On average poor mental health appeared to peak after about two years of unemployment, before getting still worse again for the very long-term unemployed.

■ The context is important. Unemployment had more of an effect on mental health in less economically developed countries and those countries with less developed protection systems (e.g. unemployment benefits) for the unemployed. Gunnell *et al.* (2009) present several pieces of evidence that show suicide rates have increased when spending on welfare provision for the unemployed has been cut in times of economic recession.

Finally, it is important to remember that not all jobs are psychologically enriching (*see* Chapter 8), so it is possible that unemployment is a less bad experience than some of the least pleasant jobs. There is also the issue of what happens when people return to work, but take less rewarding jobs than the ones they had before. This is sometimes referred to as *underemployment*. McKee-Ryan *et al.* (2009) point out that these issues mean that unemployment has an important subjective dimension: losses and recovery of well-being may hinge on how favourably or unfavourably the employee views the changes in their situation.

Key Learning Point

The impact, and length, of unemployment is determined by a number of individual differences and external factors such as labour market conditions and welfare support mechanisms.

Some psychologists have tried to identify exactly what it is about unemployment that leads people to feel psychologically bad. Jahoda (1979) wrote of the manifest function of employment (income), but also its latent functions – structuring of time, social contact outside the family, linkage to wider goals/purposes, personal status/identity and enforced activity. A person who becomes unemployed is deprived of both the manifest and the latent functions of employment, and it is this, Jahoda argued, that leads to negative psychological states. Others have seen Jahoda's approach as too limited. Warr (1987) pointed out that not all employment fosters mental health, and identified features of 'psychologically good' employment (*see* also the Vitamin Model of work stress described in Chapter 12). These included money, variety, goals, opportunity for decision-making, skill use/development, security, interpersonal contact and valued social position. This pays more attention than Jahoda to characteristics of the job itself. Warr argued that becoming unemployed would have negative psychological effects to the extent that it led to loss of these features in day-to-day life. Fryer (1998) has taken a rather different approach. He has criticised conventional treatments of unemployment for taking an overly passive view of the person. The psychological effects of unemployment are, he argues, the result of frustrated attempts to create a better future rather than memories and regrets about loss of a more satisfying past. One other interesting theoretical perspective on unemployment comes from Paul and Moser (2006) who describe the experience of being unemployed as a source of *value incongruence*. This theory suggests that people in many societies value having a job, but these values are incongruent with the reality of being unemployed. This incongruence is a source of significant emotional distress which is in turn related to the various problems with mental health that are consistently associated with unemployment. Paul and Moser (2009) argue that while the effects of unemployment are well-researched, much more research is needed to test the specific mechanisms that underpin those effects.

The psychological contract

So far in this chapter we have looked at what attitudes are, how they form, and why they are important in the workplace. By looking at turnover and unemployment we have also explored what work means to people and why it is important to them. In this section we bring these various issues together by looking at the *psychological contract*. The body of work on this topic has much to say about why employees hold certain attitudes towards their employer, why these attitudes might be linked to their behaviour, and how attitudes and behaviour are linked to what people want from their working lives.

A quite large research literature on the psychological contract has been produced in only a short time. Although there have been some debates about its usefulness (more of that later) it is currently a very important topic in work psychology. Much of the interest in the psychological contract is recent, but its roots go back a long time, it having originally been discussed by Argyris (1960). The psychological contract has been defined in several slightly different ways. We will use the following definition (Robinson and Rousseau, 1994, p. 246):

> An individual's belief regarding the terms and conditions of a reciprocal exchange agreement between that focal person and another party . . . a belief that some form of a promise has been made and that the terms and conditions of the contract have been accepted by both parties.

To add a little more detail to this definition 'psychological contract comprises subjective beliefs regarding an exchange agreement between an individual and, in organizations typically, the employing firm and its agents' (Roussseau, 2001, p. 312).

One of the reasons that the concept has been so useful is that it helps us to understand the combined effects of a lot of different psychological processes that influence employee behaviour and performance. Herriot (1992) describes psychological contracting between an individual and the organisation as 'the invisible glue which binds individuals to the organisation over time. It incorporates the parties' beliefs, values, expectations and aspirations' (p. 6).

The psychological contract should not be confused with the legally binding employment contract (although inevitably there is some overlap between the two, especially around issues such as pay and working hours). The psychological contract is of much interest to work psychologists because it is subjective. However, because it is generally not written down, this does not make it any less important. Many researchers in this field put the psychological contract at the heart of the relationship between the employee and the employer. This means that when it is working well for both parties good things happen – but when the contract breaks down, there are likely to be significant problems.

In the psychological contract there is a belief that the agreement is mutual and binding. From the employees' point of view, this is the agreement that they think they have with their employer about what they will contribute to the employer via their work, and what they can expect in return. So if the employee believes that working late will help them in the next round of promotions, they might expect that the number of times they had worked late would be viewed favourably by those making the decisions about promotions. When an employee makes these efforts they expect the employer to stick to the rules: they perceive the employer to have an obligation to give something back, to reciprocate their efforts. The word *promissory* appears quite a lot in the psychological contract research. The contract is about making and keeping promises through exchanges between the employee and the employer. The employee does something based on the employer's promise to them, and gets something back in return. As you might expect, broken promises can have a serious negative impact on any relationship.

Of course, not everyone wants the same thing from their employment. Money might be more important to some than it is to others. Some people might take a job for the training opportunities it offers. Older workers might be especially interested in the social aspects of work. The same applies to the motives and needs of employing organisation. Short-term contract workers might be hired to just do the job without being given any of the training or other benefits that went with being a permanent employee. Looking at the work of Rousseau (1990, 1995) and Herriot and Pemberton (1995) we can see that four different types of psychological exchanges/ contracts commonly operate in organisations.

Relational contracts offer the most mutual trust and stability. Employees offer loyalty, conformity to requirements, commitment to their employer's goals and trust in their employer not to abuse their goodwill. In return, the organisation offers security of employment, promotion prospects, training and development, and some flexibility about the demands made on employees if they were in difficulty. The harsh reality of the economic environment and fierce global competition are not always conducive to establishing and maintaining this type of exchange.

Transactional contracts are based more on money and well-defined specific performance terms (for both parties). These are much more like a short-term economic exchange. The employee offers longer hours, broader skills, tolerance of change and ambiguity and willingness to take more responsibility. In return the employer offers (to some) high pay, rewards for high performance and, simply, a job. This type of exchange is more common in harsh economic conditions when people are aware that they have little security of tenure.

Key Learning Point

Different employees want different things from their work. By the same token, different employers want different things from their employees. The psychological contract describes what each party promises and expects from the relationship and this contract can change and develop over time.

There are quite clearly some major differences between transactional and relational exchanges. Two other types of exchanges, transitional and balanced exchanges, sit somewhere between the two. *Transitional contracts* are typical of an eroding relationship between the employer and the employee. This can happen when the company can no longer offer promises about future employment (i.e. it is moving away from a relational contract). In a *balanced contract*, mutual expectations are flexible and dynamic, and there is a mutual understanding that performance expectations are likely to change. In this type of contract the employer will make efforts to train and support the employee when things change. This is a bit like the relational contract being enacted when things are less stable for all involved.

All of these types of exchanges can be satisfying, if they are mutually understood, accepted and everyone sticks to the deal. If you took a job thinking it offered excellent training opportunities, but the employer thought that you wanted the job just for the money, this is unlikely to result in a satisfactory outcome for either you or your new employer.

The psychological contract starts to be formed at the very early stages of the relationship between the employee and the employer, probably as soon as a prospective employee hears about a company or a job opportunity for the first time. It starts to become even more crucial during recruitment and selection as this gives both parties a chance to find out a lot more about each other. Robinson and Morrison (2000) found that problems with the psychological contract were more likely when an employee had less interaction with employer before being hired. Many researchers have found that giving prospective employees a *realistic job preview* has helped reduce levels of employee turnover near the beginning of tenure. This can be achieved through using good recruitment and selection procedures that allow prospective employees to get a good insight into the job role and the nature of the organisation they are considering coming to work for. Work sample exercises in assessment centres (*see* Chapter 5) are a very good way of giving employees some early (pre-employment) experiences of what it might be like to work for the company. Proper induction processes can also help to avoid problems with the psychological contract.

However, while important, these early interactions are not everything when it comes to establishing the psychological contract. Taris *et al.* (2006) examined the expectations of 1500 newcomers to an organisation. They found that found that unmet expectations did have an impact on important outcomes such as turnover and motivation. However, the newcomers' expectations changed over time, with some of the unmet expectations becoming less important to them as time went by after they joined the company. This shows that although a psychological contract is formed at recruitment it is fluid: employees and employers' expectations tend to change over time. One implication of this is that the contract needs to be frequently reassessed and managed, and we will return to this issue later in this section.

Much of the research into the psychological contract has looked at what happens when it is broken, or beached, or when one party 'rats' on the deal. These *breaches* can be quite common. For example, Robinson and Rousseau (1994) found that 70 of their sample of 128 managers thought that their employer had *breached* their psychological contract (i.e. what they thought they had been promised) in the first two years of employment. Breaches most commonly concerned failure to deliver on promises about training and development, pay and benefits and promotion opportunities. There are five items below (slightly) adapted from Robinson and Morrison's (2000) measure. These give a more detailed description of how employees might perceive a breach (employees would be asked to what extent they agreed with these statements):

1   Almost all the promises made by my employer during recruitment have been kept so far (agreement = no breach).

2   I feel that my employer has come through in fulfilling the promises made to me when I was hired (agreement = no breach).

3   So far my employer has done an excellent job of fulfilling its promises to me (agreement = no breach).

4   I have not received everything promised to me in exchange for my contributions (agreement = breach).

5   My employer has broken many of its promises to me even though I've upheld my side of the deal (agreement = breach).

The psychological contract concerns an individual employee's perceptions of their rights and obligations with respect to the employing organisation. When promises are broken this is referred to as a breach of the psychological contract.

The apparent frequency with which psychological contracts are breached has led psychologists to try to clarify what is coming to be called the 'violation process' (e.g. Robinson and Morrison, 2000). Figure 7.5 illustrates this. One important issue here concerns the distinction between contract breach and contract violation. The former is often thought of as the realisation that what has been promised has not materialised (i.e. a perceived discrepancy). *Violation* is often used to describe the *negative emotional reaction to a breach*. Violation is more emotionally charged than the more neutral notion of unmet expectations, and more complicated than simply asking how pleasant a person's experiences have been within a work organisation.

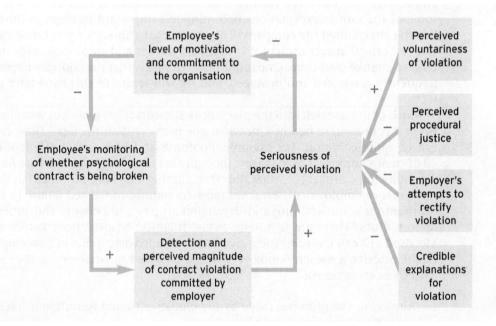

Figure 7.5   **The process of psychological contract violation**
Source: **Adapted from Rousseau (1995, p. 118), reprinted with permission. Note that this same process is depicted to illustrate features of motivation in Chapter 8.**

This distinction is important because it means that a breach could occur without there being a negative emotional reaction to it. Most researchers agree that violations occur when there is a perception that the breach was deliberate, purposeful and reflected unfair treatment (Robinson and Morrison, 2000) and carries with it a clear implication of a broken promise.

Herriot and Pemberton (1995) describe typical behavioural reactions to violation of the psychological contract as get out, get safe or get even – or, to put it another way: to leave, to stay and keep your head below the parapet, or to stay and take your revenge. In terms of attitudes to their employer, when employees felt that their employer had violated the psychological contract, they were not surprisingly inclined to feel less sense of obligation and less commitment to their employing organisation. This means that we might look at behaviours such as performance, turnover and organisational citizenship (*see* Chapter 6) and attitudes such as job satisfaction and organisational commitment when examining the impact of violations of the psychological contract.

The evidence for the impact of violations of the psychological contract continues to mount. In an authoritative meta-analysis of the research Zhao *et al.* (2007) looked at 51 well-designed studies of the consequences of psychological contract breaches and violations. The analysis revealed that the strongest links between the psychological contract and organisational outcomes occurred when employees had a strong emotional response (e.g. feelings of violation or mistrust) to the breach. As with many other issues examined in this book, how employees perceive and react to events is as important as the event itself. These reactions were particularly strongly linked to turnover intention, organisational commitment and job satisfaction. There were weaker, but significant, links to job performance and organisational citizenship behaviours. However, there was no significant link to actual turnover, most likely because turnover is a very complex, multi-causal phenomenon (as already discussed in this chapter). The type of contract breached did not seem to make too much difference to the outcomes, expect that breaches of transactional contracts had stronger links to organisational commitment than breaches of relational contracts. There is some recent evidence that age moderates the impact of a breach. Among older people, perhaps because they are better at handling their emotions, breaches are less likely to result in harm being done to trust and organisational commitment than among younger employees (Bal *et al.,* 2008).

Some of what you have read so far may leave you thinking that breaches of the psychological contract are an inevitable feature of most people's working lives. This is probably true as many organisations are faced with and respond to changing circumstances. As a result researchers have started to look at what factors determine whether a breach triggers an emotional response (violation or mistrust), and whether the negative outcomes of breaches can be averted. There is a lot of scope for individual interpretation in this process. For example, a person who starts out favourably disposed towards their employer might be less likely to notice breaches than somebody who already mistrusts the employer. They might also be less likely to construe breaches as violations.

It appears that psychological breaches can leave employees with some 'baggage' that they take forward into future employment. Robinson and Morrison (2000) found that experiences of breaches of the psychological contract with former employers were linked to the likelihood of breaches occurring with the current employer. Individual differences may also determine an individual employee's reaction to a breach. Restubog *et al.* (2007) found that breaches have bigger effects for people who attach high value to the tangible benefits of employment such as money (outcome-oriented people, or *entitled*) than it does for those that attach high value to the benefits of relationships at work (relationship-oriented people, or *benevolent*). When experiencing a breach, outcome-oriented employees tended to attempt to 'even the score' by extracting revenge. This was far less likely to be the case among the relationship-oriented employees, probably because these employees did not want to place at risk relationships with co-workers and supervisors.

Importantly for organisations, research also shows that how a breach is handled is important in determining whether it turns into a vioaltion. Lester *et al.* (2007) found that open communication with employees about the nature of the psychological contract was important to keeping the contract fulfilled. As long as employers give credible, legitimate and consistent reasons for breaches then employees appear less likely to have strong emotional reactions to breaches (i.e. they are less likely to feel the contract has been violated or to develop feelings of mistrust). Zhao *et al.* (2007) argues that employers need to guard against breaches by making efforts to keep abreast of their employees' needs. The main point underlying all this is that contract breach does not necessarily lead to reduced employee loyalty and commitment. If it is felt that the breach was neither the employer's fault, nor intended, then the impact on the employee's loyalty is likely to be small, particularly if it is put right quickly.

Key Learning Point

Interventions can stop breaches of the psychological contract leading feelings of violation or mistrust.

The concept of the psychological contract has not been accepted fully by all researchers. Some have argued that there is a danger that it is overused and that other important variables are ignored as a result (Arnold, 1996). In addition, an organisation is not a person, and therefore cannot be a party to a psychological contract. Organisations consist of many different individuals and groups, and each employee may have quite specific expectations about their rights and obligations vis-à-vis those individuals (e.g. supervisor) and groups (e.g. departments). However, Rousseau (1998) argued that the psychological contract provides a framework for better understanding some of the important psychological processes that influence individual attitudes and as a result organisational performance. It also represents a very flexible approach to understanding employee attitudes and behaviour: any aspect of the working relationship and a whole host of individual differences can shape the psychological contract. You may also think that there is some overlap with concepts of job satisfaction and organisational commitment, but if you look carefully, the underlying processes of the psychological contract are quite different (particularly the concepts of promises and reciprocity). Guest (1998) also argued that the concept is consistent with the spirit of the times (i.e. the changing nature of employment relationships); it helps to make sense of current employment relationships, and helps to highlight who has power. Perhaps the clincher is that the state of the psychological contract is linked to a range of important organisational outcomes (see Zhao *et al.*, 2007). By capturing important aspects of people's experience of work, the concept offers considerable possibilities for understanding work attitudes and behaviour.

Exercise 7.4   Mark Reason's 'tyred' psychological contract

When Mark Reason started work as a tyre-fitter for Nice New Tyres Ltd. he thought he would only be working there for a few months just to earn some money until something better came along. He didn't really know much about tyre-fitting, or the company, but the interview was easy enough, he got some training and after a short probationary period he was given a permanent contract. Months turned into years because filling in job application forms and going for interviews wasn't really his thing. Mark took on more and more responsibility, managing some junior staff and running the depot when the manager wasn't there. He worked hard at what he did, and although the pay wasn't overly generous it was fair and his colleagues were good people to be around. His manager sent him on some management training courses, telling him that he was 'clearly management material' and that he would be running a depot very soon.

Now, seven years after he started work for the company, many of his former colleagues have moved on to bigger and better things. Since the company started to struggle financially the managerial role is no longer discussed. All the training courses have stopped too. Mark often finds himself wondering what he did wrong. True, he is still paid good money for just fitting tyres, but he also gets asked to do lots of the paperwork around the place to help out his manager. He isn't paid for this and finds that he doesn't get a lot of thanks for it either, so sometimes he 'deliberately forgets' to do it. All that keeps him coming to work now is the friendly chats with customers and fact that he has a secure job when lots of people are struggling to find work.

Suggested exercises

How has Mark's psychological contract changed over the course of his employment with Nice New Tyres Ltd.? What breaches of the psychological contract can you see in the story described above? What impact might these breaches have on Mark and his relationship with his employer? Could Mark's employer have done anything different to stop these breaches or to manage the impact of the breaches?

STOP TO CONSIDER

Think about some people you know well, and who have a job at the moment. Do you think that the concept of the psychological contract would make sense to them? If you have time talk to one or two of these people about the psychological contract they have with their employer, and examine whether what they say fits with what you have read in this chapter.

Attitude change through persuasion

Throughout this chapter we have looked at some important employee attitudes and the causes and consequences of them. Changing attitudes is an important part of many people's work. Managers may seek to change the attitudes of colleagues and subordinates on issues such as marketing strategy, about how much the organisation values them or about why a breach of the psychological contract was justified. Sales staff try to persuade potential customers to hold a positive attitude to whatever they are selling. It should be noted that such attempts are ultimately aimed at changing behaviour. As we have already seen, this connection is not always simple.

We will set aside that complexity for a moment and focus on some of the factors that determine the success or otherwise of attempts by one person to change the attitudes of another. Most of this material is drawn from social psychology and what is presented here is a very simplified version of a large and diverse literature.

It is also important to remember that attempts to change people's attitudes to something they experience personally and often (such as work) solely through verbal persuasion are unlikely to be successful: as you have already seen in this chapter, many other factors influence attitudes.

Communicator credibility

The credibility of a communicator rests partly on their expertness and trustworthiness as perceived by the person on the receiving end of the communication (Hovland and Weiss, 1951). Expertness concerns how much the communicator knows about the subject of the communication. Trustworthiness usually depends mainly on whether the communicator has a record of honesty. However, the picture is not quite so simple. Sometimes a low-credibility communicator has as much persuasive effect as a high-credibility one – but not immediately; not until a few weeks later. This has been termed the *sleeper effect*, and is thought to be due to the person remembering the message but forgetting the source (Cook *et al.*, 1979). So there is hope even for unpopular politicians and propagandists!

Communicator attractiveness

Tannenbaum (1956) and others since have found that the amount of attitude change is directly related to the degree of attractiveness of the change agent. The power of attractiveness may well rest on the desire of the message receiver to be like the communicator. There is also some evidence that attractiveness is especially useful when the message is likely to be unpopular (Eagly and Chaiken, 1975), though its power can be undone if the communicator is perceived to be deliberately exploiting their attractiveness.

Key Learning Point

The perceived integrity, expertise and attractiveness of the communicator of a persuasive message partly determine whether the recipients of the message are persuaded by it.

One-sided versus two-sided arguments

Is it better to give both sides of an argument (though portraying the favoured one more convincingly), or is a one-sided message more persuasive? This issue was first examined by Yale University researchers many years ago (Hovland *et al.*, 1949) in their studies of training and indoctrination films used by the American armed forces during the Second World War. They found:

- that the two-sided presentation was more effective when the aim was to change the attitude;

- that better educated men were influenced less by the one-sided than by the two-sided presentation.

More recent research has suggested that one-sided arguments may allow the individual more time to contemplate the arguments they receive (Chattopadhyay and Alba, 1988). This may be necessary to persuade people with limited cognitive ability and/or low familiarity with the issues. Also, as Tesser and Shaffer (1990) have contended, 'perhaps the need to decide the relative merits of two sides of an unfamiliar issue leads people to concentrate on receiving the message at the expense of thinking about its implications in detail'.

Use of fear

Is the use of threat effective in changing attitudes? Janis and Feshbach (1953) found that change in attitude and behaviour tended to be greater when intensity of fear arousal was fairly low. Subsequent research has shown that moderate amounts of fear increase the effectiveness with which people process information, but high amounts of fear tend to immobilise them (Jepson and Chaiken, 1990). The amount of fear depends not only on how scary the message is, but also on how optimistic a person is about their ability to deal with the threat described in it. This is in line with Rogers and Prentice-Dunn's (1997) *protection motivation theory,* which proposes that attempts to induce fear will be successful in changing behaviour when they convince a person that:

- the problem is serious;
- the problem may affect the person;
- they can avoid the problem by taking certain specific action;
- they are capable of performing the behaviour required to avoid the problem.

This bears some resemblance to the expectancy theory of motivation (*see* Chapter 8). Protection motivation theory has received considerable support in research (e.g. Mulilis and Lippa, 1990), but offering reliable strategies to avoid the feared fate is often difficult. Many insurance companies present fear-arousing messages (e.g. about having a disabling accident), and then suggest that buying one of their insurance policies is an effective strategy. They forget that, for most people, monetary reward neither avoids such an occurrence nor fully compensates for it.

Social pressures in persuasion

Requiring people to commit themselves publicly to a change in attitude has long been used by change agents (Kiesler, 1971). As Krech *et al.* (1962) noted, 'Public commitment has been found to be an effective procedure; private commitment has been found to be ineffective.'

Research on group decision-making (*see* Chapter 13) has sought to explain why groups tend to arrive at more extreme positions than those initially held by the individual members of the group, an effect that has been labelled *group polarisation.* It seems that people are persuaded to adopt more extreme positions by hearing arguments that they regard as both valid and novel (Isenberg, 1986). As Turner (1991, pp. 67–72) pointed out, though, it is likely that attitudes are also changed by repeated exposure to arguments that people have heard before and that are therefore not novel to them. It is also possible that *social comparison processes* play a part. If a member of a group hears other group members advocating a certain position, they may draw two conclusions: first, that this position is socially acceptable, and second, that 'anything (s)he can do, I can do better', leading the person to adopt a position more extreme than the one they have just heard.

Wood (2000) has emphasised that attitude change that occurs as a result of social pressures is not necessarily superficial and temporary. We are often required to justify ourselves in public, and this tends to make us think carefully about our attitudes, and thus become more certain about what they are (Cowan and Hodge, 1996). This is one of many lines of argument which suggest that a person's attitudes at work are likely to be influenced by those of people around them.

Key Learning Point

The social context in which the persuasive message is received can affect the extent to which it is successful.

Events before the persuasive message

If the recipients of a persuasive message have been forewarned about that message, they are more likely to resist it if they feel threatened or demeaned by that attempt. Generally, people tense up (both physically and psychologically) if they are led to expect a challenge (Cacioppo and Petty, 1979). If the recipients are already amenable to being persuaded, forewarning can soften them up, and perhaps produce some attitude change even before they have heard the arguments (Hass, 1975).

Another relevant factor concerns what has sometimes been called inoculation. Some attitudes are so widely held that they are never or rarely challenged. Challenge leads the recipient to think of reasons why they were correct all along (Pfau, 1997). These reasons act as 'antibodies' against subsequent attempts at persuasion.

Overview of attitude change: central versus peripheral routes to persuasion

Petty and Cacioppo (1985) made a distinction between the central route to persuasion (which involves careful thought and weighing up of arguments) and the peripheral route, which relies more on emotional responses but relatively little thought. They argued that attitude change through the central route is longer lasting and more closely associated with behaviour than that through the peripheral route.

Persuasive messages processed through the central route need to contain strong arguments that stand up to scrutiny. People who enjoy thinking, are able to concentrate, feel involvement in the issues in question and feel personally responsible for evaluating the message are most likely to process persuasive messages by the central route. For them, the fate of the persuasive message depends more on their weighing up of the arguments than simply remembering those arguments (Cacioppo and Petty, 1989), though the latter is also important when evaluating two-sided messages (Chattopadhyay and Alba, 1988; *see also* the section One-sided versus two-sided arguments, above). A persuasive message that accurately targets the *function* served by the relevant attitude for the recipient of the message is likely to succeed. For example, someone who cares about the social consequences of their actions is more likely to respond to a persuasive message emphasising the social acceptability of the new point of view than to one which stresses how it will help make them wealthy (Lavine and Snyder, 1996).

Peripheral processing of information occurs when the recipient of the persuasive message is unwilling or unable to pay it very much attention. When this is the case, the strength of the arguments matters less, and peripheral cues matter more, in determining the success or otherwise of the attempt at attitude change. These peripheral cues include communicator attractiveness and expertise, sheer length of the message (irrespective of the quality of its content), and reactions of other recipients of the message (*see*, for example, Wood and Kallgren, 1988). It seems that peripheral processing is likely when the recipient of the message is in a good mood. Good moods seem to reduce the extent to which messages are examined critically, and weak arguments are sometimes as convincing as strong ones (Eagly and Chaiken, 1992).

Key Learning Point

How persuasive a message is depends partly on which cognitive processes are used by the recipient when thinking about it.

Clearly the distinction between central and peripheral processing is important for those who wish to change the attitudes of others. It gives some guidance about which aspects of the message, its contents and its context are important to different audiences in different situations. Whatever the route, though, it is worth remembering that persuasive messages can focus either on changing the attitude or on changing the definition and meaning of the attitude object (Wood, 2000). Changing the meaning will often automatically change the evaluation. For example, Bosveld *et al.* (1997) found that people adopted a more favourable attitude to 'affirmative action' in the workplace when it was presented in terms of equal opportunity rather than actively favouring minorities.

Exercise 7.5 Were you persuaded?

Try to think of a recent occasion when someone tried to persuade you to change your attitude to something or someone. It might have been a friend attempting to change your attitude to someone you both know, or a place such as a bar or restaurant, or a television programme. It might have been a politician making a speech. It could even have been an advertiser.

Negotiation and conflict at work

Despite the best efforts of all involved, problems with the relationships between employees and their employer do still occur, and as we have seen these can have serious consequences. Earlier in this chapter we described some of the research on turnover which shows that employees can perceive many different problems at work that lead them to start to think about leaving. Breaches of the psychological contract can lead to undesirable outcomes for all involved. Employee attitudes that are not conducive to good performance and long tenure can develop. As we have also seen the consequences of these problems are not inevitable; much depends upon how problems between employees and conflict at work are dealt with.

Negotiation is the process attempting to deal with problems at work through discussion. The most obvious form of negotiation in the workplace is that between management and employees in organisations, the latter often represented by a trade union. Psychologists have tried to describe what happens in negotiations and also in some cases to recommend strategies for success as a negotiator. They have tended to concentrate on what happens in the negotiation itself, and placed less emphasis on the economic and political context in which a negotiation takes place (Lewicki *et al.*, 1992). Although some research has involved real negotiations, much has been conducted in laboratories with students tackling standard tasks under varying conditions.

The negotiation process

As Pruitt (1981) pointed out, at certain key decision points during a negotiation, a negotiator can choose between three types of behaviour:

1   *Unilateral concession*: the negotiator lowers their demands, or agrees to something desired by an opposing negotiator.

2 *Standing firm, or contention*: the negotiator restates their demands, or refuses to give something desired by an opposing negotiator. This can involve strong uncompromising arguments in support of one's own position, and even threats.

3 *Collaboration*: the negotiator tries to work with, rather than against, opposing negotiators to find a mutually acceptable solution.

In an early and influential piece of work, Walton and McKersie (1965) distinguished between *distributive bargaining* and *integrative bargaining*, which are similar to Pruitt's competition and collaboration, respectively. In distributive bargaining the negotiators assume that there is a fixed amount of reward available, so that one negotiator's gain is another's loss, but integrative bargaining involves an attempt to increase the size of the overall reward available to both sides. One phenomenon often observed in research is that negotiators tend to treat the task as distributive even though they could gain more by taking an integrative approach. For example, suppose that negotiators A and B are trying to reach an agreement over the sale of A's house, which B wishes to buy. A wants £200,000, and B begins by offering £180,000. After some discussion, A agrees to accept £195,000 and B increases the offer to £190,000. Neither side is prepared to shift further on the price so it looks like a deal will not be struck. However, if A and B then search together for other ways of viewing the problem, they may reach an agreement. Perhaps A has little use for the carpets and curtains in the house because the one she is moving to has them fitted already. In fact, she would prefer to avoid the hassle of removing them. B on the other hand very much wants A to leave the carpets and curtains because he likes them and is too busy to arrange new ones. So A and B may agree a price of £195,000 including carpets and curtains. B considers the extra £5000 a fair price for the carpets and curtains, and A is also happy because the carpets and curtains are of no value to her, and she has got the price she wanted.

This kind of outcome, sometimes referred to as 'win–win' (Pruitt and Rubin, 1986), often depends on the negotiators having complementary priorities so that each can make concessions over issues where their subjective loss is smaller than the corresponding gain experienced by another negotiator. To engage in problem-solving implies that a negotiator has some concern for the other party's outcomes as well as their own, and can tolerate the possiblity that the other party will be seen to have got at least some of what they wanted. Indeed, a negotiator's predominant negotiating style can be predicted on the basis of the extent of their concern about outcomes of the participating parties. This is shown in Figure 7.6.

Although quite simple, Figure 7.6 has three important lessons. First, a negotiator has more options than those of conceding or not conceding. Second, a negotiator may not be concerned only with their own outcomes. Especially if one negotiator anticipates having to work with another in the future, they would be wise to pay attention to the other's wishes because this helps to maintain their relationship. Third, compromise is not in the middle of Figure 7.6 as one might expect. Instead it is near the top. This indicates that compromise requires a strong concern about the other party's outcomes. A contentious negotiator is almost as unlikely to compromise as to make a concession (Van de Vliert and Prein, 1989).

Key Learning Point

Effective negotiators pay attention to the interests of the other side as well as their own.

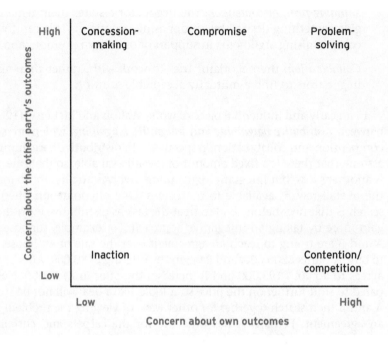

Figure 7.6   Negotiator concerns and characteristic strategies
Source: Adapted from Carnevale and Pruitt (1992), with permission from the
Annual Review of Psychology, vol. 43. © 1992 by Annual Reviews Inc.

As Carnevale and Pruitt (1992) have pointed out, whatever a negotiator's preferred or typical style, the state of the negotiation may dictate their behaviour. This
is another illustration of the fact that situation sometimes overrides personality (*see*
Chapter 1). Indeed, some research has suggested that negotiators typically behave in
a contentious fashion early in a negotiation, adopting a problem-solving approach
only when their position has been stated clearly and repeatedly. Up to a point this
seems to be a sensible strategy. Research suggests that early in negotiation, uncompromising statements by one negotiator may produce concessions, or at least a rather
lower opening bid, from the other than would otherwise have been the case (Pruitt
and Syna, 1985). However, making high initial demands *and* sticking to most of them
is a high-risk strategy because it is likely that no agreement at all will occur. In most
work settings, failing to reach agreement is unsatisfactory for both or all parties – a
so-called 'lose–lose' outcome. On the other hand, making low initial demands and
many concessions produces a quick agreement but a rather one-sided one! It may
also be a mistake to start with moderate demands and then refuse to move – the
moderation raises the expectations of the other negotiator(s) but then the inflexi-
bility frustrates them and leaves them unable to point to concessions they have
won for their supporters (Hamner, 1974). The best approach may often be to start
with high demands and make frequent concessions. Making meaningful concessions
is easier if the negotiator has some awareness of, and empathy with, the concerns of
the other party. It implies a willingness to be cooperative as opposed to (or as well
as) competitive. Deutsch (2002), in a summary of research on the social psychology
of conflict, argues that a wholly competitive approach has many negative effects,
including impairment of communication, reduced self-confidence in both self and

other party and mutual suspicion. He concludes (p. 312): 'Escalating the conflict increases its motivational significance to the participants and may make a limited defeat less acceptable and more humiliating than a mutual disaster.' Coleman and Lim (2001) make a similar point in their discussion of training people in negotiation skills.

Most theory and practice in negotiation during the late twentieth and early twenty-first centuries have stressed the importance of cooperation between negotiators where possible, based upon a concern for the other party's interests as well as one's own. A good example is so-called 'interest-based negotiation' (Fisher *et al.*, 1991). This is based on five main factors:

1 *Relationship*: a good personal relationship between the negotiators.

2 *Interests*: an understanding of what interests and concerns are most important to the other side, rather than focusing on the position they initially adopt.

3 *Options*: identifying as many options for resolution that involve mutual gain as possible.

4 *Criteria*: the use of objective criteria to evaluate possible outcomes. Criteria might include existing legislation or organisational policies.

5 *Alternatives*: an awareness of what are the alternatives to a negotiated deal, and the consequences of those alternatives.

Senger (2002) offers an interesting account from an American perspective of how interest-based negotiation operates (or does not) in various cultures. He takes most of his examples from the customer–shopkeeper negotiation, and discusses the many ways in which sellers use the five factors described above. For example, a *relationship* might be established by offering the customer a cup of tea, or free use of the shop's telephone to make a call. This can in turn create an *interest* on the part of the customer – for example an interest in repaying a favour. An illustration of *options* has been given earlier in the example of negotiation over a house sale. *Criteria* can be seen operating in the charging of higher taxi fares to tourists staying in five-star hotels than others: the criterion is the place in which they are staying, which signals their wealth. Often in buyer–seller transactions, one party will have better knowledge of *alternatives* than the other; for example, a market trader may have a pretty good idea of how much money they can typically get for a particular item, which helps the decision about whether to accept a potential customer's offer.

Senger (2002) also shows how interest-based negotiation can be manipulated. For example, one party may pretend they feel more warmly towards the other than they really do; or lie about what other customers have offered in an attempt to manipulate a potential customer's wish to appear a reasonable person. There is also the possibility that interest-based negotiation may break down if one party decides to be the ultimate hard bargainer.

Key Learning Point

Interest-based negotiation requires negotiators to think carefully and creatively about the concerns of all parties, and to focus on five concerns: relationships, interests, options, criteria and alternatives.

As Lewicki *et al.* (1992) have pointed out, much research on negotiation seems to rest on the assumption that the only negotiation worth considering occurs at the negotiating table. Yet Walton and McKersie (1965) argued that much significant negotiation occurs when negotiators try to persuade their constituents to accept a deal as the best that can be achieved, and when negotiators on the same side discuss with each other how they should respond to a certain situation. Negotiators tend to believe (sometimes correctly) that their constituents are more anxious to win than they are themselves. This makes them more inclined to engage in contentious negotiation tactics, perhaps in the real hope of getting a good deal, or perhaps just to impress their constituents even if there is no hope of further progress. On the other hand, when negotiators have to justify their behaviour to their constituents *and* when they want a continuing relationship with the other side, they are quite likely to engage in problem-solving tactics. This is presumably because problem-solving is the strategy most likely to maintain their credibility with both their constituents and the opposing negotiators.

Key Learning Point

Negotiators often have to persuade their own side that a deal is acceptable. This requirement can influence their behaviour during the negotiation itself.

Ideas from cognitive and social psychology have also contributed to our understanding of negotiator behaviour. For example, we have already seen in this chapter how people are more inclined to take a risk in the hope of avoiding a loss than in the hope of making a gain. When applied to negotiation, this means that a negotiator who perceives that they are trying to avoid a loss will be more inclined to resist concessions (thus risking failure to reach agreement) than a negotiator who construes the position as trying to make a gain (Bazerman *et al.*, 1985). Negotiators also run the risk of escalating commitment to their initial position, especially if they are inexperienced.

Negotiators also have expectations or scripts concerning how negotiations will unfold. One common element of such a script is that a concession, once made, is not withdrawn. This expectation means that such a withdrawal is less likely to happen, and that if it does happen it will be viewed with outrage.

Exercise 7.6   A negotiation at Micro

Employee relations at the Micro electronics company had reached a critical point. The company was performing well in its markets and making a good profit. In order to maintain this, managers wanted to abandon one of the company's products, for which demand was declining. This might mean some redundancies. When rumours broke out that voluntary redundancy might be available there was interest from a few people, but not enough to avoid some compulsory redundancies. At the same time, the employees who remained would undertake more varied and sometimes more skilled work. Employee attitude surveys had consistently indicated that this was what many of them wanted, and many of them claimed to want it more than an above-inflation pay rise. Perhaps swayed by this information, managers at Micro had underestimated the strength of opposition to their plans for implementing the changes they desired. Although there had not yet been industrial action, it was a clear possibility in the near future. New pay discussions were also due. Recent pay deals in similar companies to Micro had been slightly above inflation, even though all those companies faced similar dilemmas to Micro about which products to discontinue and how to manufacture the rest at the lowest possible cost. The details of those recent pay deals were described in the current issue of an industry magazine. The union negotiator, Nils Gunderson, was generally felt by union members to have achieved a poor deal in the last pay discussions two years ago. He was keen to move out of his job at Micro into a full-time union post. He had had a cordial relationship with the previous managing director, but his few encounters with the new one, Stephanie Viken, had not been so pleasant during the six months she had been in the post. Nils and Stephanie had had several arguments about relatively unimportant matters and knew little about each other as people. For her part, Stephanie was anxious to secure active union cooperation (as opposed to passive compliance) with company plans. She knew that she would need the employees on her side if the company was to remain competitive. She was also worried by the possibility that many might change to another, more militant, union.

Suggested exercises

What insights do the five factors of interest-based negotiation offer concerning (i) how Nils and Stephanie are likely to approach this negotiation, and (ii) the scope for a mutually satisfactory outcome?

Employee relations

Assessing and changing people's attitudes is an important part of employee relations processes such as negotiation. *Employee relations* have been defined by Walker (1979, p. 11) as being to do with 'the accommodation between the various interests that are involved in the process of getting work done'. This definition does not assume that the parties involved are necessarily management and other employees, nor that the latter are represented by trade unions, nor that there is necessarily conflict between the parties. However as Brotherton (2003) has pointed out, employee relations (and its earlier label industrial relations [IR]) have been dominated by research on institutions (such as government, trade unions and employers) rather than individuals. This plus the perceived tendency of psychologists to adopt a managerialist perspective has meant that psychology has been rather marginalised in the field of employee relations (see also Kelly, 1998).

Hartley (1992) has provided a helpful account of many aspects of employee relations. Figure 7.7 is an adaptation of her picture of the field.

Figure 7.7 reflects trends in many Western countries during the late twentieth and early twenty-first centuries. The references to human resource management (HRM) and employee participation and involvement reflect a decreasing emphasis

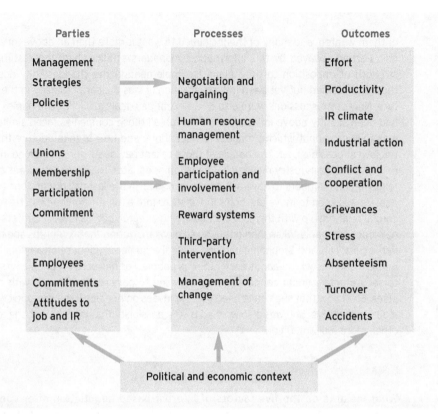

Figure 7.7   **Psychology in employee relations**
Source: Adapted from J. Hartley (1992) 'Psychology in employee relations',
in C.L. Cooper and I.T. Robertson (eds) *International Review of Industrial and
Organizational Psychology*, vol. 7. Copyright John Wiley & Sons Ltd, Wiley-
Blackwell.

on collective, formal employment relationships. Instead, as you have seen in this
chapter, there is an increasing tendency for workplace-specific employment agree-
ments, more emphasis on management for quality, training and flexibility of
employees and a greater concern with the commitment of individuals to their
employing organisation (Guest and Hoque, 1996). Attempts to increase employee
commitment and performance include share ownership, quality circles (where groups
of employees jointly review the quality of output) and empowerment. The last of
these involves trusting people to recognise and solve problems themselves rather
than referring them to someone 'higher up', or not noticing them at all. Chapter
12 shows that many employees react positively to such interventions. However,
they might not change their fundamental attitudes to managers (Kelly and Kelly,
1991). This is because employees often believe, rightly or wrongly, that powerful
groups in the organisation are still in control and might at any time choose to exert
their control in a more draconian manner.

This trend towards the individualising of employee relations (at the expense of
institutional perspectives) should mean that psychology's relevance is increasing.

Brotherton (2003) identifies three aspects of psychology for which this is particularly true:

1 Commitment, as described earlier in this chapter and in particular the circumstances in which people feel committed to both their employer and their trade union.

2 The psychological contract.

3 Social identity and social categorisation theories, which seek to explain how and when people incorporate group memberships into their personal identities.

Key Learning Point

The ways in which different power blocs in organisations relate to each other depend partly on the wider legal and cultural contexts in which the organisation operates.

We will now explore this third aspect a little more. A number of ideas from the social psychology of inter-group relations and personal identity (*see* earlier in this chapter) have been applied to the analysis of conflict in organisations. They have in common the notion that people tend to value themselves and other members of groups to which they belong more highly than members of other groups. This may be engendered by groups having conflicting goals (Sherif, 1966) or simply because our group memberships define our identity, and we are motivated to uphold the value of that identity relative to others (Tajfel, 1972). The implication of these theories is that industrial action such as strikes and overtime bans occurs either when the goals of different groups are very much in conflict and cannot readily be resolved (Sherif), or when members of a group feel that their identity is so threatened that they must make a stand (Tajfel). Note that this does not take into account an assessment of whether industrial action is likely to improve their material or psychological state, nor does it say much about how a group of people could (or should) organise and conduct industrial action. Given that industrial action is an unpleasant experience for most people involved in it, it is important for a group taking industrial action to maintain cohesion and a sense of purpose without undue escalation of commitment to an unwinnable battle.

Aspects of social identity have been used more in understanding who participates in union activities. Kelly and Kelly (1994) studied 350 union members in a UK local government organisation. They divided participation into 'easy' (e.g. reading union journals, attending union meetings) and 'difficult' (e.g. being a union delegate, speaking at branch meetings). Perhaps not surprisingly, the extent to which people engaged in either form of participation was predicted by the extent to which they identified with the union. In addition, 'easy' participation was affected by the extent to which union members had stereotypical 'us and them' perceptions of management – the more stereotypical the perceptions, the more the 'easy' participation. Interestingly, these aspects of social identity were better predictors of participation than the extent to which members felt they were badly off relative to comparison groups.

The quality of inter-group relations in the workplace, and whether poor relations lead to industrial action, depends partly on the extent to which members of the different groups have accurate perceptions of each other. Allen and Stephenson (1984) have found that when members of groups overestimate differences in attitudes and beliefs between their own group and other groups, industrial action is more likely than when the differences are underestimated. This is another illustration of the importance of social factors: not only the real difference in views, but also the perceived difference, can influence whether industrial action occurs.

Summary

In this chapter we have taken a close look at attitudes. In particular, we have focused on what they are, how they can be measured, how they can be changed and their links with behaviour. Like most social psychological phenomena, attitudes are more complicated than they seem at first sight. They have several different components which may or may not fit together nicely. A person's attitudes may predict their behaviour quite well in some circumstances, if the right attitude is assessed, and if the person's perceptions of social pressures and their own capabilities are also taken into account. Two key work attitudes are job satisfaction and organisational commitment. Job satisfaction concerns a person's evaluation of their job, while organisational commitment refers to the extent to which a person feels attached to their employing organisation. They can both be measured satisfactorily, both are influenced by the nature of the person's job, and both appear to have quite complex connections with a range of behaviours and other attitudes at work. However, they may both say more about whether a person stays in their employing organisation than about their job performance. Of course, employee turnover is complex and many other factors aside from attitudes influence this important aspect of employee behviour. The psychological contract provides a useful framework for understanding how the employment relationship develops and is maintained. It also tells us quite a lot about how attitudes develop and what work means to people. The impact that unemployment has on people shows that work fulfils a number of important psychological needs. Changing attitudes is difficult, but it is not impossible – and easier if the persuader is aware of research findings on attitude change. Resolving conflicts at work requires negotiation skills and there is quite a lot of research on how 'win–win' outcomes might be achieved.

Closing Case Study   **Staff happy with a 'duvet day'**

Sandwell Community Caring Trust looks after 350 adults and children with learning and physical disabilities, older people and their families. It is a 24-hour-a-day business. Staff agree their hours when they join, and are invited to request changes as their circumstances alter. 'If staff feel unable to cope with a specific task, they are encouraged to tell their manager,' the report said.

It's easy to see why Sandwell, based in the West Midlands, was second in this year's Sunday Times 100 Best Companies to Work For list. It came first nationally in the work-life-balance category. Sandwell's employee turnover is only 4 per cent, compared with 20 per cent or more across the care sector. Since 1997, the number of staff has gone up from 60 to 280 and business turnover has increased from £1m to £9.5m. The average time taken as sick leave is only 0.6 days a year.

Teresa Aitken, founder director of PI Costing, a niche company based in Doncaster undertaking legal services on behalf of solicitors, said trust and good communication were essential. The company offers 'duvet days'. At the discretion of the manager, staff who have worked extra hard can spend an extra hour in bed. Aitken also says if someone has finished their work in the minimum time, she is happy for them to go shopping.

Most of Aitken's 20 employees are young women. Some have had babies and want to work shorter hours, or to work several days a week from home. Homeworkers, she has found, are 20–50 per cent more productive. It can be difficult ensuring that homeworkers feel involved in the company. Small firms such as PI Costing have regular staff meetings and maintain communication in other ways. Both are also able to offer less competitive salaries because people like working for them.

In all these firms, standards are high. One individual agreed to leave Clock after abusing the system for a second time. 'This has demonstrated to all employees management's zero tolerance on breaching the trust placed on them,' the report said. And at Sandwell, where the clients are vulnerable adults and children, there is no question of shifts going uncovered.

Source: The Sunday Times, 8 July 2007 (Hofkins, D.), copyright © The Sunday Times 2007, www.nisyndication.com

Suggested exercise

Can you see evidence in this case study that employee attitudes are having a positive impact on the functioning of Sandwell Community Caring Trust? If so, which attitudes might be having this impact? What seems to be the cause of those attitudes? Perhaps you could also describe the nature of the 'typical' psychological contract that seems to be operating within this organisation. Do you think violations of the psychological contract are unlikely to occur – why?

Test your learning

Short-answer questions

1 Define three aspects of an attitude.

2 Why are attitudes useful for a person?

3 Draw a diagram to show the theory of planned behaviour, and define its key concepts.

4 Briefly describe three general phenomena that can influence job satisfaction.

5 Define organisational commitment and its component parts.

6 List the factors that can influence employee turnover.

7 What factors might lessen, or worsen, the impact of unemployment?

8 What is the psychological contract?

9 Explain what is meant by a breach of the psychological contract. How is this different from a violation of the psychological contract?

10 List the features of a persuasive message which affect the success of that message.

11 List the features of the communicator of a persuasive message which affect the success of that message.

12 Describe the main principles of interest-based negotiation.

13 Briefly describe the topics within employee relations studied by psychologists.

Suggested assignments

1 In what circumstances do attitudes determine behaviours at work?

2 Examine how much is known about what factors determine *either* job satisfaction *or* organisational commitment.

3 To what extent does the research evidence about organisational commitment suggest that managers in organisations should care about how committed their staff are?

4 'The concept of the psychological contract tells us much about the causes of problems with employee attitudes and behaviour at work.' Discuss.

5 Critically assess the proposition that compromise in negotiation is not the same as weakness.

Relevant websites

The Social Science Information Gateway (SOSIG) provides links to many sites about attitudes, and indeed to most other topics covered in this book. Go to http://www.intute.ac.uk/socialsciences/ and try typing 'attitudes' into the search box on that page. You will get brief descriptions of many sites concerned with attitudes in and out of the workplace. Many of these offer useful summaries or applications of attitude theory. For more specific items, try searching on work attitudes.

A good example of how public opinion survey companies work and present their findings can be found at http://www.yougov.co.uk/. Here you can find a summary of opinion surveys carried out recently about attitudes to topics as diverse as UK cities and tipping on holiday.

National Health Service Trusts in the UK now carry out annual staff attitude surveys. Put the phrase 'NHS attitude survey results' into an Internet search engine and you will find many of these reports. This will allow you to see the type of questions asked and how the data are analysed presented and interpreted. A summary of the findings from across all NHS Trusts can be found at: http://www.cqc.org.uk/_db/_documents/ NHSStaffSurvey_Nat_briefing_final_200904233323.pdf. The Care Quality Commission website (www.cqc.org.uk) can also be used to find specific reports published by various Trusts (via the links to Healthcare Commission Publications).

For further self-test material and relevant, annotated weblinks please visit the website at **www.pearsoned.co.uk/workpsych**

Suggested further reading

Full details for all references are given in the list at the end of this book.

1 John Meyer's chapter in the 1997 *International Review of Industrial and Organizational Psychology* provides a very thorough analysis of the literature on organisational commitment.

2 Ajzen's 2001 article in the *Annual Review of Psychology* describes the influential theory of planned behaviour, as well as other research on how attitudes work. Not an especially easy read, but very informative about attitude theory.

3 The paper by Pratkanis and Turner in the journal *Human Relations* is an excellent example of how the study of attitudes has profited from the social cognitive tradition in psychology. Elements of the paper have been briefly summarised in this chapter.

4 The paper by David Harrison, Daniel Newman and Philip Roth published in 2006 in the *Academy of Management Review* does a good job of summarising the various possible links between attitudes, individual behaviour and subsequent organisational outcomes. The introduction is particularly useful.

5 Chris Brotherton's 2003 chapter on the psychology and industrial relations in the book *Understanding Work and Employment* provides a personal and wideranging analysis of the field.

6 The book *Understanding Psychological Contracts at Work: A critical evaluation of theory and research,* by Neil Conway and Rob Briner, provides an accessible and in-depth discussion of a high-profile topic in work psychology.

CHAPTER 8

Approaches to work motivation and job design

After studying this chapter, you should be able to:

1 define the meanings and components of motivation;

2 describe three common-sense approaches to motivation;

3 describe Maslow's hierarchy of needs;

4 specify the strengths and weaknesses of need theories;

5 define the need for achievement and explain why it could affect productivity at work;

6 define valence, instrumentality and expectancy;

7 define and describe three forms of organisational justice;

8 outline the features of goals that usually enhance motivation;

9 draw a diagram describing the main features of goal-setting theory;

10 suggest how material rewards can affect motivation;

11 describe the typology of individual differences in motivation proposed by Leonard *et al.*;

12 list four techniques of job redesign;

13 draw a diagram to show the job characteristics model (JCM);

14 suggest four ways in which theory and research about the motivational features of jobs has moved beyond the JCM;

15 explain two features of Clegg and Spencer's model of work redesign that are different from other models.

Opening Case Study **Shop-floor reorganisation at Land Rover**

Marin Burela, the new head of manufacturing at Land Rover, bounces gently up and down beside the refurbished assembly line at the carmaker's plant in Solihull, England. Looking at the floor, Mr Burela points out the springy 'anti-fatigue matting' as one sign of the transformation of once dingy and cramped working conditions. 'We have made a hell of a difference here. They don't call this the Bat Cave any more,' he says.

Mr Burela is one of a corps of Ford executives dispatched to Land Rover following its €2.9bn takeover this year. He is charged with turning round the loss-making brand, abandoned by Germany's BMW after the break-up of Rover Group. 'We have got to unlock the value in our assets and get the creative juices flowing,' he says. 'It's about instilling a sense of passion in Land Rover people.'

Ford executives privately admit they were shocked by some of what they found at Solihull. The production methods on the Defender line were antiquated. Other areas were poorly lit and untidy. Given the employees' dismay after BMW's sudden withdrawal this year, part of the task before Ford has been to hide its concerns and persuade the employees that they can make better cars. The trick for Land Rover's owners has been to win employees' backing for a restructuring that begins and ends with them. Ford is trying to persuade the workforce that it believes they are a top-quality asset that was either under-used or neglected by the former owner.

To preach its message, senior managers have held a series of US-style 'town hall meetings' with 200–500 workers at a time. Workers have been urged to match the best standards of Ford's premier automotive group, which includes Jaguar, Volvo, Lincoln and Aston Martin. Executives, rarely seen on the shop floor in the past, have been instructed to walk the line. They take cars at random from the assembly line for testing; they hold impromptu meetings with groups of workers. Everyone is encouraged to be on first-name terms. 'We're looking for visual management,' says Bob Dover, the new chief executive installed at Land Rover by Ford. 'You cannot expect high standards and a sense of passion if the management is invisible or if the roof leaks and the place is a mess.'

Mr Dover, formerly chief executive of Aston Martin, wants to start by removing unused temporary buildings: 'We probably have the biggest collection of Portakabins in the Midlands,' he says. 'We could start a Portakabin museum.' That effort and the investment in facilities will be coupled to what Mr Dover calls a 'culture of openness'. 'It sounds soft and stupid but we have to start by concentrating on people.' That means changing the outlook and profile of Land Rover's staff. Mr Dover points out that Land Rover sells cars to 140 countries. 'We have to include people from different backgrounds and more women.' Part of that overhaul mirrors the transformation of Jaguar, another neglected British brand acquired by Ford.

As Jaguar, Land Rover's people are invited to sign up to a system whereby they can suggest changes in production. If a junior employee feels quality is suffering, they can stop the entire line. In future, such employees are likely to have spent time on Volvo assembly lines in Gothenburg or Jaguar factories near Coventry. 'Nothing like this has happened in Land Rover's history,' says Mr Burela. 'There is tremendous enthusiasm . . . It's changing the way we do business.'

Source: Financial Times, *27 October 2000.*

Introduction

The Ford executives in charge of the Solihull Land Rover plant back in 2000 clearly had some ideas about what would motivate employees there. We suggest you take a few minutes now to identify what they are. The senior managers were looking for 'passion' from the staff, and thought they knew how to get it, but perhaps they were less clear about what behaviour would signify passion. Also it might be asked whether a person has to exhibit passion in order to be motivated at work.

In this chapter we therefore examine the concept of motivation and explore some of its implications. We look at some conflicting so-called 'common-sense' ideas about motivation. The chapter then turns to a description and evaluation of some of the old but enduring approaches to motivation, including need theories, the motivation to manage, expectancy theory, justice theories and goal-setting. The roles of the self and personality are also considered. Both theoretical and practical issues are covered. Textbook discussions of motivation theories are sometimes described as 'a walk through the graveyard of psychology', in the sense that many of the theories are both old and lacking life. However, there have been recent attempts to integrate the most valuable parts of the various theories, and these are discussed in this chapter. The idea that jobs can be designed to be motivating is also examined: this suggests that motivation is as much a feature of the job as of the person. The topic of motivation has received huge attention from work psychologists over very many years, so it is not possible to cover every relevant theory. The earlier ones were often designed to be big theories of human nature, whereas later ones have tended to confine themselves to specific aspects of motivated behaviour. In fact, some recent approaches scarcely have the label 'motivation' at all. So although motivation continues to be a very significant concept in work psychology, its boundaries are not easy to define.

Overview of motivation

As with many important concepts in psychology, there is no single universally accepted definition of motivation. Nevertheless, the word itself gives us some clues. To use a mechanical analogy, the motive force gets a machine started and keeps it going. In legal terms, a motive is a person's reason for doing something. As Locke and Latham (2004, p. 388) put it: 'motivation refers to internal factors that impel action and to external factors that can act as inducements to action'. Clearly, then, motivation concerns the factors that push us or pull us to behave in certain ways. Specifically, it is made up of three components:

1   *Direction*: what a person is trying to do. This is also sometimes called *choice*.

2   *Effort*: how hard a person is trying. This is also sometimes called *intensity*.

3   *Persistence*: how long a person continues trying. This is also sometimes called *duration*.

In a study of bank tellers (cashiers) Gary Blau (1993) assessed *effort* by filming each teller for a day and calculating the proportion of the time they were engaged in work behaviours. He assessed *direction* using a questionnaire that asked tellers to indicate how often they engaged in each of 20 different behaviours. Blau found that both the overall effort and the type of behaviours tellers engaged in (i.e. direction) predicted the quality of their work performance. This suggests that effort and direction are indeed separable, and that both are important. Some key points should be remembered:

- People are usually motivated to do *something*. A person may try hard and long to avoid work – that is motivated behaviour! Hence we should always remember the 'direction' component.

- It is easy to make the mistake of thinking that motivation is the only important determinant of work performance. Other factors, such as ability, quality of equipment and coordination of team members' efforts also affect performance.

- Like most concepts in work psychology, motivation is abstract. It cannot be observed directly. Quite often a person's work performance is used as a measure of their motivation, but as we have just seen, many factors other than motivation influence performance. Individuals' reports of how hard they are trying (i.e. effort) are sometimes used as an indicator of motivation, but direction and persistence rarely feature (Ambrose and Kulik, 1999). This needs to change. Many people have jobs that offer choices in what to do and pay attention to (i.e. direction), and in many jobs it is necessary to keep trying over a long period in order to succeed.

One often-made distinction is between *content* theories and *process* theories of motivation. The former focus on *what* motivates human behaviour at work. The latter concentrate on *how* the content of motivation influences behaviour. In fact, most theories have something to say about both content and process, but they do vary considerably in their relative emphasis.

Key Learning Point

Motivation concerns what drives a person's choice of what to do, how hard they try and how long they keep trying. It is not the only factor that influences work performance.

Common-sense approaches to motivation

McGregor (1960), Argyris (1964), Schein (1988) and others have collectively identi-fied three broad common-sense approaches to motivation which are endorsed by different individuals or even by the same individual at different times. McGregor (1960) termed two of the three *theory X* and *theory Y*, though the reader should be clear that in neither case is the word 'theory' used in its formal academic sense. Schein (1988) added what can be called the *social* approach. In all three cases, we are essentially uncovering a general perspective on human nature. Briefly, they are as follows:

■ *Theory X*: people cannot be trusted. They are irrational, unreliable and inher-ently lazy. They therefore need to be controlled and motivated using financial incentives and threats of punishment. In the absence of such controls, people will pursue their own goals, which are invariably in conflict with those of their work organisation.

■ *Theory Y*: people seek independence, self-development and creativity in their work. They can see further than immediate circumstances and are able to adapt to new ones. They are fundamentally moral and responsible beings who, if treated as such, will strive for the good of their work organisation.

■ *Social*: a person's behaviour is influenced most fundamentally by social inter-actions, which can determine their sense of identity and belonging at work. People seek meaningful social relationships at work. They are responsive to the expectations of people around them, often more so than to financial incentives.

As you can probably see, theory X and theory Y are in most respects opposites, with the social approach different from both. Which of these common-sense ap-proaches do you find most convincing? The authors' experience with business/management undergraduates is that, if forced to choose one, about half go for the social approach, about 40 per cent for theory Y and about 10 per cent for theory X. Amongst practising managers, the overall distribution in our experience is about the same, but tends to differ between industries. The more physical the industry, the higher the proportion of theory X adherents. Which of the three approaches do you think is most evident in the opening case study of this chapter?

Key Learning Point

Common-sense views of motivation contradict each other but all have some truth.

None of these three 'common-sense' accounts is universally correct. However, as Schein (1988) pointed out, over time people may be socialised into their organisa-tion's way of thinking about motivation. Ultimately, managers can influence their staff to see motivation their way. Of course they may also attract and select staff who are already inclined to see things their way. Nevertheless, none of the approaches can be forced on all of the people all of the time. Indiscriminate use of any could have disastrous results. Hence, although each of these approaches finds some expression in theories of motivation, the match between theory and common sense is not particularly close.

So what are the theories? Let us now examine some of the most widely known and extensively researched. Bear in mind that several of the theories are old, and nowadays rarely feature in research regarded as leading edge. That does *not* mean they are useless. They contain ideas that have found expression in subsequent work, and some practising managers say they are still useful in managing their staff.

Need theories

What are they?

Need theories are based on the idea that there are psychological needs, probably of biological origin, that lie behind human behaviour. When our needs are unmet, we experience tension or disequilibrium which we try to put right. In other words, we behave in ways that satisfy our needs. Clearly the notion of need reflects the *content* of motivation as opposed to process, but most need theories also make some propositions about how and when particular needs become salient – i.e. process. The notion of need has a long history in general psychology. It has, for example, formed the basis of at least one major analysis of personality (Murray, 1938). Two major traditions have been evident in the work setting. First, there are models based on the notion of psychological growth. Second, there are various approaches which focus on certain quite specific needs.

Need theories based on psychological growth

Easily the best known of these theories is that of Abraham Maslow (1943, 1954). Maslow was a humanistically oriented psychologist who offered a general theory of human functioning. His ideas were applied by others to the work setting.

Maslow proposed five classes of human need. Briefly, these are:

1 *Physiological*: need for food, drink, sex, etc., i.e. the most primitive and fundamental biological needs.

2 *Safety*: need for physical and psychological safety, i.e. a predictable and non-threatening environment.

3 *Belongingness*: need to feel a sense of attachment to another person or group of persons.

4 *Esteem*: need to feel valued and respected, by self and significant other people.

5 *Self-actualisation*: need to fulfil one's potential – to develop one's capacities and express them.

Maslow proposed that we strive to progress up the hierarchy shown in Figure 8.1. When one need is satisfied to some (unspecified) adequate extent, the next one up the hierarchy becomes the most important in driving our behaviour.

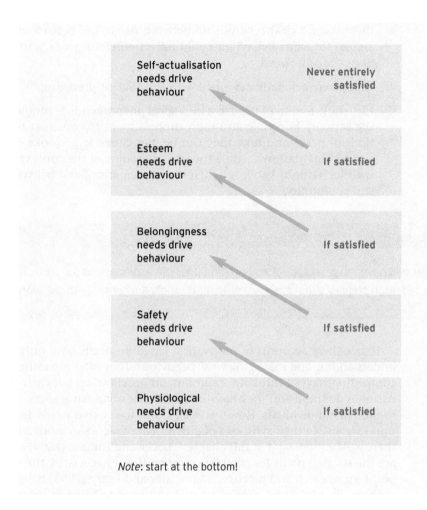

Note: start at the bottom!

Figure 8.1   **Maslow's hierarchy of needs**

Other psychologists produced rather similar analyses. For example, Alderfer (1972) proposed three classes of need: existence, relatedness and growth. Existence equated to Maslow's physiological and safety needs. Relatedness can be matched to belongingness and the esteem of others. Growth is equivalent to self-esteem and self-actualisation. Both Maslow and Alderfer made propositions about how particular needs become more or less important to the person (i.e. process), but need theories are often thought of as examples of content theories because of their emphasis on describing needs.

For some years, need theories (especially Maslow's) dominated work motivation. Unfortunately, evaluations of them (e.g. Wahba and Bridwell, 1976; Salancik and Pfeffer, 1977; Rauschenberger *et al.*, 1980) revealed a number of significant flaws, such as:

■ needs did not group together in the ways predicted;

■ the theories were unable to predict when particular needs would become important;

■ there was no clear relationship between needs and behaviour, so that (for example) the same behaviour could reflect different needs, and different behaviours the same need;

■ needs were generally described with insufficient precision;

■ the whole notion of need as a biological phenomenon is problematic. It ignores the capacity of people and those around them to construct their own perceptions of needs and how they can be met. Some (e.g. Cooke *et al.*, 2005) have argued that Maslow's whole theory is a product of the context of the Cold War, with its tensions between religion and secularism, and between individualism and conformity.

Key Learning Point

Need theories have intuitive appeal and provide possible explanations for some human behaviour, but research suggests that they are difficult to apply successfully to the work context.

Hence these accounts of motivation based on needs have only limited value in understanding and managing work behaviour. They offer interesting and intuitively compelling ways of thinking about human functioning, but their theoretical foundation is doubtful and they have offered no clear guidance to managers about how to motivate individuals. However, that is not to say that needs are unimportant or non-existent. In their synthesis of different approaches to motivation (about which there will be more later in this chapter), Locke and Latham (2004) assume that needs are the starting point for motivation, even if not necessarily the most useful focal point for research and practice. Baumeister and Leary (1995) have reviewed a wide range of literature and concluded that the need to belong is powerful and pervasive. People seem strongly driven to form social bonds and are reluctant to break them. Deprivation of frequent interactions of a positive or at least non-conflictual nature has consequences for mental and physical health. Our interpersonal relationships affect the way we think, and how we interpret the situations we encounter. Laas (2006) has argued that the leaders and goals of some (desirable) social movements reflect self-actualisation quite well, whilst others are much more about imposing one view of the world at the expense of others.

Moreover, Maslow's work has provided a clear picture of the self-actualising person. Maslow regarded self-actualisation as the pinnacle of human growth and adjustment, but argued that few of us operate at that level. The truth of this assertion is difficult to evaluate because the exact nature of self-actualisation is both disputed and ambiguous. Leclerc *et al.* (1998) tried to resolve this by developing a long list of possible descriptions of a self-actualising person and asking 30 experts on the subject to indicate whether they agree that each description is accurate. They also invited the experts to add their own descriptions if they wished. Eventually there was consensus about 36 descriptions. Some of them are shown in Table 8.1. Leclerc *et al.* emphasised that this view of self-actualisation suggests that it is not some kind of special state of being, nor is it necessarily the highest stage of being. Instead, it portrays the characteristics of people who function well in the sense that they are open to all aspects of reality, are able to understand and communicate with others, and act accordingly. These observations led Leclerc and colleagues to suggest that self-actualisation can

Table 8.1	Fifteen characteristics of self-actualising people (based on Leclerc *et al.*, 1998)

1   Have a positive self-esteem
2   Consider themselves responsible for their own life
3   Give a meaning to life
4   Are capable of establishing meaningful relationships
5   Take responsibility for their actions
6   Are aware of their feelings
7   Are capable of intimate contact
8   Have a realistic perception of themselves
9   Are capable of commitment
10 Act according to their own convictions and values
11 Are able to resist undue social pressure
12 Are capable of insight
13 Feel free to express their emotions
14 Are able to accept contradictory feelings
15 Are aware of their strengths and weaknesses

be defined as 'a process through which one's potential is developed in congruence with one's self-perception and one's experience' (pp. 78–9).

STOP TO CONSIDER

Examine Table 8.1 to see whether you think you could be described as a self-actualising person. In the opening case study to this chapter, what evidence (if any) is there that Land Rover senior managers wanted a self-actualising workforce?

Maslow's ideas still enjoy some support, and some research claims to support some of his predictions, though often the connections between what is measured in the research and Maslow's original concepts looks rather weak (e.g. Reiss and Havercamp, 2005). In our experience students can often relate to his theory. Even some of those who want to amend his theory believe that it says something profound about human nature. For example, Rowan (1998, p. 81) said 'I am merely trying to tidy up the Maslow theory, which seems to me extraordinarily useful in general.' He proposes three amendments to the need hierarchy theory:

1   There are two types of esteem needs, and they need to be separated. One is the need for the esteem and respect of other people. This is really about self-image rather than the true self, and in some ways reflects needs for relatedness. The other type of esteem is that which we give ourselves. It comes from inside the self, not from other people.

2   The need for competence should be added to the hierarchy, probably between safety and belongingness. This need reflects our desire to master certain skills and do something well for the pleasure in being able to do it. It is evident from very early in life.

3   There may be two kinds of self-actualisation. The first is where a person is able to express their real self. The second is something more mystical – a sense of closeness with God or humanity as a whole which goes beyond (transcends) the self. This distinction was evident in some of Maslow's later work, which drew open ideas from Asian psychology and religion including Taoism and Zen Buddhism (Cleary and Shapiro, 1996).

Key Learning Point

There are at least two types of esteem, and also of self-actualisation. The need for competence is an important omission from some need theories.

Achievement, power and motivation to manage

Considerable success has been enjoyed by need-based approaches to motivation which concentrate on a small number of more specific needs. Need for achievement was one of the 20 needs underlying behaviour proposed by Murray (1938). It concerns the desire 'to overcome obstacles, to exercise power, to strive to do something difficult as well and as quickly as possible' (Murray, 1938, pp. 80–81, quoted by Landy, 1989, p. 73). Typically, people with high need for achievement seek tasks that are fairly difficult, but not impossible. They like to take sole responsibility for them, and want frequent feedback on how well they are doing. Need for achievement formed the basis of McClelland's (1961) theory of work motivation. McClelland argued that a nation's economic prosperity depends partly on the level of need for achievement in its population. He based this argument on a statistical relationship between the economic performance of countries and the prominence of themes of achievement in popular children's stories in each country. He also believed that people could be trained to have high need for achievement. As for personal success, Parker and Chusmir (1991) found that people with high need for achievement tend to feel more successful regarding status/wealth, professional fulfilment and contribution to society than those with lower need for achievement.

Need for achievement has attracted considerable attention in both theoretical and applied contexts (e.g. see Beck, 1983). It is not a simple construct, however, and several attempts have been made to identify its components (e.g. Cassidy and Lynn, 1989). Sagie et al. (1996) argued that it is important to restrict analysis to the level of tasks, as opposed to wider considerations of status and power. They proposed six task preferences that signal high need for achievement:

1   Tasks involving uncertainty rather than sure outcomes.

2   Difficult tasks rather than easy ones.

3   Tasks involving personal responsibility, not shared responsibility.

4   Tasks involving a calculated risk, rather than no risk or excessive risk.

5   Tasks requiring problem-solving or inventiveness, rather than following instructions.

6   Tasks that gratify the need to succeed, rather than ensuring the avoidance of failure.

Sagie *et al.* (1996) reported a five-country study of levels of achievement motivation. People from the United States generally scored highest on most components, followed by people from the Netherlands and Israel, with those from Hungary lower and those from Japan lower again, except on the first component, where Japanese people scored close to Americans. However, it is important to remember that need for achievement is not the only route to successful work performance. Also, need for achievement may be a very Western and individualistic concept, of little relevance to some other cultures. In fact, the link that McClelland claimed between achievement themes in children's stories and national prosperity has often been questioned. For example, an analysis of economic growth over up to 50 years by Beugelsdijk and Smeets (2008) found no relationship between growth and a country's need for achievement score based on McClelland's data from the mid-twentieth century. Of course, this may be because the need for achievement data were out of date, or indeed were inaccurate from the start.

A person's need for achievement is often assessed using *projective* tests, which involve the person interpreting ambiguous stimuli. For example, a person may be asked to make up a story about what is happening in a short series of pictures. It is assumed that people *project* their personality onto the stimuli through their interpretations. This general technique is derived from psychoanalytic theory (*see* Chapter 1). Need for achievement can also be assessed in a more straightforward manner using questions about the person's behaviour, thoughts and feelings as in a personality questionnaire. Spangler (1992) reviewed the relevant literature and found that scores on most assessments of need for achievement are indeed correlated with outcomes such as career success. Also, despite the generally poor record of projective tests in psychology, projective measures of need for achievement correlated more highly with outcomes than did questionnaire measures.

Key Learning Point

Need for achievement is a sufficiently specific and valid construct to explain some aspects of work behaviour, including managerial behaviour, at least in Western contexts.

One criticism of McClelland's work is that it was always unclear exactly how need for achievement translated into economic success. McClelland himself thought that it was partly through entrepreneurial activity. There is mixed evidence on this. For example, Hansemark (2003) did not find that people with a high need for achievement were more likely than others to start up their own business. However, Rauch and Frese (2007) did find that high need for achievement was modestly associated with success amongst people who were already entrepreneurs. Another line of thinking is that need for achievement makes people more inclined to be managers. John Miner (1964) developed the concept of *motivation to manage,* and a measure of it called the Miner Sentence Completion Scale (MSCS). The seven components of motivation to manage are shown in Table 8.2. The need for power and self-control,

| Table 8.2 | Components of the motivation to manage |

Component	Meaning
Authority figures	A desire to meet managerial role requirements in terms of positive relationships with superiors
Competitive games	A desire to engage in competition with peers involving games or sports
Competitive situations	A desire to engage in competition with peers involving occupational or work-related activities
Assertive role	A desire to behave in an active and assertive manner involving activities that are often viewed as predominantly masculine
Imposing wishes	A desire to tell others what to do and to utilise sanctions in influencing others
Standing out from the group	A desire to assume a distinctive position of a unique and highly visible nature
Routine administrative functions	A desire to meet managerial role requirements of a day-to-day administrative nature

Source: Miner and Smith (1982, p. 298). Copyright © 1982 by the American Psychological Association. Adapted with permission.

and low need for affiliation probably underlie motivation to manage. So do some of the components of need for achievement.

STOP TO CONSIDER

Look again at the components of motivation to manage shown in Table 8.2. To what extent do you think they reflect what would be expected of managers across all organisational and national cultures?

Interesting studies by Miner *et al.* (1991) and Chen *et al.* (1997) investigated motivation to manage in China. They suggested that although China is a more collectivist society than Western ones, it is nevertheless sympathetic to competition and hierarchy, and that this would be one reason why the motivation to manage would be applicable there. Consistent with their arguments, they found that people in higher-level jobs scored higher on the MSCS than people in lower-level jobs. They also found that women scored no lower than men, and suggested that this might be a consequence of the assertive roles women were encouraged to take in China's cultural revolution of the late 1960s and 1970s, together with the Chinese government policy of no more than one child per family. Ebrahimi *et al.* (2001) also found no gender difference, but they did find that motivation to manage scores were generally higher in Hong Kong than in the People's Republic of China. This may have been due to the greater exposure of Hong Kong to Western influences at the time. Perhaps it would be different even a decade or so later.

Exercise 8.1   The motivation to manage

Marie Herzog is an administrative assistant at a large packaging factory in Lyons. She had previously been promoted from the factory floor and is keen to go higher. Her boss, Simone Trouchot, is not so sure – how keen is Marie? Simone made the following observations. Marie seemed rarely to impose her will on her clerical subordinates, even when they were obviously in the wrong. She got on well with the higher managers at the factory, and seemed willing to work closely to the remit they gave her. On the other hand, Marie rarely volunteered her department for trying out experimental new ideas. She seemed uncomfortable when the spotlight was turned on her and her department, even if the attention was congratulatory. Marie seemed happiest dealing with the routine administrative tasks she knew well. She was an accomplished athlete, and had recently been Lyons 400 metres champion two years in succession. Marie was extremely keen to get her department working better than other similar ones, and to ensure that she dealt with problems faster and better than others in similar jobs at the factory.

Suggested exercise

Consult Table 8.2 to judge the extent and nature of Marie Herzog's motivation to manage. Are there particular kinds of managerial roles in which she would feel particularly motivated?

Exercise 8.2   Need theory in the car factory

Look back at the opening case study of this chapter. Which of the needs described in this section do you think the Ford managers believed govern the motivation of the shop-floor workers? If possible, compare your answers with somebody else's, and discuss whether needs offer a useful guide to managers in improving motivation.

Expectancy theory: what's in it for me?

Whereas need theories place heavy emphasis on the content of motivation, expectancy theory concentrates on the process. Originally proposed by Vroom (1964), expectancy theory (also sometimes called VIE – valence, instrumentality, expectancy – theory or instrumentality theory) aimed to explain how people choose which of several possible courses of action they will pursue. This choice process was seen as a cognitive, calculating appraisal of the following three factors for each of the actions being considered:

1   *Expectancy*: if I tried, would I be able to perform the action I am considering?

2   *Instrumentality*: would performing the action lead to identifiable outcomes?

3   *Valence*: how much do I value those outcomes?

Vroom (1964) proposed that expectancy and instrumentality can be expressed as probabilities, and valence as a subjective value. He also suggested that force to act is a function of the product of expectancy, instrumentality and valence: in other words, V, I and E are multiplied together to determine motivation. This would mean that if any one of the components was zero, overall motivation to pursue that course of action would also be zero. This can be seen in Figure 8.2, where, for example, the instrumentality question is not even worth asking if a person believes they are incapable of writing a good essay on motivation.

Notice how little attention VIE theory pays to explaining *why* an individual values or does not value particular outcomes. No concepts of need are invoked to address this question. VIE theory proposes that we should ask someone how much they value something, but not bother about *why* they value it. This is an illustration of VIE theory's concentration on process, not content.

If correct, VIE theory would have important implications for managers wishing to ensure that employees were motivated to perform their work duties. They would need to ensure that all three of the following conditions were satisfied:

1   Employees perceived that they possessed the necessary skills to do their jobs at least adequately (expectancy).

Motivation to write an essay on motivation

Expectancy	X	Instrumentality	X	Valence
Question: How likely is it that I am capable of writing a good essay on motivation?		*Question:* How likely is it that I will receive rewards for writing a good essay on motivation?		*Question:* How much do I value those rewards?
Considerations: General self-efficacy Specific self-rated abilities Past experience of essay writing		*Considerations:* The weight attached to the mark in the assessment system The accuracy of the marking Likelihood of intrinsic rewards such as learning or satisfaction		*Considerations:* Importance of passing the course Interest in the subject Extent of commitment to self-development

Figure 8.2   **An example of VIE theory in action**

2   Employees perceived that if they performed their jobs well, or at least adequately, they would be rewarded (instrumentality).

3   Employees perceived the rewards offered for successful job performance to be attractive (valence).

Referring again to the Land Rover case study at the start of this chapter, to what extent do you think each of these three components of motivation was likely to have been a problem?

Key Learning Point

Expectancy theory proposes that people's choice of course of action depends upon their beliefs about (i) their own capabilities; (ii) whether the course of action will lead to rewards; and (iii) how valuable the rewards are.

Although it looks attractive, VIE theory has not done especially well when evaluated in research. Like need theories, it has rather gone out of fashion. Van Eerde and Thierry (1996) found 74 published research studies on VIE theory prior to 1990 but only 10 subsequently. Van Eerde and Thierry (1996), and also Schwab *et al.* (1979), summarised the available research and drew the following conclusions. The first four reflect badly on VIE theory as a whole. The other two are more to do with limitations of research design rather than the theory itself.

- Research studies that have not measured expectancy, or have combined it with instrumentality, have accounted for effort and/or performance better than studies that assessed expectancy and instrumentality separately.

- Behaviour is at least as well predicted by adding the three components V, I and E as it is by multiplying them.

- The theory does not work where any of the outcomes have negative valence (i.e. are viewed as undesirable) (Leon, 1981).

- The theory works better when the outcome measure is an attitude (for example intention or preference) than when it is a behaviour (performance, effort or choice).

- Self-report measures of V, I and E have often been poorly constructed.

- Most research has compared different people with each other (i.e. between-participants research design), rather than comparing different outcomes for the same person (i.e. within-participants design). The latter enables a better test of VIE theory because the theory was designed to predict whether an individual will prefer one course of action over another, rather than whether one person will favour a course of action more than another person does. Where within-participant designs are used, results tend to be more supportive of the theory.

Key Learning Point

Expectancy theory may over-complicate the cognitive processes involved in motivation, but is a helpful logical analysis of key factors in the choices made by individuals.

Expectancy theory is not quite dead and buried. It is still occasionally used in research. For example, Chiang and Jang (2008) found that expectancy, instrumentality and valence all made separate contributions to the motivation of hotel employees. However, they did not test whether multiplying the three terms together further improved prediction of motivation. Vansteenkiste *et al.* (2005) assessed the impact on people's reactions to being unemployed (e.g. general mental health) of (i) the value they placed on employment (valence) and (ii) their belief that they could get a job if they wanted to (expectancy). They found that both valence and expectancy mattered (especially valence), but multiplying them together did not improve prediction of reactions to unemployment.

Justice and citizenship theories: am I being fairly treated?

Justice theories are like expectancy theory, in that they focus on the cognitive processes that govern a person's decision whether or not to expend effort, but unlike expectancy theory they suggest that people want fairness above all. Some students and managers find it hard to believe that people might not always seek to maximise their gains, but let us suspend disbelief for the moment and consider the propositions of the original justice theory: equity theory.

Equity theory was derived from work by Adams (1965), originally in the context of interpersonal relationships. Huseman *et al.* (1987, p. 222) described the propositions of equity theory like this:

- Individuals evaluate their relationships with others by assessing the ratio of their outcomes from and inputs to the relationship against the outcome:input ratio of a comparison other.

- If the outcome:input ratios of the individual and comparison other are perceived to be unequal, then inequity exists.

- The greater the inequity the individual perceives (in the form of either over-reward or under-reward), the more distress the individual feels.

- The greater the distress an individual feels, the harder they will work to restore equity. Equity restoration techniques include altering or cognitively distorting inputs or outcomes, increasing or decreasing the amount of effort devoted to the task, acting on or changing the comparison other, or terminating the relationship.

In other words, a person is motivated to maintain the same balance between their contributions and rewards as that experienced by salient comparison person or persons.

Research way back in the 1960s and 1970s provided some support for equity theory (e.g. Pritchard, 1969), especially in laboratory-based studies where the key constructs of the theory could be controlled and measured. However, perhaps unsurprisingly, the predictions of equity theory are less often supported by research when people receive more than their share as opposed to when they receive less (Mowday, 1991). In other words, we are more likely to do something in response to feeling under-rewarded than over-rewarded. Furthermore, rather like need theories, equity theory is vague about exactly what people will do when they are dissatisfied. They might adopt any or all of the equity restoration devices listed above, and they might choose any of a number of comparison others. Equity theory is not good at specifying which restoration devices and which comparison others will be used (Greenberg, 2001). Perhaps, then, equity theory is better at providing a retrospective account of a person's motivation and behaviour than it is at predicting those things.

Like the other motivation theories discussed so far, equity theory has been researched less in recent years than in earlier ones. Nevertheless, it is still the subject of some work. It is also still frequently taught, perhaps partly because it provokes a lot of discussion about whether people really care about fairness when they are being over-rewarded. Bolino and Turnley (2008) have presented an interesting analysis of the cross-cultural applicability of equity theory. Pointing out that it originated in the US, they use cross-cultural theory to generate propositions about how equity theory might manifest differently in different parts of the world. For example, they suggest that in collectivist cultures people are likely to choose a group (e.g. people in my occupation) as their comparison other, whereas people in individualistic cultures are more likely to choose individuals (e.g. that person who started here at the same time as me).

Key Learning Point

The equity theory of motivation asserts that people are motivated by the fairness of the rewards they receive relative to the contributions they make, in comparison with other people.

Equity theory has been broadened into theories of organisational justice from the late 1980s onwards (*see*, for example, Cropanzano *et al.*, 2001; Greenberg and Colquitt, 2005). These theories focus on perceptions of fairness in the workplace. They have become very popular and widely researched, perhaps because organisational downsizing, etc. has brought issues of fairness to the fore. Equity theory refers mainly to what is called *distributive justice*: that is, whether people believe they have received (or will receive) fair rewards. However, this is only one kind of justice. There are debates about how many different kinds of workplace justice can be identified (*see* Colquitt *et al.*, 2001), but most work psychologists would say there are at least two more. *Procedural justice* reflects whether people believe that the procedures used in an organisation to allocate rewards are fair. *Interactional justice* refers to whether people believe they are treated in an appropriate manner by others at work, especially authority figures. The three forms of justice are depicted in Table 8.3.

If people believe that they are poorly paid relative to people doing similar jobs in other organisations, they may perceive distributive injustice. If at the same time they think their employing organisation is making available as much money for pay as possible, and operating fair systems to distribute them, then they may perceive procedural justice. If their bosses discuss pay openly and courteously, they may perceive interactional justice. Their satisfaction with pay would probably be low, but their commitment to their employer might well be high (McFarlin and Sweeney, 1992; Olkkonen and Lipponen, 2006).

Key Learning Point

The role of fairness and justice in motivation is becoming more prominent, and concerns a person's perceptions of the fairness of (i) who gets what, (ii) the systems used to decide who gets what and (iii) the courtesy and openness of interpersonal behaviour.

Table 8.3	Three forms of justice at work		
Distributive justice (appropriateness of outcomes)	**Procedural justice (appropriateness of the allocation process)**	**Interactional justice (appropriateness of the treatment received)**	
Appropriateness can be judged in various ways: *Equity* (as in equity theory) means that employee outcomes depend on their contributions. Alternatives include *equality* (everyone gets the same reward) and *need* (people get what they require)	This is said to depend on a number of factors: *Lack of bias* for or against any individual or group, i.e. consistent process. *Accuracy of information* used to make decisions. *Representation* for all stakeholders. *Correction* of errors or injustices via appeal or review procedure. *Ethical* codes of conduct are followed.	This has two components, which are sometimes considered two separate forms of justice. *Interpersonal* refers to the extent to which people are treated with dignity, courtesy and respect. *Informational* concerns the extent to which relevant information is shared with employees.	

Source: Adapted with permission from Cropanzano *et al.* (2007), p. 36.

Ideas about workplace justice have now been prominent for long enough to attract some close scrutiny. Helpful reviews of this field have been offered by Colquitt *et al.* (2005) and Fortin (2008). From the perspective of motivation, it is important to ask whether justice affects the direction, effort and persistence of work behaviour, and if so why? Starting with why, some people argue that justice is a moral virtue in itself, requiring no further justification other than to point out that it upholds human dignity. An alternative perspective is that being treated fairly signals that you personally are a valued member of a community, thus validating your personal and social identity. A more instrumental interpretation is that fairness enables you to control and predict what will happen to you in the future.

A lot of evidence indicates that the three forms of justice are associated with motivation and performance among other outcomes (*see* for example Folger and Cropanzano, 1998). As usual in work psychology, the number of studies in which it is clearly demonstrated that justice precedes motivation/performance rather than vice versa is limited. Even so, the evidence for the effects of justice is strong. Also, the presence of one form of justice can at least partially offset the negative effects of the lack of another form (Cropanzano *et al.*, 2007). For example, if your annual performance review does not lead to the bonus you feel you deserve (distributive injustice), if you perceive the review process as meeting the criteria for procedural justice shown in Table 8.3, your motivation will be less (or not at all) adversely affected than if you also thought the process was unjust. Another plus would be if you were given the chance to state your views (interactional justice). In fact, there is some long-established evidence that this chance to have a say seems to help even when it cannot make a difference to the outcome (Folger *et al.*, 1979). On the other hand, if people feel that in the past they have been repeatedly asked for their views and then ignored, being asked again can be more demotivating than not being asked, because it seems to be a sham and therefore a violation of interactional (and possibly procedural) justice (Folger, 1977).

STOP TO CONSIDER

From your experience of the workplace, to what extent do you think that people care about justice as a general concept, as opposed to (i) justice for themselves only and; (ii) maximising their gains? On what evidence is your answer based?

One important consequence when people in an organisation feel they have been treated justly is that they will be more willing to be 'good citizens' at work (*see* for example Liden *et al.*, 2003). Since the early 1990s, psychologists have shown a lot of interest in what have become known as organisational citizenship behaviours (OCBs) (*see* for example Moorman, 1991). This partly reflects a realisation that successful work organisations need people who help each other out in addition to doing the core tasks of their jobs well. OCBs are an interesting area for scholars of motivation, because OCBs are usually thought to be discretionary – that is, a person has choice over whether they perform them. OCBs include the following:

- *Altruism*: helping another person with a work task or problem.

- *Conscientiousness*: going well beyond minimum role requirements.

- *Civic virtue*: participation and involvement in the life of the organisation.

- *Courtesy*: preventing interpersonal problems through polite and considerate behaviour.

- *Sportsmanship*: willingness to tolerate less than ideal circumstances without complaining.

There is some reason to question whether it is appropriate to consider OCBs 'extras', over and above the job. Research by Kam *et al.* (1999) suggested that to a considerable extent bank employees across four countries felt that the five OCBs listed above were indeed part of their job. Their supervisors thought so even more! There were some differences between countries, though. Courtesy and sportsmanship were expected to a greater extent in Japan and Hong Kong than in the United States and Australia. Another common assumption about OCBs is that they enhance organisational performance. This can be questioned. Perhaps OCBs simply distract people from doing their own jobs properly. However, Podsakoff *et al.* (2009) have found that OCBs have beneficial effects on organisational performance indicators, so the fear appears to be unjustified (*see* also Chapter 6).

Key Learning Point

The motivation to perform 'good citizen' behaviours is currently a topic of considerable interest to psychologists. This motivation is enhanced by a sense of justice.

Cropanzano *et al.* (2007) offer some helpful though not particularly novel suggestions to managers about how to use insights from justice theory in managing people. For example, they highlight the importance of giving people every opportunity to show what they can do during selection and promotion processes. It is probably important both practically and morally that justice is implemented because it is valued, and not simply as a manipulation to increase employee compliance:

> Organizational justice allows managers to make tough decisions more smoothly . . . power will be used in accordance with normative principles that reflect the dignity of all involved. This is sound business advice. *It is also the right thing to do.*
> (Cropanzano et al., 2007, p. 45, italics in original)

It is important not to get too starry-eyed about justice. At any given time, even in the best-run workplaces, there will always be some people who think something is unfair. That is partly because, although people often distinguish between what is good for them and what is fair, there is some overlap between outcome favourability and distributive justice (Fortin, 2008). In other words, we tend to be more tolerant of being over-rewarded than under-rewarded. Also, the various forms of justice do tend to go together. In the performance review example above, if we do not get the outcome we think we deserve (i.e. distributive injustice), we will probably explain it in terms of something wrong with the system (i.e. procedural injustice). Finally, just as in the case of equity theory, how much justice matters and how it is interpreted may vary quite a lot between cultures (Li and Cropanzano, 2009).

Key Learning Point

Perceived justice has significant consequences for people's work motivation and performance.

Goal-setting theory: how can I achieve my aims?

The theory

This approach to motivation was pioneered in the United States by Ed Locke and his associates, starting in the 1960s and continuing with increasing strength and sophistication ever since – so much so, that by the 1990s, well over half the research on motivation published in leading academic journals reported tests, extensions or refinements of goal-setting theory.

As Locke *et al.* (1981, p. 126) put it, 'A goal is what an individual is trying to accomplish; it is the object or aim of an action. The concept is similar in meaning to the concepts of purpose and intent.' Locke drew on both academic writing on intention (Ryan, 1970) and the much more practical 'management by objectives' literature in formulating his ideas. Figure 8.3 represents goal-setting theory, and provides the key concepts for this section.

The most fundamental proposition of goal-setting theory is that in most circumstances goals that are difficult but not impossible, and that are expressed in terms of

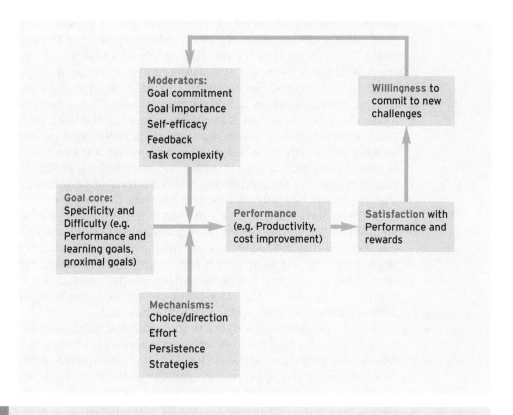

Essential elements of goal setting cycle

a clearly defined performance level, produce higher levels of performance than other kinds of goals, or an absence of goals. In particular, goals of this kind produce better performance than vague 'do your best' goals. Difficult and specific goals have this effect by focusing a person's attention on the task, increasing the amount of effort they put into it, increasing the length of time they keep trying, and encouraging the person to develop strategies for goal achievement. These fundamental ideas of goal-setting theory have of course found expression in popular management practice, particularly in the form of so-called 'SMART' – specific, measureable, agreed, realistic and time-based – goals (see for example http://www.projectsmart.co.uk/).

Over the years it has been recognised that the goal-setting process can't always be quite that simple, for two main reasons. First, people and circumstances vary, sometimes in ways which affect the goal-setting process. Second, although the words and ideas in goal-setting theory are clear enough, applying them to any work situation is more complex than it initially seems. This is not a weakness of the theory, it's just how life is!

Some of these complexities have been incorporated into the goal-setting framework, and are shown as 'Moderators' in Figure 8.3. *Goal commitment* and *goal importance* both signal that the effect of goals on behaviour and performance is likely to be much greater if the goals matter greatly to a person than if they do not. Goal commitment can be defined as an unwillingness to abandon or lower the goal (Wright *et al.*, 1994). *Self-efficacy* reflects the point from expectancy theory that a person's belief that they are capable, or can become capable, of performing the necessary behaviours is an important component of motivation. There is good evidence that self-efficacy affects the level of difficulty of goals a person will be willing to feel committed to (Wooford *et al.*, 1992), which shows that these moderators inter-relate. It also seems to be the case that people with high self-efficacy are better than those with low self-efficacy at developing new strategies in response to failure or difficulty (Latham and Pinder, 2005). The provision of *feedback* on progress towards the goal enables a person to refine their strategies. *Task complexity* matters because a task that a person perceives as complex (that is unfamiliar, multifaceted and not easily achievable) may require learning goals rather than performance goals. Put another way, it might be better to set goals about learning the nature of the task (e.g. find five different ways in which the quality of the production process can be monitored) rather than achieving a specific level of performance (e.g. make sure that the production process produces no more than 1 per cent substandard prod-uct). This reflects research which showed that on complex tasks with which people are not familiar, setting performance goals hinders their learning of the best strate-gies, because they are too focused on the outcome itself, and not enough on figur-ing out the best way to achieve it (e.g. Kanfer and Ackerman, 1989). In general, it seems that goal-setting has greater effects on performance for simple tasks than complex ones (Wood *et al.*, 1987), but nevertheless, the beneficial effect of goal-setting on complex tasks is still well worth having.

Whilst a person might well derive some intrinsic satisfaction from successful task completion, attaching tangible rewards such as a cash bonus to that achievement will substantially increase the satisfaction, and consequently willingness to take on new challenges, perhaps even more difficult than before. Locke and Latham (1990) reported that the impact of monetary reward for performance occurs either through raising goal level, or through increasing commitment to a goal – so long as the amount of money on offer is considered significant, and not tied to goals perceived as impossible. In turn, willingness to take on new challenges can affect how com-mitted the person is to a new goal, and of course over time successful performance is also likely to influence a person's sense of self-efficacy (Bandura, 1997), hence the feedback loop in Figure 8.3.

Key Learning Point

The setting of performance goals that are specific and difficult (but not impossible), and to which the person feels committed, is likely to improve their work performance. This is especially the case if the person receives feedback on progress, and rewards for successful performance.

What does research say about goal-setting? Many of the main features of the the-ory are now well-established, having been researched thoroughly (some would say exhaustively) in the 1970s to 1990s. Reviews by Locke and Latham (1990) and Mento *et al.* (1987) arrived at a number of conclusions, most of which fully or substantially supported goal-setting theory. Locke *et al.* (1981) reported that in goal-setting field experiments, the median improvement in work performance produced by goal-setting was 16 per cent. More recently, Locke and Latham (2002, p. 8) concluded that:

With goal-setting theory, specific difficult goals have been shown to increase per-formance on well over 100 different tasks involving more than 40,000 participants in at least eight countries working in laboratory, simulation and field settings. The dependent variables have included quantity, quality, time spent, costs, job behavior measures, and more. The time spans have ranged from one minute to 25 years. The effects are applicable not only to the individual but also to groups, organizational units, and entire organizations. The effects have been found using experimental, quasi-experimental, and correlational designs. Effects have been obtained whether the goals are assigned, self-set, or set participatively. In short, goal-setting is among the most valid and practical theories of employee motivation in organizational psychology.

It might be argued that Locke's enthusiasm could be partly because goal-setting theory has been a large part of his life's work, and he is therefore very motivated to see it positively. However, that would be too cynical. The evidence is more or less as he says it is, and in recent years he has shown a lot of interest in examining the less well-established areas of goal-setting and integrating it with other traditions in applied psychology, especially social cognition and self-regulation (see below).

Key Learning Point

Goal-setting theory is strongly supported by research.

Some issues around goal-setting

Locke (2000, p. 409) proposed that one way in which goals work is by unlocking or mobilising existing knowledge and skills that are relevant to the task in hand: 'It is a virtual axiom that human action is a consequence of . . . knowledge (including skill and ability) and desire'. This is a reminder of the point made near the start of third chapter that motivation does not provide a complete explanation of performance. Of course, if a person simply does not have the necessary knowledge or skill, and cannot easily acquire it, then the goal-setting process is unlikely to be successful, at least in the short-term. Therefore it could be argued that knowledge/ability should be added to Figure 8.3, even though it is partially reflected in self-efficacy, which concerns a person's beliefs about whether they have the necessary ability for the task at hand.

Key Learning Point

The impact of difficult and specific goals on a person's work performance occurs through the focusing of their strategies and intentions, and the mobilisation of their knowledge and ability.

As noted above, the notion of goal commitment has become very important in goal-setting theory. It is argued that if individuals do not feel commitment to a goal they will not exert effort in pursuit of it – even a difficult and specific one. Commitment is construed as more than simple acceptance of a goal. On the other hand, perhaps the notion of commitment is just another word for motivation – if I am committed to a goal, then that could be another way of saying I am motivated to achieve it. This means that a key focus, perhaps *the* key focus, of goal-setting theory should be how to foster goal commitment.

At one time it was argued that the best way to ensure goal commitment is to allow people to participate in discussions about what goals to set (e.g. Erez, 1986). Subsequently, however, some research suggests that often participation is not necessary. Its prime function seems to be information exchange, which can be achieved by dialogue between the person assigning a goal and the person expected to achieve it, and also by explanation of the reasons for the goals by the goal assigner. This might be the case where trust and respect are high, but that is not always the case at work. In any case, where a task is complex the goal assigner may find it difficult to specify a challenging but attainable goal without participation from those who are to try to achieve it (Haslam *et al.*, 2009).

Despite the clarity of goal-setting theory, it is not necessarily simple to implement in the workplace. In most organisations there are multiple goals to be achieved. For whole organisations, and for individuals and groups within them, there may be some conflict between goals. Achievement of one may be at the cost of another. For example, achievement of cost reductions in staff costs may be at the expense of quality of customer service. So when a manager is given goals to reduce costs by 10 per cent and to increase customer service by a similar amount, each goal on its own may be achievable but in combination they are not. This may well negate the positive effect of goal-setting. Also, in a turbulent environment, an organisation's goals and priorities may need to change at short notice. In this circumstance, and also where the tasks are inherently complex and relatively long-term (like writing this chapter!), there may be a particularly strong need to break down long-term goals into short-term (in Figure 8.3, 'proximal') ones such as 'write 3000 words that sum up the basic facts and issues in goal-setting in a scholarly but accessible way' (*see* also Fried and Slowik, 2004).

There are also other complications in applying goal-setting. These apply equally to any issue to do with managing performance, and as noted earlier are not a sign that goal-setting theory is 'wrong'. Effective goal-setting requires accurate assessment of whether a task is complex in the perception of the individual doing it, and what level of performance is difficult but not impossible for that person. If the person has a very low level of self-efficacy, it may be difficult to persuade them that even a moderate level of performance is attainable. Sometimes it takes time and trouble to provide feedback, and to link rewards reliably with performance. In this respect there are important dilemmas such as what reward, if any, to use if a person just misses a goal, or if circumstances change part-way through the process, making the goal either easier or harder to achieve. Locke and Latham (2004) offer an interesting analysis of these issues. Shaw (2004) provides a practical illustration of how goals can readily become vague aspirations rather than clear performance targets, and how this problem was addressed at Microsoft.

Key Learning Point

Although goal-setting theory is well-specified and uses well-defined concepts, successful implementation in the workplace still requires skill and sensitivity.

Exercise 8.3 Goal-setting in a car repair shop

Giovanni Russo was dissatisfied with the performance of the mechanics at his car repair workshop. He did not keep detailed records, but in his opinion too many customers brought their cars back after repair or servicing, complaining they were still not right. Others found that their cars were not ready by the agreed time. The garage had recently become the local dealer for one of the smaller car manufacturers. The mechanics had been relatively unfamiliar with cars of that make, and were still often unsure how to carry out certain repairs without frequently checking the workshop manual. Giovanni decided to introduce performance targets for the mechanics as a group. He told them that complaints and delays must be 'substantially reduced', and to sweeten the pill he immediately increased the group's pay by 8 per cent. The increase would continue as long as performance improved to what he regarded as a satisfactory extent. He promised to let the mechanics know each month whether he regarded their collective performance as satisfactory.

Suggested exercise

Use goal-setting theory and research to decide whether Giovanni Russo's attempt at goal-setting is likely to succeed.

STOP AND CONSIDER

Consider the extent to which you use goal-setting to manage and improve your own work performance. Could you use it more, or better? What special issues arise when goal-setting is used on oneself, rather than being administered by someone else?

Goals and self-regulation

Goal-setting could be criticised in its early days for being a technology rather than a theory. It successfully described how goals focus behaviour, without really addressing why or through what processes goals influenced behaviour. Starting in the 1980s, developments within the goal-setting tradition and outside it have helped progress on these issues.

Other motivation theories can also be integrated with goal-setting in order to explain further how people choose, change and implement strategies for achieving and reviewing goals (Kanfer, 1992). Social learning and social cognitive theories of *self-regulation* suggest some processes through which people do these things. Bandura (1986) argued that goals provide a person with a cognitive representation (or 'image') of the outcomes they desire. Depending on the gap between goal and the current position, the person experiences *self-reactions*. These include emotions (e.g. dissatisfaction) and self-efficacy expectations (that is, perceptions of one's ability to achieve the goal), as well as individual differences in the kind of 'self-talk' engaged in. For example, Bandura (2001) pointed out that some people respond to setbacks with thoughts that help them try again in a better way, whereas others tend to think of themselves as incapable of changing things for the better. These reactions, together with other factors, affect the level and direction of a person's future effort as well as their self-concept. For example, suppose a student is attempting to achieve the difficult task of writing a good essay in one evening's work, but by midnight only half the essay has been written. The student's self-efficacy expectations are likely to be reduced somewhat, especially if they were high to begin with. However, if self-efficacy is still fairly high, and so is dissatisfaction, the student is likely to persist until the essay is finished. If their self-efficacy has dropped a lot, or was low to start with, the student may give up even if dissatisfied with the lack of progress.

Other work relevant to the processes involved in goal-setting has been reported by Dweck (1986). She developed a theory of motivation and learning which distinguishes between *learning goal orientation* and *performance goal orientation*. Farr *et al.* (1993, p. 195) described these as follows:

> When approaching a task from a learning goal perspective, the individual's main objective is to increase his or her level of competence on a given task . . . Alternatively, when a task is approached from a performance goal orientation, individuals are primarily concerned with demonstrating their competency either to themselves or to others via their present level of task performance.

Farr *et al.* (1993) argued that people who adopt a performance goal orientation will tend to be more fearful of failure, less willing to take on difficult goals, and less receptive and able to respond constructively to feedback than those who adopt a learning goal orientation. In short, Farr and his colleagues suggested that goal-setting as a theory may be more applicable to, and useful for, learning goal-oriented people than performance goal-oriented ones. They also believed that in the long run, learning goal orientation is more likely to produce high performance and competence than performance goal orientation. They suggest that there is an increasing and ironic tendency in work organisations for goals to be set which are defined in terms of performance relative to other people, thus encouraging performance goal orientation rather than learning goal orientation.

There is quite a lot of evidence that the processes outlined in goal-setting theory do indeed apply more strongly to people with a learning goal orientation than those with a performance goal orientation (e.g. VandeWalle *et al.*, 2001). However, although goal orientations were originally conceived as a fairly constant feature of a person, akin to a personality characteristic, this has been questioned (DeShon and Gillespie, 2005). It seems that a learning goal orientation is quite easily induced in a given situation, even in those who score high on measures of dispositional performance goal orientation (Seijts and Latham, 2001).

Recently there has been increasing interest in possible subconscious influences on goal-setting processes. This is partly because goal-setting theory has placed high emphasis on conscious self-regulation and reasoning, possibly at the expense of the unconscious (Latham, 2007, Chapter 9). For example, it seems that a person's goal and/or motivation can be influenced by briefly seeing (a few hours earlier) a photograph showing someone winning a race, even though the person was not aware of the connection (Shantz and Latham, 2009).

Goal-setting theory has become increasingly integrated with social cognitive theories of self-regulation, and therefore more embedded in mainstream psychology

Self-concept and individual differences in motivation

Many of the most recent approaches to motivation have focused on how our sense of who we are, i.e. our self-concepts, personalities and values, influence the direction, effort and persistence of our behaviour (Leonard *et al.*, 1999). To some extent this is reflected in research on the role of self-efficacy and goal orientation in goal-setting described earlier in this chapter.

However, some work in this area draws on other areas of social psychology, particularly self-categorisation and social identity (Turner and Onorato, 1999; Haslam, 2004). For example, it is proposed that a person does not have just one self-concept (i.e. set of perceptions about their own nature), but many. One distinction is between *personal identity*, which represents how we see ourselves relative to others in the same social groups, and *social identity*, which is those aspects of self-concept we think we have in common with others in the same group, and which differentiate us from members of other groups (*see also* Chapter 13). We have many different personal and social identities, depending on which social group is most salient to us at any given time. Furthermore, we are motivated to behave in ways that are consistent with our identity, or perhaps in some cases our ideal self – i.e. how we would *like* to be. In a work context this might mean that if our social identity as (for example) a member of the marketing department is most salient, then we will be motivated to perform behaviours that support the value of marketing and perhaps our marketing colleagues. On the other hand, if our personal identity as an ambitious young manager is most salient, we are more likely to pursue behaviours that we see as being in our own interest, such as concentrating on our own work or making ourselves look good in front of the boss in case there is a promotion opportunity on the horizon (Haslam *et al.*, 2000; Van Knippenberg, 2000).

Leonard *et al.* (1999) suggested that our identities are composed of three elements. Traits are broad tendencies to react in certain ways. Competencies are perceptions of one's skills, abilities, talents and knowledge. Values are beliefs about desirable ways of being and/or patterns of behaviour that transcend specific situations. It is difficult to predict which of these three aspects of self will motivate behaviour at any given time. Leonard *et al.* proposed that various psychological processes involving the processing of information and integrating it with our sense of self lead to the following types of motivation:

■ **Intrinsic process motivation:** the pursuit of activities because they are fun, whether or not they help in goal attainment.

- **Extrinsic/instrumental motivation:** the pursuit of individual or group goals because they lead to rewards other than satisfaction, especially material ones.

- **External self-concept:** the pursuit of success in order to gain affirmation from others for a social identity as a member of a successful group, or a personal identity as a competent person.

- **Internal self-concept:** the pursuit of success in order that the individual is able to feel competent, irrespective of what others might think of them.

- **Goal internalisation:** the pursuit of goal-achievement for its own sake, because it is valued by the individual.

Key Learning Point

People are motivated to act in accordance with their self-concepts and identities. Different aspects of these are salient (and therefore influence their behaviour) in different situations.

Exercise 8.4 — Self and identity in motivation

Magnus Johannson was the captain of what he considered to be the best fishing crew in the Baltic Sea. Again and again his boat, *The Seagull*, brought back the highest quantity and quality catch of all the trawlers he knew about – and all the catches conformed perfectly to European Union regulations. In a very difficult era for all fishing fleets, he considered this to be a major achievement, and he valued the fact that his crew and other crews recognised it. He felt his particular talent was sensing where the best shoals of fish were likely to be, given currents and weather conditions. This was rarely the same place two days running, and sometimes Magnus's hunches proved more reliable than the ship's technical gadgets. Often his intuition about it differed from some members of his crew, but they had learned that Magnus was usually right. Indeed, it had become a standing joke on *The Seagull* that there was no point arguing with him. That was one of the things he liked best about his crew. They could laugh and joke but they still respected their captain and worked hard partly out of loyalty to him. Other crews did not seem to have that same mix of light-heartedness and purpose, as far as he could see. But Magnus sometimes felt concerned that many people with great reputations eventually fail, and he feared that a day might come when he was no longer able to find the fish or command the respect of his crew.

Suggested exercise

Which elements of the motivation themes described in the section 'self-concept and individual differences in motivation' do you think help us understand Magnus Johannson's work motivation?

Intrinsic motivation, extrinsic motivation and pay

Studies have found that when asked what motivates them at work the majority of people give answers such as variety, responsibility, recognition for achievements, interesting work and job challenge rather than pay or working conditions (e.g. Herzberg, 1966). In fact Herzberg's work has been influential in steering managers towards altering people's jobs rather than pay regimes in order to increase motivation. We discuss that view of motivation later in this chapter. It relates closely to a broad distinction between *intrinsic motivation* and *extrinsic motivation* (see also the Leonard *et al.*, 1999, analysis described above), which is often used in discussions about motivation. Ryan and Deci (2000, p. 56) defined intrinsic motivation as 'the doing of an activity for its inherent satisfactions . . . a person is moved to act for the fun or challenge entailed rather than because of external prods, pressures, or rewards'. In contrast, extrinsic motivation 'pertains whenever an activity is done in order to obtain some separable outcome' (Ryan and Deci, 2000, p. 60).

Essentially then, Herzberg argued that intrinsic motivation is more reliable and powerful than extrinsic motivation as a way of influencing behaviour at work. Intrinsic motivation has clear links with Maslow's esteem and self-actualisation needs. Some research in the 1970s suggested that high pay actually undermined intrinsic motivation by focusing a person's attention on extrinsic rewards (Deci and Ryan, 1980). More recently, however, it appears that pay can enhance intrinsic motivation, or at least not damage it, if the level of pay provides a person with information about their competencies. Damage to intrinsic motivation occurs only if the person perceives extrinsic rewards as an attempt to control their behaviour rather than to provide information about it (Deci *et al.*, 1999). The extent to which we perceive ourselves to have autonomy in pursuing extrinsic rewards, and in the way we go about it, can make a big difference. This insight has led to a more differentiated view of extrinsic motivation, which was much-needed for the analysis of work motivation. Most of us would not spend as much time doing the activities in our job if we were not paid for doing them, so extrinsic motivation must be relevant to the work context. Different forms of extrinsic motivation identified by Ryan and Deci (2000) are, in decreasing degrees of 'extrinsicness':

- *External regulation*: a person performs behaviour in order to satisfy an external demand, and experiences this as externally controlled and not what they would do by choice.

- *Introjected regulation*: similar to external regulation, except that the person has internalised the external demand enough for it to matter to their sense of self-esteem.

- *Identification*: a person accepts an external demand or reward as being of personal importance, and therefore also uses self-regulation in order to perform the required behaviours.

- *Integrated regulation*: similar to identification, but the person not only accepts external rewards or requirements as important, but also as an expression of self.

Key Learning Point

The distinction between intrinsic and extrinsic motivation is important conceptually, but in practice it is blurred, and it is important not to see intrinsic motivation as somehow morally superior to extrinsic.

The most obvious extrinsic reward is of course pay. In the case of external regulation, a person might do the work required simply because they need the pay to live. If it was a case of introjected regulation, then the person would also feel that what they earned was to some extent a reflection of their personal worth in the organisation and/or society. Identification would mean that the person viewed themself as someone who cared quite a lot about money (and would therefore work for it), whilst in the case of integrated regulation, money earned would be a central part of the person's self-concept and getting it would be an absolute necessity to retain not only a way of life but also a self-image.

Herzberg (1966) and others tend to argue that pay is not a key motivator at work, though it is acknowledged that this conclusion depends on some basic level of pay being provided in order to meet basic needs. What do the theories of motivation discussed in this chapter say about pay as a motivator? For Maslow, pay would be a motivator only for people functioning at the lower levels of the hierarchy of needs. Advocates of need for achievement point to the fact that pay and other material rewards often signal that a person is successful. So from this perspective pay is a motivator if and when it indicates that the person has succeeded in their work tasks. In expectancy theory, pay will be an effective motivator to the extent that it is desired by the person, *and* they can identify behaviours that will lead to high payment, *and* they feel capable of performing those behaviours. Igalens and Roussel (1999) reported data from a large sample of French workers which suggested that the valence of pay was much greater if good performance was rewarded by increases in salary rather than a bonus. Even then, this depended on people being able to see a connection between their efforts and successful performance. Locke and Latham (2002) provide a useful analysis of the advantages and disadvantages of different ways of achieving this connection.

From the perspective of organisational justice, people will be concerned with whether their pay is a fair reward relative to the rewards received by others. They will also want to see fair procedures for allocating pay. A common problem for performance-related pay is that these procedures are often *not* seen as fair. Bloom (1999) studied the pay of North American baseball players over the years 1985 and 1993 and found that the more equal the pay of the different players in the team, the better individuals and teams performed. This suggests that the pay of others matters as well as our own, and that having a small number of highly paid 'superstars' is not a good move.

Goal-setting theory normally involves goals that are defined in terms of a person's behaviour and/or accomplishments, not pay. Nevertheless, if there is a very clear and direct link between a person's accomplishments and pay, then specific, difficult goals defined in terms of earnings may be motivating. On the other hand, when pay is an indicator of how well a person is doing *compared with others*, we can expect it to encourage a performance goal orientation rather than a learning goal orientation. As noted above, this might be seen as a 'bad thing'.

Rynes et al. (2004) have argued forcefully that the importance of pay as a motivator is often underestimated by human resource managers. This is partly because of the work of Herzberg and Maslow, and partly because other research (e.g. Jurgensen, 1978) has asked people what motivates them at work and consistently found that pay is reported to be less important than many other things, such as job challenge, interesting work and opportunities for promotion. Rynes *et al.* argue that people's behaviour suggests that pay is more important to them than they say it is. Perhaps people do not realise the reasons for their own behaviour, or perhaps they do but are embarrassed to admit that pay matters a lot. Rynes *et al.* argue on the basis of some past research that carefully designed performance-related pay schemes can be shown to enhance performance very effectively, and that people's decisions about which job to take are often made on the basis of pay level. The importance of pay is due to its being what in behaviourist terms is called a 'generalised reinforcer'. As a Beatles song long ago pointed out, money cannot buy love, but it can buy a lot of other things, and people can use it in ways that suit them. This might include non-acquisitive purposes such as giving it away to good causes, using it to pay other people to do things you don't want to do yourself (such as home maintenance), or accessing desired leisure activities (such as joining a sports club).

Key Learning Point

Financial rewards tend to enhance performance, especially when they are seen as fair and providing accurate feedback about how well the person is doing.

Exercise 8.5   Is pay any use as an incentive?

However good the pay, it doesn't buy results

In a classic case of vanishing returns, in attempting to construct 'better incentives' and 'closer links between pay and performance', companies are expending more and more effort on trying to get right something that cannot, and should not, be done in the first place.

The catch-22 – the fatal flaw with all numerical targets and quotas – is that to be understood and acted on, incentives must be simple. But if they are that simple, in any organisation with objectives more multidimensional than a whelk stall, they are simplistic: inadequate to carry the information necessary for the accomplishment of other goals. It's impossible to specify a simple target for a complex organisation.

Simple incentives make clever companies stupid, like the banks, zapping even the instinct for self-preservation. But complex ones turn them into hotbeds of confusion, envy, fear and loathing, which is no better. Why should some people get bonuses and others not? Why is yours bigger than mine? In any organisation made up of multiple teams and interdependencies, calculating reliable attributions of responsibility for gain or loss is like counting angels on a pinhead. And trying to do it years later, with possible clawbacks depending on it, is a mathematical and legal nightmare.   ▶

Financial incentives lead to inequality in rewards – d'uh, that's what they're supposed to do. For jockeys, loggers and orange pickers that seems to result in higher performance. But it's death to the co-operation and teamwork on which overall organisational performance depends. From sports teams and university departments to publicly quoted companies, the greater the pay inequalities the worse the results, whether in terms of collaboration, productivity, financial performance or product quality. The moral of the story is that companies should be very careful what they choose to pay for – because that's what they'll get, and nothing else.

Source: Adapted from an article by Simon Caulkin, The Observer, *22 February 2009.*

Suggested exercise

To what extent does the material in this chapter on goal-setting and pay as motivators support Simon Caulkin's argument?

Motivation through job redesign

Much of the discussion so far in this chapter has suggested that motivation is a property of the person. An alternative view is that motivation (or lack of it) is inherent in the nature of jobs. This viewpoint means that we need to look less closely at the person and more closely at what it is about work that can make it motivating.

Job simplification and job enrichment

Early recommendations for how to design jobs focused on efficiency and cost reduction rather than motivation. This usually meant minimising skill requirements of jobs, maximising management control and minimising the time required to perform a task. This may appear to make good sense, especially against economic criteria. Unskilled or semi-skilled labour costs less than skilled labour, and productivity is enhanced if tasks are done quickly. However, as we shall see, jobs designed in this way frequently have human costs, and perhaps economic ones too.

This 'traditional' approach to job design stems from a philosophy called 'scientific management', or 'Taylorism', after its creator, F.W. Taylor. Taylor (1911) formulated his ideas in the United States in the early twentieth century. As a machine-shop foreman, he felt that workers consistently underproduced, and that the way to prevent this was to:

- systematically (or 'scientifically') compile information about the work tasks required;
- remove workers' discretion and control over their own activities;
- simplify tasks as much as possible;

- specify standard procedures and times for task completion;

- use financial (and *only* financial) incentives;

- by the above methods, ensure that workers could not deceive managers, or hide from them.

This of course bears a strong resemblance to the 'theory X' view of human nature (described earlier in this chapter). Observers agree that jobs in many, perhaps most, organisations are implicitly or explicitly based on Taylorism. Some argue that call centres are the most recent kind of organisation to exhibit Taylorism in a strong form (e.g. Bain *et al.*, 2002).

Key Learning Point

Scientific management, also known as Taylorism, emphasises standardised methods and minimisation of costs in the design of work.

Taylorism might make for a well-ordered world, but is it a happy and productive one? As long ago as the 1960s, a number of studies seemed to show that work organised along scientific management principles was associated with negative attitudes towards the job, as well as poor mental and/or physical health (e.g. Kornhauser, 1965; Turner and Lawrence, 1965). It was also often assumed that poor productivity would accompany such outcomes, and that simplified work actually *caused* poor mental health, motivation and satisfaction, rather than the reverse causal direction.

These studies of simplified work led to considerable concern about what came to be called *quality of working life* (QWL). Several theoretical perspectives were brought to bear on QWL. One was *job enrichment* – a concept developed through the work of Herzberg (1966) (see also the previous section of this chapter). Herzberg proposed a basic distinction between *hygiene factors* and *motivators*. Hygiene factors included pay, conditions of employment, the work environment and other features extrinsic to the work activities themselves. Motivators included job challenge, recognition and skill use – that is, features appealing to growth needs. On the basis of his data, Herzberg proposed that hygiene factors could not cause satisfaction, but that dissatisfaction could result if they were not present. On the other hand, motivators led to satisfaction: their absence produced not dissatisfaction, but a lack of satisfaction. Although Herzberg's data and conclusions can be criticised on several grounds, his recommendation that motivation and/or satisfaction can be enhanced by increasing skill use, job challenge, etc. is consistent with much subsequent work.

Another relevant theoretical tradition is *socio-technical systems* (Cherns, 1976, 1987; Heller, 1989). Arising from studies in the immediate post-1945 years, socio-technical theory emphasises the need to integrate technology and social structures in the workplace. Too often, technology is introduced with scant regard for existing friendship patterns, work groups and status differentials. Socio-technical theory attempts to rectify this, but it also makes wider propositions. For example, it states that job activities should be specified only in so far as necessary to establish the boundaries of that job. It also emphasises that boundaries should be drawn so that they do not impede transmission of information and learning, and that disruptions to work processes should be dealt with at source wherever possible, rather than by managers further removed from the situation. Such principles may seem self-evident, but close examination of many organisations will demonstrate that they are not adhered to. Socio-technical job design therefore emphasises autonomy, decision-making and the avoidance of subordinating people to machines.

Whatever their exact theoretical origin, until the early twenty-first century most attempts to redesign jobs centred on increasing one or more of the following (Wall, 1982):

- *variety* (of tasks or skills);
- *autonomy* (freedom to choose work methods, scheduling and occasionally goals);
- *completeness* (extent to which the job produces an identifiable end result which the person can point to).

This may be attempted in one or more of the following ways:

- *Job rotation*: people rotate through a small set of different (but usually similar) jobs. Rotation is frequent (e.g. each week). It can increase variety.
- *Horizontal job enlargement*: additional tasks are included in a person's job. They are usually similar to tasks already carried out. This too can increase variety.
- *Vertical job enlargement*: additional decision-making responsibilities and/or higher-level challenging tasks are included in the job. This increases autonomy, variety and possibly completeness. An increasingly commonly used term for this is *empowerment*: a person does not necessarily achieve an increase in formal status, but they are given more freedom to take decisions and implement them according to the needs of the situation at the time (Wang and Lee, 2009).
- *Semi-autonomous work groups*: similar to vertical job enlargement, but at the level of the group rather than the individual. In other words, a group of people is assigned a task and allowed to organise itself to accomplish it. Semi-autonomous workgroups have been introduced in some car factories.
- *Self-managing teams*: more often composed of managers and professionals than semi-autonomous work groups, these teams are often given considerable freedom to accomplish a group task, and perhaps even to define the task in the first place.

Key Learning Point

Job redesign can take a variety of forms and arise for many reasons (see Figure 8.4), but it has normally involved an attempt to increase the amount of variety, autonomy and/or completeness inherent in the work of one or more people.

Interest in job redesign has been stimulated in more recent years by concerns about the quality of products and services, and the needs for innovation and customer responsiveness. It is argued that well-motivated staff are particularly

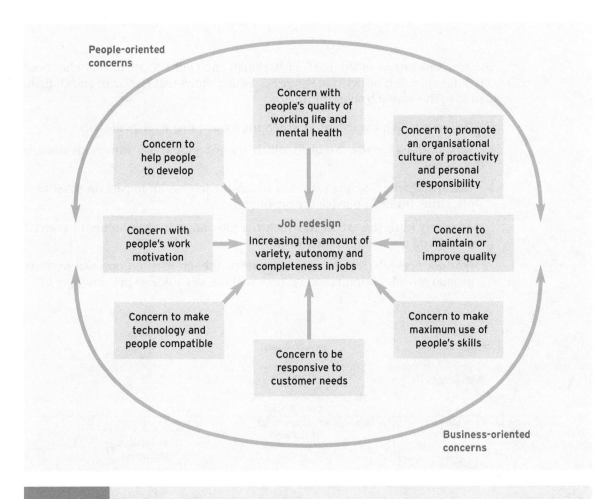

Concern with people's quality of working life and mental health

Concern to help people to develop

Concern to promote an organisational culture of proactivity and personal responsibility

Concern with people's work motivation

Job redesign
Increasing the amount of variety, autonomy and completeness in jobs

Concern to maintain or improve quality

Concern to make technology and people compatible

Concern to make maximum use of people's skills

Concern to be responsive to customer needs

People-oriented concerns

Business-oriented concerns

Figure 8.4	Concerns leading to job redesign

important for the delivery of outcomes like these (e.g. Shipton *et al.*, 2006). In other words, job redesign is part of hard-headed business strategy rather than (or as well as) a philanthropic concern with the quality of working life. At the same time, cost-cutting and efficiency are also important for organisational competitiveness, so there is much attention to practices such as the use of new technology and so-called 'just in time' and 'lean' production methods. These may not be consistent with the creation of motivating jobs, though they can have benefits for organisational productivity (Birdi *et al.*, 2008; de Treville and Antonakis, 2006).

The question of whether it is possible to design jobs that are both efficient and motivating has been investigated by Morgeson and Campion (2002). They conducted a detailed analysis of a set of jobs in one part of a pharmaceutical company and then redesigned some of them to include more 'scientific management' efficiency-based elements, some to include more variety and autonomy, and some to include more of both. They found that it was possible to increase both elements at the same time, and that this produced some small benefits for efficiency and satisfaction.

The job characteristics model

The *job characteristics model* (JCM) of Hackman and Oldham (1976, 1980) has been very influential. It is depicted in Figure 8.5, which shows that Hackman and Oldham identified five core job characteristics:

1 *Skill variety* (SV): the extent to which the job requires a range of skills.

2 *Task identity* (TI): the extent to which the job produces a whole, identifiable outcome.

3 *Task significance* (TS): the extent to which the job has an impact on other people, either inside or outside the organisation.

4 *Autonomy* (Au): the extent to which the job allows the job holder to exercise choice and discretion in their work.

5 *Feedback from job* (Fb): the extent to which the job itself (as opposed to other people) provides information on how well the job holder is performing.

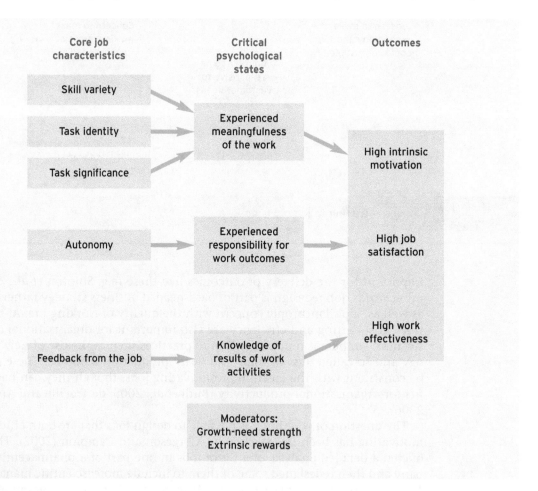

Figure 8.5   **Hackman and Oldham's job characteristics model**
Source: Adapted from J.R. Hackman and G.R. Oldham (1980), *Work Redesign*
© 1980. Reprinted by permission of Pearson Education, Inc., Upper Saddle River, NJ.

The core job characteristics are said to produce 'critical psychological states'. The first three core job characteristics are believed to influence *experienced meaningfulness of the work*. Autonomy affects *experienced responsibility for outcomes of the work*, and feedback from the job impacts on *knowledge of the actual results of the work activities*. Collectively, the critical psychological states are believed to influence three outcomes: motivation, satisfaction and work performance. This whole process is said to be moderated by several factors (*see* Figure 8.5). The most often investigated of these is growth-need strength. This refers to the importance to the individual of Maslow's growth needs (*see* earlier in this chapter). The model is said to apply more strongly to people with high growth needs than to those with low ones.

Key Learning Point

The job characteristics model specifies five features of jobs that tend to make them intrinsically motivating and satisfying.

The JCM provoked a huge amount of research, especially in the United States. This is not surprising, since it provides specific hypotheses about exactly which job characteristics matter, how they affect people's psychological states, what outcomes they produce, and which individual differences affect the whole process. Also, Hackman and Oldham produced a questionnaire called the Job Diagnostic Survey (JDS) which assesses the constructs shown in Figure 8.5. The JDS is completed by job holders.

A number of helpful observations about the JCM were made in review articles (see, for examples, Fried and Ferris, 1987; Kelly, 1993). In summary, the job characteristics identified by Hackman and Oldham did indeed usually correlate with motivation and satisfaction, though not so clearly with the performance of individuals or organisations. However, there were few studies in which attempts were made to *change* jobs so that they had more of the core job characteristics (which is, after all, the whole point of job redesign). So the correlations between job characteristics and motivation and satisfaction may not have reflected a *causal* relationship. There was also quite a lot of doubt about whether the effects on attitudes and behaviour of each core job characteristic were mediated by the critical psychological states specified by Hackman and Oldham. Indeed, in general the core job characteristics seemed to have more effect on people's attitudes to their work than on their work performance. It was also recognised that additional job characteristics may matter. Warr (1987) suggested availability of money, physical security, interpersonal contact and valued social position as likely contenders. More recently, yet more job characteristics have been identified. These are discussed a little later in this chapter.

Exercise 8.6   Bicycle assembly at Wheelspin

The Wheelspin bicycle company produces a range of bicycles for adults and children. At their factory, already-manufactured components are painted and assembled. Assembly is carried out on assembly lines which move at constant speeds. The factory manager decides which line will assemble which bicycle. Each member of staff has a specific part or parts which they screw, weld or otherwise fix onto the ▶

basic frame at a specified point on the assembly line. They carry out the same tasks about 80 times a day. Staff are recruited to a specific job: they generally remain on the same assembly line and deal with the same parts. Once every two or three months, the model being assembled changes, but generally the assembly tasks required are more or less constant. Noise levels are low enough to allow staff to chat to immediate neighbours as they work. Work quality is assessed at the end of the production line, where performance of the assembled bicycle is examined by quality control staff.

Suggested exercise

Examine the characteristics of the assembly jobs at Wheelspin. How might those characteristics be changed?

Ambrose and Kulik (1999) pointed out that research interest in the JCM decreased very markedly from about the mid-1990s. They argued that this may be appropriate, since it is now quite well understood. Nevertheless, the JCM has stood empirical testing reasonably well, especially considering the relatively large number of connections between specific variables it proposes. Even the more recent reviews acknowledge that the JCM specifies much that is important about jobs and job redesign (Parker and Wall, 1998; Humphrey *et al.*, 2007), despite a clear need to broaden the range of job characteristics beyond those specified in it.

Although the JCM is much less dominant than it used to be, it is still the basis of quite a lot of new thinking about work design. For example, Pierce *et al.* (2009) argue that the core job characteristics tend to foster a sense of *psychological ownership* for the person doing the job. The person feels psychological ownership because they have a sense of control over the job, know its 'ins and outs' very well, and find that it helps to shape a clear and positive sense of identity. Pierce *et al.* (2009) argue therefore that a sense of psychological ownership (rather than for example experienced meaningfulness of work, *see* Figure 8.5) is the key mediating variable between core job characteristics and outcomes. Like Hackman and Oldham, Pierce *et al.* list motivation, satisfaction and performance amongst the outcomes. However, they also suggest that there could be some negative outcomes as well, such as uncooperative territorial behaviours ('this is my job, don't you interfere') as a result of psychological ownership. The JCM also continues to be the foundation of some empirical research on job design (e.g. Millette and Gagne, 2008; DeVaro *et al.*, 2007).

More recent analyses of the nature of jobs

The need for employees to be responsive to customers and be willing to change and learn is said to be much greater now than it used to be. So is the need to acquire new information rapidly and share it with others who can use it. Some argue that it is better to use the term 'work', because the word 'job' implies a fixed and stable set of duties. Such constancy is rarer than it used to be. This is partly because of the pace of change in the workplace, and partly because people are often encouraged to engage in 'job crafting' (Wrzesniewski and Dutton, 2001), i.e. emphasise some parts of the job at the expense of others in order to maximise their contribution and their fit with their organisation.

Although it was quickly recognised that the JCM's list of job characteristics was not wide-ranging enough (especially given the context described in the previous paragraph), it took some time for well-developed alternative analyses to appear. The leaders in this respect are Fred Morgeson and Stephen Humphrey in the USA (Morgeson and Humphrey, 2006; Humphrey *et al.*, 2007). They argued that work redesign theory and practice needs to take into account all aspects of jobs in order to provide a sound basis for maintaining and improving the motivation, satisfaction and performance of individuals and organisations. Specifically, they make the case that:

- Whilst the JCM focuses mainly on the nature of tasks, it is also necessary to consider the *knowledge* requirements. For example, does a person's work require a deep specialist knowledge of an area? Does it require problem-solving, and are there a lot of factors to consider simultaneously? Also, whilst the JCM characteristic skill variety is important, so is task variety, and the two are not the same.

- Work is not only about tasks and knowledge. It is, for most people, also an intensely *social* activity. Therefore, a complete analysis of the nature of a person's work must include factors like the extent to which they receive social support and feedback from others, and have work which requires interaction and interdependence with others.

- The *context* in which work is carried out is also likely to be important. For example, is a person's workplace well-designed ergonomically (*see* Chapter 9)? What are the working conditions like in terms of noise, hazards etc.?

Humphrey *et al.* (2007) have reported a meta-analysis of studies that have tested the statistical relationships of work characteristics with motivation, performance and other outcomes. To the extent that they were able, they used the set of work characteristics developed by Morgeson and Humphrey (2006) for their analysis. Table 8.4 shows some of their results.

Note first of all that there are a lot of empty cells in the table, meaning that as yet there is no evidence about the associations of some of the work characteristics with outcomes. Second, note that the five JCM core job characteristics (autonomy, skill variety, task identity, task significance and feedback from the job) are all quite strongly associated with motivation, job satisfaction and organisational commitment, but not with performance (with the partial exception of autonomy). Again this illustrates the fact that motivation and performance are not always as closely connected as one might think – other factors matter too. Third, the strong relationships between the information processing and job complexity on the one hand and satisfaction on the other suggest that these two knowledge components may also be significant for motivation. Fourth, there is clear evidence that social factors are related to motivation and (even more) to satisfaction and commitment. Hence it seems that we do indeed need to move beyond the core job characteristics in order to understand how work influences motivation and other outcomes.

Key Learning Point

The core job characteristics, knowledge requirements and social features of jobs are associated with motivation. Improvements in job performance do not necessarily occur as a direct consequence of changes in job characteristics, even if motivation and/or satisfaction do improve.

	Work motivation	Work satisfaction	Work performance	Organisational commitment
Table 8.4	**Mean correlations of job characteristics with motivation, satisfaction, performance and commitment**			
Task characteristics				
Autonomy	0.27	0.37	0.14	0.30
Task variety		0.35	−0.03	
Task significance	0.30	0.31		0.34
Task identity	0.17	0.23	0.05	0.18
Feedback from job	0.29	0.33	0.09	0.29
Knowledge requirements				
Information processing		0.31		
Job complexity		0.32	−0.06	
Skill variety	0.30	0.32	−0.03	0.23
Social factors				
Interdependence	0.21	0.23		0.34
Feedback from others	0.22	0.32		
Social support	0.11	0.41		0.56
Interaction outside organisation		0.05		
Work context				
Physical demands		−0.15		
Work conditions		0.20		

Adapted with permission of American Psychological Association from Humphrey *et al.* (2007), pp. 1342–3.

STOP TO CONSIDER

What are the practical and theoretical implications if work redesign affects motivation but not performance?

Of course, these statistical associations do not prove that the work characteristics cause the so-called outcomes. Also, even if there is a causal relationship, it is not clear how it works, or whether it does so more strongly for some people than for others. As noted above, Pierce *et al.* (2009) suggest that at least some work characteristics create a sense of psychological ownership which in turn leads to the outcomes. Fried *et al.* (2007) use career theory (see Chapter 15) and suggest that some work characteristics matter more at some career stages than others. For example, they hypothesise that in their later career people become more concerned about task significance because at that stage making a positive contribution that benefits others matters a great deal to them. Of course, Hackman and Oldham also thought that their JCM would apply to some people more strongly than others – for example, those high in 'growth need strength' were expected to respond more favourably to the core job characteristics than those not so high.

Making a positive contribution that benefits others has also been the basis of some other recent thinking about work design. Arguing for the importance of social as well as task factors, Grant (2007) uses the term 'relational job design' to reflect this emphasis. Grant proposes that an important part of work motivation is, or can be, the motivation 'to make a prosocial difference' – in other words, to do things that benefit other people. In order to increase this form of motivation, Grant advocates the design of work to include frequent and in-depth contact with beneficiaries, and the opportunity to find out a lot about them. This, he says, will increase the person's perceptions of their impact on beneficiaries, and also foster a sense of commitment to them. These factors will then affect motivation to make a prosocial difference. Grant acknowledges that the notion of impact on beneficiaries overlaps with the JCM core job characteristic of task significance, but argues that his analysis is much more specific about (i) the social aspects of it and (ii) the implications for how relationships at work can and should be designed just as tasks are.

Exercise 8.7   Communication and motivation

When Alfred Josefsen, managing director of Irma, first arrived at the Copenhagen-based grocery chain, the workforce was anything but happy. Employee motivation was low and staff members were frequently leaving to go to work for other companies. 'It was a big crisis and, for the first couple of years we had to do a huge turnaround,' says Mr Josefsen.

Today, the company appears regularly on listings of best workplace awards, both in Denmark and overseas. In this year's 100 Best Workplaces in Europe, the company wins a special award for best practices in internal communication. Some 93 per cent of the company's surveyed employees believe Irma's management team is approachable ▶

and easy to talk to, while 83 per cent agree that management always informs them about corporate developments.

Mr Josefsen describes the process that was needed to get the company from its low point to this position. 'The first thing that was important was to decentralise the company and put much more decision making back to the hands of store managers,' he explains. The idea was to have each store operating more like a local grocery, competing with stores around the corner. The new approach – along with efforts to make internal communication much more informal – delivered results within a remarkably short time. 'In half a year, the atmosphere in the company was much more positive,' says Mr Josefsen.

Irma started life in 1886 as a small basement shop in Copenhagen that stocked dairy products. Today, it focuses on quality foods, pioneering the removal of trans-fats, additives and colourings from its products. It puts a large amount of organic produce on its shelves. Irma now has more than 1,700 employees working in 70 supermarkets and administrative offices. Many of them have received a visit from the managing director. Mr Josefsen likes to wander about in the company's head office and he also visits the stores themselves to talk to shop assistants and customers. It is not only Mr Josefsen who can be found in the aisles. Senior managers, too, pay regular trips to the stores and may even work in them for a day or two as 'interns'.

Cross-divisional meetings and regular workshops allow staff to come together in a professional capacity, as well as more informally at social events. At 'Strategy Days', hundreds of store-level employees get together for three days to share ideas. Mr Josefsen is frequently present at such events. 'I often walk to the side and see what's going on and usually all the people are communicating to each other very loudly,' he says. 'It's great to hear people speaking like that.'

However, perhaps the most powerful weapon in the company's communications armoury has been a short e-mail from Mr Josefsen that goes out regularly to all staff. In it, he uses personal experiences as a way of conveying key business messages.

> Six years ago, when we were having problems, I wrote a little letter and e-mailed it to the stores [he says]. This weekly letter was read by everyone in the company. They liked to hear from the managing director. When I figured out that, with one little e-mail, I could communicate with everyone, I realised that this was a fantastic tool.

> I try to be visible and in contact with people so they know that the managing director is working hard for the future of the company. My approach is value management, and you have to be in contact with people if you want to show what you're doing and that you have direction.

Source: Adapted from 'Irma: Grocery's idea bears fruit', *The Financial Times*, 18 May 2006 (Murray, S.), copyright © Sarah Murray. With permission.

Suggested exercises

1   Communication is not often talked about in motivation theory as a technique to increase motivation. Do you think Mr Josefsen's innovative ways of communicating with employees helped motivation in this case, and if so how?

2   What aspects of people's job characteristics in Irma might have been affected by the way Mr Josefsen led the company?

Twenty-first century work design

Although an expanded view of work characteristics is certainly important, an even more radical perspective is needed in order to guide the design of work in twenty-first century workplaces. Parker *et al.* (2001) have provided a careful analysis of this, and offer the following observations. Some of these observations reflect points that have already been made in this chapter, whilst others are new:

■ In an era when many jobs are less clearly defined and less closely supervised than they were, it is inappropriate to assume that jobs have characteristics that remain fixed until someone tries to redesign them.

■ There are more features of jobs that affect attitudinal and behavioural outcomes. In fact, those features probably always did matter; it is just that they are more obvious now. These include the extent to which the job is compatible with home commitments, and the various cognitive demands it makes (for example, problem-solving, vigilance). Another is whether the job requires so-called emotional labour – that is, the display of positive or negative emotion in order to, for example, empathise with customers.

■ The processes by which jobs affect people may well not be confined to motivational ones, as assumed by traditional job redesign theories. Other processes may include the extent to which a speedy response to events is possible, and also whether employees are able to use their local knowledge to solve problems as and when they arise.

■ The outcomes of job redesign should be evaluated at individual, group and organisational levels. As well as motivation, satisfaction and profitability, relevant outcomes might include creativity, innovation, customer satisfaction, accident rates, absence and turnover. Regarding creativity, Elsbach and Hargadon (2006) have argued that, at least for busy professionals, a spell of 'mindless' work during a day may help creativity because it gives them space to think. This interesting suggestion highlights the possibility that it may not be desirable for people to have 'enriched' work all day every day.

■ A much greater range of factors than those suggested in the JCM may affect the impact of job characteristics (and changes in them) on outcomes. These include the extent to which tasks within an organisation are interdependent, and the extent to which the organisation is operating in an ambiguous and/or rapidly changing environment.

■ Clearer thinking is needed about when it is best to redesign jobs at the individual level, and when at the group level. Factors such as task interdependence (see above) will probably be important here.

These points are encapsulated in Figure 8.6, which is adapted from Parker *et al.* (2001). It demonstrates how much expansion on the older models of job redesign might be required. It also suggests how difficult it might be to conduct research that includes all the relevant factors, and to provide managers with straightforward, easy to understand advice about what jobs in their organisations should look like.

Although the words used are not always the same, the model shown in Figure 8.6 encompasses many of the management techniques and terminology that have been used to try to improve individual and organisational outcomes. A good example is

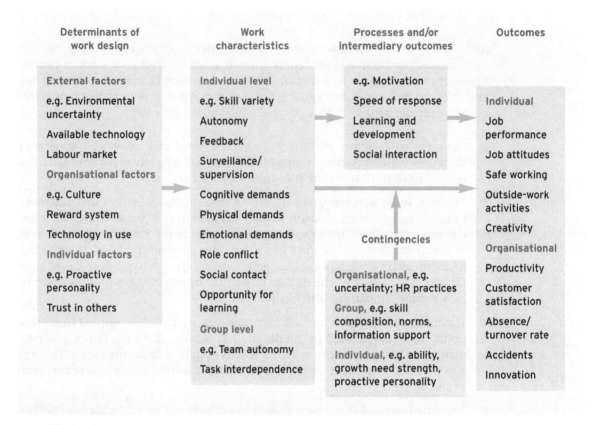

Determinants of work design	Work characteristics	Processes and/or intermediary outcomes	Outcomes
External factors e.g. Environmental uncertainty Available technology Labour market **Organisational factors** e.g. Culture Reward system Technology in use **Individual factors** e.g. Proactive personality Trust in others	**Individual level** e.g. Skill variety Autonomy Feedback Surveillance/ supervision Cognitive demands Physical demands Emotional demands Role conflict Social contact Opportunity for learning **Group level** e.g. Team autonomy Task interdependence	e.g. Motivation Speed of response Learning and development Social interaction **Contingencies** Organisational, e.g. uncertainty; HR practices Group, e.g. skill composition, norms, information support Individual, e.g. ability, growth need strength, proactive personality	**Individual** Job performance Job attitudes Safe working Outside-work activities Creativity **Organisational** Productivity Customer satisfaction Absence/ turnover rate Accidents Innovation

Figure 8.6   An elaborated model of work design
Source: Adapted, with permission, from Parker *et al.* (2001).

empowerment (Wilkinson, 1998), which refers to attempts to transfer more responsibility and scope for decision-making to people at low levels in an organisation. As Wall *et al.* (2002) have pointed out, empowerment often means increases in job control, performance monitoring, cognitive demands and possibly role conflict and social contact. It is likely to be embraced most wholeheartedly by people with a proactive personality, and perhaps have most impact in conditions of environmental uncertainty, where it is more likely that local quick decisions will be needed. Another recent management trend is towards 'high involvement work practices', which cover a mixture of human resource initiatives such as teamwork, participation in decision-making and suggestion schemes (Mohr and Zoghi, 2008). Using these practices may well have the effect of altering job characteristics (for example, feedback, task complexity and interdependence) but not explicitly under the label of work/job redesign.

Clegg and Spencer (2007) offer a new analysis of the process of work redesign that reinforces many of the arguments made by Parker *et al.* (2001). This is shown in Figure 8.7. In particular, they stress that individuals often have scope to change the nature of their work for themselves, especially if they are perceived as good and trustworthy performers. Also, they agree with Parker *et al.* (2001) that motivation may not be the only mechanism by which work characteristics affect outcomes.

Figure 8.7	A new model of the process of job design
	Source: Reproduced with permission from Clegg and Spencer (2007), p. 324.

They suggest that the opportunity to acquire new knowledge and experience may also be relevant consequences of work redesign, especially for performance.

Clegg and Spencer (2007) also go beyond Parker *et al.* (2001) in at least two ways. First, they see self-efficacy as a crucial element of the work redesign process. It is either a cause or a consequence (or both) of every element in the process except trust. For example, self-efficacy can be enhanced by changes to job content, and this self-efficacy in itself can improve performance through sheer self-belief (not through motivation, knowledge or anything else). In this respect, Clegg and Spencer are reflecting trends in the goal-setting literature, where self-efficacy is also increasingly seen as a key variable (Locke and Latham, 2002). Second, and unlike Figure 8.6, the process is circular. In Figure 8.6, the arrows are going one way only. In Clegg and Spencer's opinion, it is better to depict the process as circular, feeding on itself, as shown in Figure 8.7. This makes sense, because although it is customary to see motivation, performance, etc. as outcomes at the end of a process, they are highly likely to have their own consequences. These 'outcomes' are therefore *not* the end of a process. Instead, they are part of something ongoing. For example, a consequence of improved work performance is likely to be greater perceived competence, which in turn will increase the trust in a person and give them more scope to make more changes to their job – and so on. One implication of this is that intervention can occur at any point in the process, and may not directly involve the alteration of job characteristics. For example, a well-designed piece of skills training could increase performance, which in turn would increase perceived competence and trust, which could then lead to changes in job content through job crafting.

Recent work suggests that it is helpful to see the work redesign process as cyclical rather than linear. Changes in a person's motivation and performance can affect their job content, and the amount of trust placed in them, which in turn can again affect motivation and performance. Self-efficacy plays a central role in this process.

Integration of motivation theories

There is nowadays general agreement that whilst some motivation theories get more support from research than others, (i) nearly all of them have something to offer, and (ii) in many respects they are compatible, or at least not contradictory. As Latham and Pinder (2005, p. 507) put it:

> the antagonisms among theorists that existed throughout much of the twentieth century have either disappeared or have been minimized. Much of the energy expended on theory destruction has been replaced by theory construction aimed at building upon what is already known.

To illustrate this point, Steel and Konig (2006) have proposed temporal motivation theory (TMT), which is designed to integrate a number of theories (some covered in this chapter and some not), including some from behavioural economics. Locke and Latham (2004) attempt a similar job, mostly using theories covered in this chapter. An adaptation of their model is shown in Figure 8.8.

Locke and Latham argue that most of the links in their model have at least some research to support them, and some of the links have a great deal of research support. It would take an ambitious programme of research to test the entire model, but if the field is to make progress then such endeavours will be necessary. Some aspects

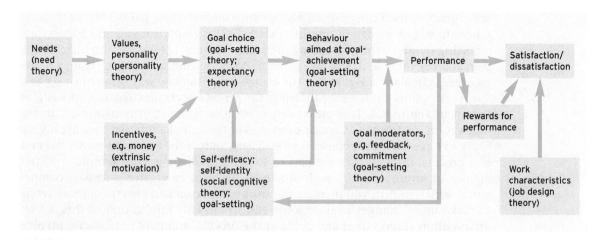

Figure 8.8   An integrated model of work motivation
Source: **Adapted with permission from Locke and Latham (2004), p. 390.**

of their model can be queried. For example, work characteristics are portrayed as affecting satisfaction but not motivation or performance. There is also a surprising lack of feedback loops – one might expect performance, rewards or satisfaction to affect goal choice and goal behaviour as well as self-efficacy. However, it is always possible to question some elements of a model as complex as this. The real challenges are to test it, improve it and use it in work settings.

Summary

Work motivation is a wide-ranging topic of considerable practical and theoretical importance. It concerns the direction, intensity and persistence of work behaviour. Some psychologists view motivation as a product of innate human needs. Others see it as a calculation based on the question 'how can I maximise my gains?' Still others take the view that we are motivated to achieve what we perceive as a fair outcome relative to that experienced by other people. Perhaps the most effective approach to motivation is goal-setting. It is based on the premise that intentions shape actions. If work goals (e.g. target levels of performance) are specific and difficult, and if they are accompanied by feedback on how well one is doing, work performance is usually enhanced. There are some circumstances, however, in which goal-setting in terms of levels of performance is less effective, especially if the task is novel and complex. The most recent analyses of motivation focus on how people allocate their cognitive resources such as attention, thinking and problem-solving to tasks, and how their self-concepts and identities influence their thought processes and are changed by their behaviour. There is also increasing interest in differences between people regarding how and why they are motivated. Another approach that has enjoyed some success is viewing motivation as something that is elicited by the right kinds of task. Here motivation is positioned as a property of the job, not the person. So the task for managers is to make jobs more motivating, not people more motivated. Early versions identified the extent to which jobs had variety and autonomy as being crucial for motivation. More recent theory and practice have broadened the range of work characteristics to include knowledge acquisition and use, the nature and extent of social interactions, and the physical conditions in which work takes place, as well as their impact on a wider range of outcomes for individual and organisation. Overall, motivation theories have done quite a good job of advancing our understanding of behaviour at work. But it is sometimes difficult to be sure about which theory is most helpful in any individual case. Recently, there are signs that an overall theory may be developed which encompasses ideas from many of the existing ones.

Closing Case Study   **An unmotivated building inspector**

Nobody at Kirraton Council planning department knew what to do about Simon Lucas. Simon was a building inspector. It was his job to approve proposals for small alterations to buildings (such as extensions and loft conversions) which did ▶

not need formal planning permission, and to check that the building work carried out was consistent with the approved plans. The trouble was, he didn't – at least, not often and not quickly. There had been a number of complaints about delays in approval of plans that were Simon's responsibility (each incoming application was assigned to one of the building inspectors for them to deal with independently). He did not seem to keep up to date with the frequent changes in building regulations, which meant that he sometimes made decisions that contradicted them. This had led to some appeals by builders and homeowners, and on three occasions the council had been forced to change its decision.

This was embarrassing and costly, and it was Simon Lucas's fault. He only rarely carried out site inspections, and even more rarely spoke directly with applicants or local residents who could be affected by a planning application. This meant that some of the less scrupulous builders got away with unauthorised changes to plans, and others who genuinely wanted his advice did not get it. This damaged the council's reputation and also increased the changes of a structurally unsound building being constructed.

However, it was difficult to point to specific rules that Simon Lucas was breaking. Council guidance was vague: plans should be dealt with 'within a few weeks'; site inspections conducted 'as and when necessary', and decisions made 'within the spirit', not the letter, of some of the less vital regulations. In any case, it wasn't always clear which of the regulations, if any, could be treated as less vital.

Simon's boss, Katherine Walker, decided that she would check his records and unobtrusively observe him at work – it was an open-plan office, so this was feasible. She discovered that Simon was 26, and had qualified as a building inspector two years earlier. Simon had been recruited by Katherine's predecessor, apparently partly because Simon had 'come up the hard way'. Rather than attending college full time to obtain the necessary qualifications, he had worked for several years as an architect's draughtsman and attended college night classes. In fact, he had been almost the last person to qualify in that way. The building inspectors' professional institute had subsequently decided that part-time study could not develop the necessary skills and knowledge for work as a qualified building inspector. Katherine knew it was true that the part-time route was often seen as 'second class'. She heard it said that this had prevented Simon from getting a job in another area of the country where he very much wanted to live. Few senior building inspectors held the view of Katherine's predecessor that Simon's route into the profession was superior to full-time study. Simon was certainly sensitive about it himself. He frequently mentioned how difficult it had been to combine study with work, but at the same time also remarked that he did not know enough about some things because his training had been 'too basic'.

Katherine observed that Simon often seemed not to be doing very much. He sat at his desk doodling quite a lot. He sometimes had to phone people more than once because he had forgotten to check something the first time. He seemed to have difficulty finding things on his shelves and desk. Sometimes he would give up after only a short and not very systematic search. He also sometimes jumped from one task to another without finishing any of them. As far as she could tell, his home life was not a particular problem. Simon was married, apparently happily, and seemed to participate in many social and leisure activities judging from his lunchtime conversations, not to mention his phone calls to squash clubs, camp sites, etc. during work time! He was especially keen on long-distance walking, and could often be seen at lunchtime reading outdoor magazines and carefully planning his walking club's next expedition. He joked to Katherine that he should have her surname because it described what he liked most.

Simon's job was relatively secure. Ultimately he could be dismissed if he demonstrated continuing incompetence, but he had successfully completed his probationary period (Katherine wasn't sure how). Because Kirraton Council covered only a small area, and because Simon's job was a specialist one, he could not be moved to another town or department. Building inspectors' pay depended on age and length of service, with slightly higher rates for those with a relevant college degree. Outstanding performance could only be rewarded with promotion, and this was extremely unlikely for anyone with less than 10 years' service. Katherine established that Simon would like promotion because of the extra money it would bring rather than the status, but he correctly perceived that he had virtually no chance of achieving it. Apart from the fact he had been at Kirraton for a relatively short time, he thought he was not scoring very well on Katherine's recently implemented building inspector performance criteria of no lost appeals, high client satisfaction, at least 15 complete projects per month, and acknowledgement of receipt of plans within four working days. This was bad for him, and also bad for the department as a whole because it affected its overall performance statistics.

The other four building inspectors were quite a close-knit group of building sciences graduates who had worked together for several years before Simon's arrival. Simon didn't really see himself as a member of the group, preferring instead to emphasise how he, unlike them, was 'on the same wavelength' as local people. He had found it hard to establish a relationship with them, and now it was even harder because they felt his apparently poor performance reflected badly on them all. They did not involve him much in their activities, nor did they appear to respect him. Simon was afraid that the others thought he wasn't doing his job properly and Katherine suspected that secretly he agreed with them. Katherine knew something had to be done, but what, and how?

Suggested exercises

1   Review the motivation theories discussed in this chapter. How would each one describe and explain the problems with Simon Lucas's motivation?

2   To what extent does each theory provide guidance to Katherine Walker about what she should do? What actions would they recommend?

3   Apply concepts from the job redesign literature to Simon's job. Do they explain why he is not motivated?

Test your learning

Short-answer questions

1 Describe the key features of the theory X and theory Y 'common-sense' views of motivation.

2 Suggest three ways in which Maslow's hierarchy of needs theory might helpfully be amended.

3 List five features of the 'self-actualising' person.

4 What are the components of the motivation to manage?

5 Define valence, instrumentality and expectancy. According to Vroom, how do they combine to determine motivation?

6 Name and define three kinds of perceived justice at work.

7 Draw a simple diagram that shows the key elements of goal-setting.

8 What are the key differences between performance goal orientation and learning goal orientation?

9 Name and define the five types of motivation suggested by Leonard *et al.* (1999).

10 Name and define four types of motivation that vary along the extrinsic–intrinsic continuum.

11 Draw a diagram which represents the main features of the job characteristics model (JCM).

12 Suggest three limitations of the JCM as a framework for job redesign.

13 Describe five characteristics of jobs not in the JCM that have been identified as being important in work redesign.

14 Briefly outline two ways in which Clegg and Spencer's (2007) model of work redesign is different from earlier ones.

Suggested assignments

1 Examine the usefulness of need theories in understanding and predicting behaviour at work.

2 In what ways, if any, do academic theories of motivation improve upon so-called 'common sense'?

3 It is often claimed that goal-setting is a theory of motivation which works. Examine whether it works better in some circumstances than others.

4 Examine the extent to which theories of motivation have or have not taken into account people's conscious sense of their own identity.

2   Gary Latham's book *Work Motivation* published in 2007 by Sage presents an historical, theoretical and practical analysis of work motivation. If this chapter has interested you, then Latham's book will be a real treat.

3   Ed Locke and Gary Latham's 2004 article attempts to specify an integrated theory of motivation. It is quite heavy going but well-written nevertheless, and a good way of expanding both your knowledge of theories and your understanding of how they might fit together.

5   When and how is pay a motivator?

6   Discuss this statement: 'The job characteristics model was a useful start as a guide to how to redesign jobs, but it was no more than a start'.

7   To what extent does Locke and Latham's (2004) attempt to provide an integrated theory of motivation do justice to the earlier theories?

Relevant websites

There are very many sites which describe training courses in motivational techniques (for managing self or others) and provide very brief accounts of some well-known motivation theories, usually the oldest and most straightforward ones. Here are a few examples:

http://www.bizhelp24.com/personal_development/motivation_theory_importance. shtml is part of a managers' self-help site. This particular item gives prominence to Herzberg's theory. It also encourages managers to take on responsibility for the motivation of the people who work for them.

A site with a lot of interesting material, including an original article by Maslow, is http://www.themanager.org/Knowledgebase/HR/Motivation.htm. This is another managers' self-help resource site.

http://changingminds.org/explanations/theories/a_motivation.htm gives an index of different theories of motivation. Clicking on a theory brings you a little more information about it.

An easy-to-understand account of the key concepts and practical uses of goal-setting can be found at http://www.mindtools.com/pages/article/newHTE_87.htm.

For further self-test material and relevant, annotated weblinks please visit the website at **www.pearsoned.co.uk/workpsych**

Suggested further reading

Full details for all references are given in the list at the end of this book.

1   Maureen Ambrose and Carol Kulik (1999) provide a good account of how various motivation theories have developed (and in some cases emerged) in recent years. It is quite a technical article, but worth the effort of reading carefully, because it presents both the fundamentals of theories and the details of how they are being extended and tested.

CHAPTER 9

Design at work

LEARNING OUTCOMES

After studying this chapter you should be able to:

1 understand the role that ergonomics has to play alongside other organisational systems (such as employee training);

2 appreciate the principles of Human Factors Integration (HFI);

3 describe the principles and process of Human-Centred Design (HCD);

4 understand the human factors issues at the various stages of the design process;

5 appreciate the changing role of the ergonomist during the various stages of work and task design.

Opening Case Study   The importance of end-user input into design

User involvement in development programmes is vital for both reducing cost and ensuring success. The Chaos Report (Standish Group, 1995) established that early user involvement was the most important factor for the success of IT projects. It was found that the highest-rated reason for why IT projects succeeded was users' involvement during the development process. Conversely, the most commonly cited reason for IT projects failing was a lack of user involvement.

An excellent example of what can go wrong was provided by the failure of the IT system responsible for allocating London's ambulances to incidents. The system was designed to improve call handling and to improve the dispatch of ambulances while also gathering data to perform several other management auditing functions, such as monitoring how the availability of resources changed over time and tracking response times. The system comprised an automatic vehicle locating system and data terminals to enable dispatch staff to communicate with ambulance crews.

As the system entered service it became apparent that there were many technical and ergonomic issues resulting in severe communication difficulties. As a result, often the dispatch system could not establish the location or the status of the ambulances under its control. The system sometimes made incorrect allocations of ambulances to incidents or failed to allocate an ambulance at all. The software responded very slowly, causing an increase in telephone and radio traffic from both frustrated ambulance crews and members of the public. On 26 and 27 October 1992 this resulted in the system slowing even further, to a completely unacceptable level. On 4 November 1992, the system failed completely after a minor programming error.

The report from the subsequent Inquiry by the Communications Directorate of the South West Thames Regional Health Authority (1993) reported that the factors underlying the failure included inadequacies in training; understaffing in the control centre; poor processes and procedures; inadequate working practices and interface problems affecting system usability. The overall management of the specification, design and procurement of the IT system was also heavily criticised.

Modern ergonomics addresses all aspects of work system design, not just the user interface: it takes a systemic approach. Problems in all of the areas criticised in the report could have been avoided with the implementation of a proper Human Factors Integration programme. The findings of the Inquiry stated that 'The next CAD [computer-aided dispatch] system must be made to fit the Service's current or future organisational structure and agreed operational practices. This was not the case with the current CAD.' The report concludes that users were not sufficiently involved in the system's development.

Sources: Communications Directorate, South West Thames Regional Health Authority (1993). Johnson (2001); Ministry of Defence, Human Factors Integration Defence Technology Centre (2006). Case Study by Chapter author.

Suggested exercise. As you read this chapter try to identify specific actions that could have been taken to avoid some of the problems identified in this Case Study.

Introduction

Ergonomics, also referred to as Human Factors (HF), is a discipline that has evolved and expanded in the last 50 years. There is no one accepted definition, however the Ergonomics Society (www.ergonomics.org.uk) describes the discipline as being concerned with 'the application of scientific information concerning humans to the design of objects, systems and environment for human use'. Ergonomics has evolved to be concerned with the design of whole systems of work, and not just simply the design of work equipment. This means that there is a great deal of overlap between what work psychologists do and what ergonomists do (their commonalities are probably more pronounced than their differences). However, as you will see in this chapter, ergonomics also encompasses elements of human physiology, anatomy and engineering system design. Furthermore, the emphasis in ergonomics is on the design of equipment, work systems and training. It is important to point out that ergonomics goes beyond the analysis of tasks and jobs; it uses work analysis as one step in the process of defining, designing and testing work equipment and systems.

Human Factors Integration (HFI) is the name often given to the contemporary approach to the specification, design and development of major equipment acquisitions, and its subsequent operational deployment. HFI is an approach is used particularly by the military and other safety-critical industries (e.g. nuclear, oil and gas industries).

The UK Ministry of Defence (MoD) specifies seven domains of HFI (Ministry of Defence, 2001) – see Table 9.1. You will notice that many aspects of HFI are also addressed in other chapters of this book (such as selection, teamwork and training). This shows that HFI is not a product that sits in isolation from the organisational context. Rather HFI is best seen as a process that considers a wide range of issues beyond the design of specific tasks and the equipment needed to carry them out (i.e. it is a process that sits within a systems engineering context).

Clearly HFI is too broad to be adequately covered in a single chapter of this text. In this chapter the focus will be placed on the process of Human-Centred Design (HCD), i.e. how we design tasks and equipment for humans. HCD is a key component of HFI: but HFI is a process that considers a much wider range of issues. Therefore, the chapter also makes frequent mention of how HFI might be influenced by the issues discussed (in detail) in the other chapters this book.

It might surprise you that no attempt will be made to outline the range of specific design solutions possible across a variety of work settings. This is because each design solution is bespoke to the application area, task, user and the environment. For example, there is no such thing as 'the best type of visual display'; there is only the best type of display for certain types of information in a certain context. Display design requires answers to questions such as 'are the values to be displayed likely to change slowly or rapidly? What degree of precision is required? How quickly must the user assimilate them?' There is always a speed vs. accuracy trade-off: displays that are designed to be read quickly will be less precise; displays that are designed to convey accurate information will take longer to read. A digital counter takes up little space and conveys precise quantitative information; however, if you use it as an altimeter in a fast military jet capable of climbing at 30,000 feet (1000 metres) per minute, the numbers on it will simply tumble in front of the pilot's eyes, making it impossible to read (Harris, 2004). However, a counter is perfectly acceptable on a photocopier if the objective of the display is to count how many copies have been made.

Table 9.1	The domains of HFI	
HFI domain	**Example issues**	**Example topics**
Staffing	How many people are required to operate and maintain the system?	Staffing levels Team organisation Job specifications
Personnel	What are the aptitudes, experience and other human characteristics?	Selection, recruitment and career development Qualifications and experience required General characteristics (e.g. size, strength, eyesight)
Training	How to develop and maintain the requisite knowledge, skills and abilities to operate and maintain the system	Identifying requirements for new skills Training courses Requirements for specialist training facilities Individual and team training Skill maintenance (e.g. refresher courses)
Human factors engineering	How to integrate human characteristics into system design to optimise performance	Equipment design Workstation/console design Workplace layout Ease of maintenance User interface design Function allocation
Health hazards	What are the hazards resulting from normal operation of the system?	Exposure to: ■ Toxic materials ■ Electric shock ■ Mechanical injury ■ Musculoskeletal injury ■ Extreme heat/cold ■ Optical hazards
System safety	How to avoid the safety risks caused by operating or maintaining the system abnormally	Sources of error Effects of misuse or abuse External and environmental hazards
Organisational and social	What is the optimum organisational configuration?	Organisational and national culture Information sharing

Source: Widdowson and Carr (2002). With permission.

Design in a sociotechnical context

It is important to recognise that all design takes place within a wider context. Simply focusing on the user interface without considering users, task requirements, organisation and/or the environmental context will usually result in substandard equipment being developed, which is also difficult to use. The Human Factors National Advisory Committee for Defence and Aerospace (2003) describes some examples of the benefits of taking a wider socio-technical/HFI approach to equipment design. For instance, the developer of an aircraft engine who adopted an HFI approach reduced the number of tools required for line maintenance of a new turbine from over 100 to just 10; fewer specialist skills were needed allowing a consolidation in the number of maintenance trades required which also resulted in a reduction in training time. What this example illustrates is that organisations can realise significant economic benefits by actively considering the wider organisational context of impact equipment redesign.

One approach to characterising the wider context within which design and operations take place is described in the five M's model (Harris and Harris, 2004; Harris and Thomas, 2005). This model shows how the operation of any commercial piece of equipment is not just about the integration of the user (*human*) and equipment (*machine*) to perform a particular task (or *mission*) within constraints imposed by the physical environment (*medium*). The societal environment (a further aspect of the *medium*) also needs to be considered, as does the role of *management* (see Figure 9.1).

Taking an HCD approach, the *human* component is the ultimate design forcing function: the designer must operate within abilities of the human operator. The *human* and the *machine* components come together to perform a *mission*. However, designers must not only work within the constraints of the technology, end-users and the physical aspects of the *medium*, they are also bound by the rules and norms of society (a further aspect of the *medium*). Performance standards for human–machine

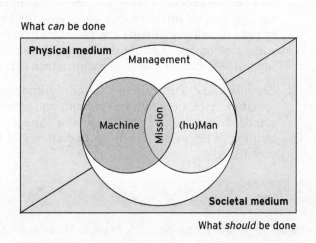

Figure 9.1   **The five M's framework**
Source: Harris and Harris (2004). With permission.

systems are primarily determined by societal norms. For example, such norms may be set by the minimum level of safety required. This can mean that designers may be more concerned with minimising operator error in the design of the controls of a nuclear reactor than they are when designing an office telephone. There may also be formal minimum standards of user competence, such as that required to obtain a licence. Fortunately, pilots need to be trained to an internationally agreed level of competence before they are allowed to fly an aeroplane. As a result, the designer may assume this level of competence when designing equipment for them to use (however, always remember that licensing only ever specifies the *minimum* level of user competence at one point in time). What the model shows is that it is not just the designer that plays an important role. *Management* must also work within these rules. Management prescribes secondary performance standards, for example through the proper selection and training of personnel who will be carrying out the task. Thus management is the key link between the human, machine, mission and medium which promotes safe and efficient operations.

Stages in design

All design has several identifiable stages. These will differ slightly in every situation, but typically cover issues such as:

- *Concept formulation.* This focuses on the identification of the need for the equipment. (What is it going to do? What are the requirements for it?)

- *Functional specification.* This focuses on the question: how is it going to do it? Typically this involves a process of breaking down the larger task that the system will perform into smaller, more manageable tasks.

- *Detailed design.* Here the functional specifications of the individual components are operationalised (or bought to life). From an HFI perspective this involves designing the user interface and identifying the logic underlying any automation of tasks. It will also involve design and implementation of other aspects of the wider system, for example the design of training for employees and logistical support (e.g. making plans for maintenance of the equipment or technology).

- *Commissioning.* Putting together all the individual components into a representative system (system integration) and establishing that it performs to the standard required. At this stage the support infrastructure (e.g. delivering training to the personnel for its operation and maintenance) also needs to be established.

Key Learning Point

The early stages of design are particularly crucial. There is a 1:10:100 rule for design costs (Pressman, 1992). For every £1 to fix a problem identified in the early design stages it will cost £10 to fix it during detailed design and development, and £100 to fix it once the system is operational. Put simply: don't skimp on front-end design activities.

Human-Centred Design

Table 9.2 describes the HCD activities within the HFI approach. As you can see, the actual design of the equipment itself occurs relatively late in the process. Table 9.2 shows that the important early activities include understanding the system requirements, its end users and the context in which it will be used. There are two very important aspects of HCD. First, it actively involves the end users of the system.

Table 9.2	HCD activities
Activity and objective	**Example activities**
Plan the human-centred process Ensure that specific HF activities are built into project plans and are sufficiently resourced.	HFI planning Requirements analysis
Understand and specify the context of use Identify the users and what they will be doing. Ensure that descriptions of users and tasks are considered as the basis for design.	Target audience description Scenario identification Task identification
Specify the user and organisational requirements Specify the characteristics required of the system which affect users and their wider organisation.	Task analysis Function allocation Ergonomics standards and guidelines User performance specification
Produce design solutions Apply HF expertise to generate design options which meet user requirements. Design iteratively using part-prototypes and prototypes as required.	Workstation design Workspace design Job/team design
Evaluate designs against user requirements Test designs against requirements by involving target users and HF specialists.	User interface prototyping User trials Human reliability assessment/formal error prediction

Source: Widdowson and Carr (2002). With permission.

Second, it is an iterative process (it is unlikely that your first design solution will be your final design!). Constant testing and refinement during the design process are essential.

All design starts with a requirements analysis. Not only does this specify what the equipment must do, it will also form the basis for verifying if the final design performs to the standards required. However, get the requirements analysis wrong (or incomplete) and, as everything else builds upon this, so everything else is subsequently mis-specified. Many major projects fail as a result of incomplete requirements analyses and/or a failure to include end users throughout the design process (Standish Group, 1995).

In HCD there are three types of requirement:

1   *Product requirements* These are the attributes of the equipment itself (e.g. any applicable design standards regarding display formats; limitations on weight if it is a person-transportable piece of equipment; integration requirements with other, existing pieces of equipment, etc.).

2   *Performance requirements* These specify the performance of the equipment and should be verifiable (e.g. usability; transaction times for set tasks; acceptable error rates, etc.).

3   *Process requirements* These define the processes to be followed during the design and development process – a critical part of any HFI plan. Typically these will specify such things as the human factors methods to be used for undertaking the formal requirements analysis; the format for reporting data; the required availability of subject matter experts and members of the target user population for undertaking design evaluations, etc.

Understanding and specifying the context of use

Formally specifying the requirements for a piece of equipment raises two important issues in the design process:

1   What are the skills, knowledge and abilities required of its end users?

2   What is the context of its use (both operational and organisational)?

In order to address these issues, an early HCD task is the production of the Target Audience Description (TAD). This document contains information such as the physical characteristics of end users (e.g. users' body size and dimension and physical strength requirements); sensory characteristics (e.g. visual and auditory capabilities); psychological characteristics (e.g. particular aptitudes and abilities; reasoning and/or decision-making skills); social and cultural characteristics (e.g. age and gender); and specific skills and qualifications (overview of target audience descriptions) (Ministry of Defence, 2000).

The TAD is a forward-looking document, anticipating demographic and cultural changes if need be. This is because many major pieces of hardware and equipment may be in service for many years (it is not uncommon for large or expensive pieces of military equipment, for example an aircraft carrier, to be in service for up to half a century). Therefore the modern ergonomist needs to be part scientist, part clairvoyant! Any TAD also needs to incorporate consideration of issues relating to initial and continuing training requirements. However, in the HCD process it is easy to concentrate entirely on the primary end user (i.e. the operator) but this can be a mistake. Good HCD is about the performance of the *whole* system. This means it is also vital to consider secondary use (and users) of the product (e.g. cleaning, maintenance and storage).

Appreciation of context is essential for successful system design, build and operation. To illustrate, as a 'rule of thumb' equipment is built from the inside outward but is maintained from the outside inward. Because of these different contexts, the requirements for efficient error-free assembly are quite different from those ensuring the maintainability of the system. Such conflicts of priority must be resolved at an early stage. If the equipment will be in service for an extended period, maintenance may take priority. However, if the equipment is relatively cheap to purchase, has a short service life, or is likely to be single-use (or disposable), error-free assembly will be of more importance.

There is no such thing as a recipe for characterising context of use. Referring back to the 5M's model (Figure 9.1) context can include the physical and societal mediums, and the domain of management. Within this latter category issues such as organisational structure, team structure and operating autonomy and independence should be considered (e.g. will the equipment be operated by a team or by an individual?). The wider aspects of the medium may include protecting the user from extremes of temperature, a hostile atmosphere, poor illumination or noise and vibration. Furthermore, the equipment may be used for protracted periods of time, at high tempo and/or when the user is under considerable stress, for example a great deal of the equipment used by anaesthetists in the modern operating theatre or by an communications operator on site at a major incident. Such issues have a profound effect on the appropriate task structure and user interface.

Key Learning Point

Actively engaging users in the design process is a crucial part of the HFI and HCD processes.

Exercise 9.1 — Different perspectives on design

When designing the wards in the new buildings of University College Hospital, London, cleaners were actively engaged in the process. Although one might immediately expect doctors and nurses to be involved in such a process, the role of cleaners is less clear. However, the input of cleaners resulted in several design changes. For example, their input led to a design decision that walls would not meet the floor at a sharp, 90 degree angle. Instead there is a large radius curve, stopping dirt gathering in the crack which harbours bacteria causing infection. As a result of this simple design modification, these wards are easier to clean and show lower reinfection rates in patients.

Suggested exercise

Think about the design of a lecture theatre. If lecturers were asked to input into the design process, what issues might they raise? As a student, what issues would you raise? Compare how the two are different and consider whether both sets of requirements could be accommodated in a single design.

Specifying user and organisational requirements

So far in this chapter the context of use and potential users have been considered, but not the actual tasks that they will perform. This is the domain of task analysis, i.e. analysing, in detail, the various operations that are required for the execution of a task. Many excellent texts are available describing task analysis in all its major forms (e.g. Diaper and Stanton, 2004; Hollnagel, 2003; Crandall *et al.*, 2006). However, as an analytical approach it can be broken down in to two principal genres: behavioural and cognitive. Behavioural forms describe the tasks and subtasks that need to be performed and their organisation. Generally these are observable, discrete operations (e.g. pull lever, push switch, turn handle, write down data, etc.).

Hierarchical task analysis (HTA) is the most common behavioural form of task analysis. HTA is based upon the principle that all large tasks are decomposable into smaller tasks capable of being organised into a hierarchy (Stanton, 2004). Since its original conception by Annett and colleagues (1971) the method has been extended and expanded to incorporate other features, such as making plans and decision events, and now also allows for the incorporation of more detailed information (e.g. by including tabular analyses specifying interface or performance requirements). An example HTA from aviation is included in Figure 9.2 (from Harris *et al.*, 2005). These

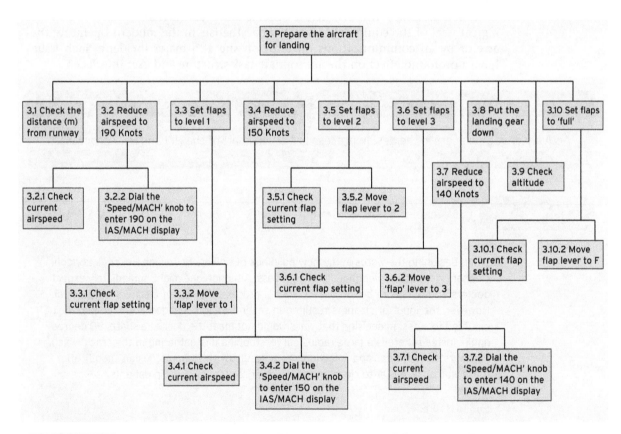

Figure 9.2   **An extract from the HTA describing the task of preparing an Airbus A320 for a CAT III autoland**
Source: **Harris *et al.* (2005).**

changes have allowed HTA to give a more complete analysis of the events occurring in the execution of a task (beyond those that can easily be observed). However, HTA can only identify task requirements and information flows. The designer must interpret this information and make decisions based upon it, for example when devising the user interface.

Many modern jobs are largely cognitive in nature, for example the supervisory control of highly automated systems, or other professions not involving high-technology equipment, such as accountancy or the law, customer services and banking. In such cases HTA may be of limited utility as it is only a formal description of the behavioural task requirements. Work in these highly automated or cognitive situations is most likely associated with situation assessment, risk management, planning, decision-making and selecting an appropriate strategy. Cognitive forms of task analysis describe the underlying cognitive skills and processes for performing a task. Crandall and colleagues (2006) suggest that cognitive task analysis (CTA) comprises three distinct stages: knowledge elicitation (extracting information to provide information on events, structures or mental models); analysis of the data (to provide structure and explanation); and knowledge representation (to depict the nature of the relationships and to help inform design and operational processes). These aspects of human functioning are more difficult for a third party to observe directly. The outputs from both forms of task analysis perform several functions in addition to providing a basis for HCD. They are also useful for specifying the attributes of personnel, forming the basis of training needs analyses and training design, informing staffing and job organisation decisions and providing a basis for performance assurance (Kirwan and Ainsworth, 1992). To some extent, CTA can be conceptualised as just one component of a larger cognitively based analytical system, work domain analysis. For example, cognitive work analysis (Vincente, 1999) is a conceptual framework to analyse both cognitively-based tasks and their context.

Key Learning Point

'Task analysis can get too detailed, and be too late [in the design process] to have an effect. Think about how much detail is needed for the people who will use the results. With a hierarchical description you can readily add detail later' (taken from *HFI Practical Guidance for IPTs*) (Ministry of Defence, 2001).

As in the case of HTA, though, CTA only provides an analysis of the cognitive work of the system operator. It does not, in itself, provide design solutions. Function allocation (FA) can be thought to be the beginning of this design process. FA is the attribution of functions to either the machine or its operator. FA should be performed while the system functions are still defined at a high level of abstraction (i.e. emphasis should be firmly placed upon defining what the system is attempting to accomplish and not *how* it is going to accomplish it). Traditionally, FA has proceeded on the simple basis of assigning a particular function to either the human operator or the machine based upon their relative strengths and weaknesses when performing this task. Parasuraman and colleagues (2000) describe automation as 'the full or partial replacement of a function previously carried out by the human operator' (p. 287). However, Hollnagel (1999) has labelled this approach 'function allocation by substitution'. Dekker and Woods (2002) have suggested that designers need to get away from this practice as it falls into the 'electric horse'[1] trap. By using this approach the automation does the same job as the human but in a slightly different way (i.e. substitution), and thus it can limit innovation. Greater benefit can often be gained by questioning some of the initial assumptions upon which the design is predicated and delivering the required capability in a different manner. Take the simple example of the airline ticket. The low-cost carriers questioned the basic assumption that a physical ticket was required. Now, all that is required is proof of identification at check-in, usually provided in the form of a passport and a cross-check with your credit card number or alpha-numeric booking reference. The function of the airline ticket has become redundant. Proof of purchase is provided in other ways.

Key Learning Point

Automation is not simply about replacing human activity with a machine performing the same job. Smart design looks at the whole system and asks 'can we do it better'? It then analyses which aspects are best done by a human and which are best performed by a machine.

Ergonomists need to be aware of already proven options for the various system components when undertaking initial design iterations. Many standards exist for HCD, ranging from very simple things (such as the arrangement of the pedals in your car) to vastly more complex standards (such as those for the design of primary flight instruments in an aircraft). ISO 13407 is an internationally recognised standard for the design processes for interactive systems. These activities largely mirror those described by Widdowson and Carr (2002) but have a greater focus on software design. The operation of the software interface and its 'look and feel' (i.e. the *product*) may be based around other 'unofficial' standards, such as the Microsoft® Office System User Interface Design Guidelines. The military have extensive standards for all aspects of HF design. One of the most comprehensive is the UK Ministry of Defence DEF-STAN 00-250 (available at www.dstan.mod.uk).[2] This standard runs to well over 1000 pages and contains information about the HF design process, interface options, HCI, etc. It is more comprehensive and contains more practical advice than any textbook on the market, and is updated relatively frequently to reflect changes in technology and the underpinning science base. Another excellent, freely available Internet resource is 'Understanding Human Factors – a guide for the railway industry' (Rail Safety and Standards Board, 2008). Compliance with standards and guidelines may be specifically written into the system design contract or may be indirectly implied via compliance with rules and regulations (e.g. the airworthiness requirements for the design of large commercial aircraft found in FAR/CS part 25). The ergonomist involved with the design of a user interface does not necessarily have a completely free hand. What should always be remembered, though, is that regulation only specifies the *minimum* performance level of the human–machine system: when done effectively HCD can help achieve far better overall system performance and produce more satisfied users.

---

[1] If you want to travel faster and carry a heavier load, making a mechanical horse is not the best way of achieving these aims – a different approach to solving the problem is required, for example designing a car!

[2] Many other standards also exist (e.g. the US military MIL-STD-1472 or US Nuclear Regulator's NUREG 0700).

Producing design solutions

It should be evident by now that the design and evaluation of human–machine interface (HMI) is only one component of the ergonomist's task. However, if you are looking for the HMI as an entity in itself, you won't find it – it doesn't really exist! Figure 9.3 shows why this is the case. On the machine output–human input *side* of the interface 'images' on the displays (hopefully) convey data/information to the operator (Figure 9.3). These images are interpreted and their content should be transformed into knowledge and understanding that allow control of the machine. On the human output–machine input *side* of the control loop, control intent from the operator needs to be translated into the desired machine output. A good control system will translate operator intent into system output in the manner desired and with minimal effort (physical or mental). A 'high-quality' HMI consists of a good 'fit' between the skills, knowledge and ability of the user and the controls and displays of the machine.

Ackoff (1989) suggested that there are five broad categories of information. These are described below, with an example to illustrate each (i.e. controlling the process in a nuclear reactor):

1   *Data.* Basic building blocks/symbols (e.g. the temperature in the primary cooling circuit in a nuclear reactor).

2   *Information.* Data that have been combined and processed to provide answers to questions concerning 'who', 'what', 'where' and 'when' (e.g. if the primary cooling circuit temperature is high, and the pressure in the steam generator is high and there is a high neutron count, then without intervention the level of criticality in the nuclear reactor will become unstable in 10 minutes).

3   *Knowledge.* This applies information to questions concerning 'how' (e.g. lowering control rods into the reactor will instantly reduce the reactivity of the reactor core and begin to lower the temperature and pressure).

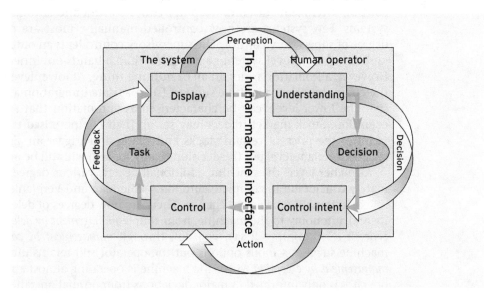

| Figure 9.3 | The concept of the human-machine interface superimposed over a representation of the classical 'perception-decision-action-feedback' control loop |

4   *Understanding.* Begins to give an appreciation concerning 'why' questions (e.g. control rods (made of neutron-absorbing material) slow the processes occurring in the reactor, thus allowing the reactor temperature to fall).

5   *Wisdom.* Which provides an evaluated understanding (e.g. without the close monitoring of the position of control rods and reactor temperatures and pressures, things could go very badly wrong!).

What can be seen from Figure 9.3 is that the HMI only provides 'data' and/or 'information' (and *perhaps* 'knowledge') but what the user requires is 'understanding'. This illustrates the importance of considering the wider design context: users often need training and supervision in order to develop the understanding wisdom to work most effectively with the technology.

Key Learning Point

Good HCD provides the user with information, not data. For example, the airworthiness regulations require aircraft flight decks to display fuel quantity and fuel flow rates. However, these data are of little use: what the pilot requires is *information* concerning what the remaining amount of fuel represents in terms of range or endurance (e.g. how many miles before the engines stop work because of lack of fuel). Information requirements are derived from the user requirements and task analyses.

The human control of many systems has changed greatly over the last half-century. Pilots do not fly the aircraft manually from London to New York (the autopilot and flight management system do it). Nuclear power plant operators do not continually control the rod positions in a reactor in response to parameter changes. Even driving a car is becoming more automated with the advent of cruise control, intelligent (distance-keeping) cruise control and automatic lane-keeping systems. Few systems are now controlled manually: most are now under some degree of supervisory control. The supervisory controller is an outer-loop controller (a setter of high-level system goals) rather than a hands-on, inner loop controller. However, automation is not an all or nothing thing. At lower levels of automation the computer offers cognitive support (such as data integration and option analysis). The lower levels can be characterised as automation that augments human cognition. Stock market traders may set up their computerised trading systems to monitor the price of certain stocks and shares and trigger an alert when a price reaches a certain level but the decision to buy (or sell) will still be made by a human.

At higher levels the machine additionally exerts various degrees of control, ultimately concluding in complete autonomy (Sheridan and Verplank, 1978). Here the role of automation begins to change. There are now degrees of delegation of authority and autonomy to the machine, from simple *management by delegation* (boss/slave type of relationship – 'I say, you do') through *management by consent* (where the machine suggests various options but the operator still retains ultimate control) to *management by exception* where the machine is operating almost autonomously. The operator is only informed of major deviations from normal operations by the system (Billings, 1997).

The higher the degree of automation the lower the operator's workload, but only when the system is operating within normal parameters. When exerting control using automation high cognitive demands are placed upon the operator, especially in the planning phases, but they are relieved of the minute-to-minute control workload. However, as a result the operator is concomitantly less aware of what the system is doing, thus when things go wrong workload can be considerably higher. For example, if the dynamic positioning system (the automatic system that keeps the ship in one place) in an oil support vessel fails, then the helmsman needs to (a) recognise that the system has failed; (b) step in and take control; (c) immediately become familiar with the strength and direction of the local currents to maintain the position of the vessel; and (d) secure the automated system. These vessels, weighing thousands of tonnes, will often be only a few metres away from a production platform. If the helmsman had been controlling the vessel manually they would have implicitly been aware of the direction and strength of the current and would have developed a 'feel' for the situation. Furthermore, they would not have also needed to take the actions required to secure the malfunctioning automated system (and perform any further diagnoses of the situation, as required). However, the human helmsman could not perform such a task to the accuracy of the automated dynamic positioning system, nor would they have the mental and physical endurance! The skill set required to control an automated system is often quite different from that required for manual control although the manual control skills are still required, but although rarely practised (see Bainbridge, 1987, for a discussion of more of these ironies of automation).

STOP TO CONSIDER

The content of this chapter has concentrated primarily upon commercial equipment where the users are selected and trained by the organisation. However, the HCD process also applies to consumer products as well (such as cars, video cameras, computer software and games consoles and even washing machines). There is great diversity of knowledge, experience and competence found within the general population. What implications might this have for the design process and the final design solution?

Modern computerised display systems offer the HMI designer new opportunities. They are essentially 'blackboards' onto which can be drawn and animated almost any display format of the designer's choosing. Computers can also integrate many data sources to provide the user with information. The ultimate objective of display design is to enhance situation awareness (SA). SA is a difficult construct to define but in this context Endsley's (1988) definition serves quite well. SA is 'the perception of elements in the environment within a volume of time and space, the comprehension of their meaning, and the projection of their status in the near future'. Endsley describes three levels of SA. Level one is based on the perception of *data*. Level two requires these *data* to be combined to provide a 'bigger picture' (*information*). Level three is achieved when the operator has *knowledge*, fully *understands* their current situation and can project ahead into the future. There are many texts that outline options for display formats: some are generic in nature (e.g. McCormick and Sanders, 1992) and others are dedicated to specific operational contexts (e.g. Rajan, 1997; Harris, 2004; Wickens *et al.*, 2004). Many of the standards cited previously contain excellent information on these topics. The key ability for the ergonomist is to be able to translate the data and information requirements elicited into design solutions.

However, most modern multifunctional interfaces now hide more information than they display. With old-style mechanical instruments this was impossible: each system parameter needed a dedicated display. Now many systems share the same display space, i.e. displays are 'moded'. For example, in the past it was typical for operators controlling chemical production processes to be faced with monitoring a plethora of mechanical gauges and dials, some of which were not even in the central control room. Today, it is common for all such data to be accessed from a small number of computer screens cited in a central control room.

With moded displays parameters are monitored automatically and failures are only drawn to the attention of the operator as required. In a system under supervisory control, targets for performance are set using one part of the HMI and then hidden while the tasks needed to achieve them are executed (their display being replaced with another component associated with system monitoring). While the manner in which the information is now conveyed may be superior to the old instrumentation, the operator now requires a great deal more knowledge about using the computerised HMI in addition to the knowledge needed to manage the system they are trying to control. For example, the chemical process operators discussed earlier now need to remember which pieces of data are hidden (e.g. the mix of chemicals in the reactor) while they are accessing information (e.g. about the temperature of the chemicals entering the reaction vessel). There is an apt, old saying: 'out of sight, out of mind'. If you can't see it, you have a good chance of forgetting about it. On an aircraft flight deck, for exactly this reason, it is mandated that certain primary flight parameters (e.g. altitude) must be displayed at all times.

This is typical of the use of all computerised systems. Using a computer requires both semantic and syntactic knowledge. Semantic knowledge refers to having some idea of what a computer can actually do (store data; retrieve data; manipulate data); syntactic knowledge encompasses the lower level operating concepts and grammars needed to operate a computer (pointing and clicking; dragging and dropping; 'opening' and 'closing' files, etc.). At an even lower level, lexical knowledge is required to learn the particular sequence of low-level actions to perform a task (Schneiderman, 1998). All of this is guided by a user's mental model of the computer/software system. This is a product of experience and training, so it needs to be recognised that HCD does not progress in isolation. Within the HFI philosophy there are intimate links to other components of the ergonomics discipline, such as the provision of education and training.

Key Learning Point

The ultimate goal in HCD is to control the system, not manage the user interface. Very 'usable' systems are not always good at helping the user achieve their goal.

Evaluating designs against user requirements

The evaluation of the HMI falls into two distinct stages. *Formative evaluation* addresses individual interface components, usually as part prototypes. These are functional prototypes of discrete parts of the HMI. *Summative evaluation* assembles all the components into a full implementation of the user interface to assess its usability as a whole. *Summative evaluation* occurs at the end of the detailed design stages. *Formative evaluation* takes place during the design evaluation/commissioning stages. These two stages require quite different approaches.

Early stage *formative evaluations* often use a simple design walk-through. This utilises a simple paper-based, page-by-page, representation of the interface, presented to typical users for comment. For example, Morley and Harris (1994) presented experienced pilots with simple paper-based, PowerPoint™ mock-ups of a new terrain awareness display, depicted in various modes of operation. These were very quick and cheap to produce and pilots were able to freely annotate these paper-based representations, giving the researchers a lasting record of points of concern to modify in the next design iteration, before progressing to the time and expense of producing a computer-based, animated prototype system. This approach is ideal as an initial 'coarse filter' for assessing the design and operating logic of an interface. If the interface passes this test, then you can go on to part-prototype the various components.

This stage of formative evaluation typically uses one (or more) of three approaches. *Experimental approaches* are the most sophisticated. These are most useful when evaluating several competing designs solutions for one aspect of the HMI using a part-prototype. If the system is implemented on a computerised, rapid prototyping system then data such as keystrokes, time, errors, etc. may be logged automatically (see Card *et al.*, 1980). This approach provides objective information about *what* people did but not *why* they did it (i.e. the focus would be on the use and the outcomes achieved when using the HMI but would yield little data about the underlying cognitive mechanisms of the process). For example, we might see that design Option 'A' led operators to make two errors per minute, whereas design Option B led operators to make 10 errors per minute, and often of a certain type. We can see Option A is better, but we can only guess at why. To evaluate the cognitive component it is necessary to supplement the experimental approach with structured questionnaires, subjective workload scales or with a full user debrief.

Observation and qualitative interviews provide data concerning what aspects of the interface users find difficult and why but provide little hard performance data. However, this approach often produces the most useful data for the first design iterations of a system. These are an excellent adjunct to experimental evaluations.

Questionnaires are the best way to evaluate the user's affective response to a system in a structured manner (e.g. to capture data about levels of frustration, workload). Again, these are especially useful when used in conjunction with other approaches.

Several textbooks describing the full range of evaluation approaches are available (e.g. Stanton *et al.*, 2005). There are also compendia describing the range of subjective measures available (e.g. Gawron, 2000). The merits of different research methods are also discussed in Chapter 1 of this text.

Key Learning Point

To evaluate against performance requirements these criteria need to be operationalised. This is sometimes not easy; for example, how would you operationalise 'promoting user understanding'? When developing performance criteria they need to be measurable in some way.

Summative evaluation is the evaluation of the *whole* system in its (almost) final form. The whole system is not just the user interface, software and hardware. It also encompasses supporting material such as manuals and training courses. The tasks undertaken during summative evaluation are representative of the tasks carried out using the whole system in everyday operation. For example, when evaluating an aircraft's flight management system, summative evaluation may be based around setting it up in flight or defining and inserting a new mid-flight. Benchmarking tests of software are also summative evaluations. These also comprise a series of representative tasks, usually undertaken by expert users so that comparisons between systems are not compounded by the effects of expertise.

There are other forms of summative evaluation. Formal test flying and certification are a form of summative evaluation that verifies the design of an aircraft against requirements of all types (both design and legislative). Large, safety-critical systems (e.g. nuclear power plants or petrochemical plants) may be subject to error analyses and probabilistic risk assessments at various stages in their design cycle using a variety of formal techniques. Probabilistic risk analysis techniques (e.g. THERP – technique for human error rate prediction (Swain and Guttman, 1983); HEART – human error assessment and reduction technique (Williams, 1986)) model a range of likely normal and non-normal scenarios that may occur when the system is in use. Typically they integrate procedures, the quality of the interface, the users' characteristics (experience, fatigue, etc.) and their working environment (noise, vibration, temperature, etc.) within a single analysis to produce an estimate of the likelihood of various anticipated failure modes. Human error identification methods (e.g. SHERPA – systematic human error reduction and prediction approach (Embrey, 1986); HET – Human Error Template (Stanton, et al., 2006)) only predict the likely error modes. These latter methods are better used during early design stages where it is quicker and cheaper to correct any HMI or procedural design flaws. Full-scale probabilistic risk-assessment techniques (e.g. THERP or HEART) need a relatively mature, near operational interface and operating concept.

However, these formal methods cannot identify all problems that reside in the depths of the systems that lie dormant until someone tries to use them. It is essential to follow up the performance of a piece of equipment when it enters service, for example using formal reporting procedures. This information will be useful when producing mid-life updates or designing the next generation of the system. Summative evaluation does not stop on release to service. For example, many software companies ask users to send program-generated errors reports over the Internet when software fails or crashes.

Summary

The modern concept of ergonomics is quite different from the old approach which was concerned only with the user interface. Ergonomics is about work systems. Although this section has concentrated on the HCD process it should be evident that this cannot be separated from other activities such as selection, training and other organisational and economic imperatives (such as the requirements to reduce staffing levels or outsource). Ergonomists that restrict themselves to the design of the user interface without considering the wider context are more likely to contribute to the problem rather than its solution. In Chapter 10 we focus on one such situation: the use of communications technology at work.

Ergonomists are often members of a larger design team and there is usually great pressure to produce 'product' – clients like to see something. However, there is an old, cautionary saying: 'there is never enough money available to design it right first time but there is always enough money to re-design it'. If the early stages of the design process (the requirements) are not right no matter how brilliant the designer is, the rest will be of poor quality. Investing money in the early stages of the design process will ultimately save money in the later stages. Therefore it appears that being an ergonomist is one of the least rewarding jobs in the world: if you get it right, no one will notice.

Closing Case Study — Driving (and stopping) on autopilot

Many modern cars have cruise control installed in them but a more advanced form of the technology, adaptive cruise control (ACC) is now available in several makes of luxury car. ACC not only controls the speed of the vehicle but when in traffic moving more slowly than the driver's selected free-traffic speed, the system keeps station (at a set following distance) from the vehicle in front. It does this with the aid of a low-powered radar system. ACC systems also have limited authority over the vehicle's brakes.

However, an even more advanced technology is also now available. Honda's advanced driver assistance system (ADAS) links ACC with a lane-keeping assistance system (LKAS). This combination keeps the vehicle centred in the roadway following a vehicle in front at a set distance without driver input to the steering wheel or throttle – almost analogous to an aircraft's autopilot system. In the ADAS system, three levels of automation are available to the driver: simple cruise control (automation has authority over the throttle); ACC (automation has authority over the throttle and brakes to keep station with the leading vehicle) and ADAS (where the vehicle has authority over throttle, brakes and steering). These modes are arranged hierarchically.

Not all automatic protections (lane keeping and/or following distance) are available in all modes and the ADAS system automatically transitions between modes at set speeds, hence protections that the driver may think are in place are actually not available. Automatic mode transitions were one of the principal concerns identified in the implementation of automation on the flight deck and have been implicated in several aviation accidents and incidents. Furthermore, these new driver aids may be supplemented with collision warning and avoidance systems (CWS/CAS).

With these systems the nature of the primary guidance of the car has changed from one of perceptual-motor control to that of hazard surveillance and automation management.

Source: Don Harris (Chapter author), using Young, Stanton and Harris (2007).

Suggested exercise

Taking a systemic, HFI approach to analysing the problem, the technology and the driver interfaces may be adequate for the job. However, have the requirements for driver training and the regulatory overview for the performance and maintenance of these highly automated systems kept pace? Is there a better way of implementing automation of this type?

Test your learning

Short-answer questions

1   Provide brief definitions of the following: human factors; human-centred design; the sociotechnical context of design; hierarchical task analysis; functional allocation.

2   Provide a brief description of the key stages in the human centred design process.

3   What are the three types of requirement in human centred design?

4   Describe Ackoff's (1989) categories of information.

5   In the human-centred design process, how are the user and organisational requirements specified?

Suggested assignments

1   How can information about end-user requirements be collected during the design process? What are the strengths and weaknesses of the various methods you have identified?

2   How can the eventual success (or failure) of a human centred design process be evaluated?

3   Discuss the impact that the wider organisational context has on the human centred design process.

Relevant websites

The website of the UK Ergonomics Society provides an excellent starting point for exploring the various issues associated with designing work and work environments. It can be found at: http://www.ergonomics.org.uk/.

The US National Institute for Occupation Safety and Health (NIOSH) publishes a number of documents about the impact of the physical aspects of work design on employees. These can be found at: http://www.cdc.gov/niosh/topics/Ergonomics/.

The Usability Professionals' Association website http://www.upassoc.org/ provides some useful definitions and examples of human-centred design. http://www.usabilitynet.org also provides some good descriptions of key elements of the human-centred design process.

For further self-test material and relevant, annotated weblinks please visit the website at **www.pearsoned.co.uk/workpsych**

Suggested further reading

Full details for all references are given in the list at the end of this book.

Excellent introductions to the use of psychology in the design of work and work environments are provided in: Noyes (2001) *Designing for Humans (psychology at work)* and Grandjean and Kroemer (1997). *Fitting the Task to the Human: A textbook of occupational ergonomics* (5th Edition).

The topic of human factors is covered in both breadth and depth in: Stanton *et al.* (2005). *Human Factors Methods: A practical guide for engineering and design.*

CHAPTER 10

Communication technology

LEARNING OUTCOMES

By the end of this chapter you should be able to:

1 identify the core features of dispersed working;

2 describe some of the challenges related to dispersed working and technology-mediated communications;

3 be aware of the relevant theories and literature that help to explain these challenges;

4 develop recommendations on how to design more effective dispersed collaborations.

Working from a distance

More and more people are now working remotely, but what happens to team dynamics when colleagues are based hundreds – or even thousands – of miles apart?

It's hard enough for people to work as a team when they are based in the same building. But for a virtual team of IT developers at Eli Lilly the challenges were much greater.

The 15-strong team was split across a larger group in the centre-west of Germany (Giessen) and two smaller satellites: one in north-east Germany (Berlin) and one in London, England. An added complication was that team members communicated with each other in English, which for many was a second language.

Small wonder, then, that despite the team's shared professional background there were misunderstandings – especially when the software developers used e-mail to convey complex information to each other. Task coordination also became a problem as new members arrived. With role boundaries not always clearly defined and the added problem of distance, uncertainty arose as to who was supposed to carry out activities such as updating the project database. Some tasks fell in the cracks because team members assumed that someone else was dealing with them.

The team responded to these problems by clarifying and modifying individuals' roles. Team-building events also helped cement working relations between colleagues based at the different locations. As one software developer said, the larger group at Giessen all knew each other well, but communications between those working at different sites could initially be a bit cold and impersonal. The team-building events, which were held around three times a year and included workshops and meetings, as well as fun activities such as go-karting, helped break the ice, and over time led to improved communications between team members. Telephone conversations between those who had met several times began to include the social chat that goes on between people who really are part of the same team.

However, there were a number of other problems that needed to be addressed.

The software developers needed to liaise with customers throughout Eli Lilly's European sites. A misunderstanding between a German developer and a Spanish customer illustrates the problem. When the customer took delivery of a product she had ordered, it turned out that there had been confusion about some of the system requirements and their cost. This was partly because of the difficulty of exchanging information about complex technical issues via telephone or e-mail. It didn't help that the customer did not share the developer's technical know-how and that they had been communicating in English, which was neither party's first language.

The IT developers also ran into difficulties when dealing with the UK-based 'server management' team, which was responsible for putting software onto the appropriate server – for example, for testing or development purposes. The development team blamed the server team for causing delays and could not understand why it took them so long to put new software on the right server, while the server team did not understand what the developers' priorities were. Their only communication was via a database, which meant that the development team did not know who was working on their request or what its status was - they just had to wait. One of the developers said that the main problem was that they did not know any of the server team and did not understand how they worked. He pointed out that if the server team had been in the next room, it wouldn't have been such a problem as they could have just gone in and asked them how they were getting on with the work.

Our interviews with people in 32 different organisations who were involved in virtual working suggests that the experience of the Eli Lilly team is typical of the growing number of people who are now collaborating with remote colleagues.

Some of these colleagues may work from home, from multiple locations, such as their cars or client offices, while others may work in a traditional office, but in a different country or region. The flexibility of these arrangements is often hailed as a good thing as it means that people are no longer constrained by where they live. Working with remote colleagues can bring diverse expertise and different local knowledge bases together, and this can have a positive impact on innovation and team effectiveness. However, lack of a common context can also create tensions.

When people work in the same place they can often get away with less than best practice, because there is a shared social system to paper over any cracks. Such colleagues usually understand each other because they come from the same or similar organisational and national backgrounds. Face-to-face communication, whether in meetings or informal corridor chats, enables them to check whether they have understood each other and put right any misunderstandings before they cause too much damage.

The organisations we studied generally agreed that the human and organisational aspects of virtual teamworking hampered effectiveness more than any inadequacies with the technology used to keep remote workers in touch with each other.

This makes it doubly important to stick to good practice and adopt a structured and planned approach to virtual working. But what is good practice for virtual work? Our research suggests that it is largely the same as for co-located working, but more so! The virtual nature of the work exacerbates many of the problems that can occur in any working environment. Those who manage virtual teams therefore need to be aware of these issues and make sure they are prepared to deal with them.

Source: Adapted from Carolyn Axtell, Jo Wheeler, Malcolm Patterson and Anna Leach (now Meachin), 'From a distance'. People Management 25 March 2004, pp. 39-40.

Suggested exercise

As you study this chapter consider the following issues:

How might this organisation (and others) enhance the effectiveness of their virtual teams? What interventions might help to tackle the two specific problems identified in this case study? Then consider some topics outside of this chapter in your answer. For example, how might selection and training be used to address some of the issues raised by this case study?

Introduction

Recent developments in information and communication technologies have transformed the way we work and play. Since the Internet was privatised and opened for commercial use in the early 1990s it has become integral to the way we live and work, providing opportunities for (amongst other things) finding information, buying products, downloading music and communicating with others (Okin, 2005). Personal computers are almost ubiquitous in the workplace, and other technologies are becoming increasingly mobile with ever smaller laptops, mobile phones, handheld computers and e-mail devices. These mobile technologies allow employees more flexibility over the location in which they work and offer the potential to be contacted and to conduct work in a range of places (cafés, trains, hotel rooms or at home) and at different times (e.g. beyond normal office hours). E-mail has also transformed the way we work, allowing written communication and attached documents to be delivered to the other side of the world about as quickly as they can be delivered to the neighbouring desk.

Such advances in technology mean that employees no longer have to be located at the main company office, or be in the same location as their colleagues. This (when coupled with the increase in globalisation) means that more and more collaborative work is being done at a distance (dispersed collaborations) via communications technologies (Duarte and Snyder, 2001). A whole range of work activities are conducted in this way from software development and aircraft design to marketing and management. Such work may cross time zones, national borders and different organisations.

In the following sections we consider such dispersed collaborations in more detail. First we will consider the core features of dispersed collaborations, and look at how they impact upon the work that employees do and the interactions that employees have with each other. Later in this chapter we examine what actions need to be taken with regard to setting up and designing these ways of working.

Core features of dispersed collaborations

Dispersion

The defining feature of a dispersed collaboration is that colleagues are split across different locations. These locations may be few or many in number, separated by only a few, or a few thousand, miles. Whilst some people may have fellow collaborators available at their own location, others may not. Thus, different collaborations may have different levels of dispersion: this has major implications for communications and their functioning in relation to their reliance on technology, the time zones and national boundaries they cross.

Technology-mediated communication

Most immediately, the obvious problem about dispersion is that at least some colleagues are not working together face-to-face and so have to collaborate and interact via communications technologies (such as telephone, e-mail, instant messaging, teleconferencing). Such technologies may be limited in their ability to convey certain types of information. This is the view taken by theories that emphasise the filtering out of social cues in communications technologies. For instance, media richness theory (Daft and Lengel, 1986) proposes that there are objective character-istics of communication media which determine their ability to carry 'rich' infor-mation (i.e. that which contains social, non-verbal and feedback cues) and thus determine the suitability of those media for certain tasks. For instance, text-based communications like e-mail might be considered a relatively 'lean' medium: recipi-ents of the message do not have the benefit of hearing the sender's voice-tone or see-ing their facial expressions to help them understand the message. Moreover, there is typically a long gap between delivering a message and receiving feedback. The tele-phone, however, is relatively 'rich' as a communication medium as 'voice-tone', hes-itation and other auditory cues can be transmitted and these can be immediately heard and responded to by the receiver (thus providing fast feedback). Face-to-face communication is considered the richest due to the high level of visual and auditory cues available.

The lack of social cues in 'lean media' can be problematic for the development of mutual understanding and good relations. Misunderstandings can occur as colleagues may interpret these 'lean' messages using different knowledge bases and may erroneously assume they have understood it the same way (Krauss and Fussell, 1990). For example, one employee may receive an e-mail about last month's sales figures and view it as an 'information update', another employee might see it as pos-itive feedback from management. Moreover, given the lack of feedback cues and false assumptions made, misunderstandings can take some time to come to light. With regard to relationship development, Sproull and Kiesler's (1986) 'lack of social context cues' hypothesis argues that the lack of social cues available in text-based media increases participant anonymity. They argue that the result is that participants pay less attention to themselves and others, resulting in a state of 'deindividuation'. The concept of deindividuation is argued to occur because in text-based electronic communications 'individuating' cues (those cues which give everyone a distinctive character, such as tone of voice, appearance, pace of speech, expression of emotion, etc.) are greatly reduced, rendering the participants relatively anonymous. This state is characterised by feeling less embarrassed or self-conscious as well as more imper-sonal and task-focused. People become less inhibited which can result in reduced politeness and increased hostility and intolerance (e.g. an employee typing some-thing in an e-mail that they would not say to the recipient face-to-face or over the telephone). As a result of this, relationship development can be impeded.

Key Learning Point

Some communications media have the capacity to deliver more social cues than others, with face-to-face communication having the richest array of cues available whereas text-based media are lean in comparison.

Whilst some research supports these theories, media richness and lack of social context cues approaches have been criticised for (i) being too technologically de-terministic and (ii) for not considering the impact of the cues remaining in the media or (iii) the possibilities of people adapting to the technology and adapting the technology to their needs. For instance, Joseph Walther (1992) proposed the social information processing (SIP) hypothesis, which states that despite there being less social information available via text-based media like e-mail, users adapt to using the social information that is available (although processing these cues is slower than face-to-face interaction). Indeed, in support of this, Walther and colleagues have found that with the social cues that are available in text-based media (such as time taken to receive a response, the style or content of the message) strong relationships can develop using this media, but they take longer to grow (e.g. Walther, 1993). The impersonal and task-focused communications suggested by the lack of social context cues hypothesis might therefore only be expected in very short-term computer-mediated collaborations.

However, other research has also found that even very early on in the communication process, few differences are found between relations in some face-to-face and computer-mediated groups (e.g. Walther and Burgoon, 1992). It also appears that relations can sometimes be more positive when computer-mediated than when face-to-face (Walther, 1995). One reason for this might be that if people expect there to be lots of future interaction right from the start, then communication is likely to become affiliative and positive almost immediately (Walther, 1994).

Another explanation for these sorts of effect is offered by the social identification/ deindividuation (SIDE) model (Lea and Spears, 1992; Spears and Lea, 1994). Earlier we examined the idea that this depersonalises communication. However, according to SIDE, deindividuation results in attention being shifted away from a focus on individual differences and towards a group identity. The limited cues that are available in the communication media (such as the department that the sender of the e-mail works within) take on relatively greater importance such that stereotypical impressions of communication partners are developed. A common group identity may be inferred from these impressions which can promote immediate attraction.

Walther also extended his SIP theory to develop the 'hyperpersonal perspective' (Walther, 1996) to take account of the more intense relationships that can develop via communications technology. Again, it is argued to be the limited cues available electronically (which may be selectively revealed by the communication partners for purposes of impression management) that take on relatively greater importance. For instance, if a remote colleague sends a speedy response to an initial e-mail, then they might create the impression of being efficient and responsive. These cues may contribute disproportionately to impressions of others in the absence of any evidence to the contrary (especially when a long-term relationship is expected and there is a shared social identity). As a result impressions of others tend to become exaggerated and 'idealised'. This effect, however, may not be very stable. For instance, one study of student teams (Walther et al., 2001) found that after hyperpersonal relations had developed via communications technology, showing photographs of team members reduced affection and affiliation within the team. Thus, whilst relations developed exclusively across communications technology may be very positive at first, they are based on limited (and perhaps biased) information and so may be rather fragile in nature.

Key Learning Point

Although there are fewer social cues available in text-based communications media like e-mail, this does not necessarily result in less positive social relations. However, these relations may be more unrealistic and fragile.

Designing for dispersion

As a result of the core features of dispersed collaborations (dispersion and technology mediation) there is a need to consider how such collaborations should be designed and implemented. However, it is the human and organisational issues, rather than the technology itself, that tend to be the most difficult to deal with in these collaborations. Naturally, the characteristics of the technology (i.e. limited cues) can exacerbate these problems. Some of the important considerations in planning for a dispersed team are outlined below.

Preparation

In line with the design of any product, spending time on the preparation stages before implementation is crucial. Similar to the notions of concept formation and functional specification discussed in Chapter 9 there needs to be clear identification of a mission (i.e. what the collaborators are going to do) and how they are going to do it: a clearly understood statement of direction is required (Duarte and Snyder, 2001). Some forethought is also required on how the task will be completed and the context in which it will be done (its functional/organisational/national context). Contextual issues concern the membership of the collaboration (and its diversity) as well as the organisational processes and structures (such as organisational philosophy, reward structures, management style). Being aware of the problems that can occur and preparing for these helps to alleviate problems later on. The following sections therefore outline the task, membership and contextual issues that need to be considered in the design of dispersed collaborations.

Key Learning Point

When designing a dispersed collaboration, preparation is key. The human and organisational issues are particularly important: just planning the technology is likely to lead to failure.

The nature of the task and dispersed collaboration

The type of task is likely to influence the ease with which the dispersed colleagues can conduct their work and so should be considered within the design of a dispersed collaboration. Tasks vary in their level of interdependence (the extent to which co-workers rely on each other's outputs to complete the task) and information requirements (e.g. cognitive, behavioural or emotional). Media richness and lack of social context cues approaches suggest that complex tasks that require a high level of information exchange, coordinated effort, consensus, negotiation, ambiguity or emotion are not suitable for 'leaner' technologies such as e-mail: instead they might require a richer media (preferably face-to-face). Simple, routine, independent and non-emotive tasks are considered to be suited to less rich technologies (e.g. Riopelle *et al.*, 2003). This line of reasoning has led many commentators to advocate that dispersed collaborations should be designed for independence (working within rather than across locations) and that where interdependence cannot be avoided, then face-to-face meetings should be encouraged (e.g. Eppinger, 2001).

The problem with this line of reasoning is that such a practice might enhance subgroup formation and conflict because it removes some of the ties across locations (*see* the next section on diversity). Interdependence and connectivity across locations might help to increase cohesion and trust within the team, particularly in the early stages of the task. Consistent with this idea, Hertel and colleagues (2004) found in a field study of dispersed teams that task interdependence was strongly related to team effectiveness in the first year of the team's life. However, once the team was established task interdependence had little impact on effectiveness. This finding suggests that it might be worth tolerating the initial process and coordination losses of high interdependence because is allows good relations to develop in the group. Interdependence can then be reduced once solid relations have developed.

It might also be the case that the team will adapt to using less rich communications media, particularly once a common language and understanding have been developed. For instance, a study of rocket engine design engineers found that at least some ambiguous tasks (such as clarifying and changing project objectives or specifications, learning about unfamiliar parts of the concept, and understanding design concerns of other team members) could be conducted via collaborative technology rather than face-to-face (Majchrzak *et al.*, 2000). This was thought to be due to the common language and understanding that had been developed in earlier face-to-face meetings. The existence of common language and understanding might mean that if interdependence is used in a mature dispersed collaboration, process losses might be less of a problem (at least for some types of task). Thus, in terms of task design for dispersed collaborations, it might be prudent to design tasks that encourage initial interdependence, but this can be relaxed later for tasks that do not adapt well to the less rich media.

Key Learning Point

There is a tension between designing for 'interdependent' work and designing for 'independent' work. Interdependent work can help to develop relations at a distance and people may adapt to using the leaner media. However, designing for independent work can help to reduce the process and coordination losses that occur when collaborating at a distance.

Diversity

One of the reasons organisations employ dispersed collaborations is to take advantage of expertise from different functions, organisations and countries. This means that such collaborations may be quite diverse. Thus, a further complication for dispersed collaborations is the addition of 'culture'; the different values, assumptions and expectations that guide human behaviour. There may be national cultural differences between colleagues as well as differences in organisational culture and functional/professional culture. These need to be understood and dealt with if the collaborators are to work together successfully (Duarte and Snyder, 2001). The different members of the collaboration may have different expectations and ways of doing things that are not compatible across the group. Moreover, there may be differences in language (not just between national languages but different uses of language across professions and even organisations). Therefore, the different cultural and language perspectives may lead those in the collaboration to make different assumptions and develop different understandings about the same information. This diversity may also affect relations because it may be harder to develop a shared social identity if other collaborators in the group are considered to be different (cf. Tajfel, 1981 – *see* also Chapter 2). Therefore, diversity can have a profound effect on how a dispersed collaboration functions. In particular, location may form the basis of social identities since those at the same location are likely to share more attributes (e.g. nationality, language, organisational culture) with each other than with team members at other locations. These may form dividing lines or 'faultlines' (cf. Lau and Murnighan, 1998) between locations splitting them into subgroups, resulting in greater conflict and lower trust between subgroups. Such processes are likely to result in performance losses, especially when the differences between the locations are greater. Polzer and colleagues (2006) found experimental support for the negative impact of these 'faultlines', with the effects being strongest when there were two subgroups of equal size and when there was national homogeneity within each subgroup. The effect was weakest when teams were fully dispersed (with each person at a different location) because subgroups could not form on the basis of shared location.

Thus, whilst there might be advantages to having diverse knowledge available within dispersed collaborations, the diversity associated with dispersion can lead to process problems due to subgroup formation. As a result, selection of dispersed colleagues should not only focus on their technical expertise but also on their ability to communicate and work within a multidisciplinary/multicultural environment. Where possible these collaborations should also be designed so that they are not split into two very different locations. In addition, efforts should be made to build relations across the potential faultlines (e.g. by highlighting and focusing on similarities across locations and maintaining a high level of communication across different sites).

Key Learning Point

Distant colleagues may be thought of as 'different' which might lead to subgroup formation. This can be problematic for collaborative relationships and so efforts need to be made to build strong relationships across locations.

Organisational context

The organisational structure(s) and processes within which the dispersed collaboration is located is also likely to have a profound impact on team functioning. For instance, Rennecker (2002) found that the local rhythms, relationships, rules, politics and resources at the different locations affected the contributions that those in each location made to the team.

First, the general organisational philosophy and culture is likely to have an impact on the success of the team. For instance, organisations that focus on technology rather than people may find their dispersed collaborations are less successful (Cramton and Webber, 2005). This is because their collaborations are likely to be structured around the technological systems rather than the social systems: what is required for success is *joint* optimisation of the technical and social systems (cf. socio-technical theory, Cherns, 1976). Moreover, people and organisational skills might be overlooked in a technically oriented organisational environment yet these skills are particularly crucial to the success of dispersed collaborations (Kirkman *et al.*, 2002). Therefore, ensuring that the organisational culture is suitable for collaborating at a distance is very important.

Second, there is a need to ensure consistency of reward structures, availability of communications technologies and managerial support at the different locations. For instance, differences in access to technology and communication transmission speeds were found to have a detrimental impact on dispersed student team functioning in a study by Cramton (2001). These differences in access led to feelings of isolation and being 'out of synch' with the rest of the team (see the Closing case study for more detail). Moreover, if reward structures are different at different locations (which might be more likely when collaborating across organisational boundaries) then this may cause feelings of inequality. In dispersed collaborations, team-based incentives and rewards might be appropriate for encouraging cooperation. In contrast, individual skill-based rewards might help to stimulate the development of the necessary skills for working at a distance (Lawler, 2003). Indeed, some support has been found for the effectiveness of team-based recognition in dispersed collaborations (Hertel *et al.*, 2004).

Third, another concern is how obligations towards the dispersed collaboration will coincide with other commitments within the organisation. For instance, there may be conflicts between commitments to the local site and commitments to distant colleagues: these conflicts can have a large impact on employee contributions to the dispersed collaboration (Axtell *et al.*, 2004). The extent to which employees are embedded within their local environment (in terms of having a lot of social and work ties) has been found to have an impact: those who are less locally embedded have been found to contribute more to their dispersed collaboration (Fleck, 2005). When collaborations cross multiple organisational units, functional groups or even different organisations these challenges may become more severe. Maintaining organisational support and resources across these different boundaries therefore requires good boundary management skills (Hertel *et al.*, 2005).

Fourth, there are different ways that the collaboration could be managed. Because they cannot see their dispersed subordinates, managers might try to control them by closely monitoring (e.g. using electronic performance data). This type of activity might be particularly evident when dispersed colleagues are conducting relatively routine tasks and in industries that already monitor employees (call centres are one such example (*see* Valsechi, 2006)). However, the types of behaviour that can be observed electronically tend to be rather limited (e.g. log-on/log-off, length of call, work rate) and it can be quite stressful for the employees (Hertel *et al.*, 2005). In the absence of such monitoring capabilities, managers might attempt to control employees through formal coordination mechanisms such as detailed project plans, deadlines, formal handover points and clear task specifications (Hinds and Bailey, 2003).

An alternative approach is to manage by trust rather than control. This type of approach emphasises the commitment of employees and allows them the autonomy to self-manage and regulate their own actions (Bell and Kozlowski, 2002). The task of management then becomes one of (participatively) setting goals and monitoring outcomes rather than processes. This type of management philosophy was examined by Hertel *et al.* (2004) who found a relationship between team perceptions of quality of goal-setting and managers' ratings of dispersed team effectiveness (good-quality goal-setting being linked to team effectiveness). However, trust and control may not be mutually exclusive philosophies. Many studies have found that having team controls (such as goal-setting and deadlines) in place can help to increase trust because such measures reduce uncertainty (e.g. Crisp and Jarvenpaa, 2000; Walther and Bunz, 2005). Thus it may be necessary to find a balance between trust and control when managing dispersed collaborations (Axtell *et al.*, 2004).

Finally, an important issue in dispersed collaborations is that of 'contextual awareness', i.e. an awareness of the situation that the distant colleague is in. People are generally very aware of the situation they themselves are in and the influence that this has on their own behaviour, but tend to underestimate the influence of the situation on other people's behaviour. When judging the cause of another person's actions people tend to overestimate the influence that the other person's disposition has on their behaviour. This is called 'the fundamental attribution error' (Ross, 1977). In part this is due to the lack of awareness of the situation the other person is in: this effect is likely to be exacerbated in dispersed teams where the other person (and their situation) is at a distance and not visible or readily accessible (Cramton, 2002). Without this contextual awareness the few cues available via communications technologies are likely to be the only ones that are used when making attributions about remote colleagues (e.g. that they did not reply to an e-mail). Therefore this behaviour may be attributed to them being lazy or rude (Cramton, 2001). A dispositional attribution is made that fails to consider the situation the remote person is in (e.g. that they are extremely busy or they did not receive the message because their technology is not working). Naturally, such negative attributions can cause relational problems.

However, Cramton and her colleagues have found that ensuring that communication partners are aware of the other person's situation can reduce these attribution errors (Cramton *et al.*, 2007) and that accompanying situational explanations with expressions of respect and concern (e.g. if someone missed a deadline) can help to repair relations (Cramton and Wilson, 2002). This research shows how important it is that dispersed collaborators learn about each other's contexts and are aware of the situation their dispersed colleagues are in. Mechanisms for doing this might include arranging visits to each other's locations, having online biographies of team members which have sections on 'work context' and ensuring that contextual issues are mentioned in other communications.

Key Learning Point

It is important not to forget the organisational context in which the dispersed collaboration is going to operate when setting up and designing it. Features such as the culture, reward structures, other organisational obligations, management philosophy and level of awareness of distant colleague's organisational contexts are all likely to have an impact on success.

Summary

More and more people are working remotely as a result of increased globalisation and advances in communications technologies. Certain challenges arise for colleagues working in this way, such as the variation in the ability of different communications technologies to transmit certain 'rich' information which can hamper relationship formation. However, people may adapt to using such media and the expectation of future communications and development of common group identities can help to override the negative impacts of leaner media. When setting up such collaborations choices need to be made about whether colleagues work interdependently across sites or independently (within site) and how to manage the diversity in the team and the organisational context in which the collaborators work. Preparation is key when designing such collaborations. Ignoring the human and social aspects and just focusing on the technical issues is bound to lead to failure.

Closing Case Study　　The importance of 'mutual knowledge'

Catherine Cramton (2001) studied a set of 13 internationally dispersed student project teams. Each team had six members with two pairs of students at two different US universities and one pair at a university located either in Canada, Australia or Portugal. Some of the students who participated were international exchange students and so there was a variety of nationalities involved. The project spanned a seven-week period.

Cramton found that failures of mutual knowledge were the most important problem faced by the teams. She identified:

1. Failure to communicate and retain contextual information about distant colleagues – e.g. the timing of the spring break was different at different universities, so some team members disappeared without warning, whilst their distant colleagues were working on things and requiring their input.

2. Unevenly distributed information – e.g. sometimes e-mails or information was sent to only part of the team which led to different perspectives on the task developing at the different locations.

3. Differences in speed of access to information – e.g. some students had 24-hour access to e-mail whereas others only had access when at their university. When using chat facilities, it was also noted that the Australian members seemed to be lagging behind in the discussion such that the exchanges between the American students kept being interrupted by messages from the Australians which referred to subjects from which they had already moved on. This caused tension and frustration within the team as the Australians' contributions were seemingly ignored because they were 'out of synch' with the rest of the team.

4. Difficulty communicating and understanding the salience of information – e.g. when writing an e-mail students tended to assume that what was salient to them in the message would be salient to others (students would differ in which topics they thought were most prominent).

5. Difficulty interpreting the meaning of silence – silence could mean all sorts of things from agreement, disagreement, indifference, away for a few days, too busy to respond, having technical problems, didn't realise a response was required, etc.

These difficulties tended to result in negative 'dispositional' attributions about remote colleagues (e.g. that they were lazy, aggressive or rude) and had a negative impact on relationships and team functioning.

Suggested exercises

What does Catherine Cramton's research tell us about how dispersed collaborations should be designed and managed within organisations?

Consider the setting for, and the participants in, this research. To what extent can we use the findings to provide guidance to commercial organisations? Which findings do you think might be most likely to transfer to organisations, and which might not?

Test your learning

Short-answer questions

1   Describe the different theoretical viewpoints regarding the impact of technology-mediated communications on dispersed working.

2   What factors contribute to misunderstandings in dispersed collaborations?

3   What are the key areas to focus on when designing for dispersion?

Suggested assignments

1   The CEO of a large multinational organisation tells you he has ensured he has the most up-to-date technology for collaboration across the different sites of his organisation. He feels that as long as the technology is right, the human and organisational factors will not be a problem. Drawing on the relevant literature in this area write a report that will convince this CEO that these factors are important and should be considered.

2   A team of employees is made up of people who work in different parts of the same building. Because of a company re-structuring half of the team members move out of the building to a new site 50 kilometres away. The team of employees still work together on the same set of tasks. What are the problems that might occur during this change? What could be done to prevent these problems from happening or to minimise their impact?

3   What can psychological theory and research tell us about how effectively people work together when most of the communication between them is technology-mediated communication?

Relevant websites

Virtual Teams: teams developed and/or operated over the Internet/Web. http://www.managementhelp.org/grp_skll/virtual/virtual.htm.

 For further self-test material and relevant, annotated weblinks please visit the website at **www.pearsoned.co.uk/workpsych**

Suggested further reading

Full details for all references are given in the list at the end of this book.

The three texts listed here all provide more detailed reviews of the issues discussed in this chapter. Virtual working raises a variety of issues in addition to the study of remote working. Therefore reading the Hislop *et al.* reference would be a good starting point, followed by one of the two other works cited.

Axtell, C., Fleck, S. and Turner, N. (2004) 'Virtual teams: collaborating across distance'.

Hertel, G., Geister, S. and Konradt, U. (2005) 'Managing virtual teams: A review of current empirical research'.

Hislop, D., Axtell, C. and Daniels, K. (2008) 'The challenge of remote working'.

CHAPTER 11

Training and development

LEARNING OUTCOMES

After studying this chapter, you should be able to:

1. identify, describe and explain the three components of the learning cycle;

2. understand how training and development activities in organisations have changed over the past 30 years;

3. describe and explain the purpose of three different levels of training needs analysis;

4. explain how learning theories can be used to inform training design;

5. identify potential barriers to the successful transfer of learning to the workplace and how these might be addressed;

6. understand the importance of training evaluation in determining the effectiveness and utility of training interventions;

7. discuss ways in which e-learning is changing how training is delivered and managed;

8. describe and evaluate two different models of training evaluation;

9. understand how training contributes to organisational learning;

10. discuss the concept of communities of practice and how these contribute to knowledge sharing in organisations.

Opening Case Study | The challenge of Generation Y

'Generation Y'ers are lifestyle-centred, impatient and socially aware. Managers see them as having "self-esteem on steroids" and confidence that exceeds their competence.' Peter Sheehan (2005)

Over the coming years Generation Y will present a significant challenge to employers across all work sectors. Also known as 'Echo Boomers' or the 'Millennium Generation', 'Gen Y' were born 1978-1989. They have new attitudes to work, bring new skills and values to the workplace, and have new expectations about how they should be treated by managers and employers. Whereas Generation X (born 1965-1976) are approaching middle years and middle organisational levels, Gen Y are now eager to stake their own claim on the workplace.

This group poses an interesting challenge to HR professionals on many fronts, but their supposed desire to advance quickly, draw information from many different sources and to learn also illustrates the increasing focus on (i) the availability of information and (ii) the acquisition of skills as key to the modern, flexible and successful worker.

However, at the very same time that Gen Y are joining the workforce, organisations are faced with a faster pace of change, and greater transition in employment trends than ever before. Major demographic change and new government legislation mean a rapidly ageing workforce. In addition, there is an increasing focus on job-change, boundaryless careers, changing psychological contracts and innovation at work (Arnold and Cohen, 2008; Jacoby, 1999; Offerman and Gowing, 1990).

The new virtual reality workplace, where jobs and work relationships can be displaced in both time and location, means that individuals who can cope with multi-tasking and flexibility are at a premium. In many ways Gen Y, who are more IT-savvy than previous generations and who often possess technical skills that far exceed those of their employers, are well placed to meet this need. Whilst they may present significant opportunities for organisations, however, they also bring important challenges. In particular, little is known about the people strategies that will be needed to maximise the potential of Gen Y in an increasingly multigenerational workforce.

Source: Prof. Jo Silvester, City University, London.

Suggested exercise

As you read this chapter think about how 'Generation Y' employees might react to the various training strategies used by employers.

Introduction

Training and development activities have the potential to benefit individuals, organisations and society as a whole. By engaging in training, an employee can develop a portfolio of skills, enhance their promotion opportunities, take part in more interesting work and move more easily between jobs and organisations. The opening case study illustrates the thirst for training among those currently entering the workforce, and the need for organisations to deliver high-quality training in order to meet the changing demands that are placed upon them. Skilled individuals perform their jobs faster and more safely, they make fewer mistakes and produce higher quality work. Therefore by offering training, organisations can benefit from increased productivity, safer work environments, improved employee well-being and lower levels of absenteeism and employee turnover. However, groups of employees such as Generation Y'ers are unlikely to be satisfied with basic on-the-job training: they are likely to be looking to the future, seeking ways to maximise their own potential. It is also important to recognise that investing in training and development is important for society as a whole. Therefore, a key question for occupational psychologists might be: how can we draw upon the drive, confidence and enthusiasm of Generation Y?

The economic competitiveness of a nation is related to its skill base. Not only is it important that organisations are able to attract and recruit skilled workers, but inward investment to a country from overseas companies can also depend upon the existence of a pool of skilled workers. For example, Japanese investment in the UK car industry during the 1990s was a good example of this. More recently Western-based companies have invested in India, exploiting the rapid growth in IT and support skills offered by Indian employees. In the case of European Union expansion, we have also seen the migration of skilled workers to countries where there are more jobs and higher wages. Today's global economy has driven an exponential growth in demand for people with high-level technical and social skills who have the ability to adapt quickly to changing circumstances and needs. For this reason governments often direct considerable efforts towards encouraging organisations to invest in the training and development of their staff. At the time of writing (2009) many governments are emphasising the need for investment in training in order to help their economies through the current global economic downturn. Efforts are also directed towards educational institutions in an attempt to ensure that students develop the skills needed for national and international economic prosperity.

The speed at which companies and markets now operate has meant that employee training and development are becoming increasingly important at a strategic level within organisations. As the opening case study shows, we have moved a long way from the traditional association between training and craft apprenticeships. As little as 30 years ago training was generally seen as a way of equipping individuals who were beginning their careers with a set of skills that were likely to remain core to their work for the rest of their working life. Organisations could afford to provide apprentices with five years of training in a specific area such as machine tooling, carpentry and precision engineering (because jobs were unlikely to change and employees were unlikely to move companies). Today apprenticeships, particularly craft apprenticeships, are hard to find. Job changes that have been driven by technological development mean that individuals must continually learn new skills, and how to use new tools and systems, just to keep up with job demands. Moreover, Generation Y individuals will not be content just to 'keep up'. The need for continual learning has been emphasised further by the evolution of flatter organisational structures. In order to progress, employees are expected to develop a diverse portfolio of skills by moving sideways and gaining skills in new roles. This means that organisations have the flexibility to move people to different positions and adapt more quickly and effectively to changing environments.

Given such widespread changes to the world of work it is not surprising that the activities of trainers and training departments have become more complex and central to organisations. Rather than providing discrete individual training courses that focus on specific needs, training departments are now primarily responsible for creating learning organisations where employees and managers engage in continual learning as part of their roles. For the purposes of this chapter we focus on 'training' in terms of the organised efforts by organisations to provide employees with structured opportunities to learn and develop within their work role. This can range from one-off courses on customer service skills, to induction training for new staff and to more comprehensive training programmes aligned to business change objectives. Therefore, learning in organisations can occur at any point – and generally does (e.g. a new team member may learn how they are expected to behave simply by observing other members). However, in this chapter, we focus on development and change that take place in a more controlled and planned fashion. Other chapters also present material of considerable importance to the training process including, in particular, job analysis (Chapters 3 and 9), performance appraisal (Chapter 6) and coaching and mentoring (Chapter 15).

Key Learning Point

Training activities are now a continual feature of organisational life.

The training cycle

Although training and development activities can benefit individuals, organisations and society as a whole, it is important to note that training per se is not necessarily beneficial. Too little, too much or the wrong type of training can cause problems. Indeed, training that is inappropriate for the specific needs of the individual or the organisation can be worse than no training at all. In short, training is only beneficial if it is based upon a needs analysis, is designed in a way that ensures this need is met, and we can only know if training is beneficial if we evaluate its success. Therefore, training needs analysis (TNA), training design (TD) and training evaluation (TE) are the three components that constitute the training cycle. Together they form a tripod that supports effective training. All three are equally vital: if one 'leg' of the tripod is poorly constructed or is missing, then the training is likely to fail. As Figure 11.1 shows, the training and development process moves from assessment of need, through programme development, to an evaluation of what has taken place.

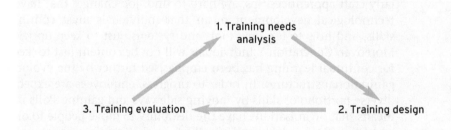

1. Training needs analysis

3. Training evaluation

2. Training design

Figure 11.1   The training cycle

This is described as a cycle, because the information gained through TE should be used to improve future training activities as part of a continuous feedback system. Each of these three elements is considered in more detail over the next sections.

Key Learning Point

Training needs analysis (TNA), training design (TD) and training evaluation (TE) constitute the three stages of the training cycle.

Training needs analysis

Before starting any systematic training or development activity, those responsible should satisfy themselves that it will produce worthwhile results. Unfortunately, a detailed analysis of training needs does not always happen. On occasions, training programmes can take on a more or less independent life of their own and can occur regardless of any clear and established need for them; managers may believe that training (any training) is simply a 'good thing', or that bringing employees together will promote team-building. An employee may also be asked to attend training because their manager has a performance objective to ensure that all employees attend five days of training per year. However, if no needs assessment has been undertaken, how do we to know that attending this training will be worthwhile? Poorly conceived training programmes can be extremely costly for organisations. Money and time are needed to develop, implement and manage the training; there may be a reduction in productivity as employees are away from their work. Not surprisingly, senior managers are likely to ask for a justification of expenses in terms of return on investment (ROI).

Exercise 11.1   The importance of training needs analysis

Mercom, a company providing telephone support for organisational clients, has received a growing number of complaints about its customer service department. The senior managers conclude that their staff lack skills, and invite an external training agency in to run a mandatory two-day training course in customer service skills. Had they had undertaken a training needs analysis, however, they would have discovered that the problem was not one of poor skills, but low morale caused by an autocratic section leader.

Suggested exercises

1   What might be the consequences of sending staff on this customer service training?

2   What could the senior managers have done to establish the reasons behind the high number of customer complaints?

3   How might you assess this section leader's training needs?

A training needs analysis (TNA) is the important first step in developing a training programme. Its primary aim is to identify the training objectives (TOs) or, in simple terms, what the training needs to achieve. Training objectives can be diverse and range from individual to organisational level. For example, an *organisational training objective* might be that all members of a marketing department should be trained in how to use a new client database system within three months. Induction training for staff working in a chain of coffee shops might include *individual training objectives* such as: trainees should be able to recognise and describe the different types of coffee on sale, or trainees should demonstrate knowledge of health and safety legislation governing the provision of hot food and drinks. As TNA is concerned with identifying what the important outcomes of a training programme *should* be: the more precisely a training need can be specified, the more focused the training can be. Thus TNA also has an important impact upon how the training is designed, delivered and evaluated. In reality, however, assessing training needs is not a mechanistic procedure: it involves a significant amount of judgement. In order to properly identify the training need, it is useful to distinguish between three basic levels of needs analysis: (1) organisational analysis, (2) job/task/role analysis and (3) person analysis.

Key Learning Point

The more precisely a training need can be specified, the more focused the training can be. Training needs can be assessed at three levels: organisational, job/task/role and person.

Organisational analysis

The purpose of undertaking a TNA at the organisational level is to understand where training activities fit into the wider organisational systems and how they relate to organisational strategy. In broad terms it asks 'what are the training needs of the whole organisation?' A first step might be to examine and discuss with senior personnel a company's strategic aims and policy statements. Organisational training needs generally exist when there is some sort of barrier hindering the achievement of organisational aims and objectives. For example, a food company establishing a new green-field production site might need to recruit 100 new employees. A merger between two organisations is likely to mean that employees will need training to use new computer systems. However, it is important to stress that such problems represent training needs *only* if the barrier to the achievement of aims and objectives is best removed by training rather than by some other activity. It is important to recognise that training is not a panacea for the challenges facing organisations. It may be more cost-effective or faster for a company to, for example, recruit individuals who already possess the required skills (Chapter 4), by redesigning the job itself (Chapter 8), by redesigning work equipment (Chapter 9) or by improving leadership (Chapter 14).

Another reason for an organisational TNA is to determine whether the organisation's investment in training provision areas across different parts of the organisation is appropriate for the organisation's needs. Senior managers usually control the level of resources devoted to training, and as such they need information about why the training is needed, together with its costs and likely ROI. Linking training interventions with corporate strategy ensures that funds invested in training are used most effectively.

Task and role analysis

Task analysis is sometimes also referred to as job or role analysis. This level of TNA is similar to job analysis (see Chapters 4 and 9). It involves determining the tasks that must be performed by an employee and the *knowledge, skills, abilities and attitudes* that they require to perform them well. In contrast to job analysis it focuses specifically on the tasks in relation to training objectives. It breaks down tasks into separate 'operations', which are defined by Annett *et al.* (1971) as 'any unit of behaviour, no matter how long or short its duration and no matter how simple or complex its structure, which can be defined in terms of its objective'. *Hierarchical task analysis* (HTA) is a technique that involves analysing and breaking down tasks into increasingly specific operations in a hierarchical fashion. HTA begins with a general description of the main operation(s) involved in the job or job components being analysed. These operations are then divided into sub-operations and, in turn, the sub-operations themselves may be subdivided. A good example of how HTA has been used to break down the components of a person working in a call centre service department can be observed by requesting information from the telephone helpline of a mobile phone company. At each level there a number of options that the customer can choose from. This represents a hierarchical decision-tree structure, with the questions representing the different questions that a receptionist might ask a customer phoning in for assistance. They can therefore be seen as sub-operations. Some of the advantages and disadvantages of this approach to analysis are also discussed in Chapter 9.

Several other analytical procedures are useful in the training needs assessment phase. Questionnaires can be used to collect relevant information from different groups of people with varying perspectives (e.g. job holders, managers or customers). The Position Analysis Questionnaire (www.paq.com) contains a number of structured questions about the nature of a job that can be used to identify the key components of the job. Interviews and discussion-based data collection procedures are also useful, and in many settings detailed observation of relevant jobs and job holders is essential. Probed-protocol analysis (see Kraiger *et al.*, 1993), is a technique that uses structured interviews to elicit information relating to training needs in roles where knowledge and cognitive skills form the basis for task performance. For example, it is difficult to observe the work undertaken by computer programmers because much of this takes place in their heads: so this type of task is not well-suited to analysis by traditional HTA methodology. In these cases probed-protocol analysis is used to elicit the main cognitive strategies that trainees will need to learn. For a more detailed review of the different techniques that can be used in task analysis *see* Patrick (1992).

Person analysis

Whereas task analysis determines the skills needed to perform a task or job, person analysis involves identifying *who needs training* and *what kind of training they require*. Person analysis may take place in response to a specific organisational need, such as determining whether a group of individuals possess specific skill levels. This might occur after a selection procedure when an applicant's performance in an assessment centre is used to identify training needs and recommendations for how a new member of staff should be trained. Person analysis is also an ongoing part of many performance management schemes. During appraisal interviews managers and employees often discuss current and future training needs: in so doing they are conducting a person-level analysis of training needs. Devolving responsibility for TNA to managers and employees is increasingly common. It is part of the philosophy of a learning organisation that argues for the need for individuals to take responsibility for their own development, supported by their line managers (*see also* Chapter 16). There are many advantages of this approach, but problems can occur if there are disagreements about the nature and importance of the learning needs, and the availability or access to appropriate training. This is one of the reasons why training managers to conduct appraisals is so important.

STOP TO CONSIDER

What might be the advantages and disadvantages of:

1 Employees identifying their own training needs?

2 Line managers identifying the training needs of their employees?

3 Senior managers identifying the training needs of their employees?

For person-level needs analysis to be targeted effectively, distinctions have traditionally been made between the development of knowledge, skills and attitudes (KSA).[1] According to this distinction, knowledge is concerned with the recall and understanding of facts and other items of information. Skills may be used with reference to the psychomotor movements involved in practical activities such as operating equipment or machinery, but may also incorporate higher-order cognitive or interpersonal processes (e.g. how to think during a complex negotiation, a sales process or a difficult customer interaction). Attitudes refer primarily to the emotional or affective feelings and views that a person has, although attitudes also have other components (*see* Chapter 7). For example, a person might be able to operate a drilling machine (skill) and might also be aware that certain safety procedures should be observed (knowledge) but feel that observing such procedures is a waste of time and unnecessary (attitude). The six types of learning identified by Gagné (1977) in Table 11.1 provide a much more comprehensive description than the KSA distinction.

To summarise, a TNA identifies the objectives of training in terms of required outcomes. It can occur at one of three levels: organisational, job or task and individual level. Training is best thought of as part of a wider system; however, organisations change, as do jobs and people. Therefore, TNA should ideally be a continuous process which feeds into the development of training programmes, ensuring that they can be adapted to the changing needs of individuals and companies.

---

[1] Rather confusingly, contemporary American industrial/organisational psychologists use the term KSAs to refer to knowledge, skills and *abilities*. As we have seen in Chapter 3, abilities (e.g. numerical reasoning, verbal reasoning, etc.) tend to be stable throughout adult life.

Table 11.1	Gagné's six types of learning: what he calls 'capabilities'

1 Basic learning

Stimulus-response associations and chains. This represents the formation of simple associations between stimuli and responses such as those that occur during classical conditioning. For example, for someone learning to drive a train, they might be told that a red signal light means stop the train: in this action there is no 'thinking' to be done.

2 Intellectual skills (divided into the following hierarchy)

(a) Discriminations, being able to make distinctions between stimulus objects or events. For example, a train driver needs to be able to reliably discriminate between red signal lights, green signal lights and red flashing signal lights (etc.).

(b) Concrete concepts, classification of members of a class by observation. For example, a train driver might need to know that lights in the driver's cab can be round, triangular, red, yellow, green, etc.

(c) Defined concepts, classification by definition (e.g. weight, speed, personality). For example, a train driver would need to know whether the speedometer was calibrated in miles per hour or kilometres per hour.

(d) Rules, use of a relation or association to govern action. For example, during their training, a train driver might be instructed never to exceed a certain speed within 500 metres of a signal.

(e) Higher-order rules, generation of new rules (e.g. by combining existing rules). To extend the train driver example, it might be that flashing red triangular lights in the cabin are warnings that something might be wrong, but that stopping the train immediately is usually unnecessary.

3 Cognitive strategy

Skills by which internal cognitive processes such as attention and learning are regulated (e.g. learning how to learn or learning general strategies for solving problems). For example, senior executives might need to learn to deal with their anxiety in some way before they can free up enough cognitive resources to gather information about a client's reaction to an important presentation.

4 Verbal information

Ability to state specific information. For example, a salesperson might need to give a clear and well-structured presentation to persuade some clients to place an order for a new product.

5 Motor skills

Organised motor acts need to be trained for many job roles. Returning to the train driver example, they might need to be trained to do several motor tasks (e.g. pull levers to control the speed of the train, watch for track-side signals, cancel or acknowledge warning signals by pressing buttons, etc.). They might also need to be trained to do several of these things in sequence or in parallel.

6 Attitude

This relates to training people to see things, people or elements of their job in a different way. For example, sales people might need to be trained to see addressing a client's concerns about a product as a vital part of the sales process.

Training design

The second component of the training cycle – training design (TD) – relates to the content of the training programme and the methods of delivering it to trainees. Whereas TNA tells us what needs to be learnt, TD is concerned with how that learning occurs and how changes in KSAs can be achieved. For example, different training media, instructional settings or the pace at which information is presented may have very different effects on the way individuals learn and the success of different programmes. As we will see, some of the most interesting research over recent years has explored the utility of e-learning facilities as part of organisational training and development activities.

TD builds upon the training aims and objectives identified by the TNA. Aims involve general statements of intent such as:

- 'This programme sets out to provide participants with "a grasp" of the basic principles of management accountancy'.

- 'The course aims to give trainees an awareness of the relevance of industrial psychology to the management process'.

By contrast, objectives are more specific and precise. They focus specifically on what trainees should be able to do as a consequence of the training. These objectives can be expressed in the following, three-component form:

1 *The criterion behaviour*: a statement of what the trainee should be able to do at the end of training. Because of this emphasis on criterion behaviour, objectives expressed in this way are often referred to as *behavioural objectives*;

2 *The conditions* under which the behaviour is to be exhibited. This might involve a specification of the equipment available to support the behaviour and the context within which it will need to occur. For example, after training, skilled craft workers will need quality tools and a might need a quiet relaxed environment in order to use their skills to the fullest;

3 *The standard of performance* of the behaviour.

It is important to recognise that whilst objectives detail what the person should be able to do at the end of training they do not describe what will happen during training. For example, the statement 'participants will gain experience of various personnel selection interviewing techniques' would not be acceptable as an objective, because it says what will happen on the course, not what the outcomes will be. An objective might be: 'participants will be able to execute a reliable, valid and fair selection interview, for three candidates who have made an application for a trainee accountancy vacancy within the organisation'. Behavioural objectives are crucial for determining whether or not the training has been effective: it is an issue that we will return to later.

Key Learning Point

Training objectives give a clear description of what the trainee should be capable of doing at the end of training.

STOP TO CONSIDER

Think about some of the training you have received (it might even be the course you are studying now). Were you given the aims and objectives for this training and did these state what you should be able to do at the end of the training? Try to identify one aim and one objective from the course to illustrate how the two concepts differ. Now consider whether the clarity of these aims and objectives has an impact on how effective the training is. Do aims and objectives make a difference to your experiences of training?

Theories of learning

Theories of learning represent ideas about how learning occurs; they feed into training practice by helping to inform choice of the most appropriate methods of instruction. This is an aspect of training where psychological research and theory have been particularly influential. Although there is no single, universally accepted theory for the learning process, there are several widely accepted underlying principles and points of agreement among psychologists. From a historical perspective the most prominent approach to learning derives from the work from the behaviourist tradition (*see* Chapter 1). According to this approach to psychology, learning results from strengthening stimulus (S)–response (R) links by reinforcing appropriate behaviour (using reward) and, in some cases, punishing inappropriate behaviour. Behaviour modification (*see* Chapter 6) has played an important role in training. However, this approach has important limitations.

The behaviourist view is that learning occurs largely through trial and error; but clearly not all learning can take place only by reinforcing S–R links: this would take too long (and in many circumstances could well be dangerous!). The approach ignores cognitive components involved in learning of new concepts. Social learning theory (SLT), developed by Bandura (1986), provided a considerable improvement to our understanding of learning by allowing a bigger role for internal, mental processes. Here cognitive processes, such as expectancies about what might happen and the capacity of individuals to learn without direct experience, are seen as having a crucial role to play in the training process. This type of training intervention requires the trainee to engage actively in, and think about, the training experience.

SLT suggests that training involves three stages. First, trainee attention is focused using a 'model' to perform the target behaviour (e.g. several real-life examples of an employee showing customer service skills). Second, learning takes place through a sequence of observations of the 'model' and the reward or punishment that they receive following their performance. Third, trainee learning is strengthened through rehearsal and practice. To illustrate what this might look like in practice, an example of this type of training intervention might include the following:

1   The trainer emphasises the importance of communication skills for teamworking success.

2   Trainees watch a video of a model effectively handling a situation involving communication of information between members of a team.

3   Key points from 2 are identified by the trainer, and group discussion takes place between the trainees and the trainer.

4   Trainees take part in a role-play with feedback from the trainer and other group members.

5   Trainees return to work to practise new behaviour with members of their own teams.

6   The trainer and trainees meet two weeks later to discuss their experiences and how they dealt with them.

Thus trainees are told why effective communication is important, they observe the required skills, then practise and receive feedback, and finally, they attempt to generalise their learning to other situations when they return to work. Research has shown that using models who are high status, the same race or gender as the trainees, and who are friendly and helpful *improves* learning (Bandura, 1977a). Training also tends to be more effective when the 'model' (i) is able to control resources that are desired by the trainees, and (ii) is seen to receive rewards for their behaviour. A good example of SLT can be found in training materials that use well-known actors and comedians to demonstrate how to, and how not to, perform work tasks like interviewing or customer service.

Baldwin (1992) makes an interesting and important observation in relation to SLT and the use of modelling in training. He argues that simply providing trainees with examples of how they should perform tasks ignores the fact that they may already have become skilled at performing them, *but in a different way* (i.e. in a way that is not desired by the organisation). For example, until the 1980s most high-street banks were bureaucratic institutions with cultures that emphasised internal procedures and systems rather than customers. Today these banks have evolved to become service-based organisations (you might have noticed that many of them now resemble retail environments, focused on customer service and sales). Employees who remained in these banks through this period had to change their attitudes and behaviour quite dramatically; particularly with respect to the way they interacted with customers. In addition to learning new skills (e.g. sales techniques), they had to 'unlearn' traditional and automated patterns of behaviour. This process of 'unfreezing' old behaviour can make change slow and particularly difficult. Yet many training programmes overlook the need to work with trainees who may arrive at training programmes 'pre-programmed' to perform in ways that are very different to the training objectives.

Despite the many positive aspects of SLT, its use can be limited because many work tasks are not suitable for behavioural modelling (Gist, 1989). Take the case of creativity and innovation. Many companies encourage their employees to come up with new ideas and ways of doing things, but it is difficult to observe the inner workings of an individual's mind when they are having an idea! Similarly, observing a model may be of little help when learning how to think strategically or how to resolve a problem in something like a piece of accounting or stock control software. As a consequence, it is perhaps not surprising that theories from cognitive psychology have become increasingly important for training design, particularly in helping to explain how a person moves from unskilled novice to expert status.

Nearly 50 years ago Fitts (1962) proposed a theory that has stood the test of time very well, and is still highly regarded by psychologists and practitioners (Table 11.2). In essence, he suggested that skill development progressed through three distinct phases: (a) a cognitive phase, (b) an associative phase and (c) an autonomous phase. Although the phases can be separated conceptually, Fitts recognised that

Table 11.2	Phases of skill development

Fitts	Anderson
Cognitive phase: learning the basic ingredients that make up skilled performance. Performance is prone to error and some lack of understanding of how to conduct task(s) may be apparent	*Declarative stage*: establishing the basic 'facts' about the tasks. The trainee is beginning to grasp what is involved in the task(s) (i.e. declarative knowledge)
Associative phase: establishment of the appropriate patterns of behaviour, underpinned by the knowledge acquired in the first phase. Initially rather a lot of errors but improvement with repeated practice	*Knowledge compilation stage*: physical mechanisms are developed for transforming the declarative knowledge into procedural knowledge (i.e. knowing how to accomplish the tasks(s))
Autonomous phase: the task(s) are performed increasingly smoothly with relatively low demands on memory or attention. Performance is very resistant to interference or stress	*Tuning stage*: performance strengthens and generalises across tasks within the relevant skill domain

Source: Fitts (1962), Anderson (1983, 1987).

there might well be some practical overlap between them. In the cognitive phase the learner is attempting to get some intellectual understanding of the tasks involved. During the cognitive stage actions are deliberate and in the forefront of consciousness, as the learner concentrates on the key features of skilled performance. For example, at this stage a novice pastry chef might concentrate on which ingredients and utensils to select, how to mix the ingredients together, how to prepare the oven and so on.

For skills that are not very easy to learn, practice is the key feature of the next (associative) phase as the learner attempts to reproduce skilful performance. During this phase there is less and less ponderous concentration on the steps involved and, usually through practice and feedback, a gradual improvement in the smoothness and accuracy of performance. So to continue with the pastry chef example, picking up utensils and mixing the ingredients becomes an increasingly smooth sequence of events. Perhaps the head chef will occasionally remind them that some mixing can be done while the oven is reaching the right temperature (especially when the restaurant is busy!).

The autonomous stage is reached as the skill becomes more and more automatic. In this phase performance of the skill requires less in the way of psychological resources, such as memory or attention, and is increasingly resistant to interference from distractions or competing activities. At this point, our hypothetical pastry chef might be able to hold a conversation with the restaurant manager and still produce a delicious pastry. You might have noticed how the skilled driver can drive a car and hold an interesting conversation at the same time. The novice driver is wise not to attempt this – or at least try not to encourage them to do so if you are the passenger!

In developing a skill the learner passes through a series of stages, with each one producing performance that is more and more automatic.

Anderson (1983, 1987) developed Fitts' ideas further, drawing upon the advances that had been made in contemporary cognitive psychology. His theory also has three stages, but an important feature of his approach is the emphasis that is placed on the distinction between *declarative* and *procedural* knowledge. Declarative knowledge is factual knowledge that may be stated (declared) and made explicit. An example of this would be a skilled counsellor who is able to provide a definition of clinical depression and list its defining symptoms. By contrast, procedural knowledge may be involved when the counsellor deals with a client who is threatening self-harm and through their intervention achieves a reduction in the frequency and severity of the client's self-harm.

Procedural knowledge is the basis for knowing how to do something, whereas declarative knowledge involves knowing that something is or is not the case. For example many people know *that* to ride, and stay on, a horse involves gripping with the knees, sitting upright, holding the reins in a particular way and maintaining balance as the horse moves. Not all of the people who know this have the procedural knowledge required to know *how* to stay on a difficult horse for any length of time. Anderson proposes that people are in the declarative stage when they start learning a new skill. Here important facts are learnt and the learner attempts to use them in working out how to conduct the tasks involved. In this stage demands on attention and memory are considerable (as you may have noticed if reading this textbook is your first experience of work psychology: although we have tried to smooth the process as much as we can). During knowledge compilation the trainee develops better and better specific procedures for conducting the tasks, and by the end of this stage the procedural knowledge (usually incorporating the application of *guiding rules*) is in place. Finally, the tuning stage is reached. This is where the underlying rules are refined and streamlined so that performance is increasingly efficient and automatic. In this stage improvements in performance are relatively small, but possibly very important, and take time to emerge.

Two psychological principles are important in the development of skilled performance: *the power law of practice* and *knowledge of results*. As you might expect, performance usually improves with practice: initial performance gains are very rapid, but tail off over time, with more practice being needed for smaller performance gains (a law of diminishing returns). However, in order for performance to develop as quickly as possible, practice needs to be accompanied by feedback on the results of the trainee's efforts. This allows the trainee to consider carefully and make sense of the feedback, so that they can adjust their approach to the task. For more detail, the interested reader is referred to Patrick (1992), who describes the psychology of training and skill acquisition in considerable detail.

STOP TO CONSIDER

Think about some of the skills that you have developed and the phases you passed through. Learning to talk is probably impossible to remember (why is this?), but learning to use a computer or a mobile phone should be easier to recall. You might be able to hold a conversation with someone while composing a text message: was this always the case? Have you learned to compose text messages more quickly? Perhaps now you don't have to think so much about where the letters and symbols are on the numbers on the keypad: why is this? What else is different from when you first started using text messages: what aspects of the task now seem more automatic? Are you satisfied that the theories of learning that you have just read about explain how your performance in this task has developed over time?

Technology and e-learning

Perhaps one of the most profound influences over the design of training in recent years has been the use of technology to support learning. According to a recent learning and development survey by the UK Chartered Institute of Personnel and Development (CIPD, 2008a), 57 per cent of the organisations they surveyed reported using e-learning, with a further 27 per cent planning to do so over the next year. Where e-learning was in use, respondents estimated that it accounted for 12 per cent of the total time devoted to training activities, and that this was likely to increase considerably over the next few years. In the US there appears to be even greater enthusiasm for e-learning: 89 per cent of companies surveyed in the 2004 Training Industry Report indicated that they already use the Internet as a method of instruction (Dolezalek, 2004).

Although there is no universally accepted definition of e-learning, most researchers and practitioners broadly agree that it relates to learning that is enabled or supported by the use of information and communications technology (ICT). As such it includes a wide variety of methods and training design, which in turn can lead to very different experiences for trainees and trainers. At one end of the spectrum, e-learning may involve a trainee being given a series of training modules on web pages, memory sticks or CD-ROMs that they are expected to work through independently, in their own time and at their own pace. At the other end, e-learning involves groups of employees in different parts of the world who are logged on in real time and who participate in a virtual classroom. Here instant messaging, web cams and e-mail are used to work on live problems with their trainer and each other. The potential advantages of e-learning for an organisation with a dispersed workforce may be obvious, but e-learning also has the advantage of allowing individuals to engage in learning at their own pace and at times that suit them best. For employees that have to travel for a large part of their job, e-learning allows the option of studying wherever they find themselves. The use of ICT also means that companies can monitor when employees log in and how effectively they engage in learning.

The CIPD (2008a) survey shows that whilst e-learning is certainly popular it is most often used to *complement* rather than replace other forms of training and development: 95 per cent of respondents agreed with the statement that 'e-learning is effective when combined with other forms of learning'. However, systematic research into how and why e-learning is effective compared to other forms of training design is still at an early stage. The combined use of e-learning and traditional face-to-face formats is known as 'blended learning', and a meta-analysis conducted by Sitzmann and colleagues (2006) revealed that blended learning resulted in *better declarative and procedural knowledge* than either classroom or web-based training alone. Other researchers have begun to look at how trainees experience e-learning and the impact of individual differences such as learning goal orientation and motivation to learn on learning and behaviour change (e.g. Gagné and Deci, 2005). Findings so far suggest that the increased control that blended learning can offer learners may benefit those who are more motivated and those who are self-directed learners. In contrast, less confident learners may not perform as well when blended learning offers less opportunity for interpersonal support (Klein *et al.*, 2006). Clearly we are witnessing the beginning of an interesting new area for researchers and practitioners, one where there is a need for more systematic study to provide evidence to inform practice. Chapter 10 also discusses the advantages and disadvantages of communicating via new technology.

Key Learning Point

E-learning allows people more flexibility over when, where and how they engage in training, but it can also depersonalise the learning experience.

Training evaluation

Training evaluation (TE), the third component of the training cycle, is concerned with establishing whether or not the training has worked. Techniques for evaluating training provide a way of examining the success of training programmes and identifying areas where change is needed. Akin to examining the validity of a selection process, training evaluation considers the validity of the training programme by assessing the extent to which trainees have reached the training objectives. However, training evaluation is usually taken to be a much broader concept than validation, as it also deals with the overall benefits of a training programme for an organisation. These might include financial benefits such as increased sales, as well as reduced absenteeism and increased organisational commitment.

Probably the most popular framework for training evaluation is that developed by Kirkpatrick (1967), involving four levels of data collection: reaction, learning, behaviour and results (Figure 11.2).

Collecting *reaction data* represents the first and minimal level of evaluation for a training programme. In Kirkpatrick's model this type of data relates to trainees' views of the training. Obviously trainees' views are valuable, but they can easily give a misleading impression of the value of a training programme and an incomplete view of training effectiveness. For example, trainees may be enthusiastic about a training programme because it provided an enjoyable break from routine, or because they found the trainer likeable and engaging. Alternatively they may provide poor reports for training where they had to work extremely hard, or where they had an unpopular instructor. None of this feedback tells us whether the training was actually effective in terms of promoting new learning. For this reason,

Level	Method of assessment
1 Reaction	Post-training feedback sheets (e.g. 'did you enjoy the training?'; 'was the training useful?')
2 Learning	Tests of knowledge acquired (e.g. a test of knowledge of the procedures for dealing with customer complaints)
3 Behaviour	Observation of skill performance and job behaviour, tests of speed and accuracy (e.g. observing an employee dealing with a customer complaint)
4 Results	Assessment of team performance, levels of absenteeism, overall organisational effectiveness, productivity and profitability (e.g. customer satisfaction with the way the employee dealt with a variety of complaints)

Figure 11.2   Kirkpatrick's levels of training evaluation

whilst most training designers ask trainees for their comments about the training (in many cases this is the only information collected), such feedback has often been dismissed as 'happy sheets'. In fact, studies have shown that there are simple ways to improve reaction level information (Brown, 2005). For example, Warr and colleagues (1999) found that including questions about how *difficult and how useful* trainees found the course were measures that *did* predict later learning and the application of skills.

Key Learning Point

Reaction-level (reactance) evaluation data can be improved by asking trainees how difficult and useful they found the training.

Level two of Kirkpatrick's framework involves collecting *learning data* and represents a considerable improvement over reaction data. Learning criteria are concerned with whether or not the trainees show evidence that they have attained the immediate learning objectives of the programme. This may involve administering pre- and post-programme written knowledge tests or tests of skills: these enable the trainer to check participants' understanding of the material covered during training. Learning results are typically collected at the end of or immediately after training, but retention of material over a longer period is also important and learning should ideally be assessed six months post-training as well.

Like reaction data, learning data are useful but incomplete. Trainees may have learned the relevant knowledge, but do they apply it? Kirkpatrick's third level of evaluation attempts to address this issue by looking at *changes in behaviour*, i.e. the extent to which trainees demonstrate the skills they have learned on the training programme once they return to work. We know that various factors can influence the transfer of learning (we discuss these in more detail in the next section), but in terms of collecting data about behaviour change, the criteria and methods used are similar to those used for assessing aspects of job performance (*see* Chapter 6). Although useful, this information should be treated with caution, because managers' ratings, for example, can be influenced by their expectation that training will be effective – particularly if it was the manager's idea that the employee should attend the training! In addition to managers' ratings, level three data might include more *objective assessments*. These might include measures of the number of mistakes an employee makes, the quality of work that they do, or the number of customer complaints they receive. However, learning a new skill often involves unlearning existing automatic behaviour, so it can take time for an individual to generalise the new skill to their workplace and move from novice to expert status. Therefore, it is just as important to decide *when* to collect behavioural data, as it is to decide *what* type of behavioural data to collect for a training evaluation.

The fourth and final level of evaluation proposed by Kirkpatrick is described as 'results' and concerns the extent to which the training has had an impact on organisational effectiveness. Although conceptually clear, results criteria are extremely difficult to assess in a controlled fashion. It can be almost impossible to determine with certainty that improved organisational effectiveness has been brought about by the effect of training, or been influenced by a combination of other factors. These might include a general improvement in the economy, an increased availability of skilled migrant workers, or the fact that the company has launched a very popular product. While managers responsible for investing in a training programme hope that it will have an ultimate impact on company effectiveness or profitability, results-level data are the most difficult to collect and interpret. Indeed, in their meta-analysis of training studies, Alliger and Janak (1997) identified only two investigations that had attempted to collect such data and relate it directly to training effectiveness.

Key Learning Point

Although important, results-level evaluation data are often difficult to collect and interpret.

Exercise 11.2 Course feedback

Universities often ask students to complete feedback sheets for the courses they have studied and the lecturers who have taught them. What type of training evaluation is this? What are its advantages and disadvantages? How might you use what you know about training evaluation to improve these feedback sheets?

Criticisms of Kirkpatrick's approach to evaluation

Kirkpatrick's model provides a popular and clear framework for evaluating training that is widely used in organisations. However, it is not without criticism. Perhaps the strongest of the criticisms has centred on his claim that the four levels are presented as hierarchical: successful learning (level 2) is seen as dependent on an individual enjoying the course (level 1). Similarly, behaviour change in the workplace (level 3) is seen as being reliant on successful acquisition of knowledge (level 2). However, in a meta-analysis of the results of training evaluation studies based on Kirkpatrick's model, Alliger and colleagues (1997) found that the associations between the four levels were consistently low. Clearly it is possible to dislike a course yet to learn some of the material. It is also possible to learn the material yet not apply it in the workplace. For example, trainees may like material and understand it perfectly well, yet be reluctant to change their behaviour when they return to work if they aren't supported to do so by managers or colleagues.

Kraiger *et al.* (1993) argue that because Kirkpatrick's model lacks specificity, it is not easy to identify which methods are best suited to assess different stages of learning. Focusing on the second level of 'learning', they propose a more detailed framework for evaluation based upon three broad, but conceptually different, categories of learning outcomes: (a) cognitive outcomes, (b) skill-based outcomes and (c) affective outcomes (Figure 11.3). Kraiger *et al.* suggest that by identifying the specific changes that should result from these categories of learning at different stages of expertise, it is possible to identify the most appropriate assessment techniques. For example, in the compilation stage skill-based learning can be assessed using methods such as targeted behavioural observation, hands-on testing and structured situational interviews. However, at the automaticity stage skill-based learning outcomes are better assessed by looking at how trainees respond to interference problems (e.g. being asked to perform a simultaneous secondary task such as talking to someone while carrying out an assembly task, or analysing data while speaking to a customer). Alternatively, affective learning outcomes can be assessed using self-report questionnaires measuring constructs such as a trainee's confidence in their ability to demonstrate a particular skill before and after training. The advantage of this model is that it allows us to investigate the causes and processes of learning in much greater detail than we might gain from Kirkpatrick's model.

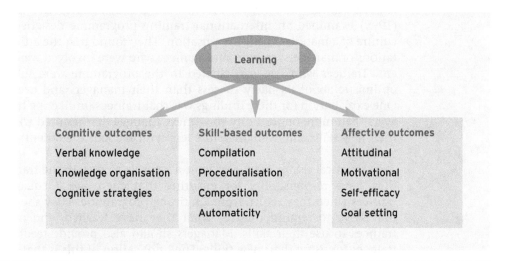

Figure 11.3 A classification scheme for learning outcomes
Source: Kraiger *et al.* (1993). Copyright © 1993 by the American Psychological Association. Adapted with permission.

Transfer of learning

Transfer of learning from a training environment back to the workplace is the third of Kirkpatrick's levels, but there is plenty of evidence that despite successfully acquiring new knowledge and skills, trainees may still not use them once they return to the workplace. Research has shown that trainee characteristics (such as aptitude, personality and motivation), training design (i.e. the use of sound principles of learning, appropriate sequencing and content), as well as the work environment, all play an important role in successful transfer (Baldwin and Ford, 1988; Colquitt *et al.*, 2000). One area of interest has focused on how trainee self-efficacy (an individual's belief in their ability to perform specific tasks) influences learning and transfer. For example, trainees with high self-efficacy generally learn new material and skills more quickly and use these skills in the workplace (Stevens and Gist, 1997). Studies have shown that self-efficacy regulates behaviour by determining task choices, effort and persistence; it concerns an individual's judgement about what they can do with the skills they possess. Low self-efficacy can therefore be seen as an individual-level barrier to successful transfer of learning.

However, there are also many organisational barriers to successful transfer including inertia, bureaucratic procedures, work overload and fear of change. Tannenbaum and Yukl (1992) found that some elements of the post-training environment can encourage (e.g. rewards, job aids, recognition), discourage (e.g. ridicule from peers, lack of management support) or even prohibit (e.g. lack of the necessary equipment) the application of new skills and knowledge. Tracey and colleagues (1995) found that organisational climate and culture were both directly related to post-training behaviours, with the social support system playing a central role in training transfer.

Perhaps not surprisingly, for training to be transferred, employees need encouragement from their managers and peers (Birdi *et al.*, 1997). However, for various reasons this may not always be forthcoming. For example, Silvester and colleagues (1999) examined an international training programme designed to change the culture of a manufacturing organisation. They found that the attitudes and expectations of managers, trainers and trainees who were involved were all quite different. Trainees who had participated in the programme were substantially more optimistic about its likely success than their managers and even their trainers. One explanation for these findings was that trainees (unlike the trainers and managers) had more opportunity to witness changes that resulted when they applied their new skills, and were therefore less cynical about the potential benefits of the training.

In practical terms, managers have a key role to play in the transfer of training: they have responsibility for ensuring that there are adequate resources for trainees when they return from a training programme. They should provide cues that serve to remind trainees what they have learned, and opportunities for trainees to use their skills. Managers should also provide feedback and reward trainees for using their new skills. The implication of this is that managers themselves may need training in order to understand the relevance and requirements of the training and how best to support transfer. For this reason, many training programmes are cascaded down organisations, with the training beginning with managers themselves.

Individual and organisational factors can serve to determine whether learning is transferred to the workplace.

Threats to accurate evaluation

Training evaluation can be complex and, in general, no single method is capable of providing detailed and comprehensive information regarding all aspects of the effectiveness of a training programme. The most successful and useful evaluation requires a multi-method approach and different types of data to build up a picture of whether a training process has achieved its objectives and how it can be improved. Anderson (2007) claims that there is a powerful need for HR professionals to be able to demonstrate the value of learning to their organisation in order to ensure the commitment of senior decision-makers to investment in training and development. Yet, Anderson goes on to point out that only a third of UK organisations seek to capture the effect of training and development on bottom line business performance. There is also little evidence that things have changed since Patrick (1992) found that, typically, only 10 per cent of companies evaluate on-the-job behaviour change and even fewer conduct longitudinal analyses of training effectiveness. There are important practical reasons for this. Individuals within the organisation may simply lack the skills necessary for conducting this type of analysis, or indeed lack interest in collecting traditional evaluation data (Anderson, 2007). There can be substantial costs associated with allocating time and resources to training evaluation that may deter investment, and few managers responsible for spending large amounts of money on a training programme want to be associated with something that hasn't worked. However, only by evaluating training is it possible to determine how best to target future investment in learning and development activities.

The problem of establishing whether training, rather than some other factor, is responsible for causing observed changes is one that makes the effective evaluation of training a technically complex and extremely time-consuming endeavour. The most thorough consideration of experimental designs that can be used by evaluators to examine the effectiveness of training programmes is presented by Cook *et al.* (1990). Fundamentally, the goal of training evaluation should be to provide the training designer with information about effectiveness that can be *unambiguously* interpreted and is *relevant* to the question of training effectiveness. To illustrate the problems involved in conducting good evaluation work we will consider some of the common difficulties that may arise. These difficulties are usually referred to as internal or external threats to *validity*, since they affect (or threaten to affect) the validity of conclusions that can be drawn from the evaluation.

The validity of training may be divided into two broad types. *Internal validity* is concerned with the extent to which the training has brought about new learning. Questions of *external validity* are to do with the extent to which the training will generalise to subsequent groups of trainees and settings.

Threats to internal validity are concerned with the factors or problems that can make it appear that a training programme has been responsible for changes in learning, behaviour or results, when in fact the changes were caused by some other factors. For example, a group of new entrants to an organisation may be given a pre-training test of knowledge of the organisation's rules and procedures. After a period of induction training (one hour per day for their first week) they may be tested again. If their test scores have improved, does this mean that the induction training was responsible? Of course not: the improved knowledge could have been gained in the six or seven hours per day spent in the organisation outside the induction course. An obvious solution to this problem is to administer the tests immediately before and after training. Would any differences now be attributable to the training? It seems more likely. However, there is the possibility that trainees might benefit from the formal training only when they have spent some of the previous day doing their normal duties in the organisation. This could be important, for instance, if, for any reason, the organisation wanted to run the induction training in one block all at once, instead of spreading it over the first week. The question here is partly one of internal validity: did the training bring about the change? It is also partly a question of external validity: will the programme be effective for different trainees in different circumstances?

Designs for training evaluation

In an attempt to control various threats to the validity of training, evaluation investigators will often make use of experimental designs. Most training evaluation has to be conducted within real organisational settings, and under these circumstances it is often not possible to obtain the conditions necessary for perfect experimental designs. In such circumstances it is common for what Campbell and Stanley (1963; *see also* Cook *et al.*, 1990) have called quasi-experimental designs to be utilised. Campbell and Stanley (1963) also described what they term pre-experimental designs. Such designs are not the strongest, but are commonplace in the training world: they produce results with so many threats to validity that they are uninterpretable and not capable of providing clear findings about training effectiveness (*see* Wexley, 1984, pp. 538–9). Two of the best-known pre-experimental designs are shown in Figure 11.4, together with more complex designs that overcome some of the problems inherent in the pre-experimental designs.

Clearly, the single-group, post-test-only design controls for none of the possible threats to internal or external validity and it is quite impossible to interpret the data. It is impossible to tell whether scores are better after training than before – let alone whether training or some other factor is responsible for any changes. The one-group, pre–post measure design goes some way towards resolving the problems by making it possible to measure *change over time*. Nevertheless, it is not possible with this design to assess whether it was the training that had caused any difference. This may only be done if there is also an untrained control group, who are similar to the trained group and whose performance has also been measured at the appropriate times. To conduct a true experiment, trainees should be assigned to the experimental and control groups on a random basis because systematic differences between groups before the experiment could otherwise bias the results. Often this degree of control is impossible in field research and the kind of quasi-experimental design shown in the non-equivalent control group example of Figure 11.4 is the best that can be done. Typically pre-existing groups in the organisation, such as all of the members of a particular job group, region or unit, form the groups. This is administratively much more

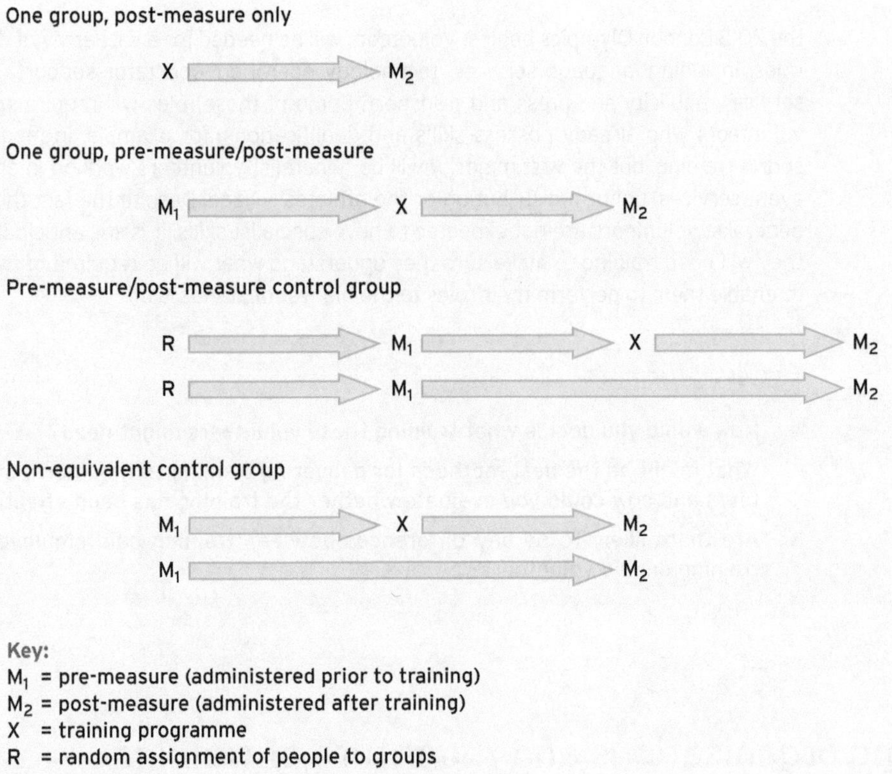

One group, post-measure only

X $\longrightarrow$ M_2

One group, pre-measure/post-measure

M_1 $\longrightarrow$ X $\longrightarrow$ M_2

Pre-measure/post-measure control group

R $\longrightarrow$ M_1 $\longrightarrow$ X $\longrightarrow$ M_2
R $\longrightarrow$ M_1 $\longrightarrow$ M_2

Non-equivalent control group

M_1 $\longrightarrow$ X $\longrightarrow$ M_2
M_1 $\longrightarrow$ M_2

Key:
M_1 = pre-measure (administered prior to training)
M_2 = post-measure (administered after training)
X   = training programme
R   = random assignment of people to groups

Figure 11.4   **Pre-experimental, experimental and quasi-experimental designs for training evaluation studies**

convenient than random assignment and does control for some of the main threats to validity. Even the pre–post measure control group design is subject to some threats to validity, and for totally unambiguous results more complex designs are needed (*see* Campbell and Stanley, 1963).

Key Learning Point

Pre-experimental designs, such as the one-group post-test-only design, are common in the training world but they are not capable of providing completely clear results.

Exercise 11.3   Training volunteers for the London 2012 Olympics

The 2008 Beijing Olympic Games were arguably a triumph of both organisation and skill. This was in no small part down to the efforts taken by the organisers of the Games to recruit and train thousands of volunteers. In 2010 the recruitment of volunteers for ▶

the 2012 London Olympics begins. Volunteers will be needed for a vast array of different roles, including language services, technology operation, spectator support, medical services, publicity and press and transport. Some of these roles will require specialist volunteers who already possess skills and qualifications, for example, in medicine or sports training, but the vast majority will be generalist volunteers working in areas like event services, uniform distribution or the athletes' village. Despite the fact that these generalist volunteers are not expected to have specialist skills, it is still anticipated that they will need training to make sure they understand what will be required of them and to enable them to perform their roles to the highest of standards.

Suggested exercises

1 How would you decide what training these volunteers might need?

2 What might be the best methods for delivering training to thousands of volunteers and how could you evaluate whether the training has been effective?

3 Are there likely to be any differences between training paid employees and training unpaid volunteers?

Learning organisations and the future of training

In preparing the new version of this chapter it has been striking how little recent research in mainstream work psychology journals is concerned with topics related to employee training and development. Perhaps these topics are seen as less exciting than topics like leadership, employee selection or innovation? Yet, step back a little to take in a slightly wider perspective and it is clear that despite this apparent lack of activity, there have been plenty of new ideas and innovations relating to organisational learning (OL) and knowledge management (KM) in fields like organisational behaviour and change. For the most part, OL and KM have received little coverage in traditional work psychology texts on training and development. Two possible reasons for this could be that (i) work psychology training and development research has usually focused on individual learning and development, and (ii) research has been driven by an emphasis on positivist empirical approaches to the evaluation of the impact of training (which as we have just seen, is quite difficult to achieve). Whereas both of these have been extremely important to developing a scientific understanding of learning and development, neither has been as successful at explaining or predicting the complex and dynamic learning systems that characterise successful organisations.

Over the past two decades training and development have increasingly been viewed as core business functions, and learning and development systems as the main mechanisms to create learning organisations. Driven by the need to deal with an increasing pace of change, unstable economies and global markets, it has been argued that organisations must learn to thrive on change, and to do this they must become learning organisations capable of adapting flexibly to changing environments and needs. Central to the concept of the learning organisation is that organisations can only adapt if their employees are also flexible and adaptive to change; therefore employees must view learning as an ongoing feature of their jobs (Burgoyne, 1999). Encouraging a positive attitude to the take-up of training opportunities can be seen as part of traditional approaches to training and development. However, what is new is the increasing focus on *capturing individual learning*, ensuring that it is (i) passed on and shared by different organisational members and groups, and (ii) used to achieve organisational benefits.

This can be illustrated by the case of companies like management consultancies, where individual employees often develop considerable knowledge and expertise relating to specific clients or subject areas. As one CEO once commented 'our most expensive assets walk out of the building every evening': this metaphor illustrates the dependency of such companies on the knowledge and expertise of key individuals. Although the company may control the content of corporate learning and development activities, they have little influence or control over the ability of the employee to learn from their experiences with clients and in different work environments. Yet this knowledge may be extremely important and valuable to the company. In such cases the employee can become more powerful and less dependent on their employer through the development of a unique knowledge base about particular clients and their needs. As a consequence, there has been growing interest in how learning and development systems can be 'turned on their head' to ensure that unstructured employee learning is transferred to the organisation through KM systems (e.g. Argote *et al.*, 2000; Goh, 2002). For example, many consultancies ask employees to write up case studies and notes about clients or specific projects: these are then made available on a central intranet for other employees to access and learn from.

In a way this illustrates a substantial shift in our way of thinking about learning and development activities. There has been a move away from seeing training as a top-down process where the organisation identifies the knowledge and skills required by an employee and controls access to them through formal, structured learning opportunities. Instead there has been growing interest in knowledge as a social construction, co-created by individuals through their interactions with one another and with the environment. Informal learning, driven by the interests and proactive engagement of an employee, is recognised as an ongoing feature of working life. This is less controllable by management, but is still key to sense-making and creating a shared understanding among work colleagues (Currie and Kerrin, 2003). Formalised training and development activities are therefore only part of the processes that define the way individuals learn within an organisation. An example of this type of learning is a community of practice.

Communities of practice

The concept of communities of practice (CoPs) has its origins in work by Etienne Wenger. It has received little attention from traditional training researchers because it epitomises the view of knowledge as a social construction. Wenger challenges the traditional psychological view of learning as an individual cognitive process (with a beginning and an end) and argues instead for a social theory of learning where knowledge is *fluid and co-created*. Wenger (1998) defines communities of practice as *groups of people who share a concern or a passion for something they do and learn how to do it better as they interact regularly*. As such, they extend beyond the workplace; for example, communities of practice might include groups of schoolchildren sharing ideas about homework on a shared website. The possibility of using communities of practice as a means for supporting individual and organisational learning has now become popular. Wenger cites the example of surgeons working together to solve the problems associated with new surgical techniques, and a group of first-time managers getting together to cope with the demands of their new role. We have seen recent examples of employees using the Internet and social networking sites to create support groups outside of the workplace. However, Wenger argues that to be defined as a community of practice a group should share certain common features: (i) there must be a network of interaction between people with a shared interest and competence in a particular area, (ii) there must be ongoing interaction, sharing of information and cooperative work to solve learning-related issues and (iii) they must be practitioners working in a similar area and therefore able to share similar experiences, stories and knowledge.

Although a number of companies have explored the possibility of creating communities of practice, there seems to have been more success with CoPs in public sector contexts. For example, in the UK, the government agency responsible for building capacity in local government, the Improvement and Development Agency (IDeA) has recently sponsored several CoPs. These have been established for professionals working in local authorities and other organisations throughout the UK as a means to share ideas and expertise. The comparative success of CoPs in the public rather than private sector may be no accident given the shared values and historical commitment to sharing knowledge and expertise among public sector organisations. In contrast, a greater emphasis on the commercialisation of knowledge and expertise particularly, but not exclusively, in the private sector can make individuals reluctant to share information that can give them a competitive advantage (i.e commercially sensitive information). Burgoyne (1999) recognised the importance of power and control in making people reluctant to share information and knowledge in learning organisations, yet the same may also be true of CoPs.

Summary

Constant social and technological change provides the context for organisational life. This coupled with individual growth and career development means that training has a key role in many organisations. The adequate analysis of training needs (at organisation, task and personal levels) provides the basis for training activities. Although the analysis of needs, together with a clear statement of training aims and objectives, is important, there is still a certain degree of judgement involved in choosing appropriate training methods. This essential subjectivity can be checked and assessed by the application of systematic procedures for evaluating the effectiveness of training. Evaluation at reaction, learning, behaviour and results levels provides a way of determining the overall value of training and assessing necessary improvements. In general, research has shown that training is an effective way of bringing about behaviour change, although there are often problems in ensuring that the potential for change provided by training activities actually transfers to the work setting. Today, many organisations are starting to see training as a continuous process of organisational learning that involves employees sharing knowledge and learning from each other. This provides a challenge for work psychologists who have traditionally seen training as a discrete intervention.

Closing Case Study   Training and organisational change

Prime TV had undergone enormous changes in the last few years. The most important of these concerned the new agreement that had been reached between management and unions. This provided a much more flexible rostering system so that unit managers could use people's time more effectively. The previous system had involved fixed rosters and set numbers of personnel for specific tasks. All this was now history and managers (in consultation with programme makers) could decide who should work on which job and how many people were needed. However, the new agreement had been achieved at a cost and it was only after severe management pressure, including threats of compulsory redundancy, that the unions finally accepted the new agreement. This had left smouldering bad feeling between many employees and the company's senior managers.

Other changes in the organisational structure of the company had also taken place. Financial controls on what was spent to make programmes were now much tighter and each department or unit was accounted for as a separate cost centre and was expected to operate at a profit by selling its services to other units within Prime TV or to outside companies.

During the period of change the human resources staff at Prime had had little opportunity to assess training needs or to organise training events – so, apart from induction training and some specialist technical training, nothing had taken place for the last five years. Kathy Lamb, the human resources manager, was well aware that this could not continue and resolved to take some positive action.

Suggested exercise

Decide what Kathy Lamb should do. Explain why.

Test your learning

Short-answer questions

1 What are the three key phases in the training system/training cycle?

2 Why is training needs analysis important and what are the levels at which this can occur?

3 Explain the function of learning objectives in the design of training.

4 Describe Anderson's three stages of skill development.

5 Explain how a consideration of individual differences in learning capabilities can help in training design.

6 Name and explain (briefly) Kirkpatrick's four levels of evaluation data.

7 How can we improve reaction level (reactance) training evaluation data?

8 Give a brief critical explanation of two designs that might be used for a training evaluation study.

9 Briefly describe the barriers to carrying out a proper evaluation of training in an organisational setting.

10 What are organisational learning and knowledge management?

11 What benefits might organisations gain from communities of practice?

Suggested assignments

1 Why is it important to position training as a central HR function linking with other selection and performance management systems?

2 Explain how you would review the training needs of an organisation and design relevant training programmes.

3 Consider what value and understanding the psychology of learning has for a training manager.

4 Traditionally, work psychologists have viewed training as a discrete set of events. To what extent does this reflect the way that knowledge and skills are developed and shared in modern organisations?

Relevant websites

The Chartered Institute of Personnel and Development offers a wide range of articles about training design, delivery and evaluation. Most are available free of charge to non-members, and offer a valuable insight into the practitioner's perspective on training: http://www.cipd.co.uk/subjects/lrnanddev/general.

An example of how training can be important in basic skills as well as high-level professional and management ones can be seen at http://www.literacytrust.org.uk/socialinclusion/adults/benefits.html. This site also shows how, at national level, economic and social policy have implications for training provided by the state and employers.

For further self-test material and relevant, annotated weblinks please visit the website at **www.pearsoned.co.uk/workpsych**

Suggested further reading

Full details for all references are given in the list at the end of this book.

John Patrick's (1992) book *Training: Research and practice* provides thorough coverage of the psychology of learning and the whole area of training. He covers operative training particularly well.

A useful human resources perspective on training is provided by Rosemary Harrison in her book *Employee Development.*

CHAPTER 12

Stress and well-being at work

LEARNING OUTCOMES

After studying this chapter, you should be able to:

1 define stress and well-being in the workplace;

2 describe some key structural models of work stress;

3 describe some key transactional models of work stress;

4 explain the core principles of positive psychology related to well-being at work;

5 identify the workplace conditions that influence employee well-being;

6 identify some of the individual differences that influence employee well-being;

7 list the possible consequences of work stress;

8 list a number of individual and organisational benefits related to positive well-being;

9 distinguish between primary, secondary and tertiary interventions designed to improve psychological well-being at work;

10 discuss the impact of different intervention strategies on psychological well-being at work;

11 describe the key steps involved in improving employee well-being and organisational health.

Opening Case Study   Workplaces cause depression
in 1 in 20 adults

A study of almost 1,000 32-year-olds in New Zealand – including everyone born in the city of Dunedin during 1972 – has revealed that having a high-stress job can double the risk of developing psychiatric problems for the first time.

It revealed that among people with no history of either depression or anxiety, 14 per cent of women and 10 per cent of men developed one or both of the disorders during the year for which they were monitored.

Around 45 per cent of these cases were directly attributable to workplace stress, scientists at King's College, London said.

They found that 15 per cent of people with the highest-stress jobs developed depression or anxiety, compared to 10 per cent of those with medium-stress jobs and 8 per cent of those with low-stress occupations.

The findings, which are published in the journal *Psychological Medicine*, suggest that workplace stress is among the biggest drivers of mental illness among employed young adults.

'Our study shows that work stress appears to bring on diagnosable forms of depression and anxiety in previously healthy young workers – in fact the occurrence is two times higher than among workers whose jobs are less demanding,' said Maria Melchior, who led the study.

'Clearly we can also deduce that work stress is associated with mental health problems of clinical significance that have health care and financial implications for wider society.'

The overall costs of mental illness to society are estimated at £12bn in lost productivity and health care, or around 1 per cent of gross domestic product, she said. The results could help employers to reduce this in the future.

The results are particularly significant because the study was carefully designed to control for the participants' background mental states, which can significantly influence their susceptibility to anxiety and depression.

As all the subjects in the cohort study have been monitored for years, their personality traits were assessed comprehensively when they were 18. The research team have used statistical methods to take these into account, so that people with negative outlooks did not skew the outcome.

In the study, a team led by Dr Melchior and Terrie Moffitt, Professor of Social Behaviour and Development at King's, gave 972 members of the Dunedin cohort detailed questionnaires about the stress they experience at work. All the participants were also assessed for major depressive disorder and generalised anxiety disorder.

Those who reported high levels of job-related stress tended to complain that they had to work at a fast pace to meet tight deadlines, with little control over their daily schedules or roles. They also said failure tended to be highly visible.

Professor Moffitt said highly stressful jobs were not always ones with extensive management responsibility, as is often assumed, and cited chefs as one of the more vulnerable professions. 'Head chefs in big restaurants are under huge time pressures and the pressure of public failure and being exposed if they screw up,' she said.

The subjects held a wide variety of jobs, including stockbroker, surgeon, helicopter pilot, primary school teacher, electrician, sheepdog trainer, dustbin man, brain surgeon, cruise ship captain, politician, police officer, laboratory technician, fish packer, forest ranger, massage therapist and journalist.

Because of the variety, it was not possible for the researchers to categorise which jobs had the highest stress levels. The research controlled for the effects of higher status jobs – previous studies have shown that people in lower status positions are more vulnerable to stress.

The scientists found that men were more vulnerable to depression as a result of work-related stress, while women are more vulnerable to anxiety.

Professor Moffitt has previously published research on the same cohort group linking a brain signalling gene to vulnerability to depression following stressful life events. The team is now planning to look at whether genes influence people's response to workplace stress.

Professor Richie Poulton of the University of Otago in New Zealand said the results have lessons for employers. 'As young adults have the highest risk of developing these conditions, it is important to alleviate work stress amongst this group, as well as directing prevention efforts towards them,' he said.

'Intervention studies show that there are at least two productive approaches to reducing work stress: it's possible to teach people to deal with distressing situations through psychological counselling or you can change the workplace in a way that decreases job demands.'

Source: The Times, 1 August 2007 (Henderson, N.), copyright © The Times 2007, www.nisyndication.com

Introduction

The health of people at work has been an important issue for psychologists for some time. As the opening case study shows, the evidence that shows work can impact upon employee health – in both a positive and negative way – continues to mount. As a result, over the last few years the management of employee well-being has become a priority issue for all types of organisations. For example, in the UK the number of organisations with an explicit strategy for managing staff well-being increased from 26 to 42 per cent in the space of just one year (CIPD, 2007b).

Until relatively recently, interest in work-related well-being has been focused on the negative effects that work can have on people. It has been argued for some time that problems such as work stress can be very damaging to individuals and organisations alike. The opening case identifies two of the serious possible consequences for individuals: *anxiety and depression*. Certain occupations, such as teaching, ambulance staff, police, social workers, etc. are believed to provide the highest stress levels (Johnson *et al.*, 2005). The case study shows that the consequences of work-related stress are not confined to certain types of jobs traditionally seen as 'stressful'. It is not only psychological health that can be damaged by work. The Whitehall II Study carried out in the UK Civil Service is a series of well-designed longitudinal investigations that have explored the relationships between job conditions and coronary heart disease (CHD) (see Ferrie *et al.*, 2005; Griffin *et al.*, 2007). A recent publication from this research looked at the link between the psychological working conditions and CHD in a cohort of over 10,000 employees (Kuper and Marmot, 2008). The results revealed that employees reporting job strain (high job demands combined with a lack of opportunities to make decisions) were at a significantly increased risk of developing CHD. It is difficult to argue that such findings are trivial.

As you might imagine, these problems with individual well-being can have consequences for organisations and the economy as a whole. The overall costs to the UK economy of mental health problems are estimated at £77 billion (Dewe and Kompier, 2008). In 2000 (when the economy was relatively healthy) one estimate put the cost of depression alone at more than £9 billion in England. Some surveys have shown that psychological problems such as anxiety and depression are the most important cause of workplace absenteeism (although musculoskeletal problems often beat them to the top of the charts). Other statistics underline the importance of mental ill health and stress at work: together they are the biggest contributor (40 per cent) to the £5 billion cost of incapacity benefit, and over half a million instances of stress-related absence from work cost UK employers a total of £3.7 billion each year (Dewe and Kompier, 2008). All of this is in addition to the 'human costs' of the problem as people experience significant personal difficulties in their own lives.

These figures paint a rather negative picture: unless work is well-managed, employees could become unhealthy. There is, however, a growing body of work that has identified the positive benefits of work to both individuals and organisations. Positive well-being focuses on issues such as positive psychological health and happiness. Much of this work examines the role of the experience of positive emotions at work in building well-being and changing the way people think and act in a healthy way (e.g. Fredrickson, 1998; Fredrickson and Joiner, 2002). The evidence is growing that well-designed and managed jobs, carried out within healthy organisations, not only reduce the risk of poor well-being, they can have a significant positive impact on employees. This is an important point: well-being at work is not just about the absence of ill-health, it is also about positive health outcomes. Some of these positive outcomes (job satisfaction, organisational commitment and employee engagement) are also discussed in Chapter 7.

Much of this chapter covers research, theory and practice on a major topic in psychological well-being at work: work-related stress. However, we also discuss the nature of well-being, health and positive emotion at work. In identifying organisational sources of stress we will look at a range of factors such as job demands, control at work, work-role problems, workplace bullying, relationships at work, career development, organisational climate and structure, and the work–home interface (*see also* Cooper *et al.*, 2001). The chapter then discusses different forms of intervention for reducing stress and promoting well-being in the workplace. It concludes by describing the concept of the healthy organisation, and the processes that organisations can use to assess and manage employee well-being.

Work-related stress

What is stress?

Stress is a word derived from the Latin word *stringere*, meaning to draw tight. Early definitions of stress drew on concepts used in physics and engineering: external forces (load) were seen as exerting pressure upon an individual, producing strain. Therefore, one could measure stress as an external stimulus to which an individual is subjected in the same way that the physical stress upon a machine could be measured (Hinckle, 1973).

Others such as Cannon (1929) defined stress in terms of the internal physiological state of subjects exposed to threatening or exciting situations (e.g. the raised adrenalin secretion that can be observed in the well-known 'fight or flight' reaction). Hans Selye (1946) provided a more elaborate model of the human response to stressors. This he called General Adaptation Syndrome. It has three stages:

1 *Alarm reaction*, in which in initial phase of lowered resistance is followed by countershock, during which the individual's defence mechanisms become active.

2 *Resistance*, the stage of maximum adaptation and, hopefully, successful return to equilibrium for the individual. If, however, the stress agent continues or the defence mechanism does not work, the individual will move on to a third stage.

3 *Exhaustion*, when adaptive mechanisms collapse.

These models of stress reflect some of what the lay person understands stress to be. They are rarely used now in work psychology, although their influence is still felt in the way we understand the causes and consequences of work stress. Stress is no longer defined in terms of the environmental pressures on a person, or its consequences for their physiological well-being (i.e. stress is not really an illness, although the lay person often uses the term in this way). Instead, contemporary theories of work-related stress describe it as the *intervening psychological processes that link exposure to work-related problems to the negative impact of those problem*s.

Most modern theories of work-related stress define it as a negative emotional state that can result from the interaction between a person and their environment. It something that is *caused or made worse* by work. Therefore stress is not high workload or work-related absence, rather it is the negative emotional state that can arise from pressures at work (e.g. high workload is a potential cause of stress) and contribute to a range of problems with psychological, physical health and organisational health (e.g. absence which is a potential consequence of stress). A stressor is any force that pushes a psychological or physical factor beyond its range of stability, producing a strain within the individual (Cooper *et al.*, 2001).

The UK Health and Safety Executive (www.hse.gov.uk/stress) definition of work stress does a good job of capturing the essence of many of the various scientific definitions of the concept: '*the process that arises where work demands of various types and combinations exceed the person's capacity and capability to cope*'.

Before we look at different theories of stress, it is important to emphasise that individual perception or *appraisal* is important in most stress theories. Two people exposed to similar working conditions can perceive them very differently. For example, some students enjoy examinations, but others (that is, probably most) find exams immensely stressful. Returning to the definition given above, stress occurs when an individual *perceives or appraises* that the various demands placed on them exceed their own view of the capacity they have to cope with them. This is important because it has significant implications for how stress at work is assessed and managed.

Key Learning Point

When perceived demands exceed the individual's perceived ability to cope, they can be said to be experiencing a negative emotional state that is referred to as stress.

Models of work stress

Most students of work psychology will encounter a rather confusing array of models and theories of work stress. Many of the models have much in common. For example, most describe stress as resulting from a lack of fit between an individual's capacity and the demands of their particular work environment. This allows us to understand better why one person seems to flourish in a certain setting, while another suffers. Most contemporary theories see the individual as an active participant in the stress process, perceiving their own situation and the demands placed on them. Some models also describe how the individual chooses and evaluates their responses to the problems they are faced with (i.e. how they cope with pressure). Some theories include a description of the impact of individual differences.

In this section, the most influential models will be described and their key features identified. To simplify things a little the various models can be split into two categories: *structural approaches* and *transactional approaches* (Cox and Griffiths, 1995).

Structural approaches

Structural approaches focus on describing the aspects of work (and the interactions between them) that are thought to lead to the negative emotional state of stress and, in turn, poor employee well-being. The various working conditions that are linked to employee health are discussed in more detail later in this chapter. However, some will be mentioned briefly now because many models have been developed on the basis that certain psychological aspects of work (sometimes rather elaborately referred to as *psychosocial working conditions*) place employees at risk.

The Demand–Control Model (Karasek, 1979) was built around two particularly important features of the work environment (naturally, you can guess what these are). Demands, as you might expect, relate to the amount of work that a person does but also include factors such as time pressures and the amount of mental and physical effort involved in the job. Karasek's definition of control includes two components: *skill discretion* (the extent to which the job allows the employee to use their skills and capabilities) and *decision latitude* (the amount of control the employee has over their work situation). By combining demands and control, four categories of job were described:

1   passive job (low demands – low control);

2   high-strain job (high demands – low control);

3   low-strain job (low demands – high control);

4   active job (high demands – high control).

Karasek and Theorell (1990) reported that employees in high-strain jobs were at a particularly increased risk of various health problems (including a range of serious psychological and physical health problems). One particularly interesting feature of this model is the positive role that control has in employee well-being. Those in active job roles were found to be the healthiest. Fox and colleagues (1993) argue that control is so important for two reasons. First because it provides employees with *opportunities to deal better* with the demands they are facing. Second because it fulfils *a basic human need* for control. Later in this chapter we discuss some examples of interventions that show the powerful effects that increasing job control can have. According to this model, a job with high demands could be healthy because of the positive effects of control. An example of this would be someone with a very high workload, having the freedom to prioritise tasks so that they could get the work done in the most efficient way.

Exercise 12.1   How stressful are these jobs?

Below is a list of job roles. Karasek and Theorell (1990) describe how a number of different jobs were categorised according to the levels of demands and control in each job. In which of the four categories of job is each job role likely to be most appropriately classified?

Call centre phone call handler; elite team-sports athlete; qualified medical doctor; shopping centre security guard; lifeguard at a swimming pool; company chief executive; supermarket checkout operator; assembly line worker; used car salesperson.

Suggested exercises

Do you think that some of these jobs could be inherently stressful?

In your current work, or in your studies, how much does having control help you when you are faced with high demands?

The model was expanded by Johnson and Hall (1988) to include social support (the Demand–Control–Support model, the DCSM). Social support is the helpful interactions with supervisors and co-workers (Daniels *et al.*, 2009). In this model, high levels of social support are thought to act as a *buffer* against the negative effects of work demands (this is similar to the effects of control). What this means is that given similar levels of demands, jobs with higher levels of social support will tend to be healthier (this means that demands, control and support might interact to predict well-being: *see* Chapter 2 for a description of interaction effects). The basic premise is that, like control, emotional support or practical help reduces the impact of high work demands on employees (O'Driscoll and Brough, 2010): this is the *strain hypothesis* (Daniels *et al.*, 2009). High control and social support when accompanied by high job demands can also help employees to learn new skills in order to adapt to the demands placed on them and lead to improved motivation and satisfaction: this is the *learning hypothesis* (De Witte *et al.*, 2007).

Reviews of these models examining the results of a large number of studies (e.g. de Lange *et al.*, 2003) tend to show that high levels of control and support often exert positive effects (although it has been found that very high levels of control are not preferred by everyone) and that high levels of demands exert negative effects on employee well-being. The evidence for *buffering* effects of social support and control in high demand situations is less consistent and clear. The stress process does not seem to be quite as simple and predictable as the models propose.

You may have noticed that these models focus on a limited range of working conditions (albeit important ones), but as we will discuss later there are many other sources of stress. Also, in these models certain combinations of working conditions are thought to be consistently 'unhealthy'. Other models have looked at a wider range of sources of stress and also placed more emphasis on employees' appraisals of the 'fit' between their own skills, abilities and preferences and the demands of the job.

Key Learning Point

Demands, control and support at work are particularly important in structural models of work stress.

The Michigan Model (Caplan *et al.*, 1975) and the Person–Environment Fit Model (French *et al.*, 1982) propose that each employee's skills, abilities, knowledge and attitudes need to be well-matched to the demands of their job. Stress is likely to occur if there is a mismatch between the person and the job, and the bigger this mismatch, the greater the stress experienced. *Subjective perceptions* of work stressors are particularly important in these models and the Michigan Model described a wide range of important job characteristics including demands, control and support but also many other factors such as job insecurity, lack of participation and role-related issues (you will read more about these later in this chapter). The core concept of lack of fit has been particularly influential in stress research partly because it allows us to consider the role of skills, ability, personality and other individual differences in the stress process. For example, the author of this chapter would find it very stressful to have to repair a broken-down car by the side of the motorway, but this is a task that a skilled mechanic with a calm approach to life would find much easier. However, it has been argued that because so many factors can influence person–environment 'fit' it is difficult to make specific predictions from these complex models that can be tested using traditional scientific methods (Mark and Smith, 2008). With its more 'testable' predictions it is perhaps understandable that the DCSM still dominates the research literature. Moreover, when using the DCSM most researchers now use questionnaire measures to examine working conditions that allow employees to express their perceptions: this is a bit like asking them to comment on their own situation in terms of person–environment fit.

Tests of structural models of work stress show that working conditions can have both positive and negative effects on the employee. This idea was extended in Warr's Vitamin Model (see Warr, 2009). In this model, working conditions, like vitamins, can have a positive impact on health, but 'mega-doses' are wasteful or in some cases harmful. This means that some working conditions will help to increase health up to some *threshold level*, at which point they will not have any more positive effects, but will not become harmful. These include factors such as levels of pay. Other factors become harmful if they are *excessive or absent*. These include factors such as demands, control and social support. Having lots of control at work might not be helpful for all employees, especially for employees who do not have sufficient knowledge, confidence or skill to exercise that control in a productive way. Similarly, being overwhelmed with support from colleagues might not be a good thing. In reviewing the evidence for the model Mark and Smith (2008) argue that more research is needed to test its predictions. Chapter 8 of this textbook describes one other model to consider – the Job Characteristics Model (Hackman and Oldham, 1980). This describes the aspects of job design that can contribute to employee well-being. Although not a 'stress theory' per se the links between job characteristics and measures of well-being can be quite strong.

Key Learning Point

The amount of 'fit' between the employee and their work environment plays an important role in determining how stressful the employee finds their job.

Transactional approaches

Structural models of work stress did much to further our understanding about how working conditions are linked to employee health. However, it seems logical to assume that the stress process does not end when there is a mismatch between the person and the environment. Through your reading of this textbook it should be clear that individuals at work react to, respond to and *transact with* the work environment (i.e. they do things that change their situation). The dynamic nature of the stress process (see Figure 12.1) was highlighted by Cummings and Cooper (1979) who argue that:

- Individuals, for the most part, try to keep their thoughts, emotions and relationships with the world in a 'steady state'.

- Each element of a person's emotional and physical state has a 'range of stability', in which that person feels comfortable. On the other hand, when forces disrupt one of these elements beyond the range of stability, the individual must act or cope to restore a feeling of comfort.

- An individual's behaviour aimed at maintaining a steady state makes up their 'adjustment process', or coping strategies. Bunce and West (1996) showed that these coping strategies can include actions taken by the individual that alter the demands of their job.

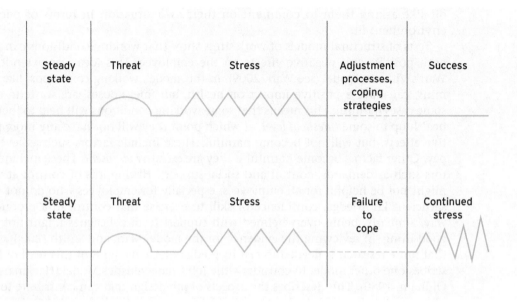

Figure 12.1   **The Cooper-Cummings framework**
Source: **Cummings, T. and Cooper, C.L. (1979) 'A cybernetic framework for the study of occupational stress',** *Human Relations,* **32, pp. 395-419. Reprinted with permission.**

Transactional models of stress (cognitive theories of stress and coping) focus more on describing the *psychological mechanisms of the stress process* (such as employees' cognitive evaluation of their working conditions, their emotional responses to their work and decision-making mechanisms relating to coping and behaviour). They are dynamic and complex models that draw in factors such as individual differences and coping styles.

Lazarus and Folkman (1984) proposed that an individual evaluates the extent to which a situation or event poses a threat to them: this is a *primary appraisal*. The appraisal might be that something was a problem (a *harm-loss* appraisal), could be a problem (a *threat* appraisal) or that the situation presents some potential for gain (a *challenge* appraisal). There is then a *secondary appraisal* where the person evaluates whether they can cope with the situation. If a person thinks they can cope with a situation they are less likely to appraise it as a threat and more likely to appraise it as a challenge. Together, these primary and secondary appraisals are the basis of what the person chooses to do in response to the situation (i.e. their *transaction* with the work environment). The appraisals are also linked to the person's emotional response and, in turn, physiological responses (such as changes in blood pressure). If threat appraisals occur often, there are likely to be negative outcomes for the employee (such as anxiety). In contrast challenge appraisals are likely to yield positive emotions and be quite motivating. As you can see, the meanings that people attach to events are extremely important in this model, and different people attach different meanings to similar events. The way people make sense of what is going on around them can be influenced by any number of individual differences (e.g. personality): these factors will be discussed later in this chapter.

Cox and MacKay's transactional model of work stress (*see* Cox, 1993, and Mark and Smith, 2008, for summaries) adds another dimension to the basic ideas of Lazarus and Folkman. It has five stages:

1   The work environment places some demands on the individual.

2   The individual evaluates/appraises these demands in relation to their coping abilities.

3   If there is a mismatch or imbalance at 2 then the individual will experience negative emotions (such being anxious) and physical changes (such as raised blood pressure). This instigates a coping response.

4   There are outcomes of the coping response (e.g. the person may be feeling less anxious, or maybe even more anxious).

5   The person appraises the effectiveness of the action taken. If they feel their action was effective, then they may become immediately less anxious and perceive similar problems as being less stressful in the future. Their actions may have even removed the source of stress. They also gain information about the effectiveness of the coping. In this model the outcomes of the individual's responses feed back into all the preceding stages of the process (i.e. it shapes what stressors they are exposed to in the future, it informs how they appraise those stressors, and how they choose to respond to them).

In this model the appraisal process is like a problem-solving cycle, and the *feedback loops* are particularly important in determining how people respond to the working conditions over a period of time. It is worth noting that this model does not suggest that the problem a person encountered is always solved by their coping responses. Some maladaptive coping responses (e.g. increased alcohol consumption) can be consequences of work stress. Some actions might help employees to reduce their exposure to stressors (e.g. by getting on with the job in hand). Cox and MacKay (1981) argue that people's choices of coping responses are not always rational and can be affected by a range of biases and individual difference variables (*see* later in this chapter). Some people might feel very able and just like to get on with things, while others may be less confident and tend to focus on managing their emotions. In addition, feedback might not always be accurate or available. For example, bosses and customers don't always tell an employee when they have done well or badly. Even if feedback is available people do not always interpret it incorrectly.

Key Learning Point

Transactional models of stress are more complex than structural models. These models have more to say about the role of perception, individual differences and coping in the experience of stress. Importantly they also describe how the individual receives feedback from the environment.

According to Cox (1993) the importance of individual appraisals means that a wide range of working conditions are potentially stressful, and that many individual difference variables can play a part in the stress process. As we will see later in this chapter, this appears to be the case.

Siegrist (1996) presented a transactional model that emphasises the importance of the balance of two factors, perceived *efforts and rewards*. According to this *Effort–Reward Imbalance (ERI)* model negative emotions are experienced when an employee perceives that their efforts are not reciprocated (in terms of money, esteem and recognition). In other words, stress arises when efforts are not appropriately rewarded, and this yields perceived unfairness. Siegrist proposes that one way that employees might respond to an imbalance is to *over commit* in a desire to obtain reward and recognition: the individual then gets into a cycle of working harder and harder, and experiencing more stress. Because it focuses on rewards, the model points to aspects of work such as career development, job security and promotion prospects as powerful sources of stress. It also places an individual difference, *self-esteem*, at the heart of the stress process. Although a relatively recent model, there is already quite a lot of evidence to support its main predictions (Tsutsumi and Kawakami, 2004).

All models of stress have something to offer, and researchers and practitioners still draw from a range of structural and transactional theories. Structural models offer relatively simple, mechanical predictions about the impact of work on employee well-being. This simplicity and the specific generalisable predictions from the models are not always borne out by research findings. However, these models have done much to further our understanding about what the major sources of work stress are and the psychological mechanisms through which they exert their effects. Transactional theories give us a more complete account of the stress process, but because they are more complex these models are more difficult to test and validate. These models do help us to see the field of enquiry should not only include employees' perceptions of working conditions, but also individual differences in how employees respond to and cope with the pressures they face at work. Some newer models attempt to combine both approaches. For example, the Demand-induced Strain Compensation Model (DISC, see de Jonge and Dormann, 2006; van Veldhoven *et al.*, 2005) suggests that stress will occur if: (i) emotional demands at work are not matched by the available emotional resources, or (ii) cognitive demands are not matched by the available cognitive resources, or (iii) that physical demands at work are not matched by the available physical resources. This model contains the reciprocal element of the ERI with some of the central tenets of the DCSM. As you will see later in this chapter, all of the models we have described have influenced how stress is identified and managed.

Key Learning Point

Most models of stress have contributed something to our current understanding of the issue. The more complex models are more difficult to test. The simpler models appear to underestimate the complexity of the stress process.

The consequences and costs of work stress

To the individual whose health or happiness has been ravaged by the effects of stress, the costs involved are only too clear. Whether manifested as minor complaints or illness, serious ailments such as heart disease, or social problems such as alcoholism and drug abuse, stress-related problems can exact a heavy price. It has also long been recognised that a family suffers indirectly from the stress problems of one of its members (e.g. through unhappy marriages or divorces). But what price do organisations and nations pay for a poor fit between people and their environments? As studies of stress-related illnesses and deaths show, stress is taking a devastatingly high toll on our combined productivity and health (Weinberg and Cooper, 2007; Palmer and Cooper, 2007).

As stress begins to take its toll on the body and mind, a variety of outcomes can result. Many of the physical and behavioural ramifications of stress listed in Table 12.1

Table 12.1	Physical and behavioural symptoms of stress	
Physical symptoms of stress	**Behavioural symptoms of stress**	**Ailments with stress aetiology**
Lack of appetite	Constant irritability with people	Hypertension: high blood pressure
Craving for food when under pressure	Feeling unable to cope	Coronary thrombosis: heart attack
Frequent indigestion or heartburn	Lack of interest in life	Migraine
Constipation or diarrhoea	Constant or recurrent fear of disease	Hayfever and allergies
Insomnia	A feeling of being a failure	Asthma
Constant tiredness	A feeling of being bad or of self-hatred	Pruritus: intense itching
Tendency to sweat for no good reason	Difficulty in making decisions	Peptic ulcers
Nervous twitches	A feeling of ugliness	Constipation
Nail-biting	Loss of interest in other people	Colitis
Headaches	Awareness of suppressed anger	Rheumatoid arthritis
Cramps and muscle spasms	Inability to show true feelings	Menstrual difficulties
Nausea	A feeling of being the target of other people's animosity	Nervous dyspepsia: flatulence and indigestion
Breathlessness without exertion	Loss of sense of humour	Hyperthyroidism: overactive thyroid gland
Fainting spells	Feeling of neglect	Diabetes melitus
Frequent crying or desire to cry	Dread of the future	Skin disorders
Impotency or frigidity	A feeling of having failed as a person or parent	Tuberculosis
Inability to sit still without fidgeting	A feeling of having no one to confide in	Depression
High blood pressure	Difficulty in concentrating	
	The inability to finish one task before rushing on to the next	
	An intense fear of open or enclosed spaces, or of being alone	

tend to be apparent *before* the onset of illness in which the experience of stress may play a part. As you can see some significant ailments may be brought on, or aggravated, by stress.

Understanding the different outcomes of stress can be challenging. Looking at Table 12.1 it is all too easy to 'medicalise' stress as an illness and make some rather alarmist predictions about its impact. Many argue that to describe stress as a medical condition is unhelpful and inaccurate, and most influential stress researchers agree on this point (despite much media reporting to the contrary). As we have already seen, established theories of stress do not conceptualise it as an illness. Through the impact of emotions on the body, stress at work can play a role in the development of a variety of important individual and organisational problems. Reviewing the stress research, Zapf and colleagues (1996) argued that working conditions have a relatively modest (albeit significant) impact on well-being because they are only one of the many factors that influence individual health. You may have guessed already that other very influential factors include socio-economic status, smoking, alcohol consumption, genetics and so on. Therefore, the relationship between the experience of stress and various outcomes (such as disease, absence, performance and turnover) is not a simple one. In Chapter 6 the complexity of measuring individual performance in terms of organisational outcomes is discussed. Similar issues apply to the measurement of organisational outcomes of work stress. Absence, for example, is the result of a complex, multifaceted process in which stress is just one potentially important factor. That said there are significant links between stressful working conditions and a variety of measures of work-related well-being.

The measures most frequently used to examine health and well-being at work can be grouped into four categories:

1 organisational measures;
2 psychological and physical health measures;
3 physiological measures;
4 measures of health-related behaviours.

Key Learning Point

The unpleasant emotion that is stress has consequences. It can have an impact on how people think and behave. In turn this can have an impact on individual well-being and the healthiness of organisations.

You will also notice that the majority of these measures are designed to detect problems rather than to measure positive aspects of well-being: this issue will be examined later in this chapter. It is important to point out that not all measures of stress outcomes correlate (*see* Chapter 2) with each other. For example, in the health care sector high levels of job satisfaction and low levels of absence are frequently found among groups of employees who report poor physical well-being (Cox *et al.*, 2002). This indicates that employees can find their job satisfying and be reluctant to take time off, while still finding the job to be exhausting. Somewhat counter-intuitively, high absence levels can be associated with good psychological health because being away from work allows the employee to escape the problems that have an adverse effect on their psychological well-being. These situation-specific nuances indicate the need to carry out a proper risk-assessment/problem analysis in an organisation in order to understand the nature of any problems and how they are linked to employee well-being. This problem-solving approach is discussed at the end of this chapter.

Organisational measures

Organisational measures include absence levels, various measures of job performance, accidents or 'near miss' incidents and actual staff turnover. Absenteeism is one of the obvious costs of stress to employers. Other causes of absence such as home and family responsibilities, personal problems, poor workplace morale, impact of long hours, lack of commitment and drink and drug problems (all of which could be classified as sources or outcomes of stress) could also be stress-related absences. This is one conclusion drawn by the UK Health and Safety Executive in 2007 which estimated that self-reported work-related stress, depression or anxiety account for 10.5 million reported lost working days per year in Britain. Perhaps an even more serious problem is that of presenteeism (Hoel *et al.*, 2003). This is when people are at work but are less productive either due to reduced commitment, motivation, satisfaction or due to physical or psychological health problems (Brun and Lamarche, 2006).

Turnover has been shown to be linked to working conditions in a number of studies (*see* Bond *et al.*, 2006, for an excellent review of this research). High rates of employee turnover can become quite expensive to a company – they raise training costs, reduce overall efficiency and disrupt other workers. Although it is hard to estimate the actual costs of labour turnover, it is thought that the cost of the loss of a member of staff is equal about five times an employee's monthly salary (Quick and Quick, 1984). The issue of staff turnover is discussed in some detail in Chapter 7.

Taris (2006) and Taris and Schreurs (2009) have tested the *happy worker = productive worker hypothesis* in many organisations. These studies were a bit different from the tests of this hypothesis cited in Chapter 7 because measures of employee well-being were included. These studies revealed significant, but *modest*, correlations between employees' work-related exhaustion and their performance. As discussed in Chapter 7, the existence of a strong relationship between *job satisfaction* and *performance* is far from certain. Cognitive performance has been used in a small number of studies of work stress (Parkes and Sparkes, 1998). Cognitive performance is often classed as an objective measure because good performance is difficult to fake. Experiments and studies have shown that, within certain limits, an individual's performance actually improves with increased levels of stress. After a point, however, stress clearly results in reduced performance. The Yerkes–Dodson law, as shown in Figure 12.2, reflects this phenomenon in medical terms. As Melhuish (1978) suggested:

> The portion of the graph between B and C represents pressures which the individual can tolerate: within these limits his health and quality of life improve with increased pressure (challenge). At C, however, increased pressure loses its beneficial effect and becomes harmful. Pressure becomes stress and in the portion C–D, health and quality of life decrease. C is the threshold (as is B, for boredom is also a potent stress and the portion B–A also represents increasing risk of stress illness).

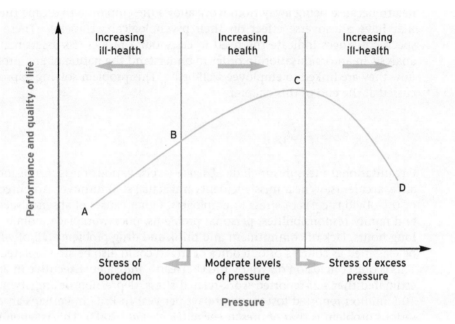

Figure 12.2 | **Medical extension of Yerkes-Dodson law**
Source: Extract from *Executive Health* by Dr Andrew Melhuish published by Random House Business Books. Used by permission of The Random House Group Limited.

The relationship between stress and performance is probably not quite as simple as this. For a short time difficult working conditions might lead to increased performance (e.g. if employees perceive that their position is under threat if they do not perform). However, in summarising the evidence O'Driscoll and Brough (2010) argue that the relationship between stress and performance tends to be more linear than the Yerkes–Dodson Law suggests (i.e. as jobs get more stressful, there is a greater impact on employee well-being and long-term productivity and performance tend to drop).

Employers are also paying directly for stress-related illnesses through workers' compensation claims (Earnshaw and Cooper, 2001). Many employers are being held responsible for employee stress due to the belief that they are doing little to cut down the stressful aspects of many jobs. This may help to explain the growth in corporate health and stress management programmes in America and elsewhere. Those employers who are at least seen to be doing something about workplace stress may be able to put forward a better defence in the courts.

According to a US government report (NIOSH, 1993), one specific type of compensation claim, 'gradual mental stress', refers to 'cumulative emotional problems stemming mainly from exposure to adverse psychosocial conditions at work . . . Emotional problems related to a specific traumatic event at work, or to work-related physical disease or injury, such as witnessing a severe accident, are not included.' According to the report, about 11 per cent of all occupational disease claims involve gradual mental stress. In the United Kingdom, because of the High Court judgement in the *John Walker vs Northumberland County Council* case in 1994, employee stress claims have been rising. There are literally hundreds of cases in the UK courts and the ones that were settled around the turn of the century averaged over £250,000 each (for details of all of these *see* Earnshaw and Cooper, 2001).

Key Learning Point

Stress has a significant cost in industrialised economies (some estimates put the cost at 10 per cent of GNP), through sickness absence, ill-health, labour turnover, decreased performance/presenteeism and litigation. However, the links between individual well-being and organisational health are not always clear.

Organisational measures are often thought to be good measures of the consequences of work stress because the data are 'objective' and are of value to the organisation. As we have seen, if absence and turnover rates are reduced, cost savings can be calculated. However, absence records are not always accurately kept. The assumption that stress levels are *always* associated with absence in every situation is not supported by the research evidence (Darr and Johns, 2008). It is also fairly obvious that employee absence behaviour is influenced by a huge range of factors (including seasonal illnesses and organisational policies for dealing with absence). In addition, Chapter 7 shows that turnover is a complex issue that is not always a result of how satisfied a person feels with their current job. Problems with the reliability, validity and sensitivity of measures of employee performance are well-documented (*see* Chapter 6). All of that aside, these organisational outcomes are important indicators of the costs of stress and the value of interventions: it is just that the quality of these data needs to be examined when they are being used as markers of the impact of stress.

Psychological data are also classified as organisational measures: these measures are sometimes referred to as being at the individual–organisation interface. These include self-report measures of job-related affect or mood (such as job satisfaction and motivation), attitudes (such as organisational commitment and intention to leave the organisation) and cognitions (such as self-efficacy). Some of these are measures of positive well-being (such as commitment) and are discussed in more detail in Chapter 7 (and later in this chapter when we examine positive well-being at work).

It is interesting to note some important trends in these data. Work has changed dramatically since the early 1990s, with more and more workplaces downsizing, merging and restructuring. The impact of these changes is reflected in the job satisfaction figures in many countries, which has been in steady decline for some time, although the UK is showing some signs recent signs of an upturn (CIPD, 2009). These changes in job satisfaction may be associated with the European workforce becoming more 'Americanised' in terms of intrinsic job insecurity, long hours and constant restructuring.

Psychological and physical health measures

Well-designed studies of the DCS model of work stress produced powerful evidence about the links between working conditions and a range of clinically diagnosed health problems (Karasek and Theorell, 1990). Morbidity (the development of serious disease, such as coronary heart disease or clinical depression) is sometimes used in long-term studies of the impact of work on health (such as the opening case study and the Whitehall II studies mentioned at the beginning of this chapter). Cooper and Quick (1999) contend that in the developed world, stress is directly implicated in four causes (heart disease, strokes, injuries and suicide), and indirectly involved in a further three (cancer, chronic liver disease and bronchial complaints such as emphysema). Stress may also play a role in the development of musculoskeletal problems through its impact on muscular tension and the body's repair mechanisms. These data can be captured through population studies (as in the opening case study) or through company records such as absence data (which may record reasons for absence) or records of referrals to occupational health departments/company doctors.

The problem with these outcome measures is that they provide indications of the impact of stress only when the problem has already taken a significant toll on the individual. In other words, they do not give a timely indication that problems are occurring. This means they are of limited use for organisations wishing to assess and manage the well-being of their employees before damage to employees sets in. This is one of the main reasons why self-report questionnaire measures of physical and psychological *symptoms* are often used. These can detect the early signs of poor health before illness becomes apparent.

There are many self-report measures of well-being and health. These measures allow an assessment of variations in employee health without the need for clinical diagnosis of disease. For example, a measure of anxiety may reveal that symptoms of anxiety are more prevalent in a specific group of workers than they are in the general working population, even if the number of employees absent from work because of stress is low. Some of these measures also have threshold scores: people scoring in excess of these levels are significantly more likely to already have a diagnosable psychological illness (e.g. clinical depression). The General Health Questionnaire (GHQ) (Goldberg and Williams, 1988) is a questionnaire that is commonly used in stress research: it measures symptoms of anxiety, depression, social dysfunction and loss of confidence. Another frequently used measure is the Brief Symptom Inventory (BSI) (Derogatis and Melisaratos, 1983) which assesses a wide range of physical and psychological symptoms although it is not specifically designed to assess work-related well-being. The General Well-being Questionnaire (GWBQ) (Cox *et al.*, 1983) is a measure designed with the assessment of work-related stress in mind: it measures symptoms of tension and exhaustion. More specific symptom reporting measures include the Beck Depression Inventory (BDI-II) (Beck, 1996), the State-Trait Anxiety Inventory (STAI) (Spielberger *et al.*, 1970) and the Maslach Burnout Inventory (MBI) (*see* Maslach and Jackson, 1981).

The MBI is interesting because it measures psychological symptoms of emotional exhaustion and cynicism that are particularly important to those in the caring professions (e.g. nurses, doctors, social workers, etc.) which are often regarded as high-stress occupations. Maslach and Jackson (1981) identified three subscales of burnout that are measured using the inventory:

1   Emotional exhaustion: *feelings of being emotionally over-stretched and exhausted by work.*

2   Depersonalisation: *an unfeeling and impersonal response to clients.*

3   Personal accomplishment: *feelings of competence and successful achievement at work.*

The use of questionnaire measures in stress research has been the subject of much controversy. Some argue that although easily gathered, self-report data can be riddled with the errors and biases that impact on human memory and judgement. Such problems are less likely to impact on verifiable 'objective' measures such as the number of days of absence, disease diagnoses, and changes in observable behaviour and physiological systems. However, if good quality measures are used, question-naires yield reliable and valid data about the immediate effects of the work envi-ronment on the individual (such as negative emotional experiences, psychological distress and dissatisfaction). It could also be argued that questionnaire measures are less contaminated by the multitude of factors that impact on organisational-level measures (e.g. absence and turnover) and measures of disease (Kompier and Kristensen, 2001). Most researchers (e.g. Cox *et al.*, 2000) agree that self-report data becomes even more powerful if secured by triangulation (*see* Chapter 2). For exam-ple, if low levels of job satisfaction are accompanied by high levels of turnover and a large number of accidents, then we might be more likely to accept that the job satisfaction data are correct and that intervention is needed.

Key Learning Point

Questionnaire measures are an extremely useful way of collecting information about phys-ical and psychological symptoms. The presence of these symptoms can indicate that stress is a problem.

Physiological measures

Changes in our physiological functioning are some of the first things that many of us notice when we experience stress. Physiological changes include elevated blood pressure, increased sweating and muscular tension. Some are less noticeable but are well-documented correlates of stress (e.g. changes in levels of the blood hormone cortisol which is important in bodily repair mechanisms). These changes can be measured and provide relatively 'instant' indications that the body is responding to changes in emotions associated with stress. For the individual employee these changes help to support coping responses (e.g. by preparing the body for increased effort in response to increased demands). However, prolonged or frequent demands on physiological systems are implicated as causes of more serious chronic health problems (such as hypertension and musculoskeletal problems). Of course, em-ployees are more likely to be willing to complete a questionnaire about their health than they are to consent to having blood samples taken from them or to have their blood pressure monitored for a 24-hour period. Collecting physiological data raises significant ethical issues. The relatively infrequent use of these measures in stress research (particularly intervention research) is probably an indication of the practi-cal and ethical problems associated with the use of these measures.

Health-related behaviours

Health-related behaviours include sleeping patterns, exercise levels and other mal-adaptive coping behaviours such as poor diet, smoking, drug and alcohol use. These data are usually captured through self-report/questionnaire measures or records from occupational health departments in organisations.

Sometimes health-related behaviours are referred to as maladaptive coping patterns (e.g. someone who drinks alcohol to excess in order to relax as a means of coping with work stress, but makes themselves ill because of their coping strategy). These behav-iours are also implicated as causes of diseases such as cancer and heart disease.

The relationship between these behaviours and working conditions is not always obvious. In a study of over 3000 employees in the United States, Gimeno *et al.* (2009) found that those in passive jobs (i.e. jobs with low demands coupled with low control) were significantly more likely than others to engage in heavy drinking (but were not likely to drink more frequently than most). Sikora *et al.* (2008) carried out a longitudinal study of alcohol use and work stress during downsizing and found that alcohol use can also be a cause of work stress (through, for example, its impact on work performance) as well as a consequence of it.

The use of maladaptive coping strategies often indicates that an employee has already been 'damaged' in some way by their work. As such these problems are often dealt with through tertiary interventions which are examined later in this chapter.

Key Learning Point

Employees may attempt to cope with stress through behaviours that are harmful to them in the long-term.

STOP TO CONSIDER

Theories and models of work stress are designed to help explain the problems with organisational and individual health you have just read about. How could you test whether these theories did help to explain these problems? Have a look back at Chapter 2 and see if any of the research methods described there could be of use. Considering this issue will help you to get a feel for how work-stress research is generally conducted.

From stress to positive well-being

Stress is a topic (or perhaps more accurately a word) that has generated huge amounts of research and media interest over many years. Yet not everyone agrees that the term is entirely helpful. This is for various conceptual and practical reasons.

In common usage the word stress tends to refer to almost anything unpleasant that happens, and/or as anything that leads a person to feel negative emotion. Many would argue this is far too broad a domain for just one word, and risks hiding important differences between different kinds of emotions. In turn, this increases the difficulty of devising research and management practices that address key issues effectively.

Much of the literature seems to construe stress as entirely negative, yet in some circumstances it is possible for both stress and positive emotions to arise from the same experience. As mentioned earlier, health care workers are often faced with heavy pressure but also experience quite high job satisfaction. Indeed, it seems that some level of challenge may even be necessary in order for other more positive things to happen, such as personal development (*see*, for example, Nicholson and West's 1988 analysis of how people react to new jobs). So as Hart and Cooper (2001) argue, it is possible to experience what we might call satisfaction and stress at the same time. This means that looking at stress would get only half the picture of a person's current experience of work.

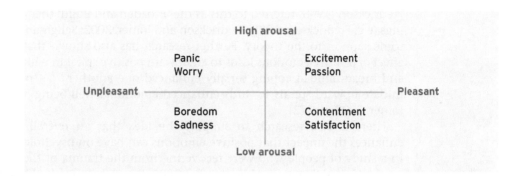

High arousal

| | Panic | | Excitement | |
| | Worry | | Passion | |

Unpleasant ————————————————————————— Pleasant

| | Boredom | | Contentment | |
| | Sadness | | Satisfaction | |

Low arousal

Figure 12.3   Four types of emotion

It is tempting to see stress as the negative end of the single dimension of well-being and/or emotion. However, many psychologists argue that this is too simplistic. It seems that the extent to which a person is experiencing pleasant emotion (*positive affect*) is more or less independent of the extent to which they are experiencing unpleasant emotion (*negative affect*). So any individual at any given moment could be high on one and low on the other, or high on both, or low on both (Agho *et al.*, 1992). It is also possible to distinguish between high arousal and low arousal. This creates four quadrants of emotion that can be experienced (see Figure 12.3). Again, this helps us gain a more complete picture of a person's work experience than simply examining 'stress'.

Although the avoidance of the negative consequences of poor well-being is still an important driver for theory, research and practice, the benefits of positive psychological well-being are becoming increasingly important to researchers and practitioners alike. Robertson and Flint-Taylor (2008) point out positive psychological well-being at work has two key components – a purposive (or *eudemonic*) element and an emotional (or *hedonic* element). The distinction between eudemonic and hedonic components of well-being dates back to Aristotle (see Boniwell and Henry, 2007). The hedonic element associates well-being with the experience of positive feelings (moods and emotions) and factors such as overall life satisfaction. Even for the most committed hedonist, day after day lounging on the yacht in the tropical sun would not produce high levels of well-being – unless there was some purpose to it – at least that's what the theory says, but it's probably worth testing for yourself! Most people feel at their very best not when totally relaxing but when something worthwhile has been achieved. For example, task significance is a key feature of the job characteristics model (*see* Chapter 8). This key principle of a worthwhile life being one that has a point or a purpose is the core of the eudemonic approach to well-being.

Ryff and Keyes (1995) present a model of positive well-being that includes six dimensions: autonomy; environmental mastery; personal growth; positive relations with others; purpose in life; and self-acceptance. At work, the eudemonic aspect of psychological well-being is exemplified by people feeling that their work activity has a clear sense of purpose.

The idea of purpose and positive emotion, as the key ingredients of positive well-being, is supported by research in the area of positive psychology. Fredrickson (1998) proposed a new theory that states that the experience of positive emotions serves to broaden the scope of people's attention, thought processes and actions; furthermore it also serves to build physical, intellectual and social resources.

Fredrickson (1998) referred to this as the 'Broaden and Build' theory. Research findings (e.g. Fredrickson, 1998; Fredrickson and Joiner, 2002; Seligman *et al.*, 2005) lend some support to the theory. Further research has also shown that the broadening effect of positive emotions leads to an upward positive spiral in which 'positive affect and broad-minded coping serially enhanced one another . . . positive emotions initiate upward spirals towards enhanced emotional well-being' (Fredrickson and Joiner, 2002, p. 172).

There is also research to support the idea that an overall *sense of purpose* enhances the impact that positive emotions can have on psychological well-being. In a study of people who were recovering from the trauma of the terrorist attacks on the United States on 11 September 2001, Fredrickson *et al.* (2003) observed the beneficial effect that positive emotions had and suggested that 'finding positive meaning may be the most powerful leverage point for cultivating positive emotions during times of crisis' (Fredrickson *et al.*, 2003, p. 374).

It would seem that a complete concept of well-being should include elements of both pleasure and purpose. As Robertson and Flint-Taylor (2008) note, this is a view of positive psychological well-being that translates very well into the organisational domain. It implies that some part of psychological well-being at work will be derived from positive feelings that are, in turn, derived from doing something that is seen as worthwhile – a perspective that is consistent with work in many related areas of work and organisational psychology, including motivation and job design. For example, goal-setting theory (Locke and Latham, 1990) involves ensuring that people have goals that are difficult but attainable – and that they are committed to attaining their goals.

Another reason for the increased interest in positive well-being at work is its potential link with desirable behaviours and attitudes at work such as engagement, commitment and organisational citizenship. The causes and consequence of the latter two are discussed in Chapter 7. Engagement is defined as 'a positive, fulfilling, work-related state of mind that is characterized by vigor, dedication, and absorption' (Schaufeli *et al.*, 2002, p. 74). Recently, a great deal has been written about the importance of developing an engaged workforce. Most of the work on engagement emphasises its potential links with beneficial organisational outcomes such as performance and reluctance to leave and the results of early research are promising (e.g. Halbesleben and Wheeler, 2008). This may be partly because, as Robinson and colleagues (2004) note, the core constructs of engagement overlap somewhat with organisational commitment (Chapter 7) and organisational citizenship (Chapter 6). In a meta-analysis of data collected from nearly 8000 separate business units in 36 companies, Harter *et al.* (2002) found significant relationships between scores on an employee questionnaire capturing elements of engagement, satisfaction and positive psychological well-being on the one hand, and business unit level outcomes (customer satisfaction, productivity, profitability, employee turnover and sickness/absence levels) on the other hand.

Wright and Cropanzano (2004) reviewed the wider body of evidence linking employee positive well-being (PWB) with performance. In conclusion they noted that

Employee PWB has both theoretical and applied relevance in today's society. Using the Positive Psychology/Positive Organizational Behavior (POB) framework, it seems evident that promoting employee PWB is an intrinsic good for which all should work. If this approach promotes better job performance, which the findings strongly suggest is the case, then so much the better.

(p. 348)

At this stage the published research is not extensive enough to clarify and confirm the relationships between these factors and individual performance and organisational success. However, the research to date and other emerging work (e.g. Robertson Cooper, 2008) suggest that both positive well-being and factors such as engagement, commitment and citizenship have an important role to play in individual performance and key organisational outcomes such as turnover, absence and productivity.

Key Learning Point

The concept of stress may be a little too narrow to capture the wide range of emotions that are generated through experiences at work. Positive well-being is not simply the absence of ill-health.

Factors linked to employee stress and well-being

In this section we examine the various working conditions and individual differences that have been shown to be implicated in work stress and employee well-being. We describe the nature of each factor and for each present some example studies that provide evidence of its importance. The research literature on these factors is so large that we focus on those factors that meta-analyses, extensive literature reviews and large-scale research studies have shown to be significantly related to some of the various outcomes of work stress described earlier in this chapter (e.g. Bonde, 2008; Bond *et al.*, 2006; Kivimäki *et al.*, 2006; O'Driscoll and Brough, 2010; Ng *et al.*, 2006; Podsakoff *et al.*, 2007). Figure 12.4 gives an overview of these factors that are included in comprehensive models of workplace stress. The exact mechanisms between the different sets of constructs shown in Figure 12.4 are still being explored but the broad links between these factors and various measures of well-being are quite well-established. As described in various models of work stress, situational and person factors interact to determine the overall levels of well-being that any individual experiences. For example, someone with the characteristics of 'hardiness' (*see* Bartone, 1989; Maddi, 2002) would be better able to withstand various situational stressors than someone who is less hardy.

The key factors that drive psychological well-being in the workplace may be very broadly grouped into factors that relate to the person, or *individual differences*, and factors that relate to the *situation* that the person is in. Individual differences include the attitudes, personality, coping strategies, and skills and abilities of the individual. Situational factors include everything that is part of the situation that the person experiences.

Key Learning Point

Aspects of the situation and individual differences are both important in determining the impact of work on individual employees.

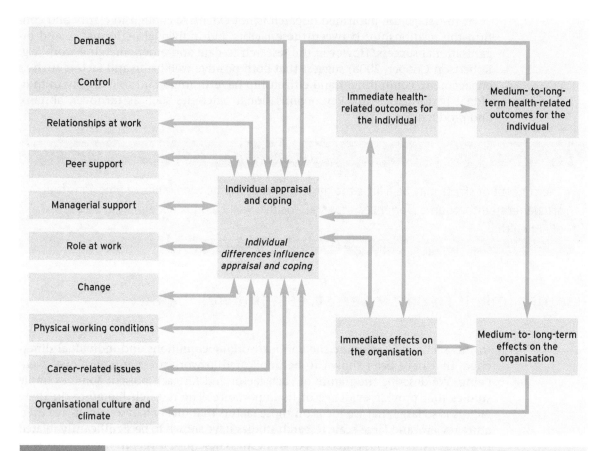

Figure 12.4	**Dynamics of work stress**

Note the use of two-way arrows in some parts of this figure, indicating that people transact with their environment. These arrows show that there is feedback into the individual appraisal throughout the process. They also show that people's perceptions/appraisals can result in them changing their environment.

Situational factors

Not all researchers agree on how situational factors should be grouped into categories. However, to use a culinary analogy, most cut the same 'cake', but choose to cut it into a slightly different number of 'slices'. As was mentioned earlier in the discussion of theories of work stress, not all situational factors are sources of stress for everybody in all workplaces. Cox *et al.* (2000) use the term *hazard* to describe situational factors of possible sources of work stress. This means that these working conditions have the *potential* to cause harm, but much can still depend on individual differences in personality, coping styles, ability and so on. In addition these factors interact, or mix, with each other, giving each workplace a unique profile of working conditions. This means that to identify the sources of work stress in any particular workplace there is a need for risk assessment/problem analysis: this is discussed at the end of this chapter. Setting that complexity aside for a moment, it is clear that some working conditions are more likely than others to be sources of work stress. One indication of this is when lots of different employees doing the job report a problem: logic suggests that individual differences are playing less of a role in the problems that lots of different people agree upon.

Key Learning Point

If there is agreement among a group of employees that a particular aspect of work is a problem, then situational factors (rather than individual differences) are more likely to be an important source of stress.

Demands

Job content and workload There are several elements of the core content of jobs that can be significant sources of work stress, and these are probably the most familiar to the lay person. These include working at a fast pace, working intensively and having to meet tight deadlines frequently. Employees are often at risk of work stress if their work is often performed under pressure, and if it contains extended periods of hard physical work or concentration with very few breaks or respite. A useful way of thinking about demands is to use the categories set out in the DISC model described earlier in this chapter: cognitive demands, emotional demands and physical demands. If any of these are excessive for an individual then there is strong evidence that problems tend to follow for both the individual and the organisation.

Two different types of work overload have been described by researchers. *Quantitative overload* refers simply to having too much work to do. In this case, too much work often leads to working long hours and the problems that go with it. *Qualitative overload* refers to work that is too difficult for an individual (French and Caplan, 1972). Repetitive routines, boring and under-stimulating work can also be a problem. Weinberg and Cooper (2007) have described this as *underload*, or not being sufficiently challenged by work. Certain workers, such as pilots, air traffic controllers and nuclear power workers, face a special aspect of work *underload*. They must deal with long periods of time in which they have little to do while facing the possibility that they may suddenly be required to spring into action in a crisis. On a smaller scale, this is also a problem for some workers with advanced manufacturing technology who (depending on how jobs are configured) may become relatively unskilled machine-minders but who nevertheless have to respond quickly if the machine malfunctions (Chase and Karwowski, 2003).

As already noted research in positive psychology (e.g. Fredrickson *et al.*, 2003) has revealed the importance that meaningfulness and a clear sense of purpose can play in supporting psychological well-being. In the workplace, 'sense of purpose' is most obviously related to the immediate job role that people hold – and the goals and objectives of that role. Goal-setting theory (see Chapter 8) shows that when people are committed to goals that are clear, specific and challenging they tend to perform well. People also tend to experience higher levels of well-being when they have a clear sense of purpose, i.e. clear, specific and challenging goals.

Emotional labour is a concept that has received much recent attention in the stress research. This is relevant in jobs (such as many forms of customer service work) where an individual must manage their emotions and their responses to the emotions of others (Morris and Feldman, 1996). One particularly stressful element of this is *emotional dissonance* that has been found to have links with several measures of employee well-being (Zapf, 2002). This is when an employee has to mask or hide their emotions (for example an airline steward who might need to appear sympathetic to the unreasonable demands of an angry passenger).

Unless the content of a job is well-designed and managed, there is a risk that several types of demands become excessive and employees will then be more likely to experience work-related stress.

Working hours The long working hours required by many jobs appear to take a toll on employee health. One early research study linked long working hours and deaths due to coronary heart disease (Breslow and Buell, 1960). This investigation of light industrial workers in the United States found that individuals under 45 years of age who worked more than 48 hours a week had twice the risk of death from coronary heart disease than did similar individuals working a maximum of 40 hours a week. Many individuals, such as executives working long hours and some medics who might have no sleep for 36 hours or more, may find that both they and the quality of their work suffer. It seems that in many Western countries the average number of hours worked per week is slowly reducing (partly due to legislation such as the European Working Time Directive). Typical working hours in some developing countries can be twice those in some of the industrialised developed countries.

It is now commonly recognised that beyond 40 hours a week, time spent working is increasingly unproductive and can create ill-health. In fact, in a meta-analytic investigation of a large number of international studies linking hours of health, it was found that consistently working long hours damaged individuals' physical and/or psychological health – and 'long' was considered any hours over 40 (Sparks *et al.*, 1997). Of course, it may not only be the long hours that create this effect. People who choose to work long hours may be especially driven individuals who are prone to health problems. Their jobs may be demanding in many different ways (for example overload, responsibility), which may lead the person to work long hours in order to complete their tasks (Burke and Cooper, 2008). This finding raises an important issue: many sources of work stress interact with and influence each other.

Shift work Many workers today have jobs requiring them to work in shifts, some of which involve working unusual or unsociable hours. Studies have found that shift work is a common occupational stress factor. It has been demonstrated that shift work has quite a profound impact on physical functioning, bringing about changes in blood temperature, metabolic rate, blood sugar levels, in addition to having an impact on sleep patterns, family and social life, mental efficiency and work motivation. In one study of nurses, for example, Demir *et al.* (2003) found that working night shifts led to exhaustion, loss of energy and 'detachment' from patients. For nurses working night shifts these problems were significantly greater than for nurses doing comparable work on day shifts.

Of course, not all shift work is the same. Shifts can start and finish at somewhat different times, they can be different lengths, and there are variations in the extent and frequency with which staff are required to change shifts. Some ways of managing shift work can be more stressful than others. The longer the work shift – for example '28 days on, 28 days off' versus '14 days on, 14 days off' – the greater its impact on employee well-being (Sutherland and Cooper, 1987). The effects of longer periods of shiftwork tend to be particularly problematical for workers who are married and have children. Fixed shifts (i.e. working just nights or just days) tend to be less unhealthy than rotating shifts (working some nights, some days, some evenings, etc.) because employees need to make less frequent and less significant changes to adapt to different working hours. However, Barnes-Farrell *et al.* (2008) in their study of shiftwork in health care workers from a number of different countries found that workers on fixed night shifts reported lower mental well-being when compared to workers on day shifts or rotating shifts (this was after the effects of age, marital status and working conditions had been controlled for). The researchers argue that the benefits of permanent night shifts may be apparent only for those employees who prefer such a work schedule.

This issue of shift length is quite complex. Shifts that are longer than the usual working day seem to have some benefits. Hoffman and Scott (2003) found that nurses working 12-hour shifts experienced no more stress than those working 8-hour shifts. Barnes-Farrell *et al.* (2008) report similar results. Mitchell and Williamson (2000) reported that power station workers on 12-hour shifts experienced fewer problems in domestic life, and better sleep and mood, than those on 8-hour shifts. However, and rather ominously, some aspects of work performance showed an increase in error rates towards the end of a 12-hour shift (somehow this brings to mind images of Homer Simpson!). The possible performance losses brought about by extended shifts are also discussed by Sparks *et al.* (2001).

Work–life interface As discussed in Chapter 1 of this textbook, there is a growing body of research and theory about how work and non-work demands interact and the consequences this interaction has for employee well-being. Home–work interface issues are usually given the label 'conflict' in the stress literature. This conflict can be in either or both of two directions: work interference with family (where the demands of work create difficulties for home life) and family interference with work (where the demands of home life create difficulties for work) (Lewis and Cooper, 2005). Large-scale reviews of research on the topic tend to identify that satisfaction at home tends to influence satisfaction at work and vice versa: this means that stress at home can influence variables such as job satisfaction (Ford *et al.*, 2007).

The interference or conflict can be manifested in a variety of ways. Most obviously, the sheer amount of time required by roles in one domain (home or work) may make it difficult to give enough time to roles in the other domain. Slightly more subtly, the amount of cognitive, emotional or physical energy required to fulfil roles in one domain may mean that insufficient energy remains for roles (including tasks and relationships) in the other. Less obviously again, the kinds of values, attitudes and behaviours required in one domain may be different from (or clash with) those required in the other. For example, a salesperson may be expected to be aggressive and dominant at work, but gentle and cooperative at home. The many human resource management practices designed to reduce home–work interface stress (e.g. workplace crèches, family leave) can help with some forms of conflict, but probably not all (Cooper and Lewis, 1993).

Time-based conflict might lead to guilt or anxiety that one is not fulfilling one's roles properly, and perhaps low satisfaction. Energy-based conflict can produce exhaustion and irritability (see Sonnentag and Niessen, 2008), while value-based conflict can lead to a sense of alienation and/or loss of self-identity.

Of course, the picture is more complicated than this. One issue is what 'home' means. Does it mean anything that is not work? If so, perhaps the term is too broad, and if not, maybe it would be more helpful to distinguish between various domestic and leisure commitments a person may have (e.g. parent, spouse, fitness fanatic, amateur photographer, etc.). Also, to some extent there are differences between cultures/countries in the importance typically assigned to work vs. home roles, and in the extent to which work and home roles are typically seen as necessarily separate or compatible. As with all work stressors, a person's appraisal of their situation is important in determining whether they see it as a problem or not, and this might be influenced by whether they are made aware that there are positive benefits to be gained from balancing different work and non-work roles (Van Steenbergen *et al.*, 2008). Sonnentag and Niessen (2008) found that individuals high in trait vigour (those with high self-esteem, high extroversion and who follow a healthy lifestyle) tend to have the most energy to deal with non-work issues after a hard day at work. So although the interface between work and other aspects of life can produce stress, there is much still to be understood about which interfaces can cause problems and why and how stress is produced (Swan and Cooper, 2005).

Key Learning Point

There are well-documented links between individual and organisational health on the one hand, and working hours, certain aspects of shift work and problems with work-life balance on the other.

Resources and communications To perform their job effectively, individuals need to feel they have the appropriate training, equipment and resources. Resources refer to knowledge, skills, ability as well as physical equipment to do the job. They also need to feel that they are adequately informed and that they are valued. A number of sources (e.g. NIOSH *et al.*, 1999; Rothmann and Cooper, 2008) have associated all or some of these factors with stress. These factors are at the heart of many contemporary theories of work stress (i.e. any that mention 'fit' between the employee's capabilities and the demands placed on them, those focus on resources, e.g. DISC, or models that focus on reward, e.g. ERI). Good-quality training and selection are rarely mentioned as stress management interventions, but they can go a long way towards ensuring that the fit between the individual employee and the demands placed upon them is maximised.

Risk and danger A job that involves risk or danger can result in poor well-being (Clarke and Cooper, 2004). When someone is constantly aware of potential danger, they are prepared to react immediately. The individual is in a constant state of arousal, as described in the 'fight or flight' syndrome. The resultant adrenalin rush, respiration changes and muscle tension are all seen as potentially threatening to long-term health. On the other hand, individuals who face physical danger – such as police, mine workers, firefighters and soldiers – often appear to have reduced stress levels. Once again training is important: those who are adequately trained and equipped to deal with emergency situations often find dealing with them a source of motivation and satisfaction.

Control

As you might expect from what you know about structural theories of work stress, control at work has received an enormous amount of attention in stress research. Control can apply to almost any aspect of work. In their widely used high-quality measure of control, Dwyer and Ganster (1991) include 22 questions for employees to measure various different aspects of control. These include:

- control over the quality of work;

- control over work pace;

- how much influence the worker has over policies and procedures;

- how much control the employee has over when they can take holidays or time off;

- control over the variety of methods used;

- control over decision-making, and so on.

Research has showed that lack of influence in the way in which work is organised and performed can be damaging to psychological and physical well-being. While low levels of control are a source of work stress, high levels of control tend to be beneficial (Weinberg and Cooper, 2007). Research shows that control is a particularly powerful predictor of employee health. In their meta-analysis, Bond and colleagues (2006) also found that high levelss of control are also associated with higher levels of job performance and lower levels of absence. In the same review it was also found that improvements in control tend to underpin the effectiveness of many stress management interventions. Whether the various aspects of control at work offset or buffer other stressors is less certain (O'Driscoll and Brough, 2010). The effects of control may also depend on whether an individual prefers to be in control or not. Meier *et al.* (2008) found that high levels of job control helped to buffer the impact of work stressors on well-being, but only for those people with an internal locus of control (*see* page 469 for a description of locus of control).

Key Learning Point

There are many different aspects of a job over which the employee may have control. There is a lot of research which shows that control at work has strong links to individual and organisational health.

Managerial support

There is a large body of evidence that shows lack of managerial support places employee well-being at risk. However, as with control, high levels of support can have significant benefits for employees. Reviews of numerous specific research studies testify to the importance of perceived supervisor support. Ng and Sorenson (2008) examined the results of 59 studies (containing a total of over 40,000 participants) and found strong relationships between this type of support and job satisfaction, commitment to the organisation and intention to stay with the organisation.

Sosik and Godshalk (2000) among others have shown that an inspiring leadership style (see Chapter 14) can significantly reduce the amount of stress experienced by subordinates. This style of leadership includes giving priority to the development needs of specific individuals, setting a personal example, and establishing clear mission for the workgroup or organisation.

Donaldson-Feilder and colleagues (2008) have conducted a thorough analysis of the managerial behaviours and how they impact on employee well-being. They say that these behaviours work through a number of mechanisms:

> Management behavior has a direct impact on staff well-being – managers can prevent or cause stress in those they manage. Managers also act as 'gatekeepers' to their employees' exposure to stressful working conditions and are vital to the identification and tackling of stress in the workplace.

(p. 11)

As a result of this research 19 categories of positive management behaviour have been identified. Four categories of behaviour are particularly important in helping employees to feel supported. They are:

- accessible/visible: has an open door policy and is in regular contact with those being managed by them;

- health and safety: takes the health and safety of the team seriously;

- feedback: providing feedback, showing gratitude and praising good work;

- individual consideration: provides regular one-to-one meetings with employees and is flexible with regard to issues affecting individual employees (e.g. work–life interface issues).

Individual differences between managers play quite a large part in determining how they behave at work. Sparks *et al.* (2001) pointed out that competitive pressures on organisations usually lead to pressure on individual managers. It now appears that managers face a new challenge: learning to manage by participation. Some managers find this hard to cope with, and many respond by behaving in unpleasant ways towards their subordinates. A boss under stress may change the nature of a subordinate's job so that it becomes more stressful – for example by supervising the subordinate much more closely (Lobban *et al.*, 1998). Management training and performance appraisal can be used to help managers recognise and manage better the impact of their behaviour on employees (Donaldson-Feilder *et al.*, 2008). Different types of managers may respond to different types of interventions. Cooper *et al.* (1993) found that there were various boss prototypes: the bureaucrat, the autocrat, the wheeler-dealer, the reluctant manager and the open manager. For example, the bureaucrat is likely to respond most positively to training that is structured, and relatively formal communication which respects established procedures.

Peer support

Both people – and our varied encounters with them – can be major sources of both stress and support (Makin *et al.*, 1996). At work, our dealings with peers can dramatically affect the way we feel at the end of the day. Very early work by Selye (1974) suggested that learning to live with other people is one of the most stressful aspects of life. This is in spite of the fact that most people, given the opportunity, seek out social contact and relationships at least some of the time. Lazarus (1966) suggested that supportive social relationships with peers, supervisors and subordinates at work are less likely to create interpersonal pressures, and will directly reduce levels of perceived job stress. Poor relationships were defined by researchers at the University of Michigan as those which include low trust, low supportiveness and low interest in listening or trying to deal with problems that confront the organisational member. Most studies show that high levels of support help to maintain good employee well-being, but that they do not always buffer the effects of other stressors (Brough *et al.*, 2009).

Stress among co-workers can arise from the competition and personality conflicts usually described as 'office politics'. Adequate social support can be critical to the health and well-being of an individual and to the atmosphere and success of an organisation (Bernin and Theorell, 2001). Because most people spend so much time at work, the relationships among co-workers can provide valuable support or, conversely, can be a huge source of stress. Most reviews (e.g. Cooper *et al.*, 2001) have concluded that mistrust of fellow workers is connected with high role ambiguity and poor communications.

In the meta-analysis by Ng and Sorenson (2008), one interesting finding was that peer support was particularly important when employees are in jobs that involve working with customers. This may be because employees in such roles share similar experiences of stressful interactions with customers and understand each other's sources of stress: this helps them to offer more effective practical help and emotional support. This camaraderie might be an important mechanism through which peer support exerts its effects.

Key Learning Point

Lack of support from managers and/or colleagues places employees at a significantly increased risk of experiencing work-related stress.

Relationships at work

As we have seen, support at work can have a significant positive impact on employees. Much attention has also been paid to what happens when relationships at work are damaging. Friction, anger and disagreements between people at work are all well-documented sources of work stress. For example sexual harassment damages organisational commitment, job satisfaction, productivity and individual psychological health (Willness *et al.*, 2007). Violence (or the threat of violence) at work is similarly problematical (*see* Kessler *et al.*, 2008). In this section we focus on one particularly well-researched problem: workplace bullying. This is not to downplay the importance of other relationship stressors, but space does not allow detailed consideration of them all.

Workplace bullying One extreme form of problems with relationships at work is workplace bullying. Some reports suggest that bullying is disturbingly common (Rayner *et al.*, 2001). Salin defines bullying as '*repeated* and *persistent negative acts* towards one or more *individual(s),* which involve *a perceived power imbalance* and create a *hostile work environment'* (2003, p. 214, emphasis in original). Workplace bullying is now recognised as a major occupational stressor, creating enormous financial and legal implications for organisations. Giga and colleagues (2008) put the annual cost of bullying-related absenteeism, turnover and productivity losses at approximately £13.75 billion (based on UK figures for 2007): 25 per cent of targets of bullying and, significantly, 20 per cent of witnesses of workplace bullying leave the organisation (e.g. Rayner *et al.*, 2002). Because of its potentially serious consequences, and because it has not been examined elsewhere in this text, we discuss the issue here in some detail. The length of the coverage given to the issue should not be taken as a measure of relative importance in comparison to other possible sources of stress.

The self-reported figures of being bullied in the previous year vary greatly, e.g. 3.5 per cent in Sweden (Leymann, 1996), 8.6 per cent in Norway (Einarsen and Skogstad, 1996), 10.1 per cent in Finland (Vartia, 1996), 28 per cent in the USA (Lutgen-Sandvik *et al.*, 2007) and 10.5 per cent in the UK (Hoel *et al.*, 2001). Some researchers argue that bullying behaviour must occur at least weekly for six months or more in order to differentiate it from social stress at work (e.g. Leymann, 1996). However, shorter durations of bullying experience, even a single incident, are associated with negative emotions (Keashly, 2001).

The impact of workplace bullying can be experienced at the individual, team and organisational levels. At the individual level impacts are: *physical*, e.g. loss of appetite, sleep problems (e.g. Einarsen, 1999); *psychological*, e.g. difficulty concentrating, anxiety, depression, suicidal thoughts (e.g. Mikkelsen and Einarsen, 2001); *social*, e.g. relationships outside of work with friends and family (e.g. Keashly and Jagatic, 2003); and *financial*, e.g. loss of employment, inability to secure another position (e.g. Einarsen and Mikkelsen, 2003).

One approach to understanding bullying has been to examine whether there are certain individual characteristics that may help to predict whether particular individuals are more likely to bully or be bullied. In terms of victims, it appears that individuals are not equally vulnerable or resilient to bullying (Rayner *et al.*, 1999), and various individual characteristics are associated with being the target of bullying, e.g. coping and conflict management skills (Einarsen *et al.*, 1994); low independence, extroversion and stability, and high conscientiousness and achievement (Coyne *et al.*, 2000); high anxiety and low social skills (Zapf, 1999).

The evidence suggests that those doing the bullying are most likely to be managers (70 per cent), followed by colleagues (37 per cent) and subordinates (12 per cent) (CIPD, 2004). However, it is very difficult to conduct research on actual bullies because people are unlikely to admit to bullying; research predominantly relies on the observations of victims and witnesses. A review of why people may bully others (Zapf and Einarsen, 2003) reported three main causes:

1   a self-regulatory process to protect or enhance self-esteem, e.g. when threatened by a high-performing subordinate;

2   the perpetrator having poor social competencies, e.g. low emotional control;

3   political behaviour to protect the individual's interests and improve their position relative to others.

However, bullying is a complex and multi-causal behaviour, influenced by the interaction between individual and organisational factors. Hence, consideration of contemporary organisational contexts is important. Workplace cultures may be becoming more aggressive, competitive and insecure. The importance of job tenure and previous experience on an individual's career potential has greatly reduced. The ability to perform multiple roles, adjust to change and meet ever-increasing targets is now more important for continued employment. Such organisational cultures create insecurity and mistrust (Peyton, 2003), which in turn are likely to influence the values and attitudes of individual employees, potentially increasing the likelihood of bullying behaviours.

Overly competitive cultures with excessive workloads and constant change can create a negative working environment that may allow bullying to flourish. Managers may adopt more autocratic styles of management to meet increasingly aggressive targets and view bullying behaviours as 'strong management' techniques (Simpson and Cohen, 2004). Hence, organisational cultures can create and sustain 'institutionalised bullying' in a variety of ways such as autocratic management style, work overload, 'blame' cultures and tolerating bullying behaviours because 'they get results' (CIPD, 2004).

In some organisations bullying behaviour is treated as acceptable and the victim is labelled as 'weak'; in others, bullying is seen as a 'personality conflict' and, again, the victim is often blamed for 'irritating' the perpetrator (Ferris, 2004). Managers and HR may see the behaviour as 'the way of life' and therefore respond inadequately to claims of bullying. In fact, rather worryingly, Ironside and Seifert (2003) suggest that bullying is now considered a basic part of management practice and that most forms are accepted as part of the daily experience of employed work.

It has been found that effective interventions for dealing with bullying require a holistic organisational response to the behaviour. This includes an understanding at all levels of an organisation that the cost of workplace bullying, in terms of reduced productivity, increased absence and turnover and low morale and well-being, greatly outweighs the short-term benefits of achieving aggressive day-to-day targets. A clear implication from the qualitative research on workplace bullying is the need for a clear and consistent understanding of what does and what does not constitute bullying. One way to achieve this is a publicised organisational policy on bullying that defines the behaviour and the informal and formal procedures for dealing with it.

Organisations should provide a range of support mechanisms available to employees experiencing bullying, whether they are victims, witnesses or accused of bullying. Such support can include more recognised routes, e.g. HR, occupational health and trade unions, but also employee assistance programmes and employee 'listener' groups. These are identified volunteer employees who provide confidential support to other employees. Another recommendation is to create a dignity at work policy that defines how people should treat others and expect to be treated. These values should be incorporated into all HR processes from recruitment and selection to performance appraisal, pay and rewards and disciplinary processes (CIPD, 2005b).Training for managers and HR on dignity at work, managing conflict and mediation can significantly help to address bullying, although as few as 30 per cent of organisations currently provide such training (CIPD, 2007a). The behaviour of line managers is a key element in tackling workplace bullying (CIPD, 2004), and skills such as communication, leadership, conflict resolution, stress management and team-building are associated with managers' effective handling of bullying.

Key Learning Point

Problems such as workplace bullying, harassment and violence at work have particularly strong links to problems of work stress. The impact of such problems on individual and organisations is very significant.

Role at work

When a person's role in an organisation is clearly defined and understood, and when expectations placed upon the individual are also clear and non-conflicting, stress can be kept to a minimum, but as researchers have clearly seen, this is not the case in many workplaces. Three critical factors – role ambiguity, role conflict and the degree of responsibility for others – are seen to be major sources of stress (O'Driscoll and Brough, 2010). Glazer and Beehr (2005) found that across a number of nations and cultures, role-related stressors in nursing were consistently linked with psychological health and organisational outcomes (such as commitment).

Role ambiguity There are two concepts with very long histories in stress research. Role ambiguity arises when individuals do not have a clear picture about their work objectives, their co-workers' expectations of them, and the scope and responsibilities of their job. Often this ambiguity results simply because a supervisor does not lay out to the employee exactly what their role is.

A wide range of events can create role ambiguity (Beehr, 1995). These include starting a new job, getting a new boss, the first supervisory responsibility, a poorly defined or unrealistic job description, or a change in the structure of the existing organisation – all of these events, and others, may serve to create a temporary state of role ambiguity. In their meta-analysis, Tubré and Collins (2000) found that role ambiguity was significantly linked to low job performance. This could be because when the role is ambiguous, employees are not sure what they need to do to get the job done, and may not even recognise when they are doing the job well.

Role conflict Role conflict exists when an individual is torn by conflicting, or irreconcilable, job demands or by doing things that they do not really want to do, or things which the individual does not believe are part of the job. Conflict situations can clearly act as stress factors upon the individuals involved. Workers may often feel themselves torn between two groups of people who demand different types of behaviour or who believe the job entails different functions. For example, Randall and colleagues (2007) describe an intervention designed to help nursing staff deal with the conflicting demands of their administrative and clinical responsibilities.

Responsibility In an organisation, there are basically two types of responsibility: responsibility for people, and responsibility for things, such as budgets, equipment and buildings. Responsibility for people has been found to be particularly stressful. Studies in the 1960s found that this was far more likely to lead to coronary heart disease than was responsibility for things (Wardwell et al., 1964). Being responsible for people usually requires spending more time interacting with others, attending meetings and attempting to meet deadlines, and thus increases the volume of work demands and change the nature of those demands.

As Ivancevich and Matteson (1980) stated:

> Part of the reason responsibility for people acts as a stressor undoubtedly results from the specific nature of the responsibility, particularly as it relates to the need to make unpleasant interpersonal decisions. Another part of the reason . . . is that people in responsibility positions lend themselves to overload, and perhaps role conflict and ambiguity as well.

Key Learning Point

A person's position within an organisation (their role) can be a major source of work stress. This is especially true if their role is not clear, it brings them into conflict with others in the organisation, or if it means their job carries with it a high degree of responsibility for people or things.

Change

Organisational change can be a source of stress for many employees. Because it is covered in depth in Chapter 16 it will not be considered in detail here. What comes through from many studies of major organisational change is that organisations need to monitor how the change process impacts on a variety of working conditions.

The other important thing to note with regard to work-related stress is that the way change is handled can make a significant difference to the impact that change has on the employee. In particular, it appears that when employees perceive that change is planned they have a more positive response to it, and that when management offer support through the change process employees experience less unpleasant uncertainty (Rafferty and Griffin, 2006). Similarly, Swanson and Power (2001) showed that social support played a key role in helping employees through a major restructuring. Kawakami *et al.* (1997) showed that the negative effects of major sudden change could be reduced through open and honest communications with employees, and the provision of ongoing support (e.g. an employee helpline).

The introduction of new technology into the work environment has required all workers, blue-collar and management, to adapt continually to new equipment, systems and ways of working. As well as the sheer amount of change, the introduction of new technology can also mean that jobs can become less fulfilling yet in some ways more demanding, thus damaging well-being, though these patterns are not inevitable (Chase and Karwowski, 2003; *see also* Chapter 9). For some, the introduction of mobile technology has also blurred the boundaries between work and home life.

Key Learning Point

Change, especially mergers and downsizing, has the potential to be very stressful for employees. However, there are ways of managing change and communicating change that can reduce its impact on individual well-being.

Physical working conditions

Our physical surroundings – noise, lighting, smells and all the stimuli that bombard our senses – can affect our moods and overall mental state, whether or not we find them consciously objectionable. Considerable research has linked working conditions to mental health. Kornhauser (1965) long ago suggested that poor mental health was directly related to unpleasant working conditions. Others have found that physical health is also adversely affected by repetitive and dehumanising work settings, such as those that often exist in fast-paced assembly lines (Weinberg and Cooper, 2007). In one study of factors associated with casting work in a steel manufacturing plant, conditions such as noise, fumes and to a lesser extent heat, together with the social and psychological consequences, including isolation and tension among workers, had significant impact on employee well-being (Kelly and Cooper, 1981).

Each occupation has its own potential environmental pressures. For example, in jobs where individuals are dealing with close detail work, poor lighting can create eye strain. On the other hand, extremely bright lighting or glare presents problems for air traffic controllers. Again, control seems to play an important part in determining how problematical these environmental factors become. As Ivancevich and Matteson (1980) stated:

> Noise, in fact, seems to operate less as a stressor in situations where it is excessive but expected, than in those where it is unexpected, or at least unpredictable. The change in noise levels more than absolute levels, seems to be the irritant. This, of course, is simply another way of saying that noise, like any stressor, causes stress when it forces us to change.

The physical design of the workplace can be another potential source of stress. If an office is poorly designed, with personnel who require frequent contact spread throughout a building, poor communication networks can develop, resulting in role ambiguity and poor relationships (*see also* Chapter 10). As Chapters 9 and 10 show, many of the problems with the design of workplaces can be minimised or eliminated through use of a design process that involves workers and puts their needs as near to the top of the agenda as is possible.

Key Learning Point

Although the physical work environment can be a source of stress, control over the work environment can help to alleviate the problem.

Career-related issues

Career-related issues are considered in considerable depth and breadth in Chapter 15. However, they are mentioned here because a host of issues can act as potential stress factors throughout one's working life. Lack of job security, fear of redundancy, obsolescence or retirement and numerous performance appraisals can cause pressure and strain. In addition, the frustration of having reached one's career ceiling or having been over-promoted can result in extreme stress. These sorts of issues are particularly important in Siegrist's (1996) ERI model discussed earlier in this chapter.

For many workers, career progression is of overriding importance. Through promotion, people not only earn more money, but enjoy increased status and new challenges. In the early years in a job, the striving and ability required to deal with a rapidly changing environment is usually rewarded by a company though monetary and promotional rewards. At middle age, however, many people find their career progress has slowed or stopped. Job opportunities may become fewer, available jobs can require longer to master, old knowledge may become obsolete and energy levels can flag. At the same time, younger competition threatens.

The transition to retirement can in itself be a stressful event. While a job is a socially defined role, retirement has been described as the 'roleless role'. The potential vagueness and lack of structure of retirement can bring problems for the ill prepared. For some individuals, becoming 'pensioners' or 'senior citizens' presents a situation in which they are uncertain about how to obtain the social rewards they value. In contrast, those individuals who have maintained balance in their lives by developing interests and friends outside their work can find retirement a liberating period in their lives. Hanisch (1994) found that people who have positive reasons for retiring (such as travel) rather than negative ones such as poor health or job dissatisfaction were more likely to plan ahead for retirement and enjoy it.

The process of being evaluated and appraised can be stressful experience for all of us (Fletcher, 2008; *see also* Chapter 6). It must be recognised that performance appraisals can be anxiety-provoking, for both the individual being examined and the person doing the judging and appraising. Particularly when poor performance is being appraised there is significant potential for conflict and damage to ongoing working relationships.

From your own experiences you may have noticed that the way in which performance is evaluated can also affect the degree of anxiety experienced. For example, taking a written examination can be a short-term stress factor, while continuous and confidential appraisals by supervisors can have a more long-term effect, depending on the structure and climate of the organisation.

Organisational culture and climate

Much has been written about organisational climate and culture (e.g. Schein, 1992; Ashkanasy and Jackson, 2001; Clegg and Cooper, 2009). There has also been quite a lot of argument concerning what is the most appropriate definition of each concept. Broadly speaking, organisational climate is about employees' perceptions of how their organisation functions, while organisational culture refers to the values, assumptions and norms that are shared by organisational members, and which influence individual and collective behaviour.

An individual is likely to experience stress if they do not share the values, etc. inherent in the employing organisation. Several factors could cause this. For example, the mismatch between individual and culture may lead the person to feel isolated and unable to communicate effectively with colleagues. It may mean that the person's role includes activities that they find distasteful, and that conflict with personal preferences (a form of role conflict – *see* above). Culture and climate can provide the conditions that lead to the growth of other problems. Willness and colleagues (2007) found that organisational climate played a significant role in the occurrence of sexual harassment at work.

'Organisational climate' can be a source of stress if a person believes that the way the organisation functions is unfair, or perhaps unclear and unpredictable (which could lead to role ambiguity). Perceived organisational support (*see* Stamper and Johlke, 2003) is defined as the extent to which employees perceive that their contributions are valued by their organisation and that the company cares about their well-being. This has been shown to have a positive impact on working conditions such role ambiguity and role conflict as well as intention to stay with the organisation.

As early as the 1940s, researchers began reporting that workers who were allowed more participation in decision-making processes produced more and had higher job satisfaction (Coch and French, 1948). They also found that non-participation at work was a significant predictor of strain and job-related stress, relating to general poor health, escapist drinking, depression, low self-esteem, absenteeism and plans to leave work. Participation in the decision-making process on the part of the individual may help increase their feeling of investment in the organisation's success, create a sense of belonging and improve communication channels within the organisation. The resulting sense of being in control seems vital for the well-being of the workforce (Bond *et al.*, 2008).

Key Learning Point

A participative organisational climate has been shown to be healthy in many organisations.

Exercise 12.2   A stressful job?

Look back over the situational factors described in this section. Now think of a job you know something about. It might be a job you have done yourself, or a job that is done by someone you know well.

Suggested exercises

What are the most likely sources of work stress in that job role? Set aside individual differences for a moment and focus on the features of that job that might place someone doing that job 'at risk' of experiencing work-related stress. Then look at the same job in a different way. What aspects of the job are likely to be sources of satisfaction or positive well-being?

Individual differences

As mentioned briefly earlier in this chapter, most models of stress construe personality as having one or more of the following roles in the stress process:

- A direct effect on stress outcomes (e.g. anxious people may be more tense across all kinds of situations, which can lead to psychological and/or physical health problems).

- A moderating effect in the stressor strain relationship. In other words, certain personality characteristics may mean that some people are more affected than others by an aspect of their work situation. So, for example, extrovert people may find a socially isolated job more stressful than introverts.

- A direct perceptual effect. Personality may have some impact on a person's perceptions of what his or her job is like. For example, people with a high need for control may be very aware of limitations on their autonomy, and rate their work autonomy low, when for most people a similar level of autonomy at work would be seen as sufficient.

There are several individual differences that are often investigated in stress research. These include:

- neuroticism/emotional instability: other similar traits have also been studied extensively such as trait anxiety (a tendency to feel higher anxiety than most people in most situations) and negative affect (i.e. the propensity to experience negative mood or emotions – this is a specific element of emotional instability);

- Type A personality;

- locus of control, self-efficacy and self-esteem;

- coping style;

- a range of demographic factors such as age, gender and length of service.

The Big Five model of personality (*see* Chapter 3) has provided a useful summarising framework for the key personality traits. One of the best-established direct relationships between personality and psychological well-being is that linking neuroticism with poorer psychological well-being. In an extensive meta-analysis DeNeve and Cooper (1998) found direct relationships between neuroticism and life satisfaction, happiness and negative affect. Positive affect was predicted equally well by extroversion and agreeableness. Grant and Langan-Fox (2007) show that the relationship between neuroticism and psychological strain was mediated by the perceived level of stress. This means that personality also plays a role in the perception of sources of stress, and that it is this perception that helps to forge the link between personality and poor psychological health.

As might be expected, studies have shown that people with high anxiety levels suffer more from role conflicts than do people who are more flexible in their approach to life. Anxiety-prone individuals experience role conflict more acutely and react to it with greater tension than people who were less anxiety-prone; and more flexible individuals respond to high role conflict with lesser feelings of tension than their more rigid counterparts (Warr and Wall, 1975).

Watson and colleagues (1988) identified two elements of mood that have been particularly influential in stress research. High negative affect refers to the propensity to feel emotions such as anger, guilt, fear and nervousness. High positive affect is the propensity to feel enthusiastic, energetic and alert. As you might expect many researchers have found these variables to influence directly the perception of sources of stress and the reporting of the consequences of work stress.

The Type A behavioural pattern is another concept that has a long history in stress research (Lee *et al.*, 1993). Many managers and other white collar and professional people who may be vulnerable to stress at work seem to display a pattern of behaviour termed Type A stress-prone behaviour (Rosenman *et al.*, 1964). The questionnaire shown in Exercise 12.3 was developed by Bortner (1969) to assess an individual's Type A behaviour. People who exhibit the Type A personality are more prone than others to the effects of stress.

There are a number of elements of cognitive style (the way people tend to think about things) that are important in the stress process. *Locus of control* refers to the extent to which a person believes they have control over their life. In many circumstances having an internal locus of control (i.e. believing one is in control) is helpful because it encourages a person to do something about their stressful situation. This is fine unless there really is not anything a person can do, in which case an internal locus of control will simply increase his or her frustration. *Self-efficacy*, a person's belief that they are capable (Bandura, 1982) and *self-esteem* (a person's feeling of their own worth) are also important. The so-called 'hardy personality' refers to a combination of internal locus of control, self-esteem, self-efficacy and motivation (especially to recover from disappointments).

In other studies, when the individual has had stronger needs for cognitive clarity or lower levels of tolerance for ambiguity, job-related stress has been found to be higher and more prolonged. Several studies (e.g. Sparks and Cooper, 1999; Cooper *et al.*, 2001) have shown that locus of control, the hardy personality and Type A behaviour are moderators between the stressors and strains in the stress process. What this means is that they alter the strength of the links between work and well-being: poor working conditions have less of an impact on someone with a hardy personality.

Exercise 12.3   Type A behavioural pattern

Fill in the following questionnaire and then score it as suggested. If you are a high Type A it means that you are very competitive, high-achieving, aggressive, hasty, impatient, time-conscious and hard driving. Type B, which is the other end of the continuum, is the opposite of this characterisation.

Circle one number for each of the statements below which best reflects the way you behave in your everyday life. For example, if you are generally on time for appointments, for the first point you would circle a number between 7 and 11. If you are usually casual about appointments you would circle one of the lower numbers between 1 and 5.

Casual about appointments	1 2 3 4 5 6 7 8 9 10 11	Never late
Not competitive	1 2 3 4 5 6 7 8 9 10 11	Very competitive
Good listener	1 2 3 4 5 6 7 8 9 10 11	Anticipates what others are going to say (nod, attempts to finish for them)
Never feels rushed (even under pressure)	1 2 3 4 5 6 7 8 9 10 11	Always rushed
Can wait patiently	1 2 3 4 5 6 7 8 9 10 11	Impatient while waiting
Takes things one at a time	1 2 3 4 5 6 7 8 9 10 11	Tries to do many things at once, thinks about what will do next
Slow deliberate talker	1 2 3 4 5 6 7 8 9 10 11	Emphatic in speech, fast and forceful
Cares about satisfying themself no matter what others may think	1 2 3 4 5 6 7 8 9 10 11	Wants good job recognised by others
Slow doing things	1 2 3 4 5 6 7 8 9 10 11	Fast (eating, walking)
Easy-going	1 2 3 4 5 6 7 8 9 10 11	Hard-driving (pushing yourself and others)
Expresses feelings	1 2 3 4 5 6 7 8 9 10 11	Hides feelings
Many outside interests	1 2 3 4 5 6 7 8 9 10 11	Few interests outside work/home
Unambitious	1 2 3 4 5 6 7 8 9 10 11	Ambitious
Casual	1 2 3 4 5 6 7 8 9 10 11	Eager

Plot total score below:

Type B   Type A
14   84   154

The higher the score on this questionnaire, the more firmly an individual can be classified as Type A. For example, 154 points is the highest possible score and indicates the
maximum Type A personality. It is important to understand that there are no distinct
divisions between Type A and Type B. Rather, people fall somewhere on a *continuum*
leaning more towards one type than the other. An average score is 84. Anyone with a
score above that is inclined towards Type A behaviour, and below that towards Type B
behaviour. What does your score say about your likely vulnerability to stress?

Source: Cooper et al. *(1988). NFER Nelson. Copyright © Previsor, UK.*

Key Learning Point

Individual differences play an important role in: (1) how people perceive their work environment and (2) their psychological and physical well-being. They can also play an important role in determining how strong the link is between (1) and (2).

How individuals cope with stress has been the focus of quite a lot of research and
practice (*see* for example Zeidner and Endler, 1996). Coping is usually defined as
the efforts people make, through their behaviour and thoughts, to alter their environment and/or manage their emotions. Coping strategies include analysing the
situation, planning a course of action, seeking information from others, seeking
support and comfort from others, relaxation techniques, counselling and using alcohol, tobacco or other drugs. Some of these place the individual's health at risk:
these are referred to as maladaptive coping strategies. Employee assistance programmes (*see* later in this chapter) are often used to help people who are placing
their health at risk in this way.

One general distinction is between *problem-focused strategies* (dealing with the
original cause of stress) and *emotion-focused strategies* (dealing with how one feels
about the stressful situation). Logically, when it is possible to change the situation,
problem-focused strategies would seem to be the better option, but research suggests
that the results of coping are hard to predict, perhaps not only because of the coping
strategy a person uses, but also because how effectively they use it, matters a lot.

Many authors argue that coping is a bit more complex than this, with there
being a range of avoidant coping strategies and a range of more active coping
strategies. Carver and colleagues (1989) presented a measure of coping with no fewer
than 16 different coping scales (including humour, denial, substance abuse, behaviour disengagement and the use of social support). This shows how many different
ways there are that people use when faced with difficult situations. Of course, a person may have a wide range of coping resources but only use some of them. Some
people may have certain resources, such as sympathetic close friends, but not use
them. Underlying this is a debate about whether people choose coping strategies
on the basis of the current situation, or their personality and prior learning. As

you will see later in this chapter, many stress management training programmes are designed to have an effect by training the individual to think or behave differently so that they use healthy and productive coping strategies (in terms of the way they think and behave) when they are faced with stressors.

A wide range of demographic factors (e.g. age, gender, tenure, etc.) have been considered in stress research. Relationships between these factors on the one hand, and the perception of stressors and employee well-being on the other hand, tend to vary from one study to another. Meta-analyses show that older workers tend to cope best with some sources of work stress (e.g. role ambiguity), and that they tend to have lower turnover and absenteeism in the face of sources of work stress than younger employees (Shirom *et al.*, 2008). This may be because older workers have had more time and experience to develop job-related skills (thus it could be that tenure, or experience, may be more important than age per se).

Exercise 12.4   Your experience of stress

Review your experience of *work* so far in your life. Consider the stressors discussed in this chapter so far, and try to decide which two or three of them have been most stressful for *you in your working life* (not why they might be stressful for other people). Then think about why you found them stressful. Was it because (i) the amount of the stressor was so great, or (ii) because the stressor stopped you achieving the most important goals of your work, or (iii) because the kind of person you are makes you vulnerable to that kind of stressor, or (iv) do you think there were some other reasons why these experiences were so stressful?

STOP TO CONSIDER

From what you have read in this chapter so far (and without reading any further!), how do you think organisations could intervene to tackle work-related stress? What strategies are available? How effective do you think each of these strategies might be? Which do you think would be a popular choice with (i) employees and (ii) senior managers? Do you think these two groups would prefer different types of interventions? If so, why?

Interventions to tackle work stress and promote employee well-being

The costs of stress indicate that the case for intervention is strong. As you have seen, there is also a considerable body of research and theory on which interventions can be based. If we know what causes work stress, then we should be able to do something about it. Government guidance and legislation in many countries now require organisations to assess and manage risks to psychological well-being (in addition to dealing with physical risks to employee health).

There are different levels of interventions that have different objectives and target different parts of the mechanisms that link work and well-being. Murphy (1988) identified three levels of intervention: (i) primary (i.e. reducing the sources of organisational stress), (ii) secondary (e.g. stress management training) and (iii) tertiary (e.g. health promotion and workplace counselling).

Key Learning Point

A useful way to view stress management is to think of interventions in terms of their objectives. These are primary prevention (e.g. dealing with the source of the stress), secondary intervention (e.g. stress management training) and tertiary (e.g. employee assistance programmes (EAPs)) rehabilitation.

Primary interventions: changing the sources of workplace stress

Primary interventions change the design, organisation and management of work. In other words they tackle the sources of work stress or attempt to 'design into the job' the sources of positive well-being. Most often they are designed to deal with problems identified by a significant proportion of employees, targeting the group-level rather than the individual employee. The logic is that this then prevents employee health being damaged by the problem, because the problem no longer exists (or is significantly reduced). A list of examples of primary interventions is shown in Table 12.2.

Elkin and Rosch (1990) summarised a useful range of possible organisation-directed strategies to reduce stress:

- redesign the task;
- redesign the work environment;
- establish flexible work schedules;
- encourage participative management;
- include the employee in career development;
- analyse work roles and establish goals;
- provide social support and feedback;
- build cohesive teams (see Chapter 13);
- establish fair employment policies;
- establish fair methods for the distribution of rewards.

Participative action research (PAR) is often the driver of primary interventions. PAR involves employees working with researchers or consultants to identify problems and design solutions. This process seems to help different stakeholders agree on the nature of the problems and to all contribute to the design of workable solutions (Heaney *et al.*, 1993). A proper risk assessment, or problem analysis, is arguably

Table 12.2	Examples of primary interventions

Tackling problems with job demands

- Jobs enrichment: the removal or automation of mundane tasks with the introduction of more complex or interesting tasks that allow individuals to make better use of their skills and abilities
- Setting up quick informal meetings to provide timely feedback and help with decision-making
- Improving the planning and forecasting of workload so that employees face more realistic deadlines
- Analysing employees' knowledge, skills and abilities to ensure that they are equipped to do the job and providing opportunities for them to develop further
- Adjusting staffing levels so that they reflect peaks and troughs in workload
- Increasing variety by, for example, allowing people to rotate around the different tasks carried out in their team
- Training specialist staff to deal with difficult or complex tasks that eat into the time, and increase the workload, of other team members
- Using information technology to reduce the cognitive load on staff, e.g. systems to help staff monitor the progress of tasks that are carried out over a number of days or weeks, or when they are dealing with many simultaneous tasks
- Allowing staff 'protected time' to deal with complex or difficult tasks that require concentration
- Setting fixed and protected break times
- Introducing flexi-time or compressed working weeks
- Establishing and communicating predictable shift patterns well in advance so that employees can be prepared for them and organise their home and leisure activities accordingly
- Allowing employees to make arrangements with colleagues whereby shifts may be swapped (but that the work is still being done)
- Ensuring that there is equity and fairness in the allocation of shifts, e.g. by allowing all staff the opportunity to, at some point, be involved in the construction of shift rotas
- Having particularly influential individuals act as role models (e.g. by having successful staff leave the office on time, or be seen to take regular breaks)

Tackling problems with control

- Reviewing, and perhaps changing, the guidance that staff are given about the completion of tasks so that they have more discretion and control about how they are completed
- Making performance feedback available quickly and in a form that can be readily used by employees to manage their own performance
- Increasing employee control over how work is allocated, e.g. through the use of self-managing teams (see Chapter 13)
- Giving staff the control and freedom to identify and rectify common problems quickly and without unnecessary approval from senior managers

Tackling problems with support

- Encouraging interaction between team members by providing them with tasks that require employees to work together with shared objectives
- Managing the workload of supervisors and managers to ensure they have adequate time to fulfil the supervisory element of their role
- Providing new employees with a proper induction, and ensuring that existing employees have easy access to information about the support available to them to help them do their job
- Introducing a mentoring process

Table 12.2   (Continued)

■ Ensuring that work schedules or the allocation of tasks do not result in individuals or groups being isolated from others in the organisation

Relationships

■ Allowing staff to 'rotate' roles to experience different jobs or tasks within their team or the organisation
■ Altering the physical layout of the workspace can have a positive impact on social relationships at work
■ Ensuring appraisal processes are of a good quality and properly implemented
■ Implementing and maintaining effective systems for dealing with bullying and harassment (*see* earlier in this chapter)
■ Ensure that staff are protected from risks of violence or threat from clients, and 'designing out' where possible elements of the job role that place them at risk
■ Allow staff to experience their colleagues' working conditions by work shadowing or job rotation so that staff appreciate the degree of interdependency that exists between them
■ Introduce handover times or overlapping shifts/work schedules to increase contact between employees

Role

■ Review, update and publicise job descriptions
■ Include the active review and clarification of roles in the performance appraisal process
■ Allow teams discretion and control over how roles and responsibilities are allocated
■ Examination of roles in relation to the current needs of the organisation and the demands of employees' jobs
■ Establish systems for employee participation in decision-making about the boundaries of job roles and responsibilities
■ Minimise the potential for competing or conflicting demands in role when designing and revising job descriptions
■ Reallocate tasks within a team to ensure that conflicting demands do not coincide for individual employees
■ Ensure that an employee's role does not result in their being in frequent conflict with colleagues, clients or members of the public – this may include job rotation – if some conflict situations are unavoidable, then the implementation of secondary and tertiary interventions is particularly important

Change

■ Opening up new lines of communication, or using new communication media, to disseminate important information about change
■ Giving a small number of staff the job of highlighting particularly important information and communicating it to staff (to avoid it being hidden within a large of amount of information routinely communicated to staff)
■ Providing training in different styles of management (*see* Chapters 14 and 16)
■ The use of newsletters and staff briefings to ensure that all staff get vital information about organisational goals, objectives and plans

Source: Adapted from *Stress Management Interventions. Performance and Well-being* (Randall, R. and Lewis, R. in ed. Donaldson-Feilder, E. 2007), with the permission of the publisher, the Chartered Institute of Personal and Development, London (www.cipd.co.uk).

a more crucial precursor to primary intervention than it is to other types of intervention. Without this assessment a suitable bespoke (tailored) intervention for tackling a problem cannot be designed (Cox *et al.*, 2000; Elo *et al.*, 2008).

When compared to stress management training and counselling, managers may think that primary interventions are not the 'easy option' for tackling stress. Designing them may take some time and involve consultation with employees. Bond *et al.* (2006) examined examples of primary interventions and concluded that they are usually not expensive and the change process, if handled correctly, need not be disruptive or lengthy. In addition, the process of involving employees in the design and implementation of primary interventions can lead to positive outcomes in itself because of its positive impact on perceptions of participation and control at work (Elo *et al.*, 2008).

There are relatively few published studies of primary interventions. As Cartwright and Cooper (1997) highlight, most workplace initiatives operate at the secondary or tertiary levels (which are discussed next in this chapter). This may be because it is not seen as the strategy of choice: many managers may think that sources of stress are resident in the individual (i.e. the result of an individual weakness, or lack of resilience) or that primary interventions are too difficult to implement.

At the start of this chapter we examined the importance of the appraisal of working conditions in numerous stress theories. These indicate that primary intervention should be an effective way of improving employee well-being in the long-term because if working conditions improve, employees no longer need to find ways of coping with the problems that are triggering their negative emotions. This logic is appealing, but is it supported by the research evidence? We now take a close look at two intervention studies that tested the effectiveness of primary interventions using very rigorous research designs.

Susan Jackson (1983) tested whether allowing hospital employees to have more input into decision-making helped them to feel more involved at work and to develop a clearer understanding of the demands of their work role. The intervention was quite simple: regular staff meetings were introduced. Researchers examined organisational records to check that meetings were happening and were being used to discuss important and relevant issues. The study was particularly powerful because the Solomon four-group design (*see* Chapter 2) was used to help rule out various alternative explanations for change that might have impacted on the results of the study. The analysis required to track the impact of the intervention through changes in working conditions to changes in well-being was very complex (structural equation modelling, again *see* Chapter 2, was used). As stress theory would predict, the meetings led to increased perceived participation and reduced problems with work roles (i.e. role conflict and ambiguity). These changes led to less emotional strain and higher job satisfaction among those involved in the meetings. The researchers were also able to show that the reductions in emotional strain were linked to lower levels of absence and lower turnover intention. However, all of this did not happen straight away: significant changes were only apparent when the intervention had been in place for six months. Findings such as these indicate that the effects of primary interventions may take time to emerge, perhaps because they work by reducing long-term exposure to chronic work stressors.

Kompier *et al.* (1998) have argued that primary interventions take time to work because they require employees to adapt to different ways of working. Initial apprehension and concern about changes to working practices may need to dissipate before the full impact of the intervention shows itself. Primary interventions can also work in unexpected ways. Susan Jackson had predicted that changes in communication and social support would be linked to improvements in employee health. In fact it was the reduction in role conflict and role ambiguity, and the increase in perceived influence, that were the most important drivers of changes in employee well-being. This illustrates that stress theories do not always allow us to make precise predictions about how interventions will work.

In the second example of a primary intervention, Bond and Bunce (2001) looked at two groups (a control group and an intervention group) employed in a UK government department. They established a series of problem-solving committee meetings in the intervention group. These committees, with help from researchers, were tasked with using their expertise of the work setting to identify interventions that would increase job control. The rationale for the intervention was based on established stress theories: it was predicted that improving control would have a positive impact on employee health and satisfaction. The committees designed and implemented a cluster of interventions that led to employees having more input into decision-making and control over their workload, and put systems in place for getting quick advice from managers about difficult or vague tasks. There were some striking outcomes. Employees from the intervention group (but not those from the control group) reported less mental ill-health, lower sickness absence and higher job performance. Data analysis also revealed that changes in perceived control in the intervention group underpinned these positive organisational outcomes.

In extending this work in another organisation, but using a similar approach to intervention, Bond *et al.* (2008) have found that an individual difference (psychological flexibility) appears to interact with the changes in control sparked by the intervention. To simplify somewhat, psychological flexibility is the extent to which a person uses thinking strategies that allow them to focus on actions (i.e. doing their job) while at the same time recognising and accepting their emotions *without* letting their emotions interfere with their performance. Bond and colleagues found that those with higher psychological flexibility tended to benefit more from the improvements to control generated by the intervention. What this shows is that individual differences can mean that the same intervention can lead to different outcomes for different employees.

Descriptions of many other primary interventions can be found in reviews of intervention research such as Cooper *et al.* (2001), Egan *et al.* (2008), Parkes and Sparkes (1998), Richardson and Rothstein (2008) and Giga *et al.* (2003).

Key Learning Point

Tackling the sources of work-related stress primary interventions could be effective in the long-term. It is important to involve employees in the design of such interventions.

Secondary interventions

While organisation-directed interventions are attempting to eliminate the source of job or organisational stress, most workplace stress initiatives have been directed at helping employees as individuals learn to cope with any stressors that occur at work. This is achieved by improving the adaptability of individuals to their environment by changing their thinking, behaviour and improving their skills. Such an approach is commonly described as 'inoculation' treatment. Inherent in this approach is the notion that the organisation and its working environment will not change, therefore the individual has to learn ways of coping that help them to 'fit' better with its demands.

Often the aim of secondary intervention is to change employees' psychological responses to difficult or stressful elements of their work. Through these changes the links between exposure to sources of stress and its negative outcomes can become weaker or disappear. The objective is to *reduce or eliminate the harm* that employees might experience without altering their exposure to sources of stress. The way employees appraise their situation is crucial in stress theories: these interventions are often designed to help employees develop the habit of appraising things more positively. Specialist expertise is needed to deliver this training (e.g. qualified counsellors or therapists). Secondary interventions are usually completed relatively quickly, with employees attending a number of short training sessions and practising their new skills between these sessions. These interventions can also be used when primary prevention is not a viable option.

Stress management training (SMT) is the most common form of secondary intervention. Generic skills are often developed through these sessions so that employees can use them to deal better with lots of different sources of stress. This includes stressors which they do not face at the time of the training but that emerge in the future (Murphy and Sauter, 2003). Cognitive behavioural interventions directly target the way employees think about their work situation and the links between their perceptions, emotions and behaviour. For this training to be effective, trainees need to work quite hard at developing new skills. There are other more passive secondary interventions where the trainee gets a bit of an 'easier ride'. Meditation and relaxation interventions focus directly on the adverse consequences of employees' reactions to stress, helping the employee to achieve a mental state that is incompatible with the experience of negative emotions.

Cognitive behavioural therapy (CBT) training is based on the concept that unhealthy human behaviour and the experience of negative emotions can be reduced by changes in cognition/appraisal. This means training people to think differently about their experiences, or to give different meanings to events. To illustrate this point, imagine you are awoken by a noise in the middle of the night. If you think that noise is a burglar then you would be anxious (and understandably so). If you heard the same noise but thought it was the neighbour's cat jumping onto your dustbin, then you might be somewhat less anxious.

Workplace CBT focuses on changing the way people perceive and attach meaning to their experiences of work (rather than to noises in the middle of the night). Usually this training will start by targeting situations that the employee has identified as being particularly stressful. In some training the employee develops the skill of attaching more positive meanings to events. This *relabelling* might involve training an employee to think of a difficult situation as a chance to deal with a *challenge* rather than as a *problem to be coped with*. Beck's CBT works by training employees to use evidence around them to critically evaluate the validity of negative thoughts (Beck, 1995). Stress inoculation training requires employees use such strategies in progressively more stressful situations.

Relaxation training is designed to train the individual to recognise when the body is becoming tense and then to think or behave in a way that relieves that tension. Physical relaxation techniques include deep breathing exercises, muscle relaxation and stretching. These methods are relatively cheap and popular with organisations. Cognitively based relaxation techniques use imagery and meditation to clear the mind of external thoughts relating to life events. *Biofeedback* is sometimes used in conjunction with relaxation training. This uses measurement devices (e.g. heart rate or blood pressure monitors) to show people their physiological responses to stress. This allows people to see if they are using the relaxation methods effectively enough to make a tangible difference.

Other possible stress management interventions include *job-related skills training* on topics such as time management and assertiveness. These can help employees to deal with some of the most difficult and stressful aspects of their job role. It is also important to remember that training to carry out core components of the job can have a significant and positive impact on the fit between the person and the demands of their role (*see* Chapter 11). These interventions are often overlooked by organisations but they can be very effective (Richardson and Rothstein, 2008). As with primary interventions, these interventions are based on the theory that a better person–environment fit is healthier.

The packaging up of several secondary interventions is quite common in stress management training. Different techniques and methods are used concurrently after an initial awareness phase where participants learn about the causes and consequences of occupational stress.

Tertiary interventions

The aim of tertiary interventions is to help those who have already been damaged by their work. In other words, these interventions are designed to rehabilitate employees after problems that have already occurred. Clearly it is better if employees are not damaged by their work, but tertiary interventions are particularly important when primary and secondary interventions are impractical (although this is rare) or when they are unlikely to be totally effective for every employee. Increasingly, these initiatives have been in the form of employee assistance programmes (EAPs) (Berridge *et al.*, 1997). The original EAPs were designed to help employees who were suffering from problems of alcohol dependency, but they are now designed to help employees who are experiencing any one of a number of different problems. Berridge and Cooper (1993) defined an EAP as:

> a programmatic intervention at the workplace, usually at the level of the individual employee, using behaviourial science knowledge and methods for the control of certain work related problems (notably alcoholism, drug abuse and mental health) that adversely affect job performance, with the objective of enabling the individual to return to making her or his full contribution and to attaining full functioning in personal life.

Most EAPs offer psychological counselling of one type or another. Usually there is a self-referral route for the employees plus the possibility of referral by line managers (training is often given to managers as to how to identify sources and symptoms of stress). These referral routes may sometimes lead to primary or secondary interventions being developed for individual employees (e.g. an employee may work with the line manager and their counsellor to redesign their workload, or may be referred to stress management or job-related skills training). EAPs come in various shapes and sizes. Randall and Lewis (2007) describe four different types of EAPs:

1 An in-house programme whereby internal counsellors or trained managers are provide support for staff.

2 An external programme whereby organisations out-source provision.

3 A consortium whereby organisations group together and establish collaborative programmes.

4 An affiliate programme, resembling the consortium approach, but coordinated by an external provider.

EAPs usually include a telephone-based or Internet-based helpline and information service. This is often used for assessing individual employees' needs, referring employees to sources of help and sometimes for short-term counselling (Employee Assistance Professionals Association, 2003). One of the key features of EAPs is that they often provide employees with support and help for non-work issues (e.g. a legal advice helpline) that can be made available to employees' relatives and retired staff. Health promotion activities (such as on-site fitness facilities, dietary control, cardiovascular fitness programmes, relaxation classes, or stress and health education) are another key feature of most stress management and EAP initiatives (Kinder *et al.*, 2008).

Key Learning Point

Tertiary interventions are designed to repair the damage. They should not be seen as a substitute for primary and/or secondary interventions.

The popularity and effectiveness of interventions

There are not lots of examples of good research into the effectiveness of primary interventions. As discussed in Chapter 2, establishing and maintaining good research designs can be very challenging in organisational settings. From a management perspective, exposing as many people as possible, as quickly as possible, to an effective intervention is the priority. This often prevents researchers from establishing control groups, making it difficult to isolate the effects of the intervention. In addition, until relatively recently, primary interventions have been far less widely used than stress management training (LaMontagne *et al.*, 2007). This situation is changing, partly because of changes in government legislation that puts the onus on employers to tackle the sources of work-related health problems. However, there remains considerable debate about the effectiveness of primary stress management interventions (Briner and Reynolds, 1999; Murphy and Sauter, 2003).

In an attempt to make sense of the available research, Richardson and Rothstein (2008) carried out a rigorous meta-analysis of the effectiveness of primary and secondary interventions. They reviewed 36 intervention studies, only five of which were primary interventions. It is worth noting that the criteria for including studies were very rigorous and the review may have excluded many less than perfect primary intervention studies that contain interesting and important findings. Setting that concern aside for a moment, the largest effects on employee well-being were found for cognitive–behavioural secondary interventions *without* other interventions. Relaxation interventions were the second most effective type of intervention.

Richardson and Rothstein (2008) note the majority of research into secondary interventions looks at the impact of intervention on psychological outcomes which may explain why they appear to be so effective. Studies that have assessed the impact of psychological counselling (Allison *et al.*, 1989; Cooper and Sadri, 1991) have shown significant improvements in the mental health of counselled employees, but little change in levels of organisational commitment. In contrast van der Klink *et al.* (2001) found that secondary interventions have little impact on levels of job satisfaction. Murphy and Sauter (2003) argue that stress management training significantly reduces symptoms of poor health but this does not lead to changes in organisational outcomes. Counselling and stress management training may have short-term effects, particularly if employees return to an unchanged work environment and its indigenous stressors. If such initiatives have little impact on improving job satisfaction, then it is more likely that the individual will adopt a way of coping that may have positive individual outcomes, but less benefit for the organisation (Cooper and Sadri, 1991).

Key Learning Point

Some secondary interventions, particularly CBT training, have been found to have quite a large short-term impact on individual psychological well-being. The impact of these interventions on long-term employee well-being and organisational health is less clear.

The choice of criteria used to measure intervention outcomes might explain at least some of the differences in intervention effectiveness. There are a small, but growing, number of studies showing primary interventions to have a significant impact on important outcomes such as absence and performance. These outcome measures can be influenced by many organisational factors unrelated to the intervention itself, which may go some way to explaining why meta-analyses show the 'average' effects for primary interventions to be small. By way of contrast, symptoms of anxiety and depression are often targeted directly in secondary interventions, and it is measures of these psychological variables that are also then used to determine intervention effectiveness.

This line of reasoning is supported by evidence that changes in self-report measures (in particular measures of working conditions) are larger than changes in other outcomes for the majority of primary intervention studies (Parkes and Sparkes, 1998). Just as secondary interventions tend to produce changes in psychological symptoms, Kompier and Kristensen (2001) have argued it is only reasonable to expect primary interventions to have consistent impact on the variables they target directly, i.e. perceived working conditions. As most theories of stress would suggest, changes in working conditions do not automatically guarantee changes in well-being. Factors such as individual differences and coping have the potential to play a role. These factors can influence the way employees perceive change and determine the *strength* of the relationship between changes in working conditions and health: those coping well may experience less benefit from a primary intervention than those who are struggling.

There is also good evidence that some working conditions have a particularly strong link to organisational outcomes, and by changing these working conditions it is possible to have a significant impact on problems such as high absence and poor performance. Perceived control at work seems to be one such working condition. Bond and colleagues (2006) found that even modest interventions to improve control tend to have a large impact especially on organisational outcomes such as job performance. In other words 'a little goes a long way' (p. 10) when enhancing job control. This does not seem to be the case for all working conditions. The same authors found that support at work was linked to performance, while problems with work roles were more closely linked to turnover intention. All of this means that it is difficult to provide a simple answer to the question 'are primary interventions effective'; certainly they can be, but much depends upon the nature of the intervention and the criteria used to evaluate it.

When reading intervention studies you will doubtless encounter many anecdotal accounts of how problems with implementing the intervention, or disruptive events occurring in the organisation diluted the impact of the intervention. However, few studies use a rigorous approach to finding out how these factors might have influenced intervention outcomes (Egan *et al.*, 2008). This raises the chance that *type III errors* (*see* Chapter 2) are being made in previous intervention research.

Process evaluation is designed to help the researcher answer questions such as 'why did the intervention work well?' and 'why did the intervention fail?'. Research into secondary intervention has shown that *session impact factors* such as the sense of comfort and belonging generated in training sessions can significantly influence intervention outcomes (Bunce, 1997). For primary interventions, process evaluation involves documenting the delivery of the intervention (implementation factors) and significant events taking place in the organisation (contextual factors). Contextual factors, such as problems with maintaining staffing levels, can make it difficult for people to find the time, energy or resources for primary intervention activities (Randall *et al.*, 2007).

There are lots of implementation and contextual factors that have been linked to intervention outcomes. Many of these were identified in a series of innovative qualitative studies carried out by Norwegian researchers (e.g. Nytrø *et al.*, 2000; Saksvik *et al.*, 2002). In the Netherlands, Kompier *et al.* (1998) examined intervention processes across a number of well-designed stress management interventions to identify the common *critical success factors* in the design and delivery of interventions.

This body of research has identified a number of process factors that appear to be important in the implementation of primary interventions. These include:

- good levels of employee involvement and participation in all aspects of the intervention process, with senior management commitment to primary intervention and a culture supportive of positive change (e.g. Kompier *et al.*, 1998; Murphy and Sauter, 2003);

- actions being taken to ensure that employees are provided with the skills, resources and support they need to extract the maximum possible benefit from the intervention (Nytrø *et al.*, 2000; Saksvik *et al.*, 2002);

- employees' readiness for change, line management support for the intervention, employee perceptions of their participation in intervention design and of the active ingredients of the intervention, i.e. whether they are aware of, or exposed to, the active ingredients of the intervention (Randall *et al.*, 2009);

- employees' perceptions of the quality of the intervention and the amount of information they are given about the intervention – for example why it is being implemented and what it is intended to achieve (Nielsen *et al.*, 2007).

You may notice that many of these features can be found in the implementation of PAR as discussed earlier in this chapter. This may be one of the reasons why such interventions, when properly delivered, appear to be particularly effective.

Key Learning Point

Primary interventions can have an impact on both individual well-being and the health of organisations. However, the processes through which they are designed and implemented play an important role in determining whether or not they are effective.

Turning to EAPs, the CIPD's 2007 Absence Management Survey showed that 31 per cent (of 819 responding organisations) operated an EAP (*see* CIPD 2007a). EAPs have proved more popular with organisations than primary-level interventions, for several reasons:

■ Cost–benefit analysis of such programmes has produced some impressive results. For example, the New York Telephone Company's 'wellness' programme designed to improve cardiovascular fitness saved the organisation $2.7 million in absence and treatment costs in one year alone (Cartwright and Cooper, 1997).

■ The professional 'interventionists' – the counsellors, physicians and clinicians responsible for health care – feel more comfortable with changing individuals than changing organisations (Ivancevich *et al.*, 1990).

■ It is considered easier and less disruptive to business to change the individual than to embark on an extensive and potentially expensive organisational development programme, the outcome of which may be uncertain (Cooper and Cartwright, 1994).

■ They present a high-profile means by which organisations can be 'seen to be doing something about stress' and taking reasonable precautions to safeguard employee health. This is likely to be important, not only in terms of the message it communicates to employees, but also to the external environment. This latter point is particularly important, given the increasing litigation fears that now exist among employers throughout the United States and Europe. It is not difficult to envisage that the existence of an EAP, regardless of whether or not an individual chooses to use it, may become an effective defence against possible legal action.

Increasingly organisations are using EAPs as safety nets to deal with the minority of problems where primary or secondary interventions do not deal with the problem. It is generally seen to be a problem when organisations over-rely on EAPs. This could mean that efforts at preventing and managing work-related problems are not taking place, or not being as effective as they could be.

Recent large-scale reviews of the research evidence have found that wellness programmes (i.e. the provision of fitness facilities and health education) significantly decrease absence and increase job satisfaction (Parks and Steelman, 2008). There is a risk that such benefits may be relatively short term, particularly if, as suggested (Ivancevich and Matteson, 1988), after a few years, 70 per cent of individuals fail to maintain a long-term commitment to exercise habits and are likely to revert to their previous lifestyle. Many EAPs also offer employees secondary interventions of the type mentioned earlier in this chapter, and therefore similar concerns have been voiced that EAP counselling interventions offer short-term gains for the individual, but have less impact on job satisfaction and performance. Lifestyle and health habits appear to have a strong direct effect on strain outcomes, in reducing anxiety, depression and psychosomatic distress, but do not necessarily moderate the stressor–strain linkage (Baglioni and Cooper, 1988). EAPs are often underused by employees who are not aware of the services on offer, or who have concerns about confidentiality (some employees become suspicious when they perceive that the employer is taking on a dual role of both manager and counselling provider).

Drawing on reviews by Murphy (1988) and French *et al.* (1997), Randall and Lewis (2007) identify that a number of features of an EAP are linked to its success:

- visible commitment and support for the EAP from senior management;

- clear, well-publicised and written agreement on the purpose, policies and procedures of the EAP, including an explicit policy on confidentiality;

- cooperation with employee representatives (e.g. trade unions);

- training of line managers to identify problems;

- frequent communication and training for employees concerning EAP services and workplace policies to employees;

- programmes that offer long-term ongoing support and referral to other agencies if necessary;

- maintenance of records to allow for programme evaluation.

Key Learning Point

Properly designed and well-managed EAPs can provide organisations with an important safety net to help employees whose health is damaged by their experiences at work.

When looking at reviews of the effectiveness of interventions it is important to remember that academics are still working with a very small (albeit increasing) number of intervention studies. Even within this small pool of research there is a great deal of variety that makes it even more difficult to draw conclusions that have a good chance of generalising across to new interventions studies. As discussed earlier in this chapter, the quality of intervention research also varies greatly. This means that there are still many uncertainties and debates about the effectiveness of interventions. What is becoming clear is that a 'one size fits all' approach to intervention is not yet available. For example, Kompier and Kristensen (2001) point out that interventions can only be effective for employees who are experiencing a problem before the intervention. Van der Hek and Plomp (1997) noted that voluntary participation in interventions does not necessarily attract the workers who are at risk. What is clear is that organisations need to follow a process that identifies the problems employees are experiencing and designing/choosing interventions that fit the particular needs of the organisation and its employees. This problem-solving approach needs to be embedded in a healthy organisation.

The healthy organisation

A healthy organisation can be defined as one characterised by both financial success (e.g. profitability) and a physically and psychologically healthy workforce, which is able to maintain over time a healthy and satisfying work environment and organisational culture, particularly through periods of market turbulence and change (Cartwright and Cooper, 2008; Hart and Cooper, 2001). Healthy work organisations are those in which:

- levels of stress are low;

- employees' organisational commitment and job satisfaction are high;

- sickness, absenteeism and labour turnover rates are below the national average;

- industrial relations are good and strikes/disputes are infrequent;

- safety and accident records are good;

- fear of litigation is absent (i.e. professional negligence, worker compensation, product liability claims, etc. are rare and insurance premiums generally are below the sector average);

- profitability and/or efficiency of resource use are good;

- impact on the physical environment is positive or neutral.

Therefore, it could be argued that the truly 'healthy' organisation, which has been successful in creating and maintain a healthy and relatively stress-free environment, will be an organisation in which stress management and counselling interventions gradually become less necessary. Such an organisation will have targeted its interventions at reducing or eliminating job and organisational stressors effectively before their longer-term consequences on employee and organisational health (in all its aspects) affect the bottom line adversely. Indeed, although organisations have recognised the benefits of providing regular health screening for employees, they have been less concerned or slower to recognise the potential diagnostic benefits of conducting regular 'stress audits' to ascertain the current state of health of their organisation as a whole (and its constituent parts), through occupational/organisational stress screening.

Key Learning Point

Dealing with the sources of stress may require a variety of interventions: these need to be tailored to the specific problems facing the organisation within the specific organisational context.

Improving psychological well-being at work: a problem-solving approach

The complexity of employee well-being often leaves organisations confused about what to do to tackle any problems they find. While research into theories and interventions has provided some tools that organisations can use, every organisation is different. Therefore any attempts at intervention need to be tailored to the particular organisational setting and the employees involved. This has led many experts to recommend that each organisation follows a *systematic problem-solving, or risk management* approach to the management of employee well-being. There is a growing body of evidence that following such a process is crucial for effective intervention (*see* Cartwright and Cooper, 1997; Cox, 1993; Cox *et al.*, 2003; Kompier *et al.*, 1998).

STOP TO CONSIDER

Organisations may often be faced with a choice between primary, secondary and tertiary interventions. What factors should be considered when they are making that choice? What, if anything, could prevent them from using their preferred intervention strategy?

Step 1: being aware and accepting that a problem exists

It is widely accepted that recognising that one has a problem is the crucial first step towards solving it. Ownership of the problem is considered to be the most significant factor in the clinical treatment of problems such as alcoholism, drug abuse or a damaging relationship. The first step in dealing with stress, therefore, requires an awareness by the individual and the organisation that stress can be a feature of modern working life. As established theories of work stress show us, at some time or other everybody is likely to experience stress at work irrespective of their position in the organisation. Stress research has also showed that stress it is not necessarily a reflection of incompetence. It is important that the individual employee is able to recognise their own stress symptomatology early in the stress process, and that the organisation seeks to create a climate which is perceived to be openly supportive rather than punitive. Helping employees to become aware of the sources and consequences of stress in their own work environment is often a first step in the design of interventions.

Organisations can tune into the problem of stress by monitoring a variety of behavioural indices. Aside from the more obvious ones such as employee turnover and absence data, other more subtle indices might include error and accident rates, insurance claims, tardiness, dips in job satisfaction and deteriorating industrial relations. Organisations can also provide training in symptom recognition and basic counselling skills for their supervisors and managers to help them to be more responsive to employee stress (see Donaldson-Feilder *et al.*, 2008). From a senior management level downwards it is important to acknowledge and communicate to employees that stress has a legitimate place on the organisation's agenda alongside other more traditional issues that fall into the category of health and safety at work (Murphy and Sauter, 2003).

Steps 2 and 3: identifying the problem/stressor and attempting to eliminate it or change it

At the individual level, stressor identification can be achieved by the maintenance of a stress diary. Experience sampling methodology (*see* Chapter 2 and Daniels *et al.*, 2009) has also been used to combine the strengths of questionnaire methods of assessment with the advantages of continuous data collection offered by diary methods. By recording on at least a daily basis the incidents, types of situation and person(s) involved that cause distress over a period of time (e.g. four weeks), this information will reveal any significant themes or common stressor patterns and help the individual to identify specific problems or problem areas. It is also useful if the individual records show how they responded to the situation at the time, whether the strategy was successful in both the short and longer term, and how, on reflection, they might have handled it better.

On the basis of this information, the individual can then move towards developing an action plan as to how they could either eliminate the source of stress or change or modify it. For example, if a boss consistently undermines you at work, you can either confront or avoid them, or consider the options for employment elsewhere. If the stressor cannot be changed, however, then the individual has to accept the situation and explore ways of coping with the situation as it is. By cataloguing current responses and ways of coping and reviewing these with the benefit of retrospection, the individual can (i) identify areas where their coping skills could be improved and (ii) develop a repertoire of successful contingency-based coping methods which can be applied to similar situations in the future. The review process is particularly important, as has been suggested, when cognitive processes are frequently impaired under stress to the extent that the range of possible alternative strategies for coping is unlikely to be fully considered or evaluated. An awareness of potential stressors can also help the individual to develop their own anticipatory coping strategies (i.e. pre-stressor).

At the organisational level, an employee survey or organisational stress audit can be used to assess and monitor employee health and well-being, and identify the sources of stress which may be operating at an organisation-wide, departmental or work group level. A range of measures can be used in such an audit. There are various measures of working conditions including the Job Content Questionnaire (see Karasek *et al.*, 1998), the Job Diagnostic Survey (Hackman and Oldham, 1980), the UK Health and Safety Executive Indicator Tool (*see* Exercise 12.5), and the Work Organisation Assessment Questionnaire (Griffiths *et al.*, 2006). Surveys can also be constructed from various reliable and valid measures of specific aspects of work such as work control (Dwyer and Ganster, 1991), supervisory support (Greenhaus *et al.*, 1990), social support (Caplan *et al.*, 1980), monotony (Melamed *et al.*, 1995) and work–family conflict (Kopelman *et al.*, 1983). One key benefit of using this survey approach is that problems that are reported by large numbers of employees are more likely to be the result of situational factors rather than individual differences. These tools may be supplemented with measures of individual differences, coping, job satisfaction, self-reported absence, intention to quit and physical and psychological health. By using various data analysis methods (e.g. correlation, analysis of variance, etc.), it is then possible to establish whether problems with working conditions are linked to poor employee well-being. Measures such as the Occupational Stress Indicator (Cooper *et al.*, 1988) or ASSET (Cartwright and Cooper, 2001) are designed to provide an all-in-one measure of various elements of the stress process: as well as examining working conditions and job satisfaction they incorporate personality measures of Type A behaviour, locus of control and employee coping strategies.

This assessment is key because different stressors are likely to suggest different organisational solutions. For example, eliminating or reducing stressors relating to factors intrinsic to the job may involve ergonomic solutions to the problem of poorly designed equipment. However, if a significant source of stress among employees relates to career issues, then this may possibly be addressed by the introduction of regular appraisals, career counselling or retraining opportunities. It may also be that different stressors operate in different parts of the organisation for different groups of employees. Some authors (e.g. Cox *et al.*, 2000) have argued that because each workplace is unique, tailored (bespoke) measures of work characteristics might be needed to capture the problems that employees are facing. At the more local workgroup level, or in small organisations, there are less formal means by which potential stress-related problems can be identified through the introduction of regular workgroup review meetings or quality circle type initiatives.

Exercise 12.5   Setting standards for stress at work

The text that follows is adapted from a Press Release from the UK Government's Health and Safety Executive (HSE), 30 October 2003.

A new practical guidance pack to enable employers and employees to develop solutions to workplace stress problems is being launched today in London. The guidance, called 'Real solutions, real people – a manager's guide to tackling work-related stress', contains examples of clear, practical measures which provide a starting point for the workforce to agree how to tackle the findings of a stress risk assessment. The guidance pack includes an introduction on how to use it, learning points, prompt cards and an action plan to record and monitor what needs to be done.

The new guidance will cover each of the following stressor areas. These are:

- demands;
- control;
- support;
- role;
- relationships;
- change.

Launching the guidance, Bill Callaghan, Chair of the Health and Safety Commission (HSC) which oversees the work of the HSE said

The Health and Safety Commission wants workplace health and safety to be a cornerstone of a civilized society and is committed to ensuring that HSE's work remains relevant to the changing world and changing economy.

'Real solutions, real people' provides a tool to help managers and staff develop solutions to tackle work-related stress that are specifically relevant to their organisation. It then encourages them to tailor their energy to the particular needs identified by risk assessment. The launch of this guidance . . . and the innovative stress management standards pilot, already well under way, are fine examples of how the HSE is seeking to help organizations reduce the incidence of occupational ill health.

The 'Real solutions, real people' conference forms part of the HSC's Priority Programme on Stress. A key element of that programme is the development of clear, agreed standards of good management practice to prevent work-related stress. Case studies from *Real Solutions, Real People* (covering each of the stressor areas) are available on HSE's website at http://www.hse.gov.uk/stress.

Since this article was published, the HSE has also launched an indicator tool (a questionnaire for employees) that organisations can use to measure the sources of work stress. This is available from the HSE website. The article by Edwards *et al.* (2008) cited in the reference list at the back of this book presents an up-to-date evaluation of the HSE's Stress Indicator tool.

Suggested exercises

Using the material in this exercise, the HSE website, and the article by Edwards *et al.* (if you have access to it) consider whether you think it is appropriate to specify acceptable standards for stress levels in an organisation, and whether the HSE is going about it in the right way. For example, do you think it is taking all major sources of stress into consideration and is it seeking to assess them correctly? Aside from using the Indicator tool, what other data should organisations also collect as part of the problem analysis?

Diagnostic stress audits can be advantageous in terms of directing organisations to areas when they can engage in interventions (be they primary, secondary or tertiary). Often a range of intervention options are available to deal with the identified problems. Generally, legal requirements mean that organisations should look to primary interventions as the preferred option. Involving various stakeholders (employees, managers, trade unions, etc.) in the intervention decision-making process is crucial: this allows the practicalities of various intervention options to be examined properly. It also allows for an intervention action plan to be devised.

Step 4: if the problem/stressor cannot be changed, then find ways of coping with it

There are likely to be certain stressors which neither the individual nor the organisation is able to change, but which have to be 'coped with' in the conventional sense of the word. For example, employees working in the emergency services are likely to be faced with distressing or upsetting situations and these cannot be designed out of the job. It is in relation to stressors of this nature that secondary and tertiary levels of intervention have a definite role to play. It is also important to recognise that not all of the stress that impacts on the workplace is necessarily or exclusively caused by the work environment. Financial crisis, bereavement, marital difficulties and other personal life events create stress, the effects of which often spill over into the workplace. Tertiary-level interventions, such as the provision of counselling services, can be extremely effective in dealing with non-work-related stress. What is important is that the options for primary intervention are discussed before secondary intervention is considered. Tertiary interventions should not be used to replace primary and secondary interventions.

Step 5: monitoring and reviewing the outcome

The final stage in any problem-solving process involves the evaluation of the implemented solution. As already discussed, the discipline of maintaining a stress diary can help the individual to review the efficacy of their own coping strategies. Similarly, stress audits can provide a baseline measure whereby the introduction of any subsequent stressor reduction technique implemented by an organisation can be evaluated. Measuring again working conditions and employee well-being can show whether interventions are having the desired effect. In addition, the more successful the organisation is in eliminating or modifying environmental stressors, the less demand there would be for stress management training and employee assistance programmes. In effect, this evaluation work is another audit and its results should be used as the stimulus for new efforts to tackle any problems that remain, or any new problems that have emerged since the original audit. This sets up a process of continuous improvement.

Key Learning Point

Managing stress at work requires a stage-by-stage approach – identifying a problem, intervening to change it or find ways of coping with it and monitoring and reviewing progress. This allows the intervention strategy to be tailored to the needs of the organisation, rather than it being determined by a generic theory that may or may not be valid in the organisation.

Exercise 12.6   Managing your stress

Here is your chance to engage in a bit of role play. Below is a description of a pretty stressful day. Imagine that you experience a day like this.

7.30 a.m. The day starts badly. You forgot to set the alarm and you're running late. You have an important client meeting at *9.30 a.m.* and you intended to get into the office early to reread the papers in preparation for the meeting. You have to stop for fuel on the way, in which further delays you. Traffic is heavy and there are roadworks on the motorway. You find yourself in a tailback of slow-moving traffic and it's at least seven kilometres until the next exit. As you're crawling along, you suddenly become aware that you have developed a flat tyre. You limp on to the hard shoulder and look at your watch. It's *8.50 a.m.* and you're still some 15 kilometres from your office. You're not going to make that meeting!

Assuming a typical response to the previous scenario, the day might continue as follows:

9.45 a.m. You eventually arrive at your office. You go to collect the file for the client meeting and the phone rings. A subordinate is having some problems accessing information on the computer; brusquely, you give hasty instructions. You then spend a further 10 minutes wading through the huge piles of paper stacked on your desk, searching for the right file. You notice a new pile of correspondence and phone messages on the desk, some marked 'urgent'. You contemplate dealing with these but you're now already 30 minutes late for this meeting. Suddenly, you realise that before you left last night your boss popped in and suggested a meeting at *10.30 a.m.* You're going to be late for that one too.

Suggested exercises

What is the most effective way of handling the various problems in the above scenario? Discuss how you would have coped with each of the problems as they occurred. Try to identify a primary, secondary and tertiary intervention that could be used to improve your day, and perhaps help prevent you from having too many more days like this in the future.

Summary

Stress has become a major issue for organisations. It is unlikely to move off the agenda as international competition increases and organisations are faced with tougher market conditions. Work psychologists are in the fortunate position that there is a lot of good theory about work stress and positive well-being that can be put to use in organisations. There is a solid body of knowledge that shows what the risks are to employee well-being, and a growing body of research that shows how the positive effects of work can be maximised. In this chapter you will have seen that much of the stress at work is caused not only by work overload and time pressures, but also by a lack of rewards and praise and, more importantly, by not providing individuals with the autonomy to do their jobs as they would like (Makin *et al.*, 1996). An important point made throughout this chapter is that different jobs have different sources of stress that affect different people in different ways.

While more research is needed to establish the relative effectiveness of different interventions, a closer inspection of primary interventions shows that many of them are features of good management practices. This suggests that employee well-being is protected when systems are in place to ensure that work is well-designed and managed. Involving employees in decision-making about primary interventions appears to be particularly important. Training employees to help them deal with unavoidable challenges at work also appears to have good outcomes, but such training must be delivered by competent practitioners and draw upon the latest advances in research. Of course, some employees may still slip through the net and tertiary interventions can help them to repair the damage done.

The assessment and management of employee well-being are not simple tasks. There are many factors to consider and these interact with each other in complex ways. However, it appears that enough is already known for work psychologists to offer clear advice to organisations about the processes that they should follow to help them develop a healthy workforce within a healthy organisation.

Closing Case Study

Somerset County Council: The business case for managing pressure and stress at work

Somerset County Council employs about 17,000 staff. In 2002 the Council decided to engage in an initiative to improve the Quality of Working Life (QWL) and well-being of their employees in order to reduce the cost of sickness absence (approximately £3.7 million in 2001/02), and to reduce their exposure to the growing risk of stress litigation and developments in legislation and case law. The Council was also aware of changes in employees' working conditions and practices associated with the impact of government-initiated Best Value reviews and wished to understand the effect that these changes were having on their employees.

The Quality of Working Life Initiative

The Council commissioned a stress audit using ASSET, a stress risk assessment tool developed by Cartwright and Cooper (2002), in order to identify the sources, locations and severity of underlying levels of stress across different staff groups.

Top management commitment was secured from the outset of the project – the Council's elected members, strategic management board and successive tiers of management across the Council were all involved in QWL initiative. Funding approval was gained at the highest levels on an ongoing basis and the QWL initiative was included in the Council's comprehensive People Strategy. The results of the stress audit provided the Council with a clear understanding of their starting position and therefore enabled accurate measurement of the achieved benefits when a subsequent survey was conducted.

The results of the stress audit were used to help construct a stress prevention strategy and action plan to address the aims, responsibilities, resources and time frames for resolving any problems identified across the organisation. Individual Directorates were given responsibility for implementation at a local level, while the central Corporate Department took responsibility for initiating Council-wide solutions.

The Council's QWL project team consisted of representatives from all major stakeholders, including trade union representation. Middle managers and employees were consulted in the process of constructing the action plan and their ideas used where relevant.

Following the audit, a broad mixture of interventions was introduced aimed at the individual, team and organisation levels. Individual interventions included skills training to help staff cope with incidents involving aggression and conflict from members of the public, while at a team level, managers have been trained to manage stress more effectively in themselves and their teams. At the organisational level, training for both managers and staff in the Council's revised performance review and development system was aimed at both developing people to deliver higher performance standards and also to reduce the opportunity for performance management creating workplace stress, if undertaken inappropriately.

Outcomes of the Quality of Working Life Initiative

In 2001/02 sickness absence levels were very high at 10.75 days lost per employee, per year. Each lost working day cost the Council approximately £800,000. In 2004/05 this figure has fallen to 7.2 days. In monetary terms, this reduction represents a total saving of approximately £2.8 million over the last three years. Provided that absence levels remain at current levels or fall still further, then annual savings will continue to grow compared against costs of absence borne by the Council in 2001/02.

In addition to the financial implications of engaging in the QWL initiative, the Council has managed to embed the practice of improving QWL into the culture of the organisation. This has helped the Council to achieve its People Strategy goals, and in particular to become an employer of choice, improve the quality of recruiting and reduce staff turnover in key areas.

Cost-Benefit Analysis of the Quality of Working Life Initiative

A cost/benefit analysis of the Council's QWL initiative over the three year period of 2002/3–2004/5 showed the process generated an annual saving of £1.3 million. The total saved on sickness absence costs over this period was £4.2 million, while the total cost of implementing the QWL initiative was £510,000. (The ASSET stress audit cost £30,000 and the QWL intervention budget accounted for the balance of £480,000.) Peter Rowe, Head of Human Resources at Somerset County Council at the time, said of the project: 'We have achieved cost saving of over £1 million per annum. We had assumed that we would need to employ more staff, but realised it would have made the problem worse.'

In addition to the cost savings identified above, the initiative reduced and re-focused the costs of the Council's Occupational Health and Counselling contracts, ensured compliance with the law, improved staff retention rates, made Council employees feel good about their employer and enabled the Council to achieve Government upper quartile sickness absence targets.

Somerset County Council's QWL initiative demonstrates how a comprehensive approach aimed at improving employee well-being can be constructed and delivered economically within a large organisation, resulting in positive change to key performance indicators as well as achieving lasting cultural change.

Source: Tasho et al. *(2005).*

Suggested exercise

What aspects of Somerset County Council's approach do you think made it so effective? Are there elements of this case study that validate the theories of work stress and the approaches to stress management described in this chapter?

Test your learning

Short-answer questions

1 What are Hans Selye's three stages of stress?

2 What are structural models of work stress?

3. What are the key predictions made by the demands–control–support model of work stress?

4 What are transactional models of work stress?

5 To what extent is absence increased by, and performance decreased by, work-related stress?

6 Which source of workplace stress, in your view, is the most damaging to the individual employee? Why?

7 Define the following: role ambiguity, role conflict and locus of control.

8 What is positive well-being?

9 List three individual difference variables that are important in the stress process.

10 Define primary, secondary and tertiary interventions.

11 What is an EAP?

12 List at least five different primary interventions that could be used to tackle five different sources of work-related stress.

13 What is more effective for tackling work stress: relaxation training or cognitive behavioural training? Briefly explain your answer.

14 What is a stress audit and what useful data might it yield?

15 Define the main features of a 'healthy organisation'.

Suggested assignments

1 What are the major sources of stress at work? Why are they stressful?

2 Compare and contrast transactional and structural theories of work stress.

3 Is the concept of stress a useful one?

4 Is it appropriate to describe stress as an illness? Explain your answer with reference to theory and research on work stress.

5 Might individual-level stress management programmes be more or less effective than organisation-oriented interventions? Explain your answer.

6 'The way a stress management intervention is implemented is just as important as the content of that intervention.' Discuss.

Relevant websites

The work on line management behaviour and work stress that is part sponsored by the CIPD can be found at http://www.cipd.co.uk/subjects/health/stress/_lnstrswrk.htm.

Practical concern with how to manage (and/or reduce) stress at work is always high, and seems to be growing. One manifestation of that is the International Stress Management Association, which can be found at http://www.isma.org.uk. This site offers links to ideas and resources for managing stress, and although it is UK-based, there are also links to equivalent sites in some other countries.

A host of resources, including the Management Standards Indicator Tool and case studies of stress management interventions can be found at the UK HSE website: www.hse.gov.uk/stress. The full research report on the Somerset County Council case study is available to download in full from the HSE website www.hse.gov.uk/research/rrhtm/rr295.htm.

 For further self-test material and relevant annotated weblinks please visit the website for this book at **www.pearsoned.co.uk/workpsych**

Suggested further reading

Full details for all references are given in the list at the end of this book.

1 *Organizational Stress: A review and critique of theory, research and application* by Cary Cooper, Philip Dewe and Mike O'Driscoll, published by Sage Publications in 2001, is a comprehensive review of theory and research in the field of organisational and occupational stress.

2 The analysis of the business case for managing work-related stress by Frank Bond and colleagues in 2006 is an excellent and accessible review of the links between sources of stress and important organisational outcomes. It can be downloaded free from the UK HSE website http://www.hse.gov.uk/research/rrpdf/rr431.pdf.

3 Richardson and Rothstein's (2008) review of stress management interventions is rather technical, but begins with some very useful information about the various interventions that are available to organisations.

4 *How to Deal with Stress* by Stephen Palmer and Cary Cooper, published by Kogan Page, 2007, explores how individuals can and should cope with stress.

5   The series of textbooks *Occupational Health Psychology: European perspectives on research, education and practice*, edited by Jonathan Houdmont and Stavroula Leka (2009), provides a range of very up-to-date articles on issues in the study of work and well-being. From 2010 this will be under the title: *Contemporary Occupational Health Psychology: Global perspectives on research and practice* (Volume 1), with the same editors, published by Wiley-Blackwell Stavroula Leka and Jonathan Houdmonts' (Eds.) textbook (2010) *Occupational Health Psychology*, published by Wiley-Blackwell is an excellent text, covering a range of issues related to health at work.

6   *Employee Mental Well-being Support* by Andrew Kinder, Rick Hughes and Cary Cooper, published by John Wiley/Blackwell, 2008, is a comprehensive review of all research on organisational employee support systems (e.g. EAPs) as well as a guide for human resource professionals about how to choose one, how to evaluate them and the costs/benefits of these for organisations.

CHAPTER 13

Groups, teams and teamwork

After studying this chapter, you should be able to:

1 outline the main features of the 'groupthink' model of group decision-making, and suggest two ways in which it may not be entirely accurate;

2 define group polarisation and explain why it occurs;

3 explain why relations between groups at work depend partly on individuals' sense of personal identity;

4 define stereotypes and specify two reasons why they can affect relations between groups at work;

5 describe the incidence of teamwork in Europe;

6 summarise how teams function;

7 explain the stages of team development;

8 describe the importance of team roles and a popular team role typology;

9 explain the ways in which the diversity within a team can affect team functioning;

10 explain some of the factors that influence team performance.

Opening Case Study   Playing the game

Team-building used to be about going to the pub on a Friday evening and helping your colleagues into a taxi when they'd had one drink too many. Gone are those days. Even team-building through paintballing is old news. These days nothing less than an African safari, hot air ballooning or sailing on the high seas will do, it seems.

The team is now the norm at work. Office life is no longer the atomised existence it once was. 'Teams have become a way of organising work,' says Rob Briner, organisational psychologist at Birkbeck College, London.

> The problem is that these teams are normally very artificial. One of the defining characteristics of a team is that you have to be interdependent, but that's rarely true of workplace teams. Part of the reason for recent interest in team-building is that these teams often aren't actually working properly.

As team-building has become the buzz word of HR departments, training providers have proliferated and their offerings diversified. Prices vary from £50 per person for a half-day activity up to several thousand pounds for week-long team-building activities overseas.

Team activities centre on forcing people into new situations. 'Getting people out of the mould and out of the existing hierarchy that they're used to is crucial,' says Alan Kiff, managing director of Campfire Adventures, which runs safaris in South Africa and dog-sledding in Finland. During week-long trips, activities include guiding a blindfold driver through an obstacle course using whistles, and doing a treasure hunt around a safari park.

Get to know your fellow workers in challenging and unfamiliar situations. Then you'll all work together better – that's the theory. But experts dispute this assumption. 'There is no strong evidence that team cohesion aids team effectiveness,' says Michael West, professor of organisational psychology and director of research at Aston University. 'People assume they work more effectively if they like the people they're with, but may simply conspire to do less work, spend longer ensuring they don't fall out, or even decide they don't like each other.'

The blame may lie with client companies and not the training providers, says Neil Russell, managing director of Eos Yacht Charters. 'Some companies really want to build a team in a genuine sense, but these are few and far between.' Many managers remain cynical about skills training and development, he says. 'People are much more into developing technical knowledge rather than teamworking skills.'

Team-building events are big business these days. And while doubts remain about the exact nature of their benefits, training providers and clients insist that they bond staff, build company loyalty and help break down barriers.

Source: Adapted from an article by Rosie Blau, 30 May 2002. 'Playing the Game (team building)', People Management, Vol. 8(II) pp. 38-9.

Introduction

The opening case study shows that teams and groups are a fashionable topic in the workplace, and allegedly a fashionable way of organising workers. However, the case study also shows that there is some scepticism about whether teams are necessarily a good way of organising work, and about whether team-building in exotic ways succeeds in enhancing team effectiveness.

In this chapter, the prevalence and impact of teamworking are examined, and some of the important psychological processes that occur in teams are identified. These include an examination of how creativity and innovation develop in teams, and the role of diversity in team membership. Teams can be argued to be a special case of groups, and this means that the research on groups can be very useful in helping us to understand teams. How we perceive and behave towards members of our own group and members of other groups has, for a very long time, been of great interest to social psychologists. Some of the key themes of that work are included in this chapter because they help us to develop a stronger understanding of how teams in organisations (*see also the prevalence of teamwork* later in this chapter).

Group decision-making

Groups versus individuals

Although many people are very cynical about the value of meetings and committees, the fact is that work tends to involve a lot of them. In work organisations most major decisions (and many lesser ones) are made by groups of people, and not by individuals. Hence the study of groups has attracted a lot of interest, an increasing proportion of which is from organisational psychologists (Guzzo and Dickson, 1996). There are some clear potential benefits of group decision-making. If handled in the right way, a decision made by a group can evoke greater commitment to it than one made by an individual: this is because more people feel a sense of involvement in the decision. On the other hand, group decisions usually consume more time (and more money) than individual ones: therefore, the enhanced quality of the decisions they make need to justify the extra costs. One often-asked question is whether individual or group decisions are superior (Davis, 1992).

One view is that 'many heads are better than one': this school of thought argues that, in groups, people can correct each other's mistakes and build on each other's ideas. An opposing view is that 'too many cooks spoil the broth', which argues that problems of communication and rivalry between group members more than cancel out any potential advantage of the increased total available knowledge, skills, abilities and other competencies.

In fact, research has shown that it is not possible to generalise about whether individuals or groups are universally better. It depends, to a large extent, on the abilities and training of the individuals and groups and on the kind of task being tackled (Hill, 1982). Examining the different activities that groups engage in allows us to better identify what it is that makes groups effective.

McGrath (1984) identified eight different types of task that groups can face. Four of these directly concern group decision-making. These are:

1   generating plans (e.g. how many new employees to hire to support expansion);

2   generating ideas (e.g. ideas for new products to help grow the business);

3   solving problems that have 'correct answers' (i.e. where the answer can be identified with a degree of certainty, for example the costs of hiring a new member of staff);

4   identifying issues that do not have a 'correct answer' at the time the decision is made (i.e. where there is considerable uncertainty over the answer, for example identifying exact levels of staff turnover in five years time).

The second and third of these provide the best opportunities for comparing group and individual performance, and these are examined in more detail below.

Brainstorming, for example, is a technique for generating ideas with which many readers will already be familiar. It was originally advocated by Osborn (1957), who argued individuals can think up twice as many ideas in a group as they could on their own, but only if those in the group agree that:

■   the more ideas they think of the better; and

■   members will be encouraged to produce even bizarre ideas, and not be ridiculed for them.

However, even if these conditions are met, groups are not always more effective than individuals during brainstorming. Some research has indicated that lone individuals who are encouraged to think of as many ideas as possible generate more ideas per individual than do groups (e.g. Lamm and Trommsdorf, 1973). A number of possible explanations have been suggested for this phenomenon. These include *evaluation apprehension*, where a person feels afraid of what others will think, despite the brainstorming instructions, and *free-riding*, where group members feel that other group members will do the work for them.

Diehl and Stroebe (1987) devised experiments to test different explanations, but their results supported a third explanation: *production blocking*. Simply, only one person at a time in a group can talk about their ideas, and in the meantime other members may forget or suppress theirs. Nevertheless, there is also clear evidence that exposure to the ideas of other people enhances creativity, especially if people are exposed to a diverse group of others (Paulus, 2000).

Taken together, the research indicates that the best brainstorming is achieved by exposing individuals to a diverse group of others, but without incurring production blocking or other negative group effects. Advances in information and communication technology can help here, by transmitting information between group members in a clear and impersonal way (e.g. Valacich *et al.*, 1994; *see also* Chapter 10 for an fuller examination of these issues). For example, it seems that groups linked by computer can produce more ideas than those meeting face-to-face, and also have greater equality of participation (Hollingshead and McGrath, 1995). However, such groups also tend to make more extreme decisions and have some hostile communications. There is more about virtual teams in Chapter 10.

Psychologists have conducted a number of experiments comparing individual and group performance on *problems with correct answers*. For example Vollrath *et al.* (1989) found that groups of people working together recognised and recalled information better than individuals. However, McGrath (1984) pointed out that there are different types of correct answers: group problem-solving processes appear to vary according to the extent to which the correct answer can be shown to be correct. This concept of 'correctness' is best explained by example.

One type of correct answer is found in 'Eureka' tasks – when the correct answer is mentioned, everyone suddenly sees that it must be right (e.g. when the group is tasked with identifying a factual answer such as the previous 12 months' production volumes). However, there are also problems where the answer can be proved correct using logic, even though its correctness is not necessarily obvious at first sight (e.g. the costs of borrowing large sums of money to take over a competitor organisation). Then there are problems where the correct (or best) answer can only be defined by experts, but whose wisdom may be challenged by a lay person (e.g. the environmental impact of an organisation's production processes).

The second type of problem is often used to investigate the complexities of group decision-making processes. One task often used in research, is the so-called 'horse-trading task'. In this task a person buys a horse for £60 and sells it for £70. Then they buy it back for £80 and again sell it for £90. How much money does the person make in the horse-trading business? Many people say £10, but the correct answer is £20 though strictly this assumes that the person does not have to borrow the extra £10 to buy back the horse, and it ignores the opportunity cost of using the £10 in that way rather than another.

Early research using problems of this kind (e.g. Maier and Solem, 1952) produced several important findings. First, lower-status group members had less influence on the group decision than higher-status ones, even when the lower-status people were correct. Second, even when at least one person in the group knew the correct answer, the group decision was by no means always correct. Third, group discussion made people more confident that the group's consensus decision was correct: unfortunately the discussion did not make a correct decision more likely! For problems like the horse-trading one, it typically needs two correct people, not one, to convince the rest of the group. Put another way, on average *the group is as good as its second-best member*. This could be taken to mean that, for solving problems with correct answers, groups are on average better than individuals, but inferior to the *best* individuals.

For problems with demonstrably correct answers, groups are (on average) as good as their second-best member. However, groups can do better or worse than this average depending on their membership and process.

However, conclusions of this kind cannot easily be generalised. In organisations, many groups are dealing with uncertainties. Many decisions made in organisations do not have a provable correct answer, or even an answer that well-qualified experts can agree on. More importantly, although organisations might find it interesting to understand how groups make decisions, they are likely to be more concerned with how they can be improved. Improving group decision-making when the group is faced with real-life issues is the focus of the next section of this chapter: it has been the subject of much popular and academic debate.

Group deficiencies and overcoming them

Some social scientists have concentrated on identifying the context within which groups are more likely to perform well (e.g. Larson and LaFasto, 1989). They point out necessities such as having group members who are knowledgeable about the problem faced; having a clearly defined and inspiring goal (*see* Locke's goal-setting theory in Chapter 8); having group members who are committed to solving the problem in the best possible way; and support and recognition from important people outside the group. Other work has attempted to identify the roles that group members should adopt in order to function effectively together. Perhaps the most influential has been Belbin (1981, 1993a), who identified the various roles required in an effective team (this work is covered in detail later in this chapter). Other observers of groups have concentrated more on procedural factors (e.g. Rees and Porter, 2001). Procedural factors include the practices of the chairperson in facilitating discussion and summing it up, ensuring that everyone has their say and that only one person speaks at a time, and making sure that votes (if taken) are conducted only when all points of view have been aired, and with clearly defined options, so that group members know what they are voting for and against.

Social psychologists have noted many features of the group decision-making process that can impair decision quality. Many of these underlie the practical suggestions already mentioned in this section that are designed to help groups avoid such pitfalls. Hoffman and Maier (1961) noted a tendency to adopt 'minimally acceptable solutions', especially where the decision task is complex. Instead of seeking the best possible solution, group members often settle on the first suggested solution that everyone considers 'good enough'. In certain circumstances this might be an advantage (e.g. in a situation where a quick, workable decision is required), but on most occasions it is probably not a good idea. Hackman (1990) pointed out that groups rarely discuss what strategy they should adopt in tackling a decision-making task (i.e. how they should go about it), but that when they do, they tend to perform better. Simply telling groups to discuss their strategy before they tackle the problem itself is usually not enough: discussion of the group's strategy has to be treated as a separate task if it is to be taken seriously and have an impact.

Motivational losses in groups can also be a problem. Experimental research has consistently shown that as the number of people in a group increases, the effort and/or performance of each one often decreases: this is the so-called *social loafing* effect (e.g. Latane *et al.*, 1979). On the other hand, this motivational loss can be avoided if individuals in the group feel that their contribution can be identified as their own, *and* that their contribution makes a significant difference to the group's performance (Williams *et al.*, 1981; Kerr and Bruun, 1983). Hence a group leader would be well advised to ensure that each group member can see the connection between the efforts of individuals and group performance (both for each individual themselves and so that they can see the contribution of other group members). Interestingly, culture may play an important role in group motivation. There is some evidence that social loafing does not occur in collectivist societies. Earley (1989) found evidence of social loafing amongst American management trainees in a management task set in a laboratory, but not amongst trainees from the People's Republic of China (even in the identical task). In collective societies, a person's sense of shared responsibility with others (in contrast with individualistic Western cultures) may explain this difference. Moreover, Erez and Somech (1996) found that differences in individualism–collectivism even within one country (Israel) made a difference to the social loafing effect (with those closest to the individualism end of the continuum being most prone to social loafing). This is a another example of the culturally specific nature of some phenomena in applied psychology.

However, social loafing appears only to occur when groups lack specific goals. As Erez and Somech pointed out, most groups in the workplace have members who: know each other, communicate with each other, have team goals that matter to them and contribute to the team in a way that means that individual performance can be identified. So social loafing may not be as widespread in the real world as it is in laboratory-based experiments: it may be the exception, not the rule, even in individualistic cultures.

Key Learning Point

Group members tend to reduce their efforts as group size increases, at least in individualistic cultures. This problem can, however, be overcome by setting teams specific goals and making team members accountable for their actions.

Another problem with group work concerns how a group reacts when things start to go wrong. It seems that groups may be even more likely than individuals to escalate their commitment to a decision (i.e. to stick to it), even if it does not seem to be working out well (Whyte, 1993). This can occur even if the majority of group members start off with the view that they will not invest any further resources in the initial decision. This essentially risky decision of the group (i.e. to persevere with a course of action even in the face of negative feedback about it) may be even more marked if the decision they are required to make is about avoiding losses rather than achieving gains. As noted earlier in this chapter, most people are more inclined to accept the risk of a big loss in the hope of avoiding a moderate loss (than they are to risk losing a moderate profit in pursuit of a big profit).

Groupthink

Janis (1972, 1982a,b) arrived at some disturbing conclusions about how some real-life policy-making groups can make extremely poor decisions that have serious repercussions around the world. He analysed the major foreign policy errors of various governments at various times in history. One of these was the 'Bay of Pigs' fiasco in the early 1960s. Fidel Castro had recently taken power in Cuba. As a response, the new US administration under President John F. Kennedy launched an 'invasion' of Cuba by 1400 Cuban exiles, who landed at the Bay of Pigs. Within two days they were surrounded by 20,000 Cuban troops, and those not killed were ransomed back to the United States at a cost of $53 million in aid.

Janis argued that this outcome was not just bad luck for the United States. Instead, such an outcome could and should have been anticipated. He suggested that in this and other fiascos, various group processes could be seen, which collectively he called *groupthink*.

According to Janis, groupthink occurs when group members' motivation for unanimity and agreement (i.e. consensus) overrides their motivation to evaluate carefully the risks and benefits of alternative decisions. This usually occurs in 'cohesive' groups, i.e. those where group members are friendly with each other, and respect each other's opinions. In such groups disagreement is construed (usually unconsciously) as a withdrawal of friendship and respect, rather than as a useful critical insight. When this is combined with (i) a group leader known (or believed) to have a position or opinion on the issues under discussion, (ii) an absence of clear group procedures for discussion and decision-making, and (iii) a difficult set of circumstances (e.g. time pressure, or high-stakes decision-making), then the group members tend to seek agreement. This leads to groupthink as shown in Figure 13.1. The symptoms can be summarised as follows:

- *Overestimation of the group's power and morality*: in groupthink, group members tend have positive opinions of each other and these are not challenged.

- *Closed-mindedness*: this can be seen through group members' efforts to downplay warnings and to stereotype other groups as inferior to their own.

- *Pressures towards uniformity*: this manifests itself through the suppression of private doubts, leading to an illusion of unanimity and the development of 'mindguards' to shield group members (especially the leader) from uncomfortable information.

Key Learning Point

Groupthink is a set of malfunctioning group processes that occur when group members are more concerned (although they may not realise it) to achieve unanimity and agreement than they are to find the best available solution to a problem or situation.

Janis (1982b) has argued that certain measures can be taken to avoid groupthink. These include:

- establishing impartial leadership (so that group members are not tempted simply to follow the leader);

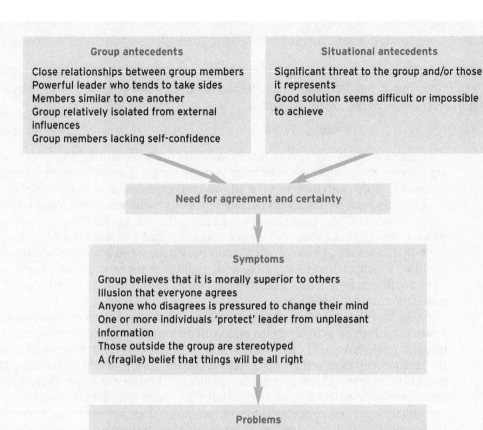

| Figure 13.1 | The Janis groupthink model |

- instructing each person in the group to give high priority to airing doubts and objections;

- having subject matter experts in attendance to raise doubts about the group's discussions and decision-making;

- including 'second chance' meetings where members express their doubts about a previously made, but not yet implemented, decision.

An overarching theme of these interventions is that groupthink can be minimised if there is a known 'group norm' that disagreeing with another group member does *not* signal disrespect or unfriendliness towards them.

Intuitively appealing as it is, Janis's work has not gone unchallenged. It has been argued that the groupthink syndrome is really simply a collection of separate phenomena that do not co-occur as neatly as Janis claims, and that these phenomena have already been separately investigated by other social scientists (Aldag and Fuller, 1993). Whyte (1989) argued that so-called groupthink is not itself a unitary phenomenon. Instead, it is a product of groups being inclined to accept risk when they perceive that losses are at stake, and of group polarisation (*see below*). In addition, Janis obtained much of his information from published retrospective accounts, which some argue may be inaccurate (i.e. what is published is not always what actually happened) and/or incomplete.

Aldag and Fuller (1993) have pointed out that some research has found that group cohesiveness actually helps open discussion of ideas (rather than inhibiting it as Janis has argued). In fact, when Mullen and Copper (1994) reviewed 66 tests of the relationship between group cohesiveness and group performance, they found that cohesiveness was, on average, a significant (though not large) aid to performance, especially when groups were small. They also found that successful group performance tended to foster cohesiveness more than cohesiveness fostered performance. This is not surprising: if we think of cohesiveness as a combination of interpersonal attraction, commitment to the task and group pride, we would reasonably expect all of these to increase when the group succeeds in its tasks.

It is worth noting that studies which have failed to replicate groupthink have been laboratory-based studies of groups that do not have the history implied by some of the antecedents listed in Figure 13.1. Park (2000) reviewed 28 tests of the groupthink model published between 1974 and 1998. Eleven of these tests were experiments using students, while most of the others were case studies of real-life events. Nine of the experiments produced partial support for the groupthink model, two produced no support and none was fully or almost fully supportive. The case studies did better: seven supported all, or nearly all, of the model, three offered partial support and three offered little or no support.

The greater support from case studies might be because the experiments were artificial situations (i.e. without the historical antecedents needed for groupthink to occur) or because data from case studies are inherently more ambiguous and open to interpretation in line with the groupthink theory. In another experiment, Park (2000) tested all the relationships between variables proposed by the groupthink model by collecting data from 64 groups of 4 students. Park found partial support for the groupthink model. Some of the key findings were:

- high group cohesiveness was associated with more symptoms of groupthink than low group cohesiveness;

- groups with members who had (on average) high self-esteem showed more symptoms of groupthink than where members had (on average) low self-esteem;

- group members' feelings of invulnerability and morality were associated with fewer symptoms of defective decision-making;

■ when the group discussion contained an incomplete survey of alternative solutions they tended to make poor-quality decisions.

You might find it helpful to refer back to Figure 13.1 and think about which of these findings are as Janis predicted, and which are not. For example, the groupthink model has little to say about the influence of individual differences such as self-esteem.

Although it has been an influential model, by no means all research into group decision-making has been designed to test the groupthink model. However, much of it has investigated phenomena similar to those identified by Janis. For example, Schulz-Hardt *et al.* (2002) found that groups of managers who had similar points of view even before they met tended to seek yet more information that supported their existing view. However, when there was genuine disagreement in initial points of view this led to the group carrying out a much more balanced search for information in their discussions. The presence of people instructed to be a 'devil's advocate' (i.e. to argue the opposite view of the group's preference whatever their own private opinion) also had some effect in reducing a group's preference for information that agreed with their initial opinions. These findings support Janis's ideas that groups where the members agree are prone to restricting their information search and that appointing a devil's advocate may go some way towards correcting that.

All of the criticisms of groupthink have some force. Nevertheless, Janis provided rich case studies which illustrate the many potential problems in group decision-making. There is now lots of well-designed research that dispels any comforting belief we might have that really important group decisions are always made rationally.

Exercise 13.1   Your experiences of group decision-making

Try to recall a time when you participated in a group that had to make a decision (for example, to choose between alternative courses of action). Bring to mind as much as you can about what happened, and then consider the following questions. If you can do so with someone else who was there, so much the better.

Suggested exercises

1   How cohesive was the group, and what consequences do you think that had for (i) the way the group went about its task and (ii) how you felt about participating?

2   Do you think the group members were (i) excited about the possibility of accomplishing something really worthwhile or (ii) fearful about making a mistake? Either way, how did that affect the discussion the group had and the decision the group made?

3   If there was a leader of the group, to what extent were they admired and trusted by the other members? What was the impact of this on how the group conducted itself?

4   To what extent were alternative options carefully considered? Think about why.

5   Finally, was the eventual decision actually implemented? Why (or why not)? Did the decision work out well, and if not, could that have been foreseen?

6   Consider how well (or not) your observations match the theory and research discussed in this chapter so far.

Key Learning Point

The groupthink model appears not to be entirely accurate, but it includes many ideas that have had a big impact on subsequent research on groups and teams.

Group polarisation

One often-voiced criticism of groups is that they arrive at compromise decisions. However, it seems that groups tend to make more extreme decisions than we might expect given the initial preferences of group members (Bettenhausen, 1991). This has most often been demonstrated with respect to risk. If the initial tendency of the majority of group members is to adopt a moderately risky decision, the eventual group decision is usually more risky than that. Conversely, somewhat cautious initial preferences of group members translate to even more cautious eventual group decisions. This is known as polarisation.

Using systematic research, psychologists have reduced eleven possible explanations for group polarisation down to two (Isenberg, 1986). The *social comparison* explanation is that we like to present ourselves in a socially desirable way, so we try to be like other group members, *only more so*. The *persuasive argumentation* explanation is that information consistent with the views held by the majority will dominate the group discussion, and (so long as that information is correct and novel) have powerful persuasive effects. Both explanations are valid, though the latter seems to exert a stronger effect. Polarisation is not in itself inherently good or bad. However, in order to benefit from group decision-making, group members need to ensure that they share all relevant information and ideas (this means that all arguments rejecting the initially favoured point of view are heard). Group members also need to avoid social conformity (one of the phenomena that Janis observed as so damaging to group decision-making). Chen *et al.* (2002) have shown that using a quantitative decision aid (e.g. a questionnaire) can reduce the impact of overly biased persuasive arguments on group members, albeit only slightly.

Key Learning Point

Contrary to popular opinion, groups often produce more extreme decisions, and fewer compromises, than do individuals working on their own.

Minority influence

Research has shown that minorities within groups only rarely convert the majority to their point of view. But how can they maximise their chances? Many people say that they should first gain the acceptance of the majority by conforming wherever possible, and *then* stick out for their own point of view on a carefully chosen crucial issue. However, research carried out by Moscovici and colleagues suggests otherwise

(Moscovici and Mugny, 1983; Moscovici, 1985). They found that, if it is to exert influence, a minority needs to *disagree* consistently with the majority, including on issues other than the one that is of particular importance to the minority group. They demonstrated that minorities do not exert influence by being liked or being seen as reasonable, but by being perceived as consistent, independent and confident. Consistent with this, Van Hiel and Mervielde (2001) found that group members believe that being *assertive and consistent is an effective strategy for minorities*, while being *agreeable is a better strategy for majority groups* than it is for minorities. If we think back to the previous section concerning group polarisation, we see that a minority can effectively limit the extent of group polarisation by expressing many arguments that oppose the majority point of view.

Much debate has centred on why and how minorities in groups exert influence (e.g. Nemeth, 1986; Smith *et al.*, 1996; McLeod *et al.*, 1997). The predominant view is that minorities and majorities exert influence in different ways. Nemeth (1986) suggested that majorities encourage convergent, shallow and narrow thinking. However, consistent exposure to minority viewpoints stimulates deeper and wider consideration of alternative perspectives. Nemeth (1986, p. 28) concluded from experimental data that:

> Those exposed to minority viewpoints . . . are more original, they use a greater variety of strategies, they detect novel solutions, and importantly, they detect correct solutions. Furthermore, this beneficial effect occurs even when the minority viewpoints are wrong.

This emphasises again that in order to reach good-quality decisions, groups need to encourage different points of view, not suppress them.

Key Learning Point

Minority views may be irritating for some group members, but their expression typically leads to better group functioning, even if they are incorrect.

Wood *et al.* (1994) reviewed 143 studies of minority influence, and found that minorities do indeed have some capacity to change the opinions of people who hear their message. This effect is even stronger if recipients of the message are not required to publicly acknowledge their change of opinion to the minority. Opinion change is also much greater on issues indirectly related to the message than it is on those directly related to it. Indeed, although the opinion of the majority usually has more effect than that of the minority, the minority exert greater influence on issues only indirectly related to the message. Ng and Van Dyne (2001) have found in an experimental study with students, that group members who (i) value collectivist beliefs (i.e. act according to social norms that emphasise interpersonal harmony) and (ii) do *not* value individualist beliefs (i.e. *do not* focus on personal goals and perspectives) are less influenced than others by minority views. This means that they tend to be more influenced by the majority, thus impairing their decision-making. Ng and Van Dyne also found that when a one-person minority happens to be the leader of the group, they have more influence than when the one-person minority is not the leader.

Exercise 13.2   A soft drink product decision

Rudi Lerner was managing director of a medium-size soft drinks company. His father had founded and then managed the business for nearly 30 years before handing over to his son four years ago. Rudi felt he knew much more about the business than his colleagues on the top management team. They agreed about that, and they liked and respected their boss as well as each other. They usually went out of their way to avoid contradicting him. On the rare occasions they did so, they received a friendly but firm reminder from the chairman that he had been in the business much longer than they had. That was true, but the team membership had not changed for five years now, so nobody was exactly ignorant. However, it was hard to argue - after all, the company had been successful relative to its competitors over the years. Rudi attributed this to frequent takeovers of competitors by people from outside the business. He rarely commissioned market research, relying instead on his 'gut feeling' and extensive prior experience. Now a new challenge faced the company: should it go into the low-calorie 'diet' drinks market, and if so, with what products? The demand for diet drinks was recent but might be here to stay.

Suggested exercise

How likely is it that Rudi and the rest of the management team will make a good decision about entering the 'diet' market? Explain your answer.

STOP TO CONSIDER

At this point in the chapter, think about how much the material you have read so far tells us about decision-making among groups of employees. Having read the sections on groupthink, polarisation and minority influence how well can we explain decision-making in work-groups using this body of knowledge? What are the issues that this literature has tackled successfully? What issues has it tackled less successfully? Also, consider the key question: under what circumstances do groups tend to make better decisions than individuals making decisions on their own?

Relations between groups at work

So far we have examined what goes on within groups that are attempting to generate ideas and/or solve problems. Another important perspective is what happens *between* groups at work (see also Chapter 10). Most workplaces are composed of a large number of overlapping groups – for example different departments, committees, occupations, locations, project teams or hierarchical levels. Some of these groups have responsibilities for making and/or implementing decisions (e.g. the management board), while others are defined simply in terms of members having something in common (e.g. accountants). Work organisations need groups to cooperate and relate well to each other, both for organisational effectiveness and for the well-being of people within them.

It is widely thought that our need for a clear and positive personal identity leads us, on occasions, to define ourselves in terms of our group membership(s): we evaluate those groups we are in positively (and, in particular, more positively than other groups that we are not in). So in effect we use the groups we belong to, to give ourselves a positive sense of who we are. These are the fundamental ideas behind social identity theory (Tajfel and Turner, 1979) and self-categorisation theory (Turner, 1999). These ideas have been applied to help us understand how groups work together in organisations.

A review of the inter-group literature by Hewstone *et al.* (2002) makes the following points:

- Usually we tend to favour the group(s) we belong to (termed the 'in-group') more than we disparage out-groups, and this often happens without us even realising it.

- Successful inter-group bias enhances self-esteem, as predicted by social identity theory. Some have also predicted that when people's self-esteem is low or threatened, they will be even keener to evaluate their in-group positively. However, there is much less evidence for this.

- Groups of high status and numerical superiority tend to show more in-group bias than those of low status and low membership numbers. However, such dominant groups may show generosity to out-group members when they see the status gap as being very wide. Low-status groups show high in-group bias when they have a chance of closing the gap and/or see their low status as unfair.

- Various methods have been tried to reduce in-group bias, on the assumption that this will improve relations between different groups. The methods include teaching people to suppress their biases; inducing them to behave positively towards out-groups so that they infer from their own behaviour that they must have a positive attitude; increasing people's knowledge about out-group members (so that they are seen as individuals more than group members); finding superordinate groups (for example, defining a group as everyone in the company) which allow people to re-categorise from out-group members to in-group members.

- In some situations, and some cultures, people tend to define themselves in terms of their group memberships. In others they do so more in terms of their characteristics as an individual (Ellemers *et al.*, 2002). So the nature and extent of in-group bias may change almost minute by minute.

Key Learning Point

Relations between groups at work are affected, often negatively, by group members' wishes to see themselves in a more positive light than members of other groups. This is a major challenge for organisations who wish to reap maximum benefits from having a diverse workforce.

An issue closely related to group membership concerns stereotypes. Stereotypes are generalised beliefs about the characteristics, attributes and behaviours of members of certain groups (Hilton and Von Hippel, 1996, p. 240). Groups can be defined on any number of criteria. Obvious possibilities are race, sex, occupation and age, but research suggests that most people do not have broad stereotypes (e.g. of all women, or all men, or all old people). Stereotypes tend to be based on rather more specific groups such as old men or old white women (Stangor *et al.*, 1992). Some stereotypes held by a person refer to quite specific groups, as in the following hypothetical examples:

- 'Employee representatives are usually people who express the most militant views.'

- 'Most nurses are caring and conscientious.'

- 'Managers in this company never tell the truth.'

- 'Accountants are always more stimulating to talk to than anybody else in the company.'

- 'Production managers usually speak their mind.'

Clearly, then, stereotypes vary in their favourability. They also differ in their extremity. The third and fourth above do not allow for any exceptions, but the others do because they refer to 'most' rather than 'all'. Often stereotypes have some validity, in the sense that *on average* members of one group differ from members of another group. On average, senior managers may be more intelligent in some respects than building site labourers. But there is equally certainly a large overlap – some building site labourers are more intelligent than some senior managers. In fact, one of the problems with stereotypes is that they lead to the overestimation of the differences between groups (Krueger, 1991).

Stereotypes of groups can develop from very limited information about them – perhaps confined to what we see on television. For example, our stereotypes about police officers may be heavily influenced by the latest television crime drama (in reality, police work is likely to be very different). Other stereotypes can arise when a generalisation is true of a very few people in one group and practically none in another group. Suppose for a moment that 1 in 500 trade union officials are members of revolutionary left-wing political groups, compared with 1 in 3000 of the general population. Would you then expect that a trade union official you were about to meet for the first time would be a revolutionary left-winger? Clearly not, the chances of this are very small. While it is more probable that they hold such views than someone who is not a trade union official, it is still not very likely. In this example, it would be inaccurate then to define trade union officials by their membership of such political groups.

Perhaps most of us like to think that we are free of stereotypes. If so, we are probably fooling ourselves. At a university where two of the authors were employed, a small number of students came each year from Norway. One of us (who shall remain nameless!) was slightly surprised that many of these students were *not* blond and tall – this was the stereotype they had of Scandinavians.

Some of the causes and consequences of stereotypes are shown in Figure 13.2, and discussion of the role of stereotypes in assessing people at work appears in Chapter 6. Devine (1989) argues that we cannot avoid starting out with stereotypes.

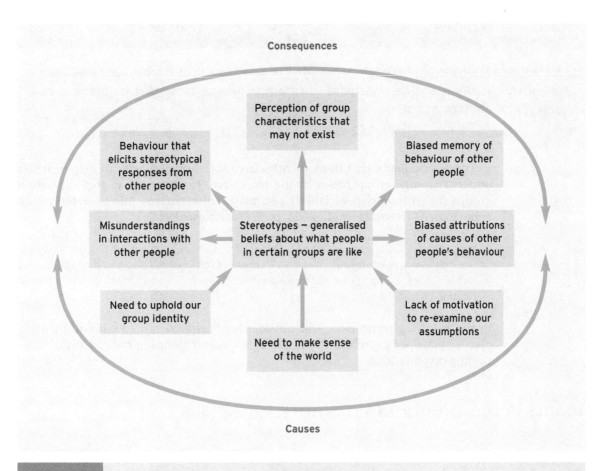

Consequences

Perception of group characteristics that may not exist

Behaviour that elicits stereotypical responses from other people

Biased memory of behaviour of other people

Misunderstandings in interactions with other people

Stereotypes – generalised beliefs about what people in certain groups are like

Biased attributions of causes of other people's behaviour

Need to uphold our group identity

Lack of motivation to re-examine our assumptions

Need to make sense of the world

Causes

Figure 13.2   Some causes and consequences of stereotypes

The difference between prejudiced and non-prejudiced individuals is that the latter *deliberately inhibit the automatically activated* stereotype and replace it with more open-minded thoughts (Devine, 1989, p. 15):

> [This] can be likened to the breaking of a bad habit . . . The individual must (a) initially decide to stop the old behavior; (b) remember the resolution, and (c) try repeatedly and decide repeatedly to eliminate the habit before the habit can be eliminated.

Other work has shown that simply instructing people to try to suppress stereotypic thoughts can actually be counterproductive. Ironically, this type of instruction itself leads people to be more conscious of the stereotype they are trying to suppress (Bodenhausen and Macrae, 1996). As Devine implied, what matters seems to be a personal commitment to changing one's perception or behaviour. Often this will involve changing one's assumptions about why a particular person is the kind of person they are – for example, by thinking about whether someone has a powerful position in an organisation because of their talent, drive and determination, rather than because they have been lucky.

Stereotypes are generalised beliefs about what people in particular groups are like. They are often inaccurate, and we sometimes use them to devalue those that we perceive as being not in our own group.

There is no doubt that these theories from social psychology can help us better understand inter-group biases in the workplace. However, what goes on within groups (i.e. intra-group variables) also plays an important role in determining behaviour. As Hewstone *et al.* (2002, p. 594) acknowledge:

> It would be a mistake, however, to consider ethnic and religious mass murder as a simple extension of intergroup bias . . . Real-world intergroup relations owe at least as much of their character to intra-group variables such as self-esteem, in-group identification . . . and group threat.

In the following sections we will consider how research carried out within workplaces has helped us to better understand teams and groups in the context of functioning organisations.

Teams in the twenty-first century workplace

The team/group distinction

Much of the previous section focused on the effectiveness of groups, mainly focusing on how they make decisions. Although very useful, a large percentage of this research has been carried out away from the organisational setting, with a focus on basic group processes. Clearly, there are other things that need to be considered when such processes take place in functioning organisations. In this section we look at how teams function from a broader perspective. You will also find relevant material in other sections of the book (e.g. Chapter 14, on leadership, has a lot to say about how to manage teams, as do the sections in Chapter 10 that deal with new methods of working and communication). Teams are increasingly common in organisations as functional boundaries break down and work is increasingly based on projects requiring input from people with different knowledge, skills, abilities and experience. The words team and group are often used interchangeably and in some cases this distinction is unimportant, but for organisational research purposes it is important to define the things being studied and teams are no exception.

A *workgroup* is characterised by being made up of individuals who:

- see themselves and are seen by others as a social entity, or unit;
- are interdependent, i.e. they rely on each other because of the tasks they perform;
- are embedded in one or more larger social systems (such as the organisation they work in);

■   perform tasks that affect others such as co-workers or customers (Guzzo and Dickson, 1996, p. 308).

Teams are different in the extent to which (i) members are interdependent (in teams levels of interdependency are very high) and (ii) the team as a whole (rather than the individuals in it) has performance goals (Sundstrom *et al.*, 1990). As Mohrman *et al.* (1995, p. 39) have put it, a team is 'a group of individuals who work together to produce products or deliver services for which they are mutually accountable'. Hackman (2002) suggested that true teams are characterised by four essential features:

1   Interdependence – team members are dependent upon each other to get things done, and the team members are not simply acting under the direction of a supervisor.

2   Membership boundaries – team members know who is part of the team (everyone knows who else carries some of the responsibility for getting things done).

3   Authority – a defined and bounded authority so that the team can manage what it does without excessive interference from, or reference to, others outside of the team. Teams are often defined according to their degree of decision-making authority (e.g. self-managing teams, semi-autonomous work groups).

4   Stability – a relatively stable membership for the lifetime of the team.

So, compared to a group, the composition of a team is relatively stable (although this stability may only last for a short period of time) and the people within it depend upon each other to achieve shared goals with the authority to act within defined boundaries. This is in contrast to assemblies of individuals (groups) where individuals rather than teams have work goals and there is much less close cooperation and interdependence. An example of a group would be all of the students studying the same course, attending the same lectures. An example of a team would be hospital employees (e.g. surgeons, anaesthetists, nurses) working together on a regular basis in an operating theatre environment. In the following sections we examine the advantages of teams (in terms of both how they benefit organisations and the individuals within them).

The prevalence of teamwork

Morita (2001) suggested that teamworking has two distinct origins. The first grew out of concern for the quality of working life in Europe (especially during the 1960s and 1970s). Teamworking was thought to provide people with more satisfying work than either working alone or in a group. The second origin was an interest in the perceived advantages of Japanese management styles, with their emphasis on multifunctional employees, loyalty to the collective and collective responsibility for the quality and quantity of work (all features of work that are important in teams). We can supplement these origins with an increased interest in the characteristics of the high-performance workplace (HPWP). Teamwork is one of several practices usually associated with the HPWP (also known as the high-commitment workplace because work practices aim to instil high levels of employee commitment). High-performance practices are implemented in an attempt to get stronger levels of employee engagement and involvement in the way that work is designed as a way of reaching higher than average levels of performance. Alongside teamwork, HPWP practices include extensive training and development, multiskilling for flexibility and performance-related pay.

So, how widespread is teamwork? The answer depends of course on how teamworking is defined, who is asked about it, and exactly how the question is asked. Perhaps the most informative analysis has been provided by Benders *et al.* (2001). Senior managers in nearly 6000 organisations in ten European countries were asked to describe the extent to which people in the largest occupational group in their workplace worked in *teams which had the authority to make their own decisions in each of the following eight areas*:

1   allocation of work;

2   scheduling of work;

3   quality of work;

4   timekeeping;

5   attendance and absence control;

6   job rotation;

7   coordination of work with other internal groups;

8   improving work processes.

Benders *et al.* decided that, in order to qualify as a 'group-based workplace' – somewhat confusingly, this means lots of employees working in teams:

■   at least four of the eight decision areas should be assigned to teams; *and*

■   at least 70 per cent of core employees should work in such groups (i.e. teams).

Only 217 workplaces (about 4 per cent of the total) met both criteria. In fact, only 1404 (24 per cent) of the workplaces assigned *any* of the eight decision areas to teams. Country by country, the 24 per cent were distributed as shown in Table 13.1.

Table 13.1	The incidence of teamworking in ten European countries	
	Percentage with at least one decision area assigned to teams	Percentage of workplaces 'team-based'
Sweden	44	11
Netherlands	38	5
France	27	5
UK	27	5
Germany	26	4
Denmark	24	3
Ireland	22	3
Italy	22	1
Portugal	6	0
Spain	4	0

Source: Adapted from Benders *et al.* (2001).

Sweden's place at the top of this table is unsurprising given its tradition of participative democracy, sociotechnical work design (*see* Chapter 8), and high-profile examples demonstrating the success of teamworking – for example Volvo. However, it is surprising that this did not spill over the border to Denmark. The low incidence of teamwork in the southern European countries is consistent with evidence that these cultures tend to emphasise status and hierarchy. Regarding which decisions teams made for themselves, improving work processes and scheduling were the most common, and job rotation, attendance and absence control the least common. Benders *et al.* note that 'headline' figures from studies of teamwork in the United States are higher than in Europe (e.g. Gittleman *et al.*, 1998, 32 per cent of workplaces using teamwork). However, on closer inspection it appears that this is partly because of differences in sampling methods and the way that questions were asked. If anything teamwork is more prevalent in Europe than in the United States. This is supported by more recent work (Blasi and Kruse, 2006; p. 572) which found that the level of adoption of self-managing teams in the 1990s was 'rather modest'.

Key Learning Point

In spite of a lot of enthusiasm for teamwork, true teamwork seems to be more the exception than the rule.

However, perhaps the stringent criteria used to identify teams underestimates the extent of organisations' efforts to implement team working. The latest (2004) Workplace Employment Relations Survey (WERS) – a very large survey of UK workplaces – shows that teamwork is the most common of the HPWP practices to be implemented (Kersley *et al.*, 2005). Almost three-quarters (72 per cent) of UK workplaces reported 'at least some of their core employees in formally designated teams'. This was very similar to the proportion in the previous 1998 WERS survey. There is some evidence of a public/private sector difference as 88 per cent of public sector workplaces claimed to be involved in teamwork compared to 68 per cent of private sector workplaces. While the WERS reported teams having a reasonable levels of responsibility for specific products and services and deciding how they can organise work, only a minority of workplaces (6 per cent) had the authority to decide who the team leader would be. Thus, organisations appear to retain a high level of control over team leader appointments.

These two large surveys suggest that UK managers report high levels if left to define teamwork for themselves: the extent of *real or true teamwork* seems considerably less. However, Scarbrough and Kinnie (2003) advise against the use of an objective definition of teamworking because the many different configurations of teamworking reflect the different work and organisational contexts in which it is attempted. Influences upon the extent of teamworking include, but are not limited to, the industrial relations context, methods of management control, the size of the organisation, the production technologies used and the extent to which they allow teamworking, the imperative for change to teamworking and the focus on teamwork in the supply chain. Given that all organisations need to exert control over employees to some extent, teamwork can be seen as a way of getting employees to control themselves while they continue to work within a framework set out by management.

How do teams work?

The input-process-output model

The classic starting point for looking at team functioning is the Input–Process–Output (I–P–O) model (McGrath, 1964). This recognises that for a given team, in a particular context, there are characteristics which can be seen as inputs that influence how the team performs (processes) and thus the final outputs. Inputs include team size, team-member diversity, structure and whether there are individual or group rewards for hitting targets. Other important input variables include the nature of the task(s) to be completed (e.g. physical or intellectual tasks, or both) and the organisational context the team is embedded in.

The interactions among the various inputs influence team processes. These include how cohesive team members feel, how well they communicate with each other and with stakeholders outside the team, how well they make decisions and how effectively team leadership occurs. Communication is influenced by the spontaneity and openness present at team meetings and may be enhanced if facilitating roles are shared rather than confined to a designated leader. While team leaders are usually appointed by the organisation this does not prevent other team members from taking leadership roles – perhaps when their specialist knowledge or personal skills can be leveraged. Another key process is decision-making (discussed earlier in this chapter) which requires the team to focus on a problem or task and deconstruct the problem/task into its components for analysis.

Naturally, outputs vary depending upon what the team exists to do. A management team could be focusing on objective, measurable targets such as income growth or cost reduction. It may also focus on introducing changes to systems or improving the efficiency of processes. Product development or customer service teams will have more clearly defined targets (e.g. to reduce the number of customer complaints filed against members of the team).

Key Learning Point

A simple model of how teams function is

Inputs → Processes → Outputs

However, the I–P–O model falls short of fully describing the complex nature of teams when they are embedded in organisational settings. It also says little about the way that teams change and evolve over time. Criticisms of the I–P–O model (Ilgen *et al.*, 2005) are:

- Many factors that influence the conversion of inputs to outputs are not processes but 'emergent cognitive or affective states' (Ilgen *et al.*, 2005, p. 520), i.e. how the team members think or feel about the problem is important, and not just the mechanics of what the team does.

- The I–P–O model implies linear paths throughout even though there are many feedback loops present. For instance, analysis of performance outputs after some intervention is an input to subsequent team processes and cognitive states and hence an input to performance at time 2.

- Relationships between the main effects in the model (e.g. the effect of team size on cohesion) are not linear as there are complex interactions between inputs and process. For example, changes in the size of the team may have an impact on how cohesive the team is. There may also be interactions between different processes, if, say, the appointment, or emergence, of a new team leader could influence the openness of team meetings.

Beyond the I–P–O model

Kozlowski and Ilgen (2006) point out that the I–P–O model was not offered as a causal model but as a way of organising the research literature that had looked at different aspects of teams. It has, however, come to be seen as a useful working model. Ilgen and colleagues go beyond the I–P–O model by proposing an 'input-mediator-output-input' (IMOI) model. Processes have been replaced by mediators to capture a wider range of variables than processes alone: mediators encompass a whole range of factors within and outside of the team that influence what the team does and the results of its efforts. The addition of 'input' to the end of the model captures the influence of feedback (i.e. the teams results being known and used to influence how it goes about its work). Removal of the hyphens in IMOI is more than just stylistic: it deliberately signifies that causal paths are more likely to be non-linear than linear.

Ilgen *et al.* (2005) propose three main stages in team functioning. The early stages of team development they called *forming*, and are described by inputs and mediators (IM). The next stage they called *functioning* which captures mediators and outputs (MO). This is followed by a *finishing* stage which captures outputs and inputs (OI). These stages are summarised below.

Forming

Forming requires three activities: trusting, planning and structuring. Trusting is about team members, collectively, believing they have the wherewithal to be effective. It also requires that team members trust each other's intentions and motives: we can all think of how we guard ourselves in the presence of people that we do not trust, particularly when they have some power over us. Guarded contributions tend to impede team performance and so a climate of psychological safety is needed.

Planning involves gathering and using information. Communication needs to be open and information needs to be shared freely (and not only when people feel under pressure to do so). With information gathered the next step is to turn it into a strategy. This calls for goals to be articulated and shared.

Structuring represents the shared mental models held by team members. The concept of mental models has helped to advance team research: they describe how people see the interrelationships that exist and who is responsible for particular outcomes. Where the mental models of team members are different, then teamwork will be compromised by differing views about how the task should be achieved (and there may be some differences about what the task actually is). Where mental models are similar then coordination is more efficient. Structuring also involves setting up a 'transactive memory': during this team members need to become aware of what is known within the team and of who knows what.

Functioning

Functioning involves *bonding, adapting and learning*. Bonding extends beyond trusting each other to reflect a genuine desire among team members to work together. It reflects concepts which have already been mentioned in this chapter including cohesion, commitment and social integration. The extent of bonding can be influenced by the diversity within the team. However, the basis of the diversity matters; personality diversity may be counterproductive if, for example, members differ widely on agreeableness (i.e. there are some people who really like a good argument, and others who will do anything they can to avoid one!). The ability to manage conflict is therefore an important aspect of team bonding.

Adapting covers two distinct concepts; the ability of a team to recognise when conditions change from being routine to being novel (and to respond when they do) and the ability to share workload among the team through mutually supporting behaviour.

Learning relates to changes in the body of knowledge that a team draws upon. One aspect of this is learning from minority and/or dissenting team members (*see also* Minority influence above). A minority in this context means people having minority views ('the lone voices'). At extremes, views that do not fit with the dominant paradigm can be suppressed to the point that the person holding them is isolated and treated as if they do not understand how complex the problem is (*see also* Groupthink above). However, teams need to hear minority opinions as they can challenge comfortable thinking. Likewise teams need to learn from the 'best' member in the team. This is not necessarily the same person all the time, but as the team's needs change so may the most knowledgeable person on a particular topic.

Finishing

This phase of decline and winding-up of a team is not well understood and we currently know very little about what happens in the end game.

Key Learning Point

In reality, there are many feedback loops operating in teams. The complexity of interactions between inputs, processes, cognitive states and outputs is very difficult to model and test.

What is teamwork?

The I–P–O and IMOI models describe how teams tackle tasks, i.e. they are descriptive. However, they are not designed to provide a detailed explanation of what effective teams do differently when compared to ineffective teams, i.e. they do not really tell us what good teamwork is. The phrase 'we need good teamwork' is so often heard in organisations that it is important we understand what good and bad teamwork are and how to identify them! Two recent studies help us to answer this question. Hoegl and Gemuenden (2001) developed a theoretical model of the quality of teamwork (and an accompanying Teamwork Quality questionnaire) comprising six dimensions:

1   Communication: good communication is frequent, spontaneous, direct between team members and open.

2   Coordination: good coordination means that there is a shared understanding of who is doing what, for whom and when.

3   Balanced contributions from members: all team members are able to input what they know.

4 Mutual support: there is collaboration and cooperation (not competition) over tasks.

5 Effort: whatever the level of effort required, it is important that team members know it and accept it.

6 Cohesion: this concerns the desire of team members to work together to stay together.

Senior and Swailes (2007) asked members of management teams to discuss examples of poor-, average- and high-performing teams in order to identify the key differences between teams performing at the three different level. Using repertory grid analysis of data they developed a seven-dimensional model of teamwork (and a Teamwork Survey that can be used to measure these seven dimensions in other teams). The seven dimensions that appeared to be linked to team performance were:

1 team purpose: goal clarity and acceptance by members;

2 team organisation: allocation of roles, responsibilities and a structure for operating;

3 leadership: the presence of appropriate leadership style and leader support for members;

4 team climate: openness, professionalism, morale, respect for differences;

5 interpersonal relations: care and support, healthy rapport, honesty and liking;

6 team communications: constructive handling of conflict, frequency of contact, coordinated communications;

7 team composition: the mix of personality and abilities and continuity of membership.

An eighth dimension reflecting the team's interaction with the wider organisation was added. This was based on previous research which shows how the impact of team is mediated by wider organisational factors such as respect for the team within the organisation, support for the team's development and the alignment of the team's objectives with organisational goals.

These models of teamwork are useful because they help us to better understand not just what teams do, but how their activities are linked to their success (or failure). They help us to understand the links between inputs, mediators and outputs. For example, measures of teamwork might help to explain why a diverse team fails to achieve its goals. Such measures can also be used in team development interventions in order to diagnose problems with team functioning (e.g. by getting people to reflect (in a structured way) on their own team and how it functions).

Putting together a good team: selecting people for teams

Knowledge, skills and abilities

Stevens and Campion (1994) argued that there is a set of individual-level competencies that influence a person's performance in teams and thus the overall team performance. Teamwork competencies, or knowledge, skills and attributes (KSAs), were proposed that covered two main areas: interpersonal knowledge and self-management. Interpersonal knowledge relates to the team member's competence when relating to others and responding to their emotions to in order to release their ideas and to maximise team members' contributions to problem-solving. More specifically, this includes:

- Conflict resolution: a person's ability to recognise it, to discourage it and where possible to use disagreement positively, e.g. by finding a constructive way forward.

- Collaborative problem-solving skills: a person's skills which are used to overcome barriers and enable the team to use the resources of all members.

- Communication skills: which include listening without evaluating, communicating openly, awareness of non-verbal cues, and the ability to engage in social conversations.

Self-management KSAs relate more to the goal-setting and the distribution of tasks within the team. More specifically, this includes:

- the team member's ability to set realistic and relevant goals for themselves, team members and for the team collectively; and

- the team member's ability to allocate work within the team to maximise the usage of the particular mix of personal skills and technical knowledge available.

Thus it follows that when selecting for teams, the extent to which potential team members already possess these KSAs needs to be considered. Fortunately, specific tests of these KSAs have been developed. The Teamwork KSA Test (Stevens and Campion, 1999) is a 35-item questionnaire embodying the KSAs listed above. However, research has shown that it had virtually the same power to predict team-related outcomes as general aptitude tests (and therefore added little extra). However, if we think of our own experience of teamwork we may remember work colleagues with potentially valuable contributions that were suppressed by their shyness, or of the dominant but not so bright colleague whose bold assertions steer the team to its final destination (a very frustrating state of affairs!). This line of thinking led Miller (2001) to point out that it is not enough for team members to possess teamwork KSAs: it is the ability to put them into practice that really matters. Although the evidence is mixed, tests such as the Teamwork KSA Test show some potential to predict individual team member behaviour and thus predict individual level effectiveness in teams (McClough and Rogelberg, 2003). Such KSAs may, therefore, be a necessary, not sufficient, requirement for effective individual performance in a team.

Team roles

Another concept of interest to teamwork theory and to the practical questions about selecting people for teams and team development programmes is that of team roles. Although several typologies of team roles exist, Meredith Belbin (1981, 1993a) developed a model that has been particularly influential and which is still widely used by organisations. He observed teams in action and concluded that that teams made up of the brightest people did not necessarily produce the best outcomes. This led him to develop a theory of team roles: he argued that a key factor behind effective teams is the presence in the team of set people who each perform

Coordinator
Calm and tolerant
Keeps team focused on
goals and encourages
individuals to
contribute

Shaper
Energetic and extrovert
Wants to achieve task goals
High need for achievement

Technical specialist
Likes to be an expert
Provides team with
specialist knowledge
and experience

Plant
Innovative and
independent
Source of imaginative
new ideas

Completer finisher
Hardworking and orderly
Ensures that detailed
aspects of group tasks are
properly planned

Monitor evaluator
Detached and intelligent
Evaluates ideas with
logic and analysis

Resource investigator
Friendly and adaptable
Gets information from
outside the group

Teamworker
Caring and diplomatic
Maintains team spirit
and provides emotional
support

Implementer
Attends to detail
Hardworking, organises
practical matters and
routine jobs

Figure 13.3   Belbin's nine team roles

specified team roles. He argued that people taking different roles needed to be appropriately combined in a team in order to achieve high performance. He identified nine roles that team members need to fulfil if the team is to be successful. These are shown in Figure 13.3.

Of course, not all teams contain nine people, each of whom takes one role. Each of us, according to the theory, has one or two preferred roles and one or two roles that we are capable of doing if no one else in the team does them better. Hence, four or five people can possess all nine roles predicted by theory. Most individuals are capable of playing more than one role and it is clear from Figure 13.3 that there are some roles that each of us would find it very difficult to fill effectively.

Key Learning Point

In theory, team members need to pool a range of different competences in order to optimise performance. However, empirical evidence for this hypothesis is limited.

Belbin developed a Team Role Self-Perception Inventory (TRSPI) and an Observer Assessment Sheet (OAS) to help identify a person's role preferences. The TRSPI gives a person's self-assessment of their role profile and should be used in conjunction with predictions from two or three others who know them, e.g. a supervisor and a colleague, via the OAS. The combined results should then be used for team development purposes. In practice, however, most situations usually only use the TRSPI, which curtails the amount of information used in development discussions.

The main value of the Inventory is to raise awareness and to provide a vocabulary with which people at work can appreciate the characteristics and strengths of others and thus talk about their teams and their roles in them. As such, it has an important developmental role.

The TRSPI, however, has attracted some rather critical psychometric evaluations that cast doubt on the reliability of the nine scales and the differences between them: this in turn cast doubt on its ability to measure stable aspects of personality. Rather, it appears that people can take on a number of different roles in a team situation. Furnham *et al.* (1993) led the charge against it but it is important to see Belbin's response to get both sides of the argument (Belbin, 1993b). Other critical assessments include Fisher *et al.* (2001) who questioned its lack of convergent and discriminant validity, i.e. that team roles did not show consistently high positive correlations with other similar constructs, or show consistently low correlations with different constructs. Anderson and Sleap (2004) questioned whether there are gender differences in the ways people respond to the Belbin questionnaire – e.g. women score significantly higher on the 'teamworker' scale. Some studies of the TRPSI have looked at reliability in different and arguably more appropriate ways, and are more supportive of its basic properties (e.g. Swailes and Aritzeta, 2006).

Key Learning Point

Team members can usually adopt two or three different roles and should appreciate the value of all the roles needed.

Virtual teams

Most of the research on teams has focused on people working in close proximity to each other, either in an organisational setting or in experimental research designs. However, as organisational structures have changed so too has the nature of teamwork in some organisations. Globalisation backed by information and communication technologies (ICT) has led to the evolution of virtual teams. These have members who are typically distributed throughout different locations and rely heavily on ICT to share information and to conference. Chapter 10 gives some details on how technology impacts on the way such teams communicate.

To what extent, say, six people in six different countries are a team is of course debatable. However, if we suspend that concern then there are some interesting questions touching on how virtual teams operate and how the competences needed for success differ, if at all, to conventional teamwork KSAs.

In relation to the competences needed, Hertel and colleagues (2006) built upon the framework of Stevens and Campion (1999) and others by proposing an additional group of competences; 'telecooperation-related KSAs'. They were conceptualised as:

- Self-management skills which are required in situations where control by a supervisor and other team members is reduced by physical separation. They include the ability to self-organise, persistence towards targets, motivation to learn in new contexts and creativity.

- Interpersonal trust: the need for this is amplified in the absence of close relationships and when the scope to intervene and help the work of a team member who is falling behind is restricted.

- Intercultural KSAs: these relate to sensitivity in dealing with other team members likely to have come from different social, educational and cultural backgrounds, a situation more likely in geographically distributed teams.

Hertel *et al.* (2006) developed a 39-item Virtual Team Competency Inventory which they argue can assist the selection of people for roles in virtual teams.

Teams: a view from the inside

Influences on members' attitudes

What does teamworking do for members' work attitudes and performance? Allen and Hecht (2004) provide an interesting counter to the thrust of much of the literature on teams. They claim that 'current beliefs in the effectiveness of teams are out of proportion to the evidence regarding their effectiveness' (p. 454). They go on to say that this state exists because teams make people more satisfied at work and raise confidence. These psychological benefits are important and are good reasons in themselves for organisations to continue using teamwork as a way or organising. However, it is useful to ask what is the evidence for these enhanced psychological states?

Rasmussen and Jeppesen (2006) reviewed 55 studies and found that teamwork generally does associate with psychological variables such as cohesion, organisational commitment and job satisfaction, although this is not always the case. Team type and size had no influence on the likelihood of the implementation of teamwork having a successful outcome. Van Mierlo *et al.* (2005) found that only job satisfaction was consistently related to self-managing teamwork.

Harley (2001) points out that on one hand there are the job redesign enthusiasts who argue that teamwork increases the amount of control people have over their work. On the other hand theorists from the 'critical management' school maintain that teamworking leads to more work and less discretion for individuals, with senior managers effectively allowing pressure and scrutiny from other team members to substitute for formal supervisory control.

Harley analysed data from the 1998 British Workplace Employee Relations Survey looking at the level of discretion (autonomy), commitment, satisfaction, stress and relations with managers. He found no significant differences between people in a team or not in a team. Harley (2001, p. 737) concluded that 'team membership does not matter much' adding:

> The results leave [both] positive and critical accounts of teamwork looking rather forlorn. While teamwork does not, according to this analysis, herald a transformation of work in which employees regain the discretion denied to them by Taylorist work organisation, nor does it appear to involve reductions in discretion and hence increased work intensification.

A possible explanation for this finding is that a large proportion of the people supposedly in teams were not really in a *true* team at all, although Harley rejects this idea. His preferred explanations are:

- that teams are managerially driven (i.e. implemented in order to raise performance) and therefore higher levels of psychological well-being and satisfaction do not necessarily occur alongside improvements in performance; or

- that teams are so widely used that their formal implementation makes little difference to the hierarchical managerial structures already found in the organisation. Therefore, on many occasions, implementing teamwork has little impact on member attitudes and behaviour.

Visions of teamwork

Some case-study based work also suggests that teamwork may have multiple and complex meanings – a team in one organisation might look very different from a team in another. This makes the overall impact of teams difficult to discern. For example, Procter and Currie (2002) studied a local branch of the United Kingdom's tax collection system, Her Majesty's Revenue and Customs. It had reduced its layers of management during the 1990s and reorganised work so that tasks were allocated to teams rather than individuals. There was a general belief that teamwork was partly intended by management to elicit more workless resources. Procter and Currie note (2002, p. 304) that in some ways teamworking had meant little substantive change in job design, but that its impact was felt in other ways:

> The range of work is little changed; employees exercise little in the way of new skills; they appear reluctant to adopt responsibility for the work of others; and the performance management system operates on the basis of individual performance. Nonetheless, teamworking appears to work in the Inland Revenue. It does so by having a team rather than an individual allocation of work, and by encouraging individual identity with the team target.

Steijn (2001) points out that one reason why some studies find little or no impact of teamworking may be that non-teamworkers in fact comprise two very different groups. One group is people who work in mundane jobs with low skill requirements and little discretion. The other is professional or craft workers who exercise both skill and discretion in pursuing their individualised un-teamlike work (i.e. their job provides for them to use skills and makes decisions, without needing to work in a team). In a survey of 800 Dutch workers, Steijn found that the mundane jobs are less pleasant for the people who do them than both professional/craft work and for those involved in teamwork. In terms of how pleasant the jobs were, professional/craft work and those done in teams differed little from each other.

A sophisticated analysis of some aspects of teamwork has been offered by Griffin *et al.* (2001). Like many others, they suggested that the introduction of teamwork reduces the role of supervisors and that this can be a difficult transition for those involved. Griffin and colleagues obtained data from nearly 5000 employees in 48 manufacturing companies in the United Kingdom, and also made their own assessments of the extent to which each company had introduced teamworking. As they hypothesised, employees' job satisfaction was influenced by the extent to which they felt their supervisors supported them, but (again as hypothesised), this effect was smaller in companies which used teamwork a lot than in those which made little use of it. In other words, teamworking does indeed reduce (but not eliminate) the impact of supervisors on their employees' job attitudes.

Overall then, the use of teamworking seemed to lead to a small reduction in job satisfaction but this was an outcome of two conflicting forces: on the one hand teamwork reduced the amount of supervisor support employees experienced, and this in turn eroded job satisfaction. On the other hand, teamwork also led to more enriched jobs (e.g. multiskilling, responsibility) which tended to increase job satisfaction. These two opposite effects occurring together may be another reason why Harley (2001) among others found little or no overall impact of teamwork on people's job attitudes. It can also be that implementing teamwork increases the autonomy of the team, while at the same time reducing the autonomy of some of the individual team members.

Key Learning Point

Teamworking appears to have a complex association with work attitudes. This is partly because the introduction of teamworking may leave some work practices unchanged, improve others and also have a negative impact on some aspects of job design. It is also partly because people who do not work in teams have many different kinds of job – some of which already contain the beneficial features of job design that teamworking may introduce.

Another important issue concerns the way people describe a team using images and concepts. This is likely to indicate quite a lot about, for example, what they expect from a team leader (*see also* Chapter 14) and their other colleagues within the team. Such images are also likely to vary somewhat between cultures. Gibson and Zellmer-Bruhn (2002) present an analysis of how employees in pharmaceutical firms in Europe, South East Asia, Latin America and the United States talk about teams. They invoke the concept of metaphor, which they define (p. 102) as 'mechanisms by which we understand our experiences. We use metaphors whenever we think of one experience in terms of another. They help us to comprehend abstract concepts and perform abstract reasoning.'

From a careful analysis of how people talked about teams, Gibson and Zellmer-Bruhn identified five types of teamwork metaphor:

1   Sports metaphor: engage in specific tasks with clear objectives and performance measurement; members have clear roles; interaction between team members is largely confined to task-related matters; relatively little hierarchy; focus on winning and losing.

2   Military metaphor: similar to sports in that the team also engages in tasks with limited scope and clear objectives, but these teams have a clear and indisputable hierarchy; the focus of the metaphor is on life, death, survival and battle.

3   Family metaphor: these teams engage in broad-ranging tasks and interact across most domains of life; they have a relatively low emphasis on goals; clear roles (e.g. 'brothers' and 'sisters') and hierarchy ('father', 'mother').

4   Community metaphor: like families, communities are broad in the scope of interactions between members. However, roles are quite informal and ambiguous; goals sometimes quite ambiguous and the team quite amorphous.

5   Associates: these teams limited activity, with interactions only in the professional domain; little hierarchy; roles may be clear but can change; ties between group members quite loose.

Where a team leader holds a teamwork metaphor that differs from those held by other team members, problems are likely to arise. For example, if the leader tends to construe a team as a sports team but the others see it more like a community, the members may feel confused or alienated by their leader's concern with meeting targets and restricting interaction to the task. Managers need to be aware of the team members' metaphor in order to manage their team effectively.

Different countries tend to exhibit somewhat different cultures (*see also* Chapter 1). This has implications for multinational companies where managers are assigned to countries other than their own, and where teams are often made up of people of various nationalities. For example, as Gibson and Zellmer-Bruhn (2002) point out, Latin American countries tend to emphasise both collectivism and status differentials, which would tend to imply a *family team metaphor*. If a leader is from a highly individualist and low power distance culture such as the United States, they may find it easier to think in terms of a sports team metaphor or the associates metaphor.

Factors influencing team performance

Teams have tasks to do and, at a simple level, team performance is simply the extent to which a task is achieved, but the extent of task achievement does not tell us anything about how the team itself performed at team level. For instance, a team aiming to improve road safety in a region may be judged by the number of accidents, injuries and fatalities on certain roads over time. While these are good indicators of road safety, even if improvements do occur those statistics do not tell us anything about team-level performance, e.g. whether the team atmosphere fostered creativity and innovation, or whether it used all of the information available to it to tackle the problem. A significant thrust of team research is about understanding the links between teamwork and team outputs. Indeed, it is important to be clear about whether team performance is being used to describe *within-team processes* or the achievement of *objective output measures*.

With that caveat in mind, researchers have devoted considerable time and effort to understanding the factors that influence team performance and the conditions under which their influence occurs. There are too many to consider all of them here, so a selection of key factors is summarised below.

Stage of team development

Teams are not fully functional from the start: anyone who follows a sports team can see that they usually need time to reach their full potential. Over time there may be changes in personnel, and the team may change in terms of how team members approach their tasks and relate to each other. One early analysis (Tuckman, 1965) suggested that teams tend to go through a series of stages in their development:

1 *Forming*: this is the stage when a team first forms, when there is typically ambiguity and confusion. The members may not have chosen to work with each other. They may be guarded, superficial and impersonal in communication and unclear about the task.

2 *Storming*: this can be a difficult stage when there is conflict between team members and some rebellion against the task as assigned. There may be jockeying for positions of power and frustration at a lack of progress in the task.

3 *Norming*: in this stage it is important that open communication between team members is established. A start is made on confronting the task in hand, and generally accepted procedures and patterns of communication are established.

4 *Performing*: having established how it is going to function, the group is now free to devote its full attention to achieving its goals. If the earlier stages have been tackled satisfactorily, the group should now be close and supportive, open and trusting, resourceful and effective.

Most teams have a limited life, so it is probably appropriate to add another stage that could be called *disbanding*. It would be important for team members to analyse their own performance and that of the group, to learn from the experience, agree whether to stay in touch and if so what that might achieve.

Understanding where a team is in terms of these stages of development might help us to understand team processes. However, not everyone agrees that these stages are either an accurate description or a desirable sequence. Teams composed of people who are accustomed to working in a certain way may jump straight to the norming stage. The members may already know each other. Even if they do not, they may be able quickly to establish satisfactory ways of interacting without conflict. In any case, many teams are required to perform right from the start, so they need to bypass the earlier stages, at least partially. West (1994, p. 98) has argued that key tasks in team start-up concern the establishment of team goals and individual tasks that are both meaningful and challenging, as well as setting up procedures for performance monitoring and review.

Key Learning Point

Some teams go through stages in their development, but many need to achieve high performance straight away, with these stages being very short-lived, or absent altogether.

Team climate

West (2002) argued that teams at work are often required both to think of new ideas and to implement them. He refers to the former as creativity and the latter as innovation and these can be seen as performance outcomes. Creativity is encouraged by diversity of perspectives in the group, coupled with participation of all members, feelings of respect for each other and expectations that it is acceptable to argue constructively with each other. These factors also help innovation. However, pressures from the environment have the opposite effect. These pressures can include uncertainty (e.g. about market conditions), probably by increasing team members' anxiety and consuming their cognitive resources. On the other hand, they may also encourage innovation because this involves action and active problem-solving to improve a possibly difficult situation.

Because of the potential pay-off from creativity and innovation (i.e. better products, services and systems) both are highly prized by organisations. In light of the widespread use of work teams and the use of teams to deliver innovative solutions, Anderson and West (1998) developed a way of measuring the climate for innovation through a Team Climate Inventory (TCI). The theoretical basis of this is a four-factor model of the drivers of work group innovation. These are:

1 Vision – this embraces the idea that clearly defined objectives lead to behaviour focused on achieving the objectives. It is broadly defined and spans the extent to which the vision is understood, valued and shared by team members.

2 Participative safety – this embraces the idea that the team climate is conducive to raising and challenging ideas and information, and to making decisions without prejudice from others. For example, if a team member felt that another would bad-mouth them to their boss then the climate for innovation would be compromised.

3 Task orientation – this concerns staying focused on the task by allocating responsibility and by evaluating and changing performance in light of progress towards agreed targets.

4 Support for innovation – the best ideas will struggle if team members do not feel that there is a genuine willingness in the workplace to change things. To be convincing, support needs to be visible (*enacted*) and not just *articulated* (for instance, by managers outside the team).

This theoretical model of is the basis of the 86-item TCI. It can be used in surveys of organisational climate, as a diagnostic tool to help understand team effectiveness and at team development events as a way of helping team members to discuss issues touching upon innovation in their own work contexts.

Team-building

Team-building and development are widely practised by organisations from junior levels of new recruits to the most senior levels of top management. This happens because organisations assume that team development is an antecedent of better team performance. Team-building is carried out on the assumption that optimal team performance occurs some time into the lifetime of a team: team development and team-building interventions are designed to move teams more quickly towards the latter stages of development. Therefore such interventions address, among other things:

- the respect for team members, their views and distinctive skills;
- team members' confidence to raise and to challenge views or information;
- the clarity of the teams' goals and priorities;
- the allocation of work within the team and relationships with others outside the team.

We may ask, given the considerable costs of conducting it, whether there is any evidence that team-building actually has any impact on team performance. In some respects, this is a question for individual organisations to answer. If an employer is convinced that in their particular context their investments are being repaid then that is enough for them. Salas *et al.* (1999) carried out a meta-analysis of team-building research. Their main findings were:

- Overall there was a non-significant effect of team-building on team performance. The effect was non-significant for objective measures of performance but a weak positive effect was found when subjective performance measures were used.
- The only component of team-building that had a significant effect was role clarification such that the more role clarification was a part of team-building the stronger the effect on performance.
- The effects of team-building on performance decreased as team size increased. Hence it may be more beneficial in smaller teams than larger teams.
- Shorter team-building interventions were more effective than longer ones.

In common with other meta-analyses the study aggregated different studies with different definitions of teams, different research settings and different measures of performance, all against a backdrop of diverse ways of attempting team-building with different development targets. This means that the findings do not necessarily apply to all team-building interventions, but they do represent interesting trends in the previous research.

Key Learning Point

This meta-analysis indicates that if team-building is attempted it is best focused on role clarification in small groups, but the final decision rests with organisations who must make their own judgements.

Team diversity

The importance of role diversity in teams and the need for effective teams to have people with differing outlooks and strengths is now generally accepted. The problem is, of course, that we may devalue characteristics we happen not to possess ourselves. While diversity in terms of occupational or organisational roles is common in teams, diversity in terms of gender, nationality, ethnicity, age or personality is perhaps less often considered. It is also difficult to manage effectively, because team members may have quite different values and expectations of how to behave. So although teams with diverse members have the *potential* to be highly effective because of the varied outlooks they possess, they often fail to achieve that potential (Kandola, 1995). Maznevski (1994) and Paulus (2000) have argued that teams need integration, and that this is more difficult to achieve as they become more diverse. Integration relies on a number of factors:

- a social reality shared by group members;
- the ability to 'decentre' – that is, see things from others' points of view;
- the motivation to communicate;
- the ability to negotiate and agree on norms of behaviour within the team;
- the ability to identify the true causes of any difficulties that arise (e.g. not blaming people for things that are not their fault);
- self-confidence of all group members.

These are good guidelines for any team, but are harder to achieve in a diverse one. Teams with diverse members must be especially careful to establish integration. How to get the best out of team member diversity has, in recent years, attracted increasing research attention. This is for good reasons. As Shaw and Barrett-Power (1998, p. 1307) have put it: 'Diversity is an increasingly important factor in organisational life as organisations worldwide become more diverse in terms of the gender, race, ethnicity, age, national origin, and other personal characteristics of their members.' This quote illustrates the fact there are many different aspects to diversity. Pelled *et al.* (1999), for example, refer to diversity in occupational backgrounds of team members, as well as diversity of race, age and tenure in the employing organisation. They suggest that functional diversity tends to lead to task-related conflict (that is, disagreement between group members about preferred solutions and methods) and that this (as long as it is handled well) helps group performance. On the other hand, diversity in race and tenure tends to lead to emotional conflict between group members, and this can undermine group performance. Jehn *et al.* (1999, p. 742) point out that 'No theory suggests that a workgroup's diversity on outward personal characteristics such as race and gender should have benefits except to the extent that diversity creates other diversity in the workgroup, such as diversity of information or perspective.'

Consistent with this assertion, Jehn *et al.* found that, among a sample of 545 employees, *informational diversity* in teams was associated with good group performance. Social *category diversity* (in the form of age and gender) made people more satisfied with their team, while *value diversity* (defined as disagreement about what the team's goals should be) tended to produce more relationship conflict within the team, and to undermine slightly the performance of the team.

Key Learning Point

There are different dimensions of diversity in teams, and each has different implications for team processes and team outputs.

A feature of society (in developed countries at least) is one of fast-changing demographics resulting in a workforce that is much more diverse (e.g. with an increasing proportion of the workforce being women, or coming from cultures or ethnic groups that have traditionally made up a very small proportion of the workforce). Work teams are often assembled by selecting a mix of individuals according to their specialist knowledge with little regard for the behaviour that they typically display. Over and above the mix of knowledge, skills and abilities that this produces, does team member diversity *in itself* have an influence on team performance? Homogeneous and heterogeneous teams may function differently through different social relations. A team of white males in their 30s is likely to function differently from a team of ethnically mixed women of different ages. Of course, as well as differences in these easily observable features, diversity also includes personality differences, team role variety, leadership skills and technical knowledge.

The theoretical background (Tziner, 1985) draws on alternative theories from social psychology. Similarity theory says that groups and teams comprising people with similar characteristics will be the most productive. This is because of the mutual attraction held by people of similar demographics, e.g. working class women relating more closely to each other than they would relate to middle class men, but the key question is: even if ties are stronger does this translate into higher performance at team level?

The alternative view says that where diverse backgrounds are combined the resulting tension will be constructive in terms of team outputs (e.g. more decision alternatives will be considered). However, equity theory describes how people adjust their inputs, up or down, to situations depending on their perceptions of their own rewards and the rewards given to others. In a team setting, individuals may lower their contribution if they see another team member as having more status due to their greater expertise or higher position in the organisation. Hence, in some circumstances heterogeneous teams could be less effective due to an unhelpful focusing on interpersonal differences.

Bowers *et al.* (2003) provide a meta-analysis which showed that, overall, the combined effects of team composition on performance were insignificant. This result took into account heterogeneity in terms of ability, sex, personality and their influence upon the quality, quantity and accuracy of team outputs. Some differences were found in that homogeneous teams performed better when task difficulty is low and heterogeneous teams performed better when task difficulty is high. So once again, we see small meta-analytic effects: it is important to be aware that these findings should not negate the view that in particular organisational contexts the diversity/performance link can be positive and quite strong (e.g. Fay *et al.*, 2006).

Key Learning Point

Research on diversity and team performance has shown some strong effects in individual studies but meta-analysis results show weak links. This may be because when the results of various studies are combined, the strong effects of diversity in some studies are offset by weak effects in other studies.

Exercise 13.3   Roles and diversity in a team

Recall your experience of working in a group or team that you used for Exercise 13.1. This time, consider the following questions:

Suggested exercises

1   How diverse were the team members in terms of (for example) age, sex, ethnic or religious affiliation, outlook, personality, past experience, social class? What consequences did the diversity (or lack of it) have for how the team went about its task, and for the final decision?

2   From the descriptions of Belbin's nine team roles above, which do you think were most often displayed by team members? Consider whether this was helpful or not, and whether more (or less) of certain roles would have been helpful.

Cognitive ability

One of the reasons why Meredith Belbin felt moved to create the TRSPI was that, as a management trainer at the time, he noticed that teams comprising the most intelligent students did not necessarily perform better than other teams of more mixed abilities. His explanation for this drew upon the presence or absence of team roles as we have seen. While general intelligence is now thought to be a good predictor of performance in a job at individual level (because higher intelligence leads to better analysis and decision-making) it does not follow that high cognitive ability at individual level translates directly into high performance at team level.

A meta-analysis of cognitive ability and team performance (Devine and Phillips, 2001) found that intelligence of team members was positively correlated with team performance for a range of tasks. However, the relationship was much weaker in real work settings than it was in experimental (laboratory) conditions. Their key finding was that the average cognitive ability of team members explained just 8.6 per cent of variance in team performance. This means that 91.4 per cent (rather a lot!) is explained by other variables than the intelligence of team members. This finding gives some support to the rather intuitive conclusions that Belbin drew from his observations over 30 years ago.

Devine and Phillips (2001) identified a number of factors that might impact on the intelligence–performance relationship. Much stronger association between intelligence and performance may be found with complex tasks: when the team needs to be good at physical work (e.g. assembly or maintenance tasks) the association could be lower than when the task is more about planning and problem-solving. In addition, over time, the association between intelligence and performance diminishes as team members get more experience of what the task needs in order for it to be done successfully. Thus, intelligence may be more influential at the start of a team's life cycle than in the mature stage. Overall, where tasks are relatively straightforward, familiar to the team and largely behavioural, intelligence and team performance are not strongly linked. Where team tasks are more complex and intellectual, then intelligence may be a much stronger predictor of performance.

This is another good example that illustrates the importance of organisational setting and context in explaining relationships among variables.

Personality in teams

Peeters and colleagues (2006) examined how team composition in terms of personality is related to performance. They hypothesised that performance agreeableness, conscientiousness, emotional stability and openness to experience would be positively associated with performance because they impact on achieving results (and, therefore, that extroversion is not related to performance). The Big Five personality dimensions were measured by the average scores in the team across all members on each dimension.

Meta-analysis showed that there was as predicted no correlation with extroversion. The expected correlation with agreeableness was found and this is presumed to derive from 'interpersonal facilitation' within the team. Conscientiousness, which has been found to correlate with individual level performance, was correlated with team performance. Contrary to predictions, there were no correlations between emotional stability or openness and performance. The type of team moderated the relationships such that positive links between agreeableness and conscientiousness and performance were only found in work teams and not in the student teams often studied by researchers. Peeters *et al.* suggest that high agreeableness and conscientiousness are viable criteria to use in the selection of team members.

STOP TO CONSIDER

We have now looked at a lot of different factors that can influence the performance of a team. At this point, to cement your knowledge of this diverse body of research, stop to consider the factors that contribute to effective/ineffective teamwork. Write a 'recipe' for a successful team, including as many factors as you possibly can. Now review the quality and quantity of the evidence presented so far: how confident can we be that if we follow this recipe we will get successful teamwork?

Participation in decision-making in organisations

Guzzo and Dickson (1996) have pointed out that improved group performance does not guarantee improved organisational performance. It depends on the appropriateness of what the group is being asked to do, and how well the efforts of different groups are coordinated. Macy and Izumi (1993) found that organisational financial performance improves most when a range of change initiatives (*see* Chapter 16) are used, such as organisational structure, technology and human resource management techniques, but team development interventions were among the more effective of those initiatives. So group interventions do appear to be useful in the wider organisational context.

Decisions in organisations can be divided into various types, and each decision has various phases (Mintzberg *et al.*, 1976; Heller and Misumi, 1987). Therefore, when we look at applying team research in its wider organisational context we need to consider the type of decision-making that teams are involved in, and at which phases of the decision-making process they have some involvement. As regards the types of decision, there are (i) operational decisions (usually with short-term effects and of a routine nature); (ii) tactical decisions (usually with medium-term effects and of non-routine nature but not going so far as reviewing the organisation's goals); and (iii) strategic decisions (usually with long-term effects and concerning the organisation's goals). In line with leadership research (*see* Chapter 14), it is also possible to distinguish between people-oriented and task-oriented decisions within each type. The phases of decision-making include (i) start-up, when it is realised that a decision is required; (ii) development, when options are searched for and considered; (iii) finalisation, when a decision is confirmed; and (iv) implementation, when the finalised decision is put into operation or fails (Heller *et al.*, 1988).

Much attention has been focused on who in organisations really makes decisions, and how their influence is distributed across the decision types and phases described above (e.g. Mintzberg, 1983; Heller *et al.*, 1988; Vandenberg *et al.*, 1999). The concept of *power* is frequently invoked. Power concerns the ability of an individual or group to ensure that another individual or group complies with its wishes. Power can be derived from a number of sources, including the ability to reward and/or punish, the extent to which a person or group is seen as expert and the amount of prestige or good reputation that is enjoyed by a person or group. These sources of power are distinct, though they tend to go together (Finkelstein, 1992). Especially if they are in short supply, individuals and groups often use *organisational politics* to maximise their chances of getting their way. Politics consists of tactics such as enlisting the support of others, controlling access to information and creating indebtedness by doing people favours for which reciprocation is expected. In extreme forms politics can also involve more deceitful activities such as spreading rumours. In general, however, the effectiveness and morality of power and politics depend on their intended goals. The distinction between the two goals of self-aggrandisement and organisational effectiveness is often blurred. After all, most of us probably construe ourselves as playing important and legitimate roles in our work organisations, and it is easy to jump from there to a belief that what is good for us must therefore also be good for the organisation.

Several large studies over the years have explored the question of who participates in organisational decisions. Heller *et al.* (1988), for example, conducted a detailed longitudinal study of seven organisations in three countries (the Netherlands, the United Kingdom and the former Yugoslavia). Not surprisingly, they found that most decision-making power was generally exercised by top management. The lower levels and works councils typically were merely informed or at best consulted. The distribution of power did, however, vary considerably between organisations and also somewhat between countries, with Yugoslavia (as it then was) generally having the most participation by people at low organisational levels, and the United Kingdom least. There was also some variation between types and phases of decision-making.

Top management was most influential in strategic decisions. Within tactical decisions, workers had quite high influence at the start-up phase of people-oriented decisions but little thereafter. This led to frustration. For tactical task-oriented decisions, they had much influence in the finalisation phase. This was often less frustrating, since the right of management to initiate decisions of this kind was rarely challenged (i.e. high legitimate power).

Senior managers are often tempted to make decisions in quite an autocratic way, involving only a few senior colleagues with little or no consultation. This is not necessarily because those managers have autocratic personalities. In fast-moving environments it may be necessary to make decisions quickly, and the participation of a large number of people slows things down. However, Ashmos *et al.* (2002) have argued for a simple management rule: use participative styles of decision-making. Although this can be time-consuming and confusing, it has a number of well-documented benefits, including:

- using the skills and knowledge available in the organisation;

- developing people's sense of involvement in the organisation;

- increasing information flow and contacts among members of the organisation;

- making decisions that reflect the real (and changing) nature of the organisation's environment.

Ashmos *et al.* argue that most organisations tend to have complex systems of rules and procedures that ensure that organisational decisions are predictable and standardised. The use of established procedures tends to eliminate real participation by organisational members. If the simple rule 'use participation' is followed, decisions are made and actions taken in less predictable and comfortable ways, but they are better suited to the specific situation. Ashmos *et al.'s* ideas are summarised in Figure 13.4. They are consistent with the proposition in the Vroom–Yetton theory of leadership (*see* Chapter 14) that participative methods are appropriate in most situations.

Key Learning Point

The amount and type of workforce participation in organisational decision-making vary between countries, between types of decision, and between phases of the decision-making processs.

Finally, examinations of strategic decision-making by senior management have been undertaken (e.g. Forbes and Milliken, 1999). Some interesting findings have emerged. For example, Papadakis and Barwise (2002) have examined strategic decisions in medium and large Greek companies. They were interested in how comprehensive and rational the decision-making process was, how hierarchically decentralised it was, how much lateral communication occurred and how political it was. They found that the personalities and other characteristics of the chief executive officer and top management team had relatively limited impact on how decisions were made. Instead, the extent to which the decision would have an impact on the firm seemed to matter. Encouragingly perhaps, higher impact was associated

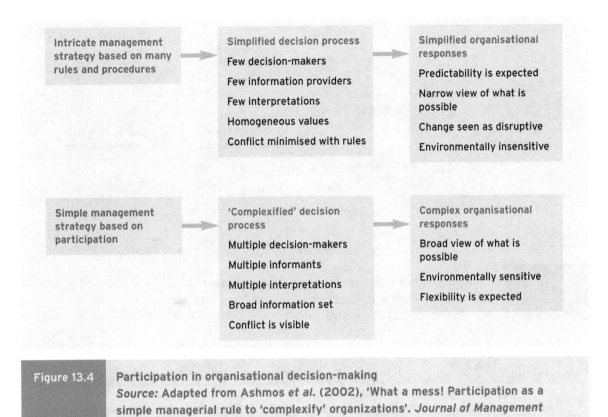

Figure 13.4   **Participation in organisational decision-making**
Source: Adapted from Ashmos *et al.* (2002), 'What a mess! Participation as a simple managerial rule to 'complexify' organizations'. *Journal of Management Studies*, 39(2), pp. 189–206, Blackwell Publishing Ltd.

with a more comprehensive process with more decentralisation (i.e. the involvement of a range of different people) and communication.

Dean and Sharfman (1996) used multiple in-depth interviews with senior managers involved in decision-making to investigate the process and outcomes of 52 strategic decisions in 24 companies. The most common types of strategic decision concerned organisational restructuring, the launch of a new product and organisational change. Their findings are summarised in Figure 13.5. The procedural rationality of the decision-making process (that is, the extent to which relevant information was sought, obtained and evaluated) had a significant impact on decision effectiveness, particularly when the business environment was changeable, requiring careful monitoring of trends. Even more important was the thoroughness and care with which the decision was implemented. This is an important reminder that managers cannot afford simply to make decisions – the decisions must be followed through. However, not everything is under decision-makers' control. The favourability of the business and industrial environment also had an impact on decision effectiveness. Political behaviour by those involved was bad for decision effectiveness. So, behaviour such as disguising one's own opinions, and complex and distracting negotiations between factions of the decision-making group, should not be accepted as an inevitable part of organisational life. They impair organisational performance, though of course they may serve the interests of individuals or subgroups.

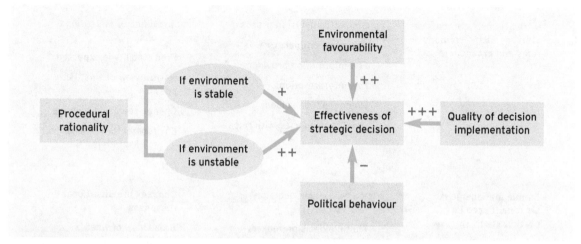

Figure 13.5   **Influences on the effectiveness of strategic decisions**
Source: From Dean and Sharfman (1996), adapted with permission.

Key Learning Point

Taking care over decision-making and implementation processes really does make a difference to organisational effectiveness.

There are also plenty of demonstrations that the biases in individual decision-making described early in this chapter occur in strategic decision-making. For example, Hodgkinson *et al.* (1999) demonstrated the tendency for people to be *risk averse* when potential gains are highlighted, but *risk-seeking* when potential losses are highlighted (this is the so-called framing bias). In two experiments Hodgkinson and colleagues asked students and bank managers to consider what they would do about a business strategy decision, where the same possible profits were described in one of two ways: either in terms of cash (highlighting the positive) or relative to a target (highlighting the negative). Negative framing led people to favour decisions that had a *low probability of a big profit and a high probability of no profit* over decisions that had a *high probability of moderate profit and a low probability of no profit*. However, this tendency was virtually eliminated if people were asked to draw a diagram representing their thinking about factors relevant to the decision (causal mapping) before making it. This leads to the optimistic conclusion that by engaging in careful thought processes we can overcome more instinctive biases in our reasoning.

There is no particular reason to believe that groups of top managers responsible for strategic decisions will behave differently from other groups. This is reinforced by Forbes and Milliken's (1999) theoretical analysis of the behaviour of company boards of directors. They make a number of propositions that are very consistent with more general theorising about groups and teams, particularly concerning the impacts of team cohesiveness and diversity. For example, they suggest that board members feeling a sense of cohesiveness is a good thing up to a point, but that too much cohesiveness impairs decision-making. This is a similar prediction to that made by Janis in his groupthink model discussed earlier in this chapter. Also, Forbes and Milliken predict that cognitive conflict (i.e. disagreements about the best solutions to problems) will increase the board's effectiveness, but reduce its cohesiveness. This is closely in line with the findings of Jehn *et al.* (1999) also noted earlier in this chapter.

Key Learning Point

Analyses of strategic decisions in organisations support the findings and perspectives of much other research on groups and teams.

STOP TO CONSIDER

Participation in decision-making is often seen as one of the major benefits of implementing teamwork. Now that you have read about participation, consider the benefits and risks of increasing levels of participation in decision-making. As you read more of this book you might also want to consider how other bodies of research help us to understand why participation might be important and beneficial. In particular think about what theories of motivation (Chapter 8), work stress (Chapter 12) and leadership (Chapter 14) tell us about the possible risks and benefits of participation in decision-making.

Topics for future research

Given the vastness of the teams literature there are many avenues where further research could increase our knowledge of them. Paris *et al.* (2000) point to the need to know more about how teams acquire knowledge and information and act on it. How do individual members contribute to information processing and the building of shared mental models? They also highlight the need to develop better ways of assessing teamwork as a way of understanding more about how teamwork affects team outputs (i.e. how the processes that take place in teams impact upon the performance of an organisation).

Guzzo and Dickson (1996) suggest that with increasing use of distributed teams better understandings of how information and communication technologies influence teamwork and team performance in virtual teams are needed. They also call for research into finding team development strategies that make a difference to effectiveness and for more studies of teams in their natural work settings, e.g. the workplace rather than artificial teams (often students) in artificial settings. This would give a better understanding of the influence of contextual variables such as the performance culture and reward practices.

We also suggest that if teamwork is to increase there is a need for a much better understanding of the social conditions and relations in the workplace that lead to the formation and functioning of real teams.

Summary

Decisions by individuals and groups are influenced by many psychological phenomena. Groups are usually more effective than the average individual but less so than the best individual in decision-making tasks. Groups can make terrible decisions, especially if characterised by problems such as the 'groupthink' syndrome. However, the research evidence about the 'typical' effectiveness of groups should not be viewed as the best that groups can do. Possible ways in which groups and teams can improve include more consideration in advance of the problem-solving strategy they wish to adopt, a clear expectation that members should challenge each other, and an understanding that such challenges do not signal hostility or disrespect. When such conditions exist, diversity within groups can have important benefits.

The extent to which employees are part of real teams seems to be relatively low overall although it does vary from country to country. The processes that occur in teams are very complex with continuous cycles of feedback and adjustment occurring rather than a simple linear pathway. Teams pass through a life cycle that involves forming, mature functioning and then winding-down. Models of teamwork emphasise the importance of factors such as goal clarity, balanced sharing of duties, open communication, good interpersonal relationships and the ability to manage conflict. Questionnaires exist to assess a person's propensity to fit with these constructs and can be used for team selection. The concept that effective teams require a balance of different team roles is popular and is the basis of much of the team development that organisations carry out.

Many organisations rely on teamwork and use it to fuel creativity and innovation in the workplace. Aside of questions about whether teams actually perform better than individuals do, the evidence that being in teams leads to higher levels of job-related attitudes (such as job satisfaction) is patchy. A long list can be made of the variables that have been used to predict team performance. They include: stage of development; climate inside the team; extent of team-building; diversity in terms of team roles, personality and gender among others; and cognitive ability.

The nature of decision-making tasks, their importance and their subject matter all have implications for the way they are handled. The amount and type of employee participation in making decisions vary widely and the ways that decisions are made and implemented do link to organisational effectiveness.

Closing Case Study   **To expand or not to expand?**

The management team of the Fastsave retail chain store company had a decision to make. Should they build a new store in Danesville, a medium-sized town in which the company owned a suitable patch of land? Fastsave was doing quite well, and had more than enough financial resources to make the necessary investment in a town that did not currently have a major supermarket. On the other hand, there were two existing large superstores within 25 kilometres. It was agreed that there was no significant danger of substantial losses: the question was more whether the time and effort involved in expansion would be worth the return.

The management team consisted of the general manager (GM), finance manager (FM), marketing manager (MM), operations manager (OM), personnel manager (PM) and company secretary (CS). Each member of the team had been supplied with reports on the demographic make-up of the town, a market research survey, detailed costings of building the store and the likely attitude of the local council planning authority.

Group members were accustomed to working together and there was rivalry (at present friendly) among them about which of them if any would succeed GM when she retired in about three years. At the outset of the meeting, GM made it clear that she would act as an impartial chairperson, and not reveal her own opinions until the end. In the past, however, she had usually been cautious about business expansions. The following extract is representative of the group's deliberations:

FM: I suspect the time is not right. We are currently upgrading six other stores, and to start a completely new one would run the risk of spreading our resources too thin. In purely financial terms we can do it, but would we do a good job?

OM: Yes, we've certainly got our hands full at present. In fact, I would be in favour of reviewing two of our already-planned store upgradings because I'm not sure they are really worth it either. Generally we're doing all right as we are - let's consolidate our position.

MM: I can't believe I'm hearing this! According to our market research report, the population of Danesville wants its own big supermarket, and what's more the 45+ age group particularly likes our emphasis on low price rather than super de luxe quality.

CS: Come on, as usual you're taking an approach which could possibly pay off but could land us in trouble . . .

MM: Like what?

CS: Well, there has been a lot of housing development in Danesville, and the local council is under pressure to preserve what it sees as the charm of the town. It would be very bad public relations to be perceived as undermining that. And having a planning application refused wouldn't be much better.

FM: That's right, and being seen as an intruder would probably reduce sales too.

PM: I can't comment on that last point, but as a general principle we should not stand still. Our competitors might overtake us. If resources are spread too thin, we can recruit more staff: we have the money, and experience suggests that the labour force in the region has the necessary skills.

FM: You've had a rush of blood to the head, haven't you? You're normally telling us how difficult it is to manage expansion of staff numbers. I must say I share the concern about a couple of our existing upgrading plans, let alone building an entirely new store. Do those stores really need refitting yet? They are doing all right.

CS: I notice that Danesville has an increasingly young, mobile population these days. In spite of the market research report, will they really be interested in a local store, especially with our position in the market?

MM: They can be made to be. Anyway, who says that a Danesville store should not go slightly more upmarket? Tesco seem to manage to have both upmarket and downmarket stores.

OM: Well yes, but I don't think we are big enough to be that versatile . . .

Suggested exercises

1   **Examine this case study from the following perspectives:**
    a.   **the likely attitude to risk**
    b.   **group polarisation**
    c.   **minority influence.**

2   **Given this examination, what do you think the group is likely to decide? What is your evaluation of that decision?**

Test your learning

Short-answer questions

1   What is groupthink?

2   What are the differences between a workgroup and a work team?

3   Summarise the I–P–O model of team functioning.

4   Suggest three possible negative consequences of stereotypes in the workplace.

5   What strategies should minorities in groups use in order to maximise their chances of influencing a group decision?

6   What is group polarisation and why does it happen?

7   List the team roles identified by Belbin and explain why they are needed for team effectiveness.

8   Briefly outline three reasons why groups sometimes make poor decisions.

Suggested assignments

1   Discuss the proposition that Janis's groupthink model adequately accounts for failures in group decision-making.

2   What gains can organisations make by organising their employees into teams? What are the risks for organisations who do this?

3   Examine the potential benefits and problems of diversity in teams.

4   To what extent is true teamwork become a normal feature of working life?

Relevant websites

A simple Google search for 'teamwork' or 'team development' leads you to many consultants' websites. They are interesting as they show how practitioners approach the topic.

The International Society for Performance Improvement, as its name suggests, is concerned with promoting techniques that will raise performance levels of individuals and organisations. It carries articles that relate to specific topics including one on virtual teams which is at http://www.pignc-ispi.com/articles/cbt-epss/virtualteam.htm.

Information about team roles and samples of the team role instruments are at http://www.belbin.com. Various documents relating to how psychometric tests can be used in team development can be found at http://www.shl.com/whatwedo/shlreports/pages/teamdevelopmentreports.aspx. The Improvement and Development Agency has a report on the composition and effectiveness of top management teams on its website at http://www.idea.gov.uk/idk/aio/5028661.

For further self-test material and relevant, annotated weblinks please visit the website for this book at **www.pearsoned.co.uk/workpsych**

Suggested further reading

Full details for all references are given in the list at the end of this book.

1   Michael West's chapter entitled 'The human team: Basic motivations and innovations' in volume 2 of the 2001 *Handbook of Industrial Work and Organisational Psychology* gives an up-to-date and scholarly but accessible review of many team processes and outcomes.

2   R. Meredith Belbin's book *Beyond the Team* (published in 2000) is a good example of a genre that attempts to use everyday language to help people understand how to make teams work.

3   Chris Brotherton's 2003 chapter on the psychology and industrial relations in the book *Understanding Work and Employment* provides a personal and wide-ranging analysis of the field.

4   Steve Kozlowski and Daniel Ilgen provide a full review of team effectiveness in their paper in *Psychological Science in the Public Interest*, 2006.

CHAPTER 14

Leadership

LEARNING OUTCOMES

After studying this chapter, you should be able to:

1. suggest reasons why leadership at work in the twenty-first century might be more challenging than ever before;

2. identify various criteria of leader effectiveness;

3. specify some common personality characteristics of leaders;

4. define the terms consideration and structure as they are used in leadership research;

5. define the key concepts and propositions of Fiedler's contingency and cognitive resource theories of leadership;

6. define five leader decision-making styles (with varying degrees of participation, and several features of the problem situation) identified by Vroom and Jago;

7. name and define four aspects of transformational leadership and two aspects of transactional leadership and examine the nature of charismatic leadership;

8. discuss the extent to which transformational and charismatic leadership influence performance at work and discuss some drawbacks of charisma and transformational leadership;

9. examine the circumstances in which leadership might be seen as relatively unimportant;

10. describe how concepts of leadership held by subordinates and in society generally give an alternative perspective on leadership;

11. explain why and in what ways effective leader behaviour may differ between countries and cultures;

12. list the cultural groupings within Europe, and describe their distinctive views of leadership.

Corporate leaders on a quest for meaning

Chief executives are reluctant to talk publicly about the difficulties of the job. In private, however, they admit to a fear of failure, qualms about their leadership style and worries about winning employees' commitment. Anonymous interviews with 30 European chief executives over the past three months reveal consistent concerns despite wide variations in culture and management style.

'The things keeping them awake at night would be to do with their own personal performance as a leader, not their business performance,' says Mike Walsh, chairman of Ogilvy Europe, Africa and Middle East, part of Ogilvy & Mather, the advertising company, which carried out the research. Strikingly, only two of the 30 had been groomed for the job, highlighting the rapid rate of CEO turnover and the difficulties, or even absence, of succession planning. While they were worried about handling external economic pressure, they felt the absence of 'textbook' solutions most acutely in relation to their personal style and effectiveness.

'Coming fresh to this role, many were tempted or persuaded to do things in which they did not believe,' says the report, *Today's CEO*.

> They learned that this did not work, primarily because the people who were expected to follow and implement such decisions could detect their lack of sincerity. The greatest mistake was to try to be something one was not: to claim to know more, do more, be more than one actually was.

The interviewees said they wanted to build relaxed, non-hierarchical working cultures, but in many cases they were part of a much larger organisation for which that was too big a step. Many needed to understand better how their employees think and feel, especially as they tried to squeeze more productivity out of them. Increasingly, they realised this need. 'There is a degree of introspection today that wasn't there three years ago, inspired by a fear of failure and loss of office', the report says.

Senior executives are increasingly searching for meaning in their lives, says Mark Watson, a coach, and director or Purple Works, a UK learning and communications group. Top jobs confer less influence and power than most people think but entail huge responsibility, and life can be a grind. 'In big organisations you're hemmed in by board committees, corporate governance protocol and expectations to perform. Many of these people also find themselves detached from the real operations.'

Source: Financial Times, *21 September 2001.*

Introduction

If the article above is to be believed, corporate leaders are not happy people. They think a lot about how they should go about being a leader. The styles they adopt are influenced by their own past experience and by the opportunities and constraints of the context. At times they feel they are expected to pay attention to the needs of others while their own needs are overlooked. They need to increase the productivity of their workgroups and organisations and they wonder how to achieve that without inducing burnout and alienation.

Many argue that demands on leaders are changing in their nature and also increasing (Dess and Picken, 2000). Work organisations are increasingly reliant upon rapid and skilful innovation and use of information at all levels. Leadership based upon monitoring and control of subordinates is often no longer appropriate or even possible. Subordinates and leaders sometimes work in different locations, which makes close supervision very difficult (*see* Chapter 10). The task of leaders, even at quite low levels in an organisation, is said to be managing continuous change and delegating responsibility while maintaining an overall sense of direction. Yet this may not come naturally to either leaders or followers. To quote an analysis of leadership from South African and American perspectives:

What is killing us is the illusion of control: that things can be predictable, consistent and forever under control. What is also killing us is that followers require their leaders to be in control, on top of things, and to take the blame when things go wrong. Nearly all the new management programmes on TQM, re-engineering, right-sizing, just-in-time, this or that, are really old wine in new bottles – more efforts to design control systems that ask the workers to try harder; do better and be even more productive.

(April et al., 2000, p. 1)

Key Learning Point

Leadership is especially challenging nowadays because of the pace of change, the illusion of control and the high expectations of followers.

In this chapter we examine some of the many academic approaches to leadership. There is quite a long history of research in this area, and it would be impossible to cover all of it. Particularly influential work will receive most attention, along with applicability in twenty-first century workplaces. In many of the early sections of this chapter you will see that we identify issues that will be discussed later in this chapter: this is because many early theories of leadership fail to account for important aspects of leadership behaviour. We also consider whether contemporary theories of leadership are successful in addressing these deficiencies. In accordance with the increasing internationalisation of the organisational realm, we will also examine the extent to which national cultures affect perceptions and impact of leaders.

Some important questions about leadership

Leadership can be considered to be the personal qualities, behaviours, styles and decisions adopted by the leader. One attempt at defining leadership in a cross-culturally valid way comes from the Global Leadership and Organisational Behavior Effectiveness (GLOBE) Project, to which we will return later. After ample discussion, scholars representing 56 countries defined leadership as 'the ability of an individual to influence, motivate, and enable others to contribute towards the effectiveness and success of the organisation of which they are members' (House *et al.*, 2004).

A leader can be defined as the 'person who is appointed, elected, or informally chosen to direct and co-ordinate the work of others in a group' (Fiedler, 1995, p. 7). This definition acknowledges that the formally appointed leader is not always the real leader, but it confines the notion of leader to a group context. If we take the word 'group' literally, this definition *excludes* leaders of larger collectives such as nations, large corporations and so on (except in so far as they lead a small group of senior colleagues, such as a cabinet of government ministers, or other members of a board of company directors). You will probably notice that this goes against how we often view leaders: we also tend to see those who are indirect supervisors at much higher levels in organisations as leaders.

When most followers do not have direct contact with the leader, the dynamics of leadership may differ from those when they do. This is an important point because many leadership theories were developed for the situation of *close supervision* rather than more distant leadership. Waldman and Yammarino (1999) have argued that similar concepts can be used to describe leadership styles in these two situations, but the ways in which followers form impressions of the leader differ. For those close to the leader, impressions are derived from day-to-day interaction. For those distant from the leader impressions depend more on leaders' stories, vision and symbolic behaviours and on how well their organisations perform.

Key Learning Point

The real leader of a group may not be the person who was formally appointed to the role.

Over the years several distinct but related questions have been asked about leaders and leadership, including:

- Who becomes a leader and how do leaders differ from other people? Can we predict the *emergence* of leadership?

- How can we describe their leadership?

It is difficult to consider these questions without bringing in the notion of effectiveness. So we can also ask questions like:

- What determines the *effectiveness* of leaders? What are effective leaders like (e.g. what characteristics do they possess, what do they do, what do they say?) and how do effective leaders differ from ineffective ones?

- What characteristics of the various situations that leaders find themselves in help or hinder a leader's effectiveness?

How can we tell whether or not leaders are effective? One method might be to assess the performance of their groups relative to other similar groups with different leaders. This assumes both that such comparison groups are available and that performance is easy to measure. However, some teams perform unique, new and knowledge-intensive tasks: this makes their performance harder to 'see'. Also, in many jobs, performance is difficult to define objectively and measure accurately in all aspects, especially in the long-term. Then there is also the problem that performance is often determined by many things other than leadership. The current state of the employment market is an obvious example of such a factor affecting performance while not being directly under the leader's control. Employees may be aware that they can get better pay for doing a similar job elsewhere, and hence underperform despite good leadership. They might also leave when there are plenty of jobs available, rendering voluntary turnover as an inaccurate measure of good leadership. Sometimes group members' satisfaction with the leader is used as a measure of leader effectiveness, but who is to say that high levels of satisfaction with the leader are always good? At times good leaders probably need to ruffle a few feathers. Although too much tends to be harmful to the organisation, some turnover might be healthy. In short, there is no perfect measure of leader effectiveness. Group performance is used most often, probably correctly, but we must remember not to expect an especially strong association with leadership: too many other factors come into play.

Key Learning Point

There is no one perfect indicator of leadership effectiveness, but the work performance of the leader's workgroup or organisation is probably the best (although the influence of other factors on workgroup performance also needs to be taken into account).

The early leader-focused approaches to leadership

You will have noticed that for many of the chapters in this book we examine the simple ideas before moving to the complex theory and research. This is the approach we will take with leadership. Most theory and practice up to the 1960s (and some since) had two key features:

1 Description of the leader in terms of their characteristics and/or behaviours rather than the dynamics of the leader's relationship with subordinates.

2 Attempts to identify the characteristics/behaviour of 'good leaders' *regardless* of the context in which they lead.

Leader characteristics

One of the questions early leadership research tried to answer was: which characteristics differentiate leaders from non-leaders, or effective leaders from ineffective ones? Some early work (reviewed by Stogdill, 1974; House and Baetz, 1979) found that leaders tended to be higher than non-leaders on:

- intelligence;
- dominance/need for power;
- self-confidence;
- energy/persistence;
- knowledge of the task.

Many other personality traits (for example good adjustment, emotional balance and high integrity) were found in some early studies to be more common among leaders than non-leaders (e.g. Bass, 1990). Although this early search for what makes a leader did yield some interesting results, researchers did not find a definitive, consistent profile of characteristics among effective leaders. Also, this research was of variable quality which made it difficult to identify reliable findings.

More recently, meta-analysis has allowed researchers to isolate the common, reliable findings from the vast amount of previous research. Judge *et al.* (2004a) reviewed a large number of studies of leadership and discovered a modest but significant overall positive correlation ($r = 0.27$) between intelligence and leadership. Meta-analysis has also helped us to better understand the relationship between personality and leadership. Judge *et al.* (2002) found that, overall, the Big Five model of personality (*see* Chapter 3) had a multiple correlation of 0.48 with leadership. This indicates that when traits are organised according to the five-factor model and they are all included, there is a moderate relationship between them and leadership. Looking at each of the Big Five in turn, this study showed that those who are more likely to emerge as leaders, and be more effective, tend also to be:

- high in extroversion, openness to experience and conscientiousness (with there being relatively small positive correlations between these and the emergence of leadership and leadership performance).
- low in neuroticism (with there being a small, negative correlation between this and leadership emergence and performance).

This comprehensive analysis of personality and intelligence concluded that no one trait stood out as the single most important determinant of effective leadership. One possible explanation that Judge *et al.* suggest for this is that traits may interact with each other to determine the quality of leadership. For example, high levels of intelligence may only lead to effective leadership if the individual also possesses the *other traits* that are also necessary to show effective leadership in any given context (Judge *et al.*, 2004b):

It is possible that leaders must possess the intelligence to make effective decisions, the dominance to convince others, the achievement motivation to persist, and multiple other traits if they are to emerge as a leader or be seen as an effective leader. If this is the case, then the relationship of any one trait with leadership is likely to be low.

(Judge et al., 2004b, pp. 549-50).

Key Learning Point

Although no single characteristic or trait fully explains leadership, personal characteristics such as intelligence and personality appear to be important for the emergence of leaders and the effectiveness of leaders.

Therefore, there is enough reliable research evidence that intelligence and sociability play a role in determining which people emerge as leaders (although as we will see later they are only part of the story). However, these same characteristics that help leaders to reach the top may also subsequently prove their undoing. For example, a high level of dominance and need for personal power may help people reach leadership positions, but once there such traits may prevent a leader maintaining good relationships with their team or superiors, and this may precipitate their removal (Conger, 1990).

In addition, the characteristics of people who attain leadership positions have been found to depend partly on their motives for being leaders, and the acceptability of those motives to those who appoint them. Research in the Netherlands compared Chief Executive Officers (CEOs) in the 'not-for-profit' sector (e.g. organisations campaigning for children's rights or environmental protection) with CEOs in the commercial sector. Those in the commercial sector scored *lower on the power motive and higher on the social responsibility motive* (De Hoogh *et al.*, 2005; De Hoogh and Den Hartog, 2008). These pieces of research also showed CEOs in the voluntary sector were also generally seen as exhibiting more power-sharing leader behaviour and less despotic leader behaviour than those in commercial organisations. These findings fit with the idea that leaders are likely to be attracted to organisations that fit their personality and values (e.g. Schneider, 1987). People with a high concern for responsibility may be more attracted to jobs in not-for-profit organisations, as they feel these organisations have a social and morally responsible orientation. Therefore, when leaders use their power for purely personal goals in such organisations, they may be perceived to be acting against the organisation's altruistic values.

A more democratic ideology, or leader motive, emphasising the decentralisation of power, fits the context of the 'not for profit' organisation. In commercial organisations top leadership positions are often where legitimate power is concentrated. In these organisations authority is generally directed downward through a hierarchy which provides a more conducive context for leaders who are motivated by, and show, dominance and personal power (De Hoogh and Den Hartog, 2008). Thus, the acceptability of leaders' motives is likely to vary in different contexts or for different 'audiences' and organisational contexts. We will return to this issue when we examine leadership in different cultures. However, it should also be noted that there are some findings that are applicable in many different organisational settings. House and Baetz (1979) have argued that the very nature of the leadership role must mean that sociability, need for power and need for achievement are at least somewhat relevant, across different organisations and organisational cultures. Two of their insights are generally accepted by many studying leadership:

1　A leader's personal characteristics must be expressed in their observable behaviour if those characteristics are to have an impact on others and their performance.

2　Different types of tasks may require somewhat different leader characteristics and behaviours.

The leadership characteristics that are desired and acceptable may vary across different organisational contexts.

Of course, one of the most evident and difficult to change personal characteristics is one's gender. It can be argued that most leadership roles are typically described in stereotypically masculine terms, which might mean that women have more difficulty in (i) being selected for leadership roles, and (ii) being seen as good leaders even when they are selected. On the other hand, one might expect women to do better precisely because only the most able ones make it to leadership roles. In a meta-analysis, Eagly *et al.* (1995) found no overall difference in leadership performance between men and women. However, men had an advantage in military and outdoor pursuits (i.e. stereotypically masculine settings), while there was no difference or a slight advantage for women in business, education and government settings. Research by Lewis (2000) suggested a rather subtle disadvantage for women leaders relative to men. Lewis asked students to view videotapes showing a male or female company chief executive displaying anger, sadness or emotional neutrality in response to a company's poor performance. The student's ratings of the leaders' effectiveness tended to be *lower* if leaders expressed emotion than if they were neutral. However, displays of anger damaged the ratings of female leaders more than they damaged those of male leaders. Lewis suggested that this result showed the importance of followers' perceptions of leaders' behaviour. In this study it was suggested that whereas a man's anger might be perceived as assertiveness, a woman's anger may be perceived as aggression or instability. Later in this chapter we will examine how leaders might be able to influence their followers' interpretation of a leader's behaviour.

Key Learning Point

Personality characteristics in themselves do not make leaders inherently effective. What matters is how those characteristics are expressed in leaders' behaviour, and how that behaviour is understood by others.

Task orientation and person orientation

In the 1950s, one research team at Ohio State University and another at Michigan University launched independent projects on leader behaviour. Rather than focusing on the *characteristics* of leaders, they focused instead on how leaders *behaved*. They did this simply by asking primarily subordinates to describe the leader's behaviour. This produced a very long initial list of leaders' behaviours, within which there seemed to be two separate groups of behaviour (i.e. two general underlying dimensions). One focused on how leaders facilitate group maintenance and the other on what leaders do to ensure task accomplishment. These were described as follows (Fleishman, 1969):

1   *Consideration*: the extent to which a leader demonstrates that they trust their subordinates, respect their ideas and show consideration of their feelings.

2   *Initiating structure*: the extent to which a leader defines and structures their own role and the roles of subordinates toward goal attainment. The leader actively directs group activities through planning, communicating information, scheduling, criticising and trying out new ideas.

The Michigan team started by classifying leaders into two groups (as effective or ineffective) and then looked for behaviours that distinguished these two groups. Behaviours associated with relationships (consideration) and task orientation (initiating structure) differentiated the effective and ineffective managers: effective managers seemed concerned about both the task and their subordinates. Based on this, Blake and Mouton's (1964) Managerial Grid (still used in some management training courses) encourages leaders to examine their own style on these two dimensions: the suggestion is that it is usually best to be high on both consideration and initiating structure.

However, when trying to achieve different outcomes, might one style be more effective than another? Meta-analysis (Judge *et al.*, 2004a) of leadership research has revealed that both consideration (correlation, $r = 0.48$) and initiating structure ($r = 0.29$) have moderately strong relationships with different leadership outcomes. Although both dimensions were related to all studied outcomes, consideration was more strongly related to follower satisfaction (both with the leader and the job), motivation and leader effectiveness. Initiating structure was slightly more strongly related to leaders' job performance and group/organisation performance. This suggests that followers may prefer considerate leaders, but seem to perform at least as well for structuring leaders (Judge *et al.*, 2004a).

This research was very useful in demonstrating what impact these leadership styles might have on followers. However, it did not show exactly *how* these styles impact on followers. It seems likely that mediating mechanisms play a role: for example, leaders' behaviour may provoke an emotional reaction among followers, or it may have some impact on followers' working conditions (Nielsen *et al.*, 2008a). Also, so far, much of the research we have discussed has assumed that there was a linear relationship between exposure to these styles of leadership and outcomes have been assumed (i.e. the more the better). However, Fleishman (1995), for example, argued for curvilinear relationships, i.e. that there are diminishing returns to the increased use of consideration and structure on the part of the leader.

In any case, structuring and consideration refer to quite specific styles of day-to-day behaviour. They give little indication of how *well* the leader structures tasks or expresses consideration. They also give no indication of how well the leader is thinking strategically about what the workgroup is trying to achieve, and by what routes. The extent to which leaders working at the highest levels of large organisations use structure and consideration with immediate subordinates may have little or no impact on the wider organisation. Later, we will return to the more strategic angle when we discuss providing an overarching vision as an important element of leadership.

Key Learning Point

Consideration and initiating structure are useful concepts that have stood the test of time in analysing leadership. However, they focus on the leader's day-to-day behaviour rather than their overall strategy.

Participation and democracy

Another behavioural style that received much attention is participation. This concerns the extent to which the leader is democratic or autocratic (i.e. has a participatory leadership style). It is clearly related to the dimensions already discussed, but not identical. For example, the definition of structure given earlier does not necessarily exclude subordinates from influencing the direction given by the leader. In discussing the nature of the democratic leadership, Gastil (1994) emphasises that it is not just a case of letting the subordinates get on with their work, rather, the three key elements of democratic leadership are:

1   *Distributing responsibility*: ensuring maximum involvement and participation of every group member in group activities and setting of objectives.

2   *Empowerment*: giving responsibility to group members, setting high but realistic goals, offering instruction but avoiding playing the role of the 'great man'. Keller and Dansereau (1995) found that use of empowerment by leaders can both help them get the performance they want from subordinates and increase subordinates' satisfaction with their leadership.

3   *Aiding deliberation*: by playing an active part in the definition and solution of group problems, without dictating solutions.

In the aftermath of the Second World War it was hoped and believed that democratic or participative leadership was superior to autocratic leadership. In fact, the evidence is that on the whole participation has only a small positive effect on performance and satisfaction of group members (Wagner, 1994). As Filley *et al.* (1976) observed, where the job to be done is clearly understood by subordinates, and within their competence, participation is not going to make much difference because there is little need for it. On the other hand, in many less straightforward situations, participation does aid group performance. This is another theme that we will return to later in this chapter when we discuss more contemporary theories of leadership.

Key Learning Point

A democratic leader is active in group affairs: they do not just sit back and let the rest of the group sort everything out.

STOP TO CONSIDER

As you will have gathered, theories that focus on leader characteristics do not provide a complete explanation of leaders' success. However, we have also seen that they do provide some useful information. At this point, if you were going to develop a selection process that would be used to identify people with strong leadership potential, what would you try to measure?

Contingency theories of leadership

The above approaches to leader behaviour contribute to our understanding of what leaders do and the effects of their behaviour. In their original forms these approaches have an important feature in common. They all describe leader behaviour without paying much attention to the situation or context in which the leader acts.

To oversimplify a little, they are stating that in order to be effective, leaders need to perform certain behaviours regardless of the context or the particular demands of the situation.

However, consideration, initiating structure and participation can all be used more flexibly. The key idea behind contingency theories is that some situations demand one kind of behaviour from leaders, while other situations may require others. Do we really need a leader high on consideration and low on structure in an emergency such as a bomb scare? Probably not – we need someone who will quickly tell us what to do. We can do without a leader who asks us, at that specific moment, how we feel about the bomb scare. On the other hand, if a leader is responsible for allocating already well-defined tasks to a group of junior managers, we might hope for some sensitive consideration of the managers' skills, preferences, career development plans, etc. You might also want to think about which types of leadership behaviour might suit different types of organisational change (*see* Chapter 16).

Contingency theories assume that optimal leader behaviour is contingent upon (i.e. depends upon) the situation. As a result, contingency theories are fairly complex. They specify not only which leader behaviours are crucial, but also which aspects of the situation matter most, and how leader behaviour and the demands of different situations interact with each other. Of course, this leaves plenty of room for disagreement between different contingency theorists. Without being exhaustive, we will examine some of the most influential and controversial contingency theories.

Key Learning Point

Contingency theories of leadership propose that different situations demand different leader behaviours.

Fiedler's contingency theory of leadership

Fred Fiedler put forward his contingency theory of leadership in the 1960s (Fiedler, 1967). Fiedler argued that leaders have fairly stable personal characteristics, leading to a characteristic behavioural style. In his view, the key personal characteristic concerns how positively leaders view their least preferred co-worker (or LPC). His questionnaire had leaders describe their least preferred co-worker on 16 dimensions, such as pleasant–unpleasant, boring–interesting and insincere–sincere. A high LPC score signifies a positive view (and a low score a negative view) of the least preferred co-worker.

Exactly what an LPC score means remains unclear. It could be quite similar to consideration (high LPC) and structuring (low LPC), though this assumes that consideration and structuring are opposite ends of the same continuum rather than independent constructs. Indeed, high LPC leaders are often referred to as person-oriented – after all, they must be if they can be positive even about people they do not like! Low LPC leaders are often thought of as task-oriented. No doubt these approaches overlap. Yet Fiedler and others have argued that LPC also reflects the leader's deeper pattern of motivation. Some suggest that LPC is strongly linked to cognitive complexity. High LPC leaders may score higher on cognitive complexity than low LPC leaders because they can differentiate between a person's inherent worth and their work performance or likeability (i.e. they have a more complex and multifaceted way of evaluating their followers).

Key Learning Point

In his original contingency theory Fiedler assumed that a leader's perception of their least preferred co-worker indicates how person-oriented the leader is.

Fiedler argued that in some situations having a high LPC leader at the helm is best, while others call for a low LPC leader. He proposed three aspects of the situation which together define its favourableness to the leader, namely:

1 Leader–member relations: whether or not subordinates trust and like their leader.

2 Task structure: are the group's tasks, goals and performance are clearly defined?

3 Position power: does the leader control rewards and punishments for subordinates?

Fiedler's research found that in highly favourable and in very unfavourable situations, group performance was better for low LPC leaders (i.e. task-oriented). In situations of moderate to quite low favourability, high LPC leaders were best (i.e. person-oriented). It is not clear why this should be. One common-sense explanation is that where the situation is good, the leader does not need to spend time on interpersonal relationships. They are already sufficient for smooth functioning. Similarly, where the situation is very bad, things are so difficult that it is not worth spending time on interpersonal relationships. Improvement would take too long even if it was possible at all. Forging ahead with the task is best. Where the situation falls between the extremes, keeping group members happy becomes more important. A leader needs high LPC to hold the group together, so that tasks can be tackled. Fiedler's theory asserts that leaders have a fairly stable LPC score, so training them to do things differently is not very useful. Instead, he argued for matching the leader to the situation and viewed placement as more useful than training (Fiedler and Chemers, 1984).

Key Learning Point

Fiedler proposed in this original contingency theory that task-oriented leaders are best in very favourable and unfavourable situations, and that people-oriented leaders are best in moderately favourable or moderately unfavourable situations.

Many problems with Fiedler's theory have been identified. Apart from the unclear nature of LPC (i.e. what factors drive a leader's LPC rating), there is doubt about whether the LPC score is indeed stable. Perhaps it depends too much on just how undesirable the leader's least preferred co-worker really is – that is, the LPC

Table 14.1	Predictions of Fiedler's contingency theory of leadership						
	Situation highly favourable						Situation highly unfavour- able
	I	II	III	IV	V	VI	VII	VIII
Leader– member relations	Good	Good	Good	Good	Poor	Poor	Poor	Poor
Task structure	Structured	Structured	Un- structured	Un- structured	Structured	Structured	Un- structured	Un- structured
Leader position power	Strong	Weak	Strong	Weak	Strong	Weak	Strong	Weak
Desirable leader LPC score	Low	Low	Low	High	High	High	High	Low

score may say more about the co-worker than the leader. Another issue concerns Fiedler's concept of the situation. For example, in the medium and long-term, leader–member relations (which Fiedler defined as a dimension of the favourable-ness of the situation) are most likely a result of the leader and subordinates' behaviours. Is it therefore valid to treat leader–member relations as part of the situation, rather than a product of the actions of leaders and followers?

Despite these doubts, Peters *et al.* (1985) reported partial support for the theory in an extensive meta-analysis. Schriesheim *et al.* (1994) also found general support by reviewing studies comparing leader performance in different situations. As predicted by Fiedler's theory, low LPC leaders did better in the two most favourable situations and the least favourable one (Table 14.1). High LPC leaders did better in moderately favourable and moderately unfavourable situations. The researchers point out that if we assume that most leadership situations are moderate, we can simply say that high LPC leaders are better, rather than going to the trouble of engineering situations to fit leader styles.

Cognitive resource theory

Fiedler built on his earlier work in his cognitive resource theory (CRT). CRT builds upon LPC theory by examining how the cognitive resources of leaders and subordinates affect group performance (e.g. Fiedler and Garcia, 1987). As Fiedler (1995, p. 7) puts it: 'the relationship between cognitive resources and leadership performance is strongly dependent on such factors as the leader's situational control over the group's processes and outcomes, and the stressfulness of the leadership situation'. Referring to situational control demonstrates the links with Fiedler's earlier theory (since situational control relates to leader–member relations, position power and task structure). The stressfulness of the situation is also linked with this because

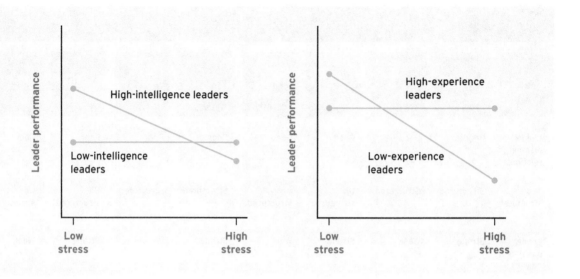

Figure 14.1   **Predictions of leader performance in Fiedler's cognitive resource therapy**

less favourable situations tend to be more stressful. Fiedler (1995) also sees stress as coming from the leader's own boss being unsupportive, hostile or over-demanding. Some of the key predictions of CRT are shown in Figure 14.1.

Fiedler argues that cognitive performance is inhibited in high-stress situations. That is, when leaders feel anxious or overloaded, they are unable to think clearly. In difficult situations they are likely to fall back on well-learned patterns of behaviour that result from their experience (Fiedler, 1996). Hence, in high-stress situations experience plays a more important role than intelligence in determining a leaders' performance.

Sternberg (1995) argues that experience is a disguised measure of so-called crystallised intelligence; that is, our store of know-how and knowledge about the world. This is essentially what Fiedler refers to when he uses the word intelligence. When a lot of our cognitive resources are being used in coping with a difficult situation, we use 'automatic' behaviour, which we can deploy without having to think too much about it. CRT theory proposes that leaders' automatic behaviour in such situations is more likely to be appropriate and effective if it is based on long experience.

Key Learning Point

Fiedler's cognitive resource theory introduces new factors about the leader and the situation. It proposes that, in difficult situations, leaders need to rely on their experience rather than their fluid intelligence.[1]

---

[1] Fluid intelligence is relatively context-free and drives logic and problem-solving. More detailed information on the distinction between crystallised and fluid intelligence can be found in Chapter 3.

Not all psychologists are convinced by CRT. Vecchio (1990, 1992) argued that there is not much empirical support for it, but Fiedler *et al.* (1992) claimed that it was simply not yet tested properly. Fiedler (1995) reports a number of studies showing results that are consistent with CRT. A recent meta-analysis examining intelligence and leadership provides support for the two moderators suggested by CRT: fluid intelligence and leadership were more strongly related when leader stress was low and when leaders exhibited directive behaviours (Judge *et al.*, 2004a).

Thus, Fiedler suggests both experience and fluid intelligence as key criteria in selecting leaders. His recent work suggests that the concept of matching leader to situation must be based on the leader's intelligence and experience as well as LPC and situational characteristics. Stress-reduction programmes are now thought to help leaders utilise their cognitive resources, and thus avoid the problems that might occur when leaders are placed in a situation where they might over-rely on 'automatic' responses.

Exercise 14.1 Using Fiedler's theories of leadership

For the last year, Debbie Walsh has been head of the ten staff of the market analysis department of a garden furniture company. The company sells its products through selected garden centres and do-it-yourself shops. The department's tasks are well established. For example, it monitors sales of each product at each outlet. It evaluates the viability of potential alternative outlets. It checks the products and prices of competitors. Debbie is a high-flyer academically, having obtained a first-class honours degree and an MBA with Distinction. The managing director has great faith in her, and has given her complete discretion over awarding salary increases to her staff and most other aspects of people management in the marketing department. This is Debbie's first marketing job: most of her previous four years' work experience were spent in general management at a knitwear company. Other staff do not resent Debbie. They feel her appointment demonstrates the truth of the company's pledge to put ability ahead of experience in promotion decisions. They may in future benefit from that policy themselves, since most of them are young and well qualified.

Debbie takes a no-nonsense approach to her work and colleagues. She responds well to business-like people who come straight to the point. She has little patience with those who are slower to get to the heart of a problem, or who do not share her objectives. Most of her present staff have a similar approach to hers. However, in one of Debbie's previous jobs her hostility toward several slow and awkward colleagues was a major factor in her decision to leave.

Suggested exercises

1 In Fiedler's terms, how favourable is Debbie Walsh's leadership situation?
2 Using Fiedler's contingency and cognitive resources theories, decide whether Debbie is well suited to her situation.

Vroom and Jago's theory of leader decision-making

Vroom and Yetton (1973) proposed a contingency theory of leader decision-making (extended by Vroom and Jago, 1988). They took a different approach from Fiedler by focusing exclusively on specific decisions, big and small, that leaders have to make.

They suggested that leaders are able to adapt their behaviour from situation to situation (remember that Fiedler's approach suggested that different leaders might be needed for different situations).

Certainly, most leaders say they do adapt their behaviour. The theory identifies five styles of leader decision-making that leaders might choose to use. The options on this 'menu' range from autocratic styles to democratic styles (*see also* the section Participation and democracy, above):

- AI: the leader decides what do to, using information already available.

- AII: the leader obtains required information from subordinates, then makes the decision about what to do. The leader may or may not tell subordinates what the problem is.

- CI: the leader shares the problem with each subordinate individually, and obtains their ideas. The leader then makes the decision.

- CII: the leader shares the problem with subordinates as a group, and obtains their ideas. The leader then makes the decision.

- GII: the leader shares the problem with subordinates as a group. They discuss options together and try to reach collective agreement. The leader accepts the decision most supported by the group as a whole.

Vroom and Jago (1988) identified some key features of situation to consider that together indicate the style a leader should adopt in that particular situation. The situational features are shown in Figure 14.2.

Also, Vroom and Jago argued that two further factors are relevant if the situational factors shown in Figure 14.2 allow for more than one recommended style to be used. These factors are (i) the importance to the leader of minimising decision time and (ii) the importance to the leader of maximising opportunities for subordinate development. Computer software has been developed that allows a leader to input answers to the questions listed in Figure 14.2. It then calculates an overall 'suitability score' for each possible style. The specific formulae are beyond our scope here, but general rules of thumb include:

- where subordinates' commitment is important, more participative styles are better;

- where the leader needs more information, AI should be avoided;

- where subordinates do not share organisational goals, GII should be avoided;

- where both problem structure and leader information are low, CII and GII tend to be best.

Key Learning Point

Vroom and Jago assume that leaders are able to alter their decision-making style to fit the situation they are in. Many factors in the situation can help determine appropriate styles, including time pressure, clarity of the decision parameters and attitudes of subordinates.

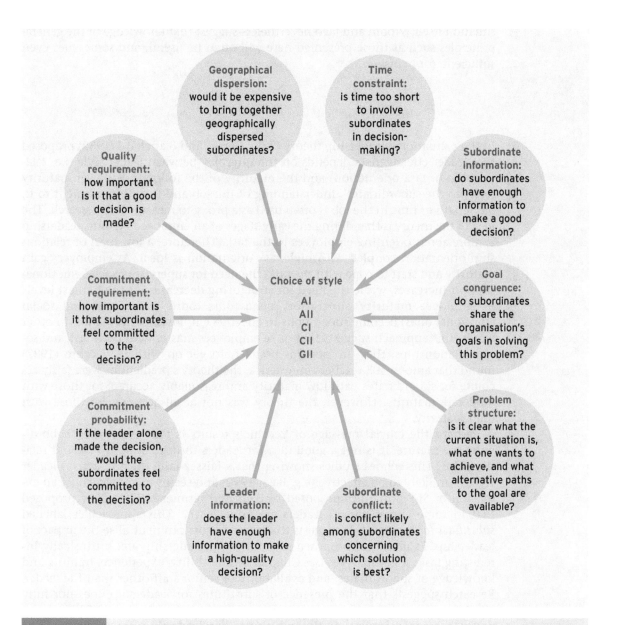

Figure 14.2   Vroom and Jago's features of leadership situations

The model has not been examined much in the published research literature. There is some evidence that the skill with which leaders put their selected style into action is at least as important as choosing an appropriate style in the first place (Tjosvold *et al.*, 1986). This suggests that it's not only what the leader does, but the way that they do it. In practice, the model's complexity makes it difficult for leaders to use quickly and easily in their everyday decision-making. Due to their subjectivity, a leader's answers to the questions posed by the model (e.g. whether subordinates share organisational values) may say as much about the leader's personality and values (i.e. how they perceive the situation) as about the reality of the situation itself. Vroom and Jago nevertheless suggest that knowledge of the general principles such as those presented here will often be useful, and sometimes even sufficient, for managers.

Other contingency approaches: is a leader really necessary?

In their situational leadership theory (SLT), Hersey and Blanchard (1982) proposed that leader effectiveness depends on the interplay between leader style (i.e. relationship or task orientation) and the maturity of the follower. Follower maturity refers to the subordinates' understanding of the job and their commitment to it, but length of time in the job is often used as a proxy to measure it in research. The idea of the theory is that during the early stages of an employee's tenure, leadership is more about orienting employees to the task. Therefore, a low level of relationship orientation coupled with high task orientation is ideal. As employees gain maturity and start to cope with the task, the need for supervisory social-emotional support increases, while the need for structuring decreases. At the highest levels of employee maturity, supervisory behaviours (both task-related and social emotional ones) become superfluous to effective employee performance. In other words, this approach suggests that once employees master with both task and social relationships, they are perhaps best left to get on with it. Vecchio (1987) found that among 303 teachers in America, the theory's predictions were fairly accurate for subordinates with low maturity and reasonably accurate for those with moderate maturity. However, the theory was not at all accurate for those with high maturity.

Perhaps the crucial message of Vecchio's results is that even when subordinates are mature, it is not a good idea for leaders to neglect both task and relationships. This echoes studies showing that a laissez-faire (or non-active) leader style is unlikely to be effective (e.g. Bass, 1990) and seems to argue against an extension of SLT principles proposed by Kerr and Jermier (1978). They proposed that in some circumstances leaders are unnecessary. This approach is labelled *substitutes for leadership*. It suggests that some factors can neutralise the impact of leadership. Examples of proposed substitutes for leadership are: intrinsically interesting tasks for employees (*see* Chapter 8); the ability, experience, training and knowledge of subordinates; and availability of senior staff other than the leader. Research suggests that the presence of substitutes for leadership does not fully eliminate effects of leadership style on satisfaction and performance. This may be partly because measures of the substitutes for leadership are not very good (Williams *et al.*, 1988). However, it also seems likely that in most situations leadership does matter. The apparent lack of efficacy of substitutes for leadership suggests either (i) that leadership tasks cannot easily be distributed around a group or (ii) that we have a psychological need for a leader: this issue we return to discuss later in this chapter.

Key Learning Point

Several contingency theories analyse leader style in terms of consideration and structuring, even if the words used are different.

STOP TO CONSIDER

Leaders may be faced with a variety of decision-making situations in their job role. To what extent do you think that contingency approaches to leadership cover all of the possible decision-making situations that a leader might be faced with? Does the research indicate that leaders can readily change their leadership styles according to the demands of the situation? Think back to the material earlier in the chapter: what personal qualities might a leader need (in terms of knowledge, personality, skills, intelligence, attitudes, etc.) in order to modify their approach as the situation demands?

Transformational leadership and charisma

The theories already discussed in this chapter show that both task- and relationship-oriented behaviours are important for effective group leadership. However, as we have highlighted, these theories did not explain the effectiveness of leaders in all situations. An important leadership function was rarely considered: leaders often provide a uniting vision, or overarching goal, for followers to strive for. In essence, much of the early research on leadership viewed the leader as a *tactician*, not as an *inspirational figure* with a strategic role. If we consider successful leaders in business and politics they are frequently portrayed as heroes and heroines who unite, inspire and motivate their followers by offering attractive strategic visions of a better tomorrow. Thus, in the 1990s, many scholars turned their attention to qualities such as vision, charisma and other related concepts. These added an important new element to the study of leadership.

What is meant by a leader's vision? Leaders often present a vision that describes a better future in ideological terms. Effective leaders tend to present a vision that is congruent with the dearly held values of followers, and this vision helps leaders to integrate and align followers' efforts. Through formulating a vision a leader interprets reality for listeners and gives meaning to events. The leader communicates this vision through words as well as deeds, modelling desired behaviour. Visionary leaders instil pride, gain respect and trust and increase a sense of optimism and hope in followers. An attractive vision of the future helps give followers a sense of vision and inspires acts as a powerful motivating force for those who share the vision (Bass, 1985; Conger, 1990; Shamir *et al.*, 1993). Earlier in this chapter we highlighted how early theories of leadership largely ignored the issue of how leaders' behaviour is perceived by followers. In contrast, the way leaders influence followers' perceptions of their behaviour is central to the theories of transformational leadership.

Theorists in this area make a clear distinction between transactional and transformational leadership (Burns, 1978; Bass, 1985, 1997). Transactional leaders try to motivate subordinates by observing their performance, identifying the rewards they desire and distributing rewards for desired behaviour. The underlying idea is that transactional leadership is based on exchanges, or transactions, with subordinates. Leaders define work goals and the behaviour deemed appropriate for reaching them. They offer clarity and the desired rewards, and in return subordinates contribute effort and skill.

Table 14.2	Components of transformational, transactional and laissez-faire leadership

The four components of transformational leadership

1 *Individualised consideration*: the leader treats each follower on their own merits, and seeks to develop followers through delegation of projects and coaching/mentoring

2 *Intellectual stimulation*: the leader encourages free thinking, and emphasises reasoning before any action is taken

3 *Inspirational motivation*: the leader creates an optimistic, clear and attainable vision of the future, thus encouraging others to raise their expectations

4 *Idealised influence*, or *charisma*: the leader makes personal sacrifices, takes responsibility for their actions, shares any glory and shows great determination

The two components of transactional leadership

1 *Contingent reward*: the leader provides rewards if, and only if, subordinates perform adequately and/or try hard enough

2 *Management by exception*: the leader does not seek to change the existing working methods of subordinates so long as performance goals are met. They intervene only if something is wrong. This can be *active* where the leader monitors the situation to anticipate problems, or *passive* where the leader does nothing until a problem or mistake has actually occurred

Laissez-faire leadership
The leader avoids decision-making and supervisory responsibility, and is inactive. This may reflect a lack of skills and/or motivation, or a deliberate choice by the leader.

Transformational leaders, on the other hand, go beyond this skilled use of inducements by developing, inspiring and challenging the intellects of followers so that they become willing to go beyond their self-interest in the service of a higher collective purpose, mission or vision. To be effective, this vision needs to be ambitious but realistic, and articulated clearly and in inspirational ways. Transformational leaders encourage followers by setting a personal example and followers become motivated and emotionally attached to the leader (Bass, 1985, 1997). Bass (1985) developed a questionnaire called the Multifactor Leadership Questionnaire (MLQ) to assess the extent to which subordinates perceive their leader to exhibit different components of transformational and transactional leadership (as well as a laissez-faire approach to leadership). The measured components are described in Table 14.2.

Key Learning Point

Transformational leadership is about inspiring and challenging subordinates, providing an overarching goal and setting a personal example.

Although the components described in Table 14.2 can be theoretically distinguished, in research in practice this is harder. Leaders' MLQ scores on the four components of transformational leadership often covary. In other words, when leaders are seen to exhibit one of these, they also tend to be rated high on the others. For example, Den Hartog *et al.* (1997) found high correlations (of 0.61 to 0.75) between the different components of transformational leadership in ratings of their leaders of about 700 people in eight Dutch organisations. Geyer and Steyrer (1998) also report similar findings in their sample of over 1400 employees of Austrian banks, as did Tracey and Hinkin (1998) in their sample of hotel employees in the United States. This shows that the components of transformational leadership tend to 'hang together' in followers' perceptions of leader behaviour.

Furthermore, contingent reward, a component of transactional leadership, also tends to go hand in hand with transformational leadership. In other words, transformational leaders also tend to administer contingent rewards. Such rewards can be tangible (e.g. money) but also intangible in nature (e.g. praise or symbolic appreciation). In some studies it seems that transformational leaders tend to also engage in active management by exception. This may be a matter of context: in a high-risk context 'good' leaders might need to or be expected to engage in monitoring.

It has often been argued over the years that transactional and transformational leadership are not mutually exclusive (e.g. Bryman, 1992), and that leaders can demonstrate one or the other, both or neither. Both and neither seem to be more common than one or the other. Therefore although they examine qualitatively different behaviours, measures of transformational and transactional behaviour are often highly correlated (e.g. Nielsen *et al.*, 2008b). Transformational leaders also tend to be perceived as executing the transactional elements of their job effectively.

Not surprisingly, the extent to which a leader is transformational seems to depend partly on his or her personality. For example, Judge and Bono (2000) found that transformational leaders tended to score higher than others on the personality traits extroversion, agreeableness and openness to experience (*see* Chapter 3). This might seem to suggest that we have come full circle back to the old trait-based approaches to leadership. However, they concluded that the connections between personality and leadership style were not strong enough to consider transformational leadership a personality-based theory: transformational leadership also appears to be about learned behaviour.

Key Learning Point

In the behaviour of real leaders, the four components of transformational leadership tend to go together with (i) each other and (ii) elements of transactional leadership.

Other work has taken a closer look at one particular element of transformational leadership: *charismatic leadership* (Conger and Kanungo, 1998). Charisma, as you might imagine, has been a difficult construct for researchers to define. It tends to be viewed by researchers as a *perception of a leader held by followers* as well as a *characteristic of the leader*. Intuitively we might think that charisma is something a leader is (or is not) born with. However, Frese and Beimel (2003) report a study which suggests that leaders can be trained to perform some of the behaviours associated with charisma. Also, as Gardner and Avolio (1998) put it, perceptions of charisma are in the eye of the beholder and thus do not always stem directly or only from the leader's behaviour. Most researchers agree that a leader is not charismatic unless described as such by their followers. Success plays a role in this: more successful leaders are often seen as more charismatic regardless of whether they had full control over getting there. For example, House *et al.* (1991) found that the perceived success of past US presidents was associated with how charismatic they were thought to be.

In order to isolate a definition of charismatic leadership, Conger *et al.* (2000) collected data from about 250 managers on five aspects of charismatic leadership in a business context. They found that there were five key elements to charismatic leadership:

1   The leader formulates a strategic vision, and articulates that vision.

2   The leader takes personal risks in pursuit of the vision.

3   The leader is sensitive to the opportunities and limitations provided by the environment (e.g. in terms of technology, money, people).

4   The leader is sensitive to others' needs.

5   The leader sometimes does unusual or unexpected things.

Although this is labelled charisma, it clearly has a wider meaning than the more specific charisma component of transformational leadership in Table 14.2. Sensitivity to others' needs resembles individualised consideration, and articulating strategic visions resembles inspirational motivation. So this model of charismatic leadership forms an alternative way of viewing transformational leadership. Rowold and Heinitz (2007) find a strong overlap between transformational leadership measured with the MLQ and charismatic leadership as measured with Conger *et al.*'s measure.

Key Learning Point

The components of charisma as defined by Conger and Kanungo go beyond the narrower charisma dimension of the Bass model. Combined, these components are similar to transformational leadership as a whole as defined by Bass.

Of course, there is great interest in whether transformational and/or charismatic leadership measurably helps improve the work performance, satisfaction, attitudes and well-being of individuals, groups and organisations, and if so how. In other words, does transformational leadership 'work'? The simple answer seems to be yes. The extent to which leaders are perceived to use elements of transformational leadership is positively correlated with subordinates' perceptions of their effectiveness, satisfaction and effort and with performance measures such as percentage of group targets reached, and supervisory evaluations of workgroup performance (e.g. Hater and Bass, 1988; Bass and Avolio, 1994). Several MLQ meta-analyses summarise the relationships of transformational, transactional and laissez-faire leadership with outcomes. Transformational leadership shows highest correlations with outcomes such as follower and leader satisfaction and effectiveness, follower motivation, leader job performance and group performance. Perhaps not surprisingly, contingent reward is positively related to a range of outcomes. Recent work also shows that inactive leaders are not, generally, effective: laissez-faire leadership was generally associated with negative outcomes. Management by exception is inconsistently related to performance criteria (e.g. Judge and Piccolo, 2004).

Geyer and Steyrer (1998) carried out a particularly well-designed study of the impact of transformational leadership. They took a careful look at the nature and measurement of transformational leadership and obtained objective measures of the performance of bank branches in Austria such as volumes of savings, loans and insurance products. They also took into account local market conditions for each branch (for example, the average income in the area). Staff then rated branch managers on the MLQ. Core transformational leadership (intellectual stimulation, inspirational motivation and charisma) was a significant predictor of branch performance. So was contingent reward, though to lesser extent. Rowold and Heinitz (2007) also found that transformational leadership shows a stronger relationship to profit than transactional leadership shows to profit.

In addition, Geyer and Steyrer found that core transformational leadership, individualised consideration and contingent reward were strongly associated with the effort that branch staff said they exerted. Passive management by exception was associated with less effort and lower branch performance. The correlations between ratings of leadership and branch performance were not especially high (around 0.25) but with a large number of branches and high volume of business, this small effect of transformational leadership could mean a big impact on profitability company-wide. The impact of transformational leadership does not appear to be limited to financial outcomes. In a longitudinal study Nielsen *et al.* (2008a) found that transformational leadership has a positive impact on employee well-being, partly due to the influence that transformational leadership behaviour has on shaping the nature of the work carried out by employees. Research by Conger *et al.* (2000) found that when followers perceive their leader as charismatic, they form more of a sense of group identity, empowerment and reverence (i.e. awe or extreme admiration) for the leader. Using a range of different measures of transformational leadership, studies find that charismatic leadership is related to top team effectiveness (De Hoogh *et al.*, 2004), followers' positive emotions (Bono and Ilies, 2006) and organisational citizenship behaviours (e.g. Den Hartog *et al.*, 2007). In the US, Waldman *et al.* (2001) and in the Netherlands, De Hoogh *et al.* (2004) found positive relationships between charismatic leadership of CEOs and financial outcomes, but only in dynamic and challenging market contexts.

Key Learning Point

Transformational and charismatic leadership tend to be associated with good performance of workgroups and organisations.

Exercise 14.2   Transactional and transformational leadership

Marc LeBlanc is manager of the claims department of a medical insurance company. He is rather unlike many of his colleagues, in that he dresses unconventionally and has long hair, which he ties into a pony tail. The department's job is to process claims by clients who have spent time in hospital. Marc considers himself scrupulously fair with his staff of 17 administrators and clerks. He thinks that if something (such as a training course) is good for one of them, then it is good for all. He has successfully resisted senior management's wish for performance-related pay, arguing that group solidarity will ensure that everyone pulls their weight.   ▶

Marc thinks of his job as making sure that the members of the department know where it is going and why. In contrast to his predecessor, he never tires of telling his staff that their job is to 'play a proper part in the client's return to good health' rather than to contest every doubt, however tiny, about a client's claim. He has been known to invite claimants to the office when he thinks they are being treated badly by the company, and to force his bosses to see them. Marc has a noticeboard for displaying complimentary letters from clients grateful for prompt and trouble-free processing of their claims. He frequently emphasises the need to look at things from the client's point of view. He tells his staff to focus on certain key aspects of the long and complicated claim form, and only briefly inspect most of the rest of it. Marc checks whether they are doing this, but only when a complaint is received from a client or the company's own internal claims auditors. In such cases he defends his staff, provided they have conformed to the department's way of doing things. He is less sympathetic if they have taken decisions about claims on other criteria, even if those claims have some unusual features.

Suggested exercises

1   Marc LeBlanc scores high on just one aspect of transformational leadership. Which one and why?

2   He scores high on one aspect of transactional leadership. Which one and why?

3   In what respects, if any, might Marc's leadership be described as charismatic?

4   The performance of the claims department could be measured with more than one criterion. Think of one respect in which Marc's style enhances the department's performance, and one respect in which his style hinders performance.

Critiquing transformational leadership

The concepts of transformational and charismatic leadership clearly represent an important advance in our understanding of how leadership can be described and of how to be an effective leader. In the complex twenty-first century world many feel we need a leader we can believe in. However, even with all this evidence to support it, this approach too has several limitations. We highlight four of these.

First, researchers have speculated, but so far scarcely investigated, whether the type of situation in which leaders and followers find themselves affects the suitability of transformational leadership. A few exceptions are starting to show that contingency models are needed for this form of leadership too. More challenging, uncertain contexts seem to offer more room for transformational leadership to have effects (e.g. Shamir and Howell, 1999). For example, several studies on charisma indicated that its effect on performance, effectiveness and organisational citizenship is context-dependent. More research on this is needed however before firm conclusions can be drawn.

Second, until recently, there seems to have been an implicit assumption that the leader is the source of most of what happens. The reality may be that followers have as much impact on the leader as the leader does on the follower. Barker (1997) noted that too much (transformational) leadership research ignores the fact that any workplace has conflict and competition. Leaders and followers do not necessarily have the same goals. Barker argues that the 'ship' in leadership has too often led to leadership being seen as a set of skills (as in craftsman*ship*) rather than a political phenomenon (as in relation*ship*).

Third, writers such as Tourish and Pinnington (2002) argue that the notion of transformational leadership moves too close to cult leaders who are revered by their followers as people who can do no wrong. Over a period of time, this may encourage authoritarianism, which is not helpful for democracy, nor for the development of employees as mature and responsible adults. For example, Kark *et al.* (2003) show how transformational leadership relates both to followers' empowerment and their dependence on the leader. Thus, although such leaders may intellectually stimulate followers and help them take responsibility they may also increase their need for leadership.

Fourth, transformational leadership glosses over the issue of whether the leader is forming and articulating an appropriate vision of the future. History tells us that some transformational leaders fail, or even cause terrible harm. In any case, followers may reject the leader's vision as being inappropriate. These concerns coupled with recent ethical scandals and sustainable management issues fuelled research on different forms of authentic and ethical leader behaviour (e.g. Avolio *et al.*, 2004; Brown and Treviño, 2006). Different theories that pay much more attention to the moral aspects of leadership emerged. Recently, researchers have begun to consider ethical leadership as a behavioural style in itself rather than focusing only on ethical aspects of other leadership styles (Brown *et al.*, 2005; De Hoogh and Den Hartog, 2008).

Brown *et al.* (2005) take a social learning approach to ethical leadership and focus on the exemplary behaviour of the leader. They define ethical leadership as 'the demonstration of normatively appropriate conduct through personal actions and interpersonal relationships, and the promotion of such conduct to followers through two-way communication, reinforcement, and decision-making' (p. 120). They find a correlation between ethical and transformational leadership, but show the two do not overlap completely (i.e. they appear to be different concepts). Others have defined ethical leadership as something more than the perceived normative appropriateness of leadership behaviour. Factors such as the leader's social influence, the purpose of the behaviour of the leader and the consequences of that behaviour for the leader and others are also important in determining ethical leadership (e.g. De Hoogh and Den Hartog, 2008; Turner *et al.*, 2002). For example, Kanungo (2001) states that the leader, in order to be ethical, must engage in virtuous acts or behaviours that benefit others, and must refrain from evil acts or behaviours that harm others.

Key Learning Point

Transformational leadership has construed the leader as a 'great person', although increasingly research is starting to pay some attention to how followers behave, ethical leadership and the impact of the situation on leader effectiveness.

Perceiving leadership

As we have seen, many leadership theories have focused on what leaders do, rather then how those actions are perceived. In recent years, increasing attention has been paid to how and when we perceive leadership to be important. A related issue is how we identify someone as a leader. Some authors have focused on these questions, using ideas from the social psychology of person perception. Other analyses recognise that leadership is partly in the eye of the beholders, something that may be particularly important for charismatic leadership. However, Meindl and colleagues go further and argue that perceptions of leadership are entirely constructed by followers and observers and have little to do with the behaviour of leaders. In an article entitled 'The romance of leadership', Meindl *et al.* (1985, p. 79) argued that:

> we may have developed highly romanticised, heroic views of leadership – what leaders do, what they are able to accomplish, and the general effects they have on our lives. One of the principal elements in this romanticised conception is the view that leadership is . . . the premier force in the scheme of organisational processes and activities.

Meindl *et al.* (1985) further argued that our conception of leadership as important and influential should lead us to consider leadership a key factor where performance is either very good or very bad. When things go really well, we attribute it to the leader's skill. When things go really badly, we blame the leader's ineptitude. But when things go averagely well, we are less likely to say it was primarily due to average leadership. This is because we have a shared understanding of leadership as a big concept which has big effects, not moderate ones. Meindl *et al.* support this claim in several ways. For example, they searched the *Wall Street Journal* (WSJ) between 1972 and 1982 for articles about 34 firms representing a range of American industries. They then related the proportion of WSJ articles about each company mentioning the leadership of top management to company performance. A higher proportion of 'leadership' articles appeared when firms were doing especially well or especially badly – particularly the former. They also conducted experiments presenting case studies of corporate success and failure, and asking participants to rate the importance of various possible causes of that success or failure, including leadership. Again, leadership was seen as a more important cause of extreme (especially good) performance than of medium performance. Pillai and Meindl (1991) expanded this and found that the charisma of the CEO in a hypothetical case study of a fast-food company was rated as very high if the case described a crisis followed by success for the company (and very low if the crisis was followed by decline).

Findings such have these have provoked some to question whether leadership can be defined objectively. Gemmill and Oakley (1992) have argued that leadership is a *culturally defined concept*. They argue that we use it to protect ourselves from anxiety brought about by uncertainty concerning what we should do ('no need to worry, the leader will decide'), and from various uncomfortable emotions and wishes that arise when people try to work together. They also argue that the cost of using the concept of leadership to organise our social world is *alienation* – that is, feeling distant from our true self and devoid of authentic relationships with others. This could be because we give too much responsibility to people we label leaders, and therefore it can feel difficult to lead purposeful lives, or to view ourselves as purposeful, *self-managing individuals*. This is a rather radical view that draws partly on psychoanalytic theory and challenges both common-sense and academic leadership theories that are well-supported by well-designed research. Most people working in organisations would probably find it difficult to agree that leadership is illusory as they take on leadership roles, or report to people in leadership positions and functions. The point that Gemmill and Oakley make is that as employees we may try to transfer responsibilities or tasks to leaders that it would be better to take on ourselves. This brings us back to a point made earlier in relation to democratic leadership: democratic leaders may have to insist that their subordinates take a share of the responsibility (Gastil, 1994).

All of this seems like good evidence for a romanticised view of leadership, where we tend to grossly overestimate its importance, but this is not necessarily true. Meindl *et al.* (1985) did not demonstrate that we are wrong to make these attributions about leadership, only that we make them. Others, such as Yukl (1998), and the numerous sources of evidence cited in this chapter, argue that the quality of leadership really does make a difference to outcomes that matter in the real world.

Key Learning Point

Leadership is partly in the eye of the beholder. We may be inclined to overestimate the impact of leaders, particularly when performance is very good or very bad. However, this does not mean that leadership is an illusory concept or unimportant.

Global leadership

The globalisation of markets brought about by communications technology and the mobility of production resources mean that more and more people work in countries and cultures that are novel to them. For many managers, this means leading people of different backgrounds and outlooks from their own. There has been much recent interest in identifying the cultural dimensions along which countries can differ: this has a number of implications for leadership that we will examine in this section. The work which started it all was carried out by Hofstede (1980, 2001), who collected data from employees of IBM across many countries. He identified four cultural dimensions:

1 *Power distance*: the extent to which members of a society accept that there should be an unequal distribution of power between its members.

2 *Uncertainty avoidance*: the extent to which members of a society wish to have a predictable environment, and have set up institutions and systems designed to achieve this.

3 *Masculinity* vs. *femininity*: a masculine society values assertion, success and achievement, while a feminine one is oriented more towards nurturing and caring.

4 *Individualism* vs. *collectivism*: the former reflects a belief that individuals should be self-sufficient while the latter emphasises people's belongingness to groups in which there is mutual support.

It would be strange if there were not differences between countries with respect to the preferred, most used and most effective leadership styles. Using Hofstede's cultural dimensions we might expect autocratic styles to be more effective in high power distance cultures than in low ones. Leaders whose style is high on structure will probably be most appreciated in high uncertainty-avoidance cultures. Dickson *et al.* (2003) provide a very informative review of research on cross-cultural leadership.

They discuss in detail some of the reasons why the dimensions of culture identified by Hofstede and others might affect which styles of leadership are expected and effective. They argue that the search for leadership styles that work across the whole world is (or should be) accompanied by more research into indigenous models (i.e. models of how leadership works in specific culture, rather then across cultures) as well as exactly how culture and leadership affect each other.

GLOBE is a long-term study concerning how societal and organisational cultures affect leadership (House *et al.*, 1999). Over 60 countries from all major regions of the world are represented, making it the most extensive investigation of cross-cultural aspects of leadership to date. The core quantitative study looks at what the images of outstanding leadership are in different cultures, and includes over 17,000 middle managers from some 800 organisations in the financial, food and/or telecommunications industries in over 60 countries. These managers were asked to describe leader *attributes* and *behaviours* that they perceived to enhance or impede outstanding leadership in their respective organisations.

What were the findings? Attributes reflecting integrity (i.e. *trustworthy, just* and *honest*) contributed to outstanding leadership in all cultures. Also, an outstanding leader in all studied cultures shows many attributes reflecting transformational leadership: these include the leader being described as *encouraging, positive, motivational, a confidence builder, dynamic* and *having foresight*. Team-oriented leadership is also universally seen as important (i.e. such a leader is effective in team-building, communicating and coordinating). Other universally endorsed attributes included *excellence-oriented, decisive, intelligent,* and a *'win–win' problem solver*. The GLOBE study also shows that several attributes are universally viewed as ineffective including: *being a loner, being non-cooperative, ruthless, non-explicit, irritable* and *dictatorial*. Interestingly, many different leadership attributes were found to be culturally contingent. In other words, a high positive rating was obtained in some and a low or even negative rating in other cultures. Examples include being *unique* (i.e. different from the 'norm'), *indirect, status-conscious, intuitive* and *habitual*. These are examples of attributes that are considered desirable for outstanding leadership in some cultures but impediments in others (Den Hartog *et al.*, 1999).

The attributes seem to reflect underlying culture differences. For instance, country means for the attribute '*Subdued*' range from 1.32 to 6.18 on a 7-point scale and for '*Enthusiastic*' from 3.72 to 6.44. Thus, in some countries acting in a subdued manner is highly relevant to being an outstanding leader and in others such an approach is described as highly inefficient. Similarly, showing enthusiasm is relevant for outstanding leadership in some, but not in other cultures. This seems to reflect cultural rules regarding the expression of emotion. In some cultures, displaying emotion is interpreted as a lack of self-control and thus perceived a sign of weakness: not showing one's emotions is the norm. In other cultures, it is hard to be an effective communicator and leader without showing emotions.

Other culture dimensions are also reflected. For instance, several of the differences in attributes seem to reflect different levels of uncertainty avoidance. People in uncertainty-avoidance cultures want things to be unambiguous, predictable and easy to interpret and in such cultures technologies, rules and rituals are used to ensure this. This is reflected in several of the cross-culturally varying attributes. For instance, the attributes *risk-taking, habitual, procedural, able to anticipate, formal, cautious* and *orderly* are seen to impede outstanding leadership in some countries and enhance it in others.

Similarly, several attributes reflect high power distance versus egalitarianism in society. For example, *status and class-conscious, elitist, domineering* and *ruler* are attributes that fit a high power distance society, but are seen in a negative light in egalitarian societies. Also, several of the attributes reflect the culture dimension of individualism, for instance, *autonomous, unique* and *independent* are more important for outstanding leaders in individualistic than in collectivist societies.

GLOBE research offers further insights into leadership perceptions across Europe. Brodbeck *et al.* (2000) have reported perceptions of what makes a good leader in 22 European and ex-Soviet countries. They asked managers to indicate the extent to which 112 words (such as *foresight, honest, logical, dynamic, bossy*) were characteristic of outstanding leaders. The 112 words were grouped into 21 scales, which were given names such as Visionary, Diplomatic, Administrative and Conflict-inducer. The researchers then searched their data for consistent patterns *both within and between* countries. There were some substantial similarities across all European countries regarding perceptions of good leadership. For example *Integrity* and *Inspirational* were seen as highly desirable leader characteristics, and *Face-saver* and *Self-centred* as highly undesirable. But there were also some differences. To a large extent these replicated other work (Ronen and Shenkar, 1985) suggesting the European cultural groupings and characteristics shown in Table 14.3. France did not fit clearly into any of the groupings.

Table 14.3	Cultural groupings in Europe	
Grouping	Countries	Five most valued leadership attributes (most important first)
1. Anglo	UK, Ireland	Performance, Inspirational, Visionary, Team integrator, Integrity
2. Nordic	Sweden, Netherlands, Finland, Denmark	Integrity, Inspirational, Visionary, Team integrator, Performance
3. Germanic	Switzerland, Germany, Austria	Integrity, Inspirational, Performance, Non-autocratic, Visionary
4. Latin	Italy, Spain, Portugal, Hungary	Team integrator, Performance, Inspirational, Integrity, Visonary
5. Central	Poland, Slovenia	Team integrator, Visionary, Administratively competent, Diplomatic, Decisive
6. Near east	Turkey, Greece	Team integrator, Decisive, Visionary, Integrity, Inspirational

Source: Adapted from Brodbeck *et al.* (2000). With permission from Professor Dr. Felix Brodbeck.

It is clear that some of the differences between clusters are quite small. Nevertheless, it is notable that, for example, the Anglo cluster is the only one to have *Performance* at the top of the list, whereas *Performance* is not even in the top 5 for the central and near east clusters. Integrator is more important in south and east Europe (i.e. clusters 4, 5 and 6) than in north and west Europe. Although not shown in Table 14.3, it is also the case that *Status consciousness* was seen as slightly unhelpful to good leadership in north and west Europe but slightly helpful in the south and east.

There is also a question of whether actual leader behaviour is interpreted differently in different cultures and countries. Some research (Smith *et al.*, 1989; Peterson *et al.*, 1993) sought to discover whether similar leader styles are described using the same dimensions across different cultures. Using data from electronics firms in the United Kingdom, the United States, Japan and Hong Kong, Smith *et al.* (1989) concluded that what they call maintenance and performance leadership styles (similar to the consideration and structuring dimensions described earlier in this chapter) do indeed exist in different cultures. However, they also stated that 'the specific behaviours associated with those styles differ markedly, in ways which are comprehensible within the cultural norms of each setting' (p. 97). For example, one of the questions asked by Smith *et al.* was: 'When your superior learns that a member is experiencing personal difficulties, does your superior discuss the matter in the person's absence with other members?' In Hong Kong and Japan, this behaviour is seen as highly characteristic of maintenance (consideration). In the United Kingdom and the United States it is not: probably most Western subordinates would regard this as 'talking about me behind my back'. Not that all other British and American perceptions were identical: as Smith *et al.* (1989) noted, in the United Kingdom, consideration can be expressed by talking about the task, but this is not so in the United States. This also holds for other behaviours and attributes. For example, Bernard Bass describes that 'Indonesian inspirational leaders need to persuade their followers about the leaders' own competence, a behaviour that would appear unseemly in Japan' (Bass, 1997, p. 132). He goes on to say that, not withstanding the fact that it can be expressed in different ways, the concept of inspiration appears 'to be as universal as the concept of leadership itself'.

Political changes in some countries, for example in Eastern Europe, also have implications for the way managers are expected to lead in different contexts. Maczynski (1997) has shown that Polish leaders' preferred problem-solving styles shifted towards more participation between 1988 and 1994: this was the time during which time communism was toppled. Smith *et al.* (1997) found some differences even between neighbouring Eastern European countries. Managers in the Czech Republic and Hungary tended to report that they made great use of their own experiences and those of others around them. This is an individualistic style consistent with those countries' long-standing links with Western Europe: it can easily be contrasted with Romanian and Bulgarian managers' self-reported reliance on widespread beliefs held in their country to guide their behaviour.

These insights are very important as work organisations become increasingly international, with employees working across national and cultural boundaries. Assuming that leaders can identify which style they wish to adopt, they need to make sure they behave in ways which are interpreted as consistent with that style. Those behaviours differ somewhat between countries and cultures. The very fact that people are willing to try to describe leaders in terms of personal characteristics supports the attributional view that we carry around in our heads conceptions of what leaders are like. It also suggests that we believe we know what a good leader is like, regardless of the situation. Nevertheless, historically the situations faced by countries may well have influenced cultural norms about what constitutes good leadership.

Key Learning Point

Both long-standing cultural differences and major social and political change can influence actual leader behaviour and the behaviour desired by subordinates.

STOP TO CONSIDER

In this chapter we have looked at a number of different approaches to leadership. From what you have read, which is the most convincing? Do the various approaches offer competing explanations of leadership (i.e. if one is valid then the other cannot be)? Or might there be elements from some approaches that overlap with others? If you were to extract the most important and most valid elements from each approach to form a 'super theory' of leadership, which elements would you select – and what would this 'super theory' look like?

Summary

This chapter has explored many approaches to leadership. Consideration, initiating structure, charisma, cognitive complexity/intelligence and participation have been identified as some key leader characteristics and behaviours. Other less discussed notions such as the extent of the leader's knowledge of the industry and organisation must not be overlooked. There is considerable overlap between the various leadership concepts, and some tidying up and increased precision is needed. The same is true of the various situational variables proposed by contingency theorists. It is therefore not surprising that several of these theories are equally (and moderately) good at explaining leadership phenomena. Several approaches contain useful practical guidance about how to go about being an effective leader. Transformational and charismatic leadership models presented a significant step forwards, but more detailed knowledge is needed. Future theory and practice in leadership need to combine concepts from the better theories in a systematic way. There is also increasing recognition that leadership is not only about leaders. It also concerns followers and their preferences, characteristics and behaviours and cultural and individual perceptions of what leaders should be as well as about the relationships between leaders and followers. Greater attention to the question of whether and how leaders can be trained or selected not only to do the desirable things, but to do them well and in an ethical and sustainable manner, is also needed.

It was a turbulent time in the health and safety department of Super Chem's Hamburg plant. The multinational chemical company had recently adopted a policy of developing managers by giving them international experience. A consequence of this policy had been that a 32-year-old Spaniard, José Alonso, had been put in charge of the department. José's German was more than adequate for the task, but this was his first assignment outside Spain, a country seen by many in the company as peripheral to its operations. He had much to learn when he first arrived, especially about German health and safety legislation. He was, however, an experienced health and safety manager, having been head of health and safety at two plants in Spain for two years each.

Almost as soon as he arrived, José was pitched into an interesting situation. Two major accidents at other plants had caused a high-level health and safety policy review. The resulting report had come out in favour of more stringent inspection and a tougher approach from company health and safety departments. The recommendations were clear and specific, and had quickly become company policy.

José knew that his presence was resented by his six staff, who had worked together for some time and tended to think alike. They felt they had more specialist knowledge than he did. Most were older than him, and they could not understand why the deputy head, Gunter Koenig, had not been promoted. Koenig himself was understandably especially bitter. José felt that he could not follow his staff around as they inspected the plant: it would look too much like snooping. On the other hand, he needed to tap into his staff's knowledge of the plant and of how things had always been done there. Existing documents were too incomplete or too out of date to be of much help.

José had reason to believe that his staff typically adopted a collaborative approach with the plant managers whose areas they inspected. They preferred to use friendly persuasion and gentle hints rather than the precise written reports and threats for non-compliance required by the new policy. It had always worked at that plant, they said, and it would continue to do so. Yet José knew that exactly the same had been said at the plants where major accidents occurred. What was worse for José was that it was fairly clear that the plant manager privately agreed with José's staff. José's position was all the more difficult because he was known to be on a two-year secondment, after which the previous head (who had herself been seconded elsewhere) was expected to return in his place. Therefore he was not in a position to exert a long-term influence on the careers of his staff. His inclination would have been to intervene in his subordinates' work only when something was clearly wrong, but the new policy did not permit that approach. José himself was answerable not only to the plant manager but also to the company health and safety chief, who was the chief proponent of the new policy.

José knew that he was not a particularly creative or imaginative individual. He enjoyed the precision and rules and regulations of health and safety work. He preferred to focus on implementing the detail of policies rather than the big picture. He was usually inclined to draw up detailed plans of work for himself and others, and to keep a careful check on implementation of those plans. He liked to formulate work plans in a collaborative manner, encouraging his subordinates to think for themselves about what was required and how best to go about it. He felt he could understand how his staff felt about his appointment as their head without their consent: he had been landed with an unwelcome boss himself a few years earlier. He did not blame them for their attitude, and, characteristically, he was always keen to emphasise what he genuinely saw as the many strengths of his subordinates. He took time to discuss their work with each of them individually and tried to assign them work that would broaden their skills.

Despite the complicated situation, José felt that his task was clear enough. A decision had to be made concerning exactly how the department's practices would need to change in order to implement the new health and safety policy. Also, it had to be made in time for a visit by the health and safety chief six weeks later.

Suggested exercises

1 Analyse this case study using Fiedler's theories. What kind of situation is it? How well suited to it is José Alonso? What should he do next? What important features of this case study, if any, are neglected by Fiedler's ideas?

2 Analyse this case study using the Vroom and Jago theory. What kind of situation is it? What should José Alonso do next? What important features of this case study, if any, are neglected by Vroom and Jago?

3 In what respects, if any, can José's leadership style be described as (i) transformational and (ii) transactional? What scope is there for him to change, and would it make any difference if he did?

4 In what respects are national and cultural differences in perceptions of leadership relevant to this case study?

Closing Case Study   Lion King and the politics of pain

Junichiro Koizumi is the most popular prime minister in Japan's history and he is turning the country's staid political world on its head. For most of the past half-century, the country's politics have been predictable and dull, with barely a change of government, let alone the earth-shaking of the past few months. Until Koizumi took power in April 2001, the possibility of the country producing an iconic statesman capable of inspiring both hope and fear was unimaginable.

When Koizumi appears in parliamentary debates, millions tune in to watch live broadcasts. When he handed out a trophy at a recent sumo tournament, he stole the show, and the following day's headlines, from the sumo champion. The prime minister is a fashion leader, too. His Armani suits and permed 'Lion King' hairstyle are the talk of afternoon TV gossip shows. Fans are so desperate for a piece of 'Jun'chan', as he is nicknamed, that schoolgirls are queuing up at his party headquarters to buy mobile phone straps decorated with little Koizumi dolls. Off-duty salarymen wear T-shirts printed with their hero's chiselled profile drawn in the style of the famous Che Guevara ▶

poster, with the message: 'It's not just my challenge, it's our challenge.' Housewives subscribe to his personal webzine, Lionheart, where he shares insights into his family life. Depicted as a cartoon cuddly, big-hearted lion, Koizumi confides that high office feels 'like being trapped in a cage'. Among Tokyo's Asian neighbours, however, his un-apologetic nationalism and mass appeal ignite fears that he may become a Japanese Hitler, a dictator who will lead the country back down the path of militarism.

Last month, Koizumi's approval ratings hit a staggering 90 per cent. Almost entirely as a result of his personal popularity, the ruling Liberal Democratic Party, which looked dead and buried at the start of the year, won a convincing victory in the upper house election. And his means of achieving such pre-eminence defy conventional political logic: Koizumi has wooed his party and the public with the bleakest of messages. Ask any Japanese citizen what words they most associate with the prime minister, and the answer will almost certainly be 'pain, pain and more pain'. Koizumi says he is willing to accept two years of recession, unemployment and bankruptcy as the price for restructuring an economy that has been described by former prime minister Yasuhiro Nakasone as 'the sick man of Asia'.

It all looked very different in 1989, when Tokyo was the envy of the world. From the ruins of the Second World War, the 'Japanese miracle' had transformed this nation of 126 million, small geographically, into the richest country on the planet. People worked hard, but in return they had the smallest gap between rich and poor in the world, the safest streets and the longest average lifespan.

Since 1989, shares on the Tokyo stock exchange have lost three-quarters of their value and land prices have more than halved. Economic growth – the *raison d'être* of postwar Japan – has virtually ground to a halt. Two years of falling prices have left the country on the edge of a deflationary spiral not seen in an industrialised nation since the great depression of the 1930s. The government has already pushed most of the emergency levers, to little effect. Even a 'money-for-nothing' policy of zero interest rates put in place by the Bank of Japan has failed to find takers.

All this would be a nightmare in any country, but it hurts more in Japan because the entire social system is built on the assumption of growth and the principle of deferred reward: men put up with low pay, long hours and short holidays; in return, they are guaranteed a job for life, steady promotion and a generous allowance when they retire. Women carry the burden in the home in return for a share of the security provided for their husbands. With a prolonged economic contraction, this unwritten contract has been broken. Faced by the trauma of restructuring, so many middle-aged salarymen are committing suicide that the average male lifespan has actually gone down.

The prime minister's family background and political record raise many questions about his claim to be a daring reformer who will shake up the country's semi-feudal political system. Like almost a third of Japanese MPs, Koizumi is a political aristocrat who inherited his father's constituency, support group and factional allegiances. He won the family seat in 1972 and has been re-elected 10 times, pushing him higher and higher up the LDP hierarchy. He has been consistently ambitious – running twice for the party leadership before this year's victory.

'He is a very unusual Japanese leader because he has a broad vision of society and culture, rather than a deep understanding of particular issues of industries', observed the governor of Okinawa, Kenichi Inamine. 'He's a weirdo', said LDP lawmaker Tanaka, before she became foreign minister and declared herself Koizumi's 'political wife'. In office, Koizumi has already shaken the old hierarchy with the formation of a cabinet that, for once, does not merely reflect the old Confucian bias towards geriatric male timeservers. In terms of sex, age and background, Koizumi has picked the most diverse administration in the country's history. Many in the cabinet stress their loyalty to the premier ahead of the party. 'I'm not doing this for LDP, I'm doing it for Koizumi', says Tanaka. For the public, this is thrilling stuff. For the first time, politics is being played out in the open rather than in smoke-filled rooms. There is a clear diversity of opinion in the cabinet and public debate about key issues. It is chaotic, exciting and not a little frightening.

It is more for his promise of economic reform than for his nationalism that the public love Koizumi. But, at times, they are disturbingly protective of their would-be saviour. Opposition politicians who dare criticise the prime minister are bombarded with hate mail. The two parties that launched the most vociferous opposition to the government's policies were almost wiped out in the last election. 'It frightens me that parties who criticise Koizumi or Tanaka during parliamentary debates receive death threats', says Kyosen Ohashi, an opposition lawmaker. 'LDP candidates think they can get elected just by posing for a campaign poster with Mr Koizumi. It is so far away from democracy that it worries me.'

Source: The Guardian, *August 2001.*

Suggested exercises

1   To what extent and in what ways can Koizumi be considered a successful leader?
2   Which leadership characteristics are most evident in this article?
3   What aspects of the situation and the followers (i.e. the Japanese population) might have contributed to perceptions of Koizumi's leadership?

Test your learning

Short-answer questions

1   Describe the strengths and weaknesses of alternative measures of leader effectiveness.
2   What are major pressures facing corporate leaders in the early twenty-first century?
3   Briefly, what factors other than the leader's personality traits influence their effectiveness?
4   Define consideration and structure.

5 Describe the key features of democratic leadership.

6 Outline the main features of Fiedler's contingency theory. Suggest two strengths and two weaknesses of the theory.

7 Outline the main features of Fiedler's cognitive resource theory.

8 List the leadership styles and problem-situation features identified in Vroom and Jago's theory of leadership.

9 Name and define four aspects of transformational leadership and two aspects of transactional leadership.

10 Describe some possible outcomes of transformational and charismatic leadership.

11 Briefly describe three or more possible weaknesses or limitations of the notion of transformational leadership.

12 Provide some examples of universally appreciated leadership characteristics and of cross-culturally contingent ones.

13 List the main cultural groupings of European countries in terms of perceptions of leadership.

Suggested assignments

1 Discuss the proposition that all of the aspects of leadership style identified in research essentially amount to person-orientation and task-orientation.

2 Examine the extent to which different contingency theories of leadership share the same key ideas.

3 Examine the implications for leadership of research which views leadership as a socially constructed phenomenon.

4 Discuss how and why leaders need to adjust their behaviour to different cultures.

5 Do theories of leadership concentrate too much on the leader as an individual?

6 Discuss the proposition that theories of leadership pay too much attention to specific aspects of the leader's behaviour, and not enough to their overall strategy.

Relevant websites

In the UK, the Council for Excellence in Management and Leadership has been working since 2000 to promote good practice – as indicated by its strap-line of 'Managers and Leaders: Raising our Game'. Its web address is http://www.managementandleadershipcouncil.org/. You can find quite a lot of useful information there, including reports prepared for the Council.

An example of how some consultancy companies promote leadership training can be found at http://www.ldl.co.uk/inspirational-leadership-management-training-course.htm. This shows the close connections between leadership and motivation, as well as the current concern with leaders who are inspirational.

One of the most influential and long-standing organisations promoting leadership research and practice is the Center for Creative Leadership, which is based in the USA but also has substantial operations in Europe (Brussels) and Asia (Singapore). Its home page is http://www.ccl.org/leadership/. There is a lot there to illustrate how ideas from theory and research are applied in management development.

For further self-test material and relevant, annotated weblinks please visit the website at **www.pearsoned.co.uk/workpsych**

Suggested further reading

Full details for all references are given in the list at the end of this book.

1 *The Nature of Leadership* edited by Antonakis, Cianciolo and Sternberg, published in 2004, is a readable overview of leadership theory which expands on many of the themes of this chapter.

2 Keith Grint's edited book published in 1997 entitled *Leadership: Classical, contemporary and critical approaches* provides a scholarly analysis of a variety of leadership theories.

3 Gary Yukl has produced a thorough text on many areas of the field called *Leadership in Organizations*. The sixth edition was published in 2006.

4 The academic journal *The Leadership Quarterly* published by Elsevier is an important source for the latest research and theorising.

CHAPTER 15

Careers and career management

After studying this chapter, you should be able to:

1 define career and list three significant features of that definition;

2 list six ways in which careers are said to have changed over the last 20 years;

3 describe the key features of so-called 'boundaryless' and protean careers;

4 name and describe the career anchors identified by Ed Schein;

5 name and define Holland's six vocational personality types, and draw a diagram to show their relationship to each other;

6 identify the conclusions that can be drawn from research on Holland's theory;

7 distinguish between different conceptions of career success;

8 name and describe four kinds of variable that may affect career success;

9 describe three styles of career decision-making;

10 name, describe and compare the stages in two developmental theories;

11 discuss whether career theories apply as well to women as they do to men;

12 name and briefly describe at least ten career management interventions that can be used in organisations;

13 explain the circumstances in which career management interventions are most likely to be successful.

Opening Case Study | Careers in changing times

The stunned expressions of employees leaving Lehman Brothers were a grim reminder of the painful consequences of redundancy, particularly for those who have experienced unemployment. 'The overwhelming sense is one of being shell-shocked,' says Gavin Cullen, who lost his job as a senior associate in equity capital markets at Deutsche Bank in London during a wave of City downsizing six years ago. 'One minute you are working 80 hours-plus a week – then, suddenly, it's gone.'

Mr Cullen went on to build a successful career as an interim change manager, working on post-merger integration with investment banks, asset management firms and wealth managers. As a self-employed consultant he still puts in long hours, but his work is more varied and he has greater control over his life. 'In a full-time role you work to a line manager. As a freelance consultant, you effectively work for senior management. If you want to take time off between assignments, you can.'

His decision to embrace self-employment is not unusual. Across Germany, the Netherlands, the US and France, between 5 and 9 per cent of small business entrepreneurs begin their enterprises in response to redundancy, according to a survey by the specialist insurer Hiscox. In the UK, almost one-fifth of entrepreneurs start out in this way. Other displaced professionals use unemployment to travel or retrain for new careers.

However, while a change of profession or a venture into entrepreneurship creates opportunities, it also carries risks. The downturn multiplies these hazards. This makes it more important than ever for the newly unemployed to weigh their options carefully.

Life-stage plays a big part in how people respond to loss of employment. As an unencumbered 31-year-old, the reaction of strategy director Cathy Bryan to the collapse of her employer, Excite UK, during the dotcom clear-out, was to take herself off to the Himalayas, where she decided to retrain as a school teacher. 'I was earning lots of money and it was fun,' says Ms Bryan, who fell into new media while working as a parliamentary researcher. 'But it didn't feel particularly worthwhile. I made hay while the sun shone. When I was made redundant, I saw that as another opportunity.'

Despite age equality laws, older professionals with ideas to offer can still fall foul of bad practice. At the age of 54, Peter Smith lost his position as director of environmental risk consulting when Arthur Andersen collapsed. In spite of finding himself apparently in demand with several large companies, he failed to clinch a job offer. When a large insurance firm invited him to a fourth discussion, having interviewed him for 11 hours already, he concluded that he was being commercially exploited. 'I realised that firms were not really interested in employing me. They were systematically passing me from pillar to post to gain more and more information about what I had worked on at Andersen.'

Rather than suffer further disappointments, he used his experience to set up CSR-Evaluator, which markets a web-based tool to help companies assess the impacts of social, environmental and economic issues on their processes and people. Clients of the business include several large corporations such as British Nuclear Fuels and Portugal Telecom.

A partnership may lower the risks of business failure. In 2003, Scott Revare was made redundant as a partner in the Kansas City office of Accenture. Rather than set up as a sole proprietor, he joined forces with an established entrepreneur with other business interests to launch Smart401k, a web-based business that advises employees on company-sponsored retirement plans. 'Having an experienced partner really cut down on the mistakes that we made. Plus, we didn't have two people dependent on the start-up for their jobs,' says Mr Revare.

Mr Revare suggests that in the current market, redundant executives thinking about setting up a business might take some form of employment while they pilot their idea on a small scale. Ultimately, he says, if you think you are cut out to be your own boss, redundancy can be the catalyst that makes it happen. 'From a job satisfaction standpoint, it's 10 times better. Whether the consequences are positive or negative, it is better to be the person who makes the decisions.'

Do people who have used redundancy to change career advise others to follow suit? Ms Bryan, the strategy director turned teacher, admits freely that the strain of mastering a new profession, coupled with loss of income and a perceived loss of status, can be demoralising. The upside, she says, is that she now works in a profession of which she is genuinely proud. 'You will have dark days, because the first few years are really tough. My advice is to hang on in there.'

Source: Financial Times, *24 September 2008.*

Introduction

This case study nicely illustrates a number of important themes in careers. Increasingly volatile labour markets mean that many people are more likely to need to change jobs and occupations. In doing so, they will need to be durable, innovative and willing to do what they can to take control of their own careers. They may well need to seek advice and support throughout their working life (not just at the start), and to view a career as part of life as a whole rather than as a separate compartment. The case study also shows that there are different ways of evaluating career success (e.g. job satisfaction vs. earnings), and that social contacts are important in gaining access to opportunities.

A distinction is often made between people who have careers and people who have jobs. Those with careers tend to be viewed as better educated, more highly paid and with better promotion prospects than those with jobs. However, this distinction between so-called careers and so-called jobs was never very helpful, and has become even less so. It can be argued that everyone has a career, but that those careers differ a great deal from each other.

In this chapter we examine alternative definitions of career, and also some of the contextual factors that affect the careers experienced by individuals. One common definition of career is as an occupation or line of work. Most young people, and nowadays some older people too, are faced with decisions about what line of work to enter. Psychologists have been very interested in that, so in this chapter we also examine alternative approaches to career choice, and some of the practical applications arising from them. But careers are not just about choosing a type of work. They also concern what happens after that – particularly changes as a person moves between jobs and grows in experience and age. We will therefore also examine starting work and subsequent work-role transitions, as well as some theories of human development over the lifespan.

Individuals and organisations are paying increasing attention to planning and managing careers. This is partly because the fast pace of economic change makes careers much less clearly defined and predictable than they once were. Ideas and perspectives from psychology play a central part in understanding and managing careers. In this chapter, the techniques that are available to help manage careers in organisations are described and analysed. Overall the chapter aims to help readers to understand career theory and practice, and to apply key concepts to their own careers and also the careers of other people.

The context of careers

Definitions

Many definitions and meanings of career have been proposed (*see* Arnold, 2001, and Inkson, 2006, for brief discussions). Many of them, including dictionary definitions, tend to focus on the idea that a career necessarily means progression to something better, and/or working in an occupation with high skill and status. This notion of career is often contrasted with that of a 'job', which is considered to have neither of those characteristics.

Nowadays most social scientists favour a more inclusive definition of career: that is, one which makes as few assumptions as possible about the observable features of a person's sequence of work experiences. For our purposes, we can consider a career as: *the sequence of employment-related positions, roles, activities and experiences encountered by a person.* This definition reflects ideas from several sources (e.g. Greenhaus *et al.*, 2000). Several points can be made about it:

■ Careers are *not* confined to professional and managerial occupations, nor to 'conventional' career paths involving increasing seniority within a single occupation and/or organisation.

■ The notion of *sequence* means 'more than one'. Instead of looking at a person's present job in isolation, we are interested in how it relates to their past and future.

■ The inclusion of *experiences* emphasises that careers are subjective as well as objective. A sequence of jobs that looks haphazard to an outside observer may make a lot of sense in the narrative the person constructs about their own life (Sugarman, 2001, Chapter 7). Also, as we will see later in this chapter, a person's subjective feeling of having been successful in their own career may differ from an objective assessment of success such as status or salary. One person may regard reaching deputy managing director as a great success, another as a disappointment.

■ The term *employment-related* means that activities such as training, education and voluntary work, as well as *un*employment, can be considered elements of a person's career. Employment includes self-employment and short-term contracts.

Key Learning Point

Careers include any sequence of work-related experiences, not just conventional or orderly ones.

Psychologists and careers

The concept of career encompasses a great many different events and experiences in a person's life. Therefore it is not surprising that applied psychologists are involved in several different ways. There is a long history of psychological theory and research in vocational guidance. This has particularly concerned helping people make good choices of occupation to enter (*see* Savickas and Baker, 2005, for a good account of this), but has also included techniques of career counselling. Psychologists have conducted a great deal of research on what predicts career success. Some of this has focused on the disadvantages often experienced by women relative to men, and by ethnic minorities relative to ethnic majorities. Combined with social psychological work on perceptions of individuals and groups, this has been extended to managing diversity; that is, ensuring that people of both genders, and all ethnic identities, sexual orientations, family structures and ages are treated fairly and have their talents and experiences appropriately used at work. Also, attempts have been made to map out the course of a person's career in terms of stages or phases, each with their own characteristics. A related body of work has focused on how people handle specific transitions from one role to another in the course of their career. There has been huge and long-lasting interest from psychologists in mentoring as a technique to facilitate careers, and to a lesser extent in other techniques such as development centres and succession planning. Rather belatedly, the interest in mentoring is now extending to coaching, though this is more apparent in practice than in theory (Palmer and Whybrow, 2006). Later in this chapter we will give some attention to all of the topics mentioned in this paragraph.

As you may have noticed, most of the psychological work on careers described above focuses on the individual person or the relationship between two people. This is typical of applied psychology more generally. It tends to neglect the impact on careers of the structure of economies and societies, including social class (Thomas, 1989). Similarly, although many careers occur in organisational settings, psychology has little to say about how organisational structures and other features can affect the careers of individuals (or indeed be affected by them). This means that psychologists tend to be somewhat marginalised in some careers research and theory, to which sociologists, economists and others make major contributions (Moore *et al.*, 2007). All of these areas of expertise offer something when examining careers: genuinely multidisciplinary thinking is needed in the analysis of careers (Arthur, 2008).

Careers lie at the intersection of individual lives and social structures. Therefore many different academic disciplines are relevant to careers.

The context of careers

Much of the careers research and practice since about 1990 has placed great emphasis on the ways in which labour markets are said to have changed, and the implications of these changes for careers. Labour economists and others argue about the extent and permanence of these changes to the context of career. However, there seems to be considerable agreement in the careers literature that compared with a generation ago, the following generalisations apply, at least in the Western world:

- *Increasing workload for individuals*, both in terms of hours worked per week, and the intensity of effort required during each working hour.

- *Organisational changes*, particularly the elimination of layers of management (delayering) and reductions in the number of people employed (downsizing).

- *More global competition*, which means that organisations in Western countries need to control costs and also make maximum use of employees' skills and ideas.

- *More team-based work*, where individuals with different types of expertise are brought together for a limited period to work on a specific project with clear goals, such as the development of a new product.

- *More short-term contracts*, where the length of a person's employment is specified at the outset. Renewal of the contract when that time has expired may be the exception, not the norm.

- *Increasingly frequent changes in the skills required in the workforce*, because of the changing requirements of work partly brought about by new technology.

- *More part-time jobs*. Most part-time jobs are occupied by women, and many part-time workers have two or more part-time jobs.

- *Changing workforces*. Relatively low birth rates and increasing longevity mean that the average age of people in work or available for it is increasing quite rapidly in most Western countries. Historic patterns of immigration and other factors mean that the workforce is more diverse in terms of ethnicity, values and gender.

- *More self-employment and employment in small organisations*. For example, nearly half of the people in work in the United Kingdom are either self-employed or work in organisations with fewer than 20 employees.

- *Working at or from home*. Advances in communications technology and cost-cutting by employers mean that more people, currently around 5 per cent of those in employment, either work at home or are permanently based there.

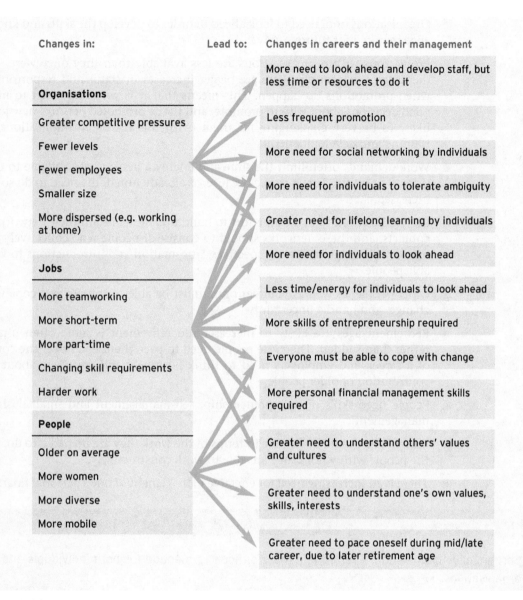

Changes in:	Lead to:	Changes in careers and their management

Organisations

Greater competitive pressures

Fewer levels

Fewer employees

Smaller size

More dispersed (e.g. working at home)

Jobs

More teamworking

More short-term

More part-time

Changing skill requirements

Harder work

People

Older on average

More women

More diverse

More mobile

More need to look ahead and develop staff, but less time or resources to do it

Less frequent promotion

More need for social networking by individuals

More need for individuals to tolerate ambiguity

Greater need for lifelong learning by individuals

More need for individuals to look ahead

Less time/energy for individuals to look ahead

More skills of entrepreneurship required

Everyone must be able to cope with change

More personal financial management skills required

Greater need to understand others' values and cultures

Greater need to understand one's own values, skills, interests

Greater need to pace oneself during mid/late career, due to later retirement age

Figure 15.1   Changes to careers and their consequences

■ *Increasing pressure on occupational and employer-based pension schemes,* owing to the ageing population and more mobility between occupations and organisations.

It is pretty clear that these labour market changes have consequences for careers. Careers are different from what they were, and also on the whole more difficult to manage. Figure 15.1 illustrates this. The characteristics of careers in the early twenty-first century include the following:

■ Individuals need to look ahead and ensure that they update their skills and knowledge in order to remain employable. One consequence is the necessity of viewing learning as lifelong, not confined to childhood and early adulthood.

■ Organisations, too, need to look ahead in order to develop the skills and knowledge required for future survival.

■ Promotions within organisations are less available than they once were, and (because of delayering) there are bigger increases in status and responsibility when promotions do happen. This means that it is very important to make good decisions about who to promote, and that a promoted person's new job is likely to be very challenging for them (with the associated implications for training and development).

■ Work demands often limit the time and energy a person has available to consider their future. This is ironic because, as already noted, the need to do so has increased.

■ Individuals need to make an effort to build up and maintain their networks of contacts, and these networks should to consist of people who collectively can offer a wide range of new perspectives, information and introductions to valuable people.

■ Older people, as well as younger ones, must be able to initiate and cope with change, and handle uncertainty.

■ Retirement ages are likely to increase, and retirement is more often phased rather than sudden. Therefore people need to pace themselves over the course of a career, and employers need to think positively and creatively about the contribution of older people.

■ People need skills of entrepreneurship, self-management and small business management.

■ Individuals should be flexible in terms of the work they are prepared to do, and the people with whom they are able to work constructively.

■ There is an increasing need for effective management of one's personal finances.

Key Learning Point

Careers have become more varied and more difficult to manage for both individuals and organisations.

It is important not to be too carried away by this narrative of change. Even though there is evidence that most of the changes described above have occurred and are occurring, they are, so to speak, 'on average'. Put another way, they do not affect everyone equally. For example, it is often said that there are no more 'jobs for life', but for many people there never were, and conversely even now some people have quite high job security. Whilst the changes described above have been experienced as change by many people born up to perhaps the early 1970s, for people younger than that, the current terrain is all they know. In the 1990s there was much concern about organisational delayering and downsizing, unexpected job insecurity and how people could cope with it (Herriot and Pemberton, 1995), but now many readers of this chapter may be surprised by how things apparently used to be.

A good example of controversy about how much things have or have not changed is the debate between Jacoby and Cappelli in the journal *California Management Review* back in 1999. Jacoby argued that, at least in the Western world, the welfare capitalist approach remains in place. There has been a 'transfer of risk' from organisations to individual employees in the sense that organisations are less likely to shield employees from economic downturns, but this trend has probably already gone about as far as it can. Jacoby also asserted that we tend to mistake cyclical change for permanent change, and to be misled by the fact that job losses in the 1990s affected the middle classes much more than those in earlier decades. Cappelli (1999) disagreed with Jacoby. He believed that there is clear evidence that jobs are becoming less secure and less stable, especially white collar and managerial ones. This means that prospects of long-term advancement within the same organisation are becoming ever slimmer. And although broad labour force statistics may suggest that change is incremental rather than fundamental, the experience of individual workers is that old assumptions can no longer be taken for granted. For example, by the 1990s it was common for organisations to be downsizing while the economy was expanding. This is a contrast that was largely unknown in earlier years.

Debates like this are important, and a long-term perspective is always valuable. However, for most of the working population, the changes debated by Jacoby and Cappelli are now part of the landscape, and are likely to reflect the environment in which the rest of their career occurs.

Key Learning Point

There is disagreement about whether or not changes in the labour market over the last 20 years reflect a fundamental and lasting shift, but for most people in the workforce, they are long-standing enough to mean that 'the way things are' is here to stay for the duration of their career.

STOP TO CONSIDER

In what ways do you see your career as different from your parents'? Does this reflect the changed landscape described above?

Career forms

It is still tempting to view careers in the narrow sense of predictable moves to jobs of increasing status, usually within a single occupation or organisation. This is what Kanter (1989) has called the *bureaucratic career*, and indeed many people do still see career in that narrow way. For example Jacoby and Cappelli (see above) both did so. Kanter (1989) also identified two other career forms. The first is *professional*, where growth occurs through development of competence to take on complex tasks rather than through promotion to another job. A person's status depends more on their reputation with other professionals or clients than on level in an organisation hierarchy. Kanter's other career form is *entrepreneurial*, which rests on the capacity to spot opportunities to create valued outputs and build up one's own organisation or operation. The experience of many people is that careers are becoming more like the professional and/or entrepreneurial form, and less like the bureaucratic form, because of the changing context discussed earlier in this chapter.

The boundaryless career

In recognition of the changing career landscape and the need for career theory to reflect it, Michael Arthur and colleagues (1999) refer to the *boundaryless career*. They define the boundaryless career in rather general fashion as 'A range of career forms that defy traditional employment assumptions' (Arthur and Rousseau, 1996, p. 3). The term 'boundaryless career' was coined as an extension of the idea of the boundaryless organisation, used by the then CEO of General Electric, Jack Welch. Since 1994 it has gained a lot of momentum and attention in career theory and practice. It clearly captures people's imagination, and resonates with what many see happening in their own careers and those of people they know. Nevertheless, the definition above is not entirely satisfactory because it says more about what the boundaryless career is not than about what it is. Arthur and Rousseau (1996) therefore developed the concept by describing six features of the boundaryless career:

1   When a career draws validation – and marketability – from outside the present employer (e.g. academic, joiner).

2   A career that moves across the boundaries of separate employers (e.g. Silicon Valley career).

3   A career which is sustained through outside networks (e.g. estate agent).

4   When traditional organisational career boundaries, notably those involving hierarchical reporting and advancement principles, are broken (e.g. some matrix organisations, project work).

5   When a person rejects existing career opportunities for personal or family reasons ('downshifting').

6   Individual interpretation – when a person perceives a boundaryless future regardless of structural constraints (those who feel they have choices, freedom, etc. notwithstanding organisational structures).

Careers are boundaryless in the sense that, either by choice or necessity, people move across boundaries between organisations, departments, hierarchical levels, functions and sets of skills. Movement across these boundaries is made easier by the fact that they are tending to dissolve anyway. Such movement is necessary for individuals to maintain their employability and for organisations to maintain their effectiveness. In some ways the boundaryless career is very similar to Kanter's notion of the professional career, because a person's marketability and affirmation are derived from outside their present employer and sustained through outside networks. Another boundary that is being broken down (in Arthur's opinion) is that between work and non-work. This is because people are increasingly likely to consider the impact of a job on their home life before taking it, and because more and more work is done at (or from) home. Arthur *et al.* (1999) found some evidence of boundaryless careers in action among a varied sample of people in New Zealand. They argue that career is a verb, not a noun: individuals are 'careering'. All this might sound very individualistic, and certainly the concept of the boundaryless career is a product of individualistic Western culture, where many situations are what Weick (1996) among others calls 'weak' – that is, they have relatively few constraints and allow individuals to express themselves. Nevertheless, Arthur *et al.* (1999) point out that successful boundaryless careering does require communion (relating closely to others, recognising interdependence) as well as agency (individual action on the environment). Indeed, there is some suggestion that the boundaryless career favours women because they are more accustomed to having to change their work and balance multiple priorities. Their orientation towards relationships, often termed 'communion', is said to be well-suited to an era of networking and teamworking. Men's orientation is more towards problem-solving and acting upon the world (often called agency), which may still be useful but not sufficient in a complex world.

Michael Arthur has done the field of careers a huge favour by developing the concept of the boundaryless career. As he must have been aware it would, the boundaryless career has provoked many questions and some of these highlight possible weaknesses and ambiguities (*see* for example Arnold and Cohen, 2008). These questions are very helpful in the further development of research and practice in careers, and are part of Arthur's contribution. Hirsch and Shanley (1996) among others have argued that although the boundaryless career might look liberating, for many people it is deeply threatening and confusing. They believe it is a recipe for the strong to prosper even more and the weak to be further disadvantaged (*see also* Pringle and Mallon, 2003). This is because much thinking around the boundaryless career seems to be based upon the assumption that people can control their own fate, at least to a reasonable extent. This may be accurate for people with qualifications and marketable skills, but might be too optimistic for others. A good illustration of this is the contrast between migrants who choose to move between countries to further their careers in highly skilled work (e.g. Tams and Arthur, 2007) versus migrants who have moved between countries because of economic necessity or sometimes persecution (e.g. Pio, 2005).

Another set of questions concerns the nature and role of boundaries. It seems that in the literature on the boundaryless career, boundaries are thought of more as barriers. That is, they are more like high and sturdy walls than lines marking the edge of a sports field. Boundaryless careers are where either these walls are dismantled, or where strong and purposeful individuals climb over them. Probably most of us could feel quite inspired by that, even though it is clear that barriers (in the form of people such as executive search consultants) do still place some constraints on the work opportunities people are and are not allowed access to (King *et al.*, 2005). Still, barriers may not be entirely undesirable to everyone – it could depend on your perspective. For people on one side of a barrier, it keeps those on the other side out. The 'frontier spirit' of the USA, where most of the thinking about boundaryless careers has developed, tends to see barriers as exclusively a bad thing. But in Europe and other parts of the world where invasions and territorial disputes are numerous through history, a firm barrier protecting the country or community can be seen as a 'must have'. An employment equivalent could be an organisation that has a policy of recruiting for desirable posts from inside: outsiders are barred from competing for them. Furthermore, boundaries (as opposed to barriers) are arguably very important to us, not expendable and undesirable. For example, without knowing where one organisation, occupation or segment of our life ends and another begins, we may find it hard to manage our lives and careers. Boundaries help us understand where we are, where we have been and where we might go in future. They contribute greatly to our cognitive maps (Hodgkinson and Healey, 2008) by which we make sense of and enact our careers. So even a career that is boundaryless in the sense that a person has worked in many different organisations derives its meaning from knowing what organisational boundaries have been crossed.

A third general issue concerns what exactly (if anything) is being recommended by advocates of the boundaryless career. Are they arguing that the boundaryless career is in some sense the right kind of career to have? If so, they are taking a *normative* perspective. Or are they merely trying to capture what careers are like these days, without putting forward opinions about how things should be? This would be a *descriptive* perspective. As noted earlier, some observers doubt whether things are really changing so much that boundaryless careers are the norm. An example is Gunz *et al.* (2000) who found plenty of evidence that bounded careers were still being pursued in the Canadian biotechnology industry. Related to this, is the boundaryless career subjective, objective or both? Briscoe *et al.* (2006) have used the term 'boundaryless mindset', which refers to a person's construal of their career as being unrestricted by boundaries. However, whilst I might think that I can move across organisational and functional boundaries if I want to, and am certainly willing to consider it, I might choose not to because I like it where I am now. So in some respects my career might look very bounded from the outside. I would reflect the sixth component of the boundaryless career described above, but probably not the others. Sullivan and Arthur (2006) have attempted to deal with this by distinguishing between physical and psychological mobility, but further clarification of this distinction is required. Underlying this is the point that the six aspects of the boundaryless career specified by Arthur and Rousseau (1996) do not necessarily work together. In other words, the boundaryless career is probably not a unitary concept after all.

Key Learning Point

The concept of the boundaryless career is a popular one, but it might overestimate the power individuals have over their own careers as well as the extent to which career forms are changing.

STOP TO CONSIDER

Look again at the six features of boundaryless careers described by Arthur and Rousseau (1996). Would you expect all these six characteristics to operate together, or are they quite independent of each other? To the extent that they are independent, what implications does this have for the concept of the boundaryless career?

The protean career

The protean career is a concept developed by American careers academic Tim Hall. Like the boundaryless career, it is intended to reflect the nature of careers today. However, its use is more overtly normative than the boundaryless career. That is,

Hall and others appear to be not only describing an approach to career, but also arguing that it is the *best* way to approach one's career. Hall originally mentioned the protean career in his 1976 book *Careers in organisations*, and he was well ahead of his time because he anticipated the trend towards self-driven careers that many people think has been necessitated by economic change. Hall developed the idea further in his 2002 follow-up book *Careers in and out of organisations* (note the nifty change of title!). Also, in recent years Hall and colleagues, especially Jon Briscoe, have been researching the protean career further (e.g. Briscoe and Hall, 2006; Briscoe *et al.*, 2006).

The protean career has been defined as 'a career based on self-direction in pursuit of psychological success in one's work' (Hall, 2002, p. 23). The word 'protean' is derived from Proteus, a sea-God in Greek mythology who could change form at will. The idea is that people can (and should) both have a coherent sense of identity, but also be able to adapt to labour market conditions. Briscoe and Hall (2006) specify that a protean career is one where the person is:

1 **values-driven**, in the sense that the person's internal values provide the guidance and measure of success for the individual's career; and

2 **self-directed** in personal and career management, having the ability to be adaptive in terms of performance and learning demands.

Table 15.1 shows how Hall contrasts the protean with the traditional career. The traditional career is clearly similar to Kanter's bureaucratic career, and represents what Hall and others believe we have left (or should leave) behind. Hall (2002; Hall and Chandler, 2005) also speaks of the 'path with a heart', which develops the notion of vocation or calling in career. This is an extension of the protean career idea

Table 15.1	The protean career vs. the traditional career	
	Protean	**Traditional**
Who is in charge?	Person	Organisation
Core values	Freedom, growth	Advancement, safety
Degree of mobility	High	Lower
Success criteria	Psychological success	Position, level, pay
Key attitudes	Work satisfaction Professional commitment	Organisational commitment

Adapted from Hall (2002).

to include a more explicit sense of (i) meaning to one's life and (ii) contribution to a community.

As with the boundaryless career, the protean career has some limitations and tensions built in. Probably because the idea has been developed in a highly free-market economy, it seems to be assumed that the values that self-directed individuals will pursue are those of freedom and growth (though this is moderated somewhat in the 'path with the heart', which allows for more communal motives). What if an individual's values are to achieve secure employment in a large organisation, and not mind what kind of work they have to do? That person's value-driven career would look very different from the pursuit of freedom and growth, but still in a sense be protean.

Although the protean image is one of freedom and autonomy, in fact Proteus was constantly being pursued, and changed form only as a desperate measure to avoid capture. This presents a rather different image – of a person trying hard to stay ahead of the labour market (hence the element of adaptability mentioned by Hall) rather than doing what helps their personal growth and development. As if to reinforce this 'other side' of the protean career, Hall's approach is firmly rooted in corporate capitalism: 'we must consider both the person's path with a heart and the employer's path to profits' (Hall, 2002, p. 303).

Key Learning Point

The protean career is one that is driven by an individual in pursuit of their own values. Therefore it is defined more in terms of what motivates it, not what it looks like from the outside.

Combining protean and boundaryless career concepts

The boundaryless and protean career concepts have both emerged from developments over the last 20 years in free-market economies. They both emphasise the less structured and less organisationally-centred nature of careers that are thought to be a consequence of socio-economic changes. Given these similarities, it is not surprising that at times they are treated as if they were the same thing. Briscoe and Hall (2006) argue that this is not the case, and have developed a matrix of combinations of boundaryless and protean elements. The two elements of boundarylessness are physical mobility and psychological mobility (Sullivan and Arthur, 2006). Physical mobility is defined as crossing boundaries such as those between occupations, organisations and status levels, whilst the psychological mobility is the perception of one's capacity to make such transitions if appropriate. The two elements of the protean career are values-driven and self-directed (see above). By breaking each of these four elements into high vs. low, there are 16 possible combinations. However, Briscoe and Hall (2006) suggest that eight of these are likely to be more plausible and commonly experienced than the other eight. An adaptation of their tabulation (Briscoe and Hall, 2006, p. 11) is shown in Table 15.2.

Time will tell whether this typology helps to advance career theory and practice. At the time of writing this, research in both the USA and Europe is being conducted to explore that question. In the meantime, it looks as if quite a lot of work is required to make some of these types easy to envisage and understand. The descriptions

Table 15.2		Eight career types based on protean and boundaryless careers			
Self-directed	Values-driven	Psychological mobility	Physical mobility	Career type	Career management characteristics of type
Low	Low	Low	Low	Lost or trapped	Waits for opportunities that help preserve status quo
Low	High	Low	Low	Fortressed	Searches for secure employment in settings that match personal values
Low	Low	Low	High	Wanderer	Accepts requests or requirements to move around but may struggle to cope
Low	High	High	Low	Idealist	Eagerly waits for the ideal opportunity to appear
High	Low	High	Low	Organisation man/woman	Actively looks for opportunities but wants a stable base
High	High	High	Low	Solid citizen	Seeks good fit with personal values and is willing to work across boundaries from a stable base
High	Low	High	High	Hired hand	Welcomes and seeks change, and adapts to new situations
High	High	High	High	Protean career architect	Proactively seeks opportunities for self-expression and service wherever they may be found

given in the right hand column of Table 15.2 illustrate the point, and even these are (in our opinion) considerably clearer than those given in Briscoe and Hall's table. Broader questions concern whether these career types are intended to describe types of career or types of person, and whether they are driven by people's characteristics or by the contexts in which their careers are occurring. For example, the extent to which a person's career shows physical mobility may be mainly due to the location and choice of opportunities available to them.

STOP TO CONSIDER

Among today's employees, which of the combinations shown in Table 15.2 would you expect to be most common, and why?

Career anchors

Another way to examine types of career is to concentrate on the subjective experience of the employee. Edgar Schein (1993) has used some research he carried out many years ago (Schein, 1978) to develop the concept of *career anchors*. This has become a very popular tool in practical career development work in recent years, though it has not sparked so much academic research. Schein defined a career anchor as

> an area of such paramount importance to a person that he or she would not give it up. The person comes to define his or her basic self-image in terms of that concern and it becomes the over-riding issue at every stage of the career.
>
> *(Schein, 1993, p. 20).*

He felt that people's anchors develop and become clear during their early career, as a result of experience and learning from it. Schein's list of alternative anchors people hold is shown in Table 15.3. We might look at the list of anchors and feel that several or even all of them are important to us, but which would win if we had to choose? Schein argues that this 'winner' is our real anchor.

Key Learning Point

Career anchors are areas of the self-concept that a person would not give up, even if faced with a difficult choice.

Career anchors consist of a mixture of abilities, motives, needs and values. They therefore reflect quite deep and far-reaching aspects of the person. It is perhaps the career anchor that a person questions when they are in the transitional periods identified by Levinson (*see* later in this chapter). Notice that career anchors do not necessarily determine the type of work or occupation a person chooses. Within any given occupation, there can be people with different anchors. One of the authors of this book regularly teaches managers and engineers in a building services company

Table 15.3	Career anchors

1 *Managerial competence.* People with this anchor are chiefly concerned with managing others. They wish to be generalists, and they regard specialist posts purely as a short-term means of gaining some relevant experience. Advancement, responsibility, leadership and income are all important.

2 *Technical/functional competence.* These people are keen to develop and maintain specialist skills and knowledge in their area of expertise. They build their identity around the content of their work.

3 *Security.* People with a security anchor are chiefly concerned with a reliable, predictable work environment. This may be reflected in security of tenure – i.e. having a job – or in security of location – wanting to stay in a particular town, for example.

4 *Autonomy and independence.* These people wish most of all to be free of restrictions on their work activities. They refuse to be bound by rules, set hours, dress codes and so on.

5 *Entrepreneurial creativity.* Here people are most concerned to create products, services and/or organisations of their own.

6 *Pure challenge.* This anchor emphasises winning against strong competition or apparently insurmountable obstacles.

7 *Service/dedication.* This anchor reflects the wish to have work that expresses social, political, religious or other values that are important to the individual concerned, preferably in organisations that also reflect those values.

8 *Lifestyle integration.* People who hold this anchor wish most of all to keep a balance between work, family, leisure and other activities, so that none is sacrificed for the sake of another.

about career development. Their dominant career anchors cover the full range shown in Table 15.3. One of the most common is service/dedication, which demonstrates that this anchor is not confined to charity and welfare work. Feldman and Bolino (2000) found in a sample of 153 self-employed people that autonomy was the most prevalent anchor, followed by entrepreneurial creativity and then security. Again this shows that not too much should be assumed about people's career anchors: small business owners may be more concerned with doing things their own way and being able reliably to provide for themselves and their families than with growing their business.

Being able to identify one's career anchor is probably important for the effective management of one's own career. It is also important that people in organisations responsible for managing careers are aware of the prevalence of the various anchors in their organisation. This might inform human resource policies such as job placement and transfer, promotion hierarchies and control systems. For example, problems are likely if there is an attempt to impose standard working hours and methods on people who most value the autonomy/independence anchor. Also, a common issue in organisations is how far up the hierarchy specialists such as scientists and engineers can rise without becoming general managers. Often the answer is not very far, which may create a problem for some talented staff who subscribe to the technical/functional competence career anchor. People with a security anchor are likely to have quite a difficult time because security is now harder to attain than it was. The technical/functional competence anchor could be a problem in organisations with project-based multidisciplinary teams, while the lifestyle integration anchor is increasingly difficult to honour when workloads are increasing (Schein, 1996). There is some research evidence to suggest that people whose anchors are compatible with their work environments are happier than those whose anchors are not compatible (e.g. Feldman and Bolino, 2000; Tan and Quek, 2001), though again we must be cautious about making assumptions regarding what types of work environment nurture what kinds of anchor.

The questions of whether just one anchor emerges, and whether it is constant through the remainder of the career, are controversial (Ramakrishna and Potosky, 2003). Perhaps this rather structured and static view is partly due to the fact that Schein's original ideas were developed in the 1970s from intensive interviews with a small number of graduates from an elite US university – in other words, people who could largely choose their own work in an era when arguably (*see* earlier in this chapter) careers unfolded in a more predictable way than they do now. However, since then Schein and others have extended that original work with bigger and broader samples (Schein, 1996).

STOP TO CONSIDER

Career anchors are usually thought of as quite independent of each other, but is this realistic? Perhaps they work together in influencing a person's career priorities. Try to think of ways in which two or more anchors may simultaneously be important for a person.

Exercise 15.1   A medical career

Rashid Kassim has been appointed a consultant doctor at a general hospital. This is the fourth hospital he has worked in since qualifying as a doctor at the age of 25. The consultant grade is the most senior type of post available for doctors who continue to specialise in clinical work as opposed to taking on major managerial responsibilities. Rashid is delighted to have achieved this promotion because he believes that the status of consultant will allow him more freedom to shape his medical work in the ways he thinks most appropriate. Also, he is very active in his professional association and believes that having the status of consultant will help him make changes that he sees as necessary. It will also make him more visible to other senior doctors, with whom it might be possible to share ideas, experiences and knowledge. And who knows, perhaps one day one of them might offer him a job!

Even now, Rashid is thinking ahead a few years, and wondering how long it will be before he gets bored. He suspects that one day he will want to move to a higher-paid consultant post in a bigger hospital attached to a university medical school. This is mainly because he would be likely to see a wider range of medical conditions, to have better equipment available and be more closely in touch with the latest developments in medical research. Still, even without moving, he might well be able to work with eminent people based elsewhere. Another factor was that soon it would be hard to move for a few years because of the stage of education his children were at.

Suggested exercise

On the basis of the information given here, try to specify the career type(s) and anchor(s) that fit Rashid Kassim's career so far. How easy is this to do? Do your conclusions depend on whether you focus mainly on the observable moves he has made and hopes to make, or on his own personal motives?

Career success

In many respects, career success is an appealing topic for work psychologists. Why is this? First, it is to do with human performance. Second, there are many potential predictors of success that can be put into box-and-arrow models and tested statistically (you will have noticed that psychologists like this kind of thing). Third, some of those potential predictors of success concern individual differences in personality or ability – another favourite area of psychologists. Fourth, how to be successful in a career is a matter of personal importance for a lot of us. Finally, some of the potential predictors of success (e.g. gender, ethnic origin, age) may have implications for organisational and societal policies regarding equality of opportunity and diversity (Nicholson and de Waal Andrews, 2005).

The nature of career success

How can we measure the success of a career? Perhaps the most obvious way is to see how high in a status hierarchy a person is, and/or how much they earn. We might also take a longer-term perspective and consider how much a person's earnings have grown over time, and/or how many steps they have risen up a hierarchy. Objectively verifiable indicators like these are indeed used in the majority of research on career success. Status and earnings are important to many people, and they reflect the distribution of material resources in societies. They are well geared to the traditional or bureaucratic concept of career. However, it is often argued that status and earnings are not centrally important to many people. Instead, subjective criteria such as career satisfaction, job satisfaction, work–life balance and feelings of personal accomplishment may be of more significance (Hall and Chandler, 2005). This is certainly consistent with protean and boundaryless careers, and of course with several career anchors. Heslin (2005) and Arthur and colleagues (2005) both provide useful discussions of career success, though the latter is a little unclear about the objective–subjective distinction. In any case, it is likely that subjective and objective success are somewhat related to each other. If we are objectively successful we will tend to feel successful (though not always), and perhaps if we feel successful we will be encouraged to take on more challenging goals that lead to greater objective achievements, as predicted by Hall and Nougaim's (1968) 'psychological success cycle'.

Some psychologists have therefore used other criteria for assessing career success. For example, there are measures available of people's feelings of career satisfaction. However, some of these measures are rather unimaginative because they tend to ask people how satisfied they are with their advancement and/or earnings, rather than tapping altogether different concepts. Research by Sturges (1999) has provided a more sophisticated analysis of the ways in which people might experience career success. She interviewed employees of a large company and obtained qualitative data about how they viewed career success. Sturges discovered that factors such as personal influence, being recognised for one's achievements, a sense of accomplishment or achievement, enjoyment, working with integrity and achieving a balance between work and non-work were frequently mentioned as criteria of career success. She discerned four groups based on different conceptions of career success, as follows:

1   **Climbers:** These people valued traditional criteria of pay and hierarchical position. They set themselves targets for achieving in these terms, and were often competitive.

2   **Experts:** These people valued doing their job well, developing expertise in what they were doing, and being appreciated for it. Personal and informal appreciation was valued much more than formal recognition via promotions and salary increases.

3   **Influencers:** These people cared most about making an impact on the organisation, either by their own efforts, or by developing other people.

4   **Self-realisers:** The focus for these people was achieving things of personal meaning to them, often in service of their own development. The kinds of achievement they were looking for were sometimes connected with good work performance in the organisation's terms, but this was rarely their main concern.

Whilst this last category is most obviously consistent with protean and boundaryless careers, none of the other three is necessarily inconsistent. Interestingly, the Climber category was dominated by men, whilst the Expert and Self-realiser categories were dominated by women. Only the Influencer group had an approximately equal split. However, Sturges' study may not have captured the widest possible range of conceptions of career success, because all her respondents were working in the same corporate setting.

Key Learning Point

There are many different criteria of career success. They vary in their relative emphasis on objective achievements, personal feelings and perceptions, and recognition from other people.

More recently, Dries and colleagues (2008) have reported an excellent study that attempts to map out the domain of career success in a comprehensive yet succinct way. They did this by interviewing people and asking them about how they saw career success. They used a technique called laddering to get at progressively more fundamental concepts of success. So, for example, if a person said that learning something new was significant to them, they were asked why it was significant. This process continued until the person could not say why something mattered to them, except that 'it just did'. All these fundamental criteria of success were reviewed by Dries and colleagues, and identical or near identical ones were eliminated. The remaining 42 were then sorted (using a Q-sort method) where career development experts were asked to sort them into piles, so that similar criteria were in the same pile. The experts were also asked to articulate what it was that criteria in the same pile had in common. These data were then pooled and subjected to multidimensional scaling (a technique that allows clusters of concepts to be identified).

Dries and colleagues found that the clusters of success criteria could be described in terms of their location on a two-dimensional diagram (see Figure 15.2). The Affect vs. Achievement dimension reflects the distinction between positive feelings and factual accomplishments. The Intrapersonal vs. Interpersonal dimension concerns on the one hand the person's self or inner world (particularly their goals, health or happiness), and on the other hand their relationships with the outside world. Using these dimensions as a framework, Dries and colleagues identified nine clusters (or

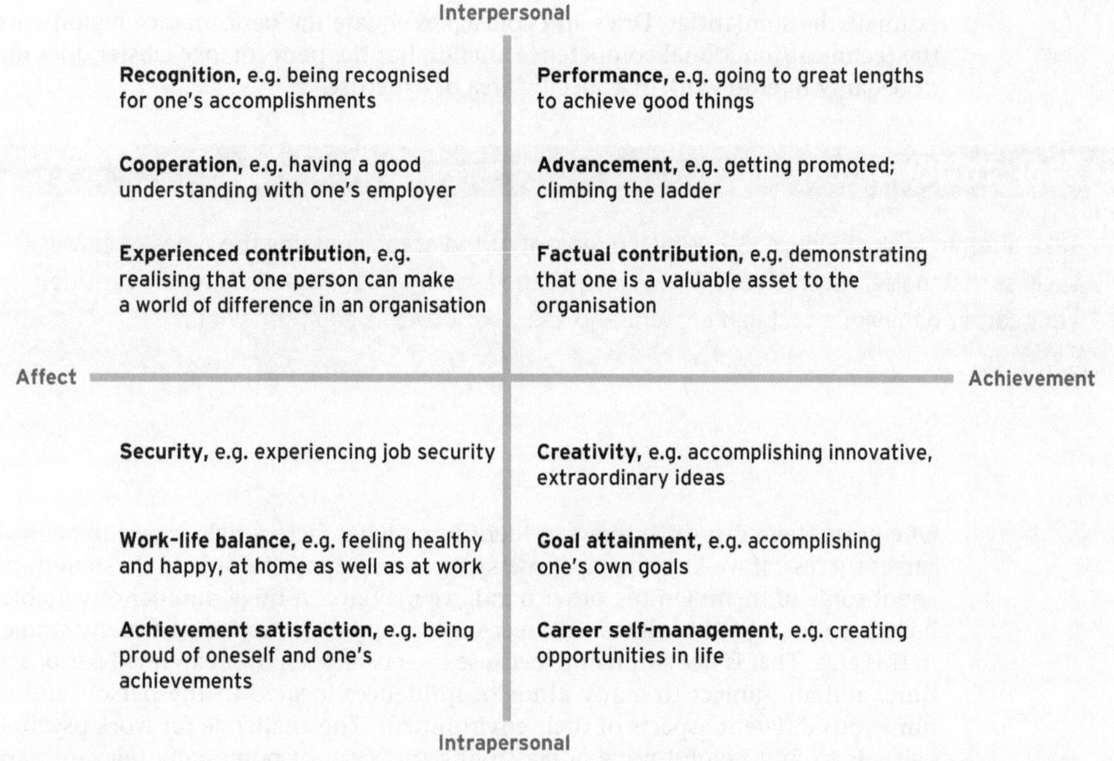

Interpersonal

Recognition, e.g. being recognised for one's accomplishments	**Performance,** e.g. going to great lengths to achieve good things
Cooperation, e.g. having a good understanding with one's employer	**Advancement,** e.g. getting promoted; climbing the ladder
Experienced contribution, e.g. realising that one person can make a world of difference in an organisation	**Factual contribution,** e.g. demonstrating that one is a valuable asset to the organisation

Affect ━━━━━━━━━━━━━━━━━━━━━━━━━━━━━━━━━━━━━━━ **Achievement**

Security, e.g. experiencing job security	**Creativity,** e.g. accomplishing innovative, extraordinary ideas
Work-life balance, e.g. feeling healthy and happy, at home as well as at work	**Goal attainment,** e.g. accomplishing one's own goals
Achievement satisfaction, e.g. being proud of oneself and one's achievements	**Career self-management,** e.g. creating opportunities in life

Intrapersonal

Figure 15.2   A mapping of career success constructs
Source: Adapted from Dries, N., Pepermans, R. and Carlier, O. (2008) 'Career success: Constructing a multidimensional model', *Journal of Vocational Behavior*, 73, 254-67.

regions as they called them). Some of these contained sub-clusters, so more than nine are shown in Figure 15.2.

Dries and her colleagues make several observations about their findings. Three of them are as follows. First, the career success criterion of salary is very difficult to place in their model. This is probably because money has many different meanings to different people. Hence salary might contribute to advancement, recognition, security and probably some other regions too. This raises the interesting possibility that as a quick measure of success, salary might be more versatile and generally applicable than it might appear. Second, in past studies of career success, measures of success have tended to fall into the interpersonal affect quadrant. However, this conclusion can be challenged because some of the categorisation of measures is questionable. For example, Dries and colleagues classify the constructs social status, recognition and reputation as interpersonal affect, when interpersonal achieve-ment seems at least as plausible as a classification. The opposite quadrant, intraper-sonal achievement, has been used relatively little. This is important, because some of the success constructs in that quadrant (such as continuous learning) seem well-suited to twenty-first-century careers, and should be used more. Third, some clear connections can be seen between clusters of success constructs and Schein's career anchors described earlier in this chapter. For example, the security cluster and the security/stability anchor are clearly similar. Nevertheless, it is easy to over-estimate the similarities. Dries and colleagues equate the performance region with the technical/functional competence anchor, but the performance cluster does not necessarily refer to work in a specific area of expertise.

STOP TO CONSIDER

Take another look at Figure 15.2. Which quadrant of the graph contains the types of career success that matter most to you? Don't just give the answer you think sounds right – consider your career behaviour past and present and see what governs your behaviour.

Predictors of career success

Of course, there is great interest in identifying what factors help a person achieve career success. If we know what those factors are, we may be able to do something about some of them. On the other hand, we may not! A huge number of variables have been found to be related to career success in one or more of the many studies in this area. That is not surprising, because careers happen over extended periods of time, and are subject to many kinds of influences located in the person and in numerous different aspects of their environment. The challenge for work psychol-ogists is to find helpful ways of classifying the array of potentially relevant vari-ables and to develop a convincing theory about how and when these variables affect career success. Bearing in mind also that career success can be construed and measured in many different ways (see above), it quickly becomes obvious that this is a huge task.

Of course, simply identifying predictors of career success does not necessarily mean that the reasons why they predict become obvious. For example a study of nearly 1400 US executives by Judge *et al.* (1995) evaluated the impact on salary, status and

Table 15.4	Which American executives are the best paid?
Predictor	**Salary value in US dollars (in mid-1990s)**
Working in consumer durables industry	54,195
Being a graduate of a top university	30,929
Being a law graduate	30,328
Being married	27,845
Having a non-working spouse	22,011
Having a high performance rating	11,816
Each 7 years of age	10,262
Ambition (per level up the hierarchy aspired to)	9238
Being male	6575
Working extra (per evening per week)	3855

Source: Based on T. Judge *et al.* (1995), reprinted with permission.
Note: the predictors' effects are *not* cumulative – for example, being a law graduate from a top university does not mean a salary advantage of over $60,000.

career satisfaction of a large range of variables. Table 15.4 shows how some of those variables affected salary. Taking them together it can be seen that the highest earners were married men in the consumer durables industry with non-employed spouses who had a degree from a top-rated American university, who desired to progress further up the hierarchy and who worked extra hours. Career satisfaction was correlated with salary showing that the subjective and objective careeers are connected. Interestingly, whites were less satisfied than people from other ethnic backgrounds, and ambitious people were less satisfied than unambitious ones, presumably because those with ambition had not yet risen as far as they wanted to. Those in the consumer durables industry tended to be more satisfied than those in entertainment/leisure, high technology, industrial manufacturing and food and beverages.

We can probably generate possible explanations for these findings quite easily, but that's the point – all too easily! For example the degree from a top-rated university might have its impact because high-paying employers only recruit from top universities, or it might be because those universities provide the best teaching and learning thus making their graduates more employable, or it might be a kind of quality label that attaches to a person and that others interpret as an easy way of knowing that this person 'must be good'. And of course it might be none of those things. Perhaps highly able people get to the top universities, so although having attended a top university looks like a cause of success it is only a correlate of success. The real cause of success might be the person's intellectual ability and/or personality/experience and/or social background that got them to that university in the first place.

Ng and colleagues (2005) have made a gallant attempt to bring this vast literature together. They report a meta-analysis of predictors of subjective and objective success based on 140 studies. As noted earlier, it is very difficult to find clear-cut and convincing ways of dividing up possible predictors into different types in order to bring order to chaos. Ng *et al.*'s approach is shown in Figure 15.3. They split predictors up into four groups. *Human capital* reflects experiences, skills, social contacts and motivations relevant to work. *Organisational sponsorship* concerns the resources invested in a person by employing organisation. *Sociodemographic* variables are inherent or at least stable features of a person's individuality. *Stable individual differences* refers to personality characteristics.

Ng *et al.* used salary and promotions as indicators of objective success and career satisfaction as an indicator of subjective success, but promotions proved quite difficult to predict, and has been omitted from Figure 15.3. Salary and career satisfaction correlated at $r = 0.3$, which supports the idea that they are connected but different. *Human capital* variables, especially education level, hours worked and work experience, were fairly good predictors of salary. They tended to be less good at predicting career satisfaction, though career planning, social capital and work centrality did so. *Organisational sponsorship* variables, on the other hand, predicted career satisfaction better than salary. However, training and development opportunities and career sponsorship predicted both, albeit more strongly for career satisfaction than salary. It is significant, and perhaps unexpected, that receiving support from one's employing organisation has a stronger impact on how one feels about one's career than on how much one earns. *Sociodemographic* variables predicted salary much better than they predicted career satisfaction. You might not be surprised to hear that white married older men tended to earn most. Slightly more optimistically, Ng *et al.* found that the salary advantage for men over women was smaller in more recent studies, suggesting that perhaps discrimination is reducing over time. *Stable individual differences* were fairly good predictors of career satisfaction. Extrovert, emotionally stable people who believed that they could influence what happened to them and were willing to take the initiative tended to be most satisfied. This suggests that there is a dispositional component to career satisfaction: some people are just more content than others. However, it does not prove the point, because this kind of person might be better than others at finding objectively better opportunities. Just one of the stable individual difference variables was a strong predictor of salary, and that was cognitive ability. This reinforces the consistent message that general intelligence is a strong predictor of performance in almost all domains (Schmidt and Hunter, 2004).

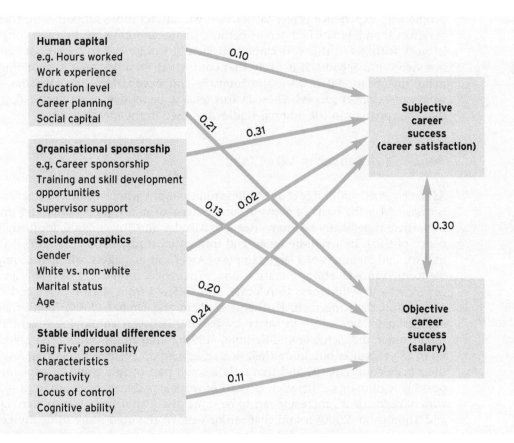

Figure 15.3 **Predictors of objective and subjective career success**
Source: Adapted from Ng, T. *et al.* (2005) 'Predictors of objective and subjective career success: A meta-analysis', *Personnel Psychology*, 58, 367–408. John Wiley and Sons. Copyright © 2005, Blackwell.
Note: The figures by the arrows from predictors to career success indicate the average correlation for predictor variables of that kind.

Key Learning Point

The stronger predictors of salary tend to be intelligence, work experience and effort, whilst the stronger predictors of career satisfaction are aspects of personality and signs of support from one's employer.

The Ng *et al.* (2005) meta-analysis provides a very helpful summary of a great deal of research. However, two important limitations should be noted. The first is that although some variables are labelled 'predictors' of career success, they are not necessarily causes of it (see the discussion above of the Judge *et al.*, 1995, study). In fact, they may not even precede the career success variables. Much of the research reviewed by Ng *et al.* was cross-sectional. It is easy to imagine that, for example, people who experience career satisfaction will attract more support from their supervisors than less satisfied people because they seem more positive and congenial to work with. So in this case career satisfaction would lead to supervisor support, not vice versa. Second, it is likely that contextual variables such as economic climate, organisational history and industry and occupation characteristics affect what causes career success. These factors tend to be hidden or unmeasured, unless they are apparent in the original studies and used in the meta-analysis.

Gender differences in career success

As the Ng *et al.* and Judge *et al.* studies studies imply, when women's career success is assessed on the basis of conventional criteria of salary progression and promotion, there is generally bad news (see also Alkadry and Tower, 2006, for further evidence of this). In a well-designed and influential study, Stroh *et al.* (1992) found that women members of a large sample of American managers, who were comparable to men in education, qualifications, experience, proportion of family income generated and willingness to relocate, still suffered from slightly less good salary progression than the men. Furthermore, Lam and Dreher (2004) found that the men gained much more in salary by moving between employing organisations than women did. Schneer and Reitman (1995) found that women MBA graduates, up to 18 years after obtaining their degree, earned on average 19 per cent less than their male counterparts, and that only a small part of this could be explained by possibly legitimate factors such as years of work experience. Even amongst women who have 'made it', there appears to be some disadvantage relative to men. Lyness and Thompson (2000) found that senior women reported more difficulty getting geographical mobility opportunities, and more concern that they did not fit the dominant culture. Lyness and Schrader (2004) examined announcements of senior job moves in the *Wall Street Journal*, and found that women's moves typically involved smaller changes of role than men's, which might well inhibit their subsequent earning power.

One way in which women's careers have traditionally differed from men's is, of course, their likelihood of being interrupted by childbearing and child-rearing, and by the fact that in most households a woman does more of the childcare and housework than a man, no matter what her employment situation. The presence of two people in a household pursuing careers (usually called dual-career couples) adds extra stresses for both partners, but again these seem to fall more on the woman than on the man (Cooper and Lewis, 1993). A variety of measures designed to help people with family responsibilities are used by some employers. One of these is the use of flexible working patterns, such as total annual working hours, which people can distribute through the year as they wish (within certain fairly broad limits). Career breaks have been used relatively extensively, most notably by financial services organisations. People can suspend their career with the organisation for several years, normally in order to make a start on raising a family. During that time they must report for refresher training for a small number of weeks per year. These may look like expensive schemes, but what evaluation evidence there is suggests that they are cost-effective for organisations because they help to retain skilled labour (the costs of lost expertise, and finding good-quality replacement staff can be enormous). On the other hand, there is some feeling that people who make use of the scheme may find that their subsequent progress is handicapped by others perceiving that they are not really serious about their career. Judiesch and

Lyness (1999) reported that leaves of absence for family responsibilities were almost always taken by women not men, and that leaves result in fewer subsequent promotions and smaller salary increases. Furthermore, these disadvantages can be very long-lasting: 25 years or more (Reitman and Schneer, 2005).

Improving your career success

An assumption behind the notions of boundaryless and protean careers is that individuals have the power to influence what happens to them, and to steer their own careers. However, many of the variables shown in Figure 15.3 might suggest otherwise. If personality and cognitive ability are quite stable, the implication is that there isn't much a person can do to change them, or indeed the sociodemographic variables. How these can be taken into account by organisations in managing careers is discussed later in this chapter. Organisational sponsorship is somewhat more under personal control, but also presumably partly dependent upon organisational policies and practices. A person's human capital seems more readily open to change by themselves. Even so, some aspects of capital, such as education and international experience, may be constrained by a person's ability, family circumstances and so on. All this serves to highlight that the rhetoric of boundaryless and protean careers may be a little too optimistic about individuals' capacity to influence their own fate.

Still, it would be discouraging to think of ourselves as helpless! The human capital variables in the Ng *et al.* study do give us some clues about how we can influence our career success, and it is probably not surprising that putting work first in your life and working long hours tends to help. Whether you want to do that is another question. Prominent in discussions of human capital is the concept of *social capital*. Its prominence is based on the 'common-sense' idea that who you know is at least as important as what you know. Social capital refers to the social resources that a person can access and utilise. In work settings, Forret and Dougherty (2001, 2004) have identified five kinds of behaviour that can enhance social capital: socialising, engaging in professional activities, maintaining contacts, participation in home community and increasing one's visibility at work. Of course, some people will find these things easier to do than others. This is partly a matter of personality, but also of social position. Much has been written about how in some work settings women and minorities tend to find it difficult to break into social networks (e.g. James, 2000; Metz and Tharenou, 2001), and there is some evidence that creating their own network can be helpful (Friedman *et al.*, 1998), though of course it risks increasing a sense of separation from other groups.

Other research in this area has used social network analysis to describe a person's social network. This maps out who an individual knows, how well and in what ways they know them and whether those people know each other. The most influential study in this tradition is by Seibert *et al.* (2001) who investigated the extent to which features of respondents' social networks affected career success. Two features were of particular interest. *Structural holes* referred to the extent to which an individual's contacts did *not* know each other (i.e. there were holes in the network) and the number of *weak ties* reflected the extent to which the person had many contacts they knew slightly, rather than a few they knew well. Social network theory suggests that the most effective networks have both of these properties because they allow the person to access many different perspectives without getting too attached to any of them. Seibert and colleagues found that the number of weak ties and structural holes both predicted the number of contacts at higher levels a person had, which in turn influenced their career satisfaction (but interestingly not so much their salary and promotions). Again, though, we must be careful when talking about cause and effect. Although Seibert and colleagues developed a sophisticated theory and tested it carefully, their data were cross-sectional. Also, they were drawn from a sample of US university graduates most of whom were working in corporate settings, so the findings may be somewhat context-specific. Some more ideas related to social factors in career success appear in the organisational career management section of this chapter.

As well as capital, the concept of career competencies is potentially useful to individuals in enhancing their career success. DeFillippi and Arthur (1996) suggested that three kinds of competence might be especially helpful in an era of boundaryless careers. 'Knowing why' concerns a person's insight into his or her career motivations and abilities. 'Knowing whom' concerns developing and using social contacts (i.e. accumulating career capital). 'Knowing how' refers to specific skills and abilities relating to one's job and career. Although some research suggests that these might be useful constructs (Eby *et al.*, 2003), at present they are poorly defined and measured. A somewhat stronger taxonomy of competencies is offered by Kuijpers and Scheerens (2006), who suggest career development ability, reflection on capacities, reflection on motives, work exploration, career control and networking.

Key Learning Point

Developing and using our career competences and social networks may be the most useful things to focus on in improving our own career success.

Exercise 15.2   Meanings of career success

Imagine your career unfolds in ways which please you. Now try to write your 'Career Epitaph' - that is, a statement about you and your career rather like the statements that sometimes appear on the headstones of graves.

Suggested exercise

Now examine your epitaph carefully. Which career forms, anchors and notions of career success are embedded in it?

Career choice

Psychologists have long been interested in how people choose an occupation, and how they can be helped to do so effectively. Here the term career is usually taken to mean occupation or line of work. Three basic requirements of effective career choice were proposed long ago by Frank Parsons (1909, p. 5, described in Sharf, 1992, Chapter 2):

1 A clear understanding of ourselves, our attitudes, abilities, interests, ambitions, resource limitations and their causes.

2 A knowledge of the requirements and conditions of success, advantages and disadvantages, compensation, opportunities and prospects in different lines of work.

3 True reasoning on the relations of these two groups of facts.

This nicely describes the nature of the task, but does not in itself help people to do it well. We now examine psychologists' attempts to take things further. An excellent overview of some of this work can be found in Savickas (2007).

John Holland's theory

John Holland developed over many years an influential theory of career choice. The most recent version can be found in Holland (1997). He summarised his approach in the preface of that book. In some ways it is a much more narrowly focused, personal and pragmatic approach than what has appeared in this chapter so far:

> I have become addicted to seeing careers from an individual's perspective – how can a person's difficulties be resolved within the present personal and environmental resources? I have neglected the restructuring of educational institutions, businesses, and public policy, although I have indicated some of the implications of the theory for these institutions. My concern for individuals has led to a related goal – to construct a formulation that can be understood and used by practitioners. Consequently, I have stuck to simple measures of all theoretical constructs. Fortunately, these simple measures usually work as well as more complex ones.
>
> *(p. vi)*

In the course of his earlier work as a careers counsellor in the United States, Holland thought he could discern six pure types of vocational personality. He also felt that he could see the roots of these types in traditional personality theory. He developed his concepts and measures of them. Subsequent work has sought to validate these, and to test Holland's hypotheses about career choice (*see below*). Very briefly, Holland's six personality types are as follows:

1 *Realistic*: outdoor-type. Tends to like, and be good at, activities requiring physical strength and/or coordination. Not keen on socialising.

2 *Investigative*: interested in concepts and logic. Tends to enjoy, and be good at, abstract thought. Often interested in the physical sciences.

3 *Artistic*: tends to use imagination a lot. Likes to express feelings and ideas. Dis-likes rules and regulations; enjoys music, drama, art.

4 *Social*: enjoys the company of other people, especially in affiliative (i.e. helping, friendly) relationships. Tends to be warm and caring.

5 *Enterprising*: also enjoys the company of other people, but mainly to dominate or persuade rather than help them. Enjoys action rather than thought.

6 *Conventional*: likes rules and regulations, structure and order. Usually well-organised, not very imaginative.

Holland proposed that the types can be arranged in a hexagon in the order described above to express their similarity to each other (*see* Figure 15.4). This ordering is usually referred to as RIASEC. Each type is placed at a corner of the hexagon. Types on opposite corners of the hexagon (i.e. three corners apart) are in many senses opposites. Types on adjacent corners (e.g. *Realistic* and *Conventional*) are quite similar to each other. Nobody exactly matches any single type, but nevertheless each of us resembles some types more than others. In fact, Holland suggests that people are most usefully described in terms of the three types they resemble most, in descending order of similarity. Hence, for example, for an ISE person, the *investigative* type comes closest to describing them, the *social* type comes next and *enterprising* third. Holland proposed that occupations can also be described in terms of the six types. He has argued that any environment exerts its influence through the people in it. Hence occupations are described in terms of the people in them, again using the three most prevalent types in descending order. In the United

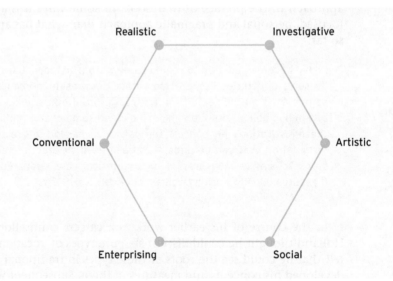

Figure 15.4	Holland's six types of vocational personality

Source: Holland (1997, p. 6). Reproduced by special permission of the publisher, Psychological Assessment Resources, Inc., from *Making Vocational Choices*, third edition, copyright 1973, 1985, 1995, 1997 by Psychological Assessment Resources, Inc. All rights reserved.

States, Holland's classification of occupations has been widely applied in, for example, the *Dictionary of Holland Occupational Codes* (Gottfredson and Holland, 1996).

Key Learning Point

John Holland has identified six vocational personality types. These types map on to different occupations.

Some of Holland's main theoretical propositions (*see* Holland, 1997, pp. 67–8) are as follows:

- People find environments satisfying when environmental patterns resemble their own personality patterns. This situation (often referred to as *congruence*) encourages stability of behaviour because people receive a lot of reinforcement of their already-preferred styles. Congruence also tends to enable a person to perform well in their work.

- Incongruent interactions stimulate change in behaviour. A person may seek a more congruent environment, remake the present one, or change to become more congruent in behaviour and/or perceptions.

- An environment expels incongruent people, seeks new congruent ones or changes its demands on inhabitants.

Holland has said he is irritated by what he sees as a lack of attention to the more dynamic social-psychological elements of his theory. However, his fundamental hypothesis is relatively straightforward and states that people will be most satisfied, and most successful, in occupations that are congruent with (i.e. match) their personality. Thus Holland's theory reflects a well-established tradition in work psychology: the matching of person and work, with the assumption that both are fairly stable over time (for example, the implications of person–environment fit for employee well-being are discussed in Chapter 12). The large volume of research on this and other aspects of Holland's theory has been reviewed by Spokane *et al.* (2000) and Arnold (2004), among others. Several conclusions can be drawn.

First, Holland's vocational personality types are a reasonably good reflection of basic personality dimensions identified in more general psychology, as indeed they should be. However, De Fruyt and Mervielde (1999) found that although Holland's interest scores did have some validity in predicting the type of occupation entered by their sample of Belgian university graduates, personality test scores added to that predictive power. This suggests that personality is tapping aspects of individuality over and above Holland's constructs.

Second, the hexagonal arrangement, whilst not a perfect representation of the relative similarities of the types, is nevertheless a good approximation for most of the voluminous data collected using Holland's measures (Tracey and Rounds, 1993). At the very least, it looks as if the circumplex arrangement of the types (that is, they can be positioned on a circle in a certain order) is accurate.

Third, and somewhat contrary to the second point above, the hexagonal arrangement may not be very generalisable across cultures. Although Leong *et al.* (1998) argued that their data from India did match the hexagon quite well, their conclusion looks rather optimistic. For example, E and R were quite similar, which might be expected in an economy where agriculture plays quite a big role in the everyday lives of much of the population. In China, Long and Tracey (2006) found that a plausible interpretation of the types was as three pairs: R/I, A/S and E/C. These could approximate to science, arts/humanities and business respectively, and may partly be a consequence of relatively early specialisation in parts of the Chinese education system.

Fourth and finally, there is some evidence that congruence is correlated with satisfaction and success, but it is surprisingly weak. Even when the correlation is observed we cannot be sure that congruence *leads* to satisfaction and success. Spokane *et al.* (2000) conducted a detailed analysis of the congruence issue. They estimated that the correlation between congruence and job satisfaction in most studies is about 0.25. They argue, correctly, that this is a strong enough relationship to take seriously. On the other hand, Young *et al.* (1998) found no significant correlations between 11 different indices of congruence and two different measures of satisfaction in data from 483 people in 172 occupations.

STOP TO CONSIDER

What might be the problems and limitations of defining congruence as the match between the vocational personality of an individual and that of the typical individual in an occupation? On what other basis might congruence be measured?

Arnold (2004) analysed fourteen possible reasons for the weak or non-existent correlations between congruence and satisfaction/performance outcomes. He grouped these under three general headings: problems with the theory; problems with research on the theory; and the nature of twenty-first-century careers. He concluded that the following three factors, all to do with the theory and research (not so much with the nature of twenty-first-century careers), were most likely to be responsible:

1 Holland's theory and measures do not adequately reflect some aspects of the person (for example, the values/anchors discussed earlier in this chapter). If aspects of the person other than those Holland includes are partly responsible for satisfaction and/or performance, then we can expect the Holland measure to show relatively weak correlations.

2 Similarly, measures of the environment might miss significant features, and in any case what is most appropriately construed as the 'environment'? Is it occupation, employing organisation, work group, industry or what? In fairness to Holland, in his occupations finder he differentiates to some extent between the same occupation in different contexts (e.g. clinical psychologist vs. organisational psychologist). However, this differentiation does not always occur, and in any case may not reflect the kinds of distinction that matter to some people. Is being a management accountant in a heavy engineering company the same as being a management accountant in a charity, for example?

3 Measures of congruence are weakened by the above two factors, and by the fact that many of them lose too much of the available data. For example, congruence indices based on three-letter codes ignore scores on the other three career-related personality types.

Key Learning Point

Congruence between person and environment, as defined in Holland's theory, is less good at predicting a person's satisfaction in an occupation than might be expected.

Holland's approach to personality assessment is a little unusual. He has developed the *Self-Directed Search* (SDS) (*see* http://www.self-directed-search.com/), which asks the respondent about their preferred activities, reactions to occupational titles, abilities, competencies and even daydreams. People can score their own SDS, establish their three-letter code, and then examine an 'occupations finder' to check which occupations might be appropriate for them. There is also a 'leisure activities finder' for people who are seeking congenial spare-time pursuits. They are encouraged to try various permutations of their three-letter code, especially if their three highest scores are of similar magnitude. All of this is unusual in a number of respects. First, it is rare for questions about both abilities and interests to be included in a vocational guidance instrument. Second, the SDS is deliberately transparent – people can see what it is getting at (Reardon and Lenz, 1998). Third, it is rare for psychologists to allow the people they assess to score and interpret their own data. Holland feels that most people simply need reassurance that their career ideas are appropriate, and that the SDS generally provides this much more quickly and cheaply than careers counselling.

More generally, there are many tests of occupational interests on the market – some paper-and-pencil, many available on the Web. Few have such a strong theoretical and empirical basis as Holland's. One that does is the *Strong Interest Inventory* (Harmon *et al.*, 1994), which has been revised to reflect the Holland types. Data from it have contributed to the classification of occupations in Holland's terms.

Key Learning Point

Holland's self-directed search makes it easy for a person to see for themself what occupations appear to be most suitable.

Theories such as Holland's describe the *content* of actual and ideal decisions, but not the *process*. How can a person make an effective career decision? Several factors are relevant.

Self-awareness and career decisions

To make sound career decisions, a person needs to have a view of their own strengths and weaknesses, values, likes and dislikes. Numerous exercises and techniques are available for this, some in published books that aim to provide a complete practical guide to making and implementing career decisions (e.g. Bolles, 2008; Lees, 2007) and others home-grown in (for example) college careers services. Most are designed to help people to examine systematically their experiences in the work setting and outside it, in order to arrive at the most accurate and complete self-assessment that their past experience allows. Research has suggested that people are not necessarily very accurate in their perceptions of their abilities (Church, 1997), though with practice and by careful comparison with other people, they can improve (Mabe and West, 1982). In Chapter 6 you will find a discussion of why self-awareness may be linked to job performance.

This notion of accuracy assumes of course that there is a 'correct' evaluation of a person, and that assessments of accuracy are derived from statistical analysis of ratings and scores. Although self-help career guides use these a bit, they aim to help a person arrive at a more holistic and descriptive sense of who they are – a qualitative rather than quantitative summary. Saying 'I'm the kind of person who likes to get out of the office and meet people, and enjoys doing different things each day' is quite different from saying 'I think my score on interpersonal skills is better than 70 per cent of the population, and my openness to experience is in the top 15 per cent', and probably more informative for making career decisions. It is also consistent with a narrative approach to careers (Sugarman, 2001), which proposes that we construct and reconstruct stories about our selves and careers that help to make sense (to ourselves and others) of our cumulative experience.

Hall (2002) stresses the importance of being guided by a clear sense of self, but also being flexible enough to change it somewhat in response to experience and the opportunities and constraints of the labour market. This is a departure from the usual psychologists' idea that individual differences are relatively fixed after a fairly early age. Hall also stresses the importance of 'psychological success' in building up a person's identity as a competent person. Objectively verifiable success in tasks leads to greater self-confidence and self-esteem, which in turn encourages the person to take on more challenging tasks, which can lead to more success, and so on.

Knowledge of occupations

Again, there are many workbooks that give guidance on how to find out about occupations (e.g. Hopson and Scally, 2000; Bolles, 2008). Various agencies (for example Connexions in the UK) and commercial companies such as CASCAiD, also provide information about what being in various occupations involves day to day (*see* http://www.connexions-direct.com/jobs4u/ and http://www.cascaid.co.uk/).

Apart from reading published information, methods include talking to a person in that occupation, and 'shadowing' such a person for a period of time in order to see what they actually do. Emphasis is placed on avoiding stereotypes of occupations, and ensuring that one pays attention not only to positions one might ultimately occupy in an occupation, but also to those one will have to fill on the way.

Often it is surprisingly difficult for people to relate what they know about occupations to what they know about self (Yost and Corbishley, 1987, Chapter 5). This is especially the case when a person is trying to choose between fairly similar occupations. As we have seen above with John Holland's theory, one advantage of the better-developed vocational measures is that they do describe people and occupations in the same language, but even then there are usually several occupations to which the person seems well suited. It is the choice between these which is often difficult.

Career exploration

Becoming aware of self and of the world of work requires exploration. Blustein (1997, p. 261) defined career (or vocational) exploration as 'encompassing those activities, directed towards enhancing the knowledge of the self and the external environment, that an individual engages in to foster progress in career development'. In early theorising, career exploration was seen as a life stage that occurs in adolescence and early adulthood (Super, 1957, *see also* next section), or as a stage in the career decision-making process (Tiedeman and O'Hara, 1963), again typically associated with youth. More recent approaches (e.g. Flum and Blustein, 2000) have construed exploration somewhat differently. They see it as a set of activities that a person can (and probably should) engage in throughout life. Also, a key outcome of exploration is the construction and reconstruction of self identity. It is not just about getting a job or choosing an occupation. Instead, exploration can be intrinsically motivated behaviour, performed for its own sake and as an expression of an individual's autonomy and curiosity. Notice that this is highly consistent with the idea that in the protean career a key developmental task is to get the right balance between identity and adaptability.

Stumpf *et al.* (1983) produced a questionnaire measure of the extent to which a person has engaged in career exploration, intends to do so and is satisfied with how they are going about it. This Career Exploration Survey (CES) has been used in a lot of subsequent research. Blustein *et al.* (1994) and Zikic and Klehe (2006) amongst others have shown that engaging in career exploration does aid progress in career decision-making. On the other hand it is difficult to identify what characteristics of a person determine the extent to which they will explore (Bartley and Robitschek, 2000). It seems that exploration of the environment helps successful job search more than exploration of self does (Werbel, 2000). This is perhaps because engaging in self-exploration signals that a person does not yet feel ready to engage in the process of making a career decision. It may also be because exploring the environment also involves some self-exploration when the person asks 'would I like it?'.

Key Learning Point

Good awareness of self and the world of work is often a consequence of willingness to engage in exploration, and a cause of successful career decisions.

Computers and career decision-making

Computer-assisted career exploration and decision-making have been available in various forms for many years, and have developed hugely (Harris-Bowlsbey and Sampson, 2001). Examples of packages available are 'Discover' in the United States, 'Adult Directions' in the United Kingdom and 'Making Better Career Decisions' (MBCD) in Israel. The most common pattern is still for users to be invited to input information about themselves, which is then matched against information about occupations held in the package's database. Some packages – for example Adult Directions – are supported by enormous amounts of regularly updated occupational information. Others are less thorough. The value of these packages depends partly on the validity and reliability of the information held and of the questions they put to users. Nevertheless, there is some evidence that people find computer-assisted careers guidance useful in many (though possibly not all) circumstances, and that it helps move them towards decision-making (Mau, 1999; Gati *et al.*, 2001, 2003). There is also some evidence that people who choose occupations suggested by these systems are more satisfied with their choices than those who do not (e.g. Gati *et al.*, 2006, in the case of MBCD).

The rapid expansion of sources of career information on the Internet makes issues of quality control even more critical. It also adds new issues such as the confidentiality of the information provided by users, and the availability of support for people who might be confused or upset by what a website 'tells' them (Sampson and Lumsden, 2000). That said, there are many interesting sites available that attempt to help people with their careers. Examples are www.Monster.com, www.Proteus-net. co.uk and www.Self-directed-search.com. As one might expect from its name the last of these specialises in Holland's theory. Another site is www.jobhuntersbible.com. This is a supplement to Richard Bolles' best-selling book *What Color is Your Parachute?* which has appeared in many editions over many years.

Decision-making styles, difficulties, and self-efficacy

Phillips *et al.* (1985) identified three styles of career decision-making: *rational*, where advantages and disadvantages of various options are considered logically and systematically, *intuitive*, where various options are considered and the decision is made on 'gut feeling', and *dependent*, where the person essentially denies responsibility for decision-making and waits for other people or circumstances to dictate what they should do. Not surprisingly, it seems that the dependent style is the least successful. The other two are about equally successful when aggregated across large numbers of individuals, though one or the other may suit any particular person best.

However, some of the findings in this area may be somewhat culture-specific. Mau (2000) compared the decision-making styles of a large sample of American and Taiwanese students. Some 32 per cent of the Taiwanese students reported a predominantly dependent style, compared with 11 per cent of the Americans. But in Taiwan, activities such as consulting parents and friends (which might be considered rather weak in the West) are normal and indeed expected activities. It may be misleading to call them dependent.

It tends to be assumed that (i) being decided about an occupation is a good thing and (ii) careers advisers and others can help people only if they know why they are undecided. The first assumption in particular can be challenged. Arnold (1990) argued that career decidedness contributed to psychological well-being only during the transition from education to work, not before. Earl and Bright (2007) found that being decided might be helpful during that transition, but having a clear sense of self was more so. Perhaps a lot depends on how a person reaches their decision. Here the long-established concept of *identity status* (Marcia, 1966) is relevant. Marcia suggested that among young people there are four possible patterns in the development of sense of self:

1   *diffusion:* general vagueness;

2   *foreclosure:* dealing with uncertainty by making quick and early decisions;

3   *moratorium:* deliberately waiting and seeing;

4   *identity achievement:* a clear sense of self based on experience and reflection.

In the context of career decision-making, it seems likely that decisions made as a consequence of foreclosure may be somewhat inappropriate, and based more on a need for certainty than careful consideration of the match between self and career.

In this case decidedness would probably not be a good thing. Conversely, someone in a state of moratorium may be undecided about a career choice, but purposefully so. This person doesn't feel ready to decide: they are not avoiding the issue, nor are they rushing to a premature conclusion. In this case, not being decided seems appropriate.

As a consequence of the second assumption described above, many attempts have been made to identify and analyse the different causes of career indecision. Various factors have been suggested, including lack on information about one's own interests, or abilities, lack of information about the world of work (specific to a work setting or more general), having two or more equally attractive choices, social pressure, e.g. from parents, lack of self-confidence, decision-making anxiety, home–work tensions and habitual indecision (*see* for example Callanan and Greenhaus, 1992; Germeijs and De Boeck, 2003).

Self-efficacy is also important in effective career decision-making. Self-efficacy had been defined as the extent to which a person believes they are capable of performing the behaviour required in any given situation (Bandura, 1977a) – in this case making an appropriate career decision. In the careers field, the concept of Career Decision-Making Self-Efficacy (CDMSE), and a measure of it, has been developed (Taylor and Betz, 1983; Betz *et al.*, 2005). CDMSE is the belief that one is able to complete successfully the tasks necessary for career decision-making, and is thought to have five components based on Crites' (1978) model of career maturity: accurate self-appraisal, gathering occupational information, goal selection, making plans for the future and problem-solving. The concept is prominent and explicit in the attempt by Lent *et al.* (1994) to combine various traditions in vocational psychology in their social cognitive theory of career interests, choice and performance. The key idea is that self-efficacy influences task performance over and above measured ability. In other words, it dictates whether people will perform as well as they are capable. There is some evidence that CDMSE does affect progress through college students' career decision-making (Taylor and Betz, 1983) and among older people too (Gianakos, 1999), though a more recent longitudinal study by Creed *et al.* (2006) found that whilst career decidedness and CDMSE did vary together, there appeared to be no causal relationship. This raises the possibility that feeling a sense of efficacy about careers and making career decisions may both be an outcome of something else. That something else could be identity status. Nauta and Kahn (2007) found that people categorised as 'identity achieved' scored significantly higher on CDMSE than people in all three other identity statuses. Nevertheless, it still seems likely that self-efficacy has some useful outcomes. For example, Saks and Ashforth (1999) found that students' sense of self-efficacy about searching for a job predicted the vigour with which they actually did so, and in turn that vigour predicted their success in getting a well-paid job. Furthermore, Donnay and Borgen (1999) found that self-efficacy in each of Holland's six areas helped to predict the occupations chosen by a large sample of American people. This was even after their Holland occupational interest scores had been accounted for. In other words, like personality, self-efficacy appears to be useful over and above John Holland's typology.

Key Learning Point

The quality of a person's style of decision-making, identity development to date and belief in their own abilities, are all likely to affect how successful their career decision-making is.

Your own career decision-making

1   How clear are you about your abilities and interests? How specific can you be about this? For example, it is not much good simply saying you like being with people. In what situations, and for what purposes do you like being with people? If you are not clear, you might like to reflect further on your past experiences, or seek new ones to find out more about yourself.

2   How much do you know about different occupations? How clear are you about what people in particular occupations actually do, and the conditions (hours, pay, environment) in which they work? If you are not clear, you might like to read more about certain occupations, and/or ask people working in them to tell you what they know.

3   What is your typical decision-making style – rational, intuitive or dependent? How successful have your decisions been in the past? If you tend to make decisions in a dependent manner, you might try to develop one of the other styles, perhaps by practising with small decisions.

4   How much have you engaged in career exploration, and how confident are you about your ability to do so? On the basis of your answers to the previous three questions you may want to consider what aspects of exploration should be your priority.

All change: approaches to lifelong career development

Development through the lifespan

Many social scientists have sought to map out human development in adulthood (*see*, for example, Perlmutter and Hall, 1992). They have often identified age-linked stages of development, each with its own specific concerns and tasks for the person. The aim is ambitious: to map out motivation and development across the whole course of life. Within the context of careers, the work of Donald Super (e.g. 1957, 1990) was influential over a long period of time. Super identified four career stages in his early work:

1   *Exploration:* of both self and world of work in order to clarify the self-concept and identify occupations which fit it. Typical ages: 15–24.

2   *Establishment:* perhaps after one or two false starts, the person finds a career field, and makes efforts to prove their worth in it. Typical ages: 25–44.

3   *Maintenance:* the concern now is to hold onto the niche one has carved for oneself. This can be a considerable task, especially in the face of technological changes and vigorous competition from younger workers. Typical ages: 45–64.

4   *Disengagement:* characterised by decreasing involvement in work and a tendency to become an observer rather than a participant. Typical ages: 65+.

Super's theory reflected some others at the time, in that he saw the late teens and twenties as a time of exploration and self-concept clarification. He viewed the following years as a time when people 'get stuck in' and make themselves indispensable. Super saw this 'getting stuck in' as achievement-oriented, though some others thought more in terms of developing a sense of involvement and belonging. Super's view of middle-age essentially concerns hanging on, while some others have placed more emphasis on creative striving.

Some older research examined whether people's career concerns do indeed match Super's stages (e.g. Veiga, 1983; Isabella, 1988). The results suggest some distinctions between stages, but they are not very clear-cut. As Hall (1986, Chapter 4) pointed out, it is difficult to identify what career stage a person is in, especially if, for example, they enter a career relatively late in life. Also, of course, the changing nature of careers makes it much more difficult to link stages with ages. In fact, Super (1980, 1990) acknowledged this, and developed a much more flexible framework for mapping a person's life and career. He identified six roles people typically perform in Western societies: homemaker, worker, citizen, leisurite, student and child. The importance of each of these roles in a person's life can rise and fall over time. Also, at any given time, a person can be at different stages (exploration, establishment, etc.) in different roles.

So the original notion of career stages has now become priorities, or concerns, that an individual may have at any point in their adult life. These insights do not in themselves create a theory, but they do help people to consider their lives in a systematic way (Super, 1990). Some self-assessment devices such as the Adult Career Concerns Inventory (Super *et al.*, 1985; Perrone *et al.*, 2003) and the Salience Inventory (Super and Nevill, 1985) have been developed to assist in this process. In spite of the increased flexibility these days around Super's ideas, his original career stages are still sometimes used to frame other thinking about careers. For example, in discussing how people become embedded in their occupations and organisations, Ng and Feldman (2007) propose somewhat different processes for the establishment, maintenance and disengagement stages. Gibson (2003) found that the ways in which people use role models to help shape their identities changed between career stages.

Key Learning Point

Donald Super proposed stage theories of career development. He later loosened the connection between ages and stages, and broadened the focus from career to other domains of life.

Of the many other attempts to map out adult life, that of Levinson and colleagues (1978) and Levinson and Levinson (1996) has been the most influential. This influence is perhaps surprising, given that in their original study (1978), Levinson and his colleagues conducted interviews (albeit in-depth ones) with only 40 American-born men between the ages of 35 and 45. Nevertheless, they came up with some interesting conclusions. They proposed that in each of three eras of adulthood (early, middle and late) there are alternating stable and transitional periods (Figure 15.5). For example, early adulthood (ages 17–40) begins with the *early adult transition* (ages 17–22), where the person seeks a niche in the adult world. Then comes a stable phase *entering the adult world* (ages 22–28), where the task is to

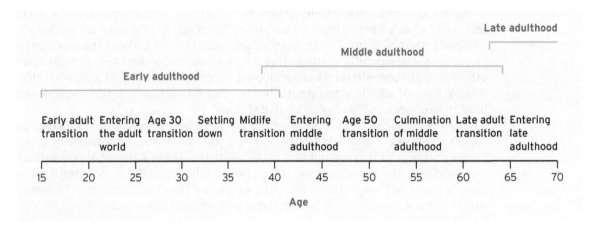

Figure 15.5   **Phases of development in adulthood**
Source: Adapted from Levinson and colleagues (1978).

explore various roles while keeping one's options open. Next, between 28 and 33, comes the *age 30 transition*, where the person appraises their experiences and searches for a satisfactory lifestyle. This is followed by a stable settling down phase, when that lifestyle is implemented. This was called Boom (Becoming One's Own Man) by Levinson, who felt that it was a key time for men to achieve in their occupational lives.

The *midlife transition* (ages 40–45) identified by Levinson has often been considered the most significant aspect of his work. He argued that the lifestyle is reappraised at this age, often with considerable urgency and emotion – so much so, that it is sometimes referred to as the 'midlife crisis'. People realise that their life is probably at least half over and this concentrates their minds on what they should be doing with the rest of it. In the eyes of their children they are now symbols of authority, old-timers. Physical signs of ageing become unmistakable. There are by now clear indications of whether or not earlier career ambitions will be achieved. These factors can lead to substantial life changes: for example, a change of career or a change of spouse. Alternatively, a commitment to the current lifestyle may be reaffirmed, and increased effort put into it. Despite the popularity of the midlife crisis concept, there is in fact little evidence that men generally find it an especially troubling time (Lawrence, 1980).

After the midlife transition comes *entering middle adulthood* (45–50), then the *age 50* transition (50–55), then the *culmination of middle adulthood* (55–60). These all concern implementing and living with midlife decisions. The *late adult transition* and *late adulthood* follow. Levinson was very clear that his stages were closely linked with age. He argued that the lives of particular individuals may look very different on the surface, but underlying them are similar personal issues (Levinson, 1986). This is a crucial point. Often, people who read about Levinson's theory dismiss it because (for example) they know many people who make changes such as moving jobs during what Levinson calls a stable period. However, according to Levinson, stable periods are stable in the sense that the person has a fairly unchanging purpose and overall pattern of life. Changing jobs does not contradict that – indeed, people may move to a new job precisely *because* the old one fails to help them achieve their stable personal goals.

Key Learning Point

Levinson proposed a closely age-linked series of phases in adult life. The phases were alternately transitional and stable in terms of tasks facing the person.

STOP TO CONSIDER

Are stage theories like those of Super and Levinson a description of human development across eras and cultures, or do they depend on certain organisational and societal structures? If so, what structures?

Developmental tasks and mid/late career

Super and Levinson's theories, and other similar ones, developed from post-Freudian analyses of the experiences and struggles people face as they go through life. Especially influential here was Erikson (1968, 1980). Erikson proposed that we journey through eight stages of psychosocial development, each with its key developmental task that must be tackled before the person is ready to move forward. A key task that many people face in the middle and later parts of their career is to pass on something of themselves and their achievements to future generations. There are signs of this concern in Levinson's ideas about the midlife crisis. This is often termed *generativity,* and the nature of this construct and its role in people's lives has been receiving some research attention (e.g. Peterson and Stewart, 1996). Related to this, in many economies ageing populations, increasing life expectancy and problems with pension provision all mean that working lives for many people will extend further into later life. So Super's characterisation of mid–late career as being about holding on to what you have and then disengaging seems a little over-simplified and out of tune with twenty-first-century careers. As well as generativity, then, we need to consider how people can keep on growing their skills, know-how and understanding at this time of life.

Clark and Arnold (2008) have investigated personal growth and generativity amongst a sample of 41 men aged 45–55 in England. Personal growth was defined in terms of (i) skills/knowledge/achievement; (ii) self-understanding/integration; and (iii) depth/quality of relationships. Generativity was defined as accomplishments and activities which reflect concern for the next and future generations, as expressed in (i) productivity; (ii) nurturance of family; (iii) care for society and its values and institutions; and (iv) leadership. They found that generativity was more on men's minds than growth, and that most growth that occurred was the first type. The third type was rare. Growth was good for psychological well-being, even though many men didn't seek it – often it came through unexpected events or crisis (but rarely a 'midlife crisis'). Most generativity occurred outside work, especially in the family setting. So-called 'mature radius' generativity (that is, generativity outside one's immediate family and friends) was associated with good psychological well-being and with growth. There were big differences in generativity and growth between occupations, which suggests that to some extent these phenomena are located as much in the day-to-day demands placed on people as in their own internal developmental path.

A more sociolinguistic way of looking at career development is to construe it as the need for a person to construct and continuously revise narratives or stories that account for their career so far, in whole or in part (*see* Sugarman, 2001). This task is ever-present throughout the career, but perhaps becomes more vital in mid- and late career. That is because by then a considerable accumulation of experiences and events requires explanation, and (according to Erikson) being able to come to terms with how one's life has been becomes an increasingly salient task. Gergen and Gergen (1988) suggested that the personal narrative we construct (the story we tell ourselves about our lives and careers) is the basic, internal structure that allows us to both experience continuity and accommodate change. In other words, we need a coherent story to tell ourselves and others, a story that accounts both for what changes and what stays the same. This story may change over time, and indeed at any given time there may be different stories for different audiences. This is not to suggest dishonesty or deception. Rather, it reflects that different audiences will be interested in different elements of the career and different ways of explaining or justifying career action. So the reasons we emphasise for leaving a job when talking with our friends may be different from those we emphasise in an interview for a new job.

Key Learning Point

As lives and careers become longer, it may be necessary to develop a more sophisticated view of the stages and concerns of mid- and late career.

Implications and critiques of stage theories

Taken at face value, these approaches to adult development have implications for career management in organisations. If people are going to work effectively, the needs and concerns of their life stage should be taken into account. Therefore, in early adulthood, people must be given the opportunity to integrate themselves into an organisation and/or career, and demonstrate their worth to themselves and others. This may involve special efforts to give the newcomer significant work assignments and social support. In mid-career, it may be necessary to provide opportunities for some people to retrain, perhaps in the light of a midlife reappraisal. They could also be given opportunities to allow them to keep up to date in their chosen field. It may also be helpful to give people in their mid- to late career a chance to act as mentor or guide to younger employees (*see* Mentoring, below) – this is, after all, a way of handing on one's accumulated wisdom and thereby making a lasting impression.

These developmental theories are all vulnerable to the accusation that they really only reflect the lives of middle-class males in Western countries in the mid- to late-twentieth century. As Sullivan and Crocitto (2007, p. 283) have put it:

> The intent of the early developmental career theories . . . . was to describe the work life of the typical post-World War II professional. At that time, the average employee was a man who worked for one or two organisations until retirement, while his wife was at home caring for their children.

Much has changed since the time these theories were developed. As noted above, many people think that work has become much less predictable, with more changing of jobs and occupations. The respective roles of women and men have changed substantially, though perhaps not fundamentally. The lifespan theories of Levinson and Super have been particularly heavily criticised for focusing on the experiences and personal concerns of men to the exclusion of those of women. For example, Bardwick (1980) and Gallos (1989), among others, argued that women focus more on attachment and affiliation in their development, in contrast to men, who emphasise separateness and achievement. Nevertheless, although some developmental issues are more problematic for women than for men, Levinson and Levinson (1996) argued that the same underlying concerns arise at the same ages for both sexes. So whereas for a man the age 30 transition might focus mainly on occupational concerns, for a woman it might concern whether and when to have children. The issues are different but the theme of fine-tuning the direction of one's life is the same (Roberts and Newton, 1987).

Whilst these traditional stage theories might be applicable to women, they may nevertheless not be the best potentially available. O'Neil and Bilimoria (2005) conducted an in-depth study of 60 women. They suggested that their careers could be divided into three quite long phases:

1   **Phase 1: idealistic achievement:** Emphasis on personal control, career satisfaction and achievement, and positive impact on others. Typically in the woman's 20s and early 30s.

2   **Phase 2: pragmatic endurance:** Doing what has to be done, whilst managing multiple relationships and responsibilities. Less personal control; more dissatisfaction especially with organisations and managers. Typically in the woman's mid-30s to late 40s.

3   **Phase 3: reinventive contribution:** To organisations, families and communities, without losing sight of self. Careers as learning opportunities and a chance to make a difference to others. Typically from around age 50 onwards.

Gersick and Kram (2002) reported a small-scale but intensive study with ten women aged 45–55 working for a large American financial company. They then cross-checked their initial findings in discussions/workshops with another 20 women in the same company. Their conclusions were somewhat similar to those of O'Neil and Bilimoria (2005), but the view of mid-career was somewhat more positive. There were trade-offs to be made between career and family. Whilst these were not always easy, for these women they often coincided with the 1970s which was an era of growing opportunity for many women. Like Levinson, Gersick and Kram noted that some issues reliably came to the fore at certain ages. For example, the career–family balance was re-evaluated around the age of 40. They noted (p. 121) that their interviewees grew up a few years after those in the Levinson and Levinson (1996) study, and this might have been crucial to their experiences of career:

Levinson (1996) portrayed women facing the same basic developmental tasks as men but [women] were hampered by external oppression and internal conflicts that make it much harder to succeed. The cohort differences we described suggest that some of the external obstacles are receding. Our participants' exuberance about career and family suggests that the internal battle is also changing. This preliminary study does not contradict Levinson's model, but it does suggest that the enduring developmental challenges for women may have less to do with overcoming [traditional gender roles] and more straightforwardly to do with individuation and relationship . . . The task of finding a life role concerns a woman's realization that she cannot build a life simply on her relationship to others as mother and wife: She must also make some decisions about where she herself wants to go and take initiatives to get there.

Exercise 15.4   Career stages

Jenny Peterson is 46 years old and had been working in the sales function of a large retailer since she was 18. She had found her early years quite difficult, and for a time wondered how she had ended up in the job. There seemed to be a lot to learn, both about the job and about life in general, especially as she married quite young and had her first child (of three) when she was 23. During those years, however, she gradually found that she could handle the tasks, and that some of them were quite enjoyable. She felt that her capacity to take advantage of new opportunities at work at that time was somewhat limited by her childcare and other home responsibilities, but would nevertheless have welcomed some chances to develop herself. By the time she was 32, she felt confident that she could cope with anything that came her way, but wondered whether she really wanted to work for the company. She thought a great deal about whether or not she liked its people and philosophy and was on the verge of leaving more than once. Over the next decade, however, she slowly but surely found herself feeling more attached to both. By her late 30s, her children were past the most dependent stage and Jenny noticed that she had more freedom and energy than many of her female colleagues who started families later than her. Suddenly more opportunities seemed to come her way, and her senior male colleagues seemed to have stopped thinking of her as a 'young mum' who would inevitably put family before work (that had never quite been the case, but somehow the men didn't seem to be able to get it out of their heads). She was now taken more seriously, and from her late 30s to mid-40s enjoyed several interesting new assignments and two promotions. Now a different matter was bothering her. Some of the younger staff seemed to know more than she did about sales techniques and marketing strategies, and she struggled to keep up with their new ideas. Was she already obsolete at age 46, she wondered?

Suggested exercise

Consider the extent to which Jenny Peterson's career so far is consistent with the lifespan analyses of career described in this section.

Key Learning Point

Women and men tend to have different developmental paths. Career theory and practice still reflect men's perspectives better than women's.

Career management in organisations

Around the end of the twentieth century, some organisations responded to the trends described earlier in this chapter by giving up any attempt to manage the careers of employees. Because traditional career paths have disappeared and organisational structures are continually changing, some senior HR managers believed (and a few still believe) that there did not seem much point in attempting corporate management of careers. The term 'self-development' is now frequently used. As the words suggest, it means that individual employees are responsible for identifying their own development needs, and for doing something about them. Making the most of this necessity to look after your own career by using your own strategies is the idea behind what is sometimes called career self-management (*see* Z. King, 2004). Refer back to the opening case study of this chapter for good illustrations of how some people approach this. However, self-development and self-management seem to mean slightly different things in different places. On the one hand, it can be quite an aggressive message: 'You're on your own; look after yourself.' Alternatively, it can be more supportive: 'Don't expect the organisation to tell you how you need to develop, but we can play a part in helping you to make and implement your own decisions.'

Hirsh and Jackson (2004) among others have argued that labour market uncertainties make it more, not less, important for organisations to participate in the management of employees' careers. True, it's not easy to anticipate every future career step and when it will happen. But complete predictability is not required for career management to be useful. Hirsh and Jackson (2004, p. 6) argue that career management should matter to organisations because:

■ Careers are the way in which people accumulate skills and knowledge that are of use to the organisation.

■ Related to this, careers are how skills and knowledge are deployed and spread in organisations.

■ The movement of people around an organisation is how its culture and values are transmitted.

■ People want to know where they stand, and clear statements about how careers will be managed helps in this.

■ Career development is a major way of attracting, motivating and retaining able employees.

An analysis of some of the techniques available and how they fit in with organisational human resource management strategies has been provided by Baruch (2004). Table 15.5 (overleaf) describes some of the interventions that can be used in organisations to manage careers. It is difficult to obtain accurate figures on which interventions are used most, though evidence from Iles and Mabey (1993) and Baruch and Peiperl (2000) is helpful. It looks as if internal vacancy advertising is nearly universal. Lateral moves and succession planning seem to be used by more than half of the organisations questioned. Perhaps surprisingly, so is counselling either by the line manager or human resources staff – though this may be slightly wishful thinking by those reporting on behalf of their organisation. Mentoring seems to be becoming increasingly common, with perhaps 50 per cent of medium to large-size organisations either running organised schemes or actively encouraging the formation of informal mentor–protégé pairings. Formal career path information is (or is said to be) provided in about one-third of organisations, which is perhaps surprising given frequent and major structural changes and the disappearance of career paths in many organisations. Self-assessment materials, development centres (which are very similar in design to the assessment centres described in Chapter 5), career planning workshops and career counselling probably feature in one quarter- or one-sixth of organisations.

Key Learning Point

There are many different career management interventions available to organisations, and some organisations use several of them.

Several of the career management interventions shown in Table 15.5 (for example, mentoring, coaching and career action centres) can be used to support self-development rather than organisational control of careers. On the whole, the interventions are used to pursue organisational goals, and in some organisations the notion of managing careers has rather come back into fashion. This is partly a reaction to the fact that the choices people make about their self-development do not necessarily serve the needs of the organisation. For example, a company's IT specialists may tend to seek training on a popular software package which helps them to maintain their employability, but which happens to be of little use to that company.

It is neither possible nor desirable to use all of the interventions in the same organisation at the same time. Hirsh *et al.* (1995) pointed out that it is much better to do a few things well than a lot badly. It is also necessary to be clear about what an intervention is designed to achieve, and on whose behalf. Possible purposes are:

- filling vacancies – that is, selecting one or more people for specific posts;

- assessment of potential, competencies, skills or interests – this might help an organisation to assess its human resources, or individuals to know how well placed they are to obtain specific jobs inside or outside the organisation;

- development of skills and competencies – in order to help an organisation to function effectively in its markets, or individuals to be more effective in future jobs;

- identification of career options – that is, what types of work or specific posts might be obtainable for one or more individuals;

- action to implement career plans.

Key Learning Point

It is important that the purpose(s) of career management interventions are clearly defined and stated.

Table 15.5	Career management interventions in organisations

1   *Internal vacancy notification.* Information about jobs available in the organisation, normally in advance of any external advertising, with a job description and some details of preferred experience, qualifications.

2   *Career paths.* Information about the sequences of jobs that people can do, or competencies they can acquire, in the organisation. This should include details of how high in the organisation any path goes, the kinds of interdepartmental transfers that are possible, and perhaps the skills/experience required to follow various paths.

3   *Career workbooks.* These consist of questions and exercises designed to guide individuals in determining their strengths and weaknesses, identifying job and career opportunities and determining necessary steps for reaching their goals.

4   *Career planning workshops.* These cover some of the same ground as workbooks, but offer more chance for discussion, feedback from others, information about organisation-specific opportunities and policies. They may include psychometric testing.

5   *Computer-assisted career management.* Various packages exist for helping employees to assess their skills, interests and values and translate these into job options. Sometimes those options are customised to a particular organisation. A few packages designed for personnel or manpower planning also include some career-relevant facilities.

6   *Individual counselling.* Can be done by specialists from inside or outside the organisation, or by line managers who have received training. May include psychometric testing.

7   *Training and educational opportunities.* Information and financial support about, and possibly delivery of, courses in the organisation or outside it. These can enable employees to update, retrain or deepen their knowledge in particular fields. In keeping with the notion of careers involving sequences, training in this context is not solely to improve performance in a person's present job.

8   *Personal development plans (PDPs).* These often arise from the appraisal process and other sources such as development centres. PDPs are statements of how a person's skills and knowledge might appropriately develop, and how this development could occur in a given timescale.

9   *Career action centres.* Resources such as literature, videos and CD-ROMs and perhaps more personal inputs such as counselling available to employees on a drop-in basis.

10 *Development centres.* Like assessment centres in that participants are assessed on the basis of their performance in a number of exercises and tests. However, development centres focus on identifying a person's strengths, weaknesses and styles for the purpose of development, instead of (or as well as) selection.

11 *Mentoring programmes.* Attaching employees to more senior ones who act as advisers, and perhaps also as advocates, protectors and counsellors.

12 *Coaching.* This is defined in various ways, and can be similar to mentoring. It usually involves one-to-one sessions between coach and 'coachee', where the former helps the latter address issues regarding adjustment and performance at work (and possibly outside it).

13 *Succession planning.* The identification of individuals who are expected to occupy key posts in the future, and who are exposed to experiences which prepare them appropriately.

14 *Job assignments/rotation.* Careful use of work tasks can help a person to stay employable for the future, and an organisation to benefit from the adaptability of staff.

15 *Outplacement.* This may involve several interventions listed above. Its purpose is to support people who are leaving the organisation to clarify and implement plans for their future.

16 *Secondment.* Individuals work temporarily in another organisation, or in another part of the same one.

Any intervention might achieve more than one purpose, but it is important to be clear about what purpose(s) it is designed for. It is also necessary, according to Hirsh *et al.* (1995), to be clear about who in the organisation is eligible to participate in interventions – preferably everyone. The operation of a career management intervention must be consistent with its goals. So, for example, it would be inappropriate for detailed feedback about performance in a development centre to be withheld from participants if an aim of the development centre was to help people identify their career options.

One reason why some HR managers are wary of these interventions is the fear that they may help people realise that they want to leave that organisation, and/or equip them to do so. A glib response to this is that if people truly do not fit with the organisation, it will be a good thing for both parties if they leave. However, given the cost and inconvenience of recruiting replacements for leavers, it is not easy to keep that in mind. Research has not yet produced a clear answer to whether the provision of career management by organisations increases employee commitment or on the other hand employees' willingness to consider leaving. There is a little evidence that both can happen simultaneously (Ito and Brotheridge, 2005). It may also be the case that where organisations both encourage people to self-manage their careers and facilitate this via career management interventions, increased loyalty can result (Sturges *et al.*, 2002).

We will now briefly describe three career management interventions that are of particular interest to work psychologists. Notice how two of them feature in the opening case study of this chapter. The interest of work psychologists in these three interventions tends to be high because each of them includes (i) some form of assessment of a person and/or (ii) the development of a relationship between two people.

Career counselling

Much of the career counselling literature focuses on young people making choices of occupation. However, career counselling is a much broader activity than that, especially in the context of organisational career interventions rather than college career services. Career counselling has been defined by Nathan and Hill (2006, p. 2) as 'a process which enables people to recognise and utilise their resources to make career-related decisions and manage career-related issues'. One might add that this process is an interpersonal one, in order to distinguish counselling from (for example) computer-aided guidance.

There are several different approaches to career counselling, some of which draw very directly on specific traditions in psychology (*see* Chapter 1; *see also* Whiston and Oliver, 2005). One approach relies heavily on the use of psychometric tests and here the counsellor tends to give advice on the basis of the test results. However, the most common approach to counselling can be described as person-centred, based loosely on Carl Rogers' humanist ideas (*see* Chapter 1). The counsellor does not generally give advice, but helps the client clarify their ideas about self and world of work by offering unconditional positive regard and asking open-ended questions. Many writers identify different phases of a counselling interaction (e.g. Reddy, 1987; Nelson-Jones, 2009; Kidd, 2006). The phases they identify tend to be fairly similar though not identical. Reddy (1987) described them as follows:

■ *Understanding*: the counsellor focuses on listening to what the client is saying, and observing the associated non-verbal behaviour. The counsellor seeks to show no more than understanding. Listening requires concentration. Normal everyday conversation often involves surprisingly little listening, so a person who is being a counsellor needs to work on it.

- *Challenging*: as Reddy (1987) pointed out, listening helps for a lot longer than one might think, but not for ever. The aim of this second phase is to help a client shift their thinking by probing for further information, challenging apparent inconsistency, summarising what the counsellor thinks the client has said, and perhaps by giving information. Suggesting interpretations and picking out themes are other possible counsellor techniques of this stage, *but not before.*

- *Resourcing*: having clarified the feeling (phase 1) and thinking (phase 2), possible decisions and plans of action often emerge. Here the counsellor's role is often to help the client to fine-tune plans, perhaps by giving coaching in job-seeking techniques, and suggesting sources of further information.

Key Learning Point

Career counselling is more about listening than giving advice. Also, it concerns any career-related issue, not just choosing an occupation.

Career counselling is offered by a number of individuals and agencies in education and private practice. It can also occur much more informally through work colleagues, friends or relatives. Some organisations offer (and pay for) career counselling for staff, normally delivered by an independent consultant who has no stake in the organisation and who can therefore work purely in the client's interest. Perhaps understandably, it is common for organisations to offer career counselling only when there is an immediate and obvious need, such as when people are being made redundant. Whatever the situation in which counselling occurs, it is important that the counsellor maintains confidentiality. Nothing that is said or done in the counselling sessions can normally be revealed to anyone else, except with the client's permission.

Evaluations of the impact of career counselling focus mainly on young people of college age. On the whole, it seems that counselling has more positive outcomes than interventions that do not use counselling, and no intervention at all (Whiston *et al.*, 2003). However, there is little published evidence about the effectiveness of counselling in organisational settings. This is probably because many organisations would want to keep such evaluations confidential, and also because it is not easy to define and measure effectiveness criteria.

Development centres

Development centres are attractive to work psychologists because of their similarity to assessment centres which are commonly used in selection. Psychologists have over many years studied the effectiveness of assessment centres and also their psychometric properties (for examples *see* Woehr and Arthur, 2003). Consequently, development centres tend to be soundly designed with exercises carefully devised to allow assessment of candidates' competencies, and well-trained assessors observing the candidates. The trickier issues concern how the development centre is used in career development. It is often said that development centres are intended to identify people's development needs rather than select them, but in reality development centres are often partly about selection. For example, they may be used to decide who gets on to a fast-track promotion scheme. This can mean that candidates try to hide their weaknesses, thus making it more difficult for assessors to identify their development needs (Woodruffe, 1993).

Studies of development centres in real organisations show that it really is difficult for assessment and development to mix if the assessment process is used to give people an overall grading, and especially if that grading affects their future prospects (Arnold, 2002). Indeed, the inclusion of an overall evaluation can affect the willingness of people attending a development centre to pay attention to, and act upon, feedback from it. This is especially the case if the evaluation is less positive than the person thought it should be (Woo *et al.*, 2008). A related issue is whether plans for personal development are drawn up after the centre sessions, and if so whether they are implemented. Carrick and Williams' (1999) review of the field suggested that this is a continuing problem because hard-pressed line managers may be unwilling to devote time and energy to developing others, and in any case may lack the skills for doing so. There may also be ambiguity concerning whose responsibility it is to implement a development plan.

Key Learning Point

It is relatively easy to design a technically sound development centre, but much more difficult to ensure that individual development plans are drawn up and implemented.

Mentoring

Mentoring has been defined in a number of ways, but perhaps the most widely quoted definition is that of Kram (1985):

> a relationship between a young adult and an older, more experienced adult that helps the younger individual learn to navigate in the adult world and the world of work. A mentor supports, guides and counsels the young adult as he or she accomplishes this important task.

Not all other definitions are quite as broad as this. They focus on the work context, not life as a whole, and often they assume that part of what the mentor does is to help the recipient of mentoring to progress up career hierarchies. However, most share Kram's assumptions that the mentor is older than the person being mentored, the person being mentored is in early career, and that mentoring is a one-to-one relationship.

Mentoring can fulfil a number of specific functions for the person being mentored (who is normally called the protégé). Kram (1985) divided these into *career functions* and *psychosocial functions*. The career functions include sponsorship, where the mentor promotes the interests of the protégé by putting them forward for desirable projects or job moves; exposure and visibility to high-ranking people;

coaching the protégé by sharing ideas and suggesting strategies; protecting the protégé from risks to their reputation; and (if the mentor is in a position to do so) providing challenging work assignments for the protégé. The psychosocial functions include acting as a role model for the protégé; providing acceptance and confirmation; frank discussion of the protégé's anxieties and fears; and friendship. Mentoring has become a popular technique for developing younger employees; so much so that claims like 'everyone needs a mentor' (Clutterbuck, 2004) are taken seriously.

Psychologists have been very keen to research mentoring, especially its impact on those who receive it. It is potentially an effective way of socialising new employees and passing on accumulated wisdom. It also offers some people in mid- or late career the chance to be a mentor, which may appeal to their career and life concerns, and can introduce a motivating new element to their job. Many studies suggest that people who have been mentored enjoy better salaries and promotion rates, at least under some circumstances (Whitley *et al.*, 1991; Aryee and Chay, 1994). Allen *et al.* (2004) and Underhill (2006) have both provided helpful meta-analyses of the relevant literature. They report that in studies that directly compared people who had received mentoring with those who had not, receipt of mentoring showed a small but statistically significant association with earnings and promotions, and a slightly bigger one with career satisfaction. Amongst those who received mentoring, similar findings were reported for the extent to which the mentor provided career support (*see* above). The provision of psychosocial support was associated with career and job satisfaction but not with earnings and promotions. The extent to which the mentor was reported to have provided the career benefits of mentoring was associated with both provisions. The benefits of mentoring seem stronger when the mentoring is informal (i.e. it happens spontaneously) rather than formal, where it happens because there is a mentoring scheme that people have to participate in (Chao *et al.*, 1992).

It is less clear whether receiving mentoring is actually what produces the benefits. There are certainly examples of mentoring failing to provide significant benefits to any of the parties involved (e.g. Arnold and Johnson, 1997). There has also been some concern that mentoring can actually cause harm – for example a mentor may stifle the protégé or have unrealistic expectations of them (Scandura, 1998). This 'dark side' of mentoring seems to be relatively rarely experienced, but it does happen (Eby and McManus, 2004). There has also been some attention to the mentor's perspective, particularly concerning what makes potential mentors more or less inclined to fulfil the role (Allen *et al.*, 1997). Perhaps the people who experience mentoring tend to have certain characteristics (for example, an ability to get themselves noticed by effective mentors, or to be selected by organisations offering mentoring) which would have brought them success even without mentoring. Some modest support for this hypothesis has been provided by Singh *et al.* (2009), who found that people who had high expectations of advancement and who took initiatives in promoting their career were more likely to report having found an informal mentor a year later.

It is likely that some mentoring schemes work better than others. It is probably important that mentors and protégés want the relationship, and they may well need training and orientation in order to make the most of it. The goals of the mentoring scheme should be clear and specific. The mentor's work performance should be assessed and rewarded partly on the basis of how effectively they are carrying out the mentoring role. The culture of the organisation should be one that values personal and professional development. Even then there is a danger that mentors will hand on outdated knowledge and skills to protégés, especially in times of rapid change.

Although interest in mentoring seems to be very long-lasting, related concepts have also received more attention in recent years. For example, some work psychologists earn their living by offering *coaching*, usually to managers. Coaching may simply be a new word for the same activities as mentoring, but it may also signal a shift to a more performance-focused approach where the emphasis is more on improving quality of work now than on long-term career or general psychological well-being. There is also a move towards considering how networks of people, not just one mentor, can help in career development (Higgins and Thomas, 2001; Molloy, 2005). In fact it is possible that people who report having a mentor also have a broad social network, the members of which contribute to the person's development (Blickle *et al.*, 2009). This could mean either that the mentor acts as a source of new contacts, or that having a mentor is simply a sign of a proactive approach to engaging others in one's development. The first possibility would mean that mentoring still played a key (mediating) role, but the second would suggest that having a mentor in itself does not contribute greatly to career development.

Key Learning Point

Mentoring has potential benefits for all parties involved, but it is not easy to achieve those benefits with an organised mentoring scheme.

Summary

Careers concern the sequence of jobs people hold, and the attitudes and behaviours associated with them. Labour market and organisational changes have made the careers experienced by many people less predictable than they once were, and a sense of injustice and broken promises is quite common among employees in work organisations. It is increasingly recognised that choices frequently have to be re-made later in careers, and that between choices many significant developments can occur. Much career development theory and practice therefore attempts to identify people's concerns at different stages of their lives, though research on career choice still tends to treat it as a choice of a type of work made by young people on the basis of their relatively static personal characteristics. Psychologists have produced helpful theories for understanding different types of people and different types of job. They have also produced some practical ways in which individuals can improve their own choice of occupation. There is also some useful guidance concerning what helps people be successful in their careers, but there is a need for more flexible thinking about what career success might mean apart from promotion and pay increases. In general, career theory tends to reflect men's perspectives better than women's. It is based on men's lives and men's values. Given the increasing frequency of job changes, there is also a lot of attention paid to how individuals and organisations can manage transitions from one job to another. Some organisations attempt to manage the career development of their employees. A number of techniques can be used to achieve this, including mentoring, careers counselling and development centres. Current trends are towards increasing flexibility of career structures, and towards identifying how career development systems can be implemented and maintained successfully within organisations.

Closing Case Study | Charity careers

There was a time when charities had to rely on inspired volunteers and passionate but not necessarily well-qualified individuals for their employment base. In recent years, this has changed and today entering the non-profit sector at graduate level is an increasingly competitive business.

For a start, the profile of the charitable sector has been rising rapidly. With figures such as Bill Gates and international celebrities such as Angelina Jolie championing causes, the sector is of intense interest to the new generation of cause-driven graduates.

'The 20-somethings and early 30-somethings are more interested in making a difference than making a fortune,' says Gib Bulloch, director of Accenture Development Partnerships, a non-profit arm of Accenture that sends select staff to work for non-profit groups in developing countries. 'They've been growing up with these issues and they want something different out of their career.'

Moreover, non-profit groups are becoming more professional and effective than their predecessors and offering better salaries. 'Charities are recognising the value of people with different skill sets,' says Salvatore LaSpada, chief executive of the UK-based Institute for Philanthropy. 'They realise they need to pay for that, so salaries are going up.'

They are also looking for a new level of skills and experience in the people they consider as employees. 'The big change is that whereas before it was dominated by passion-driven but not necessarily well-managed organizations, now they're more strategic, more skilfully using public communications and placing more emphasis on benchmarking and evaluation,' says Mr LaSpada.

For graduates, this means securing the kinds of charity jobs to which they aspire is becoming even harder. Zoe Perrott, team manager at Eden Brown, the recruitment consultancy, has been working with the charity sector for seven years. She says jobs in non-profit organizations have always been highly sought-after by graduates.

The majority of responses to Eden Brown's advertisements for non-profit jobs are from graduates, according to Ms Perrott. 'About 50 per cent have masters degrees and a lot of them are from Cambridge and Oxford,' she says. 'I've always found the sector incredibly popular with graduates. We get always about 300 CVs for every advert.'

As a result, graduates hoping to pursue a career in the non-profit sector may have to start by taking low-ranking positions and be prepared to progress slowly through the sector. 'So we might not necessarily get them their dream job but we'll give them an opportunity to go into a charity network and they then work their way up through an organization,' says Ms Perrott.

This, however, requires some tough conversations with students. 'When they're idealistic, it's very difficult,' she says. 'They come in with all these wonderful ideas but they have to start at the bottom and be prepared to do anything and everything.' Adding to the competition is the fact that, as more business people make the switch from the corporate world to the non-profit sector, charities have an expanding pool of talented and experienced recruits from which to hire their more senior staff.

Even so, the non-profit sector is approaching a leadership deficit, with baby boomers starting to retire. Mr LaSpada argues that, as a result, non-profit organizations will need to get better at helping young employees rise up through the organization. Some of the larger non-profit organizations are starting to do so. The United Nations World Food Programme, for example, has a career management framework, supported by a new IT system, that brings together its recruitment and staff development initiatives designed not only to hire people but also to establish what they are interested in and find them assignments that will prepare them for future positions in the organization.

Addaction, the leading UK drug and alcohol treatment charity, offers learning and development opportunities as well as a chance to gain professional accreditations through organizations such as the Open College Network and the Open University, with which the charity offers a Leading for Results training course for managers.

The UK's Charities Aid Foundation, which promotes the effectiveness of charities and social enterprises, has in-house training facilities. 'A great way to retain talented staff is not only to move them up the ladder within the organization,' says Mr LaSpada, 'but also to provide them with lifelong learning opportunities.'

Source: 'Charities: Passion and skills in aid of a good cause', *The Financial Times,* 13 October 2008 (Murray, S.), copyright © Sarah Murray. With permission.

Suggested exercises

1   According to this article, what career anchors might be well-suited to work in charities? Are these changing and if so, how?

2   What role do career management interventions play in charities' attempts to manage their human resources? Could this role be expanded, and if so, how?

3   In what ways does this article portray bureaucratic forms of career, and in what ways does it portray other forms?

Test your learning

Short-answer questions

1   Describe the reasons why careers are more difficult to manage than they used to be.

2   What are the distinguishing features of protean and boundaryless careers?

3   List some of the available criteria for assessing objective and subjective career success.

4   What vocational personality types have been identified by John Holland, and how are they related to each other?

5   List three limitations of Holland's theory.

6   In what ways is self-efficacy significant in career decision-making?

7 What phases of adult life were identified by Daniel Levinson, and what are the main characteristics of each stage?

8 According to Schein, what is a career anchor? List at least six of the anchors Schein proposed.

9 Define eight techniques that can be used in organisations to manage careers.

10 Define mentoring and outline its potential benefits.

11 Describe two key research findings that show how women are at a disadvantage relative to men in their careers.

Suggested assignments

1 Critically examine the extent to which labour market changes are affecting the careers that people experience.

2 Critically analyse the extent to which the concepts of the boundaryless career and the protean career are advancing our understanding of careers.

3 Discuss how the different definitions of career can influence how career success is construed.

4 Examine the extent to which John Holland's theory has improved our understanding of careers.

5 What, if anything, can career/life stage theories contribute to effective career management?

6 Using examples, examine the likely impact of career management interventions in organisations.

Relevant websites

A good example of a site geared to helping people manage their own careers (especially internationally mobile ones) is http://www.expatica.com/nl/employment.html. It gives information about the current job market in several European countries, and also advice about how to present oneself effectively across cultures, and survive and prosper when starting a new job in an unfamiliar culture.

A website to make you think about careers in diverse ways is Career-learning at http://www.hihohiho.com/. Run by UK careers expert Bill Law, it has articles and debates about the nature of careers and how they can be managed by individuals, employers and governments.

John Holland's Self-Directed Search career choice questionnaire has its own website at http://www.self-directed-search.com/. You can take a version of the SDS and see what your scores suggest about appropriate occupations for you. Beware: it does cost, though not very much. You get an on-screen report which will probably suggest more possible occupations than you expected.

Career lab is a US-based site that offers a huge range of advice, information and job opportunities. This includes some free articles by 'The Career Advisor'. http://www.careerlab.com/free.htm.

Another good example of a self-help all-purpose careers site is http://content.monster.co.uk/ (*see* the Career Advice section but there is a variety of relevant information on the www.monster.co.uk website). You can find advice about many aspects of managing your career, as well as information about various occupations. It's primarily geared to the USA, but travels relatively well.

For further self-test material and relevant, annotated weblinks please visit the website at **www.pearsoned.co.uk/workpsych**

Suggested further reading

Full details for all references are given in the list at the end of this book.

1   *The Handbook of Career Studies* (2007) edited by Hugh Gunz and Maury Peiperl, is an excellent collection of chapters which together provide a wide-ranging set of perspectives on theoretical and practical aspects of career.

2   Jeffrey Greenhaus, Gerard Callanan and Veronica Godshalk's book *Career Management*, 3rd edition, was published by Dryden Press in 2000. There is quite a strong focus on the individual as opposed to the organisation.

3   *Careers in and out of Organisations* by Douglas T. (Tim) Hall (2002) published by Sage is an overview of many themes contributing to our understanding of how people live out their careers in new and changing circumstances.

4   *Managing Careers* by Yehuda Baruch, published by Pearson Education in 2003, provides up-to-date coverage of many of the issues mentioned in this chapter, especially managing careers in global organisations.

CHAPTER 16

Understanding organisational change and culture

LEARNING OUTCOMES

After studying this chapter, you should be able to:

1 place the different approaches to change within a wider framework;

2 identify the two main approaches to organisational change;

3 describe and compare the strengths and weaknesses of the main approaches to change;

4 understand the role of culture both as an objective of, and a constraint on, change programmes;

5 identify the respective roles of managers, employees and change agents;

6 understand the difference between open-ended change and closed change;

7 appreciate how the main approaches view employee involvement and resistance;

8 explain how the different approaches view 'political' behaviour;

9 list the main reasons why change projects fail.

Nardelli's style helps to seal his fate

Four months ago, a defiant Bob Nardelli said he had no intention of resigning as chairman and chief executive of Home Depot. 'I love this company,' he told the *Financial Times*. 'I've been in business 35 years and I've never been in a company with more growth potential. As long as I have my health and support from the board I will continue.' It now seems likely that, even as Mr Nardelli spoke those words, the support of the board was already wavering. Home Depot's directors accepted his resignation, by mutual agreement, at a board meeting on Tuesday following a traumatic year for the home improvement retailer.

Mr Nardelli's departure marks a second low point for the combative executive who arrived at Home Depot from General Electric six years ago after losing out in the race to succeed Jack Welch, his mentor, as chairman of GE. His fate may have been sealed as early as last May, when he infuriated many investors by refusing to answer questions at its annual meeting about his hefty compensation package and the company's sagging share price. Mr Nardelli was already a target for shareholder activists, having received more than $120m in compensation, excluding stock options, during his first five years as chief executive, while the share price slumped. But the anger was intensified by his belligerent attitude towards rebel shareholders and activist investors who were preparing a fresh campaign against him ahead of this year's annual meeting.

Mr Nardelli arrived at Home Depot following the departure of its co-founders Bernie Marcus and Arthur Blank from management roles. His predecessors had built the company from a three-store start-up in 1979 to a $45bn chain in 2000, making it America's most rapidly-growing retailer. But the board believed the company's famously entrepreneurial *'cowboy culture'* had become a liability and turned to Mr Nardelli to bring GE-style discipline and focus to its management. Mr Nardelli's brusque, hard-driving style and his recruitment of several senior executives from GE caused tensions with managers who had grown used to the more relaxed, hands-off leadership of Mr Marcus and Mr Blank.

Source: Adapted from an article in the Financial Times, *4 January 2007, p. 22, by A. Ward.*

Introduction

The above case study illustrates three key aspects of organisational change. First, no matter how successful an organisation has been, there comes a point where there is a need for change at the top. Second, where the existing leaders have been in post for many years, a change of leadership is often accompanied by attempts to change the organisation's culture. In the case of Home Depot, there was a desire to change the entrepreneurial 'cowboy culture' which was seen as appropriate to a rapidly growing company, to a more disciplined, corporate culture suitable to a large, successful and established business. Lastly, just because there is a need to change leaders, and a desire to change culture, does not mean that these changes will be welcomed by all or lead to success. Indeed, as many writers have noted, change projects fail more often than they succeed (Beer and Nohria, 2000).

Change confronts managers with a major dilemma. On the one hand, the majority of change efforts appear to fail; on the other, if organisations do not change, they will eventually go out of business. As Turner and Crawford (1999) noted, managers have two prime tasks, managing their organisations so that they meet the needs of their stakeholders today, and reshaping their organisations in order to meet the needs of their stakeholders in the future. This is a delicate balancing act: if the wrong changes are made or if they are made at the wrong time or in an inappropriate manner, organisations may lose the ability to meet their obligations today and not develop the capabilities to meet them in future either. Therefore, the ability to identify the right changes and implement them successfully is a prime task facing managers. This applies to all forms of change. Whether change is small-scale or large-scale, strategic or operational, culture-centred or technology-focused, it needs to be planned and implemented effectively. This chapter provides a critical review of the main approaches to planning and implementing change that have been developed since the 1950s. It begins by examining the importance and complexity of organisational change and illustrates this with an examination of organisational culture. From this, it is argued that an understanding of the theory and practice of change management is crucial to organisational effectiveness and success. The chapter then goes on to review the two main approaches to organisational change: the planned approach and the emergent approach. It is shown that the planned approach, which was developed by Kurt Lewin in the 1940s and forms the core of organisation development (OD), views organisational change as essentially a process of moving from one stable behavioural state to another (through a series of iterative steps or phases). However, it will be seen that the emergent approach, which came to the fore in the 1980s, starts from the assumption that change is a continuous, open-ended and unpredictable process of aligning and realigning an organisation to its changing environment. Advocates of the emergent approach argue that it is more suitable to the turbulent environment in which firms now operate: unlike the planned approach, it recognises the need for organisations to align their internal practices and behaviour with changing external conditions. Proponents of planned change dispute this criticism and argue that as OD has developed it has come to incorporate more organisation-wide and transformational approaches to change.

The review of these two approaches will reveal that, despite the large body of literature devoted to the topic of change management, and the many tools and techniques available to change agents, there is considerable disagreement regarding the most appropriate approach. In an effort to bring clarity to the issue, the chapter concludes by presenting a *framework for change* which shows that neither the emergent nor planned approach is suitable for all situations and circumstances. Instead, it is maintained that approaches to change tend to be situation-specific and that the potential exists for organisations to influence the constraints under which they operate in order to exercise choice over what to change and how to change.

The importance of change management

Change management would not be considered particularly important if products and markets were stable and organisational change was rare. However, that is not the case, nor has it ever been so. Change is an ever-present feature of organisational life, though many leading management thinkers such as Tom Peters (1997), Rosabeth Moss Kanter (1997), John Kotter (1996) and Charles Handy (1994) do argue that the pace, magnitude and necessity of change have increased significantly over time.

Certainly, over the last 20 years, there has been much evidence that the prevalence of change is increasing (Burnes, 2004b; Carnall, 2003; Coulson-Thomas and Coe, 1991; Cummings and Worley, 2001; Ezzamel *et al.*, 1994; Jones *et al.*, 2006; Wheatley, 1992; Worrall and Cooper, 1997, 1998). Despite the increasing prevalence of change, the evidence is that it is debatable whether change actually brings benefits to organisations or to those who work in them. Indeed, there is considerable evidence to show that between 60 and 80 per cent of change efforts fail to achieve their objectives (Beer and Nohria, 2000; Jones *et al.*, 2006). Though this may seem a staggering rate of failure, studies of business process re-engineering (BPR) have shown failure rates of 70 per cent (Coombs and Hull, 1994; Hammer and Champy, 1993; Huczynski and Buchanan, 2001; Short and Venkatraman, 1992) and studies of total quality management (TQM) have revealed failure rates as high as 90 per cent (Kearney, 1992; Cruise O'Brien and Voss, 1992; Economist Intelligence Unit, 1992; Crosby, 1979; Whyte and Witcher, 1992; Witcher, 1993; Zairi *et al.*, 1994). Therefore, even well-established change initiatives, for which a great deal of information, advice and assistance are available to organisations, are no guarantee of success. This is perhaps why managers list their ability (or inability) to manage change as the number one obstacle to the increased competitiveness of their organisations (Hanson, 1993).

Key Learning Point

Effective organisational change is crucial to an organisation's competitiveness but, despite the plethora of advice available, the majority of change programmes appear to fail.

There are many reasons why change management programmes fail (Hoag *et al.*, 2002; Huczynski and Buchanan, 2001; Kotter, 1996). Though some of these are specific to the particular organisations concerned, many relate to the inadequacy or inappropriateness of the various recipes for change that are available to organisations (Burnes, 2004b). In addition, it needs to be recognised that change, even in quite small organisations, is a complex process whose consequences can be difficult to predict. Perhaps the prime example of this is culture change. Since the early 1980s, most organisations have come to believe that culture has a key role to play in achieving competitiveness (Cummings and Worley, 2001; Jones *et al.*, 2006). Not surprising, therefore, a survey by the Industrial Society (1997) in the United Kingdom found that 94 per cent of its respondents had either recently been involved in or were going through a culture change programme. To understand and illustrate why change is so complex, the following section will examine organisational culture.

Changing organisational culture

There is widespread agreement that managers and employees do not perform their duties in a value-free vacuum (Brown, 1998). Their work and the way it is done are governed, directed and tempered by an organisation's culture: this is the particular *set of values, beliefs, customs and systems unique to that organisation*. From this perspective, culture is seen as the 'glue' which holds organisations together (van den Berg and Wilderom, 2004). Though this view has been around for many years (see Blake and Mouton, 1969; Turner, 1971; Eldridge and Crombie, 1974), it was only in the 1980s, with the work of writers such as Peters and Waterman (1982) and Deal and Kennedy (1982), that culture (rather than factors such as structure, strategy or politics) came to be regarded as central to organisational success. Indeed, Hansen and Wernerfelt (1989) reported that organisational factors (i.e. culture) were twice as important in explaining the variance in profit as economic factors. So influential has this view become that, as Wilson (1992) observed, culture has come to be seen as the great 'cure-all' for the majority of organisational ills.

As Allaire and Firsirotu (1984) noted, there are many different definitions of organisational culture. Perhaps the most widely accepted definition is that offered by Eldridge and Crombie (1974, p. 78), who stated that culture refers 'to the unique configuration of norms, values, beliefs, ways of behaving and so on, that characterise the manner in which groups and individuals combine to get things done'. Culture defines how those in the organisation should behave in a given set of circumstances. It affects all, from the most senior manager to the humblest porter. Their actions are judged by themselves and others in relation to expected modes of behaviour. Culture legitimises certain forms of action and proscribes other forms.

There have been a number of attempts to identify and categorise the constituent elements of culture (e.g. Schein, 1985; Hofstede, 1990). Based on an analysis of the different definitions of culture, Cummings and Huse (1989, p. 421) produced a composite model of culture (see Figure 16.1), comprising four major elements existing at different levels of awareness:

1 *Basic assumptions*. At the deepest level of cultural awareness are unconscious, taken-for-granted assumptions about how organisational problems should be solved. They represent non-confrontable and non-debatable assumptions about relating to the environment, as well as about the nature of human nature, human activity and human relationships.

2 *Values*. The next higher level of awareness includes values about what *ought* to be in organisations. Values tell members what is important in the organisation and what they need to pay attention to.

3 *Norms*. Just below the surface of cultural awareness are norms guiding how members should behave in particular situations. These represent unwritten rules of behaviour.

4 *Artefacts*. At the highest level of cultural awareness are the artefacts and creations that are visible manifestations of the other levels of cultural elements. These include observable behaviours of members, as well as the structures, systems, procedures, rules and physical aspects of the organisation.

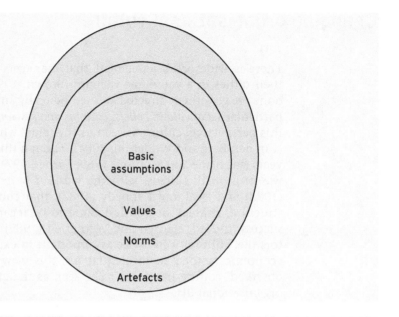

Figure 16.1   **The major elements of culture**

However, while the various hierarchical models of culture elements are useful, we should always remember that, as Brown (1995, pp. 8–9) notes, 'actual organisational cultures are not as neat and tidy as the models seem to imply'.

As well as the numerous attempts to define organisational culture, there have also been a number of attempts to categorise the various types of culture (e.g. Deal and Kennedy, 1982; Quinn and McGrath, 1985). Perhaps the best-known typology of culture, and the one that has been around the longest, is that developed by Handy (1979) from Harrison's (1972) work on 'organisation ideologies'. Handy (1986, p. 188) observed that 'There seem to be four main types of culture':

1   **Power culture.** This is frequently found in small entrepreneurial organisations such as some property, trading and finance companies. Such a culture is associated with a web-like structure with one or more powerful figures at the centre: it is these figures that wield control.

2   **Role culture.** This is appropriate to bureaucracies, and organisations with mechanistic, rigid structures and narrow jobs. Such cultures stress the importance of procedures and rules, hierarchical position and authority, security and predictability. In essence, role cultures create situations in which those in the organisation stick rigidly to their job description (role), and any unforeseen events are referred to the next layer up in the hierarchy.

3   **Task culture.** This is job- or project-oriented culture where the onus is on getting the job in hand (the task) done rather than there being a prescribed way of doing things. Such types of culture are appropriate to organically-structured organisations where flexibility and teamworking are encouraged. Task cultures create situations in which speed of reaction, integration and creativity are more important than adherence to particular rules or procedures, and where position and authority are less important than the individual contribution to the task in hand.

4   **Person culture.** This is a rare form of culture where the individual and his or her wishes are the central focus. It is associated with a minimalistic structure, the purpose of which is to assist those individuals who choose to work together. Therefore, a person culture can be characterised as a cluster or galaxy of individual 'stars'.

One of the most widely used tools for assessing culture is the Organisational Culture Inventory (OCI) (Jones *et al.*, 2006, p. 18). Instead of seeking to predefine the main forms of culture, the developers of the OCI used statistical analysis of large sets of OCI data to identify three clusters of similar cultures. These were:

1   **Constructive cultures.** Cultures in which members are encouraged to interact with others and approach tasks in ways that will help them to meet their higher-order satisfaction needs (includes achievement, self-actualisation, humanistic-encouraging and affiliative cultures).

2   **Passive/defensive cultures.** Cultures in which members believe that they must interact with people in defensive ways that will not threaten their own security (includes approval, conventional, dependent and avoidance cultures).

3   **Aggressive/defensive cultures.** Cultures in which members are expected to approach tasks in forceful ways to protect their status and security (includes oppositional, power, competitive and perfectionist cultures).

Though useful, the various attempts to provide a universal categorisation of culture types do have their critics, especially among those who point to the influence of the host society on organisational cultures (Hofstede, 1980, 1990). Nevertheless, as Burnes (2004b) notes, the debate over how to define and describe culture has significant implications for how organisations operate and are managed – but only if culture can be influenced or changed by managers. However, as Martin (1992, 2002) maintains, the literature on culture and the extent to which it can be changed is extensive and confusing with little apparent agreement.

There are those, such as Barratt (1990, p. 23) who claim that 'values, beliefs and attitudes are learnt, can be managed and changed and are potentially manipulable by management'. O'Reilly (1989) takes a similar view, arguing that it is possible to change or manage a culture by choosing the attitudes and behaviours that are required, identifying the norms or expectations that either promote or impede them, and then taking action to create the desired effect. Therefore, there is a body of opinion that sees culture as something that can be managed and changed. There are also many, many organisations in which, for a variety of reasons, senior managers have decided that their existing culture is inappropriate or even detrimental to their competitive needs and, therefore, must be changed (Deal and Kennedy, 1982; Peters and Waterman, 1982).

On the other hand, Filby and Willmott (1988) questioned the notion that management has the capacity to control culture. They point out that this ignores the way in which an individual's values and beliefs are conditioned by experience outside the workplace (e.g. through exposure to the media, through social activities, as well as through previous occupational activities). Hatch (1997, p. 235) is also very dubious about attempts to change organisational culture:

> Do not think of trying to manage culture. Other people's meanings and interpretations are highly unmanageable. Think instead of trying to culturally manage your organization, that is, manage your organization with cultural awareness of the multiplicity of meanings that will be made of you and your efforts.

A further concern expressed by a number of writers relates to the ethical issues raised by attempts to change culture (Van Maanen and Kunda, 1989; Willmott, 1995). This concern is succinctly articulated by Watson (1997, p. 278) who concludes that:

> Employers and managers engaging in these ways with issues of employees' self-identities and the values through which they judge the rights and wrongs of their daily lives must be a matter of serious concern. To attempt to mould cultures – given that culture in its broad sense provides the roots of human morality, social identity and existential security – is indeed to enter 'deep and dangerous waters' ...

A third group of writers seem to take a position somewhere in between those who see culture as something that is amenable to managerial choice and those who see it as unalterable. These writers appear to agree that culture as a whole cannot be changed but argue that certain key elements, such as norms of behaviour, can be influenced by management (Schein, 1985). This viewpoint is summed up by Meek (1988, pp. 469–70) who argues that:

> Culture as a whole cannot be manipulated, turned on or off, although it needs to be recognised that some [organisations] are in a better position than others to intentionally influence aspects of it.

Ogbonna and Harris (2002) have labelled these three groups of writers as the optimists, the pessimists and the realists. As the labels might imply, Ogbonna and Harris tend to believe that the realists have the best of the argument; culture as a whole cannot be changed but it is possible to intentionally and successfully to change key elements of it.

Nevertheless, whichever camp one falls into, there is plenty of evidence that many organisations underestimate the difficulties involved in attempting to change their culture and this leads to a high level of failure (Brown, 1995). As Jones *et al.* (2006, p. 45) observe, many culture change programmes fail because they 'ignored two critical factors: the need to generate valid data on which to base a diagnosis of change requirement, and a clear line of sight to performance outcomes'.

These comments echo the views of one of the leading writers on culture, Schein (1985). He cautions organisations to be wary of rushing into culture change programmes. He believes that before any attempt is made to change an organisation's culture, it is first necessary to understand the nature of its existing culture and how this is sustained. According to Schein, this can be achieved by analysing the values that govern behaviour and uncovering the underlying and often unconscious assumptions that determine how those in the organisation think, feel and react. His approach, therefore, is to treat the development of culture as an adaptive and tangible learning process. Schein emphasises the way in which an organisation communicates its culture to new recruits, how assumptions are translated into values and how values influence behaviour. Schein seeks to understand the mechanisms used to propagate culture, and how new values and behaviours are learned. Once these mechanisms are revealed, he argues, they can then form the basis of a strategy to change the organisation's culture: the argument is that change is likely to fail if it does not start with such an analysis.

In a synthesis of the literature on organisational culture, Hassard and Sharifi (1989, p. 11) proposed a similar approach to Schein's. In particular, they stressed the crucial role of senior managers:

> Before a major [cultural] change campaign is commenced, senior managers must understand the implications of the new system for their own behaviour: and senior management must be involved in all the main stages preceding change.
>
> In change programmes, special attention must be given to the company's 'opinion leaders'.

As we can see, most observers see organisational culture as being complex and difficult to understand. However, even among those who believe it can be changed, few appear to believe that such a change is easy or without dangers. This is perhaps why so many organisations have found successful culture change so difficult to achieve (Brown, 1998; Cummings and Worley, 2001; De Witte and van Muijen, 1999). Indeed, it is the fact that organisations are not machines but very complex social systems that makes any form of change potentially hazardous.

Key Learning Point

Organisational culture may be crucial to an organisation's performance but it is also difficult to understand and change.

Exercise 16.1   Culture is key to CPA professional development

A notable culture of development at Plante and Moran, one of the largest US accountancy and business advice firms, is a result of the degree in philosophy held by Frank Moran, one of the firm's founders. He spent a lot of time in the 1950s in conversation with Professor Harry Levinson, Harvard Business School's groundbreaking management psychologist. 'He brought a real understanding of human psychology in the workplace,' says Richard Brehler, the firm's training and education director. Mr Moran had a vision of a firm renowned for its service to clients, and for the working environment it could offer certified public accountants. He introduced the team concept, where each partner is responsible for the professional development and retention of 6 to 10 professionals, who may never work on an audit for them. The partner keeps them on track, gives them feedback where they need to improve, makes sure they get the right experiences and supervises their progress through professional development. New joiners are also assigned a 'buddy' who has been at the firm a year or two and is responsible for their introduction to the firm. 'They teach them the ropes in getting on in engagements and make sure they are introduced to the right people,' says Mr Brehler. 'They also provide informal "off-the-job" training and advice.'

The firm's investment of time and energy in its staff raises their morale, reduces turnover and improves teamwork. This makes for happier clients and an improved bottom line, which allows the company to further invest in its staff. 'We believe in "tending the orchard" by paying attention to the growth and long-term legacy of the ▶

firm, not just immediate profitability,' says Mr Brehler. 'We average a 12 per cent staff turnover rate, against 25–30 per cent in our industry. Clients like to see the same faces turning up to do their audit each year.'

The biggest challenge is the impact on staff development of automated paperless audit procedures and review. These reduce much of the human contact. 'Years ago audit teams sat across the table around the ledger sheets and had a lot of time for informal discussions, question and dialogue,' says Mr Brehler, 'but these inherent learning opportunities have disappeared. If people are not free to ask the dumb question, to expose their ignorance or to enquire, then their development is at risk.' Mr Brehler says that all CPA firms he talks to are facing the same challenges. 'We have an advantage,' he says, 'because we don't have to engender a culture of learning and professional exchange, as we have always focused on it.'

Source: From an article in the Financial Times, *12 November 2007, p. 2, by R. Newing.*

Suggested exercises

1   Using Cummings and Huse's model of culture, Figure 16.1, discuss whether Plante and Moran's staff development process can be seen as an artefact, norm, value or basic assumption.

2   What difficulties might Plante and Moran encounter if it attempted major changes to its staff development process?

3   How easy would it be for a competitor to adopt the Plante and Moran approach to staff development? What would be the main obstacles?

Despite the adverse experience of many organisations, change, of an increasingly radical form, seems to be the order of the day. Some organisations look to management gurus such as Charles Handy (1994), Rosabeth Moss Kanter (1989), John Kotter (1996) and Tom Peters (1997) for their salvation. Others seek the assistance of management consultants such as McKinsey, PricewaterhouseCoopers and KMPG. However, whether organisations seek outside advice and assistance or whether they rely on their own competence, they cannot expect to achieve successful change unless those responsible for managing it understand the different approaches on offer and can match them to their circumstances and preferences. On this basis, understanding the theory and practice of change management is not an optional extra but an essential prerequisite for survival. However, as the following examination of the two main approaches to change management will show, this is by no means an easy or straightforward exercise.

STOP TO CONSIDER

From your reading so far, what appear to be the main reasons behind the high failure rates of organisational change? Given these reasons, what are the key issues that need to be covered by theories of change in order to help organisations achieve more success when implementing change?

The planned approach to organisational change

The founding father of planned change was Kurt Lewin (Burnes, 2004a, 2007). He used the term to distinguish change that was consciously embarked upon and planned by an organisation, as opposed to types of change that might come about by accident, by impulse or which might be forced on an organisation (Marrow, 1977). Among those advocating planned change, a variety of different models of change management have arisen over the years. The planned approach to change is most closely associated with the practice of organisation development (OD), and indeed lies at the core of OD. According to French and Bell (1995, pp. 1–2):

> Organization development is a unique organizational improvement strategy that emerged in the late 1950s and early 1960s . . . [It] has evolved into an integrated framework of theories and practices capable of solving or helping to solve most of the important problems confronting the human side of organizations. Organization development is about people and organizations and people in organizations and how they function. OD is also about planned change, that is getting individuals, teams and organizations to function better.

Underpinning OD is a set of values, assumptions and ethics that emphasise its humanistic–democratic orientation and its commitment to organisational effectiveness. These values have been articulated by many writers over the years (Conner, 1977; Warwick and Thompson, 1980; Gellerman *et al.*, 1990). Hurley *et al.* (1992) found there were five clear values that OD practitioners espoused:

1   empowering employees to act;

2   creating openness in communications;

3   facilitating ownership of the change process and its outcomes;

4   the promotion of a culture of collaboration;

5   the promotion of continuous learning.

Within the OD field, there are a number of major theorists and practitioners who have contributed their own models and techniques to its advancement (e.g. Argyris, 1962; Beckhard, 1969; French and Bell, 1973; Blake and Mouton, 1976). However, despite this, there is general agreement that OD grew out of, and became the standard bearer for, Kurt Lewin's pioneering work on behavioural science in general, and his development of planned change in particular (Burnes, 2004a, 2007). Lewin was a prolific theorist, researcher and practitioner in interpersonal, group, intergroup and community relationships. The models of the change process that emerged from his work are:

■   the action research model;

■   the three-step model;

■   the phases of planned change model.

Action research

This model was designed by Lewin as a collective approach to solving social and organisational problems. Although American in origin, soon after its emergence it was adopted by the Tavistock Institute in Britain, and used to improve managerial competency and efficiency in the coal industry. Since then it has acquired a strong following on both sides of the Atlantic (French and Bell, 1984). Some comments on the methodology of action research appear in Chapter 2 of this book.

In an organisational setting, an action research project usually comprises three distinct groups: the organisation (in the form of one or more senior managers), the subject (people from the area where the change is to take place) and the change agent (a consultant who may or may not be a member of the organisation). These three distinct entities form a *learning community* in and through which the research is carried out, and by which the organisation's problem is solved (Heller, 1970).

Action research is a two-pronged process. First, it emphasises that change requires action (i.e. something needs to happen), and is directed at achieving this. Second, it recognises that successful action is based on a process of *learning* that allows those involved to analyse the situation correctly, identify all the possible alternative solutions (hypotheses) and choose the one most appropriate to the situation at hand (Bennett, 1983). The theoretical foundations of this approach lie in gestalt-field theory: this stresses that change can only successfully be achieved by helping individuals to reflect on and gain new insights into their situation (Smith *et al.*, 1982).

Although action research is highly regarded as an approach to managing change (Cummings and Huse, 1989), it is Lewin's three-step model of change that lies at the core of planned change.

Key Learning Point

Action research is concerned as much with individual and group learning as it is with achieving change.

The three-step model of change

In developing this model, Lewin (1958) noted that a change towards a higher level of group performance is frequently short-lived; after a 'shot in the arm', group behaviour may soon revert to its previous pattern. This indicates that it is not sufficient to define the objective of change solely as the achievement of a higher level of group performance: the permanence of the new level should also be included in the objective. A successful change project, Lewin (1958) argued, should involve three steps:

1   *unfreezing* the present level;

2   *moving* to the new level;

3   *refreezing* the new level.

Step 1 recognises that before new behaviour can be successfully adopted, the old has to be discarded. Only then can the new behaviour become accepted. Central to this approach is the belief that the will of the change adopter (the subject of the change) is important, both in discarding the old, 'unfreezing', and then 'moving' to the new.

Unfreezing usually involves reducing those forces maintaining the organisation's behaviour at its present level. According to Rubin (1967), unfreezing requires some form of confrontation meeting or re-education process for those involved. The essence of these activities is to enable those concerned to become convinced of the need for change. Unfreezing clearly equates with the research element of action research, just as step 2, moving, equates with the action element.

Moving, in practice, involves acting on the results of step 1. That is, having analysed the present situation, identified options and selected the most appropriate, action is then necessary to move to the more desirable state of affairs. This involves developing new behaviours, values and attitudes through changes in organisational structures and processes. The key task is to ensure that this is done in such a way that those involved do not, after a short period, revert to the old ways of doing things.

Refreezing is the final step in the three-step model and represents, depending on the viewpoint, either a break with action research or its logical extension. Refreezing seeks to stabilise the organisation at a new state of equilibrium in order to ensure that the new ways of working are relatively safe from regression. It is frequently achieved through the use of supporting mechanisms that positively reinforce the new ways of working; these include organisational culture, norms, policies and practices (Cummings and Huse, 1989).

The three-step model provides a general framework for understanding the process of organisational change. However, the three steps are relatively broad and, for this reason, have been further developed in an attempt to enhance the practicable value of this approach.

Phases of planned change

In attempting to elaborate upon Lewin's three-step model, writers have expanded the number of steps or phases. Lippitt *et al.* (1958) developed a seven-phase model of planned change, while Cummings and Huse (1989), not to be out-done, produced an eight-phase model. However, as Cummings and Huse (1989, p. 51) point out, 'the concept of planned change implies that an organization exists in different states at different times and that planned movement can occur from one state to another'. Therefore, in order to understand planned change, it is not sufficient merely to understand the processes that bring about change; there must also be an appreciation of the states that an organisation must pass through in order to move from an unsatisfactory present state to a more desired future state.

Bullock and Batten (1985) developed an integrated, four-phase model of planned change based on a review and synthesis of over 30 models of planned change. Their model describes planned change in terms of two major dimensions: change phases, which are distinct states an organisation moves through as it undertakes planned change; and change processes, which are the methods used to move an organisation from one state to another.

The four change phases, and their attendant change processes, identified by Bullock and Batten are as follows:

1   *Exploration phase*: in this state members of an organisation have to explore and decide whether they want to make specific changes in its operations and, if so, commit resources to planning the changes. The change processes involved in this phase are: becoming aware of the need for change; searching for outside assistance (a consultant/facilitator) to assist with planning and implementing the changes; and establishing a contract with the consultant which defines each party's responsibilities.

2   *Planning phase*: once the consultant and the organisation have established a contract, then the next state, which involves understanding the organisation's problem or concern, begins. The change processes involved in this are: collecting information in order to establish a correct diagnosis of the problem; establishing change goals and designing the appropriate actions to achieve these goals; and getting key decision-makers to approve and support the proposed changes.

3   *Action phase*: in this state, an organisation implements the changes derived from the planning. The change processes involved are designed to move an organisation from its current state to a desired future state, and include: establishing appropriate arrangements to manage the change process and gaining support for the actions to be taken; and evaluating the implementation activities and feeding back the results so that any necessary adjustments or refinements can be made.

4   *Integration phase*: this state commences once the changes have been successfully implemented. It is concerned with consolidating and stabilising the changes so that they become part of an organisation's normal, everyday operation and do not require special arrangements or encouragement to maintain them. The change processes involved are: reinforcing new behaviours through feedback and reward systems and gradually decreasing reliance on the consultant; diffusing the successful aspects of the change process throughout the organisation; and training managers and employees to monitor the changes constantly and seek to improve upon them.

According to Cummings and Huse (1989), this model has broad applicability to most change situations. It clearly incorporates key aspects of many other change models and, especially, it overcomes any confusion between the processes (methods) of change and the phases of change – the sequential states that organisations must go through to achieve successful change.

Key Learning Point

Both the three-step and the phases models view change as a sequential activity involving a beginning, a middle and an end.

The focus of Bullock and Batten's model, just as with Lewin's, is change at individual and group level. However, OD practitioners have recognised, as many others have, that: 'Organisations are being reinvented; work tasks are being reengineered; the rules of the marketplace are being rewritten; the fundamental nature of organisations is changing', and, therefore, OD has to adapt to these new conditions and broaden its focus out beyond individual and group behaviour (French and Bell, 1995, pp. 3–4).

From organisation development to organisation transformation

In the United States at least, OD has become a profession with its own regulatory bodies, to which OD practitioners have to belong, its own recognised qualifications, a host of approved tools and techniques and its own ethical code of practice (Cummings and Worley, 2001). The members of this profession, whether employed in academic institutions, consultancy practices or private and public organisations, exist to provide consultancy services. As with any profession or trade, unless they provide their customers with what they want, they will soon go out of business. Therefore, to appreciate the current role and approach of planned change, it is necessary to say something of how OD has responded to the changing needs of its customers.

The original focus of OD was on work groups within an organisational setting rather than organisations in their entirety, and it was primarily concerned with the human processes and systems within organisations. However, as French and Bell (1995) and Cummings and Worley (2001) noted, in recent years there has been a major shift of focus within the OD field from improving group effectiveness to transforming organisations. This move to 'transformational' OD stems from three key developments:

1 With the rise of the job design movement in the 1960s, and particularly the advent of sociotechnical systems theory, OD practitioners came to recognise that they could not solely concentrate on the work of groups and individuals in organisations but that they needed to look at other and wider systems. Gradually, OD has adopted an open systems perspective that allows it to look at organisations in their totality and within their environments.

2 OD practitioners have broadened their perspective to include organisational culture. Given that OD had always recognised the importance of group norms and values, it is a natural progression to translate this into an interest in organisational culture in general.

3 The increasing use of organisation-wide approaches to change, such as culture change programmes, coupled with increasing turbulence in the environment in which organisations operate (e.g. their marketplace and the broader national and global economy), have drawn attention to the need for OD to become involved in transforming organisations in their totality rather than focusing on changes to their constituent parts.

While these major additions to the OD repertoire are understandable, the danger is that they appear to be moving away from the commitment to individual involvement and learning that has, traditionally, been espoused by OD practitioners. This can be seen from the following five-step approach to culture change advocated by Cummings and Huse (1989, pp. 428–30):

1 *A clear strategic vision*: effective cultural change should start from a clear vision of the firm's new strategy and of the shared values and behaviour needed to make it work. This vision provides the purpose and direction for cultural change.

2 *Top management commitment*: cultural change must be managed from the top of the organisation. Senior managers and administrators need to be strongly committed to the new values and the need to create constant pressure for change.

3 *Symbolic leadership*: senior executives must communicate the new culture through their own actions. Their behaviours need to symbolise the kind of values and behaviours being sought.

4 *Supporting organisational changes*: cultural change must be accompanied by supporting modifications in organisational structure, human resource systems, information and control systems and management style. These organisational features can help to orientate people's behaviours to the new culture.

5 *Organisational membership*: one of the most effective methods for changing culture is to change organisational membership. People can be selected in terms of their fit with the new culture, and provided with an induction clearly indicating desired attitudes and behaviour. Existing staff who cannot adapt to the new ways may have their employment terminated.

Not only does Cummings and Huse's approach exclude all but senior staff from being involved in decisions about what to change and how to implement it, but also those who are deemed not to 'fit' the new culture can have their employment terminated. This all seems to be part of the growing tendency observed by French and Bell (1995, p. 351) for top managers to focus less on people-oriented values and more on 'the bottom line and/or the price of stock . . . [Consequently] some executives have a "slash and burn" mentality.' Clearly, this tendency is not conducive to the democratic and humanistic values traditionally espoused by OD practitioners. Instead, the emphasis is on the change consultant as a provider of expertise that the organisation lacks. The consultant's task is not only to facilitate but also to provide solutions. The danger in this situation is that the learner (the change adopter) becomes a passive recipient of external and, supposedly, objective data: one who has to be directed to the 'correct' solution (Cummings and Worley, 2001). This has led a number of key writers to question whether OD has lost its way as its practices have moved away from its original values (Bradford and Burke, 2004; Greiner and Cummings, 2004; Worley and Feyerherm, 2003).

As can be seen, for better or ill, OD has attempted to move considerably away from its roots in planned change and now takes a far more organisation- and system-wide perspective on change.

Exercise 16.2 Working with suppliers

When Nissan established its British car-assembly operation in the mid-1980s, it recognised that UK component suppliers fell far short of Japanese standards of quality, reliability and cost. As one means of helping suppliers to improve their capability, it established a Supplier Development Team (SDT). The aim of the SDT was to help suppliers to develop their business to the stage where they can meet Nissan's performance requirements.

Though the assistance given by the SDT to suppliers is in effect free consultancy, this is not philanthropy on Nissan's part. Nissan believes that unless its suppliers achieve world-class performance standards, it cannot produce world-beating cars. Therefore, in helping its suppliers, Nissan is helping itself.

The SDT approach is to work cooperatively with suppliers to help them identify areas for improvement, and then to assist them to develop and monitor improvement plans. The basic elements of the SDT's approach are as follows:

- Suppliers are at liberty to choose whether or not to invite the SDT into their plant.

- The SDT begins by explaining to senior managers within suppliers that its objective is to help them to develop a continuous improvement philosophy.

- The SDT seeks to train and guide a supplier's personnel to undertake change projects for themselves, rather than doing the work for them.

- The SDT insists that staff in the area where change is to take place are involved.

- The SDT seeks to promote trust, cooperation and teamworking within suppliers.

- The SDT's own members are extremely well-trained and proficient and, consequently, are able to win the confidence of the people with whom they work.

- The SDT seeks to ensure that those who carry out the improvement get the credit and praise for it, rather than seeking to take the credit itself.

It would be misleading to give the impression that Nissan was in any way 'soft' on suppliers. As Sir Ian Gibson, Nissan's then Managing Director, stated: 'Co-operative supply relationships are not an easy option, as many imagine, but considerably harder to implement than traditional buyer–seller relationships'.

Source: Adapted from Burnes (2000).

Suggested exercises

1 To what extent does Nissan's approach to supplier development fit in with the planned approach to change?

2 How does the philosophy promoted by Nissan's SDT compare to Lewin's own underlying philosophy of change?

3 Is the SDT approach compatible with 'transformational' OD?

4 What effect might a supplier's organisational culture have on the longer-term success of the SDT approach?

Planned change: summary and criticisms

Planned change is an iterative, cyclical process involving diagnosis, action and evaluation, and further action and evaluation. It is an approach that recognises that once change has taken place, it must be self-sustaining (i.e. safe from regression). The purpose of planned change is to improve the effectiveness of the human side of the organisation. Central to planned change is the emphasis placed on the collaborative nature of the change effort: the organisation, both managers and recipients of change, and the consultant jointly diagnose the organisation's problem and jointly plan and design the specific changes. Underpinning planned change, and indeed the origins of the OD movement as a whole, is a strong humanist and democratic orientation and an emphasis on organisational effectiveness (Burnes, 2004a, 2007). This fits in well with its gestalt-field orientation, seeing change as a process of learning which allows those involved to gain or change insights, outlooks, expectations and thought patterns. This approach seeks to provide change adopters with an opportunity to 'reason out' their situation and develop their own solutions (Bigge, 1982).

However, the advent of more organisation-wide approaches, which seem to be leading to a move away from OD's original focus and area of expertise (i.e. the human processes involved in the functioning of individuals and groups in organisations), coupled with a more hostile business environment, appear to be eroding the values that Lewin and the early pioneers of OD saw as being central to successful change (Bradford and Burke, 2004; Greiner and Cummings, 2004; Worley and Feyerherm, 2003).

As might be expected, these developments in OD, as well as newer perspectives on organisations, have led many to question not only particular aspects of the planned approach to change but also the utility and practicality of the approach as a whole. The main criticisms levelled against the planned approach to change are as follows.

First, as Wooten and White (1999, p. 8) observe, 'Much of the existing OD technology was developed specifically for, and in response to, top-down, autocratic, rigid, rule-based organizations operating in a somewhat predictable and controlled environment.' This may account for the assumption by many proponents of OD that, as Cummings and Huse (1989, p. 51) pointed out, 'an organization exists in different states at different times and that planned movement can occur from one state to another'. However, from the 1980s onwards in particular, an increasing number of writers argued that, in the turbulent and chaotic world in which we live, such assumptions are increasingly tenuous and that organisational change is more a continuous and open-ended process than a set of discrete and self-contained events (Nonaka, 1988; Peters, 1989; Garvin, 1993; Stacey, 2003).

Second, and on a similar note, a number of writers have criticised the planned approach for its emphasis on incremental and isolated change and its inability to incorporate radical, transformational change (Miller and Friesen, 1984; Hatch, 1997; Schein, 1985; Dunphy and Stace, 1993).

Third, the planned approach is based on the assumption that common agreement can be reached, and that all the parties involved in a particular change project have a willingness and interest in doing so. This assumption appears to ignore organisational conflict and politics, or at least assumes that problem issues can be easily identified and resolved which, as Pfeffer (1992), among many others, has shown, is not always the case.

Fourth, it assumes that one type of approach to change is suitable for all organisations, all situations and all times. Stace and Dunphy (2001) show that there is a wide spectrum of change situations, ranging from fine-tuning to corporate transformation, and an equally wide range of ways of managing these, ranging from collaborative to coercive. Though planned change may be suitable to some for these situations, it is clearly much less applicable to situations where more directive approaches may be required, such as when a crisis, requiring rapid and major change, does not allow scope for widespread involvement or consultation. This has led Dunphy and Stace (1993, p. 905) to argue that:

Turbulent times demand different responses in varied circumstances. So managers and consultants need a model of change that is essentially a 'situational' or 'contingency model', one that indicates how to vary change strategies to achieve 'optimum fit' with the changing environment.

Leading OD advocates, as might be predicted, dispute these criticisms and point to the way that planned change has tried to incorporate issues such as power and politics and the need for organisational transformation (French and Bell, 1995; Cummings and Worley, 1997). Also, as Burnes (2004a) argues, there is a need to draw a distinction between Lewin's original analytical approach to planned change and the more recent prescriptive and practitioner-oriented approaches of OD practitioners. Nevertheless, even taking these points into account, it has to be recognised that planned change was never intended to be applicable to all change situations and it was certainly never meant to be used in situations where rapid, coercive and/or wholesale change was required.

Key Learning Point

The main criticism of the planned approach is that it is not suitable for open-ended and unpredictable situations.

STOP TO CONSIDER

You will have read a number of criticisms of the planned change approach. However, what might be the merits of the planned change approach? Can it be used in some ways, in some circumstances, to help organisations implement change better? If so, under what circumstances might it be most useful?

The emergent approach to organisational change

The planned approach to change is relatively well developed and understood, and is supported by a coherent body of literature, methods and techniques. The emergent approach, on the other hand, is a relatively new concept that lacks an agreed set of methods and techniques. The proponents of the emergent approach to change view it from different perspectives and tend to focus on their own particular concerns. Therefore, they are a much less coherent group than the advocates of planned change. Rather than being united by a shared belief, they tend to be distinguished by a common disbelief in the efficacy of planned change.

Buchanan and Storey (1997, p. 127) maintain that the main criticism of planned change is its 'attempt to impose an order and a linear sequence to processes that are in reality messy and untidy, and which unfold in an iterative fashion with much backtracking and omission'. For proponents of the emergent approach, change is a continuous, dynamic and contested process that emerges in an unpredictable and unplanned fashion. As Weick (2000, p. 237) states:

Emergent change consists of ongoing accommodations, adaptations, and alternations that produce fundamental change without a priori intentions to do so. Emergent

change occurs when people reaccomplish routines and when they deal with contin-
gencies, breakdowns, and opportunities in everyday work. Much of this change goes
unnoticed, because small alternations are lumped together as noise in otherwise un-
eventful inertia . . .

The rationale for the emergent approach stems, according to Hayes (2002, p. 37),
from the belief that:

the key decisions about matching the organisation's resources with opportunities,
constraints and demands in the environment evolve over time and are the outcome of
cultural and political processes in organisations.

Pettigrew (1990a,b) has argued that the planned approach is too prescriptive and
does not pay enough attention to the need to analyse and conceptualise organisational change. He maintains that it is essential to understand the context in which
change takes place. In particular he emphasises:

- the interconnectedness of change over time (i.e. change events have causes and
consequences that are linked to each other in a complex way);

- how the context of change shapes, and is shaped by, action;

- the multi-causal and non-linear nature of change (i.e. many things impact on
change, and the change process is an complex one, rather than one that takes
place in a simple predictable sequence).

Pettigrew (1987) argues that change needs to be studied across different levels of
analysis and different time periods. This is because organisational change cuts
across functions, spans hierarchical divisions and has no neat starting or finishing
point; instead it is a 'complex analytical, political, and cultural process of challenging and changing the core beliefs, structure and strategy of the firm' (Pettigrew,
1987, p. 650).

Advocates of the emergent approach, therefore, stress the developing and unpredictable nature of change. They view change as a process that unfolds through
the interplay of multiple variables (context, political processes and consultation)
within an organisation. In contrast to what he sees as the preordained certainty of
planned change, Dawson (1994) adopted a *processual approach* to change. The
processual approach views organisations and their members as shifting coalitions
of individuals and groups with different interests, imperfect knowledge and short
attention spans. Change, under these conditions, is portrayed as a pragmatic
process of trial and error, aimed at achieving a compromise between the competitive needs of the organisation and the objectives of the various warring factions
within the organisation.

Advocates of emergent change who adopt the processual approach tend to stress
that there can be no simple prescription for managing organisational transitions
successfully, owing to temporal and contextual factors (Pettigrew, 1997). Dawson
(2003) sees change as:

a complex ongoing dynamic in which the politics, substance and context of change all
interlock and overlap, and in which our understanding of the present and expectations
of the future can influence our interpretation of past events, which may in turn shape
our experience of change.

Key Learning Point

The emergent approach challenges the view that organisations are rational entities and seeks to replace it with a view of organisations as comprising moving coalitions of different interest groups.

The rationale for the emergent approach stems from the belief that change should not and cannot be solidified, or seen as a series of linear events within a given period of time; instead, it is viewed as a continuous process. Dawson (1994) sees change as a period of organisational transition characterised by disruption, confusion and unforeseen events that emerge over long time frames. Even when changes are operational, they will need to be constantly refined and developed in order to maintain their relevance.

From this perspective, Clarke (1994) suggested that mastering the challenge of change is not a specialist activity facilitated or driven by an expert, but an increasingly important part of every manager's role. To be effective in creating sustainable change, according to McCalman and Paton (1992), managers will need an extensive and systemic understanding of their organisation's environment, in order to identify the pressures for change and to ensure that, by mobilising the necessary internal resources, their organisation responds in a timely and appropriate manner. Dawson (1994) claimed that change must be linked with the complexity of changing market realities, the transitional nature of work organisation, systems of management control and redefined organisational boundaries and relationships. He emphasises that, in today's business environment, one-dimensional change interventions are likely to generate only short-term results and heighten instability rather than reduce it.

As can be seen, though they do not openly state it, advocates of emergent change tend to adopt a contingency perspective. For them, it is the uncertainty of the environment that makes planned change inappropriate and emergent change appropriate. Stickland (1998, p. 76) extends this point by raising a question that many of those studying organisational change appear not to acknowledge: 'To what extent does the environment drive changes within a system [i.e. organisation] and to what extent is the system in control of its own change processes?' Finstad (1998, p. 721) puts this issue in a wider context by arguing that 'the organization is . . . the creator of its environment and the environment is the creator of the organization'.

This reciprocal relationship between an organisation and its environment clearly has profound implications for how managers in organisations conceptualise and manage change. It also serves to emphasise that a key competence for organisations is the ability to scan the external environment in order to identify and assess the impact of trends and discontinuities (McCalman and Paton, 1992; Stickland, 1998). This includes exploring the full range of external variables, including markets and customers, shareholders, legal requirements, the economy, suppliers, technology and social trends. This activity is made more difficult by the changing and arbitrary nature of organisation boundaries: customers can also be competitors; suppliers may become partners; and employees can be transformed into customers, suppliers or competitors.

Changes in the external environment require appropriate responses within organisations. Appropriate responses, according to the supporters of the emergent approach, should promote extensive and deep understanding of strategy, structure, systems, people, style and culture. The organisation also needs an understanding of how these factors can function either as sources of inertia that can block change, or alternatively, as levers to encourage an effective change process (Pettigrew, 1997; Dawson, 2003). A major development in this respect is the move to adopt a 'bottom-up' rather than 'top-down' approach to initiating and implementing change. This is based on the view that the pace of environmental change is so rapid and complex that it is impossible for a small number of senior managers effectively to identify, plan and implement the necessary organisational responses. The responsibility for organisational change is therefore, out of necessity, becoming more devolved.

Key Learning Point

'While the primary stimulus for change remains those forces in the external environment, the primary motivator for how change is accomplished resides with the people within the organization.'

(Benjamin and Mabey, 1993, p. 181).

Supporters of the emergent approach identify five features of organisations that either promote or obstruct success: cultures, structures, organisational learning, managerial behaviour, and power and politics.

Organisational culture

Earlier in this chapter, it was argued that organisational culture is a complex and contentious subject which can be seen both as a constraint on, and as an object of, change. In looking at culture from the emergent perspective, Johnson (1993, p. 64) has taken the view that the strategic management of change is 'essentially a cultural and cognitive phenomenon' rather than an analytical, rational exercise. Clarke (1994) stated that the essence of sustainable change is to understand the culture of the organisation that is to be changed. If proposed changes contradict cultural biases and traditions, it is inevitable that they will be difficult to embed in the organisation.

In a similar vein, Dawson (1994) suggested that attempts to realign internal behaviours with external conditions require change strategies that are sensitive to the culture of the organisation. Organisations, he points out, must be aware that the change process is lengthy, potentially dangerous and demands considerable reinforcement if culture change is to be sustained against the inevitable tendency to regress to old behaviours. Clarke (1994) also stressed that change can be slow, especially where mechanisms that reinforce old or inappropriate behaviour (such as reward, recruitment and promotion structures) continue unchallenged. In addition, if these reinforcement mechanisms are complemented by managerial behaviour that promotes risk aversion and fear of failure, a climate where people are willing to propose or undertake change is unlikely. Accordingly, as Clarke (1994, p. 94) suggested, 'Creating a culture for change means that change has to be part of the way we do things around here, it cannot be bolted on as an extra.' Therefore, for many proponents of the emergent approach to change, if an appropriate organisational culture does not exist, it is essential that one is created.

However, not all its proponents take this view. Beer *et al.* (1993) suggested that the most effective way to promote change is not by directly attempting to influence organisational behaviour or culture. Instead, they advocate restructuring organisations in order to place people in a new organisational context, which imposes new roles, relationships and responsibilities upon them. This, they believe, *forces* new attitudes and behaviours upon people. Wilson (1992, p. 91) also warns against attempting to use culture to promote change, claiming that:

> to effect change in an organization simply by attempting to change its culture assumes an unwarranted linear connection between something called organizational culture and performance. Not only is this concept of organizational culture multifaceted, it is also not always clear precisely how culture and change are related, if at all, and, if so, in which direction.

It is apparent that, while the emergent approach recognises the importance of culture to organisational change, there is a split between two groups of experts:

1. those who believe an appropriate culture can be created, where one does not exist; and

2. those who believe that attempting to change culture is something an organisation does at its peril.

Key Learning Point

Several authors propose that cultural change is at the heart of the organisational change process - but there is some debate about whether it is wise to make deliberate attempts to change culture.

Organisational structure

This is seen as playing a crucial role in defining how people relate to each other and in influencing the momentum for change (Hucynski and Buchanan, 2001; Dawson, 2003; Kotter, 1996; Hatch, 1997). Therefore, an appropriate organisation structure can be an important lever for achieving change. However, both the informal and formal aspects of organisational structure need to be recognised if structure is to be used to effect change.

The case for developing more appropriate organisational structures in order to facilitate change very much follows the arguments of the contingency theorists (Child, 1984). Those favouring an emergent approach to change point out that the last 25 years have witnessed a general move to create flatter organisational structures. The aim of this has been to increase organizational responsiveness by devolving authority and responsibility (Senior, 2002). As Kotter (1996, p. 169) remarks, the case for such structural changes is that 'An organization with more delegation, which means a flat hierarchy, is in a far superior position to manoeuvre than one with a big, change-resistant lump in the middle.'

There is an increasing trend for organisations to position themselves to respond rapidly to changing conditions by breaking down internal barriers, disseminating knowledge and developing synergy across functions. Organisations that have done this have been called *network organisations* or, to use Handy's (1989) term, 'federal' organisations. Snow *et al.* (1993) suggested that the semi-autonomous nature of each part of a network reduces the need for, and erodes, the power of centrally managed bureaucracies. This, in turn, leads to change and adaptation being driven from the *bottom up* rather than from the top down. They further argue that the specialisation and flexibility required to cope with globalisation, intense competition and rapid technological change can only be achieved by loosening: (i) the ties between the various parts of the organisation and its 'centre' and (ii) the control that the centre of the organisation has over its various parts.

Key Learning Point

Adopting an emergent approach to change may require organisations to move towards radically different structures and cultures.

Organisational learning

For advocates of the emergent approach, learning plays a key role in preparing people for, and allowing them to cope with, change (Bechtold, 1997; Senge, 2000). Put simply, this learning means 'the capacity of members of an organization to detect and correct errors and to seek new insights that would enable them to make choices that better produce outcomes that they seek' (Martin, 2000, p. 463). In many instances, a willingness to change only stems from the feeling that there is no other option. Therefore, as Wilson (1992) suggests, change can be precipitated by making impending crises real to everyone in the organisation (or perhaps even engineering crises) or encouraging dissatisfaction with current systems and procedures. The latter is probably best achieved through the creation of mechanisms by managers that allow staff to become familiar with the marketplace, customers, competitors, legal requirements, etc., in order to recognise the pressures for change.

Clarke (1994) and Nadler (1993) suggested that individual and organisational learning stems from effective top-down communication and the promotion of self-development and confidence. In turn, this encourages the commitment to, and shared ownership of, the organisation's vision, actions and decisions that are necessary to (i) respond to the external environment and (ii) take advantage of the opportunities it offers. Additionally, as Pugh (1993) pointed out, in order to generate the need and climate for change, people within organisations need to be involved in the diagnosis of problems and the development of solutions. Carnall (2003) took this argument further, maintaining that organisational effectiveness can be achieved and sustained only through learning from the experience of change.

Clarke (1994, p. 156) believed that involving staff in change management decisions was so important because it was 'stimulating habits of criticism and open debate', enabling them to challenge existing norms and question established practices. This, in turn, creates the opportunity for innovation and radical change. Benjamin and Mabey (1993) argued that such questioning of the status quo is the essence of bottom-up change. They consider that, as employees' learning becomes more valued and visible, then rather than managers putting pressure on staff to change, the *reverse* occurs. The new openness and knowledge of staff put pressure on managers to address fundamental questions about the purpose and direction of the organisation, questions which previously they might have avoided. Consequently, as Easterby-Smith *et al.* (2000) and Tsang (1997) suggest, organisational learning is neither an easy nor an uncontentious option for organisations. There is also a great diversity of opinion as to what it is and how it can be promoted, which makes organisational learning a more difficult concept to apply than many of its supporters acknowledge (Burnes *et al.*, 2003).

Key Learning Point

The emergent approach highlights the importance of employees in stimulating and influencing the change process.

Managerial behaviour

The traditional view of organisations sees managers as directing and controlling staff, resources and information. However, the emergent approach to change requires a radical change in managerial behaviour. Managers are expected to operate as facilitators and coaches who, through their ability to span hierarchical, functional and organisational boundaries, can bring together and motivate teams and groups to identify the need for, and achieve, change (Mabey and Mayon-White, 1993).

To be effective in this new role, Clarke (1994) believed that managers would require knowledge of, and expertise in, strategy formulation, human resource management, marketing/sales and negotiation/conflict resolution. However, the key to success, the decisive factor in creating a focused agenda for organisational change is, according to Clarke (1994), managers' own behaviour. If managers are to gain the commitment of others to change, they must first be prepared to challenge their own assumptions, attitudes and mindsets so that they develop an understanding of the emotional and intellectual processes involved (Boddy and Buchanan, 1992).

For supporters of the emergent approach, the essence of change is the move from the familiar to the unknown. In this situation, it is essential for managers to be able to tolerate risk and cope with ambiguity. Pugh (1993) took the view that, in a dynamic environment, open and active communication with those participating in the change process is the key to coping with risk and ambiguity. This is echoed by Clarke's (1994, p. 172) assertion that because 'top-down, unilaterally imposed change does not tend to work, bottom-up, early involvement and genuine consultation' are essential to achieving successful change. This in turn requires managers to facilitate open, organisation-wide communication via groups, individuals and formal and informal channels.

An organisation's ability to gather, disseminate, analyse and discuss information is, from the perspective of the emergent approach, crucial for successful change. The reason for this, as Wilson (1992) argued, is that to effect change successfully, organisations need consciously and proactively to move forward incrementally. Large-scale change and more formal and integrated approaches to change (such as TQM) can quickly lose their sense of purpose and relevance for organisations operating in dynamic and uncertain environments. If organisations move towards their strategic vision on the basis of many small-scale, localised incremental changes, managers have a key role to play. They must ensure that those concerned, which could (potentially) be the entire workforce, have access to and are able to act on all the available information. Also, by encouraging a collective pooling of knowledge and information in this way, a better understanding of the pressures and possibilities for change can be achieved: this should then enable managers to improve the quality of strategic decisions (Buchanan and Boddy, 1992a,b; Quinn, 1993).

As well as ensuring the free flow of information, managers must also recognise and be able to cope with resistance to change, and political intervention in it. They will, especially, need to acquire and develop a range of interpersonal skills that enable them to deal with individuals and groups who seek to block change, or manipulate change, for their own benefit (Buchanan and Boddy, 1992a,b). In addition, supporting openness, reducing uncertainty and encouraging experimentation can be powerful mechanisms for promoting change (Mabey and Mayon-White, 1993). In this respect, Coghlan (1993) and McCalman and Paton (1992) advocated the use of OD tools and techniques (such as transactional analysis, teamwork, group problem-solving, role-playing, etc.) which have long been used in planned change programmes. However, there is an enormous and potentially confusing array of these; Mayon-White (1993) and Boddy and Buchanan (1992) argued that managers have a crucial role to play in terms of identifying and applying the appropriate tools and techniques. The main objective in deploying such tools and techniques is to encourage shared learning through teamwork and cooperation. It is this that provides the framework and support for the emergence of creative solutions and encourages a sense of involvement, commitment and ownership of the change process (Carnall, 2003; McCalman and Paton, 1992).

Nevertheless, it would be naive to assume that everyone will want to work, or be able to function effectively, in such situations. The cognitive and behavioural changes necessary for organisational survival may be too large for many people, including and perhaps especially managers. An important managerial task will, therefore, be to identify sources of inertia, assess the skill mix within their organisation and, most of all, consider whether their own managerial attitudes and styles are appropriate.

Key Learning Point

The emergent approach requires a major change in the traditional role of managers. In future they will need to be facilitators and coaches rather than initiators and directors.

Power and politics

Although the advocates of emergent change tend to view power and politics from differing perspectives, they all recognise their importance and that they have to be managed if change is to be effective. Dawson (1994, p. 176), for example, concludes that: 'The central argument is that it is important to try and gain the support of senior management, local management, supervisors, trade unions and workplace employees.' Pettigrew *et al.* (1992, p. 293) state that: 'The significance of political language at the front end of change processes needs emphasizing. Closures can be labelled as redevelopments. Problems can be re-coded into opportunities with . . . broad positive visions being articulated to build early coalitions.' However, in an era in which political 'spin' is increasingly recognised and questioned, the effectiveness and integrity of such 'political language' are debatable. Kanter *et al.* (1992, p. 508) argue that the first step to implementing change is coalition-building: 'involve those whose involvement really matters . . . Specifically, seek support from two general groups: (1) power sources and (2) stakeholders.' In a similar vein, Nadler (1993) advocates the need to shape the political dynamics of change so that power centres develop that support the change rather than block it. Senior (2002), drawing on the work of Nadler (1993), proposes four steps organisations need to take to manage the political dynamics of change:

Step 1: Ensure, or develop, the support of key power groups.

Step 2: Use leader behaviour to generate support for the proposed change.

Step 3: Use symbols and language to encourage and show support for the change.

Step 4: Build in stability by using power to ensure that some things remain the same.

Key Learning Point

Though power and politics can play an influential role in managing change, other factors, such as culture, also play an influential role.

Important though power and politics are in the change process, as Hendry (1996) and Pugh (1993) argue, they are not the be all and end all of change and it is important not to focus on these to the exclusion of other important factors. Nevertheless, the focus placed on the political dynamics of change does serve to highlight the need for those who manage change to be aware of and control this dimension of the change process.

STOP TO CONSIDER

Earlier in this chapter we asked you to consider the merits of the planned change approach. Now we would like you to do the opposite with the emergent approach to change. What might be the criticisms of the emergent approach to change? In what circumstances might it not be helpful to organisations seeking to implement change better? Try to do this for yourself before moving on to the next section.

Exercise 16.3   Birth of the living company

Arie de Geus is best known for his role in the development of the concept of the 'learning organisation'. He has also produced a series of works on organisation that take a holistic view of companies and their environment. A working manager who only turned to academia late in his career, he combines pragmatism with high theory. ▶

His statement that in the future a company's only sustainable advantage may be its ability to learn became a business mantra of the 1990s.

Mr de Geus was born in Rotterdam in 1930. He joined Royal Dutch/Shell in 1951 and remained there until his retirement in 1989. Since he retired he has been a visiting fellow of London Business School and has worked with MIT's Center for Organizational Learning. Here he worked closely with Peter Senge, who cited Mr de Geus as an influence over his book, *The Fifth Discipline*. Both Mr de Geus and Prof Senge have been credited with originating the term 'learning organisation', but in fact it was first used by Tom Peters and Robert Waterman in *In Search of Excellence* nearly 10 years earlier. In Mr de Geus's view, learning and knowledge-gathering are not peripheral management activities but the very heart of management and the company that learns how to do them well can compete and win. His article 'Planning as learning', published in *Harvard Business Review* in 1988, made the learning organisation into one of the most talked-about management concepts of our time.

Mr de Geus's principal work, *The Living Company*, goes further in understanding how the learning organisation functions. He compares it to a living organism, and links its ability to learn with the extent to which it is integrated into its environment. Living organisms scour their environment for sustenance: the 'living company' uses its environment to acquire knowledge, equally important to its survival. Mr de Geus believes that companies should develop strong bonds with their customers and shareholders and develop a 'harmony of values' with them. These strong relationships enable a greater depth of learning. Learning becomes built-in, enabling companies to grow organically and even become self-aware. Companies cannot exist in isolation. The 'learning organisation' and the 'living company' are thus simultaneous concepts.

There are no hard and fast rules for creating a living company. Companies evolve and their systems for learning will change over time. Learning should always happen, though, as a natural part of business activity. Learning organisations learn as entities; effective learning is shared, not locked up in individuals. If shared effectively, the sum total of an organisation's knowledge is much greater than the pooled knowledge of individuals can ever be. The strength of the 'living company' model is not its stress on learning, but its ability to integrate key concepts: knowledge management, communication, culture, systems and ethics. The living company has been called 'the most original and innovative model of business to emerge in the latter half of the 20th century'. It offers a route to sustainable success in the 21st century, too.

Source: From an article in the Financial Times, *21 August 2003, p. 11, by M. Witzel.*

1   What is the relationship between organisational learning and organisational culture?

2   How can learning facilitate organisational change?

3   How might becoming a learning organisation help an organisation to deal with rapidly changing and diverse customer needs?

Emergent change: summary and criticisms

The proponents of emergent change are a somewhat disparate group who tend to be united more by their scepticism regarding planned change than by a commonly agreed alternative. Nevertheless, there does seem to be some agreement regarding the main tenets of emergent change, which are:

■ Organisational change is a continuous process of 'experiment' and adaptation aimed at matching an organisation's capabilities to the needs and dictates of a dynamic and uncertain environment.

■ Though this is best achieved through a multitude of (mainly) small-scale incremental changes, over time these can lead to a major reconfiguration and transformation of an organisation.

■ The role of managers is not to plan or implement change. Instead it is to create or foster an organisational structure and climate that encourages and sustains experimentation and risk-taking, and to develop a workforce that will take responsibility for identifying the need for change and implementing it.

■ Although managers are expected to become facilitators rather than doers, they also have the prime responsibility for developing a collective vision or common purpose which gives direction to their organisation, and within which the appropriateness of any proposed change can be judged.

■ The key organisational activities that allow these elements to operate successfully are: information-gathering – about the external environment and internal objectives and capabilities; communication – the transmission, analysis and discussion of information; and learning – the ability to develop new skills, identify appropriate responses and draw knowledge from their own and others' past and present actions.

Though not always stated openly, the case for an emergent approach to change is based on the assumption that all organisations operate in a turbulent, dynamic and unpredictable environment. Therefore, if the external world is changing in a rapid and uncertain fashion, organisations need to be continually scanning their environment in order to adapt and respond to changes. Because this is a continuous and open-ended process, the planned approach to change is seen as inappropriate given the unpredictable nature of the environment that organisations exist within. To be successful, changes need to emerge locally and incrementally in order to respond to and take advantage of environmental threats and opportunities.

Presented in this fashion, there is certainly an apparent coherence and validity to the emergent approach. However, it is a fragile coherence and its validity can be challenged. As far as coherence is concerned, some proponents of emergent change, especially Dawson (1994) and Pettigrew and Whipp (1993), clearly approach it from the processual perspective on organisations. However, it is not clear that Wilson (1992) and Buchanan and Boddy (1992a,b) would fully subscribe to this view. In the case of Clarke (1994) and Carnall (2003), it is clear that they do not take a processual perspective. Partly, this is explained by the fact that some of these writers (especially Wilson, 1992; Pettigrew and Whipp, 1993; Dawson, 1994) are attempting to understand and investigate change from a critical perspective, while others (notably Carnall, 2003; Boddy and Buchanan, 1992; Buchanan and Boddy, 1992a,b; Clarke, 1994) are more concerned to provide practical guidance and tools for managing change successfully. Nevertheless, these differing objectives and perspectives do put a question mark against the coherence of the emergent approach.

The validity or general applicability of the emergent approach to change depends to a large extent on whether or not one subscribes to the view that all organisations operate in a dynamic and unpredictable environment to which they continually have to adapt. Burnes (2000, 2004b) produced substantial evidence that not all organisations face the same degree of environmental turbulence and that, in any case, it is possible to manipulate or change environmental constraints. This does not necessarily invalidate the emergent approach as a whole, but it does indicate that for some organisations, the planned approach to change may be both appropriate and effective in their particular circumstances.

Obviously, the above issues raise a question mark regarding the emergent approach; however, even without reservations regarding its coherence and validity, there would still be serious criticisms of this approach. For example, a great deal of emphasis is given to creating appropriate organisational cultures; but many writers have questioned whether this is either easy or indeed possible (Filby and Willmott, 1988; Meek, 1988). Indeed, as mentioned earlier, even Wilson (1992) was sceptical about the case for viewing culture as a facilitator of change. Similar points can be made regarding the 'learning organisation' approach. As Whittington (1993, p. 130) commented:

> The danger of the purely 'learning' approach to change, therefore, is that . . . managers [and others] may actually recognize the need for change, yet still refuse to 'learn' because they understand perfectly well the implications for their power and status. Resistance to change may not be 'stupid' . . . but based on a very shrewd appreciation of the personal consequences.

A variant of this criticism relates to the impact of success on managerial learning. Miller (1993, p. 119) observed that, while managers generally start out by attempting to learn all they can about their organisation's environment, over time, as they gain experience, they 'form quite definite opinions of what works and why' and as a consequence tend to limit their search for information and knowledge. So experience, especially where it is based on success, may actually be a barrier to learning, in that it shapes the cognitive structures by which managers, and everyone else, see and interpret the world. As Nystrom and Starbuck (1984, p. 55) observed:

> What people see, predict, understand, depends on their cognitive structures . . . [which] manifest themselves in perceptual frameworks, expectations, world views, plans, goals . . . myths, rituals, symbols . . . and jargon.

This brings us neatly to the topic of the role of managers. As the above quotations indicate, they may neither welcome nor be able to accept approaches to change that require them to challenge and amend their own beliefs, especially where such approaches run counter to their experience of 'what works and why'. It is in such situations that managers may seek to use their power and political influence in an adverse manner.

Advocates of the emergent approach have undoubtedly provided a valuable contribution to our understanding of change by highlighting the neglect of these important issues. However, they have also been criticised for overstating their case. Hendry (1996, p. 621) argues that: 'The management of change has become . . .

overfocused on the political aspects of change', while Collins (1998, p. 100), voicing concerns of his own and of other researchers, argues that:

in reacting to the problems and critiques of [the planned approach], managers and practitioners have swung from a dependence on under-socialized models and explanations of change and instead have become committed to the arguments of, what might be called, over-socialized models of change.

One final and important point which needs to be considered is that, though the emergent approach offers valuable insights and guidance, it does not appear to be as universally applicable as its advocates imply. The focus of emergent change tends to be the organisation and its major subsystems rather than individuals and groups per se. It is also the case that, both implicitly and explicitly, the emergent approach advocates cooperative change rather than coercive or confrontational change. Though this is to be applauded, it is also clear that there are many situations where change is pushed through in a rapid and confrontational manner (see Edwardes, 1983; Grinyer *et al.*, 1988; Dunphy and Stace, 1992; Franklin, 1997). It is also the case that the emergent approach is specifically founded on the assumption that organisations operate in a dynamic environment that requires continuous, coherent and, over time, large-scale change. It is, then, by its own definition, not applicable to organisations operating in stable environments or to those seeking to achieve a large-scale and rapid transition from one fixed state to another. In addition, as mentioned above, if the possibility exists to manipulate environmental variables and constraints to avoid having to undertake radical change, managers may perceive this as a more attractive or viable option.

Key Learning Point

Though the emergent approach to change has apparent advantages over the planned approach, an examination of it reveals that there are question marks over its coherence, validity and applicability.

Organisational change: approaches and choices

A framework for change

As Stickland (1998, p. 14) remarks:

the problem with studying change is that it parades across many subject domains under numerous guises, such as transformation, development, metamorphosis, transmutation, evolution, regeneration, innovation, revolution and transition to name but a few.

As this chapter has shown, there are two dominant and, in the main, quite different approaches to managing change – the planned and the emergent. However, despite their contributions to assisting organisations to manage change more effectively, as has been indicated, they do not cover the full spectrum of change events organisations encounter. Indeed, given the vast array of types of organisation – operating in different industries and different countries – and the enormous variety of change situations – ranging from small to large, from technical to people – and all stages in between, *it would be surprising if just two approaches could encompass all these situations*. Nevertheless, the important point is not to be able to categorise the variety of change situations per se, but to provide a framework that matches types of change situations with the appropriate ways of managing them.

Key Learning Point

Recent approaches to change place a great deal of emphasis on the situation that the organisation is in, rather than arguing for the effectiveness of a particular approach to change across a variety of different organisations that faced with situations and challenges.

This, of course, is no small task. Dunphy and Stace (1992), for example, identify four approaches to managing change based on the degree to which employees are involved in planning and executing change, as follows: collaborative, consultative, directive and coercive. They also argue that consultative and directive approaches tend to dominate, except where rapid organisational transformations are required, when more coercive approaches come into play. Kotter (1996) takes a different view, seeing the overall direction of change as being decided by senior managers, but its implementation being the responsibility of empowered managers and employees at all levels. Storey (1992) takes yet another tack. He identifies two key dimensions. The first concerns the degree of collaboration between the parties concerned: varying from change that is unilaterally constructed by management, to change brought about by some form of joint agreement with those involved. The second dimension concerns the form that change takes: ranging from change that is introduced as a complete package, to change comprising a sequence of different individual initiatives.

We could cover many pages in this fashion, listing the various ways of managing change that writers have identified. However, the key issues are: how can these approaches be classified and what determines which approach an organisation should take and in what circumstances?

In addressing these questions Burnes (2004b) constructed *a framework for change* (*see* Figure 16.2) comprising four quadrants, each of which has a distinct focus in terms of change. The top half of the figure, Quadrants 1 and 2, represents situations where organisations need to make large-scale, organisation-wide changes to either their culture or structure. The need for these changes may be caused by the organisation's environment being turbulent or the environment may become turbulent due to the organisation's structure/culture being inappropriate. The bottom half of the figure, Quadrants 3 and 4, represents situations where organisations need to make relatively small-scale and localised adjustments to the attitudes and behaviours or tasks and procedures of individuals and groups. Such changes must be sustained and, therefore, it is crucial to ensure that the post-change environment is stable. As can be seen, the left-hand side of the figure, Quadrants 1 and 4, represents situations where the main focus of change is the human side of the organisation, i.e.

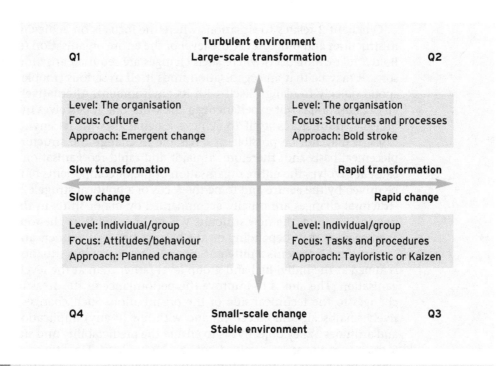

Figure 16.2   A framework for change

cultural and attitudinal/behavioural change. As argued above, these sorts of changes are likely to be best achieved through a relatively slow, participative approach, rather than a rapid and directive or coercive one. The right-hand side of Figure 16.2 represents situations where the primary focus is on achieving changes to the technical side of the organisation, i.e. structures, processes, tasks and procedures. These types of changes tend to be less participative in nature and relatively more rapid in their execution.

Key Learning Point

The nature of the change process required can be better understood by looking at the size of the change required, its intended outcomes and the organisational context of change.

Taking each of the quadrants in turn: Quadrant 1 identifies situations where the culture of an organisation is no longer appropriate for the environment in which the organisation is operating. For such relatively large-scale initiatives, where the main focus is culture change at the level of the entire organisation or large parts of it, the emergent approach (e.g. Kanter *et al.*'s Long March (Kanter *et al.*, 1992)), which emphasises both the collaborative and political dimensions of change, is likely to be most appropriate. Although the organisation may be operating in a turbulent environment and, therefore, individual elements of the cultural change may be rapid, the overall cultural transformation is likely to be a slow process.

Quadrant 2 relates to situations where the focus is on achieving major changes in structures and processes at the level of the entire organisation (e.g. Kanter *et al.*'s Bold Stroke). Situations where such changes are required arise for a variety of reasons. It may be that an organisation finds itself in serious trouble and needs to respond quickly to realign itself with its environment. Alternatively, it may be that an organisation is not experiencing a crisis, but that it perceives that it will face one unless it restructures itself to achieve a better fit with its environment. In such cases, it may not be possible or advisable to change the structure slowly or on a piecemeal basis and, therefore, a major and rapid reorganisation is necessary. Because it involves the entire organisation or major components of it, this is likely to be driven by the centre and to be the focus of a political struggle, given that major structural changes are usually accompanied by major shifts in the distribution of power. Therefore, the new structure will be imposed from the top in a directive or even coercive way, depending on the balance between winners and losers.

Quadrant 3 presents a different picture. This represents situations where change is aimed at the individual and group level rather than at the level of the entire organisation. The aim is to improve the performance of the areas involved through changes to the technical side of the organisation. Such changes tend to be relatively small-scale and piecemeal and with few (if any) implications for behaviour and attitudes. A key objective is to ensure the predictability and stability of the performance of the areas involved but at a higher level. How these changes are managed will depend on the culture of the organisation. In a traditional, bureaucratic organisation, a Tayloristic approach may be adopted, i.e. specialist managers and engineers will identify the 'best way of working' and impose it. In a more participative culture, such as a Japanese company, a more collaborative approach may be appropriate, such as a *Kaizen* initiative that brings together a team comprising workers and specialists. But either is possible and both can be achieved in a relatively speedy fashion.

Finally, Quadrant 4 covers relatively small-scale initiatives whose main objective is performance improvement through attitudinal and behavioural change at the individual and group level. As in the case of Quadrant 3, a key objective is to ensure the predictability and stability of the performance of the people involved but at a higher level. In such situations, planned change, with its emphasis on collaboration and participation, is likely to be most appropriate approach. However, because of the focus on behavioural and attitudinal change, the process may be relatively slow.

Of course, it could be argued that, at the organisational level, it is difficult to identify situations that involve solely cultural changes or involve solely structural changes. A similar comment could be made with regard to attitudinal/behavioural change and changes to tasks and procedures at the individual/group level. Such comments are valid to an extent, but the real issue is to identify the main focus of the change.

For example, writers such as Tom Peters (1997) and Rosabeth Moss Kanter (1989) argue for structural change in order to promote the cultural change they see as necessary for organisations to survive in an increasingly complex world. Therefore, though they recommend significant structural changes, these are part of the process of culture change and not an end in themselves. John Kotter (1996) advocates the need for organisations to restructure themselves on a continual basis in order to meet the challenges of the future. At different times and in different areas, he believes that this can involve all of the types of change shown in Figure 16.2. There are also many cases, as Kotter argues, where an organisation already has an appropriate culture and where changes to its overall structure, and piecemeal changes to its component parts, are seen as working with and reinforcing the existing culture rather than leading to its replacement.

Consequently, the question of whether changes can be labelled as mainly structure-oriented or mainly people-oriented is partly a matter of sequencing: what does the organisation need to do first? It is also partly concerned with the extent to which environmental turbulence has a uniform effect across an organisation. The pioneering work of James Thompson (1967) identified that different parts of an organisation, by accident or design, could experience different levels of uncertainty. On this basis, it would be perfectly feasible for some parts of an organisation to be experiencing relatively low levels of uncertainty and concentrating on small-scale, piecemeal changes whilst at the same time the overall organisation was going through a process of rapid transformation.

STOP TO CONSIDER

At this point in the chapter we are beginning to examine the merits of new approaches to understanding the change process. Earlier we asked you to consider the advantages and disadvantages of the planned and emergent approaches to change.

Now take time to consider how successful these new approaches might be in overcoming the criticisms of the planned and emergent approaches. We also saw that the planned and emergent approaches had some strengths: now consider whether these new approaches also have these same strengths.

Where does this leave us? Drawing on the work of Davenport (1993), we need to distinguish between initiatives that focus on fundamental attitudinal change and those aimed at fundamental structural change. As shown by Allaire and Firsirotu (1984), there is a strong relationship between organisational structures and organisational cultures, and so changes in one may require corresponding changes in the other. However, as they also showed, it is much easier and quicker to change structures than to change cultures. Consequently, we need to take into account the timescale for change.

Culture change, to be effective, is likely to be slow and involves incremental changes to the human side of the organisation. Also, because of its nature, it is likely to be participative and collaborative. Rapid change is only likely to be effective or necessary where the main changes are to structure, or where the organisation is in such trouble that delay is not an option (Beer and Nohria, 2000; Kanter *et al.*, 1992). In the case of structural change, this may involve some consultation but is likely to have a large element of direction from the centre. In the latter case, where the organisation is in trouble because of the urgency of the situation, change is likely to be directive and, possibly, coercive.

There is one further point that needs to be noted, and that relates to how these various approaches can be used in combination. In a manner similar to Mintzberg's (1994) definition of 'umbrella' strategies, Pettigrew *et al.* (1992, p. 297) write of instances where change is both 'intentional and emergent'. Storey (1992) identifies the need for change projects whose outlines are decided at corporate level with little or no consultation, but whose implementation comprises an interrelated series of change initiatives, some or all of which could be the product of local cooperation and consultation. Kotter (1996) takes a similar perspective. He sees strategic change as comprising a series of large and small projects aimed at achieving the same overall objectives but which are begun at different times, can be managed differently and vary in nature.

Buchanan and Storey (1997) also hint at this when criticising planned change for attempting to impose order and a linear sequence to processes that are untidy, messy, multilevel and multifunction, and that develop in an iterative and back-tracking manner. This is also identified by Kanter *et al.* (1992) when speaking of *Long Marches* and *Bold Strokes*. They argue that Bold Strokes often have to be fol-lowed by a whole series of smaller-scale changes over a more extended timescale in order to embed the changes brought about by the Bold Stroke. Beer and Nohria (2000) are even more explicit in arguing for the use of Theory E and Theory O in tandem. Similarly, Burnes (2004c) has also shown that major change projects that involve both structural and cultural change can successfully utilise both planned and emergent approaches. Consequently, when we attempt to understand, analyse or influence major change projects, we should not see them as being managed solely in a cooperative fashion or solely in a coercive fashion. Instead, they may have elements of both but at different levels, at different times and be managed by different people. They may also, indeed probably will, unfold in an unexpected way which will require rethinking and backtracking from time to time.

Key Learning Point

Change is a complex non-linear process. Attempts to better understand and manage change need to recognise this.

A framework for choice

As can be seen from Figure 16.2, what appears to be on offer is a menu approach to change whereby organisations, or more accurately those who manage them, can choose the approach that fits their circumstances. This conception of a multiplicity of approaches is in line with the call by Dunphy and Stace (1993, p. 905) for 'a model of change that is essentially a "situational" or "contingency model", one that indicates how to vary strategies to achieve "optimum fit" with the changing envi-ronment'. However, does this mean that organisations have no choice about which approach to use? We have identified situations where these various approaches seem appropriate or not, but does that mean they cannot be used in other situations and does that mean that the context cannot be changed? Supposing organisations, whose management prefer a cooperative approach, find themselves seriously out of alignment with their environment: is their only option rapid and coercive structural change? Or, alternatively, where managers prefer a more directive, less participative style, are they compelled to adopt a more participative style and culture?

These questions revolve around two issues. The first issue concerns the extent to which an organisation can influence the forces driving it to change in one direc-tion or another. If we accept that the speed and nature of the changes that organi-sations are required to make are dependent upon the nature of the environment in which they are operating, then choice will relate to the extent that organisations can influence, manipulate or recreate their environment to suit their preferred way of working. Over recent years, there has been growing support for those who argue that organisations can influence their environment, either to stabilise or to destabilise it (Morgan, 1997; Hatch, 1997; Burnes, 2004b). If this is the case, then the important question is not just how organisations can do this, but whether, finding themselves in trouble, they have the *time* to influence their environment.

This leads on to the second issue – to what extent and for how long can an organisation operate with structures, practices and cultures that are out of line with its environment? The answer to this question revolves around Child's (1972) concept of *equifinality*. Sorge (1997, p. 13) states that equifinality 'quite simply means that different sorts of internal arrangements are perfectly compatible with identical contextual or environmental states'. Put more simply, there are different ways to achieve the same end result. This does not imply that any structure is suitable for any environment. What it does suggest, though, is that total alignment between structure and environment is not always necessary. The duration for which this non-alignment is sustainable will clearly vary with the degree of non-alignment and the circumstances of the organisation in question; however, at the very least, it does offer organisations the potential to stave off realignment for some time during which they can influence or change their circumstances. It follows that Figure 16.2 depicts not only a framework for change but also a framework for choice.

It follows that the debate between planned change and emergent change is too narrow. It is too narrow in the sense that there are other approaches to change that organisations have available to them; especially it tends to ignore the more coercive and directive approaches to change that, in many organisations, may be more prevalent than more cooperative ones. It is also too narrow in the sense that it assumes that change is unidirectional, i.e. is driven by the environment. People in organisations do have the opportunity to make choices about what to change, how to change and when to change. This does not mean that all organisations will exercise such choices or that those that do will be successful. Nor does it mean that choice is not severely constrained. However, it does mean that those who do not recognise that choice exists may be putting themselves in a worse competitive position than those who do.

Key Learning Point

To understand change we need to consider the influence of the environment *and* the choices that are made by those involved in the change process.

Summary

This chapter began by examining the importance of organisational change, especially in relation to culture. It then went on to examine the merits, drawbacks and appropriateness of the planned and emergent approaches to change which have successively dominated the theory and, to a large extent, the practice of organisational change over the past 50 years. It has been argued that just as change comes in all shapes and sizes, so too do models or approaches to change. Therefore, instead of portraying the argument regarding the most appropriate approach to change as a contest between the merits of the planned and emergent approaches, a change framework has been developed (*see* Figure 16.2) which provides an overview of the range of change situations and approaches organisations face or are offered and the types of situations in which they can best be applied.

It has also been argued that the environment and other organisational constraints can be manipulated or subject to managerial choice. Consequentially, some organisations will find that the organisational adjustments required to accommodate their position on the environment continuum coincide with the dominant view in the organisation of how it should operate. In that case, whether the approach to change adopted is planned or emergent, directive or cooperative, it will fit in with both how the organisation wishes to operate and the needs of the environment. Some organisations will, obviously, find that the dominant view internally of how they should operate is out of step with what is required to align or realign them with their environment. Such organisations face a number of choices ranging from whether to attempt to change their structures, cultures or style of management to accommodate the environment, or whether to attempt to manipulate the environment and other constraints so as to align them more closely with the dominant view within the organisation of how it should operate. Still further, there will be other organisations that face severe problems either because they failed to respond quickly enough or in an appropriate manner to changes in their environment, or because the environment moved too rapidly for an incremental approach to respond adequately. Nevertheless, by showing that a more conducive environment can be brought about, the framework also provides those who wish to promote more cooperative approaches to change with the means to argue their case in situations where previously more directive and coercive measures appeared to be the only option.

The concept of a change framework that allows approaches to change to be matched to environmental conditions and organisational constraints is clearly attractive. The fact that it incorporates the potential for managers, and others, to exercise some choice or influence over their environment and other constraints allows the model to move beyond the limitations of mechanistic and rational perspectives on organisations, and into the heartland of organisational reality.

Key Learning Point

Just as organisations have choice in terms of what to change, they also have choice in what approach they adopt to change.

Closing Case Study | Team-building and problem-solving

GK Printers Limited is a small, family-run printing business. In the 1980s, in response to increased competition, it upgraded its technology and skills in order to concentrate on providing a full-range design and printing service to its customers. This enabled it to survive and prosper at a time when many companies of its size were going out of business. Nevertheless, by the mid-1990s, GK began to lose significant amounts of business. This was partly due to increased competition, but mainly it was because its customers, in seeking to cut their own costs, were reducing the size and frequency of their orders (though when orders were placed, they were often required far faster than previously). This presented a double threat to GK. First, the fall in overall volumes was having an adverse effect on turnover and profit. Second, the reduction in size of individual print runs was having an adverse effect on costs because, though the actual volume was smaller, the design, order processing and set-up costs remained constant.

Therefore, GK appeared to be faced with the dilemma of whether to increase its prices to offset rising costs (and risk more customers going elsewhere) or to maintain or reduce prices and see its profits plunge. The Marketing and Design Manager suggested that GK needed to improve on its already good level of service. In particular, it needed to cut costs in order to cut prices and improve the efficiency of its internal operations to cut delivery times. Other managers reacted negatively to this suggestion. The Marketing and Design Manager was relatively new to the company, and in some people's eyes, he lacked an in-depth knowledge of the printing industry. In addition, GK had already made significant strides in improving efficiency and cutting costs, and there was doubt as to the scope for any more real improvements in these areas.

Despite this, in the absence of any other credible suggestions, the Managing Director asked the Marketing and Design Manager to put together a plan for reducing costs and set-up times. Within a fortnight he presented his proposals to the Managing Director and other senior staff. He began by identifying what he saw as the main problems the company faced:

- Though there had been a slight decline in the number of individual orders, the actual reduction in the volume of business was much greater because customers were ordering shorter print runs.

- The result of this was that, while office staff, marketing, design, administration, etc., were as busy as ever, the print shop was short of work.

- However, though the printers were underworked, this did not provide much scope for reducing delivery times, because most of GK's lead time was accounted for by non-printing activities – especially design, which could take anything up to two weeks.

His solution was to hire more design staff. The Managing Director and other managers were taken aback by this proposal. They felt it was an outrageous piece of opportunism. The case for more design staff had been raised and rejected in the recent past. The Marketing and Design Manager's colleagues felt that he was using the company's current problems to empire-build. Not surprisingly, the meeting ended acrimoniously and no decision was taken.

The Managing Director was particularly infuriated, as he had genuinely been expecting an acceptable solution to emerge from the meeting. Instead, the friendly working atmosphere he valued had been shattered. After several weeks of indecision, during which tensions within the management team continued to rise, the Managing Director decided to seek outside assistance. He approached a contact at the local university who recommended a colleague with expertise in team-building. Though the Managing

Director was sceptical, his contact pointed out that, working together, there was enough experience in GK to solve its current dilemma. Therefore, the issue was how to bring people together, rather than seeking outside solutions.

With some misgivings, the Managing Director met with the team-builder and agreed to his suggested approach. First, all the relevant managers had to be involved. Second, the team-builder would meet each of them individually and then, as a group, would take them away from the company for two days to work on the problem. Third, each member of the team would have to agree to operate in an open and constructive fashion during the two days. Lastly, the team would agree to reach a commonly accepted solution by the end of the two days.

Although the GK management later admitted that the first day had been decidedly uncomfortable, they also agreed that the two days had been a success. The proceedings began with the team-builder reporting on his findings from the individual interviews. Though he did not reveal who said what, in a small organisation such as GK, it was relatively easy for managers to make a good guess as to the source of particular comments. This was one of the reasons why they found the first day uncomfortable.

The key issue which emerged from the team-builder's report and the subsequent discussion was the style of the Managing Director. He tended to make decisions either by himself or in consultation with one other manager. This created suspicion among managers excluded from decisions, and led to accusations of favouritism. All the managers, other than the Managing Director, favoured a more open and collective style of management.

The Managing Director was very upset and said so. He wanted, he said, to 'clear the air' there and then. However, the team-builder suggested, and agreement was eventually reached, that they should all reflect on what had been said, and return to the issue at the end of the second day. They then moved on to discuss the immediate problems facing GK: how to reverse the decline in turnover and profitability. With the delicate matter of the Managing Director's approach to decision-making out in the open, they found it much easier to reach an agreement on the way forward which they could all accept. They agreed to:

- Meet with their main customers to identify what their needs were and discuss how these could best be met.

- Review the entire production process, from order intake to dispatch, with the intention of either reducing it for all orders, or possibly shortening it for specific categories of orders.

These actions were to be carried out by two groups comprising managers and employees from the areas involved, who would report directly to the management team.

This then left the thorny issue of the Managing Director's role. Since the issue had been raised on the first day, he had spoken to the team-builder and his colleagues informally, and had come to recognise the strength of feeling on the issue, though he did not fully accept their interpretation of his actions. Nevertheless, he was prepared to try to amend his management style. He agreed that there would be regular management team meetings which would deal with all major decisions. He also agreed that he would not seek to impose a decision on the team unless the managers themselves could not reach agreement.

Six months later

The investigation of customer requirements and the order-to-dispatch process resulted in changes which brought significant improvements in the service GK could offer to its customers, and a reduction in lead times and costs. The company now offers its customers a choice of lead times and prices: normal – a two-week delivery and a 5 per cent reduction on the standard prices; accelerated – a one-week delivery charged at standard prices; and urgent – a one working day delivery charged at 10 per cent above standard prices.

In addition to these changes, the management team, after some initial difficulties (such as identifying what constituted a major decision), found that working together and having all information out in the open reduced the tension, not only between individual managers but between the individual functions as well.

Suggested exercises

1 Use the Framework for Change shown in Figure 16.1 to analyse and identify the form of change or changes described in the GK case study.

2 To what extent can the changes in how the management team operates be seen as the beginning of a cultural change or merely an adaptation within an existing culture?

3 Does the GK case study represent an example of emergent change, or of ad hoc and reactive management?

Test your learning

Short-answer questions

1 What was Kurt Lewin's main contribution to the development of organisational change?

2 How does Bullock and Batten's phases of change model differ from Lewin's three-step model?

3 What are the main advantages of the planned approach?

4 What are the main disadvantages of the planned approach?

5 What are the key components of the emergent approach?

6 How does the emergent approach view the role of organisational culture?

7 What are the main advantages of the emergent approach?

8   What are the main disadvantages of the emergent approach?

9   What are the main arguments for linking organisational culture to organisational performance?

10 What are the arguments for and implications of seeing organisations as 'societies in miniature'?

11 Explain the main components of organisational culture.

12 What are the practical benefits of the framework for change shown in Figure 16.1?

13 What factors should managers take into account, and why, when choosing an approach to change?

14 In what ways might an organisation influence its environment?

Suggested assignments

1   To what extent can it be said that, in today's rapidly changing world, the planned approach to change is no longer relevant?

2   Discuss the proposition that the emergent approach is nothing more than an attempt to provide an intellectual justification for allowing managers to adopt an ad hoc approach to change.

3   Describe and discuss the planned and emergent approaches' view of the role of managers.

4   Critically evaluate the differences between the optimists, pessimists and realists approach to culture.

5   What are the main constraints on organisations when deciding on which approach to change to adopt?

6   In what ways can the framework for change, shown in Figure 16.2, be used to increase managerial choice?

Relevant websites

The Intute website (http://www.intute.ac.uk) is a good source of links to well-known writers on the topic of change. Using the search engine on this website you can access the work of management gurus such as Peter Drucker and Tom Peters.

A short account of a practical outlook on organisational change can be found at http://www.galtglobalreview.com. Type 'change' into the search box. How well do you think what is stated here matches the content of Chapter 16?

A significant proportion of academic work on organisational change is published in the *Journal of Organizational Change Management*. The website for this journal can be found at http://www.tandf.co.uk/journals/titles/14697017.asp/. If you are a student at a university, there is a good chance that your university subscribes to this journal, in which case you will probably be able to download articles free of charge. A free sample copy can be requested.

For further self-test material and relevant, annotated weblinks please visit the website at **www.pearsoned.co.uk/workpsych**

Suggested further reading

Full details for all references are given in the list at the end of this book.

1   Bernard Burnes (2004b) *Managing Change*, 4th edition, FT/Prentice Hall: Harlow. This book provides a comprehensive review of the development of organisations and organisational change. It expands on this chapter and contains ten detailed case studies of major change projects in European companies.

2   Patrick Dawson (2003) *Reshaping Change: A processsual perspective*. Routledge: London. As the title states, this book examines the processual perspective on change which, for many people, lies at the core of the arguments for emergent change.

3   Thomas G. Cummings and Christopher G. Worley (2004) *Organization Development and Change*, 8th edition. South-Western College Publishing. The book provides a comprehensive guide to planned change and OD.

GLOSSARY OF TERMS

Action orientation   A psychological state in which a person uses self-regulatory strategies in order to achieve desired goals. Contrast with **State orientation** (*see below*).

Action research   A form of research that concentrates on solving practical problems in collaboration with the people and organisations experiencing them. For example in organisational change this is an iterative process aimed at improving organisational performance, and it involves three equal parties acting in concert: the organisation, its employees and a change agent.

Adjustment   The extent and ways in which a person is able to function effectively and happily in their environment.

Advanced manufacturing technology   Computer-controlled machinery that can perform sophisticated production activities once appropriately programmed.

Agreeableness   A positive orientation towards others, sympathetic, eager to help – preferring collaboration to conflict.

Alarm reaction   When an individual's defence mechanisms become active.

Alienation   A state of being where a person does not feel that they are in touch with their true self, nor do they experience fulfilling relationships with others.

Alternative hypothesis   (also called the *experimental hypothesis*) The hypothesis that is the alternative to the null hypothesis. The alternative hypothesis essentially proposes that 'something is going on' in the data. That is, that two or more groups of people do differ on a psychological variable, or that two or more variables are correlated with each other.

Analysis of variance   A statistical technique used to test whether two or more samples have significantly different mean scores on one or more variables.

Antecedents   Events that precede the occurrence of behaviour. In (non-behaviourist) approaches they may be seen to *cause* the behaviour.

Anxiety   *See* **Neuroticism**.

Archival data   Research information obtained from written, computerised or audiovisual sources that exist independent of the research.

Assessee   Person whose behaviour is being assessed by an assessor (either in an interview, performing a work sample task, or on the job).

Assessment centre   An assessment process that involves multiple exercises and multiple assessors to rate an assessee's performance on a series of job-related competencies.

Assessor   Person who is observing and assessing a target person's behaviour for the purposes of assessing whether they are, or are likely to be able to, perform a role effectively.

Associative phase   The second phase of skill acquisition, when the learner begins to combine the actions needed to produce skilled performance.

Attitude   A regularity in an individual's feelings, thoughts and predispositions to act towards some aspect of their environment.

Attractiveness of communicator   The extent to which a person attempting to change the attitude of another is seen as the kind of person that the recipient of the message would like to be.

Attribution   The explanation a person constructs for the nature or behaviour of another person.

Autonomous phase   The final phase of skill acquisition, when performance becomes increasingly polished. To some degree performance is automatic and control relies less and less on memory or attention.

Autonomy at work (control)   When individuals feel that they have some influence and control over their jobs.

Behavioural indicator   A description of an observable behaviour related to a specific competency.

Behaviourally anchored rating scales (BARS)   Rating scales that use anchors that describe specific behaviour. The behaviours provide anchors for a spread (good–poor) of performance standards and are derived from a systematic development procedure.

Behaviourism   An approach to psychology that concentrates on the external (to the person) conditions under which behaviour is exhibited and the observable consequences of behaviour.

Behaviourist tradition   The approach that focuses on behaviour, rather than thoughts and emotions.

Behaviour-modelling training   An approach to training in which models are reinforced for engaging in the intended behaviour.

Behaviour modification   Application of reinforcement principles to strengthen desired behaviour patterns at work.

Belongingness need   The psychological need to feel part of a group, organisation or other collective endeavour.

Bias   A psychological assessment procedure is biased if consistent errors of prediction (or classification) are made for members of a particular subgroup.

Biodata   Life history information about candidates, usually collected with the aid of a structured questionnaire. Criterion-related validity for biodata is explored by examining statistical links between biodata items and criterion measures.

Bold Strokes   These are major and rapid change initiatives which are imposed on an organisation from the top in a directive rather than participative manner.

Boundaryless career   A term given to careers that cross boundaries, for example between employers and job functions.

BPS   British Psychological Society – the governing body for psychologists in the United Kingdom.

Brainstorming   A technique for generating ideas which involves people thinking of as many things as possible that might be relevant to a given problem, however far-fetched their ideas may seem.

Bullying   Negative acts towards a person where the perpetrator has more power than the victim. The definition of bullying is complex (*see* Chapter 12) and this glossary definition is intended to capture just a couple of the main points discussed in the research.

Bureaucratic career   The term given by Kanter to a career characterised by predictable upward movement within one organisation and/or occupation.

Call centres   Work environments where computer and telephone-based technologies are used to distribute incoming calls from customers or clients to available staff.

Career   The sequence of employment-related positions, roles, activities and experiences encountered by a person.

Career anchor   The set of self-perceived skills, interests, motives and values that form a basis for a person's career preferences, and which they would not give up even if required to make a difficult choice.

Career choice   The selection made by a person of an area of work or sequence of work roles that they intend to pursue.

Career counselling   An interpersonal process that enables people to recognise and utilise their resources to make career-related decisions and manage career-related problems.

Career decision-making   The psychological processes involved in making a career choice.

Career development   The changes and adjustments experienced by a person as a consequence of a career choice.

Career exploration   The process of investigating oneself and the world of work in order to assist in career decision-making and career management.

Career management   The techniques and strategies used by individuals and organisations in seeking to optimise careers.

Career plateau   The point in a person's career when the likelihood of additional increases in responsibility is very low.

Career stage   A period of time in a person's career characterised by a particular set of concerns or motives.

Career success   The extent to which a person's career is achieving the goods that matter to the person and/or society as a whole.

Central route to persuasion   Attitude change which occurs as a result of a person carefully considering information and arguments relevant to that attitude.

Change agent   An internal or external facilitator whose role is to guide an organisation through a process of change.

Charisma   A set of attributes of leaders and/or their relationships with subordinates where the leader demonstrates and promotes a sense of pride and mission through personal example.

Chartered psychologist (C. Psychol.)   Title conferred by the BPS recognising the qualifications and experience of psychologists in the United Kingdom. Appropriately qualified work psychologists may also use the title Chartered Occupational Psychologist.

Chi-square   A statistical technique used to test whether two or more groups of people differ in the frequency with which their members fall into different categories.

Classical conditioning   A form of conditioning in which a previously neutral stimulus such as a tone (the conditioned stimulus) is repeatedly linked with the presentation of an unconditioned stimulus (such as food) so that the conditioned stimulus will, after repeated pairings, produce the unconditioned response (e.g. salivation) normally associated with the unconditioned stimulus. In other words (using this example) an animal could be conditioned to salivate at the sound of a tone.

Coaching   A form of development where one person advises and demonstrates to another on how to improve their work performance.

Cognitive ability   Also referred to as intelligence or general mental ability. Refers to the capacity of individuals to process information and use the information to behave effectively (including the capacity to learn from experience).

Cognitive phase   The first phase of skill acquisition, when the learner is developing knowledge about the task but lacks the procedural skill to carry it out.

Cognitive psychology   The branch of basic psychology that concerns the study of human perception, memory and information processing.

Cognitive resource theory   A theory of leadership proposed by Fred Fiedler which focuses on how the cognitive resources (e.g. intelligence, knowledge) of leaders influence group performance in situations of varying stress and leader control.

Cognitive task analysis (CTA)   An analysis of the underlying cognitive skills and processes required for performing a task.

Cohort effect   Lasting differences in psychological functioning between people born in different eras.

Common method variance   The extent to which people's scores on two or more psychological variables are related solely because the variables were assessed using the same research method.

Communities of practice   Groups of people who work with a common purpose or goal, that learn from each other by working together and interacting with each other.

Competency   The specific behaviour patterns (including knowledge, skills and abilities) a job holder is required to demonstrate in order to perform the relevant job tasks with competence.

Competency analysis   A person or worker-oriented approach to job analysis that focuses on identifying the relevant knowledge, skills and abilities relevant to a specific job role.

Concurrent validity   A form of criterion-related validity in which data on the predictor and criterion are obtained at the same time.

Conditioned stimulus   *See* **Classical conditioning**.

Conditions of worth   In phenomenological approaches to personality, conditions of worth are the conditions under which other people are prepared to value us as a person.

Congruence   In John Holland's theory, congruence is the extent to which a person's vocational personality matches their work environment.

Conscientiousness   A predisposition to prefer active control and organisation. A conscientious person will like to be purposeful and well-organised and see life in terms of tasks to be accomplished.

Consideration   An aspect of leadership style which reflects the extent that the leader demonstrates trust of subordinates, respect for their ideas and consideration of their feelings.

Construct validity   An indication of the extent to which the test or procedure measures the psychological construct that it is intended to measure.

Content analysis   A technique for analysing qualitative data that sorts the data, or parts of it, into different categories according to its content.

Content theories of motivation   Theories which concentrate on *what* motivates people, rather than *how* motivation works. Contrast with **Process theories of motivation** (*see below*).

Content validity   A form of validity based on a logical analysis of the extent to which a test or procedure embodies a representative sample of the behaviour from the domain being measured.

Contextual awareness   An awareness of the situation that another person (e.g. a colleague) finds themselves in.

Contiguity   The existence of only a small delay between behaviour and reinforcement (or punishment).

Contingency   This is present if reinforcement (or punishment) is given *only* when specific behaviour precedes it.

Contingency theories of leadership   These are theories of leadership that focus on how features of the situation determine what is the most effective leadership style.

Contingency theory   An approach to organisation design which rejects any universal best way and instead views organisation structures as being dependent (i.e. contingent) on the particular combination of situational variables each organisation faces. The main situational variables cited in the literature are environment, technology and size.

Control group   In an experiment investigating the impact of one or more interventions, the control group of research subjects does *not* experience an intervention. This group provides a comparison with groups which do experience an intervention.

Core job characteristics   The five aspects of jobs suggested by Hackman and Oldham as being essential in influencing satisfaction, motivation and job performance. The five are: skill variety, task identity, task significance, autonomy and feedback.

Correlation   A statistical technique used to test whether scores obtained from one sample on two variables are associated with each other, such that as scores on one variable increase, scores on the other either increase (positive correlation) or decrease (negative correlation).

Creativity   The generation of new and original ideas (contrast with **Innovation**).

Credibility of communicator   The extent to which a person attempting to change the attitude of another is seen as expert and trustworthy.

Criterion-related validity   The extent to which a predictor (e.g. a selection test score) is related to a criterion (e.g. work performance). In personnel selection, high criterion-related validity indicates that a selection measure gives an accurate indication of candidates' performance on the criterion.

Critical incident technique   A technique developed by Flanagan (1954), still widely used, to obtain information about jobs by concentrating on specific examples (incidents) of outstandingly good or poor performance.

Critical psychological states   The three immediate psychological effects of the core job characteristics, as proposed by Hackman and Oldham. The three are: experienced meaningfulness of the work, experienced responsibility for outcomes of the work and knowledge of the actual results of work activities.

Cross-sectional research   Research where data are collected at only one point in time.

Cross-validation   A research technique where a piece of research is repeated on a second sample to see if the same results as first time are obtained.

Culture   The human-generated part of the environment that is transmitted across time and generations and leads to people within that culture developing shared meanings; culture gives people 'standard operating procedures' or ways of doing things.

Cumulative trauma   The gradual build up of stress which leads to some stress-related illness or event; a term also applied to stress litigation cases.

Decision-making style   A person's normal or habitual way of going about making decisions.

Declarative knowledge   Factual knowledge that may be stated or made explicit.

Defence mechanisms   In the psychoanalytic approach to personality, these are the methods we use to deal with intrapsychic conflicts that provoke anxiety.

Demand characteristics   Features of experiments that convey clues to subjects about the hypotheses being investigated.

Democratic leadership   A leader style that encourages self-determination, equal participation and active deliberation by group members.

Dependent variable   The variable on which the impact of one or more independent variables is investigated in an experiment.

Developmental psychology   The branch of basic psychology that concerns how people develop and change throughout their life.

Development centre   A career management intervention where assessment centre methods are used to identify individual development needs and formulate development plans.

Differential validity   This would exist if there was conclusive evidence that a selection procedure had different levels of criterion-related validity for different subgroups of the population.

Discourse analysis   A technique for analysing qualitative data where the aim is to interpret what is said or written in the light of how the speaker or writer might be trying to present themself.

Dispersed collaboration   When people working together on a task are spread across different locations.

Dispositional approach to attitudes   An approach which views attitudes as determined by a person's genetic make-up or by other deep-seated stable personality characteristics.

Distributive bargaining   A form of negotiation characterised by an assumption by the negotiators that the total rewards available are fixed, so that one negotiator's gain is another's loss.

Distributive justice   Perceptions of equal treatment of different people.

Diversity   A general term given to the ways in which members of a workplace or labour force differ from one another (*see also* **Managing diversity**).

EAP   Employee assistance programme, usually referring to a counselling service provided for employees, most often by outside providers.

E-business   The procurement, production, marketing and selling of goods and services using computer communication, particularly the Internet.

Effect evaluation (or outcome evaluation)   A test of whether an intervention has resulted in change to important variables (e.g. increased performance). *See also* **Process evaluation**.

Effect size   The magnitude of an association between scores on one or more variables, or of the differences in mean scores between two or more samples.

Ego   In the psychoanalytic approach to personality, the ego is the part of the psyche that seeks to channel id impulses in socially acceptable ways.

E-learning   The use of ICT to shape the learning environment and deliver education and training interventions.

Electronic monitoring   There are different forms of electronic monitoring, which involve computers and recording instruments to observe and record an employee's performance over time. Examples include using computer programs to record the keystrokes made by an employee, or everything that is said to customers.

Emergent change   This is a bottom-up and open-ended approach that views organisations as constantly having to adjust to changing environmental circumstances.

Emotional instability   *See* **Neuroticism**.

Emotional intelligence   A set of characteristics and styles that is thought to enable a person to utilise intellect, emotion and awareness of other people in their day-to-day behaviour.

Emotional labour   The psychological effort that goes into a job that requires the worker to manage their emotions often in responses to others' (e.g. customers') displays of emotions.

Employee empowerment   The degree to which employees have a say in their jobs or the organisation they work for.

Employee relations   The accommodations made by the various parties involved in getting work done.

Empowerment   A human resource management technique that (i) increases employee involvement in (and responsibility for) decision-making and quality management, and (ii) encourages employees to learn a wide range of skills to ensure their capacity to make an effective contribution to organisational performance.

Engagement   Absorption in work, often because it is fulfilling and enjoyable.

Entrepreneurial career   The term given by Kanter to a career concerned with building one's own business through creating value through new goods or services.

Equal opportunities   The attempt to ensure that all people, no matter what their group memberships, are given a fair chance to succeed in the workplace.

Equity theory   An approach to motivation which argues that people are motivated to achieve an equitable (fair) return for their efforts in comparison with other people.

Ergonomics (human factors integration)   The application of what we know about human psychology and physiology to the design of tasks, work environments and wider organisational systems that are integral to the use of work equipment.

Escalation of commitment   A process whereby a person makes further investments in a course of action in order to justify to self and others their original decision to pursue that action.

Esteem need   The psychological need to feel respected by others and also by oneself.

Ethics   Rules of conduct that protect the well-being, dignity and other interests of people who participate in the research of work psychologists and/or use their services.

Ethnic identity   A person's image of self in terms of cultural, national or racial characteristics (*see also* **Ethnicity**).

Ethnicity   A person's cultural, national or racial group membership (*see also* **Ethnic identity**).

Exhaustion   When one's adaptive mechanisms collapse.

Expectancy   In expectancy theory, expectancy is the extent to which a person believes that they have the ability to perform certain behaviours.

Expectancy theory   An approach to motivation that focuses on the rational decision-making processes involved in choosing one course of action from alternatives.

Experiment   A research design in which the researcher controls or manipulates one or more independent variables in order to investigate their effect on one or more dependent variables.

Experimental group   The group of subjects in an experiment which experiences one or more interventions in an investigation of the impact of those interventions.

Experimental hypothesis   *See* **Alternative hypothesis**.

External validity   The extent to which one can be sure that some specific training will generalise and bring about results for subsequent groups of trainees or settings.

Extinction   This occurs when behaviour is not followed by reinforcement (or punishment). Under these circumstances operant behaviour will cease to occur.

Extrinsic motivation   The motivation to perform a task derived from rewards that are not part of the task itself (e.g. money, status). Contrast with **Intrinsic motivation** (*see below*).

Extroversion   A personality factor characterised by lively, sociable, excitable and gregarious behaviour.

Face validity   A very weak form of validity based on the extent to which a test or procedure appears to measure a particular construct.

Factor analysis   A statistical technique used to identify key factors that underlie relationships between variables.

Faith validity   A blind acceptance by users of the extent to which a selection tool is valid.

Flight-fight reaction   Individuals will choose whether to stay and fight or try to escape when confronting extreme danger or stress.

Framing effect   The impact on decision-making of the way the problem is expressed – for example either in terms of its potential losses or its potential gains.

Freudian slip   When a person accidentally says something that reflects their unconscious desires.

Functional flexibility   The name often given to the second aspect of **empowerment** described above.

Functional job analysis   An approach to job analysis that uses a standardised language and concentrates on the tasks (rather than skills) required for the job.

Fundamental attribution error   The tendency to attribute our own behaviour to more situational causes (e.g. circumstances, behaviour of others) than internal causes (e.g. personality, intentions), whilst doing the opposite when observing the behaviour of other people.

g   *See* **Cognitive ability**.

General mental ability   *See* **Cognitive ability**.

Goal commitment   In goal-setting theory, goal commitment is the extent to which a person is determined to achieve a goal.

Goal-setting theory   This approach to motivation concentrates on how goals (performance targets) can affect a person's work strategies and performance.

Grounded theory   Theory that develops during the process of data collection in a research project, and which influences data collection later in the same project.

Group   Two or more people who are perceived by themselves and others as a social entity.

Group polarisation   A phenomenon where the decision of a group after discussion is more extreme than the original preferences of individual group members.

Groupthink   A failure of group decision-making identified by Irving Janis, where the motivation of group members to seek agreement with each other exceeds their motivation to conduct a thorough and open analysis of the situation.

Hawthorne studies   A series of investigations of work behaviour conducted at the Hawthorne factory of the Western Electric Company near Chicago, USA in the 1920s.

Heuristic   General rules that people use to guide their decision-making about complex problems.

Hierarchical task analysis   A procedure for identifying the tasks involved in a job, which proceeds to increasingly detailed task units. Task breakdown ceases when predetermined criteria are satisfied, ensuring that the analysis is sufficiently detailed for the purpose in mind.

Humanism   *See* **Phenomenological approach to personality**.

Human-centred design   The process of designing tasks and equipment for humans that is guided by knowledge of the end-users' needs and capabilities.

Human-machine interface (HMI)   The fit between the skills, knowledge and ability of the user and the controls and displays of the machine.

Id   In the psychoanalytic approach to personality, the id is the part of the psyche that consists of basic instincts and drives.

Incremental validity   The importance of a variable *in addition to* other variables already accounted for.

Independent variable   A variable that is manipulated or controlled in an experiment in order to examine its effects on one or more dependent variables.

Informal assessment   Ongoing observation and assessment of individuals that occurs on a day-to-day basis which is not part of a structured system of assessment and which can be subjective and vulnerable to bias.

Innovation   The successful development of new ideas.

Instrumentality   In expectancy theory, instrumentality is the extent to which a person believes that performing certain behaviours will lead to a specific reward.

Integrative bargaining   A form of negotiation characterised by collaborative problem-solving and attempts by the negotiators to find a mutually beneficial solution.

Intelligence   *See* **Cognitive ability**.

Internal validity   The extent to which one can be confident that a specific training programme (rather than some other possible cause) has brought about changes in trainees.

Interpretative phenomenological analysis (IPA)   An approach to the collection and analysis of qualitative data. It emphasises the impact that both researcher and participant interpretations of the world have on the data collected and the results of the analysis.

Interview method   Research method where the researcher asks questions face-to-face or on the telephone with one or more subjects.

Intra-organisational (or intra-party) bargaining   The negotiations that occur between members of the same party.

Intrinsic motivation   The motivation to perform a task for rewards that are part of the task itself (e.g. interest, challenge). Contrast with **Extrinsic motivation** (*see above*).

Introversion   A personality factor characterised by a lack of enthusiasm for the company of others and a low-key, risk-averse and unexcitable approach.

Job analysis   Procedures (there is more than one way to do a job analysis) for producing systematic information about jobs, including the nature of the work performed, position in the organisation, relationships of the job holder with other people.

Job characteristics model   The name given to Hackman and Oldham's theory (*see also* **Core job characteristics** and **Critical psychological states**).

Job components inventory (JCI)   A job analysis technique developed in the United Kingdom (Banks *et al.*, 1983) which can provide profiles of the skills required for the job in question.

Job redesign   Collective name given to techniques designed to increase one or more of the variety, autonomy and completeness of a person's work tasks.

Job satisfaction   A pleasurable or positive emotional state arising from the appraisal of one's job or job experiences.

Knowledge management   A general term given to the attempt by organisations to ensure that the learning, information and experience possessed by individuals or subgroups is made available to all members.

Laissez-faire leadership   A leadership style in which the leader remains very uninvolved and passive.

Latent structure (e.g. of work performance and personality)   Personality theorists have identified five broad factors of personality that they argue encapsulate the underlying structure of personality. Certain work psychologists argue that there is a similar latent structure to work performance that comprises underlying components of work performance, common to all work roles.

Leader   The person who is appointed, elected or informally chosen to direct and coordinate the work of others in a group.

Leader-member relations   Defined as a feature of the situation in Fiedler's contingency theory of leadership, this refers to the extent to which leader and subordinates have relationships characterised by respect and mutual trust.

Learning data   Data that are concerned with the extent to which specific skills and knowledge have been attained.

Learning goal orientation   An approach people may take to a task where their main concern is to increase their level of competence on the task. Contrast with **Performance goal orientation** (*see below*).

Learning organisation   An organisation that has systems and processes in place to encourage individual learning, and ensure that it is passed on and shared by different organisational members and groups. The learning is focused on helping the organisation achieve its goals.

Least preferred co-worker (LPC)   In Fiedler's contingency theory, LPC refers to the leader's attitude towards the subordinate they like least. This attitude is assumed to reflect the leader's general orientation towards others at work.

Life stage   A period of time in a person's life characterised by a particular set of concerns or motives.

Likert scaling   A method of measuring attitudes where people respond by indicating their opinion on a dimension running from (for example) 'strongly agree' at one end to 'strongly disagree' at the other.

Locus of control   The degree to which the individual feels that they have substantial control over events (internality) or little control over events (externality).

Longitudinal research   Research where data are collected at two or more points in time, usually months or years apart.

Long Marches   Change initiatives that comprise a series of small-scale, local, incremental changes which have little overall effect in the short-term but over the long-term can transform an organisation.

Managerial grid Put forward by Blake and Mouton, this is a simple aid to assessing leadership style, based on the leader's person and task orientation.

Managing diversity The process of ensuring that all members of a workforce are treated in a way that respects their individuality, group memberships and capacity to make a contribution.

Media richness This is the theory that some ways of communicating contain more contextual information then others, and that this contextual information has an impact on how people interpret the communication.

Mediator variable A variable that acts as a link in the relationship between two other variables (i.e. it is the 'bridge' that forges the relationship between two variables).

Mentoring An approach to development in which an experienced mentor is paired with a less experienced colleague to offer career advice, support and assistance in the development of new skills.

Meta-analysis A statistical technique for aggregating data from a number of different studies in order to establish overall trends.

Mixed methods The use of different methods, often both qualitative and quantitative, in a single piece of research. If done effectively this mixing of methods can strengthen the research.

Moded displays Displays that give the user access to information as it needed, rather than displaying all the information all of the time.

Modelling The process by which one person demonstrates certain behaviours which are then learned, and may be performed, by observers.

Moderator variable A variable that alters the strength of the relationship between two other variables.

Motivating potential score Arithmetical combination of Hackman and Oldham's job characteristics designed to summarise the overall quality of a job from a psychological point of view.

Motivation The factors which determine the effort, direction and persistence of a person's behaviour.

Motivation to manage The needs and values which underlie the effort and persistence a person devotes to management tasks.

Multiple intelligences The notion that there is a range of quite separate human abilities (contrast to **Cognitive ability**).

Multiple regression A statistical technique used to identify which of two or more variables are most strongly correlated with another variable (usually called the criterion variable).

Multi-source feedback (MSF) A system of collecting performance feedback from multiple sources, usually including self, manager, subordinates, colleagues and possibly clients or customers.

Myers-Briggs type indicator (MBTI) A measure of personality that measures personality differences between people in terms of a set of four different dichotomies.

National culture   The set of values, assumptions and beliefs that are dominant in the population of a particular country.

Need   A biologically based desire that is activated by a discrepancy between actual and desired states.

Need for achievement   The desire to carry out a task as well and as quickly as possible.

Negative reinforcement   This is *not* punishment. Negative reinforcers *increase* the probability of the preceding behaviour when they are *removed* from the situation (for example, putting up an umbrella takes away the rain).

Negotiation   The process of attempting to resolve, through discussion, differences of opinion between two or more individuals or groups.

Networking   The development and maintenance of social contacts in order to increase one's learning access to information and opportunity, and to help others do the same.

Neuroticism   A predisposition to be tense and anxious. Sometimes referred to as emotional instability, or anxiety.

New technology   A generic label used to describe any form of computer-based technology.

Normal distribution   The term given to a particular distribution of scores on a variable where the distribution curve is symmetrical about the mean, with unit area and unit standard deviation.

Null hypothesis   The null hypothesis essentially proposes that 'nothing is happening' in the data. That is, that the variables measured are not correlated, or that there are no differences in mean scores between groups of people.

One-sided argument   Attempt at persuasion where all of the points made support the direction of attitude change desired by the communicator. Contrast with two-sided arguments, where points for and against the desired change are presented.

Openness to experience   A tendency to be curious about inner (psychological) and outer worlds with a willingness to entertain novel ideas and unconventional values.

Operant conditioning   A form of conditioning that shapes (operant) behaviour by the application of reinforcement, punishment or extinction.

Organisational analysis   Aims to understand where training activities fit into the wider organisational systems and how they relate to organisational strategy.

Organisational behaviour modification (OB Mod)   A systematic approach to influencing the behaviour of people in organisations which is based on the principles of conditioning.

Organisational citizenship behaviour (OCB)   Discretionary behaviour by employees that is not explicitly requested or expected by employers, but which helps to promote effective organisational functioning.

Organisational commitment   The relative strength of an individual's identification with and involvement in an organisation.

Organisational culture   The distinctive norms, beliefs, principles and ways of behaving that combine to give each organisation its distinctive character.

Organisational development (OD)   The application of behavioural science knowledge to the planned creation and reinforcement of organisational strategies, structures and processes.

Organisational justice   An approach to motivation that focuses on the extent to which people perceive that rewards are distributed fairly in their organisation, and that the process of deciding reward allocation is fair.

Organisational learning   The ability of an organisation to develop and utilise knowledge in order to create and sustain competitive advantage.

Organisational politics   Interpersonal processes used by people in an organisation to enhance or maintain their reputation.

Organisational power   The capacity of an individual or group within an organisation to make other individuals or groups do what they want them to do.

OSI   Occupational stress indicator, a measure that assesses an individual's and organisation's stress profile.

Participant observation   Research method where the researcher observes events, and perhaps asks the people involved about them, while also participating in the events.

Participants   People who contribute data in a research project (they are also sometimes called respondents or subjects, though the latter term is discouraged nowadays as being too impersonal).

Participativeness   The extent to which a leader includes their subordinates in, and allows them control over, decision-making.

Perceived behavioural control   In the theory of planned behaviour, perceived behavioural control concerns the extent to which a person believes that they can perform the behaviour required in a given situation.

Performance appraisal   A process whereby a manager (usually) observes the performance of an employee, records evidence and feeds back to them about how their performance relates to others in the group and whether it meets expected standards.

Performance goal orientation   An approach to a task where people's main concern is to demonstrate their competence to themselves and other people. Contrast with **Learning goal orientation** (*see above*).

Performance-related pay (PRP)   Where some or all of a person's pay is based on how successfully they produce results in their work.

Peripheral route to persuasion   Attitude change that occurs as a result of 'surface' features of an attempt at persuasion such as communicator attractiveness or an easily recalled slogan.

Personal identity   Aspects of our self-concept that reflect us as individuals, differentiated from others, even those in the same social group as we are (contrast with **Social identity** below).

Personality tradition   The branch of basic psychology that concerns how and why people differ from each other psychologically.

Person analysis   Involves identifying who needs training and what kind of training they need.

Person-job fit   The extent to which a person's skills, interests and needs are consistent with the requirements and rewards of their work.

Personnel specification   A representation of the demands of a job translated into human terms (i.e. a statement of the attributes needed for successful job performance).

Person-organisation fit   A term used to describe the extent to which an individual's values, interests and behaviour fits with the culture of an organisation as a whole rather than a specific role or task.

Phases of change   These are distinct states through which an organisation moves as it undertakes planned change.

Phenomenological approach to personality   An approach to personality that emphasises how personality is shaped by a person's individual interpretations, experiences and choices.

Phenomenological research   See **Social constructionist research**.

Physiological needs   The desire to avoid hunger, thirst and other unpleasant bodily states.

Physiological psychology   The branch of basic psychology that concerns the relationship between brain and body.

Planned behaviour   A theory which attempts to explain how and when attitudes determine intentions and behaviour.

Planned change   This is a generic term for approaches to change that have predetermined goals and a distinct starting and finishing point.

Position analysis questionnaire (PAQ)   A questionnaire-based procedure for job analysis which produces information about the major job elements involved, broken down into six divisions.

Position power   In Fred Fiedler's contingency theory, position power refers to the extent to which a leader is able, by virtue of their position in the organisation, to influence the rewards and punishments received by subordinates.

Positive well-being   This concept defines well-being as something that is more than just the absence of ill-health. For example, a worker may obtain pleasure from their work and develop a sense of purpose from the tasks they are engaged in.

Positivist research   In contrast to social constructionist research, positivist research takes the view that human behaviour, thoughts and feelings are substantially influenced by objectively measurable factors which exist independent of the researchers and people being researched.

Power-as-control theory   Fiske (2001) claims that powerful people at work stereotype less powerful people because they often manage large numbers of people, they have less need to make the effort to overcome stereotypes, and people who self-select for positions of power may be less motivated to individuate those lower in a hierarchy.

Practical intelligence   A view of intelligent behaviour that focuses on real-world activity, rather than controlled behaviour assessed by conventional intelligence testing.

Pragmatic science   The use of rigorous scientific methods to investigate and tackle important problems.

Predictive validity   A form of criterion-related validity in which data on the criterion are obtained after data on the predictor.

Predictor   A term sometimes used to refer to a selection procedure, on the grounds that a selection procedure is intended to *predict* candidates' job performance.

Pre-experimental design   Study design (e.g. one-shot, post-only data) that does not control for major threats to validity. The results of such designs cannot be interpreted with any certainty since many factors could have been involved in causing the observed outcomes. This design may be useful for case studies.

Primary intervention   Tackling the source of a problem.

Procedural justice   An individual's perception that the process they have been through (e.g. selection) was well-designed, appropriate and well-managed.

Procedural knowledge   The kind of knowledge that provides a basis for skilful performance; knowledge of how to do something that may be difficult to articulate.

Process evaluation   An examination of the factors that have an impact on the effects of an intervention, i.e. the focus is on why something bought about change. Contrast with **Effect evaluation** (*see above*).

Process theories of motivation   Approaches to motivation that focus on *how* motivation works, rather than *what* motivates behaviour. Contrast with **Content theories of motivation** (*see above*).

Processual approach   An approach to change that sees organisations as shifting coalitions of individuals and groups with different interests and aims, imperfect knowledge and short attention spans.

Professional career   The term given by Kanter to a career where work is primarily specialised and progress is derived from increasing challenge, competence development and personal reputation rather than promotion up a hierarchy.

Protection motivation theory   A theory proposed by Rogers (1983) to explain the effect of fear on attitude change and behaviour.

Psychoanalytic tradition   The approach to psychology that focuses on unconscious drives and conflicts as determinants of behaviour.

Psychological contract   An individual employee's beliefs about the rights and obligations of both sides in the employment relationship.

Psychology   Sometimes defined as the science of mental life, psychology concerns the systematic study of behaviour, thoughts and emotions.

Psychometric tests   Standardised procedures (often using pen and paper) embodying a series of questions (items) designed to assess key cognitive or personality dimensions. Must have acceptable levels of validity and reliability to be of value.

Psychophysiological assessment   Research method where information is obtained about some aspect of a person's neurological, physiological or medical condition.

Punishment   In the behaviourist approach to personality, punishment is the occurrence of an unpleasant stimulus or the removal of a pleasant stimulus following a specific behaviour.

Qualitative data   Information expressed in the form of words or images, rather than numbers.

Qualitative overload   Work that is too difficult for an individual.

Qualitative research   Research design where the researcher aims to obtain a detailed picture of the way in which a limited number of people interpret one or more aspects of their world, normally using words rather than numbers.

Quantitative data   Information expressed in the form of numbers.

Quantitative overload   Having too much work to do.

Quasi-experimental design   Study design that has some, but not all, of the features needed for a perfect experimental design. Such designs are often used in field settings.

Questionnaire   A written list of questions designed to obtain information about a person's life history, beliefs, attitudes, interests, values or self-concept.

Random sample   A number of people selected from a population in such a way that everyone in that population had an equal chance of being selected.

Range restriction   This arises when a limited range of scores (rather than when the full population range) is present in a sample. It can occur when the sample is biased in some way, e.g. selection scores are available *only* for people who were given jobs.

Reaction data   Data that are concerned with how trainees react to the training they have been given.

Realistic job preview   A technique used in recruitment where an organisation presents a balanced view of a job to applicants rather than only its good points. This can be done using written materials, videos or even a day or two's experience of the job itself.

Reciprocal determinism   The complex interaction between situational, personal and behavioural variables.

Reinforcement   In the behaviourist approach to personality, reinforcement is the occurrence of a pleasant stimulus (positive reinforcement) or the removal of an unpleasant stimulus (negative reinforcement) following a specific behaviour.

Reliability   An indicator of the consistency which a test or procedure provides. It is possible to quantify reliability to indicate the extent to which a measure is free from error.

Relocation   A job move within an organisation to a different location that requires a move of home.

Repertory grid technique   A method of collecting data about the way individuals view the world. It is often used to gather the views of experts, for example when analysing what constitutes effective job performance.

Respondent   A term often given to a person who provides data in psychological research, particularly a survey research sample.

Respondent conditioning   Another term for **Classical conditioning**.

Retirement   There is no single accepted definition of retirement. For most people it is the time when, having experienced a number of years of work, they withdraw from the labour market and do not intend to re-enter it.

Role ambiguity   Unclear picture of the nature of the job, its objectives, responsibilities, etc.

Role conflict   When an individual is torn by conflicting job demands.

Role innovation   The extent to which a person seeks to change the nature of their job.

Safety needs   The desire to avoid physical or psychological danger.

Sample   A number of people drawn from a defined population (e.g. all people; all females; all sales managers).

Sampling error   Fluctuations in observed results that arise when small samples are used. Any small sample may contain some unrepresentative cases, but if the sample is small these cases may have an unduly large influence on the results.

Schema   In the social cognitive tradition in psychology, a schema is an organised set of beliefs and expectations held by a person.

Science   A branch of knowledge based upon systematically collected data under controlled conditions.

Scientific management   Also called Taylorism, this is an approach to management that emphasises management control, simplification and standardisation of work activities and purely financial incentives.

Script   In the social cognitive tradition in psychology, a script is an expected sequence of events that a person associates with a particular type of situation.

Secondary intervention   Helping employees to develop skills that will enable them to cope better with a problem (e.g. stress management training).

Selection ratio   An indication of the number of positions available compared with the number of candidates. Ten candidates for every post would give a selection ratio of 1:10, i.e. 0.1.

Self-actualisation   The need to fulfil one's potential: to develop and express one's capacities.

Self-awareness   The capacity to know and understand one's own characteristics, motives and values.

Self-categorisation theory   A theory that proposes that we define who we are by placing ourselves into categories, and these categories are often social groups. We seek to defend our identity when threatened. Similar to **Social identity theory**.

Self-concept   The total set of beliefs a person holds about themself.

Self-development   An approach to staff development which places primary responsibility for identifying development needs and taking action to deal with them on the individual employee.

Self-efficacy   A person's own belief in their own ability, skills, knowledge, etc.

Self-regulation   The strategies a person uses to monitor and direct their behaviour in pursuit of a goal.

Servant leadership   An approach to leadership that portrays the leader as a helpful facilitator of others' efforts, rather than a dominant agenda-setter.

Situational interviews   A form of structured interview in which key work situations (identified through job analysis) are used to provide a basis for questioning and assessing job candidates.

Situational judgement test   A selection test that requires candidates to decide how they would behave in response to a situation described in the test. Often the test would also require the candidates to give details of their reasoning that led to their decision.

Situational leadership theory   A theory of leadership that proposes that the maturity of subordinates dictates the style a leader should adopt.

Sleeper effect   Where an attempt at attitude change produces a delayed but not an immediate effect.

Social approach   A 'common-sense' approach to motivation that argues that a person is motivated to establish and maintain meaningful social relationships.

Social cognitive theory   A theory that developed from behaviourist origins and sees the behaviourist view as incomplete, rather than wrong. In social cognitive theory internal cognitive processes (e.g. expectancies about what might happen) and external (social/situational) factors play a key role in determining behaviour.

Social cognitive tradition   The tradition in psychology that emphasises how we process information in a social context.

Social constructionist research   Research based on the assumption that there are few objective facts about the social world, and that it is therefore necessary to focus on people's subjective interpretations rather than objectively verifiable causal laws. Sometimes called phenomenological research.

Social desirability effect   The effect that occurs when a person provides biased information because of their desire to provide responses that they believe will be looked upon favourably by others. For example, more people break the speed limit when driving than admit to it when asked (even if they are not being asked by a police officer!).

Social identity   Aspects of our self-concept that reflect the general characteristics of people in the same social groups as we are, and which differentiate us from members of other group (contrast with **Personal identity** above).

Social identity theory   A theory that suggests we define ourselves largely in terms of our membership of social groups, and often tend to value our own group more than others. Similar to **Self-categorisation theory**.

Socialisation   The processes by which the person learns and adopts the behaviours, attitudes and values expected in their role.

Social loafing   The process where some members of a group do not contribute their share of effort, but still obtain the rewards of group membership.

Social psychology   The branch of basic psychology that concerns how the social world affects the behaviour, thoughts and emotions of individuals and groups.

Social support networks   Refers to informal and formal relationships which can help the individual to explore and deal with stress.

Socio-cognitive   An approach to attitudes which stresses how they are encoded in a person's memory and what functions they serve for the person.

Solomon four-group design   An experimental design that can be used to evaluate the impact of an intervention. The design uses a number of control groups to help rule out alternative explanations for change and therefore isolate the impact of the intervention.

Standard deviation   A measure of how much variability around the mean there is in a set of numerical data.

State orientation   A psychological state in which a person does *not* use self-regulatory strategies to achieve goals. Contrast with **Action orientation** (*see above*).

Statistical power   A measure of the probability that a statistically significant effect will be observed in a sample of given size if such an effect does actually exist in the population from which the sample is drawn.

Statistical significance   The probability of rejecting the null hypothesis on the basis of data obtained from a sample when it is in fact true for the population from which the sample is drawn. Psychologists are normally only willing to reject the null hypothesis if there is, at most, a 1 in 20 chance of it being true.

Stereotype   A generalised belief about what people in a particular group are like.

Strategic decision   A decision that affects the overall goals, aims or mission of an organisation.

Stress   The unpleasant, and potentially damaging, emotional state that arises when a person perceives that the demands placed upon them exceed the resources available to them to cope with those demands.

Stressor   Means the source of the stress, the cause or underlying reasons why an employee may show stress symptoms or disease.

Structural approaches to stress   Theories of stress that focus on describing the aspects of work that are the likely sources of stress.

Structural equation modelling (SEM)   A method of data analysis that can be used to examine quantitative data when there are likely to be multiple and complex relationships between the variables in the study.

Structure   Sometimes called initiating structure, this is an aspect of leadership style that reflects the extent to which the leader plans, organises and monitors the work of their group.

Structured observation   A research method where the researcher remains uninvolved in events, but records what occurs using a predetermined system.

Subjective norm   In the theory of planned behaviour, subjective norm is a combination of the (perceived) opinions of other people and the person's motivation to comply with them.

Substitutes for leadership   This term, coined by Kerr and Jermier, reflects the idea that in some circumstances the resources of a group are sufficient to make a leader unnecessary.

Superego   In the psychoanalytic tradition in psychology, the superego is the part of the psyche that concerns moral values, or conscience.

Survey   Research design where a sample of respondents/subjects provides data in a standard form on one or more variables.

Target audience description   The characteristics of the users of equipment that are considered during human-centred design.

Task analysis   involves determining what important tasks need to be performed and the KSAs that an individual requires in order to perform them.

Team   A group of people who work together towards group objectives.

Team-building   Techniques designed to enhance the effectiveness of a new or established team.

Team roles   The functions that need to be fulfilled by team members if the team is to be effective.

Technology-mediated communication   The use of the telephone, Internet, e-mail (etc.) as means of communicating.

Teleworking   Working from a remote location using information and communication technologies (ICTs).

Terminal behaviour   A statement of what the trainee should be able to do at the end of training.

Tertiary intervention   An intervention designed to help employees who have already been damaged in some way by their work (e.g. workplace counselling).

Theories of learning   Represent ideas about how learning occurs; they feed into training practice by identifying the most appropriate methods of instruction.

Theory X   A 'common-sense' approach to motivation that views people as untrustworthy, to be motivated by financial reward and punishment.

Theory Y   A 'common-sense' approach to motivation that views people as inherently trustworthy and responsible, to be motivated by challenge and responsibility.

Three-step model   This model views change as a planned and finite process which proceeds through three stages: unfreezing, moving and refreezing.

Thurstone scaling   A method of measuring attitudes where statements are graded in terms of their extremity of agreement or disagreement with a particular attitude.

Total quality management A strategic and organisation-wide approach to quality which is associated with Japanese manufacturing organisations.

Trainability tests A form of work sample test which incorporates a systematic learning period for the candidate, who is then required to attempt the task unaided.

Training Organised efforts to provide employees with structured opportunities to learn and develop within their work role.

Training design Relates to the content of the training programme and includes decisions about what information is presented to trainees and how it is presented.

Training evaluation Considers the validity of training programmes by assessing the extent to which the training objectives have been achieved.

Training objectives These define what the training needs to achieve and can include individual and organisational level objectives.

Training transfer Transfer occurs when new learning is used in new settings (e.g. on the job) beyond those employed for training purposes.

Trait A dimension upon which people differ psychologically. Traits are stable over time. This is in contrast to a state which is transient.

Trait-factor analytic theory An approach to individual differences that uses factor analysis to identify the major structural dimensions (traits) of personality.

Trait tradition The tradition in psychology that emphasises stable differences between people in their position on various personality dimensions.

Transactional leadership A leadership style originally identified by Burns (1978), in which the leader uses rewards for good performance and tends to maintain existing work methods unless performance goals are not being met.

Transactional theories of stress Theories of stress that focus on describing the psychological processes that lead to the experience of negative emotions.

Transformational leadership Another leadership style originally identified by Burns (1978), this refers to the extent to which a leader articulates a clear vision and mission, while treating individuals on their merits and encouraging free thinking.

Transition A relatively permanent move from one environment to another experienced by a person. The sequence of phases a person goes through in adjusting to a new job.

Triarchic theory of intelligence The theory that there are three facets of intelligence: analytical, creative and practical.

***t*-Test** A statistical technique used to test whether two samples have significantly different mean scores on a variable.

Type A behaviour A hard-driving, time-conscious, aggressive, impatient lifestyle.

Type I error This occurs when the null hypothesis is erroneously rejected on the basis of research data.

Type II error This occurs when the alternative hypothesis is erroneously rejected on the basis of research data.

Type III error   This occurs when a researcher erroneously concludes that an intervention is ineffective when it was the implementation of the intervention that was faulty.

Unconditional positive regard   In the phenomenological tradition in psychology, unconditional positive regard is the acceptance of one person by another, irrespective of their behaviour.

Unconditioned response   *See* **Classical conditioning**.

Unconditioned stimulus   *See* **Classical conditioning**.

Utility (financial)   A procedure for estimating the financial gain that may be derived from the improved job performance that is obtained from better personnel selection.

Valence   In expectancy theory, valence is the subjective value a person attaches to a particular reward.

Validation study   A test of whether a prediction developed from a theory or model is supported by data. A common use of this concept in work psychology is the validation of selection tests, i.e. whether the result of the selection test is related to subsequent job performance.

Validity   A general term indicating the extent to which a test or procedure measures what it is intended to measure.

Vitamin Model   This model proposes that working conditions behave like vitamins in that some are beneficial in the 'correct doses', too little of some causes problems, too much of some is 'toxic', etc.

Vroom-Jago theory of leadership   This theory assumes that leaders can vary the participativeness of their decision-making style according to the situation, and identifies key aspects of the situation.

Wash-up session   This is a meeting of the assessors at the end of an assessment centre, where the ratings for each assessee are discussed and an overall rating made.

Wellness programme   A company-wide programme to promote employee health, both physical and psychological.

Work-life integration/balance   A general term often applied to the examination of the impact of work on other aspects of a person's life (and vice versa).

Work-role transition   Any move between jobs, into a job or out of one, or any substantial change in work duties.

Work sample tests   Personnel assessment procedures that require candidates to conduct tasks that are sampled from the job(s) in question.

z-score   An individual's score on a variable expressed as the number of standard deviations above or below the mean.

REFERENCES

Abelson, R.P. (1981) 'Psychological status of the script concept', *American Psychologist*, 36, 715–29.

Ackoff, R.L. (1989) 'From data to wisdom', *Journal of Applied Systems Analysis*, 16, 3–9.

Adair, J.G. (1984) 'The Hawthorne effect: A reconsideration of the methodological artifact', *Journal of Applied Psychology*, 69, 334–45.

Adams, J.S. (1965) 'Inequity in social exchange', in L. Berkowitz (ed.), *Advances in Experimental Social Psychology*, vol. 2. New York: Academic Press.

Agho, A.O., Mueller, C.W. and Price, J.L. (1993) 'Determinants of employee job satisfaction: An empirical test of a causal model', *Human Relations*, 46, 1007–27.

Agho, A.O., Price, J.L. and Mueller, C.W. (1992) 'Discriminant validity of measures of job satisfaction, positive affectivity and negative affectivity', *Journal of Occupational and Organizational Psychology*, 65, 185–96.

Aiello, J.R. and Kolb, K.J. (1995) 'Electronic performance monitoring and social context: Impact on productivity and stress', *Journal of Applied Psychology*, 80, 339–53.

Ajzen, I. (1991) 'The theory of planned behavior', *Organizational Behavior and Human Decision Processes*, 50, 179–211.

Ajzen, I. (2001) 'Nature and operation of attitudes', *Annual Review of Psychology*, 24, 1251–63.

Ajzen, I. and Fishbein, M. (1980) *Understanding Attitudes and Predicting Social Behavior*. Englewood Cliffs, NJ: Prentice Hall.

Ajzen, I. and Fishbein, M. (2000) 'Attitudes and the attitude–behaviour relation: Reasoned and automatic process', in W. Stroebe and M. Hewstone, *European Review of Social Psychology*. Chichester: John Wiley.

Ajzen, I. and Madden, J.T. (1986) 'Prediction of goal-directed behavior: Attitudes, intentions, and perceived behavioral control', *Journal of Experimental Social Psychology*, 22, 453–74.

Akgün, A.E., Lynn, G.S. and Byrne, J.C. (2003) 'Organizational learning: A socio-cognitive framework', *Human Relations*, 56, 839–68.

Aldag, R.J. and Fuller, S.R. (1993) 'Beyond fiasco: A reappraisal of the groupthink phenomenon and a new model of group decision processes', *Psychological Bulletin*, 113, 533–52.

Alderfer, C.P. (1972) *Existence, Relatedness and Growth: Human needs in organizational settings*. New York: Free Press.

Alkadry, M.G. and Tower, L.E. (2006) 'Unequal pay: The role of gender', *Public Administration Review*, November–December, 888–98.

Allaire, Y. and Firsirotu, M.E. (1984) 'Theories of organizational culture', *Organization Studies*, 5(3), 193–226.

Allen, N.J. and Hecht, T.D. (2004) 'The "Romance of Teams": Toward an understanding of its psychological underpinnings and implications', *Journal of Occupational and Organizational Psychology*, 77(4), 439–61.

Allen, N.J. and Meyer, J.P. (1990) 'The measurement and antecedents of affective, continuance and normative commitment to the organization', *Journal of Occupational Psychology*, 63, 11–18.

Allen, P.T. and Stephenson, G.M. (1984) 'The relationship of inter-group understanding and inter-party friction in industry', *British Journal of Employee Relations*, 23, 203–13.

Allen, T.D., Eby, L.T. and Poteet, M.L. (2004) 'Career benefits associated with mentoring for protégés: A meta-analysis', *Journal of Applied Psychology*, 89, 127–36.

Allen, T.D., Poteet, M.L. and Burroughs, S.M. (1997) 'The mentor's perspective: A qualitative inquiry and future research agenda', *Journal of Vocational Behavior*, 51, 70–89.

Alliger, G.M. and Janak, E.A. (1997) 'Kirkpatrick's levels of training criteria thirty years later', *Personnel Psychology*, 41, 63–105.

Alliger, G.M., Tanenbaum, S.I., Bennett, W. Jr, Traver, H. and Shotland, A. (1997) 'A meta-analysis of the relations among training criteria', *Personnel Psychology*, 50, 341–58.

Allison, T., Cooper, C.L. and Reynolds, P. (1989) 'Stress counseling in the workplace – the Post Office experience', *The Psychologist*, 2, 384–8.

Allport, G.W. (1937) *Personality: A psychological interpretation*. New York: Holt, Rinehart and Winston.

Ambrose, M.L. and Kulik, C.T. (1999) 'Old friends, new faces: Motivation research in the 1990s', *Journal of Management*, 25, 213–92.

Anastasi, A. (1988) *Psychological Testing*. New York: Macmillan.

Anderson, J.R. (1983) *The Architecture of Cognition*. Cambridge, MA: Harvard University Press.

Anderson, J.R. (1987) 'Skill acquisition: compilation of weak-method problem solutions', *Psychological Review*, 94, 192–210.

Anderson, N. (2003) 'Applicant and recruiter reactions to new technology in selection: A critical review and agenda for future research', *International Journal of Selection and Assessment*, 11(2–3), 121–36.

Anderson, N. and Prutton, K. (1993) 'Occupational psychology in business: Strategic resource or purveyor of tests?', *The Occupational Psychologist*, 20, 3–10.

Anderson, N. and Sleap, S. (2004) 'An evaluation of gender differences on the Belbin Team Role Self-Perception Inventory', *Journal of Organizational and Occupational Psychology*, 77, 429–37.

Anderson, N., Born, M. and Cunningham-Snell, N. (2001a) 'Recruitment and selection: Applicant perspectives and outcomes', in N. Anderson, D.S. Ones, H.K. Sinangil and C. Viswesvaran (eds), *Handbook of Industrial, Work and Organizational Psychology*. Thousand Oaks, CA: Sage Publications.

Anderson, N., Herriot, P. and Hodgkinson, G.P. (2001b) 'The practitioner–researcher divide in Industrial, Work and Organizational (IWO) psychology: Where are we now, and where do we go from here?', *Journal of Occupational and Organizational Psychology*, 74, 391–411.

Anderson, N., Lievens, F., van Dam, K. and Born, M. (2006) 'A construct-driven investigation of gender differences in a leadership-role assessment center', *Journal of Applied Psychology*, 91, 555–66.

Anderson, N.R. and West, M.A. (1998) 'Measuring climate for work group innovation: Development and validation of the team climate inventory', *Journal of Organizational Behaviour*, 19, 235–58.

Anderson, V. (2007) *The Value of Learning: A new model of value and evaluation.* Report published by the Chartered Institute of Personnel Development: London.

Annett, J., Duncan, K.D., Stammers, R.B. and Gray, M.J. (1971) *Task Analysis.* Department of Employment Information Training Paper 6. London: HMSO.

Antonakis, J., Cianciolo, A.T. and Sternberg, R.J. (eds) (2004) *The Nature of Leadership.* Thousand Oaks, CA: Sage.

April, K., Macdonald, R. and Vriesendorp, S. (2000) *Rethinking Leadership.* Cape Town: University of Cape Town Press.

Argote, L., Ingram, P., Levine, J.M. and Moreland, R.L. (2000) 'Knowledge transfer in organisations: Learning from the experience of others', *Organisational Behaviour and Human Decision Processes*, 82(1), 1–8.

Argyris, C (1962) *Interpersonal Competence and Organizational Effectiveness.* Homewood, IL: Irwin.

Argyris, C. (1964) *Integrating the Individual and the Organization.* Chichester: John Wiley.

Argyris, C.P. (1960) *Understanding Organizational Behavior.* Homewood, IL: Dorsey.

Armitage, C.J. and Conner, M. (2001) 'Efficacy of the theory of planned behaviour: A meta-analytic review', *British Journal of Social Psychology*, 40, 471–99.

Arnold, J. (1990) 'From education to job markets', in S. Fisher and C.L. Cooper (eds), *On the Move: The psychological effects of change and transition.* Chichester: John Wiley.

Arnold, J. (1996) 'The psychological contract: A concept in need of closer scrutiny?', *European Journal of Work and Organizational Psychology*, 5, 511–20.

Arnold, J. (2001) 'Careers and career management', in N. Anderson, D. Ones, H. Sinangil and C. Viswesvaran (eds), *International Handbook of Work and Organizational Psychology.* London: Sage.

Arnold, J. (2002) 'Tensions between assessment, grading and development in development centres: A case study', *International Journal of Human Resource Management*, 13(6), 975–91.

Arnold, J. (2004) 'The congruence problem in John Holland's theory of vocational decisions', *Journal of Occupational and Organizational Psychology*, 77, 95–113.

Arnold, J. and Cohen, L. (2008) 'The psychology of careers in industrial-organizational settings: A critical but appreciative analysis', in G.P. Hodgkinson and J.K Ford (eds), *International Review of Industrial/Organizational Psychology*, Vol. 23, Chichester: Wiley.

Arnold, J. and Johnson, K. (1997) 'Mentoring in early career', *Human Resource Management Journal*, 7, 61–70.

Arnold, J. and Mackenzie Davey, K. (1999) 'Graduates' work experiences as predictors of organisational commitment, intention to leave, and turnover: Which experiences really matter?', *Applied Psychology: An International Review*, 48(2), 211–38.

Arthur Jr, W., Day, E.A. and Woehr, D. J. (2008) 'Mend it, don't end it: An alternate view of assessment center construct-related validity evidence', *Industrial and Organizational Psychology*, 1, 105–11.

Arthur, M.B. (2008) 'Examining contemporary careers: A call for multidisciplinary enquiry', *Human Relations*, 61, 163–86.

Arthur, M.B. and Rousseau, D.M. (1996) 'The boundaryless career as a new employment principle', in M.B. Arthur and D.M. Rousseau (eds), *The Boundaryless Career: A new employment principle for a new organizational era*. Oxford: Oxford University Press.

Arthur, M.B., Inkson, K. and Pringle, J.K. (1999) *The New Careers, Individual Action and Economic Change*. London: Sage.

Arthur, M.B., Khapova, S.N. and Wilderom, C.P.M. (2005) 'Career success in a boundaryless career world', *Journal of Organizational Behavior*, 26, 177–202.

Arvey, R.D. and Murphy, K.R. (1998) 'Performance evaluation in work settings', *Annual Review of Psychology*, 49, 141–68.

Arvey, R.D., Carter, W.G. and Buerkley, D.K. (1991) 'Job satisfaction: Dispositional and situational influences', in C.L. Cooper and I.T. Robertson (eds), *International Review of Industrial and Organizational Psychology*, 6. Chichester: John Wiley.

Aryee, S. and Chay, Y.W. (1994) 'An examination of the impact of career-oriented mentoring on work commitment attitudes and career satisfaction among professional and managerial employees', *British Journal of Management*, 5, 241–49.

Ashkanasy, N. and Jackson, C. (2001) 'Organizational culture and climate', in N. Anderson, D. Ones, H.K. Sinangil and C. Viswesvaran (eds), *Handbook of Industrial, Work and Organizational Psychology*, vol. 2. London: Sage.

Ashkanasy, N.M. and Daus, C.S. (2005) 'Rumors of the death of emotional intelligence in organizational behavior are vastly exaggerated', *Journal of Organizational Behavior*, 26, 441–52.

Ashmos, D.P., Duchon, D., McDaniel, R.R. Jr and Huonker, J.W. (2002) 'What a mess! Participation as a simple managerial rule to "complexify" organizations', *Journal of Management Studies*, 39(2), 189–206.

Atwater, L.E., Brett, J.F. and Charles, A.C. (2007) 'Multisource feedback: Lessons learned and implications for practice', *Human Resource Management*, 46, 285–307.

Atwater, L.E., Ostroff, C., Yammarino, F.J. and Fleenor, J.W. (1998) 'Self–other agreement: Does it really matter?', *Personnel Psychology*, 51, 577–98.

Austin, J.T. and Crespin, T.R. (2006) 'Problems of criteria in industrial and organizational psychology: Progress, problems and prospects', in W. Bennett Jr, C.E. Lance and D.J. Woehr (eds), *Performance Measurement: Current perspectives and future challenges*. London: Lawrence Erlbaum Associates.

Avery, D.R., McKay, P.F., Wilson, D.C. and Tonidandel, S. (2007) 'Unequal attendance: The relationships between race, organizational diversity cues and absenteeism', *Personnel Psychology*, 60, 875–902.

Avolio, B.J., Gardner, W.L., Walumba, F.O., Luthans, F. and May, D.R. (2004) 'Unlocking the mask: A look at the process by which authentic leaders impact follower attitudes and behaviors', *The Leadership Quarterly*, 15, 810–23.

Axtell, C., Fleck, S. and Turner, N. (2004) 'Virtual teams: collaborating across distance', in C.L. Cooper and I.T. Robertson (eds), *International Review of Industrial and Organisational Psychology*, vol. 19. Chichester: John Wiley.

Baglioni, A.J. Jr and Cooper, C.L. (1988) 'A structural model approach toward the development of a theory of the link between stress and mental health', *British Journal of Medical Psychology*, 61, 87–102.

Bailey, C. and Fletcher, C. (2002) 'The impact of multiple source feedback on management development: Findings from a longitudinal study', *Journal of Organizational Behavior*, 23, 853–67.

Bain, P., Watson, A., Mulvey, G., Taylor, P and Gall, G. (2002) 'Taylorism, targets and the pursuit of quantity and quality by call-centre management', *New Technology, Work and Employment*, 17, 170–85.

Bainbridge, L. (1987) 'Ironies of automation', in J. Rasmussen, K. Duncan and J. Leplat (eds), *New Technology and Human Error*, 271–83. Chichester: John Wiley.

Bakker, A.B., Demerouti, E. and Schaufeli, W.B. (2003) 'Dual processes at work in a call centre: An application of the job demands–resources model', *European Journal of Work and Organizational Psychology*, 12, 393–428.

Bal, P.M., De Lange, A.H., Jansen, P.G.W. and Van der Velde, M.E.G. (2008) 'Psychological contract breach and job attitudes: A meta-analysis of age as a moderator', *Journal of Vocational Behavior*, 72, 143–58.

Baldwin, T.T. (1992) 'Effects of alternative modelling strategies on outcomes of interpersonal-skills training', *Journal of Applied Psychology*, 77, 147–54.

Baldwin, T.T. and Ford, J.K. (1988) 'Transfer of training: A review and directions for future research', *Personnel Psychology*, 41, 63–105.

Bandura, A. (1977a) 'Self-efficacy: Toward a unifying theory of behavioral change', *Psychological Review*, 84, 191–215.

Bandura, A. (1977b) *Social Learning Theory*. Englewood Cliffs, NJ: Prentice Hall.

Bandura, A. (1982) 'The self-efficacy mechanism in human agency', *American Psychologist*, 37, 122–47.

Bandura, A. (1986) *Social Foundations of Thought and Action: A social cognitive theory*. Englewood Cliffs, NJ: Prentice Hall.

Bandura, A. (1997) *Self-efficacy: The exercise of control*. New York: Freeman.

Bandura, A. (2001) 'Social cognitive theory: an agentic perspective', *Annual Review of Psychology*, 52, 1–26.

Banks, M.H. (1988) 'Job components inventory', in S. Gael (ed.), *Job Analysis Handbook*. New York: John Wiley.

Banks, M.H., Jackson, P.R., Stafford, E.M. and Warr, P.B. (1983) 'The job components inventory and the analysis of jobs requiring limited skill', *Personnel Psychology*, 36, 57–66.

Bardwick, J. (1980) 'The seasons of a woman's life', in D. McGuigan (ed.), *Women's Lives: New theory, research and policy*. Ann Arbor, MI: University of Michigan.

Barker, R.A. (1997) 'How can we train leaders if we do not know what leadership is?', *Human Relations*, 50(4), 343–62.

Barling, J., Wade, B. and Fullagar, C. (1990) 'Predicting employee commitment to company and union: Divergent models', *Journal of Occupational Psychology*, 63, 49–61.

Barnes, C. (1991) *Disabled People in Britain: A case for anti-discrimination legislation*. London: C. Hurst and Co. Ltd.

Barnes-Farrell, J.L. (2001) 'Performance appraisal: Person perception, processes and challenges', in M. London (ed.), *How People Evaluate Others in Organizations*. London: LEA.

Barnes-Farrell, J.L., Davies-Schrils, K., McGonagle, A. *et al.* (2008) 'What aspects of shiftwork influence off-shift well-being of healthcare workers? *Applied Ergonomics*, 39, 589–96.

Barnett, R.C. and Shen, Y.C. (1997) 'Gender, high and low schedule control housework tasks and psychological distress: A study of dual earner couples', *Journal of Family Issues*, 18, 403–28.

Bar-On, R. (1997) *The Emotional Intelligence Inventory (EQ-i): Technical manual*. Toronto: Multi-Health Systems.

Bar-On, R. (2000) 'Emotional and social intelligence: Insights from the Emotional Quotient Inventory', in R. Bar-On and J.D.A. Parker (eds), *The Handbook of Emotional Intelligence*. San Francisco, CA: Jossey-Bass.

Baron, R.M., and Kenny, D.A. (1986) 'The moderator–mediator variable distinction in social psychological research: Conceptual, strategic and statistical considerations', *Journal of Personality and Social Psychology*, 51, 1173–82.

Barratt, E.S. (1990) 'Human resource management: Organisational culture', *Management Update*, 2(1), 21–32.

Barrett, P. and Sowden, P. (2000) 'Psychophysiological methods', in G. Breakwell, S. Hammond and C. Fife-Schaw (eds), *Research Methods in Psychology*. London: Sage.

Bartley, D.F. and Robitschek, C. (2000) 'Career exploration: A multivariate analysis of predictors', *Journal of Vocational Behavior*, 56, 63–81.

Bartone, P. (1989) 'Predictors of stress-related illness in city bus drivers', *Journal of Occupational Medicine*, 31, 657–63.

Bartram, D. (2000) 'Internet recruitment and selection: Kissing frogs to find princes', *International Journal of Selection & Assessment*, 8, 261–74.

Bartram, D. (2005) 'The great eight competencies: A criterion-centric approach to validation', *Journal of Applied Psychology*, 90, 1185–203.

Baruch, Y. (2003) *Managing Careers*. Harlow: Pearson Education.

Baruch, Y. (2004) 'Transforming careers – from linear to multidirectional career paths: organizational and individual perspective', *Career Development International*, 9, 58–73.

Baruch, Y. and Peiperl, M.A. (2000) 'Career management practices: An empirical survey and theoretical implications', *Human Resource Management*, 39, 347–66.

Bass, B.M. (1985) *Leadership and Performance: Beyond expectations*. New York: Free Press.

Bass, B.M. (1990) *Bass and Stogdill's Handbook of Leadership: Theory, research and managerial application*, 3rd edition. New York: Free Press.

Bass, B.M. (1997) 'Does the transactional–transformational leadership paradigm transcend organizational and national boundaries?', *American Psychologist*, 52(2), 130–39.

Bass, B.M. and Avolio, B.J. (1994) *Improving Organizational Effectiveness Through Transformational Leadership*. Thousand Oaks, CA: Sage.

Bassi, L.J. (1997) 'Harnessing the power of intellectual capital', *Training and Development*, 51, 25–30.

Bateman, T. and Strasser, S. (1984) 'A longitudinal analysis of the antecedents of organizational commitment', *Academy of Management Journal*, 27, 95–112.

Batt, R. (2000) 'Strategic segmentation in front-line services: Matching customers, employees and human "resource systems"', *International Journal of Human Resource Management*, 11, 540–61.

Baumeister, R.F. and Leary, M.R. (1995) 'The need to belong: Desire for interpersonal attachments as a fundamental human motivation', *Psychological Bulletin*, 117, 497–529.

Bazerman, M.H., Magliozzi, T. and Neale, M.A. (1985) 'Integrative bargaining in a competitive market', *Organizational Behavior and Human Decision Processes*, 35, 94–113.

Beaujean, A.A. (2005) 'Heritability of cognitive abilities as measured by mental chronometric tasks: A meta-analysis', *Intelligence*, 33, 187–201.

Bechtold, B.L. (1997) 'Chaos theory as a model for strategy development', *Empowerment in Organizations*, 5(4), 193–201.

Beck, A.T. (1996) *BDI-II, Beck Depression Inventory*. Boston, MA: Harcourt Brace.

Beck, J.S. (1995) *Cognitive Therapies: Basics and beyond*. New York: Guilford.

Beck, R.C. (1983) *Motivation: Theory and principles*. Englewood Cliffs, NJ: Prentice Hall.

Becker, T.E. and Billings, R.S. (1993) 'Profiles of commitment: An empirical test', *Journal of Organizational Behavior*, 14, 177–90.

Becker, T.E., Billings, R.S., Eveleth, D.M. and Gilbert, N.L. (1996) 'Foci and bases of employee commitment: Implications for job performance', *Academy of Management Journal*, 39, 464–82.

Beckhard, R. (1969) *Organization Development: Strategies and models*. Reading, MA: Addison-Wesley.

Beehr, T.A. (1995) *Psychological Stress in the Workplace*. London: Routledge.

Beer, M. and Nohria, N. (eds) (2000) *Breaking the Code of Change*. Boston, MA: Harvard Business School Press.

Beer, M., Eisenstat, R.A. and Spector, B. (1993) 'Why change programmes don't produce change', in C. Mabey and B. Mayon-White (eds), *Managing Change*, 2nd edition. London: Open University/Paul Chapman Publishing.

Belbin, R.M. (1981) *Management Teams: Why they succeed or fail*. London: Heinemann.

Belbin, R.M. (1993a) *Team Roles at Work: A strategy for human resource management*. Oxford: Butterworth-Heinemann.

Belbin, M. (1993b) 'A reply to the Belbin Team Role Self-Perception Inventory by Furnham, Steele and Pendleton', *Journal of Organizational and Occupational Psychology*, 66, 259–60.

Belbin, R.M. (2000) *Beyond the Team*. Oxford: Butterworth-Heinemann.

Bell, B.S. and Kozlowski, S.W.J. (2002) 'A typology of virtual teams: Implications for effective leadership', *Group and Organization Management*, 27, 14–49.

Bem, D.J. (1972) 'Self-perception theory', *Advances in Experimental Social Psychology*, 6, 1–62.

Benders, J., Huijgen, F. and Ulricj, P. (2001) 'Measuring group work; findings and lessons from a European survey', *New Technology, Work and Employment*, 16(3), 204–17.

Benjamin, G. and Mabey, C. (1993) 'Facilitating radical change', in C. Mabey and B. Mayon-White (eds), *Managing Change*, 2nd edition. London: The Open University/Paul Chapman Publishing.

Bennett, R. (1983) *Management Research*, Management Development Series no. 20. Geneva: International Labour Office.

Bennett, W., Lance, C.E. and Woehr, D.J. (2006) *Performance Measurement: Current perspectives and future challenges*. London: Lawrence Erlbaum Associates.

Bergman, M.E., Drasgow, F., Donovan, M.A. and Henning, J.B. (2006) 'Scoring situational judgment tests: Once you get the data, your troubles begin', *International Journal of Selection and Assessment*, 14, 223–35.

Bernardin, H.J., Cooke, D., Ross, S. and Villanova, P. (2000) 'Conscientiousness and agreeableness as predictors of rating leniency', *Journal of Applied Psychology*, 85, 232–36.

Bernin, P. and Theorell, T. (2001) 'Demand-control-support among female and male managers in eight Swedish companies', *Stress and Health*, 17(4), 231–43.

Berridge, J. and Cooper, C.L. (1993) 'Stress and coping in US organizations: The role of the Employee Assistance Programme', *Work and Stress*, 7, 89–102

Berridge, J., Cooper, C.L. and Highley-Marchington, C. (1997) *Employee Assistance Programmes and Workplace Counselling*. Chichester: John Wiley.

Bertua, C., Anderson, N. and Salgado, J.F. (2005) 'The predictive validity of cognitive ability tests: A UK meta-analysis', *Journal of Occupational and Organizational Psychology*, 78, 387–410.

Bettenhausen, K.L. (1991) 'Five years of group research: What we have learned and what needs to be addressed', *Journal of Management*, 17, 345–81.

Betz, N.E., Hammond, M.S. and Multon, K.D. (2005) 'Reliability and validity of five-level response continua for the career decision self-efficacy scale', *Journal of Career Assessment*, 13, 131–49.

Beugelsdijk, S. and Smeets, R. (2008) 'Entrepreneurial culture and economic growth', *American Journal of Economics and Sociology*, 67, 915–39.

Bigge, L.M. (1982) *Learning Theories for Teachers*. Aldershot: Gower.

Billings, C.E. (1997) *Aviation Automation: The search for a human-centred approach*. Mahwah, NJ: LEA.

Birdi, K., Allan, C. and Warr, P. (1997) 'Correlates and perceived outcomes of four types of employee development activity', *Journal of Applied Psychology*, 82(6), 845–57.

Birdi, K., Clegg, C., Patterson, M., Robinson, A., Stride, C.B., Wall, T.D. and Wood, S.J. (2008) 'The impact of human resource management practices on company productivity: a longitudinal study', *Personnel Psychology*, 61, 467–501.

Blackler, F. (1982) 'Organizational psychology', in S. Canter and D. Canter (eds), *Psychology in Practice*. Chichester: John Wiley.

Blackler, F. and Brown, C. (1986) 'Alternative models to guide the design and introduction of the new information technologies into work organizations', *Journal of Occupational Psychology*, 59, 287–314.

Blake, R.R. and Mouton, J.S. (1964) *The Managerial Grid*. Houston, TX: Gulf Publishing.

Blake, R.R. and Mouton, J.S. (1969) *Building a Dynamic Corporation Through Grid Organisation Development*. Reading, MA: Addison-Wesley.

Blake, R.R. and Mouton, J.S. (1976) *Organizational Change by Design*. Austin, TX: Scientific Methods.

Blasi, J.R. and Kruse, D.L. (2006) 'U.S. high performance work practices at century's end', *Industrial Relations*, 45(4), 547–87.

Blau, G. (1993) 'Operationalizing direction and level of effort and testing their relationships to individual job performance', *Organizational Behavior and Human Decision Processes*, 55, 152–70.

Blickle, G., Witzki, A. and Schneider, P.B. (2009) 'Self-initiated mentoring and career success: A predictive field study', *Journal of Vocational Behavior*, 74, 94–101.

Bloom, M. (1999) 'The performance effects of pay dispersion on individuals and organisations', *Academy of Management Journal*, 42, 25–40.

Blustein, D.L. (1997) 'A context-rich perspective of career exploration across the life roles', *Career Development Quarterly*, 45, 260–74.

Blustein, D.L., Pauling, M.L., DeMania, M.E. and Faye, M. (1994) 'Relation between exploratory and choice factors and decisional progress', *Journal of Vocational Behavior*, 44, 75–90.

Bobko, P., Roth, P.L. and Potosky, D. (1999) 'Derivation and implications of a meta-analytic matrix incorporating cognitive ability, alternative predictors, and job performance', *Personnel Psychology*, 52(3), 561–89.

Boddy, D. and Buchanan, D. (1992) *Take the Lead: Interpersonal skills for change agents*. London: Prentice-Hall.

Bodenhausen, G.V. and Macrae, C.N. (1996) 'The self-regulation of intergroup perception: Mechanisms and consequences of stereotype suppression', in C.N. Macrae, M. Hewstone and C. Stangor (eds), *Foundations of Stereotypes and Stereotyping*. New York: Guilford Press.

Bolino, M.C. and Turnley, W.H. (2008) 'Old faces, new places: equity theory in cross-cultural contexts, *Journal of Organizational Behavior*, 29, 29–50.

Bolles, R.N. (2008) *What Color is your Parachute? 2009: A practical manual for job-hunters and career changers*. Berkeley, CA: Ten Speed Press.

Bolton, G.E., Katok, E. and Ockenfels, A. (2004) 'How effective are electronic reputation mechanisms? An experimental investigation', *Management Science*, 50, 1587–602.

Bond, F.W. and Bunce, D. (2001) 'Job control mediates change in a work reorganization intervention for stress reduction', *Journal of Occupational Health Psychology*, 6, 290–302.

Bond, F.W., Flaxman, P.E. and Bunce, D. (2008) 'The influence of psychological flexibility on work redesign: Mediated moderation of a work reorganization intervention', *Journal of Applied Psychology*, 93, 645–54.

Bond, F.W., Flaxman, P.E. and Loivette, S. (2006) *A Business Case for the Management Standards for Stress*. Norwich, UK: Her Majesty's Stationery Office, Research Reports.

Bond, J.T., Galinsky, E., Kim, S.S. and Brownfield, E. (2005) *2005 National Study of Employers*. New York: Families and Work Institute.

Bonde, J.P.E. (2008) 'Psychosocial factors at work and risk of depression: a systematic review of the epidemiological evidence', *Occupational and Environmental Medicine*, 438–45.

Boniwell, I. and Henry, J. (2007) 'Developing conceptions of well-being: Advancing subjective, hedonic and hedonic theories', *Social Psychological Review*, 9, 3–18.

Bono, J.E. and Ilies, R. (2006) 'Charisma, positive emotions and mood contagion', *The Leadership Quarterly*, 17, 317–34.

Boring, E.C. (1923) 'Intelligence as the tests test it', *New Republic*, 35, 35–7.

Borman, W.C. and Motowidlo, S.J. (1997) 'Task performance and contextual performance: The meaning for personnel selection', *Human Performance*, 10, 99–109.

Bortner, R.W. (1969) 'A short rating scale as a potential measure of pattern A behaviour', *Journal of Chronic Diseases*, 22, 87–91.

Bosveld, W., Koomen, W. and Voelaar, R. (1997) 'Constructing a social issue: Effects on attitudes and the false consensus effect', *British Journal of Social Psychology*, 36, 263–72.

Bouchard, T.J. and McGue, M. (1990) 'Genetic and rearing environmental influences on adult personality: An analysis of adopted twins reared apart', *Journal of Personality*, 58, 263–92.

Boudreau, J.W. (1989) 'Selection utility analysis: A review and agenda for future research', in M. Smith and I.T. Robertson (eds), *Advances in Selection and Assessment*. Chichester: John Wiley.

Bowers, C.A., Pharmer, J.A. and Salas, E. (2003) 'When member homogeneity is needed in work teams: A meta analysis', *Small Group Research*, 31(3), 305–27.

Bowler, M.C. and Woehr, D.J. (2006) 'A meta-analytic evaluation of the impact of dimension and exercise factors on assessment center ratings', *Journal of Applied Psychology*, 91, 1114–24.

Bowling, N.A., Beehr, T.A. and Lepisto, L.R. (2006) 'Beyond job satisfaction: A five-year prospective analysis of the dispositional approach to work attitudes', *Journal of Vocational Behavior*, 69, 315–30.

Bozionelos, N. (2005) 'When the inferior candidate is offered the job: the selection interview as a political and power game', *Human Relations*, 58, 1605–31.

Bradford, D.L. and Burke, W.W. (2004) 'Introduction: Is OD in crisis?', *The Journal of Applied Behavioral Science*, 40(4), 369–73.

Brayfield, A.H. and Rothe, H.F. (1951) 'An index of job satisfaction', *Journal of Applied Psychology*, 35, 307–11.

Breckler, S.J. (1984) 'Empirical validation of affect, behavior and cognition as distinct attitude components', *Journal of Personality and Social Psychology*, 47, 1191–205.

Breslow, L. and Buell, P. (1960) 'Mortality from coronary heart disease and physical activity of work in California', *Journal of Chronic Diseases*, 11, 615–25.

Breukelen, W., Van der Vlist, R. and Steensma, H. (2004) 'Voluntary employee turnover: combining variables from the "traditional" turnover literature with the theory of planned behavior', *Journal of Organizational Behavior*, 25, 893–914.

Briner, R. and Reynolds, S. (1999) 'The costs, benefits and limitations of organizational level stress interventions', *Journal of Organizational Behavior*, 20, 647–64.

Briscoe, J.P. and Hall, D.T. (2006) 'The interplay of boundarylessness and protean careers: Combinations and implications', *Journal of Vocational Behavior*, 69, 4–18.

Briscoe, J.P., Hall, D.T. and Frautschy DeMuth, R.L. (2006) 'Protean and boundaryless careers: An empirical exploration', *Journal of Vocational Behavior*, 69, 30–47.

British Psychological Society (2006) *Code of Ethics and Conduct*. Leicester: BPS.

Brodbeck, F.C., Frese, M., Akerblom, S., Audia, G., Bakacsi, G., Bendova, H. *et al.* (2000) 'Cultural variation of leadership prototypes across 22 European countries', *Journal of Occupational and Organizational Psychology*, 73, 1–29.

Brotherton, C. (2003) 'Psychology and industrial relations', in P. Ackers and A. Wilkinson (eds), *Understanding Work and Employment*. Oxford: Oxford University Press.

Brough, P., O'Driscoll, M.P., Kalliath, T.J., Cooper, C.L. and Poelmans, S.A. (2009) *Workplace Psychological Health: Current research and practice*. Cheltenham: Edward Elgar.

Brown, A. (1995) *Organisational Culture*. London: Pitman.

Brown, A. (1998) *Organisational Culture*, 2nd edition. Harlow: FT/Prentice Hall.

Brown, D.J., Cober, R.T., Keeping, L.M. and Levy, P.E. (2006) 'Racial tolerance and reactions to diversity information in job advertisments', *Journal of Applied Social Psychology*, 36, 2048–71.

Brown, K.G. (2005) 'An examination of the structure and nomological network of trainee reactions: A closer look at "smile sheets"'. *Journal of Applied Psychology*, 90, 991–1001.

Brown, M.E. and Treviño, L.K. (2006) 'Ethical leadership: A review and future directions', *Leadership Quarterly*, 17, 595–616.

Brown, M.E., Treviño, L.K. and Harrison, D.A. (2005) 'Ethical leadership: A social learning perspective for construct development and testing', *Organizational Behavior and Human Decision Processes*, 97, 117–34.

Brun, J. and Lamarche, C. (2006) *Assessing the Costs of Work Stress*. Université Laval, Quebec, Canada. Available online at: http://www.cgsst.com/chaire/stock/eng/doc273-809.pdf

Bryman, A. (1992) *Charisma and Leadership in Organizations*. London: Sage.

Bryman, A. (2001) *Social Research Methods*. Oxford: Oxford University Press.

Bryman, A. (2006) 'Integrating quantitative and qualitative research: How is it done?', *Qualitative Research*, 6, 97–113.

Bryman, A. (2007) 'Barriers to integrating quantitative and qualitative research', *Journal of Mixed Methods Research*, 1, 8–22.

Buchanan, D. and Boddy, D. (1992a) *The Expertise of the Change Agent*. London: Prentice Hall.

Buchanan, D. and Boddy, D. (1992b) *Take the Lead: Interpersonal skills for change agents*. London: Prentice Hall.

Buchanan, D.A. and Storey, J. (1997) 'Role-taking and role-switching in organizational change: The four pluralities', in I. McLoughlin and M. Harris (eds), *Innovation, Organizational Change and Technology*. London: International Thompson.

Bullock, R.J. and Batten, D. (1985) 'It's just a phase we're going through: a review and synthesis of OD phase analysis', *Group and Organization Studies*, 10, 383–412.

Bunce, D. and West, M.A. (1996). 'Stress management and innovation interventions at work', *Human Relations*, 49, 209–32.

Bunce, D. (1997) 'What factors are associated with the outcome of individual-focused worksite stress management interventions?', *Journal of Occupational and Organizational Psychology*, 70, 1–17.

Burgoyne, J.G. (1999). 'Design of the times: A new model for the learning organisation', *People Management*, June, 38–44.

Burke, M. (2005) 'Selection utility models', in *Blackwell Encyclopedic Dictionary of Human Resource Management*. Oxford: Wiley-Blackwell.

Burke, R.J. and Cooper, C.L. (2008) *The Long Work Hours Culture: Causes, consequences and choices*. Bingley: Emerald Press.

Burnes, B. (1989) *New Technology in Context*. Aldershot: Gower.

Burnes, B. (2000) *Managing Change: A strategic approach to organisational dynamics*, 3rd edition. Harlow: FT/Prentice Hall.

Burnes, B. (2004a) 'Kurt Lewin and the planned approach to change: A re-appraisal. *Journal of Management Studies*, 41(6), 977–1002.

Burnes, B. (2004b) *Managing Change*, 4th edition. Harlow: FT/Prentice Hall.

Burnes, B. (2004c) 'Emergent change and planned change – competitors or allies? The case of XYZ Construction', *International Journal of Operations and Production Management*, 24(9), 886–902.

Burnes, B. (2007) 'Kurt Lewin and the Harwood Studies: The foundations of OD', *Journal of Applied Behavioral Science*, 43(2), 213–31.

Burnes, B., Cooper, C. and West, P. (2003) 'Organisational learning: the new management paradigm?', *Management Decision*, 41(5), 443–51.

Burns, J.M. (1978) *Leadership*. New York: Harper & Row.

Cacioppo, J.T. and Petty, R.E. (1979) 'Effects of message repetition and position on cognitive responses, recall, and persuasion', *Journal of Personality and Social Psychology*, 37, 97–109.

Cacioppo, J.T. and Petty, R.E. (1989) 'Effects of message repetition on argument processing, recall, and persuasion', *Basic and Applied Social Psychology*, 10, 3–12.

Callanan, G.A. and Greenhaus, J.H. (1992) 'The career indecision of managers and professionals: An examination of multiple subtypes', *Journal of Vocational Behavior*, 41, 212–31.

Campbell, D.T. and Stanley, J.C. (1963) *Experimental and Quasi-Experimental Designs for Research*. Chicago, IL: Rand McNally.

Campbell, J.P. (1990) 'Modelling the performance prediction problem in industrial organizational psychology', in M.D. Dunnette and L.M. Hough (eds), *Handbook of Industrial and Organizational Psychology*, 2nd edition, vol. 1. Palo Alto, CA: Consulting Psychologists Press.

Campbell, J.P. (2008) Personal web page, http://www.psych.umn.edu/people/faculty/campbell.htm, accessed 15 January 2009.

Campbell, J.P., Gasser, M.B. and Oswald, F.L. (1996) 'The substantive nature of job performance variability', in K.R. Murphy (ed.), *Individual Differences and Behavior in Organizations*. San Francisco, CA: Jossey-Bass.

Campbell, J.P., McCloy, R.A., Oppler, S.H. and Sager, C.E. (1993) 'A theory of performance', in N. Schmitt and W. Borman (eds), *Personnel Selection in Organizations*. San Francisco, CA: Jossey-Bass.

Cannon, W.B. (1929) *Bodily Changes in Pain, Hunger, Fear and Rage*. New York: Appleton.

Caplan R.D., Cobb S., French J.R.P., Van Harrison R. and Pinneau S.R. (1975) *Job Demands and Worker Health*. Cincinnati, OH: National Institute for Occupational Safety and Health.

Caplan, R.D., Cobb, S., French, J.R.P., van Harrison, R. and Pinneau, S.R. (1980) *Job Demands and Worker Health*. Ann Arbor: University of Michigan Institute of Social Research.

Cappelli, P. (1999) 'Career jobs are dead', *California Management Review*, 42, 146–67.

Card, S., Moran, T.P. and Newell, A. (1980) 'The keystroke-level model for user performance with interactive systems', *Communications of the ACM*, 23, 396–410.

Carnall, C.A. (2003) *Managing Change in Organizations*, 4th edition. Harlow: FT/Prentice-Hall.

Carnevale, P.J. and Pruitt, D.G. (1992) 'Negotiation and mediation', *Annual Review of Psychology*, 43, 531–82.

Carrick, P. and Williams, R. (1999) 'Development centres – a review of assumptions', *Human Resource Management Journal*, 9, 77–92.

Cartwright, S. and Cooper, C.L. (1997) *Managing Workplace Stress*. London: Sage.

Cartwright, S. and Cooper, C. L. (2002) *ASSET: Management guide*. Manchester: Robertson Cooper.

Cartwright S. and Cooper C.L. (2008) *The Oxford Handbook of Organizational Well Being*. Oxford: Oxford University Press.

Carver, C.S., Scheier, M.F. and Weintraub, J.K. (1989) 'Assessing coping strategies: A theoretically based approach', *Journal of Personality and Social Psychology*, 56, 267–83.

Cascio, W. (2000) 'Managing a virtual workplace', *Academy of Management Executive*, 14, 81–90.

Cassell, C. (2000) 'The business case and the management of diversity', in M.J. Davidson and R.J. Burke (eds), *Women in Management*. London: Sage.

Cassell, C. and Symon, G. (2004) *Essential Guide to Qualitative Methods in Organizational Research*. London: Sage.

Cassidy, T. and Lynn, R. (1989) 'A multifactorial approach to achievement motivation: The development of a comprehensive measure', *Journal of Occupational Psychology*, 62, 301–12.

Catalyst (1996) *Women in Corporate Leadership: Progress and prospects*. New York: Catalyst.

Cattell, R.B. (1965) *The Scientific Analysis of Personality*. Harmondsworth: Penguin.

Cattell, R.B. and Cattell, H.E.P. (1995) 'Personality structure and the new fifth edition of the 16PF', *Educational and Psychological Measurement*, 55, 926–37.

Cattell, R.B., Eber, H.W. and Taksuoka, M.M. (1970) *Handbook for the Sixteen Personality Factor Questionnaire*. Windsor: National Foundation for Educational Research.

Cervone, D. and Mischel, W. (eds) (2002) *Advances in Personality Science*. New York: Guilford Press.

Chao, G.T., Walz, P.M. and Gardner, P.D. (1992) 'Formal and informal mentorships – a comparison on mentoring functions and contrast with nonmentored counterparts', *Personnel Psychology*, 45(3), 619–36.

Chapman, M. (2000) '"When the entrepreneur sneezes, the organization catches a cold": A practitioner's perspective on the state of the art in research on the entrepreneurial personality and the entrepreneurial process', *European Journal of Work and Organizational Psychology*, 9, 97–101.

Chase, B. and Karwowski, W. (2003) 'Advanced manufacturing technology', in D. Holman, T.D. Wall, C.W. Clegg, P. Sparrow and A. Howard (eds), *The New Workplace*. Chichester: John Wiley.

Chattopadhyay, A. and Alba, J.W. (1988) 'The situational importance of recall and inference in consumer decision making', *Journal of Consumer Research*, 15, 1–12.

Chen, C., Gustafson, D.H. and Lee, Y. (2002) 'The effect of a quantitative decision aid – analytic hierarchy process – on group polarization', *Group Decision and Negotiation*, 11, 329–44.

Chen, C.C., Yu, K.C. and Miner, J.B. (1997) 'Motivation to manage: A study of women in Chinese state-owned enterprises', *Journal of Applied Behavioural Science*, 33, 160–73.

Cherns, A.B. (1976) 'The principles of sociotechnical design', *Human Relations*, 29, 783–92.

Cherns, A.B. (1987) 'Principles of sociotechnical design revisited', *Human Relations*, 40, 153–62.

Chiang, C.-F. and Jang, S. (2008) 'An expectancy model for hotel employee motivation', *International Journal of Hospitality Management*, 27, 313–22.

Child, J. (1972) 'Organizational structure, environment and performance: the role of strategic choice', *Sociology*, 6(1), 1–22.

Child, J. (1984) *Organization*. Cambridge: Harper and Row.

Church, A.H. (1997) 'Managerial self-awareness in high-performing individuals in organizations', *Journal of Applied Psychology*, 82(2), 281–92.

Church, A.H. (2000) 'Do higher performing managers actually receive better ratings? A validation of multirater assessment methodology', *Consulting Psychology Journal: Practice and Research*, 52, 99–116.

Cialdini, R.B. and Trost, M.R. (1998) 'Social influence: social norms, conformity, and compliance', in D.T. Gillbert, S.T Fiske and G. Lindzey (eds), *The Handbook of Social Psychology*, vols 1 and 2, 4th edition. Boston: McGraw-Hill.

CIPD (2004) *Managing Conflict at Work: A survey of the UK and Ireland*. London: CIPD.

CIPD (2005a) Survey Report. http://www.cipd.co.uk/subjects/perfmangmt/general/_perfmagmt.htm (accessed 15 May 2009). London: CIPD.

CIPD (2005b, revised 2009) Harassment and Bullying at Work. Available at: http://www.cipd.co.uk/subjects/dvsequl/harassmt/harrass.htm. London: CIPD.

CIPD (2007a) *Absence Management. Annual survey report*. London: CIPD.

CIPD (2007b) Employee Turnover and Retention. Available at: http://www.cipd.co.uk/subjects/hrpract/turnover/empturnretent.htm London: CIPD.

CIPD (2008a) *Labour Market Outlook: Quarterly Survey Report Spring 2008*. London: CIPD.

CIPD (2008b) 360 degree feedback. Available at: http://www.cipd.co.uk/ subjects/perfmangmt/appfdbck/360fdbk.htm London: CIPD.

CIPD (2009) *Quarterly Survey Report Spring 2009*: 'Employee outlook, employee attitudes and the recession'. London: CIPD.

Clark, M. and Arnold, J. (2008) 'The nature, prevalence and correlates of generativity among men in middle career', *Journal of Vocational Behavior*, 73, 473–84.

Clarke, A., Oswald, A. and Warr, P. (1996) 'Is job satisfaction U-shaped in age?', *Journal of Occupational and Organizational Psychology*, 69, 57–81.

Clarke, L. (1994) *The Essence of Change*. London: Prentice Hall.

Clarke, S. and Cooper, C.L. (2004) *Managing the Safety Risk of Workplace Stress*. London: Routledge.

Cleary, T.A. (1968) 'Test bias: Prediction of grades of negro and white students in integrated colleges', *Journal of Educational Measurement*, 5, 115–24.

Cleary, T.S. and Shapiro, S.I. (1996) 'Abraham Maslow and Asian psychology', *Psychologia*, 39, 213–22.

Clegg, C. and Spencer, C. (2007) 'A circular and dynamic model of the process of job design', *Journal of Occupational and Organizational Psychology*, 80, 321–39.

Clegg, S. and Cooper, C.L. (2009) *The Sage Handbook of Organizational Behavior: Macro approaches*. California and London: Sage.

Clevenger, J., Pereira, G.M., Wiechmann, D., Schmitt, N. and Harvey, V.S. (2001) 'Incremental validity of situational judgment tests', *Journal of Applied Psychology*, 86, 410–17.

Clutterbuck, D. (2004) *Everyone Needs a Mentor*, 4th edition. London: Chartered Institute of Personnel and Development.

Coch, L. and French, J.R.P. (1948) 'Overcoming resistance to change', *Human Relations*, 1, 512–32.

Coghlan, D. (1993) 'In defence of process consultation', in C. Mabey and B. Mayon-White (eds), *Managing Change*, 2nd edition. London: The Open University/Paul Chapman Publishing.

Cohen, J. (1977) *Statistical Power Analysis for the Behavioral Sciences*. London: Academic Press.

Cohen, J., Cohen, P., West, S. and Aiken, L. (2003) *Applied Multiple Regression/Correlation Analysis for the Behavioral Sciences*, 3rd edition. Mahwah, NJ: Lawrence Erlbaum Associates.

Cokley, K., Dreher, G.F. and Stockdale, M.S. (2004) 'Towards the inclusiveness and career success of African Americans in the workplace', in M.S. Stockdale and F.J. Crosby (eds), *The Psychology and Management of Workplace Diversity*. Oxford: Blackwell.

Coleman, P.T. and Lim, Y.Y.J. (2001) 'A systematic approach to evaluating the effects of collaborative negotiation training on individuals and groups', *Negotiation Journal*, 363–92.

Collins, D. (1998) *Organizational Change*. Routledge: London.

Colquitt, J.A., Conlon, D.E., Wesson, M.J., Porter, C.O. and Ng, K.Y. (2001) 'Justice at the millennium: A meta-analytic review of 25 years of organizational justice research', *Journal of Applied Psychology*, 86, 425–45.

Colquitt, J.A., Greenberg, J. and Scott, B.A. (2005) 'Organizational justice: where do we stand?', in J. Greenberg, and J.A. Colquitt, J.A. (eds), *Handbook of Organizational Justice*. Mahwah, NJ: Lawrence Erlbaum.

Colquitt, J.A., LePine, J.A. and Noe, R.A. (2000) 'Toward an integrative theory of training motivation: A meta-analytic path analysis of 20 years of research', *Journal of Applied Psychology*, 85, 678–707.

Communications Directorate, South West Thames Regional Health Authority (1993) *Report of the Inquiry into the London Ambulance Service* (February 1993). London: Communications Directorate, South West Thames Regional Health Authority.

Conger, J.A. (1990) 'The dark side of leadership', *Organizational Dynamics*, Autumn, 44–5.

Conger, J.A. and Kanungo, R.N. (1998) *Charismatic Leadership in Organizations*. London: Sage.

Conger, J.A., Kanungo, R.N. and Menon, S.T. (2000) 'Charismatic leadership and follower effects', *Journal of Organizational Behavior*, 21(7), 747–67.

Conn, S. and Rieke, M. (eds) (1994) *16PF-5. Technical manual*. Champaign, IL: Institute for Personality and Ability Testing.

Conner, P.E. (1977) 'A critical enquiry into some assumptions and values characterizing OD', *Academy of Management Review*, 2(1), 635–44.

Conte, J.M. (2005) 'A review and critique of emotional intelligence measures', *Journal of Organizational Behavior*, 26, 433–40.

Conway, J.M. (1999) 'Distinguishing contextual performance from task performance for managerial jobs', *Journal of Applied Psychology*, 84, 3–13.

Conway, N. and Briner, R.B. (2005) *Understanding Psychological Contracts at Work: A critical evaluation of theory and research*. Oxford: Oxford University Press.

Cook, J.D., Hepworth, S.J., Wall, T.D. and Warr, P.B. (1981) *The Experience of Work*. London: Academic Press.

Cook, M. (2004) *Personnel Selection: Adding value through people*, 4th edition. London: Wiley.

Cook, M. (2009) *Personnel Selection: Adding value through people*, 5th edition. Oxford: Wiley-Blackwell.

Cook, T.D. and Campbell, D.T. (1979) *Quasi-experimentation: Design and analysis issues for field settings*. Chicago, IL: Rand McNally.

Cook, T.D. and Shadish, W.R. (1994) 'Social experiments: Some developments over the past fifteen years', *Annual Review of Psychology*, 45, 545–79.

Cook, T.D., Campbell, D.T. and Peracchio, L. (1990) 'Quasi experimentation', in M.D. Dunnette and L.M. Hough (eds), *Handbook of Industrial and Organizational Psychology*. Palo Alto, CA: Consulting Psychologists Press.

Cook, T.D., Gruder, C.L., Hennigan, K.M. and Flay, B.R. (1979) 'History of the sleeper effect: Some logical pitfalls in accepting the null hypothesis', *Psychological Bulletin*, 86, 662–79.

Cooke, B., Mills, A.J. and Kelley, E.S. (2005) 'Situating Maslow in Cold War America', *Group and Organization Management*, 30, 129–52.

Coombs, R. and Hull, R. (1994) 'The best or the worst of both worlds: BPR, cost reduction and the strategic management of IT'. Paper presented to the OASIG Seminar on Organisation Change Through IT and BPR: Beyond the Hype, September, London.

Cooper, C.L. and Cartwright, S. (1994) 'Healthy mind; healthy organization – a proactive approach to occupational stress', *Human Relations*, 47, 455–71.

Cooper, C.L. and Lewis, S. (1993) *The Workplace Revolution: Managing today's dual career families*. London: Kogan Page.

Cooper, C.L. and Quick, J. (1999) *Stress and Strain*. Oxford: Health Press.

Cooper, C.L. and Sadri, G. (1991) 'The impact of stress counseling at work', in P.L. Perrewe (ed.), Handbook of job stress (special issue), *Journal of Social Behaviour and Personality*, 6, 411–23.

Cooper, C.L., Dewe, P. and O'Driscoll, M. (2001) *Organizational Stress: A review and critique of theory, research and application*. London: Sage.

Cooper, C.L., Makin, P. and Cox, C. (1993) 'Managing the boss', *Leadership and Organizational Development Journal*, 19(5), 28–32.

Cooper, C.L., Sloan, S. and Williams, S. (1987) *Occupational Stress Indicator*. Windsor: NFER/Nelson.

Cooper, C.L., Sloan, S. and Williams, S. (1988) *Occupational Stress Indicator: The manual*. Windsor: NFER/Nelson.

Coopey, J. and Hartley, J. (1991) 'Reconsidering the case for organizational commitment', *Human Resource Management Journal*, 1, 18–32.

Corr, P.J. and Gray, J.A. (1996) 'Attributional style as a personality factor in insurance sales performance in the UK', *Journal of Occupational and Organizational Psychology*, 69, 83–7.

Costa, P.T. and McCrae, R.R. (1992) *The NEO PI-R Professional Manual*. Odessa, FL: Psychological Assessment Resources Inc.

Costa, P.T. and McCrae, R.R. (2006) *Revised NEO Personality Inventory (NEO PI-R) Manual* (UK edition). Oxford: Hogrefe.

Costa, P.T., Zonderman A.B. and McCrae R.R. (1991) 'Personality, defense, coping, and adaptation in older adulthood', in E.M. Cummings, A.L. Greene and K.K. Karraker (eds), *Life-span Development Psychology: Perspectives on stress and coping*. Hillsdale, NJ: Laurence Erlbaum Associates.

Coulson-Thomas, C. and Coe, T. (1991) *The Flat Organization*. London: British Institute of Management.

Cowan, G. and Hodge, C. (1996) 'Judgements of hate speech: The effects of target group, publicness, and behavioural responses of the target', *Journal of Applied Social Psychology*, 26, 355–74.

Cox, T. (1993) *Stress Research and Stress Management: Putting theory to work*. Sudbury: HSE Books.

Cox, T. and Griffiths, A. (1995) 'The nature and measurement of work stress: theory and practice', in J.R. Wilson and E.N. Corlett (eds), *Evaluation of Human Work: A practical ergonomics methodology*. London: Taylor and Francis.

Cox, T. and MacKay, C.J. (1981) 'A transactional approach to occupational stress', in E.N. Corlett and J. Richardson (eds), *Stress, Work Design and Productivity*. Chichester: Wiley and Sons.

Cox, T., Griffiths, A.J., Barlow, C.A., Randall, R.J., Thomson, L.E. and Rial-Gonzalez, E. (2000) *Organisational Interventions for Work Stress*. Sudbury: HSE Books.

Cox, T., Griffiths, A.J. and Randall, R. (2003) 'A risk management approach to the prevention of work stress', in M.J. Schabracq, J.A.M. Winnubst and C.L. Cooper (eds), *Handbook of Work and Health Psychology*, 2nd edition. Chichester: Wiley.

Cox, T., Karanika, M., Griffiths, A. and Houdmont, J. (2007) 'Evaluating organisational-level work stress interventions: Beyond traditional methods', *Work and Stress*, 21, 348–68.

Cox, T., Randall, R. and Griffiths, A. (2002) *Interventions to Control Stress at Work in Hospital Staff*. Sudbury: HSE Books.

Cox, T., Thirlaway, M., Gotts, G. and Cox, S. (1983) 'The nature and assessment of general well-being', *Journal of Psychosomatic Research*, 27, 353–59.

Coyne, I., Seigne, E. and Randall, P. (2000) 'Predicting workplace victim status from personality', *European Journal of Work and Organizational Psychology*, 9, 335–50.

Crail, M. (2007) 'Assessment centres are worth the high cost', *Personnel Today*, 8(21), 49.

Cramton, C.D. (2001) 'The mutual knowledge problem and its consequences for dispersed collaboration', *Organization Science*, 12, 246–371.

Cramton, C.D. (2002) 'Attribution in distributed teams', in P. Hinds and S. Kiesler (eds), *Distributed Work*. Cambridge, MA: MIT Press.

Cramton, C.D. and Webber, S.S. (2005) 'Relationships among geographic dispersion, team processes and effectiveness in software development work teams', *Journal of Business Research*, 58, 758–65.

Cramton, C.D. and Wilson, J.M. (2002) 'Explanation and judgement in distributed groups: An interactional justice perspective'. Paper presented at the Academy of Management Conference, Denver, CO.

Cramton, C.D., Orvis, K.L. and Wilson, J.M., (2007) 'Situation invisibility and attribution in distributed collaborations', *Journal of Management*, 33, 525–46.

Crandall, B., Klein, G. and Hoffman, R.R. (2006) *Working Mind: A practitioner's guide to cognitive task analysis*. Cambridge, MA: MIT Press.

Creed, P.A., King, V., Hood, M. and McKenzie, R. (2009) 'Goal orientation, self-regulation strategies and job-seeking intensity in unemployed adults', *Journal of Applied Psychology*, 94, 806–13.

Creed, P., Patton, W. and Prideaux, L.A. (2006) 'Causal relationship between career indecision and career decision-making self-efficacy – a longitudinal cross-lagged analysis', *Journal of Career Development*, 33, 47–65.

Crisp, C.B. and Jarvenpaa, S.L. (2000) 'Trust over time in global virtual teams'. Research paper at the Academy of Management Meeting, Toronto, Canada, 2000.

Crites, J.O. (1978) *Theory and Research Handbook for the Career Maturity Inventory*, 2nd edition. Monterey, CA: CTB/McGraw-Hill.

Cropanzano, R., Bowen, D.E. and Gilliland, S.W. (2007) 'The management of organizational justice', *Academy of Management Perspectives*, 21(4), 34–48.

Cropanzano, R., Byrne, Z.S., Bobocel, D.R. and Rupp, D.E. (2001) 'Moral virtues, fairness heuristics, social entities and other denizens of organizational justice', *Journal of Vocational Behavior*, 58, 164–209.

Crosby, P.B. (1979) *Quality is Free*. New York: McGraw-Hill.

Cross, W.E. Jr (1995) 'The psychology of nigrescence: Revising the Cross model', in J.G. Ponterotto, J.M. Casas, L.A. Suzuki and C.M. Alexander (eds), *Handbook of Multicultural Counseling*. Thousand Oaks, CA: Sage.

Cruise O'Brien, R. and Voss, C. (1992) *In Search of Quality*. Working Paper. London: London Business School.

Cummings, T. and Cooper, C.L. (1979) 'A cybernetic framework for the study of occupational stress', *Human Relations*, 32, 395–419.

Cummings, T.G. and Huse, E.F. (1989) *Organization Development and Change*. St Paul, MN: West.

Cummings, T.G. and Worley, C.G. (1997) *Organization Development and Change*, 6th edition. Cincinnati, OH: South-Western College Publishing.

Cummings, T.G. and Worley, C.G. (2001) *Organization Development and Change*, 7th edition. Cincinnati, OH: South-Western College Publishing.

Cummings, T.G. and Worley, C.G. (2004) *Organizational Development and Change*, 8th edition. Cincinnati, OH: Southwestern College Publishing Co.

Currie, G. and Kerrin, M. (2003) 'Human resource management and knowledge management: Enhancing knowledge sharing in a pharmaceutical company', *The International Journal of Human Resource Management*, 14(6), 1027–45.

Daft, R.L. and Lengel, R.H. (1986) 'Organizational information requirements, media richness and structural design', *Management Science*, 32, 554–71.

Dambrin, C. (2004) 'How does telework influence the management–employee relationship?', *International Journal of Human Resource Development and Management*, 4, 358–74.

Daniels, K.J., Boocock, J.G., Glover, J., Hartley, R. and Holland, J. (2009) 'An experience sampling study of learning, affect and the demands control support model', *Journal of Applied Psychology*, 94, 1003–17.

Darr, W. and Johns, G. (2008) 'Work strain, health and absenteeism', *Journal of Occupational Health Psychology*, 13, 293–318.

Davenport, T.H. (1993) *Process Innovation: Re-engineering Work Through IT*. Boston, MA: Harvard Business School Press.

Davis, J.H. (1992) 'Some compelling intuitions about group consensus decisions, theoretical and empirical research, and interpersonal aggregation phenomena: Selected examples, 1950–1990', *Organizational Behavior and Human Decision Processes*, 52, 3–38.

Dawson, P. (1994) *Organizational Change: A Processual Approach*. London: Paul Chapman Publishing.

Dawson, P. (2003) *Reshaping Change: A processual perspective*. London: Routledge.

De Fruyt, F. and Mervielde, I. (1999) 'RIASEC types and big five traits as predictors of employment status and nature of employment', *Personnel Psychology*, 52, 701–27.

De Hoogh, A.H.B. and Den Hartog, D.N., (2008) 'Social responsibility, ethical leadership and performance', *Leadership Quarterly*, 19, 297–311.

De Hoogh, A.H.B., Den Hartog, D.N., Koopman, P.L., Thierry, H., Van den Berg, P.T., Van der Weide, J.G. and Wilderom, C.P.M. (2004) 'Charismatic leadership, environmental dynamism and performance', *European Journal of Work and Organizational Psychology*, 13(4), 447–71.

De Hoogh, A.H.B., Den Hartog, D.N., Koopman, P.L., Thierry, H., Van den Berg, P.T., Van der Weide, J.G. and Wilderom, C.P.M. (2005) 'Leader motives, charismatic leadership and subordinates' work attitude in the profit and voluntary sector', *Leadership Quarterly*, 16(1), 17–35.

de Jonge, J. and Dormann, C. (2006) 'Stressors, resources and strain at work: A longitudinal test of the triple-match principle', *Journal of Applied Psychology*, 91, 1359–74.

de Lange, A.H., Taris, T.W., Kompier, M.A.J., Houtman, I.L.D. and Bongers, P.M. (2003) '"The very best of the millennium": Longitudinal research and the demand-control-(support) model', *Journal of Occupational Health Psychology*, 8, 282–305.

de Treville, S. and Antonakis, J. (2006) 'Could lean production job design be intrinsically motivating? Contextual, configurational and levels-of-analysis issues', *Journal of Operations Management*, 24, 99–123.

De Witte H., Verhofstadt, E. and Omey, E. (2007) 'Testing Karasek's learning and strain hypotheses on young workers in their first job', *Work and Stress*, 21, 131–41.

De Witte, K. and van Muijen, J.J. (1999) 'Organizational culture: critical questions for researchers and practitioners', *European Journal of Work and Organizational Psychology*, 8(4), 583–95.

Deal, T. and Kennedy, A. (1982) 'Culture: A new look through old lenses', *Journal of Applied Behavioural Science*, 19(4), 497–507.

Dean, J.W. Jr and Sharfman, M.P. (1996) 'Does decision process matter? A study of strategic decision-making effectiveness', *Academy of Management Journal*, 39, 368–96.

Dean, M.A., Roth, P.L. and Bobko, P. (2008) 'Ethnic and gender subgroup differences in assessment center ratings: A meta-analysis', *Journal of Applied Psychology*, 93, 685–91.

Deci, E.L. and Ryan, R.M. (1980) 'The empirical exploration of intrinsic motivational processes', in L. Berkowitz (ed.), *Advances in Experimental Social Psychology*, vol. 13. New York: Academic Press.

Deci, E.L., Koestner, R. and Ryan, R.M. (1999) 'A meta-analytic review of experiments examining the effects of extrinsic rewards on intrinsic motivation', *Psychological Bulletin*, 125, 627–68.

DeCorte, W. (2000) 'Using order statistics to assess the sampling variability of personnel selection utility estimates', *Journal of Applied Statistics*, 27, 703–13.

DeFillippi, R.J. and Arthur, M.B. (1996) 'Boundaryless contexts and careers: a competency-based perspective', in M.B. Arthur and D.M. Rousseau (eds), *The Boundaryless Career: A new employment principle for a new organizational era*. Oxford: Oxford University Press.

Dekker, S.W.A. and Woods, D.D. (2002) 'MABA-MABA or Abracadabra?: Progress on human–automation coordination', *Cognition, Technology and Work*, 4, 240–24.

Delbridge, R, Turnbull, P. and Wilkinson, B. (1992) 'Pushing back the frontiers: Management control and work intensification under JIT/TQM factory regimes', *New Technology, Work and Employment*, 7, 97–106.

Delgado, F. (2003) 'The fusing of sport and politics: Media construction of US versus Iran at France '98', *Journal of Sport and Social Issues*, 27, 293–307.

Demir, A., Ulusoy, M. and Ulusoy, M.F. (2003) 'Investigation of factors influencing burnout levels in professional and private lives of nurses', *International Journal of Nursing Studies*, 40, 807–27.

Den Hartog D.N., De Hoogh, A.H.B. and Keegan, A.E. (2007) 'Belongingness as a moderator of the charisma–OCB relationship', *Journal of Applied Psychology*, 92(4) 1131–39.

Den Hartog, D.N., House, R.J., Hanges, P.J., Ruiz-Quintanilla, S.A. and Dorfman, P.W. (1999) 'Culture-specific and cross-culturally generalizable implicit leadership theories: Are attributes of charismatic/transformational leadership universally endorsed?', *Leadership Quarterly*, 10, 219–57.

Den Hartog, D.N., Van Muijen, J.J. and Koopman, P.L. (1997) 'Transactional versus transformational leadership: An analysis of the MLQ', *Journal of Occupational and Organizational Psychology*, 70, 19–34.

DeNeve, K.M. and Cooper, H. (1998) 'The happy personality: A meta-analysis of 137 personality traits and subjective well-being', *Psychological Bulletin*, 124, 197–229.

Derogatis L.R. and Melisaratos, N. (1983) 'The brief symptom inventory: An introductory report', *Psychological Medicine*, 13, 595–605.

DeShon, R.P. and Gillespie, J.Z. (2005) 'A motivated action theory account of goal orientation', *Journal of Applied Psychology*, 90, 1096–127.

Dess, G.G. and Picken, J.C. (2000) 'Changing roles: Leadership in the 21st century', *Organizational Dynamics*, 28(3), 18–34.

Deutsch, M. (2002) 'Social psychology's contributions to the study of conflict resolution', *Negotiation Journal*, 307–20.

DeVaro, J., Li, R. and Brookshire, D. (2007) 'Analysing the job characteristics model: new support from a cross-section of establishments', *International Journal of Human Resource Management*, 18, 986–1003.

Devine, D.J. and Philips, J.L. (2001) 'Do smarter teams do better? A meta-analysis of cognitive ability and team performance', *Small Group Research*, 32(5), 507–32.

Devine, P.G. (1989) 'Stereotypes and prejudice: Their automatic and controlled components', *Journal of Personality and Social Psychology*, 56, 5–18.

Dewe, P. and Kompier, M. (2008) *Foresight Mental Capital and Wellbeing Project. Wellbeing and work: Future challenges*. London: The Government Office for Science.

Diamantopoulos, A. and Schlegelmilch, B. (1997) *Taking the Fear out of Data Analysis*. London: Dryden Press.

Diaper, D. and Stanton, N.A. (eds) (2004) *The Handbook of Task Analysis for Human–Computer Interaction*. Mahwah, NJ: Lawrence Erlbaum Associates.

Dick, P. (2004) 'Discourse analysis', in C. Cassell and G. Symon (eds), *Essential Guide to Qualitative Methods in Organizational Research*. London: Sage.

Dickson, M.W., Den Hartog, D.N. and Mitchelson, J.K. (2003) 'Research on leadership in a cross-cultural context: Making progress, and raising new questions', *Leadership Quarterly*, 14(6), 729–68.

Diedorff, E. and Morgeson, F. (2007) 'Consensus in work role requirements: The influence of discrete occupational context on role expectation', *Journal of Applied Psychology*, 92, 1228–41.

Diehl, M. and Stroebe, W. (1987) 'Productivity loss in brainstorming groups: Toward the solution of a riddle', *Journal of Personality and Social Psychology*, 53, 497–509.

Digman, J.M. (1990) 'Personality structure: Emergence of the five-factor model', *Annual Review of Psychology*, 41, 417–40.

Dipboye, R.L. (2005) 'The selection/recruitment interview: Core processes and contexts'. In A. Evers, N. Anderson and O. Voskuijl (eds), *The Blackwell Handbook of Personnel Selection*. Malden, MA: Blackwell Publishing.

Dolezalek, H. (2004) '2004 industry report', *Training*, 41(10), 20–37.

Donaldson-Feilder, E. (2009) 'Why the business case for staff well-being is even stronger during a financial downturn', *Well-being and Performance Newsletter*, 4, July.

Donaldson-Feilder, E., Yarker, J. and Lewis, R. (2008) 'Management competencies for preventing and reducing stress at work', in J. Houdmont and S. Leka (eds), *Occupational Health Psychology: European Perspectives on Research, Education and Practice*, vol. III. Nottingham, UK: European Academy of Occupational Health Psychology and Nottingham University Press.

Donnay, D.A.C. and Borgen, F.H. (1999) 'The incremental validity of vocational self-efficacy: An examination of interest, self-efficacy and occupation', *Journal of Counseling Psychology*, 46(4), 432–47.

Dormann, C. and Zapf, D. (2001) 'Job satisfaction: A meta-analysis of stabilities', *Journal of Organizational Behaviour*, 22, 483–504.

Dries, N., Pepermans, R. and Carlier, O. (2008) 'Career success: Constructing a multidimensional model', *Journal of Vocational Behavior*, 73, 254–67.

Duarte, D.L. and Snyder, N.T. (2001) *Mastering Virtual Teams: Strategies, tools and techniques that succeed*, 2nd edition. San Francisco, CA: Jossey Bass.

Dunham, R., Grube, J.A. and Castañeda, M.B. (1994) 'Organizational commitment: the utility of an integrative definition', *Journal of Applied Psychology*, 79, 370–80.

Dunphy, D. and Stace, D. (1992) *Under New Management: Australian organizations in transition*. Roseville, NSW, Australia: McGraw-Hill.

Dunphy, D. and Stace, D. (1993) 'The strategic management of corporate change', *Human Relations*, 46(8), 905–18.

Dweck, C.S. (1986) 'Motivational processes affecting learning', *American Psychologist*, 41, 1040–8.

Dwyer, D.J. and Ganster, D.C. (1991) 'The effects of job demands and control on employee attendance and satisfaction', *Journal of Organizational Behavior*, 12, 595–608.

Eagly, A.H. and Chaiken, S. (1975) 'An attribution analysis of the effect of communicator characteristics on opinion change: The case of communicator attractiveness', *Journal of Personality and Social Psychology*, 33, 136–44.

Eagly, A.H. and Chaiken, S. (1992) *The Psychology of Attitude*s. San Diego, CA: Harcourt Brace Johanovich.

Eagly, A.H., Karau, S.J. and Makhijani, M.G. (1995) 'Gender and the effectiveness of leaders: A meta-analysis', *Psychological Bulletin*, 117, 125–45.

Earl, J. and Bright, J. (2007) 'The relationship between career decision status and important work outcomes', *Journal of Vocational Behavior*, 71, 233–46.

Earnshaw, J. and Cooper, C.L. (2001) *Stress and Employer Liability*. London: CIPD Books.

Easterby-Smith, M., Crossan, M. and Nicolini, D. (2000) 'Organizational learning: Debates past, present and future', *Journal of Management Studies*, 37(6), 783–96.

Easterby-Smith, M., Thorpe, R. and Lowe, A. (2002) *Management Research: An introduction*, 2nd edition. London: Sage.

Ebrahimi, B.P., Young, S.A. and Luk, V.M.W. (2001) 'Motivation to manage in China and Hong Kong: A gender comparison of managers', *Sex Roles*, 45, 433–53.

Eby, L.T. and McManus, S.E. (2004) 'The protégé's role in negative mentoring experiences', *Journal of Vocational Behavior*, 65, 255–75.

Eby, L.T., Butts, M. and Lockwood, A. (2003) 'Predictors of success in the era of the boundaryless career', *Journal of Organizational Behavior*, 24, 689–708.

Eby, L.T., Freeman, D.M., Rush, M.C. and Charles, L.E. (1999) 'Motivational bases of affective organizational commitment: A partial test of an integrative theoretical model', *Journal of Occupational and Organizational Psychology*, 72, 463–83.

Economist Intelligence Unit (1992) *Making Quality Work: Lessons from Europe's leading companies*. London: Economist Intelligence Unit.

Eden, M. and Chisholm, R.F. (1993) 'Emerging varieties of action research', *Human Relations*, 46, 121–42.

Edwardes, M. (1983) *Back from the Brink*. London: Collins.

Edwards, J.A., Webster, S., Van Laar, D. and Easton, S. (2008) 'Psychometric analysis of the UK Health and Safety Executive's Management Standards work-related stress Indicator Tool', *Work and Stress*, 22, 96–107.

Egan, M., Bambra, C., Petticrew, M. and Whitehead, M. (2008) 'Reviewing evidence on complex social interventions: Appraising implementation in systemic reviews of the health effects of organisational-level workplace interventions', *Journal of Epidemiology and Community Health*. Published online 21 August 2008, doi:10.1136/jech.2007.07.1233).

Einarsen, S. (1999) 'The nature and causes of bullying at work', *International Journal of Manpower*, 20, 16–27.

Einarsen, S. and Mikkelsen, E.G. (2003) 'Individual effects of exposure to bullying at work', in S. Einarsen, H. Hoel, D. Zapf and C.L. Cooper (eds), *Bullying and Emotional Abuse in the Workplace: International perspectives in research and practice*. London: Taylor and Francis.

Einarsen, S. and Skogstad, A. (1996) 'Bullying at work: Epdemiological findings in public and private organizations', *European Journal of Work and Organizational Psychology*, 5, 185–202.

Einarsen, S., Raknes, B.I. and Matthiesen, S.B. (1994) 'Bullying and harassment at work and their relationship to work environment quality: an explanatory study', *European Journal of Work and Organizational Psychology*, 5, 185–201.

Eldridge, J.E.T. and Crombie, A.D. (1974) *A Sociology of Organizations*. London: George Allen and Unwin.

Elkin, A.J. and Rosch, P.J. (1990) 'Promoting mental health at the workplace: The prevention side of stress management', *Occupational Medicine: State of the Art Review*, 5(4), 739–54.

Ellemers, N., Spears, R. and Doosji, B. (2002) 'Self and social identity', *Annual Review of Psychology*, 53, 161–86.

Ellis, C. and Sonnenfeld, J. (1994) 'Diverse approaches to managing diversity', *Human Resource Management*, 33, 79–109.

Elo, A.-L., Ervasti, J. and Mattila, P. (2008) 'Evaluation of an organizational stress management program in a municipal public works organization', *Journal of Occupational Health Psychology*, 13, 10–23.

Elsbach, K.D. and Hargadon, A.B. (2006) 'Enhancing creativity through "mindless" work: A framework of workday design', *Organization Science*, 17 470–83.

Ely, R.J. and Thomas, D.A. (2001) 'Cultural diversity at work: The effects of diversity perspectives on work group processes', *Administrative Science Quarterly*, 46, 229–73.

Embrey, D.E. (1986) 'SHERPA: A systematic human error reduction and prediction approach'. Paper presented at the International Meeting on Advances in Nuclear Power Systems, Knoxville, Tennessee.

Emmerling, R.J. and Goleman, D. (2003) 'Emotional intelligence: Issues and common misunderstandings', The Consortium for Research on Emotional Intelligence in Organizations Issues in EI (www.eiconsortium.org).

Employee Assistance Professionals Association (EAPA) (2003) *EAPA Standards and Professional Guidelines for Employee Assistance Programs*. Arlington, VA: Employee Assistance Professionals Association.

Employee Assistance Professionals Association (EAPA) (2007) *UK Purchasing Guidelines for EAPs*. Oxford: Employee Assistance Professionals Association.

Endsley, M.R. (1988) 'Design and evaluation for situation awareness enhancement', in *Proceedings of the Human Factors Society 32nd Annual Meeting*. Santa Monica, CA: Human Factors Society.

Eppinger, S.D. (2001) 'Innovation at the speed of information', *Harvard Business Review*, January, 149–60.

Equality and Human Rights Commission (2008) *Sex and Power 2008*. London: Equality and Human Rights Commission (2008). Available at http://www.equalityhumanrights.com/uploaded_files/sex_and_power_2008_word.doc.

Erez, M. (1986) 'The congruence of goal-setting strategies with sociocultural values and its effect on performance', *Journal of Management*, 12, 585–92.

Erez, M. and Somech, A. (1996) 'Is group productivity loss the rule or the exception? Effects of culture and group-based motivation', *Academy of Management Journal*, 39, 1513–37.

Erikson, E.H. (1968) *Identity, Youth and Crisis*. New York: W.W. Norton.

Erikson, E.H. (1980) *Identity and the Life Cycle*. New York: W.W. Norton.

Evers, A., Anderson, N. and Voskuijl, O. (eds) (2005) *The Blackwell Handbook of Personnel Selection*. Oxford: Blackwell Publishing.

Ewen, R.B. (2003) *An Introduction to Theories of Personality*, 6th edition. Mahwah, NJ: Lawrence Erlbaum Associates.

Eysenck, H.J. (1967) *The Biological Basis of Personality*. Springfield, IL: Charles C. Thomas.

Eysenck, H.J. and Eysenck, S.B.G. (1964) *Manual of the Eysenck Personality Inventory*. London: University of London Press.

Ezzamel, M., Green, C., Lilley, S. and Willmott, H. (1994) *Change management: Appendix 1 – A review and analysis of recent changes in UK management practices*. Manchester: Financial Services Research Centre, UMIST.

Farr, J.L., Hofman, D.A. and Ringenbach, K.L. (1993) 'Goal orientation and action control theory: Implications for industrial and organizational psychology', in I.T. Robertson and C.L. Cooper (eds), *International Review of Industrial and Organizational Psychology*, vol. 8. Chichester: John Wiley.

Fay, D., Borrill, C., Amir, Z., Haward, R. and West, M.A. (2006) 'Getting the most out of multidisciplinary teams: A multi-sample study of team innovation in health care', *Journal of Occupational and Organizational Psychology*, 79(4), 553–567.

Feldman, D.C. and Bolino, M.C. (2000) 'Career patterns of the self-employed: Career motivations and career outcomes', *Journal of Small Business Management*, 38, 53–67.

Ferguson, E. and Patterson, F. (1998) 'The Five Factor Model of personality: Openness as a distinct but related construct', *Personality and Individual Differences*, 24, 1–4.

Ferrie, J.A., Shipley, M.J., Newman, K., Stansfeld, S.A. and Marmot, M. (2005) 'Self-reported job insecurity and health in the Whitehall II study: Potential explanations of the relationship', *Social Science and Medicine*, 60, 1593–602.

Ferris, G. and Judge, T. (1991) 'Personnel human resources management: A political influence perspective', *Journal of Management*, 17, 447–88.

Ferris, G.R. and King, T.R. (1991) 'Politics in human resources decisions: A walk on the dark side', *Organizational Dynamics*, 20, 59–71.

Ferris, P. (2004) 'A personal view: A preliminary typology of organizational response to allegations of workplace bullying: see no evil, speak no evil', *British Journal of Guidance and Counselling*, 32, 389–95.

Fiedler, F.E. (1967) *A Theory of Leadership Effectiveness*. New York: McGraw-Hill.

Fiedler, F.E. (1995) 'Cognitive resources and leadership performance', *Applied Psychology: An International Review*, 44, 5–28.

Fiedler, F.E. (1996) 'Research on leadership selection and training: One view of the future', *Administrative Science Quarterly*, 41, 241–50.

Fiedler, F.E. and Chemers, M.M. (1984) *Improving Leadership Effectiveness: The leader match concept*, 2nd edition. New York: John Wiley.

Fiedler, F.E. and Garcia, J.E. (1987) *New Approaches to Effective Leadership: Cognitive resources and organizational performance*. New York: John Wiley.

Fiedler, F.E., Murphy, S.E. and Gibson, F.W. (1992) 'Inaccurate reporting and inappropriate variables: A reply to Vecchio's (1990) examination of Cognitive Resource Theory', *Journal of Applied Psychology*, 77, 372–74.

Field, A. (2009) *Discovering Statistics Using SPSS*. London: Sage.

Filby, I. and Willmott, H. (1988) 'Ideologies and contradictions in a public relations department', *Organization Studies*, 9(3), 335–51.

Filley, A.C., House, R.J. and Kerr, S. (1976) *Managerial Process and Organizational Behavior*. Glenview, IL: Scott, Foresman and Co.

Fine, S.A. and Wiley, W.W. (1974) 'An introduction to functional job analysis', in E.A. Fleishman and A.R. Bass (eds), *Studies in Personal and Industrial Psychology.* Homewood, IL: Dorsey Press.

Finegan, J.E. (2000) 'The impact of person and organizational values on organizational commitment', *Journal of Occupational and Organizational Psychology*, 73, 149–69.

Fineman, S. (2003) *Understanding Emotion at Work.* London: Sage.

Finke, R.A., Ward, T.B. and Smith, S.M. (1992) *Creative Cognition: Theory, research, and applications.* Cambridge, MA: MIT Press.

Finkelstein, S. (1992) 'Power in top management teams: Dimensions, measurement and validation', *Academy of Management Journal*, 35, 505–38.

Finstad, N. (1998) The rhetoric of organizational change', *Human Relations*, 51, 717–40.

Fisher, R., Ury, W. and Patton, B. (1991) *Getting to YES: Negotiating agreement without giving in*, 2nd edition. New York: Penguin Books.

Fisher, S.G., Hunter, T.A. and Macrosson, W. (2001) 'A validation study of Belbin's team roles', *European Journal of Work and Organizational Psychology*, 10(2), 121–44.

Fiske, S.T. (2001) 'Effects of power on bias: Power explains and maintains individual, group and societal disparities', in A.Y. Lee-Chai and J.A. Bargh (eds), *The Use and Abuse of Power: Multiple perspectives on the causes of corruption.* New York: Taylor & Francis.

Fitts, P.M. (1962) 'Factors in complex skill training', in R. Glaser (ed.), *Training Research and Education.* New York: John Wiley.

Flanagan, J.C. (1954) 'The critical incident technique', *Psychological Bulletin*, 51, 327–58.

Fleck, S.J. (2005) 'Dispersed work teams: A member level investigation'. PhD thesis, Institute of Work Psychology, University of Sheffield.

Fleishman, E.A. (1969) *Leadership Opinion Questionnaire Manual.* Henley-on-Thames: Science Research Associates.

Fleishman, E.A. (1995) 'Consideration and structure: Another look at their role in leadership research', in F. Dansereau and F. J. Yammarino (eds), *Leadership: The multi-level approaches.* Stamford, CT: JAI Press.

Fletcher, C. (1998) 'Circular argument', *People Management*, October, 46–9.

Fletcher, C. (2008) *Appraisal, Feedback and Development: Making performance review work*, 4th edition. Oxford: Routledge.

Flum, H. and Blustein, D.L. (2000) 'Reinvigorating the study of vocational exploration: A framework for research', *Journal of Vocational Behavior*, 56, 380–404.

Folger, R. (1977) 'Distributive and procedural justice: combined impact on "voice" and improvement on experienced inequity', *Journal of Personality and Social Psychology*, 35, 109–19.

Folger, R. and Cropanzano, R. (1998) *Organizational justice and human resource management.* Beverly Hills, CA: Sage.

Folger, R., Rosenfield, D., Grove, J. and Corkran, L. (1979) 'Effects of "voice" and peer opinions on responses to inequity', *Journal of Personality and Social Psychology*, 37, 2253–61.

Forbes, D.P. and Milliken, F.J. (1999) 'Cognition and corporate governance: Understanding boards of directors as strategic decision-making groups', *Academy of Management Review*, 24(3), 489–505.

Ford, M.T., Heinen, B.A. and Langkamer, K.L. (2007) 'Work and family satisfaction and conflict: A meta-analysis of cross-domain relations', *Journal of Applied Psychology*, 92, 57–80.

Forret, M.L. and Dougherty, T.W. (2001) 'Correlates of networking behavior for managerial and professional employees', *Group and Organization Management*, 26, 283–311.

Forret, M.L. and Dougherty, T.W. (2004) 'Networking behaviors and career outcomes: differences for men and women?', *Journal of Organizational Behavior*, 25, 419–37.

Fortin, M. (2008) 'Perspectives on organizational justice: Concept clarification, social context integration, time and links with morality', *International Journal of Management Reviews*, 10, 93–126.

Fox, M., Dwyer, D. and Ganster, D. (1993) 'Effects of stressful job demands and control on physiological and attitudinal outcomes in a hospital setting', *Academy of Management Journal*, 36, 289–318.

Franklin, B. (1997) *Newszak and News Media*. Arnold: London.

Fransella, F. and Bannister, D. (1977) *Manual for Repertory Grid Technique*. London: Academic Press.

Fredrickson, B.L. (1998) 'What good are positive emotions?', *Review of General Psychology*, 2, 300–319.

Fredrickson, B.L. and Joiner, T. (2002) 'Positive emotions trigger upward spirals toward emotional well-being', *Psychological Science*, 13, 172–75.

Fredrickson, B.L., Tugade, M.M., Waugh, C.E. and Larkin, G.R. (2003) 'What good are positive emotions in crises? A prospective study of resilience and emotions following the terrorist attacks on the United States on September 11th, 2001', *Journal of Personality and Social Psychology*, 84, 365–76.

French, J.R.P. and Caplan, R.D. (1972) 'Organizational stress and individual strain', in A. Marrow (ed.), *The Failure of Success*. New York: AMACOM.

French J.R.P., Caplan R.D. and Van Harrison R. (1982) *The Mechanisms of Job Stress and Strain*. New York: Wiley.

French, M.T., Dunlap, L.J., Roman, P.M. and Steele, P.D. (1997) 'Factors that influence the use and perceptions of employee assistance programs at six worksites', *Journal of Occupational Health Psychology*, 2, 312–24.

French, W.L. and Bell, C.H. (1973) *Organization Development*. Englewood Cliffs, NJ: Prentice-Hall.

French, W.L. and Bell, C.H. (1984) *Organization Development*, 4th edition. Englewood Cliffs, NJ: Prentice-Hall.

French, W.L. and Bell, C.H. (1995) *Organization Development*, 5th edition. Englewood Cliffs, NJ: Prentice-Hall.

Frese, M. and Beimel, S. (2003) 'Action training for charismatic leadership: two evaluations of studies of a commercial training module on inspirational communication of a vision', *Personnel Psychology*, 56, 671–97.

Frese, M., Fay, D., Hilburger, T., Leng, K. and Tag, A. (1997) 'The concept of personal initiative: Operationalization, reliability and validity in two German samples', *Journal of Occupational and Organizational Psychology*, 70, 139–62.

Freud, S. (1960) *The Psychopathology of Everyday Life*. London: Hogarth (first published 1901).

Fried, Y. and Ferris, G.R. (1987) 'The validity of the job characteristics model: a review and meta-analysis', *Personnel Psychology*, 40, 287–322.

Fried, Y. and Slowik, L.H. (2004) 'Enriching goal-setting theory with time: An integrated approach', *Academy of Management Review*, 29, 404–22.

Fried, Y., Grant, A.M., Leiv, A.S., Hadani, M. and Slowik, L. (2007) 'Job design in temporal context: a career dynamics perspective', *Journal of Organizational Behavior*, 28, 911–27.

Friedman, R., Kane, M. and Cornfield, D.B. (1998) 'Social support and career optimism: Examining the effectiveness of network groups among black managers', *Human Relations*, 51, 1155–77.

Friedman, R.A. and Krackhardt, D. (1997) 'Social capital and career mobility: A structural theory of lower returns to education for Asian employees', *Journal of Applied Behavioral Science*, 33, 316–34.

Frink, D.D. and Ferris, G.R. (1998) 'Accountability, impression management and goal setting in the performance evaluation process', *Human Relations*, 51, 1259–83.

Frink, D.D., Robinson, R.K., Reithel, B., Arthur, M.M., Ammeter, A.P., Ferris, G.R., Kaplan, D.M. and Morrisette, H.S. (2003) 'Gender demography and organization performance', *Group and Organization Management*, 28, 127–47.

Frone, M.R. (2002) 'Work–family balance', in J.C. Quick and L.E. Tetrick (eds), *Handbook of Occupational Health Psychology*. Washington, DC: American Psychology Association.

Fryer, D. (1998) 'Labour market disadvantage, deprivation and mental health', in P. Drenth and H. Thierry (eds), *Handbook of Work and Organizational Psychology*, vol. 2. Hove: Psychology Press/Erlbaum.

Furnham, A., Kirkcaldy, B.D. and Lynn, R. (1994) 'National attitudes to competitiveness, money and work among young people: First, second and third world differences', *Human Relations*, 47(1), 119–32.

Furnham, A., Steele, H. and Pendleton, D. (1993) 'A psychometric assessment of the Belbin Team-Role Self-Perception Inventory', *Journal of Occupational and Organizational Psychology*, 66, 245–57.

Gagné, M. and Deci, R.L. (2005) 'Self determination theory and work motivation', *Journal of Organisational Behavior*, 26, 331–62.

Gagné, R.M. (1977) *The Conditions of Learning*, 3rd edition. New York: Rinehart and Winston.

Gallos, J.V. (1989) 'Exploring women's development: Implications for career theory, practice and research', in M.B. Arthur, D.T. Hall and B.S. Lawrence (eds), *Handbook of Career Theory*. Cambridge: Cambridge University Press.

Gardner, H. (1983) *Frames of Mind: The theory of multiple intelligences*. New York: Basic Books.

Gardner, H. (1995) 'Reflections on multiple intelligences', *Phi Delta Kappan*, 77, 200–8.

Gardner, H. (2003) 'Higher education for the era of globalisation', *The Psychologist*, 16, 520–21.

Gardner, W.L. and Avolio, B.J. (1998) 'The charismatic relationship: A dramaturgical perspective', *Academy of Management Review*, 23, 32–58.

Garvin, D.A. (1993) 'Building a learning organization', *Harvard Business Review*, July–August, 78–91.

Gastil, J. (1994) 'A definition and illustration of democratic leadership', *Human Relations*, 47, 953–75.

Gati, I., Gadassi, R. and Shemesh, N. (2006) 'The predictive validity of a computer-assisted career decision-making system: A six-year follow-up', *Journal of Vocational Behavior*, 68, 205–19.

Gati, I., Kleiman, T., Saka, N. and Zakai, A. (2003) 'Perceived benefits of using an Internet-based interactive career planning system', *Journal of Vocational Behavior*, 62, 262–86.

Gati, I., Saka, N. and Krausz, M. (2001) '"Should I use a computer-assisted career guidance system?" It depends on where your career decision-making difficulties lie', *British Journal of Guidance and Counselling*, 29, 301–21.

Gawron, V.J. (2000) *Human Performance Measures Handbook*. Mahwah, NJ. Lawrence Erlbaum Associates.

Gelfand, M.J., Erez, M. and Aycan, Z. (2007) 'Cross-cultural organization psychology', *Annual Review of Psychology*, 58, 479–514.

Gellerman, W., Frankel, M.S. and Ladenson, R.F. (1990) *Values and Ethics in Organizational and Human Systems Development: Responding to dilemmas in professional life*. San Francisco, CA: Jossey-Bass.

Gemmill, G. and Oakley, J. (1992) 'Leadership: An alienating social myth?', *Human Relations*, 45, 113–29.

George, J.M. and Jones, G.R. (1997) 'Experiencing work: Values, attitudes and moods', *Human Relations*, 50, 393–416.

Gergen, K.J. and Gergen, M.M. (1988) 'Narrative and the self as relationship', in L. Berkowitz (ed.), *Advances in Experimental Social Psychology*, vol. 21. London: Academic Press.

Germeijs, V. and De Boeck, P. (2003) 'Career indecision: Three factors from decision theory', *Journal of Vocational Behavior*, 62, 11–25.

Gersick, C. and Kram, K.E. (2002) 'High-achieving women at midlife: An exploratory study', *Journal of Management Enquiry*, 11, 104–27.

Geurts, S.A. and Grundermann, R. (1999) 'Workplace stress and stress prevention in Europe', in M.A.J. Kompier and C.L. Cooper (eds), *Preventing Stress, Improving Productivity*. London: Routledge.

Geurts, S.A.E. and Demerouti, E. (2003) 'Work/non-work interface: A review of theories and findings', in M. Schabracq, J. Winnubst and C.L. Cooper (eds), *Handbook of Work and Health Psychology*. Chichester: John Wiley and Sons.

Geyer, A. and Steyrer, J.M. (1998) 'Transformational leadership and objective performance in banks', *Applied Psychology: An International Review*, 47, 397–420.

Gianakos, I. (1999) 'Patterns of career choice and career decision-making self-efficacy', *Journal of Vocational Behavior*, 54, 244–58.

Gibson, C.B. and Zellmer-Bruhn, M.E. (2002) 'Minding your metaphors: Applying the concept of teamwork metaphors to the management of teams in multicultural contexts', *Organizational Dynamics*, 31, 101–16.

Gibson, D.E. (2003) 'Developing the professional self-concept: Role model construals in early, middle and late career stages', *Organization Science*, 14, 591–610.

Giga, S.I., Hoel, H. and Lewis, D. (2008) *The Costs of Workplace Bullying*. Available at http://www.unitetheunion.com/.

Giga S.I., Noblet A.J., Faragher B. and Cooper, C.L. (2003) 'The UK perspective: A review of research on organisational stress management interventions', *Australian Psychologist*, 38, 158–64.

Gilliland, S.W. (1993) 'The perceived fairness of selection systems – an organizational justice perspective', *Academy of Management Review*, 18(4), 694–734.

Gimeno, D., Amick III, B., Barrientos-Gutiérrez, T. and Mangione, T.W. (2009) 'Work organization and drinking: An epidemiological comparison of two psychosocial work exposure models', *International Archives of Occupational and Environmental Health*, 82, 305–17.

Gioia, D.A. and Longenecker, C.O. (1994) 'Delving into the dark side: The politics of executive appraisal', *Organizational Dynamics*, 22, 47–58.

Gioia, D.A. and Manz, C.C. (1985) 'Linking cognition and behavior: A script processing interpretation of vicarious learning', *Academy of Management Review*, 10, 527–39.

Gist, M.E. (1989) 'The influence of training methods on self-efficacy and idea generation among managers', *Personnel Psychology*, 42, 787–805.

Gittleman, M., Horrigan, M. and Joyce, M. (1998) ' "Flexible" workplace practices: Evidence from a nationally representative survey', *Industrial and Labor Relations Review*, 52(1), 99–115.

Glazer, S. and Beehr, T.A. (2005) 'Consistency of implications of three role stressors across four countries', *Journal of Organizational Behavior*, 26, 467–87.

Goffin, R.D. and Gellatly, I.R. (2001) 'A multi-rater assessment of organizational commitment: Are self-report measures biased?', *Journal of Organizational Behavior*, 22, 437–51.

Goh, S.C. (2002) 'Managing effective knowledge transfer: An integrative framework and some practice implications'. *Journal of Knowledge Management*, 6(1), 23–30.

Goldberg, D.P. and Williams, P. (1988) *The User's Guide to the General Health Questionnaire*. Slough: NFER/Nelson.

Goleman, D. (1995) *Emotional Intelligence*. New York: Bantam Books.

Goleman, D. (1998) *Working with Emotional Intelligence*. New York: Bantam Books.

Goleman, D. (2001) 'An EI-based theory of performance', in C. Cherniss and D. Goleman (eds), *The Emotionally Intelligent Workplace*. San Francisco, CA: Jossey-Bass Wiley.

Gottfredson, G. and Holland, J.L. (1996) *Dictionary of Holland Occupational Codes*, 3rd edition. Odessa, FL: Psychological Assessment Resources Inc.

Gottfredson, L.S. (2002) '*g*: Highly general and highly practical'. In R.J. Sternberg and E.L. Grigorenko (eds), *The General Factor of Intelligence: How general is it?* Mahwah, NJ: Erlbaum.

Grant, A.M. (2007) 'Relational job design and the motivation to make a prosocial difference', *Academy of Management Review*, 32, 393–417.

Grant, S. and Langan-Fox, J. (2007) 'Personality and the occupational stressor–strain relationship: The role of the Big Five', *Journal of Occupational Health Psychology*, 12, 20–33.

Graves, L.M. and Powell, G.N. (1988) 'An investigation of sex discrimination in recruiters' evaluations of actual applicants', *Journal of Applied Psychology*, 73, 20–9.

Greadjean, E. and Kroemer, K.H.E. (1997) *Fitting the Task to the Human: A textbook of occupational ergonomics,* 5th edition. London: Taylor and Francis.

Greenberg, J. (2001) 'Setting the justice agenda: Seven unanswered questions about "What, Why and How"', *Journal of Vocational Behavior*, 58, 210–19.

Greenberg, J. and Colquitt, J. A. (2005) *Handbook of Organizational Justice*. Mahwah, NJ: Erlbaum.

Greene, J.C., Caracelli, V.J. and Graham, W.F. (1989) 'Toward a conceptual framework for mixed methods evaluation designs', *Educational Evaluation and Policy Analysis*, 11, 255–74.

Greenhaus, J.H. and Beutell, N.J. (1985) 'Sources and conflict between work and family roles', *Academy of Management Review*, 10, 76–88.

Greenhaus, J.H. and Parasuraman, S. (1999) 'Research on work, family and gender: Current status and future directions', in G.N. Powell (ed.), *Handbook of Gender and Work*. Thousand Oaks, CA: Sage.

Greenhaus, J.H., Callanan, G.A. and Godshalk, V. (2000) *Career Management*, 3rd edition. Orlando, FL: Dryden Press.

Greenhaus, J.H., Parasuraman, A. and Wormley, W.M. (1990) 'Effects of race on organizational experiences, job performance evaluations and career outcomes', *Academy of Management Journal*, 33, 64–86.

Greenwald, A.G., McGhee, D.E. and Schwartz, J.L.K. (1998) 'Measuring individual differences in implicit cognition: The implicit association test', *Journal of Personality and Social Psychology*, 74, 1464–80.

Greiner, L.E. and Cummings, T.G. (2004) 'Wanted: OD more alive than dead!', *The Journal of Applied Behavioral Science*, 40(4), 374–91.

Griffeth, R.W., Horn, P.W. and Gaertner, S. (2000) 'Meta-analysis of antecedents and correlates of employee turnover: Update, moderator tests and research implications for the next millennium', *Journal of Management*, 26, 463–76.

Griffin, M.A., Neal, A. and Parker, S.K. (2007) 'A new model of work role performance: positive behavior in uncertain and interdependent contexts', *Academy of Management Journal*, 50, 327–47.

Griffin, M.A., Patterson, M.G. and West, M.A. (2001) 'Job satisfaction and teamwork: The role of supervisor support', *Journal of Organizational Behavior*, 22, 537–50.

Griffin, R.W. and Bateman, T.S. (1986) 'Job satisfaction and organizational commitment', in C.L. Cooper and I.T. Robertson (eds), *International Review of Industrial and Organizational Psychology*. Chichester: John Wiley.

Griffiths, A. (1999) 'Organizational interventions: Facing the limits of the natural science paradigm', *Scandinavian Journal of Work, Environment and Health*, 25, 589–96.

Griffiths, A., Cox, T., Karanika, M., Khan, S. and Tomás, J.M. (2006) 'Work design and management in the manufacturing sector: development and validation of the Work Organisation Assessment Questionnaire', *Occupational and Environmental Medicine*, 63, 669–75.

Grint, K. (1997) *Leadership: Classical, Contemporary and Critical Approaches*. Oxford: Oxford University Press.

Grinyer, P.H., Mayes, D.G. and McKiermon, P. (1988) *Sharpbenders: The secrets of unleashing corporate potential*. Oxford: Blackwell.

Grzywacz, J.G. and Marks, N.F. (2000) 'Reconceptualising the work–family interface: An ecological perspective on the correlates of positive and negative spillover between work and family', *Journal of Health Psychology*, 5, 111–26.

Gubrium, J. and Holstein, J. (1997) *The New Language of Qualitative Method*. Oxford: Oxford University Press.

Guest, D. (1998) 'Is the psychological contract worth taking seriously?', *Journal of Organizational Behavior*, 19, 649–64.

Guest, D.E. (1997) 'Human resource management and performance: A review and research agenda', *International Human Resource Management*, 8, 263–76.

Guest, D.E. and Hoque, K. (1996) 'Human resource management and the new industrial relations', in I.J. Beardwell (ed.), *Contemporary Industrial Relations*. Oxford: Oxford University Press.

Guion, R.M. (1965) *Personnel Testing*. New York: McGraw-Hill.

Gunnell, D., Platt, S. and Hawton, K. (2009) 'The economic crisis and suicide', *British Medical Journal*, 338, 1456–7.

Gunz, H., Evans, M. and Jalland, R.M. (2000) 'Career boundaries in a boundaryless world', in M. Peiperl, M.B. Arthur, R. Goffee and T. Morris (eds), *Career Frontiers: New concepts in working lives*. Oxford: Oxford University Press.

Gunz, H.P. and Peiperl, M. (2007) *The Handbook of Career Studies*. Thousand Oaks, CA: Sage.

Gutek, B. (1995) *The Dynamics of Service: Reflections on the Changing Nature of Customer/ Provider Interactions*. San Francisco, CA: Jossey-Bass.

Gutek, B., Searle, S. and Klewpa, L. (1991) 'Rational versus gender role explanations for work/family conflict', *Journal of Applied Psychology*, 76, 560–8.

Guzzo, R.A. and Dickson, M.W. (1996) 'Teams in organizations: Recent research on performance and effectiveness', *Annual Review of Psychology*, 47, 307–38.

Hackman, J.R. (1990) *Groups that Work (and Those that Don't): Creating conditions for effective teamwork*. San Francisco, CA: Jossey-Bass.

Hackman, J.R. (2002) *Leading Teams: Setting the stage for great performance*. Boston, MA: Harvard Business School Press.

Hackman, J.R. and Oldham, G.R. (1976) 'Motivation through the design of work: Test of a theory', *Organizational Behaviour and Human Performance*, 16, 250–79.

Hackman, J.R. and Oldham, G.R. (1980) *Work Redesign*. Reading, MA: Addison-Wesley.

Halbesleben, J.R.B. and Wheeler, A.R. (2008) 'The relative roles of engagement and embeddedness in predicting job performance and intention to leave', *Work and Stress*, 22, 242–56.

Hall, D.T. (1976) *Careers in Organizations*. Glenview, IL: Scott, Foresman.

Hall, D.T. (1986) 'Breaking career routines: Midcareer choice and identity development', in D.T. Hall (ed.), *Career Development in Organizations*. London: Jossey-Bass.

Hall, D.T. (2002) *Careers In and Out of Organizations*. Thousand Oaks, CA: Sage Publications.

Hall, D.T. and Chandler, D.E. (2005) 'Psychological success: When the career is a calling', *Journal of Organizational Behavior*, 26, 155–76.

Hall, D.T. and Nougaim, K. (1968) 'An examination of Maslow's need hierarchy in an organizational setting', *Organizational Behavior and Human Decision Processes*, 3, 12–35.

Halvor Teigen, K. (1986) 'Old truths or fresh insights? A study of students' evaluations of proverbs', *British Journal of Social Psychology*, 25, 43–9.

Hammer, M. and Champy, J. (1993) *Re-engineering the Corporation*. London: Nicolas Brealey.

Hamner, W.C. (1974) 'Effects of bargaining strategy and pressure to reach agreement in a stalemated negotiation', *Journal of Personality and Social Psychology*, 30, 458–67.

Handy, C. (1979) *Gods of Management*. London: Pan.

Handy, C. (1986) *Understanding Organizations*. Harmondsworth: Penguin.

Handy, C. (1989) *The Age of Unreason*. London: Arrow.

Handy, C. (1994) *The Empty Raincoat*. London: Hutchinson.

Hanisch, K.A. (1994) 'Reasons people retire and their relations to attitudinal and behavioural correlates in retirement', *Journal of Vocational Behavior*, 45, 1–16.

Hansemark, O.C. (2003) 'Need for achievement, locus of control and the prediction of business start-ups: A longitudinal study', *Journal of Economic Psychology*, 24, 301–19.

Hansen, G.S. and Wernerfelt, B. (1989) 'Determinants of firm performance: The relative importance of economic and organizational factors', *Strategic Management Journal*, 10, 399–411.

Hanson, M.A. and Borman, W.C. (2006) 'Citizenship performance: An integrative review and motivational analysis', in W. Bennett, Jr, C.E. Lance and D.J. Wohr (eds), *Performance Measurement: Current Perspectives and Future Challenges*. London: Lawrence Erlbaum Associates.

Hanson, P. (1993) 'Made in Britain – The True State of Manufacturing Industry'. Paper presented at the Institution of Mechanical Engineers' Conference on Performance Measurement and Benchmarking, Birmingham, June.

Harley, B. (2001) 'Team membership and the experience of work in Britain: An analysis of the WERS98 data', *Work, Employment and Society*, 15(4), 721–42.

Harmon, L.W., Hansen, J.C., Borgen, F.H. and Hammer, A.L. (1994) *Strong Interest Inventory: Applications and technical guide*. Stanford, CA: Stanford University Press.

Harris, C., Daniels, K. and Briner, R. (2003) 'A daily diary study of goals and affective well-being at work', *Journal of Occupational and Organizational Psychology*, 76, 401–10.

Harris, D. (2004) 'Head down display design', in D. Harris (ed.), *Human Factors for Civil Flight Deck Design*. Aldershot: Ashgate.

Harris, D. and Harris, F.J. (2004) 'Predicting the successful transfer of technology between application areas; a critical evaluation of the human component in the system', *Technology in Society*, 26, 551–65.

Harris, D. and Thomas, L. (2005) 'The contribution of industrial and organizational psychology to safety in commercial aircraft', in G. Hodgkinson and K. Ford (eds), *International Review of Industrial and Organizational Psychology*. London: John Wiley.

Harris, D., Stanton, A., Marshall, A., Young, M.S., Demagalski, J.M. and Salmon, P. (2005) 'Using SHERPA to predict design-induced error on the flight deck', *Aerospace Science and Technology*, 9(6), 525–32.

Harris, M. (1994) 'Rater motivation in the performance appraisal context: A theoretical framework', *Journal of Management*, 20, 737–56.

Harris-Bowlsbey, J. and Sampson, J.P. (2001) 'Computer-based career planning systems: Dreams and realities', *Career Development Quarterly*, 49, 250–60.

Harrison, D.A. (2007) 'What's the difference? Diversity constructs as separation, variety or disparity in organizations', *Academy of Management Review*, 32, 1199–228.

Harrison, D.A., Newman, D.A. and Roth, P.L. (2006) 'How important are job attitudes? Meta-analytic comparisons of integrative behavioral outcomes and time sequences', *Academy of Management Journal*, 49, 305–25.

Harrison, R. (1972) 'How to describe your organization', *Harvard Business Review*, 50, September–October.

Harrison, R. (1997) *Employee Development*. London: Chartered Institute of Personnel and Development.

Hart, P.M. and Cooper, C.L. (2001) 'Occupational stress: Toward a more integrated framework', in N. Anderson, D.S. Ones, H.K. Sinangil and C. Viswesvaran (eds), *Handbook of Work, Industrial and Organizational Psychology*, vol. 2. London: Sage.

Harter, J.K., Schmidt, F.L. and Hayes, T.L. (2002) 'Business-unit-level relationship between employee satisfaction, employee engagement and business outcomes: A meta-analysis', *Journal of Applied Psychology*, 87, 268–79.

Hartley, J.F. (1992) 'The psychology of employee relations', in C.L. Cooper and I.T. Robertson (eds), *International Review of Industrial and Organizational Psychology*, vol. 7. Chichester: John Wiley.

Haslam, S.A. (2004) *Psychology in Organizations: The social identity approach*, 2nd edition. London: Sage.

Haslam, S.A., Powell, C. and Turner, J.C. (2000) 'Social identity, self-categorisation, and work motivation: Rethinking the contribution of the group to positive and sustainable organisational outcomes', *Applied Psychology: An International Review*, 49, 319–39.

Haslam, S.A., Wegge, J. and Postmes, T. (2009) 'Are we on a learning curve or a treadmill? The benefits of participative group goal setting become apparent as tasks become increasingly challenging over time', *European Journal of Social Psychology*, 39, 430–46.

Hass, R.G. (1975) 'Persuasion or moderation? Two experiments on anticipatory belief change', *Journal of Personality and Social Psychology*, 31, 1155–62.

Hassard, J. and Sharifi, S. (1989) 'Corporate culture and strategic change', *Journal of General Management*, 15(2), 4–19.

Hatch, M.J. (1997) *Organization Theory: Modern, symbolic and postmodern perspectives*. Oxford: Oxford University Press.

Hater, J. and Bass, B.M. (1988) 'Superiors' evaluations and subordinates' perceptions of transformational and transactional leadership', *Journal of Applied Psychology*, 73, 695–702.

Hausknecht, J.P., Day, D.V. and Thomas, S.C. (2004) 'Applicant reactions to selection procedures: An updated model and meta-analysis', *Personnel Psychology*, 57, 639–83.

Hayes, J. (2002) *The Theory and Practice of Change Management*. Palgrave: Basingstoke.

Health and Safety Executive (1999) *Initial Advice Regarding Call Centre Working Practices*. Sheffield: HSE.

Heaney, C., Israel, B., Schurman, S., Barker, E., House, J. and Hugentobler, M. (1993) 'Industrial relations, work stress reduction and employee well-being: A participatory action research investigation', *Journal of Organizational Behavior*, 14, 495–510.

Heller, F. (1970) 'Group feed-back analysis as a change agent', *Human Relations*, 23(4), 319–33.

Heller, F. (1989) 'Human resource management and the socio-technical approach', in G. Bamber and R. Lansbury (eds), *New Technology: International perspectives on human resources and industrial relations*. London: Unwin Hyman.

Heller, F.A. and Misumi, J. (1987) 'Decision making', in B. Bass, P. Drenth and P. Weissenberg (eds), *Advances in Organizational Psychology*. London: Sage.

Heller, F.A., Drenth, P., Koopman, P. and Rus, V. (1988) *Decisions in Organizations: A three-country comparative study*. London: Sage.

Hellervik, L.W., Hazucha, F. and Schneider, R.J. (1992) 'Behavior change: Models, methods, and a review of evidence', in M.D. Dunnette and L.M. Hough (eds), *Handbook of Industrial and Organizational Psychology*. Palo Alto, CA: Consulting Psychologists Press.

Hendey, N. and Pascall, G. (2001) *Disability and Transition in Adulthood: Achieving independent living*. London: Pavilion Publishing.

Hendry, C. (1996) 'Understanding and creating whole organizational change through learning theory', *Human Relations*, 48(5), 621–41.

Hendry, C. and Pettigrew, A. (1986) 'The practice of strategic human resource management', *Personnel Review*, 15, 3–8.

Hermelin, E. and Robertson, I.T. (2001) 'A critique and standardization of meta-analytic validity coefficients in personnel selection', *Journal of Occupational and Organizational Psychology*, 74, 153–77.

Hermelin, E., Lievens, F. and Robertson, I.T. (2007) 'The validity of assessment centres for the prediction of supervisory performance ratings: A meta-analysis', *International Journal of Selection and Assessment*, 15, 405–11.

Herriot, P. (1992) *The Career Management Challenge: Balancing individual and organizational needs*. London: Sage.

Herriot, P. and Pemberton, C. (1995) *New Deals*. Chichester: John Wiley.

Hersey, P. and Blanchard, K. (1982) *Management of Organizational Behavior*, 4th edition. Englewood Cliffs, NJ: Prentice Hall.

Hertel, G., Konradt, U. and Voss, K. (2006) 'Competences for virtual teamwork: development and validation of a web-based selection tool for members of distributed teams', *European Journal of Work and Organizational Psychology*, 15(4), 477–504.

Hertel, G., Geister, S. and Konradt, U. (2005) 'Managing virtual teams: A review of current empirical research', *Human Resource Management Review*, 15, 69–95.

Hertel, G., Konradt, U. and Orlikowski, B. (2004) 'Managing distance by interdependence: Goal setting, task interdependence and team-based rewards in virtual teams', *European Journal of Work and Organizational Psychology*, 13, 1–28.

Herzberg, F. (1966) *Work and the Nature of Man*. Cleveland, OH: World Publishing.

Heslin, P.A. (2005) 'Conceptualizing and evaluating career success', *Journal of Organizational Behavior*, 26, 113–36.

Hewstone, M., Ruibin, M. and Willis, H. (2002) 'Intergroup bias', *Annual Review of Psychology*, 53, 575–604.

Higgins, M.C. and Thomas, D.A. (2001) 'Constellations and careers: Toward understanding the effects of multiple developmental relationships', *Journal of Organizational Behavior*, 22, 223–47.

Highhouse, S. (1999) 'The brief history of personnel counseling in industrial–organizational psychology', *Journal of Vocational Behavior*, 55, 318–36.

Hill, G.W. (1982) 'Group versus individual performance: Are N1 heads better than one?', *Psychological Bulletin*, 91, 517–39.

Hilton, J.L. and Von Hippel, W. (1996) 'Stereotypes', *Annual Review of Psychology*, 47, 237–71.

Hinds, P. and Bailey, D. (2003) 'Out of sight, out of sync: Understanding conflict in distributed teams', *Organization Science*, 14, 615–32.

Hinkle, L.E. (1973) 'The concept of stress in the biological social sciences', *Stress Medicine*, 1, 31–48.

Hirsch, P.M. and Shanley, M. (1996) 'The rhetoric of boundaryless – or, how the newly empowered managerial class bought into its own marginalisation', in M.B. Arthur and D.M. Rousseau (eds), *The Boundaryless Career: A new employment principle for a new organizational era*. Oxford: Oxford University Press.

Hirsh, W. and Jackson, C. (2004) *Managing Careers in Large Organisations*. London: The Work Foundation.

Hirsh, W., Jackson, C. and Jackson, C. (1995) *Careers in Organizations: Issues for the future*, IES report 287. Brighton: Institute for Employment Studies.

Hislop, D., Axtell, C. and Daniels, K. (2008) 'The challenge of remote working', in S. Cartwright and C. Cooper (eds), *The Oxford Handbook of Personnel Psychology*. Oxford: Oxford University Press.

Hoag, B.G., Ritschard, H.V. and Cooper, C.L. (2002) 'Obstacles to effective organization change: the underlying reasons', *Leadership and Organisation Development Journal*, 23(1), 6–15.

Hodgkinson, G.P. (2003) 'The interface of cognitive and industrial, work and organizational psychology', *Journal of Occupational and Organizational Psychology*, 76, 1–25.

Hodgkinson, G.P. and Healey, M.P. (2008) 'Cognition in organizations', *Annual Review of Psychology*, 59, 387–417.

Hodgkinson, G.P. and Herriot, P. (2002) 'The role of psychologists in enhancing organizational effectiveness', in I.T. Robertson, M. Callinan and D. Bartram (eds), *Organizational Effectiveness: The role of psychology*. Chichester: Wiley.

Hodgkinson, G.P., Bown, N.J., Maule, A.J., Glaister, K.W. and Pearman, A.D. (1999) 'Breaking the frame: An analysis of strategic cognition and decision-making under uncertainty', *Strategic Management Journal*, 20(10), 977–85.

Hoegl, M. and Gemuenden, H.G. (2001) 'Teamwork quality and the success of innovative projects: A theoretical concept and empirical evidence', *Organization Science*, 12(4), 435–49.

Hoel, H., Cooper, C.L. and Faragher, B. (2001) 'The experience of bullying in Great Britain: The impact of organizational status', *European Journal of Work and Organizational Psychology*, 10, 443–65.

Hoel, H., Einarsen, S. and Cooper, C.L. (2003) 'Organisational effects of bullying', in S. Einarsen, H. Hoel, D. Zapf and C.L. Cooper (eds), *Bullying and Emotional Abuse in the Workplace: International perspectives in research and practice*. London: Taylor and Francis.

Hoffman, A.J. and Scott, L.D. (2003) 'Role stress and career satisfaction among registered nurses by work shift patterns', *Journal of Nursing Administration*, 33, 337–42.

Hoffman, B.J. and Woehr, D.J. (2006) 'Examining the relationship between person–organization fit and behavioral outcomes: A quantitative review', *Journal of Vocational Behavior*, 3, 389–99.

Hoffman, L.R. and Maier, N.R.F. (1961) 'Quality and acceptance of problem solutions by members of homogeneous and heterogeneous groups', *Journal of Abnormal and Social Psychology*, 62, 401–7.

Hofstede, G. (1980) *Culture's Consequences: International differences in work-related values*. London: Sage.

Hofstede, G. (1990) 'The cultural relativity of organizational practices and theories', in D.C. Wilson and R.H. Rosenfeld (eds), *Managing Organizations: Text, readings and cases*. London: McGraw-Hill.

Hofstede, G. (2001) *Culture's Consequences*, 2nd edition. London: Sage.

Hogarth, T., Hasluck, C., Pierre, G., Winterbottom, M. and Vivian, D. (2001) 'Work–Life Balance 2000: Results from the baseline study', in *Employment, Research Report 249*. London: DfEE.

Holland, J.L. (1997) *Making Vocational Choices: A theory of vocational personalities and work environment*, 3rd edition. Odessa, FL: Psychological Assessment Resources Inc.

Hollingshead, A.B. and McGrath, J.E. (1995) 'Computer-assisted groups: A critical review of the empirical research', in R.A. Guzzo and E. Salas (eds), *Team Effectiveness and Decision-making in Organizations*. San Francisco, CA: Jossey-Bass.

Hollnagel, E. (1999) 'From function allocation to function congruence', in S.W.A Dekker and E. Hollnagel (eds), *Coping With Computers in the Cockpit*. Aldershot: Ashgate.

Hollnagel, E. (ed.) (2003) *Handbook of Cognitive Task Design*. Mahwah, NJ: Lawrence Erlbaum Associates.

Hollway, W. (1991) *Work Psychology and Organisational Behaviour*. London: Sage.

Holman, D. (2003) 'Call centres', in D. Holman, T.D. Wall, C.W. Clegg, P. Sparrow and A. Howard (eds), *The New Workplace*. Chichester: John Wiley.

Holman, D. (2005) 'Call centres', in D. Holman, T.D. Wall, C.W. Clegg, P. Sparrow and A. Howard (eds), *The Essentials of the New Workplace: A Guide to the Human Impact of Modern Working Practices*. Chichester: John Wiley and Sons.

Holman, D., Chissick, C. and Totterdell, P. (2002) 'The effects of performance monitoring and emotional labour on well-being in call centres', *Motivation and Emotion*, 26, 57–81.

Holman, D.J., Wall, T.D., Clegg, C.W., Sparrow, P. and Howard, A. (eds) (2004) *The Essentials of the New Workplace: A guide to the human impact of modern working practices*. Chichester: John Wiley.

Hopson, B. and Scally, M. (2000) *Build Your Own Rainbow: A workbook for career and life management*. London: Management Books.

Houdmont, J. and Leka, S. (2009) *Occupational Health Psychology: European perspectives on research, education and practice*, vol. IV. Nottingham: Nottingham University Press (see also Vols I-III).

Houdmont, J., and Leka, S. (2010) *Contemporary Occupational Health Psychology: Global perspectives on research and practice*, vol. 1. London: Wiley.

Hough, L.M. and Furnham, A. (2003) 'Use of personality variables in work settings', in W.C. Borman, D.R. Ilgen, R.J. Klimoski and I.B. Weiner (eds), *Handbook of Psychology*. Hoboken, NJ: John Wiley.

Hough, L.M. and Ones, D.S. (2001) 'The structure, measurement, validity and use of personality variables in industrial, work, and organizational psychology', in N. Anderson, D.S. Ones, H.K. Sinangil and C. Viswesvaran (eds), *Handbook of Industrial, Work and Organizational Psychology*, vol. 1. London: Sage.

Hough, L.M. and Oswald, F.L. (2000) 'Personnel selection: Looking forward to the future – remembering the past', *Annual Review of Psychology*, 51, 631–64.

House, R.J. and Baetz, M.L. (1979) 'Leadership: Some empirical generalizations and new research directions', in B.M. Staw (ed.), *Research in Organizational Behavior*, vol. 1. Greenwich, CT: JAI Press.

House, R.J., Hanges, P.J., Javidan, M., Dorfman, P.W., Gupta, V. and GLOBE associates (eds) (2004) *Cultures, Leadership, and Organizations: A 62 Nation GLOBE Study*, vol. 1. Thousand Oaks, CA: Sage.

House, R.J., Hanges, P.J., Ruiz-Quintanilla, S.A., Dorfman, P.W., Javidan, M., Dickson, M. and Gupta, V. (1999) 'Cultural influences on leadership and organizatizons: Project GLOBE', in W.H. Mobley (ed.), *Advances in Global Leadership*, Stanford, CN: JAI Press.

House, R.J., Spangler, W.D. and Woycke, J. (1991) 'Personality and charisma in the US presidency: A psychological theory of leader effectiveness', *Administrative Science Quarterly*, 36, 364–96.

Hovland, C. and Weiss, W. (1951) 'The influence of source credibility on communication effectiveness', *Public Opinion Quarterly*, 15, 635–50.

Hovland, C., Lumsdaine, A. and Sheffield, F. (1949) *Experiments on Mass Communication.* Princeton, NJ: Princeton University Press.

Huczynski, A. and Buchanan, D. (2001) *Organizational Behaviour*, 4th edition. Harlow: FT/Prentice Hall.

Huffcutt, A.I. and Roth, P.L. (1998) 'Racial group differences in employment interview evaluations', *Journal of Applied Psychology*, 83, 179–89.

Huffcutt, A.I., Conway, J.M., Roth, P.L. and Stone, N.J. (2001) 'Identification and meta-analytic assessment of psychological constructs measured in employment interviews', *Journal of Applied Psychology*, 86, 897–913.

Hughes, J.L. and McNamara, W.J. (1959) *Manual for the Revised Programmer Aptitude Test.* New York: Psychological Corporation.

Hull, C.L. (1952) *A Behavior System.* New Haven, CT: Yale University Press.

Human Factors National Advisory Committee for Defence and Aerospace (2003) *Gaining Competitive Advantage Through Human Factors: A guide for the civil aerospace industry.* London: Department of Trade and Industry.

Humphrey, S.E., Nahrgang, J.D. and Morgeson, F.P. (2007) 'Integrating motivational, social and contextual work design features: A meta-analytic summary and theoretical extension of the work design literature', *Journal of Applied Psychology*, 92, 1332–56.

Hunter, J.E. and Schmidt, F.L. (2004) *Methods of Meta-analysis: Correcting error and bias in research findings*, 2nd edition. Thousand Oaks, CA: Sage.

Hunter, J.E., Schmidt, F.L. and Le, H. (2006) 'Implications of direct and indirect range restriction for meta-analysis methods and findings', *Journal of Applied Psychology*, 91, 594–612.

Hurley, R.F., Church, A.H., Burke, W.W. and Van Eynde, D.F. (1992) 'Tension, change and values in OD', *OD Practitioner*, 29, 1–5.

Hurst, J. and Baker, S. (2007) *The 24/7 Work Life Balance Survey: Executive Summary (Annual Survey): Work–Life Balance Centre.* www.24-7survey.co.uk.

Huseman, R.C., Hatfield, J.D. and Miles, E.W. (1987) 'A new perspective on equity theory: The equity sensitivity construct', *Academy of Management Review*, 12, 222–34.

Iaffaldano, M.T. and Muchinsky, P.M. (1985) 'Job satisfaction and job performance: A meta-analysis', *Psychological Bulletin*, 97, 251–73.

Ibarra, H. (1995) 'Race, opportunity, and diversity of social circles in managerial networks', *Academy of Management Journal*, 18, 673–703.

Ibarra, H. and Obodaru, O. (2009) 'Women and the vision thing', *Harvard Business Review*, January, 62–70.

Igalens, J. and Roussel, P. (1999) 'A study of the relationships between compensation package, work motivation and job satisfaction', *Journal of Organizational Behavior*, 20, 1003–25.

Iles, P. and Mabey, C. (1993) 'Managerial career development programmes: Effectiveness, availability and acceptability', *British Journal of Management*, 4, 103–18.

Ilgen, D.R., Hollenbeck, J.R., Johnson, M. and Jundt, D. (2005) 'Teams in organizations: From input–process–output models to IMOI models', *Annual Review of Psychology*, 56, 517–43.

Industrial Society (1997) *Culture Change: Managing best practice 35*. London: Industrial Society.

Inkson, K. (2006) *Understanding Careers: The metaphors of working lives*. London: Sage.

Ironside, M. and Seifert, R. (2003) 'Tackling bullying in the workplace: The collective dimension', in S. Einarsen, H. Hoel, D. Zapf and C. Cooper (eds), *Bullying and Emotional Abuse in the Workplace: International perspectives in research and practice*. London: Taylor and Francis.

Isabella, L.A. (1988) 'The effect of career stage on the meaning of key organizational events', *Journal of Organizational Behavior*, 9, 345–58.

Isenberg, D.J. (1986) 'Group polarization, a critical review and meta-analysis', *Journal of Personality and Social Psychology*, 50, 1141–51.

Ito, J.K. and Brotheridge, C.M. (2005) 'Does supporting employees'career adaptability lead to commitment, turnover, or both?', *Human Resource Management*, 44, 5–20.

Ivancevich, J.M. and Matteson, M.T. (1980) *Stress and Work*. Glenview, IL: Scott, Foresman and Co.

Ivancevich, J.M. and Matteson, M.T. (1988) 'Promoting the individual's health and well being', in C.L. Cooper and R. Payne (eds), *Causes, Coping and Consequences of Stress at Work*. Chichester: John Wiley.

Ivancevich, J.M., Matteson, M.T., Freedman, S.M. and Phillips, J.S. (1990) 'Worksite stress management interventions', *American Psychologist*, 45, 252–61.

Jackson, B.J. (2001) *Management Gurus and Management Fashions: A dramatistic enquiry*. London: Routledge.

Jackson, S.E. (1983) 'Participation in decision-making as a strategy for reducing job-related strain', *Journal of Applied Psychology*, 68, 3–19.

Jackson, S.E. and Joshi, A. (2001) 'Research on domestic and international diversity in organizations: A merger that works?', in N. Anderson, D. Ones, H. Sinangil and C. Viswesvaran (eds), *Handbook of Industrial, Work and Organizational Psychology*, vol. 2. London: Sage.

Jackson, S.E., Brett, J.F., Sessa, V.I., Cooper, D.M., Julin, J.A. and Peyronnin, K. (1991) 'Some differences make a difference: Individual dissimilarity and group heterogeneity as correlates of recruitment, promotions, and turnover', *Journal of Applied Psychology*, 76, 675–89.

Jacoby, S.M. (1999) 'Are career jobs headed for extinction?', *California Management Review*, 42, 123–45.

Jahoda, M. (1979) 'The impact of unemployment in the 1930s and the 1970s', *Bulletin of the British Psychological Society*, 32, 309–14.

James, E.H. (2000) 'Race-related differences in promotions and support: Underlying effects of human and social capital', *Organization Science*, 11, 493–508.

Janis, I. and Feshbach, S. (1953) 'Effects of fear arousing communications', *Journal of Abnormal and Social Psychology*, 48, 78–92.

Janis, I.L. (1972) *Victims of Groupthink*. Boston, MA: Houghton Mifflin.

Janis, I.L. (1982a) *Groupthink*. Boston, MA: Houghton Mifflin.

Janis, I.L. (1982b) 'Counteracting the adverse effects of concurrence – seeking in policy planning groups: Theory and research perspectives', in H. Brandstatter, J.H. Davis and G. Stocker-Kreichgauer (eds), *Group Decision Making*. London: Academic Press.

Janssens, M. and Zanoni, P. (2005) 'Many diversities for many services: Theorizing diversity (management) in service companies', *Human Relations*, 58, 311–40.

Janz, J.T. (1989) 'The patterned behaviour description interview: The best prophet of the future is the past', in R.W. Eder and G.R. Ferris (eds), *The Employment Interview: Theory, research and practice*. London: Sage.

Jarvis, W.B.G. and Petty, R.E. (1996) 'The need to evaluate', *Journal of Personal and Social Psychology*, 70, 172–94.

Jehn, K.A., Northcraft, G.B. and Neale, M.A. (1999) 'Why differences make a difference: A field study of diversity, conflict, and performance of workgroups', *Administrative Science Quarterly*, 44, 741–63.

Jenkinson, J.C. (1997) *Mainstream or Special? Educating students with disabilities*. London: Routledge.

Jepson, C. and Chaiken, S. (1990) 'Chronic issue-specific fear inhibits systematic processing of persuasive communications', *Journal of Social Behaviour and Personality*, 5, 61–84.

Johns, G. (1993) 'Constraints on the adoption of psychology-based personnel practices: Lessons from organizational innovation', *Personnel Psychology*, 46, 596–602.

Johns, G. (2001) 'In praise of context', *Journal of Organizational Behavior*, 22, 31–42.

Johns, G. (2006) 'The essential impact of context on organizational behavior', *Academy of Management Review*, 31, 386–408.

Johnson, C.W. (2001) 'A case study in the integration of accident reports and constructive design documents', *Reliability Engineering and Systems Safety*, 71(3), 311–26.

Johnson, G. (1993) 'Processes of managing strategic change', in C. Mabey and B. Mayon-White (eds), *Managing Change*, 2nd edition. London: Open University/Paul Chapman Publishing.

Johnson, J. and Hall, E. (1988) 'Job strain, work place social support and cardiovascular disease: A cross-sectional study of a random sample of the working population', *American Journal of Public Health*, 78, 1336–42.

Johnson, J.W. and Ferstl, K.L. (1999) The effects of interrater and self–other agreement on performance improvement following upward feedback. *Personnel Psychology*, 52(2), 271–303.

Johnson, P. and Cassell, C. (2001) 'Epistemology and work psychology: New agendas', *Journal of Occupational and Organizational Psychology*, 74, 125–43.

Johnson, S., Cooper, C., Cartwright, S., Donald, I., Taylor, P.J. and Millet, C. (2005) 'The experience of work-related stress across occupations', *Journal of Management*, 20, 178–87.

Jones, Q., Dunphy, D., Fishman, R., Larne, M. and Canter, C. (2006) *In Great Company: Unlocking the secrets of cultural transformation*. Sydney, Australia: Human Synergistics.

Judd, C.M., McClelland, G.H. and Culhane, S.E. (1995) 'Data analysis: Continuing issues in the everyday analysis of psychological data', *Annual Review of Psychology*, 46, 433–65.

Judge, T.A. and Bono, J.E. (2000) 'Five-factor model of personality and transformational leadership', *Journal of Applied Psychology*, 85(5), 751–65.

Judge, T.A. and Hulin, C.L. (1993) 'Job satisfaction as a reflection of disposition: A multiple source causal analysis', *Organizational Behavior and Human Decision Processes*, 56, 388–421.

Judge, T.A. and Piccolo, R. (2004) 'Transformational and transactional leadership: A meta-analytic test of their relative validity', *Journal of Applied Psychology*, 89, 755–68.

Judge, T.A., Bono, J.E., Ilies, R. and Gerhardt, M.W. (2002) 'Personality and leadership: A qualitative and quantitative review', *Journal of Applied Psychology*, 87, 765–80.

Judge, T.A., Cable, D.M., Boudreau, J.W. and Bretz, R.D. (1995) 'An empirical investigation of the predictors of career success', *Personnel Psychology*, 48, 485–519.

Judge, T.A., Colbert, A.E. and Ilies, R. (2004b) 'Intelligence and leadership: A quantitative review and test of theoretical propositions', *Journal of Applied Psychology*, 89, 542–52.

Judge, T.A., Piccolo, R.F. and Ilies, R. (2004a) 'The forgotten ones? The validity of consideration and initiating structure in leadership research', *Journal of Applied Psychology*, 89, 36–51.

Judge, T.A., Thoreson, C.J., Bono, J.E. and Patton, G.K. (2001) 'The job satisfaction–job performance relationship: A qualitative and quantitative review', *Psychological Bulletin*, 127, 376–407.

Judiesch, M.K. and Lyness, K.S. (1999) 'Left behind? The impact of leaves of absence on managers' career success', *Academy of Management Journal*, 42, 641–51.

Jung, C.G. (1933) *Psychological Types*. New York: Harcourt, Brace and World.

Jurgensen, C.E. (1978) 'Job preferences (What makes a job good or bad?)', *Journal of Applied Psychology*, 63, 267–76.

Kam, S., Hui, C. and Law, C. (1999) 'Organizational citizenship behaviour: Comparing perspectives of supervisors and subordinates across four international samples', *Journal of Applied Psychology*, 84, 594–601.

Kandola, B. and Fullerton, J. (1994) *Managing the Mosaic: Diversity in action*. London: Institute for Personnel and Development.

Kandola, R. (1995) 'Managing diversity: New broom or old hat?', in C.L. Cooper and I.T. Robertson (eds), *International Review of Industrial and Organizational Psychology*, vol. 10. Chichester: John Wiley.

Kandola, R. and Galpin, M. (2000) '360-degree feedback goes under the microscope', *Insights*, 1, 6–7.

Kanfer, R. (1992) 'Work motivation: New directions in theory and research', in I.T. Robertson and C.L. Cooper (eds), *International Review of Industrial and Organizational Psychology*, vol. 7. Chichester: John Wiley.

Kanfer, R. and Ackerman, P.L. (1989) 'Motivation and cognitive abilities: An integrative/aptitude–treatment interaction approach to skill acquisition', *Journal of Applied Psychology*, 74, 657–90.

Kanfer, R. and Ackerman, P.L. (2002) 'Non-ability influences on volition during skill training'. Paper presented as part of the symposium: New directions in research on motivational traits. Society for Industrial and Organizational Psychology 17th Annual Conference, Toronto.

Kanning, U.P., Grewe, K., Hollenberg, S. and Hadouch, M. (2006) 'From the subjects' point of view – reactions to different types of situational judgment items', *European Journal of Psychological Assessment*, 22, 168–76.

Kanter, R.M. (1989) *When Giants Learn to Dance: Mastering the challenges of strategy, management, and careers in the 1990s*. London: Unwin.

Kanter, R.M. (1997) *World Class: Thriving locally in the global economy*. New York: Simon & Schuster.

Kanter, R.M., Stein, B.A. and Jick, T.D. (1992) *The Challenge of Organizational Change: How companies experience it and leaders guide it*. New York: Free Press.

Kanungo, R.N. (2001) 'Ethical values of transactional and transformational leaders', *Canadian Journal of Administrative Sciences*, 18, 257–65.

Karasek, R. (1979) 'Job demands, job decision latitude and mental strain: Implications for job redesign', *Administrative Science Quarterly*, 24, 285–306.

Karasek, R. and Theorell, T. (1990) *Healthy Work: Stress, productivity and the reconstruction of working life*. New York: Basic Books.

Karasek, R., Brisson, C., Kawakami, N., Houtman, I., Bongers, P. and Amick, B. (1998) 'The Job Content Questionnaire (JCQ): An instrument for internationally comparative assessments of psychosocial job characteristics', *Journal of Occupational Health Psychology*, 3, 322–55.

Kark, R., Shamir, B. and Chen, G. (2003) 'The two faces of transformational leadership: Empowerment and dependency', *Journal of Applied Psychology*, 88, 246–55.

Kawakami, N., Schunichi, A., Kawashima, M., Masumoto, T. and Hayashi, T. (1997) 'Effects of work-related stress reduction on depressive symptoms among Japanese blue-collar workers', *Scandinavian Journal of Work, Environment and Health*, 23, 54–9.

Kearney, A.T. (1992) *Total Quality: Time to take off the rose-tinted spectacles*. Kempston: IFS.

Keashly, L. (2001) 'Interpersonal and systemic aspects of emotional abuse at work: The target's perspective', *Violence and Victims*, 16, 233–268.

Keashly, L. and Jagatic, K. (2003) 'US Perspectives on workplace bullying', in S. Einarsen *et al.* (eds), *Bullying and Emotional Abuse in the Workplace: International perspectives, research and practice*. London: Taylor and Francis.

Keenan, T. (1995) 'Graduate recruitment in Britain: a survey of selection methods used by organizations', *Journal of Organizational Behaviour*, 16, 303–17.

Keller, T. and Dansereau, F. (1995) 'Leadership and empowerment: A social exchange perspective', *Human Relations*, 48, 127–46.

Kelly, C. and Kelly, J.E. (1994) 'Who gets involved in collective action? Social psychological determinants of individual participation in trade unions', *Human Relations*, 47, 63–88.

Kelly, G.A. (1951) *The Psychology of Personal Constructs*, vols 1 and 2. New York: Norton.

Kelly, G.A. (1955) *The Psychology of Personal Constructs*. New York: Norton.

Kelly, J.E. (1993) 'Does job redesign theory explain job re-design outcomes?', *Human Relations*, 45, 753–74.

Kelly, J.E. (1998) *Rethinking Industrial Relations*. London: Routledge.

Kelly, J.E. and Kelly, C. (1991) '"Them and us": Social psychology and the "new employee relations"', *British Journal of Employee Relations*, 29, 25–48.

Kelly, M. and Cooper, C.L. (1981) 'Stress among blue collar workers', *Employee Relations*, 3, 6–9.

Kemp, N.J., Wall, T.D., Clegg, C.W. and Cordery, J.L. (1983) 'Autonomous work groups in a greenfield site: A comparative study', *Journal of Occupational Psychology*, 56, 271–88.

Kerr, N.L. and Bruun, S.E. (1983) 'Dispensability of member effort and group motivation losses: Free-rider effects', *Journal of Personality and Social Psychology*, 44, 78–94.

Kerr, S. and Jermier, J.M. (1978) 'Substitutes for leadership: Their meaning and measurement', *Organizational Behavior and Human Performance*, 22, 375–403.

Kersley, B., Alpin, C., Forth, J., Bryson, A., Bewley, H., Dix, G. and Oxenbridge, S. (2005) *Inside the Workplace: First findings from the 2004 Workplace Employment Relations Survey*. London: Department of Trade and Industry.

Kessler, S.R., Spector, P.E., Chang, C.H. and Parr, A.D. (2008) 'Organizational violence and aggression: Development of the three-factor violence climate survey', *Work and Stress*, 22, 108–24.

Kidd, J.M. (2006) *Understanding Career Counselling*. London: Sage.

Kiesler, C.A. (1971) *The Psychology of Commitment*. New York: Academic Press.

Kim, S. and Gefland, M.J. (2003) 'The influence of ethnic identity on perceptions of organizational recruitment', *Journal of Vocational Behavior*, 63, 396–416.

Kinder, A., Hughes, R. and Cooper C.L. (2008) *Employee Well-being Support: A workplace resource*. Chichester: John Wiley and Sons Ltd.

King, N. (1992) 'Modelling the innovation process: An empirical comparison of approaches', *Journal of Occupational and Organizational Psychology*, 65, 89–100.

King, N. (2004a) 'Using interviews in qualitative research', in C. Cassell and G. Symon (eds), *Essential Guide to Qualitative Methods in Organizational Research*. London: Sage.

King, N. (2004b) 'Using templates in the thematic analysis of text'. In C. Cassell and G. Symon (eds), *Essential Guide to Qualitative Methods in Organizational Research*. London: Sage.

King, Z. (2004) 'Career self-management: Its nature, causes and consequences', *Journal of Vocational Behavior*, 65, 112–133.

King, Z., Burke, S. and Pemberton, J. (2005) 'The "bounded" career: An empirical study of human capital, career mobility and employment outcomes in a mediated labour market', *Human Relations*, 58, 981–1007.

Kinicki, A.J., Prussia, G.E. and McKee Ryan, F.M. (2000) 'A panel study of coping with involuntary job loss', *Academy of Management Journal*, 43, 90–100.

Kipnis, D., Schmidt, S.M. and Wilkinson, I. (1980) 'Intraorganizational influence tactics: Explorations in getting one's way', *Journal of Applied Psychology*, 65, 440–52.

Kirkman, B.L., Rosen, B., Gibson, C.B., Tesluk, P.E. and McPherson, S.O. (2002) 'Five challenges to virtual team performance: Lessons from Sabre Inc.', *Academy of Management Executive*, 16, 67–79.

Kirkpatrick, D.L. (1967) 'Evaluation of training', in R.L. Craig and L.R. Bittel (eds), *Training and Development Handbook*. New York: McGraw-Hill.

Kirwan, B. and Ainsworth, L.K. (eds) (1992) *A Guide To Task Analysis*. London: Taylor and Francis.

Kivimäki, M., Virtanen, M., Elovainio, M., Kouvonen, A., Väänänen, A. and Vahtera, J. (2006) 'Work stress in the etiology of coronary heart disease – a meta-analysis', *Scandinavian Journal of Work, Environment and Health*, 32, 431–42.

Klein, H.J., Noe, R.A. and Wang, C. (2006) 'Motivation to learn and course outcomes: The impact of delivery mode, learning goal orientations and perceived barriers and enablers', *Personnel Psychology*, 59, 665–702.

Klimoksi, R. and Inks, L. (1990) 'Accountability forces in performance appraisal', *Organizational Behavior and Human Decision Processes*, 45, 194–208.

Klimoski, R.J. and Donahue, L.M. (2001) 'Person perception in organizations: An overview of the field', in M. London (ed.), *How People Evaluate Others in Organizations*. London: LEA.

Kline, P. (1993) *An Easy Guide to Factor Analysis*. London: Routledge.

Kline, P. (1999) *Handbook of Psychological Testing*, 2nd edition. London: Sage Publications.

Kline, P. (2000) *The New Psychometrics: Science, psychology and measurement*. London: Routledge.

Kluger, A. and Tikochinsky, J. (2001) 'The error of accepting the "theoretical" null hypothesis: The rise, fall and resurrection of commonsense hypotheses in psychology', *Psychological Bulletin*, 127, 408–23.

Kluger, A.N. and DeNisi, A. (1996) 'The effects of feedback interventions on performance: A historical review, a meta-analysis, and a preliminary feedback intervention theory', *Psychological Bulletin*, 119, 254–84.

Kompier, M.A.J. and Kristensen, T.S. (2001) 'Organizational work stress interventions in a theoretical, methodological and practical context', in J. Dunham (ed.), *Stress in the Workplace: Past, present and future*. London: Whurr.

Kompier, M., Geurts, S., Grundemann, R., Vink, P. and Smulders, P. (1998) 'Cases in stress prevention: The success of a participative and stepwise approach', *Stress Medicine*, 14, 155–68.

Konrad, A.M. (2003) 'Defining the domain of workplace diversity scholarship', *Group and Organization Management*, 28, 4–17.

Kopelman, R.E., Greenhaus, J.H. and Connolly, T.F. (1983) 'A model of work, family and inter-role conflict: A construct validation study', *Organizational Behavior and Human Performance*, 32, 198–215.

Kornhauser, A. (1965) *Mental Health of the Industrial Worker*. Chichester: John Wiley.

Kossek, E.E., Pichler, S.M., Meece, D. and Barratt, M.E. (2008) 'Family, friend and neighbour child care providers and maternal well-being in low income systems: An ecological and social perspective', *Journal of Occupational and Organizational Psychology*, 81, 369–2.

Kotter, J.P. (1996) *Leading Change*. Boston, MA: Harvard Business School Press.

Kozlowski, S. and Ilgen, D. (2006) 'Enhancing the effectiveness of work groups and teams', *Psychological Science in the Public Interest*, 7(3), 77–124.

Kraiger, K., Ford, J. and Salas, E. (1993) 'Application of cognitive skill based and affective theories of learning outcomes to new methods of training evaluation', *Journal of Applied Psychology*, 78, 311–28.

Kram, K.E. (1985) *Mentoring at Work: Developmental relationships in organizational life*. Glenview, IL: Scott Foresman.

Krauss, R. and Fussell, S.R. (1990) 'Mutual knowledge and communicative effectiveness', in J. Galegher, R. Kraut and C. Egido (eds), *Intellectual Teamwork: Social and technological foundations of cooperative work*. Hillsdale, NJ: Lawrence Erlbaum Associates.

Kravitz, D.A. (2008) 'The diversity–validity dilemma: Beyond selection – the role of affirmative action', *Personnel Psychology*, 61, 173–93.

Krech, D., Crutchfield, R.S. and Ballachey, E.L. (1962) *Individual in Society*. New York: McGraw-Hill.

Krueger, J. (1991) 'Accentuation effects and illusory change in exemplar-based category learning', *European Journal of Social Psychology*, 21, 37–48.

Kuijpers, M. and Scheerens, J. (2006) 'Career competencies for the modern career', *Journal of Career Development*, 32, 303–19.

Kuper, H. and Marmot, M. (2008) 'Job strain, job demands, decision latitude and risk of coronary heart disease within the Whitehall II study', *Journal of Epidemiology and Community Health*, 57, 147–53.

Laas, I. (2006) 'Self-actualization and society: A new application for an old theory', *Journal of Humanistic Psychology*, 46, 77–91.

Lam, S.S.K. and Dreher, G.F. (2004) 'Gender, extra-firm mobility and compensation attainment in the United States and Hong Kong', *Journal of Organizational Behavior*, 25, 791–805.

Lamm, H. and Trommsdorf, G. (1973) 'Group versus individual performance on tasks requiring ideational proficiency (brainstorming)', *European Journal of Social Psychology*, 3, 361–87.

LaMontagne, A.D., Keegel, T., Louie, A.M., Ostrey, A. and Landsbergis, P.A. (2007) 'A systematic review of the job-stress intervention evaluation literature, 1990–2005', *International Journal of Occupational and Environmental Health*, 13, 268–80.

Lamond, D., Daniels, K. and Standen, P. (2003) 'Teleworking and virtual organisations: The human impact', in D. Holman, T.D. Wall, C.W. Clegg, P. Sparrow and A. Howard (eds), *The New Workplace*. Chichester: John Wiley.

Lance, C.E. (2008) 'Why assessment centers do not work the way they are supposed to', *Industrial and Organizational Psychology*, 1, 84–97.

Landy, F.J. (1989) *The Psychology of Work Behavior*, 4th edition. Homewood, IL: Brooks/Cole Publishing Co.

Lansisalmi, H., Piero, J.-M. and Kivimaki, M. (2004) 'Grounded theory in organizational research', in C. Cassell and G. Symon (eds), *Essential Guide to Qualitative Methods in Organizational Research*. London: Sage.

Larson, C.E. and LaFasto, F.M.J. (1989) *Teamwork: What must go right/what can go wrong.* London: Sage.

Latane, B., Williams, K. and Harkins, S. (1979) 'Many hands make light the work: The causes and consequences of social loafing', *Journal of Personality and Social Psychology*, 37, 822–32.

Latham, G.P. (2007) *Work Motivation: History, theory, research and practice*. London: Sage.

Latham, G.P. and Pinder, C.C. (2005) 'Work motivation theory and research at the dawn of the twenty-first century', *Annual Review of Psychology*, 56, 485–516.

Latham, G.P., Skarlicki, D., Irvine, D. and Siegal, J.P. (1993) 'The increasing importance of performance appraisals to employee effectiveness in organizational settings in North America', in C.L. Cooper and I.T. Robertson (eds), *International Review of Industrial and Organizational Psychology*, vol. 8. Chichester: John Wiley.

Lau, D.C. and Murnighan, J.K. (1998) 'Demographic diversity and faultlines: The compositional dynamics of organizational groups', *Academy of Management Review*, 23, 325–40.

Lavine, H. and Snyder, M. (1996) 'Cognitive processing and the functional matching effect in persuasion: The mediating role of subjective perceptions of message quality', *Journal of Experimental Social Psychology*, 32, 580–604.

Lawler, E.E., III (2003) 'Pay systems for virtual teams', in C.B. Gibson and S.G. Cogen (eds), *Virtual Teams that Work: Creating conditions for effective virtual teams*. San Francisco: Jossey-Bass.

Lawrence, B.S. (1980) 'The myth of the mid-life crisis', *Sloan Management Review*, 4, 35–49.

Lazarus, R.S. (1966) *Psychological Stress and Coping Process*. New York: McGraw-Hill.

Lazarus, R.S. and Folkman, S. (1984) *Stress, Appraisal and Coping*. New York: Springer Publications.

Lea, M. and Spears, R. (1992) 'Paralinguistic and social perception in computer-mediated communication', *Journal of Organizational Computing*, 2, 321–41.

Leclerc, G., Lefrançois, R., Dubé, M., Hébert, R. and Gaulin, P. (1998) 'The self-actualisation concept: A contest validation', *Journal of Social Behaviour and Personality*, 13, 69–84.

Lee, C., Ashford, S.J. and Jamieson, L.F. (1993) 'The effects of Type A behaviour dimensions and optimism on coping strategy, health and performance', *Journal of Organizational Behavior*, 14, 143–57.

Lee, K. and Ashton, M.C. (2004) 'The HEXACO Personality Inventory: A new measure of the major dimensions of personality', *Multivariate Behavioral Research*, 39, 329–58.

Lee, K., Carswell, J.J. and Allen, N.J. (2000) 'A meta-analytic review of occupational commitment: Relations with person and work-related variables', *Journal of Applied Psychology*, 85, 799–811.

Lees, J. (2007) *How to Get a Job You'll Love*. Maidenhead: McGraw-Hill.

Lefkowitz, J. (1994) 'Sex-related differences in job attitudes and dispositional variables: Now you see them . . .', *Academy of Management Journal*, 37, 323–49.

Legge, K. (2003) 'Any nearer a "better" approach? A critical view', in D. Holman, T.D. Wall, C.W. Clegg, P. Sparrow and A. Howard (eds), *The New Workplace*. Chichester: John Wiley.

Lehman, D.R., Chiu, C.Y. and Schaller, M. (2004) 'Psychology and culture', *Annual Review of Psychology*, 55, 689–714.

Lent, R.W., Brown, S.D. and Hackett, G. (1994) 'Toward a unifying social cognitive theory of career and academic interest, choice and performance', *Journal of Vocational Behavior*, 45, 79–122.

Leon, F.R. (1981) 'The role of positive and negative outcomes in the causation of motivational forces', *Journal of Applied Psychology*, 66, 45–53.

Leonard, N.H., Beauvois, L.L. and Scholl, R.W. (1999) 'Work motivation: The incorporation of self-concept-based processes', *Human Relations*, 52, 969–98.

Leong, F., Austin, J. and Sakaran, U. (1998) 'An evaluation of cross-cultural validity of Holland's theory: Career choices by workers in India', *Journal of Vocational Behavior*, 52, 441–55.

Lester, S.W., Kickul, J.R. and Bergmann, T.W. (2007) 'Managing employee perceptions of the psychological contract over time: The role of employer social accounts and contract fulfillment', *Journal of Organizational Behavior*, 28, 191–208.

Levinson, D.J. with Darrow, C.N., Klein, E.B., Levinson, M.H. and McKee, B. (1978) *Seasons of a Man's Life*. New York: Knopf.

Levinson, D.J. with Levinson, J. (1996) *The Seasons of a Woman's Life*. New York: Knopf.

Lewicki, R.J., Weiss, S.E. and Lewin, D. (1992) 'Models of conflict, negotiation and third party intervention: A review and synthesis', *Journal of Organizational Behavior*, 13, 209–52.

Lewin, K. (1945) 'The Research Center for Group Dynamics at Massachusetts Institute of Technology', *Sociometry*, 8, 126–36.

Lewin, K. (1946) 'Action research and minority problems', *Journal of Social Issues*, 2, 34–6.

Lewin, K. (1958) 'Group decisions and social change', in G.E. Swanson, T.M. Newcomb and E.L. Hartley (eds), *Readings in Social Psychology*. New York: Holt, Rhinehart and Winston.

Lewis, K.M. (2000) 'When leaders display emotion: How followers respond to negative emotional expression of male and female leaders', *Journal of Organizational Behavior*, 21, 221–34.

Lewis, S. and Cooper, C.L. (2005) *Work–Life Integration: Case studies in organizational change*. Chichester and New York: John Wiley and Sons.

Lewis, S. and Taylor, K. (1996) 'Evaluating the impact of family-friendly employer policies: A case study', in S. Lewis and J. Lewis (eds), *The Work–Family Challenge: Rethinking employment*. London: Sage.

Leymann, H. (1996) 'The content and development of mobbing at work', *European Journal of Work and Organizational Psychology*, 5, 165–84.

Li, A. and Cropanzano, R. (2009) 'Do East Asians respond more/less strongly to organizational justice than North Americans? A meta-analysis', *Journal of Management Studies*, 46, 787–805.

Licht, M.H. (1997) 'Multiple regression and correlation', in L.G. Grimm and P.R. Yarnold (eds), *Reading and Understanding Multivariate Statistics*. Washington, DC: American Psychological Association.

Liden, R.C., Wayne, S.J., Kraimer, M.L. and Sparrowe, R.T. (2003) 'The dual commitments of contingent workers: An examination of contingents' commitment to the agency and the organization', *Journal of Organizational Behavior*, 24, 609–25.

Lievens, F. and Harris, M.M. (2003) 'Research on Internet recruitment and testing: Current status and future directions', in C.L. Cooper and I.T. Robertson (eds), *International Review of Industrial and Organizational Psychology*, vol. 18. Chichester: John Wiley.

Lievens, F. and Sanchez, J. (2007) 'Can training improve the quality of inferences made by raters in competency modeling? A quasi-experiment', *Journal of Applied Psychology*, 92(3), 812–19.

Lievens, F., Buyse, T. and Sackett, P. R. (2005) 'The operational validity of a video-based situational judgment test for medical college admissions: Illustrating the importance of matching predictor and criterion construct domains', *Journal of Applied Psychology*, 90, 442–52.

Lievens, F., Peeters, H. and Schollaert, E. (2008) 'Situational judgement tests: A review of recent research', *Personnel Review*, 37, 426–41.

Linley, A.P. (2006) 'Coaching research: who? what? where? when? why?', *International Journal of Evidence Based Coaching and Mentoring*, 4, 1–7.

Lippitt, R., Watson, J. and Westley, B. (1958) *The Dynamics of Planned Change*. New York: Harcourt, Brace and World.

Lobban, R.K., Husted, J. and Farewell, V.T. (1998) 'A comparison on the effect of job demand, decision latitude, role and supervisory style on self-reported job satisfaction', *Work and Stress*, 12, 337–50.

Locke, E.A. (1976) 'The nature and causes of job satisfaction', in M.D. Dunnette (ed.), *Handbook of Industrial and Organizational Psychology*. Chicago, IL: Rand McNally.

Locke, E.A. (1995) 'The micro-analysis of job satisfaction: Comments on Taber and Alliger', *Journal of Organizational Behavior*, 16, 123–5.

Locke, E.A. (2000) 'Motivation, cognition and action: An analysis of studies of task goals and knowledge', *Applied Psychology: An International Review*, 49, 408–29.

Locke, E.A. (2005) 'Why emotional intelligence is an invalid concept', *Journal of Organizational Behavior*, 26, 425–31.

Locke, E.A. and Latham, G.P. (1990) *A Theory of Goal-setting and Task Performance*. Englewood Cliffs, NJ: Prentice Hall.

Locke, E.A. and Latham, G.P. (2002) 'Building a practically useful theory of goal setting and task motivation: A 35-year odyssey', *American Psychologist*, 57 705–17.

Locke, E.A. and Latham, G.P. (2004) 'What should we do about motivation theory? Six recommendations for the twenty-first century', *Academy of Management Review*, 29, 388–403.

Locke, E.A., Shaw, K.N., Saari, L.M. and Latham, G.P. (1981) 'Goal setting and task performance 1969–1980', *Psychological Bulletin*, 90, 125–52.

London, M. (2001a) 'The great debate: Should multi-source feedback be used for administration or development only?', in D. Bracken, C. Timmreck and A. Church (eds), *The Handbook of Multi-source Feedback*. San Francisco, CA: Jossey-Bass.

London, M. (2001b) *How People Evaluate Others in Organizations*. London: Lawrence Erlbaum.

London, M. and Smither, J.W. (1995) 'Can multi-source feedback change perceptions of goal accomplishment, self-evaluations and performance related outcomes? Theory-based applications and directions for research', *Personnel Psychology*, 48, 803–39.

London, M. and Tornow, W.W. (1998a) *Maximizing the Value of 360-degree Feedback*. Greensboro, NC: Center for Creative Leadership.

London, M. and Tornow, W.W. (1998b) 'Introduction: 360-degree feedback – more than a tool!', in M. London and W.W. Tornow (eds), *Maximizing the Value of 360-degree Feedback*. Greensboro, NC: Center for Creative Leadership.

Long, L. and Tracey, T.J. (2006) 'Structure of RIASEC scores in China: A structural meta-analysis', *Journal of Vocational Behavior*, 68, 39–51.

Lord, R.G. and Maher, K.J. (1991) *Leadership and Information Processing*. Boston, MA: Routledge.

Lutgen-Sandvik, P., Tracy, S.J. and Alberts, J.K. (2007) 'Burned by bullying in the American workplace: Prevalence, perception, degree and impact', *Journal of Management Studies*, 44, 835–60.

Luthans, F. and Kreitner, R. (1975) *Organizational Behavior Modification*. Glenview, IL: Scott-Foresman.

Lyness, K.S. and Schrader, C.A. (2004) 'Moving ahead or just moving? An examination of gender differences in senior corporate management appointments', *Group and Organization Management*, 31, 651–76.

Lyness, K.S. and Thompson, D.E. (2000) 'Climbing the corporate ladder: Do female and male executives follow the same route?', *Journal of Applied Psychology*, 85(1), 86–101.

Mabe, P.A. and West, S.G. (1982) 'Validity of self-evaluation of ability: A review and meta-analysis', *Journal of Applied Psychology*, 67, 280–96.

Mabey, C. (1986) *Graduates into Industry*. Aldershot: Gower.

Mabey, C. (2001) 'Closing the circle: Participant views of a 360-degree feedback programme', *Human Resource Management Journal*, 11, 41–54.

Mabey, C. and Mayon-White, B. (1993) *Managing Change*, 2nd edition. London: Open University/Paul Chapman Publishing.

Macy, B.A. and Izumi, H. (1993) 'Organizational change, design, and work innovations: A meta-analysis of 131 North American field studies 1961–1991', in W. Passmore and R. Woodman (eds), *Research in Organizational Change and Development*, vol. 7. Greenwich, CT: JAI Press.

Maczynski, J. (1997) 'A comparison of leadership style of Polish managers before and after market economy reforms'. Paper presented at the Eighth European Congress of Work and Organizational Psychology, Verona, April.

Maddi, S. (2002) 'The story of hardiness: Twenty years of theorizing, research and practice', *Consulting Psychology Journal: Practice and Research*, 54, 175–85.

Maier, N.R.F. and Solem, A.R. (1952) 'The contribution of a discussion leader to the quality of group thinking: The effective use of minority opinions', *Human Relations*, 5, 277–88.

Majchrzak, A., Rice, R.E., King, N., Malhotra, A. and Ba, S.L. (2000) 'Computer mediated inter-organisational knowledge sharing: Insights from a virtual team innovating using a collaborative tool', *Information Resources Management Journal*, 13(1), 44–53.

Makin, P., Cooper, C.L. and Cox, C. (1996) *Organizations and the Psychological Contract*. Leicester: British Psychological Society.

Malone, J.C. and Cruchon, N.M. (2001) 'Radical behaviorism and the rest of psychology: A review/précis of Skinner's *About Behaviorism*', *Behavior and Philosophy*, 29, 31–57.

Marcia, J.E. (1966) 'Development and validation of ego-identity status', *Journal of Personality and Social Psychology*, 3, 551–8.

Mark, G.M. and Smith, A.P. (2008) 'Stress models: A review and suggested new direction', in J. Houdmont and S. Leka (eds), *Occupational Health Psychology: European perspectives on research, education and practice*, vol. III. Nottingham: Nottingham University Press.

Marrow, A.J. (1977) *The Practical Theorist: The life and work of Kurt Lewin*. New York: Teachers College Press.

Martin, J. (1992) *Cultures in Organizations: Three perspectives*. Oxford: Oxford University Press.

Martin, J. (2002) *Organizational Culture: Mapping the terrain*. London: Sage.

Martin, R. (2000) 'Breaking the code of change: observations and critique', in M. Beer and N. Nohria (eds), *Breaking the Code of Change*. Boston, MA: Harvard Business School Press.

Maslach, C. and Jackson, S.E. (1981) 'The measurement of experienced burnout', *Journal of Occupational Behavior*, 2, 99–113

Maslow, A.H. (1943) 'A theory of motivation', *Psychological Review*, 50, 370–96.

Maslow, A.H. (1954) *Motivation and Personality*. New York: Harper and Row.

Mathieu, J.E. and Zajac, D.M. (1990) 'A review and meta-analysis of the antecedents, correlates and consequences of organizational commitment', *Psychological Bulletin*, 108, 171–94.

Matthews, G. and Deary, I.J. (1998) *Personality Traits*. New York: Cambridge University Press.

Matthews, G., Deary, I.J. and Whiteman, M.C. (2003b) *Personality Traits*, 2nd edition. Cambridge: Cambridge University Press.

Matthews, G., Zeidner, M. and Roberts, R. (2003a) *Emotional Intelligence: Science and myth*. Cambridge, MA: MIT Press.

Mau, W.C. (1999) 'Effects of computer-assisted career decision making on vocational identity and career exploratory behaviors', *Journal of Career Development*, 25(4), 261–74.

Mau, W.C. (2000) 'Cultural differences in career decision-making styles and self-efficacy', *Journal of Vocational Behavior*, 57, 365–78.

Maurer, S.D., Sue-Chan, C. and Latham, G.P. (1999) 'The situational interview', in R.W. Eder and M.M. Harris (eds), *The Employment Interview Handbook*. London: Sage.

Maurer T.J., Solamon, J.M. and Lippstreu, M. (2008) 'How does coaching interviewees affect the validity of a structured interview?', *Journal of Organizational Behavior*, 29, 355–71.

Mayer, J.D. and Salovey, P. (1997) 'What is emotional intelligence?', in P. Salovey and D.J. Sluyter (eds), *Emotional Development and Emotional Intelligence: Educational implications*. New York: Basic Books.

Mayer, J.D., Caruso, D. and Salovey, P. (1999) 'Emotional intelligence meets traditional standards for an intelligence', *Intelligence*, 27, 267–98.

Mayer, J.D., Perkins, D., Caruso, D.R. and Salovey, P. (2001) 'Emotional intelligence and giftedness', *Roeper Review*, 23(3), 131–7.

Mayer, J.D., Salovey, P. and Caruso, D.R. (2000) 'Emotional intelligence as zeitgeist, as personality, and as a mental ability', in R. Bar-On and J.D.A. Parker (eds), *Handbook of Emotional Intelligence*. San Francisco, CA: Jossey-Bass.

Mayon-White, B. (1993) 'Problem-solving in small groups: Team members as agents of change', in C. Mabey and B. Mayon-White (eds), *Managing Change*, 2nd edition. London: The Open University/Paul Chapman Publishing.

Maznevski, M.L. (1994) 'Understanding our differences: Performance in decision-making groups with diverse members', *Human Relations*, 47(5), 531–52.

McCalman, J. and Paton, R.A. (1992) *Change Management: A guide to effective implementation*. London: Paul Chapman Publishing.

McClelland, D.C. (1961) *The Achieving Society*. Princeton, NJ: Van Nostrand.

McClough, A.C. and Rogelberg, S.G. (2003) 'Selection in teams: An exploration of the teamwork knowledge, skills and ability test', *International Journal of Selection and Assessment*, 11(1), 56–66.

McCormick, E.J. and Sanders, M.S. (1992) *Human Factors in Engineering and Design*, 7th edition. New York: McGraw Hill.

McCormick, E.J., Jeanneret, P. and Meacham, R.C. (1972) 'A study of job characteristics and job dimensions as based on the position analysis questionnaires', *Journal of Applied Psychology*, 36, 347–68.

McCrae, R.R. and Costa, P.T. (1990) *Personality in Adulthood*. New York: Guilford Press.

McCrae, R.R. and Costa, P.T. (1997) 'Personality trait structure as a human universal', *American Psychologist*, 52, 509–16.

McDaniel, M.A. (2005) 'Big-brained people are smarter: A meta-analysis of the relationship between *in vivo* brain volume and intelligence', *Intelligence*, 33, 337–46.

McDaniel, M.A. and Nguyen, N.T. (2001) 'Situational judgment tests: A review of practice and constructs assessed', *International Journal of Selection and Assessment*, 9, 103–13.

McDaniel, M.A., Hartman, N.S., Whetzel, D.L. and Grubb, W.L. III. (2007) 'Situational judgment tests, response instructions and validity: A meta-analysis', *Personnel Psychology*, 60, 63–91.

McDaniel, M.A., Morgeson, F.P., Finnegan, E.B., Campion, M.A. and Braverman, E.P. (2001) 'Use of situational judgment tests to predict job performance: A clarification of the literature', *Journal of Applied Psychology*, 86, 730–40.

McEntire, L. Dailey, L. Osburn, H. and Mumford, M. (2006) 'Innovations in job analysis: Development and application of metrics to analyze jobs', *Human Resource Management Review*, 16(3), 310–23.

McFarlin, D.B. and Sweeney, P.D. (1992) 'Distributive and procedural justice as predictors of satisfaction with personal and organizational outcomes', *Academy of Management Journal*, 35, 626–37.

McGrath, J.E. (1964) *Social Psychology: A brief introduction*. New York: Holt, Rinehart and Winston.

McGrath, J.E. (1984) *Groups: Interaction and performance*. Englewood Cliffs, NJ: Prentice Hall.

McGregor, D. (1960) *The Human Side of Enterprise*. New York: McGraw-Hill.

McHugh, M.F. (1991) 'Disabled workers: Psychosocial issues', in M.J. Davidson and J. Earnshaw (eds), *Vulnerable Workers*. Chichester: John Wiley.

McKay, P. and McDaniel, M.A. (2006) 'A re-examination of black–white mean differences in work performance: More data, more moderators', *Journal of Applied Psychology*, 91, 531–54.

McKee-Ryan, F.M., Virick, M., Prussia, G.E., Harvey, J. and Lilly, J.D. (2009) 'Life after the layoff: Getting a job worth keeping', *Journal of Organizational Behavior*, 30, 561–80.

McKinlay, A. (2000) 'The bearable lightness of control', in C. Prichard, R. Hull, M. Chummer and H. Willmott (eds), *Managing Knowledge: Critical investigations of work and learning*. Basingstoke: Macmillan.

McLeod, P.L., Baron, R.S., Marti, M.W. and Yoon, K. (1997) 'The eyes have it: Minority influence in face-to-face and computer-mediated group discussion', *Journal of Applied Psychology*, 82, 706–18.

Meek, V.L. (1988) 'Organizational culture: Origins and weaknesses', *Organization Studies*, 9(4), 453–73.

Meier, L.L., Semmer, N.K., Elfering, A. and Jacobshagen, N. (2008) 'The double meaning of control: Three-way interactions between internal resources, job control and stressors at work', *Journal of Occupational Health Psychology*, 13, 244–58.

Meindl, J.R., Ehrlich, S.B. and Dukerich, J.M. (1985) 'The romance of leadership', *Administrative Science Quarterly*, 30, 78–102.

Melamed, S., Ben-Avi, I., Luz, J. and Green, M.S. (1995) 'Objective and subjective work monotony: Effects on job satisfaction, psychological distress and absenteeism in blue-collar workers', *Journal of Applied Psychology*, 80, 29–42.

Melhuish, A. (1978) *Executive Health*. London: Business Books.

Mento, A.J., Steel, R.P. and Karren, R.J. (1987) 'A meta-analytic study of the effects of goal setting on task performance: 1966–1984', *Organizational Behavior and Human Decision Processes*, 39, 52–83.

Meriac, J.P., Hoffman, B.J., Woehr, D.J. and Fleisher, M.S. (2008) 'Further evidence for the validity of assessment center dimensions: A meta-analysis of the incremental criterion-related validity of dimension ratings', *Journal of Applied Psychology*, 93, 1042–52.

Metz, I. and Tharenou, P. (2001) 'Women's career advancement – the relative contribution of human and social capital', *Group and Organization Management*, 26, 312–42.

Meyer, J. (1997) 'Organizational commitment', in C.L. Cooper and I.T. Robertson (eds), *International Review of Industrial and Organizational Psychology*, 12, 175–228.

Meyer, J. (2001) 'Action research', in N. Fulop, P. Allen, A. Clarke and N. Black (eds), *Studying the Organisation and Delivery of Health Services: Research methods*. London: Routledge.

Meyer, J.P., Allen, N.J. and Smith, C.A. (1993) 'Commitment to organizations and occupations: Extension and test of a three-component conceptualization', *Journal of Applied Psychology*, 78, 538–51.

Meyer, J.P., Paunonen, S.V., Gellatly, I.R., Goffin, R.D. and Jackson, D.N. (1989) 'Organizational commitment and job performance: It's the nature of the commitment that counts', *Journal of Applied Psychology*, 74, 152–6.

Meyer, J.P., Stanley, D.J., Herscovitch, L. and Topolnytsky, L. (2002) 'Affective, continuance and normative commitment to the organization: A meta-analysis of antecedents, correlates and consequences', *Journal of Vocational Behavior*, 61, 20–52.

Micceri, T. (1989) 'The unicorn, the normal curve, and other improbable creatures', *Psychological Bulletin*, 105, 156–66.

Mikkelsen, E.G. and Einarsen, S. (2001) 'Bullying in Danish work-life: Prevalence and health correlates', *European Journal of Work and Organizational Psychology*, 10, 393–413.

Millar, M.G. and Tesser, A. (1989) 'The effects of affective–cognitive consistency and thought on attitude–behavior relations', *Journal of Experimental Social Psychology*, 25, 189–202.

Miller, D. (1993) 'The architecture of simplicity', *Academy of Management Review*, 18(1), 116–38.

Miller, D. (2001) 'Reexamining teamwork and team performance', *Small Group Research*, 32(6), 745–66.

Miller, D. and Friesen, P.H. (1984) *Organizations: A quantum view*. Englewood Cliffs, NJ: Prentice Hall.

Miller, G.A. (1966) *Psychology: The science of mental life*. Harmondsworth: Penguin.

Millette, V. and Gagne, M. (2008) 'Designing volunteers' tasks to maximize motivation, satisfaction and performance: The impact of job characteristics on volunteer engagement', *Motivation and Emotion*, 32, 11–22.

Millward, L. (2000) 'Focus groups', in G. Breakwell, S. Hammond and C. Fife-Schaw (eds), *Research Methods in Psychology*, 2nd edition. London: Sage.

Millward, L.J. (2006) 'The transition to motherhood in an organizational context: An interpretative phenomenological analysis', *Journal of Occupational and Organizational Psychology*, 79, 315–34.

Miner, J.B. (1964) *Scoring Guide for the Miner Sentence Completion Scale*. Atlanta, GA: Organizational Measurement Systems Press.

Miner, J.B. (2003) 'The rated importance, scientific validity, and practical usefulness of organizational behaviour theories: A quantitative review', *Academy of Management Learning and Education*, 2, 250–68.

Miner, J.B. and Smith, N.R. (1982) 'Decline and stabilization of managerial motivation over a 20-year period', *Journal of Applied Psychology*, 67, 297–305.

Miner, J.B., Chen, C.C. and Yu, K.C. (1991) 'Theory testing under adverse conditions: Motivation to manage in the People's Republic of China', *Journal of Applied Psychology*, 76, 343–9.

Ministry of Defence (2000) *Overview of Target Audience Descriptions*. London: Ministry of Defence.

Ministry of Defence (2001) *Human Factors Integration (HFI): Practical guidance for IPTs*. London: Ministry of Defence.

Ministry of Defence Human Factors Integration Defence Technology Centre (2006) *Cost Arguments and Evidence for Human Factors Integration*. London: Ministry of Defence.

Mintzberg, H. (1983) *Power In and Around Organizations*. Englewood Cliffs, NJ: Prentice Hall.

Mintzberg, H. (1994) *The Rise and Fall of Strategic Planning*. London: Prentice Hall.

Mintzberg, H., Raisinghani, D. and Theoret, A. (1976) 'The structure of "unstructured" decision processes', *Administrative Science Quarterly*, 21, 246–75.

Mischel, W. (1968) *Personality Assessment*. New York: John Wiley.

Mitchell, R.J. and Williamson, A.M. (2000) 'Evaluation of an 8-hour versus a 12-hour shift roster on employees at a power station', *Applied Ergonomics*, 31, 83–93.

Mobley, W.H., Horner, S.O. and Hollingsworth, A.T. (1978) 'An evaluation of precursors of hospital employee turnover', *Journal of Applied Psychology*, 63, 408–14.

Mohr, R.D. and Zoghi, C. (2008) 'High-involvement work design and job satisfaction', *Industrial and Labor Relations Review*, 61, 275–96.

Mohrman, S.A., Cohen, S.G. and Mohrman, A.M. Jr (1995) *Designing Team-based Organizations: New forms for knowledge work*. San Francisco, CA: Jossey Bass Wiley.

Molloy, J.C. (2005) 'Development networks: Literature review and future research', *Career Development International*, 10, 536–47.

Moore, C., Gunz, H. and Hall, D.T. (2007) 'Tracing the historical roots of career theory in management and organization studies', in H. Gunz and M. Peiperl (eds), *Handbook of Career Studies*. London: Sage, 13–38.

Moorman, R.H. (1991) 'Relationship between organizational justice and organizational citizenship behaviors – do fairness perceptions influence employee citizenship?', *Journal of Applied Psychology*, 76(6), 845–55.

Morgan, G. (1997) *Images of Organization*, 2nd edition. London: Sage.

Morgeson, F.P. and Campion, M.A. (2002) 'Minimizing trade-offs when redesigning work: Evidence from a longitudinal quasi-experiment', *Personnel Psychology*, 55, 589–612.

Morgeson, F.P. and Humphrey, S.E. (2006) 'The Work Design Questionnaire (WDQ): Developing and validating a comprehensive measure for assessing job design and the nature of work', *Journal of Applied Psychology*, 91, 1321–39.

Morgeson, F.P., Campion M.A., Dipboye R.L., Hollenbeck J.R., Murphy, K. and Schmitt, N. (2007a) 'Reconsidering the use of personality tests in personnel selection contexts', *Personnel Psychology*, 60, 683–729.

Morgeson, F.P., Campion, M.A., Dipboye, R.L., Hollenbeck, J.R., Murphy, K. and Schmitt, N. (2007b) 'Are we getting fooled again? Coming to terms with limitations in the use of personality tests for personnel selection', *Personnel Psychology*, 60, 1029–49.

Morita, M. (2001) 'Have the seeds of Japanese teamworking taken root abroad?', *New Technology, Work and Employment*, 16(3), 178–90.

Morley, F.J.J. and Harris, D. (1994) 'Terrain and vertical navigation displays to enhance situational awareness: a user-centred iterative design approach'. Paper presented to the Royal Aeronautical Society Conference on Controlled Flight into Terrain, 8 November 1994, London.

Morrell, K., Loan-Clarke, J. and Wilkinson, A. (2001) 'Unweaving leaving: The use of models in the management of employee turnover', *International Journal of Management Reviews*, 3, 219–44.

Morrell, K., Loan-Clarke, J. and Wilkinson, A. (2004) 'The role of shocks in employee turnover', *British Journal of Management*, 15, 335–49.

Morris, J.A. and Feldman, D.C. (1996) 'The dimensions, antecedents and consequences of emotional labour', *Academy of Management Review*, 21, 986–1010

Moscovici, S. (1985) 'Social influence and conformity', in G. Lindzey and E. Aronson (eds), *The Handbook of Social Psychology*, 3rd edition. New York: Random House.

Moscovici, S. and Mugny, G. (1983) 'Minority influence', in P.B. Paulus (ed.), *Basic Group Processes*. New York: Springer-Verlag.

Moser, K. and Schuler, H. (1989) 'The nature of psychological measurement', in P. Herriot (ed.), *Assessment and Selection in Organizations*. Chichester: John Wiley.

Mowday, R., Steers, R. and Porter, L. (1979) 'The measurement of organizational commitment', *Journal of Vocational Behavior*, 14, 224–47.

Mowday, R.T. (1991) 'Equity theory predictions of behaviour in organisations', in R.M. Steers and L.W. Porter (eds), *Motivation and Work Behavior*, 5th edition. New York: McGraw-Hill.

Mulilis, J. and Lippa, R. (1990) 'Behavioral change in earthquake preparedness due to negative threat appeals: A test of protection motivation theory', *Journal of Applied Social Psychology*, 20, 619–38.

Mullen, B. and Copper, C. (1994) 'The relation between group cohesiveness and performance: An integration', *Psychological Bulletin*, 115, 210–27.

Murphy, G.C. and Athanasou, J.A. (1999) 'The effect of unemployment on mental health', *Journal of Occupational and Organizational Psychology*, 72, 83–99.

Murphy, K. and Cleveland, J. (1995) *Understanding Performance Appraisal: Social organizational and goal-based perspectives*. London: Sage.

Murphy, K., Cleveland, J.N., Skattebo, A.L. and Kinney, T.B. (2004) 'Raters who pursue different goals give different ratings', *Journal of Applied Psychology*, 89, 158–64.

Murphy, L.R. (1988) 'Workplace interventions for stress reduction and prevention', in C.L. Cooper and R. Payne (eds), *Causes, Coping and Consequences of Stress at Work*. Chichester: John Wiley.

Murphy, L.R. and Sauter, S.L. (2003) 'The USA perspective: Current issues and trends in the management of work stress', *Australian Psychologist*, 38, 151–7.

Murphy, P.R. and Jackson, S.E. (1999) 'Managing work role performance: Challenges for twenty-first century organizations and their employees', in D.R. Ilgen and E.D. Pulakos (eds), *The Changing Nature of Performance: Implications for staffing, motivation and development*. San Francisco, CA: Jossey-Bass.

Murray, H.J. (1938) *Explorations in Personality*. Oxford: Oxford University Press.

Myors, B., Lievens, F., Schollaert, E., Van Hoye, G., Cronshaw, S.F., M ladinic, A. *et al.* (2008) International perspective on the legal environment for selection. *Industrial and Organizational Psychology: Perspectives on Science and Practice*, 1, 206–46.

Nadler, D.A. (1993) 'Concepts for the management of strategic change', in C. Mabey and B. Mayon-White (eds), *Managing Change*, 2nd edition. London: Open University/Paul Chapman Publishing.

Nagy, M.S. (2002) 'Using a single-item approach to measure facet job satisfaction', *Journal of Occupational and Organizational Psychology*, 75, 77–86.

Nathan, R. and Hill, L. (2006) *Career Counselling*, 2nd edition. London: Sage.

Nauta, M.M. and Kahn, J.H. (2007) 'Identity status, consistency and differentiation of interests and career self-efficacy', *Journal of Career Assessment*, 15, 55–65.

Nelson, D.L. and Burke, R.J. (2000) 'Women, work stress and health', in M.J. Davidson and R.J. Burke (eds), *Women in Management*. London: Sage.

Nelson-Jones, R. (2009) *Introduction to Counselling Skills*, 3rd edition. London: Sage.

Nemeth, C.J. (1986) 'Differential contributions of majority and minority influence', *Psychological Review*, 93, 23–32.

Nemetz, P.L. and Christensen, S.L. (1996) 'The challenge of cultural diversity: Harnessing adversity of views to understand multiculturalism', *Academy of Management Review*, 21, 434–62.

Ng, E.S.W. and Burke, R.J. (2005) 'Person–organization fit and the war for talent: Does diversity make a difference?', *International Journal of Human Resource Management*, 16, 1195–210.

Ng, K.Y. and Van Dyne, L. (2001) 'Individualism–collectivism as a boundary condition for effectiveness of minority influence in decision making', *Organizational Behavior and Human Decision Processes*, 84(2), 198–225.

Ng, T. and Feldman, D.C. (2007) 'Organizational embeddedness and occupational embeddedness across career stages', *Journal of Vocational Behavior*, 70, 336–51.

Ng, T. and Feldman, D.C. (2009) 'Re-examining the relationship between age and voluntary turnover', *Journal of Vocational Behavior*, 74, 283–94.

Ng, T., Eby, L.T., Sorensen, K.L. and Feldman, D.C. (2005) 'Predictors of objective and subjective career success: A meta-analysis', *Personnel Psychology*, 58, 367–408.

Ng, T., Sorensen, K. and Eby, L.T. (2006) 'Locus of control at work: A meta-analysis', *Journal of Organizational Behavior*, 27, 1057–87.

Ng, T.W. and Sorenson, K.L. (2008), 'Toward a further understanding of the relationships between perceptions of support and work attitudes', *Group and Organization Management*, 33, 243–68.

Nicholson, N. and West, M.A. (1988) *Managerial Job Change: Men and women in transition*. Cambridge: Cambridge University Press.

Nicholson, N. and de Waal-Andrews, W. (2005) 'Playing to win: Biological imperatives, self-regulation and trade-offs in the game of career success', *Journal of Organizational Behaviour*, 26, 137–54.

Nielsen, K., Randall, R. and Albertsen, K. (2007) 'Participants' appraisals of process issues and the effects of stress management interventions', *Journal of Organizational Behavior*, 28, 793–810.

Nielsen, K., Randall, R., Yarker, J. and Brenner, S.-O. (2008a) 'The effects of transformational leadership on followers' perceived work characteristics and well-being: A longitudinal study', *Work and Stress*, 22, 16–32.

Nielsen, K., Yarker, J., Brenner, S.-O., Randall, R. and Borg, V. (2008b) 'The importance of transformational leadership style for the well-being of employees working with older people', *Journal of Advanced Nursing*, 63, 465–75.

NIOSH (1993) *A National Strategy for the Prevention of Psychological Disorders in the Workplace*. Cincinnati, OH: NIOSH.

NIOSH and Sauter, S., Murphy, L., Colligan, M., Hurrel, J., Scharf, F., Sinclair, R., Grubb, Goldenhar, L., Alterman, T., Johnston, J., Hamilton, A., Tisdale, J. (1999) *Stress at Work*, available at http://www.cdc.gov/niosh/stresswk.html.

Nisbett, R. and Wilson, T. (1977) 'Telling more than we know: Verbal reports on mental processes', *Psychological Review*, 84, 231–59.

Nonaka, I. (1988) 'Creating organizational order out of chaos: Self-renewal in Japanese firms', *Harvard Business Review*, November–December, 96–104.

Novicevic, M.M. and Harvey, M.G. (2004) 'The political role of corporate human resource management in strategic global leadership development', *The Leadership Quarterly*, 15, 569–88.

Noyes, J. (2001) *Designing for Humans (Psychology at Work)*. Hove: Psychology Press.

Nystrom, P.C. and Starbuck, W.H. (1984) 'To avoid crises, unlearn', *Organizational Dynamics*, 12(4), 53–65.

Nytrø, K., Saksvik, P.Ø., Mikkelsen, A., Bohle, P. and Quinlan, M. (2000) 'An appraisal of key factors in the implementation of occupational stress interventions', *Work and Stress*, 14, 213–25.

O'Driscoll, M.P. and Brough, P. (2010) 'Work organization and health', in S. Leka and J. Houdmont (eds), *Occupational Health Psychology: A key text*. Wiley-Blackwell.

O'Neil, D.A. and Bilimoria, D. (2005) 'Women's career development phases: Idealism, endurance and reinvention', *Career Development International*, 10, 168–89.

O'Reilly, C. (1989) 'Corporations, culture and commitment', *California Management Review*, 31, 9–24.

O'Reilly, C.A. and Caldwell, D.F. (1985) 'The impact of normative social influence and cohesiveness on task perceptions and attitudes: A social information-processing approach', *Journal of Occupational Psychology*, 58, 193–206.

Offerrmann, L.R. and Gowing, M.K. (1990) 'Organizations of the future', *American Psychologist*, 45, 95–108.

Office for National Statistics (2009a) *Labour Market Statistics, March 2009*. Newport: ONS. Available at http://www.statistics.gov.uk/pdfdir/lmsuk0309.pdf.

Office for National Statistics (2009b) *Economic and Labour Market Review*, 3(2). London: Palgrave Macmillan.

Ogbonna, E. and Harris, L.C. (2002) 'Managing organisational culture: insights from the hospitality industry', *Human Resource Management Journal*, 12(1), 33–53.

Okin, J.R. (2005) *The Technology Revolution: The not-for-dummies guide to the impact, perils and promise of the internet*. Winter Harbour, ME: Ironbound Press.

Oliver, M. (1990) *The Politics of Disablement*. London: Macmillan.

Olkkonen, M.E. and Lipponen, J. (2006) 'Relationships between organizational justice, identification with organization and work unit and group-related outcomes', *Organizational Behavior and Human Decision Processes*, 100, 202–15.

Ones, D.S. and Viswesvaran, C. (1998) 'Gender, age, and race differences on overt integrity tests: results across four large-scale job applicant data sets', *Journal of Applied Psychology*, 83(1), 35–42.

Ones, D.S. and Viswesvaran, C. (2003) 'Job-specific applicant pools and national norms for personality scales: implications for range-restriction corrections in validation research', *Journal of Applied Psychology*, 88(3), 570–7.

Ones, D.S., Dilchert, S., Viswesvaran, C. and Judge, T.A. (2007a) 'In support of personality assessment in organizational settings', *Personnel Psychology*, 60, 995–1027.

Ones, D.S., Viswesvaran, C. and Dilchert, S. (2007b) 'Cognitive ability in personnel selection decisions', in A. Evers, O. Voskuijl and N. Anderson (eds), *Handbook of Selection* Oxford: Blackwell.

Organ, D.W. (1988) *Organizational Citizenship Behavior: The good soldier syndrome.* Lexington, MA: Lexington.

Organ, D.W. (1997) 'Organizational citizenship behavior: It's construct clean-up time', *Human Performance*, 10, 85–98.

Osborn, A.F. (1957) *Applied Imagination*, revised edition. New York: Scribner.

Oswald, F.L. and Converse, P.D. (2005) Correcting for reliability and range restriction in meta-analysis. Symposium presented at the 20th Annual Conference of the Society for Industrial and Organizational Psychology, (SIOP), Los Angeles, CA.

Oswald, F.L., Schmit, N., Kim, B.H., Ramsay, L.J. and Gillespie, M.A. (2004) 'Developing a biodata measure and situational judgment inventory as predictors of college student performance', *Journal of Applied Psychology*, 89, 187–207.

Palmer, S. and Cooper, C. (2007) *How to Deal with Stress.* London: Kogan Page.

Palmer, S. and Whybrow, A. (eds) (2006) *The Handbook of Coaching Psychology: A guide for practitioners.* London: Routledge.

Papadakis, V.M. and Barwise, P. (2002) 'How much do CEOs and top management matter in strategic decision-making?', *British Journal of Management*, 13(1), 83–95.

Parasuraman, R., Sheridan, T.B. and Wickens, C.D. (2000) 'A model for types and levels of human interaction with automation', *IEEE Transactions on Systems, Man and Cybernetics – Part A*, 30, 286–97.

Paris, C.R., Salas, E. and Cannon-Bowers, J.A. (2000) 'Teamwork in multi-person systems: a review and analysis, *Ergonomics*, 43(8), 1052–75.

Park, W. (2000) 'A comprehensive empirical investigation of the relationships among variables of the groupthink model', *Journal of Organizational Behavior*, 21, 873–87.

Parker, B. and Chusmir, L.H. (1991) 'Motivation needs and their relationship to life success', *Human Relations*, 44, 1301–12.

Parker, S.K. and Wall, T.D. (1998) *Job and Work Design.* San Francisco, CA: Sage.

Parker, S.K., Wall, T.D. and Cordery, J.L. (2001) 'Future work design research and practice: Towards an elaborated model of work design', *Journal of Occupational and Organizational Psychology*, 74, 413–40.

Parkes, K.R. and Sparkes, T.J. (1998) *Organizational Interventions to Reduce Work Stress: Are they effective? A review of the literature.* Sudbury: HSE Books.

Parks, K.M. and Steelman, L.A. (2008) 'Organizational wellness programs: A meta-analysis', *Journal of Occupational Health Psychology*, 13, 58–68.

Pascoe E.A and Smart Richman, L. (2009) 'Perceived discrimination and health: a meta-analytic review', *Psychological Bulletin*, 135, 531–54.

Patrick, J. (1992) *Training: Research and practice.* London: Academic Press.

Patterson, F. (2001) 'Developments in work psychology: Emerging issues and future trends', *Journal of Occupational and Organizational Psychology*, 74(4), 381–90.

Patterson, F. (2002) 'Great minds don't think alike? Person level predictors of innovation at work', *International Review of Industrial and Organisational Psychology*, 17, 115–44.

Patterson, F. (2004) 'Personal initiative and innovation', in C. Spielberger (ed.), *Encyclopaedia of Applied Psychology.* London: Elsevier.

Patterson, F. and Ferguson, E. (2007) *Selection into Medical Education and Training.* ASME monographs. Edinburgh: ASME.

Patterson, F., Baron, H., Carr, V., Plint, S. and Lane, P. (2009) 'Evaluation of three short-listing methodologies for selection into postgraduate training in general practice', *Medical Education*, 43, 50–57.

Patterson, F., Ferguson, E., Lane, P., Farrell, K., Martlew, J. and Wells, A. (2000) 'A competency model for general practice: implications for selection, training, and development', *British Journal of General Practice*, 50(452), 188–93.

Patterson, F., Ferguson, E., Norfolk, T. and Lane, P. (2005) 'A new selection system to recruit GP registrars: Preliminary findings from a validation study', *British Medical Journal*, 330, 711–14.

Patterson, F., Ferguson, E. and Thomas, S. (2008) 'Using job analyses to identify core and specific competencies for three secondary care specialties: Implications for selection and recruitment', *Medical Education*, 42, 1195–204.

Paul, K.I. and Moser, K. (2006) 'Incongruence as an explanation for the negative mental health effects of unemployment: Meta-analytic evidence', *Journal of Occupational and Organizational Psychology*, 79, 595–621.

Paul, K.I. and Moser, K. (2009) 'Unemployment impairs mental health: Meta-analyses', *Journal of Vocational Behavior*, 74, 264–82.

Paulus, P.B. (2000) 'Groups, teams, and creativity: The creative potential of idea-generating groups', *Applied Psychology: An International Review*, 49(2), 237–62.

Peeters, M., Van Tuijl, H., Rutte, C. and Reymen, I. (2006) 'Personality and team performance: A meta-analysis', *European Journal of Personality*, 20, 377–96.

Pelled, L.H., Eisenhardt, K.M. and Xin, K.R. (1999) 'Exploring the black box: An analysis of work group diversity, conflict and performance', *Administrative Science Quarterly*, 44, 1–28.

Pendry, L.F. and Macrae, C.N. (1996) 'What the disinterested perceiver overlooks: Goal-directed social observation', *Personality and Social Psychology Bulletin*, 22, 249–56.

Perlmutter, M. and Hall, E. (1992) *Adult Development and Aging*, 2nd edition. New York: John Wiley.

Perrone K.M., Gordon P.A. and Fitch J.C. (2003) 'The adult career concerns inventory: development of a short form', *Journal of Employment Counseling*, 40, 172–80.

Pervin, L.A. (1980) *Personality: Theory, assessment and research*, 3rd edition. New York: John Wiley.

Peters, L.H., Hartke, D.D. and Pohlmann, J.T. (1985) 'Fiedler's contingency theory of leadership: An application of the meta-analysis procedures of Schmidt and Hunter', *Psychological Bulletin*, 97, 274–85.

Peters, T. (1989) *Thriving on Chaos*. London: Pan.

Peters, T. (1997) *The Circle of Innovation: You can't shrink your way to greatness*. New York: Alfred A. Knopf.

Peters, T. and Waterman, R.H. (1982) *In Search of Excellence: Lessons from America's best-run companies*. London: Harper and Row.

Peterson, B.E. and Stewart, A.J. (1996) 'Antecedents and contexts of generativity motivation at midlife', *Psychology and Aging*, 11, 22–33.

Peterson, M.F., Smith, P.B. and Tayeb, M.H. (1993) 'Development and use of English versions of Japanese PM leadership measures in electronics plants', *Journal of Organizational Behavior*, 14, 251–67.

Pettigrew, A. and Whipp, R. (1993) 'Understanding the environment', in C. Mabey and B. Mayon-White (eds), *Managing Change*, 2nd edition. London: The Open University/Paul Chapman Publishing.

Pettigrew, A.M. (1987) 'Context and action in the transformation of the firm', *Journal of Management Sciences*, 24(6), 649–70.

Pettigrew, A.M. (1990a) 'Longitudinal field research on change: Theory and practice', *Organizational Science*, 3(1), 267–92.

Pettigrew, A.M. (1990b) 'Studying strategic choice and strategic change', *Organizational Studies*, 11(1), 6–11.

Pettigrew, A.M. (1997) 'What is a processual analysis?', *Scandinavian Journal of Management*, 13(40), 337–48.

Pettigrew, A.M., Ferlie, E. and McKee, L. (1992) *Shaping Strategic Change*. London: Sage.

Pettigrew, T.F. (1998) 'Intergroup contact theory', *Annual Review of Psychology*, 49, 65–85.

Petty, R.E. and Cacioppo, J.T. (1985) 'The elaboration likelihood model of persuasion', in L. Berkowitz (ed.), *Advances in Experimental Social Psychology*, vol. 19. New York: Academic Press.

Petty, R.E. and Krosnick, J.A. (1992) *Attitude Strength: Antecedents and consequences*. Hillsdale, NJ: Lawrence Erlbaum.

Peyton P.R. (2003) *Dignity at Work: Eliminate bullying and create a positive working environment*. London: Routledge.

Pfau, M. (1997) 'The inoculation model of resistance to influence', *Programme Communication Sci*, 13, 133–71.

Pfeffer, J. (1991) 'Organization theory and structural perspectives on management', *Journal of Management*, 17, 789–803.

Pfeffer, J. (1992) *Managing with Power: Politics and influence in organizations*. Boston, MA: Harvard Business School Press.

Phillips, S.D., Friedlander, M.L., Pazienza, N.L. and Kost, P.P. (1985) 'A factor analytic investigation of career decision-making styles', *Journal of Vocational Behavior*, 26, 106–15.

Pierce, J.L., Jussila, I. and Cummings, A. (2009) 'Psychological ownership within the job design context: revision of the job characteristics model', *Journal of Organizational Behavior*, 30, 477–96.

Pillai, R. and Meindl, J.R. (1991) 'The impact of a performance crisis on attributions of charismatic leadership: A preliminary study'. Paper presented at the Eastern Academy of Management, Hartford, CT.

Pio, E. (2005) 'Knotted strands: Working lives of Indian women migrants in New Zealand', *Human Relations*, 58, 1277–300.

Podsakoff, N.P., LePine, J.A. and LePine, M.A. (2007) 'Differential challenge stressor–hindrance stressor relationships with job attitudes, turnover intentions, turnover and withdrawal behavior: A meta-analysis', *Journal of Applied Psychology*, 92, 438–54.

Podsakoff, N.P., Whiting, S.W., Podsakoff, P.M. and Blume, B.D. (2009) 'Individual- and organizational-level consequences of organizational citizenship behaviors: A meta-analysis', *Journal of Applied Psychology*, 94, 122–41.

Polzer, J.T., Crisp, D.B., Jarvenpaa, S.L. and Kim, J.W. (2006) 'Extending the faultline model to geographically dispersed teams: How collocated subgroups can impair group functioning', *Academy of Management Journal*, 49, 679–92.

Port, R. and Patterson, F. (2003) 'Maximising the benefits of psychometric testing in selection', *Selection Development Review, Special issue, Test Users Conference*, 9(6), 6–11.

Posthuma, R.A., Morgeson, F.P. and Campion, M.A. (2002) 'Beyond employment interview validity: A comprehensive narrative review of recent research and trends over time', *Personnel Psychology*, 55, 1–81.

Potosky, D. and Bobko, P. (2004) 'Selection testing via the Internet: practical considerations and exploratory empirical findings', *Personnel Psychology*, 57, 1003–34.

Potter, J. (1997) 'Discourse analysis as a way of analysing naturally occurring talk', in D. Silverman (ed.), *Qualitative Research: Theory, method and practice*. London: Sage.

Pratkanis, A.R. and Turner, M.E. (1994) 'Of what value is a job attitude? A socio-cognitive analysis', *Human Relations*, 47, 1545–76.

Pressman, R.S. (1992) *Software Engineering: A practitioner's approach*. New York: McGraw-Hill.

Price, R.E. and Patterson, F. (2003) 'Online application forms: psychological impact on applicants and implications for recruiters', *Selection and Development Review*, 19(2), 12–19.

Pringle, J. and Mallon, M. (2003) 'Challenges for the boundaryless career odyssey', *International Journal of Human Resource Management*, 14, 839–53.

Pritchard, R.D. (1969) 'Equity theory: A review and critique', *Organizational Behavior and Human Performance*, 4, 176–211.

Procter, S. and Currie, G. (2002) 'How teamworking works in the Inland Revenue: Meaning operation and impact', *Personnel Review*, 31(3), 304–19.

Proudford, K.L. and Smith K.K. (2003) 'Group membership salience and the movement of conflict', *Group and Organization Management*, 28, 18–44.

Pruitt, D.G. (1981) *Negotiation Behavior*. New York: Academic Press.

Pruitt, D.G. and Rubin, J.Z. (1986) *Social Conflict: Escalation, stalemate and settlement*. New York: Random House.

Pruitt, D.G. and Syna, H. (1985) 'Mismatching the opponent's offers in negotiations', *Journal of Experimental Social Psychology*, 21, 103–13.

Ptacek, J.T., Smith, R.E. and Dodge, K.L. (1994) 'Gender differences in coping with stress: When stressor and appraisals do not differ', *Personality and Social Psychology Bulletin*, 20, 421–30.

Pugh, D. (1993) 'Understanding and managing organizational change', in C. Mabey and B. Mayon-White (eds), *Managing Change*, 2nd edition. London: Open University/Paul Chapman Publishing.

Quick, J.C. and Quick, J.D. (1984) *Organizational Stress and Preventive Management*. New York: McGraw-Hill.

Quinn, J.B. (1993) 'Managing strategic change', in C. Mabey and B. Mayon-White (eds), *Managing Change*, 2nd edition. London: Open University/Paul Chapman Publishing.

Quinn, R.E. and McGrath, M.R. (1985) 'The transformation of organizational cultures: A competing values perspective', in P.J. Frost, L.F. Moore, M.R. Louis, C.C. Lundberg and J. Martin (eds), *Organizational Culture*. Newbury Park, CA: Sage.

Rafferty, A.E. and Griffin, M.A. (2006) 'Perceptions of organizational change: A stress and coping perspective', *Journal of Applied Psychology*, 91, 1154–62.

Rail Safety and Standards Board (2008) *Understanding Human Factors: A guide for the railway industry*. London: Rail Safety and Standards Board, available at http://www.rssb.co.uk/pdf/Guide_Jun_08_screen_version.pdf.

Rajan, J. (1997) 'Interface design for safety critical systems', in F. Redill and J. Rajan (eds), *Human Factors in Safety Critical Systems*. London: Butterworth-Heinemann.

Raley, A.B., Lucas, J.L. and Blazek, M.A. (2003) 'Representation of I-O psychology in introductory psychology textbooks', *The Industrial-Organizational Psychologist*, 41, 62–6.

Ramakrishna, H.V. and Potosky, D. (2003) 'Conceptualisation and exploration of composite carer anchors: An analysis of information systems personnel', *Human Resource Development Quarterly*, 14, 199–214.

Randall, R. and Lewis, R. (2007) 'Stress management interventions', in E. Donaldson-Feilder (ed.), *Well-being and Performance*. London: CIPD.

Randall, R., Cox, T. and Griffiths, A. (2007) 'Participants' accounts of a stress management intervention', *Human Relations*, 60, 1181–209.

Randall, R., Griffiths, A. and Cox, T. (2005) 'Evaluating organizational stress-management interventions using adapted study designs', *European Journal of Work and Organizational Psychology*, 14, 23–41.

Randall, R., Nielsen, N. and Tvedt, S. (2009) 'The development of five scales to measure participants' appraisals of organizational-level stress management interventions', *Work and Stress*, 23, 1–23.

Rantanen, J., Metsäpelto, R.L., Feldt, T., Pulkkinen, L. and Kokko, K. (2007) 'Long-term stability in the Big Five personality traits in adulthood', *Scandinavian Journal of Psychology*, 48, 511–18.

Rasmussen, T.H. and Jeppesen, H.J. (2006) 'Teamwork and associated psychological factors: A review', *Work and Stress*, 20(2), 105–28.

Rauch, A. and Frese, M. (2007) 'Let's put the person back into entrepreneurship research: A meta-analysis on the relationship between business owners' personality traits, business creation and success', *European Journal of Work and Organizational Psychology*, 16, 353–85.

Rauschenberger, J., Schmitt, N. and Hunter, J.E. (1980) 'A test of the need hierarchy concept by a Markov model of change in need strength', *Administrative Science Quarterly*, 25, 654–70.

Raven, J., Raven, J.C. and Court, J.H. (1996) *Raven's Progressive Matrices, Professional Manual*. Oxford: Oxford Psychologists Press.

Rayner, C., Hoel, H. and Cooper, C.L. (2001) *Workplace Bullying: What we know, who is to blame and what we can do*. London: Taylor and Francis.

Rayner, C., Hoel, H. and Cooper, C.L. (2002) *Workplace Bullying*. London: Taylor and Francis.

Rayner, C., Sheehan, M. and Marker, M. (1999) 'Theoretical approaches to the study of bullying at work', *The International Journal of Manpower*, 20, 11–15.

Reardon, R.C. and Lenz, J.G. (1998) *The Self-directed Search and Related Holland Career Materials: A practitioner's guide*. Odessa, FL: Psychological Assessment Resources Inc.

Reddy, M. (1987) *The Managers' Guide to Counselling at Work*. Leicester: British Psychological Society.

Rees, D. and Porter, C. (2001) *The Skills of Management*. London: Thomson Learning.

Reichers, A.E. (1985) 'A review and re-conceptualization of organizational commitments', *Academy of Management Review*, 10, 465–76.

Reiss, S. and Havercamp, S.M. (2005) 'Motivation in developmental context: A new method for studying self-actualization', *Journal of Humanistic Psychology*, 45, 41–53.

Reiter-Palmon, R., Sandall, D., Buboltz, C. and Nimps, T. (2006) 'Development of an O*NET web-based job analysis and its implementation in the US Navy: Lessons learned', *Human Resource Management Review*, 16(3), 294–309.

Reitman, F. and Schneer, J.A. (2005) 'The long-term negative impacts of managerial career interruptions – a longitudinal study of men and women MBAs', *Group and Organization Management*, 30, 243–62.

Rennecker, J.A. (2002) 'The situated nature of virtual teamwork: Understanding the constitutive role of "place" in the enactment of virtual work configurations'. Paper presented at the Academy of Management Conference, Denver, CO.

Restubog, S.L.D., Bordiaw, P. and Tang, R.L. (2007) 'Behavioural outcomes of psychological contract breach in a non-western culture: The moderating role of equity sensitivity', *British Journal of Management*, 18, 376–86.

Richard, O.C. and Johnson, N.B. (1999) 'Making the connection between formal human resource diversity practices and organizational effectiveness: Behind management fashion', *Performance Improvement Quarterly*, 12, 77–96.

Richardson, K.M. and Rothstein, H.R. (2008) 'Effects of occupational stress management programs: A meta-analysis', *Journal of Occupational Health Psychology*, 13, 69–93.

Riketta, M. (2008) 'The causal relation between job attitudes and performance: A meta-analysis of panel studies', *Journal of Applied Psychology*, 93, 472–81.

Riopelle, K., Gluesing, J.C., Baba, M.L., Britt, D., McKether, W., Montplaisir, L., Ratner, H. and Wagner, K.H. (2003) 'Context, task and the evolution of technology use in global virtual teams', in C.B. Gibson and S.G. Cohen (eds), *Virtual Teams that Work: Creating conditions for effective virtual teams*. San Francisco, CA: Jossey-Bass.

Roberts, B.W., Walton, K.E. and Viechtbauer, W. (2006) 'Patterns of mean-level change in personality traits across the life course: A meta-analysis of longitudinal studies', *Psychological Bulletin*, 132, 26–8.

Roberts, P. and Newton, P.M. (1987) 'Levinsonian studies of women's adult development', *Psychology and Aging*, 2, 154–63.

Robertson Cooper (2008) *Well-being at Work: The new view*. Manchester: Robertson Cooper Ltd.

Robertson, I.T. and Flint-Taylor, J. (2008) 'Leadership, psychological well-being and organisational outcomes', in S. Cartwright and C.L. Cooper (eds), *Oxford Handbook on Organisational Well-being*. Oxford: Oxford University Press.

Robertson, I.T. and Smith, M. (2001) 'Personnel selection', *Journal of Occupational and Organizational Psychology*, 74, 441–72.

Robinson, D., Perryman, S. and Hayday, S. (2004) *The Drivers of Employee Engagement*. Brighton: Institute for Employment Studies.

Robinson, S.L. and Morrison, E.W. (2000) 'The development of psychological contract breach and violation: A longitudinal study', *Journal of Organizational Behavior*, 21, 525–46.

Robinson, S.L. and Rousseau, D.M. (1994) 'Violating the psychological contract: Not the exception but the norm', *Journal of Organizational Behavior*, 15, 245–59.

Roethlisberger, F.J. and Dickson, W.J. (1939) *Management and the Worker*. New York: John Wiley.

Rogers, C.R. (1970) *On Becoming a Person*. Boston, MA: Houghton Mifflin.

Rogers, R.W. (1983) 'Cognitive and physiological processes in fear appeals and attitude change: A revised theory of protection motivation', in J.T. Cacioppo and R.E. Petty (eds), *Social Psychophysiology*. New York: Guilford.

Rogers, R.W. and Prentice-Dunn, S. (1997) 'Protection motivation theory', in D. Gochman (ed.), *Handbook of Health Behavior Research*, vol. 1. New York: Plenham.

Ronen, S. and Shenkar, O. (1985) 'Clustering countries on attitudinal dimensions: A review and synthesis', *Academy of Management Review*, 10, 435–54.

Rosenfeld, P., Giacalone, R.A. and Riordan, C.A. (2002) *Impression Management: Building and enhancing reputations at work*. London: Thomson Learning.

Rosenman, R.H., Friedman, M. and Straus, R. (1964) 'A predictive study of CHD', *Journal of the Medical Association*, 189, 15–22.

Rosenthal, R. and DiMatteo, M.R. (2000) 'Meta analysis: Recent developments in quantitative methods for literature reviews', *Annual Review of Psychology*, 52, 59–82.

Rosenthal, R. and Rosnow, R.L. (1984) *Essentials of Behavioral Research, Methods and Data Analysis*. New York: McGraw-Hill.

Ross, L. (1977) 'The intuitive psychologist and his shortcoming: Distortions in the attribution process', *Advances in Experimental Social Psychology*, 10, 174–220.

Rothman, I. and Cooper, C.L. (2008) *Organizational Work Psychology*. London: Hodder Education

Rotundo, M. and Sackett, P. (2002) 'The relative importance of task citizenship and counterproductive performance to global ratings of job performance: A policy-capturing approach', *Journal of Applied Psychology*, 87, 66–80.

Rousseau, D.M. (1990) 'New hire perceptions of their own and their employer's obligations: A study of psychological contracts', *Journal of Organizational Behavior*, 11, 389–400.

Rousseau, D.M. (1995) *Psychological Contracts in Organizations*. London: Sage.

Rousseau, D.M. (1998) 'The "problem" of the psychological contract considered', *Journal of Organizational Behavior*, 19, 665–71.

Rousseau, D.M. (2001) 'Schema, promise and mutuality: The building blocks of the psychological contract', *Journal of Occupational and Organizational Psychology*, 74, 511–42.

Rousseau, D.M. and Fried, Y. (2001) 'Location, location, location: Contextualizing organizational research', *Journal of Organizational Behavior*, 22, 1–13.

Rowan, J. (1998) 'Maslow amended', *Journal of Humanistic Psychology*, 28, 81–92.

Rowold, J. and Heinitz, K. (2007) 'Transformational and charismatic leadership: Assessing the convergent, divergent and criterion validity of the MLQ and the CKS', *The Leadership Quarterly*, 18, 121–33.

Rubin, I. (1967) 'Increasing self-acceptance: A means of reducing prejudice', *Journal of Personality and Social Psychology*, 5, 233–38.

Ryan, A.M., Chan, D., Ployhart, R.E. and Slade, L.A. (1999) 'Employee attitude surveys in a multinational organization: Considering language and culture in assessing measurement equivalence', *Personnel Psychology*, 52, 37–58.

Ryan, R.M. and Deci, E.L. (2000) 'Intrinsic and extrinsic motivations: Classic definitions and new directions', *Contemporary Educational Psychology*, 25, 54–67.

Ryan, T.A. (1970) *Intentional Behavior*. New York: Ronald Press.

Ryff, C.D. and Keyes, C.L.M. (1995) 'The structure of psychological well-being revisited', *Journal of Personality and Social Psychology*, 69, 719–27.

Rynes, S.L., Gerhart, B. and Minette, K.A. (2004) 'The importance of pay in employee motivation: Discrepancies between what people say and what they do', *Human Resource Management*, 43, 381–94.

Rynes, S.L., McNatt, D.B. and Bretz, R.D. (1999) 'Academic research inside organisations: Inputs, processes and outcomes', *Personnel Psychology*, 52, 869–98.

Sackett, P. and Lievens, F. (2008) 'Personnel selection', *Annual Review of Psychology*, 59, 419–45.

Sackett, P.R. and Tuzinski, K.A. (2001) 'The role of dimensions and exercises in assessment centre judgements', in M. London (ed.), *How People Evaluate Others in Organizations*. London: LEA.

Sackett, P.R. and Yang, H. (2000) 'Correction for range restriction: an expanded typology', *Journal of Applied Psychology*, 85, 112–18.

Sackett, P.R., Borneman, M.J. and Connelly B.S. (2008) 'High stakes testing in higher education and employment: appraising the evidence for validity and fairness', *The American Psychologist*, 63, 215–27.

Sagie, A., Elizur, D. and Yamauchi, A. (1996) 'The structure and strength of achievement motivation: A cross-cultural comparison', *Journal of Organizational Behavior*, 17, 431–44.

Saks, A.M. and Ashforth, B.E. (1999) 'Effects of individual differences and job search behaviors on the employment status of recent university graduates', *Journal of Vocational Behavior*, 54, 335–49.

Saksvik, P.Ø., Nytrø, K., Dahl-Jørgensen, C. and Mikkelsen, A. (2002) 'A process evaluation of individual and organizational occupational stress and health interventions', *Work and Stress*, 16, 37–57.

Salancik, G.R. and Pfeffer, J. (1977) 'An examination of need satisfaction models of job attitudes', *Administrative Science Quarterly*, 22, 427–56.

Salancik, G.R. and Pfeffer, J.C. (1978) 'A social information processing approach to job attitudes and task design', *Administrative Science Quarterly*, 23, 224–53.

Salas, E., Rozell, D., Mullen, B. and Driskell, J.E. (1999) 'The effect of team building on performance – an integration', *Small Group Research*, 30(3), 309–29.

Salgado, J. (2003) 'FFM and non-FFM personality predictors of work performance', *Journal of Occupational and Organizational Psychology*, 76, 323–46.

Salgado, J.F., Anderson, N., Moscoso, S., Bertua, C. and de Fruyt, F. (2003) 'International validity generalization of GMA and cognitive abilities: A European Community meta-analysis', *Personnel Psychology*, 56, 573–605.

Salgado, J.F., Viswesvaran, C. and Ones, D. (2001) 'Predictors used for personnel selection: An overview of constructs, methods, techniques', in N. Anderson, D.S. Ones, H.K. Sinangil and C. Viswesvaran (eds), *Handbook of Industrial, Work and Organizational Psychology*. London: Sage.

Salin, D. (2003) 'Ways of explaining workplace bullying: A review of enabling, motivating and precipitating structures and processes in the work environment', *Human Relations*, 56, 1213–32.

Sampson, J.P.J. and Lumsden, J.A. (2000) 'Ethical issues in the design and use of internet-based career assessment', *Journal of Career Assessment*, 8, 21–35.

Sanchez, J. and Levine, E. (2001) 'The analysis of work in the twentieth and twenty-first centuries', in N. Anderson, D. Ones, H.K. Sinangil and C. Viswesvaran (eds), *Handbook of Industrial, Work and Organizational Psychology*, vol. 1. London and New York: Sage

Sandberg, J. (2000) 'Understanding human competence at work: An interpretative approach', *Academy of Management Journal*, 43, 9–25.

Savickas, M.L. (2007) 'Occupational choice', in H. Gunz and M. Peiperl (eds), *Handbook of Career Studies*. London: Sage.

Savickas, M.L. and Baker, D.B. (2005) 'The history of vocational psychology: Antecedents, origins and early development', in W.B. Walsh and M.L. Savickas (eds), *Handbook of Vocational Psychology*, 3rd edition. Mahwah, NJ: Erlbaum.

Sawilowsky, S.S. and Blair, R.C. (1992) 'A more realistic look at the robustness and type II error properties of the t-test to departures from population normality', *Psychological Bulletin*, 111, 352–60.

Scandura, T.A. (1998) 'Dysfunctional mentoring relationships and outcomes', *Journal of Management*, 24, 449–67.

Scarbrough, H. (2003) 'Knowledge management', in D. Holman, T.D. Wall, C.W. Clegg, P. Sparrow and A. Howard (eds), *The New Workplace*. Chichester: John Wiley.

Scarbrough, H. and Kinnie, N. (2003) 'Barriers to the development of teamworking in UK firms', *Industrial Relations Journal*, 34(2), 135–49.

Schaubroeck, J. and Kuehn, K. (1992) 'Research design in industrial and organizational psychology', in C.L. Cooper and I.T. Robertson (eds), *International Review of Industrial and Organizational Psychology*, vol. 7. Chichester: John Wiley.

Schaufeli, W.B., Salanova, M., González-Romá, V. and Bakker, A.B. (2002) 'The measurement of engagement and burnout: A two sample confirmatory factor analytic approach', *Journal of Happiness Studies*, 3, 71–92.

Schein, E.H. (1978) *Career Dynamics: Matching individual and organizational needs*. Reading, MA: Addison-Wesley.

Schein, E.H. (1985) *Organizational Culture and Leadership: A dynamic view*. San Francisco, CA: Jossey-Bass.

Schein, E.H. (1988) *Organizational Psychology*, 3rd edition. Englewood Cliffs, NJ: Prentice Hall.

Schein, E.H. (1992) *Organizational Culture and Leadership*, 2nd edition. San Francisco, CA: Jossey-Bass.

Schein, E.H. (1993) *Career Anchors: Discovering your real values*, revised edition. London: Pfeiffer and Co.

Schein, E.H. (1996) 'Career anchors revisited: implications for career development in the 21st century', *Academy of Management Executive*, 10, 80–88.

Schein, V.E. (1975) 'The relationship between sex role stereotypes and requisite management characteristics among female managers', *Journal of Applied Psychology*, 60, 340–44.

Schein, V.E., Mueller, R., Lituchy, T. and Liu, J. (1996) 'Think manager – think male: A global phenomenon?', *Journal of Organizational Behavior*, 17, 33–41.

Schippman, J.S., Ash, R.A., Carr, L., Hesketh, B., Pearlman, K. and Battista, M. *et al.* (2000) 'The practice of competency modeling', *Personnel Psychology*, 53, 703–40.

Schmidt, F.L. and Hunter, J.E. (1998) 'The validity and utility of selection methods in personnel psychology: Practical and theoretical implications of 85 years of research findings', *Psychological Bulletin*, 124, 262–74.

Schmidt, F.L. and Hunter, J. (2004) 'General mental ability in the world of work: Occupational attainment and job performance', *Journal of Personality and Social Psychology*, 86, 162–73.

Schmidt, F.L., Hunter, J.E., McKenzie, R.C. and Muldrow, T.W. (1979) 'Impact of valid selection procedures on workforce productivity', *Journal of Applied Psychology*, 64, 609–26.

Schmidt, F.L., Mack, M.J. and Hunter, J.E. (1984) 'Selection utility in the occupation of US Park Rangers for three modes of test use', *Journal of Applied Psychology*, 69, 490–97.

Schmitt, N. (1989) 'Fairness in employment selection', in J.M. Smith and I.T. Robertson (eds), *Advances in Selection and Assessment*. Chichester: John Wiley.

Schmitt, N. and Chan, D. (1998) *Personnel Selection: A theoretical approach*. Thousand Oaks, CA: Sage.

Schneer, J.A. and Reitman, F. (1995) 'The impact of gender as managerial careers unfold', *Journal of Vocational Behavior*, 47, 290–315.

Schneider, B. (1987) 'The people make the place', *Personnel Psychology*, 40, 437–53.

Schneider, B., Ashworth, S.D., Higgs, A.C. and Carr, L. (1996) 'Design, validity and use of strategically focussed employee attitude surveys', *Personnel Psychology*, 49, 695–705.

Schneider, D.J. (1991) 'Social cognition', *Annual Review of Psychology*, 42, 527–61.

Schneider, S.C. and Dunbar, R.L.M. (1992) 'A psychoanalytic reading of hostile takeover events', *Academy of Management Review*, 17, 537–67.

Schneiderman, B. (1998) *Designing the User Interface*. Reading, MA: Addison-Wesley.

Schönpflug, W. (1993) 'Applied psychology: Newcomer with a long tradition', *Applied Psychology: An International Review*, 42, 5–30.

Schriesheim, C.A., Tepper, B.J. and Tetrault, L.A. (1994) 'Least preferred coworker score, situational control, and leadership effectiveness: A meta-analysis of contingency model performance predictions', *Journal of Applied Psychology*, 79, 561–73.

Schultz, D.P. and Schultz, S.E. (2001) *Theories of Personality*, 7th edition. Belmont, CA: Wadsworth/Thomson Learning.

Schulz-Hardt, S., Jochims, M. and Frey, D. (2002) 'Productive conflict in group decision making: Genuine and contrived dissent as strategies to counteract biased information seeking', *Organizational Behavior and Human Decision Processes*, 88, 563–86.

Schwab, D.P., Olian-Gottlieb, J.D. and Heneman, H.G. (1979) 'Between subjects expectancy theory research: A statistical review of studies predicting effort and performance', *Psychological Bulletin*, 86, 139–47.

Scullen, S.E., Bergey, P.K. and Aiman-Smith, L. (2005) 'Forced distribution rating systems and the improvement of workforce potential: A baseline simulation', *Personnel Psychology*, 58, 1–32.

Secord, P.F. and Backman, C.W. (1969) *Social Psychology*. New York: McGraw-Hill.

Seibert, S.E., Kraimer, M.L. and Crant, J.M. (2001) 'What do proactive people do? A longitudinal model linking proactive personality and career success', *Personnel Psychology*, 54, 845–74.

Seijts, G.H. and Latham, G.P. (2001) 'The effect of learning, outcome and proximal goals on a moderately complex task', *Journal of Organizational Behavior*, 22, 291–307.

Seligman, M.E.P., Steen, T.A., Park, N. and Petersen, C. (2005) 'Positive psychology progress: Empirical validation of interventions', *American Psychologist*, 60, 410–21.

Selye, H. (1946) 'The General Adaptation Syndrome and the diseases of adaptation', *Journal of Clinical Endocrinology*, 6, 117.

Selye, H. (1974) *Stress without Distress*. Philadelphia, PA: J.B. Lippincott.

Semmer, N. (2003) 'Job stress interventions and organization of work', in L.Tetrick and J.C. Quick (eds), *Handbook of Occupational Health Psychology*. Washington, DC: American Psychological Association.

Semmer, N.K. (2006) 'Job stress interventions and the organization of work', *Scandinavian Journal of Work and Environmental Health*, 32, 515–27.

Senge, P.M. (2000) 'The puzzles and paradoxes of how living companies create wealth: Why single-valued objective functions are not quite enough', in M. Beer and N. Nohria (eds), *Breaking the Code of Change*. Boston, MA: Harvard Business School Press.

Senger, J.M. (2002) 'Tales of the bazaar: Interest-based negotiation across cultures', *Negotiation Journal*, 18, 233–50.

Senior, B. (2002) *Organisational Change*, 2nd edition. Harlow: FT/Prentice Hall.

Senior, B. and Swailes, S. (2007) 'Inside management teams: Developing a teamwork survey instrument', *British Journal of Management*, 18, 138–53.

Shah, S., Arnold, J. and Travers, C. (2004a) 'The impact of childhood on disabled professionals', *Children and Society*, 18, 194–206.

Shah, S., Travers, C. and Arnold, J. (2004b) 'Disabled and successful: Education in the life stories of disabled high achievers', *Journal of Research in Special Educational Needs*, 4, 122–32.

Shamir, B. and Howell, J.M. (1999) 'Organizational and contextual influences on the emergence and effectiveness of charismatic leadership', *The Leadership Quarterly*, 10, 257–83.

Shamir, B., House, R.J. and Arthur, M.B. (1993) 'The motivational aspects of charismatic leadership: A self-concept theory', *Organization Science*, 4, 1–17.

Shantz, A. and Latham, G.P. (2009) 'An exploratory field experiment of the effect of subconscious and conscious goals on employee performance', *Organizational Behavior and Human Decision Processes*, 109, 9–17.

Sharf, R.F. (1992) *Applying Career Development Theory to Counseling*. Los Angeles, CA: Brooks/Cole.

Shaw, J.B. and Barrett-Power, E. (1998) 'The effects of diversity on small work group processes and performance', *Human Relations*, 51(10), 1307–25.

Shaw, K. (2004) 'Changing the goal-setting process at Microsoft', *Academy of Management Executive*, 18(4), 139–42.

Sheehan, P. (2005) *Generation Y: Thriving and surviving with generation Y at work*. Prahan: Hardy Grant Books

Shepherd, A. (1976) 'An improved tabular format for task analysis', *Journal of Occupational Psychology*, 47, 93–104.

Shepherd, C. (2006) 'Constructing enterprise resource planning: A thoroughgoing interpretivist perspective on technological change', *Journal of Occupational and Organizational Psychology*, 79, 357–76.

Sheridan, T.B. and Verplank, W.L. (1978) *Human and Computer Control of Undersea Teleoperators. MIT, Cambridge, Man-Machine Systems Laboratory Report*. Cambridge, MA: MIT.

Sherif, M. (1966) *Group Conflict and Co-operation*. London: Routledge and Kegan Paul.

Shimmin, S. and Wallis, D. (1994) *Fifty Years of Occupational Psychology in Britain*. Leicester: British Psychological Society.

Shipton, H.J., West, M.A., Parkes, C.L., Dawson, J.F. and Patterson, M.G. (2006) 'When promoting positive feelings pays: Aggregate job satisfaction, work design features and innovation in manufacturing organizations', *European Journal of Work and Organizational Psychology*, 15, 404–30.

Shirom, A., Gilboa, S.S., Fried, Y. and Cooper, C.L. (2008) 'Gender, age and tenure as moderators of work-related stressors' relationships with job performance: A meta-analysis', *Human Relations*, 61, 1371–98.

SHL (1990) *Occupational Personality Questionnaire Manual*. Thames Ditton: Saville and Holdsworth Ltd.

Short, J.E. and Venkatraman, N. (1992) 'Beyond business process redesign: Redefining Baxter's business network', *Sloan Management Review*, Fall, 7–21.

Siegrist, J. (1996) 'Adverse health effects of high-effort/low-reward conditions', *Journal of Occupational Health Psychology*, 1, 27–41.

Sikora, P., Moore, S., Greenberg, E. and Grunberg, L. (2008) 'Downsizing and alcohol use: A cross-lagged longitudinal examination of the spillover hypothesis', *Work and Stress*, 22, 51–68.

Silverman, D. (2001) *Interpreting Qualitative Data*. London: Sage.

Silvester, J. and Anderson, N.R. (2003) 'Technology and discourse: A comparison of face-to-face and telephone employment interviews', *Special Issue on Technology & Selection: International Journal of Selection and Assessment*, 11, 206–14.

Silvester, J., Anderson, N.R., Gibb, A., Haddleton, E. and Cunningham-Snell, N. (2000) 'A cross-modal comparison of the predictive validity of telephone and face-to-face selection interviews', *International Journal of Selection and Assessment*, 8, 16–21.

Silvester, J., Anderson, N.R. and Patterson, F. (1999) 'Organisational culture change: An inter-group attributional analysis', *Journal of Occupational and Organizational Psychology*, 72, 1–23.

Silvester, J., Anderson-Gough, F.M., Anderson, N.R. and Mohammed, A.R. (2002) 'Locus of control, attributions and impression management in the selection interview', *Journal of Occupational and Organizational Psychology*, 75, 59–76.

Silvester, J., Patterson, F. and Ferguson, E. (2003) 'Comparing two attributional models of performance in retail sales: A field study', *Journal of Occupational and Organizational Psychology*, 76, 115–32.

Simonton, D.K. (2004) *Creativity in Science: Chance, logic, genius, and Zeitgeist*. Cambridge, MA: Cambridge University Press.

Simpson, R. and Cohen, C. (2004) 'Dangerous work: The gendered nature of bullying in the context of higher education', *Gender, Work and Organization*, 11, 163–86.

Singh, P. (2008) 'Job analysis for a changing workplace', *Human Resource Management Review*, 18(2), 87–99.

Singh, R., Ragins, B.R. and Tharenou, P. (2009) 'Who gets a mentor? A longitudinal assessment of the rising star hypothesis', *Journal of Vocational Behavior*, 74, 11–17.

Singh, V. and Vinnicombe, S. (2000) 'What does "commitment" really mean?: Views of UK and Swedish engineering managers', *Personnel Review*, 29(1–2), 228–54.

Sitzman, T.M., Kraiger, K., Stewart, D.W. and Wisher, R.A. (2006) 'The comparative effectiveness of web-based and classroom instruction: A meta-analysis', *Personnel Psychology*, 59, 623–64.

Skarlicki, D.P., Folger, R. and Tesluk, P. (1999) 'Personality as a moderator in the relationship between fairness and retaliation', *Academy of Management Journal*, 42, 100–8.

Skinner, B.F. (1948) *Walden Two*. New York: Macmillan.

Skinner, B.F. (1971) *Beyond Freedom and Dignity*. New York: Knopf.

Slivinski, L. W. (2008) 'A test of the relative and incremental predictive validity associated with a set of paper-and-pencil test measures and a set of situational test measures within an assessment centre', *Dissertation Abstracts International: Section B: The Sciences and Engineering*, 68, 4878.

Smith, C.A., Organ, D.W. and Near, J.P. (1983) 'Organizational citizenship behavior: Its nature and antecedents', *Journal of Applied Psychology*, 68, 653–63.

Smith, C.M., Tindale, R.S. and Dugoni, B.L. (1996) 'Minority and majority influence in freely interacting groups: Qualitative versus quantitative differences', *British Journal of Social Psychology*, 35, 137–49.

Smith, J.M. and Robertson, I.T. (1993) *The Theory and Practice of Systematic Personnel Selection*. London: Macmillan.

Smith, M., Beck, J., Cooper, C.L., Cox, C., Ottaway, D. and Talbot, R. (1982) *Introducing Organizational Behaviour*. London: Macmillan.

Smith, P.B., Kruzella, P., Czegledi, R., Tsvetanova, S., Pop, D., Groblewska, B. and Halasova, D. (1997) 'Managerial leadership in Eastern Europe: From uniformity to diversity', in R. Pepermans, A. Buelens, C.J. Vinkenburg and P.G.W. Jansen (eds), *Managerial Behaviour and Practices: European research issues*. Leuven: Acco.

Smith, P.B., Misumi, J., Tayeb, M., Peterson, M. and Bond, M. (1989) 'On the generality of leadership style measures across cultures', *Journal of Occupational Psychology*, 62, 97–109.

Smith, P.C. and Kendall, L.M. (1963) 'Retranslation of expectations: An approach to the construction of unambiguous anchors for rating scales', *Journal of Applied Psychology*, 47, 149–55.

Smith, P.C., Kendall, L.M. and Hulin, C.L. (1969) *The Measurement of Satisfaction in Work and Retirement*. Chicago, IL: Rand-McNally.

Smither, J.W., London, M. and Reilly, R.R. (2005) 'Does performance improve following multi-source feedback? A theoretical model, meta-analysis and review of empirical findings', *Personnel Psychology*, 58, 33–66.

Snow, C., Miles, R. and Coleman, H. (1993) 'Managing 21st century network organizations', in C. Mabey and B. Mayon-White (eds), *Managing Change*, 2nd edition. London: The Open University/Paul Chapman Publishing.

Solinger, O.N., Olffen, W. van and Roe, R.A. (2008) 'Beyond the three-component model of organizational commitment', *Journal of Applied Psychology*, 93, 70–83.

Sonnentag, S. and Niessen, C. (2008) 'Staying vigorous until work is over: The role of trait vigour, day-specific work experiences and recovery', *Journal of Occupational and Organizational Psychology*, 81, 435–58.

Sorge, A. (1997) 'Organization behaviour', in A. Sorge and M. Warner (eds), *The IEBM Handbook of Organizational Behaviour*. London: International Thompson Business Press.

Sosik, J.J. and Godshalk, V.M. (2000) 'Leadership styles, mentoring functions received, and job-related stress: A conceptual model and preliminary study', *Journal of Organizational Behavior*, 21, 365–90.

Spangler, W.D. (1992) 'Validity of questionnaire and TAT measures of need for achievement: Two meta-analyses', *Psychological Bulletin*, 112, 140–54.

Sparks, K. and Cooper, C.L. (1999) 'Occupational differences in the work–strain relationship', *Journal of Occupational and Organizational Psychology*, 72, 219–29.

Sparks, K., Cooper, C., Fried, Y. and Shirom, A. (1997) 'The effects of hours on work and health: A meta-analytic review', *Journal of Occupational and Organizational Psychology*, 70, 391–400.

Sparks, K., Faragher, B. and Cooper, C.L. (2001) 'Well-being and occupational health in the 21st century workplace', *Journal of Occupational and Organizational Psychology*, 74, 489–509.

Sparrow, P. (1999) 'Editorial', *Journal of Occupational and Organizational Psychology*, 72, 261–4.

Sparrow, P. (2003) 'The future of work?', in D. Holman, T.D. Wall, C.W. Clegg, P. Sparrow and A. Howard (eds), *The New Workplace*. Chichester: John Wiley.

Sparrow, P. and Hodgkinson G.P. (2002) *The Competent Organisation: A psychological analysis of the strategic management process*. Milton Keynes: Open University Press.

Spears, R. and Lea, M. (1994) 'Panacea or panopticon: The hidden power in computer-mediated communication', *Communication Research*, 21, 427–59.

Spielberger, C.D., Gorsuch, R.C. and Lushene, R.E. (1970) *Manual for the State Trait Anxiety Inventory*. Paulo Alto, CA: Consulting Psychologists Press.

Spinelli, E. (1989) *The Interpreted World*. London: Sage.

Spokane, A.R., Meir, E.I. and Catalono, M. (2000) 'Person–environment congruence and Holland's theory: A review and reconsideration', *Journal of Vocational Behavior*, 57, 137–87.

Sproull, L. and Kiesler, S. (1986) 'Reducing social-context cues: electronic mail in organizational communication', *Management Science*, 32, 1492–512.

Stace, D. and Dunphy, D. (2001) *Beyond the Boundaries: Leading and re-creating the successful enterprise*, 2nd edition. Sydney: McGraw-Hill.

Stacey, R.D. (2003) *Strategic Management and Organisational Dynamics: The challenge of complexity*. Harlow: FT/Prentice Hall.

Stamper, C.L. and Johlke, M.C. (2003) 'The impact of perceived organizational support on the relationship between boundary spanner role stress and work outcomes', *Journal of Management*, 29, 569–88.

Standish Group (1995) *The Standish Group Report*. Boston, MA: The Standish Group.

Stangor, C., Lynch, L., Duan, C. and Glass, B. (1992) 'Categorization of individuals on the basis of multiple social features', *Journal of Personality and Social Psychology*, 62, 207–18.

Stansfeld, S. and Candy, B. (2006) 'Psychosocial work environment and mental health: A meta-analytic review', *Scandinavian Journal of Work Environment and Health*, 32, 443–62.

Stanton, J.M. (2000) 'Reactions to employee performance monitoring: framework, review and research directions', *Human Performance*, 13, 85–113.

Stanton, N.A. (2004) 'The psychology of task analysis today', in D. Diaper and N.A. Stanton (eds), *The Handbook of Task Analysis for Human–Computer Interaction*. Mahwah, NJ: Lawrence Erlbaum Associates.

Stanton, N.A., Harris, D., Salmon, P., Demagalski, J.M., Marshall, A., Young, M.S., Dekker, S.W.A. and Waldmann, T. (2006) 'Predicting design-induced pilot error using HET (Human Error Template): A new formal human error identification method for flight decks', *The Aeronautical Journal*, 110(February), 107–15.

Stanton, N.A., Salmon, P.M., Walker, G.H., Baber, C. and Jenkins, D.P. (2005) *Human Factors Methods: A practical guide for engineering and design*. Aldershot: Ashgate.

Staw, B.M., Bell, N.E. and Clausen, J.A. (1986) 'The dispositional approach to job attitudes: A lifetime longitudinal test', *Administrative Science Quarterly*, 31, 56–77.

Steel, P. and Konig, C. (2006) 'Integrating theories of motivation', *Academy of Management Review*, 31, 889–913.

Steers, R.M. and Mowday, R.T. (1981) 'Employee turnover and the post decision accommodation process', in B.M. Staw and L.L. Cummings (eds), *Research in Organizational Behavior*. Greenwich, CT: JAI Press.

Steijn, B. (2001) 'Work systems, quality of working life and attitudes of workers: An empirical study towards the effects of team and non-teamwork', *New Technology, Work and Employment*, 16(3), 191–203.

Sternberg, R.J. (1985) *Beyond IQ: A triarchic theory of human intelligence*. Cambridge: Cambridge University Press.

Sternberg, R.J. (1995) 'A triarchic view of "Cognitive resources and leadership performance"', *Applied Psychology: An International Review*, 44, 29–32.

Sternberg, R.J., Forsythe, G.B., Hedlund, J., Horvath, J.A., Wagner, R.K., Williams, W.M., Snook, S.A. and Grigorenko, E. (eds) (2000) *Practical Intelligence in Everyday Life*. Cambridge: Cambridge University Press.

Stevens, C.K. and Gist, M. (1997) 'Effects of self-efficacy and goal orientation training on negotiation skill maintenance: What are the mechanisms?', *Personnel Psychology*, 50, 955–78.

Stevens, M.J. and Campion, M.A. (1994) 'The knowledge, skills and ability requirements for teamwork: Implications for human resource management', *Journal of Management*, 20, 503–30.

Stevens, M.J. and Campion, M.A. (1999) 'Staffing work teams: Development and validation of a selection test for teamwork settings', *Journal of Management*, 25, 207–28.

Stickland, F. (1998) *The Dynamics of Change: Insights into organisational transition from the natural world*. London: Routledge.

Stogdill, R.M. (1974) *Handbook of Leadership: A survey of theory and research*. New York: Free Press.

Stokes, G.S. and Reddy, S. (1992) 'Use of background data in organizational decisions', in C.L. Cooper and I.T. Robertson (eds), *International Review of Industrial and Organizational Psychology*. Chichester: John Wiley.

Storey, J. (1992) *Developments in the Management of Human Resources*. Oxford: Blackwell.

Stroh, L.K., Brett, J.M. and Reilly, A.H. (1992) 'All the right stuff: A comparison of female and male managers' career progression', *Journal of Applied Psychology*, 77, 251–60.

Stumpf, C.A., Colarelli, S.M. and Hartman, K. (1983) 'Development of the Career Exploration Survey (CES)', *Journal of Vocational Behavior*, 22, 191–226.

Sturges, J. (1999) 'What it means to succeed: Personal conceptions of career success held by male and female managers at different ages', *British Journal of Management*, 10, 239–52.

Sturges, J., Guest, D., Conway, N. and Mackenzie Davey, K. (2002) 'A longitudinal study of the relationship between career management and organizational commitment among graduates in the first ten years of work', *Journal of Organizational Behavior*, 23, 731–48.

Sugarman, L. (2001) *Life-span Development*, 2nd edition.

Sullivan, S. and Arthur, M.B. (2006) 'The evolution of the boundaryless career concept: examining physical and psychological mobility', *Journal of Vocational Behavior*, 69, 19–29.

Sullivan, S.E. and Crocitto, M. (2007) 'The developmental theories: A critical examination of their continuing impact on careers research', in H. Gunz and M. Peiperl (eds), *Handbook of Career Studies*. London: Sage.

Sundstrom, E., DeMuese, K.P. and Futrell, D. (1990) 'Work teams: Applications and effectiveness', *The American Psychologist*, 45, 120–33.

Super, D.E. (1957) *The Psychology of Careers*. New York: Harper & Row.

Super, D.E. (1980) 'A life-span, life-space approach to career development', *Journal of Vocational Behavior*, 13, 282–98.

Super, D.E. (1990) 'A life-span, life-space approach to career development', in D. Brown and L. Brooks (eds), *Career Choice and Development*, 2nd edition. San Francisco, CA: Jossey-Bass.

Super, D.E. and Nevill, D.D. (1985) *The Salience Inventory*. Palo Alto, CA: Consulting Psychologists Press.

Super, D.E., Thompson, A.S. and Lindeman, R.H. (1985) *The Adult Career Concerns Inventory*. Palo Alto, CA: Consulting Psychologists Press.

Sutherland, V. and Cooper, C.L. (1987) *Man and Accidents Offshore*. London: Lloyd's.

Swailes, S. and Aritzeta, A. (2006) 'Scale properties of the team role self-perception inventory', *International Journal of Selection and Assessment*, 14(3), 292–98.

Swain, A.D. and Guttman, H.E. (1983) *Handbook of Human Reliability Analysis with Emphasis on Nuclear Power Plant Application* (NUREG/CR-1278). Washington, DC: US Nuclear Regulatory Commission, Office of Nuclear Regulatory Research.

Swan, J. and Cooper, C.L. (2005) *Time Health and the Family: What working families want*. Working Families Publication.

Swanson, V. and Power, K.G. (2001) 'Employees' perceptions of organisational restructuring: The role of social support', *Work and Stress*, 15, 161–78.

Symon, G. and Cassell, C. (eds) (1998) *Qualitative Methods and Analysis in Organizational Research: A practical guide*. London: Sage.

Taber, T.D. and Alliger, G.M. (1995) 'A task-level assessment of job satisfaction', *Journal of Organizational Behavior*, 16, 101–21.

Tajfel, H. (1972) *Differentiation Between Social Groups: Studies in the social psychology of intergroup relations*. London: Academic Press.

Tajfel, H. (1981) *Human Groups and Social Categories*. Cambridge: Cambridge University Press.

Tajfel, H. and Turner, J. (1979) 'An integrative theory of intergroup conflict', in E.G. Austin and S. Worchel (eds), *The Social Psychology of Intergroup Relations*. Monterey, CA: Brooks-Cole.

Tams, S. and Arthur, M.B. (2007) 'Studying careers across cultures: distinguishing international, cross-cultural and globalization perspectives', *Career Development International*, 12, 86–98.

Tan, H.H. and Quek, B.C. (2001) 'An exploratory study on the career anchors of educators in Singapore', *The Journal of Psychology*, 135, 527–45.

Tannenbaum, P. (1956) 'Initial attitude toward source and concept as factors in attitude change through communication', *Public Opinion Quarterly*, 20, 413–26.

Tannenbaum, S.I. and Yukl, G.A. (1992) 'Training and development in work organisations', *Annual Review of Psychology*, 43, 399–441.

Taris, T.W. (2006) 'Burnout and objectively recorded performance: A critical review of 16 studies', *Work and Stress*, 20, 316–34.

Taris, T.W. and Schreurs, P.J.G. (2009) 'Well-being and organizational performance: An organizational-level test of the happy-productive worker hypothesis', *Work and Stress*, 23, 120–136.

Taris, T.W, Feij, J.A. and Capel, S. (2006) 'Great expectations and what comes of it: The effects of unmet expectations on work motivation and outcomes among newcomers', *International Journal of Selection and Assessment*, 14, 256–68.

Tasho, W., Jordan, J. and Robertson, I. (2005) 'Establishing the business case for investing in stress prevention activities and evaluating their impact on sickness absence levels', *RR295*. Sudbury: HSE Books.

Taylor, F.W. (1911) *Principles of Scientific Management*. New York: Harper.

Taylor, K.M. and Betz, N.E. (1983) 'Applications of self-efficacy theory to the understanding and treatment of career indecision', *Journal of Vocational Behavior*, 22, 63–81.

Tesser, A. and Shaffer, D. (1990) 'Attitudes and attitude change', in M.R. Rosenzweig and L.W. Porter (eds), *Annual Review of Psychology*, vol. 41. Palo Alto, CA: Annual Reviews Inc.

Tett, R.P. and Christiansen N.D. (2007) 'Personality tests at the crossroads: A response to Morgeson, Campion, Dipboye, Hollenbeck, Murphy and Schmitt', *Personnel Psychology*, 60, 967–93.

Thomas, R.J. (1989) 'Blue collar careers: Meaning and choice in a world of constraints', in M. Arthur, D.T. Hall and B.S. Lawrence (eds), *Handbook of Career Theory*. Cambridge: Cambridge University Press.

Thompson, E.R. (2008) 'Development and validation of an international English big-five mini-markers', *Personality and Individual Differences*, 45, 542–8.

Thompson, J. (1967) *Organizations in Action*. New York: McGraw-Hill.

Thoresen, C.J., Kaplan, S.A., Barsky, A.P., Warren, C.R. and de Chermont, K. (2003) 'The affective underpinnings of job perceptions and attitudes: A meta-analytic review and integration', *Psychological Bulletin*, 129, 914–45.

Tiedeman, D.V. and O'Hara, R.P. (1963) *Career Development: Choice and adjustment*. New York: College Entrance Exam Board.

Tippins, N.T., Beaty, J., Drasgow, F., Gibson, W.M., Pearlman K. and Segall D.O. *et al.* (2006) 'Unproctored Internet testing in employment settings', *Personnel Psychology*, 59, 189–225.

Tjosvold, D., Wedley, W.C. and Field, R.H.G. (1986) 'Constructive controversy, the Vroom–Yetton model, and managerial decision-making', *Journal of Occupational Behaviour*, 7, 125–38.

Tourish, D. and Pinnington, A. (2002) 'Transformational leadership, corporate cultism and the spirituality paradigm: an unholy trinity in the workplace', *Human Relations*, 55, 147–72.

Tracey, J.B. and Hinkin, T.R. (1998) 'Transformational leadership or effective managerial practices', *Group and Organizational Management*, 23, 220–36.

Tracey, J.B., Tannenbaum, S.I. and Kavanaugh, M.J. (1995) 'Applying trained skills on the job: the importance of the work environment', *Journal of Applied Psychology*, 80, 239–52.

Tracey, T.J. and Rounds, S.B. (1993) 'Evaluating Holland's and Gati's vocational-interest models: A structural meta-analysis', *Psychological Bulletin*, 113, 229–46.

Travers, C. and Pemberton, C. (2000) 'Think career global, but act local: Understanding networking as a culturally differentiated career skill', in M.J. Davidson and R.J. Burke (eds), *Women in Management*. London: Sage.

Trist, E.L. and Bamforth, K.W. (1951) 'Some social and psychological consequences of the long-wall method of coal getting', *Human Relations*, 4, 3–38.

Trompenaars, F. (1993) *Riding the Waves of Culture*. London: Economist Books.

Tsang, E.W.K. (1997) 'Organizational learning and the learning organization: a dichotomy between descriptive and prescriptive research', *Human Relations*, 50(1), 73–89.

Tsutsumi, A. and Kawakami, N. (2004) 'A review of empirical studies on the model of effort–reward imbalance at work: Reducing occupational stress by implementing a new theory', *Social Science and Medicine*, 59, 2235–59.

Tubré, T. and Collins, J. (2000) 'Jackson and Schuler (1985) revisited: A meta-analysis of the relationships between role ambiguity, role conflict and job performance', *Journal of Management*, 26, 155–69.

Tubré, T., Arthur, Jr, W. and Bennett, Jr, W. (2006) 'General models of job performance: Theory and practice', in W. Bennett, Jr, C.E. Lance and D.J. Wohr (eds), *Performance Measurement: Current perspectives and future challenges*. London: Lawrence Erlbaum Associates.

Tuckman, B.W. (1965) 'Development sequence in small groups', *Psychological Review*, 63, 384–99.

Turner, A.N. and Lawrence, P.R. (1965) *Industrial Jobs and the Worker*. Cambridge, MA: Harvard University Press.

Turner, B. (1971) *Exploring the Industrial Subculture*. Macmillan: London.

Turner, D. and Crawford, M. (1999) *Change Power: Capabilities that drive corporate renewal*. Sydney: Woodslane.

Turner, J.C. (1991) *Social Influence*. Buckingham: Open University Press.

Turner, J.C. (1999) 'Some current themes in research on social identity and self-categorization theories', in N. Ellemers, R. Spears and B. Doosje (eds), *Social Identity: Context, commitment, content*. Oxford: Blackwell.

Turner, J.C. and Onorato, R. (1999) 'Social identity, personality and the self-concept: A self-categorization perspective', in T.R. Tyler, R. Kramer and O. John (eds), *The Psychology of the Social Self*. Hillsdale, NJ: Erlbaum.

Turner, N., Barling, J., Epitropaki, O., Butcher, V. and Milder, C. (2002) 'Transformational leadership and moral reasoning', *Journal of Applied Psychology*, 87, 304–11.

Tyson, S. and Ward, P. (2004) 'The use of 360-degree feedback techniques in the evaluation of management learning', *Management Learning*, 35, 202–23.

Tziner, A. (1985) 'How team composition affects task performance: some theoretical insights', *Psychological Review*, 57, 1111–19.

Tziner, A., Murphy, K.R. and Cleveland, J.N. (2005) 'Contextual and rater factors affecting rating behavior', *Group and Organization Management*, 30, 89–98.

UK Labour Force Survey (2007) *2007 Annual Survey of Pay and Earnings*. London: National Statistics, available at: http://www.statistics.gov.uk/pdfdir/ashe1107.pdf.

Underhill, C.M. (2006) 'The effectiveness of mentoring programs in corporate settings: A meta-analytical review of the literature', *Journal of Vocational Behavior*, 68, 292–307.

Valacich, J.S., Dennis, A.R. and Connolly, T. (1994) 'Idea generation in computer-based groups: A new ending to an old story', *Organizational Behavior and Human Decision Processes*, 57, 448–67.

Valsecchi, R. (2006) 'Visible moves and invisible bodies: The case of teleworking in an Italian call centre', *New Technology Work and Employment*, 22, 123–38.

Van de Vliert, E. and Prein, H.C.M. (1989) 'The difference in the meaning of forcing in the conflict management of actors and observers', in M.A. Rahim (ed.), *Management Conflict: An interdisciplinary approach*. New York: Praeger.

Van den Berg, P. and Wilderom, C. (2004) 'Defining, measuring and comparing organizational culture', *Applied Psychology: An International Review*, 53, 575–82.

Van der Hek, H. and Plomp, H.N. (1997) 'Occupational stress management programmes: A practical overview of published effect studies', *Occupational Medicine*, 47, 133–41.

Van der Klink, J.J.L., Blonk, R.W.B., Schene, A.H. and van Dijk, F.J.H. (2001) 'The benefits of interventions for work-related stress', *American Journal of Public Health*, 91, 270–6.

Van Eerde, W. and Thierry, H. (1996) 'Vroom's expectancy models and work related criteria: A meta-analysis', *Journal of Applied Psychology*, 81, 575–86.

Van Harreveld, F., van der Plight, J., de Vries, N.K. and Andreas, S. (2000) 'The structure of attitudes: Attribute importance, accessibility, and judgement', *British Journal of Social Psychology*, 39, 363–80.

Van Hiel, A. and Mervielde, I. (2001) 'Preferences for behavioral style of minority and majority members who anticipate group interaction', *Social Behavior and Personality*, 29(7), 701–10.

Van Knippenberg, D. (2000) 'Work motivation and performance: A social identity perspective', *Applied Psychology: An International Review*, 49, 357–71.

Van Knippenberg, D. and Schippers, M.C. (2007) 'Work group diversity', *Annual Review of Psychology*, 58(1), 515–41.

Van Maanen, J. and Kunda, G. (1989) 'Real feelings: Emotional expression and organizational culture', in B. Staw and L. Cummings (eds), *Research in Organizational Behavior*, 11. Greenwich, CT: JAI Press.

Van Veldhoven, M.J.P.M., Taris, T.W., De Jonge, J., Broersen, S. (2005) 'The relationship between work characteristics and employee health and well being: How much complexity do we really need?', *International Journal of Stress Management*, 12, 3–28.

Vandenberg, R.J., Richardson, H.A. and Eastman, L.J. (1999) 'The impact of high involvement work processes on organizational effectiveness: A second-order latent variable approach', *Group and Organization Management*, 24(3), 300–39.

Vandenberghe, C. and Bentein, K. (2009) 'A closer look at the relationship between affective commitment to supervisors and organizations and turnover', *Journal of Occupational and Organizational Psychology*, 82, 331–48.

VandeWalle, D.M., Cron, W.L. and Slocum, J.W. (2001) 'The role of goal orientation following performance feedback', *Journal of Applied Psychology*, 86, 629–40.

Van Mierlo, H., Rutte, C.G., Kompier, M., Doorewaard, H. (2005) 'Self managing teamwork and psychological well-being: review of a multilevel research domain', *Group and Organization Management*, 30, 211–35.

Van Steenbergen, E.F., Ellemers, N., Haslam, S.A. and Urlings, F. (2008) 'There is nothing either good or bad but thinking makes it so: Informational support and cognitive appraisal of the work–family interface', *Journal of Occupational and Organizational Psychology*, 81, 349–67.

Vansteenkiste, M., Lens, W., De Witte, H. and Feather, N.T. (2005) 'Understanding unemployed people's job search behaviour, unemployment experience and well-being: A comparison of expectancy-value theory and self-determination theory', *British Journal of Social Psychology*, 44, 269–87.

Vartia, M. (1996) 'The sources of bullying: psychological work environment and organizational climate', *European Journal of Work and Organizational Psychology*, 5, 215–37.

Vecchio, R.P. (1987) 'Situational leadership theory: An examination of a prescriptive theory', *Journal of Applied Psychology*, 72, 444–51.

Vecchio, R.P. (1990) 'Theoretical and empirical examination of cognitive resource theory', *Journal of Applied Psychology*, 75, 141–47.

Vecchio, R.P. (1992) 'Cognitive resource theory: Issues for specifying a test of the theory', *Journal of Applied Psychology*, 77, 375–76.

Veiga, J.F. (1983) 'Mobility influences during managerial career stages', *Academy of Management Journal*, 26, 64–85.

Verkuyten, M. (1998) 'Attitudes in public discourse: Speakers' own orientations', *Journal of Language and Social Psychology*, 17(3), 302–22.

Vernon, H.M. (1948) 'An autobiography', *Occupational Psychology*, 23, 73–82.

Vernon, P.A., Petrides, K.V., Bratko, D. and Scherner, J.A. (2008) 'A behavioral genetic study of trait emotional intelligence', *Emotion*, 8, 635–42.

Villanova, P. and Bernardin, H.J. (1991) 'Performance appraisal: The means, motive and opportunity to manage impressions', in R.A. Giacalone and P. Rosenfeld (eds), *Applied Impression Management*. Newbury Park, CA: Sage Publications.

Vince, R. (2002) 'The politics of imagined stability: A psychodynamic understanding of change at Hyder plc', *Human Relations*, 55, 1189–208.

Vincente, K.J. (1999) *Cognitive Work Analysis: Toward safe, productive and healthy computer-based work*. Mahwah, NJ: Lawrence Erlbaum.

Vinnicombe, S. and Colwill, N.L. (1996) *The Essence of Women in Management*. Englewood Cliffs, NJ: Prentice Hall.

Viswesvaran, C. (2003) 'Introduction to special issue: Role of technology in shaping the future of staffing and assessment', *International Journal of Selection and Assessment*, 11(2–3), 107–12.

Viswesvaran, C. and Ones, D.S. (2000) 'Perspectives on models of job performance', *International Journal of Selection and Assessment*, 8, 216–25.

Viswesvaran, C., Schmidt, F. and Ones, D. (2005) 'Is there a general factor in ratings of job performance? A meta-analytic framework for disentangling substantive and error influences', *Journal of Applied Psychology*, 90, 108–31.

Vollrath, D.A., Sheppard, B.H., Hinsz, V.B. and Davis, J.H. (1989) 'Memory performance by decision-making groups and individuals', *Organizational Behavior and Human Decision Processes*, 43, 289–300.

Voskuijl, O. (2005) 'Job analysis: Current and future perspectives', in A. Evers, N. Anderson and O. Voskuijl (eds), *The Blackwell Handbook of Personnel Selection*. Oxford: Blackwell Publishing.

Vroom, V.H. (1964) *Work and Motivation*. Chichester: John Wiley.

Vroom, V.H. and Jago, A.G. (1988) *The New Leadership: Managing participation in organizations*. Englewood Cliffs, NJ: Prentice Hall.

Vroom, V.H. and Yetton, P.W. (1973) *Leadership and Decision Making*. Pittsburgh, PA: Pittsburgh Press.

Wagner, J.A. (1994) 'Participation's effects on performance and satisfaction: A reconsideration of research evidence', *Academy of Management Review*, 19, 312–30.

Wahba, M.A. and Bridwell, L.B. (1976) 'Maslow reconsidered: A review of research on the need hierarchy theory', *Organizational Behaviour and Human Performance*, 15, 212–40.

Waldman, D.A. and Yammarino, F.J. (1999) 'CEO charismatic leadership: Levels-of-management and levels-of-analysis effects', *Academy of Management Review*, 24, 266–85.

Waldman, D.A., Ramirez, G.G., House, R.J. and Puranam, P. (2001) 'Does leadership matter? CEO leader attributes and profitability under conditions of perceived environmental uncertainty', *Academy of Management Journal*, 44, 134–43.

Walker, A. (1982) *Unqualified and Unemployed*. Basingstoke: Macmillan/National Children's Bureau.

Walker, A.G. and Smither, J.W. (1999) 'A five-year study of upward feedback: What managers do with their results matters', *Personnel Psychology*, 52, 393–423.

Walker, K.F. (1979) 'Psychology and employee relations: A general perspective', in G.M. Stephenson and C.J. Brotherton (eds), *Employee Relations: A social psychological approach*. Chichester: John Wiley.

Wall, T.D. (1982) 'Perspectives on job redesign', in J.E. Kelly and C.W. Clegg (eds), *Autonomy and Control in the Workplace*. London: Croom Helm.

Wall, T.D. and Wood, S.J. (2005) 'The romance of human resource management and business performance and the case for big science', *Human Relations*, 58(4), 429–62.

Wall, T.D., Clegg, C.W. and Kemp, N.J. (1987) *The Human Side of Advanced Manufacturing Technology*. Chichester: John Wiley.

Wall, T.D., Cordery, J.L. and Clegg, C.W. (2002) 'Empowerment, performance and operational uncertainty: A theoretical integration', *Applied Psychology: An International Review*, 51, 146–69.

Walther, J.B. (1992) 'Interpersonal effects in computer-mediated interaction: a relational perspective', *Communication Research*, 19, 52–90.

Walther, J.B. (1993) 'Impression development in computer-mediated interaction', *Western Journal of Communication*, 57, 381–98.

Walther, J.B. (1994) 'Anticipated ongoing interaction versus channel effects on relational communication in computer-mediated interaction', *Human Communication Research*, 20, 473–501.

Walther, J.B. (1995) 'Relational aspects of computer-mediated communication: Experimental observations', *Organization Science*, 6, 186–203.

Walther, J.B. (1996) 'Computer-mediated communication: Impersonal, interpersonal and hyperpersonal interaction', *Communication Research*, 23, 3–43.

Walther, J.B. and Burgoon, J.K. (1992) 'Relational communication in computer mediated interaction', *Human Communication Research*, 19, 50–88.

Walther, J.B. and Bunz, U. (2005) 'The rules of virtual groups: Trust, liking and perform-ance in computer-mediated communication', *Journal of Communication*, 55, 828–46.

Walther, J.B., Slovacek, C. and Tidwell, L.C. (2001) 'Is a picture worth a thousand words? Photographic images in long-term and short-term virtual teams', *Communication Research*, 28, 105–34.

Walton, R. and McKersie, R. (1965) *A Behavioral Theory of Labor Negotiations: An analy-sis of a social interaction system*. New York: McGraw-Hill.

Wanberg, C.R., Kammeyer-Mueller, J. and Shi, K. (2001) 'Job loss and the experience of unemployment: International research and perspectives', in N. Anderson, D.S. Ones, H.K. Sinangil and C. Viswesvaran (eds), *Handbook of Work, Industrial and Organizational Psychology*, vol. 2. London: Sage.

Wang, G.P. and Lee, P.D. (2009) 'Psychological empowerment and job satisfaction; an analysis of interactive effects', *Group and Organization Management*, 34, 271–96.

Wardwell, W., Hyman, I.M. and Bahnson, C.B. (1964) 'Stress and coronary disease in three field studies', *Journal of Chronic Disease*, 17, 73–4.

Warr, P. and Wall, T. (1975) *Work and Well-Being*. Harmondsworth: Penguin.

Warr, P., Allen, C. and Birdi, K. (1999) 'Predicting three levels of training outcome', *Journal of Occupational and Organisational Psychology*, 72, 351–76.

Warr, P., Cook, J. and Wall, T. (1979) 'Scales for the measurement of some work atti-tudes and aspects of psychological well-being', *Journal of Occupational Psychology*, 52, 129–48.

Warr, P.B. (1987) *Work, Unemployment and Mental Health*. Oxford: Oxford University Press.

Warr, P.B. (2008) 'Work values: Some demographic and cultural correlates', *Journal of Occupational and Organizational Psychology*, 81, 751–75.

Warr, P.B. (2009) 'Environmental "vitamins", personal judgments, work values and happiness', in S. Cartwright and C.L. Cooper (eds), *The Oxford Handbook of Organisa-tional Well-Being*. Oxford: Oxford University Press.

Warwick, D.P. and Thompson, J.T. (1980) 'Still crazy after all these years', *Training and Development Journal*, 34, 16–22.

Wasti, S.A. and Can, Ö. (2008) 'Affective and normative commitment to organization, supervisor, and coworkers: Do collectivist values matter?', *Journal of Vocational Behavior*, 73, 404–13.

Watson, D., Clark, L.A. and Tellegen, A. (1988) 'Development and validation of brief measures of positive and negative affect: The PANAS scales', *Journal of Personality and Social Psychology*, 54, 1063–70.

Watson, T.J. (1997) *Sociology, Work and Industry*, 3rd edition. London: Routledge.

Webster, J. and Starbuck, W.H. (1988) 'Theory building in industrial and organisational psychology', in C.L. Cooper and I.T. Robertson (eds), *International Review of Indus-trial and Organizational Psychology*, vol. 3. Chichester: John Wiley.

Weekley, J.A. and Ployhart, R.E. (eds) (2006) *Situational Judgment Tests: Theory, measure-ment and application*. San Francisco, CA: Jossey Bass.

Weick, K. (1996) 'Enactment and the boundaryless career: Organizing as we work', in M.B. Arthur and D.E. Rousseau (eds), *The Boundaryless Career*. Oxford: Oxford University Press.

Weick, K.E. (2000) 'Emergent change as a universal in organisations', in M. Beer and N. Nohria (eds), *Breaking the Code of Change*. Boston, MA: Harvard Business School Press.

Weinberg, A. and Cooper, C.L. (2007) *Surviving the Workplace: A guide to emotional well-being*. London: Thomson.

Weirsma, U. and Latham, G.P. (1986) 'The practicality of behavioural expectation scales and trait scales', *Personnel Psychology*, 39, 619–28.

Welbourne, T.M., Cycyota, C.S. and Ferrante, C.J. (2007) 'Wall Street reaction to women in IPOs', *Group and Organization Management*, 32, 524–47.

Wenger, E. (1998) *Communities of Practice: Learning, meaning and identity*. Cambridge: Cambridge University Press.

Werbel, J.D. (2000) 'Relationships among career exploration, job search intensity and job search effectiveness in graduating college students', *Journal of Vocational Behavior*, 57, 379–94.

Werner, J.M. and Bolino, M.C. (1997) 'Explaining US courts of appeals decisions involving performance appraisal: Accuracy, fairness and validation', *Personnel Psychology*, 50, 1–24.

Wernimont, P.F. and Campbell, J.P. (1968) 'Signs, samples and criteria', *Journal of Applied Psychology*, 52, 372–76.

West, M.A. (1994) *Effective Teamwork*. Leicester: British Psychological Society.

West, M.A. (2002) 'Sparkling fountains or stagnant ponds: An integrative model of creativity and innovation implementation in work groups', *Applied Psychology: An International Review*, 51(3), 355–87.

West, M.A. and Farr, J.L. (1990) 'Innovation at work'. In M.A. West and J.L. Farr (eds), *Innovation and Creativity at Work: Psychological and organizational strategies*. Chichester: Wiley.

Westman, M., Etzion, D. and Gattenio, E. (2008) 'International business travels and the work–family interface: A longitudinal study', *Journal of Occupational and Organizational Psychology*, 81, 459–80.

Wexley, K.N. (1984) 'Personnel training', *Annual Review of Psychology*, 35, 519–51.

Wheatley, M. (1992) *The Future of Middle Management*. London: British Institute of Management.

Whiston, S.C. and Oliver, L.W. (2005) 'Career counseling process and outcome', in W.B. Walsh and M.L. Savickas (eds), *Handbook of Vocational Psychology*, 3rd edition. Mahwah, NJ: Erlbuam.

Whiston, S.C., Brecheisen, B.K. and Stephens, J. (2003) 'Does treatment modality affect career counselling effectiveness?', *Journal of Vocational Behavior*, 62, 390–410.

Whitley, W., Dougherty, T.W. and Dreher, G.F. (1991) 'Relationship of career mentoring and socioeconomic origin to managers' and professionals' early career progress', *Academy of Management Journal*, 34, 331–51.

Whitmore, J. (2004) *Coaching for Performance: Growing people, performance and purpose*, 3rd edition. London: Nicholas Brearley Publishing.

Whittington, R. (1993) *What is Strategy and Does it Matter?* London: Routledge.

Whyte, G. (1989) 'Groupthink reconsidered', *Academy of Management Review*, 14, 40–56.

Whyte, G. (1993) 'Escalating commitment to individual and group decision making: A prospect theory approach', *Organizational Behavior and Human Decision Processes*, 54, 430–55.

Whyte, J. and Witcher, B. (1992) *The Adoption of Total Quality Management in Northern England*. Durham: Durham University Business School.

Wickens, C.D., Ververs, P.M. and Fadden, S. (2004) 'Head up displays', in D. Harris (ed.), *Human Factors for Civil Flight Deck Design*. Aldershot: Ashgate.

Widdowson, I. and Carr, J. (2002) *Human Factors Integration: Implementation in the onshore and offshore industries* (HSE Research Report 001). London: HSE Publications.

Wilkinson, A. (1998) 'Empowerment theory and practice', *Personnel Review*, 27, 40–56.

Williams, J.C. (1986) 'HEART: A proposed method for assessing and reducing human error'. Paper presented at the Ninth Advances in Reliability Technology Symposium, University of Bradford.

Williams, K., Harkins, S. and Latane, B. (1981) 'Identifiability as a deterrent to social loafing: Two cheering experiments', *Journal of Personality and Social Psychology*, 40, 303–11.

Williams, K.Y. and O'Reilly, C.A. (1998) 'Demography and diversity in organizations: A review of 40 years of research', *Research in Organizational Behavior*, 20, 77–140.

Williams, M.L., Podsakoff, P.M., Todor, W.D., Huber, V.L., Howell, J.P. and Dorfman, P.W. (1988) 'A preliminary analysis of the construct validity of Kerr and Jermier's "substitutes for leadership" scales', *Journal of Occupational Psychology*, 61, 307–34.

Williams, R. (2002) *Managing Employee Performance: Design and implementation in organizations*. London: Thomson Learning.

Willig, C. (2008) *Introducing Qualitative Research in Psychology*, 2nd edition. Maidenhead: Open University Press.

Willmott, H. (1995) 'Strength is ignorance; slavery is freedom: Managing culture in modern organizations', *Journal of Management Studies*, 30, 511–12.

Willness, C.R., Steel, P. and Lee, K. (2007) 'A meta-analysis of the antecedents and consequences of workplace sexual harassment', *Personnel Psychology*, 60, 127–62.

Wilson, D.C. (1992) *A Strategy of Change: Concepts and controversies in the management of change*. London: Routledge.

Winefield, A.H. (1995) 'Unemployment: Its psychological costs', in C.L. Cooper and I.T. Robertson (eds), *International Review of Industrial and Organizational Psychology*, vol. 10. Chichester: Wiley.

Witcher, B. (1993) *The Adoption of Total Quality Management in Scotland*. Durham: Durham University Business School.

Woehr, D.J. and Arthur, W. (2003) 'The construct-related validity of assessment center ratings: A review and meta-analysis of the role of methodological factors', *Journal of Management*, 29, 231–58.

Wohlers, A.J. and London, M. (1989) 'Ratings of managerial characteristics: Evaluation difficulty, co-worker agreement and self-awareness', *Personnel Psychology*, 42, 235–61.

Wong, C.S., Hui, C. and Law, K.S. (1998) 'A longitudinal study of the job perception–job satisfaction relationship: A test of the three alternative specifications', *Journal of Occupational and Organizational Psychology*, 71(2), 127–46.

Woo, S.E., Sims, C.S., Rupp, D.E. and Gibbons, A.M. (2008) 'Development engagement within and following developmental assessment centers: considering feedback favourability and self-assessor agreement', *Personnel Psychology*, 61, 727–59.

Wood, R., Mento, A. and Locke, E.A. (1987) 'Task complexity as a moderator of goal effects', *Journal of Applied Psychology*, 72, 416–25.

Wood, W. (2000) 'Attitude change: Persuasion and social influence', *Annual Review of Psychology*, 51, 539–70.

Wood, W. and Kallgren, C.A. (1988) 'Communicator attributes and persuasion: Recipients' access to attitude-relevant information in memory', *Personality and Social Psychology Bulletin*, 14, 172–82.

Wood, W., Lundgren, S., Ouellette, J.A., Busceme, S. and Blackstone, T. (1994) 'Minority influence: A meta-analytic review of social influence processes', *Psychological Bulletin*, 115, 323–45.

Woodruffe, C. (1993) *Assessment Centres: Identifying and developing competence*, 2nd edition, London: Institute of Personnel and Development.

Wooford, J.C., Goodwin, V.L. and Premack, S. (1992) 'Meta-analysis of the antecedents of personal goal level and of the antecedents and consequences of goals commitment', *Journal of Management*, 18, 595–615.

Wooten, K.C. and White, L.P. (1999) 'Linking OD's philosophy with justice theory: Postmodern implications', *Journal of Organizational Change Management*, 12, 7–20.

Worley, G.W. and Feyerherm, A.E. (2003) 'Reflections on the future of organization development', *The Journal of Applied Behavioral Science*, 39(1), 97–115.

Worrall, L. and Cooper, C.L. (1997) *The Quality of Working Life: The 1997 survey of managers' changing experiences*. London: Institute of Management.

Worrall, L. and Cooper, C.L. (1998) *The Quality of Working Life: The 1998 survey of managers' changing experiences*. London: Institute of Management.

Wright, P., Ferris, S.P., Hiller, J.S. and Kroll, M. (1995) 'Competitiveness through management of diversity: Effects on stock price evaluation', *Academy of Management Journal*, 38(1), 272–87.

Wright, P.M. and Dyer, L. (2001) *People in the e-Business: New challenges, new solutions*. Ithaca, NJ: Center for Advanced Human Resource Studies, Cornell University.

Wright, P.M., O'Leary-Kelly, A.M., Cortina, J.M., Klein, H.J. and Hollenbeck, J. (1994) 'On the meaning and measurement of goal commitment', *Journal of Applied Psychology*, 79, 795–803.

Wright, T.A. and Cropanzano, R. (2004) 'Psychological well-being and job satisfaction as predictors of job performance', *Journal of Occupational Health Psychology*, 5, 84–94.

Wright, T.A. and Staw, B.M. (1999) 'Affect and favourable work outcomes: Two longitudinal tests of the happy-productive worker thesis', *Journal of Organizational Behavior*, 20, 1–23.

Wright, V. (1991) 'Performance-related pay', in F. Neale (ed.), *The Handbook of Performance Management*. London: CIPD.

Wrzesniewski, A. and Dutton, J.E. (2001) 'Crafting a job: Revisioning employees as active crafters of their work', *Academy of Management Review*, 26, 179–201.

Yost, E.B. and Corbishley, M.A. (1987) *Career Counseling*. London: Jossey-Bass.

Young, G., Tokar, D.M. and Subich, L.M. (1998) 'Congruence revisited: Do 11 indices differentially predict job satisfaction and is the relation moderated by person and situation variables?', *Journal of Vocational Behavior*, 52, 208–23.

Young, M.S., Stanton, N.A. and Harris, D. (2007) 'Driving automation: Learning from aviation about design philosophies', *International Journal of Vehicle Design*, 45(3), 323–38.

Yukl, G.A. (1998) *Leadership in Organizations*, 4th edition. Upper Saddle River, NJ: Prentice Hall.

Yukl, G. (2006) *Leadership in Organizations*, 6th edition. Englewood Cliffs, NJ: Prentice Hall.

Yun, G.J., Donahue, L.M., Dudley, N.M. and McFarland, L.A. (2005) 'Rater personality, rating format and social context: Implications for performance appraisal ratings', *International Journal of Selection and Assessment*, 13, 97–107.

Zairi, M., Letza, S. and Oakland, J. (1994) 'Does TQM impact on bottom line results?', *TQM Magazine*, 6(1), 38–43.

Zapf, D. (1999) 'Organizational work group related and personal causes of mobbing/bullying at work', *International Journal of Manpower*, 20, 70–85.

Zapf, D. (2002) 'Emotion work and psychological well-being: A review of the literature and some conceptual considerations', *Human Resource Management Review*, 12, 237–68.

Zapf, D. and Einarsen, S. (2003) 'Individual antecedents of bullying: victims and perpetrators', in S. Einarsen, H. Hoel, D. Zapf and C.L. Cooper (eds), *Bullying and Emotional Abuse in the Workplace: International perspectives in research and practice*. London: Taylor and Francis.

Zapf, D., Dormann, C. and Frese, M. (1996) 'Longitudinal studies in organizational stress research. A review of the literature with reference to methodological issues', *Journal of Occupational Health Psychology*, 1, 145–69.

Zatzick, C.D., Elvira, M.E. and Cohen, L.E. (2003) 'When is more better? The effects of racial composition on voluntary turnover', *Organization Science*, 14, 483–96.

Zeidner, M. and Endler, N.S. (1996) *Handbook of Coping: Theory, research, applications*. Oxford: John Wiley.

Zeidner, M., Roberts, R.D. and Matthews, G. (2008) 'The science of emotional intelligence: Current consensus and controversies', *European Psychologist*, 13, 64–78.

Zhao, H., Wayne, S.J., Glibkowski, B.C. and Bravo, J. (2007) 'The impact of psychological contract breach on work-related outcomes: A meta-analysis', *Personnel Psychology*, 60, 647–80.

Zhou, J. and Shalley, C.E. (2008) *Handbook of Organizational Creativity*. Hove: Psychology Press.

Zikic, J. and Klehe, U. (2006) 'Job loss as a blessing in disguise: The role of career exploration and career planning in predicting reemployment quality', *Journal of Vocational Behavior*, 69, 391–409.

Zimmerman, R.D. (2008) 'Understanding the impact of personality traits on individuals' turnover decisions: a meta-analytic path model', *Personnel Psychology*, 61, 309–48.

INDEX

Note: **bold** page numbers denote glossary entries.

F

M

T